T0181105

Lecture Notes in Computer Science 12661

More information about this subseries at http://www.springer.com/series/7412

Alberto Del Bimbo · Rita Cucchiara ·
Stan Sclaroff · Giovanni Maria Farinella ·
Tao Mei · Marco Bertini ·
Hugo Jair Escalante · Roberto Vezzani (Eds.)

Pattern Recognition

ICPR International Workshops and Challenges

Virtual Event, January 10–15, 2021
Proceedings, Part I

 Springer

Editors
Alberto Del Bimbo ⓘ
Dipartimento di Ingegneria
dell'Informazione
University of Firenze
Firenze, Italy

Stan Sclaroff ⓘ
Department of Computer Science
Boston University
Boston, MA, USA

Tao Mei
Cloud & AI, JD.COM
Beijing, China

Hugo Jair Escalante ⓘ
Computational Sciences Department
National Institute of Astrophysics,
Optics and Electronics (INAOE)
Tonantzintla, Puebla, Mexico

Rita Cucchiara ⓘ
Dipartimento di Ingegneria "Enzo Ferrari"
Università di Modena e Reggio Emilia
Modena, Italy

Giovanni Maria Farinella ⓘ
Dipartimento di Matematica e Informatica
University of Catania
Catania, Italy

Marco Bertini ⓘ
Dipartimento di Ingegneria
dell'Informazione
University of Firenze
Firenze, Italy

Roberto Vezzani ⓘ
Dipartimento di Ingegneria "Enzo Ferrari"
Università di Modena e Reggio Emilia
Modena, Italy

ISSN 0302-9743   ISSN 1611-3349 (electronic)
Lecture Notes in Computer Science
ISBN 978-3-030-68762-5   ISBN 978-3-030-68763-2   (eBook)
https://doi.org/10.1007/978-3-030-68763-2

LNCS Sublibrary: SL6 – Image Processing, Computer Vision, Pattern Recognition, and Graphics

This Springer imprint is published by the registered company Springer Nature Switzerland AG
The registered company address is: Gewerbestrasse 11, 6330 Cham, Switzerland

Foreword by General Chairs

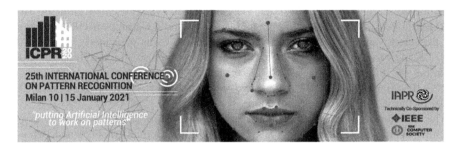

It is with great pleasure that we welcome you to the post-proceedings of the 25th International Conference on Pattern Recognition, ICPR2020 Virtual-Milano. ICPR2020 stands on the shoulders of generations of pioneering pattern recognition researchers. The first ICPR (then called IJCPR) convened in 1973 in Washington, DC, USA, under the leadership of Dr. King-Sun Fu as the General Chair. Since that time, the global community of pattern recognition researchers has continued to expand and thrive, growing evermore vibrant and vital. The motto of this year's conference was *Putting Artificial Intelligence to work on patterns*. Indeed, the deep learning revolution has its origins in the pattern recognition community – and the next generations of revolutionary insights and ideas continue with those presented at this 25th ICPR. Thus, it was our honor to help perpetuate this longstanding ICPR tradition to provide a lively meeting place and open exchange for the latest pathbreaking work in pattern recognition.

For the first time, the ICPR main conference employed a two-round review process similar to journal submissions, with new papers allowed to be submitted in either the first or the second round and papers submitted in the first round and not accepted allowed to be revised and re-submitted for second round review. In the first round, 1554 new submissions were received, out of which 554 (35.6%) were accepted and 579 (37.2%) were encouraged to be revised and resubmitted. In the second round, 1696 submissions were received (496 revised and 1200 new), out of which 305 (61.4%) of the revised submissions and 552 (46%) of the new submissions were accepted. Overall, there were 3250 submissions in total, and 1411 were accepted, out of which 144 (4.4%) were included in the main conference program as orals and 1263 (38.8%) as posters (4 papers were withdrawn after acceptance). We had the largest ICPR conference ever, with the most submitted papers and the most selective acceptance rates ever for ICPR, attesting both the increased interest in presenting research results at ICPR and the high scientific quality of work accepted for presentation at the conference.

We were honored to feature seven exceptional Keynotes in the program of the ICPR2020 main conference: David Doermann (Professor at the University at Buffalo), Pietro Perona (Professor at the California Institute of Technology and Amazon Fellow at Amazon Web Services), Mihaela van der Schaar (Professor at the University of Cambridge and a Turing Fellow at The Alan Turing Institute in London), Max Welling (Professor at the University of Amsterdam and VP of Technologies at Qualcomm), Ching Yee Suen (Professor at Concordia University) who was presented with the IAPR 2020 King-Sun Fu Prize, Maja Pantic (Professor at Imperial College UK and AI Scientific Research Lead at Facebook Research) who was presented with the IAPR 2020 Maria Petrou Prize, and Abhinav Gupta (Professor at Carnegie Mellon University and Research Manager at Facebook AI Research) who was presented with the IAPR 2020 J.K. Aggarwal Prize. Several best paper prizes were also announced and awarded, including the Piero Zamperoni Award for the best paper authored by a student, the BIRPA Best Industry Related Paper Award, and Best Paper Awards for each of the five tracks of the ICPR2020 main conference.

The five tracks of the ICPR2020 main conference were: (1) Artificial Intelligence, Machine Learning for Pattern Analysis, (2) Biometrics, Human Analysis and Behavior Understanding, (3) Computer Vision, Robotics and Intelligent Systems, (4) Document and Media Analysis, and (5) Image and Signal Processing. The best papers presented at the main conference had the opportunity for publication in expanded format in journal special issues of *IET Biometrics* (tracks 2 and 3), *Computer Vision and Image Understanding* (tracks 1 and 2), *Machine Vision and Applications* (tracks 2 and 3), *Multimedia Tools and Applications* (tracks 4 and 5), *Pattern Recognition Letters* (tracks 1, 2, 3 and 4), or *IEEE Trans. on Biometrics, Behavior, and Identity Science* (tracks 2 and 3).

In addition to the main conference, the ICPR2020 program offered workshops and tutorials, along with a broad range of cutting-edge industrial demos, challenge sessions, and panels. The virtual ICPR2020 conference was interactive, with real-time live-streamed sessions, including live talks, poster presentations, exhibitions, demos, Q&A, panels, meetups, and discussions – all hosted on the Underline virtual conference platform.

The ICPR2020 conference was originally scheduled to convene in Milano, which is one of the most beautiful cities of Italy for art, culture, lifestyle – and more. The city has so much to offer! With the need to go virtual, ICPR2020 included interactive **virtual tours** of Milano during the conference coffee breaks, which we hoped would introduce attendees to this wonderful city, and perhaps even entice them to visit Milano once international travel becomes possible again.

The success of such a large conference would not have been possible without the help of many people. We deeply appreciate the vision, commitment, and leadership of the ICPR2020 Program Chairs: Kim Boyer, Brian C. Lovell, Marcello Pelillo, Nicu Sebe, René Vidal, and Jingyi Yu. Our heartfelt gratitude also goes to the rest of the main conference organizing team, including the Track and Area Chairs, who all generously devoted their precious time in conducting the review process and in preparing the program, and the reviewers, who carefully evaluated the submitted papers and provided invaluable feedback to the authors. This time their effort was considerably higher given that many of them reviewed for both reviewing rounds. We also want to acknowledge the efforts of the conference committee, including the Challenge Chairs, Demo and Exhibit Chairs, Local Chairs, Financial Chairs, Publication Chair, Tutorial Chairs, Web Chairs, Women in ICPR Chairs, and Workshop Chairs. Many thanks, also, for the efforts of the dedicated staff who performed the crucially important work behind the scenes, including the members of the ICPR2020 Organizing Secretariat. Finally, we are grateful to the conference sponsors for their generous support of the ICPR2020 conference.

We hope everyone had an enjoyable and productive ICPR2020 conference.

Rita Cucchiara
Alberto Del Bimbo
Stan Sclaroff

Preface

The 25th International Conference on Pattern Recognition Workshops (ICPRW 2020) were held virtually in Milan, Italy and rescheduled to January 10 and January 11 of 2021 due to the Covid-19 pandemic. ICPRW 2020 included timely topics and applications of Computer Vision, Image and Sound Analysis, Pattern Recognition and Artificial Intelligence. We received 49 workshop proposals and 46 of them have been accepted, which is three times more than at ICPRW 2018. The workshop proceedings cover a wide range of areas including Machine Learning (8), Pattern Analysis (5), Healthcare (6), Human Behavior (5), Environment (5), Surveillance, Forensics and Biometrics (6), Robotics and Egovision (4), Cultural Heritage and Document Analysis (4), Retrieval (2), and Women at ICPR 2020 (1). Among them, 33 workshops are new to ICPRW. Specifically, the ICPRW 2020 volumes contain the following workshops (please refer to the corresponding workshop proceeding for details):

- CADL2020 – Workshop on Computational Aspects of Deep Learning.
- DLPR – Deep Learning for Pattern Recognition.
- EDL/AI – Explainable Deep Learning/AI.
- (Merged) IADS – Integrated Artificial Intelligence in Data Science, IWCR – IAPR workshop on Cognitive Robotics.
- ManifLearn – Manifold Learning in Machine Learning, From Euclid to Riemann.
- MOI2QDN – Metrification & Optimization of Input Image Quality in Deep Networks.
- IML – International Workshop on Industrial Machine Learning.
- MMDLCA – Multi-Modal Deep Learning: Challenges and Applications.
- IUC 2020 – Human and Vehicle Analysis for Intelligent Urban Computing.
- PATCAST – International Workshop on Pattern Forecasting.
- RRPR – Reproducible Research in Pattern Recognition.
- VAIB 2020 – Visual Observation and Analysis of Vertebrate and Insect Behavior.
- IMTA VII – Image Mining Theory & Applications.
- AIHA 2020 – Artificial Intelligence for Healthcare Applications.
- AIDP – Artificial Intelligence for Digital Pathology.
- (Merged) GOOD – Designing AI in support of Good Mental Health, CAIHA – Computational and Affective Intelligence in Healthcare Applications for Vulnerable Populations.
- CARE2020 – pattern recognition for positive teChnology And eldeRly wEllbeing.
- MADiMa 2020 – Multimedia Assisted Dietary Management.
- 3DHU 2020 – 3D Human Understanding.
- FBE2020 – Facial and Body Expressions, micro-expressions and behavior recognition.
- HCAU 2020 – Deep Learning for Human-Centric Activity Understanding.
- MPRSS - 6th IAPR Workshop on Multimodal Pattern Recognition for Social Signal Processing in Human Computer Interaction.

- CVAUI 2020 – Computer Vision for Analysis of Underwater Imagery.
- MAES – Machine Learning Advances Environmental Science.
- PRAConBE - Pattern Recognition and Automation in Construction & the Built Environment.
- PRRS 2020 – Pattern Recognition in Remote Sensing.
- WAAMI - Workshop on Analysis of Aerial Motion Imagery.
- DEEPRETAIL 2020 - Workshop on Deep Understanding Shopper Behaviours and Interactions in Intelligent Retail Environments 2020.
- MMForWild2020 – MultiMedia FORensics in the WILD 2020.
- FGVRID – Fine-Grained Visual Recognition and re-Identification.
- IWBDAF – Biometric Data Analysis and Forensics.
- RISS – Research & Innovation for Secure Societies.
- WMWB – TC4 Workshop on Mobile and Wearable Biometrics.
- EgoApp – Applications of Egocentric Vision.
- ETTAC 2020 – Eye Tracking Techniques, Applications and Challenges.
- PaMMO – Perception and Modelling for Manipulation of Objects.
- FAPER – Fine Art Pattern Extraction and Recognition.
- MANPU – coMics ANalysis, Processing and Understanding.
- PATRECH2020 – Pattern Recognition for Cultural Heritage.
- (Merged) CBIR – Content-Based Image Retrieval: where have we been, and where are we going, TAILOR – Texture AnalysIs, cLassificatiOn and Retrieval, VIQA – Video and Image Question Answering: building a bridge between visual content analysis and reasoning on textual data.
- W4PR - Women at ICPR.

We would like to thank all members of the workshops' Organizing Committee, the reviewers, and the authors for making this event successful. We also appreciate the support from all the invited speakers and participants. We wish to offer thanks in particular to the ICPR main conference general chairs: Rita Cucchiara, Alberto Del Bimbo, and Stan Sclaroff, and program chairs: Kim Boyer, Brian C. Lovell, Marcello Pelillo, Nicu Sebe, Rene Vidal, and Jingyi Yu. Finally, we are grateful to the publisher, Springer, for their cooperation in publishing the workshop proceedings in the series of Lecture Notes in Computer Science.

December 2020

Giovanni Maria Farinella
Tao Mei

Challenges

Competitions are effective means for rapidly solving problems and advancing the state of the art. Organizers identify a problem of practical or scientific relevance and release it to the community. In this way the whole community can contribute to the solution of high-impact problems while having fun. This part of the proceedings compiles the best of the competitions track of the *25th International Conference on Pattern Recognition (ICPR)*.

Eight challenges were part of the track, covering a wide variety of fields and applications, all of this within the scope of ICPR. In every challenge organizers released data, and provided a platform for evaluation. The top-ranked participants were invited to submit papers for this volume. Likewise, organizers themselves wrote articles summarizing the design, organization and results of competitions. Submissions were subject to a standard review process carried out by the organizers of each competition. Papers associated with seven out the eight competitions are included in this volume, thus making it a representative compilation of what happened in the ICPR challenges.

We are immensely grateful to the organizers and participants of the ICPR 2020 challenges for their efforts and dedication to make the competition track a success. We hope the readers of this volume enjoy it as much as we have.

November 2020
Marco Bertini
Hugo Jair Escalante

ICPR Organization

General Chairs

Rita Cucchiara	Univ. of Modena and Reggio Emilia, Italy
Alberto Del Bimbo	Univ. of Florence, Italy
Stan Sclaroff	Boston Univ., USA

Program Chairs

Kim Boyer	Univ. at Albany, USA
Brian C. Lovell	Univ. of Queensland, Australia
Marcello Pelillo	Univ. Ca' Foscari Venezia, Italy
Nicu Sebe	Univ. of Trento, Italy
René Vidal	Johns Hopkins Univ., USA
Jingyi Yu	ShanghaiTech Univ., China

Workshop Chairs

Giovanni Maria Farinella	Univ. of Catania, Italy
Tao Mei	JD.COM, China

Challenge Chairs

Marco Bertini	Univ. of Florence, Italy
Hugo Jair Escalante	INAOE and CINVESTAV National Polytechnic Institute of Mexico, Mexico

Publication Chair

Roberto Vezzani	Univ. of Modena and Reggio Emilia, Italy

Tutorial Chairs

Vittorio Murino	Univ. of Verona, Italy
Sudeep Sarkar	Univ. of South Florida, USA

Women in ICPR Chairs

Alexandra Branzan Albu	Univ. of Victoria, Canada
Maria De Marsico	Univ. Roma La Sapienza, Italy

Demo and Exhibit Chairs

Lorenzo Baraldi   Univ. Modena Reggio Emilia, Italy
Bruce A. Maxwell   Colby College, USA
Lorenzo Seidenari   Univ. of Florence, Italy

Special Issue Initiative Chair

Michele Nappi   Univ. of Salerno, Italy

Web Chair

Andrea Ferracani   Univ. of Florence, Italy

Corporate Relations Chairs

Fabio Galasso   Univ. Roma La Sapienza, Italy
Matt Leotta   Kitware, Inc., USA
Zhongchao Shi   Lenovo Group Ltd., China

Local Chairs

Matteo Matteucci   Politecnico di Milano, Italy
Paolo Napoletano   Univ. of Milano-Bicocca, Italy

Financial Chairs

Cristiana Fiandra   The Office srl, Italy
Vittorio Murino   Univ. of Verona, Italy

Contents – Part I

**AIHA 2020 - International Workshop on Artificial Intelligence
for Healthcare Applications**

CADL2020 - Workshop on Computational Aspects of Deep Learning

3DHU 2020 - 3D Human Understanding

Workshop on 3D Human Understanding (3DHU)

3DHU is a forum for researchers and practitioners working in the field of 3D vision. The goal of this workshop was to bring together and unify research efforts in the field of 3D human understanding, spanning a variety of both theoretical and applicative topics.In the context of human analysis, there are several technical problems that are still open and that this workshop aimed to address.

The significant recent advancements in research fields such as robotics, autonomous driving, or human-machine interaction strongly renewed the interest in understanding the 3D world. In this context, interpreting the behavior of humans represents a crucial step towards the development of systems able to naturally blend into the real world. Other than that, 3D data represents a richer source of information compared to 2D images or video sequences, andthe development of new affordable and accurate 3D acquisition sensors is making the application of machine learningalgorithms possible in real scenarios, further posing new challenges and practical issues.

The first edition of the International Workshop on 3D Human Understanding (3DHU) was held in Milan, Italy, in conjunction with the 25th edition of the International Conference on Pattern Recognition (ICPR). The format of the workshop included two invited speakers and paper presentations.

We received 10 submissions for review. After a thorough and accurate peer review process, 7 papers were accepted for presentation and publication in the proceedings. In particular, 5 out of the 7 accepted papers were full-length papers. The review process focused on the quality of the papers and their scientific soundness. In compliance with the main conference protocol, we adopted a single-blind review policy, and each paper was reviewed by a minimum of 2 independent, expert reviewers. After collecting the reviews, final decisions were taken as the result of chairs' discussion.

The accepted papers represented an interesting mix of contributions. They covered a wide range of topics, spanning from 3D face recognition and re-identification, to body shape and silhouette reconstruction from single images, 3D body pose estimation, action recognition or pedestrian trajectory prediction in the context of autonomous driving. Other significant contributions such as new datasets were also accepted.

The workshop program was completed by two invited talks, given by, respectively, Prof. Anup Basu from the University of Alberta, and Dr. Federico Tombari, from the Technische Universität of Munich.

A special issue related to the workshop topics has been organized in partnership with MDPI Journal of Imaging.

January 2021

Organization

3DHU Workshop Chairs

Claudio Ferrari	University of Florence, Italy
Stefano Berretti	University of Florence, Italy
Giuseppe Lisanti	University of Bologna, Italy
Liming Chen	Ecole Centrale Lyon, France
Di Huang	Beihang University, China
Xiaoming Liu	Michigan State University, Michigan (USA)

Technical Program Committee

Djamila Aouada	SnT, University of Luxembourg, Luxembourg
Silvia Biasotti	CNR-IMATI, Italy
Guido Borghi	University of Bologna, Italy
Maxime Devanne	Université Haute-Alsace, France
Hassen Drira	IMT Lille-Douai, France
Leonardo Galteri	University of Florence, Italy
Anis Kacem	SnT, University of Luxembourg, Luxembourg
Iacopo Masi	University of Rome, Italy
Joao Cardia Neto	FATEC Catanduva, Brazil
Riccardo Spezialetti	University of Bologna, Italy
Claudio Tortorici	Technology Innovation Institute, Abu Dhabi
Pavan Turaga	Arizona State University, Arizona
Naoufel Werghi	Khalifa University, Abu Dhabi

Additional Reviewer

Matteo Bruni	University of Florence

Sponsors

MDPI Journal of Imaging cooperated with the workshop as media partner.

Subject Identification Across Large Expression Variations Using 3D Facial Landmarks

SK Rahatul Jannat, Diego Fabiano, Shaun Canavan[✉], and Tempestt Neal

University of South Florida, Tampa, FL 33620, USA
{jannat,dfabiano,scanavan,tjneal}@usf.edu

Abstract. In this work, we propose to use 3D facial landmarks for the task of subject identification, over a range of expressed emotion. Landmarks are detected, using a Temporal Deformable Shape Model and used to train a Support Vector Machine (SVM), Random Forest (RF), and Long Short-term Memory (LSTM) neural network for subject identification. As we are interested in subject identification with large variations in expression, we conducted experiments on 3 emotion-based databases, namely the BU-4DFE, BP4D, and BP4D+ 3D/4D face databases. We show that our proposed method outperforms current state of the art methods for subject identification on BU-4DFE and BP4D. To the best of our knowledge, this is the first work to investigate subject identification on the BP4D+, resulting in a baseline for the community.

1 Introduction

Broadly, face recognition can be categorized as holistic, hybrid matching, or feature-based [38]. Holistic approaches look at the global similarity of the face such as a 3D morphable model (3DMM) [2]; hybrid matching make use of either multiple methods [14] or multiple modalities [17]; feature-based methods look at local features of the face to find similarities [40]. The work proposed in this paper can be categorized as feature-based. Due to its non-intrusive nature and wide applicability in security and defense related fields, face recognition has been actively researched by many groups in recent decades.

Since some of the earlier methods for face recognition [31,37], to more recent works within the past 10 years [7,35] 2D face recognition has been an actively researched field. With the recent advances in deep neural networks, we have seen significant jumps in performance [12,18,22,24,28,33]. Liu et al. [21] proposed the angular softmax that allows convolutional neural networks (CNN) the ability to learn angularly discriminative features. This was proposed to handle the problem where face features are shown to have a smaller intra-class distance compared to inter-class distance. Recently, Tuan et al. [30] proposed regressing 3D morphable model shape and texture parameters from a 2D image using a CNN. Using this approach, they were able to obtain a sufficient amount of training data

© Springer Nature Switzerland AG 2021
A. Del Bimbo et al. (Eds.): ICPR 2020 Workshops, LNCS 12661, pp. 5–13, 2021.
https://doi.org/10.1007/978-3-030-68763-2_1

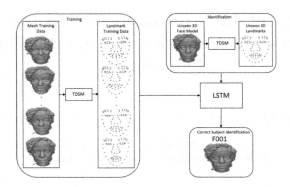

Fig. 1. Overview of proposed method. Example is showing an unseen 3D mesh model of subject 'F001' from BP4D+ [39], who is correctly identified based on training a LSTM [13] from 3D facial data detected from a TDSM.

for their network showing promising results. Zhu et al. [41] proposed a high-fidelity pose and expression normalization method that made use of a 3DMM to generate natural, frontal facing, neutral face images. Using this method, they achieved promising results in both constrained and unconstrained environments (i.e. wild settings). Although performance has been increasing and groups have been actively working on 2D subject identification, there are still some challenges such as pose and lighting. 3D faces can help to minimize these challenges [25], and in recent years, this research has made significant strides [11,12,26] due to the development of powerful, high-fidelity 3D sensors.

Echeagaray-Patron et al. [11] proposed a method for 3D face recognition where conformal mapping is used to map the original face surfaces onto a Riemannian manifold. From the conformal and isometric invariants that they compute, comparisons are then made. This method was shown to have invariance to both expression and pose. Lei et al. [20] proposed the Angular Radial Signature for 3D face recognition. This signature is extracted from the semi-rigid regions of the face, followed by mid-level features being extracted from the signature by Kernel Principal Component Analysis. These features were then used to train a support vector machine showing promising results when comparing neutral vs. non-neutral faces. Berretti et al. [1] proposed the use of 3D Weighted Walkthroughs with iso-geodesic facial strips for the task of 3D face recognition. They achieved promising results on the FRGC v2.0 [23] and SHREC08 [10] 3D facial datasets. Using multistage hybrid alignment algorithms and an annotated face model, Kakadiaris et al. [15] used a deformable model framework to show robustness to facial expressions when performing 3D face recognition.

Motivated by the above works, we propose to use 3D facial landmarks for subject identification across large variations in expression. We track the facial landmarks using a Temporal Deformable Shape Model (TDSM) [6]. See Fig. 1 for an overview of the proposed approach. The rest of the paper is organized as follows. Section 2 gives a brief overview of the TDSM algorithm, Sect. 3 details our experimental design and results, and we conclude in Sect. 4.

2 Temporal Deformable Shape Model

The Temporal Deformable Shape Model (TDSM) models the shape variation of 3D facial data. Given a sequence of data (i.e. 4D), it also models the implicit constraints on shape that are imposed (e.g. small changes in motion and shape). To construct a TDSM, a training set of 3D facial landmarks is required. First, the 3D facial landmarks are aligned using a modified version of Procrustes analysis [5]. Given a training set of size L 3D faces, where each face has N facial landmarks (aligned with Procrustes analysis), a parameterized model S is constructed, $S = F_1^1, ..., F_N^1, ..., F_1^m, ..., F_N^m$. F_i^m is the ith landmarks of the mth 3D face in the training set, where $F_i^m = (x_i^m, y_i^m, z_i^m)$ and $1 \leq m \leq L$. From this model, principal component analysis (PCA), is then applied to learn the modes of variation, V, of the training data.

Given the parameterized model, S, and the modes of variation, V, to detect 3D facial landmarks, an offline weight vector, w, is constructed that allows for new face shapes to be constructed, by a linear combination of landmarks as $S = \bar{s} + Vw$ where $\bar{s}$ is the average face shape. These constructed face shapes are constrained to be within the range $-2\sqrt{\lambda_i} \leq w_i \leq 2\sqrt{\lambda_i}$, where w_i is the ith weight in the range, and λ_i is the ith eigenvalue from PCA. This constraint is imposed to make sure the new face shape is a 3D face.

To fit (i.e. detect landmarks) to a new input mesh, an offline table of weights (w) is constructed with a uniform amount of variance. The Procrustes distance, D, is then computed between each face shape (referred to as an instance of the TDSM) and the new input mesh. The smallest distance is considered the best detected landmarks. Note that this is not meant to be an exhaustive overview of a TDSM, therefore we refer the reader to the original work [6] for more details.

3 Experimental Design and Results

Using a TDSM, we detected 83 facial landmarks on 3 publicly available 3D emotion-based face databases: BU4DFE [34], BP4D [36], and BP4D+ [39]. From these facial landmarks, we then conducted subject identification experiments, where the landmarks are used as training data for 3 machine learning classifiers. Using these 83 facial landmarks we have also reduced the dimensionality of the 3D faces from over 30,000 3D vertices, while still retaining important features for subject identification. This allows us to reduce storage requirements, as well as processing time of the 3D face, which can be limitations of 3D face recognition [3,16]. An overview of the databases and the experimental design is detailed in the following subsections.

3.1 3D Face Databases

One of the main goals of this work is to show subject identification across large variations in expression. Considering this, we evaluated 3 large, state-of-the-art 3D emotion-based face databases with a total of 282 subjects across all 3.

BU-4DFE [34]**:** Consists of 101 subjects displaying 6 prototypical facial expressions plus neutral. The dataset has 58 females and 43 males, including a variety of racial ancestries. The age range of the BU-4DFE is 18–45 years of age.

BP4D [36]**:** Consists of 41 subjects displaying 8 expressions plus neutral. It consists of 23 females and 18 males; 11 Asian, 4 Hispanic, 6 African-American, and 20 Euro-American ethnicities are represented. The age range of the BP4D is 18–29 years of age. This database was developed to explore spatiotemporal features in facial expressions. Due to its large variation in expression, it is a natural fit for our subject identification study.

BP4D+ [39]**:** Consists of 140 subjects (82 females and 58 males) ages 18–66. This data corpus consists of ethnic and racial ancestries that include African American, Caucasian, and Asian each with highly varied emotions. These emotions are elicited through tasks designed to elicit dynamic emotions in the subjects such as disgust, sadness, pain, and surprise resulting in a challenging dataset. Like the BP4D database, this dataset was also designed to study emotion classification. Its diversity and number of subjects, as well as large variations in expressions, make it a natural fit for our study.

3.2 Experimental Design

To conduct our experiments, we detected 83 facial landmarks on the 3D data using a TDSM. Given 3D facial landmarks, we then translated them so that the centroid of the face is located at the origin in 3D space to align the data. The translated 3D facial features were then used for subject identification. Each of the 3D facial landmarks (x, y, z coordinates) are inserted into a new feature vector. For all 83 landmarks, this gives us a feature vector of size $83 \times 3 = 249$. This feature vector is used to train classifiers for subject identification. To ensure our results were not classifier specific, we trained a support vector machine (SVM) [32], random forest (RF) [4], and Long short-term memory (LSTM) neural network [13]. Our network consists of one short-term memory layer with a look back of two faces (estimated landmarks), followed by 0.5 dropout, and a fully connected layer for classification. The softmax activation function was used, along with the RMSprop [29] optimizer with a learning rate of 0.0001.

For each classifier, each subject's identity was used as the class (each 3D face is labeled with a subject id). Accurate results on an SVM, RF, and LSTM show the robustness of the 3D facial landmarks to multiple machine learning classifiers. We conducted one-to-many subjection identification, where all subjects were in both the training and testing sets. These sets were split based on time (i.e. different sections of the sequences available in the datasets) so consecutive (i.e., similar) frames did not appear in both sets.

3.3 Subject Identification Results

We achieved an average subject identification accuracy of 99.9%, on random forest and support vector machine, and 99.93% for an LSTM, across all databases.

Table 1. Subject identification accuracies for the 3 tested datasets and classifiers.

	BU4DFE	BP4D	BP4D+
SVM	99.9%	99.9%	99.9%
RF	100%	99.9%	99.8%
LSTM	100%	99.9%	99.9%

Table 2. Subject identification accuracies(percentage) for faces with simulated occlusion. Key: TR: Top Right; TL: Top Left; LR: Lower Right; LL: Lower Left.

	BP4D				BP4D+			
	TR	TL	LR	LL	TR	TL	LR	LL
RF	**99.7**	**99.7**	**99.7**	**99.7**	**99.3**	**99.3**	**99.6**	**99.5**
SVM	95.1	96.8	93.4	87.5	98.8	99.1	97.5	94.8

As can be seen in Table 1, an SVM, RF, and LSTM can accurately identify subjects from the BU4DFE, BP4D, and BP4D+ datasets achieving a max accuracy of 100% on BU4DFE, and a minimum accuracy of 99.8% on BP4D+. All three of the tested classifiers achieved consistent results across all three datasets, showing these results are not classifier dependent. As each of the datasets contain large variations in expression, these results show the detected 3D landmarks have robustness to expression changes for the task of subject identification.

3.4 Subject Identification with Occluded Faces

Along with subject identification using all 83 landmarks, we also tested on a smaller number of facial landmarks to simulate occluded faces. For these experiments, we split the 3D facial landmarks (i.e. face) into 4 quadrants (Fig. 2) and detected a smaller number of landmarks (top right: 23; top left:23; lower right: 20; lower left: 17) using a TDSM. We then ran the same experiments for each quadrant. As shown in Sect. 3, the results are not classifier specific, as the random forest, SVM, and LSTM network have similar results. Due to this we only used a random forest and support vector machine for these experiments.

When testing on simulated occluded faces on BU4DFE, both the random forest and SVM achieved 99.9% accuracy in all four quadrants, showing robustness to occlusion. Testing on BP4D, the random forest achieved an average accuracy of 99.7% across the four quadrants, and SVM achieved an average accuracy of 93.2% across the four quadrants. On BP4D+, random forest and SVM achieved an average accuracy of 99.4% and 97.5%, respectively across the four quadrants. These results detail the expressive power of the detected 3D facial landmarks to reliably identify subjects under extreme conditions. See Table 2 for individual quadrant accuracies for BP4D and BP4D+ (BU4DFE not shown as all quadrants had same accuracy of 99.9% for both classifiers).

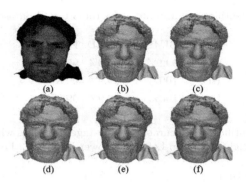

Fig. 2. Detected landmarks (BP4D [36]) used for subject ID (original 3D mesh shown only for display purposes). (a) 83 landmarks with texture (note: texture is shown for display purposes only showing robustness to facial hair); (b) 83 landmarks; (c) top left quadrant; (d) top right quadrant; (e) lower left quadrant; and (f) lower right quadrant.

Table 3. State-of-the-art comparisons.

Method	BU4DFE	BP4D
Proposed Method (RF)	**100%**	**99.9%**
Proposed Method (LSTM)	**100%**	**99.9%**
Proposed Method (SVM)	99.9%	**99.9%**
Sun et al. [27]	98.61%	N/A
Fernandes et al. [19]	96.71%	N/A
Canavan et al. [8]	92.7%	93.4%

3.5 Comparisons to State of the Art

We compared our proposed method to the current state of the art on BU-4DFE [34] and BP4D [36] (see Table 3 for both). To the best of our knowledge this is the first study to perform subject identification on BP4D+ [39]; therefore, we did not have any works to compare against resulting in a baseline for the community. In these comparisons, it is important to note that Canavan et al. [8] used 1800 and 2400 frames from BU-4DFE and BP4D, respectively, for their experiments. We used all data in both datasets (60402 and 367474 respectively). The work from Sun et al. [27] also requires both spatial and temporal information to achieve their results of 98.61%, and while our approach can incorporate temporal information (e.g. LSTM), it can also identify a subject based on one frame of data, which is useful when temporal information is not available.

4   Conclusion

We have shown 3D facial landmarks can be used for subject identification across large variations in expression. We validated our approach on three 3D emotion-based face databases (BU4DFE [34], BP4D [36], and BP4D+ [39]), using a random forest, support vector machine, and long short-term neural network. The proposed method outperforms current state of the art on 2 publicly available 3D face databases achieving a max identification accuracy of 100% on BU-4DFE and 99.9% on BP4D. To the best of our knowledge, this is the first work to report subject identification results on the BP4D+. We have also shown the detected landmarks can be used for subject identification in the presence of facial occlusion (simulated). We will further investigate this robustness to expression and occlusion in future work, by investigating other state-of-the-art 3D face emotion datasets such as 4DFab [9], which was also designed with biometrics studies in mind, as well as large variations in expression.

We are also interested in emotion-invariant multimodal subject identification. In this paper, we have shown that 3D landmarks are invariant to large expression changes for the task of subject identification. Since facial expressions are often physiological responses to emotion, emotion-invariant identification can have a broad range of applications such as medicine and healthcare (e.g., identifying individuals despite expressions of pain). Multimodal approaches are generally more accurate due to the fusion of heterogeneous data, each contributing identifying information. Considering this, we hypothesize a multimodal approach will significantly advance research on emotion-invariant subject identification while yielding new insight on the impact of emotion on novel modalities such as smartphone sensor data (e.g., accelerometer and touch measurements) and other unconstrained and transparently acquired data. Such approaches will be valuable for continuous subject identification.

References

1. Berretti, S., Del Bimbo, A., Pala, P.: 3D face recognition using isogeodesic stripes. IEEE Trans. PAMI **32**(12), 2162–2177 (2010)
2. Blanz, V., Vetter, T.: Face recognition based on fitting a 3D morphable model. IEEE Trans. PAMI **32**(12), 1063–1074 (2003)
3. Bowyer, K., Chang, K., Flynn, P.: A survey of approaches and challenges in 3D and multi-modal 3D+ 2D face recognition. CVIU **101**(1), 1–15 (2006)
4. Breiman, L.: Random forests. Mach. Learn. **45**(1), 5–32 (2001)
5. de Bruijne, M., et al.: Adapting active shape models for 3D segmentation of tubular structures in medical images. In: BICIPMI
6. Canavan, S., Zhang, X., Yin, L.: Fitting and tracking 3D/4D facial data using a temporal deformable shape model. In: ICME (2013)
7. Canavan, S., et al.: Evaluation of multi-frame fusion based face classification under shadow. In: ICPR, pp. 1265–1268 (2010)
8. Canavan, S., et al.: Landmark local on 3D/4D range data using a shape index-based stat shape model with global and local constraints. CVIU **139**, 136–148 (2015)

9. Cheng, S., et al.: 4DFAB: a large scale 4D database for facial expression analysis and biometric applications. In: CVPR, pp. 5117–5126 (2018)
10. Daoudi, M., et al.: SHREC 2008-shape retrieval contest of 3D face scans (2008)
11. Echeagaray-Patron, B., Kober, V., Karnaukhov, V., Kuznetsov, V.: A method of face recognition using 3D facial surfaces. J. CTE **62**(6), 648–652 (2017)
12. Emambakhsh, M., Evans, A.: Nasal patches and curves for expression-robust 3D face recognition. IEEE Trans. PAMI **39**(5), 995–1007 (2016)
13. Hochreiter, S., Schmidhuber, J.: LSTM. Neural computation **9**(8), 1735–1780 (1997)
14. Huang, J., Heisele, B., Blanz, V.: Component-based face recognition with 3D morphable models. In: ICAVPA (2003)
15. Kakadiaris, I., et al.: 3D face recognition. In: BMVC (2006)
16. Kakadiaris, I., et al.: 3D face recognition in the presence of facial expression: an annotated deformable model approach. IEEE Trans. PAMI **29**(4), 640–649 (2007)
17. Kakadiaris, I.O.: Multimodal face recognition: combination of geometry with physiological information. In: CVPR, vol. 2, pp. 1022–1029 (2005)
18. Kemelmacher-Shlizerman, I., et al.: In: CVPR, pp. 4873–4882 (2016)
19. Fernandes, S.L., Bala, G.J.: 3D and 4D face recognition: a comprehensive review. Recent Pat. Eng. **8**(2), 112–119 (2014)
20. Lei, Y., et al.: An efficient 3D face recognition approach using local geometrical signatures. Pattern Recogn. **47**(2), 509–524 (2014)
21. Liu, W., et al.: SphereFace: deep hypersphere embedding for face recognition. In: CVPR, pp. 212–220 (2017)
22. Parkhi, O., et al.: Deep face recognition. In: BMVC (2015)
23. Phillips, P., et al.: Overview of the face recognition grand challenge. In: CVPR (2005)
24. Saragih, J., Lucey, S., Cohn, J.: Deformable model fitting by regularized landmark mean-shift. Int. J. Comput. Vis. **91**(2), 200–215 (2011)
25. Singh, S., Prasad, S.: Techniques and challenges of face recognition: a critical review. Procedia Comput. Sci. **143**, 536–543 (2018)
26. Soltanpour, S., Boufama, B., Wu, Q.J.: A survey of local feature methods for 3D face recognition. Pattern Recogn. **72**, 391–406 (2017)
27. Sun, Y., Yin, L.: 3D spatio-temporal face recognition using dynamic range model sequences. In: CVPRW (2008)
28. Sun, Y., et al.: Deep learning face representation by joint identification-verification. In: Advances in Neural Information Processing Systems, pp. 1988–1996 (2014)
29. Tieleman, T., Hinton, G.: Lecture 6.5-rmsprop: divide the gradient by a running average of its recent magnitude. COURSERA **4**(2), 26–31 (2012)
30. Tran, A.T., et al.: Regressing robust and discriminative 3D morphable models with a very deep neural network. In: CVPR, pp. 5163–5172 (2017)
31. Turk, M., Pentland, A.: Face recognition using Eigenfaces. In: CVPR, pp. 586–591 (1991)
32. Vapnik, V.: The support vector method of function estimation. In: Nonlinear Modeling, pp. 55–85 (1998)
33. Wen, Y., et al.: A discriminative feature learning approach for deep face recognition. In: ECCV, pp. 499–515 (2016)
34. Yin, L., et al.: A high-red 3D dynamic facial expression database. In: FG (2008)
35. Zhang, L., et al.: Sparse representation or collaborative representation: which helps face recognition? In: ICCV, pp. 471–478 (2011)
36. Zhang, X., et al.: BP4D-spontaneous: a high-resolution spontaneous 3D dynamic facial expression database. Image Vis. Comput. **32**(10), 692–706 (2014)

37. Zhao, W., et al.: Discriminant analysis of principal components for face recognition. In: Face Recognition, pp. 73–85 (1998)
38. Zhao, W., et al.: Face recognition: a literature survey. ACM Comput. Surv. **35**(4), 399–458 (2003)
39. Zheng, Z., et al.: Multimodal spontaneous emotion corpus for human behavior analysis. In: CVPR (2016)
40. Zhong, C., et al.: Robust 3D face recognition using learned visual codebook. In: CVPR (2007)
41. Zhu, X., et al.: High-fidelity pose and expression normalization for face recognition in the wild. In: CVPR, pp. 787–796 (2015)

3D Human Pose Estimation Based on Multi-Input Multi-Output Convolutional Neural Network and Event Cameras: A Proof of Concept on the DHP19 Dataset

Alessandro Manilii[1], Leonardo Lucarelli[1], Riccardo Rosati[1(✉)], Luca Romeo[1,2],
Adriano Mancini[1], and Emanuele Frontoni[1]

[1] Department of Information Engineering (DII), Università Politecnica delle Marche,
Via Brecce Bianche, 12, 60131 Ancona, Italy
r.rosati@pm.univpm.it
[2] Computational Statistics and Machine Learning and Cognition,
Motion and Neuroscience, Istituto Italiano di Tecnologia, Genova, Italy

Abstract. Nowadays Human Pose Estimation (HPE) represents one of the main research themes in the field of computer vision. Despite innovative methods and solutions introduced for frame processing algorithms, the use of standard frame-based cameras still has several drawbacks such as data redundancy and fixed frame-rate. The use of event-based cameras guarantees higher temporal resolution with lower memory and computational cost while preserving the significant information to be processed and thus it represents a new solution for real-time applications. In this paper, the DHP19 dataset was employed, the first and, to date, the only one with HPE data recorded from Dynamic Vision Sensor (DVS) event-based cameras. Starting from the baseline single-input single-output (SISO) Convolutional Neural Network (CNN) model proposed in the literature, a novel multi-input multi-output (MIMO) CNN-based architecture was proposed in order to model simultaneously two different single camera views. Experimental results show that the proposed MIMO approach outperforms the standard SISO model in terms of accuracy and training time.

Keywords: Human Pose Estimation · Event cameras · Multi-Input multi-Output convolutional neural network

1 Introduction

Human pose estimation (HPE) is a traditional computer vision challenge aiming at generating 2D or 3D human skeleton from single or multiple view of one or more subjects. This tasks need great computational capacity to achieve good performance since big amount of data need to be processed. Standard approaches rely on RGB [5] or RGB-D camera with several applications in different scenarios including retail [18,19], people counting, person re-identification [11], clinical

A. Del Bimbo et al. (Eds.): ICPR 2020 Workshops, LNCS 12661, pp. 14–25, 2021.
https://doi.org/10.1007/978-3-030-68763-2_2

monitoring [16] and rehabilitation [6,7]. Event cameras represent a great solution, guaranteeing high temporal resolution, high dynamic range and fewer storage requirements [3]. These cameras, such as the Dynamic Vision Sensor (DVS), reduce the amount of data recording only changes in pixel intensity values: this produces asynchronous streams of events and it avoids the redundancy caused by fixed and insignificant background information. Moreover, they also prevents problems such as fixed frame rate which does not change if the registered object is static or in movement, producing higher quality output. In this scenario, the DVS 3D Human Pose dataset (DHP19) [4], the first DVS dataset for 3D human pose estimation, could represent the benchmark for future works in real-time context in which lightness and speed are crucial features. The aim of this work is to explore the dataset by evolving the single-input single-output (SISO) approach proposed in [4] with a novel multi-input multi-output (MIMO) Convolutional Neural Network (CNN) model able to improve generalization performance by simultaneously modeling two different views. In particular, the model learns simultaneously the human pose from different views (cameras) thus leading to the simultaneous HPE for each different camera. We introduce a detailed and reproducible experimental setup procedure of our proposed model by tuning the optimal hyperparameters and selecting the best confidence threshold strategy. The main contribution of the work is the proposal of a MIMO strategy based on CNN model that allows to (i) improve the generalization performance and (ii) to reduce the computation effort in terms of training time[1].

The paper is organized as follows: Sect. 2 provides a description of the state-of-the-art about HPE task and CNN approaches applied to event cameras datasets. Section 3 gives details on the DHP19 dataset, the preprocessing steps applied and the proposed MIMO approach, which is the main core of this work. In Sect. 4, a comparative evaluation of our approach with the state-of-the-art is offered. Finally, in Sect. 5, discussion and conclusions about future directions for this field of research are drawn.

2 Related Work

2.1 HPE Datasets

Until today, there are multiple existing datasets for 3D HPE recorded using frame-based cameras. Between these, the most used are HumanEva [21], Human3.6M [9] and MPI-INF-3DHP [15]. All of them include a whole-body recording obtained with multiple cameras on different subjects, performing different movements. Moreover, they include ground-truth 3D pose recording from a motion capture system. However, state-of-the-art contributions on HPE through innovative datasets are not many. In literature, there are only two works related to human gestures or body movements recorded through event-based cameras

---

[1] The code to reproduce all results is available at the following link: https://github.com/AlessandroManilii/3D_HumanPoseEstimation_event-based_dataset.

[2,8], but the only dataset built for HPE purpose with whole-body joints position is the one introduced in [4] and described in Sect. 3.1.

2.2 CNN Architectures

In the literature, a wide use of CNN has been made to solve the HPE task based on standard RBG images [17,22,23]. CNNs have been applied to the output of event-based cameras only to solve classification problems as in [2,12,13] or regression problems using independently different input and generating single output in [14]. Differently from the state of the art work we formulate the HPE using a MIMO strategy based on CNN models. As we shall see in the experimental results, our model performs favorably with respect to the SISO strategy proposed in [4].

3 Materials and Methods

DHP19 is the first human pose dataset with data collected from DVS event-based cameras. This specific feature implies a more complex preprocessing step in order to generate a standard frame from a sequence of events, but it introduces great enhancements, i.e. avoiding redundancy and saving space for more information, making the dataset more valuable. For the HPE task, the baseline approach is the same described in [4], in which a single CNN is used for each camera to predict joints' positions in 2D. Instead in the multi-view approach, two frames from different cameras but related to the same time instant are given as input to the network, and multiple outputs are returned as a couple of heatmaps representing estimated 2D joints positions for the two frames. For both methods, the final 3D pose estimation is inferred from 2D predictions using triangulation and knowing the position of the camera. A detailed description of the dataset contents, the instruments used, the preprocessing steps and the network architectures is provided below.

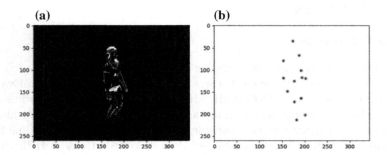

Fig. 1. a) Example frame generated from DVS events for subject 2, movement 9 of DHP19 dataset and b) the relative joint labels obtained as described in Sect. 3.2.

3.1   Dataset

DHP19 contains the records of 17 subjects, 12 females and 5 males who perform specific movements in a recording volume of $2 \times 2 \times 2$ m^3 in a therapy environment. All 33 movements, grouped in 5 sessions, can be categorized in upper-limb movements (1, 2, 5, 6, 15–20, 27–33), lower-limb movements (3, 4, 7, 8, 23–26), and whole-body movements, and they are performed by each subject 10 times consecutively. The subject position is represented through 13 labeled joints positions corresponding to the head, both shoulder, both elbow, hands, left/right hip, both knees and feet as can be seen in Fig. 1. In our experiments, subjects 1–9 (52% of the dataset) were used as training set, subjects 10–12 (18% of the dataset) as validation set and remaining subjects 13–17 (30%) as testing set.

3.2   Preprocessing and Frame Generation

Data have been acquired with the simultaneous use of 4 Dynamic and Active Pixel Vision Sensor (DAVIS) cameras [10], a complex version of standard DVS with a resolution of 260×344 pixels, and Vicon motion capture system for ground-truth recording, made of 10 Bonita Motion Capture (BMC) infrared (IR) cameras. An event $e = (x, y, t, p, c)$ is made of: position (x, y) in pixel array, time t in microsecond, polarity of the brightness change p and camera ID (0–3) c. In order to make use of pre-existent frame-based deep learning algorithms for event cameras, we applied the same preprocessing steps and transformed event stream into frames as in [4]. For this purpose, a fixed amount of events (about $7.5k$ per camera) are grouped in each frame, which is finally normalized in the range [0,255]. Instead, labels are constructed knowing initial and final event timestamps for each generated frame calculating the average position in that time window. The last step consists of mapping the obtained 3D label position into frame space, rounding to the nearest pixel, making use of projection matrices for each camera view. The projected 2D labels represent the absolute position in pixel space. Finally, a smoothing filter is applied on each heatmap through Gaussian blurring with a sigma of 2 pixels.

3.3   Baseline: Single-Input Single-Output (SISO) Architecture

In this approach, a single CNN takes as input one frame at a time and so, for each camera, a different output for the same time instant is obtained. Input image is downsampled and then upsampled to produce a heatmap of the same size: the output of the network is an array of shape (260, 344, 13), where the 13 heatmaps represent the probability for each joint to be in a certain position among all 260×344 (frame size) possibilities. The training points are a sequence of frames picked up from a different subject, session, movement and from the two cameras. To get the final prediction, the position corresponding to the max value is taken and then compared with the label through mean squared error. A detailed description of model architecture and methods used for training and testing is provided in the following paragraphs.

Model Architecture. CNN is organized in 18 convolutional layers as shown in Table 1. Each layer is followed by Rectified Linear Unit (RELU) activation and it has a variable number of 3×3 filters from 16 to 64 contributing to a total amount of about 220k trainable parameters. A bidimensional max-pooling allows decreasing computational cost and affecting possible overfitting. In order to reproduce the baseline results in [4], we implemented their architecture considering the same setting for each layer parameter (i.e. number of filters, kernel size, strides, dilation rate).

Table 1. SISO model architecture

Layer	Out dimension	Stride	Dilatation
(1) Conv2D	(260, 344, 16)	1	1
MaxPooling2D	(130, 172, 16)	1	1
(2) Conv2D	(130, 172, 16)	1	1
(3) Conv2D	(130, 172, 32)	1	1
(4) Conv2D	(130, 172, 32)	1	1
MaxPooling2D	(65, 86, 32)	1	1
(5) Conv2D	(65, 86, 64)	1	2
(6) Conv2D	(65, 86, 64)	1	2
(7) Conv2D	(65, 86, 64)	1	2
(8) Conv2D	(65, 86, 64)	1	2
(9) Conv2DTc	(130, 172, 32)	2	1
(10) Conv2D	(130, 172, 32)	1	2
(11) Conv2D	(130, 172, 32)	1	2
(12) Conv2D	(130, 172, 32)	1	2
(13) Conv2D	(130, 172, 32)	1	2
(14) Conv2DTc	(260, 344, 16)	2	1
(15) Conv2D	(260, 344, 16)	1	1
(16) Conv2D	(260, 344, 16)	1	1
(17) Conv2D	(260, 344, 16)	1	1
(18) Conv2D	(260, 344, 13)	1	1

3.4   Proposed Approach: Multiple-Input Multiple-Output (MIMO) Architecture

In order to deeply adapt model architecture to the multi-view case-study, we implemented a multi-input and multi-output (MIMO) CNN, which employs shared layers. In particular, as shown in Fig. 2, the network takes as input two frames of the same instant time respectively from cameras 2 and 3 and it outputs 13 heatmaps, one per joint, for each one as in single-input CNN. In single-input approach, the same layers were trained on both cameras and the batches are made up of a casual sequence of frames picked up from a different subject, session, movement. Differently, in this case, the not-shared layers are only trained on a specific camera view, generating batches as a sequence of a couple of frames always related to two different cameras and randomly put in sequence.

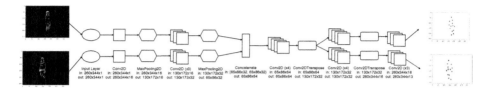

Fig. 2. Multi-Input Multi-Output (MIMO) model architecture.

Model Architecture. As shown in Fig. 2, CNN is constituted by two separate single input heads and output tails that share a group of central layers. The shared layers are the four convolutional layers (5–8) and the transposed convolution one (9) indicated in Table 1. These layers are updated on frames of both cameras while the others are only related to images from a specific cam. Where the two branches are separated (Conv2DTranspose layer), the bank of filters are duplicated. The increased number of layers due to this new configuration rises the number of trainable parameters from 220k to 310k.

3.5   3D Human Pose Estimation

There are different approaches for reconstructing 3D HPE from 2D HPE belonging to different multi-camera views [1,20]. The method we have chosen for 3D triangulation is the same described in [4]. Firstly the model predicts 2D joints position, then the triangulation method is applied to project the 2D prediction on the 3D space knowing the position of the camera, as represented in Fig. 3.

3.6   Experimental Procedure

Training Setting. The SISO model was trained for 20 epochs using a batch size of 64 and a variable learning rate of 10e-3 for the first 10 epochs, of 10e-4 from epoch 11 to 15 and of 10e-5 from 16 to 20. Mean Squared Error (MSE) and RMSProp are used respectively as cost function and optimizer. The training phase took about 80 h on an NVIDIA RTX-2080 Ti. As regards the MIMO model, the training procedure and network parameters remain the same described for SISO to perform a fair comparison between the two approaches, except for the batch size equal to 32 in order to generate batches with the same number of frame used for the single-input model. In this case, the training time was about 70 h: this lower execution time with respect to the single-input approach is due to the implementation of multi-input approach which, for each couple of frames given in input, decrease the total amount of training points.

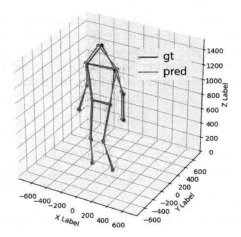

Fig. 3. Ground-truth and prediction overlapping in 3D space.

Testing. After the preprocessing step, we tested the models on the same test subjects (13–17) with and without confidence threshold in the range [0.1–0.5]. The confidence threshold mechanism works comparing the max value of the heatmap with the set threshold for each joint and, in case the condition isn't satisfied, the last valid joint position is taken. This can lead to taking better or worst prediction depending on which is the average max value in the output heatmaps: this is the reason why using a higher confidence threshold does not improve performance, as shown by the results in following paragraphs. We first tested the model trained by [4] in order to reproduce their own results, then the SISO and MIMO models trained from scratch.

Evaluation Metric. For evaluation purposes the mean per joint position error (MPJPE) metric is used, expressed with the following formula:

$$MPJPE = \frac{1}{J} \sum_{i}^{J} \left\| x_i - \hat{x}_i \right\| \tag{1}$$

where i represent a different joint at every iteration, ranging in the interval [1,J], J is the number of joints, x is the ground-truth absolute position acquired by the Vicon system and $\hat{x}$ is the predicted absolute position.

4   Results

In Sect. 4.1 the validation results are reported, while in Sects. 4.2 and 4.3 we reported the results related to 2D pose estimation and 3D pose estimation respectively.

4.1   Validation Results

Despite we use MSE as validation loss for both models, it's more explanatory to calculate MPJPE on the validation subjects in order to analyze how training performance evolves during epochs. Figures 4 represents the trend of the MPJPE through the 20 epochs respectively for the single-input model and the multi-input model, calculated with the corresponding optimal confidence threshold identified in the next sections. We can notice how both models converge and the trend follows the learning rate scheduler.

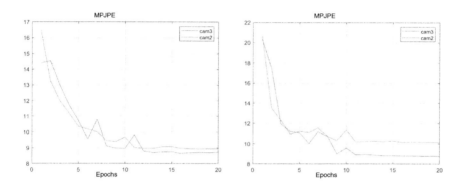

Fig. 4. MPJPE trend for a) SISO model and b) MIMO model for camera 2 and camera 3 through the 20 epochs.

4.2   2D Pose Estimation

Table 2 shows the testing results in terms of MPJPE values for different confidence thresholds for the pre-trained model introduced in [4] and the models described in Sects. 3.3 and 3.4. The MPJPE are averaged over all the testing subjects (subject 13, 14, 15, 16 and 17). The optimal threshold for 2D pose estimation is calculated as a function of the average max of the predicted value for each pixel. In fact, a higher threshold means that a large number of predictions are discarded and for each one of them this mechanism takes as an actual prediction the last one (in terms of time) that has satisfied the threshold's condition. Hence, a higher confidence threshold means a higher probability that the temporal gap between the current prediction and the last good one is elevated. On the other hand, a lower confidence threshold may lead to a higher sparsity of the heatmap values and to a higher uncertainty of the prediction. The extracted SISO model results reveals a difference with respect to the baseline results reported in [4]. For the baseline model, the best results correspond to the confidence threshold equal to 0.3, with a relative improvement (compared to no-confidence results) of 6% and 12% for cameras 2 and 3 respectively. Results of the SISO model are worse compared to the baseline results, with an average

MPJPE increment of 30%. This may be due to a different set of training parameters or a different type of data normalization made by authors in [4]. However, the MIMO model leads to an average improvement of the 2D HPE results of 3.5% compared to SISO model (referring to the value corresponding to the best confidence threshold of each model).

Table 2. Summary table comparing MPJPE score on test subjects for the baseline pre-trained model, the SISO model and the MIMO model, all trained on the two frontal cameras (camera 2 and 3) and tested with various confidence thresholds. In bold the best-selected confidence threshold used for 3D projection.

Conf. Thr	None	0.01	0.1	0.3	0.4
Baseline					
Cam 2	7.70	7.55	7.42	**7.22**	7.26
Cam 3	7.92	7.69	7.25	**6.91**	6.98
SISO					
Cam 2	11.47	11.12	**10.56**	11.09	11.65
Cam 3	10.86	10.72	**10.16**	10.36	10,77
MIMO					
Cam 2	10.49	**10.40**	11.82	14.85	16.54
Cam 3	9.64	**9.58**	10.51	13.75	15.93

4.3   3D Pose Estimation

Table 3 summarises the 3D pose estimation results. For all the models, the best results are obtained for the second section (precisely movements 9–14, 21, 22), which correspond to movements where the human shape is entirely visible in the DVS frames. The pre-trained baseline model, with a confidence threshold of 0.3, reaches the averaged MPJPE of 80,31 mm. The MIMO model obtains an improvement (118.23 mm vs 115.48 mm respectively) of 2.5% in terms of 3D MPJPE with respect to the standard SISO model.

The increased number of layers due to this new configuration rises the number of trainable parameters from 220k (for a single network) to 308k. However, the computation effort in terms of the training time of the MIMO is reduced by 10% compared to the SISO model. This fact can be explained by the lower number of training images (the half compared to SISO) required by MIMO for learning simultaneously the pose from two different cameras instead of aggregating the data acquired from the two cameras.

Table 3. Averaged 3D MPJPE (in mm) of the 5 testing subject through the 5 sessions for different CNNs. In bold the overall mean of the 3D MPJPE for each model.

\	Subj. 13	Subj. 14	Subj. 15	Subj. 16	Subj. 17	Subj. Mean
Baseline						
Session 1	84,67	95,87	86,74	125,37	107,41	90,95
Session 2	40,69	53,29	48,65	72,88	79,43	66,43
Session 3	91,80	134,50	104,70	125,16	134,74	124,79
Session 4	77,57	101,05	105,97	92,53	99,63	80,53
Session 5	75,70	107,24	106,48	147,81	111,46	113,84
Session Mean	60,44	80,91	75,85	92,12	86,22	**80,31**
SISO						
Session 1	175,96	190,79	166,43	202,26	175,70	150,09
Session 2	64,21	73,77	68,12	101,60	102,92	87,17
Session 3	162,35	186,77	171,70	214,22	182.45	209,74
Session 4	129,42	147,47	149,90	135.82	123.36	116,29
Session 5	147,47	198,07	177.16	240,46	180,28	198,40
Session Mean	95,27	121,50	116,74	136,84	116,08	**118,23**
MIMO						
Session 1	147,02	168,42	179,63	173,78	263,26	165,38
Session 2	55,70	61,70	60,24	93,12	104,13	85,06
Session 3	149,17	166,00	150,37	216,58	191,38	183,94
Session 4	131,73	142,51	154,79	126,71	129,93	115,48
Session 5	144,58	161,27	124,75	224,25	177,62	174,22
Session Mean	96,90	101,78	107,61	127,60	126,65	**115,48**

5   Conclusions

In this work we improve the single-input single-output (SISO) approach proposed in [4] with a novel multi-input multi-output (MIMO) Convolutional Neural Networks (CNN) model able to improve the generalization performance of HPE by simultaneously modeling two different views of event cameras. Starting from the experimental procedure presented in [4] we tried to reproduce their experimental results implementing the same SISO CNN based model. However, the baseline results extracted by [4] seems to be not fully reproducible. The incongruences found between the SISO and baseline results on DHP19 dataset reported in the paper may be due to several reasons. The more reasonable one regards the training hyperparameters, especially for SISO model in which CNN architecture has not to be modified. For example, the setting of different batch size or learning rate schedule, according to the evaluation metrics trend among epochs, could lead to a difference in performance. Other reasons could be linked to the data generator mechanism, which may lead to a different training procedure, or to another kind of output normalization.

Our Experimental results on the DHP19 dataset demonstrated how the novel MIMO approach allows improving the generalization performance of 2D and 3D HPE while reducing the computation effort in terms of training time. This can be explained by considering that the two inputs (event camera views) given to the model share the same discriminative features since they correspond to 2 different points of view of the same instant of time. Thus the use of shared layers may encourage this relatedness by increasing generalization performance, as well as guaranteeing lower training time.

Future works could be related to exploring different training hyperparameters, by also selecting the optimal number of shared layers. Finally, another interesting future direction could be addressed to (i) extend the MIMO strategy by converting the 2D CNN into 3D CNN for obtaining a direct 3D HPE (ii) to impose kinematic constraints to refine the overall 3D HPE. Accordingly, recurrent 3D CNN can be investigated in order to learn spatio-temporal features by modeling sequential temporal relationships among weights.

References

1. Amin, S., Andriluka, M., Rohrbach, M., Schiele, B.: Multi-view pictorial structures for 3d human pose estimation. In: 24th British Machine Vision Conference, pp. 1–12. BMVA Press (2013)
2. Amir, A., et al.: A low power, fully event-based gesture recognition system. In: 2017 IEEE Conference on Computer Vision and Pattern Recognition (CVPR), pp. 7388–7397 (2017)
3. Brandli, C., Berner, R., Yang, M., Liu, S.C., Delbruck, T.: A 240× 180 130 DB 3 μs latency global shutter spatiotemporal vision sensor. IEEE J. Solid-State Circuits **49**(10), 2333–2341 (2014)
4. Calabrese, E., et al.: Dhp19: dynamic vision sensor 3d human pose dataset. In: Proceedings of the IEEE/CVF Conference on Computer Vision and Pattern Recognition (CVPR) Workshops, June 2019
5. Cao, Z., Simon, T., Wei, S., Sheikh, Y., et al.: Openpose: realtime multi-person 2d pose estimation using part affinity fields. IEEE Trans. Pattern Anal. Mach. Intell. **42**(5), 1146-1161 (2019)
6. Capecci, M., et al.: A tool for home-based rehabilitation allowing for clinical evaluation in a visual markerless scenario. In: 2015 37th Annual International Conference of the IEEE Engineering in Medicine and Biology Society (EMBC), pp. 8034–8037. IEEE (2015)
7. Capecci, M., et al.: The kimore dataset: kinematic assessment of movement and clinical scores for remote monitoring of physical rehabilitation. IEEE Trans. Neural Syst. Rehabil. Eng. **27**(7), 1436–1448 (2019)
8. Hu, Y., Liu, H., Pfeiffer, M., Delbruck, T.: DVS benchmark datasets for object tracking, action recognition, and object recognition. Front. Neurosci. **10**, 405 (2016). https://doi.org/10.3389/fnins.2016.00405, https://www.frontiersin.org/article/10.3389/fnins.2016.00405

9. Ionescu, C., Papava, D., Olaru, V., Sminchisescu, C.: Human3.6m: large scale datasets and predictive methods for 3D human sensing in natural environments. IEEE Trans. Pattern Anal. Mach. Intell. **36**(7), 1325–1339 (2014)
10. Lichtsteiner, P., Posch, C., Delbruck, T.: A 128×128 120 DB 15μ s latency asynchronous temporal contrast vision sensor. IEEE J. Solid-State Circuits **43**(2), 566–576 (2008)
11. Liciotti, D., Paolanti, M., Frontoni, E., Mancini, A., Zingaretti, P.: Person re-identification dataset with RGB-D camera in a top-view configuration. In: Nasrollahi, K., Distante, C., Hua, G., Cavallaro, A., Moeslund, T.B., Battiato, S., Ji, Q. (eds.) FFER/VAAM -2016. LNCS, vol. 10165, pp. 1–11. Springer, Cham (2017). https://doi.org/10.1007/978-3-319-56687-0_1
12. Liu, H., Moeys, D.P., Das, G., Neil, D., Liu, S., Delbrück, T.: Combined frame- and event-based detection and tracking. In: 2016 IEEE International Symposium on Circuits and Systems (ISCAS), pp. 2511–2514 (2016)
13. Lungu, I., Corradi, F., Delbrück, T.: Live demonstration: convolutional neural network driven by dynamic vision sensor playing roshambo. In: 2017 IEEE International Symposium on Circuits and Systems (ISCAS), p. 1 (2017)
14. Maqueda, A.I., Loquercio, A., Gallego, G., García, N., Scaramuzza, D.: Event-based vision meets deep learning on steering prediction for self-driving cars. CoRR abs/1804.01310 (2018), http://arxiv.org/abs/1804.01310
15. Mehta, D., Rhodin, H., Casas, D., Sotnychenko, O., Xu, W., Theobalt, C.: Monocular 3D human pose estimation using transfer learning and improved CNN supervision. CoRR abs/1611.09813 (2016), http://arxiv.org/abs/1611.09813
16. Moccia, S., Migliorelli, L., Carnielli, V., Frontoni, E.: Preterm infants' pose estimation with spatio-temporal features. IEEE Trans. Biomed. Eng. **67**(8), 2370–2380 (2019)
17. Newell, A., Yang, K., Deng, J.: Stacked hourglass networks for human pose estimation. In: Leibe, B., Matas, J., Sebe, N., Welling, M. (eds.) ECCV 2016. LNCS, vol. 9912, pp. 483–499. Springer, Cham (2016). https://doi.org/10.1007/978-3-319-46484-8_29
18. Paolanti, M., Romeo, L., Liciotti, D., Pietrini, R., Cenci, A., Frontoni, E., Zingaretti, P.: Person re-identification with RGB-D camera in top-view configuration through multiple nearest neighbor classifiers and neighborhood component features selection. Sensors **18**(10), 3471 (2018)
19. Paolanti, M., Romeo, L., Martini, M., Mancini, A., Frontoni, E., Zingaretti, P.: Robotic retail surveying by deep learning visual and textual data. Robot. Auton. Syst. **118**, 179–188 (2019)
20. Rhodin, H., Robertini, N., Casas, D., Richardt, C., Seidel, H., Theobalt, C.: General automatic human shape and motion capture using volumetric contour cues. CoRR abs/1607.08659 (2016), http://arxiv.org/abs/1607.08659
21. Sigal, L., Balan, A., Black, M.J.: HumanEva: synchronized video and motion capture dataset and baseline algorithm for evaluation of articulated human motion. Int. J. Comput. Vision **87**(1), 4–27 (2010)
22. Sun, K., Xiao, B., Liu, D., Wang, J.: Deep high-resolution representation learning for human pose estimation. In: Proceedings of the IEEE Conference on Computer Vision and Pattern Recognition, pp. 5693–5703 (2019)
23. Toshev, A., Szegedy, C.: Deeppose: human pose estimation via deep neural networks. In: Proceedings of the IEEE Conference on Computer Vision and Pattern Recognition, pp. 1653–1660 (2014)

Image-Based Out-of-Distribution-Detector Principles on Graph-Based Input Data in Human Action Recognition

Jens Bayer[1,2]($\boxtimes$) (ID), David Münch[1,2] (ID), and Michael Arens[1,2] (ID)

[1] Fraunhofer Center for Machine Learning, Karlsruhe, Germany
[2] Fraunhofer IOSB, Gutleuthausstraße 1, 76275 Ettlingen, Germany
jens.bayer@iosb.fraunhofer.de

Abstract. Living in a complex world like ours makes it unacceptable that a practical implementation of a machine learning system assumes a closed world. Therefore, it is necessary for such a learning-based system in a real world environment, to be aware of its own capabilities and limits and to be able to distinguish between confident and unconfident results of the inference, especially if the sample cannot be explained by the underlying distribution. This knowledge is particularly essential in safety-critical environments and tasks e.g. self-driving cars or medical applications. Towards this end, we transfer image-based Out-of-Distribution (OoD)-methods to graph-based data and show the applicability in action recognition.

The contribution of this work is (i) the examination of the portability of recent image-based OoD-detectors for graph-based input data, (ii) a Metric Learning-based approach to detect OoD-samples, and (iii) the introduction of a novel semi-synthetic action recognition dataset.

The evaluation shows that image-based OoD-methods can be applied to graph-based data. Additionally, there is a gap between the performance on intraclass and intradataset results. First methods as the examined baseline or ODIN provide reasonable results. More sophisticated network architectures – in contrast to their image-based application – were surpassed in the intradataset comparison and even lead to less classification accuracy.

Keywords: Human action recognition · OoD-detection · GCN

1 Introduction

Modern deep convolutional neural networks are able to recognize objects in images [30], segment areas pixel wise [15], and even generate realistic looking photos [24,36]. Despite their superb capabilities in those areas, they are not able to expose their own lack of knowledge. As some studies have found out, the confidence of a network in its output is as high for irrelevant or non-human understandable input data as for in-distribution input data [18,33,41]. As a

© Springer Nature Switzerland AG 2021
A. Del Bimbo et al. (Eds.): ICPR 2020 Workshops, LNCS 12661, pp. 26–40, 2021.
https://doi.org/10.1007/978-3-030-68763-2_3

result, there are numerous approaches [11,18,26,29,31] detecting so called out-of-distribution (OoD) data.

To the best of our knowledge there are no OoD-detection methods explicitly designed for use with graph-based data nor have the existing methods been investigated on graph-based data. This work investigates the applicability of OoD-detection methods on graph-based input data. To be more specific, graph-based action recognition is examined. Since human skeleton graphs can be easily generated from RGB images [6,35], depth data [34], and even RF-signals [46], the representation of the dynamics of human actions can be captured without the high computational cost of optical flow or problems regarding poor visual conditions. The contribution of this work is: (i) the examination of the portability of ODIN [29] and the confidence learning approach from [11], when using graph-structured input data in an action recognition task. As a baseline, the softmax output comparison proposed in [18] is used. Additionally, (ii) a Metric Learning-based approach detecting OoD-samples is developed. (iii) To ensure to have a controlled and repeatable evaluation environment, a novel semi-synthetic action recognition dataset is also introduced.

In the following section an overview of related work on both graph-based structured action recognition and OoD-detection is given. The baseline method and the examined methods are explained in Sect. 3. The semi-synthetic dataset and the quantitative evaluation are presented in Sect. 4.

2   Related Work

Both in action recognition and outlier detection there is a large number of related work. We focus on skeleton-based action recognition as well as deep neural network outlier detection approaches. However, additional information regarding action recognition can be found in the surveys [28,37,44]. A good overview on outlier detection is given by [3,21,47]. Recognizing actions based on image data is one way to solve action recognition tasks. Another strategy uses skeleton data which can be extracted by a 2D or 3D pose estimator such as Stacked Hourglass Networks [32], PersonLab [35], or OpenPose [6]. The extracted landmarks can be seen as human joints and form the nodes of a skeleton graph (Fig. 5). Based upon a time series of this graph input data, there are several ways on how to recognize an action.

On one hand, shallow methods [10,25,34] use handcrafted features of the skeleton graphs to analyze and classify a given time series of graph input data. On the other hand, deep learning models [12,39,40,45] are trained in an end-to-end manner.

For the detection of OoD-samples, there are numerous detection methods which [21] categorizes into statistical [1,9,16,22,27,38,42], machine learning [13, 14], and neural network [4,11,18,23,26,29,31] based methods.

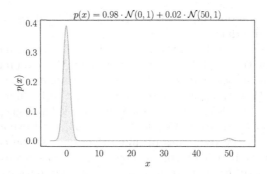

Fig. 1. A clear definition of OoD-data is mandatory. For example, values in the range $x = [47, 53]$ are explainable by the given distribution but significantly less common then values in the range $x = [-3, 3]$.

3   Out-of-Distribution Detectors

First, a clear definition of OoD-Samples is necessary. As shown in Fig. 1, the naïve definition of OoD-Samples, saying that they are not explainable by an underlying learned distribution, is somewhat difficult. Even if the values between 47 and 53 are explainable by the given distribution, the likelihood of having a sample in this range is negligibly small. Therefore, in-distribution samples must be *significantly* explainable by the learned distribution. Otherwise, they are out-of-distribution.

OoD-Samples can be categorized into three main types: novelties, anomalies and outliers. Novelties are samples, sharing some common space with the trained distribution, e.g. unseen classes. Anomalies are not related with the trained distribution [31]. Credit card fraud or system failures are prominent examples of anomalies of high interest [8]. Plain outliers are neither part of a new class nor part of an anomaly. They simply lie on or beyond the decision borders for their classes as a result of bad data or insufficient training.

The experimental setup of this work can be seen as novelty detection problem: A predetermined single class is excluded during the training and only present during the test phase. The predetermined class can be seen as the OoD-class and should be detected by the system.

3.1   Baseline

The most basic way of detecting an OoD-sample is presented in [18]. Given a pre-trained classifier which uses a softmax output layer, this method simply checks the maximum softmax output against a predefined threshold. If the maximum is greater than the threshold, the classification is continued. Otherwise, the input is labeled as out-of-distribution.

3.2   Out-of-DIstribution Detector for Neural Networks

Instead of using the default softmax output, ODIN [29] uses the tempered soft-max [20]

$$\sigma_T(x)_c = \frac{e^{(x_c/T)}}{\sum_{j \in \mathcal{C}} e^{(x_j/T)}}, \quad c \in \mathcal{C} \tag{1}$$

during the test phase. The higher the temperature parameter T, the more equally distributed is its output among all available classes $\mathcal{C}$ (see Fig. 2). As a result, a high temperature parameter during the test phase forces the network to be confident in its classification decision. Otherwise, the maximum softmax output is oppressed by the resulting almost equal distributed class probabilities.

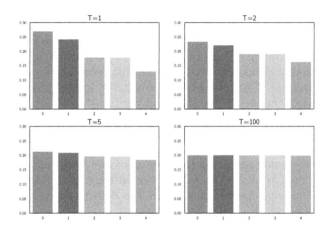

Fig. 2. Tempered softmax applied to the same input with different values for T. The higher the temperature parameter, the more equally distributed is the output.

3.3   Learning Confidence for OoD Detection

A more sophisticated method is presented in [11] and changes the underlying network architecture by adding a confidence branch. This branch enables the network to output a degree of confidence γ for a given input instead of just declaring an input sample as in- or out-of-distribution. As a result, the training procedure changes as follows: The classification output o is interpolated with the one-hot encoded ground truth y,

$$o' = \gamma \cdot o + (1 - \gamma) \cdot y \tag{2}$$

where the degree of interpolation is the confidence of the network for the given input. In order to prevent the network from always stating a low confidence and therefore get a low classification loss, a weighted confidence loss

$$L_\gamma = -\lambda \cdot log(\gamma) \tag{3}$$

is added to the classification loss. The weight λ of the confidence loss is defined by a budget parameter β and is adjusted whenever the weights are updated: If the confidence loss is greater than β, λ is increased and the system is punished more for low confidences. Otherwise, λ is decreased and the system is getting punished less as a result of having a high confidence.

3.4   Metric Learning-Based Approach

Metric learning encourages samples with the same class to be close in an embedding space while simultaneously ensuring a margin to samples with different classes. A dense and pure region in the embedding space can therefore be seen as a more safe and confident region in comparison to a sparse and mixed region. Our approach follows this idea and enables the network to approximate the density and pureness of regions in the embedding space. More precisely, the underlying network changes in the following way: A Metric Learning layer ($f(x)$ in Fig. 3) is inserted between the base network and the classification layer. Additionally, a branch for learning the confidence, by approximating either the *density* or *entropy* in the learned manifold is added. The Metric Learning Layer is trained with the contrastive loss [17]. Based on the resulting embeddings, the classification branch is trained with the cross-entropy loss. The loss function of the confidence branch depends on whether the density or entropy of the local neighborhood of a sample should be approximated.

The local neighborhood

$$n_{\mathcal{B}}(x) = \{y \mid d(f(x), f(y)) < m\}, \qquad x, y \in \mathcal{B}, \ m \in \mathbb{R}^+ \tag{4}$$

of a sample x in a batch $\mathcal{B}$ is given by all other samples in the batch where the (Euclidean) distance $d(.,.)$ to the corresponding embedding is lower than a predefined margin m.

Density Approximation. The density of the area around a given sample x

$$\rho_{\mathcal{B}}(x) = \frac{|n_{\mathcal{B}}(x)|}{|\mathcal{B}|} \tag{5}$$

is the number of elements in the local neighborhood, normalized by the batch size. Using the calculated density as the ground truth, the network learns to approximate the density but still lacks of the information about the pureness of the area. In an unclear decision region, the network should be able to give additional information, especially in terms of decision confidence. The entropy addresses this issue.

Entropy Approximation. The entropy (Eq. 6) and the Gini impurity (Eq. 7) are both common criteria for the splits in a decision tree. Both are used to measure the information gain or impurity for an optimal split and can be seen as a metric for the purity of the local neighborhood $n_\mathcal{B}(x)$.

$$H(Y) = -\sum_{c \in \mathcal{C}} p(c \mid Y) \cdot log(p(c \mid Y)) \tag{6}$$

$$G(Y) = 1 - \sum_{c \in \mathcal{C}} p(c \mid Y)^2 \tag{7}$$

where C is the set of all available classes and Y the given local neighborhood. The approach is similar to the density approximation but requires a few tweaks in the ground truth calculation. Since the entropy (Gini impurity) reaches its maximum (minimum) if all samples belong to the same class, a weighting term needs to take care of empty neighborhoods. This refers especially to neighborhoods consisting only of the processed sample itself. The weighting term

$$\omega_\mathcal{B}(x) = \frac{(|n_\mathcal{B}(x)| - 1) \cdot |\mathcal{B}|}{1 + \sum_{z \in \mathcal{B}} |n_\mathcal{B}(z)|} \tag{8}$$

for a sample x weights neighborhoods according to their size. After applying the weighting term, the resulting loss

$$L_H = \frac{1}{|\mathcal{B}|} \cdot \sum_{x \in \mathcal{B}} |\gamma - \omega_\mathcal{B}(x) \cdot H(n_\mathcal{B}(x))| \tag{9}$$

for the entropy approximation is the mean of the absolute differences between the calculated ground truth values for the batch $\mathcal{B}$ and the networks confidence output γ.

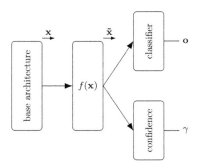

Fig. 3. Metric Learning-based approach to detect in- and out-of-distribution samples. The base network is extended by a Metric Learning layer ($f(x)$) as well as a confidence layer.

4   Evaluation

The following section first describes the pipeline and introduces the novel semi-synthetic dataset. Afterwards the evaluation metrics are explained. Finally, the results are presented in a quantitative way.

4.1   Pipeline

Figure 4 shows the basic pipeline of the system, which is basically the same as the one presented in [45] except for the OoD-detector. Given a video input, single frames are extracted and analyzed by a 2D pose estimator (e.g. OpenPose [6]). The resulting sequence of skeleton data is then propagated through a graph CNN (e.g. ST-GCN [45]) resulting in a regularized high-level representation of the input data. Based on this extracted high-level representation, the OoD-detectors are examined and the classification is done.

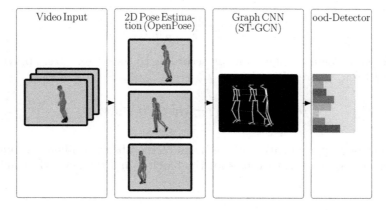

Fig. 4. Basic pipeline for all experiments. First, the video input is divided into single frames. Those frames are then analyzed by an 2D pose estimator (e.g. OpenPose). The resulting skeleton sequences are then propagated through a graph CNN (e.g. ST-GCN) and finally analyzed by an OoD-detector.

4.2   Semi-synthetic Dataset

To obtain reproducible results, we introduce a novel semi-synthetic dataset. The dataset provides a controllable environment and is based on skeleton data of the CMU Graphics Lab Motion Capture Database [7]. This skeleton data is used to animate a human 3D model [43]. The resulting sequences are rendered with Blender [5] from 144 different camera settings. This can be seen as data augmentation and enables a scale and viewpoint invariance of the network [2,19]. Each rendered RGB image has a resolution of 640×480px, depth data in the form of a

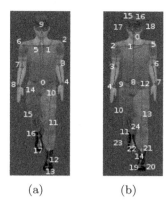

(a)   (b)

Fig. 5. Available skeleton data in the novel semi-synthetic dataset: 18 node ground truth data (a) and 25 node OpenPose generated data (b).

corresponding 640×480px 16bit-grayscale image (Fig. 6) and an 18 node ground truth skeleton (Fig. 5). In addition, the 25 node skeletons, which were generated by OpenPose, are also part of the dataset. Currently, there are 32 different classes of actions in 109 sequences.

To verify the results and be able to check on interdataset OoD-samples, the NTU-RGB+D [39] dataset is used additionally. It contains 60 action classes, presented in RGB videos with a resolution of 1920×1080px each, recorded from three different viewpoints. In addition, the dataset contains the depth data for each frame. Compared to the short basic actions of the novel synthetic dataset, the NTU-RGB+D dataset contains more complex actions in which several persons may be involved.

4.3   Metrics

There are four established metrics used for the comparison of the different approaches [11,18,29]. The first one is the false positive rate (FPR) when the true positive rate (TPR) is fixed at 0.95. The second one is the detection error at the same fixed true positive rate. The area under the receiver-operator characteristic (AUROC) and the area under the precision-recall curve (AUPR) are the last two.

FPR at 0.95 TPR. The FPR at 0.95 TPR measures the false positive rate when the true positive rate is fixed at 0.95.

Detection Error. The detection error

$$P_e = 1/2(1 - TPR + FPR) \tag{10}$$

(a)   (b)   (c)

Fig. 6. Example image of a sequence of the semi-synthetic dataset: The same image as (a) RGB image, (b) depth image and (c) RGB image with a modified background.

measures the misclassification probability when the true positive rate is fixed at 0.95. We assume, that the occurrence of a positive and a negative sample has the same probability in the test set.

AUROC. The receiver-operator characteristic compares the true positive rate of a classifier with the corresponding false positive rate. The area under the receiver-operator characteristic is a threshold independent metric, measuring the overall performance of a classifier.

AUPR. Another threshold independent metric is the area under the precision-recall curve. Unlike the AUROC, the AUPR is more sensitive to imbalanced datasets which is a desirable feature when examining OoD-detectors. Since the inlier and outliers can both be handled as positives in the AUPR calculation, a AUPR-IN and AUPR-OUT score is given respectively.

4.4   Experimental Setup

This work distinguishes between an intraclass and intradataset OoD-detection. For the intraclass case, only the semi-synthetic dataset is taken into account. For each of the 32 different classes and each detector, a network is trained. In each training, a single class represents the OoD-class and is excluded from the training whilst the other 31 classes are in-distribution classes and included in the training. For the intradataset case, the trained networks from the intraclass OoD-detection were investigated on how good they distinguish between the 31 semi-synthetic (inlier) classes and the NTU-RGB+D plus the selected semi-synthetic (outlier) classes.

The data is split according to a stratified cross-validation into a test- and training set in a ratio of 1:4. As data augmentation, the skeleton graphs are modified by the following pipeline: First, the sequence is randomly cropped to a sequence of 20 consecutive graphs. Then a Gaussian noise ($\mu = 0, \sigma = 0.005$) is added to the node values. After this, there is a 50% chance that nodes will be set to zero (dropout) and a 50% chance that a vertical and horizontal mirroring is applied. The noise as well as the application of dropout and the mirroring is fix for a whole sequence.

For the graph analysis, ST-GCN with the spatial configuration partitioning strategy and random initialization has been chosen [45]. Adam was used as optimizer with its default parameters except for the initial learning rate. Unless otherwise stated out, the networks are trained over 100 epochs with a batch size of 512 and an initial learning rate of 0.001 and shrinks all 30 epochs by a factor of 10.

The evaluation follows the procedure described in [18]. First the test set is separated into correctly and incorrectly classified examples. From the two resulting groups, the AUROC and AUPR scores are calculated. Afterwards, the confidence threshold is estimated in such a way, that the true positive rate of the correctly classified examples drops to 0.95. Based on this threshold, the FPR 95 and detection error is calculated. Since there are 32 different classes and therefore 32 trained networks for a given method, the results are averaged and the corresponding standard deviation is given.

Baseline and ODIN. The baseline method and ODIN do not require a modification of the existing network and can therefore be examined without retraining.

Learning Confidence. The batch size is set to 512 and the budget parameter is set to 0.3.

Metric Learning. The training of the Metric Learning approach is divided into three parts. First the Metric Learning layer is trained. Based on the embedding, the classifier and OoD-detector are trained, while the weights of the Metric Learning layer are being held fixed. The Metric Learning layer is trained over 200 epochs. The learning rate shrinks every 80 epochs by a factor of 10. The layer maps the input onto a 256 dimension output. The classification layer and the confidence layer are then both separately trained over 50 epochs with an initial learning rate of 0.0001 and a reduction every 20 epochs by a factor 10.

4.5   Results

In the following, the results are presented in quantitative terms. Since the baseline and ODIN can be used without any modifications of the architecture, they are additionally evaluated on the learning confidence and metric learning networks. The temperature parameter is displayed logarithmically on the x-axis. The plotted curves are the mean values with the standard deviations for each of the 32 trained networks. To give a hint where the value 0.95 resides, each of the plots contain a dotted red line. Tables 1 and 2 provide results of the intraclass and intradataset evaluation. For both tables, the up/down arrows indicate if a higher or lower value is desired.

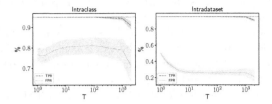

Fig. 7. Baseline and ODIN Results: TPR and FPR for different temperature parameters. At $T = 100$, the TPR is no longer fixed at 0.95, which leads to a better FPR but also allows more errors.

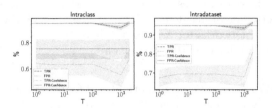

Fig. 8. Learning Confidence Results: It is noticeable, that the FPR as well as the TPR increase for $T = 2000$, which is a strange behavior compared to the other plots.

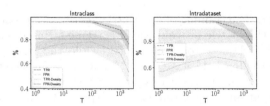

Fig. 9. Metric Learning Results: Density approximation. The intraclass and intradataset FPR values for the density approach differ primarily in the standard deviation.

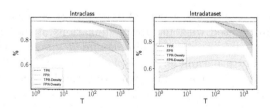

Fig. 10. Metric Learning Results: Entropy approximation. As the density approximation, the FPR values of the entropy approach differ primarily in the standard deviation.

Baseline and ODIN. The results for the baseline as well as ODIN are shown in Fig. 7. The parameter $T = 1$ equals the baseline. In the intraclass OoD-detection, the FPR reaches its minimum at a temperature parameter of $T = 1.6$. For temperature parameter values above 100, the required TPR of 0.95 cannot be guaranteed and are therefore not taken into account. Compared to the results in [29], the curve has an unusual course for a rising temperature parameter in the intraclass case. Instead of a lower FPR with a rising temperature parameter, the FPR raises after $T = 1.6$. The curve of the intradataset, on the other hand, shows a similar course as the results in [29].

Learning Confidence. Figure 8 shows the results of the confidence learning approach. The intradataset ODIN curve vary heavily from the ones, depicted in Fig. 7. It should also be noted, that for the intradataset case the method performs significantly worse than ODIN, even if ODIN operates on the modified network architecture. Another remarkable problem is, that the average accuracy in Table 1 has dropped from 0.74 ± 0.03 (base architecture) down to 0.62 ± 0.09 (learning confidence).

Metric Learning. Our proposed density and entropy approximating Metric Learning approaches were investigated and result in almost identical plots (Figs. 9, 10). The ODIN FPR curves of the metric learning results in the intraclass case have some similarities with the intraclass curve of the base architecture: The lowest FPR is reached at $T = 1$ and raises until The TPR curve drops at $T = 100$. In comparison to the learning confidence approach and in terms of the intraclass case, both Metric Learning approaches perform worse than the learning confidence or ODIN. In terms of the intradataset case, they perform better than the learning confidence approach but also have a higher variance. The average accuracies of the density and entropy classifiers are 0.648 ± 0.12 and 0.647 ± 0.12 and outperform the learning confidence ones (0.62 ± 0.09).

The experiments showed that the OoD-detector method ODIN outperforms the more sophisticated confidence learning and the metric learning based methods. For the intraclass case, ODIN and the learning confidence approach are comparable, but ODIN has a significant higher accuracy. For the intradataset case, ODIN outperforms all other methods by far. The superiority of ODIN is of particular interest as the confidence learning method outperforms ODIN in the original paper in nearly every case. Our presented metric learning based methods beat the confidence learning method only in the intradataset case.

Table 1. Intraclass comparison: Training and test use the same dataset. A single class is excluded from the training and serves as OoD-class in the test phase.

Method	FPR 95 ↓	AUROC ↑	AUPR-IN ↑	AUPR-OUT ↑	ERR ↓	ACC ↑
Baseline	0.77 ± 0.10	0.77 ± 0.10	0.94 ± 0.08	0.30 ± 0.21	0.41 ± 0.05	0.74 ± 0.03
ODIN	0.76 ± 0.10	**0.77 ± 0.10**	**0.94 ± 0.07**	0.30 ± 0.21	0.41 ± 0.05	**0.74 ± 0.03**
Confidence	**0.76 ± 0.22**	0.76 ± 0.15	0.94 ± 0.08	**0.35 ± 0.27**	**0.40 ± 0.11**	0.62 ± 0.09
Density	0.81 ± 0.23	0.65 ± 0.23	0.89 ± 0.15	0.29 ± 0.27	0.43 ± 0.12	0.65 ± 0.12
Gini	0.80 ± 0.25	0.67 ± 0.23	0.89 ± 0.13	0.29 ± 0.27	0.43 ± 0.13	0.65 ± 0.12

Table 2. Intradataset comparison: Training on the semi-synthetic dataset, test on the NTU-RGB+D dataset.

Method	FPR 95↓	AUROC ↑	AUPR-IN ↑	AUPR-OUT ↑	ERR ↓	ACC ↑
Baseline	0.50 ± 0.06	0.88 ± 0.02	0.74 ± 0.05	0.95 ± 0.01	0.27 ± 0.03	0.74 ± 0.03
ODIN	**0.26 ± 0.07**	**0.94 ± 0.02**	**0.85 ± 0.08**	**0.98 ± 0.00**	**0.15 ± 0.04**	**0.74 ± 0.03**
Confidence	0.91 ± 0.08	0.53 ± 0.04	0.16 ± 0.03	0.88 ± 0.03	0.48 ± 0.04	0.62 ± 0.09
Density	0.84 ± 0.16	0.49 ± 0.18	0.25 ± 0.16	0.82 ± 0.10	0.45 ± 0.08	0.65 ± 0.12
Gini	0.83 ± 0.18	0.52 ± 0.18	0.26 ± 0.17	0.84 ± 0.10	0.44 ± 0.09	0.65 ± 0.12

5   Conclusion

The evaluation shows that OoD-methods can successfully be applied to graph-based data. Their behavior is however different as on image-based data. In conclusion, we have shown with our novel semi-synthetic dataset, that applying ODIN on graph-based data is currently the best OoD-method.

Our presented metric learning based method is able to embed high-level features into a manifold and learns to approximate the density or entropy of an embedded sample. To further increase the OoD-detection performance, it is crucial to find a good embedding for in-distribution data and a training strategy, that prepares the network for possible the out-of-distribution data.

Acknowledgements. This work was developed in Fraunhofer Cluster of Excellence "Cognitive Internet Technologies".

Portions of the research in this paper used the NTU-RGB+D Action Recognition Dataset made available by the ROSE Lab at the Nanyang Technological University, Singapore.

References

1. Allan, J., Carbonell, J., Doddington, G., Yamron, J., Yang, Y.: Topic Detection and Tracking Pilot Study. Topic Detection and Tracking Workshop Report (2001)
2. Bayer, J., Münch, D., Arens, M.: Viewpoint Independency for Skeleton Based Human Action Recognition. Tech. rep, Fraunhofer IOSB, Ettlingen (2020)
3. Bhosale, S.V.: Holy Grail of Outlier Detection Technique: A Macro Level Take on the State of the Art. IJCSIT (2014)
4. Bishop, C.M.: Novelty detection and neural network validation. IEE Proc. Vision Image Signal Process. **141**(4), 217–222 (1994)

5. Blender Online Community: Blender - a 3D modelling and rendering package (2019)
6. Cao, Z., Simon, T., Wei, S.E., Sheikh, Y.: Realtime multi-person 2D pose estimation using part affinity fields. In: CVPR 2017-Janua, pp. 1302–1310 (2017)
7. Carnegie Mellon Graphics Lab: CMU Graphics Lab Motion Capture Database
8. Chandola, V., Banerjee, A., Kumar, V.: Anomaly detection. ACM Comput. Surv. **41**(3), 1–58 (2009)
9. Dasgupta, D., Forrest, S.: Novelty detection in time series data using ideas from immunology. In: The 8th International Conference on Intelligent Systems, pp. 82–87 (1999)
10. Devanne, M., Wannous, H., Berretti, S., Pala, P., Daoudi, M., Del Bimbo, A.: 3-D human action recognition by shape analysis of motion trajectories on riemannian manifold. IEEE Trans. Cybern. **45**(7), 1340–1352 (2015)
11. DeVries, T., Taylor, G.W.: Learning confidence for out-of-distribution detection in neural networks. arXiv preprint arXiv:1802.04865 (2018)
12. Du, Y., Wang, W., Wang, L.: Hierarchical recurrent neural network for skeleton based action recognition. In: CVPR (2015)
13. Ester, M., Kriegel, H.P., Sander, J., Xu, X.: Others: a density-based algorithm for discovering clusters in large spatial databases with noise. KDD **96**, 226–231 (1996)
14. John, G.H.: Robust decision trees: removing outliers from databases. In: KDD, pp. 174–179 (1995)
15. Garcia-Garcia, A., Orts-Escolano, S., Oprea, S., Villena-Martinez, V., Martinez-Gonzalez, P., Garcia-Rodriguez, J.: A survey on deep learning techniques for image and video semantic segmentation. Appl. Soft Comput. J. **70**, 41–65 (2018)
16. Grubbs, F.E.: Procedures for detecting outlying observations in samples. Technometrics **11**(1), 1–21 (1969)
17. Hadsell, R., Chopra, S., LeCun, Y.: Dimensionality reduction by learning an invariant mapping. In: CVPR, vol. 2, pp. 1735–1742. IEEE (2006)
18. Hendrycks, D., Gimpel, K.: A baseline for detecting misclassified and out-of-distribution examples in neural networks. In: ICLR (2017)
19. Hilsenbeck, B., Münch, D., Kieritz, H., Hübner, W., Arens, M.: Hierarchical hough forests for view-independent action recognition. In: 2016 23rd International Conference on Pattern Recognition (ICPR), pp. 1911–1916 (2016)
20. Hinton, G., Vinyals, O., Dean, J.: Distilling the Knowledge in a Neural Network. arXiv preprint arXiv:1503.02531 (2015)
21. Hodge, V.J., Austin, J.: A survey of outlier detection methodologies. Artif. Intell. Rev. **22**(2), 85–126 (2004)
22. Laurikkala, J., Juhola, M., Kentala, E.: Informal identification of outliers in medical data. In: IDAMAP, vol. 1, pp. 20–24 (2000)
23. Japkowicz, N., Myers, C., Gluck, M.: A novelty detection approach to classification. In: IJCAI, pp. 518–523, Montreal (1995)
24. Karras, T., Laine, S., Aila, T.: A style-based generator architecture for generative adversarial networks. In: CVPR (2019)
25. Kerola, T., Inoue, N., Shinoda, K.: Spectral graph skeletons for 3D action recognition. In: Cremers, D., Reid, I., Saito, H., Yang, M.-H. (eds.) ACCV 2014. LNCS, vol. 9006, pp. 417–432. Springer, Cham (2015). https://doi.org/10.1007/978-3-319-16817-3_27
26. Kliger, M., Fleishman, S.: Novelty Detection with GAN. arXiv preprint arXiv:1802.10560 (2018)
27. Knox, E.M., Ng, R.T.: Algorithms for mining distance based outliers in large datasets. In: VLDB, pp. 392–403. Citeseer (1998)

28. Kong, Y., Fu, Y.: Human action recognition and prediction: a survey. arXiv preprint arXiv:1806.11230 (2018)
29. Liang, S., Li, Y., Srikant, R.: Enhancing the reliability of out-of-distribution image detection in neural networks. In: ICLR (2018)
30. Liu, L., Ouyang, W., Wang, X., Fieguth, P., Chen, J., Liu, X., Pietikäinen, M.: Deep learning for generic object detection: a survey. Int. J. Comput. Vision **128**(2), 261–318 (2019). https://doi.org/10.1007/s11263-019-01247-4
31. Masana, M., Ruiz, I., Serrat, J., van de Weijer, J., Lopez, A.M.: Metric learning for novelty and anomaly detection. In: BMVC (2018)
32. Newell, A., Yang, K., Deng, J.: Stacked hourglass networks for human pose estimation. In: Leibe, B., Matas, J., Sebe, N., Welling, M. (eds.) ECCV 2016. LNCS, vol. 9912, pp. 483–499. Springer, Cham (2016). https://doi.org/10.1007/978-3-319-46484-8_29
33. Nguyen, A., Yosinski, J., Clune, J.: Deep neural networks are easily fooled: High confidence predictions for unrecognizable images. In: CVPR, pp. 427–436 (2015)
34. Papadopoulos, G.T., Axenopoulos, A., Daras, P.: Real-time skeleton-tracking-based human action recognition using kinect data. In: Gurrin, C., Hopfgartner, F., Hurst, W., Johansen, H., Lee, H., O'Connor, N. (eds.) MMM 2014. LNCS, vol. 8325, pp. 473–483. Springer, Cham (2014). https://doi.org/10.1007/978-3-319-04114-8_40
35. Papandreou, G., Zhu, T., Chen, L.-C., Gidaris, S., Tompson, J., Murphy, K.: PersonLab: person pose estimation and instance segmentation with a bottom-up, part-based, geometric embedding model. In: Ferrari, V., Hebert, M., Sminchisescu, C., Weiss, Y. (eds.) Computer Vision – ECCV 2018. LNCS, vol. 11218, pp. 282–299. Springer, Cham (2018). https://doi.org/10.1007/978-3-030-01264-9_17
36. Pidhorskyi, S., Adjeroh, D.A., Doretto, G.: Adversarial latent autoencoders. In: CVPR (2020)
37. Poppe, R.: A survey on vision-based human action recognition. Image Vis. Comput. **28**(6), 976–990 (2010)
38. Seheult, A.H., Green, P.J., Rousseeuw, P.J., Leroy, A.M.: Robust regression and outlier detection. J. Royal Stat. Soc. Ser. A (Stat. Soc.) **152**(1), 133 (1989)
39. Shahroudy, A., Liu, J., Ng, T.T., Wang, G.: Ntu rgb+d: a large scale dataset for 3d human activity analysis. In: CVPR (2016)
40. Si, C., Jing, Y., Wang, W., Wang, L., Tan, T.: Skeleton-based action recognition with spatial reasoning and temporal stack learning. In: Ferrari, V., Hebert, M., Sminchisescu, C., Weiss, Y. (eds.) ECCV 2018. LNCS, vol. 11205, pp. 106–121. Springer, Cham (2018). https://doi.org/10.1007/978-3-030-01246-5_7
41. Szegedy, C., et al.: Intriguing properties of neural networks. In: ICLR (2014)
42. Tax, D., Ypma, A., Duin, R.: Support vector data description applied to machine vibration analysis. In: Proceedings of 5th Annual Conference of the Advanced School for Computing and Imaging, pp. 15–23 (1999)
43. The MakeHuman team: MakeHuman. www.makehumancommunity.org. Accessed 15 Nov 2020
44. Turaga, P., Chellappa, R., Subrahmanian, V.S., Udrea, O.: Machine recognition of human activities: A survey. TCSVT **18**(11), 1473–1488 (2008)
45. Yan, S., Xiong, Y., Lin, D.: Spatial temporal graph convolutional networks for skeleton-based action recognition. In: AAAI, pp. 7444–7452 (2018)
46. Zhao, M., et al.: Through-wall human pose estimation using radio signals. In: CVPR (2018)
47. Zimek, A., Filzmoser, P.: There and back again: outlier detection between statistical reasoning and data mining algorithms (2018)

A Novel Joint Points and Silhouette-Based Method to Estimate 3D Human Pose and Shape

Zhongguo Li[✉], Anders Heyden, and Magnus Oskarsson

Lund University, Lund, Sweden
{zhongguo.li,anders.heyden,magnus.oskarsson}@math.lth.se

Abstract. This paper presents a novel method for 3D human pose and shape estimation from images with sparse views, using joint points and silhouettes, based on a parametric model. Firstly, the parametric model is fitted to the joint points estimated by deep learning-based human pose estimation. Then, we extract the correspondence between the parametric model of pose fitting and silhouettes in 2D and 3D space. A novel energy function based on the correspondence is built and minimized to fit a parametric model to the silhouettes. Our approach uses comprehensive shape information because the energy function of silhouettes is built from both 2D and 3D space. This also means that our method only needs images from sparse views, which balances data used and the required prior information. Results on synthetic data and real data demonstrate the competitive performance of our approach on pose and shape estimation of the human body.

Keywords: 3D human body · Joint points · Silhouettes · SMPL · Pose estimation · Shape estimation

1 Introduction

Estimation of 3D human body models from images is an important but challenging task in computer vision. In many practical fields, for instance, video games, VR/AR, E-commerce and biomedical research, 3D human body models are needed and play vital roles. However, the human body in real scenes naturally exhibits many challenging properties, such as non-rigid motion, clothes and occlusion. These factors make it difficult to accurately and efficiently estimate the 3D human body model from images, and many approaches have been proposed to obtain 3D human body models during the past decades.

Time-of-flight cameras, and other types of hardware solutions, can provide depth information and have been one of the solutions to the reconstruction of 3D human bodies [11,18,23,27,31]. More specifically, depth cameras are utilized to capture RGB images and the corresponding depth images of the scenes. The 3D meshes of each view can be computed from the RGB-D images and the complete

© Springer Nature Switzerland AG 2021
A. Del Bimbo et al. (Eds.): ICPR 2020 Workshops, LNCS 12661, pp. 41–56, 2021.
https://doi.org/10.1007/978-3-030-68763-2_4

3D model can be estimated by fusing the 3D meshes of each view. The process of fusion is often implemented using the Iterated Closest Point (ICP) algorithm [11] or other similar improved algorithms, which often are computation-consuming. Since these methods only can handle rigid scenes well, research on dynamic scenes has been explored [18, 23, 27, 31]. However, compared to ordinary cameras, the cameras with depth sensors are still expensive and calibration of the depth camera can also be complicated.

With the development of deep learning architectures, 3D human body models can be estimated by optimization- [1, 5] or regression-based methods [12, 13]. For methods based on optimization, prior information, for example, human poses and silhouettes can be estimated by deep neural networks. The 3D model can then be obtained by fitting the parametric human body model to the prior information. The regression-based methods use deep neural networks to directly estimate the parameters of the given parametric human body model from images, by training the deep neural networks [12, 13, 24]. Both approaches have been explored extensively and have achieved good performance in 3D human body reconstruction. However, regression-based methods require a large amount of data to train the neural network. This often requires much work and it is difficult, and sometimes expensive, to generate the dataset. Compared to regression-based methods, the human pose estimation and semantic segmentation based on deep neural networks have been well developed and many pre-trained models can be utilized directly. This means that prior information in optimization-based methods can be more easily estimated through deep neural networks. For these reasons, our choice of method, proposed in this paper, is also optimization-based.

In this paper, the goal is to estimate the 3D human body from images. Since this is a very complex problem and one single image can only provide limited prior information, a number of images taken from different view-points are used in our paper. The human pose estimation based on deep neural network [3] is adopted to estimate the joint points of the human body in the multiple-view images. The Skinned multi-person linear model (SMPL) [16], which is widely used in the methods based on optimization, is the parametric human body model also used in our paper. Then, an energy function is established based on the predicted joint points and the SMPL. By minimizing the energy function, we can achieve an estimated 3D human body model which has a pose consisted with the observed images. Afterwards, the silhouettes are exploited to improve the shape of the estimated human body model. Through building the correspondence edges between the estimated human body model and the given silhouettes from 2D and 3D space, the energy function for the silhouettes is constructed. The shape parameters of the human body model are obtained by optimizing the energy function. The final 3D human body model is generated by the estimated pose and shape parameters after pose fitting and shape fitting. The experiments on synthetic data and a public real dataset validate the performance of our method.

In summary, the contribution of our method consists of two parts. Firstly, an improved energy function for silhouettes is constructed from 2D and 3D perspectives to estimate the parameters of shape. Secondly, a small number of images (four in our experiments) from different views are applied in our method, which balances the number of images and the prior information.

2   Related Work

In order to obtain 3D human body models from images, researchers have explored a large number of methods from hardware and software during the past decades. These work can be basically categorized according to whether a parametric human body model is adopted in the methods. For the approaches which do not depend on any parametric human body model, the 3D reconstruction of the human body is mainly implemented from RGB-D images captured by depth cameras. In contrast to the above methods, the approaches based on a parametric human body model often attempt to estimate the pose and shape from common RGB images. We call the two categories *parametric model-free* and *parametric model based* methods, respectively.

Parametric model-free methods often reconstruct 3D human body models from RGB-D images, which means that these methods often require depth cameras. KinectFusion [11] was the typical work which used a Kinect depth camera to reconstruct the 3D meshes of an indoor scene with static objects. However, KinectFusion was mainly aiming at reconstructing rigid objects rather than dynamic scene like a moving human body. In order to tackle non-rigid reconstruction, DynamicFusion [18], VolumeDeform [10], KillingFusion [23] were proposed over the next several years. These methods can handle reconstruction of non-rigid and moving objects, but they typically only obtain good performance for partial body or small slow moving objects. Yu et al. proposed BodyFusion [30] and DoubleFusion [31] to reconstruct the whole 3D human body model for moving persons with high accuracy. One common thing in all of the above work is that they utilize one single Kinect to recover the 3D human body model. In order to improve the accuracy more, some methods based on multiple Kinects [6,29] were proposed to reconstruct 3D geometry, which was more complicated to set than single a Kinect. In addition, commercial depth [27] cameras have also been used as a tool to reconstruct 3D models. The core idea of the parametric-model free methods is that they utilized depth cameras to capture RGB-D images and fused the meshes of each view to obtain the final 3D model. Although the work has achieved good performance for 3D reconstruction of human body, cameras with depth sensor are still inconvenient in many applications.

Parametric model based methods often tackle the problem through fitting a parametric human body model to prior information of the given images. The parametric human body model is often trained by a dataset and is defined as a function of variables which can represent prior information like pose and shape. The parametric models such as SCAPE [2] and SMPL [16] have been used in many methods. Recently, an improved model called SMPL-X was proposed by considering the motion of face and hands [19]. With the development of deep learning, some methods exploited deep neural networks to regress the parameters of the parametric model, hence we call them regression based methods. In [12], the pose and shape parameters of the SMPL model were estimated by training a deep encoder network. In [24], the loss function of mesh was added to further finetune the mesh of the 3D model. In [20], the pose and shape parameters were separately trained in two pipelines to make the result better. Nikos et al. [13] used the output of deep neural network to initialize the SMPL model and then supervise the training process of deep neural networks through the SMPL model. In [21], texture was utilized to capitalize on the appearance constancy of images from different viewpoints. Although these methods have achieved competitive results, collecting datasets for training is still cumbersome work and training the network is also time-consuming. Another way to solve the problem is to fit the parametric human body model to prior information through optimizing an error function (optimization based methods). Early work [22] used SCAPE to estimate the articulated pose and non-rigid shape. In [8], silhouettes and joint points were manually obtained and the SCAPE model was fitted to the priori clues to estimate the parameters of SCAPE. In [4,26], RGB-D images were utilized to estimate the parameters of SCAPE model. Xu et al. [28] scanned a template as the parametric model and used it to fit the prior information through optimizing an energy function. Bogo et al. [5] proposed a method called SMPLify in which the joint points were predicted by human pose estimation based on a deep neural network, and then SMPL was fitted to the estimated joint points. Moreover, silhouettes [1] and multiple images with different views [9,15] were introduced as prior information for the SMPL model. Overall, optimization based methods are often easier to implement, since it is unnecessary to create datasets and to do training.

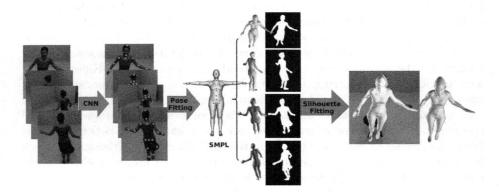

Fig. 1. The overview of our method.

3   Method

In this section we present a method to obtain a 3D human body model from a small number of images taken from different view-points based on the SMPL model, using the joint points and silhouettes as input. The overview of the proposed method is shown in Fig. 1.

3.1   Parametric Human Body Model

The parametric human body model in our method is called SMPL, and it is learned from an aligned human body dataset [16]. SMPL is defined as a function of pose $\theta \in \mathbb{R}^{3 \times 24}$ and shape $\beta \in \mathbb{R}^{1 \times 10}$ of the human body. The output of the function is a mesh with $V = 6890$ vertices and $F = 13776$ faces. This means that we can generate different 3D human bodies as long as we can get proper parameters of θ and β. There are 24 joint points in SMPL and each of them is represented as the rotation vector in terms of the root point, i.e., the i-th joint point is represented as $\theta_i \in \mathbb{R}^3$. The shape parameters β are the first 10 coefficients of the principle components of the training dataset.

3.2   Pose Fitting

In the following, we explain the pose fitting in our method between SMPL and estimated joint points. For given multiple-view RGB images, the joint points are predicted by a CNN-based human pose estimation method [3]. In order to ensure the accuracy of human pose estimation, we firstly use Cornernet [14] to detect the bounding box of the person, and then use the image with bounding box into [3] to predict the joint points. Note that the order of the output of [3] is different from the order of joints of SMPL. For given N images from different views, the joint points are defined as $J_{2d}^{(i)}, i = 0, ..., N-1$. For the SMPL model, the joint points J_S are in 3D space and J_S is a function of pose θ and shape β. Suppose that the camera transformation matrix is $\Pi_i = (R_i, t_i)$ for the i-th camera. The projected 2D joint points of the SMPL model on the image plane can be represented as $\Pi_i(J_S(\theta, \beta))$. Therefore, the energy function to fit the SMPL model using joint points is defined as

$$E(\theta, \beta, \boldsymbol{R}, \boldsymbol{t}) = E_{jt}(\theta, \beta, R, t) + \omega_\theta E_\theta(\theta) + \omega_\beta E_\beta(\beta), \tag{1}$$

where E_{jt} is the joint points term and $E_\theta(\theta), E_\beta(\beta)$ are the regularization term for θ, β. ω_θ and ω_β are the weights of the regularization terms. $\boldsymbol{R}$ is $\{R_1, R_2, R_3\}$ and $\boldsymbol{t}$ is $\{t_1, t_2, t_3\}$. The joint points term E_{jt} measures the difference between all of the joint points $J_{2d}^{(i)}$ and $\Pi_i(J_S(\theta, \beta))$

$$E_{jt}(\theta, \beta, \boldsymbol{R}, \boldsymbol{t}) = \sum_{i=0}^{N-1} \rho \left(J_{2d}^{(i)} - \Pi_i(J_S(\theta, \beta)) \right), \tag{2}$$

where ρ is the Geman-McClure function [7] and is defined as $\rho(x) = x^2/(\sigma^2 + x^2)$. Here σ is a constant and it is set as 100. Geman-McClure function can better deal with large noise and outliers. The regularization term for θ is defined as

$$E_\theta(\theta) = \alpha \sum_{i=55,58,15,12} exp(\theta_i), \tag{3}$$

where α is a constant which is set as 10 and the $55th$, $58th$, $15th$, and $12th$ elements in $\boldsymbol{\theta}$ are the joint points on the left and right elbows and knees. This can avoid the arms and legs to exhibit strange bending. The regularization term of β is defined as

$$E_\beta(\boldsymbol{\beta}) = \sum_{i=0}^{9} \beta_i. \tag{4}$$

The advantage of our method is that the camera parameters are also regarded as variables. After the optimization, the rotation and translation of the cameras will also be estimated. Therefore, through the minimization of the energy function, the pose, shape parameters of the SMPL model and the camera parameters can be obtained.

3.3   Shape Fitting

The following section will describe the progress of shape fitting in our method. Since joint points mainly provide information about human pose in the first step, the silhouettes are used in this part to improve the estimation of shape. Here we assume that the silhouettes have been given. Now let us revisit the SMPL model concerning the vertex position. As shown in [16], the vertex of SMPL is transformed as

$$\boldsymbol{t}_i = \sum_{k=1}^{K} \omega_{k,i} G'_k(\boldsymbol{\theta}, J(\boldsymbol{\beta})) \left(\bar{\boldsymbol{t}} + B_S(\boldsymbol{\beta}) + B_P(\boldsymbol{\theta}) \right). \tag{5}$$

In addition, since the rotation R and translation t of the camera are estimated after pose fitting, the positions of the cameras can be computed as $c = -R^T t$. Thus, we can define a ray from the camera c to the vertex $\boldsymbol{t}_i$ of the transformed SMPL model as $\boldsymbol{r}$, as shown in Fig. 2. Then, for the untransformed SMPL model, the corresponding ray is

$$\boldsymbol{r}' = \left[\sum_{k=1}^{K} \omega_{k,i} G'_k(\boldsymbol{\theta}, J(\boldsymbol{\beta})) \right]^{-1} \boldsymbol{r} - B_P(\boldsymbol{\theta}). \tag{6}$$

We would like to find the correspondence between $\boldsymbol{r}'$ and the boundary points of the observed silhouette. This ray can be decomposed using Plucker coordinates $(\boldsymbol{r}'_m, \boldsymbol{r}'_n)$. Given the silhouette of the image, we can find the boundary points $\boldsymbol{v}$ of the silhouette and then backproject $\boldsymbol{v}$ to $\boldsymbol{V}$ in the camera coordinates since we have estimated the camera parameters. Then, the distance from the points to the ray can be computed

Fig. 2. An example of correspondence between silhouette and SMPL model in 2D and 3D space. The left is the 3D correspondence and the right is the 2D correspondance between SMPL and silhouettes. The red points are SMPL vertices and the blue points are the corresponding points on silhouettes. (Color figure online)

as $d = \boldsymbol{V} \times \boldsymbol{r}'_n - \boldsymbol{r}'_m$. Those points and rays whose distance is smaller then a threshold are regarded as corresponding pairs. These pairs are defined as a set

P which is the correspondence in 3D space. On the other hand, the vertices of SMPL model intersected by ray r' can be projected to the image plan as v' using the camera parameters. The point set v and v' are defined as Q, which is the correspondence in 2D space. Figure 2 shows one example of the correspondence on the SMPL vertices and the silhouettes in 2D and 3D space. We can see that the correspondence in this case seems to be correct and can provide additional information for the shape fitting. Overall, the energy function using silhouettes is defined as

$$E(\boldsymbol{\beta}) = E_{silh}(\boldsymbol{\beta}) + E_{reg}(\boldsymbol{\beta}). \tag{7}$$

The silhouette term $E_{silh}(\boldsymbol{\beta})$ is constructed by using the set P and Q and is defined as

$$E_{silh}(\boldsymbol{\beta}) = \sum_{(\boldsymbol{V},r) \in P} \rho(\boldsymbol{V} \times \boldsymbol{r}'_n - \boldsymbol{r}'_m) + \sum_{(v,v') \in Q} \rho(\boldsymbol{v} - \boldsymbol{v}'), \tag{8}$$

where $\boldsymbol{V} \times \boldsymbol{r}'_n$ is the cross product of $\boldsymbol{V}$ and $\boldsymbol{r}'_n$, ρ is the Geman-McClure function as (2). The first part of E_{silh} measures the difference of 3D points of backprojected silhouette boundary and rays, while the second part shows the difference of 2D silhouette points and projected SMPL vertices. Therefore, the silhouette term considers the silhouette information from both 3D and 2D perspective in contrast to the paper [1].

The regularization term is defined based on the SMPL model with zero pose, i.e., $\boldsymbol{\theta} = \boldsymbol{0}$. This is because this part only focuses on the shape estimation. Then, the SMPL model is computed as $t(\beta, D) = \bar{t} + B_S\beta + D$, where D is the offset given by the SMPL model. The regularization term contains the Laplacian term E_L as well as the body model term E_B and it is represented as in [1]

$$E_{reg}(\boldsymbol{\beta}) = \omega_L E_L + \omega_B E_B, \tag{9}$$

where ω_L and ω_B are the weights. The Laplacian term E_L is defined as

$$E_L = \sum_{i=1}^{N} ||L(\boldsymbol{t}_i) - \delta_i||^2, \tag{10}$$

where L is the Laplace operator and $\delta_i = L(\boldsymbol{t}_i(\boldsymbol{\beta}, 0))$. This term enforces smooth deformation. The body model term E_B is represented as

$$E_B = \sum_{i=1}^{N} ||\boldsymbol{t}_i(\boldsymbol{\beta}, D) - \boldsymbol{t}_i(\boldsymbol{\beta}, 0)||^2. \tag{11}$$

Through minimizing (7), the shape parameters can be estimated and the final results are obtained.

3.4   Optimization

After building the energy functions based on joint points and silhouettes, we need to optimize the energy functions. We have used Python to implement our optimization method. The energy functions in (1) and (7) are minimized by Powell's dogleg method which is provided in the Python modules called OpenDR [17] and Chumpy. For four images with different views, it takes about 2 min to obtain the final estimation of the 3D human body.

Table 1. The values of parameters for the optimization.

	Synthtic dataset						Real dataset					
	Pose fitting			Shape fitting			Pose fitting			Shape fitting		
k	ω_θ	ω_β	σ	ω_L	ω_B	σ	ω_θ	ω_β	σ	ω_L	ω_B	σ
1	91.0	100	100	6.5	0.9	0.05	91.0	100	100	6.5	0.9	0.08
2	91.0	50	100	5.25	0.75	0.03	91.0	50	100	5.25	0.75	0.04
3	47.4	10	100	4	0.6	0.01	47.4	10	100	4	0.6	0.03
4	4.78	5	100				4.78	5	100			

The parameters used during the optimization are shown in Table 1. In the following experiments, we mainly used a synthetic dataset and a real dataset to evaluate our approach. Table 1 gives the parameters that we used in the experiments for the two datasets. For pose fitting, we assume that the focal length of the camera is known, but the translation and rotation of the camera are unknown. We initialize the rotation matrix as the identity matrix. The translation vector is initialized according to the torso length of SMPL model and the torso length of human body in the images. The weights ω_θ and ω_β in the energy function are decreased gradually after some iterations or when the value of the energy function is smaller than a threshold. For the silhouettes based energy function, we assume that the ground truth of the silhouettes are given. The weights ω_L, ω_B and the parameter σ in Geman-McClure function are decreased gradually after some iterations or when the value of the function is smaller than a threshold.

4   Experiments

In this section, the experiments to evaluate our proposed method are presented. We firstly introduced the datasets which were used in the experiments. Then, we discussed the effect of joint points on pose fitting and the influence of silhouettes on shape fitting, respectively. Besides, we also evaluated the pose fitting and shape fitting on the final estimation. Finally, we compared our method to several previous approaches on the datasets to validate the advantage of our approach.

4.1   Datasets

To evaluate our approach for a variety of poses and shapes, we generated a synthetic dataset and also used a public real dataset. The synthetic dataset

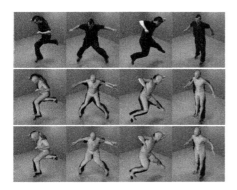

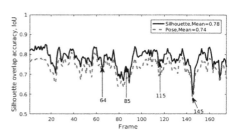

Fig. 3. Comparison of pose fitting and shape fitting. From top to bottom: Original images, results after pose fitting and results after shape fitting. From left to right: the 64th, 85th, 115th and 145th frames.

Fig. 4. Quantitative comparison of IoU of the pose fitting and shape fitting on the *Bouncing*.

consisted of 50 male and 50 female 3D human bodies which were created by the SMPL model. We set all the human bodies as "A" pose through giving the same pose parameters of the SMPL model, while the shape of each human body was different by varying the shape parameters of the SMPL model. For each 3D human body, we used four cameras from different views to project the 3D model into four 2D images. Since the 3D joint points of the SMPL model relied on the pose and shape parameters, the ground truth of 2D joint points and silhouettes can also be obtained when we projected the SMPL model.

The real dataset [25] consists of ten image sequences. Each sequence was captured by eight cameras in an indoor scene. Four images which are taken by the 2nd, 4th, 6th and 8th cameras are adopted in our experiments. Note that there are two marches and squats in the dataset, so we evaluate the results of march1 and squat2, i.e, the experiments are implemented based on eight image sequences. We predicted the bounding box of the person through Cornernet [14], and then estimated the joint points of the dataset through the method in [3]. In terms of the silhouettes, the ground truth was given in this dataset. However, the silhouettes can be extracted through threshold and filter since the background can be easily removed. In practice, semantic segmentation can be used for silhouettes extraction. Silhouette segmentation is not the key problem in our method, So we directly use the ground truth of silhouettes as in [1].

The metric for quantitatively comparison is the intersection over union (IoU) between the ground truth (GT) of silhouettes and the silhouettes of the estimated human body model from multiple views. Note that the GT of silhouettes here is used for computing the IoU, which has no relationship with the silhouettes in the optimization. This is because the silhouettes for optimzation can use the GT of silhouettes or be obtained by some other segmentation algorithms.

4.2   Evaluation of Pose Fitting and Shape Fitting

We use the real data to evaluate the performance of pose fitting and shape fitting on the final results. The qualitative and quantitative results of pose fitting and shape fitting for *Bouncing* from the real dataset are shown in Fig. 3 and Fig. 4, respectively. The results in Fig. 3 are the frames of 64, 85,115 and 145, which is pointed out in Fig. 4. We can see that the human bodies after shape fitting are better fitted to the original images. Even for the 145th frame which has the lowest IoU due to the effect of pose fitting, the final human body is better than the result only relying pose fitting. The IoU of silhouettes from four views of the image sequence *Bouncing* are shown in Fig. 4. It is shown from the figure that the IoU after silhouette fitting is higher than the IoU only using pose fitting for most frames in the sequence. The mean IoU after shape fitting is 0.78, while the mean IoU only using pose fitting is 0.74, which shows that shape fitting is a step to improve the accuracy of human body reconstruction.

4.3   Comparison to Previous Approaches

In this section we evaluate our method on both the synthetic and real dataset. We compared to three previous approaches: SMPLify [5], SMPLify4 [15] and VideoAvatar [1]. Figure 5 qualitatively shows the comparison of two examples from the synthetic data. The areas indicated by red rectangles show that our method can better recover the shape of the human body model than the other three methods. The estimated human body models (pink models) by our method better fitted to the original human body models (white models). Especially for VideoAvatar, since our method established the energy function of silhouettes in 2D and 3D space, the results using four images are better than VideoAvatar which used 120 images from different view-points to obtain the 3D human body model. Figure 6 shows the results of our method from the other three view-points of the male and female model in Fig. 5. Although the areas indicated by read circles are still not accurate enough, the results are satisfying.

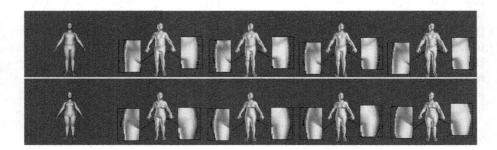

Fig. 5. Two results on the synthetic data of one view. From left to right: the original images, SMPLify [5], SMPLify4 [15], VideoAvatar [1] and our method. (Color figure online)

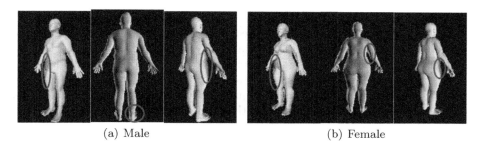

(a) Male   (b) Female

Fig. 6. The results of the other three views obtained by our method. (Color figure online)

Figure 7 shows the IoU of silhouette overlap of our methods compared to the other three methods on the synthetic dataset. The IoU of silhouette overlap is computed based on the silhouette of the projected 3D human body model and the corresponding ground truth of silhouette. The IoU for SMPLify is calculated based on one view-point, while the IoU of the other methods is based on four view-points. Although the results of some samples for SMPLify are better, the accuracy of our method is still higher than the results of the other three methods for the most samples in the dataset. Since SMPLify only adopts one image, the optimization is not sensitive to the initialization, which is the reason that the results of SMPLify on some samples are better. Compared to the SMPLify4 [15], our method introduced silhouette after the joint points optimization, and thus, the results of our method are better on the synthetic dataset. In addition, for VideoAvatar [1] which also uses silhouettes, our results are still better. The reason could be that the energy function of silhouette in VideoAvatar was only built from 3D space. In VideoAvatar, the 3D model was acquired from a video stream containing 120 frames from multiple viewpoints. By contrast, the improved energy function of silhouettes in our method considers both 2D and 3D, which ensures that our method have good performance only using four images.

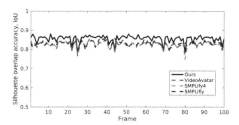

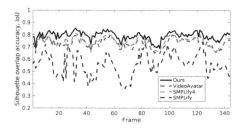

Fig. 7. The comparison of IoU of silhouette overlap between our method and other methods on the synthetic dataset.

Fig. 8. The comparison of IoU of silhouette overlap between our method and other methods on the *Crane* image sequence in read dataset.

In the following, we evaluate our method on the data [25]. Firstly, we show the IoU of silhouette overlap for image sequence *Crane* in Fig. 8 by comparing to SMPLify [5], SMPLify4 [15], VideoAvatar [1]. Note that the IoU of SMPLify is also computed based on four images to reflect the accuracy of the 3D models. We can see that our method obtains higher accuracy than the other three methods for the most samples in this image sequence. Furthermore, Table 2 gives the average of IoU of silhouettes overlap for the eight different actions in the dataset. It shows that our method achieves the best performance comparing to other three previous methods based on that the IoU of our method is the highest. The results of SMPLify are worst, while the SMPLify4 and VideoAvatar have almost the same performance and they are better than SMPLify. The results of *Handstand* are not good because the pose estimation for the images in the sequence is not good. The pretrained model in human pose estimation of [3] cannot achieve good estimation for human body with handstand. Even in this case our results are still the best comparing to other methods. Overall, our method has competitive performance among these approaches according to Table 2.

Examples from *Swing, Crane, Samba* and *Bouncing* are shown in Fig. 9. The figure gives the qualitative results of the three previous methods and our method from one view. We can see from the figure that the shape of our method gives a better fit to the original images, which can be seen from the parts that are zoomed in. More specifically, the *Bouncing* results of SMPLify are not correct. This is because using only a single RGB image gives a too high uncertainty concerning the spatial information. Compared to SMPLify4 and VideoAvatar, which are shown in the second and third columns in Fig. 9, the shapes of our method provides a better fit to the original images. This demonstrates the effectiveness to use the energy function based on silhouettes from 2D and 3D space. Therefore, our method achieves a good estimation not only for the pose but also for the shape of the human body. We also provide the results obtained by our method from the other three views in Fig. 10. It demonstrates that the results

Table 2. The mean IoU of silhouette overlap of the 8 image sequence in the real dataset.

	Frames	SMPLify [5]	SMPLify4 [15]	VideoAvatar [1]	Ours
Swing	150	0.5649	0.7570	0.7573	**0.7748**
Crane	175	0.5558	0.7425	0.7296	**0.7900**
Bouncing	175	0.5660	0.7367	0.7337	**0.7811**
Jump	150	0.5664	0.7078	0.7035	**0.7590**
Samba	175	0.5255	0.7544	0.7559	**0.7734**
Handstand	175	0.5384	0.6131	0.6118	**0.6504**
March	250	0.5224	0.6930	0.6887	**0.7227**
Squat	250	0.5256	0.7316	0.7304	**0.7726**

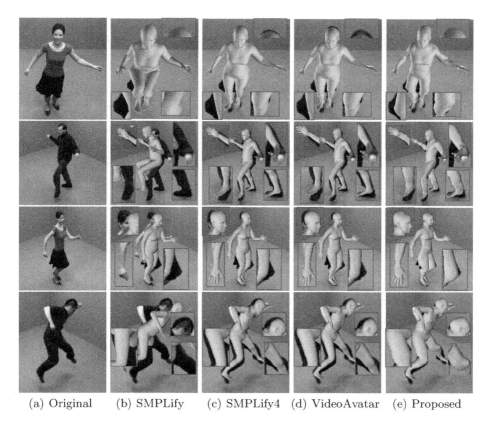

(a) Original   (b) SMPLify   (c) SMPLify4   (d) VideoAvatar   (e) Proposed

Fig. 9. The results of *Swing, Crane, Samba and Bouncing* from top to down. The original images and the results of SMPLify [5], SMPLify4 [15], VideoAvatar [1] and proposed method are shown in (a), (b), (c), (d) and (e).

from other views are correct, which means that the 3D model estimated by our method has better accuracy.

5   Conclusion

We propose a novel method for 3D human pose and shape estimation using joint points and silhouettes based on SMPL model from four-view images. Our method consists of two steps: joint points based fitting and silhouettes based fitting. The joint points of the images were firstly predicted by deep learning-based human pose estimation. Then, the pose and shape parameters of a SMPL model were estimated by fitting the SMPL model to the joint points of the four images simultaneously. Furthermore, we identified the corresponding points on the edge of silhouettes and the SMPL model to build a novel energy function from 2D and 3D space. The shape parameters of SMPL were improved by minimizing the novel energy function. Our method not only estimated the pose of the human body, but also obtained better shape appearance of the human body (Fig. 9).

The experiments on synthetic and real data indicate that our approach can obtain better human body shape comparing to the previous methods.

The limitation of our method is that we strongly depend on the estimated joint points and silhouettes, which may result in that the estimation of pose and shape is not correct when the joint points or silhouettes are not predicted correctly. In addition, the texture of the images is not mapped to the 3D model, which makes the appearance not realistic enough in some cases. Overall, our method can be used in many practical fields such as VR video games or biomedical research.

Fig. 10. The results of *Swing, Crane, Samba and Bouncing* from other three views obtained by our method.

Acknowledgements. We would like to appreciate the support from ELLIIT, eSSENCE and the China Scholarship Council (CSC) for our research.

References

1. Alldieck, T., Magnor, M., Xu, W.P., Theobalt, C., Pons-Moll, G.: Video based reconstruction of 3d people models. In: CVPR, pp. 8387–8397 (2018)
2. Anguelov, D., Srinivasan, P., Koller, D., Thrun, S., Rodgers, J., Davis, J.: Scape: shape completion and animation of people. ACM Trans. Graph. **24**, 408–416 (2005)
3. Xiao, B., Wu, H., Wei, Y.: Simple baselines for human pose estimation and tracking. In: Ferrari, V., Hebert, M., Sminchisescu, C., Weiss, Y. (eds.) ECCV 2018. LNCS, vol. 11210, pp. 472–487. Springer, Cham (2018). https://doi.org/10.1007/978-3-030-01231-1_29
4. Bogo, F., Black, M.J., Loper, M., Romero, J.: Detailed full-body reconstructions of moving people from monocular RGB-D sequences. In: ICCV, pp. 2300–2308 (2015)
5. Bogo, F., Kanazawa, A., Lassner, C., Gehler, P., Romero, J., Black, M.J.: Keep It SMPL: automatic estimation of 3d human pose and shape from a single image. In: Leibe, B., Matas, J., Sebe, N., Welling, M. (eds.) ECCV 2016. LNCS, vol. 9909, pp. 561–578. Springer, Cham (2016). https://doi.org/10.1007/978-3-319-46454-1_34
6. Dou, M.S., et al.: Fusion4d: real-time performance capture of challenging scenes. ACM Trans. Graph. **35**, 114:1–114:13 (2016)
7. Geman, S., McClure, D.: Statistical methods for tomographic image reconstruction. Bull. Int. Stat. Inst. **52**, 5–21 (1987)
8. Guan, P., Weiss, A., Bălan, A.O., Black, M.J.: Estimating human shape and pose from a single image. In: ICCV, pp. 1381–1388 (2009)
9. Huang, Y., et al.: Towards accurate marker-less human shape and pose estimation over time. In: 2017 International Conference on 3D Vision (3DV), pp. 421–430 (2017)

10. Innmann, M., Zollhöfer, M., Nießner, M., Theobalt, C., Stamminger, M.: VolumeDeform: real-time volumetric non-rigid reconstruction. In: Leibe, B., Matas, J., Sebe, N., Welling, M. (eds.) ECCV 2016. LNCS, vol. 9912, pp. 362–379. Springer, Cham (2016). https://doi.org/10.1007/978-3-319-46484-8_22

11. Izadi, S., et al.: Kinectfusion: real-time 3d reconstruction and interaction using a moving depth camera. In: Proceedings of the 24th Annual ACM Symposium on User Interface Software and Technology (UIST), pp. 559–568 (2011)

12. Kanazawa, A., Black, M.J., Jacobs, D.W., Malik, J.: End-to-end recovery of human shape and pose. In: CVPR, pp. 7122–7131 (2018)

13. Kolotouros, N., Pavlakos, G., Black, M.J., Daniilidis, K.: Learning to reconstruct 3d human pose and shape via model-fitting in the loop. In: ICCV, pp. 2252–2261 (2019)

14. Law, H., Deng, J.: Cornernet: detecting objects as paired keypoints. Int. J. Comput. Vision, 1–15 (2019)

15. Li, Z., Heyden, A., Oskarsson, M.: Parametric model-based 3d human shape and pose estimation from multiple views. In: 21st Scandinavian Conference on Image Analysis (SCIA), pp. 336–347 (2019)

16. Loper, M., Mahmood, N., Romero, J., Pons-Moll, G., Black, M.J.: Smpl: a skinned multi-person linear model. ACM Trans. Graph. **34**, 248:1–248:16 (2015)

17. Loper, M.M., Black, M.J.: OpenDR: an approximate differentiable renderer. In: Fleet, D., Pajdla, T., Schiele, B., Tuytelaars, T. (eds.) ECCV 2014. LNCS, vol. 8695, pp. 154–169. Springer, Cham (2014). https://doi.org/10.1007/978-3-319-10584-0_11

18. Newcombe, R.A., Fox, D., Seitz, S.M.: Dynamicfusion: reconstruction and tracking of non-rigid scenes in real-time. In: CVPR, pp. 343–352 (2015)

19. Pavlakos, G., Choutas, V., Ghorbani, N., Bolkart, T., Osman, A., Tzionas, D., Black, M.J.: Expressive body capture: 3d hands, face, and body from a single image. In: CVPR, pp. 10975–10985 (2019)

20. Pavlakos, G., Zhu, L.Y., Zhou, X.W., Daniilidis, K.: Learning to estimate 3D human pose and shape from a single color image. In: CVPR, pp. 459–468 (2018)

21. Pavlakos, G., Kolotouros, N., Daniilidis, K.: Texturepose: Supervising human mesh estimation with texture consistency. In: ICCV pp. 803–812 (2019)

22. Sigal, L., Balan, A., Black, M.J.: Combined discriminative and generative articulated pose and non-rigid shape estimation. In: NIPS, pp. 1337–1344 (2008)

23. Slavcheva, M., Baust, M., Cremers, D., Ilic, S.: Killingfusion: on-rigid 3d reconstruction without correspondences. In: CVPR, pp. 5474–5483 (2017)

24. Varol, G., Ceylan, D., Russell, B., Yang, J., Yumer, E., Laptev, I., Schmid, C.: BodyNet: volumetric inference of 3D human body shapes. In: Ferrari, V., Hebert, M., Sminchisescu, C., Weiss, Y. (eds.) ECCV 2018. LNCS, vol. 11211, pp. 20–38. Springer, Cham (2018). https://doi.org/10.1007/978-3-030-01234-2_2

25. Vlasic, D., Baran, I., Matusik, W., Popović, J.: Articulated mesh animation from multi-view silhouettes. ACM Trans. Graph. **27**, 97:1–97:9 (2008)

26. Weiss, A., Hirshberg, D., Black, M.J.: Home 3D body scans from noisy image and range data. In: ICCV, pp. 1951–1958 (2011)

27. Xu, L., Su, Z., Han, L., Yu, T., Liu, Y., FANG, L.: Unstructuredfusion: Realtime 4d geometry and texture reconstruction using commercial rgbd cameras. IEEE Trans. Pattern Anal. Mach. Intell., 1 (2019)

28. Xu, W.P., et al.: Monoperfcap: human performance capture from monocular video. ACM Trans. Graph. **37**, 27:1–27:15 (2016)

29. Ye, G., Liu, Y., Hasler, N., Ji, X., Dai, Q., Theobalt, C.: Performance capture of interacting characters with handheld kinects. In: Fitzgibbon, A., Lazebnik, S., Perona, P., Sato, Y., Schmid, C. (eds.) ECCV 2012. LNCS, vol. 7573, pp. 828–841. Springer, Heidelberg (2012). https://doi.org/10.1007/978-3-642-33709-3_59

30. Yu, T., et al.: Bodyfusion: real-time capture of human motion and surface geometry using a single depth camera. In: ICCV, pp. 910–919 (2017)

31. Yu, T., et al.: Doublefusion: real-time capture of human performances with inner body shapes from a single depth sensor. In: CVPR, pp. 7287–7296 (2018)

Pose Based Trajectory Forecast of Vulnerable Road Users Using Recurrent Neural Networks

Viktor Kress[1]([envelope]), Stefan Zernetsch[1], Konrad Doll[1], and Bernhard Sick[2]

[1] University of Applied Sciences Aschaffenburg, Aschaffenburg, Germany
{viktor.kress,stefan.zernetsch,konrad.doll}@th-ab.de
[2] University of Kassel, Kassel, Germany
bsick@uni-kassel.de

Abstract. In this work, we use Recurrent Neural Networks (RNNs) in form of Gated Recurrent Unit (GRU) networks to forecast trajectories of vulnerable road users (VRUs), such as pedestrians and cyclists, in road traffic utilizing the past trajectory and 3D poses as input. The 3D poses represent the postures and movements of limbs and torso and contain early indicators for the transition between motion types, e.g. *wait*, *start*, *move*, and *stop*. VRUs often only become visible from the perspective of an approaching vehicle shortly before dangerous situations occur. Therefore, a network architecture is required which is able to forecast trajectories after short time periods and is able to improve the forecasts in case of longer observations. This motivates us to use GRU networks, which are able to use time series of varying duration as inputs, and to investigate the effects of different observation periods on the forecasting results. Our approach is able to make reasonable forecasts even for short observation periods. The use of poses improves the forecasting accuracy, especially for short observation periods compared to a solely head trajectory based approach. Different motion types benefit to different extent from the use of poses and longer observation periods.

Keywords: 3D human trajectory forecast · 3D body pose · Vulnerable road users

1 Introduction

1.1 Motivation

In future, autonomous or partly automated systems such as automated vehicles or robots will operate in areas shared with humans. In order to achieve safe, efficient, and comfortable movements of autonomous systems, it is necessary for them to understand and forecast human behavior. For example, an autonomous vehicle must ensure the safety of vulnerable road users (VRUs), but at the same time it should not stop each time a pedestrian is standing at

A. Del Bimbo et al. (Eds.): ICPR 2020 Workshops, LNCS 12661, pp. 57–71, 2021.
https://doi.org/10.1007/978-3-030-68763-2_5

the side of the road, which disrupts the traffic flow. Based on reliable trajectory forecasts, autonomous vehicles can plan their own movements and initiate countermeasures, such as emergency braking, in case of dangerous situations. While many research studies use the motion state, i.e. positions or velocities, for forecasting, it is shown in [19] and [8] that poses contain additional clues for trajectory forecasting. To be able to forecast the trajectories after a short time in case of suddenly appearing VRUs, we combine Gated Recurrent Unit (GRU) networks with the use of poses. The GRU networks provide initial forecasts after a short time period, which are then successively improved as the observation period of the VRUs increases. In contrast, other methods often require a constant observation period, so that no trajectory forecast can be made until the respective VRU has been observed for a sufficient time.

1.2   Related Work

Regarding pose estimation, there has been great research activity and progress in recent years, mainly by using Convolutional Neural Networks (CNNs). However, there are only few works with specific implementations for the transportation domain. Kress et al. [11] adapted general methods for 2D and 3D pose estimation of pedestrians and cyclists from a moving vehicle in urban traffic. Here, a 2D pose describes the positions of several joints in the two-dimensional coordinate system of an image, while 3D poses describe the joint positions in a three-dimensional coordinate system including depth. The proposed system was evaluated on a dataset recorded specifically for this purpose in realistic road traffic showing advantages of the 3D pose estimation method compared to distance measurements of single joints by means of a stereo camera. In [21], general 2D human pose estimation methods were transferred to the intelligent vehicle domain and evaluated on a newly introduced 2D pose dataset of VRUs.

Research using poses for trajectory forecasting and intention detection is still limited. In this context, we define intention detection as classification of motion behavior of VRUs in classes such as *walking*, *standing*, or *crossing* for pedestrians. Image based 2D poses are mainly utilized for intention detection. In [6] and [4], pose based intention detection of pedestrians to cross the street is performed with help of a Random Forest from a moving vehicle. This approach is extended in [5] to recognize arm signals of cyclists. On the other hand, 3D poses are used both for intention detection and trajectory forecasting. In [16], several balanced Gaussian process dynamical models (GPDMs) were trained based on 3D poses for the motion types *walk*, *stop*, *start*, and *wait* of pedestrians. Trajectory forecasting was performed with the most similar model for the respective pedestrian behavior. However, the system was mainly trained and evaluated on a dataset recorded indoors, which does not represent the diversity of real road traffic. In [12], a method for pose based detection of starting intentions of cyclists is presented. An additional use of 3D poses led to better results compared to a solely head trajectory based approach. 3D poses are used for trajectory forecasting of pedestrians and cyclists in [13]. Once again, 3D poses improve the trajectory forecasts especially for starting and stopping VRUs.

Not much research has been dedicated to the effects of varying observation periods on trajectory forecasting of VRUs. In [17], relatively long observation periods were investigated and datasets focusing on human interactions instead of traffic scenarios were used. According to [14], 2 s contain enough cues to predict motions in road traffic. However, this refers to all kinds of agents and not specifically to cyclists and pedestrians, while [10] focused on long-term forecasts. In [13], three selected observation periods were handled by training three Multilayer Perceptrons (MLPs) separately.

Recurrent Neural Networks (RNNs) are widely used for trajectory forecasting of VRUs. For example, the authors of [1] forecasted the trajectories of pedestrians in crowded spaces with help of a pooling based Long Short-Term Memory (LSTM) network, which particularly considers their interactions. Pool et al. [15] proposed an architecture based on GRUs for trajectory forecasting of cyclists incorporating contextual features such as hand signals. However, RNNs have not been used for trajectory forecasting of VRUs with entire 3D body poses.

1.3   Main Contributions and Outline of This Article

To the best of our knowledge, this is the first time GRUs are used in combination with 3D body poses for trajectory forecasting of cyclists and pedestrians. We focus on forecasting future trajectories based on different and especially short observation periods of the VRU's behavior while other methods often require constant observation periods. This aspect is not sufficiently considered in existing literature. In particular, we analyze the effects of short observation periods on the forecast accuracy. This is motivated by the fact that VRUs in road traffic can become visible from the perspective of an approaching vehicle only a short time before potentially dangerous situations occur. This can be due to occlusions, such as parked cars, especially in inner-city areas. In such a case, a forecast must be made quickly in order to have sufficient time for reactions.

This work is structured as follows: In Sect. 2 we discuss our method. In particular, we take a closer look at the used dataset (Sect. 2.1), our GRU architecture (Sect. 2.2), and the training as well as the evaluation methodology (Sect. 2.3). Next, we present our results in Sect. 3, before summarizing the key findings and giving an outlook on future work (Sect. 4).

2   Method

2.1   Data Acquisition and Preprocessing

To our knowledge there is no public dataset available containing trajectories and 3D poses of pedestrians and cyclists recorded in real road traffic. Therefore, we created a dataset, which was recorded from a moving vehicle in inner-city traffic covering a variety of roads, intersections, different seasons, times of the day, and weather conditions. The dataset is not limited to a specific scenario but covers actual road traffic. Some of the recorded VRUs were instructed to follow certain routes, while the remaining VRUs were uninstructed. The sensor setup consists of a stereo camera with a resolution of 1024×544 px, a frame rate of 25 fps, a base length of 21 cm, and a system for localizing the vehicle. The head trajectories of the VRUs were measured by means of the stereo camera and a Kalman tracker while compensating the vehicle's own motion. Only VRUs closer than 25 m to the vehicle were tracked. 2D poses were estimated in the images with help of the CNN proposed in [2]. Afterwards, corresponding 3D poses were reconstructed by the algorithm described in [20]. In order to give an impression of the dataset, Fig. 1 shows exemplary images from our dataset and the corresponding estimated 3D poses of a pedestrian in the images. The 3D poses are presented from different perspectives, which do not correspond to the perspective of the respective image. A detailed description and evaluation of the methodology used for trajectory measurement and pose estimation can be found in [11] and [13]. The use of 3D poses instead of 2D poses or other image-based methods is motivated by their independence from the perspective of the recording camera. In particular, the 3D poses, in contrast to 2D poses, allow the compensation of the vehicle's own motion. The appearance of a VRU in the image can change considerably both by motion of the VRU and the vehicle. In contrast, 3D poses and the implicitly contained body orientations can be transformed into an independent coordinate system if the vehicle's motion is known. This makes a trajectory forecast based on different observation periods possible, since the underlying data refer to a single coordinate system. Therefore, a comparison of our approach with solely image-based methods, which usually require stationary cameras, is not feasible.

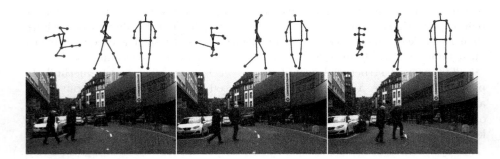

Fig. 1. Exemplary images (bottom) of our dataset taken from an approaching vehicle and the estimated 3D poses (top) of the left person. For each image the 3D pose is shown from above, perpendicular to the movement direction and from the front.

Figure 2 shows the distribution of the temporal lengths of the trajectories recorded and tracked with help of the camera during driving in inner-city traffic for cyclists and pedestrians. We define a trajectory as a continuous recording of a motion sequence of a single person. The distribution illustrates the high number of short trajectories for both, cyclists and pedestrians. The distribution for cyclists also includes longer trajectories compared to pedestrians. One reason for this is that cyclists share the road with cars and are, therefore, less frequently affected by occlusions. On the other hand, the longer trajectories are caused by cyclists riding in front of the vehicle. Of course, these records are influenced by numerous factors, such as the detection range of the sensor, the quality of the tracking system and the speed of the vehicle. However, we do not expect a fundamental change of the trajectory length due to these factors. Hence, we conclude that the behavior of VRUs is mainly observed in form of short trajectories from a vehicle in real road traffic and that we need to deal with them.

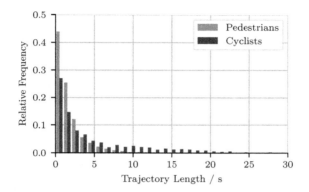

Fig. 2. Distribution of the trajectory lengths of cyclists and pedestrians recorded during driving in inner-city traffic.

During evaluation (Sect. 3.2) we investigate the effects of different observation periods as input data for the forecasting model ranging between 0.04 s and 0.96 s. Hence, in this work we never use longer observation periods than 0.96 s as input for our trajectory forecasting models. For a fair evaluation of the effects of different observation periods, we assure that the dataset is the same for all considered observation periods by only considering trajectories longer than 0.96 s. As a result, the dataset consists of 1605 trajectories of cyclists and 2977 trajectories of pedestrians including 3D poses corresponding to accumulated temporal lengths of approximately 362 min and 161 min, respectively. The dataset may contain several trajectories of the same person, e.g., if this person enters the field of view of the sensor several times or is temporarily occluded by other objects.

In Sect. 3.2, the trajectory forecasts are evaluated separately for the motion types *wait*, *start*, *move*, and *stop*. At any time the VRU has one of the four motion types. The transition between the motion types *wait* and *start* is defined by the initial movement of the wheels for cyclists while for pedestrians the first heel off is crucial. Accordingly, the transition between the motion types *stop* and *wait* is determined by the last movement of the wheels and the heel strike of the dragged foot. Both transitions were labelled manually, whereas the *start* and *stop* phases were determined by an algorithm according to the acceleration. The end of the *start* phase and the beginning of the *stop* phase are detected if the acceleration drops below a certain percentage of the maximum absolute acceleration of the respective VRU. These empirically determined thresholds are 10% for cyclists and 30% for pedestrians. Additionally, cyclists are evaluated according to the manually labelled motion types *turn left* and *turn right*. Given the predominantly short trajectories of pedestrians in our dataset, these motion types are difficult to identify for pedestrians even for humans. Therefore, the trajectory forecasts of pedestrians are not evaluated according to the motion types *turn left* and *turn right*. None of the motion types are used during training. Instead, they are only intended to provide a deeper insight during evaluation.

In the following we train different models for pedestrians and cyclists, in each case using 80% of the trajectories for training and 20% for testing. The training data are further divided into four equally sized folds for hyperparameter optimization via cross-validation. The motion types are distributed as equally as possible. To ensure rotational invariance, the trajectories of the training dataset are rotated randomly and artificially duplicated by a factor of 3 through data augmentation via repeated random rotation.

For trajectory forecasting at current time c we consider n past time steps as input for our models. The motion type at the current time also determines to which motion type the forecast is assigned during evaluation. For each input time t_i with index i in $[c - (n - 1), c]$ corresponding to the times $T_i = \{-(p - 0.04\,\text{s}), ..., -0.04\,\text{s}, 0.00\,\text{s}\}$ with the observation period p we concatenate a feature vector I_i consisting of the head velocities $v_{x,i}$ and $v_{y,i}$ in x and y direction of the ground plane, which are calculated by means of the difference quotient of the head trajectory points, and the three-dimensional coordinates of thirteen joint positions representing the 3D pose of the VRU. The pose contains the head as well as shoulders, elbows, wrists, hips, knees and feet each for the left and right side of the body (Fig. 1). The origin of the coordinate system in x and y direction is in the head position of the VRU and the z direction (height) of the hip is 0. All poses are further scaled such that all hips have the same width. Summarizing, we use a feature vector $I_i = [v_{x,i}, v_{y,i}, x_{Head,i}, y_{Head,i}, z_{Head,i}, ..., z_{LFoot,i}]$ for each input time t_i as input for the forecasting models. Beforehand, the feature vectors are normalized over all training samples using the statistical z-transformation. As baseline we also train models using the head velocities excluding the poses as input and refer to these models as solely head based.

2.2   Network Architecture

The network architecture is composed of multiple stacked layers of GRU cells [3] and a fully connected output layer (fcn). The use of RNNs is primarily motivated by their ability to process observation periods of varying lengths, a capability many other methods do not provide and which is important for our application. All GRU cells use Rectified Linear Unit (ReLU) as activation function. The

number of GRU layers and the number of units in each GRU cell (dimensionality of hidden and output states) are hyperparameters, which are selected during
hyperparameter optimization (Sect. 3.1). The feature vector I_i of the respective time serves as input for the first GRU layer. In order to combine multiple
feature vectors of an observation period, the network is unrolled through time
as shown in Fig. 3. The framed GRU cells and fcn layers share their trainable

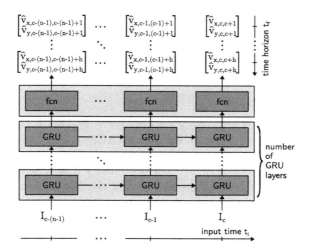

Fig. 3. Network architecture, unrolled through time, which forecasts velocities for h
future time indices for each input time t_i. The framed fcn layers as well as the GRU
cells share their trainable parameters.

parameters. The network outputs h forecasted velocities in x and y direction for
2.52 s ($h = 63$ time steps) into the future corresponding to the time horizons
$t_f \in T_f = \{0.04\,\text{s}, 0.08\,\text{s}, ..., 2.25\,\text{s}\}$. A forecast is produced for each input time t_i.
During evaluation, observation periods of any duration can be fed into the net-
work where only the output at current time c matters. The network is trained by
backpropagation through time [18,22] and minimizing the loss function in Eq. 2,
which considers the forecasts for each input time t_i. The core of the loss function
consists of the Mean Squared Error (MSE) (Eq. 1), which is calculated individually for the forecasts at each input time t_i and each forecasted time horizon t_f.
Thereby, M is the number of sequences and $\hat{v}_x$, $\hat{v}_y$, v_x, and v_y represent the
forecasted and ground truth velocities in the two directions, respectively. Since
the forecasted time horizons for each input time t_i overlap each other, there
are multiple forecasts for one point in time indicated by the input time t_i as
index of the forecasted $\hat{v}_x$ and $\hat{v}_y$ velocities. However, there is only one ground
truth velocity at any given time calculated by the sum of the negative input
time t_i and forecasted time horizon t_f. Forecasted velocities are only considered
in the error if there is a ground truth velocity available. This way, even short
trajectories can be utilized for training.

$$MSE_{t_i,t_f} = \frac{1}{M} \sum_{m=1}^{M} \left(\left(\hat{v}_{x,m,t_i,t_f} - v_{x,m,t_i+t_f} \right)^2 + \left(\hat{v}_{y,m,t_i,t_f} - v_{y,m,t_i+t_f} \right)^2 \right)$$

$$(1)$$

The MSE is normalized and averaged over the forecasted time horizon t_f and subsequently averaged over all forecasts made for each input time t_i (Eq. 2). We favor the MSE of the velocities in the loss function over the physically interpretable average Euclidean error (AEE) of positions used later during evaluation because it is less prone to unstable gradients.

$$L = \frac{1}{|T_i|} \sum_{t_i \in T_i} \frac{1}{|T_f|} \sum_{t_f \in T_f} \frac{MSE_{t_i,t_f}}{t_f}$$

$$(2)$$

2.3   Evaluation Method

We evaluate the forecasts separately for different observation periods p ranging from 0.04 s up to 0.96 s. Therefore, we use the AEE, which calculates the average Euclidean distance between forecasted and ground truth position for each forecasted time horizon t_f (Eq. 3). The forecasted positions are obtained by integrating the forecasted velocities and adding the last known position of the respective VRU.

$$AEE_{t_f} = \frac{1}{M} \sum_{m=1}^{M} \sqrt{ \left(\hat{x}_{m,0,t_f} - x_{m,t_f} \right)^2 + \left(\hat{y}_{m,0,t_f} - y_{m,t_f} \right)^2 }$$

$$(3)$$

Finally, we use the average specific AEE (ASAEE) [7] to evaluate the forecasts over the entire forecast time horizon. This metric normalizes and averages the AEE regarding the forecasted time horizon t_f (Eq. 4).

$$ASAEE = \frac{1}{|T_f|} \sum_{t_f \in T_f} \frac{AEE_{t_f}}{t_f}$$

$$(4)$$

3   Experimental Results

3.1   Hyperparameter Optimization

In total, we train four networks for cyclists and pedestrians using poses and solely the head velocities as inputs. We utilize adaptive moment estimation (Adam) [9] as optimizer and perform parameter sweeps for hyperparameter optimization. We conduct a four fold cross-validation and apply early stopping as regularization technique. Table 1 shows the investigated hyperparameters. Each parameter sweep is followed by a training of the network with the lowest value of the loss function on the entire training dataset. The best configuration of each of the four networks is used for the evaluation. Each of them has two GRU layers. However, the number of units in each GRU cell differs. For the pose based method the numbers of units are 100 and 150, while for the solely head based approach the numbers are 100 both for cyclists and pedestrians, respectively.

Table 1. The used parameters for the parameter sweeps.

Parameter	Values
Number of GRU layers	2, 1
Number of units in each GRU cell	150, 100, 50, 25

3.2 Test Results

In the following, the forecast results of the best networks for the pose and solely head based method are presented both for cyclists and pedestrians. All results were obtained using the corresponding separate test dataset. The inference time of our GRU networks using poses and an Nvidia Titan X (Pascal) over the entire observation period of 0.96 s, i.e. 24 forecasts, is 17 ms. Furthermore, we compare the results with the model from [13]. Therefore, the model, which also uses 3D poses, was trained on our dataset for the three observation periods 0.08 s, 0.52 s, and 0.96 s separately, as it is not able to handle different observation periods. For these networks the inference time equals 0.8 ms. Table 2 shows the forecast errors for cyclists in form of the ASAEE for the three observation periods differentiated according to the motion types *wait, start, move, stop, turn left*, and *turn right*. Furthermore, Figs. 4(a) and Fig. 4(b) illustrate the forecast errors of our pose based and solely head based method over the observation period p. The corresponding results for pedestrians are shown in Table 3, Fig. 5(a), and Fig. 5(b). Apart from short observation periods, the largest forecast errors occur for the motion types *turn left, turn right, start* and *stop*. This is reasonable, since these types of movements are characterized by major changes in velocities and directions. In contrast, the smallest errors occur for *waiting* cyclists and pedestrians, as their positions remain the same.

Table 2. ASAEE in $\frac{cm}{s}$ for cyclists, structured by motion type, observation period p and model.

p	Model	Wait	Start	Move	Stop	Turn left	Turn right
0.08 s	[13]	24.3	67.6	66.0	**61.3**	**76.8**	**87.4**
	Head	**21.4**	78.4	72.6	62.1	95.9	105.1
	Pose	23.8	**67.4**	**65.6**	62.4	79.6	88.7
0.52 s	[13]	16.6	49.0	41.1	**39.6**	59.6	62.7
	Head	**12.6**	56.8	41.8	45.0	64.9	79.2
	Pose	16.1	**46.0**	**38.4**	41.3	**56.2**	**58.6**
0.96 s	[13]	16.8	47.6	39.0	**38.9**	55.6	60.5
	Head	**12.6**	52.9	39.6	42.0	59.1	72.1
	Pose	16.1	**44.1**	**37.0**	40.1	**54.1**	**56.5**

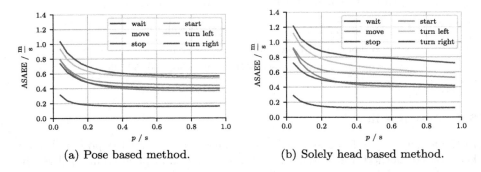

(a) Pose based method.   (b) Solely head based method.

Fig. 4. ASAEE forecast error for cyclists over the observation period p separated according to motion types.

Table 3. ASAEE in $\frac{cm}{s}$ for pedestrians, structured by motion type, observation period p and model.

p	Model	Wait	Start	Move	Stop
0.08 s	[13]	60.2	**60.1**	61.9	58.6
	Head	**59.4**	93.7	89.4	61.3
	Pose	60.3	63.8	**61.3**	**57.2**
0.52 s	[13]	**39.0**	51.6	48.0	47.9
	Head	40.6	57.1	46.5	47.1
	Pose	41.3	**45.9**	**43.3**	**46.2**
0.96 s	[13]	**35.6**	54.7	46.7	45.2
	Head	35.8	56.0	41.6	43.7
	Pose	37.8	**47.3**	**40.0**	**42.9**

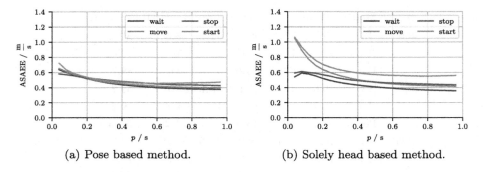

(a) Pose based method.   (b) Solely head based method.

Fig. 5. ASAEE forecast error for pedestrians over the observation period p separated according to motion types.

Compared to the solely head based method, the use of poses leads to an overall improvement in the forecast results. With an observation period of 0.96 s, the error is reduced by 8.8 $\frac{cm}{s}$, 50. $\frac{cm}{s}$, and 15.6 $\frac{cm}{s}$ for cyclists and the motion types *starting, turn left* and *turn right*, while similar results are achieved for the motion types *move, stop*, and *wait*. For *starting* pedestrians the error is reduced by 8.7 $\frac{cm}{s}$ by using poses. Altogether, the results for pedestrians and cyclists are similar, except for the motion type *wait*.

As expected, the forecast accuracy deteriorates with shorter observation periods (Figs. 4(a), 4(b), 5(a) and 5(b)). However, the GRU still provides reasonable forecasts. In particular, the forecast error increases slowly with decreasing observation period. All motion types benefit from longer observation periods.

For shorter observation periods, the forecasts profit from the additional information provided by poses. For instance, with an observation period of 0.08 s the poses reduce the error for *moving, starting*, and *stopping* pedestrians by 28.1 $\frac{cm}{s}$, 29.9 $\frac{cm}{s}$, and 4.1 $\frac{cm}{s}$, respectively. However, the error for *waiting* pedestrians increases slightly by 1.0 $\frac{cm}{s}$. It is worth noting that the forecast error for *starting* pedestrians increases not until the observation period is shorter than 0.40 s when using poses. For *moving, starting*, and *turning* cyclists, improvements of 6.9 $\frac{cm}{s}$, 11.0 $\frac{cm}{s}$, and 16.3 $\frac{cm}{s}$ are achieved. On the other hand, the error for *stopping* and *waiting* cyclists increases by 0.2 $\frac{cm}{s}$ and 2.4 $\frac{cm}{s}$. A deterioration of the forecasts for cyclists by more than 5% on the entire test dataset is only reached for observation periods shorter than 0.48 s (Fig. 4(a)). For pedestrians this threshold is exceeded after 0.06 s (Fig. 5(a)).

Compared to the model from [13], our GRU network achieves slightly better results for both cyclists and pedestrians. In addition, our model is able to handle arbitrary observation periods and offers a first forecast already after an observation period of 0.04 s.

To gain a deeper insight into the effects of different observation periods on the forecasts, Fig. 6 and Fig. 7 show error ellipses for cyclists and pedestrians, respectively. The ellipses represent the mean and the standard deviation of the difference between forecasted and ground truth positions in longitudinal and lateral direction. Therefore, the forecasts and ground truth trajectories were first aligned based on the pose orientations of the VRUs. The forward directions are indicated by arrows. Each ellipse shows the forecasting error of the pose based method for a forecasted time horizon of 1.00 s for different observation periods. From largest to smallest, the ellipses correspond to the observation periods 0.04 s, 0.16 s, 0.28 s, 0.40 s, 0.52 s, 0.64 s, 0.76 s, and 0.88 s. A positive deviation means that the velocities are overestimated in the respective direction, while a negative one corresponds to an underestimation of the velocities. First of all, it is again apparent that the errors for longer observation periods differ only slightly and only increase considerably for short observation periods. In addition, the figures visualize the errors separately for the lateral and longitudinal direction, which usually equals the direction of movement. Especially for cyclists, the error is larger in longitudinal direction. Furthermore, an overestimation of the velocities in longitudinal direction in case of *stopping* VRUs and an underestimation in case

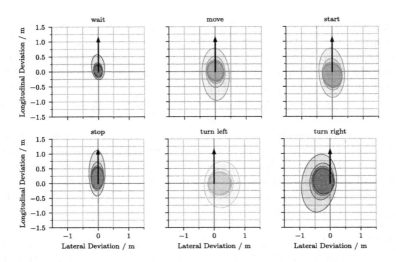

Fig. 6. Error ellipses for cyclists of the pose based method representing the mean and standard deviation of the divergence between forecasted and ground truth positions for a forecasted time horizon of 1.0 s. The positions have been aligned according to the pose orientations and the forward directions are indicated by arrows. From largest to smallest, the ellipses in each plot correspond to observation periods of 0.04 s, 0.16 s, 0.28 s, 0.40 s, 0.52 s, 0.64 s, 0.76 s, and 0.88 s.

of *starting* VRUs is apparent. This effect is intensified for shorter observation periods. In contrast, the ellipses for *waiting* and *moving* VRUs are concentric for longer observation periods. However, this changes with shorter observation periods. The networks seem to have more and more difficulties to distinguish between *waiting* and *starting* as well as between *moving* and *stopping* VRUs. Accordingly, the forecasted velocities are too high for *waiting* and too low for *moving* VRUs. The error ellipses of the motion types *turn left* and *turn right* of cyclists indicate an underestimation of the change of direction. This effect increases for shorter observation periods. The asymmetry to the longitudinal axis of the error ellipses of the motion types *wait* and *move* of pedestrians indicates a slight imbalance in the dataset.

Figure 8 shows examples of trajectory forecasts of a cyclist based on different observation periods in order to give an impression of their influence. The head trajectory of which a respective part is used as input for our GRU network is shown in black, the ground truth trajectory in red and the forecasts are colorized according to the observation period. The 3D poses which are also part of the input are not shown. In total, the trajectories are forecasted 2.52 s into the future. As can be seen, the forecast of both velocity and direction is difficult with an observation period of 0.04 s. However, the forecasts improve considerably with slightly longer observation periods and continue to improve. With an observation period of 0.84 s, the forecast is accurate in direction and speed.

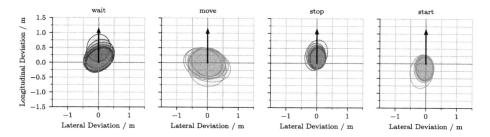

Fig. 7. Error ellipses for pedestrians of the pose based method.

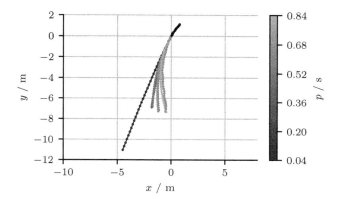

Fig. 8. Exemplary trajectory forecasts of a turning cyclist based on poses and varying observation periods. The various forecasts are based on different observation periods and are colored accordingly using the color scale on the right. The input is represented by the head trajectory (black) while the 3D poses are not shown. The ground truth trajectory is plotted in red. Each time interval between two consecutive points is 0.08 s. (Color figure online)

4   Conclusions and Future Work

In this article, we presented an approach for forecasting trajectories of cyclists and pedestrians with help of a GRU network. In particular, we investigated the effects of short observation periods on the forecasting results. We compared our approach with a state-of-the-art method which also uses 3D poses. Our approach reduced the forecasting error and is moreover capable of handling observation periods of any duration so that an initial forecast can be made quickly after the detection of the VRU. Furthermore, we investigated the effects of using 3D poses compared to trajectory forecasting solely based on head velocities. Our approach is able to make reasonable forecasts even with short observation periods which is important for an application in real road traffic with numerous occlusions and limited field of view. The use of poses improved the forecasting accuracy especially for short observation periods. The results were evaluated separately for the motion types *wait, start, move, stop, turn left*, and *turn right*. The largest forecast errors occur for the motion types *start, stop, turn left*, and *turn right*, as these contain major changes in direction and speed. For very short observation periods, it is difficult to distinguish between *waiting* and *starting*, and between *moving* and *stopping* VRUs.

In future work we will extend our dataset including poses and investigate different network architectures. Further, we will adapt the pose and GRU based approach to detect the motion types of pedestrians and cyclists, such as *moving, starting* or *bending in* and investigate the effects of occluded poses on the forecasting and detection results. This is crucial, as VRUs are often partially occluded in road traffic. Finally, we aim to combine our approach with additional contextual information about the environment of the VRU to improve trajectory forecasting. For example, this may include information on obstacles, the course of roads or pavements, and zebra crossings.

Acknowledgment. This work was supported by "Zentrum Digitalisierung.Bayern". In addition, the work is backed by the project DeCoInt², supported by the German Research Foundation (DFG) within the priority program SPP 1835: "Kooperativ interagierende Automobile", grant numbers DO 1186/1-2 and SI 674/11-2.

References

1. Alahi, A., Goel, K., Ramanathan, V., Robicquet, A., Fei-Fei, L., Savarese, S.: Social LSTM: human trajectory prediction in crowded spaces. In: IEEE Conference on Computer Vision and Pattern Recognition (CVPR), pp. 961–971. Las Vegas (2016)
2. Cao, Z., Simon, T., Wei, S.E., Sheikh, Y.: Realtime multi-person 2D pose estimation using part affinity fields. In: IEEE Conference on Computer Vision and Pattern Recognition (CVPR), pp. 1302–1310. Honolulu (2017)
3. Cho, K., et al.: Learning phrase representations using RNN encoder-decoder for statistical machine translation. In: Conference on Empirical Methods in Natural Language Processing (EMNLP), pp. 1724–1734. ACL (2014)
4. Fang, Z., López, A.M.: Is the pedestrian going to cross? answering by 2D pose estimation. In: IEEE Intelligent Vehicles Symposium (IV), Changshu, pp. 1271–1276 (2018)
5. Fang, Z., López, A.M.: Intention recognition of pedestrians and cyclists by 2D pose estimation. IEEE Trans. Intell. Transp. Syst. **21**, 1–11 (2019)
6. Fang, Z., Vázquez, D., López, A.M.: On-board detection of pedestrian intentions. Sensors **17**(10), 2193 (2017)
7. Goldhammer, M.: Selbstlernende Algorithmen zur videobasierten Absichtserkennung von Fußgängern. Ph.D. thesis, University of Kassel (2016)
8. Hubert, A., Zernetsch, S., Doll, K., Sick, B.: Cyclists' starting behavior at intersections. In: IEEE Intelligent Vehicles Symposium (IV), pp. 1071–1077. Los Angeles (2017)
9. Kingma, D.P., Ba, J.: Adam: a method for stochastic optimization. In: International Conference on Learning Representations (ICLR), San Diego (2015)
10. Kitani, K.M., Ziebart, B.D., Bagnell, J.A., Hebert, M.: Activity forecasting. In: Fitzgibbon, A., Lazebnik, S., Perona, P., Sato, Y., Schmid, C. (eds.) ECCV 2012. LNCS, vol. 7575, pp. 201–214. Springer, Heidelberg (2012). https://doi.org/10.1007/978-3-642-33765-9_15

11. Kress, V., Jung, J., Zernetsch, S., Doll, K., Sick, B.: Human pose estimation in real traffic scenes. In: IEEE Symposium Series on Computational Intelligence (SSCI), Bangalore, pp. 518–523 (2018)
12. Kress, V., Jung, J., Zernetsch, S., Doll, K., Sick, B.: Pose based start intention detection of cyclists. In: IEEE Intelligent Transportation Systems Conference (ITSC), Auckland, pp. 2381–2386 (2019)
13. Kress, V., Zernetsch, S., Doll, K., Sick, B.: Pose based trajectory forecast of vulnerable road users. In: IEEE Symposium Series on Computational Intelligence (SSCI), Xiamen, pp. 1200–1207 (2019)
14. Lee, N., Choi, W., Vernaza, P., Choy, C.B., Torr, P.H.S., Chandraker, M.: DESIRE: distant future prediction in dynamic scenes with interacting agents. In: IEEE Conference on Computer Vision and Pattern Recognition (CVPR), pp. 2165–2174 (2017)
15. Pool, E.A.I., Kooij, J.F.P., Gavrila, D.M.: Context-based cyclist path prediction using Recurrent Neural Networks. In: IEEE Intelligent Vehicles Symposium (IV), pp. 824–830 (2019)
16. Quintero, R., Parra, I., Fernández-Llorca, D., Sotelo, M.A.: Pedestrian path, pose, and intention prediction through gaussian process dynamical models and pedestrian activity recognition. IEEE Trans. Intell. Transp. Syst. **20**(5), 1803–1814 (2019)
17. Radwan, N., Valada, A., Burgard, W.: Multimodal interaction-aware motion prediction for autonomous street crossing. arXiv:1808.06887 (2019)
18. Rumelhart, D.E., Hinton, G.E., Williams, R.J.: Learning internal representations by error propagation In: Parallel Distributed Processing: Explorations in the Microstructure of Cognition, vol. 1, pp. 318–362. MIT Press, Cambridge (1986)
19. Schneemann, F., Heinemann, P.: Context-based detection of pedestrian crossing intention for autonomous driving in urban environments. In: IEEE/RSJ International Conference on Intelligent Robots and Systems (IROS), Daejeon, pp. 2243–2248 (2016)
20. Tome, D., Russell, C., Agapito, L.: Lifting from the deep: Convolutional 3d pose estimation from a single image. In: IEEE Conference on Computer Vision and Pattern Recognition (CVPR), pp. 5689–5698. Honolulu (2017)
21. Wang, S., et al.: Leverage of limb detection in pose estimation for vulnerable road users. In: IEEE Intelligent Transportation Systems Conference (ITSC), pp. 528–534 (2019)
22. Werbos, P.J.: Backpropagation through time: what it does and how to do it. Proc. IEEE **78**(10), 1550–1560 (1990)

Towards Generalization of 3D Human Pose Estimation in the Wild

Renato Baptista[✉], Alexandre Saint[✉], Kassem Al Ismaeil[✉],
and Djamila Aouada[✉]

Interdisciplinary Center for Security, Reliability and Trust (SnT),
University of Luxembourg, Luxembourg, Luxembourg
{renato.baptista,alexandre.saint,kassem.alismaeil,djamila.aouada}@uni.lu

Abstract. In this paper, we propose 3DBodyTex.Pose, a dataset that addresses the task of 3D human pose estimation in-the-wild. Generalization to in-the-wild images remains limited due to the lack of adequate datasets. Existent ones are usually collected in indoor controlled environments where motion capture systems are used to obtain the 3D ground-truth annotations of humans. 3DBodyTex.Pose offers high quality and rich data containing 405 different real subjects in various clothing and poses, and 81k image samples with ground-truth 2D and 3D pose annotations. These images are generated from 200 viewpoints among which 70 challenging extreme viewpoints. This data was created starting from high resolution textured 3D body scans and by incorporating various realistic backgrounds. Retraining a state-of-the-art 3D pose estimation approach using data augmented with 3DBodyTex.Pose showed promising improvement in the overall performance, and a sensible decrease in the per joint position error when testing on challenging viewpoints. The 3DBodyTex.Pose is expected to offer the research community with new possibilities for generalizing 3D pose estimation from monocular in-the-wild images.

Keywords: 3D human pose estimation · 3DBodyTex.Pose · Synthetic data · In-the-wild

1 Introduction

In the past couple of years, human pose estimation has received a lot of attention from the computer vision community. The goal is to estimate the 2D or 3D position of the human body joints given an image containing a human subject. This has a significant number of applications such as sports, healthcare solutions [3], action recognition [3,6], and animations.

Due to the recent advances in Deep Neural Networks (DNN), the task of 2D human pose estimation a great improvement in results [4,5,14]. This has been mostly achieved thanks to the availability of large-scale datasets containing 2D annotations of humans in many different conditions, e.g., in the wild [2]. In contrast, advances in the task of human pose estimation in 3D remains limited. The

© Springer Nature Switzerland AG 2021
A. Del Bimbo et al. (Eds.): ICPR 2020 Workshops, LNCS 12661, pp. 72–81, 2021.
https://doi.org/10.1007/978-3-030-68763-2_6

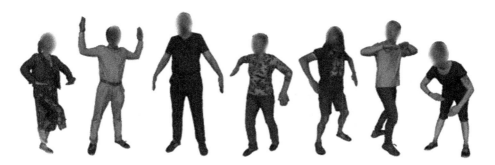

Fig. 1. Examples of the 3D body scans used to generate in-the-wild images with 2D and 3D annotations of humans.

main reasons are the ambiguity of recovering the 3D information from a single image, in addition to the lack of large-scale datasets with 3D annotations of humans, specifically considering in-the-wild conditions. Existent datasets with 3D annotations are usually collected in a controlled environment using Motion Capture (MoCap) systems [9], or with depth maps [7,17]. Consequently, the variations in background and camera viewpoints remain limited. In addition, DNNs [28] trained on such datasets have difficulties generalizing well to environments where a lot of variation is present, e.g., scenarios in the wild.

Recently, many works focused on the challenging problem of 3D human pose estimation in the wild [16,18,26,27]. These works differ significantly from each other but share an important aspect. They are usually evaluated on the same dataset that has been used for training. Thus, it is possible that these approaches have been over-optimized for specific datasets, leading to a lack of generalization. It becomes difficult to judge on the generalization, and more precisely for in-the-wild scenarios where variations coming from the background and camera viewpoints are always present.

In order to address the aforementioned challenge, this paper presents a new dataset referred to as *3DBodyTex.Pose*. It is an original dataset generated from high-resolution textured 3D body scans, similar in quality to the ones contained in the 3DBodyTex dataset introduced in [19] and later on presented in the *SHARP2020* challenge [20,21]. 3DBodyTex.Pose is dedicated to the task of human pose estimation. Synthetic scenes are generated with ground-truth information from real 3D body scans, with a large variation in subjects, clothing, and poses (see Fig. 1). Realistic background is incorporated to the 3D environment. Finally, 2D images are generated from different camera viewpoints, including challenging ones, by virtually changing the camera location and orientation. We distinguish extreme viewpoints as the cases where the camera is, for example, placed on top of the subject. With the information contained in 3DBodyTex.Pose, it becomes possible to better generalize the problem of the 3D human pose estimation to in-the-wild images independently of the camera viewpoint as shown experimentally on a state-of-the-art 3D pose estimation approach [27]. In summary, the contributions of this work are:

(1) 3DBodyTex.Pose, a synthetic dataset with 2D and 3D annotations of human poses considering in-the-wild images, with realistic background and standard to extreme camera viewpoints. This dataset will be publicly available for the research community.

(2) Increasing the robustness of 3D human pose estimation algorithms, specifically [27], with respect to challenging camera viewpoints thanks to data augmentation with 3DBodyTex.Pose.

The rest of the paper is organized as follows: Sect. 2 describes the related datasets for the 3D human pose estimation task. Section 3 provides details about the proposed 3DBodyTex.Pose dataset and how it addresses the challenges of in-the-wild images and extreme camera viewpoints. Then, Sect. 4 shows the conducted experiments, and finally Sect. 5 concludes this work.

2   Related Datasets

Monocular 3D human pose estimation aims to estimate the 3D joint locations from the human present in the image independently of the environment of the scene. However, usually not all camera viewpoints are taken into consideration. Consequently, the 3D human body joints are not well estimated for the cases where the person is not fully visible or self-occluded. In order to use such images for training, labels for the position of the 2D human joints are needed as ground-truth information [2,10]. Labeling such images from extreme camera viewpoints is an expensive and difficult task as it often requires manual annotation. To overcome this issue, MoCap systems can be used for precisely labeling the data. However, they are used in a controlled environment such as indoor scenarios. The Human3.6M dataset [9] is widely used for the task of 3D human pose estimation and it falls under this scenario. It contains 3.6M frames with 2D and 3D annotations of humans from 4 different camera viewpoints. The HumanEva-I [23] and TotalCapture [24] datasets are also captured in indoor environments. HumanEva-I contains 40k frames with 2D and 3D annotations from 7 different camera viewpoints. TotalCapture contains approximately 1.9M frames considering 8 camera locations where the 3D annotations of humans were obtained by fusing the MoCap with inertial measurement units. Also captured within a controlled environment, the authors of [13] proposed the MPII-INF-3DHP dataset for 3D human pose estimation which was recorded in a studio using a green screen background to allow automatic segmentation and augmentation. Consequently, the authors augment the data in terms of foreground and background, where the clothing color is changed on a pixel basis, and for the background, images sampled from the internet are used. Recently, von Marcard *et al.* [11] proposed a dataset with 3D pose in outdoor scenarios recorded with a moving camera. It contains more than 51k frames and 7 actors with a limited number of clothing style.

An alternative proposed with SURREAL [25] and exploited in [15], is to generate realistic ground-truth data synthetically. SURREAL places a parametric body model with varied pose and shape over a background image of a scene to

Table 1. Comparison of datasets for the task of 3D human pose estimation. ($\star$) indicates that clothing was synthetically added to the dataset.

	3DBodyTex. Pose (Ours)	HumanEva-I	Human3.6M	MPII-INF-3DHP	TotalCapture	3DPW	SURREAL
# of subjects	405	4	11	8	5	7	n/a
# of samples	81k	40k	~3.6M	>1.3M	~1.9M	>51k	~6.5M
Ground-truth pose	2D+3D	2D+3D	2D+3D	3D	3D	3D	2D+3D
Real people	Yes	Yes	Yes	Yes	Yes	Yes	No
Background	Indoor & outdoor	Indoor	Indoor	Green screen	Indoor	Outdoor	Indoor
Clothing	Realistic	Realistic	Realistic	Realistic$^{(\star)}$	No	Limited	No
# of total camera viewpoints	200	7	4	14	8	n/a	n/a
# of challenging viewpoints	70	0	0	3	0	n/a	n/a

simulate a monocular acquisition. Ground-truth 2D and 3D poses are known from the body model. To add realism, the body model is mapped with clothing texture. A drawback of this approach is that the body shape lacks details.

The 3DBodyTex dataset [19] contains static 3D body scans from people in close-fitting clothing, in varied poses and with ground-truth 3D pose. This dataset is not meant for the task of 3D human pose estimation. However, it is appealing for its realism: detailed shape and high-resolution texture information. It has been exploited for 3D human body fitting [22] and it could also be used to synthesize realistic monocular images from arbitrary viewpoints with ground-truth 2D and 3D poses. The main drawback of this dataset is the fact that it contains the same tight clothing with no variations.

3   Proposed 3DBodyTex.Pose Dataset

In contrast with 3DBodyTex, the new 3DBodyTex.Pose dataset contains 3D body scans that are captured from 405 subjects in their own regular clothes. From these 405 subjects, 204 are females and 201 are males. Having different clothing style from different people adds more variation to the dataset when considering in-the-wild scenarios. Figure 1 shows a couple of examples of 3D body scans with different clothing. In this work, the goal is to use the 3D body scans to synthesize realistic monocular images from arbitrary camera viewpoints with its corresponding 2D and 3D ground-truth information for the task of 3D human pose estimation. The principal characteristics of 3DBodyTex.Pose are compared to state-of-the-art datasets in Table 1.

The 3DBodyTex.Pose dataset aims to address the challenges of in-the-wild images and the extreme camera viewpoints. Given that the only input is the set of 3D scans, we need to estimate the ground-truth 3D skeletons, to synthesize the monocular images from challenging viewpoints and to simulate an in-the-wild environment. These three stages are detailed below.

Ground-Truth 3D Joints. To estimate the ground-truth 3D skeleton, we follow the automatic approach of 3DBodyTex [19] where body landmarks are first detected in 2D views before being robustly aggregated into 3D positions. Hence, for every 3D scan we have the corresponding 3D positions of the human body joints that is henceforth used as the ground-truth 3D skeleton.

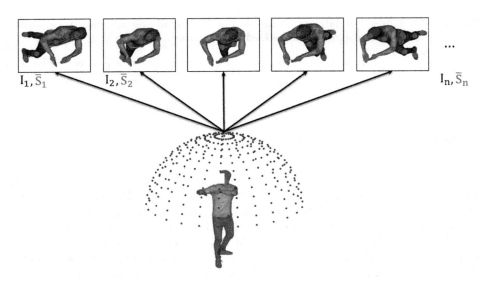

Fig. 2. Extreme camera viewpoints images (top row) from a single 3D body scan. The blue dots represent the camera locations for each camera viewpoint. Better visualized in color. (Color figure online)

Challenging Viewpoints. We propose to change the location and orientation of the camera in order to create monocular images where also extreme viewpoints are considered, see Fig. 2. Considering a 3D body scan $P \in \mathbb{R}^{3 \times K}$, where K is the number of vertices of the mesh, the 3D skeleton with J joints $S \in \mathbb{R}^{3 \times J}$, and also the homogeneous projection matrix M_n for the camera position n, we can back-project the 3D skeleton into the image I_n by

$$\bar{S}_n = M_n \cdot S, \tag{1}$$

where $\bar{S}_n \in \mathbb{R}^{3 \times J}$ represents the homogeneous coordinates of the projected 3D skeleton into the image plane I_n, corresponding to a 2D skeleton. In this way, we are able to generate all possible camera viewpoints around the subject and easily obtain the corresponding 2D skeleton. In summary, each element of the 3DBodyTex.Pose is composed of image I_n, 2D skeleton $\bar{S}_n$, and 3D skeleton S in the camera coordinate system.

In-the-Wild Environment. In order to address the challenge of the in-the-wild images with ground-truth information for the task of 3D human pose estimation, we further propose to embed the 3D scan in an environment with cube mapping [8] which in turns adds a realistic background variation to the dataset. An example texture cube is shown in Fig. 3(a). The six faces are mapped to a cube surrounding the scene with the 3D body scan at the center, see Fig. 3(b). Realistic textures cubes are obtained from [1].

(a)   (b)

Fig. 3. (a) Example of an unfolded cube projection of a 3D environment (extracted from [1]). (b) Example of a 3D body scan added to the 3D environment of a realistic scene.

To have variation in the data, for each image, we randomly draw a texture cube, a camera viewpoint and a 3D scan. The proposed 3DBodyTex.Pose dataset provides reliable ground-truth 2D and 3D annotations with realistic and varied in-the-wild images while considering arbitrary camera viewpoints. Moreover, it offers a relatively high number of subjects in comparison with state-of-the-art 3D pose datasets, refer to Table 1. It also offers richer body details in terms of clothing, shape, and the realistic texture. Figure 4 shows the data generation overview.

4 Experimental Evaluation

In what follows, we use the approach proposed by Zhou *et al.* [27] to showcase the impact of the 3DBodyTex.Pose dataset in improving the performance of 3D pose estimation in the wild. We note that, in a similar fashion, 3DBodyTex.Pose can be used to enhance any other existent approach. Our goal is to share this new dataset with the research community and encourage (re-)evaluating and (re-)training existent and new 3D pose estimation approaches especially considering in-the-wild scenarios with a special focus on extreme viewpoints.

4.1 Baseline 3D Pose Estimation Approach

The work in [27] aims to estimate 3D human poses in the wild. For that, the authors proposed to couple together in-the-wild images with 2D annotations with indoor images with 3D annotations in an end-to-end framework. The authors provided the code for both training and testing the network.

The network proposed in [27] consists of two different modules: (1) 2D pose estimation module; and (2) depth regression module. In the first module, the

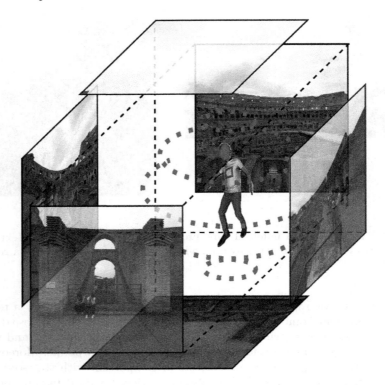

Fig. 4. Data generation overview. The 3D body scan is placed in the center of the cube mapping environment. Different camera viewpoints (in red) are considered in order to capture the scene from multiple angles. Better visualized in color. (Color figure online)

goal is to predict a set of J heat maps by minimizing the L^2 distance between the predicted and the ground-truth heat maps where only images with 2D annotations were used (MPII dataset [2]). Secondly, the depth regression module learns to predict the depth between the camera and the image plane by using the images where 3D annotations are provided (Human3.6M dataset [9]). Also within the second module, the authors proposed a geometric constraint which serves as a regularization for depth prediction when the 3D annotations are not available. At the end, the network is built in a way that both modules are trained together.

4.2   Data Augmentation with 3DBodyTex.Pose

We propose to retrain the network presented in [27] by adding the 3DBody-Tex.Pose data to the training set originally used in [27]. Specifically, 60k additional RGB images from 3DBodyTex.Pose and their corresponding 2D skeletons were used to increase the variation coming from realistic background and camera viewpoints.

Table 2. Quantitative results of the MPJPE in millimeters on the Human3.6M dataset following the same protocol as in [27]. The average column represents the average error value of all actions in the validation set.

Methods	Average (mm)
Zhou *et al.* [27]	64.9
Zhou *et al.* [27] ++ (Ours)	**61.3**
Martinez *et al.* [12]	62.9
Rogez *et al.* [18]	61.2
Yang *et al.* [26]	<u>58.6</u>

Table 3. Results of the MPJPE while testing on challenging camera viewpoints only.

Methods	Average (mm)
Zhou *et al.* [27]	292
Zhou *et al.* [27] ++ (Ours)	**267**

We first follow the same evaluation protocol as in [27] by testing on the Human3.6M dataset [9], and using the Mean Per Joint Position Error (MPJPE) in millimeters (mm) as an evaluation metric between 3D skeletons. Table 2 shows the results of retraining [27] by augmenting with 3DBodyTex.Pose (**Zhou et al.** [27] ++) along with other reported state-of-the-art results as a reference. Without using 3DBodyTex.Pose, the average error between the estimated 3D skeleton and the ground-truth annotation is 64.9 mm, and when retrained with the addition of our proposed dataset, the error decreases to 61.3 mm. This result is a very promising step towards the generalization of 3D human pose estimation for in-the-wild images. Despite the fact that testing in Table 2 is on Human3.6M (indoor scenes only), retraining with 3DBodyTex.Pose helps bring the performance of [27] closer to the top performing approaches [18,26] and even beating others, i.e., [12].

As one of the aims of this paper is to mitigate the effect of challenging camera viewpoints, we tested the performance of [27] on a new testing set containing challenging viewpoints only. These were selected from the 3DBodyTex.Pose dataset and reserved for testing only[1]. Table 3 shows that adding the 3DBody-Tex.Pose to the training set in the network of [27] performs better when testing with challenging viewpoints only. Note that the relative high values of the errors, as compared to Table 2, are due to the fact that the depth regression module is learned with the 3D ground-truth poses of the Human3.6M dataset only.

5   Conclusion

This paper introduced the 3DBodyTex.Pose dataset as a new original dataset to support the research community in designing robust approaches for 3D human

---

[1] Never seen during training.

pose estimation in the wild, independently of the camera viewpoint. It contains synthetic but realistic monocular images with 2D and 3D human pose annotations, generated from diverse and high-quality textured 3D body scans. The potential of this dataset was demonstrated by retraining a state-of-the-art 3D human pose estimation approach. There is a significant improvement in performance when augmented with 3DBodyTex.Pose. This opens the door to the generalization of 3D human pose estimation to in-the-wild images. As future work, we intend to increase the size of the dataset covering more camera viewpoints and realistic backgrounds, and by adding different scaling factors with respect to the camera location in order to increase the generalization over the depth variation.

Acknowledgements. This work was funded by the National Research Fund (FNR), Luxembourg, under the projects C15/IS/10415355/3DACT/Bjorn Ottersten and AFRPPP/11806282. The authors are grateful to Artec3D, the volunteers, and to all present and former members of the CVI^2 group at SnT for participating in the data collection. The experiments presented in this paper were carried out using the HPC facilities of the University of Luxembourg.

References

1. Humus Cubemap. http://www.humus.name/index.php?page=Textures. Accessed 29 Jan 2020
2. Andriluka, M., Pishchulin, L., Gehler, P., Schiele, B.: 2D human pose estimation: new benchmark and state of the art analysis. In: CVPR (2014)
3. Baptista, R., et al.: Home self-training: visual feedback for assisting physical activity for stroke survivors. CMPB **176**, 111–120 (2019)
4. Cao, Z., Hidalgo, G., Simon, T., Wei, S.E., Sheikh, Y.: OpenPose: realtime multi-person 2D pose estimation using part affinity fields. arXiv:1812.08008 (2018)
5. Chu, X., Yang, W., Ouyang, W., Ma, C., Yuille, A.L., Wang, X.: Multi-context attention for human pose estimation. In: CVPR (2017)
6. Demisse, G.G., Papadopoulos, K., Aouada, D., Ottersten, B.: Pose encoding for robust skeleton-based action recognition. In: CVPRW (2018)
7. D'Eusanio, A., Pini, S., Borghi, G., Vezzani, R., Cucchiara, R.: Manual annotations on depth maps for human pose estimation. In: Ricci, E., Rota Bulò, S., Snoek, C., Lanz, O., Messelodi, S., Sebe, N. (eds.) ICIAP 2019, Part I. LNCS, vol. 11751, pp. 233–244. Springer, Cham (2019). https://doi.org/10.1007/978-3-030-30642-7_21
8. Greene, N.: Environment mapping and other applications of world projections. IEEE CG&A **6**(11), 21–29 (1986)
9. Ionescu, C., Papava, D., Olaru, V., Sminchisescu, C.: Human3.6m: large scale datasets and predictive methods for 3D human sensing in natural environments. IEEE TPAMI **36**(7), 1325–1339 (2014)
10. Johnson, S., Everingham, M.: Clustered pose and nonlinear appearance models for human pose estimation. In: BMVC, vol. 2, p. 5. Citeseer (2010)
11. von Marcard, T., Henschel, R., Black, M.J., Rosenhahn, B., Pons-Moll, G.: Recovering accurate 3D human pose in the wild using IMUs and a moving camera. In: Ferrari, V., Hebert, M., Sminchisescu, C., Weiss, Y. (eds.) ECCV 2018, Part X. LNCS, vol. 11214, pp. 614–631. Springer, Cham (2018). https://doi.org/10.1007/978-3-030-01249-6_37

12. Martinez, J., Hossain, R., Romero, J., Little, J.J.: A simple yet effective baseline for 3D human pose estimation. In: ICCV (2017)

13. Mehta, D., et al.: Monocular 3D human pose estimation in the wild using improved CNN supervision. In: 3DV (2017)

14. Newell, A., Yang, K., Deng, J.: Stacked hourglass networks for human pose estimation. In: Leibe, B., Matas, J., Sebe, N., Welling, M. (eds.) ECCV 2016, Part VIII. LNCS, vol. 9912, pp. 483–499. Springer, Cham (2016). https://doi.org/10. 1007/978-3-319-46484-8_29

15. Pavlakos, G., Zhu, L., Zhou, X., Daniilidis, K.: Learning to estimate 3D human pose and shape from a single color image. In: CVPR (2018)

16. Pavllo, D., Feichtenhofer, C., Grangier, D., Auli, M.: 3D human pose estimation in video with temporal convolutions and semi-supervised training. In: CVPR (2019)

17. Pini, S., D'Eusanio, A., Borghi, G., Vezzani, R., Cucchiara, R.: Baracca: a multi-modal dataset for anthropometric measurements in automotive. In: International Joint Conference on Biometrics (IJCB) (2020)

18. Rogez, G., Weinzaepfel, P., Schmid, C.: LCR-Net++: multi-person 2D and 3D pose detection in natural images. IEEE TPAMI **42**(5), 1146–1161 (2019)

19. Saint, A., et al.: 3DBodyTex: textured 3D body dataset. In: 3DV (2018)

20. Saint, A., Kacem, A., Cherenkova, K., Aouada, D.: 3DBooSTeR: 3D body shape and texture recovery. In: Bartoli, A., Fusiello, A. (eds.) ECCV 2020. LNCS, vol. 12536, pp. 726–740. Springer, Cham (2020). https://doi.org/10.1007/978-3-030-66096-3_49

21. Saint, A., et al.: SHARP 2020: the 1st shape recovery from partial textured 3D scans challenge results. In: Bartoli, A., Fusiello, A. (eds.) ECCV 2020. LNCS, vol. 12536, pp. 741–755. Springer, Cham (2020). https://doi.org/10.1007/978-3-030-66096-3_50

22. Saint, A., Shabayek, A.E.R., Cherenkova, K., Gusev, G., Aouada, D., Ottersten, B.: Bodyfitr: robust automatic 3D human body fitting. In: ICIP (2019)

23. Sigal, L., Balan, A.O., Black, M.J.: HumanEva: synchronized video and motion capture dataset and baseline algorithm for evaluation of articulated human motion. IJCV **87**(1–2), 4 (2010)

24. Trumble, M., Gilbert, A., Malleson, C., Hilton, A., Collomosse, J.: Total capture: 3D human pose estimation fusing video and inertial sensors. In: BMVC, vol. 2, p. 3 (2017)

25. Varol, G., et al.: Learning from synthetic humans. In: CVPR (2017)

26. Yang, W., Ouyang, W., Wang, X., Ren, J., Li, H., Wang, X.: 3D human pose estimation in the wild by adversarial learning. In: CVPR (2018)

27. Zhou, X., Huang, Q., Sun, X., Xue, X., Wei, Y.: Towards 3D human pose estimation in the wild: a weakly-supervised approach. In: ICCV (2017)

28. Zhou, X., Sun, X., Zhang, W., Liang, S., Wei, Y.: Deep kinematic pose regression. In: Hua, G., Jégou, H. (eds.) ECCV 2016, Part III. LNCS, vol. 9915, pp. 186–201. Springer, Cham (2016). https://doi.org/10.1007/978-3-319-49409-8_17

Space-Time Triplet Loss Network for Dynamic 3D Face Verification

Anis Kacem[1(✉)], Hamza Ben Abdesslam[1], Kseniya Cherenkova[1,2], and Djamila Aouada[1]

[1] SnT, University of Luxembourg, Luxembourg, Luxembourg
{anis.kacem,djamila.aouada}@uni.lu
[2] Artec3D, Luxembourg, Luxembourg
kcherenkova@artec-group.com

Abstract. In this paper, we propose a new approach for 3D dynamic face verification exploiting 3D facial deformations. First, 3D faces are encoded into low-dimensional representations describing the local deformations of the faces with respect to a mean face. Second, the encoded versions of the 3D faces along a sequence are stacked into 2D arrays for temporal modeling. The resulting 2D arrays are then fed to a triplet loss network for dynamic sequence embedding. Finally, the outputs of the triplet loss network are compared using cosine similarity measure for face verification. By projecting the feature maps of the triplet loss network into attention maps on the 3D face sequences, we are able to detect the space-time patterns that contribute most to the pairwise similarity between different 3D facial expressions of the same person. The evaluation is conducted on the publicly available BU4D dataset which contains dynamic 3D face sequences. Obtained results are promising with respect to baseline methods.

Keywords: Dynamic 3D face recognition · Triplet loss · Convolutional Neural Networks

1 Introduction

Automatic recognition of faces is a non-intrusive technology that, if performed accurately, can open the door to many innovative applications and revolutionize the interactions of humans with infrastructures and services. However, the aforementioned revolution can only be possible if users are allowed to be in free motion and their faces to express their natural emotions in unconstrained environments. Recently, the advances in 3D scanning technologies have made the face recognition task more robust to head pose variations and illumination changes than standard 2D images [16]. There are, today, impressive 3D face recognition software that work well. What they lack is the use of 3D face

This work was funded by the National Research Fund (FNR), Luxembourg, under the project reference CPPP17/IS/11643091/IDform/Aouada.

deformations due to facial expressions in a dynamic face recognition scenario. Indeed, most of state-of-the-art approaches proposed to filter the facial expressions out [2,9,10,12]. This could be a logical option, since it allows to obtain neutral templates that can be efficiently matched with new queries. However, this may lead to ignoring informative patterns that can be present in the facial deformations. Indeed, recent studies in cognitive science have shown a strong positive correlation between face emotion recognition and face identity recognition [8,18]. This means that for humans, both tasks share a common processing mechanism. Taking this direction, the authors in [21] investigated the use of 3D face deformations by extracting local 3D dynamic spatio-temporal features with Hidden Markov Models (HMMs). Other ideas were presented in [1] where curvatures of 3D faces along sequences were mapped into subspaces using k-Singular Value Decomposition (k-SVD) then analyzed in the Grassmann manifold for face recognition. More recently, the authors in [7] proposed a new large-scale 3D dynamic face dataset with various expressions and exploited dense shape deformation for dynamic face recognition. This dataset has not yet been made public. Their method was based on fitting a 3D morphable model and retaining only the expression parameters which were used within a Long Short Term Memory (LSTM) network for sequence classification. Their results indicated that the use of dynamic expression sequences in a biometric scenario is worth investigating. Despite their promising results, the aforementioned works included the 3D face deformations in their analysis without expressing what makes them useful for face recognition.

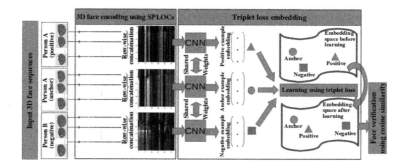

Fig. 1. Overview of the proposed approach

The aim of this work is to investigate the use of 3D face deformations for face recognition. Specifically, we propose a new interpretable dynamic-based 3D face verification approach exploiting local 3D face deformations. As a first step, a new representation of static 3D faces is employed. Instead of considering global deformations for 3D face representation as in previous works [7,10] through morphable models, we use localised deformations. This is performed using Sparse Localised deformation Components (SPLOCs) [14] which encode the local deformations of

3D faces with respect to a mean face. Then, the proposed static representations of 3D face frames are stacked into 2D arrays for temporal modeling of the 3D face sequences. In addition, we propose a new embedding of the dynamic 3D face sequences represented by the 2D arrays using a Triplet Loss (TL) network. Despite its impressive performance in 2D face recognition [19], to the best of our knowledge, this work is the first to use these networks for 3D face recognition. By coupling the proposed space-time representation using SPLOCs with the proposed TL network, we are able to localise the relevant space-time patterns for face recognition in the input 3D face sequences under different face expressions. Experiments are conducted on a publicly available dataset showing promising results. The rest of the paper is organized as follows: Sect. 2 presents the proposed static 3D face representation based on localised deformation components. The triplet loss embedding of the dynamic 3D face sequences and the visualization of attention maps are explained in Sect. 3. In Sect. 4, we report the obtained results for face verification. Finally, Sect. 5 concludes the paper.

2   Proposed Static 3D Face Representation

The first step of our approach is to find a static representation for each frame of the 3D face sequences. Let us consider a set of m face meshes $\{F_i\}_{i=1}^m$. Each of them is represented by n vertices $[f_1, f_2, \ldots, f_n]$ where f_i denotes the 3D coordinates of the vertex i. We assume that all the 3D face meshes are cropped, have the same number of vertices, and each vertex from each 3D face mesh has its corresponding vertex in all the other meshes. A mean face $\tilde{F} = \left[\tilde{f}_1, \tilde{f}_2, \ldots, \tilde{f}_n\right]$ can be computed by averaging the vertices over all meshes. By stacking the vertices of all meshes in a row-wise fashion then subtracting the mean shape, we obtain a data matrix $\mathcal{F} \in \mathbb{R}^{m \times 3n}$. Our goal is to find a lower-dimensional representation for each 3D face mesh F_i. A widely used technique for this purpose in 3D face analysis is that of shape morphable model [4,5], which linearly encodes each 3D face with respect to a specific basis as follows, $F_i = \tilde{F} + \sum_{j=1}^K w_{ij} d_j$, where $w_{ij} \in \mathbb{R}$ denotes the weight of the face mesh F_i along the deformation vector $d_j \in \mathbb{R}^{3n}$ with respect to the mean shape $\tilde{F}$. In order to identify the deformation vectors and weights related to the data stacked in $\mathcal{F}$ (from which the mean shape was subtracted), one should find an approximate matrix factorisation of the form $\mathcal{F} = WD$, where $D = [d_1; d_2; \ldots; d_K] \in \mathbb{R}^{K \times 3n}$ is the deformation matrix with respect to the mean face $\tilde{F}$ and $W = [(w_{11}, \cdots, w_{1K}); \ldots; (w_{m1}, \cdots, w_{mK})] \in \mathbb{R}^{m \times K}$ is the weight matrix. A common technique for solving this problem is through Principal Component Analysis (PCA). PCA results in deformation vectors that involve all original variables allowing the deformation of every vertex in each deformation vector d_j. This makes the deformation vectors scattered and not able to identify the local deformations of the data. We are interested in finding the most informative local regions of the face for face recognition under different expressions, hence it is more advantageous to deal with spatially localised deformations.

The authors in [14] proposed such a method called SPLOCs for estimating spatially localised deformation components using a variant of Sparse PCA. In their work, the deformation vectors d_j are sparse (*i.e.*, some vertices are not deforming in some deformation vectors). The matrix factorization problem is seen as a joint regularized minimization,

$$\underset{W,D}{\operatorname{argmin}} \|\mathcal{F} - WD\|_F + \mathcal{R}(D) \quad \text{s.t. } 0 \leq W_{i,j} \leq 1, \tag{1}$$

where $\|.\|_F$ denotes the Frobeinus norm and $\mathcal{R}(D)$ is a regularization term on D inducing sparsity on it. For more details about the regularization term and the optimization, readers are referred to [14]. In what follows, we represent each 3D face mesh $F_i \in \mathbb{R}^{3n}$ by its weights $w_i \in \mathbb{R}^K$, where K denotes the number of deformation components.

3 Dynamic 3D Face Embedding

For temporal modeling of the 3D face sequences, we propose to represent them using 2D arrays by stacking in a row-wise fashion the weights of each frame of the sequence. By doing so, a 3D face sequence $S_F = [F_1, F_2, \ldots, F_s]$ is represented by a single 2D array of size $s \times K$ that can be assimilated to a gray scale image, $I = [w_{11}w_{12} \ldots w_{1K}; w_{21}w_{22} \ldots w_{2K}; \ldots; w_{s1}w_{s2} \ldots w_{sK}]$, where s denotes the number of frames of the sequence S_F and K the number of deformation components. The representation of the 3D facial sequences with 2D arrays (images) opens the gate to the use of standard Convolutional Neural Networks (CNNs) which have achieved impressive performance in image-based face recognition [6,15,19]. An example of these CNNs is given by the TL network [19]. This network is formed by three CNN branches sharing the same weights as depicted in Fig. 1; one branch takes as input an anchor array I_a^i, the second takes as input a positive array example I_+^i (*i.e.*, array of the same person with different facial expression), and the last one takes as input a negative example I_-^i (*i.e.*, array of a different person). The TL aims to find an embedding ϕ such that the distance between positive pairs and a specific margin is smaller than the distance between negative pairs. The loss function to be minimized can be formulated as,

$$L = \sum_{i=1}^{n_{\mathcal{T}}} \max(\|\phi(I_a^i) - \phi(I_+^i)\|_2 - \|\phi(I_a^i) - \phi(I_-^i)\|_2 + \alpha, 0), \tag{2}$$

where $n_{\mathcal{T}}$ is the number of possible array triplets in the training set and $\alpha > 0$ is a margin that is enforced between positive and negative pairs. We use the online triplet selection method called *batch hard* introduced in [11] where only the hardest positive and the hardest negative samples within the batch are selected. By coupling the SPLOCs representation with the proposed TL network, it would be possible to localise the relevant space-time patterns for face recognition in the input 3D face sequences under different face expressions. This could be achieved by projecting the Feature Maps of the TL network into attention maps on the input images produced by SPLOCs as explained earlier. Such process has already been studied in [20] on standard RGB images within an image retrieval context, where it was possible to highlight the regions of input images that contribute most to pairwise similarity in a similarity network. By doing so, we are able to locate the frames and the local deformation components that make two different facial expressions belong to the same person. In order to reconstruct the attention maps from the images produced by SPLOCs to the 3D face sequences, we weight the magnitudes of the deformation components by the attention values mapped in SPLOCs images and plot these magnitudes as color maps on the vertices of the 3D face frames.

4   Experimental Results

4.1   Dataset and Experimental Setup

To evaluate the proposed method, we use the BU4D dataset [22] which was designed for dynamic facial expression recognition. It contains 606 dynamic 3D face sequences collected from 101 subjects, each of them conveying the six basic facial expressions (*i.e.*, happiness, fear, anger, disgust, sadness, and surprise). We use this dataset for face recognition purpose since we are interested in identifying the relevant patterns of facial expressions for face identity recognition. All the 3D faces are cropped, aligned, and put in correspondences with respect to universal template (*e.g.*, mean face) using the fitting method of Li *et al.*, [13]. Furthermore, we divide the dataset into two splits in a subject-independent manner by randomly selecting half of the subjects for training, and the remaining subjects for testing. This results in two folds; in one fold, 306 3D face sequences are considered for training and 294 3D face sequences for testing, in the other fold, the training set and the testing set are switched. In order to generate the 2D arrays (*i.e.*, images) from the 3D face sequences as stated in Sect. 3, the number of deformation components K and the number of frames s should be fixed in advance. We found out that using PCA and SPLOCs, 28 components were enough to keep $\simeq 98\%$ of the variance of the data. Regarding the number of frames, we selected 28 frames from each 3D face sequence by keeping one frame and skipping three from each sequence. The same procedure was conducted on each training sequence by shifting two frames for data augmentation. By doing so, we derived two 2D images from each 3D face sequence, each of them is of size 28×28. The architecture of the network used for evaluation consists of three blocks. The first two blocks have two convolutional layers followed by a max-pooling layer and the third one is formed by a convolutional layer and two fully connected layers. The dimension of the output is 64. We use the Adam optimizer for optimization and a batch size of 64. The margin α defined in Eq. (2) is set to 1.5.

4.2   Face Verification Results

The used evaluation criteria of the verification performance are, the Area Under Curve (AUC) of the ROC curve, the Equal Error Rate (EER), and

Table 1. Comparison of the obtained results with baseline methods.

Method	AUC (%)		EER (%)		TAR@1%FAR (%)	
	Fold 1	Fold 2	Fold 1	Fold 2	Fold 1	Fold 2
PCA + DTW	76.45	79.32	31.3	27.56	28.75	32.58
SPLOCs + DTW	78.65	80.81	27.18	23.6	31.56	34.38
PCA + TL	94.58	93.83	13.34	15.62	61.5	58.76
SPLOCs + TL	**97.3**	**98.54**	**8.9**	**5.97**	**67.56**	**73.97**

the True Acceptance Rate (TAR) at a False Acceptance Rate (FAR) of 1% (TAR@1%FAR). For more details about these metrics, readers are referred to [17]. Note that we use the cosine similarity measure on the output embedding vectors of the triplet loss network to compare and match face sequences. Using the experimental settings explained in the previous section, the AUC on first fold is 97.3% and is slightly better on the second fold reaching 98.54%. The (TAR@1%FAR) for the first fold is 67.56% and 73.97% for the second fold. Finally, we found an EER of 8.9% on the first fold and 5.97% on the second one.

Comparison with Baseline Methods: In Table 1, we compare our method with representative baseline methods. Firstly, we compare the obtained results with SPLOCs and Triplet Loss (TL) to those obtained using SPLOCs and Dynamic Time Warping (DTW) [3]. When using DTW, the SPLOCs weights are seen as time-series and not converted into 2D arrays, hence the triplet loss embedding is discarded. It can be observed that in this case the performance dramatically decreases on the two folds with $\simeq 20\%$ in terms of AUC and EER, and more than 30% in terms of TAR@1%FAR. This result shows the importance of the triplet loss embedding. Second, we compare the performance of the face encoding step using SPLOCs with that of PCA which result in global deformation components. It can be observed in Table 1 that PCA with DTW results in lower performance than SPLOCs with DTW. Using triplet loss embedding on the 3D face encoded using PCA, the performance highly increases but remains lower than the one using SPLOCs. This could be explained by the fact that spatially localised components describe better the deformation of the 3D faces with respect to the mean face and result in more discriminative representations. To the best of our knowledge, only [21] and [1] have reported face recognition results on the BU4D dataset. In these works, the authors did not report face verification results but reported the recognition accuracy. In order to compare with these methods, we trained the TL network on Fold 1 then fine-tuned it on Fold 2 using one expression per subject by adding a softmax layer and finally tested it on the remaining expressions of Fold 2. The same procedure was conducted after switching the two folds. Using this protocol, we obtained an average accuracy of 96.82% compared to 84.13% obtained by [1] and 94.87% reported in [21].

Visualization of the Attention of TL Network: In Fig. 2, we show five frames corresponding to four facial expressions picked from two different persons of the BU4D dataset. The two first rows correspond to person A, while the last two rows correspond to a different person B. Using the visualization method explained in Sect. 3, each facial expression is compared to another different facial expression of the same person and the resulting attention maps are mapped using color maps on the 3D face frames. Here, a blue color means that the attention value is small while the red color denotes a high attention value. Unsurprisingly, a high attention is observed on the nose tip and the chin in almost all the cases. This could be explained by the fact that these parts are generally not subject to strong motions when conveying facial expressions. In the first column, we compare for the two persons the happiness expression with the sadness expression and vice versa. We can observe that the attention of the network is different from person A to person B when comparing the same expressions. This suggests that the captured patterns are not specific to facial expressions but are more linked to the identity of the persons. We can also see this behavior in the second column of Fig. 2, where we compare other facial expressions. On one hand, when comparing disgust to surprise for person A, we can observe low attention values around the eyebrows and the cheeks, which is similar to the comparison of happiness to sadness for person A. On the other hand, high attention values can be observed around the eyebrows and the upper corners of the mouth when comparing fear to surprise for person B, again similarly to the comparison of happiness and sadness for person B. Note that we did not consider two deformation components that showed artifacts due to fitting issues.

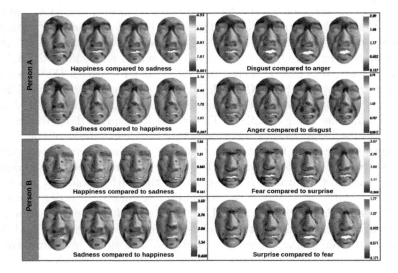

Fig. 2. Visualization of the attention of the TL network on the 3D face deformations. Best viewed in color. (Color figure online)

5   Conclusions and Future Works

In this paper, we proposed a novel method for dynamic 3D face verification. The 3D faces were encoded into low-dimensional vectors with respect to spatially localised deformation components using SPLOCs. They are then used to train a triplet loss network with the aim of learning a metric for face verification. Thanks to the localised deformation components and the triplet loss network, we were able to locate common space-time patterns within different facial expressions of the same person. The proposed method was evaluated on a publicly available dataset and showed promising results. As future works, we will apply the proposed method on a large-scale dataset which should be more suitable for training the triplet loss network. We will also combine the localised space-time patterns with an expression-invariant method for a more robust recognition system.

References

1. Alashkar, T., Amor, B.B., Daoudi, M., Berretti, S.: A Grassmann framework for 4D facial shape analysis. Pattern Recogn. **57**, 21–30 (2016)
2. Amberg, B., Knothe, R., Vetter, T.: Expression invariant 3D face recognition with a morphable model. In: 2008 8th IEEE International Conference on Automatic Face & Gesture Recognition. IEEE (2008)
3. Berndt, D.J., Clifford, J.: Using dynamic time warping to find patterns in time series. In: KDD Workshop, Seattle, WA (1994)
4. Blanz, V., Vetter, T., et al.: A morphable model for the synthesis of 3D faces. In: SIGGRAPH (1999)
5. Booth, J., Roussos, A., Zafeiriou, S., Ponniah, A., Dunaway, D.: A 3D morphable model learnt from 10,000 faces. In: CVPR, pp. 5543–5552 (2016)
6. Chen, J.C., Patel, V.M., Chellappa, R.: Unconstrained face verification using deep CNN features. In: 2016 WACV. IEEE (2016)
7. Cheng, S., Kotsia, I., Pantic, M., Zafeiriou, S.: 4DFAB: a large scale 4D database for facial expression analysis and biometric applications. In: CVPR (2018)
8. Connolly, H.L., Young, A.W., Lewis, G.J.: Recognition of facial expression and identity in part reflects a common ability, independent of general intelligence and visual short-term memory. Cogn. Emot. **33**(6), 1119–1128 (2019)
9. Drira, H., Amor, B.B., Srivastava, A., Daoudi, M., Slama, R.: 3D face recognition under expressions, occlusions, and pose variations. IEEE TPAMI **35**, 2270–2283 (2013)
10. ter Haar, F.B., Veltkamp, R.C.: Expression modeling for expression-invariant face recognition. Comput. Graph. **34**, 231–241 (2010)
11. Hermans, A., Beyer, L., Leibe, B.: In defense of the triplet loss for person re-identification. arXiv preprint arXiv:1703.07737 (2017)
12. Kim, D., Hernandez, M., Choi, J., Medioni, G.: Deep 3D face identification. In: 2017 IEEE IJCB (2017)
13. Li, H., Sumner, R.W., Pauly, M.: Global correspondence optimization for non-rigid registration of depth scans. Comput. Graph. Forum **27**(5), 1421–1430 (2008)
14. Neumann, T., Varanasi, K., Wenger, S., Wacker, M., Magnor, M., Theobalt, C.: Sparse localized deformation components. ACM Trans. Graph. (TOG) **32**(6), 1–10 (2013)

15. Parkhi, O.M., Vedaldi, A., Zisserman, A., et al.: Deep face recognition. In: BMVC (2015)
16. Petrovska-Delacrétaz, D., Chollet, G., Dorizzi, B.: Guide to Biometric Reference Systems and Performance Evaluation. Springer, London (2009). https://doi.org/10.1007/978-1-84800-292-0
17. Poh, N., Chan, C., Kittler, J., Fierrez, J., Galbally, J.: Description of metrics for the evaluation of biometric performance. Biometrics Evaluation and Testing (2012)
18. Redfern, A.S., Benton, C.P.: Representation of facial identity includes expression variability. Vision Res. **157**, 123–131 (2019)
19. Schroff, F., Kalenichenko, D., Philbin, J.: FaceNet: a unified embedding for face recognition and clustering. In: CVPR (2015)
20. Stylianou, A., Souvenir, R., Pless, R.: Visualizing deep similarity networks. In: 2019 IEEE WACV (2019)
21. Sun, Y., Chen, X., Rosato, M., Yin, L.: Tracking vertex flow and model adaptation for three-dimensional spatiotemporal face analysis. IEEE Trans. Syst. Man Cybern. Part A Syst. Hum. **40**(3), 461–474 (2010)
22. Yin, L., Sun, X.C.Y., Worm, T., Reale, M.: A high-resolution 3D dynamic facial expression database. In: IEEE International Conference on Automatic Face and Gesture Recognition, vol. 126 (2008)

AIDP - Artificial Intelligence for Digital Pathology

Preface

Since the introduction of slide scanners around the year 2000, whole-slide imaging has become increasingly common, so moving modern pathology practice toward a digital workflow. Digital Pathology carries out multiple advantages, including ease of slides and cases sharing, organization of archived digitized slides, and extraction of complex data in a highly reproducible fashion via specialized software. The emergence of Artificial Intelligence in health care, the reduced costs of digital data, and the availability of usable digital images are now in alignment to provide exciting solutions for Digital Pathology with good accuracy for diagnosis and predic-tion of the disease. In particular, Machine Learning and other Artificial Intelligence derived methods raised for image feature extraction, segmentation, classification, recognition, and clinical outcomes prediction, promise to provide pathologists with a number of useful tools not only from a diagnostic perspective (reducing/eliminating inter- and intra-observer variations in diagnosis), but also for research applications (understanding the biological mechanisms of the disease process). However, Digital Pathology has yet to fully benefit from the vast amount of infor-mation virtual slides carry out, since whole-slide images show challenging difficulty to be processed in their entirety from a computational point of view. With this mis-sion, the workshop was aimed at sharing the innovative ideas and AI algorithms in the field Digital Pathology, which had potential to solve still open problems, to enhance pathology workflows and to improve patient outcomes. In recent years, the increase of AI algorithms for Digital Pathology has resulted in a growing number of work-shops at the main conferences on related topics. The main goal of the 1st International Workshop on Artificial Intelligence for Digital Pathology (AIDP) was to exploit and to discuss the state-of-the-art on the possible roles of AI for the Digital Pathology workflow, the limits of current AI techniques and new possible uses of AI methods that have not yet been explored. Even if, there al-ready were conferences devoting attention to Digital Pathology, the AIDP workshop was mostly focused on the profitable connection between AI and Digital Pathology.

The format of the workshop included a keynote followed by technical presenta-tions. All submitted papers have undergone to a single blind reviewing process by at least two referees with an acceptance rate of 55%. The review process focused on the qual-ity of the papers, their scientific novelty and applicability to existing pathology work-flow. The organizers would like to thank the speakers who participated in the 1st AIDP workshop and the program committee whose members made the workshop possible with their rigorous and timely review process.

The 1st International Workshop on Artificial Intelligence for Digital Pathology was held in conjunction with the 25th International Conference on Pattern Recognition (ICPR 2020). The workshop consisted in a half-day event. Even if originally planned to be held in Milan (Italy), it has been turned to a virtual event because of SARS-CoV-2 pandemia. After the opening by the organizers, the professor Nasir Rajpoot given his invited talk, in which he presented his research results on digital pathology. Sub-sequently, six oral presentations have been held by the authors of the accepted papers on the main rolling themes in digital pathology.

This workshop aimed to be an international forum where not only researchers, but also companies have had the opportunity to share a common vision on the state of the art in the field of Digital Pathology. In particular, AIDP have had a dual purpose. On one hand, to explore the potential that AI techniques like Machine Learning had to improve pathology workflows. On the other hand, to understand how research outcomes can be exploited to foster international cooperation projects and to develop new tools to make available to pathologists.

January 2021

Nadia Brancati
Giuseppe De Pietro
Maria Frucci
Maria Gabrani
Daniel Riccio

Organization

General Chairs

Nadia Brancati	ICAR-CNR, Italy
Giuseppe De Pietro	ICAR-CNR, Italy
Maria Frucci	ICAR-CNR, Italy
Maria Gabrani	IBM Research, Swithzerland
Daniel Riccio	University of Naples Federico II, Italy

Program Committee Chair

Antonio Foncubierta Rodriguez	IBM Research, Swithzerland

Program Committee

Gloria Bueno	UCLM, Ciudad Real, Spain
Gerardo Botti	NCI-IRCCS Fondazione G.Pascale, Naples, Italy
Pau-Choo Chung	National Cheng Kung University, Taiwan
Vincenzo Della Mea	University of Udine, Udine, Italy
Cesare Furlanello	Fondazione Bruno Kessler, Trento, Italy
Marcial García-Rojo	SESCAM, Jerez, Spain
Orcun Goksel	ETH Zurich, Switzerland
April Khademi	Ryerson University, Toronto, Canada
Jin Tae Kwak	Sejong University, Seoul
Geert Litjens	Radboud University Medical Center, Nijmegen, The Netherlands
Francesco Martino	University of Naples Federico II, Naples, Italy
Francesco Merolla	University of Molise, Campobasso, Italy
Henning Müller	Institute of Information Systems, HES-SO Valais-Wallis, Switzerland
Pushpak Pati	IBM Research, Zurich, Swithzerland
Josien P. W. Pluim	Eindhoven University of Technology, The Netherlands
Marcel Prastawa	Icahn School of Medicine at Mount Sinai, New York, USA
Talha Qaiser	University of Warwick, Coventry, UK

Noise Robust Training of Segmentation Model Using Knowledge Distillation

Geetank Raipuria, Saikiran Bonthu, and Nitin Singhal$^{(\boxtimes)}$

AIRA MATRIX Pvt. Ltd., Mumbai, India
{geetank.raipuria,saikiran.bonthu,nitin.singhal}@airamatrix.com

Abstract. Deep Neural Networks are susceptible to label noise, which can lead to poor generalization. Degradation of labels in a Histopathology segmentation dataset can be especially caused due to the large inter-observer variability between expert annotators. Thus, obtaining a clean dataset may not be feasible. We address this by using Knowledge Distillation as a learned Label Smoothening Regularizer which has a denoising effect when training on a noisy dataset. To show the effectiveness of our approach, an evaluation is performed on the Gleason Challenge dataset which has high discordance between expert pathologists. Based on the reported experiments, we show that the distilled model achieves significant performance gain when training on the noisy dataset.

Keywords: Label-noise · Segmentation · Knowledge distillation · Transfer learning

1 Introduction

Deep Learning has seen successful applications in numerous domains, including histopathology. The superior performance of these complex models comes with the expensive cost of precisely annotating a large-sized dataset. Specifically, histopathology data is required to be annotated by expert pathologists with numerous years of experience in the domain. However, even when annotated by experts, the process is complex due to factors including complex cell morphology, intra-class and inter-observer variability. A common issue occurs with tissues with similar morphology that may get incorrectly annotated due to a difference in expert opinion as well as human error. Inevitably, this leads to corrupted annotations, especially for the segmentation which requires pixel-level labels.

Deep learning models can learn corrupted labels in the data, infact deep learning models have shown to have sufficient capacity to memorize entire datasets including random noise [1,2], leading to poor generalization. Furthermore, in histopathology, tissue classes often have small inter-class variance, making deep learning models even more susceptible to noise. This can lead to errors in the diagnostic decision and impact patient care. To improve the model performance, it is important to explore techniques that make them robust to data noise.

© Springer Nature Switzerland AG 2021
A. Del Bimbo et al. (Eds.): ICPR 2020 Workshops, LNCS 12661, pp. 97–104, 2021.
https://doi.org/10.1007/978-3-030-68763-2_8

Label Smoothing Regularizer (LSR) has been shown to have a denoising effect when training with corrupted labels [3], for object recognition task. This results in a significant improvement in model performance. Furthermore, [4] demonstrated that Knowledge Distillation (KD) [5] at high temperatures, which acts as a learned LSR, achieves higher performance when training a student model and is a better choice for model regularisation. We leverage these findings and use KD as a learned LSR to improve model performance on a noisy segmentation dataset.

We compare the performance of segmentation models trained with and without distillation using a noisy dataset. Unlike the typical distillation setup for model compression, our student model is a cumbersome network with a small (Reverse-KD) or same network (Self-KD) as the teacher. Based on the experiments, we show that distillation substantially improves the performance of the model using both Reverse as well as Self KD, Reverse-KD performing marginally better.

The contributions of this paper are as follows:

1. We use knowledge distillation for training a segmentation model on a noisy dataset and achieve significant performance gain.
2. We show that Reverse-KD and Self-KD are effective in improving the performance of a cumbersome model under noisy data.

2   Related Work

2.1   Noise Robust Training

Label noise in deep learning is a long-existing problem. A common approach is to treat noisy samples differently from cleaner samples. This can be done by reweighing the corrupted samples. [6] uses a meta-learning algorithm to assign weights to samples in a mini-batch using their gradient directions. [7] iteratively learns noisy labels and discriminative features in a closed-loop, reweighing the noisy samples. [8] uses a mentor network in a curriculum learning setup to reweigh data samples for training a student network. [9] uses two concurrent models that cross-trained by selectively feeding data to each other based on the loss function. These are different from the proposed distillation approach as we do not try to reweigh the samples rather smoothen the labels.

Another direction of work assumes having a small clean dataset in addition to a larger noisy dataset. [10] distills knowledge learned from the clean dataset to facilitate learning from a larger noisy dataset, guided by a knowledge graph. [11] also uses a small clean dataset to relabel noisy data under a meta-reweighting framework. However, in histopathology, noise is prevalent in the entire dataset due to the nature of the data and annotation process. It is thus difficult to obtain a cleaner set of data.

Adapting a loss function to improve generalization on a noisy dataset has also been explored. [12] showed that the mean absolute value of error (MAE loss), l_1 norm between prediction and labels, is robust to data noise. However,

MAE leads to increased training time and reduced accuracy [13]. [14] used a combination of dice coefficient loss and MAE loss to improve performance on a noisy dataset.

2.2 Knowledge Distillation

Knowledge Distillation (KD) is an effective way to transfer knowledge from an ensemble or a large model into a smaller compressed model [5,15]. Distillation works by providing additional supervision to the student model from the teacher model. The supervision signal from the teacher helps the student model mimic the behavior of the teacher model. KD has been effective for semantic segmentation tasks [16,17] as well, to obtain a compressed efficient model.

Recent work [4] has shown in addition to transferring knowledge, KD acts as a learned LSR by regularization of soft targets. Specifically, KD is a special case of LSR such that the smoothening distribution is learned rather than being uniform and predefined like in LSR. At higher temperatures, the distribution of the teacher's soft targets is similar to the uniform targets of LSR. Furthermore, [18] has empirically shown KD is effective in improving learning under label noise for image classification tasks. We exploit this relation between KD and LSR to train a student model with noisy data, to achieve better generalization.

3 Method

We apply the KD technique to train a model using a noisy dataset. The teacher model would provide learned Label Smoothening Regularization, which would result in a denoising effect during the training of the student model.

The training setup consists of a student network and a teacher network. In addition to multiclass cross-entropy loss, the student model is trained with supervision from the teacher model such that the student model learns to mimic the output class probabilities of the teacher. Following [5], we use Kullback–Leibler (KL) divergence between the output class probabilities of teacher and student models as the supervisory signal.

$$L_{KL} = \frac{1}{wh} \sum \mathbf{KL}(p_i^S || p_i^T), \tag{1}$$

where $w \times h$ is the feature map size, p_i^S and p_i^T are the pixel class probabilities of the student and teacher models.

The class probabilities are calculated using softmax function, given by the following equation

$$p_i = \frac{exp(z_i/\tau)}{\sum exp(z_i/\tau)} \tag{2}$$

where z_i are class logits and τ is the temperature. Higher value of τ smoothens the class probability distribution.

The combined loss function for training is given by

$$L = L_{CE}(S) + \lambda L_{KL}(S, T) \tag{3}$$

where L_{CE} is the cross-entropy loss and λ is the parameter to weight the two loss components.

Typically, KD is used for distilling knowledge from a large cumbersome model to a smaller compressed model. However, such a setup is not suitable for this work, as we intend to improve the performance of an existing cumbersome model. Recently, [4] has shown a student model to effectively improve performance when distilling knowledge from a teacher with the same architecture or even a smaller teacher model. We follow this to train a state-of-the-art segmentation model under Self-KD and Reverse-KD settings. We compare the performance of both these distillation settings with the model trained without distillation on a noisy dataset. Details of the teacher-student models are provided in Sect. 4.2.

4   Experiments

4.1   Datasets

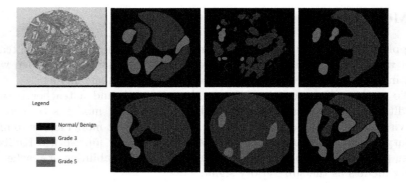

Fig. 1. Gleason TMA Annotations by six pathologist showing high discordance.

The dataset consists of 244 H&E stained Tissue Micro Array (TMA) images, collected from the Gleason 2019 MICCAI challenge [19]. The challenge dataset aims to classify prostate TMA cores as one of the four classes - benign, grade 3, 4, and 5 Gleason patterns. Six expert pathologists independently reviewed the images and provided pixel-level annotations. Importantly, annotations of all six are provided along with the TMA images, to be used for training prediction models.

However, there is high discordance in pixel-level annotations between six pathologists, a sample annotation by six pathologists can be seen in Fig. 1. There

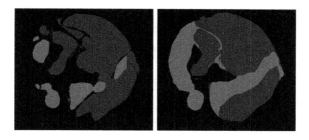

Fig. 2. Comparison of methods for combining expert annotations, left: majority voting annotation, right: STAPLE annotation

is not only disagreement between pathologists on marking the boundaries of the class, but also on the presence of a class in the image itself. Furthermore, erroneous categorization between Gleason patterns 4 and 5 is a common problem in Prostate Gleason studies [20].

The annotations by the pathologists can be combined using two approaches, majority voting and STAPLE algorithm based label fusion approach [21]. Majority voting simply uses the most common annotation for each pixel, whereas STAPLE uses the expectation-maximization algorithm to compute a probabilistic estimate of the ground truth segmentation using a collection of annotations from 6 pathologists. Figure 2 shows the ground truth annotation obtained using both these approaches. Using either of these methods leads to corrupted labels that are difficult to denoise.

We divide the dataset into 172 training images and 72 validation images and apply the STAPLE algorithm based label fusion approach to effectively generate ground truth annotations from 6 different pathologists. For training the deep learning model, patches of size 1024×1024 pixels were extracted from (5120×5120) TMA core images .

4.2   Implementation Details

We use DeepLabV3+ [22] with ResNet-101 [23] backbone as our student model. Under self-distillation (Self-KD), the same model architecture is first trained independently and then used to provide supervision to the student model. Whereas, in the case of reverse-KD, we use a ResNet-101 encoder appended with a 1×1 convolution for pixel classification - $teacher_{simple}$ as teacher model, Also, in $teacher_{simple}$, instead of using max-pooling, dilated convolution is used in the last two ResNet blocks. In both setups, the teacher model is trained using cross-entropy loss.

Both the student and teacher models were trained using SGD, with cosine learning rate decay and an initial learning rate of 0.007. The models are trained with a batch size of 8, with an input image dimension of 1024×1024. The models are trained for 75 epochs. We find $\lambda = 2$ works well and balances the contribution of the two components of the student training. The temperature (τ) value of 5 was found to be the most effective for distillation.

The code was implemented in PyTorch, and the models are trained on a Nvidia V100 GPU.

4.3   Evaluation

To we evaluate the performance of KD loss we compare the distilled model with models trained on baseline Cross Entropy (CE) loss, Dice loss and Noise Reducing Dice Loss (NR-Dice)[14]. Table 1 shows the evaluation results.

Table 1. Dice score on Gleason validation dataset

	Background	Begnin	Grade 3	Grade 4	Grade 5	Mean
CE	92.04	83.14	78.26	76.62	56.37	77.29
Dice	**92.10**	**83.59**	78.93	76.88	58.44	77.98
NR-Dice	91.96	83.46	79.76	76.95	60.56	78.53
Self-KD	90.26	82.03	79.52	**77.03**	**73.23**	80.41
Reverse-KD	90.61	82.29	**80.30**	76.94	72.76	**80.58**

CE loss tends to fit noisy data as it focuses on low probability examples which includes incorrectly classified noise labels. Similarly, Dice loss focuses on non overlapping region between prediction and (noisy) ground truth making it sensitive to noise. Dice loss obtains slightly better results than CE Loss due to its robustness in dealing with imbalance in class distribution.

On the other hand, MAE loss calculates the absolute difference in probability between the prediction and the ground truth. This allows it to treat all examples more equally, making it more robust to data noise. NR-DICE combines both Dice loss and MAE, resulting in improved model performance than CE loss as well as Dice loss.

KD loss captures the information loss between the ground truth and the predicted probability distribution at raised temperatures. Using higher temperatures causes the probabilities to smoothen out and reduces the emphasis on a single class. This benefits generalization when training on noisy datasets as the importance of the incorrect ground truth class is relatively reduced. Both the distillation setups - Self-KD and Reverse-KD outperform the models trained without KD loss, which shows its effectiveness.

It is interesting to see that Grade 4 and 5 especially show improvement as the model improves robustness to noise. This can be explained by the fact that label noise is known to be higher between the three grades compared to benign vs cancerous [24], also ground truth miscategorization between Gleason patterns of Grade 4 and 5 is common [20]. As a result, the noise robustness benefits Grade 4 and 5 classes more than Benign and Grade 3 classes.

5   Conclusion

In this paper, we show the effectiveness of using knowledge distillation in improving the performance of a state-of-the-art segmentation model when training with noisy data. Knowledge distillation acts as a learned label smoothening regularizer to provide a denoising effect on training, which allows for better generalization of the model. Furthermore, to train a cumbersome state-of-the-art model we use self-distillation and reverse-distillation. We evaluate our proposed approach on the Gleason Challenge dataset. Using both distillation setups, the model achieves better performance than the model trained without distillation.

References

1. Zhang, C., Bengio, S., Hardt, M., Recht, B., Vinyals, O.: Understanding deep learning requires rethinking generalization (2018)
2. Arpit, D., et al.: A closer look at memorization in deep networks. arXiv preprint arXiv:1706.05394 (2017)
3. Lukasik, M., Bhojanapalli, S., Menon, A.K., Kumar, S.: Does label smoothing mitigate label noise? arXiv preprint arXiv:2003.02819 (2020)
4. Yuan, L., Tay, F.E.H., Li, G., Wang, T., Feng, J.: Revisiting knowledge distillation via label smoothing regularization. In: Proceedings of the IEEE/CVF Conference on Computer Vision and Pattern Recognition, pp. 3903–3911 (2020)
5. Hinton, G., Vinyals, O., Dean, J.: Distilling the knowledge in a neural network. arXiv preprint arXiv:1503.02531 (2015)
6. Ren, M., Zeng, W., Yang, B., Urtasun, R.: Learning to reweight examples for robust deep learning. arXiv preprint arXiv:1803.09050 (2018)
7. Wang, Y., et al.: Iterative learning with open-set noisy labels. In: Proceedings of the IEEE Conference on Computer Vision and Pattern Recognition, pp. 8688–8696 (2018)
8. Jiang, L., Zhou, Z., Leung, T., Li, L.J., Fei-Fei, L.: Mentornet: learning data-driven curriculum for very deep neural networks on corrupted labels. In: International Conference on Machine Learning, pp. 2304–2313 (2018)
9. Han, B., et al.: Co-teaching: robust training of deep neural networks with extremely noisy labels. In: Advances in Neural Information Processing Systems, pp. 8527–8537 (2018)
10. Li, Y., Yang, J., Song, Y., Cao, L., Luo, J., Li, L.J.: Learning from noisy labels with distillation. In: Proceedings of the IEEE International Conference on Computer Vision, pp. 1910–1918 (2017)
11. Zhang, Z., Zhang, H., Arik, S.O., Lee, H., Pfister, T.: Distilling effective supervision from severe label noise. In: Proceedings of the IEEE/CVF Conference on Computer Vision and Pattern Recognition, pp. 9294–9303 (2020)
12. Ghosh, A., Kumar, H., Sastry, P.S.: Robust loss functions under label noise for deep neural networks. arXiv preprint arXiv:1712.09482 (2017)
13. Wang, X., Hua, Y., Kodirov, E., Robertson, N.M.: Imae for noise-robust learning: mean absolute error does not treat examples equally and gradient magnitude's variance matters. arXiv preprint arXiv:1903.12141 (2019)
14. Wang, G., et al.: A noise-robust framework for automatic segmentation of covid-19 pneumonia lesions from CT images. IEEE Trans. Med. Imaging **39**(8), 2653–2663 (2020)

15. Gou, J., Yu, B., Maybank, S.J., Tao, D.: Knowledge distillation: a survey. arXiv preprint arXiv:2006.05525 (2020)
16. Xie, J., Shuai, B., Hu, J.F., Lin, J., Zheng, W.S.: Improving fast segmentation with teacher-student learning. arXiv preprint arXiv:1810.08476 (2018)
17. Liu, Y., Chen, K., Liu, C., Qin, Z., Luo, Z., Wang, J.: Structured knowledge distillation for semantic segmentation. In: Proceedings of the IEEE Conference on Computer Vision and Pattern Recognition, pp. 2604–2613 (2019)
18. Sarfraz, F., Arani, E., Zonooz, B.: Knowledge distillation beyond model compression. arXiv preprint arXiv:2007.01922 (2020)
19. Gleason 2019 Challenge (2020). Accessed 10 Oct 2020
20. Nagpal, K., et al.: Development and validation of a deep learning algorithm for improving gleason scoring of prostate cancer. NPJ Dig. Med. 2(1), 1–10 (2019)
21. Warfield, S.K., Zou, K.H., Wells, W.M.: Simultaneous truth and performance level estimation (staple): an algorithm for the validation of image segmentation. IEEE Trans. Med. Imaging 23(7), 903–921 (2004)
22. Chen, L.-C., Zhu, Y., Papandreou, G., Schroff, F., Adam, H.: Encoder-decoder with atrous separable convolution for semantic image segmentation. In: Proceedings of the European Conference on Computer Vision (ECCV), pp. 801–818 (2018)
23. He, K., Zhang, X., Ren, S., Sun, J.: Deep residual learning for image recognition. In: Proceedings of the IEEE Conference on Computer Vision and Pattern Recognition, pp. 770–778 (2016)
24. Nir, G., et al.: Automatic grading of prostate cancer in digitized histopathology images: Learning from multiple experts. Med. Image Anal. 50, 167–180 (2018)

Semi-supervised Learning with a Teacher-Student Paradigm for Histopathology Classification: A Resource to Face Data Heterogeneity and Lack of Local Annotations

Niccolò Marini[1,2(✉)], Sebastian Otálora[1,2], Henning Müller[1,3], and Manfredo Atzori[1]

[1] Institute of Information Systems, HES-SO (University of Applied Sciences and Arts Western Switzerland), 3960 Sierre, Switzerland
niccolo.marini@hevs.ch
[2] Centre Universitaire d'Informatique, University of Geneva, 1227 Carouge, Switzerland
[3] Medical Faculty, University of Geneva, 1211 Geneva, Switzerland

Abstract. Training classification models in the medical domain is often difficult due to data heterogeneity (related to acquisition procedures) and due to the difficulty of getting sufficient amounts of annotations from specialized experts. It is particularly true in digital pathology, where models do not generalize easily. This paper presents a novel approach for the generalization of models in conditions where heterogeneity is high and annotations are few. The approach relies on a semi-supervised teacher/student paradigm to different datasets and annotations. The paradigm combines a small amount of strongly-annotated data, with a large amount of unlabeled data, for training two Convolutional Neural Networks (CNN): the teacher and the student model. The teacher model is trained with strong labels and used to generate pseudo-labeled samples from the unlabeled data. The student model is trained combining the pseudo-labeled samples and a small amount of strongly-annotated data. The paradigm is evaluated on the student model performance of Gleason pattern and Gleason score classification in prostate cancer images and compared with a fully-supervised learning approach for training the student model. In order to evaluate the capability of the approach to generalize, the datasets used are highly heterogeneous in visual characteristics and are collected from two different medical institutions. The models, trained with the teacher/student paradigm, show an improvement in performance above the fully-supervised training. The models generalize better on both the datasets, despite the inter-datasets heterogeneity, alleviating the overfitting. The classification performance shows an improvement both in the classification of Gleason pattern at patch level ($\kappa = 0.6129 \pm 0.0127$

Both authors contributed equally to this work. S. Otálora thanks to Colciencias for partially funding his Ph.D. studies through the call "756 - Doctorados en el exterior".

A. Del Bimbo et al. (Eds.): ICPR 2020 Workshops, LNCS 12661, pp. 105–119, 2021.
https://doi.org/10.1007/978-3-030-68763-2_9

from $\kappa = 0.5608 \pm 0.0308$) and at in Gleason score classification, evaluated at WSI-level $\kappa = 0.4477 \pm 0.0460$ from $\kappa = 0.2814 \pm 0.1312$).

Keywords: Digital pathology · Deep learning · Semi-supervision · Prostate cancer

1   Introduction

The lack of large datasets with local annotations and the highly-heterogeneous data represents a critical challenge for developing machine learning algorithms that generalize well in the digital pathology domain [8], despite the increasing amount of datasets available with repositories such as TCGA (The Cancer Genome Atlas).

Machine learning algorithms, particularly Convolutional Neural Networks (CNNs), are the state-of-the-art for analyzing digital pathology images [23,35] (such as whole slide images, WSIs, or tissue-micro-arrays, TMAs). CNN models usually require large datasets with local annotations to train robust models [17] that generalize well to unseen data [6]. The annotation of digital pathology images is a time-consuming and expensive process that requires medical experts, such as the pathologists. Therefore, only a small amount among the publicly available datasets is locally annotated, e.g. the Camelyon dataset [22].

Despite the small amount of datasets that are locally annotated, an increasing number of histopathological images datasets is available, e.g. The Cancer Genome Atlas (TCGA)[1]. Most of these datasets come without local annotations (strong annotations) of the region of interest for the diagnosis. Some of these datasets are released with medical reports and some are unlabeled. The reports include the final diagnosis, among other information, that can instead be used as weak annotations for digital pathology images.

The amount of strongly-annotated data is much smaller than the unlabeled and weakly-annotated data. This fact constitutes a challenge for training supervised CNN models in a fully-supervised fashion. Furthermore, histopathological images that come from different sources are highly-heterogeneous, as a consequence of the acquisition procedures applied to the samples. Hematoxylin and eosin (H&E) represent the golden standard for staining the samples within a WSI [10]. Although H&E is a standard, their preparation procedures are not fully standardized, often leading to inter-dataset heterogeneity [19,37]. This heterogeneity leads to models that are more prone to overfit, compared with models trained in conditions where the inter-dataset heterogeneity is not present. Therefore, many CNN models, trained to analyze histopathological images, face a decrease in their performance when they are tested on data originated from a different source, as shown in previous works [32,33].

Despite the lack of large datasets that are locally annotated and the highly-heterogeneous data, new methods were proposed recently for training the models

---

[1]   https://www.cancer.gov/about-nci/organization/ccg/research/structural-genomics/tcga. Retrieved 9th of March, 2020.

with small datasets of local annotations, showing partial success, such as semi-supervised learning [3,11,14,20,21,24,26,28,31,38], active learning [27,29,30,39] and weakly supervised learning [1,4,6,18,25,32,36]. This paper represents a novelty in a domain where there is a lack of large datasets with local annotations and the data are highly heterogeneous. The semi-supervised teacher/student paradigm [13,20,31,32] is applied to the digital pathology task of prostate cancer classification, using two datasets.

Table 1. State-of-the-art works for Gleason patterns and Gleason scoring deep learning models. In Classes column, GP = Gleason patterns, GS = Gleason score, Low risk GS = GS6 and GS7, High risk GS = GS8, GS9, GS10.

Reference	Classes	Results	Dataset	Annotations
Arvaniti [2]	Benign, GP3, GP4, GP5	$\kappa = 0.53$	886 TMAs	Strong
Ström [32]	GP1, GP2, GP3, GP4, GP5	$\kappa = 0.67$	6682 WSIs	Strong
Ström [32]	Benign vs cancer	AOC = 0.99	6682 WSIs	Strong
This work	Benign, GP3, GP4, GP5	$\kappa = 0.61$	886 TMAs	Strong
			301 WSIs	Weak
Arvaniti [2]	GS6, GS7, GS8, GS9, GS10	$\kappa = 0.75$	886 TMAs	Strong
Arvaniti [1]	GS6, GS7, GS8, GS9, GS10	AUC = 0.88	886 TMAs	Strong
			447 WSIs	Weak
Jimenez-del-Toro [36]	Low risk vs high risk	ACC = 0.78	235 WSIs	Weak
Otálora [25]	GS6, GS7, GS8, GS9, GS10	$\kappa = 0.44$	341 WSIs	Weak
Bulten [4]	GS6, GS7, GS8, GS9, GS10	$\kappa = 0.72$	1243 WSIs	Strong
				Weak
Campanella [6]	Benign vs cancer	AUC = 0.98	24859 WSIs	Weak
This work	GS6, GS7, GS8, GS9, GS10	$\kappa = 0.44$	886 TMAs	Strong
			301 WSIs	Weak

Prostate cancer (PCa) is the fourth most frequent cancer in the entire human population[2]. Prostate cancer is diagnosed using the Gleason grading system, which is based on two steps: first, the identification of Gleason patterns, second the computation of the Gleason Score. The identification of Gleason patterns is made to estimate the aggressiveness of cancer. The tissue structures in a sample are distinguished in different Gleason patterns, according to their cell abnormality and their gland deformation. The Gleason patterns range from 1 to 5. According to the guidelines described by the Union for International Cancer Control and the World Health Organization/International Society of Urological Pathology, the Gleason score is computed by evaluating the most diffused primary and secondary patterns. Typically, malignant prostate cancer has a Gleason score ranged from 6 to 10. The recent advancements in the digital pathology cancer prostate classification task are summarized in the Table 1.

---

[2] https://www.wcrf.org/dietandcancer/cancer-trends/worldwide-cancer-data. Retrieved 16th of March, 2020.

In this paper, two highly-heterogeneous datasets are used for training the models: a small strongly-labeled dataset with pixel-wise annotations and a large unlabeled dataset of whole slide images. The strongly-annotated dataset is the Tissue Micro-Arrays Zurich dataset (TMAZ). The non locally annotated dataset is a cohort of The Cancer Genome Atlas PRostate ADenocarcinoma (TCGA-PRAD).

The approach proposed follows the teacher/student paradigm and consists of two models: a high-capacity model, called *teacher model*, and a smaller model, called the *student model*. The teacher model generates pseudo-labeled examples from the unlabeled data. The student model is trained combining the pseudo-labeled examples and the strongly-annotated data.

The teacher and the student models are implemented using large pre-trained models and following the paradigm constraints. The teacher model must be a high-capacity model, while the student model must be efficient at test time. The teacher model is a high-capacity ResNexT based model (22 million of parameters), pre-trained with a dataset of one billion natural images retrieved from Instagram [38]. The model is trained with the strongly-annotated data and it creates the pseudo-labeled examples annotating the unlabeled data. The student model is a DenseNet121, pre-trained with ImageNet weights. The student architecture is a small model, compared with the model used for implementing the teacher. The model is trained first with the pseudo-labeled data and then fine-tuned with the strongly-annotated data. The models' performance is compared with the fully-supervised learning of the student model, considered as the baseline. The teacher/student paradigm, as shown in the experimental results, performs better than the fully-supervised CNN (trained only with strongly-annotated data), both at the Gleason pattern level and at the Gleason score level. The approach allows leveraging large unlabeled datasets as a source of supervision for training CNN models in digital pathology. This work is included in a bigger study on semi-supervised and semi-weakly supervised learning approaches, partly presented in Otálora et al. [26]. The difference between the approaches regards the steps included in order to train the teacher model: while the semi-weakly supervised learning approach previously described includes additional training components based on weak labels from the WSI, the semi-supervised approach described in this paper does not use any labels from the WSI dataset.

2   Methods

2.1   Datasets

Two open-access datasets are adopted for the evaluation of the teacher/student paradigm. They are highly heterogeneous, which makes them similar to real clinical classification problems, and they are pre-processed with the same approach. In both datasets, the images are pre-processed dividing them into patches and removing the background regions. The images are divided into tiles of 750 × 750 pixels, and then they are resized to 224 × 224 pixels to fit as input to the

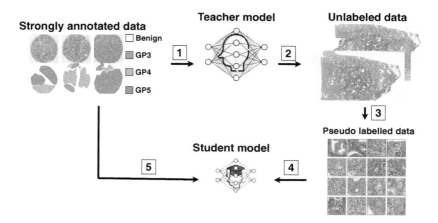

Fig. 1. Overview of the teacher/student training model. In step one, the teacher is trained with strongly-annotated data. In step two, the teacher predicts the class probabilities for the unlabeled data. In step three, the samples with the highest probabilities are selected (pseudo-labeled data). In step four, the student model is trained using the pseudo-labeled data. In step five, the student model is trained using the strongly-annotated data.

chosen networks. Only the patches extracted from tissue regions are selected (background regions are non-informative). The HistoQC tool [16] is used for generating tissue masks of the images that come without local annotations so that only patches that include tissue are extracted. The two datasets are the tissue microarray dataset (TMAZ) released by Arvanity et al. [2] and a cohort of the TCGA-PRAD dataset[3]. The TMAZ includes 886 prostate TMA core images with pixel-wise annotations, made by pathologists. Each TMA core has a size of 3100^2 pixels, scanned at 40x resolution (0.23 microns per pixel). The arrays are scanned at the same medical center, the University Hospital of Zurich (NanoZoomer-XR Digital slide scanner, Hamamatsu). The TMAZ includes four classes: benign, Gleason pattern 3, Gleason pattern 4, Gleason pattern 5. It is split into three partitions: the training partition is composed of 508 cores, the validation partition is composed of 133 cores, and the test partition of 245 cores. The partitions of the dataset are shown in the left part of Table 2. From each TMAZ core, 30 patches are randomly extracted. The number of patches to extract is chosen considering the trade-off between the patch size and the whole tissue covered within the TMA. The number of patches for each class is summarized in Table 3.

TCGA-PRAD[4] is a data repository including up to 490 tissue slides of digitized prostactectomies (made up of $100'000^2$ pixels), preserved with paraffin embeddings or frozen tissues, with no pixel-wise annotations. The cohort of

---

[3] https://www.cancer.gov/about-nci/organization/ccg/research/structural-genomics/tcga. Retrieved 9th of March, 2020.

[4] https://portal.gdc.cancer.gov/projects/TCGA-PRAD. Retrieved March 1, 2020.

Table 2. Number of TMA cores in the TMAZ dataset (left) and WSIs in the TCGA-PRAD dataset (right) for each Gleason score.

Class/Partition	Train	Valid	Test	Total class
Benign	61; −	42; −	12 ; −	115; −
GS6	158; 13	35; 20	79; 5	272; 38
GS7: 3 + 4	47; 42	14; 10	28; 6	89; 58
GS7: 4 + 3	18; 30	11; 14	23; 11	52; 55
GS8	119; 37	15; 12	84; 13	218; 62
GS9& GS10	105; 49	16; 28	19; 11	140; 88
Total	508; 171	133; 84	245; 46	886; 301

Table 3. Number of patches for each Gleason pattern in the TMAZ dataset.

Class/Partition	Training	Validation	Test
Benign	1830	1260	127
GP3	5992	1352	1602
GP4	4472	831	2121
GP5	2766	457	387
Total	15060	3900	4237

the TCGA-PRAD dataset used in this work includes only 301 WSIs from the original dataset, preserved only with paraffin embeddings sections. The WSIs come without pixel-wise annotations and are paired with their primary and secondary Gleason pattern within the corresponding pathology report. The WSIs in the cohort are collected from 20 medical centers. This large number of medical centers leads to a highly heterogeneous WSIs. The dataset is split into three partitions (as shown in the right part of Table 2): the training set is composed of 171 WSIs, the validation set composed of 84 WSI, and the test set composed of 46 WSIs. In this paper, the TCGA-PRAD patches are annotated with pseudo-labels by the teacher model. It predicts a probability vector for each of the patches within the WSIs. The probability vectors are sorted in descending order by the class probabilities and the top-ranked K patches are selected. Different values of K are tested for the training partitions of pseudo-labeled data. They vary between 1000 and 10'000 patches per class and they are explored increasing the value of 1000 patches per class, between two consecutive K values. Therefore 1000 patches per class are included in the first subset and 2000 per class in the second one. The validation and test partition include both 8000 patches (2000 samples for each class).

2.2   Teacher/Student Paradigm

The presented semi-supervised learning approach is a pipeline based on teacher/student paradigm [13,20]. Figure 1 shows an overview of the training schema. The paradigm includes two distinct CNNs, called respectively the teacher model and the student model. The teacher model is a high-capacity neural network, trained to annotate pseudo-labeled examples from the unlabeled data. The pseudo-labels are the labels predicted by a model, in this case, the teacher model [20]. They are assigned considering the prediction vector and selecting the class with the maximum predicted probability. The pseudo-labels do not come from experts, therefore some of them match with the correct class (relevant labels) and some of them do not (noisy labels) [14,38]. Noisy labels can compromise the learning process [14]. The choice to use high-capacity models permits to better separate noisy labels from relevant labels [14]. Furthermore, high-capacity models can better leverage a large amount of data [38]. The teacher model annotates unlabeled data with pseudo-labels that are used for training the student model. The annotation process is made predicting the class probabilities of unlabeled data [20]. The relevant samples are labeled with the highest probabilities for separating them from noisy examples. The student model is a smaller (compared to the teacher) neural network, trained using a combination of pseudo-labeled and strongly-annotated data. The choice to use a smaller network is made so that the model can be highly efficient at test time, but guaranteeing performance comparable to the teacher [12].

The training schema is composed of a pipeline of operations that are summarized here:

1. train the teacher with strongly-annotated data;
2. predict pseudo-labeled data;
3. select pseudo-labeled data;
4. train the student with pseudo-labeled data;
5. fine-tune the student with strongly-annotated data.

In the first step of the training schema, the teacher model is trained with strongly-annotated data. Thus, it learns how to select relevant examples from the unlabeled data. In the second step, the teacher annotates unseen data, generating a prediction vector of the class probabilities from a softmax layer. In the third step, the teacher selects the pseudo-labeled samples to present to the student model. The samples selected are the ones with the highest probability of belonging to a class. The vectors are sorted in descending order by the class probability. K samples per class are selected from the highest-ranked ones [38]. In this step, it is essential to minimize the number of noisy samples selected [14]. Therefore, the right K value must be selected. However, this value is not possible to be identified a priori. In the fourth step, the student model is trained using the pseudo-labeled data. In this step, it is possible to explore different K values. Therefore, the model is trained with different subsets of pseudo-labeled data, each one including a different number of pseudo-labels per class. Among these models, the one that shows the best performance is the one trained with the subset with fewer noisy labels. Indeed, this subset includes the smallest number of noisy labels, compared with the others. In the fifth step, the student model is fine-tuned using the strongly-annotated data. The learning paradigm is tested on the student model. The model is tested in two different steps of the pipeline and it is compared with fully-supervised learning approach. Firstly, it is tested after the training with only the pseudo-labeled data (Fig. 1, step 4). Secondly, it is tested after the training with the pseudo-labeled and the fine-tuning with the strongly annotated data (Fig. 1, step 5). In the fully-supervised learning approach, the student model is trained only with strongly-annotated data.

2.3   Implementation

The teacher model is Resnext50_32x4d, while the student model is DenseNet121 [15]. Both networks are implemented in PyTorch (version 1.1.0) and trained on the Cartesius cluster infrastructure, provided by the SURFsara HPC (High-Performance Computing) centre[5], using Tesla K40m GPUs. Both the architectures are trained with the same strategy to set the hyperparameters. In order to avoid overfitting, class-wise data augmentation is applied during the training, with a probabilistic rate. The strategy for training the models regards the hyperparameters of the network, the weights used for initializing the models and the replacement of the last layer. Both models are trained ten different times, in order to avoid the non-deterministic effects caused by the stochastic gradient descent and the data augmentation pipeline. The average and standard deviation of the models are reported. The teacher model used for annotating the unlabeled data is the one that shows the best performance in the TMAZ validation set among the ten repetitions. The student model, selected to be fine-tuned with strongly annotated data, is the one that shows the best performance on the TMAZ validation set among the ten repetitions. Each of these training repetitions is trained for 15 epochs with a batch size of 32 samples. The hyperparameters adopted are the same for both models: they are optimized using Adam optimizer with a learning rate of 0.001 and a decay rate of 10^{-6}. Both the models are initialized with pre-trained weights. The teacher model has the initialized weights pre-trained with the YFCC100M dataset [34], which includes almost 1 billion Instagram images [38]. The student model has the initialized weights pre-trained with ImageNet images [9]. In both models, the architecture is changed for adapting the problem to the number of classes. The last layer of the original network architecture (1000 nodes) is changed with a new dense layer of four nodes (the number of classes in this classification problem). A class-wise data augmentation (CWDA) solution is applied during the training phase of the CNNs. The class-wise data augmentation consists of three operations, applied in order to avoid overfitting. The operations of the pipeline are rotation, flipping and colour augmentation, implemented with the Albumentations open-source library [5]. They are applied to the training images with a probability of 0.5 on each batch. The unbalanced distribution of the classes, combined with the small

---

[5] https://userinfo.surfsara.nl/systems/hpc-cloud. Retrieved 7th of February, 2020.

amount of data, can lead to overfitting. Class-wise data augmentation (CWDA) is applied to reduce the effect of unbalanced classes on training. It is implemented by the GitHub open access repository of Ufoyn[6].

3   Results

The models trained with the teacher/student paradigm perform better than the one trained with the fully-supervised training. The performance is evaluated with the weighted Cohen κ-score. The models are trained to classify the Gleason patterns and the Gleason score of histopathological image patches. The Gleason patterns are evaluated on images with annotations manually made by a pathologist, while the Gleason score on the diagnosis included in the medical report. The performance is evaluated on the student model and compared with a fully-supervised learning approach.

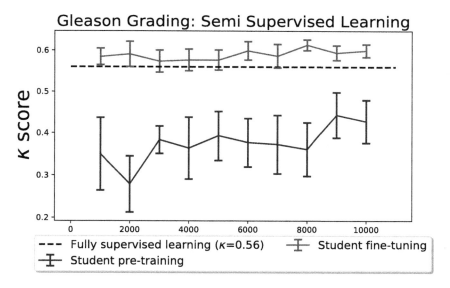

Fig. 2. Results of the student model average performance, trained with the semi-supervised approach, evaluated at the patch level, using the TMAZ test set. They are measured by the κ-score as a function of the amount of pseudo-labeled data used to train the student model.

The performance is measured by the weighted Cohen κ-score as a function of the amount of pseudo-labeled examples (per class) used for training the student model. The weighted Cohen κ-score is a metric for measuring agreement between raters. The quadratically weighted κ is adopted for penalizing stronger

---

[6] https://github.com/ufoym/imbalanced-dataset-sampler. Retrieved 6th of February, 2020.

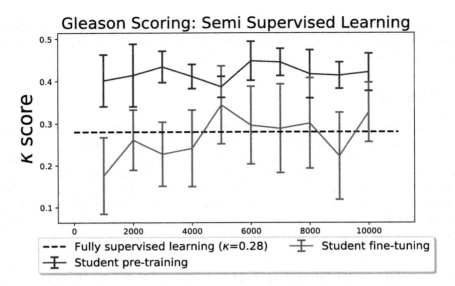

Fig. 3. Results of the student model average performance, trained with the semi-supervised approach, evaluated at the WSI level, using the TCGA-PRAD test set. They are measured by the κ-score as a function of the amount of pseudo-labeled data used to train the student model.

predictions far from their real class. The Gleason score classification is evaluated at the WSI level, while Gleason pattern classification is evaluated at the patch-level. The Gleason score is measured by the aggregation of Gleason patterns at the patch level, using a majority voting system and the rules of the American Urology Association[7]. In this paper, the majority voting system is applied only on 1000 patches per WSI, selected with the Blue-ratio technique [7]. Blue-ratio permits to avoid the extraction of patches with a small number of nuclei, such as the ones that contain stroma or fat. The student models are tested also using the Wilcoxon Rank-Sum test, in order to determine if they have the same probabilistic distribution (null hypothesis) of the models trained with the fully-supervised approach. The null hypothesis is tested positive when the p-value > 0.05, while it is tested negative when the p-value < 0.05. Figures 2 and 3 show the performance of the training/student semi-supervised paradigm. In both figures, three curves are present. The blue curve represents the performance measured after training the student model with pseudo-labeled data. The green curve represents the performance measured after training the model with pseudo-labeled data and then fine-tuning it with strongly-annotated data. The dashed black line represents the performance of the fully-supervised training of the student

---

[7] https://www.auanet.org/education/auauniversity/education-products-and-resources/pathology-for-urologists/prostate/adenocarcinoma/prostatic-adenocarcinoma-gleason-grading-(modified-grading-by-isup). Retrieved 5th of February, 2020.

model. The classification performance of Gleason patterns in the TMAZ dataset is presented in Fig. 2, while the classification performance of Gleason scores in TCGA-PRAD is presented in Fig. 3. In Fig. 2, the performance is measured on the TMAZ test set at the patch level. The baseline models (student model trained only with strongly–annotated data) reached a $\kappa = 0.5608 \pm 0.0308$. Each curve has a peak value since the curves are not monotonically increasing. The performance of the student model trained only with pseudo-labeled data (blue curve) is below the baseline, for each one of the amounts of samples per class tested. The peak value is $\kappa = 0.4434 \pm 0.0547$, reached with the pseudo-labeled training partition with 9000 patches pseudo-labeled per class. The performance of the student model trained with pseudo-labeled and fine-tuned with strongly-annotated data (green curve) exceeds the baseline, for each one of the amounts of pseudo-labeled data tested. The peak value is $\kappa = 0.6129 \pm 0.0127$, reached with the pseudo-labeled training partition with 8000 patches pseudo-labeled per class. Therefore, the model trained with pseudo-labeled and fine-tuned with strongly-annotated data exceeds the baseline by 0.052 in κ. The improvement obtained is statistically significant (p-value $= 0.005$ for the peak value). In Fig. 3, the performance is measured on the TCGA-PRAD test set at the WSI level. The baseline models (student model trained only with strongly–annotated data) reached a $\kappa = 0.2814 \pm 0.1312$. Each curve has a peak value since the curves are not monotonically increasing. The performance of the student model trained only with pseudo-labeled data (blue curve) exceeds the baseline, for each one of the amounts of pseudo-labeled data tested. The peak value is $\kappa = 0.4478 \pm 0.0460$, reached with the pseudo-labeled training partition with 6000 patches pseudo-labeled per class. The improvement obtained is statistically significant (p-value $= 0.012$ for the peak value). The lowest performance exceeds the baseline by 0.09 in κ, where the model is trained with 5000 pseudo-labeled samples per class. The performance of the student model trained with pseudo-labeled and fine-tuned with strongly-annotated data (green curve) exceeds the baseline, only for a range (from 5000 to 8000) of pseudo-labeled samples per class tested. The peak value is $\kappa = 0.3438 \pm 0.0924$, reached with the pseudo-labeled training partition with 5000 patches pseudo-labeled per class. The improvement obtained is not statistically significant (p-value $= 0.200$ for the peak value). Therefore, the baseline is exceeded by 0.062 in κ using the semi-supervised learning. The student model trained with the semi-supervised approach, in both the steps of the pipeline tested, exceed the baseline. The student model trained with pseudo-labeled data exceeds the baseline by 0.166 in κ. The student model trained with pseudo-labeled and fine-tuned with strongly-annotated data exceeds the baseline by 0.062 in κ. The results are summarized in Table 4.

Table 4. Performance measured for the semi-supervised approach, evaluated in κ−score. If the result is statistically significant (compared with the baseline), an asterisk (*) is reported close to the value.

Dataset	Fully-supervised	Student pre-training	Student fine-tuning
TMAZ	0.5608 ± 0.0308	0.4434 ± 0.0547	**0.6129 ± 0.0127***
TCGA-PRAD	0.2814 ± 0.1312	**0.4477 ± 0.0460***	0.3437 ± 0.0923

4 Discussion

The teacher/student paradigm permits to leverage on a large amount of the unlabeled data for training a more robust CNN model and improving its performance in Gleason grading and Gleason scoring classification. The performance classification of the models trained with the paradigm is improved compared to a fully-supervised training schema. A trade-off is identified between the number of pseudo-labeled samples used for training and the model's classification performance. The paradigm permits to face the heterogeneity between datasets, limiting the overfitting. As expected, in both the Gleason grading and the Gleason scoring, the models trained combining pseudo-labels and strongly-annotated data improve the performance, compared with the fully-supervised schema. This is explainable considering that the amount of data used (combining pseudo-labels and strongly-annotated) is increased. However, the metric curves are not monotonically increasing. A peak value in *kappa* is identified for each of the approaches tested. This peak value allows exploring the best P parameter for the paradigm. P represents the amount of pseudo-labeled samples per class in a subset. The subset that reaches the peak value has less noisy pseudo-labels, compared with the other subsets. The higher the peak value, the fewer noisy labels are included in pseudo-label samples. Therefore, the higher the peak value, the higher is the performance. The paradigm can alleviate overfitting caused by heterogeneity between datasets, although models tend to adapt their weights to the data with which they are trained (as it was expected). The results show that a model, trained on a dataset, does not generalize well for a different dataset. It is a consequence of the inter-dataset heterogeneity. This effect happens for both the datasets. The student model trained with the TMAZ patches reaches good results in its own set, but it fails to generalize in the TCGA-PRAD test partition, where it obtains some of the worst results (dashed line on Fig. 3). The student model, trained with the pseudo-labeled samples, reaches the best results in TCGA-PRAD test set, but it fails to generalize in the TMAZ test partition, where it reaches the worst results (blue curve in Fig. 2). The inter-dataset heterogeneity is the reason why the student model, trained only with pseudo-labeled data, performs better on TCGA-PRAD dataset, compared with the same model trained combining pseudo-labeled and strongly-annotated data. However, training the model combining the different data sources alleviates the overfitting. On the TMAZ dataset, the model trained with both the dataset obtains the best performance ($\kappa = 0.6129 \pm 0.0127$), but it does not generalize well for the TCGA-PRAD dataset. The model's performance is better than the fully-supervised training of the student. However, the same model, trained only with pseudo-labeled data, exceeds this performance by 0.096 in κ.

5 Conclusion

In this paper, the classification of prostate cancer tissue is tackled with a novel approach, based on the semi-supervised teacher/student paradigm for training CNNs. It permits face data heterogeneity and alleviates the difficulty of obtaining a sufficient amount of locally annotated data for training the models. The approach is compared with a fully-supervised CNN learning approach. The teacher/student paradigm improves the performance of a CNN prostate cancer classification at the patch level and the WSI level. Therefore, it is possible to adopt it to leverage a large amount of unlabeled data and then improve the fully supervised classification performance of CNNs. Furthermore, the teacher/student paradigm permits to face the heterogeneity of the datasets used for training the models. It permits to generalize better in datasets that come from different medical sources, reducing the effects caused by the overfitting. In the future works, the teacher/student paradigm will be tested on different types of biopsy tissues, with larger values of K parameter and testing more training steps and within the pipeline. The code and all the pre-trained models are made publicly available on Github (https://github.com/ilmaro8/Semi_Supervised_Learning). The pseudo-labeled data are available from the corresponding author on request.

References

1. Arvaniti, E., Claassen, M.: Coupling weak and strong supervision for classification of prostate cancer histopathology images. In: Medical Imaging Meets NIPS Workshop, NIPS 2018 (2018)
2. Arvaniti, E., et al.: Automated Gleason grading of prostate cancer tissue microarrays via deep learning. Sci. Rep. **8**, 1–11 (2018)
3. Bagherzadeh, J., Asil, H.: A review of various semi-supervised learning models with a deep learning and memory approach. Iran J. Comput. Sci. **2**(2), 65–80 (2018). https://doi.org/10.1007/s42044-018-00027-6
4. Bulten, W., et al.: Automated deep-learning system for Gleason grading of prostate cancer using biopsies: a diagnostic study. Lancet Oncol. **21**(2), 233–241 (2020)
5. Buslaev, A., Parinov, A., Khvedchenya, E., Iglovikov, V.I., Kalinin, A.A.: Albumentations: fast and flexible image augmentations. ArXiv e-prints (2018)
6. Campanella, G., et al.: Clinical-grade computational pathology using weakly supervised deep learning on whole slide images. Nat. Med. **25**(8), 1301–1309 (2019)
7. Chang, H., Loss, L.A., Parvin, B.: Nuclear segmentation in H&E sections via multi-reference graph cut (MRGC). In: International Symposium Biomedical Imaging (2012)
8. Cheplygina, V., de Bruijne, M., Pluim, J.P.: Not-so-supervised: a survey of semi-supervised, multi-instance, and transfer learning in medical image analysis. Med. Image Anal. **54**, 280–296 (2019)

9. Deng, J., Dong, W., Socher, R., Li, L.J., Li, K., Fei-Fei, L.: ImageNet: a large-scale hierarchical image database. In: 2009 IEEE Conference on Computer Vision and Pattern Recognition, pp. 248–255. IEEE (2009)

10. Fischer, A.H., Jacobson, K.A., Rose, J., Zeller, R.: Hematoxylin and eosin staining of tissue and cell sections. Cold Spring Harb. Protoc. **2008**(5), pdb-prot4986 (2008)

11. Foucart, A., Debeir, O., Decaestecker, C.: Snow: semi-supervised, noisy and/or weak data for deep learning in digital pathology. In: 2019 IEEE 16th International Symposium on Biomedical Imaging (ISBI 2019), pp. 1869–1872. IEEE (2019)

12. Guo, T., Xu, C., He, S., Shi, B., Xu, C., Tao, D.: Robust student network learning. IEEE Trans. Neural Netw. Learn. Syst. **31**(7), 2455–2468 (2019)

13. Hady, M.F.A., Schwenker, F.: Semi-supervised learning. In: Bianchini, M., Maggini, M., Jain, L. (eds.) Handbook on Neural Information Processing. Intelligent Systems Reference Library, vol. 49, pp. 215–239. Springer, Heidelberg (2013). https://doi.org/10.1007/978-3-642-36657-4_7

14. Han, B., et al.: Co-teaching: robust training of deep neural networks with extremely noisy labels. In: Advances in Neural Information Processing Systems, pp. 8527–8537 (2018)

15. Huang, G., Liu, Z., Weinberger, K.Q.: Densely connected convolutional networks. CoRR abs/1608.06993 (2016). http://arxiv.org/abs/1608.06993

16. Janowczyk, A., Zuo, R., Gilmore, H., Feldman, M., Madabhushi, A.: HistoQC: an open-source quality control tool for digital pathology slides. JCO Clin. Cancer Inf. **3**, 1–7 (2019)

17. Komura, D., Ishikawa, S.: Machine learning methods for histopathological image analysis. Comput. Struct. Biotechnol. J. **16**, 34–42 (2018)

18. van der Laak, J., Ciompi, F., Litjens, G.: No pixel-level annotations needed. Nat. Biomed. Eng. **3**, 1–2 (2019)

19. Larson, K., Ho, H.H., Anumolu, P.L., Chen, T.M.: Hematoxylin and eosin tissue stain in Mohs micrographic surgery: a review. Dermatol. Surg. **37**(8), 1089–1099 (2011)

20. Lee, D.H.: Pseudo-label: the simple and efficient semi-supervised learning method for deep neural networks. In: Workshop on Challenges in Representation Learning, ICML, vol. 3, p. 2 (2013)

21. Li, J., et al.: An EM-based semi-supervised deep learning approach for semantic segmentation of histopathological images from radical prostatectomies. Comput. Med. Imaging Graph. **69**, 125–133 (2018)

22. Litjens, G., et al.: 1399 H&E-stained sentinel lymph node sections of breast cancer patients: the CAMELYON dataset. GigaScience **7**(6), giy065 (2018)

23. Litjens, G., et al.: A survey on deep learning in medical image analysis. Med. Image Anal. **42**, 60–88 (2017)

24. Lu, M.Y., Chen, R.J., Wang, J., Dillon, D., Mahmood, F.: Semi-supervised histology classification using deep multiple instance learning and contrastive predictive coding. arXiv preprint arXiv:1910.10825 (2019)

25. Otálora, S., Atzori, M., Khan, A., Jimenez-del Toro, O., Andrearczyk, V., Müller, H.: A systematic comparison of deep learning strategies for weakly supervised Gleason grading. In: Medical Imaging 2020: Digital Pathology, vol. 11320, p. 113200L. International Society for Optics and Photonics (2020)

26. Otálora, S., Marini, N., Müller, H., Atzori, M.: Semi-weakly supervised learning for prostate cancer image classification with teacher-student deep convolutional networks. In: Cardoso, J., et al. (eds.) IMIMIC/MIL3ID/LABELS -2020. LNCS, vol. 12446, pp. 193–203. Springer, Cham (2020). https://doi.org/10.1007/978-3-030-61166-8_21

27. Otálora, S., Perdomo, O., González, F., Müller, H.: Training deep convolutional neural networks with active learning for exudate classification in eye fundus images. In: Cardoso, M.J., et al. (eds.) LABELS/CVII/STENT-2017. LNCS, vol. 10552, pp. 146–154. Springer, Cham (2017). https://doi.org/10.1007/978-3-319-67534-3_16

28. Peikari, M., Salama, S., Nofech-Mozes, S., Martel, A.L.: A cluster-then-label semi-supervised learning approach for pathology image classification. Sci. Rep. **8**(1), 1–13 (2018)

29. Raczkowski, L., Mozejko, M., Zambonelli, J., Szczurek, E.: ARA: accurate, reliable and active histopathological image classification framework with Bayesian deep learning. Sci. Rep. **9**(1), 1–12 (2019)

30. Shao, W., Sun, L., Zhang, D.: Deep active learning for nucleus classification in pathology images. In: 2018 IEEE 15th International Symposium on Biomedical Imaging (ISBI 2018), pp. 199–202. IEEE (2018)

31. Shaw, S., Pajak, M., Lisowska, A., Tsaftaris, S.A., O'Neil, A.Q.: Teacher-student chain for efficient semi-supervised histology image classification. arXiv preprint arXiv:2003.08797 (2020)

32. Ström, P., et al.: Pathologist-level grading of prostate biopsies with artificial intelligence. arXiv preprint arXiv:1907.01368 (2019)

33. Tellez, D., et al.: Quantifying the effects of data augmentation and stain color normalization in convolutional neural networks for computational pathology. Med. Image Anal. **58**, 101544 (2019)

34. Thomee, B., et al.: The new data and new challenges in multimedia research. CoRR abs/1503.01817 (2015). http://arxiv.org/abs/1503.01817

35. Jimenez-del-Toro, O., Otálora, S., Atzori, M., Müller, H.: Deep multimodal case–based retrieval for large histopathology datasets. In: Wu, G., Munsell, B.C., Zhan, Y., Bai, W., Sanroma, G., Coupé, P. (eds.) Patch-MI 2017. LNCS, vol. 10530, pp. 149–157. Springer, Cham (2017). https://doi.org/10.1007/978-3-319-67434-6_17

36. del Toro, O.J., et al.: Convolutional neural networks for an automatic classification of prostate tissue slides with high-grade Gleason score. In: Medical Imaging 2017: Digital Pathology, vol. 10140, p. 101400O. International Society for Optics and Photonics (2017)

37. Tsujikawa, T.: Robust cell detection and segmentation for image cytometry reveal Th17 cell heterogeneity. Cytom. Part A **95**(4), 389–398 (2019)

38. Yalniz, I.Z., Jégou, H., Chen, K., Paluri, M., Mahajan, D.: Billion-scale semi-supervised learning for image classification. arXiv preprint arXiv:1905.00546 (2019)

39. Zhou, Z., Shin, J., Zhang, L., Gurudu, S., Gotway, M., Liang, J.: Fine-tuning convolutional neural networks for biomedical image analysis: actively and incrementally. In: Proceedings of the IEEE Conference on Computer Vision and Pattern Recognition, pp. 7340–7351 (2017)

Self-attentive Adversarial Stain Normalization

Aman Shrivastava[1], William Adorno[1], Yash Sharma[1], Lubaina Ehsan[1],
S. Asad Ali[2], Sean R. Moore[1], Beatrice Amadi[3], Paul Kelly[3,4], Sana Syed[1(✉)],
and Donald E. Brown[1(✉)]

[1] University of Virginia, Charlottesville, VA, USA
{as3ek,wa3mr,ys5hd,ss8xj,deb}@virginia.edu
[2] Aga Khan University, Karachi, Pakistan
[3] University of Zambia School of Medicine, Lusaka, Zambia
[4] Queen Mary University of London, London, England

Abstract. Hematoxylin and Eosin (H&E) stained Whole Slide Images
(WSIs) are utilized for biopsy visualization-based diagnostic and prognostic assessment of diseases. Variation in the H&E staining process
across different lab sites can lead to important variations in biopsy image
appearance. These variations introduce an undesirable bias when the
slides are examined by pathologists or used for training deep learning
models. Traditionally proposed stain normalization and color augmentation strategies can handle the human level bias. But deep learning models
can easily disentangle the linear transformation used in these approaches,
resulting in undesirable bias and lack of generalization. To handle these
limitations, we propose a Self-Attentive Adversarial Stain Normalization (SAASN) approach for the normalization of multiple stain appearances to a common domain. This unsupervised generative adversarial
approach includes self-attention mechanism for synthesizing images with
finer detail while preserving the structural consistency of the biopsy features during translation. SAASN demonstrates consistent and superior
performance compared to other popular stain normalization techniques
on H&E stained duodenal biopsy image data.

Keywords: Stain normalization · Adversarial learning

1 Introduction

Histopathology involves staining patient biopsies for microscopic inspection to
identify visual evidence of diseases. The most widely used stain in histopathology
is the Hematoxylin and Eosin (H&E) stain [4]. Hematoxylin has a deep blue-
purple color and stains acidic structures such as nucleic acids (DNA in cell
nuclei). While Eosin is red-pink, and stains basic structures such as nonspecific
proteins in the cytoplasm and the stromal matrix. Staining is crucial as it enables
visualization of the microscopic structural features in the biopsy. The process

A. Del Bimbo et al. (Eds.): ICPR 2020 Workshops, LNCS 12661, pp. 120–140, 2021.
https://doi.org/10.1007/978-3-030-68763-2_10

of staining is followed by glass biopsy slide creation and eventually digitization into Whole Slide Images (WSIs) using digital scanners.

Computer vision is becoming increasingly useful in the field of histology for computed-aided diagnosis and discovering information about histopathological microscopic cellular [13]. Tremendous potential has been shown for training deep learning algorithms on these datasets for diagnosis and visual understanding of diseases requiring histopathological assessment. Convolution Neural Networks (CNNs) have been successfully reported for biopsy-based diagnosis of breast cancer and enteropathies among others [15,33]. The performance and fairness of such data-driven methods is dependent on the data used for training. Therefore, it is imperative for the training data to be free of any bias that might skew the models. A common source of such bias is significant stain color variation among images. This is due to the discrepancies in the manufacturing protocol and the raw materials of the staining chemicals [1] across different sites where the biopsy slides are prepared. Multiple H&E stain distributions within the CNN input data can lead to biased predictions where the results are influenced by color differences rather than microscopic cellular features of interest for clinical diagnostic interpretation. Additionally, it causes difficulty for a trained model to make predictions on a biopsy WSI with a new stain appearance that is not represented in the data used to train the model.

To overcome these issues, researchers have developed stain normalization techniques to convert all input images to an equivalent color distribution. Some of the most popular stain normalization techniques depend on a qualitatively chosen target image that represents an ideal color appearance [10,16,28]. The input (source) image is normalized to match the stain profile of the chosen target image. The obvious downside to this approach is that the normalization is highly dependent on the color distribution of a single image. Rather than using just one target image to represent an entire stain distribution, an alternative approach to consider an entire set of images that share the same stain distribution as the target domain has been suggested [9,24]. A mapping function can then be learned to translate images from a particular source domain to a target domain. This problem can be modelled as an unsupervised image-to-image translation task [14].

Recently, Generative Adversarial Networks (GANs) have been shown to demonstrate exceptional results in unpaired image translation tasks [11,34,38]. However, the challenge posed by the stain normalization task is to ensure the preservation of fine details and microscopic structural properties that are crucial for the correct disease assessment. Additionally, since the biopsy slides can be sourced from multiple sites, the framework needs to be capable of mapping multiple stain distributions to a common target distribution.

In this paper, we propose a novel adversarial approach that can execute *many-to-one* domain stain normalization. A custom loss function, structural cycle-consistency loss, is designed to make sure that the structure of the image is preserved during translation. Self-attention [19] is used to ensure that highly detailed microscopic features can be synthesized in the image. Our approach and other leading stain normalization techniques are compared on duodenum biopsy image data that was used to diagnose Celiac or Environmental Enteropathy disease in children, and on MITOS-ATYPIA Challenge dataset consisting of H&E stained WSI slides scanned by two scanners: Aperio Scanscope XT and Hamamatsu Nanozoomer 2.0-HT. SAASN demonstrated superior performance in preserving the structural integrity of images while transferring the stain distribution from one domain to the other.

2   Related Work

The earliest methods that attempted stain normalization were primarily simple style transfer techniques. Histogram specification mapped the histogram statistics of the target image with the histogram statistics of the source [3]. This approach only works well if the target and source images have similar color distributions. Forcing the normalization of the source image to match the histogram statistics of the target can create artifacts which can alter the structural integrity. As demonstrated by Reinhard [21], color transfer with histogram specification can also be performed in a decorrelated CIELAB color space which is designed to approximate the human visual system.

For H&E stained histology images, the presence of each stain or the lack thereof at each pixel should represent the most appropriate color space. Considering this, researchers developed stain normalization methods that outperformed the histogram specification technique by leveraging stain separation. These techniques start with converting an RGB image into Optical Density (O_D) as $O_D = log\frac{I_0}{I}$, where I_0 is the total possible illumination intensity of the image and I is the RGB image. Color Deconvolution (CD) is made easier in the OD space, because the stains now have a linear relationship with the OD values. The CD is typically expressed as $O_D = VS$, where V is the matrix of stain vectors and S is the stain density map. The stain density map can preserve the cell structures of the source image, while the stain vectors are updated to reflect the stain colors of the target image.

In Macenko [16], stain separation is computed using singular value decomposition on the OD tuples. Planes are created from the two largest singular values to represent H&E stains. One useful assumption with this approach is that the color appearance matrix is non-negative, this is the case because a stain value of zero would refer to the stain not being present at all. The approach by Vahadane [28] also includes the non-negative assumption, as well as, a sparsity assumptions, which states that each pixel is characterized by an effective stain that relates to a particular cell structure (nuclei cells, cytoplasm, etc.). Stain separation is generated with Sparse Non-negative Matrix Factorization (SNMF) where the sparsity acts as a constraint to greatly reduce the solution space [23]. SNMF is calculated using dictionary learning via the SPAMS package.

While Macenko and Vahadane are both unsupervised techniques, supervised approaches to this problem have also been studied. Khan [10] applies a relevance vector machine or a random forest model to classify each pixel as hematoxylin, eosin or background. The authors provide a pre-trained model for cases which is only useful if the color distribution of new source images is close to the color distribution of their training data. Training a new model would require a training set with pixel level annotations for each stain. After the stain separation, the color of the target image is mapped with a non-linear spline. The non-linear mapping approach can lead to undesirable artifacts and this normalization approach is more computationally costly than the unsupervised approaches.

Recently, techniques for stain normalization have progressed to include non-linear approaches [2,9,10,24,36]. The StainGAN [24] approach applied the CycleGAN framework for *one-to-one* domain stain transfers. In a *one-to-one* stain transfer situation, the cycle-consistency loss is calculated by taking the $L1$ distance between the cycled image and the ground truth. In a *many-to-one* situation, the cycled image will likely have a different color appearance than the original image. Therefore, a new loss function that focuses on image structure and not the color differences is required.

Biopsy WSIs contain repetitive patterns across the image in the form of recurring cell structures, stain gradients, and background alike. During translation, these spatial dependencies can be used to synthesize realistic images with finer details. Self-attention [19] exhibits impressive capability in modelling long-range dependencies in images. SAGAN [37] demonstrated the use of self-attention mechanism into convolutional GANs to synthesize images in a class conditional image generation task. We incorporate these advances in SAASN to enable it to efficiently find spatial dependencies in different areas of the image.

3   Approach

The general objective of the proposed framework is to learn the mapping between stain distributions represented by domains X and Y. Since the aim of the approach is to normalize stain patterns across the entire dataset, one of these domains can be considered as the target domain (say Y). The task is then to generate images that are indistinguishable the target domain images based on stain differences. The stain normalization task desires translation of images to a singular domain of stain distribution. This allows us to have multiple sub-domains in domain X representing different stain patterns. The overall objective then becomes to learn mapping functions $G_{YX} : X \rightarrow Y$ and $G_{XY} : Y \rightarrow X$ given unpaired training samples $\{x_i^k\}_{i=1}^N$, $x_i^k \in X^{(k)} \in X$, $k \in [1, K]$ where K denotes the number of sub-domains in X and $\{y_j\}_{j=1}^M$, $y_j \in Y$. The distribution of the training dataset is denoted as $x \sim p(x \mid k)$ and $y \sim p(y)$. Additionally, two discriminator functions D_X and D_Y are used. D_X is employed to distinguish mapped images $G_{XY}(y_i)$ from x_i while in a similar fashion D_Y is used to distinguish $G_{YX}(x_i)$ from y_i. As illustrated in Fig. 1, the mapping function G_{XY} will map images from domain Y to a previously undefined sub-domain $\hat{X}$ whose boundary is defined by the optimization function and the training data distributions in domain X. The overall optimization function used to train the

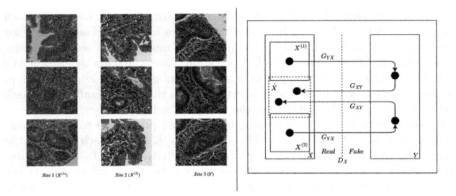

Fig. 1. (Left) H&E stained duodenal biopsy patches created from whole slide images sourced from different locations. **(Right)** Visual example of a *many-to-one* stain transfer network. Two different stains are present as inputs within X: $X^{(1)}$ and $X^{(2)}$. Both of these domains are translated to Y with G_{XY}. To complete the cycle, G_{YX} returns the image back to the X domain, but it can no longer be mapped directly to the input sub-domains $X^{(1)}$ or $X^{(2)}$ from which it originated. Instead, the image is mapped back to $\hat{X}$ which is represents a new domain of stain appearance.

designed framework includes a combination of *adversarial loss* [5], *cycle consistency loss* [38], *identity loss* [26], *structural cycle consistency loss* based on the *structural similarity index* [32] and a *discriminator boundary control* factor.

Adversarial loss is used to ensure that the stain distribution of the generated images matches the distribution of the real (ground truth) images in that domain. The objective for the mapping function $G_{YX} : X \rightarrow Y$ and the corresponding discriminator D_Y is defined as:

$$\mathcal{L}_{adv}^Y = \mathbb{E}_{y \sim p_{(y)}}[\log D_Y(y)] + \mathbb{E}_{x \sim p_{(x|k)}}[\log(1 - D_Y(G_{YX}(x)))] \tag{1}$$

Here G_{YX} tries to generate images that are indistinguishable from images in domain Y and consequently fool the discriminator D_Y, i.e. the generator G_{YX} tries to minimize the given objective function while the discriminator D_Y tries to maximize it. Similarly the objective for the reverse mapping function $G_{XY} : Y \rightarrow X$ is defined. The presence of multiple distinct stain distributions in the domain X can make it challenging for the discriminator D_X to learn the decision boundary surrounding the domain X. This can especially pose a challenge when there is an overlap or proximity in the stain distribution of one of the sub-domains of X and the target domain Y in the high-dimensional space. Therefore, to make sure that the decision boundary learned by D_X does not include sections of the target domain Y, a **discriminator boundary control** factor is added to the optimization function as follows:

$$\mathcal{L}_{adv}^X = \mathbb{E}_{x \sim p_{(x|k)}}[\log D_X(x)] + \mathbb{E}_{y \sim p_{(y)}}[\log(1 - D_X(G_{XY}(y)))] \\ + \mathbb{E}_{y \sim p_{(y)}}[\log(1 - D_X(y))] \tag{2}$$

Cycle consistency loss [38] is implemented to reconcile with the unpaired nature of the task. To overcome the lack of a ground truth image for a fake image generated in a particular domain, the image is mapped back to its original domain using the reverse mapping function. The reconstructed image is then compared to the original source image to optimize the mapping function as follows:

$$\mathcal{L}_{cyc} = \mathbb{E}_{x \sim p(x|k)} \left[\left\| G_{XY}(G_{YX}(x)) - x \right\|_1 \right] + \mathbb{E}_{y \sim p(y)} \left[\left\| G_{YX}(G_{XY}(y)) - y \right\|_1 \right] \quad (3)$$

Structural cycle consistency loss is added to the objective function to alleviate the shortcomings of the cycle consistency loss for *many-to-one* translation. In a *many-to-one* situation, the cycled images are likely to have a distinct color distribution than any of the sub-domains. Therefore minimizing the $L1$ distance between original and the cycled image alone is not an effective way to ensure cycle consistency. We use a color agnostic structural dissimilarity loss based on the Structural Similarity (SSIM) index [32] as follows:

$$\mathcal{L}_{scyc} = \frac{1 - SSIM\left(G_{XY}(G_{YX}(x)), x\right)}{2} + \frac{1 - SSIM\left(G_{YX}(G_{XY}(y)), y\right)}{2} \quad (4)$$

Additionally, to ensure that the the mapping learnt by the generator does not result in the loss of biological artifacts, the structural dissimilarity loss is also computed between the mapped and the original image:

$$\mathcal{L}_{dssim} = \frac{(1 - SSIM\left(G_{YX}(x), x\right))}{2} + \frac{(1 - SSIM\left(G_{XY}(y), y\right))}{2} \quad (5)$$

where

$$SSIM(a, b) = \frac{(2\mu_a\mu_b + C_1) + (2\sigma_{ab} + C_2)}{(\mu_a^2 + \mu_b^2 + C_1)(\sigma_a^2 + \sigma_b^2 + C_2)} \quad (6)$$

where μ, σ are the respective means and standard deviations of the windows (a and b) of the fixed size $N \times N$ that strides over the input image. C_1 and C_2 are stabilizing factors that prevent the denominator from disappearing. These measures are calculated for multiple corresponding windows of gray-scaled input images and aggregated to get the final measure. Gray-scaled inputs are used to focus on structural differences between images and not changes in color.

Identity loss [26] is utilized to regularize the generator and preserve the overall composition of the image. The generators are rewarded if a near identity mapping is produced when an image from the respective target domain is provided as an input image. In other words, when an image is fed into a generator of its own domain, the generator should produce an image that is nearly identical to the input. This is enforced by minimizing the $L1$ distance of the resulting image with the input image as follows:

$$\mathcal{L}_{id} = \mathbb{E}_{y \sim p(y)} \left[\left\| G_{YX}(y) - y \right\|_1 \right] + \mathbb{E}_{x \sim p(x|k)} \left[\left\| G_{XY}(x) - x \right\|_1 \right] \quad (7)$$

The overall objective function then becomes:

$$\mathcal{L}(G_{YX}, G_{XY}, D_X, D_Y) = \mathcal{L}_{adv}^Y + \mathcal{L}_{adv}^X + \alpha * \mathcal{L}_{cyc} + \beta * \mathcal{L}_{scyc} + \gamma * \mathcal{L}_{dssim} + \delta * \mathcal{L}_{id} \quad (8)$$

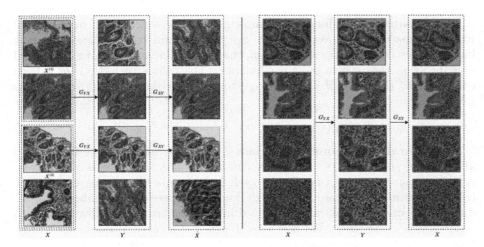

Fig. 2. *Left*: Results when mapping was done from two sub-domains of X to Y. Patches from both domains $X^{(1)}$ and $X^{(2)}$ are translated to domain Y using G_{YX}. These generated images are then translated back to a new domain defined by a G_{XY} as a combination of stain distributions of sub-domains of X. Patches on either end of the second column are real images from domain Y and have been added to visually show the performance of G_{YX}. *Right*: Results when mapping was learnt using a single domain in X to Y.

where parameters α, β, γ and δ manage the importance of different loss terms. The parameters in the generators and the discriminators are tuned by solving the above objective as:

$$G_{YX}^{*}, G_{XY}^{*} = \arg \min_{G_{YX}, G_{XY}} \max_{D_X, D_Y} \mathcal{L}(G_{YX}, G_{XY}, D_X, D_Y) \qquad (9)$$

In the following sections, we describe the implementation and compare our results with other current state-of-the-art methods of color normalization with both multiple ($K = 2$) and single ($K = 1$) sub-domains in X (Fig. 2).

4   Dataset and Implementation

4.1   Dataset

For this paper, the algorithm was evaluated on two datasets: 1) duodenal biopsy patches were extracted from 465 high resolution WSIs from 150 H&E stained duodenal biopsy slides (where each glass slide could have one or more biopsies). The biopsies were from patients with Celiac Disease (CD) and Environmental Enteropathy (EE). The biopsies were from children who underwent endoscopy procedures at either Site 1 (Aga Khan University, Pakistan, 10 children, n = 34 WSIs), Site 2 (University Teaching Hospital, Zambia, 16 children, n = 19 WSIs), or Site 3 (University of Virginia Childrens Hospital, 63 children, n = 236

WSIs; and 61 healthy children, n = 173 WSI). It was observed that there was a significantly large stain variation between images originating from different sites. While images from Site 1 were different tones of dark blue, images from Site 3 were more pink with images from Site 2 lying somewhere in the middle of this spectrum. Our approach and other competing methods were performed on 500×500 pixel patches generated from the images, which were further resized to 256×256 pixel to marginally reduce the resolution. In the multi-sub-domain setup, patches from Site 1 (sub-domain $X^{(1)}$) and Site 2 (sub-domain $X^{(2)}$) were both considered to be in domain X and patches from Site 3 to be in domain Y. While in single sub-domain training setup, patches from Site 1 were considered to be in domain X and Site 3 to be in domain Y. For training both X and Y had 16000 patches where $X^{(1)}$ contributed 10817 and $X^{(2)}$ 5183 patches. Testing metrics were computed on 1500 patches in each sub-domain.

2) The algorithm was also evaluated on a publicly available MITOS-ATYPIA 14 challenge dataset[1] to demonstrate performance on a *one-to-one domain* set-up. Dataset consists of 1136 frames at x40 magnification which are stained with standard H&E dyes. Same tissue section has been scanned by two slide scanners: Aperio Scanscope XT and Hamamatsu Nanozoomer 2.0-HT. For evaluating the model, 500×500 patches were generated from whole slide images of both scanners resized to 256×256. 23000 patches were used for training the model and 9600 patches were used for evaluation. It was ensured distinct WSIs were used for training and validation to avoid any type of bias and leak.

4.2   Network Architecture

The generator network is a modified **U-Net** [22] which has been shown to generate excellent results in image translation tasks [8]. U-Net is encoder-decoder network [6] that uses skip connections between layers i and $n - i$ where n is the total number of layers in the network. In previous encoder-decoder architectures [20,31,35]. The input is passed through a series of convolutional layers that downsample the input until a bottleneck is reached after which the information is upsampled to generate an output of the desired dimensions. Therefore, by design all information passes through the bottleneck. In the stain normalization task, input and output of the network share a lot of general information that might get obscured through the flow of such a network. Skip connections in a U-Net solve this problem by circumventing the bottleneck and concatenating the output from the encoder layers to the input of the corresponding decoder layers.

The discriminator is a 4 block CNN, which eventually outputs the decision for each image. Every convolutional block in both the generator and the discriminator is a module consisting of a convolution-normalization-ReLU layers in that order. Both instance [27] and batch [7] normalization were used; and batch normalization was empirically chosen for the final network. The convolutional layers have a kernel size of 4 and stride 2, with the exception of the last layer in the discriminator which operates with stride 1.

---

[1] https://mitos-atypia-14.grand-challenge.org/.

Self-attention layers [19] were added after every convolutional block in both the generator and the discriminator network. The self-attention mechanism complements the convolutions by establishing and leveraging long range dependencies across image regions. It help the generator synthesize images with finer details in regions based on a different spatial region in the image. Additionally the discriminator with self-attention layers is able to enforce more complex structural constraints on input images while making a decision. As described in SAGAN [37], a non-local network [30] was used to apply the self-attention computation. The input features $x \in \mathbb{R}^{C \times N}$ are transformed using three different learnable functions $q(x), k(x), v(x)$ analogous to query, key and value setup in [29] as follows:

$$q(x) = W_q x; \qquad k(x) = W_k x; \qquad v(x) = W_v x \qquad (10)$$

where $W_q \in \mathbb{R}^{\bar{C} \times C}$, $W_k \in \mathbb{R}^{\bar{C} \times C}$, and $W_v \in \mathbb{R}^{\bar{C} \times C}$. Also, C is the number of channels, $N = height * width$ of the feature map from the previous layer and $\bar{C}$ is an adjustable parameter. For our model, $\bar{C}$ was set as $C/8$. The attention map is further calculated as:

$$\begin{aligned} \alpha_{j,i} &= softmax(k(x_i)^T g(x_j)) \\ &= \frac{\exp\left(k(x_i)^T g(x_j)\right)}{\sum_{i=1}^{N} \exp\left(k(x_i)^T g(x_j)\right)} \end{aligned} \qquad (11)$$

where $\alpha_{j,i}$ represents the attention placed on location i while synthesizing location j. The ouput $o \in \mathbb{R}^{C \times N}$ is calculated as:

$$o_j = \sum_{i=1}^{N} \alpha_{j,i} v(x_i) \qquad (12)$$

The output o is then scaled and added to the initial input to give the final result,

$$y_i = \mu o_i + x_i \qquad (13)$$

where μ is a learnable parameter that is initialized to 0.

Spectral normalization when applied on the layers of the discriminator network has been shown to stabilize the training of a GAN [18]. Moreover, based on the findings about the effect of a generator's conditioning on its performance, Zhang [37] argue that while training a self-attention based GAN, both the generator and the discriminator can benefit from using spectral normalization. Therefore, a spectral normalization (with spectral norm of all weight layers as 1) was added to all the networks.

4.3   Training Details

The parameter values of $\alpha = 10$, $\beta = 10$, $\gamma = 10$ and $\delta = 0.1$ were empirically chosen after experimentation for the evaluation model. Across all experiments,

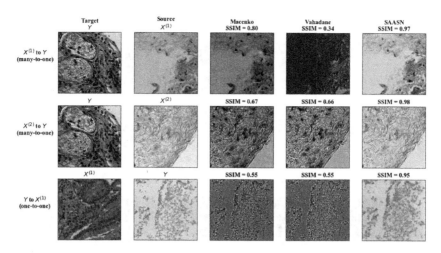

Fig. 3. Visual comparison of performance in cases where Macenko and Vahadane techniques struggle to properly transfer stain in each scenario. The target image only applies to the Macenko and Vahadane techniques.

we used the Adam optimizer [12] with a learning rate of 0.0002 and batch size 16. The model was trained for the first 50 epochs with a fixed learning rate and the next 50 epochs while linearly decaying the learning rate to 0. Instead of updating the discriminator with an image generated form the latest generator, a random image selected from a buffer of 50 previously generated images was used to perform the update cycle [25]. Least-squares adversarial loss inspired from LSGAN [17] was used instead of the described cross-entropy loss for some experiments. The least-squares loss stabilized the training but there was no significant visual difference in the results produced.

5   Results and Evaluation

To demonstrate the value of each introduced term in the designed loss function, an ablation study was performed. A competitive version of StainGAN [24] was also implemented based on the information given in the paper. It was observed that the addition of self-attention layers helped the model to generate more vibrant results that preserved medically significant artifacts. For instance, the red blood cells in the second row of Fig. 4 get visually merged with the surrounding cells when self-attention is not used. The ablation study shows that with the cycle consistency loss alone the forward mapping function (G_{XY}) is suppressed from providing a *many-to-one* mapping as the generated domain ($\hat{X}$) from the inverse function (G_{YX}) will overlap more with the dominant domain in the training set. Addition of the structural cycle consistency loss term alleviates this issue as it is stain agnostic and a combination of the said losses gives a more compelling result.

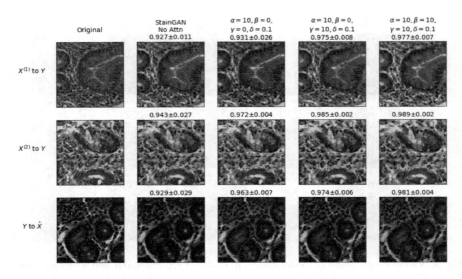

Fig. 4. Visual and quantitative comparison of performance between StainGAN and ablation study on SAASN. The numbers indicate the overall mean ± standard deviation of the SSIM index for the transformation. All models were trained in a *many-to-one* setup.

To evaluate the stain transfer, the Structural Similarity (SSIM) index is again utilized. SSIM is calculated by comparing the normalized image with the original. Both images are converted to gray-scale before beginning SSIM calculations. Our approach is compared to two of the most popular unsupervised stain normalization techniques, Macenko [16] and Vahadane [28]. The popular supervised approach by Khan [10] could not be tested due to lack of pixel-level labeling in our data. These results are compiled in Table 1 for duodenal biopsy dataset and in Table 2 for MITOS-ATYPIA dataset. For the $X^{(1)}$ to Y and the $X^{(2)}$ to Y stain transfers, the values for SAASN are higher than the other two normalization techniques and the variance is significantly smaller. This demonstrates that SAASN is not only better at preserving structure, but also consistently transfers stain without major anomalies. The traditional approaches (Vahadane and Macenko) approaches can struggle if the source has a much different stain distribution than the target. This can lead to the stains appearing in the wrong areas on the normalized image. SAASN is able to leverage information from entire stain domains and therefore is not as affected by this issue. These results demonstrate that SAASN can be trusted to produce consistent stain transfers on a robust set of stain patterns in WSI patches.

In addition to assessing the structure-preserving ability of the stain normalization methods, visual comparisons are essential to ensure that the stains have transferred properly. In Fig. 3, results are displayed for the three stain transfers in duodenal biopsy dataset. The images with the smallest $L2$-norm for combined Macenko and Vahadane SSIM values were selected to demonstrate the

Table 1. Mean ± Standard deviation of the SSIM index values for normalization across domains. For StainGAN and SAASN all values are computed for a *many-to-one* setup on the first dataset.

Method	$X^{(1)}$ to Y	$X^{(2)}$ to Y	Y to $X^{(1)}$
Vahadane	0.861 ± 0.108	0.919 ± 0.029	0.932 ± 0.033
Macenko	0.942 ± 0.033	0.934 ± 0.022	0.941 ± 0.020
StainGAN	0.927 ± 0.011	0.943 ± 0.027	0.929 ± 0.021
SAASN	**0.977 ± 0.007**	**0.989 ± 0.002**	**0.981 ± 0.004**

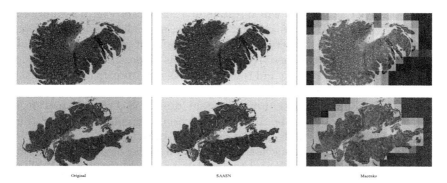

Fig. 5. Normalized Whole Slide Image using ours and traditional approaches. Macenko was chosen because it performed better than Vahadane on our dataset. The target slide for Macenko was empirically selected to give the best translation.

performance of SAASN. For $X^{(1)}$ to Y and $X^{(2)}$ to Y, the same target image from domain Y is used. For Y to $X^{(1)}$, a target image from domain $X^{(1)}$ is used. The three selected source images are similar in that they all have a large majority of pixels containing connective tissue or background. The unsupervised approaches can struggle executing color deconvolution on these types of images. This is apparent in the Macenko and Vahadane normalizations shown in Fig. 3. The stains are either inverted (hematoxylin-like color transferred to the

Table 2. Mean ± Standard deviation of the SSIM index values for normalization across domains. For StainGAN and SAASN all values are computed for the *one-to-one* setup on the second dataset.

Method	Aperio to Hamamatsu	Hamamatsu to Aperio
Vahadane	0.971 ± 0.031	0.955 ± 0.038
Macenko	0.968 ± 0.034	0.956 ± 0.039
StainGAN	0.967 ± 0.009	0.947 ± 0.032
SAASN	**0.995 ± 0.001**	**0.996 ± 0.001**

background) or confusing connective tissue as an actual cell structure. Meanwhile, SAASN did not have difficulty identifying the connective tissue or background pixels in the source image.

A similar analysis was also performed using the highest $L2$-norm values. These are the examples where the traditional methods performed the best[2]. Vahadane and Macenko are able to maintain structure, but may not visually match the target distribution or the proper background pixel color.

Stain normalization is crucial for bias-free visual examination of Whole Slide Images (WSIs) and diagnosis by medical practitioners in control trial settings. WSIs have very large dimensions and cannot be normalized without resizing to a computationally tractable size which results in a significant loss in resolution. To normalize WSIs, they must be split into patches, normalized and then stitched back together. Traditional methods perform computations for transformation independently on these patches. As a result, it is impossible to reconstruct a WSI that has a consistent stain and is indistinguishable from an original image in the target domain. As demonstrated in Fig. 5, for our method, since the trained weights of the mapping function are constant during this transformation, the reconstructed WSI could not be distinguished from original images and thus is easier for medical professionals to hold diagnosis trails.

In order to a validate a successful translation three medical professionals, including a board-certified pathologist, completed a blind review of 10 WSIs normalized via traditional and our method as shown in Fig. 5. The pathologist confirmed that medically relevant cell types (polymorphonuclear neutrophils, epithelial cells, eosinophils, lymphocytes, goblet cells, paneth cells, neuroendocrine cells) were not lost during translation. The pathologist further observed that our method was able to completely preserve the structure and the density of all of these cell types which traditional methods only partially preserved. Specifically, the eosinophilic granules in paneth cells, neuroendocrine cells and eosinophils were not appreciated in traditionally stain normalized WSIs which made it difficult to differentiating these cells from each other. cifically, the eosinophilic granules in paneth cells, neuroendocrine cells and eosinophils were not appreciated in traditionally stain normalized WSIs which made it difficult to differentiating these cells from each other.

A   Conclusions

The proposed framework is successful in effective translation of the stain appearance of histopathological images while preserving the biological features in the process. This setup was specifically designed to accommodate a *many-to-one* stain transfer situation in which multiple stains are converted to a common domain. SAASN is compared to other leading stain normalization techniques on pathology images in both *one-to-one* and *many-to-one* setup. SAASN consistently performed successful stain transfers even when the other techniques failed

---

[2] Please refer to https://github.com/4m4n5/saasn-stain-normalization and additional materials for implementation and additional results.

due to large variations between the source and target image stains and unconventional input image structures. Results also show that SAASN outperformed traditional methods at preserving the cellular structures. We contend that the proposed unsupervised image to image translation approach can be successfully applied to general *many-to-one* image translation problems outside the medical domain as well.

B   Additional Results

We trained and tested the model in both a *one-to-one* ($K = 1$) and *many-to-one* ($K = 2$) setup. In this section we demonstrate the model performance, on test datasets, for visual inspection (Fig. 7, 8, 9 and 10).

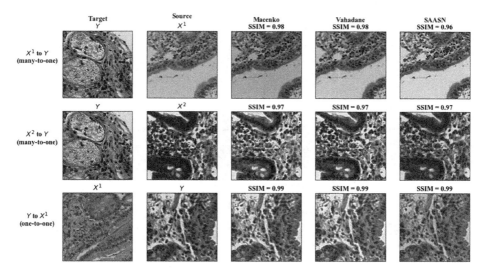

Fig. 6. Visual comparison of performance in cases where Macenko and Vahadane techniques perform very well according to a combined SSIM index. The target image only applies to the Macenko and Vahadane techniques. The main results section included a visual comparison of SAASN stain transfers with the worst performing Macenko and Vahadane images based on SSIM. Alternatively, SAASN is also compared to the best SSIM indexes for the other two techniques. Figure 6 displayed the top three images in each stain transfer scenario based on the highest $L2$-norm of Macenko and Vahadane SSIM results. For the $X^{(1)}$ to Y transfer, SAASN was the only technique that properly maintained a whitish/gray background pixel color. For the $X^{(2)}$ to Y transfer, Macenko appeared to create a new stain distribution that was not close to the desired target image. All three normalizations performed well in the *one-to-one* transfer. The comparison in Fig. 6 demonstrates that SAASN can perform better at preserving structure and properly transferring stain domains, because both areas are incorporated into the network's loss functions.

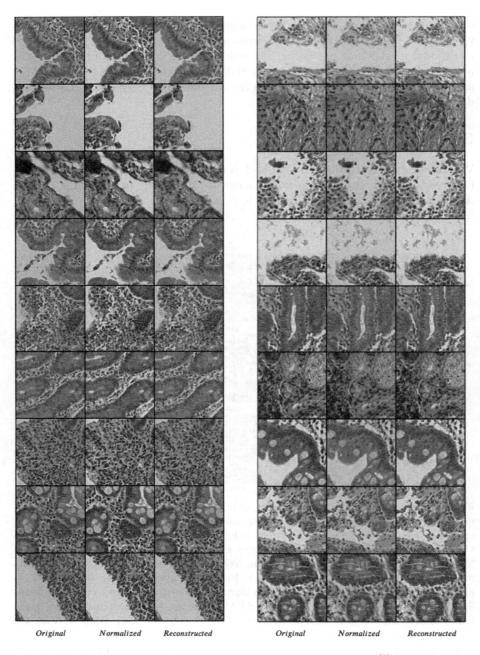

Original	*Normalized*	*Reconstructed*	*Original*	*Normalized*	*Reconstructed*

Fig. 7. *One-to-one* (K = 1) model. **Left:** Translation from domain $X^{(1)}$ to Y and back to domain $X^{(1)}$. **Right:** Translation from domain Y to $X^{(1)}$ and back to Y.

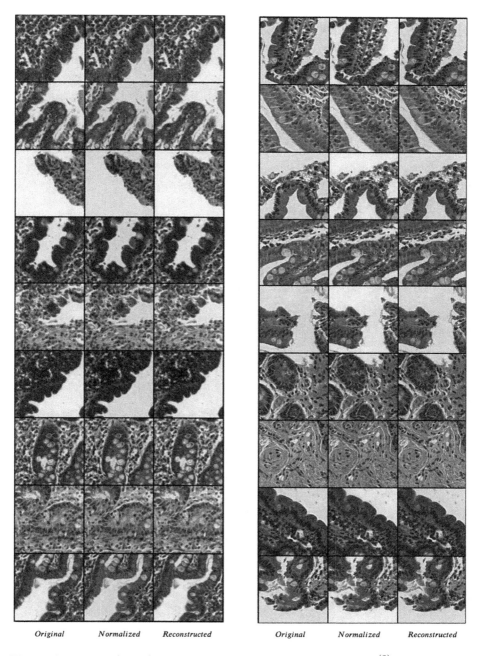

Original   Normalized   Reconstructed   Original   Normalized   Reconstructed

Fig. 8. *One-to-one* (K = 1) model. **Left:** Translation from domain $X^{(2)}$ to Y and back to domain $X^{(2)}$. **Right:** Translation from domain Y to $X^{(2)}$ and back to Y.

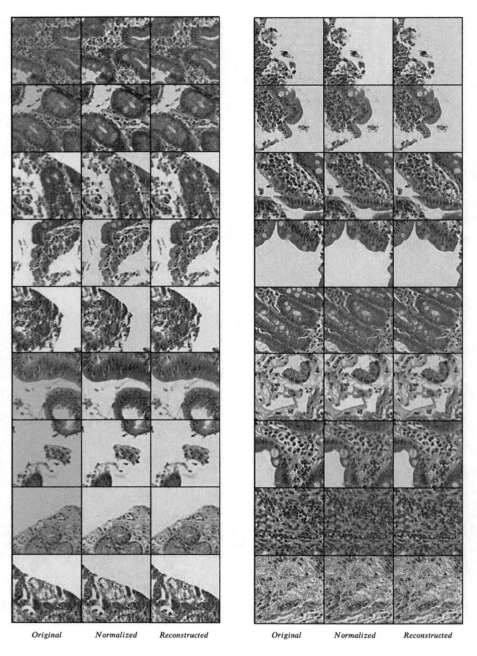

| Original | Normalized | Reconstructed | | Original | Normalized | Reconstructed |

Fig. 9. *Many-to-one* (K = 2) model. **Left:** Translation from domain X to Y and back to domain $\hat{X}$. **Right:** Translation from domain Y to $\hat{X}$ and back to Y.

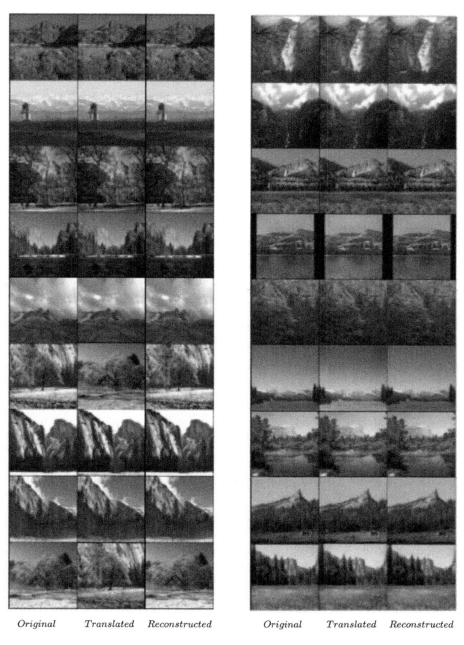

| Original | Translated | Reconstructed | | Original | Translated | Reconstructed |

Fig. 10. The model was also trained on Yosemite summer to winter dataset from the CycleGAN paper. **Left:** Translation from winter to summer and back to winter. **Right:** Translation from summer to winter and back to summer. The model was trained with the same parameters as for the stain normalization task.

References

1. Bejnordi, B.E., Timofeeva, N., Otte-Höller, I., Karssemeijer, N., van der Laak, J.A.: Quantitative analysis of stain variability in histology slides and an algorithm for standardization. In: Medical Imaging 2014: Digital Pathology, vol. 9041, p. 904108. International Society for Optics and Photonics (2014)
2. BenTaieb, A., Hamarneh, G.: Adversarial stain transfer for histopathology image analysis. IEEE Trans. Med. Imaging **37**(3), 792–802 (2017)
3. Coltuc, D., Bolon, P., Chassery, J.M.: Exact histogram specification. IEEE Trans. Image Process. **15**(5), 1143–1152 (2006)
4. Fischer, A.H., Jacobson, K.A., Rose, J., Zeller, R.: Hematoxylin and eosin staining of tissue and cell sections. Cold Spring Harbor Protoc. **2008**(5), pdb-prot4986 (2008)
5. Goodfellow, I., et al.: Generative adversarial nets. In: Advances in Neural Information Processing Systems, pp. 2672–2680 (2014)
6. Hinton, G.E., Salakhutdinov, R.R.: Reducing the dimensionality of data with neural networks. Science **313**(5786), 504–507 (2006)
7. Ioffe, S., Szegedy, C.: Batch normalization: accelerating deep network training by reducing internal covariate shift. arXiv preprint arXiv:1502.03167 (2015)
8. Isola, P., Zhu, J.Y., Zhou, T., Efros, A.A.: Image-to-image translation with conditional adversarial networks. In: Proceedings of the IEEE Conference on Computer Vision and Pattern Recognition, pp. 1125–1134 (2017)
9. Janowczyk, A., Basavanhally, A., Madabhushi, A.: Stain normalization using sparse autoencoders (stanosa): application to digital pathology. Comput. Med. Imaging Graph. **57**, 50–61 (2017)
10. Khan, A.M., Rajpoot, N., Treanor, D., Magee, D.: A nonlinear mapping approach to stain normalization in digital histopathology images using image-specific color deconvolution. IEEE Trans. Biomed. Eng. **61**(6), 1729–1738 (2014)
11. Kim, T., Cha, M., Kim, H., Lee, J.K., Kim, J.: Learning to discover cross-domain relations with generative adversarial networks. In: Proceedings of the 34th International Conference on Machine Learning, vol. 70, pp. 1857–1865. JMLR. org (2017)
12. Kingma, D.P., Ba, J.: Adam: a method for stochastic optimization. arXiv preprint arXiv:1412.6980 (2014)
13. Litjens, G., et al.: A survey on deep learning in medical image analysis. Med. Image Anal. **42**, 60–88 (2017)
14. Liu, M.Y., Breuel, T., Kautz, J.: Unsupervised image-to-image translation networks. In: Advances in Neural Information Processing Systems, pp. 700–708 (2017)
15. Liu, Y., et al.: Detecting cancer metastases on gigapixel pathology images. Technical report, arXiv (2017) https://arxiv.org/abs/1703.02442
16. Macenko, M., et al.: A method for normalizing histology slides for quantitative analysis. In: 2009 IEEE International Symposium on Biomedical Imaging: From Nano to Macro, pp. 1107–1110. IEEE (2009)
17. Mao, X., Li, Q., Xie, H., Lau, R.Y., Wang, Z., Smolley, S.P.: Least squares generative adversarial networks. In: Proceedings of the IEEE International Conference on Computer Vision, pp. 2794–2802 (2017)
18. Miyato, T., Kataoka, T., Koyama, M., Yoshida, Y.: Spectral normalization for generative adversarial networks. arXiv preprint arXiv:1802.05957 (2018)
19. Parikh, A.P., Täckström, O., Das, D., Uszkoreit, J.: A decomposable attention model for natural language inference. arXiv preprint arXiv:1606.01933 (2016)

20. Pathak, D., Krahenbuhl, P., Donahue, J., Darrell, T., Efros, A.A.: Context encoders: Feature learning by inpainting. In: Proceedings of the IEEE Conference on Computer Vision and Pattern Recognition, pp. 2536–2544 (2016)
21. Reinhard, E., Adhikhmin, M., Gooch, B., Shirley, P.: Color transfer between images. IEEE Comput. Graph. Appl. **21**(5), 34–41 (2001)
22. Ronneberger, O., Fischer, P., Brox, T.: U-Net: convolutional networks for biomedical image segmentation. In: Navab, N., Hornegger, J., Wells, W.M., Frangi, A.F. (eds.) MICCAI 2015. LNCS, vol. 9351, pp. 234–241. Springer, Cham (2015). https://doi.org/10.1007/978-3-319-24574-4_28
23. Roy, S., kumar Jain, A., Lal, S., Kini, J.: A study about color normalization methods for histopathology images. Micron **114**, 42–61 (2018)
24. Shaban, M.T., Baur, C., Navab, N., Albarqouni, S.: Staingan: stain style transfer for digital histological images. In: 2019 IEEE 16th International Symposium on Biomedical Imaging (ISBI 2019), pp. 953–956. IEEE (2019)
25. Shrivastava, A., Pfister, T., Tuzel, O., Susskind, J., Wang, W., Webb, R.: Learning from simulated and unsupervised images through adversarial training. In: Proceedings of the IEEE Conference on Computer Vision and Pattern Recognition, pp. 2107–2116 (2017)
26. Taigman, Y., Polyak, A., Wolf, L.: Unsupervised cross-domain image generation. arXiv preprint arXiv:1611.02200 (2016)
27. Ulyanov, D., Vedaldi, A., Lempitsky, V.: Instance normalization: the missing ingredient for fast stylization. arXiv preprint arXiv:1607.08022 (2016)
28. Vahadane, A., et al.: Structure-preserving color normalization and sparse stain separation for histological images. IEEE Trans. Med. Imaging **35**(8), 1962–1971 (2016)
29. Vaswani, A., et al.: Attention is all you need. In: Advances in Neural Information Processing Systems, pp. 5998–6008 (2017)
30. Wang, X., Girshick, R., Gupta, A., He, K.: Non-local neural networks. In: Proceedings of the IEEE Conference on Computer Vision and Pattern Recognition, pp. 7794–7803 (2018)
31. Wang, X., Gupta, A.: Generative image modeling using style and structure adversarial networks. In: Leibe, B., Matas, J., Sebe, N., Welling, M. (eds.) ECCV 2016. LNCS, vol. 9908, pp. 318–335. Springer, Cham (2016). https://doi.org/10.1007/978-3-319-46493-0_20
32. Wang, Z., Bovik, A.C., Sheikh, H.R., Simoncelli, E.P., et al.: Image quality assessment: from error visibility to structural similarity. IEEE Trans. Image Process **13**(4), 600–612 (2004)
33. Wei, J.W., Wei, J.W., Jackson, C.R., Ren, B., Suriawinata, A.A., Hassanpour, S.: Automated detection of celiac disease on duodenal biopsy slides: a deep learning approach. J. Pathol. Inform **10**, 7 (2019)
34. Yi, Z., Zhang, H., Tan, P., Gong, M.: Dualgan: unsupervised dual learning for image-to-image translation. In: Proceedings of the IEEE International Conference on Computer Vision, pp. 2849–2857 (2017)
35. Yoo, D., Kim, N., Park, S., Paek, A.S., Kweon, I.S.: Pixel-level domain transfer. In: Leibe, B., Matas, J., Sebe, N., Welling, M. (eds.) ECCV 2016. LNCS, vol. 9912, pp. 517–532. Springer, Cham (2016). https://doi.org/10.1007/978-3-319-46484-8_31
36. Zanjani, F.G., Zinger, S., Bejnordi, B.E., van der Laak, J.A., de With, P.H.: Stain normalization of histopathology images using generative adversarial networks. In: 2018 IEEE 15th International Symposium on Biomedical Imaging (ISBI 2018), pp. 573–577. IEEE (2018)

37. Zhang, H., Goodfellow, I., Metaxas, D., Odena, A.: Self-attention generative adversarial networks. arXiv preprint arXiv:1805.08318 (2018)
38. Zhu, J.Y., Park, T., Isola, P., Efros, A.A.: Unpaired image-to-image translation using cycle-consistent adversarial networks. In: Proceedings of the IEEE International Conference on Computer Vision, pp. 2223–2232 (2017)

Certainty Pooling for Multiple Instance Learning

Jacob Gildenblat[1], Ido Ben-Shaul[1(✉)], Zvi Lapp[1], and Eldad Klaiman[2]

[1] SagivTech Ltd., Ra'anana, Israel
{jacob,ido,zvi}@sagivtech.com
[2] Roche Innovation Center Munich, Munich, Germany
eldad.klaiman@roche.com

Abstract. Multiple Instance Learning is a form of weakly supervised learning in which the data is arranged in sets of instances called bags with one label assigned per bag. The bag level class prediction is derived from the multiple instances through application of a permutation invariant pooling operator on instance predictions or embeddings. We present a novel pooling operator called **Certainty Pooling** which incorporates the model certainty into bag predictions resulting in a more robust and explainable model. We compare our proposed method with other pooling operators in controlled experiments with low evidence ratio bags based on MNIST, as well as on a real life histopathology dataset - Camelyon16. Our method outperforms other methods in both bag level and instance level prediction, especially when only small training sets are available. We discuss the rationale behind our approach and the reasons for its superiority for these types of datasets.

Keywords: Deep learning · Multiple instance learning · Certainty · Digital pathology

1 Introduction

Multiple instance learning (MIL) is a form of weakly supervised learning where training instances are arranged in sets called bags, and a label is provided for the entire bag [2] while the labels of the individual instances in the bag are not known. Weakly annotated data is especially common in medical imaging [10] where an image is typically described by a single label (e.g. benign/malignant) or a Region Of Interest (ROI) is roughly given.

We assume the case where a binary label is assigned to every bag in the dataset. The most common binary MIL assumption, is that the bag label is positive if at least one of the instances contains evidence for the label, and is negative if all of the instances do not contain evidence for the label. More formally, every bag is composed of a group of instances $\{x_1, ..., x_K\}$, where K is the size of the bag. K can vary between the bags. A binary label $Y \in \{0, 1\}$ is associated with every bag. The MIL assumption can then be written in this form:

© Springer Nature Switzerland AG 2021
A. Del Bimbo et al. (Eds.): ICPR 2020 Workshops, LNCS 12661, pp. 141–153, 2021.
https://doi.org/10.1007/978-3-030-68763-2_11

$$Y = \left\{ \begin{array}{cc} 0, \text{ iff } y_k = 0, \text{ } for \text{ } k \in \{1 \ldots K\} \\ 1, \qquad otherwise \end{array} \right\} \tag{1}$$

In MIL a pooling operator is typically applied to aggregate the instance embeddings or predictions to create a bag output. Common choices for pooling operators are max-pooling Eq. (2), or mean-pooling Eq. (3).

$$Z_m = \max_{k \in \{0 \ldots K\}} (h_{km}), \tag{2}$$

$$Z_m = \frac{1}{K} \sum_{k=1}^{K} h_{km}, \tag{3}$$

where Z_m is the bag level prediction, h_{km} is the instance prediction value and $k \in \{0 \ldots K\}$ and m are the instance and bag indices respectively.

A more general formulation has been proposed in [6] by assigning every instance a learned attention weight Eq. (4).

$$Z_m = g(\sum_{k=1}^{K} a_{km} e_{km}), \tag{4}$$

where Z_m is the bag level prediction, g is the bag level classifier, e_{km} is the instance embedding, a_{km} is the instance attention value and $k \in \{0 \ldots K\}$ and m are the instance and bag indices respectively.

Recently there has been increased usage of MIL on large datasets, especially in the field of computational pathology [6,8,12]. In the MIL setting for computational pathology, whole slide images (WSIs) are given a global label (e.g. "Tumor" if tumor cells exist in this WSI and "Normal" otherwise.). Instances are then extracted from the slides by sampling image tiles from the WSI with or without overlap. Instances (tiles) are then grouped into bags where every bag contains the tiles extracted from a specific slide and has that slide's global label.

In some cases just a small portion of the instances contains evidence for the global slide label, e.g. when the tumor is localized in a small part of the biopsy, which is usually the case. The interpretability of MIL algorithms is based on the ability to identify predictive instances in the bag [6]. In addition, the sizes of the bags can be very large. For example, in the case of digital pathology, some slides in full resolution can have tens of thousands of instances extracted from them. These factors form a challenging MIL setting. As the bags grow larger, the ability of the network to correctly classify the bag is diminished and tightly linked to the selected pooling function. In the case of a low evidence ratio bag (i.e. a bag with a small number of positive instances compared to the total number of instances), if mean-pooling is used, a large negative instance population in the bag will overshadow the positive instances and create a false negative global bag level prediction. On the other hand, if max-pooling is used, a single negative instance with a high prediction value can corrupt the resulting global bag level prediction and create a false positive result. This is magnified by the unstable nature of deep learning models, where a small change in the input image can trigger a very different output [14]. Given this setting, a large bag that contains many visually similar looking instances, might result in very different embeddings or predictions for each of them. Therefore pooling functions are a key element in any MIL algorithm.

In this paper we propose a novel pooling strategy for MIL that addresses the shortcomings of the current pooling functions and deals with the underperformance of MIL in the case of bags with low evidence ratio. We test and compare our method against baseline pooling methods i.e. max and mean pooling, as well as a state of the art MIL pooling method, namely Attention Pooling MIL. We conduct the algorithm tests and comparisons on both a controlled MNIST based dataset and a real life pathology image dataset - Camelyon16. Additionally, we explore the effect of dataset size on performance metrics of different MIL algorithms and evaluate performance on both datasets by examining bag level prediction and instance level prediction.

2   Related Work

In the context of digital pathology, an example of a recent use-case of MIL combined with deep learning for classification of prostate cancer Hematoxylin & Eosin (H&E) stained WSIs is described in [1]. A huge dataset of 12,000 slides were extracted into 12,000 bags, with 1,000 instances per bag on average. Resnet18 pre-trained on Image Net was used to extract feature embeddings for the instances. Then a classification neural network with fully connected layers was trained on these embeddings using the max pooling operator (selecting the instance with the highest score for the cancer category).

The Attention Pooling MIL method [6] is a state of the art MIL algorithm that uses a neural network to assign an attention weight score for every instance. These weights can then be used to aggregate the embeddings of the instances into a global slide embedding (by multiplying every embedding by its weight, and then summing over all embeddings). In the MNIST based experiments presented in [6], the bags used have an evidence ratio of 10%.

Measuring certainty in deep learning networks, by Monte-Carlo (MC) dropout was introduced in [4]. In MC dropout, dropout is applied in test time, and a forward pass is performed multiple times in order to capture the certainty of the model predictions. In [7] certainty was used for multi-task learning by weighting individual task losses to create a global loss function. During the training, tasks with lower certainty receive weaker gradients.

We propose an MIL approach that uses the MC-dropout Mean-STD method for certainty calculation and generates weaker gradients during training for instances the model is not sure about. To the best of our knowledge this is the first work describing using certainty in the context of MIL algorithms.

3   Proposed Method

We formulate a new certainty based pooling function, which we call Certainty Pooling, that aggregates over the bag instances using the certainty score of the individual instances. We define X_k to be the vector of MC dropout predictions

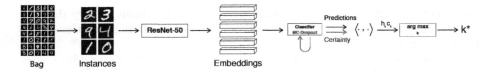

Fig. 1. Visual representation of the proposed method and model architecture.

for instance k. In Eq. 5 we define the instance certainty C_k as the inverse standard deviation of X_k.

$$C_k = C(X_k) = \frac{1}{\sigma(X_k) + \epsilon}, \tag{5}$$

where σ is the standard deviation operator and ϵ is a small number that prevents division by zero.

In Certainty Pooling Eq. (6), we define the global bag level prediction Z_m as the prediction value of the instance having the highest certainty weighted model output.

$$Z_m = h_{k^*m} \;\; where \;\; k^* = argmax(C_k \cdot h_{km}), \tag{6}$$

where k^* is the index of the instance having the highest certainty weighted model output.

Additionally, a visual representation of the proposed method and model architecture is presented in Fig. 1.

4 Experiments

4.1 Low Evidence Ratio MNIST-Bags

The aim of this experiment is to test our method in a controlled dataset scenario where the bag evidence ratio is known and to compare it with current baseline and state of the art MIL methods. In order to make a fair comparison, we use the MNIST-Bags dataset proposed in [6]. In this dataset, the bags are made of instances that are MNIST digits, where the bags can have a varying size. Bags containing the digit 9 are labeled as positive bags and bags without the digit 9 are labeled negative. In the originally proposed dataset bag evidence ratio was 10%, i.e. on average 10% of the instances in the positive bags are 9. With a dataset size of 200 bags and the setting used in [6], both the Attention Pooling MIL and our method achieve near 100% AUC.

In order to test and compare the behavior of the methods in low bag evidence ratio scenarios we explore a similar but more challenging dataset in which the evidence ratio is only 1%. We select a constant bag size of 100 instances and define positivity in the same way. Positive bags contain exactly a single instance 9, and negative bags do not contain any instances of 9. We explore the effect of the number of bags in the training set on the performance for the different methods. We use a validation set of 1000 bags and test our models on a testing

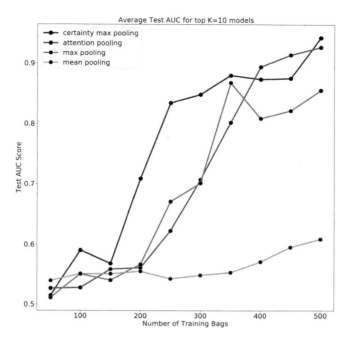

Fig. 2. Testing dataset bag prediction AUCs for models trained with different sizes of low evidence ratio MNIST bag datasets. In all experiments we consider the average of the top K = 10 runs.

dataset of 1000 bags. In all training and validation datasets, as well as in the testing dataset, exactly one half of the bags are positive.

We use the same network architectures as defined in [6] and only replace the attention network with the proposed certainty based calculation.

In order to account for the stochastic nature of deep neural network (DNN) convergence, we repeat the experiment 20 times with different random seeds for every algorithm and training set size, and take the average of the top K = 10 results. The best model is selected for each method based on its performance on the validation dataset.

As a metric, we use the AUC value. We measure and compare the AUC of the bag level prediction, as well as instance level prediction on the testing set for the different sizes of training sets in each of the tested methods.

The performance of our method compared to the benchmark methods on a low evidence ratio task with different sizes of training datasets is shown in Fig. 2. The graph shows how our method outperforms classical pooling methods as well as the benchmark Attention Pooling MIL method in most cases, and especially in small dataset sizes.

Some insights regarding the nature of stochasticity of these methods can be seen in Fig. 2. We find that the comparison between the Attention Pooling MIL and the Certainty Pooling MIL results is especially revealing. One can observe that with a very low number of bags in training set (50–150) both methods are rarely able to generate a good model for the testing set. In the interval between 200 and 300 training set bags Certainty Pooling seems to have more and higher results compared to the other methods. With training set sizes of 350 to 500 bags, Attention Pooling MIL results become comparable and even slightly better than Certainty Pooling. These observations could mean that in the case of low evidence ratio datasets where not enough data is available, Certainty Pooling can provide a better model where other methods encounter difficulties.

Instance level prediction AUC is a practical way to assess the performance of the trained classifier on the instance level. This metric is calculated by using the instance level labels and predictions. This enables a comparison at test time of the different methods without dependence on the MIL pooling methods and shows how well the MIL training was able to learn a meaningful representation of the positive instances. In Fig. 3, we show the average instance prediction AUC values for the top $K = 10$ models for all the test dataset instances based on the instance level labels (e.g. label is positive if instance is the digit 9 and negative otherwise). It can be observed that our method yields better results in both instance level prediction as well as bag level prediction. Given that all the compared methods were using the exact same network architecture, this might imply that training with Certainty Pooling provides more meaningful gradients during training and is therefore able to train a better instance level model predictor.

In Fig. 4, we show an example visualization of the instance prediction values assigned to different instances in selected bags for the Attention Pooling MIL method and the Certainty Pooling method based on one of the conducted experiments with a middle range training dataset size of 300 bags. For each method we choose the model parameters based on the best validation score from all experiments run on the selected dataset size. The first digit in each row is a 9 which is the positive instance, while the other instances are negative instances presented in descending order of their prediction value. We can observe that the differences between the prediction value for the positive and negative instances are much larger with the Certainty Pooling MIL than the Attention Pooling MIL algorithm, demonstrating the ability of our method to better train a classifier to select key instances.

Figure 5 shows the distribution of instance predictive values for the entire MNIST-Bags testing dataset for Certainty Pooling vs. Attention Pooling. The graph further illustrates how for Certainty Pooling, the instance prediction values for the negative and positive labels are much better separated than for Attention Pooling. This clarifies the better instance prediction AUC values observed for Certainty Pooling in comparison to the other methods, as can be seen in Fig. 3.

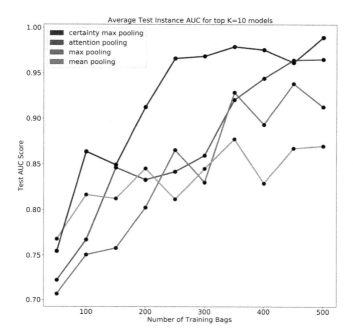

Fig. 3. Average instance prediction AUC values for the top $K = 10$ models.

4.2 Camelyon16 Lymph Node Metastasis Detection Challenge

In this experiment we evaluate and compare our proposed method to other MIL methods on a challenging real life dataset. The Camelyon16 dataset consists of 400 H&E stained WSIs taken from sentinel lymph nodes, which are either healthy or exhibit metastases of some form. In addition to the WSIs, the dataset contains both slide level annotations, i.e. healthy or contains-metastases and pixel level segmentation masks per slide denoting the metastases.

We use the 270 WSIs in the Camelyon16 training set for training and 130 WSIs from the Camelyon16 test set for testing our algorithm. We investigate the effect of dataset sizes on algorithm performance in the real-life dataset paradigm, we conduct multiple experiments, each with a different training set size. In order to do this, we randomly select a fraction of the training dataset slides in 10% increments between 50% and 100% and use only that selection for model training. From the selected dataset slides we holdout 25% of the slides as a validation set, and use only the global slide labels for training.

We extracted 256×256 non-overlapping tiles at $20\times$ resolution which is the working magnification used by clinical pathologists to review slides. Simple image processing based tissue detection was applied to discard background (white) tiles. The tiles in each slide were grouped into a bag, where every bag contains only tiles from one specific WSI. In Histology applications, a step called stain normalization is typically applied to normalize tissue staining in different slides

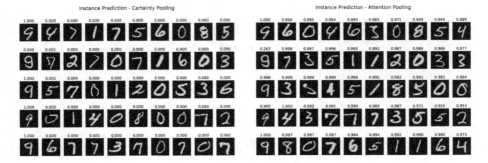

Fig. 4. Example instance level prediction values for Certainty Pooling MIL (left) and Attention Pooling MIL (right). The positive instance followed by the highest value instances in the bag ordered in descending order are presented and the value above each image represents the prediction value for that instance.

[9, 11]. We apply a simple stain normalization step, by normalizing the mean and standard deviation of the LAB color space channels to be the same as in a reference image from the Camelyon16 training set [13].

The resulting training/validation dataset contains roughly 4 million instances (tiles) in 270 bags (slides). Similar to [1] we avoid learning directly on the instance images because of the computational cost and instead we first extract 2048 length features for every instance using Resnet50 [5] pre-trained on ImageNet.

The prediction network we used consists of 5 fully connected (FC) layers. The first hidden layer has 1024 neurons, and every layer following has half the amount of the previous. We introduce a dropout layer with 50% dropout after each FC layer and ReLU activation. We set the learning rate to 0.01. For Attention Pooling MIL we used the attention network architecture suggested in [6], but increased the number of neurons to 1024 in the hidden layers, to fit the higher complexity of this data. In all cases, an Adam optimizer was used with default parameters.

Similar to [3], we randomly select 128 instances from every bag during training in each epoch as an augmentation strategy. We found this largely improved results and prevented quick over-fitting on the training set. We train the different models for 1000 epochs and selected a model that performed best on a held out validation set. We test the selected model on the Camelyon16 test set tiled and generated in a similar fashion. During testing, no instance sampling is performed and the full bag is analysed. As described in the competition instructions, we report the AUC metric on the Camelyon16 test set for the global labels.

In order to account for the stochastic nature of deep neural network (DNN) convergence, we repeat each experiment 20 times with different random seeds for every algorithm and training set size. We try to reduce the prohibitively long duration of the multiple seed experiments by checking the validation set AUC score, every 5 epochs and randomly sampling 20,000 tiles from each slide in the validation set to compute the slide prediction. We run the training for

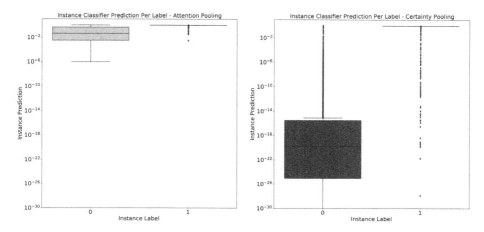

Fig. 5. Distribution of instance level prediction values for Attention Pooling MIL (left) and Certainty Pooling MIL (right) on the entire MNIST-Bags testing dataset.

1000 epochs and select the best model for each method based on its performance on the validation dataset. The average of the top $K = 10$ results is presented in Fig. 6. Our method achieves top bag level AUC results in all datapoints compared to both the baseline MIL pooling methods and the benchmark Attention Pooling MIL method.

Additionally we calculate the instance level prediction AUC for each method by using the Camelyon16 WSI mask annotations to label each tile. Due to the inherent huge imbalance of the instance labels, i.e. only 42 of the 137 slides are positive, and among these slides less than 6% are positive instances. The instance level prediction AUC is computed for each positive slide separately and averaged across slides. instance level prediction AUC is defined only for positive slides since only they contain both positive and negative tiles.

It is interesting to note that from the testing set, only 17 out of 42 positive slides have an evidence ratio higher than 1% and only 7 above 5%, meaning the majority of test set slides have an evidence ratio of much less than 1%.

The average top $K = 10$ instance level prediction AUC per method on the testing set are displayed in Fig. 7. Our method achieves top instance AUC results in all datapoints compared to both the baseline MIL pooling methods and the benchmark Attention Pooling MIL method.

In Fig. 8 a gallery of top predicted instances for 5 positive (Tumor labeled) slides from the Camelyon16 testing set are presented for Certainty Pooling MIL and Attention-MIL. It is visible in the galleries that while Certainty Pooling produces a classifier that retrieves only tumor labeled tiles in the top-10 tiles per slide for the example slides, the Attention-MIL trained classifier does not perform as well on the instance level.

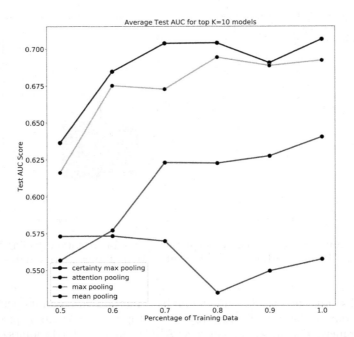

Fig. 6. Camelyeon16 testing set average top $K = 10$ global bag prediction AUCs for different training dataset sizes.

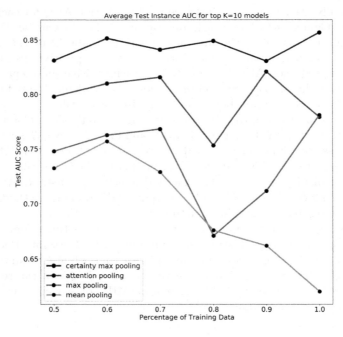

Fig. 7. Camelyeon16 testing set average top $K = 10$ global instance prediction AUCs for different training dataset sizes.

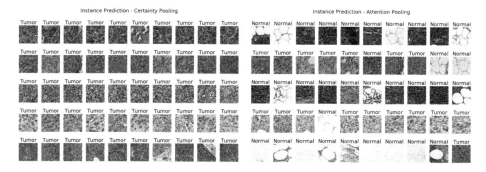

Fig. 8. Example instance level prediction tiles for Certainty Pooling MIL (left) and Attention Pooling MIL (right). The top instances sorted by predicted instance (tile) value for 5 "Tumor" labeled slides. Above each tile the instance level label from the Camelyon16 mask labels.

5 Conclusions

In this paper, we introduce a novel MIL pooling function based on network certainty measures. Our method is based on calculation of the instance classifier network certainty and then weighting instance predictions by their associated certainty.

We test our methods on a "controlled" MNIST based dataset which is a modification of the MNIST-Bags dataset that creates a very challenging setting, which we call "Low Evidence Ratio MNIST-Bags", as well as on the Camelyon16 "real-life" histology dataset which has over 4 million instances and a low evidence ratio. Certainty Pooling improves both Bag Level Prediction and Instance Level Prediction in both experiments.

We argue our method is able to train a more interpretable model in terms of key instance retrieval. We demonstrate this by looking at top prediction instances and show that our method presents more relevant instances with high value prediction. Our method also improves results in MIL settings where the ratio of instances containing evidence is low. As MIL is increasingly being applied on challenging datasets with limited size, we believe the improvements presented can have a real impact on the quality and interpretability of trained MIL networks.

We rationalize the approach of choosing certainty as a weighing factor for the pooling operation as follows. First, we argue that the learned model tends to be more certain about predictive instances than about non-predictive instances. One possible explanation for this is that since non-predictive instances appear both in positive and negative bags (e.g. digits 0–8 in MNIST and normal tissue or background tiles in Camelyon16), they receive contradicting gradients during training, causing a divergence in the network trained with Dropout layers. This in turn creates fluctuations in the predicted instance value during inference with Dropout and causes a large variance in the instance prediction values. We interpret this variance as model uncertainty in the prediction of this instance and use it to weigh the contribution of the instance on the bag prediction.

We think it is natural to decrease the contribution of instances the model is not sure about, especially in the scenario of large bags where there are many opportunities for mistakes that can affect the bag prediction. When the instance attention levels are directly learned as with Attention Pooling MIL, there is no direct control over which instances will achieve high attention values.

Our method provides a simple way to dynamically weigh instances in an explainable way without learning the weight via another neural network. By doing this we believe our method bridges the gap between traditional mean and max pooling operators and more advanced learned weighting mechanisms such as attention.

Future work will include hyper-parameter optimizations, working image resolution and resolution combinations as well as investigation into the limits of dataset sizes and evidence ratio for training certainty based MIL algorithms. We also plan to investigate the advantages of more sophisticated color normalization schemes in this scenario.

References

1. Campanella, G., Silva, V.W.K., Fuchs, T.J.: Terabyte-scale deep multiple instance learning for classification and localization in pathology. arXiv preprint arXiv:1805.06983 (2018)
2. Carbonneau, M.A., Cheplygina, V., Granger, E., Gagnon, G.: Multiple instance learning: a survey of problem characteristics and applications. Pattern Recogn. **77**, 329–353 (2018)
3. Couture, H.D., Marron, J.S., Perou, C.M., Troester, M.A., Niethammer, M.: Multiple instance learning for heterogeneous images: training a CNN for histopathology. In: Frangi, A.F., Schnabel, J.A., Davatzikos, C., Alberola-López, C., Fichtinger, G. (eds.) MICCAI 2018. LNCS, vol. 11071, pp. 254–262. Springer, Cham (2018). https://doi.org/10.1007/978-3-030-00934-2_29
4. Gal, Y., Islam, R., Ghahramani, Z.: Deep bayesian active learning with image data. In: Proceedings of the 34th International Conference on Machine Learning, vol. 70, pp. 1183–1192. JMLR. org (2017)
5. He, K., Zhang, X., Ren, S., Sun, J.: Deep residual learning for image recognition. In: Proceedings of the IEEE Conference on Computer Vision and Pattern Recognition, pp. 770–778 (2016)
6. Ilse, M., Tomczak, J.M., Welling, M.: Attention-based deep multiple instance learning. arXiv preprint arXiv:1802.04712 (2018)
7. Kendall, A., Gal, Y., Cipolla, R.: Multi-task learning using uncertainty to weigh losses for scene geometry and semantics. In: Proceedings of the IEEE Conference on Computer Vision and Pattern Recognition, pp. 7482–7491 (2018)
8. Klaiman, E., et al.: Prediction of biomarker status, diagnosis and outcome from histology slides using deep learning-based hypothesis free feature extraction. J. Clin. Oncol. **37**(15_suppl), 3140 (2019)
9. Macenko, M., et al.: A method for normalizing histology slides for quantitative analysis. In: 2009 IEEE International Symposium on Biomedical Imaging: From Nano to Macro, pp. 1107–1110. IEEE (2009)
10. Quellec, G., Cazuguel, G., Cochener, B., Lamard, M.: Multiple-instance learning for medical image and video analysis. IEEE Rev. Biomed. Eng. **10**, 213–234 (2017)

11. Reinhard, E., Adhikhmin, M., Gooch, B., Shirley, P.: Color transfer between images. IEEE Comput. Graph. Appl. **21**(5), 34–41 (2001)
12. Rony, J., Belharbi, S., Dolz, J., Ayed, I.B., McCaffrey, L., Granger, E.: Deep weakly-supervised learning methods for classification and localization in histology images: a survey. arXiv preprint arXiv:1909.03354 (2019)
13. Ruifrok, A.C., Johnston, D.A., et al.: Quantification of histochemical staining by color deconvolution. Anal. Quant. Cytol. Histol **23**(4), 291–299 (2001)
14. Zheng, S., Song, Y., Leung, T., Goodfellow, I.: Improving the robustness of deep neural networks via stability training. In: Proceedings of the IEEE Conference on Computer Vision and Pattern Recognition, pp. 4480–4488 (2016)

Classification of Noisy Free-Text Prostate Cancer Pathology Reports Using Natural Language Processing

Anjani Dhrangadhariya[1][(✉)] [ORCID], Sebastian Otálora[1] [ORCID], Manfredo Atzori[1] [ORCID], and Henning Müller[2] [ORCID]

[1] University of Applied Sciences Western Switzerland (HES-SO), Sierre, Switzerland
anjani.dhrangadhariya@hevs.ch
[2] University of Geneva (UNIGE), Geneva, Switzerland

Abstract. Free-text reporting has been the main approach in clinical pathology practice for decades. Pathology reports are an essential information source to guide the treatment of cancer patients and for cancer registries, which process high volumes of free-text reports annually. Information coding and extraction are usually performed manually and it is an expensive and time-consuming process, since reports vary widely between institutions, usually contain noise and do not have a standard structure. This paper presents strategies based on natural language processing (NLP) models to classify noisy free-text pathology reports of high and low-grade prostate cancer from the open-source repository TCGA (The Cancer Genome Atlas). We used paragraph vectors to encode the reports and compared them with n-grams and TF-IDF representations. The best representation based on distributed bag of words of paragraph vectors obtained an f_1-score of 0.858 and an AUC of 0.854 using a logistic regression classifier. We investigate the classifier's more relevant words in each case using the LIME interpretability tool, confirming the classifiers' usefulness to select relevant diagnostic words. Our results show the feasibility of using paragraph embeddings to represent and classify pathology reports.

Keywords: Pathology reports · Natural language processing · Paragraph embeddings

1 Introduction

Pathologists examine tissue via a microscope or in a digital image looking for specific cell and gland morphologies that resemble cancer or healthy tissue. After careful examination, they summarize their findings in a free-text report, as shown in Fig. 1. Pathology reports include a diagnosis or a score in a grading/staging

Supported by University of Applied Sciences Western Switzerland (HES-SO), Sierre, Switzerland.

system, despite being an inherently complex and uncertain process [13]. The outcomes are often discussed in tumor boards or given to oncologists and referring clinicians to decide on the best treatment options for the patient.

While free-text reporting has been the main approach in clinical practice for decades (sometimes helped by speech recognition), structured reporting is gaining importance in clinical practice, as it allows to improve quality parameters in diagnostic practice, including timeliness, accuracy, completeness, conformance with current agreed standards, consistency and clarity in communication. In addition, structured approaches can be fundamental (e.g. for cancer registries) for population-level quality monitoring, benchmarking, interventions and benefit analyses in public health management [6].

Automatic analysis and classification of reports can allow to enhance the practice of pathologists. First, it is a possible way to create structured reports from free text ones, in order to standardize previously diagnosed cases for monitoring, benchmarking and benefit analyses in public health management. Second, it can allow to retrieve similar cases in proprietary databases [16], enabling pathologists to navigate repositories of images for clinical decision support and teaching. In such situations, the comparison with visually similar cases is fundamental to reduce the risk of misinterpretations in the diagnosis and provide high quality teaching guidelines. Finally, it can allow faster preparation of multi-center and population-level studies, which require a single agreed international and evidence-based standard to ensure interoperability and comparability [6].

Manually extracting information from free-text pathology reports is an expensive and time-consuming process since they vary widely between institutions, usually contain noise and do not have a standard structure. Still, manual extraction is the most common practice when structured reports are not available, since free-text reports are in most cases extremely noisy and the design and creation of tools that automatically extract information from pathology reports is not straightforward [3,12,18]. With the advent of digital pathology and structured reporting, there is an increasing interest in automatic analysis of pathology reports [2,7,14,22,23].

Natural Language Processing (NLP) tools are used extensively to analyze clinical health records automatically [7,11,23]. While there has been an increase in the use of recurrent neural networks [7] and word2vec embeddings [17] to represent the content of reports, the use of deep learning techniques has not yet fully penetrated clinical NLP [21]. Particularly, with the recently proposed distributed representations of words and documents [8], and transformer networks that have outperformed traditional NLP approaches in many NLP tasks and benchmarks [19], the evidence on the applicability to clinical and pathology text remains under-explored.

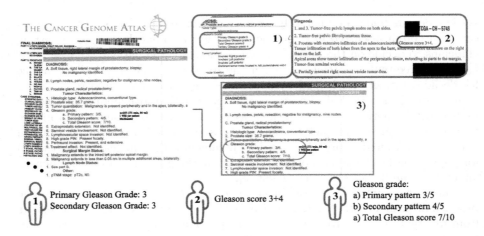

Fig. 1. Snippets of three pathology reports from the TCGA-PRAD repository. The variation in the diagnosis text makes it difficult to manually develop specified rules to extract these important parts of the report automatically.

2   Related Work

There are machine learning and NLP approaches in the literature that classify and extract clinical information from pathology reports [7] automatically. The tasks' performance varies widely and depends mainly on the database's size and how structured the reports are. In the work of Yala et al. [23], each of the sentences in a large dataset of more than 90,000 breast cancer pathology reports is represented with an n-gram. Each report is classified independently into 20 categories, with an average accuracy of 97%. In the work of Qiu et al. [14], the authors use a CNN to automatically extract ICD-O-3 topographic codes from a corpus of breast and lung cancer pathology reports, obtaining a micro-F score of 0.811 and outperforming conventional NLP strategies. Gao et al. [7] used hierarchical attention networks to model free-text pathology reports and extract from them information, including primary tumor sites and histological grades, obtaining macro F-scores of 0.852 and 0.708 respectively in a set of 942 pathology reports. In the work of Alawad et al. [1], the authors used a multitask CNN for classifying histological grade, type, laterality, and primary cancer site in a dataset of 95231 pathology reports, achieving a macro-F measure of 0.766 in the grading task. Similar studies usually lack an in-depth analysis of the classifier's more relevant words, besides reporting the model's quantitative performance. This paper investigates the use of paragraph vectors to represent and classify high and low-grade prostate pathology reports. We encode the reports using distributed representations of sentences and compare it to standard NLP techniques. Our results show that our approach is better than conventional and TF-IDF by 0.23 in AUC, reaching an F-score of 0.858 and an AUC of 0.854. We also analyze the more relevant words qualitatively for classifying the reports in each class, finding them similar to the words that pathologists use the diagnosis of Gleason grading.

3   Methods

This section describes the pathology report corpus used, the pre-processing steps and the classification approach. Figure 2 gives an overview of our approach used to automatically classify pathology reports into high-grade vs. low-grade prostate cancer.

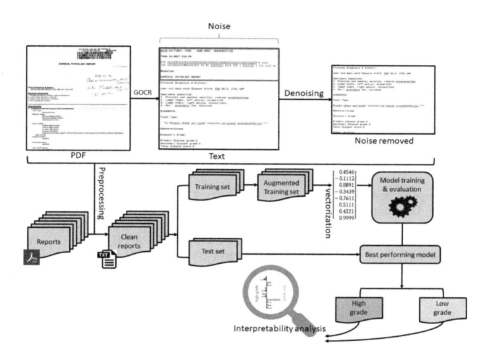

Fig. 2. Our approach

3.1   Corpus

The approach described in this paper uses publicly available prostate adenocarcinoma clinical pathology reports from The Cancer Genome Atlas (TCGA) Pan-Cancer dataset[1]. The clinical report corpus originally consisted of 494[2] reports out of which 404 non-empty reports were selected for further analysis. These reports were varying in length (see Fig. 5), unstructured free-text (see Fig. 1)

---

[1] https://portal.gdc.cancer.gov/projects/TCGA-PRAD.

[2] http://www.cbioportal.org/study/clinicalData?id=prad_tcga_pan_can_atlas_2018.

scanned copies of the original documents available as Portable Document Format (PDF). An unstructured report in contrast to a structured report is not divided into self-explanatory sections. The corpus documents were manually labelled with two class labels: high-grade (Gleason Score > 7) and low-grade (Gleason Score < 6,7) using the diagnosis information from them. This separation has clinically relevant patient stratification [10]. After manual classification, 171 reports were identified as high-grade prostate cancer and 233 reports were identified as low-grade prostate cancer creating a slight class imbalance (refer Fig. 5).

3.2   Corpus Preprocessing

Any text corpus requires thorough preprocessing before it can be used for any downstream NLP task. Text preprocessing primarily includes 1) conversion of immutable text documents to machine readable, 2) filtering of useless and noisy parts from the data, and 3) removal of uninformative filler words. The following preprocessing steps were performed before the feature extraction.

1. PDF to text: The PDF documents were converted into editable and searchable text files using GOCR, an open-source optical character reader (OCR) data suite[3].

2. Fixed-pattern noise removal: Next, the most apparent noise elements following a known pattern, like a trail of hyphens (-), pipes (|), asterisks (*), patient identifiers (for e.g., Patient ID: QUID : 70DD94DF - 1301 . 40FC-A52B - 43E2229563E3), sample identifiers (for e.g., TCGA- ZG-A9NI - 91A-PR), and HEX NULL characters (e.g. <0x0C>, <0x0F>) were automatically removed. Fully automatic filtering can miss some noise. Denoising these documents was an important preprocessing step.

3. Stop-word removal: The most frequent, noisy tokens were automatically removed using a set of predefined English language stop-words provided by NLTK (Natural Language ToolKit)[4] along with the corpus-specific stop-words and punctuation, listed in Table 1.

3.3   Data Augmentation

Class imbalance often reduces the classifier performance, so in the present work it was addressed by oversampling through back-translation text augmentation technique. Augmentation and oversampling using back-translation process involves augmenting the minority class by translating a document to a language other than the source language and then translating it back to the source language [20]. Here the documents were translated from the source language English

---

[3] http://jocr.sourceforge.net/.
[4] https://www.nltk.org/api/nltk.tokenize.html.

Table 1. List of the additional corpus-specific stop-words removed from the pathology reports.

Stop-words			Punctuation				
Report	Reviewed	Surgical	;	#	[]	'	
Electronically	Approved	Signed	:	()	?	/	&
Pathology	Page	Redacted	,	_	!	\	"

to German and back using the Google translate python package[5]. German was used as a target language for augmentation because it has a high lexical similarity with English (a similarity coefficient of 0.60) thereby adding variability to the oversampled text without altering its meaning [5].

The corpus was split into training and test sets. After splitting, the training set was oversampled to equally learn both the classes during training. Table 2 gives a summary of the corpus used in our experiments.

Table 2. Number of reports per class after train-test split and oversampling.

Partition/Class	Train	Test
High-Grade	186	47
Low-Grade	186	34

3.4   Document Representation

In natural language classification problems, it is important to represent the text documents in machine understandable form. Text representation or vectorization methods convert text documents into fixed-length numeric vectors understood by NLP systems. Two types of numeric representations were extracted from the documents, each one encoding different levels of information. These text representation methods were: I) Count-based vectors, and II) Semantic vectors.

Count Vectors: Count vectors encode text as word counts or frequency. Term Frequency - Inverse Document Frequency (TF-IDF) is weighted, sparse, word frequency encoding for numeric text representation. TF-IDF is a multiplication between term frequency (TF) matrix and inverse document frequency (IDF) matrix. Term frequency of a word W is defined as the word count of W for the document D divided by the number of words N in D. IDF of a word W is defined as logarithm of the total number of documents divided by the number of documents containing W. tf-idf increases weight for the meaningful words in the corpus and reduces the weight for filler words like a, an, the, in, if, *etc* [4].

---

[5] https://pypi.org/project/googletrans/.

Semantic Vectors: Count vectors not only lose the word order and semantic information but also suffer high-dimensionality and sparsity. To take into account semantics of the text, document-level, semantic, dense paragraph vectors were extracted. Paragraph vectors are generated in an unsupervised manner and learn a distributed representation for pieces of text along with distributed representation for the individual words. These vectors learn to associate words with document identifiers rather than with the other words in the context. This work used two kinds of paragraph vectors: 1) a distributed memory model of paragraph vectors (PV-DM) and 2) a distributed bag of words model of paragraph vectors (PV-DBOW) [8]. PV-DM and PV-DBOW vectors were generated for the training documents on fly during the experiments using the gensim functionality[6].

3.5 Document Classification

After feature extraction for each document, L2 normalization for each feature vector was computed. All the labelled documents were used to train and evaluate multiple classifiers (Logistic Regression (LR), Support Vector Machines (SVMs) with linear kernel and K-nearest neighbour (KNN)) in order to separate the reports into high *vs.* low-grade prostate cancer. Grid search was used to explore and identify best performing parameters for these classifiers and feature vector combinations. The model performance was evaluated on an independent held-out test set.

3.6 Experimental Setup

Twelve experiments were conducted each combining the above-mentioned feature vector-classifier combination. Grid search was used to identify the best feature vector, hyperparameters and classifier combination in the training set using ROC AUC (Receiver Operating Curve; Area Under Curve) as a guiding metric. The macro-F1 score, Precision, Recall and ROC AUC measures were used. Random seed for the experiments was set to 42.

Hyperparameter Space for Count Vectors: The tf-idf vectors were extracted and an n-gram space with n ranging from 1 to 10 was explored. Too frequently or too infrequently appearing terms were controlled.

Hyperparameter Space for Semantic Vectors: For the semantic paragraph vectors, vector dimensions of 100, 300, and 500 with window sizes 2, 3 and 5. The paragraph vectors were trained for epochs 20, 30 and 50 along with the above vector dimension and window size combination.

---

[6] https://radimrehurek.com/gensim/models/doc2vec.html.

4   Results

Table 3 reports classification results for the best feature vector classifier combination. Paragraph vectors capture better discriminatory information between the classes compared to the count vectors as seen from the ROC AUC scores. PV-DBOW - logistic regression has the best ROC AUC score of 85.4% compared to the other feature vector classifier combinations. Compared to SVM classifier combined with paragraph vectors, LR offers gains in precision by 2.6%, while the recall values for both the classifiers remain identical (79.4%). Paragraph vectors achieve this best ROC AUC score for the denoised, augmented and class-balanced training documents, but training with noisy documents leads to a massive drop in ROC AUC by 11.5%. Training these noisy documents without any oversampling leads to a further drop in ROC AUC by 2.6%. The confusion matrix for both the best performing feature vector - classifier combination is shown in Fig. 3. The hyperparamters for the best performing feature vectors are shown in Table 4. For the tf-idf vectors, KNN classifier offers overall better macro precision and recall compared to the other classifiers.

Table 3. The table shows the results for the best classifier-feature vector combination (see Sect. 3.6).

| Feature-classifier | Class "High-grade" | | | Macro average | | | |
	Precision	Recall	F1	Precision	Recall	F1	ROC AUC
tf-idf-LR	0.630	0.500	0.554	0.657	0.644	0.645	0.645
tf-idf-SVM	0.655	0.559	0.603	0.683	0.683	0.675	0.673
tf-idf-KNN	0.739	0.500	0.596	0.723	0.686	0.689	0.686
PV-DBOW-KNN	0.826	0.559	0.667	0.784	0.737	0.743	0.737
PV-DBOW-SVM	0.844	**0.794**	0.818	0.850	0.844	0.847	0.843
PV-DBOW-LR							
- Denoised oversampled	**0.870**	**0.794**	**0.830**	**0.866**	**0.854**	**0.859**	**0.854**
- noisy reports	0.847	0.579	0.688	0.767	0.739	0.732	0.739
- no oversampling	0.735	0.658	0.694	0.716	0.714	0.713	0.713

Table 4. The table shows the parameter settings used for the best feature vector-classifier combination (refer Sect. 3.6).

Features	Classifier	Vector parameters
tf-idf	KNN	n-gram 10, max df 0.7, min df 0.0
PV-DBOW	LR	window size 5, vector dimension 300, Epochs 20

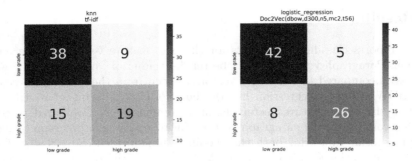

Fig. 3. Confusion matrix for best count vector classifier combination vs. best semantic vector classifier combination

5   Discussion and Analysis

The Corpus Characteristics: The corpus with pathology reports consisted of highly variable length reports (Fig. 4). These are unstructured reports without any explicit demarcation or order for different sections like patient history, diagnosis, conclusion and summary. Figure 5 shows a histogram of the number of reports against report length measured in number of characters. The smallest report had 485 characters while the longest one had 11440. Additionally, except diagnosis section, not all reports were complete and comprehensive lacking one or the other above mentioned sections. The reports originated from heterogeneous sources and were available in the PDF format. Upon conversion from PDF to text format using open-source OCR software, further added to the noise to the already heterogeneous corpus. All these issues made the preprocessing and classification process rather challenging.

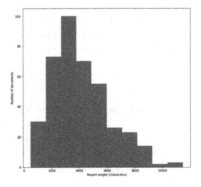
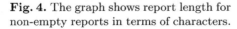
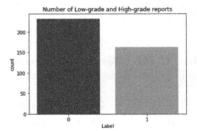

Fig. 4. The graph shows report length for non-empty reports in terms of characters.

Fig. 5. Histogram showing class imbalance in the corpus. "0" corresponds to class low-grade prostate cancer and "1" correspond to class high-grade prostate cancer.

Interpretation: Paragraph vectors (refer Paragraph 3.4) used in our work are representations generated in unsupervised manner using shallow neural networks. Such representations are not interpretable and are considered as black-box representations. In order to inspect if the best performing paragraph vector representations did capture relevant hints for classifying the documents into high *vs.* low-grade prostate cancer, we used LIME (Local Interpretable Model-Agnostic Explanations) [15]. LIME abstracts the behavior of a black-box system around individual predicted instances in the form of interpretable natural language units (bag of words) i.e. the words. It generates explanations by training a locally-faithful interpretable linear model for individual predicted instances by tweaking its feature values and observing the output. LIME was used to extract six explanations for each class from the individual reports in the test set. Figures 6, 7, 8, and 9 show LIME explanations for the high-grade and low-grade prostate cancer classes on the test instances.

Figure 6 shows a high-grade instance with LIME explanations for both the classes. LIME picks up the numbers "4", "5", and "9" from the text which forms the part of gleason score phrase. Total gleason grading score of "9" is one of the strongest clues to classify the diagnosed prostate cancer into high-grade.

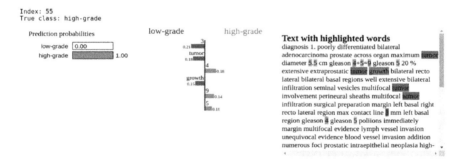

Fig. 6. LIME explanation for a high-grade report instance from the test set.

In Figure 7, we present a contradictory example where for a high-grade prostate cancer report, LIME confidently picks up rather irrelevant terms (right, left, prostatic, etc.) for the low-grade class instead.

Figure 8 shows low-grade instance with LIME explanations for the low-grade class. One of the relevant explanation for classification into low-grade are the numbers "3", "4", and "7". These numbers form part of the total gleason score term for low-grade prostate cancer. The model, however, does not pick any word explanations from the class high-grade and also picks other irrelevant explanations like the term "prosectomy" and "excision".

Figure 9 shows a low-grade instance with several strong explanations. For the class low-grade, several relevant clues are picked up; the tumor histologic grade term "g3" and the numbers "3" and "4". It can be noticed that these numbers

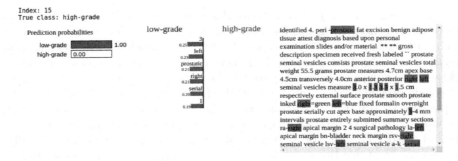

Fig. 7. LIME explanation for a high-grade report instance from the test set.

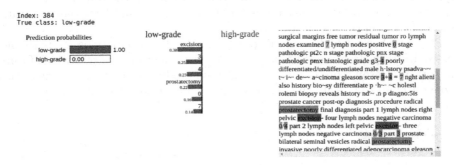

Fig. 8. LIME explanation for a low-grade report instance from the corpus.

form part of the Gleason grade phrases and are present in the reports as "gleason grade $3+3$", "gleason grade $3+4$", "primary gleason grade 3", "secondary gleason grade 4" depicting an overall low-grade Gleason score.

From each example LIME explanation demonstrated here, it has to be noted that the paragraph representation model picks several strong informative terms for each class but also picks up many irrelevant words with high confidence and

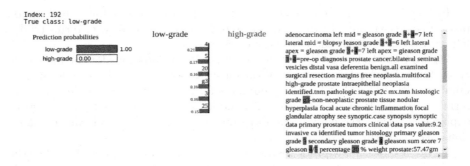

Fig. 9. A strong LIME explanation for a low-grade report instance from the corpus.

misses out on rather strong diagnosis information terms. LIME explanations warrant further inspection with respect to the hyper-parameters like the number of explanations generated, number of neighbouring samples used to generate explanations, random seed used, and distance metric [9].

6   Conclusions and Future Work

We presented an approach for classification of noisy, heterogeneous pathology reports corpus into high-grade prostate cancer and low-grade prostate cancer using two levels of textual information. Semantic information proved to be more discriminatory between the classes compared to the count information. These pathology reports included unstructured complex information that is spread over long segments of text. Our results and interpretability analysis suggest not only the feasibility, but also reliability of using paragraph vectors to represent and classify prostate pathology reports into high- vs. low-grade prostate cancer.

Each report consists of multiple tumor staging terms, clinical measurements, prostrate tissue anatomy information and their combination with negation terms. We hypothesize that this problem of extracting information from pathology reports might be better suited as an entity recognition problem. Extracting semantically inclined entities could help fine-grained classification of these rather noisy, heterogeneous reports. The noisy and denoised prostrate cancer pathology report corpus, the source code to reproduce our experiments and the python notebook to explore interpretability analysis can be found on Github: https://github.com/anjani-dhrangadhariya/pathology-report-classification.git.

Acknowledgement. This project has received funding from the European Union's Horizon 2020 research and innovation program under grant agreement No 825292 ExaMode. Sebastian Otálora thanks Minciencias through the call 756 for PhD studies.

References

1. Alawad, M., et al.: Automatic extraction of cancer registry reportable information from free-text pathology reports using multitask convolutional neural networks. J. Am. Med. Inform. Assoc. **27**(1), 89–98 (2020)
2. Baranov, N.S., et al.: Synoptic reporting increases quality of upper gastrointestinal cancer pathology reports. Virchows Archiv **475**(2), 255–259 (2019)
3. Campanella, G., et al.: Clinical-grade computational pathology using weakly supervised deep learning on whole slide images. Nat. Med. **25**(8), 1301–1309 (2019)
4. Dhrangadhariya, A., Jimenez-del Toro, O., Andrearczyk, V., Atzori, M., Müller, H.: Exploiting biomedical literature to mine out a large multimodal dataset of rare cancer studies. In: Medical Imaging 2020: Imaging Informatics for Healthcare, Research, and Applications, vol. 11318, p. 113180A. International Society for Optics and Photonics (2020)
5. Eberhard, D.M., Simons, G.F., Fennig, C.D.: Ethnologue: Languages of the World, 23rd edn. Sil International, Dallas (2020). https://www.ethnologue.com/language/de

6. Ellis, D., Srigley, J.: Does standardised structured reporting contribute to quality in diagnostic pathology? the importance of evidence-based datasets. Virchows Archiv **468**(1), 51–59 (2016)
7. Gao, S.: Hierarchical attention networks for information extraction from cancer pathology reports. J. Am. Med. Inform. Assoc. **25**(3), 321–330 (2018)
8. Le, Q., Mikolov, T.: Distributed representations of sentences and documents. In: International Conference on Machine Learning, pp. 1188–1196 (2014)
9. Madhyastha, P., Jain, R.: On model stability as a function of random seed. arXiv preprint arXiv:1909.10447 (2019)
10. Narain, V., Bianco Jr., F.J., Grignon, D.J., Sakr, W.A., Pontes, J.E., Wood Jr., D.P.: How accurately does prostate biopsy gleason score predict pathologic findings and disease free survival? The Prostate **49**(3), 185–190 (2001)
11. Olago, V., Muchengeti, M., Singh, E., Chen, W.C.: Identification of malignancies from free-text histopathology reports using a multi-model supervised machine learning approach. Information **11**(9), 455 (2020)
12. Otálora, S., Atzori, M., Khan, A., Jimenez-del Toro, O., Andrearczyk, V., Müller, H.: A systematic comparison of deep learning strategies for weakly supervised gleason grading. In: Medical Imaging 2020: Digital Pathology, vol. 11320, p. 113200L. International Society for Optics and Photonics (2020)
13. Pena, G.P., Andrade-Filho, J.S.: How does a pathologist make a diagnosis? Arch. Pathol. Lab. Med. **133**(1), 124–132 (2009)
14. Qiu, J.X., Yoon, H.J., Fearn, P.A., Tourassi, G.D.: Deep learning for automated extraction of primary sites from cancer pathology reports. IEEE J. Biomed. Health Inf. **22**(1), 244–251 (2017)
15. Ribeiro, M.T., Singh, S., Guestrin, C.: "Why should i trust you?" explaining the predictions of any classifier. In: Proceedings of the 22nd ACM SIGKDD International Conference on Knowledge Discovery and Data Mining, pp. 1135–1144 (2016)
16. Schaer, R., Otálora, S., Jimenez-del Toro, O., Atzori, M., Müller, H.: Deep learning-based retrieval system for gigapixel histopathology cases and the open access literature. J. Pathol. Inform. **10** (2019)
17. Jimenez-del-Toro, O., Otálora, S., Atzori, M., Müller, H.: Deep multimodal case-based retrieval for large histopathology datasets. In: Wu, G., Munsell, B.C., Zhan, Y., Bai, W., Sanroma, G., Coupé, P. (eds.) Patch-MI 2017. LNCS, vol. 10530, pp. 149–157. Springer, Cham (2017). https://doi.org/10.1007/978-3-319-67434-6_17
18. del Toro, O.J., et al.: Convolutional neural networks for an automatic classification of prostate tissue slides with high-grade gleason score. In: Medical Imaging 2017: Digital Pathology, vol. 10140, p. 1014000. International Society for Optics and Photonics (2017)
19. Vaswani, A., et al.: Attention is all you need. In: Advances in Neural Information Processing Systems, pp. 5998–6008 (2017)
20. Wang, Y., Liu, F., Verspoor, K., Baldwin, T.: Evaluating the utility of model configurations and data augmentation on clinical semantic textual similarity. In: Proceedings of the 19th SIGBioMed Workshop on Biomedical Language Processing, pp. 105–111 (2020)
21. Wu, S., et al.: Deep learning in clinical natural language processing: a methodical review. J. Am. Med. Inform. Assoc. **27**(3), 457–470 (2020)
22. Xiao, C., Choi, E., Sun, J.: Opportunities and challenges in developing deep learning models using electronic health records data: a systematic review. J. Am. Med. Inform. Assoc. **25**(10), 1419–1428 (2018)
23. Yala, A., et al.: Using machine learning to parse breast pathology reports. Breast Cancer Res. Treat. **161**(2), 203–211 (2017)

AI Slipping on Tiles: Data Leakage in Digital Pathology

Nicole Bussola[1,2]([✉]), Alessia Marcolini[3], Valerio Maggio[4], Giuseppe Jurman[1], and Cesare Furlanello[3]

[1] Fondazione Bruno Kessler, Trento, Italy
{bussola,jurman}@fbk.eu
[2] University of Trento, Trento, Italy
[3] HK3 Lab, Milan, Italy
{alessia.marcolini,cesare.furlanello}@hk3lab.ai
[4] University of Bristol, Bristol, UK
valerio.maggio@bristol.ac.uk

Abstract. Reproducibility of AI models on biomedical data still stays as a major concern for their acceptance into the clinical practice. Initiatives for reproducibility in the development of predictive biomarkers as the MAQC Consortium already underlined the importance of appropriate Data Analysis Plans (DAPs) to control for different types of bias, including data leakage from the training to the test set. In the context of digital pathology, the leakage typically lurks in weakly designed experiments not accounting for the subjects in their data partitioning schemes. This issue is then exacerbated when fractions or subregions of slides (i.e. "tiles") are considered. Despite this aspect is largely recognized by the community, we argue that it is often overlooked. In this study, we assess the impact of data leakage on the performance of machine learning models trained and validated on multiple histology data collection. We prove that, even with a properly designed DAP (10×5 repeated cross-validation), predictive scores can be inflated up to 41% when tiles from the same subject are used both in training and validation sets by deep learning models. We replicate the experiments for 4 classification tasks on 3 histopathological datasets, for a total of 374 subjects, 556 slides and more than $27,000$ tiles. Also, we discuss the effects of data leakage on transfer learning strategies with models pre-trained on general-purpose datasets or off-task digital pathology collections. Finally, we propose a solution that automates the creation of leakage-free deep learning pipelines for digital pathology based on `histolab`, a novel Python package for histology data preprocessing. We validate the solution on two public datasets (TCGA and GTEx).

Keywords: Reproducibility · Deep learning · Digital pathology

---

N. Bussola and A. Marcolini—Joint first author.
G. Jurman and C. Furlanello—Joint last author.

A. Del Bimbo et al. (Eds.): ICPR 2020 Workshops, LNCS 12661, pp. 167–182, 2021.
https://doi.org/10.1007/978-3-030-68763-2_13

1   Introduction

Bioinformatics on high-throughput omics data has been plagued by uncountable issues with reproducibility since its early days; Ioannidis and colleagues [1] found that almost 90% of papers in a leading journal in genetics were not repeatable due to methodological or clerical errors. Although the landscape seems to have improved [2], and broad efforts have been spent across different biomedical fields [3], computational reproducibility and replicability still fall short of the ideal. Lack of reproducibility has been linked to inaccuracies in managing batch effects [4,5], small sample sizes [6], or flaws in the experimental design such as data normalization simultaneously performed on development and validation data [7,8]. The MAQC-II project for reproducible biomarker development from microarray data demonstrated, through a community-wide research effort, that a well-designed Data Analysis Plan (DAP) is mandatory to avoid selection bias flaws in the development of models for high-dimensional datasets [9].

Among the various types of selection bias that threaten the reproducibility of machine learning algorithms, *data leakage* is possibly the most subtle one [10]. Data leakage refers to the use of information from outside the training dataset during model training or selection [11]. A typical leakage occurs when data in the training, validation and/or test sets share indirect information, leading to overly optimistic results. For example, one of the preclinical sub-dataset in the MAQC-II study consisted of microarray data from mice triplets. These triplets were expected to have an almost identical response for each experimental condition, and therefore they had to be kept together in DAP partitioning to circumvent any possible leakage from training to internal validation data [9].

The goal of this study is to provide evidence that similar issues are still lurking in the grey areas of preprocessing, ready to emerge in the everyday practice of machine learning for digital pathology. The BreaKHis [12] dataset, one of the most popular histology collection of breast cancer samples, has been used in more than 40 scientific papers to date [13], with reported results spanning a broad range of performance. In a non-negligible number of these studies, overfitting effects due to data leakage are suspected to impact their outcomes.

Deep learning pipelines for histopathological data typically require Whole Slide Images (WSIs) to be partitioned into multiple patches (also referred to as "tiles" [14]) to augment the original training data, and to comply with memory constraints imposed by GPU hardware architectures. For example, a single WSI of size $67,727 \times 47,543$ pixels can be partitioned in multiple 512×512 tiles, which are randomly extracted, and verified such that selected subregions preserve enough tissue information. These tiles are then processed by data augmentation operators (e.g. random rotation, flipping, or affine transformation) to reduce the risk of overfitting. As a result, the number of multiple subimages originating from the very same histological specimen is significantly amplified [15,16], consequently increasing the risk for data leakage. Protocols for data partitioning (e.g. a repeated cross-validation DAP) are not naturally immune against replicates, and so the source originating each tile should be considered to avoid any risk of bias [17].

In this work, we quantify the importance of adopting *Patient-Wise* split procedures with a set of experiments on digital pathology datasets. All experiments are based on DAPPER [18], a reproducible framework for predictive digital pathology composed of a deep learning core ("backbone network") as feature encoder, and multiple task-related classification models, i.e. Random Forest or Multi-Layer Perceptron Network (see Fig. 1). We test the impact of various data partitioning strategies on the training of multiple backbone architectures, i.e. DenseNet [19], and ResNet models [20], fine-tuned to the histology domain.

Our experiments confirm that train-test contamination (in terms of modeling) is a serious concern that hinders the development of a dataset-agnostic methodology, with impact similar to the lack of standard protocols in the acquisition and storage of WSIs in digital pathology [21]. Thus, we present a protocol to prevent data leakage during data preprocessing. The solution is based on `histolab`, an open-source Python library designed as a reproducible and robust environment for WSI preprocessing, available at https://github.com/histolab/histolab. The novel approach is demonstrated on two public large scale datasets: GTEx [22] (i.e. non-pathological tissues), and TCGA [23] (i.e. cancer tissues).

2   Data Description

We tested our experimental pipeline on three public datasets for image classification in digital pathology, namely GTEx [22], Heart Failure (HF) [24], and BreaKHis [12]. Descriptive statistics of the datasets are reported in Table 1, and Fig. 1.

The GTEx Dataset. The current release of GTEx (v8) includes a total of 15,201 H&E-stained WSIs, retrieved with an Aperio scanner (20× native magnification) and gathered from a cohort of 838 nondiseased donors[1]. In this work, we consider a subset of 265 WSIs randomly selected from 11 histological classes, for a total of 83 subjects. From this subset, we randomly selected a balanced number of WSIs per tissue: adrenal gland ($n = 24$); bladder ($n = 19$); breast ($n = 26$); liver ($n = 26$); lung ($n = 21$); ovary ($n = 26$); pancreas ($n = 26$); prostate ($n = 24$); testis ($n = 26$); thyroid ($n = 26$); uterus ($n = 21$).

We implemented a data preprocessing pipeline to prepare the tile dataset from the GTEx collection. First, the tissue region is automatically detected in each WSI; this process combines the *Otsu-threshold* binarization method [25] with the dilation and hole-filling morphological operations. A maximum of 100 tiles of size 512×512 is then randomly extracted from each slide. To ensure that only high-informative images are used, tiles with tissue area that accounts for less than the 85% of the whole patch are automatically rejected. At the end of this step, a total of 26,174 random tiles is extracted from the WSIs, each available at different magnification levels (i.e., $20\times, 10\times, 5\times$). In this paper we limit experiments and discussions to tiles at $5\times$ magnification, with no loss of generality.

---

[1] https://gtexportal.org/home/releaseInfoPage.

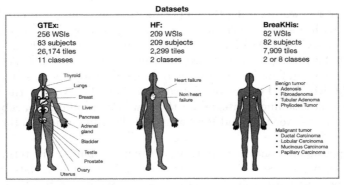

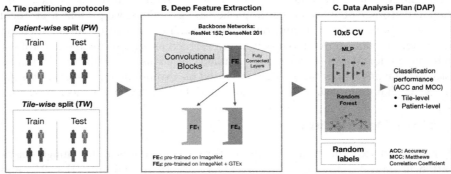

Fig. 1. Experimental environment for evaluation of data leakage impact on machine learning models in digital pathology. (A) Tile datasets are split into train/test set following either the *Tile-Wise* or the *Patient-Wise* protocol; (B) the train set is used to train a backbone network for feature extraction, using different transfer learning strategies; (C) machine learning classifiers on the deep features are evaluated within the Data Analysis Plan.

Table 1. Statistics of the datasets considered in this study.

Dataset	Subjects	WSIs	WSIs per subject			Tiles	Tiles per subject		
			Min	Max	Median		Min	Max	Median
GTEx	83	265	1	7	3	26, 174	1	700	300
HF	209	209	1			2, 299	11		
BreaKHis	82	82	1			2, 013	9	62	21

The HF Dataset. The Heart Failure collection [24] originates from 209 H&E-stained WSIs of the left ventricular tissue, each corresponding to a single subject. The learning task is to distinguish images of *heart failure* ($n = 94$) from those of *non-heart failure* ($n = 115$). Slides in the former class are categorized according to the disease subtype: ischemic cardiomyopathy ($n = 51$); idiopathic dilated cardiomyopathy ($n = 41$); undocumented ($n = 2$). Subjects with no heart failure are further grouped in: normal cardiovascular function ($n = 41$); non-HF and no other pathology ($n = 72$); non-HF and other tissue pathology ($n = 2$). WSIs in this dataset have been acquired with an Aperio ScanScope at 20× native magnification, and then downsampled at 5× magnification by authors. From each WSI, 11 non-overlapping patches of size 250 × 250 were randomly extracted. The entire collection of 2,299 tiles is publicly available on the Image Data Resource Repository[2] (IDR number: idr0042).

The BreaKHis Dataset. The BreaKHis histopathological dataset [12] collects 7,909 H&E-stained tiles (size 700 × 460) of malignant or benign breast tumour biopsies. Tiles correspond to regions of interest manually selected by expert pathologists from a cohort of 82 patients, and made available at different magnification factors, i.e., 40×, 100×, 200×, 400×) [12]. To allow for a more extensive comparison with the state of the art, only the 200× magnification factor will be considered in this paper. The BreaKHis dataset currently contains 4 histological distinct subtypes of benign, and malignant tumours, respectively: Adenosis ($n = 444$); Fibroadenoma ($n = 1,014$); Tubular Adenoma ($n = 453$); Phyllodes Tumor ($n = 569$); Ductal Carcinoma ($n = 3,451$); Lobular Carcinoma ($n = 626$); Mucinous Carcinoma ($n = 792$); Papillary Carcinoma ($n = 560$). This dataset is used for two classification tasks: (BreaKHis-2) binary classification of benign and malignant tumour samples; (BreaKHis-8) classification of the 8 distinct tumour subtypes.

3   Methods

The pipeline used in this work is based on the DAPPER framework for digital pathology [18], extended by (i) integrating specialised train-test splitting protocols, i.e. *Tile-Wise* and *Patient-Wise*; (ii) extending the feature extractor component with new backbone networks; (iii) applying two transfer learning strategies for feature embedding. Figure 1 shows the three main blocks of the experimental environment defined in this paper: (A) dataset partition in train and test set; (B) feature extraction procedure with different transfer learning strategies; (C) the DAP employed for machine learning models.

A. Dataset Partitioning Protocols. The tile dataset is partitioned in the *training* set and *test* set, considering 80% and 20% split ratio for the two sets, respectively. We compare two data partitioning protocols to investigate the impact of a train-test contamination (Fig. 1A): in the *Tile-Wise* (TW) protocol, tiles are randomly split between the training and the test sets, regardless of the original WSI. The *Patient-Wise* (PW) protocol splits the tile dataset strictly ensuring that all tiles extracted from the same subject are found either in the training or the test set. To avoid other sources of leakage due to class

---

[2] http://idr.openmicroscopy.org/.

imbalance [26], the two protocols are both combined with stratification of samples over the corresponding classes, and any class imbalance is accounted for by weighting the error on generated predictions.

B. Deep Learning Models and Feature Extraction. The training set is then used to train a deep neural network for feature extraction (Fig. 1B), i.e. a "backbone" network whose aim is to learn a vector representation of the data (*features embedding*). In this study, we consider two backbone architectures in the residual network (ResNet) family, namely ResNet-152 [20] and DenseNet-201 [19]. Given that the DenseNet model has almost the double of parameters[3], and so a higher footprint in computational resources, diagnostic experiments and transfer learning are performed only with the ResNet-152 model. Similarly to [16], and [18], we started from off-the-shelf version of the models, pre-trained on ImageNet, and then fine-tuned to the digital pathology domain using transfer learning. Specifically, we trained the whole network for 50 epochs with a learning rate $\eta = 1e-5$, and Adam optimizer [27], in combination with the categorical cross-entropy loss. The β_1 and β_2 parameters of the optimizer are respectively set to 0.9 and 0.999, with no regularization. To reduce the risk of overfitting, we use train-time data augmentation, namely random rotation and random flipping of the input tiles.

The impact of adopting a single or double-step transfer learning strategy in combination with the *Patient-Wise* partitioning protocol is also investigated in this study. Two sets of features embeddings (FE) are generated: FE_1, backbone model fine-tuned from ImageNet; FE_2, backbone model sequentially fine-tuned from ImageNet and GTEx.

C. Classification and Data Analysis Plan (DAP). The classification is finally performed on the feature embedding within a DAP for machine learning models (Fig. 1C). In this work, we compare the performance of two models: Random Forest (RF) and Multi-Layer Perceptron Network (MLP). In particular, we apply the 10×5-fold CV schema proposed by the MAQC-II Consortium [9]. In the DAP setting, the input datasets are the two separate training and test sets, as resulted from the 80–20 train-test split protocol. The test set is kept completely unseen to the model, and only used for the final evaluation. The training set further undergoes a 5-fold CV iterated 10 times with a different random seed, resulting in 50 separated internal *validation* sets. These validation sets are generated adopting the same protocols used in the previous train-test generation, namely *Tile-Wise* or *Patient-Wise*. The overall performance of the model is evaluated across all the iterations, in terms of average Matthews Correlation Coefficient (MCC) [28] and Accuracy (ACC), both with 95% Studentized bootstrap confidence intervals (CI). Moreover, results have been reported both at tile-level and at patient-level, in order to assess the ability of machine learning models to generalise on unseen subjects (see Sect. 4).

---

[3]   DenseNet-201: ∼12M parameters; ResNet-152: ∼6M parameters.

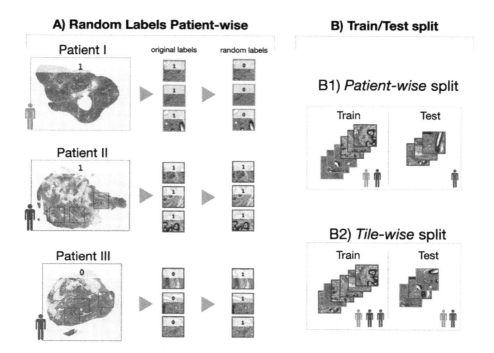

Fig. 2. Random Labels experimental settings. A) The labels of the extracted tiles are randomly shuffled consistently with the original patient. B) The train/test split is then performed either *Patient-Wise* or *Tile-Wise*.

As an additional caution to check for selection bias, the DAP integrates a *random labels* schema (RLab) (Fig. 2). In this setting, the training labels are randomly shuffled and presented as reference ground truth to the machine learning models. In particular, we consistently randomize the labels for all the tiles of a single subject, thus they would all share the same random label (Fig. 2A); then we alternatively use the *Patient-Wise* (Fig. 2B1) or the *Tile-Wise* (Fig. 2B2) splits within the DAP environment. Notice that an average MCC score close to zero ($MCC \approx 0$) indicates a protocol immune from sources of bias, including data leakage; we focus on the RLab validation to emphasise evidence of data leakage derived from the TW and the PW protocols.

Performance Metrics. Several patient-wise performance metrics have been defined in the literature [12,24,29]. Two metrics are considered in this study: (1) *Winner-takes-all* (WA), and (2) *Patient Score* (PS).

In the WA metric, the label associated to each patient corresponds to the majority of the labels predicted for their tiles. With this strategy, standard metrics based on the classification confusion matrix can be used as overall performance indicators. In this paper, ACC is used for comparability with the PS

metric. The PS metric is defined for each patient [12] as the ratio of the N_c correctly classified tiles over the N_P total number of tiles per patient, namely $PS = \frac{N_c}{N_P}$. The overall performance is then calculated using the *global recognition rate* (RR), defined as the average of all the PS scores for all patients:

$$RR = \frac{\sum PS}{|P|}$$

In this paper, the WA metric and the PS metric are used for comparison of patient-level results on the HF dataset and the BreaKHis dataset, respectively.

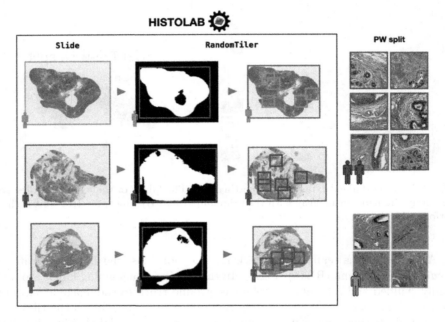

Fig. 3. Workflow of the proposed protocol against data leakage in digital pathology, using the histolab software. The documentation of histolab is available at http://histolab.readthedocs.io.

Preventing Data Leakage: The `histolab` Library. As a solution to the data leakage pitfall, we have developed a protocol for image and tile splitting based on `histolab`, an open source software recently developed for reproducible WSI preprocessing in digital pathology. This library implements a tile extraction procedure, whose reliability and quality result from robust design, and extensive software testing. A high level interface for image transformation is also provided, making `histolab` an easy-to-adopt tool for complex histopathological pipelines.

In order to intercept data leakage conditions, the protocol is designed to create a data-leakage free collection (tile extraction with the *Patient-Wise* split) that can be easily integrated in a deep learning workflow (Fig. 3). The protocol is

Table 2. DAP results for each classifier head, using the *Tile-Wise* partitioning protocol, and the FE_1 feature embedding with the ResNet-152 as backbone model. The average cross validation metrics (MCC_v and ACC_v) with 95% CI are reported for each classification task, along with metrics on the test set (MCC_t and ACC_t). The *Others* column reports the highest accuracy achieved among the compared papers.

Dataset	MLP MCC_v	MCC_t	RF MCC_v	MCC_t	MLP ACC_v	ACC_t	RF ACC_v	ACC_t	Others ACC_t
GTEx	0.999 (0.999, 0.999)	0.998	0.999 (0.999, 0.999)	0.997	0.999 (0.999, 0.999)	0.999	0.999 (0.999, 0.999)	0.998	–
HF	0.959 (0.956, 0.963)	0.956	0.956 (0.953, 0.959)	0.960	0.980 (0.978, 0.982)	0.978	0.978 (0.977, 0.980)	0.980	–
BreaKHis-2	0.989 (0.987, 0.991)	0.988	0.990 (0.988, 0.992)	0.994	0.995 (0.994, 0.996)	0.994	0.996 (0.995, 0.997)	0.997	0.993 [30]
BreaKHis-8	0.945 (0.942, 0.949)	0.922	0.929 (0.925, 0.932)	0.921	0.959 (0.956, 0.962)	0.940	0.946 (0.943, 0.949)	0.940	0.985 [31]

already customized for standardizing WSI preprocessing on GTEx and TCGA, two large scale public repositories that are widely used in computational pathology. The code can be also adapted to rebuild the training and test datasets from GTEx used in this study, thus extending the HINT collection presented in [18].

4   Results

Data Leakage Effects on Classification Outcome. The results of the four classification tasks using the ResNet-152 pre-trained on ImageNet as backbone model (i.e. feature vectors FE_1) are reported in Table 2 and Table 3, with the *Tile-Wise* and the *Patient-Wise* partitioning protocols, respectively. The average cross validation MCC_v and ACC_v with 95% CI are presented, along with results on the test set (i.e. MCC_t, and ACC_t). State of the art results (i.e. *Others*) are also reported for comparison, whenever available.

Table 3. DAP results for each classifier head, using the *Patient-Wise* partitioning protocol, and the FE_1 feature embedding with the ResNet-152 as backbone model. The average cross validation metrics (MCC_v and ACC_v) with 95% CI are reported for each classification task, along with metrics on the test set (MCC_t and ACC_t). The *Others* column reports the highest accuracy achieved among the compared papers.

Dataset	MLP MCC_v	MCC_t	RF MCC_v	MCC_t	MLP ACC_v	ACC_t	RF ACC_v	ACC_t	Others ACC_t
GTEx	0.998 (0.998, 0.998)	0.998	0.997 (0.997, 0.997)	0.997	0.998 (0.998, 0.998)	0.998	0.997 (0.997, 0.998)	0.997	–
HF	0.852 (0.847, 0.858)	0.856	0.848 (0.836, 0.860)	0.833	0.927 (0.924, 0.929)	0.915	0.924 (0.918, 0.930)	0.915	0.932 [24]
BreaKHis-2	0.695 (0.665, 0.724)	0.801	0.709 (0.671, 0.746)	0.863	0.870 (0.856, 0.882)	0.924	0.876 (0.859, 0.892)	0.946	0.973 [29]
BreaKHis-8	0.561 (0.529, 0.594)	0.541	0.594 (0.562, 0.631)	0.471	0.679 (0.655, 0.703)	0.644	0.701 (0.681, 0.732)	0.600	0.973 [29]

As expected, estimates are more favourable for the *TW* protocol (Table 2) with respect to the *PW* one (Table 3), both in validation and in test and consistently for all the datasets. Moreover, the inflation of the *Tile-Wise* estimates is amplified in the multi-class setting (see BreaKHis-2 vs BreaKHis-8). Notably, these results are comparable with those in the literature, suggesting the evidence of a data leakage for studies adopting the *Tile-Wise* splitting strategy. Results on the GTEx dataset do not suggest significant differences using the two protocols; however both MCC and ACC metrics lie in a very high range. Analogous results (not reported here) were obtained using the DenseNet-201 backbone model, further confirming the generality of the derived conclusions.

Random Labels Detects Signal in the *Tile-Wise* split. A data leakage effect is signalled for the *Tile-Wise* partitioning with a MCC consistently positive in the RLab validation schema (Sect. 3). For instance, as for BreaKHis-2 coupled with MLP, $MCC_{RL} = 0.354$ $(0.319, 0.392)$ in the *Tile-Wise* setting, to be compared with $MCC_{RL} = -0.065$ $(-0.131, 0.001)$ using the *Patient-Wise* protocol. Full MCC_{RL} results considering 5 trials of the RLab test are reported in Table 4, with corresponding ACC_{RL} values also included for completeness. Notably, all the tests using the *Patient-Wise* split perform as expected, i.e. with median values near 0, whereas results of the *Tile-Wise* case exhibit a high variability, especially for the BreaKHis-2 dataset (Fig. 4).

Table 4. Random Labels (RLab) results using the ResNet-152 as backbone model, and *Tile-Wise* and *Patient-Wise* train-test split protocols. The average MCC_{RL} and ACC_{RL} with 95% CI are reported.

Dataset	MCC_{RL}		ACC_{RL}	
	TW	*PW*	*TW*	*PW*
HF	0.107	0.004	0.553	0.502
	(0.078, 0.143)	(−0.042, 0.048)	(0.534, 0.570)	(0.474, 0.530)
BreaKHis-2	0.354	−0.065	0.637	0.560
	(0.319, 0.392)	(−0.131, 0.001)	(0.613, 0.662)	(0.506, 0.626)
BreaKHis-8	0.234	0.013	0.318	0.097
	(0.173, 0.341)	(−0.042, 0.065)	(0.215, 0.506)	(0.056, 0.143)

Benefits of Domain-Specific Transfer Learning. The adoption of the GTEx domain-specific dataset for transfer learning (Table 5) proves to be beneficial over the use of ImageNet only (Table 3). Notably, the *Patient-Wise* partitioning protocol with the FE_2 embedding have comparable performance with FE_1 and the inflated TW splitting (Table 2). However, minor improvements are achieved on the BreaKHis-8 task, with results not reaching state of the art. It must be observed that the BreaKHis dataset is highly imbalanced in the multiclass task. As a countermeasure, authors in [34,35] adopted a balancing strategy

Table 5. DAP results for each classifier head, using the *Patient-Wise* partitioning protocol, and the FE_2 feature embedding with ResNet-152 as backbone model. The average cross validation MCC_v and ACC_v with 95% CI are reported, along with results on the test set (i.e. MCC_t, and ACC_t). The *Others* column reports the highest accuracy achieved among the compared papers.

Dataset	MLP		RF		MLP		RF		Others
	MCC_v	MCC_t	MCC_v	MCC_t	ACC_v	ACC_t	ACC_v	ACC_t	ACC_t
HF	0.956 (0.952, 0.960)	0.964	0.955 (0.943, 0.958)	0.950	0.978 (0.976, 0.980)	0.982	0.977 (0.975, 0.979)	0.978	0.932 [24]
BreaKHis-2	0.864 (0.839, 0.888)	0.948	0.912 (0.892, 0.932)	0.961	0.941 (0.930, 0.952)	0.980	0.963 (0.955, 0.971)	0.984	0.973 [29]
BreaKHis-8	0.573 (0.539, 0.602)	0.478	0.586 (0.552, 0.621)	0.482	0.685 (0.661, 0.712)	0.603	0.699 (0.675, 0.724)	0.606	0.973 [29]

during data augmentation, which we did not introduce here for comparability with the other experiments.

To verify how much of previous domain-knowledge can be still re-used for the original task, we devised an additional experiment on the GTEx dataset: on the *Feature Extractor* component (i.e. Convolutional Layers) of the model trained on GTEx and fine-tuned on BreaKHis-2, we add back the MLP classifier of the model trained on GTEx. Notably, this configuration recover high predictive performance (i.e. $MCC_t = 0.983$) on the classification task after only a single epoch of full training on GTEx.

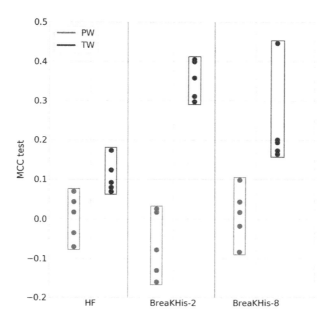

Fig. 4. MCC_{RL} results on the test set. TW: *Tile-Wise*, PW: *Patient-Wise*.

Table 6. Patient-level results for each classifier head, using the *Patient-Wise* and *Tile-Wise* partitioning protocols, and the FE_1 feature embedding with the ResNet-152 backbone model. The average cross-validation Patient-level accuracy with 95% CI (ACC_v), and corresponding scores on the test set (ACC_t), are reported. The *Others* column reports the highest accuracy achieved among the compared papers.

Dataset	Metric	Partitioning protocol	MLP		RF		Others
			ACC_v	ACC_t	ACC_v	ACC_t	ACC_t
HF	WA	TW	0.984 (0.982, 0.987)	0.995	0.984 (0.981, 0.986)	0.995	–
		PW	0.981 (0.975, 0.986)	0.951	0.977 (0.971, 0.983)	0.927	0.940 [24]
BreaKHis-2	PS	TW	0.995 (0.994, 0.996)	0.997	0.997 (0.996, 0.998)	0.998	0.872 [32]
		PW	0.864 (0.851, 0.877)	0.885	0.883 (0.869, 0.898)	0.893	0.976 [29]
BreaKHis-8	PS	TW	0.963 (0.960, 0.967)	0.950	0.957 (0.955, 0.959)	0.962	0.964 [33]
		PW	0.687 (0.667, 0.709)	0.752	0.705 (0.685, 0.728)	0.725	0.967 [29]

Patient-Level Performance Analysis. We report patient-wise performance using the ResNet-152 backbone model with either the FE_1 feature embedding and both *Tile-Wise* and *Patient-Wise* protocols (Table 6), or with the FE_2 strategy and the *Patient-Wise* split (Table 7).

Table 7. Patient-level results for each classifier head, with the *Patient-Wise* partitioning protocol and the FE_2 feature embedding with the ResNet-152 model. The average cross-validation Patient-level accuracy with 95% CI (ACC_v) and corresponding scores on the test set (ACC_t) are reported. The *Others* column reports the highest accuracy achieved among the compared papers.

Dataset	Patient-level metric	MLP		RF		Others
		ACC_v	ACC_t	ACC_v	ACC_t	ACC_v
HF	WA	0.992 (0.989, 0.995)	0.976	0.989 (0.984, 0.992)	0.976	0.940 [24]
BreaKHis-2	PS	0.941 (0.930, 0.951)	0.971	0.958 (0.948, 0.968)	0.991	0.976 [29]
BreaKHis-8	PS	0.691 (0.669, 0.716)	0.721	0.699 (0.676, 0.723)	0.724	0.967 [29]

5   Discussion

We report here a short description of the approach employed by comparable studies on the same datasets considered in this work; we refer to a *Patient-Wise* partitioning protocol when the authors clearly state the adoption of a train-test split consistent with the patient, or when the code is provided as reference. Notice that the different accuracy scores obtained for deep learning models applied on the same data can be explained by the adoption of diverse experimental protocols (e.g. preprocessing, data augmentation, transfer learning methods).

Nirschl et al. [24] train a CNN on the HF dataset to distinguish patients with or without heart failure. They systematically apply the *Patient-Wise* rule for the initial train-test split (50–50) and for the training partition into three-folds for cross-validation. Data augmentation strategies are also applied, including random cropping, rotation, mirroring, and staining augmentation. As for the BreaKHis dataset, Alom et al. [29] use a 70–30 *Patient-Wise* partitioning protocol to train a CNN with several (not specified) hidden layers, reporting average results from 5-fold cross-validation. Further, the authors apply augmentation strategies (i.e., rotation, shifting, flipping) to increase the dataset by a factor of 21× for each magnification level. The work of Han et al. [34] propose a novel CNN adopting a *Tile-Wise* partition with the training set accounting for the 50% of the dataset. Data augmentation (i.e. intensity variation, rotation, translation, and flipping) is used to adjust for imbalanced classes. Jiang et al. [30] train two different variants of the ResNet model to address the binary and the multi-class task, for each magnification factor. They adopt a *Tile-Wise* partitioning protocol for the train-test split, using 60% and 70% of the data in the training set for BreaKHis-2 and BreaKHis-8, respectively. Data augmentation is also exploited in the training process, and experiments are repeated 3 times.

Other authors employed a similar protocol to address the BreaKHis-8 task by training a CNN pretrained on ImageNet: Nawaz et al. [33] implemented a DenseNet-inspired model, while Nguyen et al. [36] choose a custom CNN model, instead. Both studies use a *Tile-Wise* partition on the BreaKHis dataset (70–30 and 90–10, respectively), and do not apply any data augmentation. Xie et al. [32] adapt a pre-trained ResNet-V2 to the binary and multiclass tasks of BreaKHis, at different magnification factors, using a 70–30 *Tile-Wise* partition. Data augmentation has been applied to balance the least represented class in BreaKHis-8. Jannesary et al. [31] used a 90–10 *Tile-Wise* train-test split with data augmentation (i.e. resizing, rotations, cropping and flipping) to fine-tune a ResNet-V1 for binary and multi-class prediction. Moreover, experiments in [31] were performed combining images at different magnification factors in a unified dataset. Finally, both [37] and [38] used a *Tile-Wise* train-test split for prediction of malignant vs benign samples using a pre-trained CNN and [38] also employed data augmentation (rotation and flipping).

6   Conclusions

Possibly even more than other areas of computational biology, digital pathology faces the risk of data leakage. The first part of this study clearly demonstrates the impact of weakly designed experiments with deep learning for digital pathology. In particular, we found that the predictive performance estimates are inflated if the DAP does not flawlessly concentrate the subject and/or the tissue specimen from which tiles are extracted either in the training or test datasets. Fortunately, many studies already adopt the correct procedure [12,16,17,24,34,35]. However, we argue that this subtle form of selection bias still constitutes a threat to reproducibility of AI models that may have affected a considerable number of works. Indeed, a significant number of studies considered in this work do not explicitly mention the patient-wise strategy [30–33,39,40]. We encourage the community to adopt our code (https://github.com/histolab/histolab/tree/master/examples) as a launchpad for reproducibility of AI pipelines in digital pathology.

References

1. Ioannidis, J.P.A., et al.: Repeatability of published microarray gene expression analyses. Nat. Genet. **41**(2), 149 (2009)
2. Iqbal, S.A., et al.: Reproducible research practices and transparency across the biomedical literature. PLoS Biol. **14**(1), e1002333 (2016)
3. National Academies of Sciences, Engineering, and Medicine, Policy and Global Affairs. Reproducibility and Replicability in Science. National Academies Press (2019)
4. Leek, J.T., et al.: Tackling the widespread and critical impact of batch effects in high-throughput data. Nat. Rev. Genet. **11**(10), 733 (2010)
5. Moossavi, S., et al.: Repeatability and reproducibility assessment in a large-scale population-based microbiota study: case study on human milk microbiota. bioRxiv:2020.04.20.052035 (2020)
6. Turner, B.O., et al.: Small sample sizes reduce the replicability of task-based fMRI studies. Commun. Biol. **1**(1), 1–10 (2018)
7. Barla, A., et al.: Machine learning methods for predictive proteomics. Briefings Bioinform. **9**(2), 119–128 (2008)
8. Peixoto, L., et al.: How data analysis affects power, reproducibility and biological insight of RNA-seq studies in complex datasets. Nucleic Acids Res. **43**(16), 7664–7674 (2015)
9. The MAQC Consortium: The MAQC-II project: a comprehensive study of common practices for the development and validation of microarray-based predictive models. Nat. Biotechnol. **28**(8), 827–838 (2010)
10. Ching, T., et al.: Opportunities and obstacles for deep learning in biology and medicine. J. Roy. Soc. Interface **15**(141), 20170387 (2018)
11. Saravanan, N., et al.: Data wrangling and data leakage in machine learning for healthcare. Int. J. Emerg. Technol. Innov. Res. **5**(8), 553–557 (2018)
12. Spanhol, F.A., et al.: A dataset for breast cancer histopathological image classification. IEEE Trans. Biomed. Eng. **63**(7), 1455–1462 (2016)
13. Shahidi, F., et al.: Breast cancer classification using deep learning approaches and histopathology image: a comparison study. IEEE Access **8**, 187531–187552 (2020)
14. Cohen, S.: Artificial Intelligence and Deep Learning in Pathology. Elsevier, Amsterdam (2020)
15. Komura, D., et al.: Machine learning methods for histopathological image analysis. Comput. Struct. Biotechnol. J. **16**, 34–42 (2018)
16. Mormont, R., et al.: Comparison of deep transfer learning strategies for digital pathology. In: Proceedings of the 2018 IEEE Conference on Computer Vision and Pattern Recognition Workshops (CVPRW), pp. 2343–234309. IEEE (2018)

17. Marée, R.: The need for careful data collection for pattern recognition in digital pathology. J. Pathol. Inform. **8**(1), 19 (2017)
18. Bizzego, A., et al.: Evaluating reproducibility of AI algorithms in digital pathology with DAPPER. PLOS Comput. Biol. **15**(3), 1–24 (2019)
19. Huang, G., et al.: Densely connected convolutional networks. In: Proceedings of the 2018 IEEE Conference on Computer Vision and Pattern Recognition (CVPR), pp. 2261–2269. IEEE (2018)
20. He, K., et al.: Deep residual learning for image recognition. In: Proceedings of the 2016 IEEE Conference on Computer Vision and Pattern Recognition (CVPR), pp. 770–778. IEEE (2016)
21. Barisoni, L., et al.: Digital pathology and computational image analysis in nephropathology. Nat. Rev. Nephrol. **16**, 669–685 (2020)
22. The GTEx Consortium: The genotype-tissue expression (GTEx) project. Nat. Genet. **45**(6), 580–585 (2013)
23. Tomczak, K., et al.: The cancer genome atlas (TCGA): an immeasurable source of knowledge. Contemp. Oncol. **19**(1A), A68 (2015)
24. Nirschl, J.J., et al.: A deep-learning classifier identifies patients with clinical heart failure using whole-slide images of H&E tissue. PLOS ONE **13**(4), e0192726 (2018)
25. Otsu, N.: A threshold selection method from gray-level histograms. IEEE Trans. Syst. Man Cybern. **9**(1), 62–66 (1979)
26. Raschka, S.: Model evaluation, model selection, and algorithm selection in machine learning. arXiv:1811.12808v3 (2020)
27. Kingma, D.P., et al.: Adam: a method for stochastic optimization. In: Published as a conference paper at ICLR 2015. arXiv:1412.6980 (2014)
28. Jurman, G., et al.: A comparison of MCC and CEN error measures in multi-class prediction. PLOS ONE **7**(8), 1–8 (2012)
29. Alom, M.Z., Yakopcic, C., Nasrin, M.S., Taha, T.M., Asari, V.K.: Breast cancer classification from histopathological images with inception recurrent residual convolutional neural network. J. Digital Imaging **32**(4), 605–617 (2019). https://doi.org/10.1007/s10278-019-00182-7
30. Jiang, Y., et al.: Breast cancer histopathological image classification using convolutional neural networks with small SE-ResNet module. PLOS ONE **14**(3), e0214587 (2019)
31. Jannesari, M., et al.: Breast cancer histopathological image classification: a deep learning approach. In: Proceedings of the 2018 IEEE International Conference on Bioinformatics and Biomedicine (BIBM), pp. 2405–2412 (2018)
32. Xie, J., et al.: Deep learning based analysis of histopathological images of breast cancer. Front. Genet. **10**, 80 (2019)
33. Nawaz, M., et al.: Multi-class breast cancer classification using deep learning convolutional neural network. Int. J. Adv. Comput. Sci. Appl. **9**(6), 316–332 (2018)
34. Han, Z., et al.: Breast cancer multi-classification from histopathological images with structured deep learning model. Sci. Rep. **7**(1), 4172 (2017)
35. Alom, M.J., et al.: Advanced deep convolutional neural network approaches for digital pathology image analysis: a comprehensive evaluation with different use cases. arXiv:1904.09075 (2019)
36. Nguyen, P.T., et al.: Multiclass breast cancer classification using convolutional neural network. In: Proceedings of the 2019 International Symposium on Electrical and Electronics Engineering (ISEE), pp. 130–134. IEEE (2019)
37. Deniz, E., Şengür, A., Kadiroğlu, Z., Guo, Y., Bajaj, V., Budak, Ü.: Transfer learning based histopathologic image classification for breast cancer detection. Health Inf. Sci. Syst. **6**(1), 1–7 (2018). https://doi.org/10.1007/s13755-018-0057-x

38. Myung, J.L., et al.: Deep convolution neural networks for medical image analysis. Int. J. Eng. Technol. **7**(3), 115–119 (2018)
39. Pan, X., et al.: Multi-task deep learning for fine-grained classification/grading in breast cancer histopathological images. In: Lu, H. (ed.) ISAIR 2018. SCI, vol. 810, pp. 85–95. Springer, Cham (2020). https://doi.org/10.1007/978-3-030-04946-1_10
40. Shallu, R.M.: Breast cancer histology images classification: training from scratch or transfer learning? ICT Exp. **4**(4), 247–254 (2018)

AIHA 2020 - International Workshop on Artificial Intelligence for Healthcare Applications

Preface

AIHA is a forum of researchers working on artificial intelligence applications in healthcare. Most of the medical data collected from healthcare systems are recorded in digital format. The increased availability of these data has enabled a number of artificial intelligence applications. Specifically, machine learning can generate insights to improve the discovery of new therapeutics tools, to support diagnostic decisions, to help in the rehabilitation process, to name a few. Researchers coupled with expert clinicians can play an important role in turning complex medical data (e.g., genomic data, online acquisitions of physicians, medical imagery, electrophysiological signals, etc.) into actionable knowledge that ultimately improves patient care. In the last years, these topics have drawn clinical and machine learning research which ultimately led to practical and successful applications in healthcare. The scientific objective of the workshop is to present the most recent advances in artificial intelligence techniques for healthcare applications including, but not limited to, automatic diagnosis support systems, automatic disease prediction, assisted surgery, and medical image analysis.

Due to the COVID-19 pandemic, the 2020 edition of the AIHA workshop was held fully virtual in conjunction with the 25th Internal Conference of Pattern Recognition. The format of the workshop includes oral and poster presentations of the accepted papers, and a keynote held by Prof. Nico Karssemeijer, in which he gave a talk entitled "AI Applications for Early Detection and Diagnosis of Breast Cancer". In his presentation, an overview of the state of art was presented, focusing both on the technology and validation in clinical practice. The overview included a variety of applications ranging from breast cancer risk assessment, early detection, and diagnosis using a multi-modal approach.

This year we received 41 submissions for reviews. After an accurate and thorough single-blind peer review process involving two reviewers for each submission, we selected 32 papers for presentation at the workshop. The review process focused on the quality of the papers, their scientific novelty, technical soundness, and relevance with the topics of the workshop. The acceptance of the papers was the result of the workshop organizers' discussion and agreement based on reviewers' reports and their self-assigned expertise rating. Due to the overall high quality of submissions, the acceptance rate was 78%. The accepted articles represent an interesting mix of (i) machine and deep learning techniques for automatic disease diagnosis and prediction and medical image segmentation and classification, (ii) computer vision techniques for assisted surgery, pose estimation, and fall detection, (iii) electrophysiological signal processing, and (iv) handwriting analysis for neurodegenerative diseases assessment.

We would like to thank the AIHA 2020 Program Committee, whose members made the workshop possible with their rigorous and timely review process, and ICPR 2020 for hosting the workshop and our emerging community.

Organization

AIHA Chairs

Alessandro Bria	University of Cassino and Southern Lazio, Italy
Nicole Dalia Cilia	University of Cassino and Southern Lazio, Italy
Francesco Fontanella	University of Cassino and Southern Lazio, Italy
Claudio Marrocco	University of Cassino and Southern Lazio, Italy

Program Committee

Berdakh Abibullaev	University of Houston, USA
Kassem Al Ismaeil	University of Luxembourg, Luxembourg
Djamila Aouada	University of Luxembourg, Luxembourg
George Azzopardi	University of Groningen, Netherlands
Giuseppe Boccignone	University of Milan, Italy
Daniele Cafolla	I.R.C.C.S. INM Neuromed, Italy
Stefano Cagnoni	University of Parma, Italy
Lorenzo Carnevale	I.R.C.C.S. INM Neuromed, Italy
Albert Comelli	Fondazione Ri.MED, Italy
Jesus G. Cruz-Garza	University of Houston, USA
Vittorio Cuculo	University of Milan, Italy
Claudio De Stefano	University of Cassino and Southern Latium, Italy
Moises Diaz	University of Las Palmas de Gran Canaria, Spain
Luc Evers	Radboud UMC, Netherlands
David Fofi	Université de Bourgogne, France
Adrian Galdran	University of Bournemouth, UK
Donato Impedovo	University of Bari, Italy
Guillaume Lemaître	Inria, France
Xavier Lladó	University of Girona, Spain
Angelo Marcelli	University of Salerno, Italy
Joan Mart	University of Girona, Spain
Robert Mart	University of Girona, Spain
Murad Mengjhani	University of Columbia, USA
Mario Merone	University Campus Bio-Medico of Rome, Italy
Pablo Mesejo	University of Granada, Spain
Mario Molinara	University of Cassino and Southern Latium, Italy

Arnau Oliver	University of Girona, Spain
Antonio Parziale	University of Salerno, Italy
Carlo Sansone	University of Naples Federico II, Italy
Alessandra Scotto Di Freca	University of Cassino and Southern Latium, Italy
Rosa Senatore	University of Salerno, Italy
Steven Shepard	University of California, USA
Desirè Sidibè	University Evry Val d'Essonne, France
Omar Tahri	University of Burgundy, France
Francesco Tortorella	University of Salerno, Italy
Gennaro Vessio	University of Bari, Italy

Additional Reviewers

Vincenzo Dentamaro
Mohamed Adel Mohamed Ali

Predictive Medicine Using Interpretable Recurrent Neural Networks

André Ferreira[1]([✉]) [iD], Sara C. Madeira[2] [iD], Marta Gromicho[3] [iD],
Mamede de Carvalho[3,4] [iD], Susana Vinga[1,5] [iD], and Alexandra M. Carvalho[1,6] [iD]

[1] Instituto Superior Técnico, Universidade de Lisboa, Lisbon, Portugal
andre.c.n.ferreira@tecnico.ulisboa.pt
[2] LASIGE, Faculdade de Ciências, Universidade de Lisboa, Lisbon, Portugal
[3] IMM, Faculdade de Medicina, Universidade de Lisboa, Lisbon, Portugal
[4] Department of Neurosciences and Mental Health, CHULN, Lisbon, Portugal
[5] INESC-ID, Rua Alves Redol, 9, 1000-029 Lisboa, Portugal
[6] Instituto de Telecomunicações, Av. Rovisco Pais 1, 1049-001 Lisboa, Portugal

Abstract. Deep learning has been revolutionizing multiple aspects of our daily lives, thanks to its state-of-the-art results. However, the complexity of its models and its associated difficulty to interpret its results has prevented it from being widely adopted in healthcare systems. This represents a missed opportunity, specially considering the growing volumes of Electronic Health Record (EHR) data, as hospitals and clinics increasingly collect information in digital databases. While there are studies addressing artificial neural networks applied to this type of data, the interpretability component tends to be approached lightly or even disregarded. Here we demonstrate the superior capability of recurrent neural network based models, outperforming multiple baselines with an average of 0.94 test AUC, when predicting the use of non-invasive ventilation by Amyotrophic Lateral Sclerosis (ALS) patients, while also presenting a comprehensive explainability solution. In order to interpret these complex, recurrent algorithms, the robust SHAP package was adapted, as well as a new instance importance score was defined, to highlight the effect of feature values and time series samples in the output, respectively. These concepts were then combined in a dashboard, which serves as a proof of concept in terms of a AI-enhanced detailed analysis tool for medical staff.

Keywords: Deep learning · Interpretability · Recurrent neural network · EHR · Disease progression · Data visualization

---

Supported by the Portuguese Foundation for Science and Technology (Fundação para a Ciência e a Tecnologia – FCT) through UIDB/50008/2020 (Instituto de Telecomunicações), UIDB/50021/2020 (INESC-ID) and UIDB/00408/2020 (LASIGE Research Unit), and projects MATISSE (DSAIPA/DS/0026/2019), PREDICT (PTDC/CCI-CIF/29877/2017), PERSEIDS (PTDC/EMS-SIS/0642/2014) and NEUROCLINOMICS2 (PTDC/EEI-SII/1937/2014).

A. Del Bimbo et al. (Eds.): ICPR 2020 Workshops, LNCS 12661, pp. 187–202, 2021.
https://doi.org/10.1007/978-3-030-68763-2_14

1   Introduction

Through deep learning models, academia and industry alike have disrupted a wide variety of areas. However, compared to previous machine learning models, these high-performing yet more complex deep learning models are less intuitive, in terms of interpreting their outputs. This observation started a performance and interpretability tradeoff, as while in some cases one might desire accuracy above all, in other, more critical scenarios, it is also very important to validate and understand how the model gets to each result.

One case where interpretability matters particularly is in healthcare. When a decision can define recovery or deteriorating health, life or death, any error can result in serious consequences. So, each decision must be carefully thought of, neatly planned out and made with thorough understanding of the situation. Medics cannot afford to just blindly trust an algorithm, no matter how good it claims to be. This difficult interpretability of deep learning models is likely why AI has not yet been massively integrated into healthcare systems worldwide. Traditional machine learning models, with relatively low accuracy, do not represent enough value, while deep learning cannot be trusted.

Towards reaching an AI approach that can be considered for integration in a healthcare system, several steps need to be taken. This work hopes to push in that direction, by contributing in key areas and showcasing the potential of it. To do so, the main objectives have been defined as:

- Training machine learning models that excel in the prediction of disease progression, based on Electronic Health Records (EHR) data.
- Find or develop an adequate interpretability technique to allow for model validation and output explainability.
- Create a prototype of a platform that can allow for intuitive interaction with the trained models, gathering insights from it and interpreting its outcomes.

2   Related Work

Over the last few years, there has been an increasing number of papers published on deep learning applied to EHR data [1,3,4,6,11–13]. These tend to focus mostly on these models' main advantage, the gain in performance. After an initial study [4] proved the abilities of Recurrent Neural Networks (RNN) in medical time series contexts, a slew of other papers started following the same steps, with some variations to try to achieve state-of-the-art. However, despite the critical case of healthcare, these studies do not usually give due priority to interpretability of the models. For instance, in the DeepCare paper [11], they present an interesting custom model, that is based on Long Short Term Memory (LSTM) with incorporation of elapsed time between samples, as well as embedding layers and an intriguing targeting of intervention data. Yet they do not offer any explanation of the model's outputs. Later, in 2018, a team at Google AI developed a model ensemble, composed of RNNs, Time Aware Neural Networks and boosted decision trees, which achieved state-of-the-art results on the predictions of mortality, readmission, long stay and discharge diagnosis. While they did not ignore the interpretability factor, the authors only interpreted part of the model with its attention mechanism, which only allows to see what was highlighted by the model, not more specifically how each data point impacted the outcomes. A paper that put a more serious focus on output explanations was the RETAIN [3] paper that managed to make a model where feature contribution scores, i.e. how each feature impacts the output, could be calculated analytically. Furthermore, in its follow up paper RetainVis [6], the authors presented a dashboard that showcased how medical staff could interact with these analysis, see relevant instances in the patients' time series, and gather insights from the model. However, both of these papers' interpretability approach relies on a very specific and complex model architecture, which would not work for other, potentially better performing models.

3   Background

3.1   Recurrent Neural Networks (RNN)

Recurrent Neural Networks [10] are the backbone of sequential or temporal classification and prediction problems and, as seen in the literature review, EHR problems are no exception. The way it works is that, by receiving a sequential input, each vector in the sequence is fed into a block of this neural network, which is usually referred to as a cell. Then, this cell computes a vector h_t, based on the current input x_t and the previous cell's h_{t-1}, and sends it to the next cell, the one that gets the next vector in the input sequence. These h values are called hidden memories, as they accumulate information from previous inputs. From this hidden memories, an output can be calculated, using for instance a Softmax activation function to obtain a classification probability, as seen in the following equation:

$$\begin{cases} h_t = \sigma(Ux_t + Wh_{t-1}) \\ y_t = Softmax(Vh_t) \end{cases} \tag{1}$$

It is also worth noting that multiple layers of RNN can be stacked on top of each other, with the possibility of them having opposite directions, in terms of the recurrent connection that traverses the input sequence, which creates a bidirectional RNN.

3.2   Long Short-Term Memory (LSTM)

In order to fix the vanilla RNN's problem with vanishing and exploding gradients, research has been made on possible modifications of this recurrent architecture. One of the most famous variations is the Long Short-Term Memory [5]. It solves the gradient issues by creating what is sometimes referred to as a "gradient highway", a recurrent connection that avoids repeated multiplications by the same weight matrix over and over again. Instead, in the LSTM, the hidden memories are calculated through pointwise multiplications and additions, which change along the sequence according to the inputs, as seen in the following equations:

$$
\begin{cases}
i_t = \sigma(W_i h_{t-1} + U_i x_t) \\
f_t = \sigma(W_f h_{t-1} + U_f x_t) \\
o_t = \sigma(W_o h_{t-1} + U_o x_t) \\
\widetilde{C}_t = tanh(W_g h_{t-1} + U_g x_t) \\
C_t = \sigma(f_g \odot C_{t-1} + i_t \odot \widetilde{C}_t) \\
h_t = tanh(C_t) \odot o_t
\end{cases}
\tag{2}
$$

3.3   LSTM with Varying Timestamps

We now know about RNN and LSTM models, which have the ability to hold memory of previous instances, with longer memory in LSTM models, granting them an advantage over other models when handling sequential data. However, these models do not have any built-in procedure to tackle varying time differences between samples. Time variation between samples can be particularly important, as a sample very far away from the last one should take past information less into account, several frequent samples can indicate a more severe status or the presence in a certain type of medical unit, among others. So, we need to find a way to include information of time variation between samples, from here on out also referred to as Δt, in these recurrent models. To the models that include this information somehow, we can classify as "Time Aware Models".

A straightforward solution to this problem is to simply add a Δt feature to the model. This technique requires minimal intervention in the models' overall structure, with just the addition of more weights regarding the Δt feature. Hopefully, in a well optimized model and with enough data, it will make the model learn how to handle the time differences in the current prediction or regression task.

Meanwhile, there has been research [2,11] to modify the LSTM architecture, aiming to have a better integration of time variation between the samples of a sequence. One of these modified versions is referred to in the paper of Inci M. Baytas et al. [2] as MF1-LSTM, which stands for Modified Forget Gate LSTM. After the usual calculations, it multiplies the forget gate's output by $g(\Delta t)$ such as $f_t = g(\Delta t) * f_t$. In this paper, we use $g(\Delta t) = \max\left(1, \frac{1}{\Delta t}\right)$, with normalized Δt. The intention here was as to avoid attributing too much importance and possibly even saturation-prone high values to samples that are very close in time.

With a similar logic, there is the MF2-LSTM model type. Instead of scaling the forget gate's output, it directly alters its formula by introducing parametric time weight such as $f = \sigma\left(W_f x_t + U_f h_{t-1} + Q_f q_{\Delta t} + b_f\right)$. Similarly to the original paper, we use $q_{\Delta t} = \left(\frac{\Delta t}{15}, \left(\frac{\Delta t}{90}\right)^2, \left(\frac{\Delta t}{180}\right)^3\right)$, with unnormalized Δt, with a notion of short, medium and long time differences.

Then there is T-LSTM, a model proposed in [2]. It preserves the original LSTM structure, but adds more steps when defining the previous cell state c_t.

So now, it replaces LSTM's direct connection of c_{t-1} with c_{t-1}^*, according to the following equations:

$$
\begin{cases}
c_{t-1}^S = \tanh\left(W_d c_{t-1} + b_d\right) \\
\hat{c}_{t-1}^S = c_{t-1}^S * g(\Delta t) \\
c_{t-1}^T = c_{t-1} - c_{t-1}^S \\
c_{t-1}^* = c_{t-1}^T + \hat{c}_{t-1}^S
\end{cases}
\tag{3}
$$

3.4   SHAP Values

In 2017, Scott Lundberg and Su-In Lee published the paper "A Unified Approach to Interpreting Model Predictions" [9]. As the title suggests, they proposed a new method to interpret machine learning models that unifies previous ones. They found out that many interpretability methods follow the same core logic: learn a simpler explanation model from the original one, through a local linear model.

For each sample x that we want to interpret, using model f's output, we train a linear model g, which locally approximates f on sample x. However, the linear model g does not directly use x as input data. Rather, it converts it to x', which represents which features are activated (for instance, $x'_i = 1$ means that we're using feature i, while $x'_i = 0$ means that we're "removing" feature i). As such, and considering that we have M features and $M + 1$ model coefficients (named ϕ), we get the following equation for the interpreter model:

$$
g(z') = \phi_0 + \sum_{i=1}^{M} \phi_i z'_i.
\tag{4}
$$

And, having the mapping function h_x that transforms x' into x, the interpreter model should locally approximate model f by obeying to the following rule, whenever we get close to x' (i.e. $z' \approx x'$):

$$
g(z') \approx f(h_x(z')), \text{ if } z' \approx x'.
\tag{5}
$$

Knowing that the sample x that we want to interpret naturally has all features available (in other words, x' is a vector of all ones), this local approximation dictates that the sum of all ϕ should equal the model's output for sample x:

$$
\sum_{i=0}^{M} \phi_i = f(x).
\tag{6}
$$

Each coefficient ϕ, being this a linear model, relates to each feature's importance on the model. For instance, the bigger the absolute value of ϕ_i is, the bigger the importance of feature i is on the model. Naturally, the sign of ϕ is also relevant, as a positive ϕ corresponds to a positive impact on the model's output (the output value increases) and the opposite occurs for a negative ϕ. An exception here is ϕ_0, which assumes the average model output on all the data.

SHAP has multiple explainers, i.e. algorithms to estimate SHAP values. The single most important SHAP explainer for this work, as it is currently the only one suited for interpreting recurrent neural networks, is the Kernel Explainer. It relies in a linear model that locally approximates the original model as an interpreter, and uses the simplified input x'. Furthermore, it does not assume any specific model component or characteristics, which makes it model-agnostic. The linear model's loss function has a specific weighting $\pi_x(z')$ that is applied on the training samples, which fulfills SHAP properties and gives more value to combinations of small and large numbers of active feature values.

Another particularly relevant estimator, considering its usability in one of this work's baseline models, is the Tree Explainer [7,8]. Following the same basic structure of SHAP values, it optimizes part of the calculation for tree-based models such as decision trees, random forests and gradient boosted trees. Without going into more details, considering its optimizations, the Tree Explainer can do a complete calculation of SHAP values in a considerably faster way than the model-agnostic Kernel Explainer.

4   Methodology

4.1   Data

The main dataset which this paper addresses is the Portuguese ALS dataset, a collection of data from Amyotrophic Lateral Sclerosis (ALS) patients, collected between 1995 and 2018 in the Translational Clinic Physiology Unit, Hospital de Santa Maria, IMM, Lisbon. The dataset contained 1110 patients and a variety of feature types, both static and temporal, categorical and numerical, and from multiple topics, ranging from demographics and family history to genetic and respiratory data. A particularly relevant column is the date of Non-Invasive Ventilation (NIV), as it is the source from which we extract the label. The goal is to predict the use of NIV anytime over the next 90 days.

4.2   Data Utils Package

Along the work done for this paper, a toolbox was developed, which encompassed and standardized the core data science pipelines that were needed: the Data Utils package. It is divided on multiple modules, each one addressing a different type of tasks. These can be seen as separate core parts of a data science pipeline, ranging from the usual data preprocessing to training neural networks. While it mostly relies on well known best practises, such as normalization, model versioning and hyperparameter tuning, there are also some less common intuitions builtin. One of them is the embedding in a multivariate time series context.

Deep learning models cannot handle categorical features directly. So, we need to find a way to convert them into a numerical representation, be it binary, integer or float. A straightforward solution is to apply one hot encoding, where each category is converted into its own binary feature, which indicates if that category is present in the sample or not. However, using embedding layers instead can lead to better results. As such, a solution was developed inside Data Utils.

The method relies on a pre-existing PyTorch function, which is the embedding bag. It is essentially an embedding layer but with an averaging operation on top, in case we have multiple categories to embed. It is however optimized for unidimensional sequences. So, we first one hot encode the categorical features then, for those that we want to embed, the embedding pipeline multiplies each one hot encoded column with its index, counting only the columns that originated from the same categorical feature. This way, we can feed sequences of keys to the embedding bag, which it can encode and return the average of embeddings, row by row. Inside Data Utils, the code then handles all the intermediate steps required to integrate these lists of embeddings into the data and remove the former one hot encoded columns.

4.3   Interpretability

The Kernel Explainer, a SHAP values estimator addressed in Sect. 3.4, is referred to as being model-agnostic, being able to interpret any machine learning model. However, this very advantage of being agnostic, with virtually no assumptions regarding the model that it will explain, can be a disadvantage. Some specific machine learning models, including RNNs, do need a special treatment, which is not builtin. When applied to RNNs, the resulting sum of the SHAP coefficients does not match with the model output, which breaks Eq. 6. This is due to the fact that the Kernel Explainer always tries to explain each sample individually, separate from all the others. As we are using a RNN, which accumulates memory from previous instances in its hidden state, it will consider the samples as being separate sequences of one single instance, eliminating the use of the model's memory. In order to fix this issue, SHAP's code had to be changed, so that it includes the option to interpret recurrent models on multivariate sequences. There were more subtle changes needed, but the core changes can be summarized by changing KernelSHAP's iteration through data so as to preserve the model's hidden memory throughout the sequences. By going sequence by sequence, instead of sample by sample, we can maintain the flow of the RNN-type model's hidden state. We can now recover the local accuracy property (Eq. 6), where the sum of SHAP values equals the machine learning model's output.

The typical KernelSHAP approach can be unpractical because of its slowness. A computationally heavy part of the process is the iteration through multiple combinations of samples from the background data, when training the interpreter model. So, if we could reduce the number of samples used, we would be able to get a speedup. Now the question is if we could represent the missing features by just a single reference value. And a hint for the answer lies on of SHAP's formulas, of the marginal expectation $f_x(h_x(z')) \approx f([z_S, E[z_{\bar{S}}]])$. If we are integrating over samples to get the expected values of the missing features, it seems reasonable to directly use the average values of those features as a reference value. And this is even easier to do if, in the preprocessing phase, we normalized the data into z-scores:

$$z = \frac{x - \mu}{\sigma}. \tag{7}$$

This way, we just need to use an all zeroes vector as the sole background sample, as zero represents each feature's average value.

Similarly to the approach discussed in Sect. 4.2, the interpretability pipelines were wrapped in methods inside a package, called Model Interpreter, so as to facilitate and standardize its use. However, it does not only include the custom SHAP approach mentioned before, but also adds a new process. In a multivariate time series context, SHAP values only lead to feature importance, without interpreting the relevance of instances, i.e. individual samples in a time series, as a whole. An instance importance score was missing, so we needed to define one. An initial approach comes rather naturally: just remove the instance of which we want to get an importance score and see how it affects the final output. To do this, we subtract the original output by the output of the sequence without the respective instance. So, considering N as the index of the last instance of the sequence, i as the index of the instance that we are analysing and S as the set of instances in the sequence, we get the following formula:

$$occlusion\_score = output_S^N - output_{S \setminus i}^N. \tag{8}$$

When keeping track of something along time, such as a patient's disease progression, there tend to be certain moments where something new happens that can have repercussions or be repeated in the following events. For instance, if we were predicting the probability of worsening symptoms, we could have a patient that starts very ill but, after successful treatment, gets completely cured, with a low probability of getting sick again. If we were to only apply the previous method of instance occlusion, all instances of the patient after the treatment could receive similar scores, although it is clear that the moment that he received the treatment is, in fact, the crucial one. In order to address this, we can take into account the variation in the output brought in by the instance. That is, we compare the output at the instance being analyzed (i) with the one immediately before it ($i - 1$), like if we were calculating a derivative:

$$outvar\_score = output_S^i - output_S^{i-1}. \tag{9}$$

Of course, the occlusion score might still be relevant in many scenarios, so the ideal solution is to combine both scores in a weighted sum. Considering the more straightforward approach of occlusion, and some empirical analysis, the weights were picked to be 0.7 for occlusion and 0.3 for output variation. And since these changes in the output can be somewhat small, we should also apply a nonlinear function on the result, so as to amplify high scores. For that, I have chosen the $tanh$ function, as it keeps everything in the range of -1 to 1, and added a multiplier of 4 inside, so that a change of 25% points in the output gets very close to the maximum score of 1. In summary, we can define the instance importance score as:

$$inst\_score = tanh(4 \times [w \times occlusion\_score \\ + (1 - w) \times outvar\_score]). \tag{10}$$

4.4   Dashboard

A dashboard was developed, composed of four major components: performance; dataset overview; feature importance; detailed analysis. As Fig. 1 shows, its homepage begins with two dropdown boxes, where the user is prompted to select a dataset and a model to analyse. After both are selected, each component's preview card loads a subset of information, related to that part's intent. At first glance, we can already see in the homepage the current model's accuracy, AUC and F1 metrics on the test set of the chosen dataset, some demographics and label balance information of the dataset, the model's three most influential features, an overview of four patients' time series and the importance of each of their samples. We can then click on any preview card's "expand" button to go into its associated page or use the dashboard's banner to do so.

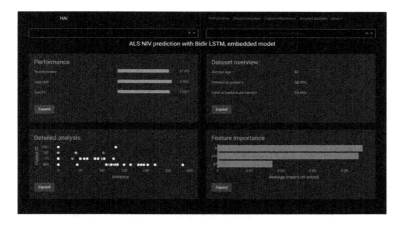

Fig. 1. The dashboard homepage, when selecting "ALS" as the dataset and "LSTM, embedded" as the model.

Most of the pages serve somewhat self-contained information. In "Performance" we can compare models by their architecture and metrics; "Dataset overview" dives into the chosen dataset, showing information such as data size and demographics; "Feature importance" displays aggregate SHAP values, which paints a picture of how important each feature usually is for the model's output. Then, the "Detailed analysis" page connects all the ideas into a deeper visualization experience. It contains several distinct yet interconnected cards, so let us go one by one. Looking at Fig. 2, in the first card, we can see an instance importance plot. It is inspired by the RetainVis paper [6], which has its own dashboard with a "patients list" segment, in which we can see each patient's time series and their clinical visits, colored according to their impact on the final output (red indicates an positive impact in the output and blue indicates a negative impact). The main difference here is that while in the "RetainVis" paper the instance importance scores are calculated based on sums of attention values, which are incorporated on their specific model architecture, in here we use the formula that was described in Sect. 4.3, which can be applied to any sequential machine learning model. Through this graph, we can see all patients' disease progression, identify interesting samples and select one for further examination. As one sample is hovered or click on in the instance importance plot, all of the remaining page updates according to it. On the right, we can see an indication of whether or not that sample's patient used NIV in the end of his or her time series, as well as the model's final output predicting exactly this NIV usage. On the left side of the page, we have a card that lists the patient's most salient feature values, according to their SHAP values. This can give a fast reveal of the patient's main characteristics and symptoms along its medical history. Meanwhile, in the middle of the page, we have a feature importance visualization, which indicates how each feature value in the selected sample pushed the output from the average, expected value to the sample's output value. Once again, a red color means that the feature value was responsible for an increase in the output, while blue refers to a decrease. The size of the horizontal bar is equivalent to the magnitude of that output change. On the bottom right corner of the page, we have also a "Edit sample" button. By clicking on it, a new card emerges from bellow, with a table that shows the selected sample's values. With this table, we can edit the sample as much as we want and, when we click on "Stop editing", the data and the whole page is updated.

Fig. 2. HAI dashboard's detailed analysis page, where every patient's time series can be inspected. In this screenshot, the option to edit the selected sample is activated.

4.5   Reproducibility

The models were trained in Google Cloud's AI Platform, using n1-highmem-4 instances, with 4 vCPUs, 26 GB RAM and 1 NVIDIA Tesla T4 GPU.

In the list bellow you can find the links to the repositories and packages that were developed during the study:

– Preprocessing and training on the Portuguese ALS dataset: https://github. com/AndreCNF/FCUL_ALS_Disease_Progression
– Preprocessing and training on the eICU dataset: https://github.com/ AndreCNF/eICU-mortality-prediction
– Data Utils package: https://github.com/AndreCNF/data-utils
– Model Interpreter package: https://github.com/AndreCNF/model-inter preter
– Custom SHAP package: https://github.com/AndreCNF/shap
– HAI dashboard: https://github.com/AndreCNF/hai-dash

5   Results

5.1   Model Performance

Before diving into the results, it is important to note that all models were trained using common hyperparameters. This setting, shown in Table 1, was determined according to the best performing RNN model from an hyperparameter tuning procedure. From the same model, which had an embedding layer that learned its weights alongside it, the embedding layer was attached to all the models that relied on embeddings, with this layer frozen to avoid further changes to it. By fixing the main hyperparameters like this, we guarantee a fairer comparison between the models, without interference from different parameters, which we do not intend to analyse in detail. Additionally, all the deep learning based models have a fully connected layer which transforms a sample's hidden state, from its recurrent cell, into the output score.

Table 1. Common model hyperparameters.

Hyperparameter	Value
n_hidden	653
n_layers	2
$p\_dropout$	0.4250806721766345
$embedding\_dim^a$	7

[a] Only used when the model has an embedding layer.

Another relevant detail to consider is that, as the models' performance is dependant on their initial random state, each model was trained three times, on different random seeds, with the results presented on Table 2, showing the average and standard deviation across these experiments. With this approach, we can reduce the "luck" element out of the randomness of model initialization, getting a fairer comparison between the models based on their core characteristics.

The first observation that we might get from the results of Table 2, where the models' average test AUC are shown in a descending order, is how not only are the intrinsically time-aware models MF1-LSTM, MF2-LSTM and T-LSTM not in the top of the table, but they are in fact at the bottom, with some of the worse performance. One of the reasons might be because of added parameters, which for a small dataset such as the Portuguese ALS one, it might be too much to allow for proper learning.

Although they do not reach the top of the ranking, logistic regression and specially XGBoost have results comparable to unidirectional recurrent models, which can be surprising as they only analyse sample by sample, without handling the sequential nature of the data. This can be because the problem might be somewhat easy to solve, perhaps due to a couple of features that have a strong connection with the label, the NIV treatment (as we will see in the interpretation results of Sect. 5.2).

Table 2. Model performance results, indicated through test AUC. The presented values correspond to the average and standard deviation over three different trained models for each type.

Model	Avg. Test AUC	Std. Test AUC
Bidir.[a] LSTM, Δt^b	**0.937**	0.026
Bidir.[a] LSTM, embed	0.927	0.026
Bidir.[a] LSTM	0.916	0.016
Bidir.[a] LSTM, embed, Δt^b	0.915	0.021
Bidir.[a] RNN, embed, Δt^b	0.897	0.022
XGBoost	0.833	0.036
LSTM, embed, Δt^b	0.822	0.035
RNN	0.797	0.015
LSTM	0.793	0.023
Logistic regression	0.782	0.003
MF1-LSTM	0.675	0.028
MF2-LSTM	0.669	0.024
T-LSTM	0.649	0.023

[a] Bidirectional recurrent model.
[b] Time aware model which uses elapsed time information as a feature.

We can then see that the best performing models are all bidirectional. It is more predictable, contrary to the previous observations, not only because of other cases where bidirectionality was a key factor but also due to the clear advantage in its logic. It has advantages such as being able to extract more insights from the added direction and, in a more subjective way, we can view it as more similar to human behaviour, where we sometimes check a sequence of events from the most recent one to the oldest.

Each artificial neural network can have several add-ons, as if pieces which can be added or removed according to the desired behaviour. Comparing all the models' performances, between those that are equal except with the variation of having or not a given component, we can see the average impact of each component on Fig. 3. This plot really emphasizes the considerable benefit of making a model be bidirectional, adding an average of more than 0.1 to the test AUC. LSTMs also show an improvement over traditional RNNs, although not on the scale that one would expect, considering the better handling of gradients as explained in Sect. 3.2. Besides the previously mentioned hypothesis of dominant features, the sequences are very short, averaging on just six samples per patient. This way, there is less risk of vanishing or exploding gradients and so RNNs could be good enough, without running into many memory issues. Meanwhile, the time awareness (i.e. adding time variation between samples as a feature) and embedding have an even smaller scale of effect, with the latter even having a negative contribution to the performance, on average. The time difference between instances adds more parameters to the model and, as the data has short sequences and we suspect of features that have a strong correlation with the label, it seems reasonable that it does not have a big payoff in the current use case. Meanwhile, the embedding layer could also not be of particular relevance as there is only one categorical feature and, once again, there is a subset of other features which tend to outshine all the others.

Having all the flaws and surprises in consideration, it is still noteworthy to see the impressive performance of the top models, sustained mainly by bidirectional LSTMs, which reach almost the maximum possible value of test AUC (which would be 1). There is no clear, specific winning combination, considering the standard deviation of the performances and the comparably small difference between the average metrics, but it becomes clear the advantage of recurrent neural networks, in particular those of type LSTM, and of these being bidirectional.

5.2   Model Interpretation

Observing the feature importance plots, such as that of Fig. 4, it becomes clear right away that, as suspected, there is a small subset of features that have a large impact on the models' output. For the LSTM and RNN models, features $3r$ and $p10$ have a contribution that, on average, is over two times larger than the third most influential feature, with an increasing distance to the remaining ones. On the XGBoost models, even just the $3r$ feature seems to be enough to decide most predictions, with an average SHAP value that is several times larger than that of all the other features. This might be the main reason why the top performing models are so good and even most of the baselines have considerable performance, since just one or two features are usually so decisive. It is also interesting to observe that, being both $3r$ and $p10$ features related to

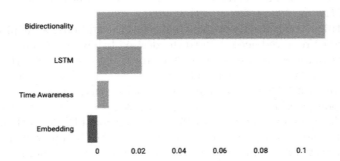

Fig. 3. The average performance impact of each model component, indicated through test AUC. These only apply to comparisons between LSTM and RNN models. As in other plots, the red color indicates an increase, in this case of the test AUC metric, while the blue color corresponds to a decrease. (Color figure online)

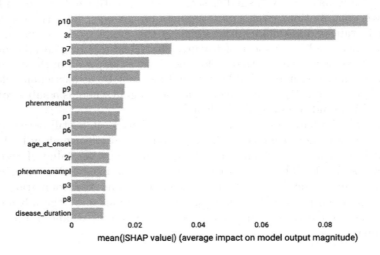

Fig. 4. Feature importance of model bidirectional LSTM, time aware.

respiratory symptoms, it makes sense that they have a high correlation with the use of NIV, the label of this machine learning task, since it constitutes respiratory support. Other features, such as the also respiratory symptoms related r and $2r$, motor capabilities related $p7$ and $p5$, and the patient's age are also top impactful features that are common to multiple models. These are not only subjectively seen as a proxy to ALS disease progression, but also can be seen directly from the data as clearly having different patterns depending on whether the patient is on NIV or not.

The similarities between the feature importance summary of different models, including with the XGBoost which uses a more optimized version of SHAP, helps to validate the robustness of the implemented feature importance approach. In particular, it supports the custom SHAP version that was developed in this paper, which made some adaptations to make it compatible with RNN-based models.

6   Conclusions

This study's accomplishments can be summarized in three parts:

– **Performance:** Deep learning models were trained to predict NIV in ALS patients, with the top performing models surpassing the baseline by a significant margin, i.e. over 0.1 increase in the average test AUC. This performance boost was demonstrated to be mainly caused by the bidirectionality and use of LSTM cells in the artificial neural networks.
– **Interpretability:** Kernel SHAP, a robust technique for the explanation of model outputs, was adapted to RNN-based models, including possible variations, such as bidirectionality. This represents an important step to truly make Kernel SHAP a model-agnostic method and towards the interpretation of recurrent models. There was also an introduction to a new instance importance score, which allows us to interpret how each sample influenced a sequence's final output, based on its impact on the model's outputs.
– **Usability:** A dashboard was developed, as a prototype of what a real healthcare solution could be like, integrating the concepts that this paper addresses.

This paper was focused on a relatively small and disease specific dataset. As future work, given enough time and resources, it could be scaled up to larger, more complex scenarios. With larger datasets, we could have a better test to embedding and time variation concepts, as well as get a more interesting case to compare deep learning sequential models to traditional ones. It would also be more interesting to address such datasets that contain more treatment data. With this kind of data, model interpretation, as it was performed in this paper, could be more useful in the sense of optimizing the patients' treatment.

Above all, without dismissing the progress so far and the usefulness of current approaches, we should remain sceptic and continue to improve the interpretation of models, in a time when machine learning keeps on entering our lives and we are asked to trust the models.

References

1. Avati, A., Jung, K., Harman, S., Downing, L., Ng, A., Shah, N.H.: Improving Palliative Care with Deep Learning (2017). http://arxiv.org/abs/1711.06402

2. Baytas, I.M., Xiao, C., Zhang, X., Wang, F., Jain, A.K., Zhou, J.: Patient subtyping via time-aware LSTM networks. In: Proceedings of the 23rd ACM SIGKDD International Conference on Knowledge Discovery and Data Mining, vol. 10 (2017). https://doi.org/10.1145/3097983.3097997, http://biometrics.cse.msu.edu/Publications/MachineLearning/Baytasetal_PatientSubtypingViaTimeAwareLSTMNetworks.pdf
3. Choi, E., Bahadori, M.T., Kulas, J.A., Schuetz, A., Stewart, W.F., Sun, J.: RETAIN: an interpretable predictive model for healthcare using reverse time attention mechanism (2016). http://arxiv.org/abs/1608.05745
4. Choi, E., Bahadori, M.T., Schuetz, A., Stewart, W.F., Sun, J.: Doctor AI: predicting clinical events via recurrent neural networks (2015). http://arxiv.org/abs/1511.05942
5. Hochreiter, S., Schmidhuber, J.: Long short-term memory. Neural Comput. 9(8), 1735–1780 (1997). https://doi.org/10.1162/neco.1997.9.8.1735, http://www.mitpressjournals.org/doi/10.1162/neco.1997.9.8.1735
6. Kwon, B.C., et al.: RetainVis: visual analytics with interpretable and interactive recurrent neural networks on electronic medical records. IEEE Trans. Vis. Comput. Graph., 1 (2018). https://doi.org/10.1109/TVCG.2018.2865027, https://ieeexplore.ieee.org/document/8440842/
7. Lundberg, S.M.: From local explanations to global understanding with explainable AI for trees. Nat. Mach. Intell. 2(1), 2522–5839 (2020)
8. Lundberg, S.M., Erion, G.G., Lee, S.I.: Consistent Individualized Feature Attribution for Tree Ensembles (2018)
9. Lundberg, S.M., Lee, S.I.: A unified approach to interpreting model predictions. In: Guyon, I., et al. (eds.) Advances in Neural Information Processing Systems, vol. 30, pp. 4765–4774. Curran Associates, Inc. (2017). http://papers.nips.cc/paper/7062-a-unified-approach-to-interpreting-model-predictions.pdf
10. Jordan, M.I.: Attractor dynamics and parallelism in a connectionist sequential machine. In: Diederich, J. (ed.) Artificial Neural Networks, pp. 112–127. IEEE Press (1990). http://dl.acm.org/citation.cfm?id=104134.104148
11. Pham, T., Tran, T., Phung, D., Venkatesh, S.: Predicting healthcare trajectories from medical records: a deep learning approach. J. Biomed. Inf. 69, 218–229 (2017). https://doi.org/10.1016/j.jbi.2017.04.001, https://linkinghub.elsevier.com/retrieve/pii/S1532046417300710
12. Rajkomar, A., et al.: Scalable and accurate deep learning for electronic health records (2018). https://doi.org/10.1038/s41746-018-0029-1, http://arxiv.org/abs/1801.07860
13. Suresh, H., Hunt, N., Johnson, A., Celi, L.A., Szolovits, P., Ghassemi, M.: Clinical Intervention Prediction and Understanding using Deep Networks (2017). http://arxiv.org/abs/1705.08498

Automated Detection of Adverse Drug Events from Older Patients' Electronic Medical Records Using Text Mining

Nicola Colic[1,3]([✉]) [iD], Patrick Beeler[4,5], Chantal Csajka[6,7,8], Vasiliki Foufi[9],
Frederic Gaspar[6,7,8], Marie-Annick Le Pogam[10], Angela Lisibach[6,7,8],
Christian Lovis[9], Monika Lutters[1], and Fabio Rinaldi[2,3] [iD]

[1] Department of Computational Linguistics, University of Zurich, Zurich, Switzerland
nicola.colic@uzh.ch
[2] Dalle Molle Institute for Artificial Intelligence Research (IDSIA),
Lugano, Switzerland
[3] Swiss Institute of Bioinformatics, Lausanne, Switzerland
[4] Division of Occupational and Environmental Medicine, Epidemiology,
Biostatistics and Prevention Institute, University of Zurich and University
Hospital Zurich, Zurich, Switzerland
[5] Center for Research and Innovation in Clinical Pharmacy Sciences,
University of Lausanne and University Hospital Lausanne, Lausanne, Switzerland
[6] School of Pharmaceutical Sciences, University of Geneva, Geneva, Switzerland
[7] Institute of Pharmaceutical Sciences of Western Switzerland, University of Geneva,
Geneva, Switzerland
[8] Division of Medical Information Sciences, Geneva University Hospitals,
Geneva, Switzerland
[9] Center for Primary Care and Public Health, Unisanté, University of Lausanne,
Lausanne, Switzerland
[10] Clinical Pharmacy, Cantonal Hospital Baden, Baden, Switzerland

Abstract. The Swiss Monitoring of Adverse Drug Events (Swiss-MADE) project is part of the SNSF-funded Smarter Health Care initiative, which aims at improving health services for the public. Its goal is to use text mining on electronic patient reports to automatically detect adverse drug events automatically in hospitalised elderly patients who received anti-thrombotic drugs. The project is the first of its kind in Switzerland: the data is provided by four hospitals from both the German- and French-speaking part of Switzerland, all of which had not previously released electronic patient records for research, making extraction and anonymisation of records one of the major challenges of the project.

In this paper, we describe the part of the project concerned with the de-identification and annotation of German data obtained from one of the hospitals in the form of patient reports.

All of these reports are automatically de-identified using a dictionary-based approach augmented with manually created rules, and then automatically annotated. For this, we employ our entity recognition pipeline

Supported by the SNSF under NRP74 and the SNF Requête no 407440$_1$67381/1.

A. Del Bimbo et al. (Eds.): ICPR 2020 Workshops, LNCS 12661, pp. 203–211, 2021.
https://doi.org/10.1007/978-3-030-68763-2_15

called OGER (OntoGene Entity Recognizer), also a dictionary-based approach, augmented by an adapted transformer model to obtain state of the art performance, to detect drug, disease and symptom mentions in these reports. Furthermore, a subset of reports are manually annotated for drugs and diagnoses by a medical expert, serving as a validation set for the automatic annotations.

Keywords: Biomedical text mining · Entity recognition · Adverse drug events

1   Introduction

Adverse drug events (ADE) are the second most frequent source of complications in hospitals. They increase patient morbidity and hospital costs, and in many cases, could be easily prevented [8,14]. Elderly patients especially suffer frequently from ADEs, and are more severely affected by them [11]. Given our ageing population, the problem of preventable ADEs in older patients is particularly relevant nowadays.

Apart from other factors, ADEs can occur as a result of previously unknown adverse interactions between drugs and diseases, or drugs and drugs; and inappropriate prescription [1]. Antithrombotic drugs are particularly widely used in elderly patients to treat coronary problems and thrombosis, but have been shown to be also associated with hemorrhages and thromboses, making them an important subject for study.

In the SwissMADE project, electronic free text discharge summaries of patients hospitalised for longer than 24 h between 2015 and 2016, aged 65 and older, and who received at least one antithrombotic drug during their stay are considered.

The data are obtained from four hospitals: the Lausanne University Hospital (CHUV) and the Geneva University Hospitals (HUG) for the French speaking part, and the Cantonal Hospital Baden (KSB) and University Hospital Zurich (USZ) for the German speaking one. The extraction and processing of data was performed separately and locally at each institution for the French and German data, but following the same methodology. All data contain structured sections as well as unstructured, free text sections which are mined using natural language processing techniques.

We describe in this paper our work in de-identifying and processing, that is, automatically and manually annotating, the reports extracted from USZ, which is a set of 18 000 patient reports conforming to the criteria described above.

2   Methods

2.1   De-Identification

None of the hospitals had previously used electronic patient records for research. The documents thus had to be extracted from the database of medical records, and de-identified, that is, to have all instances of information that could allow the identification of the people or institution involved removed, in order to be allowed to leave the hospitals for processing. This was particularly necessary for the USZ data, which was not processed by the hospital itself, but by the University of Zurich.

The American Health Insurance Portability and Accountability Act (HIPAA) lays out a set of data items, called Personal Health Information (PHI), that allow identification of patients, and thus need to be removed in de-identification; and has become the *de facto* standard for this task. While machine learning approaches for de-identification are promising, the legally critical nature of this task favours dictionary-based approaches and approaches based on manual rules on grounds of their easy comprehensibility and traceability [12].

At USZ, independently of the SwissMADE project, a separate de-identification project was conducted with the goal to establish a pipeline that de-identifies electronic records for research. The SwissMADE project served as a first use case for this separate de-identification project.

The approach used by this separate de-identification project relies on three parts:

1. Firstly, from the hospital database a list of names of all the patients, medical staff and hospital units is generated and normalised. This list is then used as a dictionary to find occurrences of PHI in the medical documents.
2. Secondly, using a set of manually annotated records, rules were manually constructed to remove information such as street names, zip codes etc.
3. Thirdly, PHI which has been removed as described above is replaced by plausible alternatives. This approach has the advantage of allowing PHI missed in step 2 to *hide in plain sight* since in the final de-identified report PHI missed in step 2 and PHI replaced in step 3 cannot be distinguished. For the replacement, manually created rules are used that draw on the dictionary created in step 1.

For comparison, at the KSB a similar approach was used based on previous work done by the University of Mainz, which also uses a combination of dictionary and manually created rules [9].

2.2   Manual Annotation

For annotations of the reports, a schema and guidelines were created and validated by all the project participants to ensure consistent annotations across the entire project. While an initial schema covered a variety of entities, a first annotation attempt on a small data set of discharge summaries across the different hospitals showed that the number of entities increased the complexity of the annotation task dramatically. Therefore, the annotation schema has been simplified and at this step, only two entities are manually annotated: potential ADEs in relation to hemorrhagic and thromboembolic events, and drugs.

From the data at USZ, a subset of 600 reports was selected and is being manually annotated by medical experts according to the schema using GATE[1], an open source text processing software.

2.3 Automatic Annotation

The reports contain a structured section in which medical staff write their findings in a standardised manner. However, this structured section does not always perfectly match the diagnoses described in the free text. For this reason, the structured sections' diagnoses were aggregated across all reports, and used as a dictionary in order to find as many variations of diagnoses and symptoms in all reports using OGER.

For the drugs, the BioTermHub (BTH)[2] was used to generate a dictionary. The BTH queries various public repositories of drug lists such as RxNorm and CTD to create a single, canonical dictionary [2].

Both dictionaries were used then by OGER[3], our own dictionary-based entity recognition pipeline to automatically annotate drugs and diagnoses in the free text. Results are post-filtered using a machine learning algorithm for false positives, which frequently limit dictionary-based approaches' performance [6].

Furthermore, a set of regular expression-based rules was created to extract drug administrations as described in Sect. 2.7.

From these automatic annotations, their validity will be evaluated against the manually created corpus; and statistically relevant co-occurrences will be calculated at a later stage.

2.4 OGER and BioBERT

Finding occurrences of entities in free text and mapping them to canonical identifiers is usually performed in consecutive steps. Recently, however, we performed those two steps simultaneously, and were able to show that it outperforms the traditional approach [4]. We used the pre-trained language model BioBERT, trained on almost 100 manually annotated medical articles (CRAFT corpus). We evaluated this work on the CRAFT corpus, and obtained F1-scores between 0.74 and 0.92, depending on the type of entity.

OGER is a dictionary-based look-up tool using efficient fuzzy matching [6] and uses a dictionary of relevant entities and their canonical ID. Its performance replies on the dictionary's quality and extent, which manually or automatically curated ontologies such as CHEBI provide. It thus requires no training, and can detect entities that an example-based system would miss if they are not present in the training data, provided they are present in the dictionary.

---

[1] https://gate.ac.uk/.

[2] http://www.ontogene.org/resources/termdb.

[3] https://pub.cl.uzh.ch/projects/ontogene/oger/.

2.5   BioBERT

The multi-layer transformer BERT is trained on Wikipedia and BookCorpus [3] to predict probabilities of two sentences following each other and randomly blacked out words, thus building a language model that may be fine-tuned for various tasks, such as named entity recognition [7] and linking, or adapted for different domains by training it further. In the case of BioBERT, BERT was trained on PubMed articles, adapting it to biomedical applications [10,13].

We trained BioBERT on CRAFT, thus building an ID and span prediction model. The ID model works like a classical named entity recogniser, but extends the output tag set to all possible concept IDs. The span model outputs IOBES labels (for Inside, Outside, Beginning, Ending and Single Elements), and the entities found thus receive their IDs from OGER.

The ID model thus predicts spans and IDs directly, which would make using other methods unnecessary. However, it only predicts concepts seen during training and doesn't perform well in situations where a word has a meaning in both the domain and general language (for example, *I* in *hexokinase I*). The span model and OGER help to compensate these drawbacks (Fig. 1).

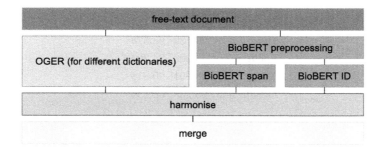

Fig. 1. Overall structure of the general OGER and BioBERT pipeline

2.6   Harmonisation and Merging

When span or ID annotations of BioBERT and OGER conflict or overlap, our previous research [5] revealed that the best strategy for merging is dependent on the type of the entity. We use the strategies described there to decide on the final output. If a span annotation from BioBERT is selected, the ID provided by OGER is used as a label (see Sect. 2.5).

2.7   Drug Administration

For the extraction of drugs, a set of 35 manually created rules were created that find in the free-text mentions of drugs and, in particular, their concentrations as well as form of administration. These rules are regular expressions that mirror the way drug administrations are described. Due to the tools medical staff use to write free-text reports, such drug administration mentions appear in a somewhat standardised manner and can be found with relative ease. These rules are used to augment the results obtained from OGER as described in Sect. 2.3 and can be found online[4].

3   Results

3.1   De-Identification

The dataset of 18 000 electronic patient discharge summaries that have been extracted from USZ for the SwissMADE project have been de-identified and evaluated on a test set of 400 manually de-identified reports (see Table 1).

Table 1. Recall and precision values over different categories of PHI for the pipeline that deidentified the patient reports at USZ.

Type	Recall	Precision
Age	94.452	95.206
Contact	99.133	99.154
Date	99.139	98.576
Location	85.208	84.304
Name	98.991	90.818
Occupation	55.238	60.559

3.2   Lexico-Semantic Resources

From a test subset of the 18 000 discharge summaries' structured sections, two dictionaries have been created:

- A drug dictionary, listing 178 variations of drug names mapped to 132 unique ATC codes.
- A symptoms dictionary, with 628 variations of diagnoses and symptoms mapped to 201 unique ICD-10 codes.

3.3   Automatic Annotation

We generate dictionaries for finding symptoms and drugs from the structured sections of the reports; but also augment the drugs dictionary from publicly available resources using our BioTerm Hub. These dictionaries are used by OGER as described in Sect. 2.3. The manual annotation of the reports, however, requires

---

[4] https://git.io/JTq6V.

medical expertise. Even though the data is anonymised, legal barriers make it difficult to transfer the data to external project partners where such expertise is available. Because of this, we must leave a thorough evaluation for the future.

The examples below, however, demonstrate how the annotated reports are visualised; and how the annotations are stored. As Fig. 2 shows, annotations are stored in an XML format that is obtained by converting GATE's own format. The annotations in that example represent the automatic output of the rules described in Sect. 2.7.

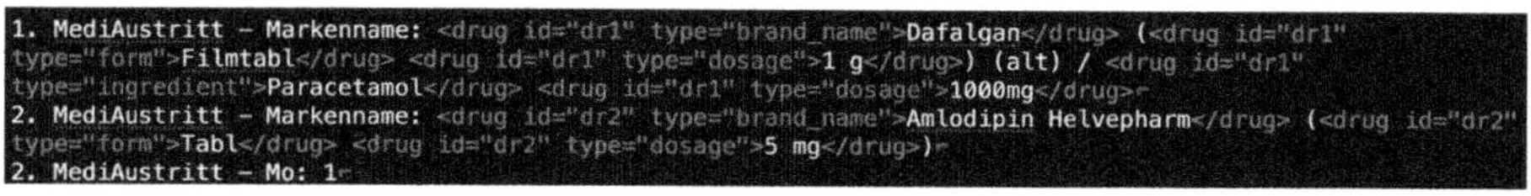

```
1. MediAustritt - Markenname: <drug id="dr1" type="brand_name">Dafalgan</drug> (<drug id="dr1"
type="form">Filmtabl</drug> <drug id="dr1" type="dosage">1 g</drug>) (alt) / <drug id="dr1"
type="ingredient">Paracetamol</drug> <drug id="dr1" type="dosage">1000mg</drug>
2. MediAustritt - Markenname: <drug id="dr2" type="brand_name">Amlodipin Helvepharm</drug> (<drug id="dr2"
type="form">Tabl</drug> <drug id="dr2" type="dosage">5 mg</drug>)
2. MediAustritt - Mo: 1
```

Fig. 2. XML format to store both manual and automatic annotations. The figure above shows an automatically annotated sample report.

The annotations can be easily visualised, as Fig. 3 shows. Note that in the report shown there, the dates had been previously identified by the anonymisation pipeline and replaced by plausible dates, while maintaining the distance between the dates within the report. Likewise, clinics and locations (such as *Wald* in the example) were automatically replaced by places from a list of likely alternatives.

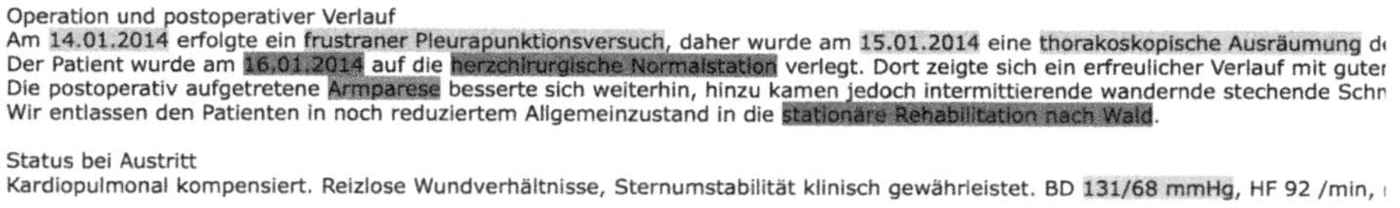

Operation und postoperativer Verlauf
Am 14.01.2014 erfolgte ein frustraner Pleurapunktionsversuch, daher wurde am 15.01.2014 eine thorakoskopische Ausräumung d
Der Patient wurde am 16.01.2014 auf die herzchirurgische Normalstation verlegt. Dort zeigte sich ein erfreulicher Verlauf mit guter
Die postoperativ aufgetretene Armparese besserte sich weiterhin, hinzu kamen jedoch intermittierende wandernde stechende Schn
Wir entlassen den Patienten in noch reduziertem Allgemeinzustand in die stationäre Rehabilitation nach Wald.

Status bei Austritt
Kardiopulmonal kompensiert. Reizlose Wundverhältnisse, Sternumstabilität klinisch gewährleistet. BD 131/68 mmHg, HF 92 /min,

Fig. 3. Visualisation of annotations in the browser for various types. In this case, in green are marked surgeries and interventions and their corresponding dates, in yellow patient stays; in orange symptoms and in red measurements. This segment is the result of an exploratory manual annotation including more types that were later discarded.

4 Discussion

SwissMADE served as a first project to pave the path in Switzerland for patient record-based research, establishing collaboration between hospitals and research groups as well as procedures for how to make available electronic patient records to researchers.

The detection of ADEs is a complex task both for the human annotators and automatic systems. This is mainly due to the semantic ambiguities of the medical concepts and the complexity of medical free-text data, but also due to the fact that training of models and their evaluation relies on manual annotations, which are time-consuming and costly to obtain.

Leveraging the vast amount of electronic patient records data bears the promise to improve quality of such automatic annotations; and machine learning approaches such as the one used in the OGER and BioBERT pipeline presented here are the most propitious methods. Our research is one of the first forays into how this can be done under Switzerland's legal and multilingual circumstances, and also points to the importance and difficulty of obtaining manual annotations by experts to train and evaluate machine learning approaches.

References

1. Alhawassi, T.M., Krass, I., Bajorek, B.V., Pont, L.G.: A systematic review of the prevalence and risk factors for adverse drug reactions in the elderly in the acute care setting. Clin. Interventions Aging **9**, 2079 (2014)
2. Basaldella, M., Furrer, L., Tasso, C., Rinaldi, F.: Entity recognition in the biomedical domain using a hybrid approach. J. Biomed. Seman. **8**(1), 51 (2017)
3. Devlin, J., Chang, M.W., Lee, K., Toutanova, K.: BERT: pre-training of deep bidirectional transformers for language understanding. arXiv preprint arXiv:1810.04805 (2018)
4. Furrer, L., Cornelius, J., Rinaldi, F.: UZH@CRAFT-ST: a sequence-labeling approach to concept recognition. In: Proceedings of The 5th Workshop on BioNLP Open Shared Tasks, pp. 185–195 (2019)
5. Furrer, L., Cornelius, J., Rinaldi, F.: Parallel sequence tagging for concept recognition. arXiv preprint arXiv:2003.07424 (2020)
6. Furrer, L., Jancso, A., Colic, N., Rinaldi, F.: Oger++: hybrid multi-type entity recognition. J. Cheminform **11**(1), 7 (2019)
7. Hakala, K., Pyysalo, S.: Biomedical named entity recognition with multilingual BERT. In: Proceedings of The 5th Workshop on BioNLP Open Shared Tasks, pp. 56–61. Association for Computational Linguistics, Hong Kong (2019). https://doi.org/10.18653/v1/D19-5709, https://www.aclweb.org/anthology/D19-5709
8. Krähenbühl-Melcher, A., Schlienger, R., Lampert, M., Haschke, M., Drewe, J., Krähenbühl, S.: Drug-related problems in hospitals. Drug Saf. **30**(5), 379–407 (2007)
9. Lablans, M., Borg, A., Ückert, F.: A restful interface to pseudonymization services in modern web applications. BMC Med. Inf. Decis. Mak. **15**(1), 2 (2015)
10. Lee, J., et al.: BioBERT: a pre-trained biomedical language representation model for biomedical text mining. Bioinformatics **36**(4), 1234–1240 (2020)
11. Mallet, L., Spinewine, A., Huang, A.: The challenge of managing drug interactions in elderly people. Lancet **370**(9582), 185–191 (2007)
12. Meystre, S.M., Friedlin, F.J., South, B.R., Shen, S., Samore, M.H.: Automatic de-identification of textual documents in the electronic health record: a review of recent research. BMC Med. Res. Methodol **10**(1), 70 (2010)

13. Sun, C., Yang, Z.: Transfer learning in biomedical named entity recognition: an evaluation of BERT in the PharmaCoNER task. In: Proceedings of The 5th Workshop on BioNLP Open Shared Tasks, pp. 100–104. Association for Computational Linguistics, Hong Kong (2019). https://doi.org/10.18653/v1/D19-5715, https://www.aclweb.org/anthology/D19-5715
14. de Vries, E.N., Ramrattan, M.A., Smorenburg, S.M., Gouma, D.J., Boermeester, M.A.: The incidence and nature of in-hospital adverse events: a systematic review. BMJ Qual. Saf. **17**(3), 216–223 (2008)

Length of Stay Prediction for Northern Italy COVID-19 Patients Based on Lab Tests and X-Ray Data

Mattia Chiari[1]([✉]), Alfonso E. Gerevini[1], Roberto Maroldi[1,2], Matteo Olivato[1], Luca Putelli[1], and Ivan Serina[1]

[1] Università degli Studi di Brescia, Brescia, Italy
{m.chiari017,alfonso.gerevini,roberto.maroldi,m.olivato,l.putelli002,
ivan.serina}@unibs.it
[2] ASST Spedali Civili di Brescia, Brescia, Italy

Abstract. The recent spread of COVID-19 put a strain on hospitals all over the world. In this paper we address the problem of hospital overloads and present a tool based on machine learning to predict the length of stay of hospitalised patients affected by COVID-19. This tool was developed using Random Forests and Extra Trees regression algorithms and was trained and tested on the data from more than 1000 hospitalised patients from Northern Italy. These data contain demographics, several laboratory test results and a score that evaluates the severity of the pulmonary conditions. The experimental results show good performance for the length of stay prediction and, in particular, for identifying which patients will stay in hospital for a long period of time.

1 Introduction

In these days one of the primary challenges addressed by AI and machine learning is to help hospitals and doctors in dealing with the spread of COVID-19, which has lead to substantial impact in our society putting a strain on healthcare, economy and societies around the world with more than 38 million cases at October 2020. This challenge has been met on various different levels in the last few months [8, 26, 29]. With our work, we want to address the problem of hospital overloads and, for this reason, we focused on predicting the length of stay (LOS) for hospitalised patients. This work was made possible thanks to a strict collaboration with *Spedali Civili di Brescia*, one of the hospitals that had more COVID-19 patients in Italy. Knowing in advance which patients will stay in the hospital for a longer period of time can help doctors to manage resources proactively and to avoid overloads as much as possible. Therefore, predicting the length of stay can help the hospital in managing limited healthcare resources [26].

Our data include patients demographic information such as sex and age, ten different laboratory tests values and an innovative score (designed and used in *Spedali Civili di Brescia* [4]) for assessing the severity of the pulmonary conditions and the progression of COVID-19 based on chest X-ray. Important data

© Springer Nature Switzerland AG 2021
A. Del Bimbo et al. (Eds.): ICPR 2020 Workshops, LNCS 12661, pp. 212–226, 2021.
https://doi.org/10.1007/978-3-030-68763-2_16

such as patients medical treatments and comorbidities or regarding COVID-19 related symptoms could not be included in our models due to their unavailability.

Our previous work [8] was also based on patients hospitalised in *Spedali Civili di Brescia* for predicting the mortality risk in different times during the hospitalisation and it obtained promising results. In this work, we present another approach for predicting also the length of stay, with a particular focus on finding which patients require an hospital bed for more than two weeks.

All our datasets are created using raw data from more than 1000 patients. Given that we want to evaluate the patient conditions at different times during his hospitalisation, we build different datasets that represent a "snapshot" of the progression of the disease after a certain amount of days from the start of the recovery. In our experiments we consider 2, 4, 6, and 8 days from the start of the recovery. For each of these datasets we build a different model to predict the length of stay. This allows us to handle temporal dependencies between each set and to provide a more accurate prediction over time. Moreover a significant change in length of stay prediction could help doctors to understand the effectiveness of certain treatments or the impact of certain events in specific patients.

While building our dataset we have to deal with some issues related to the real-world context from which the data are retrieved. These issues include missing and outdated values. In order to improve the performance of our models we also added some custom features. To help doctors understand how many patients will stay longer than 2 weeks in the hospital we also classified the prediction results using a threshold that is set at 16 days from the admission date.

To solve our learning task we have tested several machine learning algorithms. Algorithms based on ensembles of regression trees (Random Forest and Extra Trees) obtain the best performance in terms of MAE over a test set of more than 150 patients. Furthermore our models obtain good performance also for identifying, in a binary classification task based on the LOS prediction, the patients who are going to stay more than two weeks.

In the following, after discussing related work, we describe our data sets, we present our prediction models and their experimental evaluation, and finally we give conclusions and mention future work.

2   Related Work

Artificial Intelligence and Machine Learning can help dealing with COVID-19 in different aspects, such as evaluating in advance the most severe patients, predicting the mortality risk, the length of stay or the need of intensive-care. However, given that the pandemic outbreak has started only few months ago, most works are still preliminary, and there isn't a clear description of the developed techniques and of their results (often only pre-printed and not properly peer-reviewed).

A preliminary study is presented in [13]. Given a set of only 53 patients with mild symptoms and their lab tests, comorbidities and treatment, the authors train several machine learning models (Logistic Regression, Decision Trees, Random Forests, Support Vector Machines, KNN) to predict if a patient will be subject to more sever symptoms, obtaining a prediction accuracy score of up to 0.8 using 10-fold cross validation. The generalisability and strength of these results are questionable, given the very small set of considered patients. A more sound analysis is shown in [28] that uses lab tests for predicting the mortality risk, along with symptoms and comorbidities for 485 patients in the region of Wuhan, China. After training a XGBoost algorithm and evaluating its performance, the authors select the most important features and train a single decision tree which can be used by the physicians as a simplified and understandable version of the model.

Ensemble of decision trees are the main model used in our previous work [8] (also based on patients hospitalised in *Spedali Civili di Brescia*) for predicting the mortality risk at different times during the stay. This study monitors the progression of COVID-19 considering lab tests and their trends in terms of improvement, stable conditions or worsening and it introduces an innovative technique for recognising the less reliable predictions made by the system.

The problem of predicting the length of stay for patients from a statistical point of view is the focus of [3] and [15], two pre-printed works published in the last months. The first one focuses on English patients data collected in the national Surveillance System database (CHESS) and uses techniques such as Accelerated Failure Time and Truncation Correction Method. The work in [15] describes a tool made in Singapore that combines the length of stay prediction with the fatality rate, the hospital capacity and other features for building a bed resource plan in best-case, base-case and worst-case scenarios.

Machine learning techniques are used in [20] for predicting the length of stay, alongside with a survival analysis, for a dataset made by more than 1,000 patients. The authors compare the results of traditional statistic methods with Support Vector Machines and Gradient Boosting algorithms. Given the difficulty to obtain complete data in an emergency situation, the authors also deal with missing exams results and no comorbidities information.

Different AI and machine learning techniques have been developed for prognosis and disease progression prediction in the context of diseases different from COVID-19 [6,7,16–19,22–24,27]. The survey in [1] presents a review of statistical and ML systems for predicting the length of stay and the mortality risk for hospitalised patients. In particular, the work by Harutyunyan et al. [10] covers several clinical problems such as mortality risk, length of stay prediction and possible decompensation and creates a multitask learning algorithm based on LSTM neural networks.

An overview of the issues and challenges for applying ML in a critical-care context is available in [14]. This work stresses the need to deal with corrupted data, like missing values, imprecision, and errors that can increase the complexity of prediction tasks.

Lab test findings and their variation over time are the main focus of the work by Hyland et al. [12], which describes a system that processes these data to generate an alarm predicting if a patient will have a circulatory failure 2 h in advance.

3   Available Data Sources

During the COVID-19 outbreak, from February to April 2020 in hospital *Spedali Civili di Brescia* more than two thousand patients were hospitalised. During their hospitalisation, the medical staff performed several exams to them in order to monitor their conditions, checking the response to some treatments, verifying the need to transfer a patient to the ICU, etc. We consider data from a total of more than 1,000 hospitalised patients in April 2020; for each of these patients, the specific data that were made available to us are:

Table 1. Lab tests performed during the hospitalisation. In the second column, we show the range which is considered clinically normal for a specific exam. In the third column, we show the median value extracted considering the lab test findings for our set of patients.

Lab test	Normal range	Median value
C-Reactive Protein (PCR)	≤ 10	34.3
Lactate dehydrogenase (LDH)	[80, 300]	280
Ferritin (Male)	[30, 400]	1030
Ferritin (Female)	[13, 150]	497
Troponin-T	≤ 14	19
White blood cell (WBC)	[4, 11]	7.1
D-dimer	≤ 250	553
Fibrinogen	[180, 430]	442
Lymphocite (over 18 years old patients)	[20, 45]	1.0
Neutrophils/Lymphocites	[0.8, 3.5]	4.9
Chest XRay-Score (RX)	< 7	8

- the age and sex;
- the values and dates of several lab tests (see Table 1);
- the scores (each one from 0 to 18), assigned by the physicians, assessing the severity of the pulmonary conditions resulting from the X-ray exams [4];
- the values and dates of the throat-swab exams for COVID-19;
- the length of stay (LOS), calculated as the number of days between the date of admission and the date of release. In Fig. 1 we show the distribution of the LOS in our dataset. The median value is 14 days.

Table 1 specifies the considered lab tests, their normal range of values, and their median values in our set of patients. We had no further information about symptoms, their timing, comorbidities, generic health conditions or clinical treatment. Moreover, we have no CT images or text reports associated with the X-ray exams. The available information about whether a patient was or had been in ICU was not clear enough to be used. Finally, of course, also the names of the patient and of the involved medical staff names were not provided.

3.1   Data Quality Issues

When applying machine learning to raw real-world data, there are some non-trivial practical issues to deal with, such as the quality of the available data and related aspects, that in biomedical applications are especially important given the very sensitive domain [11].

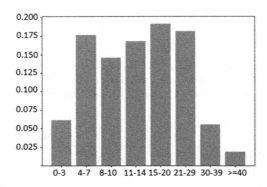

Fig. 1. Length of stay distribution histogram in our dataset. On the x-axis, we indicate the range of days of stay in hospital. On the y-axis, we indicate the fraction of patients.

In our case, the most important issue is that the lab tests and X-ray exams are not performed at a regular frequency due, e.g., to the different kinds and timing of the relative procedures, the need of different resources (X-Ray machines, lab equipment, technical staff, etc.), or to the different severity of the health conditions of the patients. For example, in our data we see that a patient can be tested for PCR everyday and not be subject to a Ferritin exam for two weeks. This leads to the need of handling the issues *missing values* and *outdated values*. When we consider a snapshot of a patient at a certain day, we have a missing value for a lab test (or X-ray) feature if that test (X-ray) has not been performed. We have an outdated value for a feature if the corresponding lab test (X-ray) was performed several days earlier: since in the meanwhile the disease has progressed, the findings of the lab test could be inconsistent with the current conditions of the patient, and so they could mislead the prediction.

Data quality issues arise especially for those patients who were hospitalised in the period of the highest emergency, when several hundreds of patients were in the hospital at the same time causing a significant overload for the staff.

Moreover, the length of the hospitalisation period can sensibly differ from one patient to another (from few days to two months), due to different reasons including the novelty and the characteristics of the disease or the absence of an effective treatment. Therefore, the number of performed lab tests and relative findings significantly varies among the considered set of patients (from only three to hundreds).

4   Datasets for Training and Testing

In our previous work [8] we show our ability to recognise with good results the patients at death risk, in this new study we concentrate our efforts for predicting the length of stay (LOS). This allows to integrate the two systems in a single tool that can provide both the predictions to the physicians. For building our training and test sets, we use only the patients who were released alive.

The LOS prediction is done at different days of the patient hospitalisation, according to the current patient conditions reflected by the available lab findings and X-ray scores. In this section, we describe the specific extracted features and the (training and testing) datasets that we built for this purpose.

4.1   Pre-processing and Feature Extraction

The issues presented in Sect. 3.1 compel us to a robust pre-processing phase with the goal of extracting features in order to summarise the patients conditions and process them by machine learning algorithms.

Given that we have no information about the survival or the decease of a patient after a transfer (which can be due to limited availability of beds or ICU places), we exclude also from our training and test set the 142 patients which were admitted in *Spedali Civili di Brescia* and then transferred to another hospital. However, the 74 patients who were transferred to a rehabilitation centre can be considered not at risk of death; therefore we include them in our datasets and consider the transferred patients as released alive.

Patient Snapshot and Feature Engineering. In order to provide a prediction for a patient at different hospitalisation times, we introduced the concept of **patient snapshot** to represent the patient health conditions at a given day.

In this snapshot, for each lab test of Table 1, we consider its most recent value. In the ideal case, we should know the lab test findings at every day. However, as explained in Sect. 3.1, in a real-world context the situation is very different. For example, in our data if we consider to take a snapshot of a patient 14 days after the admission into the hospital, we have cases with very recent values of PCR, LDH or WBC (obtained one or a few days before), very old values for Fibrinogen or Troponin-T (obtained the first day of the hospitalisation) and even no value for Ferritin.

Given the difficulty to set a predefined threshold that separates recent and old values of the lab tests (e.g., for Fibrinogen and Troponin-T), we choose to always use the most recent value, even if it could be outdated. In order to allow the learning algorithm to capture that a value may not be significant to represent the current status of the patient (because too old), we introduce a feature called **ageing** for each test finding. If a lab test has been performed at a day d_0, and the snapshot of a patient is taken at day d_1, the ageing is defined as the number of days between d_1 and d_0. If there is no available value for a lab test, its ageing is considered a missing value.

Monitoring the conditions of a patient means knowing not only the patient status at a specific time, but also how the conditions evolve during the hospitalisation. For this purpose, we introduce a feature called **trend** that is defined as follows. For each lab test, if there is no available value for a lab test or if the patient has not performed the lab test at least two times, the trend is a *missing value* Otherwise, we consider a set of points (d, v), where d is the date of the lab test and v is its value and we calculate a simple linear regression, representing the trend as a line $y = ax + b$. Our trend feature is the angular coefficient a. In order to ensure the reliability of the calculated trend, we have to consider only strongly correlated values by checking if the Pearson Correlation Coefficient of the linear regression is above 0.7 in the case of positive trend or less then -0.7 in the case of negative trend. If the Pearson Coefficient doesn't denote a strong correlation, then we remove lab values from the trend calculation until it does. This can be done in two ways:

- **short trend**: which is the coefficient of the linear regression computed starting from the last exam and going backwards in time adding older exams until the correlation constraint remains true;
- **long trend**: which is the coefficient of the linear regression firstly computed with all the lab values and then progressively removing the the oldest ones until the remaining values are in strong correlation.

To summarise, for each lab test in a patient snapshot, we have the most recent finding and the relative ageing and trends, as well as the static features **age** and **sex**.

4.2 Training and Test Sets Generation

In this section we describe how we generated the training and test sets for the purpose of predicting, at different days from the start of the patient hospitalisation, the length of her/his stay.

First we used stratified sampling for selecting *80% of the patients for training* the models and *20% for testing* them. Then, we created specific training and test sets for each element in a sequence of times when the model is used to make the prediction[1]:

- **2 days** of hospitalisation. We include all the patients' snapshots containing the first values for each lab test conducted in the first two days after the hospital admission. Note that if a patient has performed a lab test more than once in the first two days, the snapshot will consider the oldest value. In fact, the purpose of the model we want to build is to provide the prediction as soon as possible, with the first information available. Furthermore, in these snapshots the ageing and trend values are not included.

---

[1] We chose 2, 4, 6, 8, 10 days after the hospitalisation but any other sequence could be considered.

– **4 days**, **6 days** and **8 days** of hospitalisation. In these cases, the corresponding snapshots also contain the ageing and trend features (both *short* and *long*), and the lab values will be the most recent ones in the available data.

It is important to observe, that while the datasets of the latter days will contain more information about the single patients (more lab tests findings, less missing values), the overall number of patients in the datasets decreases with the prediction day increase. This is due to the fact that more patients are released or die within longer periods of hospitalisation, and therefore such patients are not included in the corresponding datasets. In Table 2 we report the number of samples contained in training and testing set for each dataset.

Finally, note that the splitting between training and testing of the data is done only once considering all patients. Thus if, for instance, a patient belongs to the training set of 2 days, then he does not belong to the test set of the following days.

5   Machine Learning Algorithms

In this section, we briefly describe the machine learning algorithms used in our prognosis prediction system.

Table 2. Number of training and test samples for each considered snapshot

	Training set	Test set
2days	667	170
4days	637	160
6days	596	149
8days	524	132

5.1   Regression Algorithms

Decision Trees. Decision Trees [25] are one of the most popular learning methods for solving classification and regression tasks. In a decision tree, the root and each internal node provides a condition for splitting the training samples into two subsets depending on whether the condition holds for a sample or not. In our context, for each numerical feature f, a candidate splitting condition is $f \leq C$, where C is called *cut point*. The final splitting condition is chosen by finding the f and C values providing the best split according to one of some possible measures like Mean Square Error (MSE) and Mean Absolute Error (MAE).

A subset of samples at a tree node can either be split again by further feature conditions forming a new *internal node*, or form a *leaf node* with a specific prediction value.

Random Forests. Random Forests (RF) [5] is an ensemble learning method [30] that builds a number of decision trees at training time. For building each individual tree of the random forest, a randomly chosen subset of the data features is used. While, in the standard implementation of random forests the final prediction value is provided using the statistical mode of the class values predicted by each individual tree, in the well-known tool Scikit-Learn [21] that we used for our system implementation, the output value is obtained by averaging the values provided by all trees.

Extra Trees. Extremely Randomised Trees (Extra Trees or ET) [9] are another ensemble learning method based on decision trees. The main differences between Extra Trees and Random Forests are:

- In the original description of Extra Trees [9] each tree is built using the entire training dataset. However in most implementations of Extra Trees, including Scikit-Learn [21], the decision trees are built exactly as in Random Forests.
- In standard decision trees and Random Forests, the cut point is chosen by first computing the optimal cut point for each feature, and then choosing the best feature for branching the tree; while in Extra Trees, first we randomly choose k features and then, for each chosen feature f, the algorithm randomly selects a cut point C_f in the range of the possible f values. This generates a set of k couples $\{(f_i, C_i) \mid i = 1, \ldots, k\}$. Then, the algorithm compares the splits generated by each couple (e.g., under split test $f_i \leq C_i$) to select the best one using a split quality measure such as the MAE or others.

5.2 Hyperparameter Search

Most machine learning algorithms have several hyperparameters to tune such as, for instance, in a Random Forest the number of decision trees to create and their maximum depth. Since in our application handling the missing values is an important issue, we also used a hyperparameter that represents this with three possible settings: a missing value is set to either the average value, the median value or a special constant (-1).

In order to find the best performing configuration of the hyperparameters, we used the Random Search optimisation approach [2], which consists of the following main steps:

1. We divide our training sets into k folds, with either $k = 10$ or $k = 5$, depending on the dimension of the considered dataset.
2. For each randomly selected combination of hyperparameters, we run the learning algorithm in k-fold cross validation.
3. For each fold, we evaluate the performance of the algorithm with that configuration using the RMSE.
4. The overall evaluation score of the k-fold cross validation for a configuration of the parameters is obtained by averaging the scores obtained for each fold.
5. The hyperparameter configuration with the best overall score is selected.

6 Experimental Evaluation and Discussion

In this section, we evaluate the performance the of the machine learning models that we built. Our system is implemented using the Scikit-Learn [21] library for Python, and the experimental tests were conducted using a Intel(R) Xeon(R) Gold 6140M CPU @ 2.30 GHz. Regarding the training time, including the hyperparameter search over 4096 random configurations and the optimisation of the uncertainty threshold, for any specific dataset, the overall training time is between 20 and 30 min.

The performance of the learning algorithms with the relative optimised hyperparameters was evaluated using the test set in terms of Mean Absolute Error (MAE). However, these metrics, taken as a single value, can be misleading. For example predicting 5 days instead of 10 produces the same MAE as predicting 20 instead of 25. In a more practical point of view, we aim to create a system which identifies which patients have a long stay and has a good exactness for those who don't. Then, for evaluating the prediction of the length of stay we consider also how the system identifies the patients who are staying definitely more than two weeks (16 days), independently from how many days he or she has already spent in the hospital. We consider the prediction correct if the prediction and the ground truth are both over or under a threshold $threshold_{days}$. This threshold is calculated as:

$$threshold_{days} = 16 - number\_of\_days$$

For example, for the 2days dataset, the $threshold_{days}$ is 14.

Predicting if a patient stays in the hospital more than two weeks can be seen as a binary classification problem and we evaluate the performance of our models in terms of Precision, Recall and F-Score, which are the most used evaluation metrics for classification tasks.

Table 3. Detailed performance of our prediction models in terms of Mean Absolute Error (MAE) over the test set. We also computed the error for the patients that stayed less than a week (MAE 0-7), less than 2 weeks (MAE 7-14) and over 2 weeks (MAE $\geq$ 14)

Dataset	MAE	MAE 0-7	MAE 7-14	MAE $\geq$ 14
2days	4.962	3.921	4.962	7.001
4days	4.479	3.453	4.728	7.156
6days	4.783	3.529	4.745	7.503
8days	4.115	3.647	4.609	7.447

6.1 Results

Table 4. Precision (P), Recall (R) and F1-Score (F1) for the binary classification task defined as identifying those patients who stays in the hospital more than two weeks.

Dataset	P	R	F1
2days	80.0	75.2	75.7
4days	78.1	75.9	76.1
6days	79.3	78.2	78.2
8days	78.7	78.8	78.7

In Table 3 we show the results of the regression task for predicting the length of stay in terms of Mean Absolute Error. For each dataset (at 2 days, after 4, 6 or 8 days) we want to evaluate our performance in terms of MAE for different kinds of situations considering:

- the entire test set, i.e. all the patients (MAE);
- the patients whose conditions are improving and which are going to be released in the following week (MAE 0-7);
- the patients who are going to stay at least for another week but no more than two (MAE 7-14);
- the patients with more severe conditions and which are going to require at least another two weeks of hospitalisation (MAE $\geq$ 14).

For all the considered datasets, the overall error is always between 4 and 5 days. The most problematic situation is clearly for the 2days dataset, which means predicting the LOS only using the first data available. However, after just a few days of hospitalisation we can see some improvements and the MAE reaches 4.11 after 8 days.

This metric is clearly influenced by the presence of patients who stay in the hospital for more than two weeks or even a month (see also Fig. 1). In these cases, predicting the exact LOS after just a few days of hospitalisation is a very complex task and MAE is over 7 for all the considered datasets. On the other hand, for the patients who are going to be released between the next 7 and 14 days, we have a MAE between 4 and 5 days for each dataset. The best result is obtained after 8 days (4.61), mainly because, after this amount of time, the model can exploit more data for giving the prediction.

We have a significantly lower error for those patients who are going to be released in the following week. For example, considering those patients who have already stayed in the hospital for 4 days and they are going to be released in the following week, we are able to predict their LOS with a MAE of 3.45. We have similar results for the 6days and 8days datasets.

In Table 4 we show the results of the binary classification problem created for recognising those patients who are going to stay more than 15 days as described

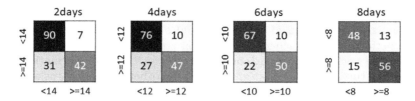

Fig. 2. Confusion matrices at different days for the prediction of the length of stay of our test set. For each matrix of 4 numbers, on the main diagonal we have the correct predictions (*under the threshold* on the top-left corner, *over the threshold* on the bottom-right corner, on the anti-diagonal we have the incorrect predictions.

in Sect. 6. The results for this task are quite promising, with a F1-Score always higher than 75%.

Given that more time has passed from the admission date, the 6days and 8days datasets contain more thorough information. For this reason we can see how F1-Score and Recall measures improve over time. In fact, the 8days dataset has the best overall performances (P 78.8%, R 78.7% and F1 78.8%). Despite the issues in dealing with partial information, 2days has the best performance in terms of Precision (80.0%).

In Fig. 2, we show the confusion matrices for the binary classification task. As you can see, we have some issues for not recognising patients with a LOS over the threshold for the 2days and 4days datasets, with respectively 31 and 27 errors. However, these errors decrease in the other datasets, who can exploit more data. In general, if the system predicts that a patient is staying more than two weeks, its predictions is very reliable, with only 7 errors for the 2days dataset and a maximum of 13 for 8days.

7   Conclusions and Future Work

We have presented a system for monitoring and evaluating the prognosis of COVID-19 patients focusing on the prediction of their length of stay. We built and engineered some datasets from lab test and X-ray data of more than 1000 patients in an hospital in Northern Italy that was severely hit by COVID-19. Our predictive system uses Random Forest and Extra Trees and works at different times during the hospitalisation.

The experimental results for our system are quite promising, with an overall MAE always less than 5 days. In particular, we obtain the best results in terms of mean absolute error for predicting the LOS for those patients who stays in the hospital for a shorter period of time. Besides, our system has good performance in recognising those patients who are going to need hospitalisation for more than two weeks, with an F1-Score higher than 75% even after performing just a few exams.

We also remind that these results are obtained without knowing any information about clinical treatment or administration of drugs. Therefore, there is room for improvement. We are confident that having more information, such as patient comorbidities, clinical treatments and administered drugs will help to improve performance, reducing the regression error.

For future work we plan to extend our datasets with more information (both additional features and patients) and to address other prediction tasks such as the need of ICU beds and critical hospital resources. Moreover, we are analysing the importance of the features used in our models, and we intend to investigate additional learning techniques such as Recurrent Neural Networks for better taking into account the progress of the disease.

Acknowledgements. The work of the first author has been supported by Fondazione Garda Valley.

References

1. Awad, A., Bader–El–Den, M., McNicholas, J.: Patient length of stay and mortality prediction: a survey. Health Serv. Manag. Res. **30**(2), 105–120 (2017). https://doi.org/10.1177/0951484817696212, pMID:28539083
2. Bergstra, J., Bengio, Y.: Random search for hyper-parameter optimization. J. Mach. Learn. Res. **13**(Feb), 281–305 (2012)
3. Bindu, V., et al.: Hospital length of stay for COVID-19 patients: data-driven methods for forward planning. BMC pre-print (2020)
4. Borghesi, A., Maroldi, R.: COVID-19 outbreak in Italy: experimental chest X-ray scoring system for quantifying and monitoring disease progression. La radiologia medica **125**(5), 509–513 (2020). https://doi.org/10.1007/s11547-020-01200-3
5. Breiman, L.: Random forests. Mach. Learn. **45**(1), 5–32 (2001). https://doi.org/10.1023/A:1010933404324
6. Gerevini, A.E., et al.: Automatic classification of radiological reports for clinical care. In: ten Teije, A., Popow, C., Holmes, J.H., Sacchi, L. (eds.) AIME 2017. LNCS (LNAI), vol. 10259, pp. 149–159. Springer, Cham (2017). https://doi.org/10.1007/978-3-319-59758-4_16
7. Gerevini, A.E., et al.: Automatic classification of radiological reports for clinical care. Artif. Intell. Med. **91**, 72–81 (2018). https://doi.org/10.1016/j.artmed.2018.05.006
8. Gerevini, A.E., Maroldi, R., Olivato, M., Putelli, L., Serina, I.: Prognosis prediction in covid-19 patients from lab tests and x-ray data through randomized decision trees. In: Bach, K., Bunescu, R.C., Marling, C., Wiratunga, N. (eds.) Proceedings of the 5th International Workshop on Knowledge Discovery in Healthcare Data co-located with 24th European Conference on Artificial Intelligence, KDH@ECAI 2020, Santiago de Compostela, Spain & Virtually, 29–30 August 2020. CEUR Workshop Proceedings, vol. 2675, pp. 27–34. CEUR-WS.org (2020). http://ceur-ws.org/Vol-2675/paper4.pdf
9. Geurts, P., Ernst, D., Wehenkel, L.: Extremely randomized trees. Mach. Learn. **63**(1), 3–42 (2006). https://doi.org/10.1007/s10994-006-6226-1
10. Harutyunyan, H., Khachatrian, H., Kale, D.C., Ver Steeg, G., Galstyan, A.: Multitask learning and benchmarking with clinical time series data. Sci. Data **6**(1), 1–18 (2019)

11. Hasan, S., Padman, R.: Analyzing the effect of data quality on the accuracy of clinical decision support systems: a computer simulation approach. In: AMIA Annual Symposium Proceedings, vol. 2006, p. 324. American Medical Informatics Association (2006)
12. Hyland, S., et al.: Early prediction of circulatory failure in the intensive care unit using machine learning. Nat. Med. **26**, 1–10 (2020). https://doi.org/10.1038/s41591-020-0789-4
13. Jiang, X., et al.: Towards an artificial intelligence framework for data-driven prediction of coronavirus clinical severity. CMC Comput. Mater. Continua **63**, 537–51 (2020)
14. Johnson, A.E., Ghassemi, M.M., Nemati, S., Niehaus, K.E., Clifton, D.A., Clifford, G.D.: Machine learning and decision support in critical care. Proc. IEEE **104**(2), 444–466 (2016)
15. Lam, S.W.S., et al.: Towards health system resiliency: an agile systems modelling framework for bed resource planning during COVID-19. BMC pre-print (2020)
16. Mehmood, T., Gerevini, A., Lavelli, A., Serina, I.: Leveraging multi-task learning for biomedical named entity recognition. In: Alviano, M., Greco, G., Scarcello, F. (eds.) AI*IA 2019. LNCS (LNAI), vol. 11946, pp. 431–444. Springer, Cham (2019). https://doi.org/10.1007/978-3-030-35166-3_31
17. Mehmood, T., Gerevini, A., Lavelli, A., Serina, I.: Multi-task learning applied to biomedical named entity recognition task. In: Bernardi, R., Navigli, R., Semeraro, G. (eds.) Proceedings of the Sixth Italian Conference on Computational Linguistics, Bari, Italy, 13–15 November 2019. CEUR Workshop Proceedings, vol. 2481. CEUR-WS.org (2019). http://ceur-ws.org/Vol-2481/paper47.pdf
18. Mehmood, T., Gerevini, A.E., Lavelli, A., Serina, I.: Combining multi-task learning with transfer learning for biomedical named entity recognition. In: Cristani, M., Toro, C., Zanni-Merk, C., Howlett, R.J., Jain, L.C. (eds.) Knowledge-Based and Intelligent Information & Engineering Systems: Proceedings of the 24th International Conference KES-2020, Virtual Event, 16–18 September 2020. Elsevier (2020). Procedia Comput. Sci. **176**, 848–857. https://doi.org/10.1016/j.procs.2020.09.080
19. Mehmood, T., Serina, I., Lavelli, A., Gerevini, A.: Knowledge distillation techniques for biomedical named entity recognition. In: Basile, P., Basile, V., Croce, D., Cabrio, E. (eds.) Proceedings of the 4th Workshop on Natural Language for Artificial Intelligence (NL4AI 2020) co-located with the 19th International Conference of the Italian Association for Artificial Intelligence (AI*IA 2020), Anywhere, 25th-27th November 2020. CEUR Workshop Proceedings, vol. 2735, pp. 141–156. CEUR-WS.org (2020). http://ceur-ws.org/Vol-2735/paper53.pdf
20. Nemati, M., Ansary, J., Nemati, N.: Machine-learning approaches in COVID-19 survival analysis and discharge-time likelihood prediction using clinical data. Patterns **1**(5), 100074 (2020).https://doi.org/10.1016/j.patter.2020.100074, http://www.sciencedirect.com/science/article/pii/S2666389920300945
21. Pedregosa, F., et al.: Scikit-learn: machine learning in Python. J. Mach. Learn. Res. **12**, 2825–2830 (2011)
22. Putelli, L., Gerevini, A., Lavelli, A., Serina, I.: The impact of self-interaction attention on the extraction of drug-drug interactions. In: Proceedings of the Sixth Italian Conference on Computational Linguistics (2019)

23. Putelli, L., Gerevini, A.E., Lavelli, A., Olivato, M., Serina, I.: Deep learning for classification of radiology reports with a hierarchical schema. In: Cristani, M., Toro, C., Zanni-Merk, C., Howlett, R.J., Jain, L.C. (eds.) Knowledge-Based and Intelligent Information & Engineering Systems: Proceedings of the 24th International Conference KES-2020, Virtual Event, 16–18 September 2020. Elsevier (2020). Procedia Comput. Sci. **176**, 349–359. https://doi.org/10.1016/j.procs.2020.08.045
24. Putelli, L., Gerevini, A.E., Lavelli, A., Serina, I.: Applying self-interaction attention for extracting drug-drug interactions. In: Alviano, M., Greco, G., Scarcello, F. (eds.) AI*IA 2019. LNCS (LNAI), vol. 11946, pp. 445–460. Springer, Cham (2019). https://doi.org/10.1007/978-3-030-35166-3_32
25. Rokach, L., Maimon, O.: Data Mining with Decision Trees: Theory and Applications. World Scientific Publishing Co., Inc., River Edge (2008)
26. van der Schaar, M., Alaa, A.: How artificial intelligence and machine learning can help healthcare systems respond to COVID-19 (2020). https://www.vanderschaar-lab.com/covid-19/
27. Toninelli, G., Gerevini, A., Serina, I., Vaglio, M., Badilini, F.: Study of ECG quality using self learning techniques. In: Computing in Cardiology, CinC 2014, Cambridge, Massachusetts, USA, 7–10 September 2014, pp. 577–580. www.cinc.org (2014). http://www.cinc.org/archives/2014/pdf/0577.pdf
28. Yan, L., et al.: An interpretable mortality prediction model for COVID-19 patients. Nat. Mach. Intell., 1–6 (2020)
29. Yan, L., Zhang, H.T., Xiao, Y., Wang, M., et al.: Prediction of criticality in patients with severe covid-19 infection using three clinical features: a machine learning-based prognostic model with clinical data in Wuhan. medArxiv preprint (2020)
30. Zhou, Z.H.: Ensemble Methods: Foundations and Algorithms, 1st edn. Chapman & Hall/CRC, Boca Raton (2012)

Advanced Non-linear Generative Model with a Deep Classifier for Immunotherapy Outcome Prediction: A Bladder Cancer Case Study

Francesco Rundo[1(✉)], Giuseppe Luigi Banna[2], Francesca Trenta[3], Concetto Spampinato[4], Luc Bidaut[5], Xujiong Ye[5], Stefanos Kollias[5], and Sebastiano Battiato[3]

[1] STMicroelectronics, ADG Central R&D, Catania, Italy
francesco.rundo@st.com
[2] Medical Oncology Department, Queen Alexandra Hospital, Portsmouth, UK
giuseppe.banna@nhs.net
[3] IPLAB Group, University of Catania, Catania, Italy
francesca.trenta@unict.it, battiato@dmi.unict.it
[4] PerCeiVe Lab, University of Catania, Catania, Italy
cspampin@dieei.unict.it
[5] Computer Science Department, University of Lincoln, Lincolnshire, UK
{LBidaut,XYe,skollias}@lincoln.ac.uk

Abstract. Immunotherapy is one of the most interesting and promising cancer treatments. Encouraging results have confirmed the effectiveness of immunotherapy drugs for treating tumors in terms of long-term survival and a significant reduction in toxicity compared to more traditional chemotherapy approaches. However, the percentage of patients eligible for immunotherapy is rather small, and this is likely related to the limited knowledge of physiological mechanisms by which certain subjects respond to the treatment while others have no benefit. To address this issue, the authors propose an innovative approach based on the use of a non-linear cellular architecture with a deep downstream classifier for selecting and properly augmenting 2D features from chest-abdomen CT images toward improving outcome prediction. The proposed pipeline has been designed to make it usable over an innovative embedded Point of Care system. The authors report a case study of the proposed solution applied to a specific type of aggressive tumor, namely Metastatic Urothelial Carcinoma (mUC). The performance evaluation (overall accuracy close to 93%) confirms the proposed approach effectiveness.

Keywords: Cellular non-linear network · Deep convolutional network · Immunotherapy · Radiomics

© Springer Nature Switzerland AG 2021
A. Del Bimbo et al. (Eds.): ICPR 2020 Workshops, LNCS 12661, pp. 227–242, 2021.
https://doi.org/10.1007/978-3-030-68763-2_17

1   Introduction

Immunotherapy is now considered the last frontier of the cancer treatment, and it is based on the revolutionary concept of curing tumors as if they were an infection, that is "arming" the patient's immune system in such a way as to recognize cancer cells and destroy them [1,36]. Cancer cells are normally recognized by the immune system, which triggers an attack by T lymphocytes. However, this body defense mechanism is not always effective because cancer cells are able to implement a whole series of escape strategies. One of these benefits from the immune system's self-regulation mechanism through a series of proteins that act as "accelerators" or "brakes" on T cells [1,12,36,39]. A promising immunotherapy strategy is based on the inhibition of "Immunological Checkpoints" (ICIs), i.e., on the use of specific antibodies to re-enable the immune system (previously disabled by the cancer cells) and thus increase the ability of T lymphocytes to deal with tumors [1,12,36]. Specifically, in this contribution, we will focus on ICIs-based immunotherapy treatments that act on the PD-1 receptor [12]. Scientific studies have shown that cancer cells "defend" themselves from T lymphocytes using a molecule present on their membrane, called PD-L1, which binds to the lymphocyte PD-1 receptor to disable the protective action of the T lymphocytes. The ICIs anti PD-1/PD-L1 immunoherapy treatment aims to inhibit the action of PD-1/PD-L1 receptors that prevent T lymphocytes from recognizing and destroying cancer cells [12,39]. In this work, we studied this mechanism in the specific case of metastatic bladder cancer (specifically metastatic Urothelial Carcinoma (mUC)) [39]. According to recent studies, urothelial carcinoma is one of the most aggressive cancers involving the urinary system [1]. This carcinoma causes about 165.000 death every year [16]. Several clinical trials confirmed that platinum-based chemotherapy is the current gold standard for the treatment of mUC [39]. However, the scientific community has investigated the dynamic of the patient's long-term survival rate with bladder cancer treated with chemotherapy or immunotherapy through the so-called Progression-Free Survival (PFS) rate [11]. Another relevant discriminative index is the Overall Survival (OS) rate, a quantitative measure of the treatment effectiveness [11]. Regarding high-dose chemotherapy treatment, the median OS ranges between 12 and 15 months for a cisplatin-based regimen and about 9 months for a carboplatin-based regimen [32]. In both cases, significant toxicity is associated with chemotherapy treatments. In this context, immunotherapy has emerged as a new standard of care considering that ICIs drugs such as *Atezolizumab* and *Pembrolizumab* both showed a median OS of more than 10 months in both cases, but with a significant reduction in collateral effects compared to the chemotherapy treatments [5,28]. Despite the effectiveness of immunotherapy compared to chemotherapy, only about 20%–30% of patients have a positive response [2,27,33]. Therefore, the development of discriminative bio-markers suitable to identify the patients who could benefit from immunotherapy is the mainstream of the research activity herein described. Recently, as predictive immunotherapy outcome bio-markers the scientific community has focused its research efforts on analyzing visual features from medical images as well as PD-L1 expression level or such blood indexes as the neutrophil to lymphocytes ratio [4]. From imaging component, such clinical trials have been increasingly linked to the Radiomics research field [4, 18, 23, 37]. Radiomics is a relatively new encompassing concept in the medical field that refers to the quantitative analysis of large sets of biomedical multi-modal data for early disease prediction, treatment outcome estimation, etc. In this paper, we propose an innovative and less invasive (by comparison to biopsies) pipeline based on a deep learning algorithm for classifying visual features extracted from radiological images (chest-abdomen CT-scan) of patients with a bladder cancer diagnosis. Through this pipeline and using a specifically configured Cellular Non-Linear (or Neural) Network (CNNs), CT cancer lesions will be properly identified and augmented. Additionally, the overall pipeline was designed to be implemented over an embedded hardware accelerated Point of Care.

2   Related Works

A fundamental step in predicting specific medical treatment outcomes is designing a proper quantitative data processing pipeline of the disease in the metastatic stage. To this end, several approaches based on Machine and Deep Learning solutions have been proposed in scientific literature [18, 20, 37]. In [37], the authors evaluated the performance of several Machine Learning (ML) algorithms to predict the mortality after a radical cystectomy in a large dataset of bladder cancer patients. The results have shown that the Regularized Extreme Learning Machine outperformed other methods in terms of accuracy. Garapati et al. [18] applied some of the most common ML algorithms (e.g., Linear Discriminant Analysis (LDA), Support Vector Machine (SVM), Random Forest (RAF), etc.) to analyze CT-scan urography of each recruited patient belonging to a clinical study of 84 subjects. The reported evaluation confirmed that SVM achieved impressive results [18]. Other ML methods (e.g., K-Nearest, AdaBoost, SVM, etc.) have been proposed for bladder cancer disease estimation [20]. Specifically, the method proposed in [20] described an interesting approach for predicting cancer recurrence and survival in recruited treated patients from multi-modal data analysis (imaging, surgical findings, etc.). The reported results (Specificity and Sensitivity higher than 70%) confirmed that the proposed algorithm provided positive evidence about the effectiveness of the Radiomics applied in medical oncology. With the massive amounts of multi-source medical data being collected from clinical studies, the learning model paradigm has significantly changed, providing different and more efficient data processing approaches. Different solutions for cancer image-lesion segmentation enabling 2D or 3D convolution networks have been proposed in scientific literature [8, 19, 20, 26, 34]. The performance indicators related to the segmentation stage of metastatic lesions from CT imaging are significant and promising, although it refers to lesions of the same type (visceral or lymphatic) [8, 19, 20, 26, 34]. Further interesting deep pipelines for estimating the response to such cancer treatments based on quantitative data analysis can be found in [7, 22, 38]. The Deep Learning architecture proposed in [38] is a modified version of the AlexNet backbone [22]. The authors applied the proposed deep architecture to learn visual features from segmented CT slices in order to assess the chemotherapic treatment. The experimental results pointed out the effectiveness of the proposed deep network on estimating treatment outcome [38]. In [7], the authors implemented a Deep Learning pipeline for immunotherapy outcome prediction in bladder cancer subjects. The pipeline is composed of two stages. Specifically, the first stage focused on CT-scans primary cancer-lesion segmentation. The second block deals with treatment response prediction through deep architecture. The performance is promising i.e., specificity at 81% (DL-CNN) and sensitivity of 66.7% (RF-ROI) in a dataset of 82 patients with bladder cancer [7]. In [30], the authors introduced a novel deep pipeline for detecting immunotherapy outcomes using artificial intelligence technology. More in detail, the authors implemented a deep classifier of visual features generated by a stack of encoders. With an accuracy of 86.05%; Specificity of 89.29%, and Sensitivity of 80.00%, the proposed pipeline showed promising results as embedded systems for immunotherapy outcome prediction in bladder cancer patients. The pipeline herein described outperforms the previous solution implemented by the authors, confirming the progress in classification performance [30].

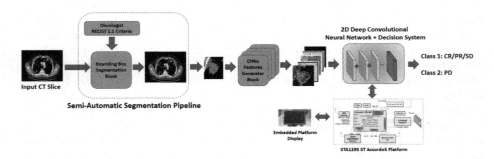

Fig. 1. The proposed immunotherapy treatment outcome prediction pipeline.

3   The Proposed Deep Network Framework

In Fig. 1, we reported the overall scheme of the proposed deep pipeline. The system allows the prediction of the ICIs immunotherapy treatment outcome of patients diagnosed with metastatic bladder cancer. The approach explores radiomics applied to the quantitative analysis of selected chest-abdomen CT-scan imaging cancer lesions. The selection of the CT-scan lesions is made by the experienced oncologists/radiologists following the RECIST 1.1 guideline [14]. Unlike most of the scientific similar pipelines [7] the proposed approach works both by analyzing primary lesion images (bladder) as well as through metastatic lesion images (visceral or lymph-nodes). This feature makes the method herein described particularly robust and efficient in the medical field. Firstly, the proposed semi-automatic pipeline performs a bounding box segmentation of the

CT lesion identified by the experienced physicians, which defines the Region of Interest (ROI) to which the proposed predictive pipeline is applied. Those ROI images have different biologically visual features as they have been extracted from various body-sites of mUC metastasis (lungs, abdominal organs, bladder, lymph nodes, etc.). This data variability makes this a challenging dataset and makes it difficult to build a fully automatic semantic segmentation pipeline. The segmented ROIs (CT lesions) will be further processed by ad-hoc configured and extended 2D Cellular Non-Linear Network (2D-CNN), which generates a series of augmented domain-agnostic features to be properly classified by downstream 2D Deep classifier (2D-DNN). The designed 2D-DNN will be able to discriminate augmented visual features for predicting correlated patients who potentially show some response to immunotherapy treatment (CR: Complete response/PR: Partial response/SD: Stable disease) by those who instead have a progression of the disease (PD: progressive disease). Several 2D-DNN backbones have been tested preferring deep architectures with medium-low complexity to make the overall pipeline portable on embedded platforms based on STA1295 ASIL-B certified hardware architecture[1]. The following sections provide a detailed description of the proposed solution.

3.1   The Bounding Box Segmentation Block

This block performs a semi-automatic CT-scan lesion segmentation driven by experienced oncologists/radiologists. Specifically, starting from the whole chest-abdomen CT scan of each patient, the oncologist/radiologist manually selected a target characteristic cancerous lesion according to RECIST revision 1.1 criteria [14]. Nowadays, all CT scanner imaging software allows the automatic selection of a ROI according to certain spatial, dimensional, or morphological criteria. After this selection, a MxN bounding box ROI around (centered), the lesion is automatically extracted by our proposed segmentation software. The dimensional setup (M, N) can ranges, and it does not affect the overall pipeline performance as the segmented lesion will be further re-scaled according to the input size of the downstream 2D-DNN classifier. In our case, we have chosen to segment with a $64x64$ bounding box ROI. Below is a brief reference to the RECIST 1.1 guideline [14]. With the term RECIST, we refer to an official deterministic methodology to evaluate the cancer treatment outcome in solid tumours [14]. The RECIST criteria, as of interest in this research work, includes the following items:

- Measurable lesion (target lesion): a lesion that can be accurately measured with longest diameter (in one dimension) ≥ 20 mm (CT scan imaging);
- A sum of the longest diameter (LD) for all CT image target lesions will be computed and reported as the baseline for the follow-up evaluations.

The RECIST 1.1 guideline consequently specifies how to classify the patient's response to a specific cancer therapy:

---

[1] https://www.st.com/en/automotive-infotainment-and-telematics/sta1295.html.

- A patient shows a complete response (CR) to the medical treatment if all identified target lesions disappear at the end-treatment CT imaging.
- A patient shows a partial response (PR) if the target lesions (LD sum) are reduced by at least 30%.
- A patient shows a progressive disease (PD) if the LD sum increases by, at least, 20%;
- A patient instead reports stable disease (SD) if no significant increase or decrease is observed on the target lesions.

This work as well as the clinical trial to which it refers, provide results based on RECIST 1.1 guideline [14].

3.2   The 2D-CNN Features Generative Model

This block performs further processing of the collected ROIs in order to leverage discriminating visual features. The proposed generative model is based on properly configured and extended version of 2D Cellular Non-linear Networks (CNNs). The Cellular Neural (or Nonlinear) Network (CNN) theory is briefly outlined.

L.O Chua and L. Yang firstly proposed the first architecture of the CNN[10]. The CNN can be defined as high speed local interconnected computing array of analog processors called "cells" [10]. The basic unit of CNN is the cell. The CNN processing is configured through the instructions provided by the so-called cloning templates [10]. Each cell of the CNN may be considered a dynamical system arranged into a topological 2D or 3D structure. The CNN cells interact with each other within its neighborhood configured by a heuristically ad-hoc defined radius [10]. Each CNN cell has an input, a state, and an output, a functional mapping of the state (usually through PieceWise Linear function). Some stability results and consideration about the dynamics of the CNNs are reported in [3,10]. We highlight that the used 2D-CNN is a *transient-response* CNN. In these architectures, the transformation of the input data is performed and time-limited at the transient stage, that is, in the phase in which each single cell of the CNN dynamically evolves from the initial state along the trajectory that converges to the CNN steady-state [3,10]. In this way we are able to extract intermediate 2D-CNN transformation features of the input which will be used as augmented generated features. In the CNN paradigm, we can hypothesize the dependence between state, input, output, and neighborhood in different ways considering that CNN is a "Universal Machine" [9,17]. Therefore, we proceed with an extended mathematical representation of a generative model based on CNNs. The CNN can be considered as a system of cells (or non-linear neurons) defined on a normed-space S_N (grid structure), which is a discrete subset of R^n (generally $n \leq 3$) with distance function d: $S_N \rightarrow N$ (N is the set of positive integer numbers). Cells are indexed in a space-set L_i. Neighborhood function $N_r(.)$ of a k-th cell can be defined as follows:

$$N_r : L_i \rightarrow L_i^\beta$$
$$N_r(k) = \{l|d(i,j) \leq r\} \tag{1}$$

where β depends on r (neighborhood radius) and on space geometry of the grid. The CNNs can be implemented as a single layer or multi-layers so that the cell grid can be e.g., a planar array (with rectangular, square, octagonal geometry) or a k-dimensional array (usually $k \geq 3$), generally considered and realized as a stack of k-dimensional arrays (layers). Therefore, CNN can be represented as a time-continuous - space-discrete system whose dynamic is well defined by the spatio-temporal evolution of the cells. The following mathematical model defines the dynamic of an extended CNN cell:

$$
\partial x_j/\partial t = g[x_j\,(t)]
$$

$$
+ \sum_{\gamma \in N_r(i)} \aleph_{\vartheta_j}(x_j|_{(t-\tau,t]}, y_\gamma\,|_{(t-\tau,t]}; p^A_{\,j})
$$

$$
+ \sum_{\gamma \in N_r(j)} \mathcal{B}_{\varphi_j}(x_j|_{(t-\tau,t]}, u_\gamma\,|_{(t-\tau,t]}; p^B_{\,j}) \tag{2}
$$

$$
+ \sum_{\gamma \in N_r(j)} \mathbb{C}_{\rho_j}(x_j|_{(t-\tau,t]}, x_\gamma\,|_{(t-\tau,t]}; p^C_{\,j})
$$

$$
+ I_j(t)
$$

$$
y_{j(t)} = \psi(x_j|_{t-\tau,t}) \tag{3}
$$

In Eq. 2, x, y, u, I_j denote cell state, output, input, and bias respectively while j and γ are cell indices; g is a local instantaneous feedback function, N_r define the neighborhood function while p^A, p^B and p^C are arrays of ad-hoc configurable parameters, notation $z|T$ denotes the restriction of function $z()$ to interval T of its argument, $\aleph_{\vartheta_j}$ is the neighborhood feedback functional (one out of several applicable, identified by index ϑ_j), and in the same way $\mathcal{B}_{\varphi_j}$ is the input functional, $\mathbb{C}_{\rho_j}$ is the cell-state functional. The term I_j represents ad-hoc defined bias. The function ψ defines the mathematical correlation between the state and the output of the cell. Applying a linear re-mapping and extension of the model reported in Eqs. (2)–(3), the following CNN cell generative dynamical model is proposed:

$$
C\frac{dx_{ij}(t)}{dt} = -\frac{1}{R_x}x_{ij}
$$

$$
+ \sum_{C(k,l) \in N_r(i,j)} A(i,j;k,l)y_{kl}(t)
$$

$$
+ \sum_{C(k,l) \in N_r(i,j)} B(i,j;k,l)u_{kl}(t)
$$

$$
+ \sum_{C(k,l) \in N_r(i,j)} C(i,j;k,l)x_{kl}(t) \tag{4}
$$

$$
+ \sum_{C(k,l) \in N_r(i,j)} D(i,j;k,l)(y_{ij}(t), y_{kl}(t))
$$

$$
+ I
$$

$$
1 \leq i \leq M, 1 \leq j \leq N
$$

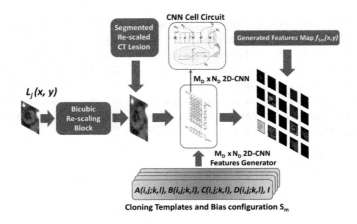

Fig. 2. The proposed 2D-CNN generative model

$$y_{ij}(t) = \frac{1}{2}(|x_{ij}(t) + 1| - |x_{ij}(t) - 1|) \tag{5}$$

$$N_r(i,j) = \{C_r(k,l); (max(|k-i|, |i-j|) \leq r)\} \\ (1 \leq k \leq M, 1 \leq l \leq N)) \tag{6}$$

In Eqs. (4)-(6) the $Nr(i,j)$ represents the neighborhood of each CNN cell $C(i,j)$ with radius r. The terms x_{ij}, y_{ij}, u_{ij}, and I defines the state, the output, the input and the bias of the cell $C(i,j)$ respectively. The terms $A(i,j;k,l)$, $B(i,j;k,l)$, $C(i,j;k,l)$, $D(i,j;k,l)$ are the cloning templates which define the CNN processing. Specifically, $D(i,j;k,l)$ represents the extended non-linear space-invariant cloning template applied to the proposed 2D-CNN model [29]. More details about CNN non-linear cloning templates in [29]. As described in [9,17,24] through the cloning template configurations (matrix coefficients), a specific CNN generative features model will be enabled. In Eqs. (4)–(6), the spatial CNN dimension is defined by (M, N) setup. R_x is ad-hoc defined coefficient (correlated to the hardware implementation of the CNN cell), which was set to 1. The workflow of the implemented CNN generative features model is showed. We fed the input and the state of the 2D-CNN with the segmented ROI lesion described in the previous section. According to the used downstream 2D-DNN input size ($M_D x N_D$), we perform a preliminary bi-cubic re-scaling of the segmented ROI to $M_D x N_D$ size. Consequently, an $M_D x N_D$ 2D-grid CNN was implemented. More in detail, each of the resized $M_D x N_D$ segmented ROI will be fed in the input u_{ij} and state x_{ij} of $M_D x N_D$ 2D grid-CNN i.e., each input and state of the CNN cells will be bound to the corresponding pixel of the selected re-sized input visual lesion (i.e., gray level intensity as the CT input ROI lesion is a single layer gray-level image). In Fig. 2, we report the described workflow.

Analytically, if we indicate with $L_j(x,y)$ the j-th visual segmented resized gray-level ROI image fed as input (u_{ij}) and state (x_{ij}) of the $M_D x N_D$ CNNs

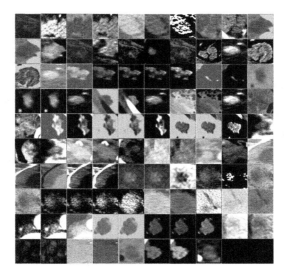

Fig. 3. A collection of the 2D-CNN generated features

grid, the image processing task driven by the configured generative model as per Eqs. (4)–(6) will be performed. Therefore, for each designed setup S_m of the cloning templates $A(i, j; k, l)$, $B(i, j; k, l)$, $C(i, j; k, l)$, $D(i, j; k, l)$, and bias I (generative model), a specific visual feature $f_{Sm}(x, y)$ of the input ROI $L_j(x, y)$ will be generated. After several tests, we decided to use m = 97 different generative models i.e., 97 different configurations of 3 x 3 cloning template matrices and biases (1 x 1), in order to generate corresponding 97, augmented visual features for each segmented resized ROI $L_j(x, y)$. Through ad-hoc heuristically implemented unsupervised approach aiming to minimize the loss of the downstream 2D-DNN Classifier (maximize the discrimination accuracy), we have selected the generative models. Basically during the training, with a random-driven searching algorithm, we selected the 3 x 3 cloning templates and bias configurations S_m, which actually produced an improvement in the discriminatory performance of the 2D-DNN classifier. The designed generative models (cloning templates and biases) as well as the adopted transient configuration of the used 2D-CNN can be downloaded from ad-hoc designed web page[2]. In Fig. 3 a collection of such 2D-CNN generated features is reported. The reported features are associated to different CT cancer native lesion types i.e. visceral, lymph-nodes, etc.

3.3   The 2D-DNN Classifier with Decision System

This block aims to learn the 2D-CNN generated augmented features to properly classify the patients eligible for immunotherapy treatment. Figure 4 shows the

---

[2] https://iplab.dmi.unict.it/immunotherapy/.

underlying backbone of the proposed deep architecture. Different 2D deep classifiers were investigated to test the computational complexity over the implemented embedded hardware Point of Care and determine those that provide the best predictive performance. Specifically, the following 2D deep classifier backboes have been validated: ResNet-18, VGG-19, Xception, MobileNetV2, GoogleNet, AlexNet [25]. Finally a NasNetMobile based 2D Deep Classifier has been tested [40]. For each patient, the RECIST 1.1 compliant target CT lesions (ROIs) are selected by the introduced semi-automatic segmentation block. The re-scaled ROIs are augmented through the proposed 2D-CNN generative engine. The generated augmented features maps will then be classified by the 2D-DNN, which provides a probability estimation of belonging to class 1 (CR/PR: complete or partial response to immunotherapy treatment or SD: stable disease) or class 2 (PD: progressive disease). As reported in Fig. 4 in the last block, there is also a Decision System. This layer aims of collecting the classifications of the single augmented visual 2D-CNN generated feature. As previously described, for each patient, a set of $m = 97$ visual features will be generated by the 2D-CNN generative model. Therefore, each of the feature images thus generated will be classified by 2D-DNN as belonging to class 1 or 2. Consequently, it is needed to know which is the main (statistically more representative) classification of the generated features associated with the patient whose CT visual lesion they refer to. The task of the Decision System, for each patient, is to determine the main 2D-DNN classification rate of the CNNs generated features. This predominant classification will be the definitive classification of the patient. Analytically, the Decision Layer will produce the following output:

$$D_k = \xi_c(C_{DNN}(f_{Sm})); \quad C_{DNN}(f_{Sm}) = \{1, 2\} \tag{7}$$

Equation (7) shows the mathematical model of the Decision Layer. The function ξ_c will analyze the 2D-DNN classification C_{DNN} rate of the f_{Sm} generated features ($m = 97$) related to the k-th patient, determining the class (1 or 2) that statistically is most represented. The output class of the Decision System (ξ_c) becomes the definitive classification (immunotherapy outcome prediction) related to the analyzed patient.

4   Experimental Results

We retrospectively analysed a dataset of 106 mUC cancer lesions (cases) extracted from the chest-abdomen CT scans of trial-recruited patients with histologically confirmed bladder cancer. Patients with multiple non-overlapped RECIST-compliant lesions have been analysed for each target lesion detected on CT examination. The recruited patients had histologically confirmed bladder cancer (mUC) progressing after platinum-based chemotherapy and were treated with a PD-L1 ICIs immunotherapy agent in the second-line setting. All patients provided written informed consent to their participation in clinical trials covered by IRB "Catania 1 Ethical Committee" Nr. D4191C00068 and MO29983. For

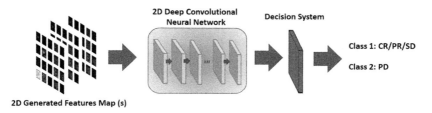

2D Generated Features Map (s)

Fig. 4. The proposed immunotherapy outcome deep predictor.

each recruited patient, a chest-abdomen CT-scan was performed (at the diagnostic phase) for disease staging. CT imaging was performed by using a GE multi-slice (64 slices) CT scanner with a slice thickness of 2.5 mm; working current in the range 10–700 mA; working voltage: 120 kV; pitch: 0.98. Clinical and personal history data complemented each CT scan. The target of the proposed pipeline is to examine the use of augmented CT image features at the time of bladder cancer diagnosis to predict the outcome of the immunotherapy treatment. Some statistical information about the recruited dataset is shown. About 30% of the patients were under the age of 60. 91% of patients were male, with the remaining 9% female. About 33% of subjects had lymph node metastases, while the remaining 67% had various visceral metastatic lesions. 43 cases (target lesions) showed a complete/partial response or a disease stabilization following immunotherapy treatment (CR/PR/SD: Class 1), while 63 cases experienced disease progression despite anti-PD-L1 drug treatment (PD: Class 2). The dataset was splitted as follows: 76 target lesions (28 of Class 1 and 48 of Class 2) were used for training and validation sessions, while the remaining 30 CT images (15 of Class 1 and 15 of Class 2) were used as test set. The lesions thus collected in both training and testing were then augmented through the proposed generative model based on 2D-CNN. Therefore, considering that for each CT image lesion a generative engine of $m = 97$ CNN models setup (3×3 cloning templates and 1×1 biases) has been defined, the augmented dataset will be composed of a total of 7372 (76×97) image features (2716 images of Class 1; 4656 images of Class 2) for the training and validation set and 2910 image features (1455 images for each class) for the test set. The proposed pipeline has been developed in MATLAB rev. 2019b full toolboxes running on a server with Intel 16-Cores and NVIDIA GeForce RTX 2080 GPU. We used Deep Learning and custom matCNN Matlab toolboxes for implementing the proposed 2D-DNN and 2D-CNN generative models, respectively. The matCNN MATLAB library can be downloaded from this web-page (See footnote 2). The initial boundary conditions, transient setup and environment configuration are included in the matCNN materials downloadable from the designed web page (See footnote 2). We used the following learning parameters for all the tested 2D-DNN model backbones: a mini-batch size of 10, initial learning rate set to 3e-4, max epochs set to 900 and the stochastic gradient descent with momentum (SGDM) algorithm as learning optimizer. We have configured a 2D-CNN $M_d x N_d$ grid according to the input image size of the

Table 1. 2D-DNN Performance Benchmark - 2D-CNN Dataset Augmentation Model

2D-Deep classifier backbone	Metrics			
	Accuracy	*Sensitivity*	*Specificity*	*Input size*
ResNet-18	93.33%	93.33%	93.33%	224 × 224
VGG-19	93.33%	100.00%	86.66%	224 × 224
XCeption	86.66%	93.33%	80.00%	299 × 299
MobileNetV2	83.33%	100.00%	66.66%	224 × 224
GoogleNet	86.66%	86.66%	86.66%	224 × 224
AlexNet	83.33%	80.00%	86.66%	227 × 227
NasNetMobile	76.66%	80.00%	73.33%	224 × 224
Previous [30]	86.05%	80.00%	89.29%	40 × 40

tested 2D-DNN classifier, as reported in Table 1. We configured the 2D-CNN with 3 x 3 cloning templates and 1 x 1 biases (97 different setups) downloadable from this web-page (See footnote 2). Table 1 reports the overall performance of the tested 2D-DNN architectures with 2D-CNN augmentation. To validate the performance of the proposed pipeline, we used classical metrics such as Accuracy, Sensitivity and Specificity. We considered as "True Positive" the correct classification of a patient who had shown a certain response to immunotherapy treatment (complete response (CR), partial (PR) or stable disease (SD)) and had been previously classified by our pipeline as belonging to Class 1. Conversely, we considered as "True Negative" a patient who was previously classified as belonging to Class 2 and then, following treatment, did not show any response to the immunotherapy drug (i.e., the progression of the disease (PD)). The "False Negative" and "False Positive" values were computed accordingly. Table 1 represents the results (in test set) in terms of accuracy, sensitivity and specificity, using each selected 2D-DNN classifier with a CT image dataset augmented trough the proposed 2D-CNN generative model. Although some architectures show 100% in terms of sensitivity, the deep architectures showed acceptable performance even in specificity are preferred. An interesting trade-off in classification performance (accuracy, sensitivity, specificity) was obtained by ResNet-18 (Accuracy: 93.33% Sensitivity: 93.33% and Specificity 93.33%) and VGG-19 (Accuracy: 93.33% Sensitivity: 100.00% and Specificity 86.66%). All performance results are reported in Table 1. Specifically, the values of accuracy, sensitivity and specificity refer to the overall classification of the generated features performed by the Decision System as reported in Eq. (7) (ξ_c output). Table 1 analysis confirms that despite the reduced architectural complexity of the tested classifier backbones (due to hardware limitation of the underlying embedded Point of Care), the overall prediction performances are very promising.

The contribution of the 2D-CNN generative model is confirmed trough the benchmarks reported in Table 2. We reports the comparison results of the

Table 2. 2D-DNN Performance Benchmark - Classical Dataset Augmentation Method

Deep classifier backbone	Metrics		
	Accuracy	*Sensitivity*	*Specificity*
ResNet-18	86, 66%	100.00%	78.66%
VGG-19	73.33%	86.66%	60.00%
3D-DenseNet	83.33%	86.66%	80.00%
ResNet-101	76.66%	80.00%	73.33%

most performer architectures reported in Table 1 (ResNet-18 and VGG-19) but without 2D-CNN generative model and by using classic input augmentation approaches [35]. The results in terms of overall performance were significantly lower than the same architectures trained with a dataset augmented through 2D-CNN. Although ResNet-18 grew in sensitivity compared to the same architecture with the 2D-CNN generative model (100% compared to 93.33%), it considerably under-performed in specificity (78.66% compared to 93.33%), thus limiting the overall performance of the pipeline. VGG-19 also showed significantly lower performance than the same with the upstream 2D-CNN generative model. Even the comparison with more complex 3D and 2D architectures (3D-DenseNet [6] with classification stage and 16 CT slices as input temporal depth and 2D ResNet-101) tested without the use of the 2D-CNN generative model (see Table 2), confirmed the valid contribution in performance of the 2D-CNN generative model.

5   Conclusion and Discussion

This study reports an innovative pipeline to investigate the use of augmented CT image features for predicting ICIs immunotherapy treatment outcome in patients with bladder cancer diagnosis. Many of the investigated scientific approaches show limited performance and high invasiveness [21,36]. For these reasons, we analyzed the challenge of finding a non-invasive image-based, highly discriminative predictive biomarker. As confirmed in [13], a novel mechanism of ICIs treatment with immune and T cell activation leads to unusual patterns of response on CT imaging. Therefore, a pipeline which learns image-features from chest-abdomen CT of mUC-diagnosed patients was investigated. Additionally due to the low availability of labeled clinical data, an extended 2D-CNN generative model was validated. As confirmed by experimental results reported in Table 1 and 2, the proposed pipeline shows very promising performances both in terms of accuracy, sensitivity and specificity. The improved performance stems from the combination of a deep high-capability classifier and 2D-CNN augmented training set [15]. The proposed 2D-CNN augmentation pipeline enables the downstream 2D-DNN to perform a greater and deeper exploration of the segmented RECIST 1.1 chest-abdomen CT image-lesions identifying a more discriminative visual patterns in originally limited clinical dataset. The proposed pipeline has been validated over all recruited RECIST 1.1 compliant lesions. This confirms that the method is not strongly influenced by the lesion selection made by the radiologist/oncologist, i.e. by the experience of the involved physicians. The implemented pipeline was designed for the embedded STA1295 platform with OpenCV and YOCTO Linux O.S. (See footnote 1). Careful studies are underway to equip the proposed pipeline with a fully automatic segmentation block. We are investigating an enhanced GradCAM [31] driven algorithm which embed RECIST 1.1 guideline allowing automatic CT ROIs segmentation based on visual explainable features. Moreover, such enhanced adaptive Deep GAN architecture was investigated as generative model.

References

1. Alsaab, H.O., et al.: PD-1 and PD-L1 checkpoint signaling inhibition for cancer immunotherapy: mechanism, combinations, and clinical outcome. Front. Pharmacol. **8**, 561 (2017)
2. Apolo, A.B., et al.: Avelumab, an anti-programmed death-ligand 1 antibody, in patients with refractory metastatic urothelial carcinoma: results from a multicenter, phase Ib study. J. Clin. Oncol. **35**(19), 2117 (2017)
3. Arena, P., Baglio, S., Fortuna, L., Manganaro, G.: Dynamics of state controlled CNNs. In: 1996 IEEE International Symposium on Circuits and Systems. Circuits and Systems Connecting the Worl (ISCAS 1996), vol. 3, pp. 56–59. IEEE (1996)
4. Banna, G.L., et al.: The promise of digital biopsy for the prediction of tumor molecular features and clinical outcomes associated with immunotherapy. Front. Med. **6**, 172 (2019)
5. Bellmunt, J., et al.: Pembrolizumab as second-line therapy for advanced urothelial carcinoma. N. Engl. J. Med. **376**(11), 1015–1026 (2017)
6. Bui, T.D., Shin, J., Moon, T.: 3D densely convolutional networks for volumetric segmentation (2017). http://arxiv.org/abs/1709.03199
7. Cha, K.H., et al.: Bladder cancer treatment response assessment in CT using radiomics with deep-learning. Sci. Rep. **7**(1), 1–12 (2017)
8. Cha, K.H., et al.: Urinary bladder segmentation in CT urography using deep-learning convolutional neural network and level sets. Med. Phys. **43**(4), 1882–1896 (2016)
9. Chua, L.O., Roska, T.: The CNN universal machine. i. the architecture. In: Proceedings of Second International Workshop on Cellular Neural Networks and their Applications (CNNA 1992), pp. 1–10. IEEE (1992)
10. Chua, L.O., Yang, L.: Cellular neural networks: theory. IEEE Trans. Circuits Syst. **35**(10), 1257–1272 (1988)
11. Santis De, M., et al.: Randomized phase II/III trial assessing gemcitabine/carboplatin and methotrexate/carboplatin/vinblastine in patients with advanced urothelial cancer who are unfit for cisplatin-based chemotherapy: EORTC study 30986. J. Clinical Oncol. **30**(2), 191 (2012)
12. Ding, X., et al.: Clinicopathological and prognostic value of PD-L1 in urothelial carcinoma: a meta-analysis. Cancer Manage. Res. **11**, 4171 (2019)
13. Dromain, C., Beigelman, C., Pozzessere, C., Duran, R., Digklia, A.: Imaging of tumour response to immunotherapy. Eur. Radiol. Exp. **4**(1), 2 (2020)
14. Eisenhauer, E.A., et al.: New response evaluation criteria in solid tumours: revised recist guideline (version 1.1). Eur. J. Cancer **45**(2), 228–247 (2009)

15. Rundo, F., Conoci, S., Banna, G.L.: Image processing method, corresponding system and computer program product (2018)
16. Ferlay, J., et al.: Cancer incidence and mortality worldwide: sources, methods and major patterns in GLOBOCAN 2012. Int. J. Cancer **136**(5), E359–E386 (2015)
17. Fortuna, L., Arena, P., Balya, D., Zarandy, A.: Cellular neural networks: a paradigm for nonlinear spatio-temporal processing. IEEE Circuits. Syst. Mag. **1**(4), 6–21 (2001)
18. Garapati, S.S., et al.: Urinary bladder cancer staging in CT urography using machine learning. Med. Phys. **44**(11), 5814–5823 (2017)
19. Gordon, M., et al.: Segmentation of inner and outer bladder wall using deep-learning convolutional neural network in CT urography. In: Proceedings of Medical Imaging 2017: Computer-Aided Diagnosis. International Society for Optics and Photonics, vol. 10134, p. 1013402 (2017)
20. Hasnain, Z., et al.: Machine learning models for predicting post-cystectomy recurrence and survival in bladder cancer patients. PloS one **14**(2) (2019)
21. Havel, J.J., Chowell, D., Chan, T.A.: The evolving landscape of biomarkers for checkpoint inhibitor immunotherapy. Nat. Rev. Cancer **19**(3), 133–150 (2019)
22. Krizhevsky, A., Sutskever, I., Hinton, G.E.: Imagenet classification with deep convolutional neural networks. In: Advances in Neural Information Processing Systems, pp. 1097–1105 (2012)
23. Lambin, P., et al.: Radiomics: extracting more information from medical images using advanced feature analysis. Eur. J. Cancer **48**(4), 441–446 (2012)
24. Lee, C.C., de Gyvez, J.P.: Color image processing in a cellular neural-network environment. IEEE Trans. Neural Networks **7**(5), 1086–1098 (1996)
25. Liu, W., Wang, Z., Liu, X., Zeng, N., Liu, Y., Alsaadi, F.E.: A survey of deep neural network architectures and their applications. Neurocomputing **234**, 11–26 (2017). https://doi.org/10.1016/j.neucom.2016.12.038. https://www.sciencedirect.com/science/article/abs/pii/S0925231216315533
26. Ma, X., et al.: 2D and 3D bladder segmentation using u-net-based deep-learning. In: Medical Imaging 2019: Computer-Aided Diagnosis. International Society for Optics and Photonics, vol. 10950, p. 109500Y (2019)
27. Massard, C., et al.: Safety and efficacy of durvalumab (MEDI4736), an anti-programmed cell death ligand-1 immune checkpoint inhibitor, in patients with advanced urothelial bladder cancer. J. Clinical Oncol. **34**(26), 3119 (2016)
28. Powless, T., et al.: Atezolizumab versus chemotherapy in patients with platinum-treated locally advanced or metastatic urothelial carcinoma (IMvigor211): a multicentre, open-label, phase 3 randomised controlled trial. The Lancet **391**(10122), 748–757 (2018)
29. Roska, T., Chua, L.O.: Cellular neural networks with nonlinear and delay-type template elements. In: IEEE International Workshop on Cellular Neural Networks and their Applications, pp. 12–25 (1990)
30. Rundo, F., Spampinato, C., Banna, G.L., Conoci, S.: Advanced deep learning embedded motion radiomics pipeline for predicting anti-PD-1/PD-L1 immunotherapy response in the treatment of bladder cancer: preliminary results. Electronics **8**(10), 1134 (2019)
31. Selvaraju, R.R., Cogswell, M., Das, A., Vedantam, R., Parikh, D., Batra, D.: Grad-cam: Visual explanations from deep networks via gradient-based localization. In: 2017 IEEE International Conference on Computer Vision (ICCV), pp. 618–626 (2017)
32. Seront, E., Machiels, J.P.: Molecular biology and targeted therapies for urothelial carcinoma. Cancer Treat. Rev. **41**(4), 341–353 (2015)

33. Sharma, P., et al.: Efficacy and safety of nivolumab monotherapy in metastatic urothelial cancer (mUC): Results from the phase I/II checkmate 032 study (2016)
34. Shkolyar, E., et al.: Augmented bladder tumor detection using deep learning. Eur. Urol. **76**(6), 714–718 (2019)
35. Shorten, C., Khoshgoftaar, T.M.: A survey on image data augmentation for deep learning. J. Big Data **6**, 1–48 (2019)
36. Spencer, K.R., Wang, J., Silk, A.W., Ganesan, S., Kaufman, H.L., Mehnert, J.M.: Biomarkers for immunotherapy: current developments and challenges. Am. Soc. Clinical Oncol. Educ. book **36**, e493–e503 (2016)
37. Wang, G., Lam, K.M., Deng, Z., Choi, K.S.: Prediction of mortality after radical cystectomy for bladder cancer by machine learning techniques. Comput. Biol. Med. **63**, 124–132 (2015)
38. Wu, E., et al.: Deep learning approach for assessment of bladder cancer treatment response. Tomography **5**(1), 201 (2019)
39. Zhou, T.C., Sankin, A.I., Porcelli, S.A., Perlin, D.S., Schoenberg, M.P., Zang, X.: A review of the PD-1/PD-L1 checkpoint in bladder cancer: from mediator of immune escape to target for treatment. In: Urologic Oncology: Seminars and Original Investigations. vol. 35, pp. 14–20. Elsevier (2017)
40. Zoph, B., Vasudevan, V., Shlens, J., Le, Q.V.: Learning transferable architectures for scalable image recognition (2017)

Multi-model Ensemble to Classify Acute Lymphoblastic Leukemia in Blood Smear Images

Sabrina Dhalla[✉], Ajay Mittal, Savita Gupta, and Harleen Singh

University Institute of Engineering and Technology, Panjab University, Chandigarh, India
dhallasabrina@gmail.com

Abstract. Acute Lymphoblastic Leukemia (ALL) is one of the most commonly occurring type of leukemia which poses a serious threat to life. It severely affects White Blood Cells (WBCs) of the human body that fight against any kind of infection or disease. Since, there are no evident morphological changes and the signs are pretty similar to other disorders, it becomes difficult to detect leukemia. Manual diagnosis of leukemia is time-consuming and is even susceptible to errors. Thus, in this paper, computer assisted diagnosis method has been implemented to detect leukemia using deep learning models. Three models namely, VGG11, ResNet18 and ShufflenetV2 have been trained and fine tuned on ISBI 2019 C-NMC dataset. Finally an ensemble using weighted averaging technique is formed and evaluated as per the criteria of binary classification. The proposed method gave an overall accuracy of 87.52% and F1-score of 87.40%. Thus, it outperforms most of the existing techniques for the same dataset.

Keywords: Leukemia · White Blood Cells · Deep learning · Ensemble

1 Introduction

Leukemia, being a potentially deadly disease is known to cause thousands of deaths as per the reports of National Cancer Institute [1]. It is majorly found in adults over 55 years and children under 15 years of age every year. In United States alone, 61,780 cases of leukemia were detected in 2019, accounting for 3.5% of all cancer cases in the country. It is also ranked at 7th position amongst all the cancers in India as per the reports of Global Cancer Observatory [2], listing around 42,055 cases in 2019. Although exact cause for leukemia is not known, plausible factors include smoking, genetic flaws, therapies involving contact with radiations or some other certain chemicals. Symptoms of leukemia, such as, loss in weight, migraine, pain in joints, absence of vitality and immunity loss develop within few days after the original cells begin to die. Leukemia can be comprehensively classified in two categories- lymphocytic (or "lymphoblastic")

© Springer Nature Switzerland AG 2021
A. Del Bimbo et al. (Eds.): ICPR 2020 Workshops, LNCS 12661, pp. 243–253, 2021.
https://doi.org/10.1007/978-3-030-68763-2_18

and myelogenous (or "myeloid") [3]. Under lymphocytic leukemia, cancer cells develop in the marrow cells that grow up to form lymphocytes. Contrary to it, malignant growth cells develop in the marrow cells that normally go on to form Red Blood Cells (RBCs), platelets and different type of WBCs in myelogenous leukemia. Both these categories can be further sub divided into two categories-acute and chronic. While acute leukemia is characterised by fast growth of the blast cells resulting in over-growth of immature cells, progress of cancer cells is somewhat moderate in chronic leukemia and it causes overgrowth of matured cells.

The initial stage of leukemia can be detected by a blood test that shows an abnormal white cell count, followed by confirmatory bone marrow tests. Such diagnostic treatments require highly specialized manpower and high-end systems for testing purposes. Thus, it becomes imperative to automate the process of leukemia detection and diagnosis to overcome limitations of manual screening. Computer aided diagnostic tools help with the analysis of triage and can reduce the clinical burden. In this paper, we propose the classification of microscopic blood smear images into acute lymphoblastic leukemia (ALL) or normal cell images. In order to achieve this objective, three pre-trained convolutional neural networks (CNN), a class of deep learning (DL) models namely VGG11, ResNet18 and ShufflenetV2 are deployed. These data-driven models can self discover patterns and attributes from the image data.

The organization of the paper is as follows. Related work which have been previously worked upon is presented in Sect. 2. Section 3 focuses on the materials required for the implementation and the steps of methodology adopted. Results of the experiments conducted have been discussed in Sect. 4. The last section i.e. Sect. 5 covers the conclusion and future scope of the research.

2   Prior Art

Extensive work has already been done on various datasets to detect ALL in blood smear images. The process of detection of malignant cells can be broadly classified in two ways: traditional machine learning and deep learning methods. Machine learning methods use semi-automated feature extraction method in order to extract features of blast cells and its components. Scotti [4], who has greatly contributed in this area, processed and classified ALL using morphological features of images. Selection of the features play a vital role in determining accuracy of the model as a whole. Classifiers such as linear Bayes (LB) normal classifier, k-nearest neighbour (k-NN), Neural Networks (NNs). have been compared to identify their capability for blast cells identification. NNs achieved the least mean error of 0.0133% whereas LB took the least processing time.

Rawat [5] fed a total of 331 features (shape and texture) calculated using 420 images dataset to genetic algorithm. Then these features were experimented on SVMs of varied kernels to detect the best possible kernel in order to differentiate between normal, ALL and acute myeloid leukemia (AML). Gaussian radial basis kernel (RBF) SVM achieved accuracy of 99.5%, nearly outperforming all the other kernels. Images of cells from ALL-IDB1 [6] were processed and segmented to extract sub-images of cells by Putzu et al. in [7,8]. Chromatic and texture feature along with SVM were used for the purpose of binary classification. Results were then validated by 10-fold cross validation to cross-check model's accuracy, which is approximated to 92%. Madhloom et al. [9] obtained 260 images of ALL and normal cells from the medical centres. An extensive search was carried on the feature selection process. Total of 30 features calculated were ranked using Fisher's Discrimination Ratio (FDR) based on the co-relation amongst features. It was then followed by exhaustive search to select the best three features to feed classifier. k-NN was applied on the feature set using Euclidean distance and accuracy of 92.5% was achieved. However, authors suggested on using SVMs or NN for superior results. Bhattacharjee et al. [10] compared artificial NN, k-NN and SVM over the dataset along with the usage of cross validation. Since the dataset was small, k-NN gave the optimised results in short span of time.

Fatma et al. [11] used feed-forward type of NN in which no cycle is directly formed between the layers or neurons and information flows from one layer to next layer only. Total number of images used were 50, out of which 38 were used for training and 12 for testing. Although the overall process achieved accuracy of 91%, author explained the need of larger image dataset to further improve the results. Parvaresh et al. [12] utilised Discrete Wavelet Transform in order to extract features from image dataset. It was followed by a heuristic algorithm known as Chain Tabu in order to select the features which were dissimilar in nature. Feature vector was thus passed to Multi-Layer Perceptron (MLP) for classification. It includes group of neurons stacked vertically and layers in forward direction. Interconnection between the layers helped to pass the information with the help of ADAM optimiser in this case. An accuracy of 98.88% was obtained using ALL-IDB2 [6], which consists of 260 images in total.

Apart from using these classifiers individually, Mohapatra et al. [13] used combination of numerous algorithms to form their ensemble. Total of 44 features which include shape, texture and color properties of cells were extracted. T-test, a statistical approach was used to rank the importance of various features and hence, select them. In order to take advantage of diverse architectures, bagging method was employed for the ensemble and labels were generated by majority voting principle. It was observed that ensemble of Naive Bayes, KNN, MLP and SVM topped all the performance metrics in comparison with the independent results.

After careful observation, it was noted that the machine learning algorithms were applied on data-sets which had small number of images, typically in hundreds. In order to learn more complex patterns in data-set and enhance the learning process, deep learning models have a hand over machine learning algorithms. Contrary to machine learning, deep learning methods perform end-to-end feature extraction, selection and classification process [14]. Convolution Neural Networks (CNN) have also shown quite impressive results in image recognition, object detection and localization [15,16]. Thanh et al. [17] used ALL-IDB1 [6] dataset and created their own CNN consisting of 7 layers. The initial five layers recognised and learnt the best features in the images. During this learning phase, ReLU was used as an activation function. Last two helped in the classification of images on the basis of feature vector learnt. It was also proved by the author that CNN algorithms outperformed the methods which learn features manually by achieving accuracy of 96.43%. Ghosh et al. [18] did not code from scratch and utilised a pre-trained CNN called AlexNet. This network was used in the feature extraction part and later layers were modified as per the ALL-IDB [6] dataset used. Author claims accuracy of more than 97% for leukemia images which is qualitatively better than the work issue prior to it. To the best of our knowledge and analysis, ALL-IDB [6] has been used popularly in majority papers. This dataset however, is not suitable for deep learning applications which require huge amounts of labelled data to perform end-to-end tasks. Hence, our study focuses on using the large-scale clinical dataset [19] to evaluate performance of deep learning models in real.

3   Materials and Methods

3.1   Dataset

In this work, C-NMC dataset [19] is used which consists of total 15,135 RGB images. These .bmp images have resolution of 450 × 450 pixels and labels are provided in .csv format. The labels consist of data of 118 patients in general. Each image consists of one cell with no background. This dataset is publically available after ALL Challenge of ISBI took place in 2019 to classify acute leukemic images. Furthermore, labels have been categorised into-Train, Pre-test and Final-test categories.

3.2   Methodology

1. Pre-processing: The data-set utilised for the process is imbalanced in nature as ratio of ALL and normal cell images is 2:1. Such a biased ratio will train model in such a way that it will favour class with higher images. This can be avoided in either of two ways- oversampling of less samples or undersampling of abundant samples. In our research, oversampling was performed to approximately balance ratio of both the classes. Another pre-processing technique which is commonly seen useful in deep learning methods is data augmentation. It helps the model to learn all the relevant features in images and to classify them more robustly. Since model is trained on microscopic single celled images, augmentation methods applied are vertical flips, horizontal flips and random rotations only as in Fig. 1.

2. Network training: For the CNNs to train optimally, large amounts of annotated data is needed. Under the scenarios where the availability of data is limited such as medical data, transfer learning strategy is applied. CNN models which are pre-trained on huge image datasets, e.g ImageNet [20], are utilized to learn the generic features and in-turn apply them to target images. The method of using pre-trained weights is a good way of initialising weights

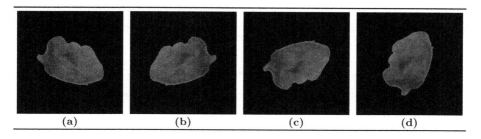

| (a) | (b) | (c) | (d) |

Fig. 1. Data Augmentation (a) Original Image, (b) Horizontal Flip, (c) Vertical Flip, (d) Random Rotate

and are known to perform better than random initializations. Hence, after the data-set is prepared three popular pre-trained CNN models were fine-tuned. First one is VGG11 [21], which is very popular sequential model. It consists of total 11 layers out of which 7 are convolution layers and 5 are max pooling layers. These are followed by fully connected layers and sigmoid function in the end. Second model used in the research is Shufflenet V2 [22]. It is extremely light-weight model and is well known for its property of dealing with bottlenecks. Also, the usage of point-wise group convolution in the network makes it very efficient in detecting all the required features in an image. Last model is known as ResNet 18 [23]. Unlike plain networks like VGG, it consists of residual block also known as identity block. There are skip connections or a shortcuts in between the networks which allow information to flow easily by bypassing the data along with normal CNN flow.

After the models are selected, dataset is divided in the ratio 80:20 for training and testing. It is then fed to models individually. In addition to this, an ensemble has been created using these architectures as in Fig. 2. It is a process of combination of various models in order to improve results of overall predictions. Weighted ensemble technique, which assigns weights to results of each model has been applied in the study. Variety of weights were used and optimised ranging from 0 to 1 for each of them. After larger number of settings, chosen weights are 0.5, 0.4, 0.1 for ResNet18, VGG11 and ShuffleNet V2 respectively.

Learning rate of value 0.0001 has been chosen and reduce on plateau learning decay has been scheduled at 0.1. Binary cross-entropy loss as per Eq. (1) has been used to optimise the gradients during training. Batch size is set to 16 so that all the samples can fit into the memory available. Implementation of all the models has been done in PyTorch, open source machine learning library with the help of NVIDIA Tesla K80 GPU having 12 GB RAM.

$$E_{\text{entropy}} = -\sum_{n}^{N} [t_k^n \ln y_k^n + (1 - t_k^n) \ln(1 - y_k^n)] \tag{1}$$

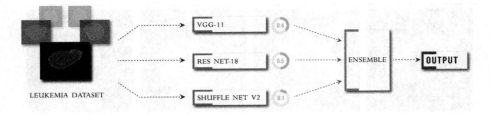

Fig. 2. Workflow illustrated

Table 1. Performance metrics of individual models and model ensemble.

Model	Test accuracy (0-Hem)	Test accuracy (1-all)	Test accuracy (Overall)	Specificity	Sensitivity	F-score
Vgg11	76.08%	90.65%	85.59%	85.44%	85.59%	85.47%
Resnet18	78.24%	88.84%	85.16%	85.13%	85.16%	85.14%
ShuffleNetV2	70.52%	90.16%	83.34%	83.11%	83.34%	83.09%
Ensemble	**78.55%**	**92.29%**	**87.52%**	**87.40%**	**87.52%**	**87.40%**

4   Results and Discussion

Various performance metrics have been summarised in Table 1. Accuracy and loss for all training and validation experiments have been represented graphically in Fig. 4. It can be observed from the training graphs that all the respectively networks have converged well. Also, the minimised validation loss proves that hyper parameters have finely tuned.

For the purpose of testing, total of 1867 images were fed to the base networks and ensemble network. Confusion matrices for all the networks were obtained and are displayed in Fig. 3. Comparison between Receiver Operating Characteristic (ROC) curves of all the architectures has been shown in Fig. 5. Curves which are

Table 2. Comparison of recent works on leukemia

Reference	Accuracy	Specificity	Sensitivity	F-score
Honnalgere et al. [24]	–	–	–	80.79%
Shah et al. [25]	86.13%	–	–	83.12%
Ding et al. [26]	–	–	86.53%	86.74%
Kulhalli et al. [27]	–	–	–	72%
Khan et al. [28]	–	–	–	83.17%
Li et al. [29]	–	–	85%	84%
Proposed method	87.52%	87.40%	87.52%	87.40%

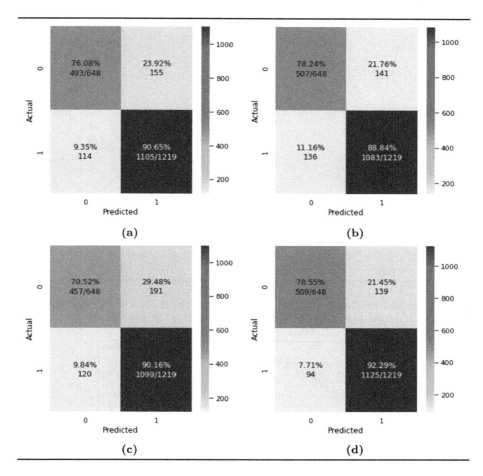

Fig. 3. Confusion Matrix for (a) VGG11, (b) ResNet18, (c) ShuffleNetV2, (d) Ensemble

elevated more towards high left boundary are considered to be more well-defined and accurate.

It illustrates that the respective fine-tuned models have converged efficiently. Since, accuracy alone can not prove the viability of the model, various other metrics such as sensitivity, specificity and f1-score have been calculated for the same. These help in analysing credibility of the results and in checking how well hyperparameters have been optimised. Values of sensitivity, specificity and f-score for VGG11 are 85.59%, 85.44% and 85.47%. For ResNet18 and ShufflenetV2, values for sensitivity, specificity and f-score are 85.16%, 85.13%, 85.14% and 83.34%, 83.11%, 83.09% respectively. The ensemble architecture shows an increment in all these values when compared to base models. In order to compare the results

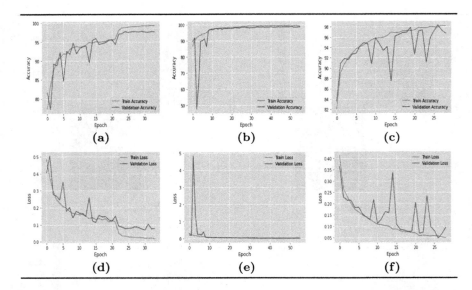

Fig. 4. Train and validation accuracy of (a) VGG11, (b) ResNet18, (c) ShuffleNetV2, Train and validation loss of (d) VGG11, (e) ResNet18, (f) ShuffleNetV2

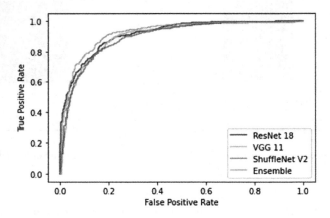

Fig. 5. ROC curve for different architectures as mentioned in labels

of model in true sense, prior work on same data-set has been examined and summarised in Table 2. By comparing the value of all the metrics, it can be inferred that ensemble model increases the overall efficiency.

5   Conclusion

In this paper, a deep learning based ensemble method is proposed in order to classify image dataset into normal and blast cells. The architecture structured three pre-trained models which were fine-tuned and fused together to make the model more efficient and robust. The ensemble learning helps decrease the variance of various models by optimally combining results of individual models and reduces sensitivity towards the training data. The most important part of the ensemble is manually optimisation of various hyper-parameters in the model. Although, this proposed method outperforms many of the state-of-art methods for ISBI C-NMC dataset, yet performance is still not at par to be used practically. As a part of future work, ensemble model is intended to be improved. Since, the accuracy is low for the class which has lower number of samples, it is advised to focus on data balancing problem. Various techniques such as metric learning or siamese network can be experimented with for the same. Other than this, light weight models such as DenseNet, SqueezeNet will form a part of future endeavours so that model can be deployed using less computational resources.

References

1. National Cancer Institute (2018)
2. The Global Cancer Observatory (2018)
3. Markiewicz, T., Osowski, S., Marianska, B., Moszczyński, L.: Automatic recognition of the blood cells of myelogenous leukemia using SVM. In: Proceedings of the International Joint Conference on Neural Networks, vol. 4, pp. 2496–2501 (2005). https://doi.org/10.1109/IJCNN.2005.1556295
4. Scotti, F.: Automatic morphological analysis for acute leukemia identification in peripheral blood microscope images. In: CIMSA. 2005 IEEE International Conference on Computational Intelligence for Measurement Systems and Applications, pp. 96–101. IEEE (2005)
5. Rawat, J., Singh, A., Bhadauria, H.S., Virmani, J., Devgun, J.S.: Computer assisted classification framework for prediction of acute lymphoblastic and acute myeloblastic leukemia. Biocybern. Biomed. Eng. **37**(4), 637–654, 2017. https://doi.org/10.1016/j.bbe.2017.07.003. ISSN 02085216
6. Labati, R.D., Piuri, V., Scotti, F.: ALL-IDB: the acute lymphoblastic leukemia image database for image processing. In: 2011 18th IEEE International Conference on Image Processing, pp. 2045–2048. IEEE (2011)
7. Putzu, L., Di Ruberto, C.: White blood cells identification and classification from leukemic blood image. In: International Work-Conference on Bioinformatics and Biomedical Engineering, pp. 99–106. Copicentro Editorial (2013)
8. Putzu, L., Caocci, G., Di Ruberto, C.: Leucocyte classification for leukaemia detection using image processing techniques. Artif. Intell. Med. **62**(3), 179–191 (2014)
9. Madhloom, H.T., Kareem, S.A., Ariffin, H.: A robust feature extraction and selection method for the recognition of lymphocytes versus acute lymphoblastic leukemia. In: 2012 International Conference on Advanced Computer Science Applications and Technologies (ACSAT), pp. 330–335. IEEE (2012)
10. Bhattacharjee, R., Saini, L.M.: Robust technique for the detection of acute lymphoblastic leukemia. In: 2015 IEEE Power, Communication and Information Technology Conference (PCITC), pp. 657–662. IEEE (2015)
11. Fatma, M., Sharma, J.: Identification and classification of acute leukemia using neural network. In: 2014 International Conference on Medical Imaging, m-Health and Emerging Communication Systems (MedCom), pp. 142–145. IEEE (2014)

12. Parvaresh, H., Sajedi, H., Rahimi, S.A.: Leukemia diagnosis using image processing and computational intelligence. In: 2018 IEEE 22nd International Conference on Intelligent Engineering Systems (INES), pp. 000305–000310. IEEE (2018)
13. Mohapatra, S., Patra, D., Satpathy, S.: An ensemble classifier system for early diagnosis of acute lymphoblastic leukemia in blood microscopic images. Neural Comput. Appl. **24**(7), 1887–1904 (2013). https://doi.org/10.1007/s00521-013-1438-3
14. LeCun, Y., Bengio, Y., Hinton, G.: Deep learning. Nature **521**(7553), 436–444 (2015)
15. Krizhevsky, A., Sutskever, I., Hinton, G.E.: ImageNet classification with deep convolutional neural networks. Commun. ACM **60**(6), 84–90 (2017)
16. Redmon, J., Divvala, S., Girshick, R., Farhadi, A.: You only look once: unified, real-time object detection. In: Proceedings of the IEEE Conference on Computer Vision and Pattern Recognition, pp. 779–788 (2016)
17. Thanh, T.T.P., Vununu, C., Atoev, S., Lee, S.-H., Kwon, K.-R.: Leukemia blood cell image classification using convolutional neural network. Int. J. Comput. Theory Eng. **10**(2), 54–58 (2018)
18. Ghosh, A., Singh, S., Sheet, D.: Simultaneous localization and classification of acute lymphoblastic leukemic cells in peripheral blood smears using a deep convolutional network with average pooling layer. In: 2017 IEEE International Conference on Industrial and Information Systems (ICIIS), pp. 1–6. IEEE (2017)
19. SbiLab. https://competitions.codalab.org/competitions/20395
20. Deng, J., Dong, W., Socher, R., Li, L.-J., Li, K., Fei-Fei, L.: ImageNet: a large-scale hierarchical image database. In: 2009 IEEE conference on Computer Vision and Pattern Recognition, pp. 248–255. IEEE (2009)
21. Simonyan, K., Zisserman, A.: Very deep convolutional networks for large-scale image recognition. arXiv preprint arXiv:1409.1556 (2014)
22. Ma, N., Zhang, X., Zheng, H.-T., Sun, J.: ShuffleNet V2: practical guidelines for efficient CNN architecture design. In: Ferrari, V., Hebert, M., Sminchisescu, C., Weiss, Y. (eds.) Computer Vision – ECCV 2018. LNCS, vol. 11218, pp. 122–138. Springer, Cham (2018). https://doi.org/10.1007/978-3-030-01264-9_8
23. He, K., Zhang, X., Ren, S., Sun, J.: Deep residual learning for image recognition. In: Proceedings of the IEEE Conference on Computer Vision and Pattern Recognition, pp. 770–778 (2016)
24. Honnalgere, A., Nayak, G.: Classification of normal versus malignant cells in B-all white blood cancer microscopic images. In: Gupta, A., Gupta, R. (eds.) ISBI 2019 C-NMC Challenge: Classification in Cancer Cell Imaging. LNB, pp. 1–12. Springer, Singapore (2019). https://doi.org/10.1007/978-981-15-0798-4_1
25. Shah, S., Nawaz, W., Jalil, B., Khan, H.A.: Classification of normal and leukemic blast cells in B-all cancer using a combination of convolutional and recurrent neural networks. In: Gupta, A., Gupta, R. (eds.) ISBI 2019 C-NMC Challenge: Classification in Cancer Cell Imaging. LNB, pp. 23–31. Springer, Singapore (2019). https://doi.org/10.1007/978-981-15-0798-4_3
26. Ding, Y., Yang, Y., Cui, Y.: Deep learning for classifying of white blood cancer. In: Gupta, A., Gupta, R. (eds.) ISBI 2019 C-NMC Challenge: Classification in Cancer Cell Imaging. LNB, pp. 33–41. Springer, Singapore (2019). https://doi.org/10.1007/978-981-15-0798-4_4
27. Kulhalli, R., Savadikar, C., Garware, B.: Toward automated classification of B-acute lymphoblastic leukemia. In: Gupta, A., Gupta, R. (eds.) ISBI 2019 C-NMC Challenge: Classification in Cancer Cell Imaging. LNB, pp. 63–72. Springer, Singapore (2019). https://doi.org/10.1007/978-981-15-0798-4_7

28. Khan, M.A., Choo, J.: Classification of cancer microscopic images via convolutional neural networks. In: Gupta, A., Gupta, R. (eds.) ISBI 2019 C-NMC Challenge: Classification in Cancer Cell Imaging. LNB, pp. 141–147. Springer, Singapore (2019). https://doi.org/10.1007/978-981-15-0798-4_15
29. Liu, Y., Long, F.: Acute lymphoblastic leukemia cells image analysis with deep bagging ensemble learning. In: Gupta, A., Gupta, R. (eds.) ISBI 2019 C-NMC Challenge: Classification in Cancer Cell Imaging. LNB, pp. 113–121. Springer, Singapore (2019). https://doi.org/10.1007/978-981-15-0798-4_12

MIINet: An Image Quality Improvement Framework for Supporting Medical Diagnosis

Quan Huu Cap[1,2]([⊠]), Hitoshi Iyatomi[2], and Atsushi Fukuda[1]

[1] Aillis Inc., Tokyo, Japan
{quan.cap,atsushi.fukuda}@aillis.jp
[2] Graduate School of Science and Engineering, Hosei University, Tokyo, Japan
iyatomi@hosei.ac.jp

Abstract. Medical images have been indispensable and useful tools for supporting medical experts in making diagnostic decisions. However, taken medical images especially throat and endoscopy images are normally hazy, lack of focus, or uneven illumination. Thus, these could difficult the diagnosis process for doctors. In this paper, we propose MIINet, a novel image-to-image translation network for improving quality of medical images by unsupervised translating low-quality images to the high-quality clean version. Our MIINet is not only capable of generating high-resolution clean images, but also preserving the attributes of original images, making the diagnostic more favorable for doctors. Experiments on dehazing 100 practical throat images show that our MIINet largely improves the mean doctor opinion score (MDOS), which assesses the quality and the reproducibility of the images from the baseline of 2.36 to 4.11, while dehazed images by CycleGAN got lower score of 3.83. The MIINet is confirmed by three physicians to be satisfying in supporting throat disease diagnostic from original low-quality images.

Keywords: Medical image improvement · Throat image diagnosis · Image-to-image translation · Generative adversarial networks

1 Introduction

Medical images provide a lot of useful information and visual insight into different hidden body organs. They are very effective for helping doctors in making correct diagnoses or can be used as valuable reference resources for better treatment. Moreover, with the rapid development of artificial intelligence (AI), many breakthrough applications have been built on top of medical images data [11,13,24,27,32].

However, obtaining medical images especially endoscopic or throat images is never an easy task. In practice, those images normally contain noise, hazy, uneven illumination, lack of focus, etc., due to many difficult shooting conditions inside the body. Thus, these could greatly affect the medical diagnostic process.

© Springer Nature Switzerland AG 2021
A. Del Bimbo et al. (Eds.): ICPR 2020 Workshops, LNCS 12661, pp. 254–265, 2021.
https://doi.org/10.1007/978-3-030-68763-2_19

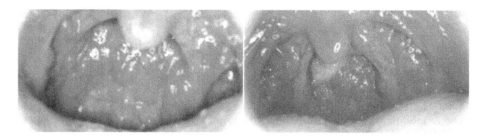

Fig. 1. Two examples of throat images with undesirably quality (out of focus (left) or hazy (right)).

Several studies applying machine learning techniques for diagnosing endoscopic and throat images have been reported that their systems are highly sensitive to the image conditions [1,14,15,29,30]. Poor image quality could easily lead to a misdetection, making it a very challenging task.

We are developing a special camera device for supporting doctors in diagnosis oral and throat diseases. We also experienced that the inside environment of patient's palate contains many negative factors that reduce the quality of images such as the hazy caused by patient's breath on camera or the lack of focus. Figure 1 illustrates examples of throat images with undesirably quality and this is an obstacle for doctors from making medical decisions. Therefore, a method to improve the quality of medical image to support the diagnosis is essential. We believe that this problem can be addressed by applying image dehazing technique.

Recent works have been utilizing a deep learning method called convolutional neural networks (CNNs) and shown tremendous success for recovering image quality from very dense haze and noise. Those dehazing techniques can be divided into two major approaches: the supervised approach [4,20,26,33,35] and the unsupervised approach [9,10,16,34]. The former normally achieves compelling results thanks to the modeling power of CNNs. However, they require a large amount of paired ground-truth images for supervision which is almost unavailable to obtain in reality. The latter offers more practical settings for image dehazing by removing the need of paired label training data. They are all built on the success of CycleGAN [37], which is a generative adversarial network (GAN) [12] based image-to-image translation method. CycleGAN introduced the cycle-consistency constraint that generated image from a domain should be identical to its original form when transforming it back.

Despite their impressive results, there are two main problems of these methods when applying to our practical throat images data. Firstly, supervised and several unsupervised studies were still built based on the assumption that hazy images (training data) have unique haze and are generated by the atmosphere scattering model [22,23]. For this reason, they may not be practical in scenarios when the disturbance deviates from prior assumptions (e.g., when shooting environment changed, such as differences in equipment, camera-setting or protocols). Secondly, naïve CycleGAN is reported to not work well on high-resolution data [21] and it

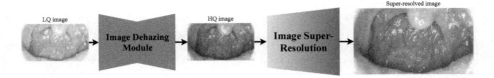

Fig. 2. The schematic of our MIINet. Given a low-quality input image, the image dehazing module will transform it into a high-quality clean image. The image super-resolution module then enlarges the clean image to obtain a high-resolution result.

does not generate sufficient resolution output for our purposes. We should note that the literature [10] suggested to use the Laplacian upscaling for the output of CycleGAN to obtain higher resolution results. However, the obtained images are normally overly smooth and sometimes fails to accurately represent detailed structures. Therefore, these abovementioned problems will make it difficult for doctors to diagnose through throat images. A framework that generates clean throat images with high-resolution from original low-quality (LQ) images could be a great tool for supporting doctors in making medical decisions.

In this paper, we propose a medical image improvement framework named MIINet for helping doctors to make medical diagnostic decisions. Our MIINet consists of two modules: the image dehazing module (IDM) and the image super-resolution (ISR) module. The IDM is developed based on the CycleGAN [37] model with the aims of translating images from LQ domain to high-quality (HQ) domain. In this work, we introduce a new loss term based on the perceptual loss function [17] with the aims to preserve original input image attributes such as structure, color, texture. This function is essential since that original information is crucial in medical diagnosis. Besides the IDM, we introduce a CNN-based image super-resolution (ISR) module to enlarge the output from our IDM, obtaining high-resolution results. The ISR module acts as an optional module when doctors need to enlarge images for more diagnosis details.

Our contributions can be summarized as follows:

- We propose the MIINet that improves the quality of practical LQ throat images while preserving the structure of the involved areas.
- Our MIINet with the introduction of the ISR module is able to produce high-resolution throat images, making the disease diagnosis more favorable for doctors.
- The dehazed throat images obtained by our MIINet shows a significantly higher of the mean doctor opinion score (MDOS) of 4.11 compared to the original LQ images of 2.36, in assessing the quality and the reproducibility of the images.

2   Proposed Method – MIINet

The proposed MIINet consists of two modules: (1) image dehazing module (IDM), and (2) image super-resolution (ISR) module. Figure 2 shows the

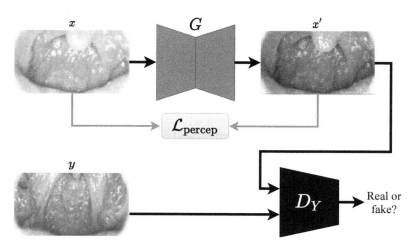

Fig. 3. Dataflow of the translation $X{\to}Y$ from low-quality image (domain X) to high-quality image (domain Y).

schematic of our framework. Given an input of original LQ throat image, our IDM will calibrate and convert that image into a HQ clean image. Since the output of our IDM is relatively small size, it will be fed to the ISR to enlarge into higher resolution with 4× upscaling, this will help doctors to have a better visual inspection.

2.1 The Image Dehazing Module – IDM

Our IDM is an improved version of CycleGAN [37] for unpaired throat image improvement. It consists of a mapping function $G : X{\to}Y$ that translates image from source domain (X) to target domain (Y), and an invert mapping function $F : Y{\to}X$ to enforce the cycle-consistency. Corresponding to two generators are the two adversarial discriminators D_X and D_Y, where D_X is trying to discriminate the real image $x \in X$ from the generated image $F(y)$ with $y \in Y$. Similarly, D_Y distinguishes the real image y from the generated image $G(x)$. In this work, we assume X is the LQ image domain while Y is the HQ image domain.

Figure 3 shows the dataflow of the translation from $X{\to}Y$. Given a LQ image x, the generator G will transform it into a HQ clean image x'. Then, the image $y \in Y$ and x' are then fed into the discriminator D_Y. Note that the translation $Y{\to}X$ is symmetric to the translation $X{\to}Y$.

Based on the GAN literature [12], the adversarial losses for both mapping functions $G : X{\to}Y$ and $F : Y{\to}X$ are $\mathcal{L}_{\mathrm{adv}}(G, D_Y)$ and $\mathcal{L}_{\mathrm{adv}}(F, D_X)$, respectively. Where:

$$\mathcal{L}_{\mathrm{adv}}(G, D_Y) = \mathbb{E}_{y\sim p_{\mathrm{data}}(y)}[(D_Y(y) - 1)^2] + \mathbb{E}_{x\sim p_{\mathrm{data}}(x)}[(D_Y(x'))^2], \quad (1)$$

and

$$\mathcal{L}_{\mathrm{adv}}(F, D_X) = \mathbb{E}_{x\sim p_{\mathrm{data}}(x)}[(D_X(x) - 1)^2] + \mathbb{E}_{y\sim p_{\mathrm{data}}(y)}[(D_X(y'))^2]. \quad (2)$$

Note here that $x' = G(x)$ and $y' = F(y)$. The cycle consistency loss $\mathcal{L}_{\text{cyc}}(G, F)$ is formulated as follows:

$$\mathcal{L}_{\text{cyc}}(G, F) = \mathbb{E}_{x \sim p_{\text{data}}(x)}[|F(G(x)) - x|_1] + \mathbb{E}_{y \sim p_{\text{data}}(y)}[|G(F(y)) - y|_1]. \quad (3)$$

As we mentioned before that preserving the original attributes of input images (i.e., structure, texture, color) is crucial in medical diagnosis. Therefore, we introduce a new loss term based on the perceptual loss $\mathcal{L}_{\text{percep}}$ [17]. To ensure that the attributes of original input and output are as similar as possible, we minimize the L1 distance between the features extracted by a CNN model of both input and generated image. Based on our preliminary experiments, we use the 2nd pooling layer of the ImageNet [7] pre-trained VGG16 [28] model to extract the features. The $\mathcal{L}_{\text{percep}}$ will be defined as:

$$\mathcal{L}_{\text{percep}}(G, F) = \mathbb{E}_{x \sim p_{\text{data}}(x)}[|\phi(G(x)) - \phi(x)|_1] + \quad (4)$$
$$\mathbb{E}_{y \sim p_{\text{data}}(y)}[|\phi(F(y)) - \phi(y)|_1],$$

where $\phi(\cdot)$ is the features extracted from the VGG16 model. Finally, our final objective function can be summed up as:

$$\mathcal{L}(G, F, D_X, D_X) = \mathcal{L}_{\text{adv}}(G, D_Y) + \mathcal{L}_{\text{adv}}(F, D_X) + \quad (5)$$
$$\lambda \mathcal{L}_{\text{cyc}}(G, F) + \beta \mathcal{L}_{\text{percep}}(G, F),$$

where λ, β are the coefficient to control the balance of different loss terms.

2.2   The Image Super-Resolution Module - ISR

Our ISR module is a GAN-based single image super-resolution (SISR) model, which aims to learn an end-to-end mapping function to recover a high-resolution (HR) image from a single low-resolution (LR) image [8,19,31]. Many SISR models have also been proposed and widely used in many practical applications ranging from medical imaging [6,36], security and surveillance [3], satellite imaging [25], to agriculture [5].

In this work, we propose an SISR module namely throat image super-resolution (ISR) for enlarging the resolution of the clean throat image output from our IDM. Our ISR module is built based on an excellent SR model so-called ESRGAN [31] which generates realistic perceptual quality results and achieved impressive performances in many benchmarks [2]. Similar to ESRGAN, our ISR module consists of two networks: a generator S which generates super-resolved images from LR images and a discriminator D_{SR} that discriminates the HR image from the super-resolved ones. We use the architecture of the generator S, the loss functions, and the hyperparameters as same as in ESRGAN literature. For the discriminator D_{SR}, we design our network to take the input of 224×224 instead of the original 128×128 as in ESRGAN since this setting helps our model gains slightly better performance based on our preliminary experiments. The two networks are then trained together in an alternating manner to solve a minimax problem [12]. For more technical training details, please refer to the original ESRGAN article [31].

3   Experimental Results

3.1   Throat Image Dataset

In this work, we collected 1,600 throat images from over 160 patients in which contain both ill-conditioned images and clean images. They were taken by a special camera designed for throat diagnosis and each of which has the size of 1920 × 1080 pixels. Experts were asked to manually inspect and carefully select 200 images with hazy and lack of focus (see Fig. 1) as low-quality images and we refer it as the "LQ Throat" dataset. Note that those images are the most difficult cases for physicians to diagnose. From this "LQ Throat" dataset, 100 images are used for training and the others 100 are for testing. The rest 1,400 images are clean and high-quality. We refer it as the "HQ Throat" dataset.

3.2   Training the IDM

Since the number of images between the two datasets "LQ Throat" and "HQ Throat" is quite different from each other. We randomly selected 100 images from "HQ Throat" dataset (i.e., same amount as the "LQ Throat" test dataset) to train our IDM. We then combined and applied different data augmentation techniques such as horizontal flip, random scale, random resize on both datasets beforehand. Since the IDM (or other image-to-image translation GAN models such as CycleGAN) cannot handle high-resolution data due to the limitation of available GPU memory, we resized input images to the size of 480 × 270 pixels before training. As a result, each dataset has 2,300 images after data augmentation.

We applied the same training procedures as described in CycleGAN [37] to train our MIINet. The Adam optimizer [18] was used to train the network. We set the λ and β in Eq. (5) equal to 10.0 and 1.5, respectively. The training process finished after 400 epochs. Please refer to [37] for more training details.

3.3   Training the ISR Module

In this paper, we built our ISR module for super-resolving the output from the IDM. The scaling factor of ×4 was used for enlarging HR from LR throat images. We used the "HQ Throat" dataset described in Sect. 3.1 to train our ISR model. During the training, the HR images were obtained by randomly cropping from training images with the size of 224 × 224. The LR images are 1/4× down-sampled from HR images using bicubic interpolation. We randomly applied Gaussian blur to the LR images with the standard deviation $\sigma = 5$ as we observed this helped our ISR module to generate better visual results. Note here again that this ISR module acts as an optional module when doctors need to enlarge images for more diagnosis details. Since the HR (clean) version of the input LR throat images is unavailable, we do not report the numerical results of our ISR module in this paper. The training details are the same as in the ESRGAN literature [31] and was completed after 400 epochs.

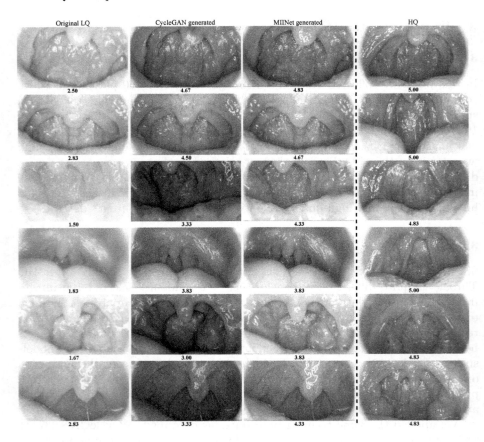

Fig. 4. Visual comparison among original LQ throat images, generated images by CycleGAN and MIINet, and the HQ images evaluated with MDOS. The above HQ images are unrelated with the rest of the images, and we evaluated them as a reference in our experiment.

3.4   The Mean Doctor Opinion Score

Since there are no quantitative metrics for assessing the throat image quality for diagnostic purposes, we introduce a new evaluation criteria called mean doctor opinion score (MDOS) based on the mean opinion score to evaluate the quality of throat images. Specifically, only experienced doctors were requested to give the scores. We asked each doctor to assess a given image under two aspects: *the quality* (i.e., how good is this image for diagnosis?) and *the reproducibility* (i.e., how good is this image in preserving the structure, texture, color from the original throat image?). We should note that scores for original LQ and HQ throat images are given based on the quality aspect only.

We asked three specialized doctors to assign a score from 1 (bad quality) to 5 (excellent quality) to the throat images. The doctors rated three versions of

Table 1. The mean doctor opinion score (MDOS) results among original and generated throat images (100 images each; ranging from 1 to 5; higher is better)

	Original LQ	CycleGAN generated	(proposed) MIINet generated	HQ
MDOS	2.36 ± 0.54	3.83 ± 0.62	4.11 ± 0.50	4.76 ± 0.20

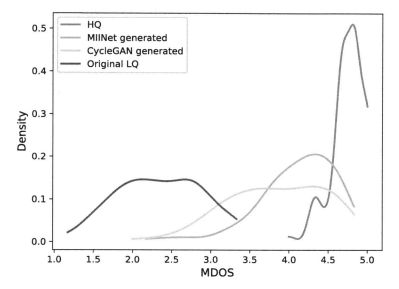

Fig. 5. Line distributions of the mean doctor opinion score (MDOS) among original LQ throat images, generated images by CycleGAN and MIINet, and the HQ images. Each line represents the scores distribution from 100 images.

each image on 100 test images from the "LQ Throat" dataset (i.e., original LQ throat images, generated images by CycleGAN and MIINet, respectively) and an addition 100 HQ images. Each doctor thus rated 400 instances.

3.5 Results

For comparison purposes, we also trained a CycleGAN model and evaluated its dehazed images. Comparisons of original LQ images, generated images by CycleGAN and MIINet, and HQ images are shown in Fig. 4. Our proposed MIINet successfully generates clean versions from original LQ images and have a much better capability of preserving the original attributes (i.e., structure, color, texture) than the CycleGAN model. Note here that the HQ images provided in the examples have no association with the rest of the images, and we evaluated them as a reference for a better intuitive understanding about the MDOS in our experiment. Our MIINet also significantly improved the MDOS from the LQ images and is better than CycleGAN as shown in Table 1 and Fig. 5.

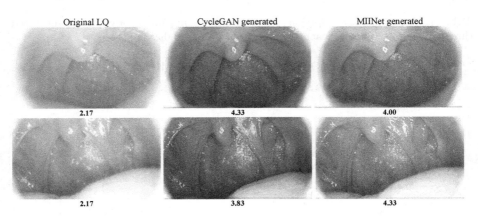

Original LQ   CycleGAN generated   MIINet generated

2.17   4.33   4.00

2.17   3.83   4.33

Fig. 6. Example of better visual results from CycleGAN than our MIINet.

4 Discussion

We confirm the effectiveness of our MIINet for supporting doctors in image-based throat diagnosis by using the MDOS testing. From the results in Figs. 4, 5 and Table 1, it is clear that the original LQ images yield the lowest MDOS since they are affected by negative factors such as hazy, uneven illumination, lack of focus etc., making it difficult for doctors to make their decisions.

As for the result of CycleGAN, even it improves a much better visual quality than original LQ images, there is a significant difference in scores distribution in comparison with our MIINet (see Fig. 5) since the CycleGAN could not preserve the original attributes (i.e., structure, color, texture) of LQ throat images. Visual results from Fig. 4 show that CycleGAN either changes the color or generates much different structure and shape from input images. This is because the original CycleGAN only learns to generate images that look close to the samples from the target domain but has no mechanisms to preserve those original attributes. We should note that the color distribution of the "HQ Throat" dataset is quite different from the "LQ Throat" dataset. Thus, CycleGAN generated outputs that have similar color as the target domain. Keeping the similar structure and color is very important for doctors to make their decisions and therefore, the generated images from CycleGAN are not preferable.

From doctor's feedback, generated images by MIINet are recommended to support throat diagnosis. Thanks to the introduction of the perceptual loss, our MIINet not only learns to generate compelling quality images but also helps preserving the originality from inputs, significantly improved the MDOS from original LQ images from 2.36 to 4.11.

Although our system has achieved a promising result, there are several cases when CycleGAN generates slightly better visual focus images than our MIINet as shown in Fig. 6. This is the trade-off of adding the perceptual loss into the objective function of CycleGAN. MIINet is forced to keep the characteristics of original inputs while CycleGAN has more freedom to generate close outputs to the "HQ Throat" dataset. Despite that fact, it is worth to mention that the MDOS of MIINet generated images in most cases are higher than CycleGAN since the original attributes have been preserved. For better medical decisions, doctors recommend utilizing both results from CycleGAN and MIINet when diagnosing throat images if necessary. Moreover, proposing more objective quantitative evaluations beside the MDOS metric for our framework could be useful and we intend to develop it in future works.

5   Conclusion

In this paper, we proposed the medical image improvement method (MIINet) to improve the quality of throat images for supporting in making medical diagnosis. With the introduction of the simple but effective perceptual loss, our MIINet largely improved the quality of original LQ throat images and achieved a promising result on the real-world throat images dataset. From the results, we believe that our proposed MIINet method could be a useful tool for supporting doctors in making medical decisions and has a potential impact on different types of medical images.

Acknowledgment. This work was done while the first author did a research internship at Aillis Inc., Japan. We would like to thank all researchers, specially doctor Sho Okiyama, Memori Fukuda, Kazutaka Okuda for their valuable comments and feedback.

References

1. Askarian, B., Yoo, S.C., Chong, J.W.: Novel image processing method for detecting strep throat (streptococcal pharyngitis) using smartphone. Sensors **19**(15), 3307 (2019)
2. Blau, Y., Mechrez, R., Timofte, R., Michaeli, T., Zelnik-Manor, L.: The 2018 PIRM challenge on perceptual image super-resolution. In: Leal-Taixé, L., Roth, S. (eds.) ECCV 2018. LNCS, vol. 11133, pp. 334–355. Springer, Cham (2019). https://doi.org/10.1007/978-3-030-11021-5_21
3. Bulat, A., Tzimiropoulos, G.: Super-fan: integrated facial landmark localization and super-resolution of real-world low resolution faces in arbitrary poses with GANs. In: Proceedings of the IEEE Conference on Computer Vision and Pattern Recognition, pp. 109–117 (2018)
4. Cai, B., Xu, X., Jia, K., Qing, C., Tao, D.: DehazeNet: an end-to-end system for single image haze removal. IEEE Trans. Image Process. **25**(11), 5187–5198 (2016)
5. Cap, Q.H., Tani, H., Uga, H., Kagiwada, S., Iyatomi, H.: Super-resolution for practical automated plant disease diagnosis system. In: The 53rd Annual Conference on Information Sciences and Systems, pp. 1–6 (2019)
6. Dalca, A.V., Bouman, K.L., Freeman, W.T., Rost, N.S., Sabuncu, M.R., Golland, P.: Medical image imputation from image collections. IEEE Trans. Med. Imaging **38**(2), 504–514 (2018)
7. Deng, J., Dong, W., Socher, R., Li, L.J., Li, K., Fei-Fei, L.: ImageNet: a large-scale hierarchical image database. In: Proceedings of the IEEE Conference on Computer Vision and Pattern Recognition, pp. 248–255 (2009)

8. Dong, C., Loy, C.C., He, K., Tang, X.: Image super-resolution using deep convolutional networks. IEEE Trans. Pattern Anal. Mach. Intell. **38**(2), 295–307 (2015)
9. Dudhane, A., Murala, S.: CDNet: single image de-hazing using unpaired adversarial training. In: Proceedings of the IEEE Winter Conference on Applications of Computer Vision, pp. 1147–1155 (2019)
10. Engin, D., Genç, A., Kemal Ekenel, H.: Cycle-dehaze: enhanced CycleGAN for single image dehazing. In: Proceedings of the IEEE Conference on Computer Vision and Pattern Recognition Workshops, pp. 825–833 (2018)
11. Esteva, A., et al.: Dermatologist-level classification of skin cancer with deep neural networks. Nature **542**(7639), 115–118 (2017)
12. Goodfellow, I., Pouget-Abadie, J., Mirza, M., Xu, B., Warde-Farley, D., Ozair, S., et al.: Generative adversarial nets. In: Advances in Neural Information Processing Systems, pp. 2672–2680 (2014)
13. Gulshan, V., et al.: Development and validation of a deep learning algorithm for detection of diabetic retinopathy in retinal fundus photographs. JAMA **316**(22), 2402–2410 (2016)
14. He, J.Y., Wu, X., Jiang, Y.G., Peng, Q., Jain, R.: Hookworm detection in wireless capsule endoscopy images with deep learning. IEEE Trans. Image Process. **27**(5), 2379–2392 (2018)
15. Hirasawa, T., et al.: Application of artificial intelligence using a convolutional neural network for detecting gastric cancer in endoscopic images. Gastric Cancer **21**(4), 653–660 (2018). https://doi.org/10.1007/s10120-018-0793-2
16. Huang, L.Y., Yin, J.L., Chen, B.H., Ye, S.Z.: Towards unsupervised single image dehazing with deep learning. In: Proceedings of the IEEE International Conference on Image Processing, pp. 2741–2745 (2019)
17. Johnson, J., Alahi, A., Fei-Fei, L.: Perceptual losses for real-time style transfer and super-resolution. In: Leibe, B., Matas, J., Sebe, N., Welling, M. (eds.) ECCV 2016. LNCS, vol. 9906, pp. 694–711. Springer, Cham (2016). https://doi.org/10.1007/978-3-319-46475-6_43
18. Kingma, D.P., Ba, J.: Adam: a method for stochastic optimization. In: International Conference on Learning Representations, pp. 1–15 (2015)
19. Ledig, C., et al.: Photo-realistic single image super-resolution using a generative adversarial network. In: Proceedings of the IEEE Conference on Computer Vision and Pattern Recognition, pp. 4681–4690 (2017)
20. Li, B., Peng, X., Wang, Z., Xu, J., Feng, D.: AOD-Net: all-in-one dehazing network. In: Proceedings of the IEEE International Conference on Computer Vision, pp. 4770–4778 (2017)
21. Li, M., Huang, H., Ma, L., Liu, W., Zhang, T., Jiang, Y.: Unsupervised image-to-image translation with stacked cycle-consistent adversarial networks. In: Ferrari, V., Hebert, M., Sminchisescu, C., Weiss, Y. (eds.) ECCV 2018. LNCS, vol. 11213, pp. 186–201. Springer, Cham (2018). https://doi.org/10.1007/978-3-030-01240-3_12
22. Narasimhan, S.G., Nayar, S.K.: Chromatic framework for vision in bad weather. In: Proceedings of the IEEE Conference on Computer Vision and Pattern Recognition, vol. 1, pp. 598–605 (2000)
23. Narasimhan, S.G., Nayar, S.K.: Vision and the atmosphere. Int. J. Comput. Vision **48**(3), 233–254 (2002). https://doi.org/10.1023/A:1016328200723
24. Rajpurkar, P., et al.: CheXNet: radiologist-level pneumonia detection on chest x-rays with deep learning. arXiv:1711.05225 (2017)
25. Rangnekar, A., Mokashi, N., Ientilucci, E., Kanan, C., Hoffman, M.: Aerial spectral super-resolution using conditional adversarial networks. arXiv:1712.08690 (2017)

26. Ren, W., et al.: Gated fusion network for single image dehazing. In: Proceedings of the IEEE Conference on Computer Vision and Pattern Recognition, pp. 3253–3261 (2018)

27. Ronneberger, O., Fischer, P., Brox, T.: U-Net: convolutional networks for biomedical image segmentation. In: Navab, N., Hornegger, J., Wells, W.M., Frangi, A.F. (eds.) MICCAI 2015. LNCS, vol. 9351, pp. 234–241. Springer, Cham (2015). https://doi.org/10.1007/978-3-319-24574-4_28

28. Simonyan, K., Zisserman, A.: Very deep convolutional networks for large-scale image recognition. In: International Conference on Learning Representations, pp. 1–14 (2015)

29. Takiyama, H., et al.: Automatic anatomical classification of esophagogastroduodenoscopy images using deep convolutional neural networks. Sci. Rep. **8**(1), 1–8 (2018)

30. Tobias, R.R.N., et al.: Throat detection and health classification using neural network. In: International Conference on Contemporary Computing and Informatics, pp. 38–43 (2019)

31. Wang, X., et al.: ESRGAN: enhanced super-resolution generative adversarial networks. In: Leal-Taixé, L., Roth, S. (eds.) ECCV 2018. LNCS, vol. 11133, pp. 63–79. Springer, Cham (2019). https://doi.org/10.1007/978-3-030-11021-5_5

32. Yala, A., Lehman, C., Schuster, T., Portnoi, T., Barzilay, R.: A deep learning mammography-based model for improved breast cancer risk prediction. Radiology **292**(1), 60–66 (2019)

33. Yang, D., Sun, J.: Proximal Dehaze-Net: a prior learning-based deep network for single image dehazing. In: Ferrari, V., Hebert, M., Sminchisescu, C., Weiss, Y. (eds.) ECCV 2018. LNCS, vol. 11211, pp. 729–746. Springer, Cham (2018). https://doi.org/10.1007/978-3-030-01234-2_43

34. Yang, X., Xu, Z., Luo, J.: Towards perceptual image dehazing by physics-based disentanglement and adversarial training. In: Proceedings of the AAAI Conference on Artificial Intelligence, pp. 7485–7492 (2018)

35. Yuan, K., Wei, J., Lu, W., Xiong, N.: Single image dehazing via NIN-DehazeNet. IEEE Access **7**, 181348–181356 (2019)

36. Zhao, X., Zhang, Y., Zhang, T., Zou, X.: Channel splitting network for single MR image super-resolution. IEEE Trans. Image Process. **28**(11), 5649–5662 (2019)

37. Zhu, J.Y., Park, T., Isola, P., Efros, A.A.: Unpaired image-to-image translation using cycle-consistent adversarial networks. In: Proceedings of the IEEE International Conference on Computer Vision, pp. 2223–2232 (2017)

Medical Image Tampering Detection: A New Dataset and Baseline

Benjamin Reichman[1], Longlong Jing[1], Oguz Akin[2], and Yingli Tian[1(✉)]

[1] The City University of New York, New York, NY 10031, USA
ytian@ccny.cuny.edu
[2] Memorial Sloan-Kettering Cancer Center, New York, NY 10065, USA

Abstract. The recent advances in algorithmic photo-editing and the vulnerability of hospitals to cyberattacks raises the concern about the tampering of medical images. This paper introduces a new large scale dataset of tampered Computed Tomography (CT) scans generated by different methods, LuNoTim-CT dataset, which can serve as the most comprehensive testbed for comparative studies of data security in healthcare. We further propose a deep learning-based framework, ConnectionNet, to automatically detect if a medical image is tampered. The proposed ConnectionNet is able to handle small tampered regions and achieves promising results and can be used as the baseline for studies of medical image tampering detection.

Keywords: Tamper detection · Healthcare data security · Medical imaging · CT scans · Deep learning

1 Introduction

As a non-invasive process, medical imaging plays essential roles in diagnosis and treatment of diseases by creating visual representations of the interior of a body or the function of some organs or tissues such as the commonly used Magnetic Resonance Imaging (MRI) and CT imaging. While machine learning and artificial intelligence technologies are developed for many online applications of medical imaging analysis [11,22], data security (i.e. vulnerability) becomes a main concern [13]. Patients' medical images can be accessed and manipulated by attackers for multitude of reasons, including financial gain through holding the real data ransom or through insurance fraud [15].

Image tampering can take on many forms. The simplest methods just perform copy-move tampering, resampling, sharpening, blurring, and compression. More intricate methods use classical inpainting algorithms such as Navier-Stokes inpainting, image melding, or patchmatch [3,5,7]. More recent deep learning-based methods use Generative Adversarial Networks (GANs) to generate or change the content of images with high visual realism [12,17]. All these methods can be applied to medical images [10,15,20]. Unlike natural scene images which contains rich texture and color information in high resolutions, most medical

© Springer Nature Switzerland AG 2021
A. Del Bimbo et al. (Eds.): ICPR 2020 Workshops, LNCS 12661, pp. 266–277, 2021.
https://doi.org/10.1007/978-3-030-68763-2_20

images are gray scale with relatively low resolutions which makes the detection of tampered images more challenging for human beings as well as for algorithms.

Some approaches have been proposed to detect non-medical tampered images. Bayar and Stamm proposed a convolutional neural network (CNN) based method to suppress the image content and emphasize the relationship of a pixel with its neighbor [4]. Rao and Ni developed a CNN-based approach to guide the network to detect copy-move tampering by initializing the first layer to only contain high-pass filters [19]. Recently, a few GAN tampering detection methods were reported. Marra *et al.* tested ideas from different areas of tampering detection [14]. Cozzolino *et al.* developed an encoder-decoder network with a latent space that, during training, manually separated the untampered images from the tampered images [6]. Wang *et al.* trained a ResNet-50 to predict whether an image is forged or not [21].

For medical imaging, recently Mirsky *et al.* proposed a deep generative network, CT-GAN, to generate tampered images by producing and inserting visually realistic patches into medical CT images [15]. These images have been reviewed by radiologists in both an open and blind trial respectively and demonstrated misdiagnosis [15]. Although there are some studies exploring medical image tampering detection such as embedding extra information (watermark) into images before transmission [2,8,16] as well as non-intrusive techniques to detect image forgery [10,18,20], currently there is no existing method to detect the more advanced and realistic tampered medical images generated by deep learning methods.

This paper attempts to detect realistic tampered medical images in lung cancer CT scans (see examples in Fig. 1.) To the best of our knowledge, this is the first work to study how to prevent deep learning based medical image tampering. The contributions of this paper are summarized in the following three aspects: (1) We generate a large-scale dataset consisting of $7,202$ total tampered CT scans with $356,217$ slices by different tampering methods including copy-move forgery, classical inpainting, and deep inpainting. This dataset will serve as the most comprehensive testbed for comparative studies of data security in healthcare and directly benefit the research of the medical image analysis community. We will release the dataset and annotations of the forged regions through our research website; (2) We propose a novel framework, ConnectionNet, to detect tampered images by effectively propagating fine-grained features to the decision function; (3) Experimental results demonstrate that our proposed ConnectionNet is effective at detecting tampered images generated by different methods.

2   Tampered Medical Image Dataset Generation

Medical image tampering detection is a burgeoning field. However, researchers create and conduct experiments on their own private datasets [10,20]. The CT-GAN tampered dataset is generated by a GAN for testing and evaluation of tampered images [15], but it is small and only contains 41 CT scans and 821 CT

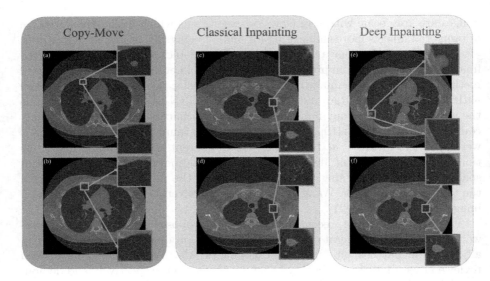

Fig. 1. Examples of our collected LuNoTim-CT dataset which contains tampered lung cancer CT slices generated by three methods: Copy-move, classical inpainting, and deep inpainting. The green patches are original while the red patches are tampered. (a) copying outer lung tissue and moving it into the inner lung; (b) copying inner lung tissue and moving it to another location in the inner lung; (c) removing a nodule by navier-stokes inpainting; (d) removing a nodule by patchmatch inpainting; (e) adding a nodule by deep inpainting; and (f) removing a nodule by deep inpainting. Note that each tampered slice is only changed in one or more small regions. (Color figure online)

slices. To train deep learning-based tampered image detection methods, large-scale datasets are needed for networks to capture the real distribution of the data. Therefore, we have generated a large-scale dataset, LuNoTim-CT (Lung Nodule Tampered Images), consisting of $7,225$ scans with $356,217$ CT slices (see details in Table 1) which can serve as the most comprehensive testbed for comparative studies of data security in healthcare. The LuNoTim-CT dataset will be released through our research website[1].

Our LuNoTim-CT dataset is generated based on the LIDC-IDRI dataset [1], which contains $1,020$ lung CT scans with 883 of them having lung nodules. The CTs in our dataset are tampered by three different tampering methods including copy-move, classical inpainting, and deep inpainting by removing and adding nodules from/to the original CT scans in the original LIDC-IDRI dataset. For each tampered slice, only one tampering method is used at once while the same CT scan can be tampered by different tampering methods at different time. The scans that are excluded from the dataset are the ones where the random process repeatedly led to unrealistic tamperings, either due to what the random process decided or the output of the algorithms used. On average

---

[1] http://media-lab.ccny.cuny.edu/wordpress/datecode.

about 50 slices are tampered per CT scan. There are no restrictions to how many regions are tampered in one slice, however, tampered regions should not overlap if there is more than one region. In particular, the copy-move tampering method is employed to add tampered regions. The classical inpainting tampering method is used to remove nodules in CT slices. The deep inpainting tampering method is employed to do both adding and removing. It is worth noting that only the slices with nodules present in the base LIDC-IDRI dataset can have nodules removed, thus limiting the total number of slices with removals in our database. For adding, there is no such limitation. Some examples of tampered images generated by different methods in our dataset can be found in Fig. 1.

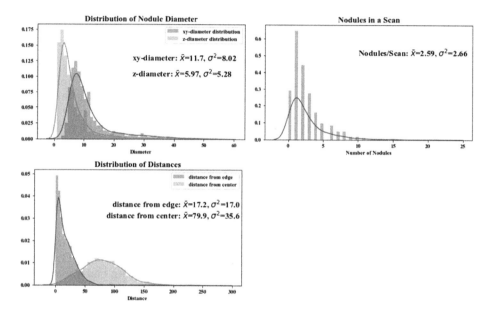

Fig. 2. The statistics of nodule size, number, and location in the LIDC-IDRI dataset which are used as guidance to generate our tampered medical image LuNoTim-CT dataset. Left: Nodule size (unit: pixels); Middle: Number of nodules per scan; Right: Nodule location with distance in pixels.

Tampering Location and Size Selection. To generate realistic fake nodules in lung CT scans, we first calculate the statistics of the nodule size, location, and the number of successive slices a nodule appears in the LIDC-IDRI dataset as shown in Fig. 2. There are on average 2 nodules per CT scan and each nodule may appear on six slices. In addition, we observe that more nodules are located closer to the boundary of the inner lung regions. Then guided by the distributions of size and location, a diverse set of forged nodules are generated in three ways: a) removing the existing nodules; b) randomly adding nodules; and c) randomly moving normal tissue to different areas of the CT slice.

Copy-Move Tampering (CMT). The copy-move tampering method copies an area of an image and moves it to another area. In our LuNoTim-CT dataset, two strategies of copy-move forgeries are performed: 1) moving an outer non-nodule lung area to an inner lung region [see Fig. 1(a)]. As these tampered regions are sufficiently different, it is possible to be observed by human eyes. 2) moving an inner non-nodule lung area to a different position of the inner lung [see Fig. 1(b)]. Since the textures of inner lung regions are self-similar, this type of tampering would be much harder to observe. In both strategies the boundary between the copied patch and its neighborhood is not changed which may presents edge artifacts. The average size of a patch that was copied and moved is between 17×17 pixels. Note that these patches helps disassociate the occurrence of tampering from those of lung nodules. The copy-move method contributes $3,823$ scans ($124,367$ tampered slices) where non-nodule areas are changed.

Classical Inpainting Tampering (CIT). Inpainting algorithms are a class of algorithms that fill in missing patches of an image. Two classical inpainting algorithms are employed to generate tampered CT slices by removing lung nodules: Navier-Stokes inpainting and PatchMatch guided inpainting. Navier-Stokes inpainting is a physics based algorithm that uses ideas of flow from fluid dynamics to propagate the gradient of image intensity smoothly into the inpainted area [5] [see Fig. 1(c)]. PatchMatch inpainting uses a random algorithm to efficiently find patches of images that are similar [3]. Patches with nodules are substituted with similar patches without nodules [see Fig. 1(d)]. The average size of tampered regions is 31×31. The two classical inpainting methods generated $1,753$ CT scans with $29,132$ tampered slices where nodules are removed.

Deep Inpainting Tampering (DIT). Deep inpainting uses deep neural networks to determine how a missing patch of an image should be filled. Compare to copy-move and classical inpainting methods, deep inpainting generates more realistic tampered regions which are harder to detect. In our paper, CT-GAN, a method verified to cause misdiagnosis by radiologists, is employed to add and remove nodules [15]. CT-GAN combines GAN with additive white gaussian noise to blend the generated patch which is further blended by combining the GAN generated cuboid with the original cuboid [15]. The average patch size for these blending procedures is 50×50. Deep inpainting method contributes 758 scans where nodules ($77,898$ slices) are removed and 891 scans ($124,495$ slices) where nodules are added.

In order to verify that the generated dataset is similar to the original dataset that it is based on, Principal Component Analysis (PCA) is applied to image patches from both the generated LuNoTim-CT dataset and the original LIDC-IDRI dataset. PCA aims to find the orthogonal vectors of the training data that explains the most amount of variance between samples [9]. The PCA model was trained using patches from both datasets with the goal of reducing a patch to data along two orthogonal vectors. Then samples from different parts of the LuNoTim-CT and the LIDC-IDRI datasets that were withheld during training were inputted to the PCA model to visualize where in the reduced, two dimen-

Table 1. Amount of CT scans and slices generated by different methods in our LuNoTim-CT dataset. "CMT": Copy-Move Tampering; "CIT": Classical Inpainting Tampering; and "DIT": Deep Inpainting Tampering.

Tampering method	Adding		Removing	
	# CT scans	# CT slices	# CT scans	# CT slices
CMT	3,823	124,692	–	–
CIT	–	–	1,753	29,132
DIT	891	124,495	758	77,898
Total	4,714	249,187	2,511	107,030

sional space they would appear. The results shown in Fig. 3 show that there is a high degree of overlap between the untampered and the tampered datasets. The CT-GAN added portion of the dataset overlaps the most with the untampered dataset, whereas the narrowest overlap comes from the Patchmatch and Navier-Stokes portion of the dataset.

Fig. 3. The overlap of the untampered slices and the tampered slices is demonstrated in two dimensions reduced by applying PCA. The highest degree of overlap is observed for tampered CTs with added patches, whereas the narrowest overlap in the removal part of the dataset.

3   Framework for Medical Tampering Detection

3.1   Architectures

A natural choice for the network $F(x|\theta)$ would be a classification network. The vanilla VGG network makes predictions based on high-level features (fixed dimension vectors) which are extracted by hierarchical convolution layers. The max-pooling layer and global average pooling layer helps the network to capture high-level global features, but leaves low-level features ignored. However, detecting tampering artifacts requires the network to identify tiny regions (size) from a full size image. To augment the capability of capturing fine-grained features, as shown in Fig. 4, we propose ConnectionNet to forward the fine-grained features from shallow layers to the fully-connected layers to aid in prediction.

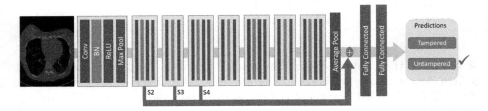

Fig. 4. The proposed framework of ConnectionNet for tampered medical image detection. The backbone of the network is VGG-11. S_n indicates a skip connection that forwards the nth convolutional layer to a 1×1 convolution layer that is then sent to an average pooling layer. These fine-grained features from these skip connections are then appended to the output of the network's average pooling layer.

3.2   Model Parameterization

Let $\mathcal{D} = \{(X_1, y_1), (X_2, y_2), ..., (X_n, y_n)\}$ denotes training data of size N, and the i-th datapoint (X_i, y_i) indicate an image from the dataset and its corresponding label represent whether it is tampered or not. The ConnectionNet, $F(x|\theta)$, takes an input image x and predicts if it is tampered by optimizing the parameters of the network θ using D. Cross-entropy loss is employed to optimize the network. Given a medical image x_i, the cross entropy loss is formulated as:

$$loss(x_i|\theta) := -\sum_i (y_i \log(F(x_i|\theta)) + (1 - y_i) \log(1 - F(x_i|\theta))). \quad (1)$$

Given a set of N training pairs $D = \{x_i\}_{i=0}^N$, the overall training loss function is defined as:

$$loss(D) = \min_\theta \frac{1}{N} \sum_{i=1}^N loss(x_i|\theta). \quad (2)$$

4   Experiments and Results

4.1   Experimental Setup

The dataset was split in a 64%-16%-20% scheme for training, validation, and testing, respectively. In our experiments, Stochastic Gradient Descent (SGD) optimizer is used with an initial learning rate of 0.001, a momentum of 0.9, and weight decay of 0.0005. It is trained over 30 epochs using a batch size of 6, evenly sampling from the tampered and untampered dataset. To thoroughly evaluate the performance, we evaluated the models using different criteria including precision, accuracy, recall, and Area Under the Curve (AUC).

4.2   Ablation Study of Backbone Networks

Table 2. Using VGG as a backbone network results in better performance in all metrics except AUC other than the ResNet backbone, therefore, it is adopted as the backbone of our framework.

Backbone	Input	Accuracy	Precision	Recall	F1 Score	AUC
Baseline networks						
VGG	512×512 Image	**0.83**	**0.88**	**0.73**	**0.80**	0.59
ResNet-18	512×512 Image	0.67	0.72	0.57	0.63	**0.75**
ResNet-50	512×512 Image	0.798	0.87	0.66	0.75	0.51

As shown in Table 2, for full resolution images (512×512), ResNet50 outperforms ResNet18 by more than 10% on the DIT portion of the dataset. The VGG network achieves better performance than ResNet in all metrics including classification accuracy, precision, recall, and F1 score. In the ImageNet dataset, the performance of VGG is 68.9% while the performance of ResNet is 76% which is almost 7% higher than the VGG network. This observation indicates that ResNet is more powerful on natural images, however, for medical image tampering detection, VGG significantly outperforms ResNet.

Different from natural image tampering, only one or more small regions are tampered (usually about 50×50 pixels) in each image in our tampered medical image LuNoTim-CT dataset. To capture global features, the current mainstream neural networks employ a max-pooling layer or stride convolution to extract high-level invariant features. With these networks, the information of the tampered region is overwhelmed in the global features. So we tested another straightforward method by training and testing networks with patches cropped from the images. As shown in Table 2, the patch-based method has a relatively high accuracy from being able to identify untampered images, but has very low precision and recall compared to the full resolution method. Thus, a patch-based approach is not optimal in this situation.

4.3   Results of Our Framework

As shown in Table 3 by forwarding the features from the second-convolution layer to the fully connected layer, the recall of the VGG-S2 network significantly improved by 7%. The VGG-S2S3S4 network greatly improves on the precision (+8%) and AUC (+0.32) of the vanilla VGG network while also slightly increasing the overall accuracy (+1%) and F1 score (+2%).

Table 3. The ConnectionNet model achieves a much higher AUC, precision, and recall, depending on the amount and location of skip connections, all while maintaining a similar accuracy to VGG.

Backbone	Input	Accuracy	Precision	Recall	F1 score	AUC
VGG	512 × 512 Image	0.83	0.88	0.73	0.80	0.59
VGG-S1	512 × 512 Image	0.79	0.84	0.72	0.77	0.87
VGG-S2	512 × 512 Image	0.82	0.81	**0.83**	0.82	0.91
VGG-S1S2	512 × 512 Image	0.81	0.82	0.80	0.81	0.90
VGG-S2S3S4	512 × 512 Image	**0.84**	**0.96**	0.72	**0.82**	**0.91**

4.4   Generalizability of the ConnectionNet

Table 4. All networks trained on the DIT portion of the dataset and tested on the CMT, CIT, and DIT datasets generalize pretty well by keeping the same level accuracy, precision, and recall while increasing in the AUC metric. Varying ConnectionNet networks outperform VGG in the different metrics used.

Backbone	Input	Accuracy	Precision	Recall	F1 score	AUC
VGG	512 × 512 Image	0.83	0.90	0.75	0.82	0.90
ResNet-18	512 × 512 Image	0.70	0.74	0.62	0.68	0.78
ResNet-50	512 × 512 Image	0.81	0.90	0.71	0.79	0.89
VGG-S1	512 × 512 Image	0.82	0.85	0.79	0.82	0.90
VGG-S2	512 × 512 Image	0.81	0.79	**0.83**	0.81	0.90
VGG-S1S2	512 × 512 Image	0.83	0.83	0.82	**0.83**	**0.91**
VGG-S2S3S4	512 × 512 Image	**0.85**	**0.96**	0.72	0.82	**0.91**

We further evaluate the generalizability of the proposed ConnectionNet on tampered medical images generated by different methods. ConnectionNet is trained only on the DIT portion of the dataset and tested on the three types of tampered images including DIT, CMT, and CIT. As shown in Table 4, our proposed method performs consistently well and improves on vanilla VGG by 2% in terms of accuracy on a testing set that consists of three different tampering methods. Compared to vanilla VGG, the recall of our VGG-S1S2 and the precision of our VGG-S2S3S4 is significantly higher than other networks. The consistency of the VGG-S1S2 and VGG-S2S3S4 across the different datasets shows that the proposed framework has strong generalization ability across different types of tampering. Table 5 shows the results of the proposed framework and baselines across each section of the dataset. We observe that the lowest accuracy and recall occur when tumors are added to CT scans as opposed to when tumors are removed from CT scans. This suggests that it is more difficult to spot when elements are added to a CT scan than when they are removed. As shown in Fig. 3, the portion of the dataset where elements are added has a high degree of overlap (less distinguishable) with the untampered portion of the dataset. On the other hand, the removed portion of the dataset has a narrower range of overlap with the untampered portion of the dataset (more distinguishable).

Table 5. Granular accuracy/recall results of each network on each section of the dataset.

Backbone	Untampered scans	CT-GAN A	CMT	CT-GAN R	PatchMatch	Navier-Stokes R	Overall
VGG	0.83/**0.75**	0.78/0.64	**0.83/0.76**	0.90/**0.89**	0.89/**0.86**	0.87/0.82	0.83/**0.75**
VGG-S1S2	**0.88**/0.72	0.75/**0.65**	0.78/0.69	0.89/0.85	0.85/0.80	0.91/**0.88**	0.84/0.72
VGG-S2S3S4	0.85/0.73	**0.79**/0.62	**0.83**/0.70	**0.92**/0.88	**0.90**/0.84	**0.92**/0.86	**0.85**/0.73

5 Conclusion

This paper tackles the important medical data security problem of how to detect realistic tampered medical images generated by advanced deep learning methods. We have generated a large scale dataset of tampered chest CT scans and proposed the ConnectionNet framework for detecting tampered CT slices. Our ConnectionNet framework achieves better accuracy and a higher AUC score than the vanilla VGG network. This demonstrates that propagating fine-grained features to the decision function is an effective way to learn the small scale features that helps to detect the removed patches. Our future work includes extending the dataset to more different types of images in addition to CT scans, conducting independent evaluations by radiologists, and further improve the accuracy of unauthorized alteration detection in medical images.

Acknowledgements. This work was supported in part by National Science Foundation under award numbers IIS-1400802 and IIS-2041307, Memorial Sloan Kettering Cancer Center Support Grant/Core Grant P30 CA008748, and Intelligence Community Center of Academic Excellence (IC CAE) at Rutgers University.

References

1. Armato III, S.G., et al.: The lung image database consortium (LIDC) and image database resource initiative (IDRI): a completed reference database of lung nodules on CT scans. Med. Phys. **38**(2), 915–931 (2011)

2. Arsalan, M., Malik, S.A., Khan, A.: Intelligent reversible watermarking in integer wavelet domain for medical images. J. Syst. Softw. **85**(4), 883–894 (2012)
3. Barnes, C., Shechtman, E., Finkelstein, A., Goldman, D.B.: PatchMatch: a randomized correspondence algorithm for structural image editing. ACM Trans. Graph. (Proc. SIGGRAPH) **28**(3), 24 (2009)
4. Bayar, B., Stamm, M.C.: A deep learning approach to universal image manipulation detection using a new convolutional layer. In: Proceedings of the 4th ACM Workshop on Information Hiding and Multimedia Security, pp. 5–10 (2016)
5. Bertalmio, M., Bertozzi, A.L., Sapiro, G.: Navier-stokes, fluid dynamics, and image and video inpainting. In: Proceedings of the 2001 IEEE Computer Society Conference on Computer Vision and Pattern Recognition. CVPR 2001, vol. 1, p. I-I. IEEE (2001)
6. Cozzolino, D., Thies, J., Rössler, A., Riess, C., Nießner, M., Verdoliva, L.: ForensicTransfer: weakly-supervised domain adaptation for forgery detection. arXiv preprint arXiv:1812.02510 (2018)
7. Darabi, S., Shechtman, E., Barnes, C., Goldman, D.B., Sen, P.: Image melding: combining inconsistent images using patch-based synthesis. ACM Trans. Graph. (TOG) (Proceedings of SIGGRAPH 2012) **31**(4), 82:1–82:10 (2012)
8. Das, S., Kundu, M.K.: Effective management of medical information through ROI-lossless fragile image watermarking technique. Comput. Methods Programs Biomed. **111**(3), 662–675 (2013)
9. Geladi, P., Isaksson, H., Lindqvist, L., Wold, S., Esbensen, K.: Principal component analysis of multivariate images. Chemometr. Intell. Lab. Syst. **5**(3), 209–220 (1989). https://doi.org/10.1016/0169-7439(89)80049-8, http://www.sciencedirect.com/science/article/pii/0169743989800498
10. Ghoneim, A., Muhammad, G., Amin, S.U., Gupta, B.: Medical image forgery detection for smart healthcare. IEEE Commun. Mag. **56**(4), 33–37 (2018)
11. Gong, E., Pauly, J.M., Wintermark, M., Zaharchuk, G.: Deep learning enables reduced gadolinium dose for contrast-enhanced brain MRI. J. Magn. Reson. Imaging **48**(2), 330–340 (2018)
12. Goodfellow, I., et al.: Generative adversarial nets. In: Advances in Neural Information Processing Systems, pp. 2672–2680 (2014)
13. Jalali, M.S., Kaiser, J.P.: Cybersecurity in hospitals: a systematic, organizational perspective. J. Med. Internet Res. **20**(5), e10059 (2018)
14. Marra, F., Gragnaniello, D., Cozzolino, D., Verdoliva, L.: Detection of GAN-generated fake images over social networks. In: 2018 IEEE Conference on Multimedia Information Processing and Retrieval (MIPR), pp. 384–389. IEEE (2018)
15. Mirsky, Y., Mahler, T., Shelef, I., Elovici, Y.: CT-GAN: malicious tampering of 3D medical imagery using deep learning. In: 28th {USENIX} Security Symposium ({USENIX} Security 2019), pp. 461–478 (2019)
16. Nyeem, H., Boles, W., Boyd, C.: A review of medical image watermarking requirements for teleradiology. J. Digit. Imaging **26**(2), 326–343 (2013). https://doi.org/10.1007/s10278-012-9527-x
17. Pathak, D., Krahenbuhl, P., Donahue, J., Darrell, T., Efros, A.A.: Context encoders: feature learning by inpainting. In: Proceedings of the IEEE Conference on Computer Vision and Pattern Recognition, pp. 2536–2544 (2016)
18. Qureshi, M.A., Deriche, M.: A bibliography of pixel-based blind image forgery detection techniques. Sig. Process. Image Commun. **39**, 46–74 (2015)
19. Rao, Y., Ni, J.: A deep learning approach to detection of splicing and copy-move forgeries in images. In: 2016 IEEE International Workshop on Information Forensics and Security (WIFS), pp. 1–6. IEEE (2016)

20. Ulutas, G., Ustubioglu, A., Ustubioglu, B., Nabiyev, V.V., Ulutas, M.: Medical image tamper detection based on passive image authentication. J. Digit. Imaging **30**(6), 695–709 (2017). https://doi.org/10.1007/s10278-017-9961-x
21. Wang, S.Y., Wang, O., Zhang, R., Owens, A., Efros, A.A.: CNN-generated images are surprisingly easy to spot... for now. arXiv preprint arXiv:1912.11035 (2019)
22. Yi, X., Walia, E., Babyn, P.: Generative adversarial network in medical imaging: a review. Med. Image Anal. **58**, 101552 (2019)

Deep Learning for Human Embryo Classification at the Cleavage Stage (Day 3)

Astrid Zeman[1] , Anne-Sofie Maerten[1](✉) , Annemie Mengels[2], Lie Fong Sharon[2], Carl Spiessens[2], and Hans Op de Beeck[1]

[1] Department Brain & Cognition & Leuven Brain Institute, KU Leuven, 3000 Leuven, Belgium
annesofie.maerten@kuleuven.be
[2] Leuvens Universitair Fertiliteitscentrum, UZ Leuven, 3000 Leuven, Belgium

Abstract. To date, deep learning has assisted in classifying embryos as early as day 5 after insemination. We investigated whether deep neural networks could successfully predict the destiny of each embryo (discard or transfer) at an even earlier stage, namely at day 3. We first assessed whether the destiny of each embryo could be derived from technician scores, using a simple regression model. We then explored whether a deep neural network could make accurate predictions using images alone. We found that a simple 8-layer network was able to achieve 75.24% accuracy of destiny prediction, outperforming deeper, state-of-the-art models that reached 68.48% when applied to our middle slice images. Increasing focal points from a single (middle slice) to three slices per image did not improve accuracy. Instead, accounting for the "batch effect", that is, predicting an embryo's destiny in relation to other embryos from the same batch, greatly improved accuracy, to a level of 84.69% for unseen cases. Importantly, when analyzing cases of transferred embryos, we found that our lean, deep neural network predictions were correlated (0.65) with clinical outcomes.

Keywords: Deep learning · Visual expertise · Embryology

1 Introduction

In the context of in vitro fertilization, embryo assessment is used to determine the health of each sample and ultimately the destiny of every embryo: to be transferred, discarded or cryogenically preserved. Embryo assessment requires visual expertise, which is acquired through visual learning over extensive training [1].

Embryo quality assessment is carried out over multiple days and stages. From a clinical perspective, assessments that are carried out on day 3 are particularly important, since this is when embryos are traditionally transferred [2]. At this stage, the cleavage stage, the most relevant scoring dimensions are the number and size of cells (blastomeres) and the degree of fragmentation (Fig. 1). These three variables are shown to be useful predictors of embryo viability [3]. An ideal embryo at day 3 would have eight, equally-sized blastomeres with less than 10% fragmentation (Fig. 1A) [4]. Embryos that divide

---

A. Zeman and A.-S. Maerten–Equal contribution.

© Springer Nature Switzerland AG 2021
A. Del Bimbo et al. (Eds.): ICPR 2020 Workshops, LNCS 12661, pp. 278–292, 2021.
https://doi.org/10.1007/978-3-030-68763-2_21

slowly and fail to reach the 8-cell stage at day 3 (Fig. 1B) or divide too fast (Fig. 1C) are likely to have reduced success in implantation [4]. In addition, the degree and pattern of fragmentation, defined as anuclear, membrane-bound extra-cellular cytoplasmic structures, is negatively correlated with pregnancy and implantation (Fig. 1D) [5]. Unequally sized blastomeres (referred to as asymmetry) may reflect an unequal partitioning of proteins, mRNA and mitochondria during cell division, potentially impairing further embryo development and leading to chromosomal aberrations (Fig. 1E) [6].

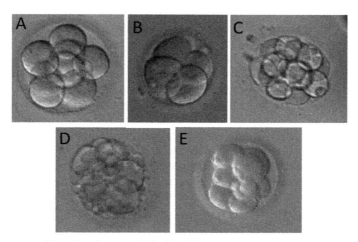

Fig. 1. Examples of Day 3 embryos. A) Ideal healthy embryo. B) and C) illustrate low and high scores on number of blastomeres. D) High fragmentation. E) High asymmetry.

Previously, there have been multiple attempts at automating morphological scoring or the classification of embryos. Recent studies have recruited deep convolutional neural networks (CNNs) to grade the appearance characteristics of embryos [7] or predict embryo quality [8, 9]. Iwata et al. [8] implemented a CNN to discriminate good- from poor- quality embryos, using a limited dataset of only 118 embryos, 90 of which were used for training, and 10 for validation. Each embryo was photographed using high-resolution, time-lapsed images taken every 2 min, resulting in 2000 photographs per embryo. Their network reached a validation accuracy of 80% on good-quality embryos (4 out of 5). Kragh et al. [7] used time-lapse images of 8664 embryos to train a recurrent neural network (RNN) to grade the inner cell mass and trophectoderm, two relevant scoring dimensions at the blastocyst stage (day 5). First, they trained multiple CNNs on static images, created by combining three grayscale microscopic images at different focal depths into a single 'rgb' image. Then, these CNNs were incorporated into a single RNN, which represented temporal information for each of the time-lapse image sequences. As such, the network was trained on images at 3 different focal depths and multiple different timepoints for each embryo. The RNN could predict the inner cell mass and trophectoderm score with an accuracy of 71.9% and 76.4% respectively, whereas embryologists scored 65.1% and 73.8%. In addition, the network could predict pregnancy outcome to the same level of accuracy as embryologists. To date, Khosravi et al. [9] have reported the highest prediction accuracy of any study so far, at 96.94%. They trained a CNN using 12,001 images from 1674 embryos (good and poor quality) and evaluated performance on 1930 images from 283 embryos, taking the majority vote for images of the same embryo. The performance reported in this study is based on relatively easy cases of high- and low-quality embryos at a day 5 blastocyst stage, excluding fair-quality cases that are the most difficult to categorize.

In our study, we focused on assessing embryos at a day 3 stage, given its importance from a clinical perspective [2]. In contrast to other studies, we had access to a much larger dataset than has ever been previously published – stacked tiff images from 38,000 embryos, with each layer of the stack corresponding to a different focal depth plane. We aimed to classify embryos of any quality at the cleavage stage (day 3). Specifically, we addressed the following questions: a) What is the highest performance that can be achieved by assessing samples in standalone fashion, using only technician scores? b) How well does the state-of-the-art CNN model perform on our data, given only middle-slice images from the stacked tiff images? c) What is the highest CNN performance that we can achieve, by assessing samples in standalone fashion, using only the middle slice of each embryo? d) Do multiple slices improve performance of our CNN? e) Does the implementation of a CNN with multiple branches, one for each dimension in the technician score, improve performance? f) Does performance improve if we no longer assess images in a standalone fashion, and by how much? h) Do CNN predictions correlate with real-world pregnancy outcomes, i.e. implantation rate?

2 Method

2.1 Images

The current study was approved by the Ethical Committee of UZ Leuven. We sourced approximately 38,000 records with technician scores from hospital UZLeuven, where each record corresponds to multiple images at varying focal depth of a single embryo. These records were taken at day 3, when the destiny of each embryo was also determined. Example images from our dataset are shown in Fig. 1. At this time period, the zygote has not yet become a blastocyst, which usually occurs around day 5 and is typically the stage that is used in automated systems for evaluating cell destiny.

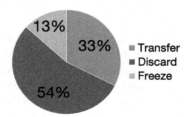

Fig. 2. Cell destiny over full dataset. 20.72k embryos are discarded, 12.38k are transferred, and 5.08k are cryogenically frozen.

Our main aim in this first study was to predict the transfer versus discard decision for each embryo. We first excluded all "freeze" decisions in our dataset. Then we randomly excluded part of the "discard" cases in order to ensure a balanced dataset (Fig. 2). Our secondary aim was to investigate whether CNNs were able to predict technician scores, and so potentially use this information for discard versus transfer decisions. In predicting technician scores, we also excluded records with missing values. Ultimately, we used 20.30k embryos for training, 1.79k for testing and 1.79k for validation, resulting in an 85:7.5:7.5 split.

For each embryo, we had z-stack images in tiff format taken with Evidence software (IHMedical). The embryos were imaged using a Zeiss Axiovert Observer Z1 microscope with 20x magnification. Hoffman modulation contrast (HMC) microscopy was used to increase contrast. The images were taken with a CCD camera (Sony ICX285) with a resolution of 1392 × 1040 for each slice in a z-stack. Given that the images were taken over a time span of more than 5 years, the exact number of focal planes in the third dimension (stack size) varied considerably from a single slice to 144 slices, with the majority of cases falling somewhere in between. We investigated two different image formats to present to the networks: 1. Only the middle slice of the stack and 2. a multi-slice format. All images were resized and cropped to 256 × 256 pixels and stored in jpg format. For the multi-slice images, we opted to select 3 slices (including the middle transversal) and store these as a three-channel 'rgb' image, similar to the method reported in Kragh et al. [7]. Because the stack size varied per record, selecting consistent slice indices across embryos would not result in the selection of slices with an equal distance between them. Furthermore, the outer slices were low in structure and often contained very little information due to blurring. Therefore, we aimed to include slices that would maximize the combined information in the three-channel images. We calculated the correlation between the middle slice and all other slices and averaged these correlations across embryos with the same stack size (referred to as a 'group'). Figure 3 shows that these group-averaged correlations followed a peak-shaped distribution. Based on these group-averaged curves, we computed the slice indices that determined which slices to include for an embryo belonging to a certain group. First, we computed the value halfway between the peak and asymptote for both tails. Second, we selected the slice index that was closest to the halfway point for each tail. Lastly, we averaged these two indices for the final slice selection, to ensure that slices were equidistant from the middle on both sides of the curve.

To assess the viability of combining 3 focal point images as separate channels within a single 'rgb' image, we also assessed performance when separating the 3 focal point images into three separate images, resulting in a dataset 3 times as large. Thus, we trained the networks on a dataset of 20.30k middle slice images, a dataset of 20.30k rgb images and a larger dataset of 60.90k training images. This allowed for performance to be compared across these different image formats.

2.2 State-of-the-Art CNN Model: STORK

The CNN model with the highest accuracy so far, in predicting embryo destiny, is named STORK [9]. The model assesses embryos at the blastocyst stage (day 5), using records with multiple (up to 7) focal points at different depths per embryo. Architecturally, the main variant of STORK is an implementation of Google's Inception v1 model [10]. STORK is trained using 12,001 images, of which 6000 are sourced from 877 good

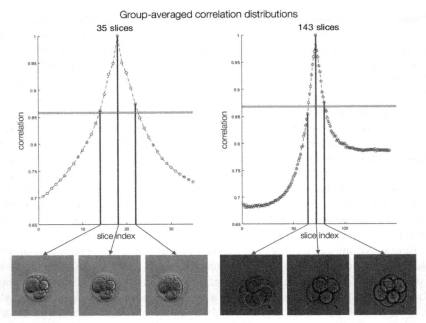

Fig. 3. Method to select 3 slices for the three-channel images, from the raw, multi-slice images. Group-averaged curves are shown for stacks with 35 (left) or 143 (right) slices. Each data point (blue open circle) represents the average correlation of a slice at a given index with the middle slice, for stacks of the same size. Red lines indicate the average halfway point between the peak and asymptotes of each curve. Blue lines connect the three selected values on the curve to the three corresponding indices from one example embryo. (Color figure online)

quality embryos, and 6001 images are from 887 poor quality embryos. STORK then classifies an image as "poor" or "good", indicating the pregnancy likelihood.

The authors report that STORK was able to reach 96.94% accuracy in its assessment of easy cases (good and poor-quality embryos). In regard to difficult cases (fair quality embryos), STORK classified these as 82% good quality (526 embryos) and 18% poor quality (114 embryos). These STORK classifications showed a statistically significant difference when mapped to pregnancy outcomes, with embryos classified as poor-quality showing a lower likelihood of positive live birth (50.9%), compared to those classified as good quality (61.4% positive live birth).

We trained the STORK architecture for 50k iterations (490 epochs), using the same training regime as Khosravi et al. [9], on our dataset of day 3 embryos, to see how this state-of-the-art model performs on classification at the cleavage stage.

2.3   Our CNN Models

We opted for a leaner approach, using relatively shallower networks, to predict embryo destiny. We opted for two different architectures. The first network was the standard Alexnet architecture [11], an 8 layer, serially connected architecture, with 5 convolutional layers followed by 3 fully-connected ones (Fig. 4A). The output is the probability of a discard or transfer destiny. The second network is a branched network, with the input feeding into three separate, parallel architectures. The output of each branch represents each of the three technician scores (number of blastomeres, fragmentation and asymmetry). Each branch has 8 serially connected layers, with 5 convolutional followed by 3 fully-connected (Fig. 4B). Both networks had a dropout rate of 0.4 in the first two fully-connected layers (of each branch) and were trained for 250 epochs with SGD as optimizer and MSE as loss function. The learning rate was set to 0.05 with a decay of 0.001 and momentum of 0.9. In addition, we employed data augmentation, such as rotations and brightness shifts, to account for strong variations in luminance of the images in our dataset. Alternatively, we tried mean-centering the luminance of our images, which yielded similar results. Because the data augmentation method does not require image-preprocessing, we opted for this approach. Additionally, we explored slight variations in network architecture (varying the number of filters per convolutional layer), training regime (Adam as optimizer, cross-entropy as loss function) and datasplit (randomly dividing the train, validation and test set for different runs) and achieved comparable results for all these variations. This suggests that our results are fairly robust. The networks were implemented using the Keras framework with Tensorflow 2.0 [12].

2.4   Implantation Rate

The implantation rate was calculated per embryo score, on data acquired between 2010 and 2017 at the fertility center at UZLeuven. Calculations were based on all fresh single embryo transfers within this time period. The implantation rate is defined as the number of gestational sacs observed, divided by the number of embryos transferred (usually expressed as a percentage) [13]. We included embryo scores with at least 50 transfers. The total number of transfers used for this calculation was 4483.

3   Results

All our model implementations resulted in similar performance levels on training, validation and test sets. Consequently, we report solely the test set performance, unless stated otherwise.

3.1   Regression Model of Technician Scores for Standalone Cases

We first analyzed the relationship between cell destiny (transfer vs discard) and the three technician scores of asymmetry, fragmentation and number of blastomeres. We implemented a method akin to a regression model, by training a shallow neural network with a single hidden layer (128 nodes) to predict the cell destiny, given the three scores as input. Validation performance reached 82.96% and test performance reached 83.64%. This provided us with a ceiling value of performance when assessing each embryo individually, if a deep network would be able to glean all technician scores from the images. Another interpretation of these results, is that 17.04% of decisions cannot be explained by these 3 values alone.

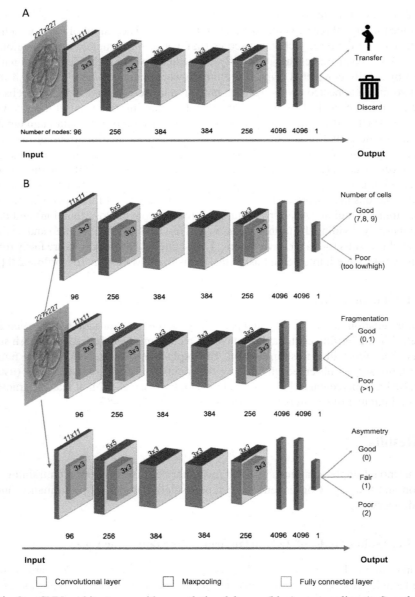

Fig. 4. Our CNN architectures, with convolutional layers (blue), maxpooling (red) and fully connected (green). A. Simple 8-layer network (Alexnet) trained to predict the destiny of an embryo; B. Branched network trained to predict the relevant scoring dimensions used to assess embryo-quality at day 3. Input dimensions and filters are shown in italics and the number of filters or nodes within a layer is shown below each layer representation. (Color figure online)

Note that the technician scores of asymmetry, fragmentation and number of blastomeres are not entirely independent. The number of cells is negatively correlated with fragmentation ($\rho = -0.38$, p $< .05$), meaning that a higher number of cells in an embryo is often accompanied by a lower degree of fragmentation. In addition, fragmentation is positively correlated with asymmetry ($\rho = 0.26$, p $< .05$), meaning that the more fragments, the more asymmetrical cells are within an embryo. Lastly, the number of cells and asymmetry are not correlated with one another ($\rho = -0.008$, p $= 0.21$).

3.2 STORK Performance on Middle Slice and Multi-slice Images

We applied STORK [9] to our data, using only the middle slice of each record. In this way, we were able to assess the robustness of a previously successful technique, that can be considered as the state-of-the-art. To iterate the differences between our data and that which has been used to train STORK, our images are not time-lapsed (only a single snapshot is taken) and our data is taken at a day 3 instead of a day 5 stage. So, it is unclear how this network architecture would perform on day 3 images that have an important place in clinical practice. In addition, we trained on all images, not only good- and poor-quality cases, and we did not perform any pre-processing. We achieved 68.48% accuracy using the STORK architecture on our middle slice images. This accuracy is averaged across 5 runs in which STORK was trained from scratch. The standard deviation across these runs was 1.79, which gives an indication of the order of magnitude that performance differences should have to consider them meaningful.

In addition to this attempt with middle-slice images, we also trained and tested STORK on 3-focal point images, resulting in a test performance of 67.40%. When separating the 3 focal point images into 3 separate images, and training on a dataset 3 times as large, performance was at 66.58% and by incorporating the majority vote (as was done originally in STORK) performance rose slightly to 68.12%. These results indicate that training on a dataset three times as large does not necessarily improve performance, compared to using only the middle focal point.

3.3 CNN Performance on Middle Slice and Multi-slice Images in Standalone Fashion

Using our simple implementation (8-layer CNN), we first assessed performance on middle slice images. The 8-layer CNN achieved 75.24% accuracy, with a standard deviation of 1.31 over 5 runs. When combining multiple focal points into a multi-slice image, performance was roughly equivalent, at 75.06%. When separating the three focal point images into separate images, and training on a dataset three times as large, performance was at 75.98%, and by incorporating a majority vote for each embryo, performance rose slightly to 76.27%. Given these results, we see that performance based on the simplest input implementation was not markedly improved by more complex input formats, when considering the standard deviation across multiple runs. Importantly, this performance of an 8-layer CNN is much better than what we obtained with STORK, with on average a 7% improvement (Fig. 5).

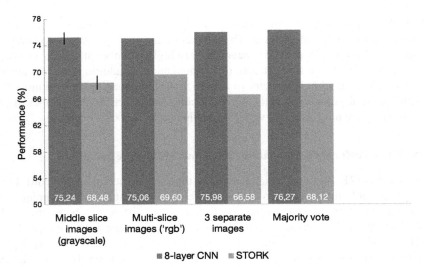

Fig. 5. Performance comparison of the single-branch, 8-layer CNN and STORK. Results on the left (Middle slice images, Multi-slice images) were obtained by training on 20.30k images. Results on the right (3 separate images, Majority vote) were obtained by training on 60.90k images.

3.4 CNN Performance on Individual Technician Scores

We trained a multi-branch CNN to determine which features the network was capable of learning, by testing predictions for each of the technician scores of fragmentation, asymmetry and number of blastomeres. The output of each branch was i) a binary prediction of the number of cells (7,8,9 vs less/more) ii) a ternary prediction of asymmetry (0 vs 1 vs 2) iii) a binary prediction of fragmentation (0,1 vs > 1). These category boundaries were chosen to maintain a relatively balanced dataset given the frequencies of the different values. In each of these aforementioned output cases, the first value indicates higher embryo viability compared to latter values.

The branched model predicted the number of cells at 76.48%, fragmentation at 84.07% and asymmetry at 41.69%, when training and testing on middle slice images. This indicated that the model was able to predict two out of three technician scores fairly well, but did not successfully predict asymmetry. Note that the asymmetry prediction is still above chance, since the ternary decision for asymmetry means that chance level is at 33.33%, versus 50% for the binary decisions related to fragmentation and cell number. Overall, the performance of the multi-branch CNN on the individual dimensions was not markedly better than performance of the leaner, single-branch architecture that immediately predicted the transfer/discard decision, which motivated us to do further tests with the single-branch, 8-layer CNN.

3.5 Batch Effect

Typically, there are multiple embryos collected from a single patient in the same procedure that are processed in parallel. We refer to such a set of embryos as a batch. The embryo that is judged to be the most viable in the batch will be selected for transfer. Therefore, batch context is highly relevant for the destiny of each embryo. Excellent embryos may not be transferred, if the batch consists of many viable embryos. Alternatively, relatively poor embryos may be transferred, if the batch consists of only poor-quality embryos. Taking such batch information into account may improve performance, since we would no longer assess images in a standalone fashion.

To investigate the batch effect, we paired together two images from the same batch that had different destinies (i.e. one was transferred and one was discarded), and compared predictions for each of these two cases using the 8-layer CNN. In other words, we assessed how often the network predicted a 'transfer' outcome with a higher probability for the first example in each pair. As such, predictions for each embryo were judged in a relative context according to each pairing, rather than defining a transfer outcome based on individual probabilities being greater than 0.5. Here we imposed a constraint for the network to make a binary decision, to allow for performance comparison with standalone assessment. In our dataset, however, the batch size varied from a single embryo to 29 embryos.

Taking each of the held-out test images, these were paired with other test images (78 unique cases), validation images (169 cases) and training images (1829 cases), given the restriction that a discarded embryo could only be paired with one that is transferred. Training, validation and test performance all reached a similar level, indicating that the network did not overfit to our training data. We therefore included pairs containing training and validation images, in order to have a substantial number of pairs. For each of these scenarios, the linear regression model we trained achieved 96.84% for test-test pairs, 96.45% for test-val pairs and 96.06% for test-train pairs. The 8-layer CNN achieved 82.28% accuracy for test-test pairs, 85.80% for test-val pairs and 84.86% for test-train pairs. These results show a marked improvement compared to standalone image assessment.

3.6 Performance on Easy Decisions

Not all outcome decisions are the same, in that some cases are more difficult than others. There are cases where an embryo will clearly be transferred (e.g. has 8 blastomeres, no asymmetry and no fragmentation), and cases where an embryo is clearly rejected (contains less than 5 blastomeres). In addition, there are many cases in between these two extremes, where the decision is much more difficult. We sought to assess performance of the 8-layer CNN for so called "easy" cases, in order to better determine how our model performed against STORK's reported performance of 96.94% accuracy. We selected test images that would constitute obvious discard decisions, with cell count of less than 5, that would be considered to be of "poor-quality". We also selected test images that were obvious transfer decisions, having an ideal 8 cells with no fragmentation and no asymmetry, being of "good-quality". Note that this selection of easy cases is fairly restricted, and that the inclusion criteria of easy cases by Khosravi et al. [9] are likely to be different from ours. From our test image set, 344 images were obvious discard cases and 71 were obvious transfer cases. Our 8-layer CNN implementation decides 95.93% discard for obvious discard cases and 85.92% transfer for obvious transfer cases. The actual technician decision for these two easy sets was 92.73% discard and

97.18% transfer. Averaging performance over all test cases, our model achieved 94.22%. Figure 6 illustrates the 8-layer CNN results for these easy cases.

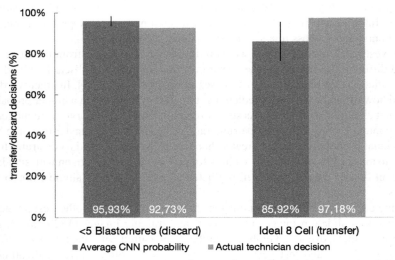

Fig. 6. The performance of an 8-layer CNN for "easy" cases in dark blue, expressed as the proportion of discard decisions (left, less than 5 blastomeres) or transfer decisions (right, embryo has 8 cells with no fragmentation and no asymmetry). Error bars represent 95% confidence intervals. The bars in light blue reflect the proportion of cases in which this expected decision was made by the technician. (Color figure online)

3.7   Pregnancy Outcomes

We analyzed whether CNN predictions correlated with real-world pregnancy outcomes, namely implantation rate. The implantation rate was based on clinical data of the same fertility center for a range of score combinations (number of cells, fragmentation and asymmetry). The result is shown in the figure below (Fig. 7.). Note that the majority of predictions of the model were above 50% (with the exception of 3 cases), indicating a bias towards a transfer result. This reflects real world outcomes, given that implantation rates can only be computed for scoring combinations that have been transferred relatively frequently, and therefore might constitute a clear transfer decision for both technicians and the network. The correlation between the average model predictions per scoring group and the implantation rate was R = 0,6451, accounting for an explained variance of R^2 = 4,4162. Due to the "restriction of range" phenomenon, the correlation reported here is a lower estimate than the actual real correlation, when taking the entire dataset. However, such a 'real' correlation could only be measured in an experiment in which embryos of all possible score combinations would be transferred, which for obvious reasons is not an ethical experiment as many score combinations would rarely result in pregnancy.

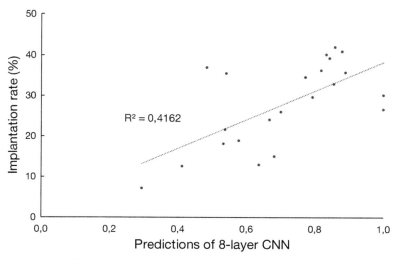

Fig. 7. Model prediction (% transfer decisions) vs implantation rate per scoring group. The correlation between these two sets of values is 0.6451. The linear fit to these data points has an explained variance (R^2) of 0.4162.

4   Discussion and Conclusion

We successfully applied deep neural networks to classifying images of embryos taken at the cleavage stage (day 3). Our findings suggest that (i) relatively simple deep nets provide good performance for this task, (ii) it is important to incorporate the batch effect (iii) some cases are harder than others to classify, both for the networks and for human technicians, and (iv) predictions of the model are related to clinical implantation rates.

Automating embryo quality assessment using deep learning allows the computation of scoring dimensions or embryo destiny based on images alone, omitting the need to score each embryo by observation. This automated quality assessment is especially relevant for IVF treatments, were the success rate and inter-observer reliability are relatively low [1]. One could argue that simpler computer vision or image processing techniques can be used to compute each of the three scoring variables. These can then be passed on to the simple regression model we trained (see Sect. 3.1). This would probably result in similar performance levels. That being said, deep learning is elegant because the whole process is implemented in one architecture and the architecture is "off the shelf" rather than adapted per application domain.

It is relevant to highlight that we obtained good performance with a relatively simple deep net of only 8 layers. Using an architecture of this depth is relatively common in several domains, since the publication of Krizhevsky et al. [11]. Obviously, there are many more advanced architectures available. While some include hundreds of layers, the most relevant one to apply to the field of embryology was the inception v1 architecture used by Khosravi et al. [9], which is also often used for medical image analysis [14, 15]. Somewhat surprisingly, this benchmark model did not perform as well as the simpler 8-layer network on day 3 embryos. It is not guaranteed that this is a mere consequence of network architecture. There are many choices that need to be made when training such complex models with a high number of parameters. We adopted the same training regime as Khosravi et al. to train STORK on our dataset, and did not further explore other options (other than varying the learning rate). Further exploration of different training regimes might yield better results. In addition, there were several differences between our use of STORK and the original implementation (apart from the dataset). First, the images in our dataset were not preprocessed and we did not exclude certain cases based on predefined exclusion criteria (as opposed to the data used by Khosravi et al.). Second, our dataset consisted of snapshot images, whereas the original STORK implementation was trained on time-lapse image sequences. These differences might explain why our implementation of STORK did not perform well. That being said, at the very least, we can say that it is not trivial to achieve good results with more complex architectures. When researchers find that simpler models do better, it is tempting to suggest that this is due to the complexity of the problem. While a network that is too simple will not learn the problem, a network with too many parameters will fail because some parameters will remain underspecified given the amount of available training data [16]. Our dataset of over 20k images is already very large relative to other published attempts. Therefore, it might be better to not exaggerate the size and depth of a network. For our problem at hand, an 8-layer network proved to be a good choice.

Given this architecture, we tried several variations in the format of our training data (one versus multiple focal points) and decision structure (training on technician decision or on the dimensions that underlie this decision). None of these variations mattered a lot, which is why we provide most information on the simplest case, namely training with single-slice images to predict the technician decision.

What mattered much more, was how we characterized performance. It is hard to capture performance with one single number. Instead, we provided multiple measurements of performance. The lowest performance we reported, of 75.24%, was obtained when we attempted to predict the technician's decision out of context and included all possible test cases, hard as well as easy ones. As is evident, technicians reach their decision based upon contextual information from a batch of embryos. In that context, the decision, to transfer an embryo or discard it, depends on the quality of the other embryos in that particular batch. When we incorporate this batch context, performance rises from 75.24% to 84.65%. Comparing our results to others reported in the literature, it is important to note that we considered all embryos in our dataset that were transferred or discarded, whereas the 96.94% performance obtained by Khosravi et al. [9] omitted fair-quality cases. Looking at network performance for extremely easy cases, we note that these were associated with more extreme performance levels of our 8-layer network implementation, suggesting that we might reach performance levels around 90% when we restrict our dataset by excluding fair-quality embryos.

From a medical perspective, it is particularly relevant to implement deep learning for embryo assessment at day 3, which is earlier than previous AI applications in the field. Embryos are traditionally transferred on day 3, making this an important developmental stage. Over the past decade there has been a move to transferring embryos in a later stage, i.e. on day 5 or 6. However studies on obstetric and perinatal outcomes show contradictory results on preterm delivery after extended embryo culture until day 5 or 6

[17, 18]. Another disadvantage of extended cultures is that it might be accompanied with increased costs. As such, automating embryo-quality assessment at an earlier stage of development would be valuable to reduce extended embryo culture. This shift to an earlier stage leads to a very different set of relevant dimensions. While the relevant scoring variables on day 5 (inner cell mass, trophectoderm) require mostly texture processing, the scoring of day 3 embryos relies largely on holistic processing (counting the number of blastomeres and judging their size). Several studies suggest that CNNs might perform better on texture processing compared to shape processing [19–22], making this shift from day 5 to day 3 in automating embryo-quality a challenging task.

There are several avenues of work that are important to follow-up in order to resolve remaining questions. There were many details and choices in our procedure that had not been fully explored, such as, the exact CNN architecture used, the training parameters, the choice of focal planes (see Fig. 3), and the possible inclusion of freeze decisions. In addition, previous studies have used time-lapsed videos [7–9], which would allow to directly compare the different stages in terms of ease of training, test performance, and clinical relevance, as well as comparing the benefit of time-lapsed videos over using individual time points. In such a project, it will be a challenge to obtain an image set with multiple time points that is as large as our current dataset. For that reason, it will also be important in the future to characterize how the performance of deep nets depends on the size of the image set involved in training. A further question concerns the generalizability of findings and trained deep nets across clinical centers. Our image set was obtained at one clinical center using the microscopes of one company, and from a clinical perspective it is very important to follow up with training regimes using images from multiple centers, in the hopes of guaranteeing and improving generalization across centers. Our procedures did not involve screening or selection of images based on image quality, so our findings already represent performance under the presence of representative levels of noise. Still, we did not incorporate variations in image quality and other image properties between clinical sites. Lastly, given that there is low inter-and intra-observer reliability between embryologists [1], obtaining scores from multiple embryologists for each embryo in the dataset could further improve automated quality assessment [7, 9].

Acknowledgments. This work was supported by KU Leuven Research Council (grant C14/16/031) and FWO-Flanders through the Excellence Of Science program (EOS grant HUMVISCAT). The authors thank Suzy Pellens for useful discussions and the reviewers for their helpful suggestions and comments.

References

1. Paternot, G., Devroe, J., Debrock, S., D'Hooghe, T.M., Spissens, C.: Intra-and inter-observer analysis in the morphological assessment of early-stage embryos. Reprod. Biol. Endocrinol. **7**(1), 105 (2009)
2. Glujovski, D., Farqubar, C.: Cleavage-stage or blastocyst transfer: what are the benefits and harms? Fertil. Steril. **106**(2), 244–250 (2016)
3. Van den Bergh, M., Ebner, K.: Atlas of Oocytes, Zygotes and Embryos in Reproductive Medicine. Cambridge University Press, Cambridge (2012)

4. Balaban, B., et al.: Alpha scientists in reproductive medicine and ESHRE special interest group of embryology. The Istanbul consensus workshop on embryo assessment. In: Proceedings of an Expert Meeting. Hum. Reprod., pp. 1270–1283, Istanbul (2011)
5. Alikani, M., Cohen, J., Tomkin, G., Garrisi, G.J., Mack, C., Scott, R.T.: Human embryo fragmentation in vitro and its implications for pregnancy and implantation. Fertil. Steril. **71**(5), 836–842 (1999)
6. Embryology, ESHRE Special Interest Group: Istanbul consensus workshop on embryo assessment: proceedings of an expert meeting. Reprod. Biomed. Online **22**(6), 632–646 (2011)
7. Kragh, M.F., Rimestad, J., Berntsen, J., Karstoft, H.: Automating grading of human blastocysts from time-lapse imaging. Comput. Biol. Med. **115**, 103494 (2019)
8. Iwata, K., et al.: Deep learning based on images of human embryos obtained from high-resolution time-lapse cinematography for predicting good-quality embryos. Fertil. Steril. **110**(4), e213 (2018)
9. Khosravi, P., et al.: Deep leaning enables robust assessment and selection of human blastocysts after in vitro fertilization. NPJ Digital Med. **2**(1), 1–9 (2019)
10. Szegedy, C., et al.: Going deeper with convolutions. In: Proceedings of the IEEE conference on computer vision and pattern recognition and pattern recognition, pp. 1–9 (2015)
11. Krizhevsky, A., Sutskever, I., Hinton, G.E.: Imagenet classification with deep convolutional neural networks. In: Advances in Neural Information Processing Systems, pp. 1097–1105 (2012)
12. Chollet, F., Keras: Github repository (2015). https://github.com/fchollet/keras
13. Zegers-Hochschild, F., et al.: International committee for monitoring assisted reproductive technology; world health organization. International committee for monitoring assisted reproductive technology (ICMART) and the world health organization (WHO) revised glossary of ART terminology. Fertil. Steril. **92**(5), 1520–1524 (2009)
14. Habibzadeh, M., Jannesari, M., Rezaei, Z., Baharvand, H., Totonchi, M.: Automatic white blood cell classification using pre-trained deep learning models: ResNet and inception. In: Tenth International Conference on Machine Vision, p. 1069612. International Society for Optics and Photonics (2017)
15. Khosravi, P., Kazemi, E., Imielinski, M., Elemento, O., Hajirasouliha, I.: Deep convolutional neural networks enable discrimination of heterogeneous digital pathology images. EBioMedicine **27**, 317–328 (2018)
16. Goodfellow, I., Bengio, Y., Courville, A., Bengio, Y.: Deep Learning. MIT press, Cambridge, Massachusetts (2016)
17. Maheshwari, A., Kalampokas, T., Davidson, J., Bhattacharya, S.: Obstetric and perinatal outcomes in singleton pregnancies resulting from the transfer of blastocyst-stage versus cleavage-stage embryos generated through in vitro fertilization treatment: a systematic review and meta-analysis. Fertil. Steril. **100**(6), 1615–21.e1–10 (2013)
18. Marconi, N., Raja, E.A., Bhattacharya, S., Maheshwari, A.: Perinatal outcomes in singleton live births after fresh blastocyst-stage embryo transfer: a retrospective analysis of 67 147 IVF/ICSI cycles. Hum. Reprod. **34**(9), 1716–1725 (2019)
19. Geirhos, R., Rubisch, P., Michaelis, C., Bethge, M., Wichmann, F.A., Brendel, W.: ImageNet-trained CNNs are biased towards texture; increasing shape bias improves accuracy and robustness. arXiv preprint arXiv:1811.12231 (2018)
20. Gatys, L., Ecker, A.S., Bethge, M.: Texture synthesis using convolutional neural networks. In: Advances in Neural Information Processing Systems, pp. 262–270 (2015)
21. Brendel, W., Bethge, M.: Approximating CNNs with bag-of-local-features models works surprisingly well on ImageNet. arXiv preprint arXiv:1904.00760 (2019)
22. Ballester, P., de Araujo, R.M.: On the performance of GoogLeNet and Alexnet applied to sketches. In: Thirtieth AAAI Conference on Artificial Intelligence (2016)

Double Encoder-Decoder Networks for Gastrointestinal Polyp Segmentation

Adrian Galdran[1](✉), Gustavo Carneiro[2], and Miguel A. González Ballester[3,4]

[1] Department of Computing and Informatics, Bournemouth University, Poole, UK
agaldran@bournemouth.ac.uk
[2] Australian Institute for Machine Learning, University of Adelaide,
Adelaide, Australia
[3] BCN Medtech, Department of Information and Communication Technologies,
Universitat Pompeu Fabra, Barcelona, Spain
[4] ICREA, Barcelona, Spain

Abstract. Polyps represent an early sign of the development of Colorectal Cancer. The standard procedure for their detection consists of colonoscopic examination of the gastrointestinal tract. However, the wide range of polyp shapes and visual appearances, as well as the reduced quality of this image modality, turn their automatic identification and segmentation with computational tools into a challenging computer vision task. In this work, we present a new strategy for the delineation of gastrointestinal polyps from endoscopic images based on a direct extension of common encoder-decoder networks for semantic segmentation. In our approach, two pretrained encoder-decoder networks are sequentially stacked: the second network takes as input the concatenation of the original frame and the initial prediction generated by the first network, which acts as an attention mechanism enabling the second network to focus on interesting areas within the image, thereby improving the quality of its predictions. Quantitative evaluation carried out on several polyp segmentation databases shows that double encoder-decoder networks clearly outperform their single encoder-decoder counterparts in all cases. In addition, our best double encoder-decoder combination attains excellent segmentation accuracy and reaches state-of-the-art performance results in all the considered datasets, with a remarkable boost of accuracy on images extracted from datasets not used for training.

Keywords: Polyp segmentation · Colonoscopy · Colorectal Cancer

1 Introduction

The large bowel within the human gastrointestinal tract can be affected by different diseases, among which, Colorectal Cancer (CRC) is particularly concerning. CRC represents the second most common cancer type in women and

A. Del Bimbo et al. (Eds.): ICPR 2020 Workshops, LNCS 12661, pp. 293–307, 2021.
https://doi.org/10.1007/978-3-030-68763-2_22

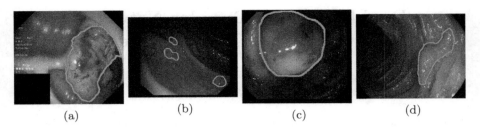

(a)   (b)   (c)   (d)

Fig. 1. Polyp visual aspects have a wide variety in terms of shape and color. Four different polyps sampled from the different databases considered in this work: (a) Kvasir-Seg [19], (b) CVC-ClinicDB [5], (c) CVC-ColonDB [4], (d) ETIS [29].

third most common for men [15]. Gastro-intestinal polyps are known precursors of this type of cancer [34], being present in almost half of the patients over 50 undergoing screening colonoscopies [31]. This kind of lesions show a wide range of shapes and visual appearances, as shown in Fig. 1, turning its identification and segmentation into a challenging problem.

Treatment of CRC starts with the detection of colorectal paraneoplastic lesions, performed during colonoscopy screenings. In this endoscopic procedure, a flexible tube with a light camera mounted on its tip is introduced through the rectum to find and sample (or resect) polyps from the colon. Early detection of CRC has been demonstrated to substantially increase 5-year survival rates, with screening programs enabling even pre-symptomatic treatment [31]. Unfortunately, it is estimated that around 6–27% of polyps are missed during a colonoscopic examination [1]. It has been recently shown in [25] that up to 80% of missed lesions could be avoided with real-time computer-aided colonoscopic image analysis and decision support systems. Therefore, computer-aided polyp detection has been extensively explored as a complementary tool for colonoscopic procedures to improve detection rates, enable early treatment, and increase survival rates.

The most relevant computer-aided tasks related to polyp analysis in endoscopic imaging are: 1. Polyp Detection: Deciding if polyps appear in an endoscopic frame [6]. 2. Polyp Classification: Assigning polyps to a range of subcategories or degrees of malignancy [7]. 3. Polyp Localization: finding the position (usually in terms of a bounding box) of polyps within a frame [38]. 4. Polyp Segmentation: delineating the exact polyp contour in a given endoscopic frame [35].

This work is concerned with the task of polyp segmentation, which has attracted much attention in recent years. Polyp segmentation is typically achieved by means of encoder-decoder architectures composed a pair of Convolutional Neural Networks (CNN). The main variation across different works is the design of such architectures. For instance in [14] an encoder-decoder network containing multi-resolution, multi-classification, and fusion sub-networks was proposed, and in [32] several combinations of different encoder and decoder architectures were explored. In [12] an architecture in which there is a shared encoder

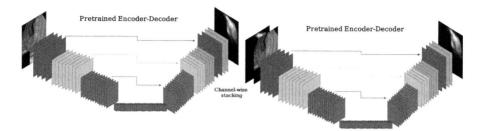

Fig. 2. Pre-trained Double Encoder-Decoder Network for Polyp Segmentation. The second network receives as input the original colonoscopic frame concatenated with the prediction of the first network; we conjecture that this allows the second network to better focus on interesting areas of the image, improving its segmentation accuracy.

and two mutually depending decoders that model polyp areas and boundaries respectively is introduced, whereas in [22] ensembles of instance-segmentation architectures like Mask-RCNN were studied, and in [11] parallel reverse attention layers are proposed to better capture the relationship between polyp areas and their boundaries. Two-stage detection/segmentation pipelines, in which a first an object detector roughly locates a polyp and then an encoder-decoder CNN delineates its margins have also been explored, e.g. in [21]. Alternative loss function have also been studied, e.g. in [32]. A recent review of these and other approaches can be found in [31].

The approach proposed here consists of stacking two segmentation networks in a sequential manner, where the second network receives as input the concatenation of the prediction from the first one with the original frame, as shown in Fig. 2. This way, the output of the first network acts as an attention mechanism that provides the second network with a map of interesting locations on which the second network should focus. It should be noted that iterative segmentation networks have been proposed in other contexts recently, such as the method by Li et al. [23], which proposes stacking a large U-Net with N−1 smaller U-Nets for the task of retinal vessel segmentation. The main difference compared with our technique is that in [23] the subsequent small U-Nets do not process the input image, but rather the candidate segmentation only. Also for retinal vessel segmentation, the recent paper by Galdran et al. [13] makes use of two consecutive U-Nets, but their focus is on building compact models for a substantially simpler task, not benefiting from using pre-trained CNN. The Double-UNet, introduced in [18], holds also some similarities with our proposed approach, but in their approach the output of the first network is multiplied by the input image (instead of concatenated), potentially discarding useful information, which may not be recovered, for the second network. In addition, the backbone encoder for Double-Unet is a VGG-19 [30], which is currently not competitive with the state-of-the-art classification networks that have been proposed in recent years.

In this work, we propose a framework for semantic segmentation based on the sequential use of two encoder-decoder networks. Extensive experimental results with three different pre-trained encoders and decoders on a recently proposed polyp segmentation dataset [19] show that our double encoder-decoder networks provide a boost in performance over their single encoder-decoder in all cases. In addition, results across different combinations of encoders show substantial robustness and consistency. Our best model is re-trained on a common polyp segmentation benchmark in order to enable comparison with the state-of-the-art, attaining results that considerably improve upon several recent approaches, with remarkable performance on three unseen datasets, where our approach achieves a performance boost in terms of Dice score of 1.52%, 5,29%, and 12,07% when compared to the second best considered method.

2   Methodology

2.1   Double Autoencoders

Dense semantic segmentation tasks that produce per-pixel predictions are typically approached with an encoder-decoder network [3,33,36]. In this context, the encoder can be regarded as a feature extractor that downsamples spatial resolution and increases the number of channels by learning convolutional filters. After the image has been encoded into a low-dimensional representation, the decoder upsamples this representation back to the original input size, thereby generating a pixel-wise prediction. Typically, skip connections are added to map information from the encoder to the decoder [27]. Double encoder-encoders are a direct extension of encoder-decoder architectures in which two encoder-decoder networks are sequentially combined. Denoting by x the input RGB image, $E^{(1)}$ the first network, and $E^{(2)}$ the second network, in a double encoder-decoder, the output $E^{(1)}(x)$ of the first network is provided to the second network together with x so that it can act as an attention map that allows $E^{(2)}$ to focus on the most interesting areas of the image:

$$E(x) = E^{(2)}(x, E^{(1)}(x)), \tag{1}$$

where x and $E^{(1)}(x)$ are stacked so that the input to $E^{(2)}$ has four channels instead of the three channels corresponding to the RGB components of x. This is illustrated in Fig. 2. There are some choices to be made in this framework, specifically about the structure of the encoder and decoder sub-networks within $E^{(1)}$ and $E^{(2)}$. Note that $E^{(1)}$ and $E^{(2)}$ do not need to share the same architecture, although in this work we restrict ourselves to this case to simplify the exposition. In the next two sections we describe different alternatives that we will thoroughly explore in our experiments.

2.2   Pretrained Encoders

Double encoder-decoder networks contain two sub-networks $E^{(1)}$ and $E^{(2)}$, each of which have an encoder branch that can be chosen as any Convolutional Neural Network designed for classification purposes. Image representations obtained at the end of this branch are expected to be useful to classify objects within the image and to segment objects when iteratively upscaled in the decoder branch. In particular, it is favorable to select top-performer architectures that have been shown to work well for natural image classification tasks, since we can then re-use the weights of the decoder. This experimentally leads to faster convergence, requires less training data and leads to better generalization. In this work we consider three such architectures, which we briefly review below. These range from more compact models to larger, more powerful architectures, to better illustrate the benefits of double encoder-decoder networks under different scenarios.

MobileNet V2. MobileNet is a mobile architecture specifically designed to maximize compactness, speed, and efficiency [28] to enable its deployment on mobile devices. The main feature of this network is that it implements efficient depthwise separable convolutions to reduce computational load. Later improved versions of this architecture adopt "inverted residual" blocks on which shortcut connections are established between "thin" activation volumes that contain less features, considerably reducing memory constraints. In addition, interleaved non-linearities within narrow layers of the network are avoided, which is shown to further decrease computational demands.

Resnet34. Residual Network architectures (ResNets) were first introduced in [16], and have since then become the default networks for Computer Vision tasks, due to their excellent complexity versus performance trade-off. ResNets popularized the notion of skip-connections, which were the main ingredient of residual blocks: a series of convolutions are applied to the input of a particular network layer, but a by-pass is added to the input so that information can flow unaltered up to the output of the block. This improves the training process of very deep networks, helping to avoid vanishing gradient problems. Although large ResNet architectures with up to 152 layers have been proposed, as well as improved versions like ResNext [37], we limit our experiments to a relatively small ResNet variant, namely ResNet34. This provides a nice intermediate stage in between the compactness of MobileNet and the complexity of Dual-Path-Networks, which we describe next.

Dual-Path Networks. Dual Path Networks (DPNs) were presented in [10], and they provide an hybrid design that merges different aspects of Residual Networks and Densely Connected CNNs (DenseNets, [17]). As described above, ResNets employ skip-connections within each single residual block to enable better information flow. DenseNets in turn introduce these paths between all residual blocks, concatenating input and output features from different network levels. The authors analyze both architectures and discover that residuals path implicitly favor features re-usage, but are limited in exploring new features, whereas DenseNets are better at exploring new features but suffer from heavy feature redundancy. This observation leads to the proposal of a combined architecture that is shown to outperform both ResNets and DenseNets in a variety of computer vision tasks.

2.3 Decoders

It is common in semantic segmentation architectures to decouple the design of the encoder and the decoder, as this provides a better understanding of each component [36]. In addition, it is usual to adopt pretrained encoders as described above, which leaves some design freedom to focus on specific characteristics of encoders that may allow for better reconstruction and upsampling techniques. We review below the three encoder architectures that we will be using in our experimental evaluation.

U-Net Decoder. We first adopt the encoder branch of the widely popular U-Net architecture, one of the first CNNs designed for image segmentation, with particular success in biomedical imaging [27]. U-Net was among the first architecture designs to introduce the idea of an encoding (downsampling) branch followed by a decoding (upsampling) branch, with skip connections mapping intermediate activation from one branch to the other. This was shown to improve gradient flow during backpropagation and iterative weight updating, being also useful for recovering high-resolution information from the downsampling branch and adding it to the upsampling activations. The decoder branch of the U-Net features transposed convolutions as the most distinctive characteristic.

DeepLab. The first version of this architecture was presented in [8], with the main feature being that atrous convolution that were leveraged to gain control on the resolution at which feature responses are computed by the network. Further improvements have been introduced to this architecture later on, and in this work we adopt DeepLab V3 [9], which differs form DeepLab V1 on that atrous spatial pyramid pooling and batch-norm layers are adopted to increase long-range information modeling and improve training efficiency.

Feature-Pyramid Networks. FPNs were introduced in [24]. The authors proposed to build segmentation predictions not only in the last layer of the decoder but also at intermediate layers. These predictions range from low to high-resolution, and are combined into a single segmentation only at the end of the forward pass, in order to compare it to the ground-truth. This multi-scale approach is shown to effectively re-use information from all layers of the decoder, and results in increased performance.

2.4 Training Details

All the models trained in this work follow the same protocol. We optimize network weights to minimize the cross-entropy loss using standard Stochastic Gradient Descent with a learning rate of $l = 0.01$ and a batch-size of 4. The learning

Table 1. Description of each of the datasets considered in this paper. The first two are employed for training purposes. We use the five of them to assess performance on images similar/different to the training set.

Dataset	Characteristics & Challenges
KVasir-Seg [19]	Large scale (n = 1000), diverse, includes multi-polyp cases Varying resolution from 487×332 to 1920×1072 pixels
CVC-ClinicDB [5]	n = 612 images of resolution 388×284 from 31 sequences Different polyp categories and sizes, substantial specularities
CVC-ColonDB [4]	n = 300 images from 15 short sequences, 574×500 resolution Great variability in types of polyp and appearances
ETIS-LaribPolypDB [29]	n = 196 still images with a resolution of 1225×966 Contains 44 different polyps from 34 sequences
EndoScene [34]	n = 912, combination of CVC-ColonDB + CVC-ClinicDB Images of varying resolutions, only part of the test set used

rate is decayed following a cosine law from its initial value to $l = 1e - 8$ during 25 epochs, which defines a training cycle. We then repeat this process for 20 cycles, restarting the learning back at the beginning of each cycle. Images are re-scaled to 640×512, which respects the predominant rectangular aspect ratio in most polyp segmentation datasets, and during training they are augmented with standard techniques (random rotations, vertical/horizontal flipping, contrast/saturation/brightness changes). The mean Dice score is monitored on a separate validation set and the best performing model is kept for testing purposes. For testing, we generate four different versions of each image by horizontal/vertical flipping, predict on each of them, and average the results.

3   Experimental Results

This section describes our experimental analysis on the performance of the proposed approach to polyp segmentation. We first describe the data and the performance metrics used to validate our technique. We then develop an analysis of the accuracy of different combinations of encoders and decoders, comparing the performance on the Kvasir dataset [19] of a standard encoder-decoder network with that of its double encoder-decoder counterpart. Next we re-train the best model in a large-scale experiment and comprehensively analyze its performance when compared to other recent polyp segmentation methods on five different databases.

3.1   Data and Evaluation Metrics

It is certainly complicated to compare different approaches for polyp segmentation, as no clear evaluation protocol has emerged from the literature. This would involve clearly defining training and test subsets from the different publicly available datasets, as well as defining proper evaluation metrics.

In order to provide a fair comparison, we propose the following experimental setup. For the first set of experiments, we consider the KVasir-seg database [19], which we split into 90% training and 10% test images. In this dataset, we carry out ablation experiments to find out which is the best encoder-decoder combination, and to demonstrate that double encoder-decoders offer superior performance. For the second part of this section, where we compare our approach against the state-of-the-art in a large-scale experiment, we follow closely the data source definitions provided in [11]. This involves up to five different databases that are described in Table 1. The considered training set is the union of two subsets of KVasir-seg [19] and CVC-Clinic-DB [5], containing 90% of the data. From this training set, a validation set is separated before training is carried out. To evaluate the performance of our models, we use the remaining 10% of both datasets as test sets, which allow us to assess performance when test data is similar to training data. In addition, we use the three other datasets shown in Table 1 to assess performance on data that comes from a different source: CVC-ColonDB [4], ETIS-LaribDB [29], EndoScene [34]. Note that the training/test splits are exactly the same[1] as in [11]. In particular, we only use the part of the EndoScene test set that does not belong to CVC-ClinicDB, which is used for training, referred to as CVC-300 below. All other performance results are also extracted from [11], which ensures a correct comparison of all approaches.

Regarding performance metrics, a consensus has not been reached yet in the literature [32]. We therefore follow the recommendation in [19] and compute Dice and Intersection over Union (IoU) scores on each binary prediction of a given test set, and report their averages across all images. Note that this is different from [11], where the probabilistic (grayscale) predictions are used to derive an overall Dice and IoU score: if predictions are considered to be discretized in 8-bits, for each threshold in a predefined range $\{0, 1, ..., 255\}$ a score is computed. Then the mean score is kept for each image, and the average of these is reported as the final performance. This is different from conventional performance metrics reported in other papers, and we prefer to follow the simpler approach of employing binary predictions to compute a single Dice and IoU score, as the binary segmentation is the most relevant outcome of a polyp segmentation pipeline, and it does not appear to be suitable to test a method on thresholds that are never going to be used in clinical practice. Nevertheless, as in [11], in order to also assess the quality of the probabilistic predictions, we report Mean Absolute Error computed as the average of the absolute value of pixelwise differences between the binary ground-truth and the grayscale predicted segmentation.

---

[1] All data, training/test splits, and results of other compared methods were directly downloaded from https://github.com/DengPingFan/PraNet.

Table 2. Performance analysis of different combinations of pretrained encoders and decoders on the Kvasir databaset. Bold numbers indicate performance improvements of double encoder-decoders upon their single encoder-decoder counterparts.

Decoder →	U-Net [27]			DeepLab [9]			FP-Net [24]		
Encoder ↓	DICE	IOU	MAE	DICE	IOU	MAE	DICE	IOU	MAE
MobileNet [28]	88.59	82.87	3.65	88.87	82.88	3.79	89.15	83.14	3.61
MobileNet×2	88.80	83.24	3.68	90.23	84.80	3.59	90.73	85.53	3.17
Perf. Diff.	**+0.21**	**+0.37**	+0.03	**+1.36**	**+1.96**	−0.20	**+1.58**	**+2.39**	−0.44
Resnet34 [16]	89.72	84.28	3.24	89.26	83.66	3.31	89.90	84.76	3.00
Resnet34×2	90.13	84.77	3.09	90.39	85.30	3.12	90.70	85.55	3.01
Perf. Diff.	**+0.41**	**+0.49**	−0.15	**+1.13**	**+1.64**	−0.19	**+0.80**	**+0.79**	+0.01
DPN [10]	89.72	83.91	3.19	90.23	84.83	3.25	89.96	84.61	3.04
DPN×2	90.21	85.10	3.25	91.21	86.16	2.84	91.97	87.05	2.65
Perf. Diff.	**+0.49**	**+1.19**	+0.06	**+0.98**	**+1.33**	−0.39	**+2.01**	**+2.44**	−0.39

In order to generate binary segmentations from probabilistic predictions and calculate Dice/IOU scores, we use a simple adaptive thresholding algorithm [26], which is a popular approach in polyp segmentation [2], followed by morphological hole filling. The same binarization scheme is applied to the grayscale predictions of the compare methods, which were provided by the authors of [11].

3.2   Autoencoders vs. Double Autoencoders

We first train each of the combinations of pretrained encoders and decoders that we described in Sects. 2.2 and 2.3 on the K-Vasir dataset. Our aim with this set of experiments is to investigate if using double encoder-decoders brings performance improvements.

Table 2 reports the results of our experiments with different encoders and decoders. The main pattern arising is that double encoder-decoders do provide a performance boost in every considered case. Although the improvement is varying, there is no single case in which single encoder-decoder networks outperform their doubled counterparts. In addition, we can see that Feature-Pyramid networks (FP-Net) are the best decoder for this particular problem, surpassing the performance of U-Net and DeepLab for whichever considered encoder network. For the particular case of FP-Net encoders, it is also interesting to note that the lightweight MobileNet encoder achieves a better performance when compared to the heavier ResNet34 encoder. It is also worth noting that Dual Path Networks (DPN) stand out as the best pretrained encoder for all the considered decoders. In the remaining of this section, we select the DPN+FP-Net combination, and evaluate the performance of a double encoder-decoder network against other recent polyp segmentation techniques.

Table 3. Performance of the best double encoder-decoder model (DPN68×2) compared to other approaches on the test set of the KVasir-Seg and CVC-Clinic databases. Models were learned on the combination of the training set of both datasets.

	KVasir			CVC-Clinic		
	DICE	IOU	MAE	DICE	IOU	MAE
U-Net/MICCAI'15 [27]	83.00	75.91	5.47	84.39	77.70	1.92
ResUNet-mod [20]	79.09	42.87	–	77.88	45.45	–
ResUNet++ [20]	81.33	79.27	–	79.55	79.62	–
SFA/MICCAI'19 [12]	73.10	61.87	7.54	70.61	61.26	4.16
U-Net++/TMI'20 [39]	83.21	75.60	14.95	81.20	74.67	7.97
PraNet/MICCAI'20 [11]	90.37	84.79	2.96	90.72	85.89	**0.93**
DPN68×2	**91.70**	**86.74**	**2.68**	**91.61**	**86.65**	1.42

3.3 Comparison with Recent Techniques

In this section we re-train the best double encoder-decoder network (referred to as DPN68 × 2) on the dataset employed in [11] following the same train/test split. This training set derived from the Kvasir and CVC-Clinic databases is used to optimize the double DPN68 × 2 architecture, and we conduct two types of experiments. First, we test the resulting model on data similar to the training distribution by computing performance (separately) on the KVasir and the CVC-Clinic test sets. Second, we use the ColonDB and ETIS databases, which contain relatively dissimilar colonoscopic frames, to assess the generalization ability of our approach. Following [11], we also include in this experiment the CVC-300 database, although this dataset contains part of the test set of CVC-Clinic, and it represents therefore an easier problem.

In both cases, we compare the performance of our technique with a) two popular medical image segmentation architectures, namely U-Net [27] and its extensions U-Net++ [39], and b) three architectures specifically developed for polyp segmentation techniques, ResUnet++ [20], SFA [12], and PraNet [11].

Results of the first of our experiments are reported in Table 3. It can be seen that the DPN68×2 architecture improves the performance of all other approaches, achieving top performance by a wide margin with respect to most considered methods. The second best approach is the recently introduced PraNet CNN, which attains a performance relatively close to the one of DPN68×2, although still slightly inferior.

It is however on our second experiment that reveals most remarkable performance differences between our approach and PraNet and the other considered techniques. The results displayed in Table 4 show that the generalization capability of our DPN68 × 2 model is much larger than previous approaches: when compared to the second best model (again PraNet), it attains an increase 5.29 in DICE score in the CVC-ColonDB and 12.07 Dice score in the ETIS databases. This margin is even larger for other methods, which clearly signals to DPN68×2 being substantially more competitive when using unseen data that is far away from the training distribution. On the CVC-300 database, which is more similar to the training data, DPN68×2 still surpasses all other methods, although with a smaller difference.

Table 4. Performance of the best double encoder-decoder model (DPN68×2) compared to other approaches on the ColonDB, ETIS, and CVC-300 databases.

	ColonDB			ETIS			CVC-300		
	DICE	IOU	MAE	DICE	IOU	MAE	DICE	IOU	MAE
U-Net/MICCAI'15	53.91	46.28	5.86	44.02	36.72	3.62	73.99	65.30	2.21
SFA/MICCAI'19	45.90	33.83	7.46	29.88	21.82	4.55	46.90	32.95	6.51
U-Net++/TMI'20	51.73	43.37	7.42	48.05	40.15	4.52	74.79	65.89	3.36
PraNet/MICCAI'20	72.42	65.11	4.31	64.12	57.98	3.11	87.63	80.35	0.99
DPN68×2	**77.71**	**69.81**	**3.97**	**76.19**	**68.43**	**1.68**	**89.15**	**82.56**	**0.90**

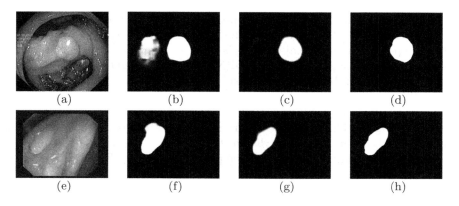

(a)   (b)   (c)   (d)

(e)   (f)   (g)   (h)

Fig. 3. (a), (e): Polyps extracted from the Kvasir-Seg and CVC-Clinic databases. Segmentations produced by (b), (f): PraNet, (c), (g): DPN68×2. (d), (h): Ground-truth

3.4 Qualitative Analysis

In this section, we visually analyze some of the segmentation results obtained on the different test data when compared with other approaches.

Figure 3 shows two challenging cases of polyps extracted from the Kvasir and CVC-Clinic databases (test set associated to the training set), while Fig. 4 displays two polyps extracted from the test set of ColonDB and ETIS (dissimilar data). We also show the results produced by the second best technique, PraNet.

In the Kvasir example, it can be appreciated that DPN68×2 succeeds to properly segment the polyp appearing in the center of the frame in Fig. (3a), whereas PraNet is probably confused by the specularities present in the image

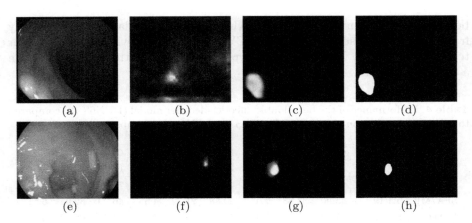

Fig. 4. (a), (e): Polyps extracted from the CVC-ColonDB and ETIS databases. Segmentations produced by (b), (f): PraNet, (c), (g): DPN68×2. (d), (h): Ground-truth

and oversegments this example, as shown in Figs. (3b) and (3c). As for the CVC-Clinic example in Fig. (3e), the polyp appearing to the left of the frame is reasonably segmented by both methods. However, the confounding artifact above the polyp due to optical blurring is wrongly segmented by PraNet as part of the anomaly, as seen in (Fig. 3f); DPN68×2 is also slightly confused, but it assigns much less probability to the pixels pixels related to the blurring artifact in Fig. (3g).

A challenging example extracted from the CVC-ColonDB is shown in the top row of Fig. 4. This low-contrast frame leads to a wrong prediction in the PraNet case shown in Fig. (4b), whereas the DPN68×2 model has no trouble in accurately delineating the borders of the polyp in Fig. (4c). Finally, an example from the ETIS database is shown in the bottom row of Fig. 4. This is a hardly visible polyp, and PraNet erroneously locates it to the right of the image, while DPN68×2, even if producing some oversegmenting, avoids this confusion.

4   Discussion and Conclusion

In this work we have analyzed double decoder-encoder networks for the task of polyp segmentation on endoscopic images. The encoder of the first network generates an attention map that indicates the second network the most interesting areas of the image. Double encoder-decoders leverage state-of-the-art encoder pretrained large natural image databases. We have shown that they provide a clear advantage over their single encoder-decoder counterparts. Comprehensive experimental results also show that a double encoder-decoder with a DPN encoder and a FP-Net decoder attains state-of-the-art on common benchmarks, with particularly good results on data that is visually dissimilar to the training images. Future steps involve the investigation of more efficient combination of the two building blocks of double encoder-decoders. It is reasonable to expect that smaller networks can already generate a suitable attention map that can be employed by the second network to achieve similar results at a reduced computational load.

References

1. Ahn, S.B., Han, D.S., Bae, J.H., Byun, T.J., Kim, J.P., Eun, C.S.: The miss rate for colorectal adenoma determined by quality-adjusted, back-to-back colonoscopies. Gut and Liver **6**(1), 64–70 (2012)
2. Akbari, M., et al.: Polyp segmentation in colonoscopy images using fully convolutional network. In: 2018 40th Annual International Conference of the IEEE Engineering in Medicine and Biology Society (EMBC), pp. 69–72, July 2018. ISSN: 1558–4615
3. Badrinarayanan, V., Kendall, A., Cipolla, R.: SegNet: a deep convolutional encoder-decoder architecture for image segmentation. IEEE Trans. Pattern Anal. Mach. Intell. **39**(12), 2481–2495 (2017)
4. Bernal, J., Sánchez, J., Vilariño, F.: Towards automatic polyp detection with a polyp appearance model. Pattern Recogn. **45**(9), 3166–3182 (2012)
5. Bernal, J., Sánchez, F.J., Fernñndez-Esparrach, G., Gil, D., Rodríguez, C., Vilariño, F.: WM-DOVA maps for accurate polyp highlighting in colonoscopy: validation vs. saliency maps from physicians. Comput. Med. Imaging Graph. **43**, 99–111 (2015)
6. Bernal, J., et al.: Comparative validation of polyp detection methods in video colonoscopy: results from the MICCAI 2015 endoscopic vision challenge. IEEE Trans. Med. Imaging **36**(6), 1231–1249 (2017)
7. Carneiro, G., Pu, L.Z.C.T., Singh, R., Burt, A.: Deep learning uncertainty and confidence calibration for the five-class polyp classification from colonoscopy. Med. Image Anal. **62**, 101653 (2020)
8. Chen, L.C., Papandreou, G., Kokkinos, I., Murphy, K., Yuille, A.L.: DeepLab: semantic image segmentation with deep convolutional nets, atrous convolution, and fully connected CRFs. IEEE Trans. Pattern Anal. Mach. Intell. **40**(4), 834–848 (2018)
9. Chen, L.C., Papandreou, G., Schroff, F., Adam, H.: Rethinking atrous convolution for semantic image segmentation. arXiv:1706.05587 [cs], December 2017
10. Chen, Y., Li, J., Xiao, H., Jin, X., Yan, S., Feng, J.: Dual path networks. In: Proceedings of the 31st International Conference on Neural Information Processing Systems. NIPS 2017, pp. 4470–4478. Curran Associates Inc., Red Hook, NY, USA, December 2017
11. Fan, D.-P., et al.: PraNet: parallel reverse attention network for polyp segmentation. In: Martel, A.L., et al. (eds.) MICCAI 2020. LNCS, vol. 12266, pp. 263–273. Springer, Cham (2020). https://doi.org/10.1007/978-3-030-59725-2_26
12. Fang, Y., Chen, C., Yuan, Y., Tong, K.: Selective feature aggregation network with area-boundary constraints for polyp segmentation. In: Shen, D., et al. (eds.) MICCAI 2019. LNCS, vol. 11764, pp. 302–310. Springer, Cham (2019). https://doi.org/10.1007/978-3-030-32239-7_34
13. Galdran, A., Anjos, A., Dolz, J., Chakor, H., Lombaert, H., Ayed, I.B.: The little w-net that could: state-of-the-art retinal vessel segmentation with minimalistic models. arXiv:2009.01907, September 2020

14. Guo, Y., Bernal, J., Matuszewski, B.J.: Polyp segmentation with fully convolutional deep neural networks-extended evaluation study. J. Imaging **6**(7), 69 (2020)
15. Haggar, F.A., Boushey, R.P.: Colorectal cancer epidemiology: incidence, mortality, survival, and risk factors. Clin. Colon Rectal Surg. **22**(4), 191–197 (2009)
16. He, K., Zhang, X., Ren, S., Sun, J.: Deep residual learning for image recognition. In: 2016 IEEE Conference on Computer Vision and Pattern Recognition (CVPR), pp. 770–778, June 2016. ISSN: 1063–6919
17. Huang, G., Liu, Z., Van Der Maaten, L., Weinberger, K.Q.: Densely connected convolutional networks. In: 2017 IEEE Conference on Computer Vision and Pattern Recognition (CVPR), pp. 2261–2269, July 2017. ISSN: 1063–6919
18. Jha, D., Riegler, M., Johansen, D., Halvorsen, P., Johansen, H.D.: DoubleU-Net: a deep convolutional neural network for medical image segmentation. In: 2020 IEEE 33rd International Symposium on Computer-Based Medical Systems (CBMS) (2020)
19. Jha, D., et al.: Kvasir-SEG: a segmented polyp dataset. In: Ro, Y.M., et al. (eds.) MMM 2020. LNCS, vol. 11962, pp. 451–462. Springer, Cham (2020). https://doi.org/10.1007/978-3-030-37734-2_37
20. Jha, D., Smedsrud, P.H., Riegler, M.A., Johansen, D., Lange, T.D., Halvorsen, P., Johansen, H.D.: ResUNet++: an advanced architecture for medical image segmentation. In: 2019 IEEE International Symposium on Multimedia (ISM), pp. 225–2255, December 2019
21. Jia, X., et al.: Automatic polyp recognition in colonoscopy images using deep learning and two-stage pyramidal feature prediction. IEEE Trans. Autom. Sci. Eng. **17**(3), 1570–1584 (2020)
22. Kang, J., Gwak, J.: Ensemble of instance segmentation models for polyp segmentation in colonoscopy images. IEEE Access **7**, 26440–26447 (2019)
23. Li, L., Verma, M., Nakashima, Y., Nagahara, H., Kawasaki, R.: IterNet: retinal image segmentation utilizing structural redundancy in vessel networks. In: The IEEE Winter Conference on Applications of Computer Vision (WACV), March 2020
24. Lin, T.Y., Dollár, P., Girshick, R., He, K., Hariharan, B., Belongie, S.: Feature pyramid networks for object detection. In: 2017 IEEE Conference on Computer Vision and Pattern Recognition (CVPR), pp. 936–944, July 2017. ISSN: 1063–6919
25. Lui, T.K., et al.: New insights on missed colonic lesions during colonoscopy through artificial intelligence-assisted real-time detection (with video). Gastrointest. Endosc. **93**(1), 193–200.e1 (2021). https://www.sciencedirect.com/science/article/pii/S0016510720342668
26. Otsu, N.: A threshold selection method from gray-level histograms. IEEE Trans. Syst. Man Cybern. **9**(1), 62–66 (1979)
27. Ronneberger, O., Fischer, P., Brox, T.: U-Net: convolutional networks for biomedical image segmentation. In: Navab, N., Hornegger, J., Wells, W.M., Frangi, A.F. (eds.) MICCAI 2015. LNCS, vol. 9351, pp. 234–241. Springer, Cham (2015). https://doi.org/10.1007/978-3-319-24574-4_28
28. Sandler, M., Howard, A., Zhu, M., Zhmoginov, A., Chen, L.C.: MobileNetV2: inverted residuals and linear bottlenecks. In: 2018 IEEE/CVF Conference on Computer Vision and Pattern Recognition, pp. 4510–4520, June 2018. ISSN: 2575–7075
29. Silva, J., Histace, A., Romain, O., Dray, X., Granado, B.: Toward embedded detection of polyps in WCE images for early diagnosis of colorectal cancer. Int. J. Comput. Assist. Radiol. Surg. **9**(2), 283–293 (2013). https://doi.org/10.1007/s11548-013-0926-3

30. Simonyan, K., Zisserman, A.: Very deep convolutional networks for large-scale image recognition. In: International Conference on Learning Representations (2015)
31. Sánchez-Peralta, L.F., Bote-Curiel, L., Picón, A., Sánchez-Margallo, F.M., Pagador, J.B.: Deep learning to find colorectal polyps in colonoscopy: a systematic literature review. Artif. Intell. Med. **108**, 101923 (2020)
32. Sánchez-Peralta, L.F., Picón, A., Antequera-Barroso, J.A., Ortega-Morán, J.F., Sánchez-Margallo, F.M., Pagador, J.B.: Eigenloss: combined PCA-based loss function for polyp segmentation. Mathematics **8**(8), 1316 (2020)
33. Tian, Z., He, T., Shen, C., Yan, Y.: Decoders Matter for Semantic Segmentation: Data-Dependent Decoding Enables Flexible Feature Aggregation, pp. 3126–3135 (2019)
34. Vázquez, D., et al.: A benchmark for endoluminal scene segmentation of colonoscopy images. J. Healthc. Eng. **2017**, 4037190 (2017)
35. Wickstrøm, K., Kampffmeyer, M., Jenssen, R.: Uncertainty and interpretability in convolutional neural networks for semantic segmentation of colorectal polyps. Med. Image Anal. **60**, 101619 (2020)
36. Wojna, Z.: The devil is in the decoder: classification, regression and GANs. Int. J. Comput. Vis. **127**(11), 1694–1706 (2019). https://doi.org/10.1007/s11263-019-01170-8
37. Xie, S., Girshick, R., Dollár, P., Tu, Z., He, K.: Aggregated residual transformations for deep neural networks. In: 2017 IEEE Conference on Computer Vision and Pattern Recognition (CVPR), pp. 5987–5995, July 2017. ISSN: 1063–6919
38. Zhang, R., Zheng, Y., Poon, C.C.Y., Shen, D., Lau, J.Y.W.: Polyp detection during colonoscopy using a regression-based convolutional neural network with a tracker. Pattern Recogn. **83**, 209–219 (2018)
39. Zhou, Z., Siddiquee, M.M.R., Tajbakhsh, N., Liang, J.: UNet++: redesigning skip connections to exploit multiscale features in image segmentation. IEEE Trans. Med. Imaging **39**(6), 1856–1867 (2020)

A Superpixel-Wise Fully Convolutional Neural Network Approach for Diabetic Foot Ulcer Tissue Classification

Rania Niri[1]([✉]), Hassan Douzi[1], Yves Lucas[2], and Sylvie Treuillet[2]

[1] IRF-SIC Laboratory, Ibn Zohr University, Agadir, Morocco
rania.niri@edu.uiz.ac.ma, h.douzi@uiz.ac.ma
[2] PRISME Laboratory, Orleans University, Orleans, France
{yves.lucas,sylvie.treuillet}@univ-orleans.fr

Abstract. Accurate assessment of diabetic foot ulcers (DFU) is primordial to provide an efficient treatment and to prevent amputation. Traditional DFU assessment methods used by clinicians are based on visual examination of the ulcer by estimating the surface and analyzing tissue conditions. These manual methods are subjective and make direct contact with the wound, resulting in high variability and risk of infection. In this research work, we propose a novel smartphone-based skin telemonitoring system to support medical diagnoses and decisions during DFU tissues examination. The database contains 219 images, for effective tissue identification and annotation of the ground truth, a graphical interface based on superpixel segmentation method has been used. Our method performs DFU assessment in an end-to-end style comprising automatic ulcer segmentation and tissue classification. The classification task is performed at a patch-level, superpixels extracted with SLIC are used as input for the training of the deep neural network. State-of-the-art deep learning models for semantic segmentation have been used to perform tissue differentiation within the ulcer area into three classes (Necrosis, Granulation and Slough) and have been compared to the proposed method. The proposed superpixel-based method outperforms classic fully convolutional network models while improving significantly the performance on all the metrics. Accuracy and DICE index are improved from 84.55% to 92.68% and from 54.31% to 75.74% respectively for FCN-32. The results reveal robust tissue classification effectiveness and the potential of our system to monitor DFU healing over time.

Keywords: Deep learning · Fully convolutional networks · Superpixel segmentation · Diabetic foot ulcer · Tissue classification · Slic

1 Introduction

Diabetes is a chronic disease characterized by abnormally high levels of glucose in the blood. At present, almost half a billion people worldwide suffers from

A. Del Bimbo et al. (Eds.): ICPR 2020 Workshops, LNCS 12661, pp. 308–320, 2021.
https://doi.org/10.1007/978-3-030-68763-2_23

diabetes. Poorly managed diabetes leads to several complications including cardiovascular disease, kidney disease, eye complications, nephropathy, lower limb ulcers, etc. Diabetic foot ulcers (DFU) are the most chronic and severe complication of diabetes associated with neurological disorders and peripheral vascular disease leading to millions of amputations every year. A lower limb is lost to amputation every 30 s somewhere in the world due to diabetes [4]. This diabetes related complication has a significant impact on individuals' life quality and imposes a high social and economic cost. However, if an appropriate management of these ulcers is achieved, lower limbs amputation can be delayed or prevented altogether. Diabetic foot ulcers should be regularly checked by healthcare professionals for clinical care and to evaluate the healing progress. In standard clinical practice, the examination of ulcers is mainly based on physical measurements and visual assessment of the skin tissues [5]. Manual methods rely on the use of a simple ruler to measure ulcer perimeter (length and width), an outline over a transparent sheet to calculate the surface area and physiological serum for volume estimation [14]. Moreover, these methods are invasive and in direct contact with the wound bed which carries high risk of infection. On the other hand, analyzing color and proportion of the tissues help to determine the healing progress of the ulcer and provide quantitative measurement without contact. Within the ulcer boundaries, visual inspection is based on red-yellow-black color evaluation model corresponding respectively to the different tissues: granulation, slough and necrosis [30] (see Fig. 1).

The principal objective of this work is to develop an automatic smartphone-based system for ulcer segmentation and tissue identification. This work is part of the STANDUP project [1] which aims to prevent diabetic foot ulceration in an early stage and to monitor in an efficient way the ulcer healing over time. In order to provide a robust tissue classification, we propose a novel superpixel-based approach for automatic tissue analysis using deep learning methods.

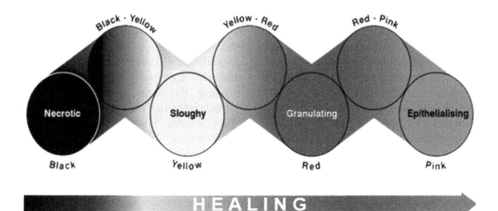

Fig. 1. The wound healing continuum (WHC) [13]

The final system can serve as effective tool to support medical diagnoses and decisions during DFU examination to ensure an accurate management of lower limb lesions. Moreover, this methodology is applicable to other wound conditions such as pressure injuries, surgical and traumatic wounds, venous ulcers, etc.

2   Related Work

In recent years, the use of smartphones and imaging technology in daily clinical practice, especially towards wound and DFU assessment has increased considerably. Clinicians can obtain additional information about the wound characteristics from digital image processing to improve diagnostic accuracy. Several image processing studies have addressed wound segmentation using different approaches. Mainly, these methods are based on supervised traditional machine learning (ML) especially SVM classifiers. ML algorithms require handcrafted features extracted from images using different texture and color descriptors followed by SVM [26,29]. Nevertheless, descriptors can be influenced by image resolution and require a color correction step using a reference pattern inserted in the field of view. Although their performance, ML methods are not robust enough due to their reliance on the handcrafted features. Recent approaches involve more sophisticated methods such as deep learning. Including convolutional neural networks (CNN) for classification or fully convolutional neural networks (FCN) for semantic segmentation. The training of these networks requires the use of a large labeled dataset. In [25], Wang et al. proposed a new deep learning architecture based on en-coder-decoder to perform wound segmentation using 650 images from NYU database [22]. On a different approach, Goyal et al. [11] developed a new DL model called DFUNet to classify DFU sub-images into normal and abnormal skin using 397 images. The proposed network DFUNet outperforms GoogLeNet in all the evaluation metrics. In a recent work [12], the same authors used a two-tier transfer learning model combining R-CNN with Inception-V2 to localize DFU with a precision of 91.8%.

Regarding tissue classification, most of the methods found in the literature use traditional machine learning algorithms. Mukherjee et al. [16] performed wound tissue classification using five color and ten textural features followed by a 3rd polynomial kernel SVM. In a different approach, Hazem et al. [28] proposed a multi-view tissue classification using 3D model and SVM. Due to the lack of annotated images in the biomedical field and especially for chronic wounds (CW), few studies have been conducted using DL methods for wound tissue classification. In [10], the authors used 30 wound images to perform tissue segmentation using the fully convolutional net-work U-net designed for small medical image databases [20]. The network was initialized with a pre-trained VGG-16 [8]. The results show an accuracy of 94% and 96% after a color space reduction. Zahia et al. [31] presented an approach to handle small datasets in DL through patch-level tissue classification. Their approach was based on partitioning 22 images into small 5×5 patches that have been used to train the proposed convolutional network. The achieved performance was relatively high with an accuracy of 92.01%. Similarly, Nejati et al. [17] performed tissue classification on a patch-level but with combining ML and DL methods. The dataset contains 350 images partitioned into 20×20 patches. AlexNet has been used for feature extraction and SVM to classify each patch into the corresponding tissue class.

Unlike existing approaches using square patches, we used homogeneous superpixels instead. Superpixels have more perceptual meaning since pixels belonging to a given superpixel share similar tissue properties. In a recent work [7], Blanco et al. proposed a superpixel-driven method called QTDU using the CNN ResNet for dermatological wounds tissue classification. The method, outperformed different machine learning approaches. In contrast, our premise is to perform superpixel-based diabetic foot ulcer tissue classification at pixel-level using fully convolutional neural networks for a more accurate and precise tissue identification.

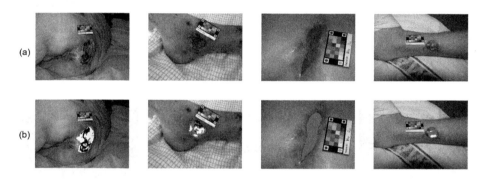

Fig. 2. Some images from ESCALE database (a) and corresponding ground-truth (b).

3   Proposed Method

Our approach is divided into two steps: first, the automatic extraction of the ulcer area eliminates all background elements that may threaten the classification. This ulcer segmentation is useful for perimeter and surface assessment based on a pattern included in the field of view for fixing the image scale factor. Secondly, tissue classification is performed to identify the different tissues within the ulcer area after superpixel extraction.

3.1   Image Acquisition and Data Annotation

A database of diabetic foot ulcer images has been constituted in two hospital centers, Hospital Nacional Dos de Mayo (Lima, Peru) and CHRO Hospital (Orleans, France). The acquisition protocol consists on capturing free-handedly a set of images using a smartphone camera while framing the ulcer area from a point of view as frontal as possible. Chronic wound images from ESCALE database [27] were also added to the training set. The images are with different resolutions, acquired using different cameras and under different illumination conditions. The whole database comprises 219 images with variety of types of chronic wounds including leg ulcers, diabetic ulcers, bed sores, etc. The database has been labeled by medical experts into three main types of tissues using the graphical interface proposed in [18] based on the red-yellow-black usual model. Figure 2 shows some examples of wound images multi-class annotation.

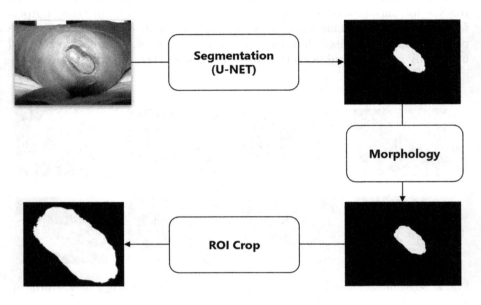

Fig. 3. Diabetic foot ulcer segmentation framework

3.2   Ulcer Segmentation and Superpixels Extraction

The first stage of our method is ROI extraction. This step is meant to extract the ulcer area from healthy skin and to eliminate background elements. The background removal aims to highlight the tissues features inside the wound bed in order to simplify the classification task. The segmentation was performed using U-net, which achieved an accuracy of 94.96% and a Dice score of 97.25% [19]. To refine the segmentation results, we combined different morphological operations (i.e., erosion, dilation, opening, and closing) [24]. Then, the non-ulcer region has been represented by a white background in the original images and corresponding ground-truth. Mainly, the wound area especially for DFUs represents less than 30% in most images. Hence, using the entire image as input for the training of the network is unnecessary. Therefore, we cropped the ROI in all images and their annotations to focus the training on the wound area only (see Fig. 3).

To extract superpixels from the segmented wound, we adopted simple linear iterative clustering (SLIC) [2] which relies on k-means method to generate an efficient image partition into homogeneous clusters by combining (R,G,B,X,Y) five-dimensional color and image plane space. Superpixel extraction from the ROI was provided using the zero-parameter version of the SLIC algorithm called SLICO. Instead of using the same compactness parameter initialized by the user for all superpixels in the image, this method adaptively changes the compactness parameter for each superpixel depending on its texture [3]. The result is regularly shaped superpixels regardless of the texture while conserving a high computational efficiency. The obtained superpixel segmentation map is then applied to the ground truth image in order to generate the annotation label of each sub-image. After superpixels split, only the ones corresponding to a single tissue and their corresponding label were conserved and all totally white superpixels were removed for an efficient training. Finally, the superpixels were cropped and resized to 224×224 resolution (see Fig. 4).

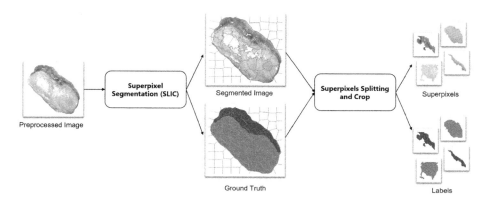

Fig. 4. Superpixel extraction from the segmented DFU image using SLIC

3.3 Superpixel-Based Tissue Classification

Our objective is to classify DFU tissue at a pixel level into three main classes combining deep neural networks and superpixels. The segmentation was performed using the state-of-the-art deep neural networks for semantic segmentation called as Fully Convolutional Neural Networks. These networks replace the fully connected layers in the classification models with convolutional layers which allow a pixel-wise prediction. A class label is assigned to each pixel of the image. The typical architecture for semantic segmentation is encoder-decoder and it consists of an encoder network followed by the corresponding decoder. U-Net [20], SegNet [6] and FCN-Net [15] are the most used algorithms for semantic segmentation in the field of medical images. U-Net proposed by Ronneberger et al. is specially designed for small databases segmentation and produces precise segmentation using few images for training. SegNet is an encoder-decoder network identical to the convolutional layers in VGG16 [23] adapted for semantic segmentation, the encoder network is considerably reduced which make it computationally efficient. FCN-32, FCN-16, and FCN-8 are the three main variants of FCN-Net based on a pre-trained VGG16 network as encoder. FCN-32 is same as VGG16 in which fully connected layer of VGG16 is replaced by a 1×1 convolution. FCN-16 and FCN-8 additionally work on low-level features by adding decoder layers to the network in order to produce more precise segmentation.

The generated superpixels with SLIC were used as input to feed these fully convolutional neural network models. (Figure 5) illustrates the proposed framework based on an FCN-32 architecture. In the model training, we adopted a large-scale dataset with over 5000 wound superpixel and corresponding ground truth without any data augmentation. The output of the proposed method is a semantic segmentation of each superpixel. The model evaluation for DFU tissue classification of an entire image is done into three steps. Initially, the ulcer is segmented and split into superpixels similarly as presented in the previous section. Then, the generated superpixels and their corresponding labels are cropped and resized. Secondly, each superpixel will be given to the trained network for prediction to get the segmentation map. Thirdly, a class label will be assigned to each superpixel depending on its dominant color (red, yellow or black). The non-tissue superpixels such as bones will be classified as unknown and represented by a white color. Finally, an output image will be reconstructed based on the superpixel classification and the final result is a segmentation map of the different tissues inside the wound bed.

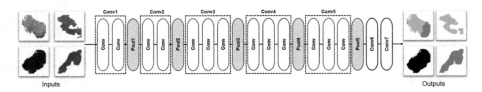

Fig. 5. Overview of the proposed fully convolutional network architecture based on super-pixels

4   Results

4.1   Performance Metrics

We evaluated the performance of the proposed method at pixel level using the most common metrics in the field of medical image segmentation. These metrics are accuracy, sensitivity, specificity, precision, and dice similarity coefficient (DICE) [9]. The formulas are defined respectively as the following:

$$Accuracy = \frac{TP + TN}{TP + FP + TN + FN} \tag{1}$$

$$Sensitivity = \frac{TP}{TP + FN} \tag{2}$$

$$Specificity = \frac{TN}{TN + FP} \tag{3}$$

$$Precision = \frac{TP}{TP + FP} \tag{4}$$

$$DICE = \frac{2TP}{2TP + FP + FN} \tag{5}$$

Where TP, FP, TN and FN stand for the number of the true positive, false positive, true negative and false negative classified pixels.

Table 1. Number of superpixels for the training and testing set

	Training	Testing
Granulation	2872	762
Slough	1897	594
Necrosis	463	155
Unknown	24	19

4.2 Experimental Results

The database containing the generated superpixels and their labels was divided into training and testing set. The partition percentage was around 75% for the training, and 25% for the testing as shown in (Table 1). The evaluation aimed at quantifying the improvement of the of state-of-the-art FCNs using the proposed superpixel based approach (Spx) in comparison to their classic version and determining the most suitable network to perform tissue identification of diabetic foot ulcers. Accordingly, The different models have been trained on the same chronic wound database and tested using only DFU images. The methods were implemented in Keras with TensorFlow backend using the stochastic gradient descent (SGD) optimizer [21], a learning rate of 0.01 and a batch-size of 32. The FCN methods were trained for 200 epochs while the Superpixel-based ones were trained for 50 epochs due to computational resources limitation and memory constraint.

Table 2 lists the segmentation results of all the tested methods regarding the accuracy, sensitivity, specificity, precision and DICE. The proposed superpixel-based approach outperformed all the state-of-the-art methods. It shows a higher performance for all the computed metrics. As we can see, the results were considerably improved by the usage of superpixels instead of the whole image as training set. This demonstrates the effectiveness of combining SLIC superpixels and FCN as it is capable of performing a more precise semantic segmentation of tissues.

Table 2. Tissue segmentation results of FCNs vs. Spx-based FCNs

	Accuracy	Sensitivity	Specificity	Precision	DICE
SegNet	58.6%	36.4%	82.2%	43.7%	33.2%
Spx-SegNet	**79.2%**	**65.9%**	**93.3%**	**72.2%**	**67.1%**
UNet	69.56%	55.1%	87.6%	68.7%	57.5%
Spx-UNet	**80.75%**	**68.3%**	**94%**	**74.8%**	**69.2%**
FCN8	69.37%	61%	90%	63%	60.3%
Spx- FCN8	**81.92%**	**74.5%**	**93.6%**	**78.7%**	**73.7%**
FCN16	72%	57.7%	90.6%	62.9%	56.1%
Spx- FCN16	**83.67%**	**75.4%**	**94.2%**	**76.9%**	**75.5%**
FCN32	84.55%	54.68%	89.32%	62.08%	54.31%
Spx- FCN32	**92.68%**	**74.53%**	**94.39%**	**78.07%**	**75.74%**

Table 3. Classification results for each tissue using the proposed Spx-FCN32 method

	Sensitivity	Specificity	Precision	DICE
Necrosis	51.55%	99.01%	70.94%	59.71%
Slough	84.63%	91.89%	71.48%	77.50%
Granulation	69.68%	95.81%	76.01%	72.71%

To choose the most suitable network, we selected the best performances of Table 2. Spx-FCN16 and Spx-FCN32 achieved the best results for all the computed metrics, SPX-FCN32 was slightly better than Spx-FCN16 regarding Sensitivity, Specificity, precision and DICE and it achieved a higher accuracy. A fusion of superpixels and FCN-32 improved accuracy by 8.13% to reach 92.68% and led to a high DICE score of 75.74% instead of 54.31%. Figure 6 shows some examples of DFU tissue segmentation output for both approaches. We also investigated how the method performed on each tissue type. Detailed classification results for necrotic, granulation, and slough tissues using the superpixel-based FCN-32 variant can be seen on Table 3. The results on specific tissue types indicate that necrotic class performance is inferior when compared to slough or granulation tissue. Necrosis appears to be the most difficult to be identified by the network. This could be justified by the number of superpixels per class during the training phase which lead to wrong pixel classification of this tissue. Necrosis represents only 9% of the training set comparing to 54% for granulation and 36% for slough. Therefore, the performance results for non-necrotic classes is reliable and reflect a significant improvement in wound tissue segmentation. Unlike the existing methods in literature which deal with slough tissue due to the different textures related to it, our method is capable of segment it with the highest DICE score of 77.5%.

Moreover, by observing the qualitative results (see Fig. 6), we can clearly notice that the method based on superpixels produces an accurate segmentation with a very high precision regarding the three classes (Granulation, Necrosis and Slough). The tissue segmentation precision was significantly improved using superpixels instead of the entire image to train the FCN-32 network. In addition,

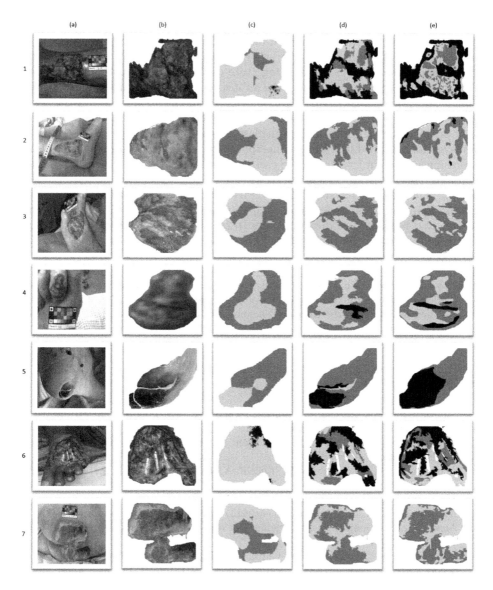

Fig. 6. DFU tissue segmentation results: (a) original image, (b) segmented image, (c) output of FCN-32, (d) output of the proposed Spx-FCN32, and (e) Ground truth.

the identification of non-tissue pixels corresponding to bones inside the ulcer area (see Fig. 6, sample 6), is a statement of our method robustness.

5 Conclusion

We presented a novel approach for automatic diabetic foot ulcer segmentation and tissue classification. The proposed classification method was performed by a superpixel-based semantic segmentation using fully convolutional networks. The experimental tests show that the proposed image segmentation method exhibits higher performance than the existing state-of-the-art FCN methods regarding all the metrics and demonstrate the robustness of our method especially for slough and granulation tissue. Furthermore, we intend to expand our database by acquiring new high-quality wound images with different tissue types in order to improve tissue identification for all classes especially necrotic one. In addition, our system is embedded into a smartphone with add-on temperature sensor. Assessing the wound temperature can help to localize sign of deep inflammation and infection and to identify the DFU type (neuroischemic or neuropathic) as well. The proposed system could be used by clinicians during diabetic foot examination for an accurate and complete assessment from ulcer delineation, surface and temperature measurements to tissue area identification and analysis. This system can be extended to the assessment of chronic wounds such as burn wounds, pressure injuries, etc.

Acknowledgments. This research work is supported by the European Union's Horizon 2020 under the Marie Sklodowska-Curie grant agreement No. 777661. The authors express their gratitude to the Hospital Nacional Dos de Mayo in Peru, the CHRO Hospital in France and especially to Evelyn Gutiérrez for their cooperation in collecting diabetic foot images.

References

1. Standup: Smartphone thermal analysis for diabetic foot ulcer prevention and treatment (2018). https://standupproject.eu/
2. Achanta, R., Shaji, A., Smith, K., Lucchi, A., Fua, P., Süsstrunk, S.: Slic superpixels. Technical report (2010)
3. Achanta, R., Shaji, A., Smith, K., Lucchi, A., Fua, P., Süsstrunk, S.: Slic superpixels compared to state-of-the-art superpixel methods. IEEE Trans. Pattern Anal. Mach. Intell. **34**(11), 2274–2282 (2012)
4. Aguiree, F., et al.: Idf diabetes atlas (2013)
5. Alexiadou, K., Doupis, J.: Management of diabetic foot ulcers. Diab. Ther. **3**(1), 4 (2012)
6. Badrinarayanan, V., Kendall, A., Cipolla, R.: Segnet: a deep convolutional encoder-decoder architecture for image segmentation. IEEE Trans. Pattern Anal. Mach. Intell. **39**(12), 2481–2495 (2017)
7. Blanco, G., et al.: A superpixel-driven deep learning approach for the analysis of dermatological wounds. Comput. Methods Programs Biomed. **183**, 105079 (2020)

8. Deng, J., Dong, W., Socher, R., Li, L.J., Li, K., Fei-Fei, L.: Imagenet: a large-scale hierarchical image database. In: 2009 IEEE Conference on Computer Vision and Pattern Recognition, pp. 248–255. IEEE (2009)
9. Dice, L.R.: Measures of the amount of ecologic association between species. Ecology **26**(3), 297–302 (1945)
10. Godeiro, V., Neto, J.S., Carvalho, B., Santana, B., Ferraz, J., Gama, R.: Chronic wound tissue classification using convolutional networks and color space reduction. In: 2018 IEEE 28th International Workshop on Machine Learning for Signal Processing (MLSP), pp. 1–6. IEEE (2018)
11. Goyal, M., Reeves, N.D., Davison, A.K., Rajbhandari, S., Spragg, J., Yap, M.H.: DFUNet: convolutional neural networks for diabetic foot ulcer classification. IEEE Trans. Emerg. Topics Comput. Intell. **4**, 728–739 (2018)
12. Goyal, M., Reeves, N.D., Rajbhandari, S., Yap, M.H.: Robust methods for real-time diabetic foot ulcer detection and localization on mobile devices. IEEE J. Biomed. Health Inform. **23**(4), 1730–1741 (2018)
13. Gray, D., White, R., Cooper, P., Kingsley, A.: Understanding applied wound management. WOUNDS UK **1**(1), 62 (2005)
14. Jørgensen, L.B., Sørensen, J.A., Jemec, G.B., Yderstræde, K.B.: Methods to assess area and volume of wounds-a systematic review. Int. Wound J. **13**(4), 540–553 (2016)
15. Long, J., Shelhamer, E., Darrell, T.: Fully convolutional networks for semantic segmentation. In: Proceedings of the IEEE Conference on Computer Vision and Pattern Recognition, pp. 3431–3440 (2015)
16. Mukherjee, R., Manohar, D.D., Das, D.K., Achar, A., Mitra, A., Chakraborty, C.: Automated tissue classification framework for reproducible chronic wound assessment. BioMed Rese. Int. **2014**, 1–9 (2014)
17. Nejati, H., et al.: Fine-grained wound tissue analysis using deep neural network. In: 2018 IEEE International Conference on Acoustics, Speech and Signal Processing (ICASSP), pp. 1010–1014. IEEE (2018)
18. NIRI, R., Lucas, Y., Treuillet, S., Douzi, H.: Smartphone-based thermal imaging system for diabetic foot ulcer assessment. In: Journées d'Etude sur la TéléSanté. Sorbonne Universités, Paris, France, May 2019. https://hal.archives-ouvertes.fr/hal-02161044
19. Rania, N., Douzi, H., Yves, L., Sylvie, T.: Semantic segmentation of diabetic foot ulcer images: dealing with small dataset in DL approaches. In: El Moataz, A., Mammass, D., Mansouri, A., Nouboud, F. (eds.) ICISP 2020. LNCS, vol. 12119, pp. 162–169. Springer, Cham (2020). https://doi.org/10.1007/978-3-030-51935-3_17
20. Ronneberger, O., Fischer, P., Brox, T.: U-Net: convolutional networks for biomedical image segmentation. In: Navab, N., Hornegger, J., Wells, W.M., Frangi, A.F. (eds.) MICCAI 2015. LNCS, vol. 9351, pp. 234–241. Springer, Cham (2015). https://doi.org/10.1007/978-3-319-24574-4_28
21. Ruder, S.: An overview of gradient descent optimization algorithms. arXiv preprint arXiv:1609.04747 (2016)
22. Silberman, N., Hoiem, D., Kohli, P., Fergus, R.: Indoor segmentation and support inference from RGBD images. In: Fitzgibbon, A., Lazebnik, S., Perona, P., Sato, Y., Schmid, C. (eds.) ECCV 2012. LNCS, vol. 7576, pp. 746–760. Springer, Heidelberg (2012). https://doi.org/10.1007/978-3-642-33715-4_54
23. Simonyan, K., Zisserman, A.: Very deep convolutional networks for large-scale image recognition. arXiv preprint arXiv:1409.1556 (2014)
24. Sreedhar, K., Panlal, B.: Enhancement of images using morphological transformation. arXiv preprint arXiv:1203.2514 (2012)

25. Wang, C., et al.: A unified framework for automatic wound segmentation and analysis with deep convolutional neural networks. In: 2015 37th Annual International Conference of the IEEE Engineering in Medicine and Biology Society (EMBC), pp. 2415–2418. IEEE (2015)
26. Wang, L., Pedersen, P.C., Agu, E., Strong, D.M., Tulu, B.: Area determination of diabetic foot ulcer images using a cascaded two-stage SVM-based classification. IEEE Trans. Biomed. Eng. **64**(9), 2098–2109 (2016)
27. Wannous, H., Lucas, Y., Treuillet, S., Albouy, B.: A complete 3D wound assessment tool for accurate tissue classification and measurement. In: 2008 15th IEEE International Conference on Image Processing, pp. 2928–2931. IEEE (2008)
28. Wannous, H., Treuillet, S., Lucas, Y.: Robust tissue classification for reproducible wound assessment in telemedicine environments. J. Electron. Imaging **19**(2), 023002 (2010)
29. Wantanajittikul, K., Auephanwiriyakul, S., Theera-Umpon, N., Koanantakool, T.: Automatic segmentation and degree identification in burn color images. In: The 4th 2011 Biomedical Engineering International Conference, pp. 169–173. IEEE (2012)
30. Young, T.: Accurate assessment of different wound tissue types. Wounds Essentials **10**(1), 51–4 (2015)
31. Zahia, S., Sierra-Sosa, D., Garcia-Zapirain, B., Elmaghraby, A.: Tissue classification and segmentation of pressure injuries using convolutional neural networks. Comput. Methods Programs Biomed. **159**, 51–58 (2018)

Fully vs. Weakly Supervised Caries Localization in Smartphone Images with CNNs

Duc Duy Pham[1(✉)], Jonas Müller[1], Piush Aggarwal[2], Amit Khatri[3],
Mayank Sharma[3], Torsten Zesch[2], and Josef Pauli[1]

[1] Intelligent Systems, University of Duisburg-Essen, Duisburg, Germany
{duc.duy.pham,jonas.mueller,josef.pauli}@uni-due.de
[2] Language Technology Lab, University of Duisburg-Essen, Duisburg, Germany
{piush.aggarwal,torsten.zesch}@uni-due.de
[3] Department of Paedodontics and Preventive Dentistry, UCMS and GTB Hospital,
Delhi, India
{Khatriamit,Mayank}@ucms.ac.in

Abstract. While in developed countries routine dental consultations
are often covered by insurance, access to prophylactic dental examinations is often expensive in developing countries. Therefore, sufficient oral
health prevention, particularly early caries detection, is not accessible to
many people in these countries, yet. This observation is, however, contrary to the accessibility of smartphone technology, as smartphones have
become available and affordable in most countries. Their technology can
be utilized for low-cost initial caries inspection to determine the necessity
for a subsequent dental examination. In this paper we address the specific problem of caries detection in smartphone images. Fully supervised
methods usually require tedious location annotations, whereas weakly
supervised approaches manage to address the detection task with less
complex labels. To this end, we propose a weakly supervised caries detection strategy with local constraints and investigate its caries localization
capabilities compared to a superior fully supervised Faster R-CNN approach as upper baseline. Our proposed strategy shows promising initial
results on our in-house smartphone caries data set.

Keywords: Caries detection · Caries detection in smartphone
images · Weakly supervised detection · Local constraints

1 Introduction

1.1 Medical Motivation

There are many infectious diseases that are responsible for the decay of tooth
enamel. Dental caries is considered as one of those diseases that create cavities and even affect inner tooth layers such as dentin and fuels further decay

© Springer Nature Switzerland AG 2021
A. Del Bimbo et al. (Eds.): ICPR 2020 Workshops, LNCS 12661, pp. 321–336, 2021.
https://doi.org/10.1007/978-3-030-68763-2_24

of the tooth pulp [9]. In more serious cases bacteria may infect periodontal ligament, bone or gum cells, which results in dental abscess. A patient infected from caries feels pain, when the affected area comes in contact with hot, cold or sweet substances. Nearly 90% of adults, and 60–90% of school children, have had cavities before.[1] That this infection is not limited to adults can be observed in France for instance, as one-third of children with age less than 6 years to 50% of children with age less than 12 years are found infected with this disease. Similar trends are observed in Canada [2]. Malnutrition and inadequate eating habits during weaning in young kids cause 'early childhood caries'. The disease shows its dominant effect on children, especially from developing countries. The limited or non-existent access to precautionary oral screenings for children with low socio-economic background is also considered a public health problem, as early detection of caries certainly limits the progress of this disease [28, 29]. Dental caries is a global oral health problem which can be effectively prevented and controlled through a combination of individual, community and professional efforts. The global distribution of dental caries has shown distinctive variations [34]. The low ratio of skilled dentist to affected patients (1:12500) is a major motivation towards the introduction of technological aspects in the detection of caries [5]. Computer aided tools not only assist the dentists in accelerating the caries detection and diagnosis process, but may also be helpful in reducing human errors. Existing technical systems for the detection of tooth decay are based on standardized imaging techniques, such as X-Ray. Access to the technology required for this is not common, especially in developing countries. However, smartphone technology has become available and affordable in most countries [23]. This technology can be utilized for affordable initial caries inspection to determine the necessity for a subsequent dental examination. Therefore, this work investigates the possibility of caries localization in smartphone images with both fully supervised and weakly supervised object detection methods.

1.2   Technical Motivation

Fully supervised object detection methods usually require the exact locations of the object of interest's bounding box for training. Therefore, a bounding box annotation is required for each caries occurrence. Establishing these fully informative annotations (FIA) is often tedious and costly, particularly for large data sets, in which the target object may appear multiple times within one image. Weak supervision on the other hand poses a more time-efficient but more challenging option to address object detection with less informative annotations. To this end, we consider image-level annotations (ILA), in which only the image label but no information about the caries location is available. Furthermore, we also consider mouth region annotations (MRA), in which a bounding box of the mouth region is given additionally to the ILAs, as weak annotations. Although information about exact locations and the number of occurrences within each image is nevertheless missing, these are still time-efficient to produce. These

---

[1] https://www.nidcr.nih.gov/research/data-statistics/dental-caries.

MRAs are represented as binary rectangular masks. In total we compare three approaches using Convolutional Neural Networks (CNNs): one fully supervised method with FIAs and two weakly supervised strategies with ILAs and MRAs, respectively. Particulary, we use Ren et al.'s Faster R-CNN [26] for the fully supervised case with FIAs. For the weakly supervised cases we train a CNN classifier with the ILAs and MRAs, respectively, and leverage the activation maps within the CNN to locate possible caries occurrences. This is a challenging task as the caries regions may appear at multiple and different locations, different scales and under a variety of viewpoints.

1.3   Contributions

In this paper we make the following contributions. Firstly, we apply deep learning strategies on the use case of caries detection in smartphone images to foster an increased usage of recent research developments in real world health applications. For this we propose a weakly supervised caries detection pipeline and furthermore demonstrate the efficacy of adding location constraints to the weak supervision. Finally, we compare a fully supervised approach to our weakly supervised methods on our in-house data set which is collection of colour images of dental tooth caries.

The remainder of the paper is structured as follows. Section 2 discusses the related work and Sect. 3 deals with the methodology. Section 4 describes the experiments, while Sect. 5 discusses the results. Section 6 concludes the paper with suggestions for future work.

2   Related Work

Primarily, the detection of dental caries has been a visual process, principally based on visual-tactile examination and radio-graphic examination [33]. Using these methods, caries can only be diagnosed by a dental health professional. Due to the asymptomatic initiation and progression of the dental caries, patients often fail to consult a dentist in time, resulting in dental caries progression to an irreversible loss of the dental hard tissue [17]. Ali et al. [1] and Choi et al. [6] make use of neural networks to automatically detect caries areas within X-ray images. Casalegno et al. [4] make use of near-infrared transillumination imaging instead of X-ray to extract caries regions by means of a U-Net like [27] deep learning architecture. Kositbownchai et al. [18] also train a neural network to detect artificial dental caries using images from a charged coupled device (CCD) camera and intra-oral digital radiography. For their evaluation only teeth with artificial caries are considered, which usually have different properties than naturally affected ones. Similar to our contribution, Datta et al. [7] use RGB images to detect caries regions, however, by means of traditional image processing methods, i.e. image enhancement, transforming the images into HIS color space and clustering in this color space. In contrast to our case. their images were captured with a specialized camera for the oral cavity and allows similar lighting conditions and viewpoints across the data set. Saravanan et al. [30] propose a strategy to detect dental caries in its early stage using histogram and power spectral analysis. In this method, the detection of tooth cavities is done based on the region of concentration of pixels with regard to the histogram and based on the magnitude values with regard to the spectrum. Zhang et al. [36] and Liang et al. [20] propose deep learning-based localization systems for cavity detection and integrate theirs systems into smartphone applications. Liu et al. [22] explore the applicability of in-home dental healthcare by presenting a complete IoT system, in which deep learning is used for object localization. Most of these contributions have in common, that either full supervision or traditional unsupervised image processing is applied to detect the caries region.

Regarding weakly supervised methods related work can be generally categorized into multiple instance learning (MIL) based methods [3,35], CNN based approaches [24] and a combination of both [19]. In MIL based approaches, an image is usually considered to be a bag of instances, where the object locations represent the instances. The aim is usually to alternatively learn a discriminative representation by means of the image-level annotation, which is then used to detect positive object instances in positive images. In this paper, however, we mainly focus on a solely CNN based approach for weakly supervised object detection, that makes use of insights in the field of explainability of classification CNNs. We particularly make use of so called class activation maps (CAMs).

3   Methods

3.1   Fully Supervised Object Detection

For the fully supervised scenario with fully informative annotations (FIAs) of the caries' bounding boxes within each image, we make use of a variant of region based convolutional neural networks (R-CNNs), as first proposed by Girshick et al. in 2014 [14]. The basic idea is to propose regions of interest (RoIs), i.e. possible object regions within the input image (e.g. by selective search), which are then classified by a CNN to predict the class labels (including background) for the proposed RoIs. The concept of R-CNNs builds the foundation of various subsequent object detection algorithms.

Faster R-CNN. For our use case of caries detection in smartphone images, we make use of Ren et al.'s Faster R-CNN approach [26]. It is based on Girshick's work on Fast R-CNN [13], an improvement of the initial R-CNN proposal [14]. In contrast to these initial R-CNN iterations, Ren et al. formulate an end-to-end strategy, in which the region proposal is carried out by a CNN. The general pipeline is depicted in Fig. 1. First the input image is processed by a pre-trained CNN, e.g. by Simonyan and Zisserman's VGG-16 [32] or He et al.'s ResNet-50 [16], to extract the image's latent features with their last convolutional layer. Then, a region proposal network (RPN) processes the feature map stack to propose possible RoIs. For this the RPN learns to classify whether so called

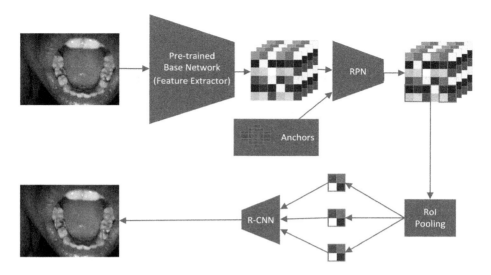

Fig. 1. Scheme of the Faster R-CNN architecture, as proposed by Ren et al. [26]

anchors, i.e. bounding boxes with specific size and aspect ratio for each image position, are possible object regions or not. Additionally, the RPN learns to refine the anchor boundaries. Since the proposed regions of the RPN may be of different size, a RoI pooling layer transforms the proposed regions to a uniform size. A RoI pooling layer is able to reduce a region of arbitrary size to a pre-defined size by using as many pools on the input region as the pre-defined size suggests. The uniformly sized RoIs are then passed to the R-CNN to be classified. A particular advantage of the Faster R-CNN approach is the end-to-end architecture and the network's capability to locate even small objects, such as caries cavities.

3.2 Weakly Supervised Localization

For the weakly supervised case we only utilize image-level annotations (ILAs) to predict possible caries locations within the input image. We propose using Zhou et al.'s class activations mappings (CAMs) [37], which were originally introduced to visually inspect and explain the decision processes of specifically designed classification CNNs. Since training classification CNNs only requires ILAs, this strategy is applicable for this scenario. The basic idea of CAMs is to inspect the influence of each feature map and their activations after the CNN's last convolutional layer. To do so Zhou et al. require the CNN to contain a global average pooling (GAP) layer, followed by a fully connected (FC) layer after the last convolutional layer. According to the weights of the FC, it is then possible to retrieve the importance of each feature map after the CNN's last convolutional layer. The weighted sum of these feature maps results in a CAM for each class, visualizing which regions of the image were responsible for the class assignment.

For the caries localization task, we treat the activated regions of the CAM as possible caries locations.

Gradient-Weighted Class Activation Mapping. We propose using a more general extension of CAMs, presented in Selvaraju et al.'s work on gradient-weighted class activation mappings (Grad-CAMs) [31]. Let F_k denote the k-th feature map of a feature map stack, with $k \in \{0, 1, \dots, K\}$, where $K + 1$ denotes the number of feature maps in that stack. The general idea is that the partial derivative of the model output y^c for a class c with respect to a feature map's pixel position (i, j), i.e. $\frac{\partial y^c}{\partial F_k(i,j)}$, corresponds to the local influence for the class assignment to c. Therefore, the global average over the partial derivatives of y^c with respect to all pixel positions of a feature map F_k determines the approximated influence of F_k on the class assignment of class c to the input image, i.e.:

$$\alpha_k^c := \frac{1}{WH} \sum_i \sum_j \frac{\partial y^c}{\partial F_k(i,j)}, \tag{1}$$

where W, H denote width and height of F_k, respectively. Selvaraju et al. [31] propose computing the Grad-CAM for a class c by means of the weighted sum over all feature maps, where the weights are determined by the influence in Eq. 1, followed by a ReLU activation, i.e.:

$$A_{Grad-CAM}^c := ReLU \left(\sum_k \alpha_k^c F_k \right). \tag{2}$$

The ReLU activation helps to only consider regions, which have a positive impact on the assignment to the class c.

Proposed Caries Detection Pipeline. As Grad-CAMs offer the possibility to visualize the image regions, which are responsible for the class prediction, we propose extracting these regions as possible caries areas. First we train a ResNet-50 [16] classifier, pretrained on ImageNet [8] to differentiate between caries and non-caries images. Then we calculate the class activation map $A_{Grad-CAM}^{caries}$ for the caries class. Figure 2 depicts the subsequent generation of bounding boxes, based on the Grad-CAM pipeline. We apply Otsu thresholding [25] on $A_{Grad-CAM}^{caries}$ to generate a binary mask, that only keeps relevant activation positions. By point-wise multiplication (Hadamard product) we isolate the relevant activation locations. Afterwards we apply Gaussian blurring as pre-processing, to smooth the activation landscape for a subsequent extraction of local maxima. These are used as seed points for a random walk algorithm to segment the remaining image following Grady's contribution [15]. Based on the segmentation results the bounding box limits for predicted caries locationas can finally be established.

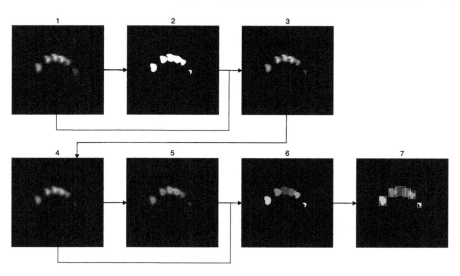

Fig. 2. Bounding box extraction process from Grad-CAM. (1) Grad-CAM, (2) mask after Otsu thresholding, (3) Hadamard product, (4) smoothed by Gaussian blur, (5) extraction of local maxima, (6) random walk segmentation, (7) extracted bounding boxes

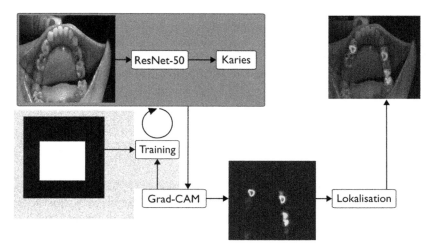

Fig. 3. Scheme of proposed weakly supervised pipeline with local constraints. The extension with additional local constraints only differs from the original proposal during training, as depicted by the blue background. (Color figure online)

Extension with Location Constraints. To improve the localization capabilities of the proposed pipeline, we additionally consider annotations of the mouth region (MRAs), as these are fast and easy to produce. These auxiliary location constraints are injected into the classification network only during training by extending the classification loss function by a localization constraint term $\mathcal{L}_{constraint}$. Let M denote a binary mask, indicating the mouth region. Then the localization constraint term for class c is defined as

$$\mathcal{L}_{constraint} := \sum_{(i,j)} A^c_{Grad-CAM}(i,j) \cdot (1 - M(i,j)), \tag{3}$$

punishing any activation outside the mouth area. The pipeline and its difference to the originally proposed procedure are depicted in Fig. 3. While in our original proposal the Grad-CAM is only computed during inference, in the extension the current Grad-CAM and the location constraints are also taken into account during training.

3.3   Implementation

For the Faster R-CNN implementation we use the Tensorflow Object Detection API.[2] We use ResNet-50 [16], pre-trained on ImageNet [8] with an input size of 1024×1024 as the base network for feature extraction. The RPN is empirically configured for anchors with scales of $0.25, 0.5, 1.0, 2.0$ and aspect ratios of $0.5, 1.0, 2.0$, resulting in 12 different anchor variations per location. For training we use a batch size of 16 and employ a momentum optimizer with cosine learning rate decay, initialized with a base rate of 0.1. Due to the given implementation we set a maximal number of training iteration steps of 15000 instead of setting a maximal number of epochs. The proposed weakly supervised methods are implemented in Tensorflow 2.0. We train the model with a batch size of 8 for maximally 100 epochs, employing the RMSprop optimizer with a learning rate of 0.001 and early-stopping.

4   Experiments

4.1   Data

For the experiments we used our in-house data set where annotations were done by the Department of Paedodontics and Preventive Dentistry. It consists of 387 smartphone images of the oral cavity, from which 220 are of patients with caries and 167 images show healthy teeth. From the 220 caries images, for 93 images the exact caries locations were annotated with bounding boxes (FIAs), whereas the remaining images only have image-level annotations (ILAs). The mouth region annotations (MRAs) were created for all 387 images. For image collection, a OnePlus 7 pro smartphone composite camera[3] system was used, consisting of three different $(48, 16, 8)$ mega pixels cameras. All images were taken while considering the normal picture taking behavior of a user. For example, the camera is focused on the tooth cavities (if apparent) and pictures are taken in zoom

---

[2] https://github.com/tensorflow/models/tree/master/research/object_detection.
[3] https://oneplus.com/de/7pro#/specs.

out mode. For both patients with healthy and patients with caries affected teeth the camera focus was set on the oral cavity. The patients were asked to keep still to avoid blurry images. Depending on the exposure of the patient to natural light, we also used artificial light of the smartphone to increase visibility if necessary. The field of view and the perspective of the images vary, depending on the position of the carious lesions.

4.2   Evaluation

The evaluation was conducted in a hold-out manner, in which we divided the data set into non-overlapping training, validation and testing set with a ratio of approximately 60 : 20 : 20. The training set is used for training, the validation set for monitoring and the testing set for the evaluation. First we present our classification results to inspect the performance of the base classifiers for the classification task. Then we investigate the caries localization performances. It needs to be noted that for training the Faster R-CNN approach we could only apply caries images with FIAs (and all non-caries images without location information), which have also been divided in the aforementioned ratio. Therefore, we used all testing images for the classification evaluation, whereas only testing images with FIAs (and all non-caries testing images) were considered for the object detection evaluation. The Faster R-CNN system is used as a baseline to estimate the upper bound for the localization task, as it is to be expected that a fully supervised system yields better results than weakly supervised approaches. In the following we will denote the weakly supervised caried detection method as **WSCDM** and its extension with local constraints as **WSCDM-LC**. Both systems are trained with ILAs and WSCDM-LC additionally with MRAs.

Classification Performance. Since the weakly supervised strategy is based on a base classificaton CNN, it is crucial to analyse whether the base classifier yields reasonable results. To evaluate the classification performance of the ResNet-50 base networks, that were trained with and without local constraints, we make use of the metrics precision, recall and the F1-Score. Also, in order to draw comparisons between the classification capabilities of the proposed weakly supervised systems and the fully supervised object detection approach, we interpreted images with caries location predictions of Faster R-CNN as positives, whereas images without any predictions as negatives. Table 1 shows the achieved results of the three systems on the unseen testing set in comparison.

It is noticeable that both WSCDMs achieve a precision of 1, which means that both systems have predicted zero false positives on the test data set. This implicates a general low false positive rate for the ResNet-50 classifiers. However, Faster R-CNN yields the highest recall, which is favorable in terms of clinical applicability, as this implicates the lowest false negative rates, thus less prone to oversee caries images. Regarding F1-Score it is observable that WSCDM-LC obtains the best results.

Table 1. Achieved classification results regarding precision, recall, and F1-Score of fully and weakly supervised systems on test set.

Metric	Faster R-CNN	WSCDM	WSCDM-LC
Precision	0.61	1.00	1.00
Recall	0.90	0.76	0.86
F1-score	0.73	0.86	0.92

Localization Performance. For a comparison of the localization capabilities, we employ the mean average precision (mAP) as performance metric. To discuss the mAP, we first need to consider the computation of the precision-recall curve.

We assume any bounding box prediction that has an intersection over union (IoU) with a ground truth annotation over 0.5 as a true positive, and any prediction, that achieves a maximal IoU of below 0.5 with any available ground truth bounding box as a false positive. We iterate over all predictions of the network, ranked by network confidence, and calculate precision and recall based on the already considered predictions. For the first iteration, a very low recall value is expected, as the number of true positives only yields a small fraction of all possible positives within the test data set. For precision, however, we would either get 1 or 0, as all of the predictions so far (i.e. the first and highest ranked prediction) are either correct or not. While the recall value can only rise or stay the same with each additionally considered prediction, the precision value rises with correct and decreases with wrong additional predictions.

For each network prediction we get a precision-recall pair, which can be visualized in a precision-recall curve. Usually the precision values of each recall level are adapted in a way, that the resulting curve is monotonically decreasing with ascending recall. This is accomplished by using the maximally achieved precision in all *higher* recall levels. The resulting precision-recall curves of our experiments are shown in Fig. 4. The average precision (AP) basically approximates the area under the curve. Since this procedure can be done for multiple classes, the mAP is often defined to be the mean AP over all classes. However, the precise definition and also the calculation of AP is often dependent on the context. In this work we refer to the mAP definitions of the Pascal VOC [10–12] and COCO challenges [21]. Table 2 shows the various achieved mAP values for each system. For the COCO definition the values after @ denote the considered IoU threshold(s). It is observable that the fully supervised Faster R-CNN achieves the best results across all considered mAP definitions. It is also notable that except for the Pascal VOC2007 case the location constraint extension yields better results than the original WSCDM for the remaining mAP definitions.

5   Discussion

The results of our conducted experiments show, that the baseline fully supervised Faster R-CNN approach yields the best caries localization results on our

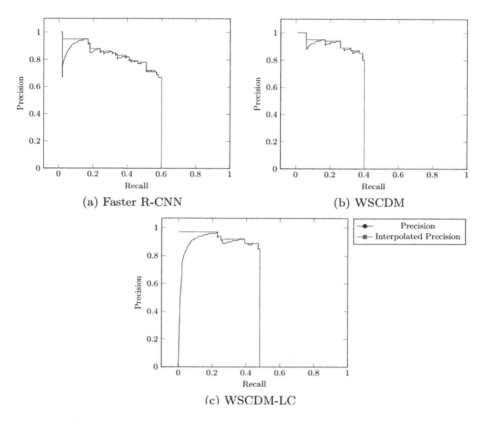

(a) Faster R-CNN

(b) WSCDM

(c) WSCDM-LC

Fig. 4. Precision-Recall-Curves for IoU level of 0.5

Table 2. Detection results of caries locations on test set regarding Pascal VOC 2007 & 2012 and COCO mAP.

		Faster R-CNN	WSCDM	WSCDM-LC
Pascal VOC	2007	.55	.43	.43
	2012	.53	.41	.45
COCO	@[.5 : .05 : .95]	.46	.29	.34
	@.5	.53	.42	.45
	@.75	.51	.38	.45

test data set. This outcome was to be expected, as the annotations contain more complex information than the image-level and mouth region annotations. However, our proposed weakly supervised strategies nevertheless achieve promising detection results, although the gap to the fully supervised Faster R-CNN upper baseline can only be partially reduced by our proposed additional location constraint. Figure 5 shows the location predictions of the systems for exemplary

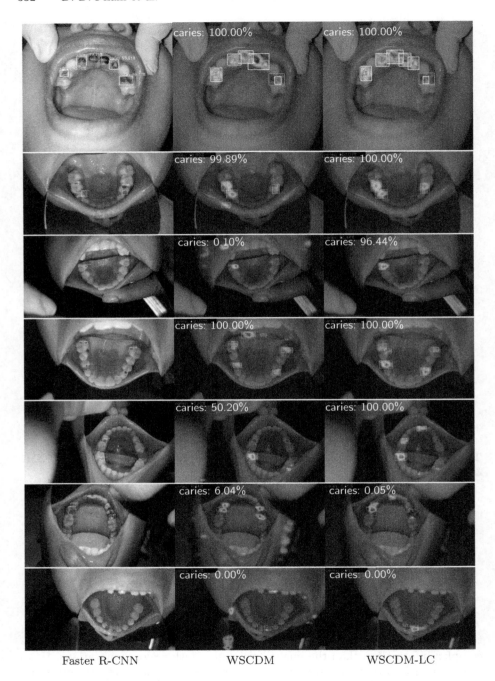

Faster R-CNN   WSCDM   WSCDM-LC

Fig. 5. Example predictions on test set. Ground truth bounding box in green, predictions in white. First row image was cropped to keep patient's anonymity. (Color figure online)

test images. The predicted bounding boxes are depicted as white, whereas the ground truth bounding boxes are shown in green. The activations maps of the weakly supervised systems is overlayed and the confidence of the base classifiers of the weakly supervised systems is depicted in the upper left corner. In the first row it is observable, that surprisingly the location prior during training seems to help in differentiating different instances, which WSCDM fails to achieve. The additional coarse location information, possibly fosters some reallocation of made available network resources. Rows 2–4 depict example images, in which WSCDM-LC show more intuitive activation maps focused within the mouth region, whereas in these cases WSCDM shows multiple activations in non-caries regions. This indicates a superior detection performance of WSCDM-LC compared to WSCDM, underlined by most mAP results in Table 2. In particular, row 3 shows an image, for which the base classifier of the WSCDM predicts a false negative, whereas the semantically more meaningful activation map of WSCDM-LC seems to help in an improved classification, which is also suggested in the overall superior classification results in Table 1. However, although row 1 suggests that the location constraint helps in differentiating adjacent instances, row 4 shows a drawback of the additional location constraint. For strong activations our bounding box extraction strategy captures a larger area, as the neighborhood of a strong activation usually also shows strong activations. In this case the strong activation results in a bounding box prediction, that is larger than the desired ground truth. Row 5 shows an example test image, in which all systems, including Faster R-CNN, yield a false positive prediction in the bottom left area. A closer inspection shows, that all 3 systems have detected a caries region, which was not annotated in the ground truth data, as the predicted region is labeled as caries in the dentist's mirror, but not on the actual tooth. The last two rows show difficult examples, in which the base classifiers of the weakly supervised systems both predict false negatives. Therefore no bounding boxes are generated. However, when inspecting the activation maps, it is still noteworthy, that WSCDM-LC shows more intuitive activation locations than WSCDM. Furthermore, it is noteworthy for the last row, that (although miss-classifying) WSCDM-LC shows clear activations in very difficult caries areas, which even Faster R-CNN fails to detect. Overall, it is notable that although expensive FIAs result in most convincing detection results using a fully supervised system like Faster R-CNN, affordable ILAs also result in promising detection results with a weakly supervised Grad-CAM based strategy. These can be improved by means of location constraints such as MRAs, which are also easy and fast to acquire. Since CAMs have been mostly used for visually inspecting classification networks, that are often trained on images containing only one object, it is a promising observation, that nevertheless multiple instances of the same class can be located, and that incorporation of MRAs even helps in differentiating adjacent instances.

6   Conclusion

In this paper we apply both fully supervised and weakly supervised deep learning strategies to detect caries regions in smartphone camera images. For the weakly supervised case we propose a Grad-CAM based approach, in which the activation maps are used to locate the caries areas. We furthermore extend this pipeline by incorporating location priors in terms of additional mouth region annotations during training. On our in-house data set we demonstrate that both fully supervised and weakly supervised methods show promising detection results, although the gap between these approaches can only be partly reduced by means of mouth region annotations. Interestingly, the additional location constraints not only focus the activations within the mouth region, but also help in better classification of the base network and they seem to improve differentiation between adjacent instances. In the future we aim to extend and improve our smartphone caries in-house data set. We expect to increase the number and variability of training samples and intend to create location annotations, that also differentiate between different caries severity stages, that may be more challenging to detect and classify. We aim to publish this multi-label data set in the near future.

References

1. Ali, R.B., Ejbali, R., Zaied, M.: Detection and classification of dental caries in X-ray images using deep neural networks. In: International Conference on Software Engineering Advances (ICSEA), p. 236 (2016)
2. Badet, C., Richard, B.: Étude clinique de la carie. EMC - Dentisterie 1(1), 40–48 (2004). https://doi.org/10.1016/j.emcden.2003.11.003, http://www.sciencedirect.com/science/article/pii/S1762566103000096
3. Bilen, H., Pedersoli, M., Tuytelaars, T.: Weakly supervised detection with posterior regularization. In: Proceedings of the British Machine Vision Conference. BMVA Press (2014).https://doi.org/10.5244/C.28.52
4. Casalegno, F., et al.: Caries detection with near-infrared transillumination using deep learning. J. Dent. Res. 98(11), 1227–1233 (2019)
5. Chen, T.C., Hsu, T.C.: A gas based approach for mining breast cancer pattern. Expert Syst. Appl. 30(4), 674–681 (2006). 10.1016/j.eswa.2005.07.013, http://www.sciencedirect.com/science/article/pii/S0957417405001557
6. Choi, J., Eun, H., Kim, C.: Boosting proximal dental caries detection via combination of variational methods and convolutional neural network. J. Sign. Process. Syst. 90(1), 87–97 (2018)
7. Datta, S., Chaki, N.: Detection of dental caries lesion at early stage based on image analysis technique. In: 2015 IEEE International Conference on Computer Graphics, Vision and Information Security (CGVIS). IEEE, November 2015. https://doi.org/10.1109/cgvis.2015.7449899
8. Deng, J., Dong, W., Socher, R., Li, L.J., Li, K., Fei-Fei, L.: ImageNet: a large-scale hierarchical image database. In: CVPR09 (2009)
9. Diniz, M.B., de Almeida Rodrigues, J., Lussi, A.: Traditional and novel caries detection methods. In: Li, M.Y. (ed.) Contemporary Approach to Dental Caries, chap. 6. IntechOpen, Rijeka (2012).https://doi.org/10.5772/38209

10. Everingham, M., Van Gool, L., Williams, C.K.I., Winn, J., Zisserman, A.: The PASCAL Visual Object Classes Challenge 2012 (VOC2012) Results. http://www.pascal-network.org/challenges/VOC/voc2012/workshop/index.html, May 2012

11. Everingham, M., Gool, L.V., Williams, C.K.I., Winn, J., Zisserman, A.: The Pascal visual object classes (VOC) challenge. Int. J. Comput. Vis. **88**(2), 303–338 (2009). https://doi.org/10.1007/s11263-009-0275-4

12. Everingham, M., Van Gool, L., Williams, C.K., Winn, J., Zisserman, A.: The PASCAL visual object classes challenge 2007 (VOC2007) results (2007)

13. Girshick, R.: Fast R-CNN. In: Proceedings of the IEEE International Conference on Computer Vision, pp. 1440–1448 (2015)

14. Girshick, R., Donahue, J., Darrell, T., Malik, J.: Rich feature hierarchies for accurate object detection and semantic segmentation. In: Proceedings of the IEEE Conference on Computer Vision and Pattern Recognition, pp. 580–587 (2014)

15. Grady, L.: Random walks for image segmentation. IEEE Trans. Pattern Anal. Mach. Intell. **28**(11), 1768–1783 (2006)

16. He, K., Zhang, X., Ren, S., Sun, J.: Deep residual learning for image recognition. In: 2016 IEEE Conference on Computer Vision and Pattern Recognition (CVPR), pp. 770–778 (2016)

17. Hummel, R., Akveld, N., Bruers, J., van der Sanden, W., Su, N., van der Heijden, G.: Caries progression rates revisited: a systematic review. J. Dental Res. **98**(7), 746–754 (2019). https://doi.org/10.1177/0022034519847953, http://journals.sagepub.com/doi/10.1177/0022034519847953

18. Kositbowornchai, S., Siriteptawee, S., Plermkamon, S., Bureerat, S., Chetchotsak, D.: An artificial neural network for detection of simulated dental caries. Int. J. Comput. Assist. Radiol. Surg. **1**(2), 91–96 (2006). https://doi.org/10.1007/s11548-006-0040-x

19. Li, D., Huang, J.B., Li, Y., Wang, S., Yang, M.H.: Weakly supervised object localization with progressive domain adaptation. In: Proceedings of the IEEE Conference on Computer Vision and Pattern Recognition (CVPR), June 2016

20. Liang, Y., et al.: OralCam: enabling self-examination and awareness of oral health using a smartphone camera. In: Proceedings of the 2020 CHI Conference on Human Factors in Computing Systems, pp. 1–13 (2020)

21. Lin, T.Y., et al.: Microsoft COCO: common objects in context. In: Fleet, D., Pajdla, T., Schiele, B., Tuytelaars, T. (eds.) ECCV 2014. LNCS, vol. 8693, pp. 740–755. Springer, Cham (2014). https://doi.org/10.1007/978-3-319-10602-1_48

22. Liu, L., Xu, J., Huan, Y., Zou, Z., Yeh, S.C., Zheng, L.R.: A smart dental health-IoT platform based on intelligent hardware, deep learning, and mobile terminal. IEEE J. Biomed. Health Inform. **24**(3), 898–906 (2019)

23. Mayes, J., White, A., Byrne, M., Mogg, J.: How smartphone technology is changing healthcare in developing countries. J. Global Health Columbia Univ. **6**(2), 36–38 (2016)

24. Oquab, M., Bottou, L., Laptev, I., Sivic, J.: Is object localization for free?-weakly-supervised learning with convolutional neural networks. In: Proceedings of the IEEE Conference on Computer Vision and Pattern Recognition, pp. 685–694 (2015)

25. Otsu, N.: A threshold selection method from gray-level histograms. IEEE Trans. Syst. Man Cybern. **9**(1), 62–66 (1979)

26. Ren, S., He, K., Girshick, R., Sun, J.: Faster R-CNN: towards real-time object detection with region proposal networks. In: Advances in Neural Information Processing Systems, pp. 91–99 (2015)

27. Ronneberger, O., Fischer, P., Brox, T.: U-Net: convolutional networks for biomedical image segmentation. In: Navab, N., Hornegger, J., Wells, W.M., Frangi, A.F. (eds.) MICCAI 2015. LNCS, vol. 9351, pp. 234–241. Springer, Cham (2015). https://doi.org/10.1007/978-3-319-24574-4_28

28. Rosenblatt, A., Zarzar, P.: Breast-feeding and early childhood caries: an assessment among Brazilian infants. Int. J. Paediat. Dent./Br. Paedodontic Soc. Int. Assoc. Dentistry Child. **14**, 439–45 (2004). https://doi.org/10.1111/j.1365-263X.2004.00569.x

29. Reisine, S., Douglass, J.M.: Psychosocial and behavioral issues in early childhood caries. Community Dent Oral Epidemiol (1998). https://doi.org/10.1111/j.1600-0528.1998.tb02092.x

30. Saravanan, T., Raj, M., Gopalakrishnan, K.: Identification of early caries in human tooth using histogram and power spectral analysis. Middle - East J. Sci. Res. **20**, 871–875 (2014). https://doi.org/10.5829/idosi.mejsr.2014.20.07.226

31. Selvaraju, R.R., Cogswell, M., Das, A., Vedantam, R., Parikh, D., Batra, D.: Grad-CAM: visual explanations from deep networks via gradient-based localization. In: Proceedings of the IEEE International Conference on Computer Vision, pp. 618–626 (2017)

32. Simonyan, K., Zisserman, A.: Very deep convolutional networks for large-scale image recognition. In: International Conference on Learning Representations (2015)

33. Srilatha, A., Doshi, D., Kulkarni, S., Reddy, M., Bharathi, V.: Advanced diagnostic aids in dental caries - a review. J. Glob. Oral Health **2**, 118–127 (2020). https://doi.org/10.25259/JGOH_61_2019

34. Baelum, V., van Palenstein Helderman, W., Hugoson, A., Yee, R., Fejerskov, O.: A global perspective on changes in the burden of caries and periodontitis: implications for dentistry. J. Oral Rehabil., 872–940 (2007). https://doi.org/10.1111/j.1365-2842.2007.01799.x

35. Wan, F., Liu, C., Ke, W., Ji, X., Jiao, J., Ye, Q.: C-MIL: continuation multiple instance learning for weakly supervised object detection. In: Proceedings of the IEEE Conference on Computer Vision and Pattern Recognition, pp. 2199–2208 (2019)

36. Zhang, Y., et al.: A smartphone-based system for real-time early childhood caries diagnosis. In: Hu, Y., et al. (eds.) ASMUS/PIPPI-2020. LNCS, vol. 12437, pp. 233–242. Springer, Cham (2020). https://doi.org/10.1007/978-3-030-60334-2_23

37. Zhou, B., Khosla, A., Lapedriza, A., Oliva, A., Torralba, A.: Learning deep features for discriminative localization. In: Proceedings of the IEEE Conference on Computer Vision and Pattern Recognition, pp. 2921–2929 (2016)

Organ Segmentation with Recursive Data Augmentation for Deep Models

Muhammad Usman Akbar[1,2(✉)], Muhammad Abubakar Yamin[1,2],
Vittorio Murino[1,3,4], and Diego Sona[1,5]

[1] Pattern Analysis and Computer Vision, Istituto Italiano di Tecnologia,
Genova, Italy
muhammad.akbar@iit.it
[2] Department of Electrical, Electronics and Telecommunication Engineering,
Università di Genova, Genova, Italy
[3] Huawei Technologies Ltd., Ireland Research Center, Dublin, Ireland
[4] Department of Computer Science, Università di Verona, Verona, Italy
[5] Neuroinformatics Laboratory Fondazione Bruno Kessler, Trento, Italy
https://pavis.iit.it/

Abstract. The precise segmentation of organs from computed tomography is a fundamental and pivotal task for correct diagnosis and proper treatment of diseases. Neural network models are widely explored for their promising performance in the segmentation of medical images. However, the small dimension of available datasets is affecting the biomedical imaging domain significantly and has a huge impact in training of deep learning models. In this paper we try to address this issue by iteratively augmenting the dataset with auxiliary task-based information. This is obtained by introducing a recursive training approach, where a new set of segmented images is generated at each iteration and then concatenated with the original input data as organ attention maps. In the experimental evaluation two different datasets were tested and the results produced from the proposed approach have shown significant improvements in organ segmentation as compared to a standard non-recursive approach.

Keywords: Deep learning · Recursive training · Diverse features · Organ segmentation

1 Introduction

Computed tomography (CT) is a widely used medical imaging technique to examine the human body, because it contains a great amount of detailed information. For example, in abdomen imaging, multiple organs can be easily detected, including liver, kidney, spleen, galbladder, different kind of hard and soft tissues, vascular structures and many more. Automatic segmentation of organs and other parts in human body is a crucial component in the design of a computer-aided diagnosis system. Despite intensive studies on semi-automatic and automatic

© Springer Nature Switzerland AG 2021
A. Del Bimbo et al. (Eds.): ICPR 2020 Workshops, LNCS 12661, pp. 337–343, 2021.
https://doi.org/10.1007/978-3-030-68763-2_25

methods, segmentation is still considered a challenge that needs to be addressed before any deployment of these methodologies in a clinical environments. Many state-of-the-art methods have been introduced for organ segmentation in CT scans, which include thresholding of pixel values, region-based methods, graph cut, etc. Recently, deep learning models have shown exceptional performance with semantic segmentation [5]. Hence, deep-learning models have a significant potential to revolutionize medical imaging as well. A vast number of deep learning methodologies are being developed specifically for biomedical imaging to perform classification [3,10], organ and lesions detection [8,9,11] and segmentation of organs [6,12]. Recently, Convolution Neural Networks have been proved to be more effective in segmenting bladder and several digestive organs [15] as compared to the old traditional methodologies.

As there are a lot of benefits there are challenges as well. An important challenge in this domain is the lack of datasets large enough to allow proper training of these models. A common approach to address this issue is data augmentation, which consists in the introduction of new data derived from various transformation of the original data. A completely different approach has been introduced with the concept of auto context learning [13], where auxiliary information is introduced enriching the original data. A similar approach has been used in [1] and [2], where additional preliminary solution to a task is used to simplify the problem and boost the model performance where the problem is more complex.

In a similar way, we propose a recursive pipeline that improves the segmentation of the input image recursively. During the training phase the original dataset is recursively augmented with auxiliary preliminary segmentation at each iteration and the newly augmented data is added to the pool of training data. Here, the auxiliary data is the segmentation produced by the model in the previous iteration which is concatenated as a second channel. This new enriched data is added to the original dataset to refine segmentation in the next iteration increasing the number of samples at each iteration, during training. Adding this auxiliary information to the original data has shown multiple benefits which include better accuracy and fast learning.

2   Dataset

To evaluate the proposed solution we used two publicly available dataset. The first dataset is CHAOS[1], which contains CT scans from 20 subjects and the ground truth for liver segmentation is available. The second dataset is of abdomen images in SYNAPSE[2] [7], which consists of CT scans of 30 healthy subjects along with ground truth for segmentation of 13 different classes corresponding to different abdomen organs are available. Pre-processing was performed on both datasets to make them optimal for the deep model. Gray values were truncated between -350 and 350. The volumes were then clipped to focus on the abdomen only and re-sampled to size 256 x 256. The two datasets were

---

[1] https://chaos.grand-challenge.org/Data/.
[2] https://www.synapse.org/#!Synapse:syn3193805/wiki/217789.

used separately in such a way that training, validation and test subject were always the same across trials for a fair comparison.

3   Proposed Methodology

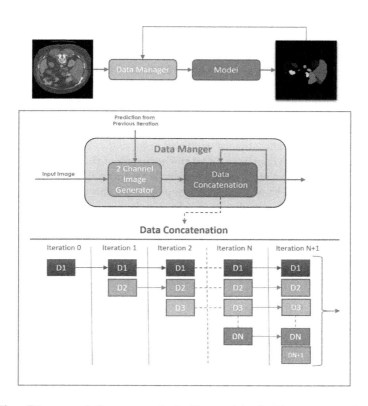

Fig. 1. Flow Diagram of the proposed pipeline and in depth representation of Data manager.

In this paper we propose a pipeline that uses a recursive approach when processing the data. The idea is inspired from auto context learning [13] where the proposed methodology first learns a classifier on local image patches and then the probability maps learned by the classifier are used as context information, in addition to the original image patches, to train a new classifier iterating towards the final prediction.

Inspired by the above approach, we propose an iterative approach where we train the model iterating over a growing dataset. After each fitting of the model, the original input images are augmented concatenating to each image the produced segmentation as a second channel. In the next iteration, the training data is composed of all the previous dataset augmented with the newly enriched images, thus increasing the size of dataset at each iteration. The process, which is represented in Fig. 1, continues until the model does not improve the performance anymore. This makes the dataset grow linearly at each iteration, introducing small variability in the data distribution, which helps the model concentrate more where the problem is more difficult.

More specifically, the model input is made by two channels. One channel contains the image that need to be segmented. The second channel instead contains the additional information that in our case is the segmentation determined by the model in the previous iteration. In the first iteration (iteration 0) the second channel contains the replica of the first channel. The advantage of such approach is that at each iteration the model is provided with a refined information on the task. Attaching a segmentation map to the image is like providing a sort of attention information on where the objects are [1,14]. This allows the model to concentrate the learning on most ambiguous fine grain information, which usually is located near the objects' contour.

The training process continues until the accuracy of the computed predictions on the entire training set stabilise and there is no more improvement. The same number of iterations is then used when deployed on the test dataset.

The proposed pipeline is shown in Fig. 1, where it can be seen that, before being processed by the deep model, input images are manipulated by the *Data Manager*. It pairs the image with a second channel containing the auxiliary information. During training the generated pair is dynamically added to the training dataset.

4   Experimental Setup

The main advantage of the proposed approach is that it is very general and independent of the used model. Indeed, any model performing image segmentation can be used in the proposed framework. Since the input is augmented without changing its original structure, the same architecture with the same structure is used for all iterations.

In all our experiments we used FC-DenseNet103 [4]. This model has transition down and transition up layers. Feature maps are extracted in the dense block of transition down layer. It uses pre-activation layers, where ReLU, convolution, max pooling and Batch normalization are performed on the input slice of 256 x 256. Up-sampling is performed in transition up layer where input is up sampled and concatenated with the skip connections and finally segmentation is computed using soft-max layer. It is to note here that the pipeline is trained and evaluated in iterations and this same model explained above is used in all the iterations and no changes have been made in the structure of the model.

The model was trained from scratch in all iterations, in order to better fit the model to the new augmented data. All experiments were performed with cross-validation. In particular, CHAOS dataset was divided into a training set with 14 subjects, a validation set with 2 subjects and 4 subject were used for testing purpose. In a similar way, SYNAPSE dataset was divided into 24 subjects used for training, 2 subjects for validation and 4 subjects for testing purpose. The test and validation data were never mixed up with the training data to avoid biases. For evaluation purpose, we used Dice score in Eq. (1) to measure accuracy of segmented organs in all iteration so to observe the evolution of segmentation performance.

$$DSC = \frac{2|X \cap Y|}{|X| + |Y|} \tag{1}$$

5   Results and Discussion

The results for CHAOS dataset with a single organ segmentation task are shown in Table 1. Even if the task is easy, still, at each iteration the Performance of the model slightly increases. The results for SYNAPSE dataset with a multi-organ segmentation task can be observed in Table 2. In this dataset organs have different sizes and the results show that the proposed methodology was helpful in increasing the accuracy of the model for all organs. This is particularly evident for small organs which are usually more difficult to detect and segment. The dice score for only three iterations are shown for both dataset because after third iteration the results are stable and there is no evident increase in the accuracy. It is to be noted that the results shown in both tables are the average dice score for the respective test subjects.

Table 1. Results for CHAOS dataset. Average Dice score computed with cross-validation over all subjects. The first three iterations are shown.

Class	I-1	I-2	I-3
Liver	0.9670	0.9710	0.9714

In all our experiments we noted that the first iteration takes most of the time for training and then all following iterations require much less time and they converge in fewer epochs. This because the auxiliary information, which acts as an "organs attention mask" simplifies the task, suggesting to the later models in the loop where the organs are. These models just need to learn how to do a better identification of correct contours, improving the segmentation performance. From another perspective, iterating the data augmentation we create a sequence of specialized machines that learn how to extract the best information from the preceding machines.

Table 2. Results for SYNAPSE dataset. Average cross-validation Dice score computed over all subjects

Class	I-1	I-2	I-3
Spleen	0.9938	0.9939	0.9939
R. Kidney	0.8463	0.8675	0.8689
L. Kidney	0.8767	0.8878	0.8906
Gallbladder	0.8467	0.8647	0.8698
Esophagus	0.2847	0.3257	0.3259
Liver	0.9337	0.9444	0.9471
Stomach	0.5808	0.5884	0.5896
Aorta	0.7612	0.7866	0.7889
Inferior Vena Cava	0.8468	0.8554	0.8557
Portal & Splenic Veins	0.7123	0.7124	0.7248
Pancreas	0.3368	0.4148	0.5029
R. Adrenal Gland	0.4186	0.4736	0.4912
L. Adrenal Gland	0.3977	0.4331	0.4381

6   Conclusion

In this paper we have proposed a pipeline that can be built around any segmentation model, which aim is to improve the segmentation performance. The proposed framework, repeatedly process the input data concatenated with the segmentation obtained from last trained version of the model. This newly enriched data is then added to the training dataset in a data augmentation framework. This allows to iteratively refine the segmentation, processing the data from the rough representation of segmented organs to the fine grain details of organs' contours.

The proposed framework was tested on two different datasets for the task of organ segmentation from CT scans. In both experiments the results have shown that the approach systematically improves the performance of a plain model.

References

1. Akbar, M.U., Aslani, S., Murino, V., Sona, D.: Multiple organs segmentation in abdomen CT scans using a cascade of CNNs. In: Ricci, E., Rota Bulò, S., Snoek, C., Lanz, O., Messelodi, S., Sebe, N. (eds.) ICIAP 2019. LNCS, vol. 11751, pp. 509–516. Springer, Cham (2019). https://doi.org/10.1007/978-3-030-30642-7_46
2. Chen, H., et al.: A recursive ensemble organ segmentation (reos) framework: application in brain radiotherapy. Phys. Med. Biol. **64**(2), 025015 (2019)
3. Gerazov, B., Conceicao, R.C.: Deep learning for tumour classification in homogeneous breast tissue in medical microwave imaging. In: IEEE EUROCON 2017–17th International Conference on Smart Technologies, pp. 564–569. IEEE (2017)

4. Jégou, S., Drozdzal, M., Vazquez, D., Romero, A., Bengio, Y.: The one hundred layers tiramisu: fully convolutional densenets for semantic segmentation. In: Proceedings of the IEEE Conference on Computer Vision and Pattern Recognition Workshops, pp. 11–19 (2017)
5. Long, J., Shelhamer, E., Darrell, T.: Fully convolutional networks for semantic segmentation. In: Proceedings of the IEEE Conference on Computer Vision and Pattern Recognition, pp. 3431–3440 (2015)
6. Mansoor, A., Cerrolaza, J.J., Perez, G., Biggs, E., Nino, G., Linguraru, M.G.: Marginal shape deep learning: applications to pediatric lung field segmentation. In: Medical Imaging 2017: Image Processing. vol. 10133, p. 1013304. International Society for Optics and Photonics (2017)
7. Pawlowski, N., et al.: DLTK: state of the art reference implementations for deep learning on medical images. arXiv preprint arXiv:1711.06853 (2017)
8. Sevastopolsky, A.: Optic disc and cup segmentation methods for glaucoma detection with modification of u-net convolutional neural network. Pattern Recogn. Image Anal. **27**(3), 618–624 (2017)
9. Shahab, A., et al.: Multi-branch convolutional neural network for multiple sclerosis lesion segmentation. NeuroImage **196**, 1–15 (2019)
10. Shen, W., Zhou, M., Yang, F., Yang, C., Tian, J.: Multi-scale convolutional neural networks for lung nodule classification. In: Ourselin, S., Alexander, D.C., Westin, C.-F., Cardoso, M.J. (eds.) IPMI 2015. LNCS, vol. 9123, pp. 588–599. Springer, Cham (2015). https://doi.org/10.1007/978-3-319-19992-4_46
11. Shin, H.C., Orton, M.R., Collins, D.J., Doran, S.J., Leach, M.O.: Stacked autoencoders for unsupervised feature learning and multiple organ detection in a pilot study using 4d patient data. IEEE Trans. Pattern Anal. Mach. Intell. **35**(8), 1930–1943 (2012)
12. Sun, C., et al.: Automatic segmentation of liver tumors from multiphase contrast-enhanced ct images based on fcns. Artif. Intell. Med. **83**, 58–66 (2017)
13. Tu, Z.: Auto-context and its application to high-level vision tasks. In: 2008 IEEE Conference on Computer Vision and Pattern Recognition, pp. 1–8. IEEE (2008)
14. Wang, Y., Zhou, Y., Shen, W., Park, S., Fishman, E.K., Yuille, A.L.: Abdominal multi-organ segmentation with organ-attention networks and statistical fusion. Med. Image Anal. **55**, 88–102 (2019)
15. Zou, Y., Li, L., Wang, Y., Yu, J., Li, Y., Deng, W.: Classifying digestive organs in wireless capsule endoscopy images based on deep convolutional neural network. In: 2015 IEEE International Conference on Digital Signal Processing (DSP), pp. 1274–1278. IEEE (2015)

Pollen Grain Microscopic Image Classification Using an Ensemble of Fine-Tuned Deep Convolutional Neural Networks

Amirreza Mahbod[1]([✉]), Gerald Schaefer[2], Rupert Ecker[3], and Isabella Ellinger[1]

[1] Institute for Pathophysiology and Allergy Research, Medical University of Vienna, Vienna, Austria
[2] Department of Computer Science, Loughborough University, Loughborough, U.K.
[3] Research and Development Department, TissueGnostics GmbH, Vienna, Austria

Abstract. Pollen grain micrograph classification has multiple applications in medicine and biology. Automatic pollen grain image classification can alleviate the problems of manual categorisation such as subjectivity and time constraints. While a number of computer-based methods have been introduced in the literature to perform this task, classification performance needs to be improved for these methods to be useful in practice.

In this paper, we present an ensemble approach for pollen grain microscopic image classification into four categories: Corylus Avellana well-developed pollen grain, Corylus Avellana anomalous pollen grain, Alnus well-developed pollen grain, and non-pollen (debris) instances. In our approach, we develop a classification strategy that is based on fusion of four state-of-the-art fine-tuned convolutional neural networks, namely EfficientNetB0, EfficientNetB1, EfficientNetB2 and SeResNeXt-50 deep models. These models are trained with images of three fixed sizes (224×224, 240×240, and 260×260 pixels) and their prediction probability vectors are then fused in an ensemble method to form a final classification vector for a given pollen grain image.

Our proposed method is shown to yield excellent classification performance, obtaining an accuracy of 94.48% and a weighted F1-score of 94.54% on the ICPR 2020 Pollen Grain Classification Challenge training dataset based on five-fold cross-validation. Evaluated on the test set of the challenge, our approach achieves a very competitive performance in comparison to the top ranked approaches with an accuracy and weighted F1-score of 96.28% and 96.30%, respectively.

Keywords: Pollen grain images · Microscopic images · Deep learning · Image classification · Transfer learning

---

This research has received funding from the Austrian Research Promotion Agency (FFG), No. 872636. We thank Nvidia corporation for their generous GPU donation.

A. Del Bimbo et al. (Eds.): ICPR 2020 Workshops, LNCS 12661, pp. 344–356, 2021.
https://doi.org/10.1007/978-3-030-68763-2_26

1   Introduction

Palynology is the scientific study of pollen grains which are produced by plants for the purpose of reproduction. Nowadays, pollen grain classification is a valuable tool for various applied sciences including systematics and forensics [16]. In the medical context, pollens are among the most common triggers of seasonal allergies. Allergic diseases have become a major public health problem. The World Health Organization (WHO) estimates that worldwide 400 million people suffer from allergic rhinitis [7]. In Europe, the prevalence of pollen allergy in the general population is about 40% [11]. Clinicians and patients may be able to anticipate the onset of pollen-related allergy symptoms by monitoring pollen levels [2].

The performance of any pollen counter (human or machine) depends on two key tasks: finding the pollen grains by discriminating pollen from non-pollen, and pollen grain classification. Traditionally, pollen grain classification involves observation and discrimination of features by a highly qualified palynologist. While this is an accurate and effective method, it takes considerable amounts of time and resources [36]. Therefore, automatic recognition of pollen species by means of computer vision is of major importance in modern palynology [18].

Automatic computer-based pollen grain image classification methods have been proposed in several studies with the aim of reducing human interaction in the analysis procedure [18]. Similar to other image classification tasks, machine learning-based approaches have shown a better performance for pollen grain image classification compared to conventional techniques [1,33].

Most of the classical approaches for pollen grain image classification make use of feature extraction and subsequent training of a classifier such as a multi-layer perceptron or a support vector machine. Well-known image features used for this task include morphological features [40], texture features [12] and hybrid features [4]. However, due to the similar morphological appearance of pollen grains and various artefacts that may present, deriving well-working hand-crafted features is a challenging task.

Deep learning approaches and more specifically convolutional neural networks (CNNs) [24] allow for a more suitable solution for distinguishing different types of pollen grains compared to earlier approaches. These deep models can be trained end-to-end without the use of hand-crafted features and can be applied directly on raw or pre-processed images [1,9,15,33].

Since the number of labelled pollen grain images in publicly available datasets is too small to train a CNN from scratch, transfer learning can be employed. Here, pre-trained CNNs can be used as optimised deep feature extractors or they can be fine-tuned to solve the classification task. Standard pre-trained CNNs such as AlexNet [22] or VGGNet [35] have been used for these purposes [1,30,33,34]. However, the performance of such approaches still needs to be improved to be useful for practical applications.

In this paper, we present an ensemble method for multi-class pollen grain microscopic image classification. Based on our earlier work on various medical image classification tasks and recent advances in transfer learning [25,27,28,42], we develop a classification method which exploits four state-of-the-art pre-trained CNNs fine-tuned with pollen grain images at three different image resolutions. We then fuse the prediction vectors from different models in an ensemble strategy to form the final classification vector. Evaluated on the training set and the test set of the ICPR 2020 Pollen Grain Classification Challenge[1], our proposed method provides excellent classification performance, achieving weighted F1-scores of 94.54% and 96.30% on the challenge training and test set, respectively.

2   Materials and Methods

2.1   Dataset

While a number of earlier datasets exist for pollen grain image classification, such as the POLEN23E dataset [33] or the dataset from Ranzato *et al.* [32], which contain 805 and 1,429 pollen grain images, respectively, in this paper, we use the ICPR 2020 Pollen Grain Classification Challenge dataset[2], which is one the biggest publicly available datasets for this task [1]. It contains 11,279 microscopic training image of size 84×84 pixels in RGB format. The images belong to one of four classes, namely Corylus Avellana well-developed pollen grain (normal pollen), Corylus Avellana anomalous pollen grains (anomalous pollen), Alnus well-developed pollen grains (Alnus), and non-pollen (debris), example of which are shown in Fig. 1. There are 1,566 normal pollen images, 773 anomalous pollen images, 8,216 Alnus images, and 724 debris images. In addition to the raw images, segmentation masks of the pollen grains are also provided by the challenge organisers, but we do not make use of these. A test set of 1,991 images (without segmentation masks) has also been released but labels for these images are kept private by the challenge organisers.

2.2   Pre-processing

We apply two pre-processing steps. First, we subtract the mean intensity RGB values of the ImageNet dataset [10] from all training and test images. Then we resize all images to a fixed size of 260×260 pixels.

2.3   Pre-trained CNNs

There are a number of well-established pre-trained CNNs that can be employed for fine-tuning. Recently developed deep neural networks that are widely used for various transfer learning applications include but are not limited to residual networks and their derivatives such as ResNeXt or wide ResNet [17,41], DenseNets with various depths such as Densenet-121 or DenseNet-169 [20], squeeze and excitation networks that can be also combined with other models such as SeResNeXt

---

[1] https://iplab.dmi.unict.it/pollenclassificationchallenge.

[2] https://iplab.dmi.unict.it/pollenclassificationchallenge/train.zip.

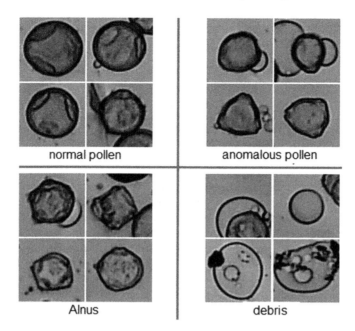

normal pollen   anomalous pollen

Alnus   debris

Fig. 1. Example images from the ICPR 2020 Pollen Grain Classification Challenge.

or SeResNet [19], GoogLeNet and its derivatives such as Inception [37,38] and EfficientNet [39] models which yield state-of-the-art performance on ImageNet classification tasks. As mentioned above, some earlier pre-trained CNNs such as AlexNet and VGGNet have already been used for pollen grain image classification. However, their performance can be improved by employing more advanced architectures which for other tasks have shown superiority over AlexNet and VGGNet.

In our approach, we exploit four recently developed yet already well-established pre-trained CNNs from the EfficientNet [39] and SeResNeXt [19] families as they have shown excellent performance in, for example, classification of skin lesions and ophthalmological image classification [27,29,42].

The backbone model of the SeResNeXt network is ResNet. ResNet models consist of special building blocks, called residual blocks, that alleviate the vanishing gradient problem by connecting the input and output of each residual block. Thus, the network depth can be increased to yield a better classification performance with deeper models. ResNet-50, ResNet-101, and ResNet-152 are the three most used variations, while ResNeXt is a modified architecture whose residual blocks are wider compared to ResNet through multiple parallel pathways similar to the inception module in the GoogLeNet family. SeResNeXt incorporates the squeeze and excitation blocks from [19] into the model, while SeResNeXt-50 and SeResNeXt-101 are the best-known models of the family.

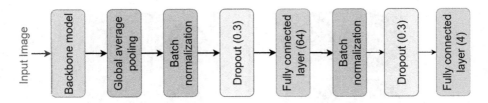

Fig. 2. Overview of the fine-tuning approach. The backbone model is either Efficient-NetB0, EfficientNetB1, EfficientNetB2 or SeResNeXt-50.

In general, by solving the vanishing gradient issue by some techniques such as skip or dense connections, the performance of a CNN can be improved by increasing the network depth, width, or input image resolution. In the design of many former CNNs such as ResNet or wide ResNet, only one aspect of the model is increased which leads to a better classification performance (e.g., DenseNet-169 outperforms DenseNet-121 as it is deeper). In contrast, in the EfficientNet architecture, all three aspects of the models are increased systematically and by a constant factor. This leads to eight different architectures, EfficientNetB0 to EfficientNetB7, that have various depths, widths and pre-defined input image sizes (from 224×224 to 600×600 pixels) while being computationally less expensive compared to other well-known CNNs.

We use three variations of EfficientNet, namely EfficientNetB0, Efficient-NetB1, and EfficientNetB2, as well as the SeResNeXt-50 model for fine-tuning. We choose the shallower versions of the EfficientNet family networks to prevent over-fitting to the limited training data available. All four utilised networks are initially trained on natural images with image sizes between 224×224 to 260×260 pixels

2.4   Fine-Tuning

We apply a similar approach for fine-tuning the networks as in our work on skin lesion classification [26–28]. The general scheme for fine-tuning the pre-trained networks is depicted in Fig. 2.

First, fully connected (FC) layers of the original networks are removed. Then, we apply two blocks of batch normalisation, drop out layers (with a drop factor of 0.3) and FC layers (with 64 and 4 nodes in the first block and second block, respectively). We train the models with three different images sizes, namely 224×224, 240×240, and 260×260 pixels. For the two smaller sizes (i.e. 224×224 and 240×240 pixel images), random cropping within the 260×260 pixel images is performed during training and testing. We use a global average pooling layer just before the first batch normalisation layer to prevent dimensionality mismatch for different image sizes.

The weights of the newly added FC layers are initialised using the Xavier method [14] and the weight factors are kept ten times larger compared to all other learnable weights in the models. We fine-tune the network with the Adam

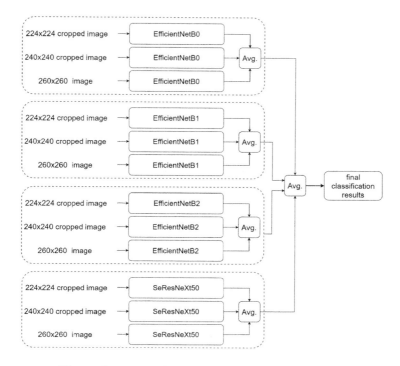

Fig. 3. Overview of the proposed ensemble strategy.

optimiser [21] with an initial learning rate of 0.001. We halve the learning rate after every seven epochs and train the networks in total for 40 epochs. To deal with the imbalanced dataset set, we use a weighted focal loss function [23] with weights of 7.20, 14.59, 1.37, and 15.57 for the normal pollen, anomalous pollen, Alnus pollen, and debris, respectively.

As in [27], we use various augmentation techniques in the training and testing phases to prevent over-fitting. For training augmentation, we use random cropping (for the models trained with 224×224 and 240×240 pixels images), adaptive histogram equalisation (with a probability of 0.1), random cut-out (with a probability of 0.1), random brightness and contrast shifts (with a probability of 0.4), random horizontal and vertical flipping (with a probability of 0.5), and random rotations (0, 90, 180 and 270 degrees, with a probability of 0.5).

In the inference phase, we use 25-folds test time augmentation with the same augmentation methods as described for training. We monitor the prediction probability vectors for each augmented image. If the maximum value in a prediction vector is below 0.5, we disregard that prediction vector and take the average over the rest of the prediction vectors for a specific test image.

2.5 Fusion

To improve the classification performance, we employ an ensemble strategy as shown in Fig. 3.

In our fusion scheme, first, the results from the five folds for each image size and for each network are fused. Then, the results from three different image sizes for a specific model architecture are combined and finally the classification probability vectors of the four model architectures (i.e., EfficientNetB0, EfficientNetB0, EfficientNetB0, and SeResNeXt-50) are fused to form the final classification prediction. From the final prediction for each image, we chose the element with maximum probability to determine the image class. Fusion of multiple models is performed by taking the average over their classification prediction vectors.

2.6 Evaluation

As evaluation measures, we use accuracy, balanced accuracy [3], which is defined as the average recall over all classes, and the weighted F1 score [5], which is calculated as the F1 score for each class weighted by its number of true samples. The latter is also the main evaluation measure that is used in the ICPR challenge.

2.7 Implementation

We use the Keras[3] (version 2.3.1) and Tensorflow[4] (version 1.14) deep learning frameworks for algorithm development and employ the implementation available at[5] and[6] to extract the backbone pre-trained models. All experiments are conducted using a single workstation with an Intel Core i7-8700 3.20 GHz CPU, 32 GB of RAM and a Titian V Nvidia GPU card with 12 GB of installed memory.

3 Results

Since the ground truth of the test data is kept private by the challenge organisers, in developing our model and for showing the effectiveness of the our ensemble approach, we use five-fold cross-validation (5CV) based on the ICPR challenge training data. That is, the training data is split into five folds and four of these are used for training while the fifth is utilised for testing. This is repeated five times so that each test fold is used once and the obtained results are averaged.

Table 1 shows the 5CV results for each network architecture and each input image size.

The results in Table 2 give the performance of the classification models obtained by fusing networks trained at the three different image sizes. The final row in Table 2 shows the final fusion performance, derived from fusion of 12 (3 image sizes × 4 architectures) sub-models.

---

[3] https://keras.io/.

[4] https://www.tensorflow.org/.

[5] https://github.com/qubvel/classification_models.

[6] https://github.com/qubvel/efficientnet.

Table 1. 5CV results [%] based on different input crop sizes and different network architectures.

Network	Image size	Accuracy	Balanced accuracy	Weighted F1
EfficientNetB0	224 × 224	92.48	92.20	92.66
EfficientNetB0	240 × 240	91.96	92.22	92.18
EfficientNetB0	260 × 260	93.07	92.18	93.20
EfficientNetB1	224 × 224	93.01	92.11	93.16
EfficientNetB1	240 × 240	94.06	92.68	94.13
EfficientNetB1	260 × 260	93.20	92.60	93.34
EfficientNetB2	224 × 224	92.74	92.03	92.91
EfficientNetB2	240 × 240	92.68	92.38	92.84
EfficientNetB2	260 × 260	93.18	92.17	93.31
SeResNeXt-50	224 × 224	92.00	91.84	92.20
SeResNeXt-50	240 × 240	92.40	91.81	92.57
SeResNeXt-50	260 × 260	91.50	91.49	91.74

Table 2. 5CV results [%] based on network fusion with different input image sizes and fusion of all architectures.

Network	Image size	Accuracy	Balanced accuracy	Weighted F1
EfficientNetB0	All sizes	93.35	92.75	93.47
EfficientNetB1	All sizes	94.26	92.83	94.34
EfficientNetB2	All sizes	93.61	92.52	93.72
SeResNeXt-50	All sizes	93.45	92.38	93.56
All networks	All sizes	94.48	93.22	94.54

We also compare the obtained results with other state-of-the-art classification models for pollen grain images. In particular, we compare with the results reported in [1] where both classical feature extraction-based methods and deep learning models were evaluated. The investigated techniques include histogram of oriented gradients (HOG) [8] and local binary pattern (LBP) [31] features, and multi-layer perceptron (MLP) [13] and support vector machine (SVM) [6] classifiers, while the explored deep learning models include AlexNet [22] and VGG [35].

The results are listed in Table 3. It should be noted that the results in [1] are obtained based on a fixed split into 85% training data and 15% test data and that this split is not publicly available. In contrast, we perform 5CV to evaluate our method, and thus use slightly less training data while ensuring that all available data is used once for testing.

Examples of correctly and incorrectly classified images from the training data (by the full fusion approach) are shown in Fig. 4 and Fig. 5, respectively.

As the final experiment, we extend our fusion approach to combine the output of all 5CV results in the ensemble strategy to investigate the performance of the model for the 1,991 test images of the ICPR challenge. Hence, instead of combining 12 sub-models, we fuse the results of all 60 sub-models (5CV × 3 image sizes × 4 architectures). The results for this (evaluated by the challenge organisers) and comparison to the top three performers of the ICPR challenge are shown in Table 4.

Table 3. Comparison to other state-of-the-art methods from [1] based on the ICPR 2020 Pollen Grain Classification Challenge training data.

Approach type	Features/Model	Accuracy	Weighted F1
Classical machine learning	HOG features + RBF SVM	86.58	85.66
Classical machine learning	HOG features + MLP	84.93	84.31
Classical machine learning	LBP features + MLP	80.02	77.64
Deep learning	AlexNet + augmentation	89.63	88.97
Deep learning	Small VGG + augmentation	89.73	89.14
Deep learning	Our approach	94.48	94.54

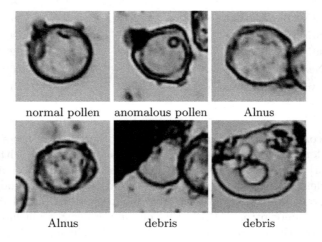

normal pollen   anomalous pollen   Alnus

Alnus   debris   debris

Fig. 4. Examples of correctly classified images.

4   Discussion

The results in Table 1 show that all networks deliver very good classification performance, while EfficientNetB1 is slightly superior compared to the rest and SeResNeXt-50 is slightly worse.

Looking at Table 2, we can see that fusing the results from different image sizes improves the classification performance for all four models. The performance is further slightly improved when the results from different model architectures are also fused (final row of Table 2).

The comparison between our proposed method and other state-of-the-art techniques in Table 3 demonstrates a clear superiority of our approach over the other classification models. While, as mentioned, the training/test configuration we employ is somewhat different from that of the other methods, it represents arguably a harder test, yet as the results in the table clearly indicate we achieve significantly better results both in terms of accuracy and weighted F1 score. In addition, the techniques reported in [1] utilise the segmentation masks (which are only available for the training dataset of the challenge) to obtain segmented images. In contrast, our approach uses only the raw images as input and is segmentationless.

Finally, the results in Table 4 shows the performance of our proposed method on the actual test data of the ICPR challenge. By comparing the 5CV results (last row of Table 3) and the challenge results (last row of Table 4), performance

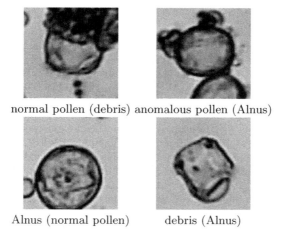

normal pollen (debris)   anomalous pollen (Alnus)

Alnus (normal pollen)   debris (Alnus)

Fig. 5. Examples of incorrectly classified images. The ground truth class is mentioned first and the predicted class in (brackets).

Table 4. Results on ICPR Challenge test data of our extended fusion approach and the top three performers of the challenge.

Method/Team	Accuracy	Weighted F1
Zhangbaochang	97.53	97.51
Fang Chao	97.34	97.30
Penghui Gui	97.29	97.26
Our approach	96.28	96.30

improvement in both accuracy and weighted F1 score can be observed. Compared to the top performers of the ICPR challenge our approach delivers very competitive performance with slightly inferior results (by 1.25% and 1.21% in terms of accuracy and weighted F1 score, respectively). Further details of the test set results can be found on the challenge website[7]. Note that the details of the other approaches have not been disclosed at the time of writing this paper.

5   Conclusions

In this paper, we have proposed an effective approach to classify pollen grain microscopic images to four pollen grain types. We exploit several fine-tuned convolutional neural networks at various image sizes and combine them in a simple yet effective fusion framework. Our approach does not require segmentation and we have demonstrated excellent classification results on the challenge's training and test data sets. The performance can be potentially further improved by incorporating other network architectures or other image resolutions or by more sophisticated ensembling methods.

References

1. Battiato, S., Ortis, A., Trenta, F., Ascari, L., Politi, M., Siniscalco, C.: Detection and classification of pollen grain microscope images. In: Conference on Computer Vision and Pattern Recognition Workshops (2020)
2. Biedermann, T., Winther, L., Till, S.J., Panzner, P., Knulst, A., Valovirta, E.: Birch pollen allergy in Europe. Allergy **74**(7), 1237–1248 (2019). https://doi.org/10.1111/all.13758
3. Brodersen, K.H., Ong, C.S., Stephan, K.E., Buhmann, J.M.: The balanced accuracy and its posterior distribution. In: International Conference on Pattern Recognition, pp. 3121–3124 (2010). https://doi.org/10.1109/ICPR.2010.764
4. Chica, M.: Authentication of bee pollen grains in bright-field microscopy by combining one-class classification techniques and image processing. Microsc. Res. Tech. **75**(11), 1475–1485 (2012). https://doi.org/10.1002/jemt.22091
5. Chinchor, N.A., Sundheim, B.: Message understanding conference (MUC) tests of discourse processing. In: Spring Symposium on Empirical Methods in Discourse Interpretation and Generation, pp. 21–26 (1995)
6. Cortes, C., Vapnik, V.: Support-vector networks. Mach. Learn. **20**(3), 273–297 (1995). https://doi.org/10.1007/BF00994018
7. Cruz, A.A.: Global Surveillance, Prevention and Control of Chronic Respiratory Diseases: A Comprehensive Approach. World Health Organization, Geneva (2007)
8. Dalal, N., Triggs, B.: Histograms of oriented gradients for human detection. In: Computer Society Conference on Computer Vision and Pattern Recognition. vol. 1 (2005)
9. Daood, A., Ribeiro, E., Bush, M.: Pollen grain recognition using deep learning. In: Bebis, G., Boyle, R., Parvin, B., Koracin, D., Porikli, F., Skaff, S., Entezari, A., Min, J., Iwai, D., Sadagic, A., Scheidegger, C., Isenberg, T. (eds.) Advances in Visual Computing, pp. 321–330. Springer International Publishing, Cham (2016). https://doi.org/10.1007/978-3-319-50835-1_30

---

[7] https://iplab.dmi.unict.it/pollenclassificationchallenge/results.

10. Deng, J., Dong, W., Socher, R., Li, L.J., Li, K., Fei-Fei, L.: ImageNet: a large-scale hierarchical image database. In: Conference on Computer Vision and Pattern Recognition, pp. 248–255 (2009). https://doi.org/10.1109/CVPR.2009.5206848
11. D'Amato, G., et al.: Allergenic pollen and pollen allergy in Europe. Allergy **62**(9), 976–990 (2007). https://doi.org/10.1111/j.1398-9995.2007.01393.x
12. Fernandez-Delgado, M., Carrion, P., Cernadas, E., Galvez, J., Sa-Otero, P.: Improved classification of pollen texture images using SVM and MLP. In: International Conference on Visualization, Imaging and Image Processing. vol. 2 (2003)
13. Gardner, M.W., Dorling, S.: Artificial neural networks (the multilayer perceptron) - a review of applications in the atmospheric sciences. Atmos. Environ. **32**(14–15), 2627–2636 (1998)
14. Glorot, X., Bengio, Y.: Understanding the difficulty of training deep feedforward neural networks. In: International Conference on Artificial Intelligence and Statistics, pp. 249–256 (2010)
15. Goncalves, A.B., et al.: Feature extraction and machine learning for the classification of Brazilian Savannah pollen grains. PloS One **11**(6), e0157044 (2016). https://doi.org/10.1371/journal.pone.0157044
16. Halbritter, H., et al.: Palynology: history and systematic aspects. Illustrated Pollen Terminology, pp. 3–21. Springer, Cham (2018). https://doi.org/10.1007/978-3-319-71365-6_1
17. He, K., Zhang, X., Ren, S., Sun, J.: Deep residual learning for image recognition. In: Conference on Computer Vision and Pattern Recognition, pp. 770–778 (2016)
18. Holt, K.A., Bennett, K.D.: Principles and methods for automated palynology. N. Phytol. **203**(3), 735–742 (2014). https://doi.org/10.1111/nph.12848
19. Hu, J., Shen, L., Sun, G.: Squeeze-and-excitation networks. In: Conference on Computer Vision and Pattern Recognition, pp. 7132–7141 (2018)
20. Huang, G., Liu, Z., Van Der Maaten, L., Weinberger, K.Q.: Densely connected convolutional networks. Conf. Comput. Vis. Pattern Recogn. **1**, 4700–4708 (2017)
21. Kingma, D.P., Ba, J.: Adam: A method for stochastic optimization. arXiv preprint arXiv:1412.6980 (2014)
22. Krizhevsky, A., Sutskever, I., Hinton, G.E.: ImageNet classification with deep convolutional neural networks. In: Advances in Neural Information Processing Systems, pp. 1097–1105 (2012)
23. Lin, T.Y., Goyal, P., Girshick, R., He, K., Dollár, P.: Focal loss for dense object detection. In: International Conference on Computer Vision, pp. 2980–2988 (2017)
24. Litjens, G., et al.: A survey on deep learning in medical image analysis. Med. Image Anal. **42**, 60–88 (2017)
25. Mahbod, A., Ellinger, I., Ecker, R., Smedby, Ö., Wang, C.: Breast cancer histological image classification using fine-tuned deep network fusion. In: Campilho, A., Karray, F., ter Haar Romeny, B. (eds.) ICIAR 2018. LNCS, vol. 10882, pp. 754–762. Springer, Cham (2018). https://doi.org/10.1007/978-3-319-93000-8_85
26. Mahbod, A., Schaefer, G., Ellinger, I., Ecker, R., Pitiot, A., Wang, C.: Fusing fine-tuned deep features for skin lesion classification. Computer. Med. Imaging Graph. **71**, 19–29 (2019). https://doi.org/10.1016/j.compmedimag.2018.10.007
27. Mahbod, A., Schaefer, G., Wang, C., Dorffner, G., Ecker, R., Ellinger, I.: Transfer learning using a multi-scale and multi-network ensemble for skin lesion classification. Comput. Methods Programs Biomed. **193**, p. 105475 (2020). https://doi.org/10.1016/j.cmpb.2020.105475
28. Mahbod, A., Schaefer, G., Wang, C., Ecker, R., Dorffner, G., Ellinger, I.: Investigating and exploiting image resolution for transfer learning-based skin lesion classification. In: 25th International Conference on Pattern Recognition (2020)

29. Mahbod, A., Tschandl, P., Langs, G., Ecker, R., Ellinger, I.: The effects of skin lesion segmentation on the performance of dermatoscopic image classification. Comput. Methods Programs Biomed. **197**, 105725 (2020). https://doi.org/10.1016/j.cmpb.2020.105725

30. Menad, H., Ben-Naoum, F., Amine, A.: Deep convolutional neural network for pollen grains classification. In: 3rd Edition of the National Study Day on Research on Computer Sciences. CEUR Workshop Proceedings, vol. 2351 (2019)

31. Ojala, T., Pietikainen, M., Maenpaa, T.: Multiresolution gray-scale and rotation invariant texture classification with local binary patterns. IEEE Trans. Pattern Anal. Mach. Intell. **24**(7), 971–987 (2002)

32. Ranzato, M., Taylor, P., House, J., Flagan, R., LeCun, Y., Perona, P.: Automatic recognition of biological particles in microscopic images. Pattern Recogn. Lett. **28**(1), 31–39 (2007)

33. Sevillano, V., Aznarte, J.L.: Improving classification of pollen grain images of the POLEN23E dataset through three different applications of deep learning convolutional neural networks. PloS One **13**(9), e0201807 (2018). https://doi.org/10.1371/journal.pone.0201807

34. Sevillano, V., Holt, K., Aznarte, J.L.: Precise automatic classification of 46 different pollen types with convolutional neural networks. PLoS One **15**(6), e0229751 (2020). https://doi.org/10.1371/journal.pone.0229751

35. Simonyan, K., Zisserman, A.: Very deep convolutional networks for large-scale image recognition. arXiv preprint arXiv:1409.1556 (2014)

36. Stillman, E., Flenley, J.R.: The needs and prospects for automation in palynology. Quat. Sci. Rev. **15**(1), 1–5 (1996)

37. Szegedy, C., et al.: Going deeper with convolutions. In: Conference on Computer Vision and Pattern Recognition, pp. 1–9 (2015)

38. Szegedy, C., Vanhoucke, V., Ioffe, S., Shlens, J., Wojna, Z.: Rethinking the inception architecture for computer vision. In: Conference on Computer Vision and Pattern Recognition, pp. 2818–2826 (2016)

39. Tan, M., Le, Q.V.: EfficientNet: Rethinking model scaling for convolutional neural networks. arXiv preprint arXiv:1905.11946 (2019)

40. Travieso, C.M., Briceño, J.C., Ticay-Rivas, J.R., Alonso, J.B.: Pollen classification based on contour features. In: International Conference on Intelligent Engineering Systems (2011). https://doi.org/10.1109/INES.2011.5954712

41. Xie, S., Girshick, R., Dollár, P., Tu, Z., He, K.: Aggregated residual transformations for deep neural networks. In: Conference on Computer Vision and Pattern Recognition, pp. 5987–5995 (2017)

42. Zhang, Z.: Deep-learning-based early detection of diabetic retinopathy on fundus photography using efficientnet. In: International Conference on Innovation in Artificial Intelligence, pp. 70–74 (2020). https://doi.org/10.1145/3390557.3394303

Active Surface for Fully 3D Automatic Segmentation

Albert Comelli[1]([✉]) [iD] and Alessandro Stefano[2] [iD]

[1] Ri.MED Foundation, Palermo, Italy
acomelli@fondazionerimed.com
[2] Institute of Molecular Bioimaging and Physiology, National Research Council (IBFM-CNR),
Cefalù, Italy

Abstract. For tumor delineation in Positron Emission Tomography (PET) images, it is of utmost importance to devise efficient and operator-independent segmentation methods capable of reconstructing the 3D tumor shape.

In this paper, we present a fully 3D automatic system for the brain tumor delineation in PET images. In previous work, we proposed a 2D segmentation system based on a two-steps approach. The first step automatically identified the slice enclosing the maximum tracer uptake in the whole tumor volume and generated a rough contour surrounding the tumor itself. Such contour was then used to initialize the second step, where the 3D shape of the tumor was obtained by separately segmenting 2D slices. In this paper, we migrate our system into fully 3D. In particular, the segmentation in the second step is performed by evolving an active surface directly in the 3D space. The key points of such advancement are that it performs the shape reconstruction on the whole stack of slices simultaneously, leveraging useful cross-slice information. Additionally, it does not require any specific stopping condition, as the active surface naturally reaches a stable topology once convergence is achieved.

Performance of this approach is evaluated on the same dataset discussed in our previous work to assess if any benefit is achieved migrating the system from 2D to 3D. Results confirm an improvement in performance in term of dice similarity coefficient (89.89%), and Hausdorff distance (1.11 voxel).

Keywords: Active surface · Automatic 3D segmentation · Positron Emission Tomography

1 Introduction

Positron Emission Tomography (PET) is a crucial methodology towards precise radiation therapy treatment planning also to identify the most aggressive areas within the tumour. In the era of "dose painting", PET conveys valuable guidance for targeting tumours more efficiently, escalating the radiation dose. Additionally, radiomics feature extraction from PET imaging depends on a reliable tumour volume segmentation [1–4]. It is a necessary prerequisite for obtaining accurate and reproducible PET parameters associated with the cancer tissue [5, 6]. Nevertheless, delineating the volume of the tumour in PET images

© Springer Nature Switzerland AG 2021
A. Del Bimbo et al. (Eds.): ICPR 2020 Workshops, LNCS 12661, pp. 357–367, 2021.
https://doi.org/10.1007/978-3-030-68763-2_27

is still considered a challenging task [7, 8]. Despite manual segmentation is a common choice in the clinical practice, it is time-consuming and dependent on the expertise and clinical specialization of the physician. Concerning computer-aided segmentations, several automatic or semi-automatic algorithms have been proposed so far [9–16]. Among them, active contours (AC) [17–19] leverage a silhouette initially placed around the tumour, which deforms and moves to fit the tumour boundaries. Such iterative evolution of the contour is obtained by minimizing a real-valued multi-parameter energy function. The lower the energy, the better the segmentation. In our recent study [20], we devised an algorithm for the semi-automatic tumour segmentation that became fully automatic in the case of brain lesions [21]. In the specific, 11C-labeled Methionine (MET) PET imaging shows great sensitivity and specificity in the discrimination between healthy versus brain cancer tissues. In this way, PET conveys complementary information to the anatomical information derived from Magnetic Resonance Imaging (MRI) or Computerized Tomography (CT) [22, 23], and under favourable conditions, it may even outperform them [24]. Starting from our 2D study [21], we implement a fully 3D automatic system. In the previous study, the system performed the segmentation by individuating an operator-independent rough contour surrounding the tumour. This initial contour (mask) was located on an automatically selected PET slice. Once the initial mask was identified, it was sent to an enhanced local active contour segmentation algorithm. In the specific, it was leveraged a slice-by-slice marching algorithm coupled with a suitable stopping condition, while segmentation on single slices was achieved through the active contour. The main motivation to previous work was to obtain efficient, repeatable and real-time PET segmentations. Another technical aspect is worthy of note: in PET images, the planar resolution is greater than the vertical one and this physical aspect could introduce an artificial preferential direction in the segmentation. For these reasons, the slice-by-slice marching approach represented an efficient simplification moving an important step toward 3D segmentation. Nevertheless, the slice-by-slice marching approach does not consider what is happening in the PET slices above and below. This approach is efficient as long as the tumour section changes continuously between slices. In other cases, to remove this limitation, a fully 3D implementation is recommended [25].

For this reason, we propose a segmentation based on the evolution of a 3D active surface (i.e. truly 3D). Summarizing, we have 1) created a new 3D initialization process, 2) replaced the slice-marching active contour with the evolution of an active surface, 3) reformulated the energy functional of the active surface to work efficiently in 3D. In the last step, the energy function is adapted to PET imaging field and designed in such a way that its minimum corresponds to the best possible segmentation. To assess the performance of the system and to verify its suitability as medical decision tool in clinical practice, we considered the same patient dataset of our previous work [21] by comparing the gold standards, provided by three physicians, and the contours corresponding to the intersection of the active surface with the PET slices. As a final note, while in our previous study we demonstrated that the proposed approach was very efficient on phantom experiments and performed better than several other state-of-the-art methods, the present paper aims to show the improved performance obtained migrating the system from 2D into 3D. As such we deemed unnecessary the validation on phantom experiments and comparison with other methods.

2   Materials and Methods

2.1   Patient Dataset and PET Protocol Acquisition

In [21], we performed an investigation on phantom experiments, demonstrating that the algorithm was extremely accurate. The only place where we expect some room for improvement is the clinical cases. Consequently, in this study, performance evaluation was performed considering the only real clinical cases. In the specific, ten patients with brain metastases have been retrospectively considered. Patients were referred to diagnostic PET/CT scan before radiotherapy treatment (Gamma-Knife treatment) within the same department using the same equipment. Tumour segmentation was performed off-line without influencing the treatment protocol or patient management. No sensitive patient data were accessed. As such, the institutional hospital medical ethics review board approved the study protocol and all patients involved were properly informed re-leased their written consent.

Patients fasted 4 h before the PET examination and successively were intravenously injected with MET. The PET oncological protocol started 10 min after the injection and it concerned the only brain area. Acquisitions were performed using the Discovery 690 PET/CT scanner (General Electric Medical Systems, Milwaukee, WI, USA). The PET protocol included a SCOUT scan at 40 mA, a CT scan at 140 keV and 150 mA (10 s), and 3D PET scans. The 3D ordered subset expectation maximization algorithm was used to PET image reconstruction. Each PET image consisted of 256×256 voxels with a grid spacing of 1.17 mm^3 and thickness of 3.27 mm^3. Consequently, the size of each voxel was $1.17 \times 1.17 \times 3.27$ mm^3.

2.2   Overview of the Proposed System

The present system inherits several features from the system described in our previous work [21]. In this section, we highlight the key novelty aspects introduced. In previous work, the first step was the automatic identification of the optimal starting 2D mask surrounding the tumour using the region growing method. This mask was used as input for the subsequent steps of the system, where the segmentation process was performed combining a local region-based active contour algorithm, appropriately modified to support PET images. In the specific, PET images were pre-processed into standardized uptake value (SUV) images to normalize the voxel activity and to take into account the functional aspects of the disease. Among PET quantification parameters, SUV is the most widely used in clinical routine. The obtained mask was then propagated to the adjacent slices using a slice-by-slice marching approach. Propagation was performed in parallel both upward and downward until a suitable stopping condition was met (automatic detection of the tumour-free slice). Finally, a user-independent three-dimensional volume was obtained. The 3D shape corresponded to the assembly of all the contours produced on every slice. Details can be found in [21].

The present system inherits the same pre-segmentation design (from PET images to SUV images) while the fine segmentation is achieved evolving one whole active surface which intersects and segments all PET slices at once, replacing the slice-marching active contour. To initialize the 3D algorithm a 3D shape is required, instead of the 2D mask of the previous work. To generate a suitable initial shape, the 2D mask is transformed in an ellipsoid enclosing the tumour. It is worthy of note that a regular surface, such as the ellipsoid, used as starting condition helps the stability of the evolution of the active surface. Also, we reformulate the energy function to work efficiently in the 3D space. Figure 1 compares the 2D system proposed in [21] and the new 3D implementation discussed here to highlight differences and improvements. A more detailed explanation is reported in the following sections.

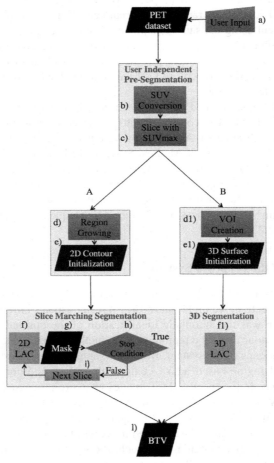

Fig. 1. A comparison of the two-step PET segmentation algorithm from our previous work (A) and the new implementation introduced here (B). The new implementation substitutes the slice-wise active contour and the slice-by-slice marching approach (blocks d, e, f, g, h, and i,) with a fully 3D shape evolution (blocks d1, e1, and f1). In this way, cross-slice information that was previously overlooked is now fully leveraged. The block 'e' was modified to provide a 3D shape as initialization (block e1). Further, the shape evolution can run to convergence (i.e. to a stable shape) without the need of an artificial stopping condition (block h).

Ellipsoid Identification. To obtain a fully automatic segmentation, the initial 3D mask enclosing the tumour must be obtained without any operator intervention. Con-sequently, the system identifies the PET slice containing the maximum SUV in the whole PET volume by taking advantage of the great sensitivity and specificity of the MET radiotracer in the discrimination between healthy and tumour tissues [26]. Once the current slice with maximum SUV has been identified, an automatic procedure identifies the mask surrounding the tumour. The voxel containing the maximum SUV is used as target seed for a rough 2D segmentation based on the region growing method [21]. It is noteworthy that this method is used only to obtain a rough estimate of the tumour contour. Starting from this 2D rough segmentation, the major axes of the contour are used to obtain an ellipsoid which contains the tumour. This 3D shape is fed into the next logical block of the system where the delineation takes place through the fully 3D active surface methodology.

The Fully 3D Active Surface. Starting from the model proposed by Lankton et al. [17] where the local active contour was applied via independent segmentation of 2D slices, we designed a procedure which achieves the simultaneous segmentation of all PET slices by evolving a single surface within the corresponding 3D space. The ellipsoid obtained by the pre-segmentation step is used as input and evolved to minimize the energy 'E' and consequently to fit the tumour silhouette.

The functional energy E is defined as:

$$E = \int_S \left(\int_{R_{\text{in}}} \chi_l(x, s)(SUV(x) - u_l(s))^2 dx + \int_{R_{\text{out}}} \chi_l(x, s)(SUV(x) - v_l(s))^2 dx \right) dS$$

where:

- S is the active surface (3D) and dS is the surface area measure
- s is the surface parameter (2D)
- x is a point within the 3D volume and dx the volume measure
- R_{in} and R_{out} are the 3D regions inside and outside the surface respectively
- $\chi_l(x, s)$ is the indicator function of a local neighbourhood around the surface point $S(s)$. We choose these neighbourhoods to be spheres of radius l centred around each point of the surface S. Note that the function $\chi_l(x, s)$ evaluates to 1 in a local neighbourhood around each surface point S(s) and 0 elsewhere.

$$\chi_l(x, s) = \begin{cases} 1 & when \, x \in l - ball(C(s)); \\ 0 & otherwise; \end{cases}$$

- $u_l(s)$ and $v_l(s)$ are the local mean $SUVs$ within the intersections of this local neighbourhood with the volumes R_{in} and R_{out} inside and outside the surface respectively.

$$u_l(s) = \frac{S_{I_1}(s)}{V_{I_1}(s)}, \quad v_l(s) = \frac{S_{E_1}(s)}{V_{E_1}(s)}$$

$$S_{I_1}(s) = \int_{R_{\text{in}}} \chi_I(x, s)SUV(x)dx, \; S_{E_1}(s) = \int_{R_{\text{out}}} \chi_I(x, s)SUV(x)dx$$

$$V_{I_1}(s) = \int_{R_{\text{in}}} \chi_I(x, s)dx, \; V_{E_1}(s) = \int_{R_{\text{out}}} \chi_I(x, s)dx$$

The shape of the surface S then divides each such local region into interior local points and exterior local points following the surface's segmentation of the SUV. The local means are specified in terms $S_{I_1}(s)$, $S_{E_1}(s)$, $V_{I_1}(s)$, and $V_{E_1}(s)$ which represent the local sums of SUVs and the volumes of their respective portions of the local neighbourhood $\chi_1(x, s)$ inside and outside the curve (within R_{in} and R_{out}). More precisely, the local interior region may be expressed as $R_{in} \cap \chi_1(x, s)$ and the local exterior region as $R_{out} \cap \chi_1(x, s)$.

2.3 Performance Evaluation

In PET images, the only valid ground truth can be obtained using histopathology analysis [7]. Obviously, after radiotherapy, such as Gamma Knife, the actual gold-standard is impossible to retrieve. Consequently, we use manual delineations performed by three clinicians with different expertise as a substitute for ground truth. Nevertheless, manual segmentations performed by different operators are different. For this reason, we used the software STAPLES [27] to generate a consolidated reference for each clinical case, starting from the three different segmentations, and to evaluate the performance of the proposed system.

We used performance parameters widely used for shape comparison in biomedical imaging studies [12]:

- The dice similarity coefficient (DSC) to measure the spatial overlap between the reference volume and the segmented one. it ranges between 0% (no overlapping) and 100% (perfect overlapping):

$$DSC = \frac{2 \times TP}{2 \times TP + FP + FN} \times 100\% \tag{1}$$

The overlap between the two contours were measured according to true positive (TP), false positive (FP), true negative (TN) and false negative (FN) voxels.

- The Hausdorff distance (HD) to measure the most mismatched pair of voxels, one belonging to the boundary of the reference volume and the other belonging to the segmented boundary:

$$HD = max\{h(A, B), \; h(B, A)\} \tag{2}$$

where h(A,B) is the directed Hausdorff distance:

$$h(A, B) = max_{a \in A} \left\{ min_{b \in B} \sqrt{\sum_{k=1}^{n} (a_k - b_k)^2} \right\} \tag{3}$$

These parameters take into account the similarity of the contours at each slice providing an evaluation of the similarity of the overall 3D shape to the gold standard.

3 Results

To assess the performance of the implemented 3D system, 10 clinical cases of oncological patients with brain metastases were considered. We compared the gold standards (see Sect. 2.3) with the contours obtained by intersecting the active surface with the planes defined by the PET slices. For each clinical case, we computed DSC and HD, and we compared them with the corresponding results of the previous study [21]. The following Table 1 gives the performance evaluation for the patient dataset. The 3D system showed a mean DSC of 89.89 ± 2.60%, and the 2D system of 88.35 ± 2.37%. Despite a 1.54% improvement of the DSC, a statistically significant difference (at 95%) was not obtained, probably due to small number of patients.

Table 1. Performance evaluation comparison between 2D [21] and 3D systems.

	2D		3D	
Brain cancer	DSC	HD	DSC	HD
#1	91.70%	0.62	92.90%	0.53
#2	85.50%	1.54	85.90%	2.28
#3	84.70%	1.91	87.90%	1.01
#4	85.20%	2.37	89.70%	1.14
#5	89.40%	0.79	91.40%	0.46
#6	90.00%	1.40	91.20%	1.10
#7	87.10%	1.54	88.70%	0.98
#8	91.70%	1.54	92.10%	1.63
#9	88.70%	1.81	87.20%	1.39
#10	89.50%	0.66	91.90%	0.55
Mean	88.35%	1.42	89.89%	1.11
± std	2.60%	0.57	2.37%	0.56
± CI (95%)	1.61%	0.36	1.47%	0.35
± CV	2.94%	0.41	2.64%	0.51

Figure 2 reports the qualitative comparison between 2D and 3D segmentations and the gold-standard.

(a)   (b)

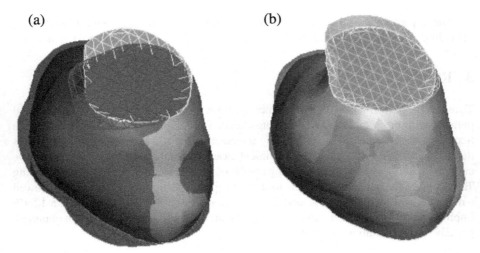

Fig. 2. An example showing the difference between the segmentations based on the active surface and the slice-marching approach is proposed. In (a) segmentations based on slice-marching (red contours) and the gold standards (yellow contours) are superimposed. Surfaces are rendered with a certain degree of transparency to emphasize volume intersections. In the same way, the proposed active surface segmentation (green contours) and the gold standard (yellow contours) are shown in (b). (For interpretation of the references to color in this figure legend, the reader is referred to the web version of this article.) (Color figure online)

4 Discussions

Inclusion of PET imaging in the treatment of oncological patients can convey several benefits. In the specific, functional volume identification is a crucial step toward person-alized medicine. For this reason, many PET segmentation algorithms have been proposed [9–11, 16, 28]. In this study, we upgraded our previous 2D system based on the active contour and slice-marching [21] to fully 3D system based on the active surface. Some aspects are worthy of note.

First, the present study describes a modification to our previous study to leverage a 3D shape evolution capable of segmenting the PET slices all at once, and therefore capable of leveraging additional cross-slice information that was not used at all before. Moving toward fully 3D, some adaptations of the pre-segmentation algorithm were mandatory. We implemented a simple and fast solution for the initialization purpose, based on geometric considerations, identifying an ellipsoid following the main axes of 2D mask surrounding the tumour to roughly including the most of the high uptake tissue. The ellipsoid provided a reasonable and reliable initialization despite its simplicity.

Second, a significant benefit of the active surface over the slice marching approach is that it does not require any stopping condition [21], as the tumour boundaries are naturally managed in the vertical direction as well (i.e. the direction perpendicular to the PET slices).

Third, the previous system [21] was already efficient on phantom experiments. Now, we expect an improvement in the clinical data side. Consequently, in this study, the performance comparisons are performed considering the only real clinical dataset making the use of phantoms unnecessary to the purposes of this study. The quantitative validation was not just to test the performance of the model itself, but to assess if the migration into 3D yielded a practical benefit. Similarly, while in the previous work, the slice-by-slice marching approach showed better performance than several other state-of-the-art methods (i.e. the original local active contour method [17], the region growing method re-implemented by us [29], the original enhanced random walks method described in [30], and the fuzzy C-means clustering method re-implemented by us [31]), the present paper aims to demonstrate the improved performance obtained migrating the system from 2D to 3D. As such we deemed unnecessary a thorough comparison with other state-of-the-art methods. The desired improvements were confirmed in terms of DSC, and HD values motivating the investment made in terms of time in revamping an existing 2D segmentation system into a fully 3D system. The 3D approach not only removes some limitations of the 2D system but it also improves the segmentation. Furthermore, in terms of computational complexity, the difference between the two approaches was minimal with a segmentation time < 1 s for both implementations.

Finally, the inclusion of machine learning components [32–35] and anatomical information from MRI or CT images will be reserved for future developments.

Acknowledgments. We would like to thank Dr. Samuel Bignardi, Prof. Anthony Yezzi, Dr. Giorgio Russo, Dr. Maria Gabriella Sabini, and Dr. Massimo Ippolito, who provided crucial suggestions and high quality observations during the preparation of this study. Additionally, we would like to acknowledge our family, for their unceasing encouragement.

References

1. Stefano, A., et al.: A preliminary PET radiomics study of brain metastases using a fully automatic segmentation method. BMC Bioinformatics **21**, 325 (2020). https://doi.org/10.1186/s12859-020-03647-7
2. Hatt, M., Tixier, F., Visvikis, D., Cheze Le Rest, C.: Radiomics in PET/CT: more than meets the eye? J. Nucl. Med. **58**, 365–366 (2017). https://doi.org/10.2967/jnumed.116.184655
3. Vernuccio, F., Cannella, R., Comelli, A., Salvaggio, G., Lagalla, R., Midiri, M.: Radiomica e intelligenza artificiale: nuove frontiere in medicina. Recenti Prog. Med. **111**, 130–135 (2020). https://doi.org/10.1701/3315.32853
4. Gallivanone, F., Interlenghi, M., D'Ambrosio, D., Trifirò, G., Castiglioni, I.: Parameters influencing PET imaging features: a phantom study with irregular and heterogeneous synthetic lesions. Contrast Media Mol. Imaging **2018** (2018). https://doi.org/10.1155/2018/5324517
5. Cegla, P., Kazmierska, J., Gwozdz, S., Czepczynski, R., Malicki, J., Cholewinski, W.: Assessment of biological parameters in head and neck cancer based on in vivo distribution of 18F-FDG-FLT-FMISO-PET/CT images. Tumori (2019). https://doi.org/10.1177/0300891619868012.
6. Banna, G.L., et al.: Predictive and prognostic value of early disease progression by PET evaluation in advanced non-small cell lung cancer. Oncology **92**, 39–47 (2017). https://doi.org/10.1159/000448005

7. Hatt, M., et al.: The first MICCAI challenge on PET tumor segmentation. Med. Image Anal. **44**, 177–195 (2018). https://doi.org/10.1016/j.media.2017.12.007

8. Hatt, M., Lee, J.A., Schmidtlein, C.R., Lu, W., Jeraj, R.: Classification and evaluation strategies of auto-segmentation approaches for PET: report of AAPM task group no. 211. Med Phys. **44**, e1–e42 (2017)

9. Berthon, B., et al.: Toward a standard for the evaluation of PET-auto-segmentation methods following the recommendations of AAPM task group no. 211: requirements and implementation. Med. Phys. (2017). https://doi.org/10.1002/mp.12312

10. Guo, Z., Guo, N., Gong, K., Zhong, S., Li, Q.: Gross tumor volume segmentation for head and neck cancer radiotherapy using deep dense multi-modality network. Phys. Med. Biol. (2019). https://doi.org/10.1088/1361-6560/ab440d

11. Guo, Z., Guo, N., Li, Q., Gong, K.: Automatic multi-modality segmentation of gross tumor volume for head and neck cancer radiotherapy using 3D U-Net. Presented at the (2019). https://doi.org/10.1117/12.2513229

12. Foster, B., Bagci, U., Mansoor, A., Xu, Z., Mollura, D.J.: A review on segmentation of positron emission tomography images. Comput. Biol. Med. **50**, 76–96 (2014). https://doi.org/10.1016/j.compbiomed.2014.04.014

13. Im, H.-J., Bradshaw, T., Solaiyappan, M., Cho, S.Y.: Current methods to define metabolic tumor volume in positron emission tomography: which one is better? Nucl. Med. Mol. Imaging **52**(1), 5–15 (2017). https://doi.org/10.1007/s13139-017-0493-6

14. Angulakshmi, M., Lakshmi Priya, G.G.: Automated brain tumour segmentation techniques—a review. Int. J. Imaging Syst. Technol. (2017). https://doi.org/10.1002/ima.22211

15. Comelli, A.: Fully 3D active surface with machine learning for PET image segmentation. J. Imaging. **6**, 113 (2020). https://doi.org/10.3390/jimaging6110113

16. Sbei, A., ElBedoui, K., Barhoumi, W., Maktouf, C.: Gradient-based generation of intermediate images for heterogeneous tumor segmentation within hybrid PET/MRI scans. Comput. Biol. Med. **119**, 103669 (2020). https://doi.org/10.1016/J.COMPBIOMED.2020.103669

17. Lankton, S., Nain, D., Yezzi, A., Tannenbaum, A.: Hybrid geodesic region-based curve evolutions for image segmentation. In: Hsieh, J., Flynn, M.J. (eds.) Medical Imaging 2007: Physics of Medical Imaging. p. 65104U. International Society for Optics and Photonics (2007). https://doi.org/10.1117/12.709700

18. Comelli, A., et al.: Active contour algorithm with discriminant analysis for delineating tumors in positron emission tomography. Artif. Intell. Med. **94**, 67–78 (2019). https://doi.org/10.1016/j.artmed.2019.01.002

19. Comelli, A., et al.: K-nearest neighbor driving active contours to delineate biological tumor volumes. Eng. Appl. Artif. Intell. **81**, 133–144 (2019). https://doi.org/10.1016/j.engappai.2019.02.005

20. Comelli, A., et al.: A smart and operator independent system to delineate tumours in positron emission tomography scans. Comput. Biol. Med. **102**, 1–5 (2018). https://doi.org/10.1016/j.compbiomed.2018.09.002

21. Comelli, A., Stefano, A.: A fully automated segmentation system of positron emission tomography studies. In: Zheng, Y., Williams, B.M., Chen, Ke. (eds.) MIUA 2019. CCIS, vol. 1065, pp. 353–363. Springer, Cham (2020). https://doi.org/10.1007/978-3-030-39343-4_30

22. Muccio, C.F., Tedeschi, E., Ugga, L., Cuocolo, R., Esposito, G., Caranci, F.: Solitary cerebral metastases vs. high-grade gliomas: usefulness of two MRI signs in the differential diagnosis. Anticancer Res. (2019). https://doi.org/10.21873/anticanres.13677

23. Stefano, A., et al.: A fully automatic method for biological target volume segmentation of brain metastases. Int. J. Imaging Syst. Technol. **26**, 29–37 (2016). https://doi.org/10.1002/ima.22154

24. Levivier, M., et al.: Integration of the metabolic data of positron emission tomography in the dosimetry planning of radiosurgery with the gamma knife: early experience with brain tumors. Techn. Note. J. Neurosurg. **93**(Suppl 3), 233–238 (2000). https://doi.org/10.3171/jns.2000.93.supplement

25. Comelli, A., et al.: Development of a new fully three-dimensional methodology for tumours delineation in functional images. Comput. Biol. Med. **120** (2020). https://doi.org/10.1016/j.compbiomed.2020.103701

26. Stefano, A., et al.: An automatic method for metabolic evaluation of Gamma knife treatments. In: Murino, V., Puppo, E. (eds.) ICIAP 2015. LNCS, vol. 9279, pp. 579–589. Springer, Cham (2015). https://doi.org/10.1007/978-3-319-23231-7_52

27. Warfield, S.K., Zou, K.H., Wells, W.M.: Simultaneous truth and performance level estimation (STAPLE): an algorithm for the validation of image segmentation. IEEE Trans. Med. Imaging. **23**, 903–921 (2004). https://doi.org/10.1109/TMI.2004.828354

28. Huang, B., et al.: Fully automated delineation of gross tumor volume for head and neck cancer on PET-CT using deep learning: a dual-center study. Contrast Media Mol. Imaging. (2018). https://doi.org/10.1155/2018/8923028

29. Day, E., et al.: A region growing method for tumor volume segmentation on PET images for rectal and anal cancer patients. Med. Phys. **36**, 4349–4358 (2009). https://doi.org/10.1118/1.3213099

30. Stefano, A., et al.: An enhanced random walk algorithm for delineation of head and neck cancers in PET studies. Med. Biol. Eng. Comput. **55**(6), 897–908 (2016). https://doi.org/10.1007/s11517-016-1571-0

31. Belhassen, S., Zaidi, H.: A novel fuzzy C-means algorithm for unsupervised heterogeneous tumor quantification in PET. Med. Phys. **37**, 1309–1324 (2010). https://doi.org/10.1118/1.3301610

32. Cuocolo, R., et al.: Machine learning applications in prostate cancer magnetic resonance imaging. Eur. Radiol. Exp. **3**, 35 (2019). https://doi.org/10.1186/s41747-019-0109-2

33. Comelli, A., Stefano, A., Benfante, V., Russo, G.: Normal and abnormal tissue classification in positron emission tomography oncological studies. Pattern Recogn. Image Anal. **28**, 106–113 (2018). https://doi.org/10.1134/S1054661818010054

34. Comelli, A., et al.: Tissue classification to support local active delineation of brain tumors. In: Zheng, Y., Williams, B.M., Chen, Ke. (eds.) MIUA 2019. CCIS, vol. 1065, pp. 3–14. Springer, Cham (2020). https://doi.org/10.1007/978-3-030-39343-4_1

35. Agnello, L., Comelli, A., Ardizzone, E., Vitabile, S.: Unsupervised tissue classification of brain MR images for voxel-based morphometry analysis. Int. J. Imaging Syst. Technol. **26**, 136–150 (2016). https://doi.org/10.1002/ima.22168

Penalizing Small Errors Using an Adaptive Logarithmic Loss

Chaitanya Kaul[1]([✉]) [iD], Nick Pears[2] [iD], Hang Dai[3] [iD],
Roderick Murray-Smith[1] [iD], and Suresh Manandhar[4] [iD]

[1] School of Computing Science, University of Glasgow, Glasgow G12 8RZ, UK
{Chaitanya.Kaul,Roderick.Murray-Smith}@glasgow.ac.uk
[2] Department of Computer Science, University of York, York YO10 5DD, UK
nick.pears@york.ac.uk
[3] MBZUAI, Masdar City, Abu Dhabi, United Arab Emirates
hang.dai@mbzuai.ac.ae
[4] NAAMII, Katunje, Bhaktapur, Kathmandu, Nepal
suresh.manandhar@naamii.org.np

Abstract. Loss functions are error metrics that quantify the difference between a prediction and its corresponding ground truth. Fundamentally, they define a functional landscape for traversal by gradient descent. Although numerous loss functions have been proposed to date in order to handle various machine learning problems, little attention has been given to enhancing these functions to better traverse the loss landscape. In this paper, we simultaneously and significantly mitigate two prominent problems in medical image segmentation namely: i) class imbalance between foreground and background pixels and ii) poor loss function convergence. To this end, we propose an Adaptive Logarithmic Loss (ALL) function. We compare this loss function with the existing state-of-the-art on the ISIC 2018 dataset, the nuclei segmentation dataset as well as the DRIVE retinal vessel segmentation dataset. We measure the performance of our methodology on benchmark metrics and demonstrate state-of-the-art performance. More generally, we show that our system can be used as a framework for better training of deep neural networks.

Keywords: Semantic segmentation · Class imbalance · Loss functions · U-Net · FocusNet

1 Introduction

With advances in technology, deep convolutional networks have become a fast and accurate means to carry out semantic segmentation tasks. They are widely used in most applications in 2D and 3D medical image analysis. The networks effectively learn to label a binary mask as 0, for every background pixel and

C. Kaul and R. Murray-Smith—Acknowledge support from the iCAIRD project, funded by Innovate UK (project number 104690).

© Springer Nature Switzerland AG 2021
A. Del Bimbo et al. (Eds.): ICPR 2020 Workshops, LNCS 12661, pp. 368–375, 2021.
https://doi.org/10.1007/978-3-030-68763-2_28

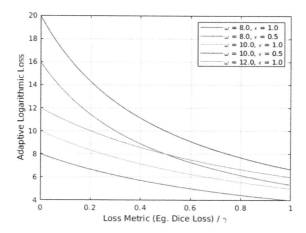

Fig. 1. The plot shows the value of the derivative of our loss against the value of the Dice Loss that it optimizes. It can be seen that for smaller values of the loss metric, a larger loss is backpropagated. γ is fixed empirically based on initial experiments to any value on the x-axis.

as 1 for the foreground. Historically, the Binary Cross Entropy loss emerged as the loss function of choice for this per-pixel labelling task. It generally works well for classification and segmentation tasks, as long as the labels for all classes are balanced. If one class dominates over the other, the imbalance results in the network predicting all outputs to be the dominant class, due to convergence to a non optimal local minimum. Some recently proposed loss functions such as the dice loss and the Focal Loss [7] tackle this problem by weighting some outputs more than others. Other losses such as the Generalized Cross Entropy Loss [11] have been shown to be robust to noisy labels. General evaluations of these losses is done by calculating the overall overlap between the ground truth and the prediction. The most basic form of such a metric is the Jaccard Index. In contrast, the Dice Index assigns a higher weight to the true positives, and is given by the formula: $DI = \frac{2|G \cap P|}{|G| + |P|}$ where G is the ground truth mask and P is the predicted mask. Due to its high weight on the true positives, DI is also widely used as a loss function. The Tversky Index [9] is another proposed metric, that adds further weight to the false positives and false negatives to get better predictions. These similarity metrics are generally converted to loss functions by optimizing over a sum of their class-wise difference from the optimal value. Their general form is $L = \sum_c (1 - M)$ where the metric, M, can be the Jaccard, Dice or the Tversky Index. The subscript indicates a summation over the number of classes, c. Although many loss functions have also been proposed [5,10,12] as weighted combinations of these losses, none of the existing losses in medical image segmentation explicitly account for both class imbalance, as well as network convergence, even though methods to tackle such problems exist in other computer vision applications [4]. In this paper, we propose to enhance the properties of the Dice Loss using our methodology. We conduct an extensive hyperparameter search for our loss and empirically show that our technique leads to better convergence of the dice loss under even less optimal settings of the hyperparameters. We compare with state-of-the-art for the same problems, and show performance gains over them. We use the U-Net [8], and FocusNet [6] architectures to compare results. Our enhancement experiments with the Dice Loss due to its popularity in medical image segmentation tasks, but in theory, any loss function could be used here. The rest of the paper is organized as follows. In Sect. 2, we discuss our loss function. Section 3 describes our evaluation. Results are presented in Sect. 4 and we conclude with Sect. 5.

2   Adaptive Logarithmic Loss

We motivate the need for our loss based on the properties a good loss function should possess. Once a loss function computes the error between the label and the ground truth values, the error is backpropagated though a network in order to make it learn. This fundamental task is generally conducted well by all loss functions, though some tend to converge faster than the others. Empirically, Tversky Loss converges in lesser epochs compared to the earlier proposed losses such as CE or the Jaccard Loss. A good loss function should not take too long to converge. It is an added bonus if it speeds up convergence. Secondly, a loss function should be able to adapt to the loss landscape closer to convergence. Keeping these points in mind, we construct a loss function that can both, converge at a faster rate, as well as adaptively refine its landscape when closer to convergence. The formula for this adaptive loss is given by,

$$ALL(x) = \begin{cases} \omega \ln(1 + \frac{|DL|}{\epsilon}) & |DL| < \gamma \\ |DL| - C & \text{otherwise} \end{cases} \tag{1}$$

where $C = \gamma - \omega \ln(1 + (\frac{\gamma}{\epsilon}))$ is used to make the loss function differentiable and smooth at $|DL| = \gamma$ and DL is the computed dice loss. γ, ω and ϵ are hypermarameters of this loss function. Further, as the dice loss lies between $[0, 1]$, we experiment with values of γ that are $[0, 1]$ to find the optimal threshold to shift to a smoother log based loss for convergence close to the minima. As log is a monotonic function, it smoothens the convergence. The derivative of this loss can be computed via the chain rule. It is visually shown in Fig. 1. Differentiating a function of a function results in the product of two derivatives. This results in, $[ALL(DL(\cdot))]' = ALL'(DL) \times DL'(\cdot)$, where the plot of $ALL'(DL)$ is shown in Fig. 1. Hence, given any loss as input to our adaptive function, it's derivative will be multiplied by a smooth differentiable function that would in turn remove any discontinuities. After experimentation, we observed negligible computational overhead compared to other loss functions for computing our loss. We found the optimal values for the hyperparameters to be, $\gamma = 0.1$, $\omega = 10.0$ and $\epsilon = 0.5$. The loss is mainly sensitive to the value of γ, while ω and ϵ can be kept constant (as we observed little change in the value of the loss across these two parameters once they had been optimally set).

Table 1. Optimizing the values of ω and ϵ over the corresponding Jaccard Index (%). Values are averages of 3 runs. Experiments conducted with constant $\gamma = 0.1$. JI with baseline Dice Loss = 71.36. Results obtained using FocusNet.

ϵ	ω					
	6	8	10	12	14	16
0.3	81.43	81.48	81.51	81.59	81.90	81.67
0.5	81.97	81.57	**82.43**	82.24	81.58	81.07
1.0	81.78	82.11	81.84	81.73	82.21	81.96
2.0	81.75	81.99	82.18	81.58	81.71	81.63

Table 2. Optimizing the values of γ over the Jaccard Index (%). Values are averages of 3 runs. Experiments conducted with constant values of $\omega = 10$, $\epsilon = 0.5$. JI with baseline Dice Loss = 71.36. Results obtained using FocusNet.

γ	0.08	0.10	0.12	0.15	0.20	0.30
JI	81.60	**82.43**	81.54	81.51	80.85	80.97

3 Evaluation

The experiments for our methodology are conducted with two architectures. We use the benchmark U-Net [8] and the attention based FocusNet [6]. A generic U-Net is enhanced with batch normalization, dropout and strided downsampling to improve on it's performance. The FocusNet architecture used is exactly the same as proposed in [6]. We use 3 datasets that exhibit varying class imbalance for our experiments, to study the effect of our loss on them. The ISIC 2018 skin cancer segmentation dataset [3], the data science bowl 2018 cell nuclei segmentation dataset, and the DRIVE retinal vessel segmentation dataset [2] are used. We do not apply any pre-processing excepting resizing the images to a constant size and scaling the pixel values between [0, 1]. For the DRIVE dataset, we extract 200,000 small patches from the images (mostly within the field of view, along with some edge cases) to construct our dataset. The images for the ISIC 2018 dataset were resized to 192 × 256, keeping with the aspect ratio of the training set. The images for the cell nuclei segmentation task were resized to 128 × 128. The patches extracted from the DRIVE dataset were of the size 48 × 48. The data for all experiments is divided into a 80:20 split. To keep the evaluation fair, we do not use any augmentation strategies as different augmentations can effect performances differently. We apply a grid search style strategy to find the optimal hyperparameters of our loss, where we first run some initial tests to see the behaviour of the loss given some hyperparameters, and then tune them. Initially, we set $\gamma = 0.1$ and tuned the values of ω and ϵ to their optimal settings. Then, we use the empirically estimated ω and ϵ to find the optimal value for γ. The values obtained are shown in Table 1 and 2. From the tables we can see that the loss is not affected a lot by changes in ω or ϵ, but even small changes in γ can cause significant changes in the loss value. This is graphically verified via the derivative of the loss in Fig. 1 where we can see that for small values of γ, the penalty for getting a prediction wrong is a lot larger. All experiments were run using Keras with a TensorFlow backend. Adam with a learning rate of 1e−4 was used. A constant batch size of 16 was used throughout. Our implementation of the loss will be available on GitHub. The experiments were run for a maximum of 50 epochs. To evaluate the performance of our loss, we compute the intersection over union (IoU) overlap, recall, specificity, F-measure and the area under the receiver operator characteristics curve (AUC-ROC) of the corresponding network predictions trained on various loss functions.

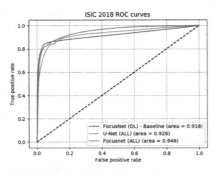

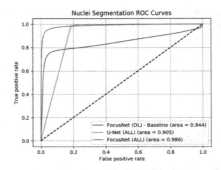

(a) Skin cancer segmentation ROC.   (b) Cell nuclei segmentation ROC.

Fig. 2. Our loss has a better Area Under the ROC curve than the baseline in both cases. When the imbalance is higher (Fig. 2b), our loss provides a much more robust and significant Area Under the ROC curve than the baseline, demonstrating a superior convergence. The curves are plotted for the best performing models for our experiments on the tasks.

4   Results

We compare the performance of our loss (Table 3) with the Jaccard Loss (JL), Dice Loss (DL), Tversky Loss (TL) [9], Focal Loss (FL) [7] and the Combo Loss (CL) [10]. The ISIC 2018 dataset shows the least imbalance and hence the results are fairly even for this dataset, though our loss does manage to get the best in class IoU. This is also exhibited in Fig. 2a where we plot the ROC curves. FocusNet with the ALL gets the best area under the curve. We also compared FocusNet trained with the ALL against the recently proposed Focal Tversky Loss [1] for the ISIC 2018 dataset. We used the same train-test split as their implementation based on their open sourced GitHub code and averaged our results over 3 runs. Our loss outperforms their architecture trained on their loss by 1.53% on the Dice Index. We also report a better precision and recall than their methodology. The results for this experiment are shown in Table 4. The nuclei segmentation dataset exhibits more class imbalance, and in such a case our loss shows significantly superior performance compared to all the other losses. We get significant gains over the baseline AUC as shown in Fig. 2b.

Table 3. Segmentation results for the three datasets. All values in the ISIC 2018 experiments, Data Science Bowl and the DRIVE retinal blood vessel segmentation datasets are averaged over 5, 3 and 2 runs respectively to average out the effects of random weight initialization as much as possible. The values reported are all in %. Here, [8] and [6] are the U-Net and the FocusNet architectures respectively, with the relevant loss function. TNR is the True Negative Rate (Specificity).

Method	ISIC 2018			Data science bowl 2018			DRIVE		
	Recall	TNR	Jaccard	Recall	TNR	Jaccard	F1	Recall	Jaccard
[8] (JI)	78.62	85.21	72.96	76.27	81.29	73.64	78.46	73.28	65.37
[8] (DL)	76.12	83.74	69.34	74.92	82.85	64.57	78.94	74.10	67.79
[8] (TL)	80.82	86.98	74.18	79.21	85.81	77.72	79.89	74.47	66.18
[8] (FL)	**83.76**	**89.85**	**79.17**	78.27	86.88	78.82	80.07	75.65	68.96
[8] (CL)	82.19	87.96	75.87	77.34	85.63	78.24	79.26	74.33	67.42
[8] (**ALL**)	83.56	88.47	77.69	**79.88**	**87.27**	**79.71**	**81.41**	**75.83**	**69.23**
[6] (JI)	80.13	86.17	72.28	77.12	84.19	74.97	77.87	73.28	64.67
[6] (DL)	80.78	85.81	71.92	78.37	84.92	77.82	77.86	73.98	64.71
[6] (TL)	84.86	90.62	77.63	79.64	88.27	77.28	81.31	74.19	68.66
[6] (FL)	86.19	**93.95**	82.78	79.26	89.17	78.73	81.28	**76.89**	69.57
[6] (CL)	84.82	86,19	78.63	80.65	87.34	79.35	78.64	74.18	68.34
[6] (**ALL**)	**86.62**	92.78	**82.84**	**82.51**	**90.86**	**81.37**	**82.17**	76.13	**70.96**

Table 4. Experiments run for the ISIC 2018 dataset training-validation-test split in [1]. Our reported values (in %) are averaged over 3 runs. 'M' denotes Multi Scale Input. 'D' denotes deep supervision.

Method	Dice	Precision	Recall
U-Net (FTL)	82.92	79.74	92.61
Att-U-Net+M+D (FTL)	85.61	85.82	89.71
FocusNet (**ALL**)	**87.14**	**88.11**	**90.47**

FocusNet with just the Dice Loss suffers from poor convergence and does not get competitive results. We do not compare the DRIVE dataset by the AUC or accuracy as these metrics are fairly saturated for this dataset and do not offer any statistically significant insights. It is interesting to note that we do get an improved F-measure score and the best in class IoU, which given the large number of patches extracted, is statistically significant. Overall, our loss shows significantly better performance than the baseline Dice Loss for all three datasets, which means that it manages to optimize the loss to a significantly better minimum on the loss landscape leading to a more optimal solution. In all cases, the trend shown by our loss is to converge to within delta of the optimal solution and then refine the convergences using the adaptive strategy. Without the adaptive strategy, our loss often gets stuck in local minimum, which reiterates the importance of having such a piece-wise continuous loss. The other loss functions (especially Dice Loss) exhibit slightly unstable convergence. We observed that our loss mostly converged faster than JL, DL, TL and CL. FL convergence is at par with our loss, while TL converges more smoothly. We verify

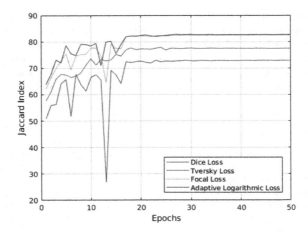

Fig. 3. Comparing the influence of different loss functions on FocusNet. The plot shows the validation Jaccard Index on the ISIC 2018 dataset vs the number of epochs.

this visually by plotting the behaviour of the losses against the number of epochs (see Fig. 3). Compared to the other losses, we observed no extra computational overhead and the need to tune just one hyperparameter during training. This coupled with a better handling of class imbalance makes our loss a superior choice for such class of problems.

5   Conclusion

In this paper, we proposed an enhanced loss function that potentially constructs a loss landscape that is easier to traverse via backpropagation. We tested our approach on 3 datasets that show varied class imbalance. As the imbalance in the data increases, our loss provides a more robust solution (along with better convergence) to this prominent problem compared to other state-of-the-art loss functions. We base our conclusions on carefully constructed evaluation metrics for each task that show significantly superior performance in favour of our loss compared to the baseline.

References

1. Abraham, N., Khan, N.M.: A novel focal tversky loss function with improved attention u-net for lesion segmentation. In: 2019 IEEE 16th International Symposium on Biomedical Imaging (ISBI 2019), pp. 683–687 (2019). https://doi.org/10.1109/ISBI.2019.8759329
2. Staal, J., et al.: Ridge based vessel segmentation in color images of the retina. IEEE Trans. Med. Imaging **23**(4), 501–509 (2004)
3. Codella, N.C.F., et al.: Skin lesion analysis toward melanoma detection 2018: A challenge hosted by the international skin imaging collaboration (ISIC). CoRR abs/1902.03368 (2019). http://arxiv.org/abs/1902.03368

4. Feng, Z., Kittler, J., Awais, M., Huber, P., Wu, X.: Wing loss for robust facial landmark localisation with convolutional neural networks. In: 2018 IEEE/CVF Conference on Computer Vision and Pattern Recognition, pp. 2235–2245 (2018). https://doi.org/10.1109/CVPR.2018.00238

5. Isensee, F., et al.: Abstract: nnU-Net: self-adapting framework for U-net-based medical image segmentation. Bildverarbeitung für die Medizin 2019. I, pp. 22–22. Springer, Wiesbaden (2019). https://doi.org/10.1007/978-3-658-25326-4_7

6. Kaul, C., Manandhar, S., Pears, N.: Focusnet: an attention-based fully convolutional network for medical image segmentation. In: 2019 IEEE 16th International Symposium on Biomedical Imaging (ISBI 2019), pp. 455–458 (2019). https://doi.org/10.1109/ISBI.2019.8759477

7. Lin, T., Goyal, P., Girshick, R., He, K., Dollár, P.: Focal loss for dense object detection. IEEE Trans. Pattern Anal. Mach. Intell. **42**(2), 318–327 (2020). https://doi.org/10.1109/TPAMI.2018.2858826

8. Ronneberger, O., Fischer, P., Brox, T.: U-Net: convolutional networks for biomedical image segmentation. In: Navab, N., Hornegger, J., Wells, W.M., Frangi, A.F. (eds.) MICCAI 2015. LNCS, vol. 9351, pp. 234–241. Springer, Cham (2015). https://doi.org/10.1007/978-3-319-24574-4_28

9. Salehi, S.S.M., Erdogmus, D., Gholipour, A.: Tversky loss function for image segmentation using 3D fully convolutional deep networks. In: Wang, Q., Shi, Y., Suk, H.-I., Suzuki, K. (eds.) MLMI 2017. LNCS, vol. 10541, pp. 379–387. Springer, Cham (2017). https://doi.org/10.1007/978-3-319-67389-9_44

10. Taghanaki, S.A., et al.: Combo loss: handling input and output imbalance in multi-organ segmentation. Comput. Med. Imaging Graph. **75**, 24–33 (2019)

11. Zhang, Z., Sabuncu, M.: Generalized cross entropy loss for training deep neural networks with noisy labels. In: Bengio, S., Wallach, H., Larochelle, H., Grauman, K., Cesa-Bianchi, N., Garnett, R. (eds.) Advances in Neural Information Processing Systems, vol. 31, pp. 8778–8788. Curran Associates, Inc. (2018). http://papers.nips.cc/paper/8094-generalized-cross-entropy-loss-for-training-deep-neural-networks-with-noisy-labels.pdf

12. Zhu, W., et al.: Anatomynet: deep learning for fast and fully automated whole-volume segmentation of head and neck anatomy. Med. Phys. **46**(2), 576–589 (2019). https://doi.org/10.1002/mp.13300, https://aapm.onlinelibrary.wiley.com/doi/abs/10.1002/mp.13300

Exploiting Saliency in Attention Based Convolutional Neural Network for Classification of Vertical Root Fractures

Zhenxing Xu[1], Peng Wan[1], Gulibire Aihemaiti[2], and Daoqiang Zhang[1(✉)]

[1] MIIT Key Laboratory of Pattern Analysis and Machine Intelligence,
College of Computer Science and Technology,
Nanjing University of Aeronautics and Astronautics, Nanjing, China
dqzhang@nuaa.edu.cn
[2] Affiliated Stomatology Hospital of Medical School, Nanjing University,
Nanjing, China

Abstract. Cone-beam computed tomography (CBCT) is widely used in clinical diagnosis of vertical root fractures (VRFs) which presents as crack on the teeth. However, manually checking the VRFs from a larger number of CBCT images is time-consuming and error-prone. Although the Convolutional Neural Networks (CNN) have achieved unprecedented progress in natural image recognition, end-to-end CNN is unsuitable to identify VRFs due to crack appears to be multi-scales and their complex relationships with surroundings tissues. We proposed a novel Feature Pyramids Attention Convolutional Neural Network (FPA-CNN), which incorporates saliency mask and multi-scale feature to boost the classification performance. Saliency map is viewed as spatial probability map where a person might look first to make a discriminative conclusion. Therefore it plays a role of high-level hint to guide the network focusing on the discriminative region. Experimental results demonstrate that our proposed FPA-CNN overcomes the challenge arised from multi-scale crack and complex contextual relationships.

Keywords: Vertical root fractures · Attention · Weakly supervised

1 Introduction

Cone-beam computed tomography (CBCT) is the most sensitive imaging technique with the lowest medical exposure in diagnosing incomplete vertical root fracture (VRFs) among the common radiological examinations [19]. The early detection of VRFs is important to prevent extensive and additional damages to the periodontal tissues and also unnecessary treatment and costs [25]. Unfortunately, clinical examination provides limited information for VRF detection and is based on unspecific signs and symptoms [3]. The radiologic evaluation of VRFs may be improved by the use of tridimensional imaging such as cone-beam computed tomographic (CBCT) imaging [4,21].

© Springer Nature Switzerland AG 2021
A. Del Bimbo et al. (Eds.): ICPR 2020 Workshops, LNCS 12661, pp. 376–388, 2021.
https://doi.org/10.1007/978-3-030-68763-2_29

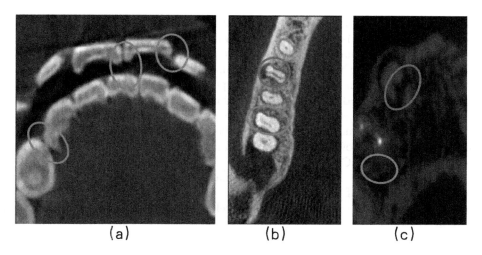

(a) (b) (c)

Fig. 1. The CBCT image samples. The co-occurrences of multi-scale crack in different regions makes the classification difficult to CNNs. The red circles denote the VRFs region, while the green circles denote the healthy tissue that is prone to be identified as VRFs. (a) is located in cross area between upper and lower jaw, which shows that there are many cracks which should not be identified as VRFs. (b) and (c) show that there exist confused cracks in various scales. (Color figure online)

Manually checking the existence of the VRFs from CBCT images one by one is time-consuming and error-prone. Hence, it is practically meaningful to develop an automatic method for checking the VRFs via CBCT images. Deep Convolutional Neural Network (CNN) is a special type of Neural Networks. CNN have proven to be useful models for tackling a wide range of visual tasks such as classification [13,30], Segmentation [20,26] and Objection Detection [24]. The powerful learning capability of CNN is due to the use of hierarchical feature extraction layers which obtain semantics from input images.

The challenge of identifying VRFs in CBCT images is arised from multi-scale cracks and complex contextual relationships. As shown in Fig. 1. Crack in neighbouring teeth and rows of teeth is similar to the real VRFs in a range of scales. Therefore, high spatial resolution and strong semantic information are required to achieve this challenge. However, the spatial resolution and semantic information compete with each other. Hence, the traditional end-to-end CNN is unsuitable for this problem.

Most successful CNNs perform outstandingly under the supervised learning framework, which require ground-truth labels to be given for a big training data. The pixel-level, region-level and image-level ground-truth are fed into the CNNs to process Segmentation, Detection, and classification model building respectively. Recently, weakly supervised learning has made big progress. These works use low-level ground-truth at train stage, and predict the high-level label, e.g. Additional informations such priori knowledge, reasonable constraint, and partial labels are exploited for achieving the goal. Among the these researches about weakly supervised learning, many works indicate that CNN trained for classification using image-level label has the power of locating. This means CNN implicitly learns how to extract the discriminate region for classification task. This is also the reason why these weakly supervised learning CNN should initialize from a well trained classification CNN instead of initializing it from scratch. As mentioned above, the classification CNN designed for nature image recognition can not work normally on this problem. Well trained classification CNN implies high-level knowledge. In reverse, can some high-level hint help training a good classification CNN?

In this paper, we exploit the coarse image saliency in guiding the CNN to learning the feature of VRFs. We build some coarse image saliency in which there are pixels labelled as seed. After that, a level-set method are applied to generate a more reasonable image saliency from seed pixels. Then, these image saliency actor as high-level hint, which guides the region based attention module to learning the saliency features. Finally, the saliency is used as soft attention probability mask to let the classification submodule focusing on discriminative regions. All in all, We proposed a Feature Pyramids Attention Convolutional Neural Network (FPA-CNN) which incorporates saliency mask to boost the classification performance in our challenging dataset.

The rest of paper is organized as follows. We first review some related works, and clarify the difference from ours in Sect. 2. And then we introduce database used in our study, later present the FPA-CNN in Sect. 3. In Sect. 4, we evaluate the performance of our method by comparing with several state-of- the-art CNN architecture.

2   Relate Work

2.1   VRFs Recognition

In literature, the neural network is introduced for detecting vertical root fracture in ex-Vivo [12]. They use extracted premolars with no carious lesions as study object and the adjacent anatomic structures are ignored. Johari [10] takes almost the same routine with additional denoising method. The main difference between their work and ours are that all the CBCT images in our dataset are captured in-vivo. So our images contains the whole jaw and are affected by artifacts. What's more, the difference between individuals can not be ignored. In contrast to FPA-CNN, their work focus on images which contains only one tooth. As far as we know, these has not been exploiting by preview works.

2.2   CNN Based Image Classification

Starting with LeNet-5 [14] and AlexNet [13], convolutional neural networks (CNN) have typically a standard structure, stacked convolutional layers are followed by one or more fully-connected layers. There are many state-of-the-art

CNN perform well on nature images. [28] and [6] boost the CNN classification capability using deeper hierarchical layers and the shortcut structures. [9, 29, 30] make a tradeoff on width and depth of the network. And features from various receptive field are fused to get better discriminate feature. Hu et al. [7] propose a mechanism that allows the network to perform feature recalibration, which can learn global information to selectively emphasise informative features and suppress less useful ones. Huang et al. [8] connects each layer to every other layer in a feed-forward fashion, which result in significant improvements at the cost of more graphic memory at training stage.

Although large scaled CNN requires a great amount of data, we can transfer the CNN pretrained on large dataset to a domain which has a small amount of data. Our FPA-CNN use a pretrained resnet50 as our basic networks to extract the shared features for next feature pyramids module and region based attention module.

2.3   Weakly Supervised Learning

Weakly Supervised Learning in CNN. Weakly supervised learning is an umbrella term covering a variety of studies that attempt to construct predictive models by learning with weak supervision [34]. Here we focus on a specified situation where region-level or pixel-level information are implicitly learnt using image-level labels. Zhou et al. [33] indicate classification CNN is able to localize the discriminative image regions on a variety of tasks despite not being trained for them. This localization ability can even be improved by using global average pooling layer, global max pooling layer [32], or log-sum-exp pooling layer [23]. Recently, Zhu et al. [35] designs a network module, Soft Proposal(SP), which can be plugged into any standard convolutional architecture to introduce the nearly cost-free object proposal.

This sounds free ability of classification CNN make many weakly supervised learning possible. Ahn et al. [1] learning instance segmentation with image-level class labels as supervision. They combine the localization ability of classification CNN and traditional image processing methods to generates pseudo instance segmentation labels of training images. Then the pseudo instance segmentation are used to train a fully supervised model. Joon et al. [22] add extra information called 'seed' into the processing of generating pseudo. Furthermore they use the region proposed by well trained classification CNN as a binary mask segmenting the one object a person is most likely to look first. Image saliency has multiple connotations. Binary mask is just one kind of definition. In this paper, we view image saliency as a spatial probability map of where a person might look first to make a discriminative conclusion, which is similar to [31].

Propagating Labels. Inspired by [31], we define image saliency as a spatial probability map of most discriminative region. The saliency map can be generated by classification CNN in a weakly supervised method mentioned as above, or it can also be labeled by human which is also called 'seed'. One simple way to propagate the label from known pixel to unknown pixel is to merge the pixel into super pixel. This process is very similar with clustering algorithm, and the 'distance' is defined as the similarity between pixels. [2,5,27] can take full use of neighbouring information around the pixel to group pixels. There are many works combining the CNN and information propagated on image saliency [16,22,35]. However these works only take the information around the label into account.

In this paper we utilize the active contour model [11], also called snakes to propagate the information from the local seed to the whole image, which considers the global information in image. Early active contour models are formulated in terms of a dynamic parametric contour $C(s,t) : [0,1] \times [0,\infty] \to R^2$ with a spatial parameter s in $[0,1]$ which parameterizes the points in the contour, and a temporal variable $t \in [0,\infty]$. The active contour model given in a level set formulation is called an implicit active contour or geometric active contour model, which is able to handle topological changes, such as splitting and merging, in a natural and efficient way. So we take distance regularized level set (DRLS) [15] method as our information propagation method. The details will be explained in next section.

3   Materials and Method

3.1   VRFs DataSets

The data is collected randomly from patients in cooperative stomatological hospital, which guaranteeing the practical usage of final models driven by it. The data desensitization is also applied for privacy protection. The dataset was consist of 9219 CBCT images coming from 37 subjects. There are about 250 images per subject, which generated by scanning in vertical directions. Among those, there are only 1868 positive instance, in which there exist VRFs. By the time we trained the networks, and is growing bigger. We aim to label at least 5k positive instance regardless of the negative quantity. Patients are in sitting position and keep the mandible parallel with ground during the scanning. All image is collected by a NewTom VG with 110kv of X-ray tube voltage, and 0.125mm of reconstructed resolution. Traditional techniques of image enhancement such as Gaussian filter and histogram equalization are applied to highlight the fractures for next labelling work.

At the labelling stage, dentists label each image that exists VRFs as positive instance. What's more, there are about 18 subjects have the scribble on the teeth. These scribble indicating the image saliency, i.e. the spatial probability map of most discriminative region. Most important of all, these scribble is easily obtained and can be done by non-professional person. Three typical types of weak supervision [34]: incomplete supervision, where only a subset of training data is given with labels; inexact supervision, where the training data are given with only coarse-grained labels; and inaccurate supervision, where the given labels are not always ground-truth. Scribble labels used in our datasets play a role of incomplete supervision. That means the scribble only indicating the partial discriminative region, so the level-set is applied to propagate the information

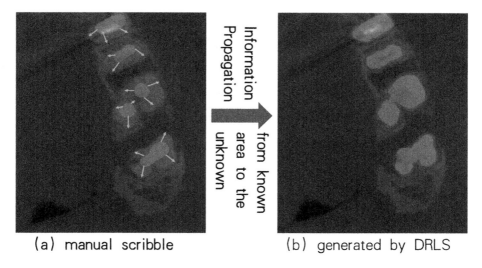

(a) manual scribble   (b) generated by DRLS

Fig. 2. The information propagation and subjects difference. (a) the red regions are labeled manually, indicating the discriminative regions. However, only partial of regions are labeled. So the level-set are applied to propagate the information from the known regions to unknowns. The yellow arrows show the directions of information propagation (b) shows the results generate image saliency. Notice that all the teeth have been marked by the generate labels, which will guide the network to checking the existence of VRFs. Comparing to Fig. 1 this fig also shows the differences between the subjects (The contrast of images from different subject varies), which increase the difficulty of VRFs recognition. (Color figure online)

from local to global. What's more, there are only 50% of images have scribbled labels, which can also be viewed as incomplete supervision. So regularized level set is applied to propagate information from the partial labels to global images. These generated saliency plays a role as high-level hint in our FPA-CNN to guides the networks choose the right discriminative regions. Figure 2 shows this process of the labeling and the generated saliency map in our dataset.

3.2 Feature Pyramids Attention Convolutional Neural Network

In order to incorporate the generated saliency and recognize the various scales of VRFs. We propose a novel classification network FPA-CNN. There are two important modules. One of which is feature pyramids module, the other is soft attention module. ResNets [6] are adopted as our backbone, on which the modules are attached. The FPA-CNN structure can be seen in Fig. 3.

Feature Pyramids Module. The feature pyramids [17] are a basic module in recognition systems for detecting objects at different scales. As mentioned above, The co-occurrences of crack in different scales requires network has well

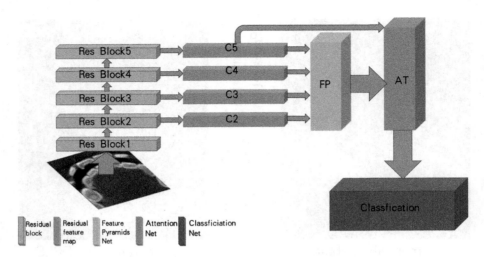

Fig. 3. FPN-CNN overview. ResNets are adopted as backbone, on which the feature pyramids module and attention module are attached. At last the processed feature maps are fed into classification net.

perception in multi spatial resolution. So we add Feature pyramids module to our backbone network to get a feature extracter that can handle the various scales of VRFs.

There are two significant information flow in feature pyramids. The bottom-up pathway is the feedforward computation of the backbone ConvNet, which computes a feature hierarchy. Specifically, for ResNets there five residual block. Denoting the output of these residual blocks as C_1, C_2, C_3, C_4, C_5 for conv1, conv2, conv3, conv4, and conv5 outputs, which have strides of $2, 4, 8, 16, 32$ pixels with respect to the input image. However, only C_2, C_3, C_4, C_5 are used to generate the final feature maps, in consideration of graphic memory ($C1's$ feature map consumes a lot).

The topdown pathway fuses the low-level features and high-level features. The low-level features have strong spatially resolution, while the high-level features have strong semantically information. The high-level feature maps is then merged with the corresponding low-level map (which undergoes a 1×1 convolutional layer to reduce channel dimensions) by upsampling followed by element-wise addition. Additional 3×3 convolution is applied on each merged map to generate the final feature map set P_2, P_3, P_4, P_5. This set of fusion feature maps makes perception in multi resolution possible. The details of feature pyramids module is shown in Fig. 4.

Saliency Driven Attention. VRFs can been view as cracks in teeth. In the mean while, there are a large number of regions seem look crack, e.g. the regions between teeth and healthy tissue (green circles in Fig. 1 picture (b)) Attention module helps later classifier overcoming these confusing regions.

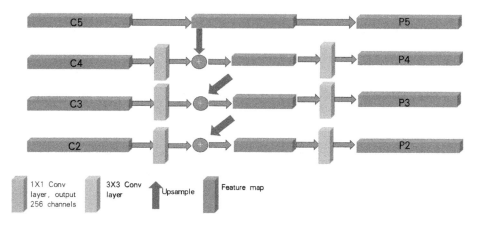

Fig. 4. Feature pyramids module. The fusion feature maps makes perception in multi resolution possible.

Attention module is actually a small network. It uses the feature maps C_5 as its's input features. It's output is spatial probability map of where a person might look first to make a discriminative conclusion, that is the image saliency. C_5 undergoes a 3×3 convolutional layer to get the context information around the pixels, then followed by a 1×1 convolutional layer to reduce channel dimensions.

The final outputs has two channels presenting the degree of confidence that the region should be a discriminative area. A spatial probability map A_1 is obtained by Softmax layer regularizing the outputs. This A_1 indicates the most discriminative regions on which the classification decision should be made.

Features Aggregation. The classification subnet combines the outputs from feature pyramids module and attention module. The attention output A_1 is applied to each features in P_2, P_3, P_4, P_5 by element-wise multiplication. Upsampling is applied if the size of two features dismatch in shape. In $A1$ Those discriminative regions have a higher weights, so the multiplication of A_1 and P_n where $n \in 2, 3, 4, 5$ is actually a soft attention which emphasize the focus regions and reserve the less importance regions. And we denote the results of multiplication as P_2', P_3', P_4', P_5' Then a ROI max pooling [24], also called adaptive max pooling, is applied to each feature map in P_2', P_3', P_4', P_5' to get the same features shape in regardless of inputs size. Finally, The results of pooling are concatenated and flatted before sent to the full connected layer. This is shown in Fig. 5.

Joint Training. FPA-CNN has two kinds of loss items. Attention loss measures difference between the generated discriminative regions from level-set and those from attention net. Due to there are only 50% images have supervision information from level-set method, the attention loss is optional. Classification loss is the main loss, which guides the FPA-CNN to learning the proper information.

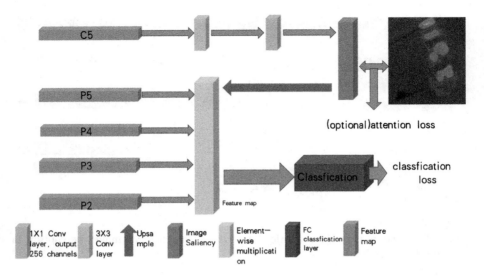

Fig. 5. Attention module and classification. The attention module generates the image saliency, which is used on the inputs of classification net as soft attention.

What's more, the classification loss can affect the attention module, thus the generated image saliency mainly incorporates the classification information and the supervision image saliency for attention module only play a role of assistant at the very begin of trainning.

4   Experiments

we compare our FPA-CNN with ResNets [6], InceptionV3 [30] by calculating the Area Under Curve (AUC) of Precision-Recall (PR) Curve. The reason why we choose PR curve is that we only care about identifying the VRFs. Even if the image do not contains the VRFs, there is no promise that other symptom do not exist. Therefor PR curve is a good choice due to it focus itself on single class. First of all, we present some experimental setting. The learning rate and weights decay are 10^{-5} and 10^{-2} respectively for next experiments. Stochastic Gradient Descent with momentum 0.9 is applied as our optimizer. What's more, we train each networks until the classification loss value on testing dataset doesn't descend for 5 epoch to avoid over-fitting. As for the spliting of dataset, we split the dataset into training part and testing part in two way. The one is splitting at image level which is a general way in nature image domain, the other is splitting at subject level which considers the differences between subjects and the image similarity from same subject. Due to the images from the same subject are actually continuous in spatially, splitting at image level will implicitly introduce the information of training dataset to testing. When there comes a new subject, the network fail. Splitting at subject level is suitable for this special dataset.

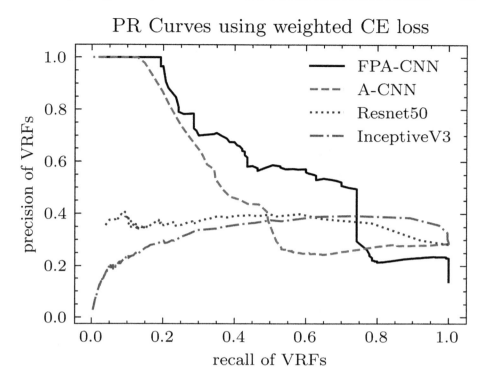

Fig. 6. Network Precision-Recall curve

In the next experiments, we pick 33 subjects from 37 as training data and the remains used as testing data.

Another key points is that dataset is unbalance, so the image containing the VRFs is in the minority. In order to elimination arised from the imbalance data, we choose the weighted cross entropy and focal loss [18] as our classification loss. The positive and negative have the coefficients of 0.9 and 0.1 respectively in weighted cross entropy. And the hyperparameter γ in focal loss is 2, which is a relatively moderate. Table 1 shows this two kinds of loss function. We observe that the weighted cross entropy performs better than focal loss, therefore we adopt the weighted CE loss as out standard function loss for next experiments.

Figure 7 shows the network PR curve on test dataset. A-CNN's structure is the similar to FPA-CNN except features pyramids module. Although Resnet50 and InceptionV3 seem to have a little discriminative capability, the 26% is almost reaching the positive rate in test dataset. This result indicates that Resnet50 and InceptionV3 has almost no discriminative capability on test dataset. A-CNN makes a big progress with the help of region proposal attention module. However this discriminative capability stay in a narrow interval, and there is a steep drop in PR curve. The FPA-CNN gain a relative wider range of discriminative probability, due to the feature pyramids module provides a multi-scale adaptive

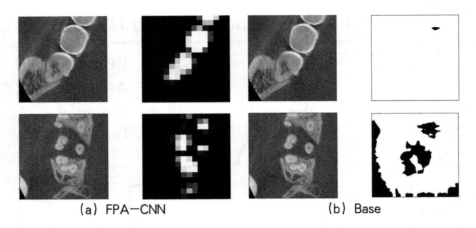

(a) FPA—CNN   (b) Base

Fig. 7. Attention regions for classification decision

features. Then we compare the focusing regions of network, Fig. 6 shows the saliency image of discrimination, from which we find a possible explanation of the poor performance of Resnet50 and InceptionV3. In contrast to original version, our FPA-CNN focus on the suitable regions which enhances the useful features as well as reduces the misleading information introduced by backgrounds.

Table 1. The AUC results on different loss function

Method	Base	Focal Loss	Weighted CE
Resnet50	0.327	0.332	0.365
InceptionV3	0.315	0.323	0.334
FPA-CNN	**0.565**	**0.573**	**0.592**

References

1. Ahn, J., Cho, S., Kwak, S.: Weakly supervised learning of instance segmentation with inter-pixel relations. In: Proceedings of the IEEE Conference on Computer Vision and Pattern Recognition (CVPR), pp. 2209–2218 (2019)
2. Boykov, Y.Y., Jolly, M.P.: Interactive graph cuts for optimal boundary & region segmentation of objects in nd images. In: Proceedings eighth IEEE International Conference on Computer Vision (ICCV), vol. 1, pp. 105–112. IEEE (2001)
3. Cohen, S., Berman, L.H., Blanco, L., Bakland, L., Kim, J.S.: A demographic analysis of vertical root fractures. J. Endodontics **32**(12), 1160–1163 (2006)
4. Corbella, S., Del Fabbro, M., Tamse, A., Rosen, E., Tsesis, I., Taschieri, S.: Cone beam computed tomography for the diagnosis of vertical root fractures: a systematic review of the literature and meta-analysis. Oral Surg. Oral Med. Oral Pathol. Oral Radiol. **118**(5), 593–602 (2014)

5. Felzenszwalb, P.F., Huttenlocher, D.P.: Efficient graph-based image segmentation. Int. J. Comput. Vision **59**(2), 167–181 (2004)
6. He, K., Zhang, X., Ren, S., Sun, J.: Deep residual learning for image recognition. In: Proceedings of the IEEE conference on Computer Vision and Pattern Recognition (CVPR), pp. 770–778 (2016)
7. Hu, J., Shen, L., Sun, G.: Squeeze-and-excitation networks. In: Proceedings of the IEEE conference on Computer Vision and Pattern Recognition (CVPR), pp. 7132–7141 (2018)
8. Huang, G., Liu, Z., Van Der Maaten, L., Weinberger, K.Q.: Densely connected convolutional networks. In: Proceedings of the IEEE Conference on Computer Vision and Pattern Recognition (CVPR), pp. 4700–4708 (2017)
9. Ioffe, S., Szegedy, C.: Batch normalization: ccelerating deep network training by reducing internal covariate shift. arXiv preprint arXiv:1502.03167 (2015)
10. Johari, M., Esmaeili, F., Andalib, A., Garjani, S., Saberkari, H.: Detection of vertical root fractures in intact and endodontically treated premolar teeth by designing a probabilistic neural network: an ex vivo study. Dentomaxillofacial Radiol. **46**(2), 20160107 (2017)
11. Kass, M., Witkin, A., Terzopoulos, D.: Snakes: active contour models. Int. J. Comput. Vision **1**(4), 321–331 (1988)
12. Kositbowornchai, S., Plermkamon, S., Tangkosol, T.: Performance of an artificial neural network for vertical root fracture detection: an ex vivo study. Dent. Traumatol. **29**(2), 151–155 (2013)
13. Krizhevsky, A., Sutskever, I., Hinton, G.E.: Imagenet classfication with deep convolutional neural networks. In: Advances in Neural Information Processing Systems (NIPS), pp. 1097–1105 (2012)
14. LeCun, Y., Bottou, L., Bengio, Y., Haffner, P.: Gradient-based learning applied to document recognition. Proc. IEEE **86**(11), 2278–2324 (1998)
15. Li, C., Xu, C., Gui, C., Fox, M.D.: Distance regularized level set evolution and its application to image segmentation. IEEE Trans. Image Process. **19**(12), 3243–3254 (2010)
16. Lin, D., Dai, J., Jia, J., He, K., Sun, J.: Scribblesup: scribble-supervised convolutional networks for semantic segmentation. In: Proceedings of the IEEE Conference on Computer Vision and Pattern Recognition (CVPR), pp. 3159–3167 (2016)
17. Lin, T.Y., Dollár, P., Girshick, R., He, K., Hariharan, B., Belongie, S.: Feature pyramid networks for object detection. In: Proceedings of the IEEE Conference on Computer Vision and Pattern Recognition (CVPR), pp. 2117–2125 (2017)
18. Lin, T.Y., Goyal, P., Girshick, R., He, K., Dollár, P.: Focal loss for dense object detection. In: Proceedings of the IEEE International Conference on Computer Vision (ICCV), pp. 2980–2988 (2017)
19. Long, H., et al.: Diagnostic accuracy of CBCT for tooth fractures: a meta-analysis. J. Dent. **42**(3), 240–248 (2014)
20. Long, J., Shelhamer, E., Darrell, T.: Fully convolutional networks for semantic segmentation. In: The IEEE Conference on Computer Vision and Pattern Recognition (CVPR), June 2015
21. Ma, R., Ge, Z., Li, G.: Detection accuracy of root fractures in cone-beam computed tomography images: a systematic review and meta-analysis. Int. Endod. J. **49**(7), 646–654 (2016)
22. Oh, S.J., Benenson, R., Khoreva, A., Akata, Z., Fritz, M., Schiele, B.: Exploiting saliency for object segmentation from image level labels. In: 2017 IEEE Conference on Computer Vision and Pattern Recognition (CVPR), pp. 5038–5047. IEEE (2017)

23. Pinheiro, P.O., Collobert, R.: From image-level to pixel-level labeling with convolutional networks. In: Proceedings of the IEEE Conference on Computer Vision and Pattern Recognition (CVPR), pp. 1713–1721 (2015)
24. Ren, S., He, K., Girshick, R., Sun, J.: Faster R-CNN: towards real-time object detection with region proposal networks. In: Advances in Neural Information Processing Systems (NIPS), pp. 91–99 (2015)
25. Rivera, E., Walton, R.: Cracking the cracked tooth code: detection and treatment of various longitudinal tooth fractures. Am. Assoc. Endodontists Colleagues Excellence News Lett. **2**, 1–19 (2008)
26. Ronneberger, O., Fischer, P., Brox, T.: U-Net: convolutional networks for biomedical image segmentation. In: Navab, N., Hornegger, J., Wells, W.M., Frangi, A.F. (eds.) MICCAI 2015. LNCS, vol. 9351, pp. 234–241. Springer, Cham (2015). https://doi.org/10.1007/978-3-319-24574-4_28
27. Rother, C., Kolmogorov, V., Blake, A.: Grabcut interactive foreground extraction using iterated graph cuts. ACM Trans. Graph. (TOG) **23**(3), 309–314 (2004)
28. Simonyan, K., Zisserman, A.: Very deep convolutional networks for large-scale image recognition. arXiv preprint arXiv:1409.1556 (2014)
29. Szegedy, C., et al.: Going deeper with convolutions. In: Proceedings of the IEEE conference on Computer Vision and Pattern Recognition (CVPR), pp. 1–9 (2015)
30. Szegedy, C., Vanhoucke, V., Ioffe, S., Shlens, J., Wojna, Z.: Rethinking the inception architecture for computer vision. In: Proceedings of the IEEE Conference on Computer Vision and Pattern Recognition (CVPR), pp. 2818–2826 (2016)
31. Yamada, K., Sugano, Y., Okabe, T., Sato, Y., Sugimoto, A., Hiraki, K.: Can saliency map models predict human egocentric visual attention? In: Koch, R., Huang, F. (eds.) ACCV 2010. LNCS, vol. 6468, pp. 420–429. Springer, Heidelberg (2011). https://doi.org/10.1007/978-3-642-22822-3_42
32. Zhou, B., Khosla, A., Lapedriza: Learning deep features for discriminative localization. In: Proceedings of the IEEE Conference on Computer Vision and Pattern Recognition (CVPR), pp. 2921–2929 (2016)
33. Zhou, B., Khosla, A., Lapedriza, A., Oliva, A., Torralba, A.: Object detectors emerge in deep scene CNNs. arXiv preprint arXiv:1412.6856 (2014)
34. Zhou, Z.H.: A brief introduction to weakly supervised learning. Nat. Sci. Rev. **5**(1), 44–53 (2018)
35. Zhu, Y., Zhou, Y., Ye, Q., Qiu, Q., Jiao, J.: Soft proposal networks for weakly supervised object localization. In: Proceedings of the IEEE International Conference on Computer Vision, pp. 1841–1850 (2017)

UIP-Net: A Decoder-Encoder CNN for the Detection and Quantification of Usual Interstitial Pneumoniae Pattern in Lung CT Scan Images

Rossana Buongiorno[1]([✉]), Danila Germanese[1], Chiara Romei[2], Laura Tavanti[3], Annalisa De Liperi[2], and Sara Colantonio[1]

[1] Institute of Information Science and Technologies (ISTI), National Research Council (CNR), Pisa, Italy
rossanabuongiorno@gmail.com
[2] 2nd Radiology Unit, Pisa University Hospital, Pisa, Italy
[3] Pulmonary Unit, Pisa University Hospital, Pisa, Italy

Abstract. A key step of the diagnosis of Idiopathic Pulmonary Fibrosis (IPF) is the examination of high-resolution computed tomography images (HRCT). IPF exhibits a typical radiological pattern, named Usual Interstitial Pneumoniae (UIP) pattern, which can be detected in non-invasive HRCT investigations, thus avoiding surgical lung biopsy. Unfortunately, the visual recognition and quantification of UIP pattern can be challenging even for experienced radiologists due to the poor inter and intra-reader agreement.

This study aimed to develop a tool for the semantic segmentation and the quantification of UIP pattern in patients with IPF using a deep-learning method based on a Convolutional Neural Network (CNN), called UIP-net. The proposed CNN, based on an encoder-decoder architecture, takes as input a thoracic HRCT image and outputs a binary mask for the automatic discrimination between UIP pattern and healthy lung parenchyma. To train and evaluate the CNN, a dataset of 5000 images, derived by 20 CT scans of different patients, was used. The network performance yielded 96.7% BF-score and 85.9% sensitivity. Once trained and tested, the UIP-net was used to obtain the segmentations of other 60 CT scans of different patients to estimate the volume of lungs affected by the UIP pattern. The measurements were compared with those obtained using the reference software for the automatic detection of UIP pattern, named Computer Aided Lungs Informatics for Pathology Evaluation and Rating (CALIPER), through the Bland-Altman plot. The network performance assessed in terms of both BF-score and sensitivity on the test-set and resulting from the comparison with CALIPER demonstrated that CNNs have the potential to reliably detect and quantify pulmonary disease in order to evaluate its progression and become a supportive tool for radiologists.

Keywords: Deep-learning · Convolutional Neural Network · Idiopatic Pulmonary Fibrosis

© Springer Nature Switzerland AG 2021
A. Del Bimbo et al. (Eds.): ICPR 2020 Workshops, LNCS 12661, pp. 389–405, 2021.
https://doi.org/10.1007/978-3-030-68763-2_30

1   Introduction

The term *Interstitial Lung Diseases* (ILDs) refers to a large group of lung disorders, most of which cause scars of the interstitium, usually referred to as pulmonary fibrosis. Fibrosis reduces the ability of the air sacs to capture and carry oxygen into the bloodstream, leading to a progressive loss of the ability to breathe. Although ILDs are rare if taken individually, together they represent the most frequent cause of non-obstructive chronic lung disease. The Idiopatic Pulmonary Fibrosis (IPF) is a chronic, progressive fibrosing interstitial pneumonia, which is classified among the ILDs with the poorest prognosis [1]. The high variability and unpredictability of IPF course have traditionally made its clinical management hard. The recent introduction of antifibrotic drugs has opened novel therapeutic options for mild to moderate IPF [2]. In this respect, treatment decisions highly rely on the assessment and quantification of IPF impact on the interstitium and its progression over time. High-Resolution Computed Tomography (HRCT) has demonstrated to have a key role in this frame, as it represents a non-invasive diagnostic modality to evaluate and quantify the extent of lung interstitium interested by IPF [3]. In fact, IPF shows a typical radiological pattern, called Usual Interstitial Pneumonia (UIP) pattern, whose presence is usually assessed by radiologists to diagnose IPF. The HRCT features that characterize the UIP pattern are the presence and positioning of specific lung parenchymal anomalies, known as *honeycombing*, *ground-glass opacification* and *fine reticulation* [4]. These anomalies appear in the HRCT scans with specific textural characteristics that are detected via a visual inspection of the imaging data. Assessing the diffusion of these anomalies is instrumental to understand the impact of IPF and to monitor its evolution over time. Quantitative and reliable approaches are in high demand in this respect, as the visual examination by radiologists suffers, by its nature, of poor reproducibility [5].

To overcome this issue, much research is being conducted to develop new techniques for automatic detection of lung diseases that may support radiologists during the diagnostic pathway, particularly in HRCT image analysis.

CALIPER (*Computer Aided Lung Informatics for Pathology Evaluation and Rating*) is a software tool developed by the Biomedical Imaging Resource Laboratory at the Mayo Clinic for the automatic detection and quantification of CT anomalies in HRCT images of ILDs [10]. CALIPER uses histogram signatures to characterize and quantify parenchymal disease on HRCT and it was developed using pathologically confirmed imaging data evaluated by expert radiologist consensus. It is currently considered as the most viable instrument by radiologists. Nevertheless, it is not an open-source tool and its performance varies based on the acquisition context, thus on CT scanners and protocols and on the spatial kernel used by the image reconstruction algorithm.

This study aims to provide a tool for UIP pattern recognition based on a low-cost and real-time Machine Learning (ML) method to obtain UIP-pattern volume measurements based on a different approach than CALIPER, in the attempt to eventually overcome the aforementioned limits. The method relies on a fully-convolutional neural network (CNN), called UIP-net, which takes as input a lung HRCT image and returns the corresponding binary map discriminating disease and normal tissue. This preliminary work firstly investigates whether CALIPER might be reproduced, to open the way to further investigation on many different scenarios (e.g., using UIP-net on images acquired by different scanners and reconstructed with different spatial kernels), possibly leveraging an unsupervised approach towards more generalizable results.

The paper is organized as follows: Sect. 2 describes the state of the art in the field of ML techniques applied to the detect UIP pattern and IPF biomarkers from lung HRCT scans; in Sect. 3 the UIP-net, that is the CNN here proposed for the detection of UIP patterns, is presented; then, in Sect. 4 the experimental setup and results provided by the UIP-net are described. Finally, Sect. 5 concludes the paper.

2   State of the Art

Modern CT scanners allow for assessing anatomical and physiological properties providing high-definition volumetric images with an excellent spatial and temporal resolution. Computerized algorithm for HRCT image analysis, namely quantitative CT (QCT), gives a non-invasive mean for direct visualization, characterization and quantification of anatomic structures in order to obtain rapid and reproducible digital IPF biomarkers [6]. Indeed, several studies showed that QCT may overcome the issue of the inter-observer variability and could provide more consistent prognostic indexes. Furthermore, QCT may allow to extract CT features that are not visually recognisable and to objectively keep track of the disease progression [7]. The most relevant QCT methods for the assessment of ILD in patients with IPF are based on densitometric and local histogram analysis and textural analysis.

CT histogram provides a distribution of X-ray attenuation allowing the calculation of mean value, skewness and kurtosis that may give a measure of the extent of fibrosis. For example, both kurtosis and skewness showed correlation with functional test such as Forced Vital Capacity (FVC) [8]. It was demonstrated also that mean value, skewness and kurtosis are correlated with survival in patient with ILDs [9]. However, this approach is not sufficient to quantify the extent of every single interstitial lung abnormalities in patient with IPF, therefore more sophisticated textural analysis have been implemented.

Texture analysis consists in the quantitative description of the structural arrangement of pixels of different intensities and their relationship to the surrounding environment. Given the heterogeneity of lung parenchyma both in healthy subjects and in the presence of IPF, a correct interpretation of HRTC images may rely on texture analysis.

CALIPER (*Computer-Aided Lung Informatics for Pathology Evaluation and Rating*) can be considered as the most performing method based on texture analysis for IPF pattern visualization. This tool integrates a texture matching method with the analysis of histogram features of voxels for the automated lung parenchymal characterization and quantification of pulmonary disease on HRCT images. This process automatically labels each pixel as belonging to one of seven specific parenchymal patterns: normal, ground-glass opacity (GGO), reticular density, honeycombing, and mild, moderate, or severe low-attenuation areas (see Fig. 1). It has been demonstrated that compared to visual scoring, CALIPER results are strongly correlated with functional tests [11], overall survival and decline of pulmonary capacity [12,13].

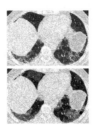

Fig. 1. HRCT image of UIP with CALIPER characterization. Top: Reticulation, groundglass opacity with a honeycomb cyst in the left lower lobe. Bottom: Color overlay image highlighting parenchymal patterns characterized by CALIPER: normal lung (light and dark green), ground-glass opacity (yellow), reticulation (orange), and honeycombing (red). (Color figure online)

2.1 Deep Learning and Convolutional Neural Networks

The discussed methods, based on histogram and texture analysis, involve *hand-crafted* features, that means manually engineered features, which are fed to machine learning classifiers to locally recognize patterns in lung tissue. More recently, advanced AI techniques, such as Deep Learning, outperformed such methods by adopting *learned features*, that are automatically obtained from the layers of the neural network thus overcoming the issues related to human bias.

Deep learning has achieved impressive results in several medical image classification tasks but only few methods have been proposed for IPF radiological pattern classification through Convolutional Neural Networks (CNNs).

Walsh et al. used a pre-trained Neural Network (NN) for the discrimination of UIP and not-UIP patterns, with training data labelled by expert radiologists [14]. Anthimopoulos et al. designed and tested a CNN for the classification of 7 anomalies within 2-D patches of HRCT images: healthy, GGO, micronodules, consolidation, reticulation, honeycombing, combination of GGO and reticulation [15], as shown in Fig. 2. The proposed CNN reached an accuracy of 85% showing the potential of CNNs in IPF pattern recognition. Also Kim et al. developed a CNN for the classification of lung tissue in 2-D images; in this specific case, CNN outperformed a Support Vector Machine classification algorithm [16].

Several studies focused on the development of deep neural networks also for segmentation tasks. Anthimopoulos et al. designed a network that outperformed the traditional classification methods with less computational power and few segmentation errors [14, 16, 17]. Agarwala et al. pre-trained a P-net using daily photographs and after a fine-tuning, the parameters of the network have been modified in order to optimize the performance on thoracic HRCT images including only ILD manifestations [18]. The network had good capacity in detecting fibrosis and emphysema even if the number of labelled patches used as training data was exiguous. Although the reported deep neural networks provided good results, they were not able to overcome the issues related to texture recognition of UIP patterns in HRCT images. The work reported in this paper aimed to design a CNN for the detection of UIP patterns preserving texture details during image processing. The network, named UIP-net, exploits the descriptive capability of neural networks to improve the diagnostic accuracy compared to the existing methods for quantitative image analysis of IPF. The network has been trained and tested on a dataset of 5000 images. In addition, according to the opinion of an expert radiologist, it provided acceptable results compared to CALIPER.

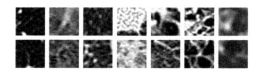

Fig. 2. Healthy tissue and typical ILD patterns from left to right: healthy, GGO, micronodules, consolidation, reticulation, honeycombing, combination of GGO and reticulation [15].

3   Data and Methods

3.1   Data

For the training and test of UIP-net, 20 HRCT volumetric scans of patients with IPF from the 2nd Radiology Unit database of Pisa University Hospital were used. Each scan had about 250 slices with 512×512 pixels per slice, thus the dataset had a total of about 5000 images. The scans were acquired using the same CT scan (Siemens Sensation 64) and acquisition protocol. Each slice had the same pixel spacing of 0.7 mm.

First of all, CT scans were processed by CALIPER in order to obtain the *ground truth*. CALIPER provided colour images with the segmentation of the areas corresponding to the parenchymal anomalies characteristic of the UIP pattern: yellow for Ground Glass Opacity (GGO), orange for reticulation and red for honeycombing, as shown in Fig. 1. The colour images returned by CALIPER were imported in Matlab®(version R2019b) for obtaining the corresponding binary masks. These masks had pixels values equals to 0 or 1 if belonging to normal tissue or to UIP patterns, respectively. They represented the desired outputs of UIP-net: that means, UIP-net was trained to provide a binary mask for each gray-level input image with pixels equals to 0 or 1 if belonging to normal tissue or disease, respectively.

In order to test the usefulness of UIP net in quantifying the volume of the disease, another 60 CT scans of different patients and acquired with the same scanner were used. Also these scans had gray-scale slices with 512×512 pixels per slice.

3.2 Methods

Data Pre-processing. In order to reduce the computational complexity of training and improve the speed of convergence of the model, the original images were pre-processed using Matlab®.

Nonetheless, no filtering was applied for preserving the intensity difference of adjacent pixels. On the other hand, to optimize the amount of data to be analyzed, the number of nonzero pixels was decreased through a Fuzzy c-means (FCM) algorithm. Two clusters were defined: the background (with the abdomen) and the foreground (i.e., the lungs). Pixels with a probability greater than 70% to belong to background were set to zero, those with a probability greater than 70% to belong to foreground were kept unchanged. After that, both the images and the ground truth were cropped for reducing the size of the Field of View (FOV). Thus, pre-processed images had 492×492 pixels with nonzero values only within the lungs (see Fig. 3).

Fig. 3. On the left: an example of pre-processed cropped image with non-zeros pixels only within the lungs. On the right: an example of the ground truth obtained from CALIPER.

UIP-Net Architecture. First, in order to design the optimal architecture of UIP-net, the problem was carefully analyzed and the requirements of the model were defined:

1. Since UIP patterns are characterized by typical textural features, the network should preserve the excellent image quality, in term of spatial resolution and bit depth, and be able to capture texture details;
2. The network should reduce data loss during training;
3. The network should be trainable and provide good results even:
   (a) with few examples because big datasets are not always available;
   (b) with few computational resources to make the network an accessible tool.

On the basis of these assumptions, UIP-net was inspired by [19] and designed with an Encoder-Decoder structure as in Fig. 4. With respect to [19], the design of UIP-net architecture provides for:

1. the suppression of batch-normalization and pooling layers in order to prevent an excessive loss of information;
2. fewer layers to reduce the number of operations performed on the images;
3. the introduction of the tanh activation function for the last layer (instead of the softmax), in order to improve the speed of convergence of the model and make the network stable against sudden changes of the input.

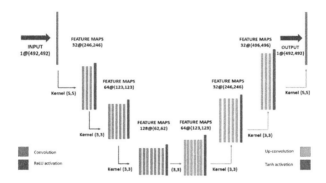

Fig. 4. UIP-net architecture.

The input layer of the UIP-net takes a 492×492 image and is followed by three convolutional layers and three de-convolutional layers. The size of receptive field was set to 3×3 for each layer, except for the first and the last one that have 5×5 kernel, in order to capture characteristic local structure of texture. Each convolutional layer doubles the number of features maps outputted. Thus, the first, the second and the third layers return 32, 64 and 128 features maps, respectively. On the other hand, two of the three de-convolutional layers produce 64 and 32 feature maps, while the third one keeps the same number of features maps, changing only the size of images. The last convolutional layer, finally, merges all the features maps into one with 492×492 pixels. Therefore, the output layer returns a binary mask with the segmentation of UIP patterns detected in the input image, keeping the same size. Each layer has a ReLU activation function, except the last one which, as mentioned above, has tanh activation.

Since no pooling was carried out between the convolutional layers to prevent loss of information, the stride was set to 2 in order to halve the size of the image after each layer. The padding was set to $\frac{k-1}{2}$ with k equal to the size of kernel (i.e 5×5 for the first and last layers, 3×3 for the others).

Training Method. The UIP-net was trained by minimising the binary cross-entropy using Adam optimizer.

After some experiments, it was proved that the network works well with default values, namely the learning rate equal to 0.001, the exponential decay rates for the moving average of the gradient equal to 0.9, and the squared gradient equal to 0.999.

Furthermore, Dice score monitored the network performances during training, comparing the segmentation made by UIP-net (S) with the ground truth (G), according to Eq. 1.

$$D = \frac{2S \cap G|}{|S| + |G|} \tag{1}$$

Finally, the weight updates were performed in mini-batches and the number of samples per batch was set to 10.

4   Experimental Setup and Results

4.1   Experimental Setup

The number of HRCT scans available for the training set was set to 13. Since each scan had about 215 slices, the training set consisted of about 3200 examples. Nevertheless, in order to avoid overfitting, it was necessary to establish how many images were strictly necessary.

Also the number of the epochs was set in order to stop training once the model performance stops improving on a validation set.

Thus, the validation set used for the fine tuning of the hyper-parameters was made up of 30% the examples, randomly extracted from the training set at each epoch.

A total of 20 trainings were carried-out:

1. 200, 400, 800, 1600, 3200 samples were fed to UIP-net for the same number of epochs;
2. UIP-net was trained for 50, 100, 150, 200 epochs keeping unchanged the number of examples.

Loss function and Dice score were monitored during training in order to choose both the correct number of examples and epochs.

As shown in Fig. 5, the best model was the one trained by 800 samples for 50 epochs, with a binary cross-entropy on training and validation set of 0.14 and 0.097 respectively, and a Dice score of 0.81 and 0.78, respectively.

For this model, a 5-fold cross validation scheme was adopted to ensure the validity of the results. On average over all folds, the number of slices was 640 images for training and 160 for testing, while Dice score was 76.19% with a deviation standard of 3.54%.

The discussed method was implemented using Keras and TensorFlow framework and coded in Python 3.7.

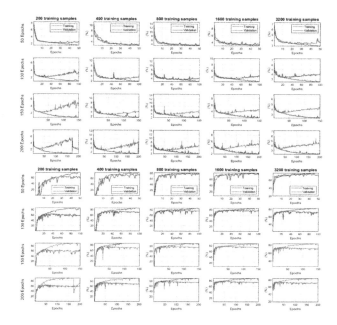

Fig. 5. Loss function (top) and Dice score (bottom) during training.

4.2   Results

The performances of the network were evaluated on the test set, consisting of 7 HRCT scans, with 1800 images in total. A quantitative performance analysis was performed, followed by qualitative assessment according to the opinion of an expert radiologist on the predicted segmentation (see Fig. 6).

Finally, 60 HRCT scans were used to compute the volume of UIP pattern detected by the UIP-net. The measurements were then compared with those obtained with CALIPER.

Fig. 6. On the left: original input image with ground truth overlapped (yellow). On the right: original input image with predicted segmentation of UIP-patterns overlapped (red). The predicted segmentations outputted by the network were assessed both quantitatively and qualitatively. (Color figure online)

Quantitative Analysis. The quantitative evaluation measures were: Dice and Boundary F1 (BF) contour matching score (BF-score), sensitivity and specificity.

BF score is a metric that tends to correlate better with human qualitative assessment than Dice score. It measures how close the predicted boundary of an object matches the ground truth boundary. The BF score is defined as the harmonic mean of the precision (P) and recall (R) values calculated within a distance error tolerance (typically 0.75% of the image diagonal [20]) to decide whether a point on the predicted boundary has a match on the ground truth boundary or not. BF-score can be defined through P and R according to the following Eq. (2):

$$BF = \frac{2PR}{(P+R)} \tag{2}$$

Sensitivity and specificity could be defined on the basis of true/false positive and true/false negative, as shown in Eq. (3) and (4).

$$Sensitivity = \frac{TP}{(TP+FN)} \tag{3}$$

$$Specificity = \frac{TN}{(TN+FP)} \tag{4}$$

In Table 1 evaluation measures on the test set are shown, with maximum values highlighted in green and minimum in red, while in Table 2 mean value and standard deviation of all HRCT scans of the test set are shown.

Table 1. Quantitative evaluation measures on test set.

	P1	P2	P3	P4	P5	P6	P7
Dice	74.94%	73.3%	61.58%	59.4%	58.4%	57%	56.65%
BF-score	78.96%	72.9%	81.16%	78.68%	81.32%	75%	83.73%
Sens	83.52%	83.51%	84.57%	74.46%	80.39%	74%	77.03%
Spec	98.75%	98.33%	97.98%	98.7%	99%	99%	98.17%

Table 2. Mean value and standard deviation of evaluation measures

	Dice	BF-score	Sensitivity	Specificity
Mean value	63.1%	78.8%	79.6%	98.5%
Standard deviation	7%	3%	4.4%	0.4%

Qualitative Assessment. For a more comprehensive evaluation process, the performance of UIP-net was assessed through a qualitative visual analysis of the predicted segmentation performed by an expert radiologist. This showed that, compared to the ground truth (see Fig. 7):

1. UIP-net detected some patterns missed by CALIPER expecially where the amount of diseased tissue is high (see Fig. 7);
2. UIP-net detected lung disease in the intestine and labelled vessels and airways as lung tissue. On the contrary, CALIPER manages to discriminate both vessels and airways.

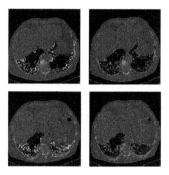

Fig. 7. On the left: the ground truth. On the right: UIP-net predicted segmentations. At the top: in the blue boxes, there are pixels detected by UIP-net but ignored by CALIPER. At the bottom: on the left, the arrows point to the vessels segmented by CALIPER, but ignored by UIP-net; on the right, the red box highlights the intestine mistakenly segmented by UIP-net. (Color figure online)

In order to evaluate how the discussed issues affect the quantitative measures of the performance of UIP-net, a post-processing step was carried-out.

Firstly, false detections in the intestine were removed using the method proposed by Ross et al. [21] that allows to obtain masks containing only lungs. Briefly, this involves initial gray level thresholding using Otsu's method followed by morphological closing to fill in high attenuating areas within the lung field. In order to properly label airways outside the lung field, component region growing was applied. Once the region of the trachea is determined, an initial threshold and seed location are selected to initialize the region growing algorithm to extract the airway tree. The obtained masks contain lungs without airways but with vessels. Thus, in order to extract vessels from lungs, the method proposed by Sato et al. [22] was used. This involves 3-D line enhancement filtering with which accomplishes the following:

1. Recovery of line structures of various width, especially thin structures;
2. Removal of the effects of non-linear structures and of noise and artifacts.

Both methods were implemented using 3-D Slicer software and Chest Imaging Platform (CIP) framework. Once binary masks of the whole lungs and vessels were obtained, they were combined in order to get another one with only lungs which allowed to keep only segmented pixels belonging to lungs, thus removing those belonging to vessels and intestine (see Fig. 8).

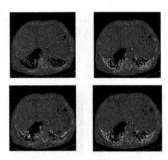

Fig. 8. On the top: predicted segmentations of UIP-net before (left) and after (right) post-processing. On the bottom: ground truth (left) compared to predicted segmentation of UIP-net after post-processing (right).

The same quantitative evaluation measures described in Sect. 4.2 were then computed (see Table 3 with maximum values highlighted in green and minimum in red).

Table 3. Quantitative evaluation measures after post-processing.

	P1	P2	P3	P4	P5	P6	P7
Dice	84.43%	77.4%	65.77%	62.28%	75.43%	60.1%	64.58%
BF-score	96.07%	96.1%	96.71%	91%	93.6%	89.2%	94.14%
Sens	75%	84%	85.87%	76.3%	80.7%	75%	78.1%
Spec	100%	98.33%	98.66%	99.2%	99.3%	99%	98.87%

In Table 4 mean values with standard deviations of evaluation measures before post-processing and after post-processing are compared.

Volume Estimation and Comparison with CALIPER. In order to evaluate the reliability of UIP-net in quantifying the volume of diseased tissue in the lungs, 60 HRCT scans were used. The scans were provided as input to the network to segment the UIP pattern. The segmentations were then imported in 3D-Slicer and, through CIP framework, the measures of volume of diseased tissue in each scan (in cm^3) were computed. The comparison with those estimated

Table 4. Mean value and standard deviation of evaluation measures before and after post-processing

	Dice	BF-score	Sensitivity	Specificity
Before post-processing	63.10% ± 7%	78.8% ± 3%	79% ± 4.4%	98.5% ± 0.4%
After post-processing	70% ± 9%	93.8 ± 2.8%	79.2 ± 4.4%	99 ± 0.5%

by CALIPER was done through the Bland-Altman plot (see Table 5 and Fig. 9) since it provides a visual representation of the agreement between two different methods.

The difference between UIP-net and CALIPER were acceptable: in Fig. 9 can be seen that most measures fall in the range between the lower and the upper Limit Of Agreement (LOA).

Table 5. Mean value (bias) and standard deviation of raw differences calculated between the measurements of volume obtained with UIP-net and CALIPER. Lower and Upper Limit of Agreement (LOA) were mean ± 1.96 × standard deviation. Bias, lower LOA and upper LOA are shown on Bland-Altman plot as dashed lines.

	Raw differences (cm^3)	Lower LOA	Upper LOA
UIP pattern volume	69.18041 ± 584.6433	−1076.72	1215.081

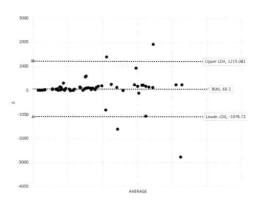

Fig. 9. Bland-Altman Plot. Average and raw differences between UIP-net and CALIPER measurements (x-axis and y-axis respectively). The dashed lines indicate the lower and the upper LOA.

4.3   Discussion

Quantitative analysis of predicted segmentation of UIP-net and volume estimates followed by comparisons with CALIPER highlighted some aspects.

First of all, the lower values of Dice score, which was less correlated with human visual opinion than the others evaluation measures, could be due to the inhomogeneities of ILD. Indeed, Dice score works best with the segmentation of compact diseases like nodules, but ILD is mostly uneven within the lungs (Fig. 10).

On the other hand, BF-score was always consistent with visual assessment and took higher values than Dice score. At last, although specificity had always highest values, it is not clear if such measure is accurate. As mentioned above, IPF is heterogeneously distributed within the lungs and tends to be present mostly in the middle and lower lung fields, so the many null pixels of apical slices of the same scan, might unbalance the measures (Fig. 10). On the contrary, sensitivity can be taken as a reference measure and it had similar values to BF-score.

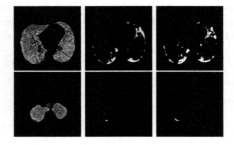

Fig. 10. On the top: an example of sparsity of the segmentation. On the bottom: an example of images with null pixels which unbalance the value of specificity. Original image (left), ground truth (center), predicted segmentation (right).

Overall, the UIP-net demonstrated good performance metrics and these results are encouraging. BF-score after post-processing reached a maximum of 83.73%. The post-processing results demonstrated that the misclassification of vessels and intenstine mostly affected the performance. In fact, all the computed indices increase: Dice score increases of 7%, while BF-score increases of 15% reaching a maximum of 96.71%. Thus, finer pre-processing can solve the issue.

Another consequence of a wrong pre-processing can be seen in Fig. 11: some pixels belonging to the abdomen were mistaken for belonging to the lungs and appear on the final image given as input to UIP-net. Consequenlty, UIP-net analyze them and find the disease. This fact is reflected on the outliers in red of Fig. 9 which represent the increased amount of diseased tissue detected.

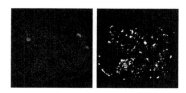

Fig. 11. Original image after an incorrect pre-processing (left): the abdomen are mistaken for lungs by the clustering algorithm. Segmentation mask outputted by UIP-net on the right.

5   Conclusion

In this work, a CNN named UIP-net was proposed for the detection of UIP patterns in HRCT images. A novel architecture was designed in order to preserve fine details of the texture, thus taking advantage of the excellent quality of the images, both in term of spatial resolution and bit depth.

Future works will consist in:

1. Validating the current version of the UIP-net on additional data.
2. Modifying the network in order to:
   - take into account the 3-D nature of the UIP pattern;
   - provide a differential characterization of UIP patterns (e.g. to discriminate between honeycombing and GGO).
3. Improving the generalizability and reliability of the CNN testing it on images belonging to different acquisition contexts. In this work, only images acquired with the same scanner and reconstructed with B60 kernel were involved.
4. Investigating unsupervised and label-independent learning, to boost UIP-net's performance and generalization ability on data not human-annotated.
5. Using the UIP-net to detect also HRCT manifestations of other diseases, first of all those produced by Covid-19.

Acknowledgment. The authors express all their gratitude to Brian J. Bartholomai from the Division of Radiology and Ronald Karwoski from Biomedical Imaging Resource of Mayo Clinic, MN, USA. Thanks to their useful support, it was possible to obtain the labelled images outputted by CALIPER used as ground truth. Without CALIPER, it would not have been possible to train the novel network proposed in this work.

References

1. Walsh, S.L.F.: Imaging biomarkers and staging in IPF. Curr. Opin. Pulm. Med. **24**, 445–452 (2018)
2. Kim, H.J., Perlman, D., Tomic, R.: Natural history of idiopathic pulmonary fibrosis. Respir. Med. **109**, 661–670 (2015)
3. Hansell, D.M., Goldin, J.G., King, T.E., et al.: CT staging and monitoring of fibrotic interstitial lung diseases in clinical practice and treatment trials: a position paper from the Fleischner Society. Lancet Respir. Med. **3**, 483–496 (2015)

4. Ragu, G., et al.: Diagnosis of idiopathic pulmonary fibrosis, an Official ATS/ERS/JRS/ALAT clinical practice guideline. Am. J. Respir. Crit. Care Med. **198**, e44–e68 (2018)

5. Walsh, S.L., Calandriello, L., Sverzellati, N., et al.: Interobserver agreement for the ATS/ERS/JRS/ALAT criteria for a UIP pattern on CT. Thorax **71**, 45–51 (2016)

6. Goldin, J.G.: Computed tomography as a biomarker in clinical trials imaging. J. Thorac Imaging **28**, 291–297 (2013)

7. Jacob, J., Bartholmai, B.J., Rajagopalan, S., Kokosi, M., Nair, A., Karwoski, R., et al.: Mortality prediction in idiopathic pulmonary fibrosis: evaluation of computerbased CT analysis with conventional severity measures. Eur. Respir. J. **49** (2017)

8. Kim, H.J., et al.: Comparison of the quantitative CT imaging biomarkers of idiopathic pulmonary Fibrosis at baseline and early change with an interval of 7 months. Acad. Radiol. **22**, 70–80 (2015)

9. Best, A.C., et al.: Idiopathic pulmonary fibrosis: physiologic tests, quantitative CT indexes, and CT visual scores as predictors of mortality. Radiology **246**, 935–940 (2008)

10. Xiaoping, W., et al.: Computed tomographic biomarkers in idiopathic pulmonary fibrosis the future of quantitative analysis. Am. J. Respir. Crit. Care Med. **199**, 12–21 (2018)

11. Jacob, J., et al.: Mortality prediction in idiopathic pulmonary Fibrosis: evaluation of computerbased CT analysis with conventional severity measures. Eur. Respir. **49** (2017)

12. Moua, T., et al.: Can progression of fibrosis as assessed by computer-aided lung informatics for pathology evaluation and rating (CALIPER) predict outcomes in patients with idiopathic pulmonary Fibrosis. Chest **140** (2011)

13. Jacob, J., Bartholmai, B.J., Rajagopalan, S., et al.: Serial automated quantitative CT analysis in idiopathic pulmonary fibrosis: functional correlations and comparison with changes in visual CT scores. Eur. Radiol. **28**(3), 1318–1327 (2017). https://doi.org/10.1007/s00330-017-5053-z

14. Walsh, S.L.F., Calandriello, L., Silva, M., Sverzellati, N.: Deep learning for classifying Fibrotic lung disease on high-resolution computed tomography: a case-cohort study. Lancet Respir. Med. **6**, 837–845 (2018)

15. Anthimopoulos, M., Christodoulidis, S., Ebner, L., Christe, A., Mougiakakou, S.: Lung pattern classification for interstitial lung diseases using a deep convolutional neural network. IEEE Trans. Med. Imaging **35** (2016)

16. Kim, G.B., Jung, K.H., Lee, Y., et al.: Comparison of shallow and deep learning methods on classifying the regional pattern of diffuse lung disease. J. Digit. Imaging **31**(4), 415–424 (2017). https://doi.org/10.1007/s10278-017-0028-9

17. Ronneberger, O., Fischer, P., Brox, T.: Convolutional networks for biomedical image segmentation. In: Medical Image Computing and Computer-Assisted Intervention (2015)

18. Agarwala, S., Kale, M., Kumar, D., et al.: Deep learning for screening of interstitial lung disease patterns in high-resolution CT images. Clin. Radiol. **75** (2020)

19. Liu, F., Zhou, Z., Jang, H., Samsonov, A., Zhao, G., Kijowski, R.: Deep convolutional neural network and 3D deformable approach for tissue segmentation in musculoskeletal magnetic resonance imaging. Magn. Reson. Med. **79**, 2379–2391 (2018)

20. Csurka, G., Larlus, D.: What is a good evaluation measure for semantic segmentation? IEEE Trans. Pattern Anal. Mach. Intell. **26** (2013)

21. Ross, J.C., Nakajima, S., Shiraga, N., et al.: Lung extraction, lobe segmentation and hierarchical region assessment for quantitative analysis on high resolution computed tomography images. In: Yang, G.-Z., Hawkes, D., Rueckert, D., Noble, A., Taylor, C. (eds.) MICCAI 2009. LNCS, vol. 5762, pp. 690–698. Springer, Heidelberg (2009). https://doi.org/10.1007/978-3-642-04271-3_84

22. Sato, Y., Nakajima, S., Shiraga, N., et al.: Three-dimensional multi-scale line filter for segmentation and visualization of curvilinear structures in medical images. Med. Image Anal. **2**, 143–168 (1998)

Don't Tear Your Hair Out: Analysis of the Impact of Skin Hair on the Diagnosis of Microscopic Skin Lesions

Alessio Gallucci[1(✉)], Dmitry Znamenskiy[2], Nicola Pezzotti[1,2], and Milan Petkovic[1,2]

[1] Eindhoven University of Technology, Eindhoven, The Netherlands
{a.gallucci,n.pezzotti,m.petkovic}@tue.nl, {nicola.pezzotti,
milan.petkovic}@philips.com
[2] Philips Research, Eindhoven, The Netherlands
dmitry.znamenskiy@philips.com

Abstract. Recent work on the classification of microscopic skin lesions does not consider how the presence of skin hair may affect diagnosis. In this work, we investigate how deep-learning models can handle a varying amount of skin hair during their predictions. We present an automated processing pipeline that tests the performance of the classification model. We conclude that, under realistic conditions, modern day classification models are robust to the presence of skin hair and we investigate three architectural choices (Resnet50, InceptionV3, Densenet121) that make them so.

Keywords: Dermatology · Imaging · Hair detection · Skin lesion · Melanoma · Deep learning · Augmentations

1 Introduction

Skin cancer is the most common cancer in the U.S. [1], and, the number of treated adults has increased over time, from 3.4 million in the 2002–2006 period to 4.9 million in the 2007–2011 period [2]. Usually, screening and diagnosis are primarily carried by clinical visual inspection and, if necessary, by biopsy. There is an urge to automate and facilitate this procedure with image-based screening since early detection is crucial for treatment options [3]. Deep convolutional neural networks (CNN) have demonstrated great potential for solving various vision tasks [4] and recently reached dermatologists performance in suspicious skin lesions classification [5]. To support early diagnosis, effective and computationally efficient models can be deployed on smartphone devices to enable a first level of patient-driven screening. In this setting, the models have to deal with much less controlled conditions than in a laboratory environment. In this paper, we investigate the effect that a varying amount of skin hair have on the classification accuracy of deep learning classifiers. We present an automated testing pipeline that, while currently focused on testing for the impact of skin hair, we plan to extend to other type of unforeseen circumstances, e.g., different camera models, light conditions and resolutions.

© Springer Nature Switzerland AG 2021
A. Del Bimbo et al. (Eds.): ICPR 2020 Workshops, LNCS 12661, pp. 406–416, 2021.
https://doi.org/10.1007/978-3-030-68763-2_31

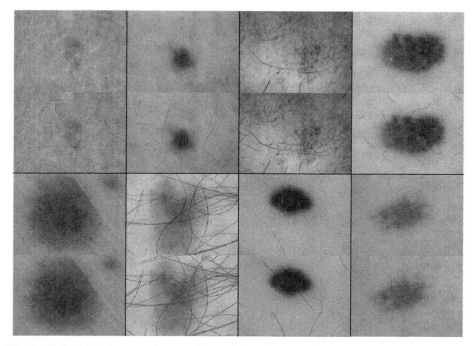

Fig. 1. Eight skin hair annotation samples, each showing the original image (upper half) and the annotated version (lower half).

To perform such analysis, we first segment skin hair in images depicting small skin patches. These patches often contain skin lesions and we evaluate whether the learned segmentation helps to improve the robustness of the skin lesion classification. This work is motivated by the need to create and validate a screening approach that does not require removing skin hair. If feasible, such an approach has several benefits in a professional healthcare setting, it can improve patient comfort, save time in the screening procedure, and improve diagnosis since the presence of hair can help differentiate skin lesions [6]. Moreover, it can allow the development of a first round of user-driven screening on, for example, smartphone devices.

The contribution of this paper is twofold; we first present an approach for the segmentation of hairs in existing skin image patches. This segmentation approach gives us realistic hair patterns that can be used to test for the robustness of skin lesions classifiers. Our second contribution is a set of image augmentation strategies, based on our first contribution, that form a testing pipeline for the robustness of skin lesions classifiers. More specifically, for the first contribution we have developed an algorithm for the hair segmentation based on the state-of-the-art architecture for biomedical segmentation U-NET [7]. Since we needed data for training, which was difficult to find in open source datasets, we contributed to the enrichment of the public benchmark dataset HAM10000 [8] by annotating skin hair. Figure 1 shows eight examples out of 75 annotated images, now published at https://doi.org/10.4121/uuid:9ed94e25-8b74-4807-b84a-

2c54ec9d96f0. Note that the resolution of each image is of 600×450 pixels, highlighting the challenge of such a manual segmentation and the benefit that our segmentation network can provide to the research community.

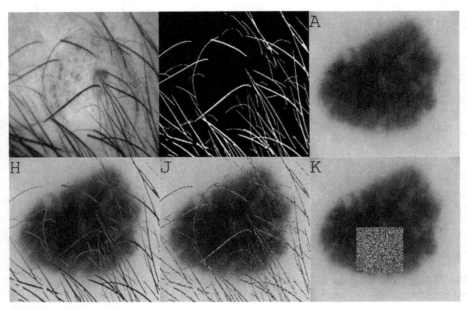

Fig. 2. Top left is the input hair image. Top center the segmentation of hair. Top right an input image to be classified as nevi or melanoma. The bottom row shows the hair with their original color, transplanting hair with random pattern color and finally masking flat squares of equal area. We excluded scaling, sheer and rotation for visualization purposes.

As second contribution, we evaluate a new testing pipeline, relying on realistic image augmentations strategies, see Fig. 2, for the skin condition classification task. We first consider a basic augmentation strategy with small rotation, sheer and scaling. Our main contribution, however, is to build on top of our segmentation approach, by adding realistic hair obtained from different skin images. In this approach, hereinafter referred to as "virtual hair transplantation", we tested the addition of hair patterns in different positions, orientations and color. We test our method on the binary classification task of nevi versus melanoma with respectively 4522 and 12875 images taken from the datasets HAM10000 [8], BCN20000 [9] and MSK [10].

2   Related Work for Hair Detection

Multiple techniques are available to check and find hair on the human body. Most of them are relatively old, relying on the manual counting and traditional image processing techniques. The manual counting by visual inspection with a naked eye or lens is the oldest, but still in use in many professional practices. The accuracy of this technique is naturally susceptible to loss of the instant local attention by the expert, which is influenced by tiredness, random gaze trajectory, and other psychophysical factors. Second, there are automatic systems present on the market like Chowis [11]. While Chowis mention the use of AI, they do not disclose the actual methods used in the products.

Other approaches relying on the traditional image processing have been used in the prior art to provide hair segmentation. Hoffmann [12] presents an automated system to detect hair loss and hair thinning conditions. Vallotton and Thomas [13] developed an approach for measuring body hair. They iteratively merge small line segments to account for curly variations. They only addressed cases in which the hairs are darker than the skin, though their algorithm can be easily modified to predict the opposite. In [14, 15], Shih and Lin proposed an unsupervised approach to count hair. The authors mainly used traditional computer vision techniques to detect lines. This approach, while good in a controlled image acquisition environment, suffers from different light conditions and perspective distortions. Besides, a slight change in the acquiring device implies the need for re-tuning the numerous parameters of the computer vision algorithm. Lim et al. [16], developed an automatic hair counting system to evaluate laser hair removal. They also validated their performance in clinical trials. They collected images from the thighs of five volunteers with Fitzpatrick skin type III–IV. Their percentage error was <5% in each subject.

All the mentioned techniques may work on a dataset, but they are not easily generalizable and not easy to replicate, for example, when considering different skin types or hair colour. Since we were not aware of prior art on the use of neural networks for hair detection, we experimented with U-NET architecture which is widely used for biomedical image segmentation [17]. We did not try any other segmentation techniques or architecture since U-NET provided good hair segmentation sufficient for the virtual "hair transplantation" augmentation. Note that several hair segmentation techniques based on deep learning exist but are not focused on segmenting the individual hair but rather on the segmentation and color detection from frontal face pictures.

3 Methods

In this section, we define the methodologies for the hair segmentation problem and for the skin lesion augmentations used to solve the binary lesion classification task.

3.1 Hair Segmentation

We have randomly selected 75 images to annotate from dataset [8] where we have first deleted all duplicates lesions. The implementation and definition of U-NET are taken from [18]. For the training of the network, we used the popular dice loss [19] (which is equal to 1 – dice coefficient) where we included a 'smooth' normalization parameter S = 0.0001 in the definition of the dice coefficient DSC, as presented in [20]:

$$\text{dice loss } (A, \ B) = 1 - DSC = 1 - \frac{2|A \cap B| + S}{|A| + |B| + S},$$

where A is the binary ground truth annotation and B is the binarized prediction. We used the Jaccard index as the primary measure to evaluate the performance of similarity between binary label A and predicted segmentation map B:

$$J(A, B) = \frac{|A \cap B|}{|A \cup B|}.$$

For each training strategy, the last transformation in the data generator is a spatial reduction with random crops of 128×128, which also removes, in the case of rotated images, the black margins. The input resolution of each image for this task is 600×450. After training, we generate the hair segmentation mask y for all skin lesions x in the combined datasets D.

3.2 Augmentations

Using the hair segmentation mask, the hair can be copy-pasted from one image to another. Later, we make use of this mask in our testing pipeline to add hair from another image in the classification mask. Given an image x in the dataset D, we defined four different augmentation strategies to test for the skin lesion classification task.

The first strategy A is simply the identity or no augmentation, where the input image remains the same. The second is the basic augmentation strategy, denoted in the following by F where the input image x is randomly rotated by an angle $\theta \in [-20, +20]$, scaled by a factor between 0.8 and 1.2 and undergo a shear transform with parameter $(0.05, 0.05)$. The three later strategies always add to F. Strategy H adds the transform that transplants hairs from image x_H with the corresponding hair mask y_H, where the image uniformly sampled from the dataset D. We define the strategy J as replacing x_H with x_R an image of the same size containing only random pixels. Finally, we define strategy K which adds, after augmentation F, a square containing random pixels with the size $e = sqrt(\sum y_H)$ where y_H is the hair segmentation mask of randomly chosen images from dataset D, so that the area of the square equals the total area of the segmentation mask. The above transformations can be notated as:

$$A: x = x$$

$$F: x = F(x)$$

$$H: x = F(x(1 - y_H) + x_H y_H)$$

$$J: x = F(x(1 - y_H) + x_R y_H)$$

$$K: x = F(x(1 - y_K) + x_R y_K)$$

where x_R is the image consisting of the random pixel values of the same size as x, and all multiplications are considered pixel-wise. We have to note that before applying the transplantation, we rotate the input image $x_H (x_R)$ by random $\theta \in [-180, +180]$ to get the rotation augmentation. One can see that the hair augmentation strategy 'H', when compared to J and K, is a smooth and soft way to perform a natural augmentation of the skin background in the skin lesion dataset. Moreover, this makes the prediction more robust to hair presence, as we will see below. The average area covered by hair is low and that less than 10% of images are covered by more than 5% of hair.

3.3 Skin Lesion Classification

As network architecture, we selected the state of the art Resnet50 [21] (achieves dermatologist level performance in [22]), InceptionV3 [23] (achieves dermatologist level performance in [6]), and Densenet [24] (best performing according to [25]). All the network are pre-trained on ImageNet [26] and fine-tuned for the skin lesion classification task. For the training with strategy H, in the augmentation phase as a hair source, we considered all input images. Figure 3 shows the distribution of the relative hair density in the test set. The hot pixels sum per image is computed as the sum of the segmentation before applying the binary threshold. We can see that the average area covered by hair is low and that less than 10% of images are covered by more than 5% of hair.

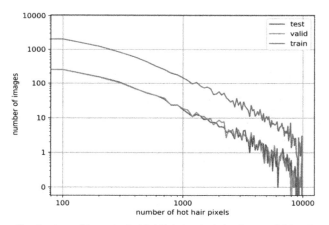

Fig. 3. Average distribution of hot pixels highlighting hair in the ten-fold train, validation and test set (images with resolution 224 × 224). On the y-axis the number of images and on the x-axis the number of hot pixels. Both axes are in log scale.

We train all the networks for 100 epochs using the Adam optimizer [27] and learning rate 1e−4. For each combination of strategy and architecture, we randomly split D in train, validation and test set with each containing respectively 80%, 10%, and 10% of the images. We repeat all procedure 10 times to reach the final test set error.

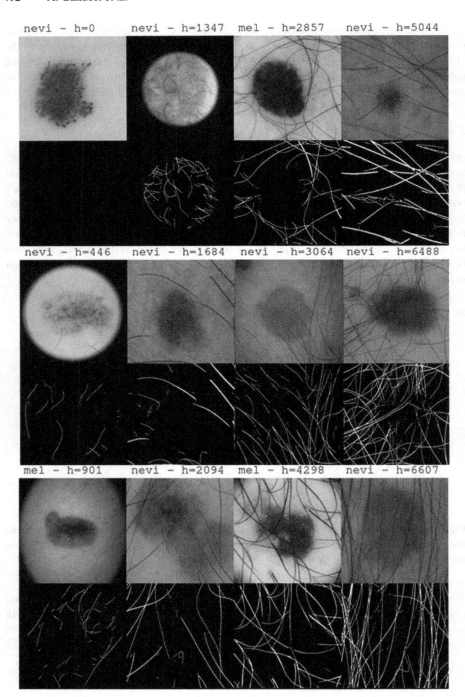

Fig. 4. Examples of images with relative predicted hair. On top the label and the number of hot pixels in the 224 × 224 resized version of the input image.

Table 1. Test set accuracy metrics for the three different architectures and the four different augmentations plus no augmentation A. The standard deviation is the result of 10 iterations of the experiment. The total number of images in the set is 1740 with 516 average hot hair pixels.

	Resnet50	InceptionV3	Densenet121
A	0.8855 ± 0.0061	0.9016 ± 0.0093	0.9052 ± 0.0078
F	0.9155 ± 0.0096	0.9259 ± 0.0064	0.9175 ± 0.0083
H	0.9161 ± 0.0090	0.9233 ± 0.0070	0.9224 ± 0.0066
J	0.9147 ± 0.0091	0.9220 ± 0.0074	0.9238 ± 0.0079
K	0.9172 ± 0.0058	0.9217 ± 0.0050	0.9228 ± 0.0086

4 Results

In this section, we present the results for the two described problems: the preliminary task of hair segmentation and the evaluation of skin classification when applying the different augmentation techniques.

4.1 Hair Segmentation

Due to the limited dataset size, 75 annotated images, the hair segmentation task was relatively fast to accomplish but still resulting in a sufficient basis for the added augmentations. The parameters used for training are learning rate 0.01, epochs 500, batch size 8. The test set includes 12 images, and the resolution for testing is the original one. The trained U-NET achieves Jaccard value 0.51 with a discrete recall of 0.66 and accuracy 0.98. Therefore, the visual inspection, see Fig. 4, offers promising results as a starting point to carry on the following skin classification analysis using hair augmentation. Cross-validation and a bigger dataset would be a possible next step to consolidate the hair segmentation results.

4.2 Skin Lesion Classification

The results presented in Table 1, overall shows the hair augmentation H does not essentially improve the performance of the models. Table 1 presents the average accuracy of ten repetitions of the experiment as introduced in the relative method section. In particular, H is not underperforming compare to the base F and the other color and shape pattern J, K. But when considering Densenet121 we see that H, J and K have positive regularization effect since they improve the accuracy compared to the baseline F. Apart from this difference, all three models show similar accuracies, with Resnet50 behind by only 1%

In Table 2, 3, we present the accuracy when considering only images with moderate and densely crowded skin hair presence. We believe that the increase in overall accuracy across compared to Table 1 is random. Even though the standard deviation increases, due to the lower number of images selected, the overall accuracy does not decrease when augmenting the images.

Table 2. Same as Table 1 but considering only moderate to densely crowded hair images. Only images containing minimum 1500 hot hair pixels (average 3412 ± 79) with 153 ± 9 images in total.

	Resnet50	InceptionV3	Densenet121
A	0.8953 ± 0.0176	0.9017 ± 0.0158	0.9161 ± 0.0161
F	0.9238 ± 0.0088	0.9323 ± 0.0112	0.9325 ± 0.0191
H	0.9264 ± 0.0089	0.9271 ± 0.0123	0.9298 ± 0.0187
J	0.9223 ± 0.0165	0.9258 ± 0.0244	0.9334 ± 0.0152
K	0.9297 ± 0.0140	0.9299 ± 0.0173	0.9353 ± 0.0109

Table 3. Same as Table 1 but considering only densely crowded hair images. Only images containing minimum 4000 hot hair pixels (average is 6011 ± 240) with 42 ± 6 images in total.

	Resnet50	InceptionV3	Densenet121
A	0.9199 ± 0.0261	0.9053 ± 0.0239	0.9315 ± 0.0281
F	0.9370 ± 0.0345	0.9557 ± 0.0310	0.9413 ± 0.0267
H	0.9510 ± 0.0294	0.9360 ± 0.0302	0.9398 ± 0.0334
J	0.9309 ± 0.0284	0.9232 ± 0.0398	0.9385 ± 0.0301
K	0.9408 ± 0.0264	0.9305 ± 0.0353	0.9355 ± 0.0379

5   Conclusions and Future Work

The results show that the presence of hair in skin images has little effect on the prediction of skin lesions. A practical consequence of this discovery can lead towards improving patient comfort and efficiency of screening, while opening the door to the investigation of a first-level screening performed by the user on mobile devices. We also show that the problem of hair segmentation on the skin images can be solved easily and robustly with deep learning.

For future work, we suggest to consider for the virtual 'hair transplantation' only images with sufficient hair density and consider improving the quality of the hair inpainting with skin color normalization which can reduce the visibility of the generated artefacts, or consider inpainting techniques based on the Generative Adversarial Networks, see [28, 29]. Finally, the proposed augmentation strategy of virtual 'hair transplantation' can be evaluated versus a more straightforward strategy where the real hairs are replaced with the random line patterns of the same area.

References

1. Stern, R.S.: Prevalence of a history of skin cancer in 2007: results of an incidence-based model. Arch. Dermatol. **146**(3), 279–282 (2010)

2. Guy Jr, G.P., Machlin, S.R., Ekwueme, D.U., Yabroff, K.R.: Prevalence and costs of skin cancer treatment in the US, 2002–2006 and 2007–2011. Am. J. Prev. Med. **48**(2), 183–187 (2015)
3. Smith, R.A., et al.: Cancer screening in the United States, 2018: a review of current American Cancer Society guidelines and current issues in cancer screening. CA. Cancer J. Clin. **68**(4), 297–316 (2018)
4. Krizhevsky, A., Sutskever, I., Hinton, G.E.: 2012 AlexNet. Adv. Neural Inf. Process. Syst. 1–9 (2012). https://doi.org/10.1016/j.protcy.2014.09.007
5. Brinker, T.J., et al.: A convolutional neural network trained with dermoscopic images performed on par with 145 dermatologists in a clinical melanoma image classification task. Eur. J. Cancer **111**, 148–154 (2019). https://doi.org/10.1016/j.ejca.2019.02.005
6. Huang, A., Kwan, S.-Y., Chang, W.-Y., Liu, M.-Y., Chi, M.-H., Chen, G.-S.: A robust hair segmentation and removal approach for clinical images of skin lesions. In: 2013 35th Annual International Conference of the IEEE Engineering in Medicine and Biology Society (EMBC), pp. 3315–3318 (2013)
7. Ronneberger, O., Fischer, P., Brox, T.: U-Net: convolutional networks for biomedical image segmentation. In: Navab, N., Hornegger, J., Wells, W.M., Frangi, A.F. (eds.) MICCAI 2015. LNCS, vol. 9351, pp. 234–241. Springer, Cham (2015). https://doi.org/10.1007/978-3-319-24574-4_28
8. Tschandl, P., Rosendahl, C., Kittler, H.: The HAM10000 dataset, a large collection of multisource dermatoscopic images of common pigmented skin lesions. Sci. Data **5**, 180161 (2018)
9. Combalia, M., et al.: BCN20000: Dermoscopic lesions in the wild. arXiv Preprint arXiv: 1908.02288 (2019)
10. Codella, N., et al.: Skin lesion analysis toward melanoma detection 2018: a challenge hosted by the international skin imaging collaboration (ISIC), p. 12 (2019). https://arxiv.org/abs/1902.03368
11. Chowis (2019). https://chowis.com/hair-ai-diagnostic-technology/
12. Hoffmann, R.: TrichoScan Ein neues Werkzeug fr die digitale Haarzhlung. Der Hautarzt **12**(53), 798–804 (2002)
13. Vallotton, P., Thomas, N.: Automated body hair counting and length measurement. Skin Res. Technol. **14**(4), 493–497 (2008). https://doi.org/10.1111/j.1600-0846.2008.00322.x
14. Shih, H.-C.: An unsupervised hair segmentation and counting system in microscopy images. IEEE Sens. J. **15**(6), 3565–3572 (2014)
15. Shih, H.-C., Lin, B.-S.: Hair segmentation and counting algorithms in microscopy image. In: 2015 IEEE International Conference on Consumer Electronics (ICCE), pp. 612–613 (2015)
16. Lim, H., et al.: Development of a novel automated hair counting system for the quantitative evaluation of laser hair removal. Photomed. Laser Surg. **35**(2), 116–121 (2017). https://doi.org/10.1089/pho.2016.4140
17. Litjens, G., et al.: A survey on deep learning in medical image analysis. Med. Image Anal. **42**, 60–88 (2017)
18. Buda, M., Saha, A., Mazurowski, M.A.: Association of genomic subtypes of lower-grade gliomas with shape features automatically extracted by a deep learning algorithm. Comput. Biol. Med. **109**, 218–225 (2019)
19. Sudre, C., Li, W., Vercauteren, T., Ourselin, S., Jorge Cardoso, M.: Generalised dice overlap as a deep learning loss function for highly unbalanced segmentations. In: Cardoso, M.J., et al. (eds.) DLMIA/ML-CDS -2017. LNCS, vol. 10553, pp. 240–248. Springer, Cham (2017). https://doi.org/10.1007/978-3-319-67558-9_28
20. Iglovikov, V., Mushinskiy, S., Osin, V.: Satellite imagery feature detection using deep convolutional neural network: a Kaggle competition. arXiv Preprint arXiv:1706.06169 (2017)

21. He, K., Zhang, X., Ren, S., Sun, J.: Deep residual learning for image recognition. In: Proceedings of the IEEE Conference on Computer Vision and Pattern Recognition, pp. 770–778 (2016)
22. Esteva, A., et al.: Dermatologist-level classification of skin cancer with deep neural networks. Nature **542**(7639), 115 (2017)
23. Szegedy, C., Vanhoucke, V., Ioffe, S., Shlens, J., Wojna, Z.: Rethinking the inception architecture for computer vision. In: Proceedings of the IEEE conference on computer vision and pattern recognition, pp. 2818–2826 (2016)
24. Huang, G., Liu, Z., Van Der Maaten, L., Weinberger, K.Q.: Densely connected convolutional networks. In: Proceedings of the IEEE Conference on Computer Vision and Pattern Recognition, pp. 4700–4708 (2017)
25. Perez, F., Vasconcelos, C., Avila, S., Valle, E.: Data augmentation for skin lesion analysis. In: Stoyanov, D., et al. (eds.) CARE/CLIP/OR 2.0/ISIC -2018. LNCS, vol. 11041, pp. 303–311. Springer, Cham (2018). https://doi.org/10.1007/978-3-030-01201-4_33
26. Russakovsky, O., et al.: ImageNet large scale visual recognition challenge. Int. J. Comput. Vision **115**(3), 211–252 (2015). https://doi.org/10.1007/s11263-015-0816-y
27. Kingma, D.P., Ba, J.: Adam: a method for stochastic optimization. arXiv Preprint arXiv:1412.6980 (2014)
28. Goodfellow, I., et al.: Generative adversarial nets. In: Advances in Neural Information Processing Systems, pp. 2672–2680 (2014)
29. Isola, P., Zhu, J.-Y., Zhou, T., Efros, A.A.: Image-to-image translation with conditional adversarial networks. In: Proceedings of the IEEE Conference on Computer Vision and Pattern Recognition, pp. 1125–1134 (2017)

Deep Learning Based Segmentation of Breast Lesions in DCE-MRI

Roa'a Khaled⬤, Joel Vidal⬤, and Robert Martí[(✉)]⬤

Computer Vision and Robotics Institute, University of Girona, Girona, Spain
`robert.marti@udg.edu`

Abstract. Dynamic Contrast Enhanced Magnetic Resonance Imaging (DCE-MRI) is a popular tool for the diagnosis of breast lesions due to its effectiveness, especially in a high risk population. Accurate lesion segmentation is an important step for subsequent analysis, especially for computer aided diagnosis systems. However, manual breast lesion segmentation of (4D) MRI is time consuming, requires experience, and it is prone to interobserver and intraobserver variability. This work proposes a deep learning (DL) framework for segmenting breast lesions in DCE-MRI using a 3D patch based U-Net architecture. We perform different experiments to analyse the effects of class imbalance, different patch sizes, optimizers and loss functions in a cross-validation fashion using 46 images from a subset of a challenging and publicly available dataset not reported to date, that is the TCGA-BRCA. We also compare the proposed U-Net framework with another state-of-the-art approach used for breast lesion segmentation in DCE-MRI, and report better segmentation accuracy with the proposed framework. The results presented in this work have the potential to become a publicly available benchmark for this task.

Keywords: Breast Cancer · DCE-MRI · Breast lesions segmentation · 3D U-Net

1 Introduction

The spread of Breast Cancer (BC) is one of the main health challenges in the world. According to the American Cancer Society (ACS), BC is the most common cancer among women in the US (excluding skin cancer) and the second cause of cancer deaths (after lung cancer) [6]. Despite that, BC death rate has dropped by 40% from 1989 to 2017 and is continuously decreasing [6], which can be attributed to the early detection and the expanding access to high-quality prevention and treatment services, particularly imaging modalities.

Although mammography (and digital breast tomosynthesis) is widely available as the main screening modality due to its high sensitivity and specificity in the screening population, other modalities such as ultrasound and MRI are an important complement to mammography in specific circumstances, such as high risk or younger women [12].

© Springer Nature Switzerland AG 2021
A. Del Bimbo et al. (Eds.): ICPR 2020 Workshops, LNCS 12661, pp. 417–430, 2021.
https://doi.org/10.1007/978-3-030-68763-2_32

Dynamic contrast enhanced (DCE) MRI is one of the mostly used MRI techniques to diagnose BC as it visualizes both physiological tissue characteristics and anatomical structures. This MRI technique aims to observe and quantify the contrast enhancement over time. Hence, one scan is acquired before the administration of a contrast agent and one or more scans are acquired afterwards (usually 3 to 5 volumes referred to as post-contrast volumes). The degree of contrast enhancement depends on vascular characteristics such as concentration of blood vessels and their permeability, which are related to cancer tissues.

Nevertheless, the analysis of 4D volumes of DCE-MRI data is time consuming and requires experienced radiologists. Many image analysis methods have been developed to automatically extract features and help to interpret DCE-MRI scans. The extraction of these features requires the lesions to be accurately segmented first. Therefore, the accurate segmentation of breast lesions in DCE-MRI is a critically significant task for automated BC analysis, diagnosis and treatment follow-up [15]. Manual segmentation is time-consuming and error-prone, hence automating this task could help radiologists to reduce their workload and to improve diagnosis accuracy. In that sense, automatic breast lesion segmentation based on DCE-MRI remains a challenging problem and an active area of research.

In this work we propose an automated segmentation method for breast lesions in DCE-MRI using a ROI guided, 3D patch based U-Net framework. The contribution of this work is the analysis of different aspects such as class imbalance, patch sizes, optimizers and loss functions in a U-Net framework. We use 46 images from a subset of a challenging and publicly available dataset, that is the TCGA-BRCA [4], which has not reported to date for lesion segmentation. We have compared our proposed U-Net framework with more complex recent methods such as hierarchical U-Nets [15] showing better results of the proposed method with the TCGA-BRCA dataset. The results presented in this work have the potential to become a publicly available benchmark for this task.

The remainder of this paper is structured as follows: Sect. 2 outlines some related works in the literature. In Sect. 3 we introduce our proposed method. Section 4 reports and discusses the results we obtained. Finally, in Sect. 5 we present our conclusions and future work.

2   State of the Art

Several automatic segmentation methods have been proposed to replace manual segmentation. Most of the existing studies on DCE-MRI adopt a semi-supervised approach to overcome the challenge of identifying breast lesions from confounding organs or vessels [15]. In those methods, the lesion regions had to first be manually defined by a radiologist in order to make the automatic segmentation task easier [13, 17].

Supervised approaches include both traditional machine learning and deep learning (DL) approaches. With respect to the traditional machine learning approaches, many studies propose a similar framework based on selecting a set of meaningful features which are then used in the segmentation model [8]. In DL based approaches (unlike traditional approaches), feature extraction and model training are both treated as one learning framework and the segmentation task is performed in an end-to-end manner. These approaches have recently achieved state-of-the-art performance in medical imaging analysis. However, there are very few works addressing breast lesion segmentation in DCE-MRI using DL methods. In these works, SegNet [1] and U-Net [11] models were mostly used, with U-Net being more popular. For instance, Chen et al. proposed a stacking of three parallel ConvLSTM networks (to extract temporal and 3D features) over a 4-layer U-Net to perform the segmentation [3]. In [16] both 2D and 3D U-Net frameworks were proposed and evaluated using binary cross-entropy as a loss function. The 3D U-Net performed slightly better in terms of dice coefficient and yielded less false positives. However, the slices used in this study were selected only from the second-post contrast scan. Moreover, the U-Net models were fed by images of lesion bounding boxes instead of the full size of the MRI.

In [7] the authors proposed two DL approaches by using both SegNet and U-Net. The binary cross entropy loss function was also used. In this study, U-Net outperformed SegNet. One of the limitations of this study is that 2D slices were used as inputs instead of 3D volumes which is a clear limitation as lesion segmentation is regarded as a 3D segmentation problem. Another limitation of this study is that the ground truth labels were provided by only one radiologist, an evaluation which could be affected by reader variability.

In [10] the authors proposed U-Net method exploiting the well-known Three Time Points approach (3TP). The 3TP approach was proposed by Degani et al. who showed that breast lesion analysis can be improved by focusing on just three well defined temporal acquisitions (t0 = pre-contrast, t1 = 2 min after contrast agent injection, t2 = 6 min after contrast agent injection) [5]. In [10], images acquired at the three specific time points were fed to the network in order to take into account the DCE-MRI fundamental characteristics. Segmentation was performed slice-by-slice, considering the three temporal acquisitions of the same slice as channels within the image and using a dice based loss function.

Despite the promising results in existing works, the problems of both class imbalance and confounding regions are rarely taken into account in most of the existing DL based methods [15]. In that sense Zhang et al. proposed a mask-guided hierarchical learning (MHL) framework using U-Net [15]. First, the pre-contrast volumes were used as input to a U-Net model to generate 3D breast masks as the region of interest (ROI), so that confounding regions from input DCE-MRI were removed. Then a two-stage U-Net model was used to perform coarse-to-fine segmentation. In the first stage the post-contrast volumes and the difference volumes (between post-contrast and pre-contrast) were used along with the generated breast masks as inputs to a first stage U-Net to generate over-segmented lesion-like regions. Also, to handle the class-imbalance problem, a dice-sensitivity-like loss function was proposed. In the second stage, an additional U-Net was used to refine the segmentation results of the previous stage, using a dice-like loss function and a reinforcement sampling strategy.

3 Materials and Methods

We propose an automated method for segmenting breast lesions in DCE-MRI based on a 3D patch based U-Net. In order to tackle the problems of class imbalance and confounding regions, we performed balanced patch sampling restricted by an automatically extracted ROI to ensure that the two classes are equally distributed in the training set and to avoid having patches from confounding regions. Moreover, different aspects have been investigated, such as the optimizers, loss functions and patch sizes.

3.1 Data

The dataset used in this work is a subset of the TCGA-BRCA collection, which was collected by the TCGA Breast Phenotype Research Group and made available in The Cancer Imaging Archive (TCIA) [4]. The data subset we used consists of 46 cases (with the Tissue Source Site code BH) all of them diagnosed with BC (breast invasive carcinoma). Scans were acquired at the University of Pittsburgh Medical Center (1999–2004) prior to any treatment. MRIs were acquired using a standard double breast coil on a 1.5T GE whole body MRI system (GE Medical Systems, Milwaukee, Wisconsin, USA). The imaging protocols included one pre-contrast and four to six post-contrast volumes obtained using a T1-weighted 3D spoiled gradient echo sequence with a gadolinium-based contrast agent (Omniscan; Nycomed-Amersham, Princeton, NJ). Typical in-plane resolution was 0.53–0.86 mm, and typical spacing between slices was 2–3 mm.

Each breast MRI examination was independently reviewed by three expert board-certified breast radiologists and each primary breast lesion was then automatically segmented in 3D.

It is important to mention that most of the cases had multiple lesions according to the reviewer radiologists, however the Ground Truth (GT) was obtained only from the primary lesion since the purpose of the TCGA/TCIA study was to map the radiomics (phenotypes) of the primary lesion to the corresponding clinical, histopathology, and genomics data.

3.2 Pre-processing

Prior to feeding input volumes to the network, the following pre-processing steps were performed:

- ROI masks generation in order to exclude confounding organs. This was performed using a simple landmark detection method in which we detected the skin-air boundary between the two breasts and then excluded non-breast part of the volume that lies beyond the detected landmark.
- Zero padding with padding width equal to half of the patch size.
- Zero-mean unit-variance intensity normalization.
- Balanced patch extraction in order to tackle the class imbalance problem.

ROI Masks Generation. As mentioned earlier, confounding background such as vessel structures and organs in DCE-MRI makes the task of breast lesion segmentation more challenging. Therefore, it is important to generate a region of interest (ROI) that includes the breast only. Based on the fact that breasts have regular morphological shapes and relatively fixed position on MRI images, we detected a landmark at the breast-air boundary between the two breasts and then excluded parts of the volume that lie beyond the detected landmark. This was done by first obtaining the voxels at the intersection line of mid-sagittal and mid-transverse planes (located between two breasts) and then detecting the local maxima of intensities across those voxels. Then local maxima were filtered (using empirically chosen values of height and distance between each two local maxima) such that the location of the first detected local maximum (anterior to posterior direction) corresponds to the required landmark slice. Figure 1(a) to (c) illustrates the steps followed to detect the required landmark. Accordingly, the remaining part (coronal slices) starting from few slices (empirically chosen) after that landmark were set to zero while other parts were set to one in order to generate the 3D binary mask, Fig. 1(d) shows the generated ROI mask overlaid on an example case.

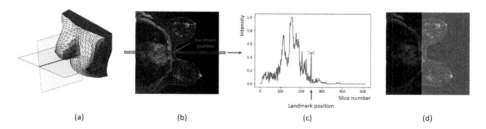

Fig. 1. Illustration of ROI mask generation method. (a) 3D representation of breast with mid-sagittal and mid-transverse planes intersection. (b) Intersection line in a 2D example slice. (c) Detection of breast-air boundary landmark. (d) Obtained ROI mask overlaid on an example slice.

Patch Sampling. A common approach to extract patches from images is uniform sampling, in which patches are extracted from all parts of an image uniformly with a certain step between each two consecutive patches. However, in the context of lesion segmentation the number of voxels in the lesion region (positive class) is much smaller than that in the background (negative class). This leads to a very common issue of class imbalance where only a small number of the extracted patches will be taken from the lesion class and hence yielding a poor performance of the network. This common issue has been addressed in several studies on lesion segmentation of different organs [2,14]. In our work, we utilized a ROI restricted balanced sampling technique in which negative and positive patches were equally extracted. Additionally, negative patches were extracted only within the ROI we generated to avoid extracting patches from region of confounding organs and to make sure they are located within the breast region.

3.3   Segmentation Algorithm

In this work we adopt a 3D U-Net architecture. U-Net is an encoder-decoder architecture originally designed for biomedical electron microscopy (EM) images multi-class pixel-wise semantic segmentation [11,18]. The architecture we deployed is illustrated in Fig. 2. Every level in the contracting path consists of:

- $(3 \times 3 \times 3)$ convolution with zero-padding $= 1$ in order to maintain the output shapes.
- Rectified Linear Unit (ReLU) activation.
- $(2 \times 2 \times 2)$ max-pooling with stride $= 2$ for down-sampling.

Then they are followed by a latent level which consists of a $(3 \times 3 \times 3)$ convolution with zero-padding $= 1$ followed by a rectified Linear Unit (ReLU) activation. Similarly, every level in the expanding path consists of:

- $(2 \times 2 \times 2)$ up-convolution with stride $= 2$.
- Concatenation with feature-map from the corresponding level of the contracting path.
- $(3 \times 3 \times 3)$ convolution with zero-padding $= 1$ in order to maintain the output shapes.
- Rectified Linear Unit (ReLU) activation.

Finally, there is a $(1 \times 1 \times 1)$ output convolution layer with two output channels followed by a softmax layer that returns probabilities for each class.

Unless otherwise stated in the experiments, the framework is based on using a binary cross-entropy loss function, AdaDelta optimizer and a probability threshold of 0.5 to generate the final segmentation. Moreover, three input volumes were fed to the U-Net: pre-contrast, last post-contrast and the subtraction between them (i.e. $post - pre$). A total of 4,000 balanced patches of the size (32, 32, 32) were extracted with a sampling step of (32, 32, 32).

4   Results and Discussion

Different experiments were performed in order to evaluate different aspects of our algorithm such as thresholds, optimizers, loss functions and patch sizes. Additionally, we compared the performance of our proposed architecture to another U-Net based architecture, that is a two hierarchical U-Nets method proposed in [15]. All experiments were performed using 5 fold cross-validation across the provided 46 cases in order to obtained lesion segmentation results for each of the 46 cases. In each fold 20 epochs were performed. Dataset was splitted such that in each fold 9 cases were used for testing (10 cases in the last fold) and the remaining cases were shuffled and divided into 80% for training and 20% for

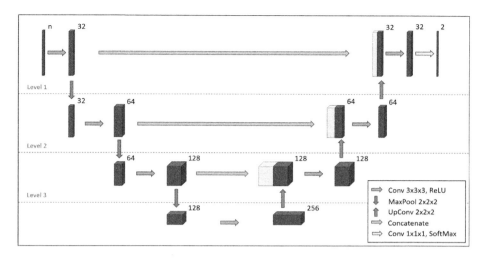

Fig. 2. The deployed 3D U-Net architecture.

evaluation. As evaluation criteria, we used the commonly used Dice Similarity Coefficient (DSC) described in Eq. 1.

$$DSC = \frac{2TP}{2TP + FP + FN} \tag{1}$$

where TP, FP and FN refer to True Positive, False Positive and False Negative respectively. However, since the annotations provided (GT) have only the main lesion segmented for each case and most cases were denoted by radiologists as having multiple lesions (multi-centric or multi-focal), the obtained DSC values might not adequately evaluate the performance of the algorithm because other (non-primary) lesions could be incorrectly considered as FPs (even though they are correctly detected by our algorithm). Therefore we computed a second dice which evaluates how good the main lesion was segmented, regardless of the presence of any other lesions (secondary lesions). To do this, we first detected the largest three connected components (CCs) in the obtained segmentation. Then we obtained the distances between their centroids and centroid of the lesion in the GT. Finally we kept only the nearest CC to the segmented lesion in GT. In all experiments discussed in the following subsections DSC_1 denotes the normal dice (without post-processing) and DSC_2 denotes the dice of main lesions only. However, it is important to mention that GT is never used for performing post-processing. This was used just to obtain a better indication of the performance considering the problematic (incomplete) GT we had and that secondary lesions will be miss-classified as FPs.

4.1 Experiment 1: Threshold

Thresholding is needed in order to binarize the output probability map and generate a segmented volume. We studied the effect of different thresholds on both the overall dice (DSC_1) and the main lesion dice (DSC_2), as shown in Table 1.

Table 1. DSC values (mean±std) obtained using different thresholds.

Threshold	DSC_1	DSC_2
0.9	0.490 ± 0.273	0.545 ± 0.288
0.5	$\mathbf{0.508 \pm 0.275}$	0.576 ± 0.291
0.4	0.500 ± 0.271	0.569 ± 0.301
0.3	0.499 ± 0.271	0.573 ± 0.302
0.2	0.032 ± 0.120	$\mathbf{0.581 \pm 0.295}$

As we can see from Table 1, the threshold parameter is not particularly critical, since robust results were obtained along a large threshold range (0.3 to 0.9). Even though main lesions were segmented well when using lower threshold values (0.2) and a higher value of DSC_2 was obtained, this resulted in low value of DSC_1 caused by the high FPs. Therefore, a threshold value of 0.5 was used in our proposed algorithm as well as in all experiments discussed in the following subsections.

4.2 Experiment 2: Optimizer

Experiments were performed to compare the performance of AdaDelta optimizer to another optimizer (Adam). These two optimizers are extensively used as they are adaptive, which means no tuning of the learning rate is required (unlike in gradient descent's algorithms). Tuning the learning rate is not a trivial task and highly affects the speed and performance. In both optimizers a fixed number of previous gradients are used during training and hence the problem of vanishing learning rate is avoided. The difference between them is that in AdaDelta the sum of gradients is recursively defined as a decaying average of past squared gradients while in Adam it is defined as an exponentially decaying average of past gradients (similar to momentum).

Table 2 shows the obtained results. Adam optimizer is reported as the one with faster convergence and better performance in most cases, however as we can see from Table 2, in our case better results were obtained using AdaDelta optimizer.

Table 2. DSC values (mean±std) obtained using two different optimizers.

Optimizer	DSC_1	DSC_2
AdaDelta	**0.508 ± 0.275**	**0.576 ± 0.291**
Adam	0.367 ± 0.289	0.552 ± 0.302

4.3 Experiment 3: Loss Function

In the existing literature, several loss functions have been proposed for lesion segmentation tasks. Binary cross-entropy loss is one of the most commonly used. It evaluates the class predictions for each voxel individually and then averages over all voxels, being all voxels and labels of equal importance in the training process. However, in the case of unbalanced labels this could bias the training towards the dominant class. This problem is a typical issue in lesion segmentation as voxels in the background (negative class) outnumber voxels in lesion regions (positive class). Other loss functions have been proposed to overcome this issue. for instance, Long et al. proposed a weighted cross entropy loss by weighting each class in order to avoid the class imbalance issue [9]. Ronneberger et al. proposed a loss weighting scheme for each pixel such that higher weight is assigned to pixels at the contour of segmented objects [11]. Zhang et al. proposed the dice-sensitivity-like loss defined as a combination of dice and sensitivity [15]. Dice coefficient, unlike other measurements (such as the traditional overall accuracy, mean squared error, or cross-entropy) highly focuses on the lesion class and penalizes the missed voxels as well as false positives. Sensitivity adds an additional bias towards detection of lesion (positive) voxels and therefore addresses the issue of imbalance by shifting the focus toward the minority class (lesion voxels). However, this could also lead to an increase of false positive detections, as stated in [15].

Here we compare the performance of the cross-entropy loss function with other loss functions: Dice loss (defined as $1 - DSC$), a combination (summation) of both dice and binary cross-entropy and finally the dice-sensitivity loss proposed in [15]. Table 3 shows the obtained results, where the best DSC was obtained using the cross-entropy loss. Although one would expect segmentation related loss functions (e.g. Dice loss) to obtain better results as in [15], our experiments show that more generic losses (i.e cross-entropy) outperforms the other losses. These results will be further investigated in the future using larger number of cases.

4.4 Experiment 4: Patch Size

Several studies have been published to investigate the effect of the patch size in patch based neural networks, showing that larger patches may improve the segmentation results in terms of robustness (i.e. finding difficult lesions), as the network can capture more contextual information. However, larger patches involve

Table 3. DSC values (mean±std) obtained using different loss functions.

Loss function	DSC_1	DSC_2
Cross entropy	**0.508 ± 0.275**	**0.576 ± 0.291**
Dice	0.470 ± 0.294	0.505 ± 0.309
Dice+cross entropy	0.472 ± 0.309	0.521 ± 0.313
Dice sensitivity	0.471 ± 0.314	0.524 ± 0.336

longer computational times especially for training time and potentially less accurate segmented contours. Accordingly, we compared the performance of four different patch sizes: (32, 32, 32), (32, 32, 16), (16, 16, 16), and (16, 16, 8). The obtained results are reported in Table 4.

Table 4. DSC values (mean±std) obtained using different patch sizes.

Patch size	DSC_1	DSC_2
(32, 32, 32)	0.508 ± 0.275	0.576 ± 0.291
(32, 32, 16)	**0.511 ± 0.266**	0.608 ± 0.273
(16, 16, 16)	0.474 ± 0.263	0.630 ± 0.276
(16, 16, 8)	0.398 ± 0.250	**0.643 ± 0.276**

Several observations can be made from Table 4. Patch sizes of (32, 32, 32) and (32, 32, 16) performed better in terms of general dice (DSC_1), with average dice values of 0.508 and 0.511 respectively. The slightly better performance when using patch size of (32, 32, 16) compared to (32, 32, 32) can be attributed to the pixel size of our scans, which is larger across the axial dimension (2 mm) compared to coronal and sagittal (ranging from 0.5078 mm to 0.7813 mm). We can also observe that in terms of segmenting the main lesion only (i.e. values of DSC_2), the patch sizes (16, 16, 8) and (16, 16, 16) performed better. However the general dice (DSC_1) was lower in this case which indicates that more FPs were detected. This might be explained by the fact that many cases had small lesions which were better segmented using smaller patch size and the contours of other lesions in general were segmented better, but this caused more FPs to be also detected. Finally, and taking into account both dice scores, both patch sizes of (32, 32, 16) and (16, 16, 16) can be considered as having a good overall performance.

4.5   Implementation Details

The proposed architecture was implemented in Python 3.7.4 using the Pytorch 1.4.0 machine learning framework. All python scripts were executed on Ubuntu on a 256 GB RAM server with a Nvidia GeForce RTX 2080 GPU.

4.6   Discussion

In this subsection we compare results obtained using our proposed framework with another approach that is based on Zhang et al. work. In that other approach we used two hierarchical U-Net stages in which we used dice-sensitivity loss in the first stage and dice loss in the second stage, as proposed by Zhang et al. [15]. It is important to note that we used our proposed basic U-Net architecture

Table 5. DSC values (mean±std) obtained using different U-Net based approaches.

Network	Patch size	DSC_1	DSC_2
Basic U-Net	(32, 32, 32)	$\mathbf{0.508 \pm 0.275}$	0.576 ± 0.291
Basic U-Net	(16, 16, 16)	0.474 ± 0.263	$\mathbf{0.630 \pm 0.276}$
Two hierarchical U-Nets	(32, 32, 32)	0.482 ± 0.294	0.581 ± 0.301

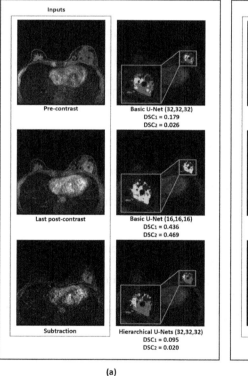
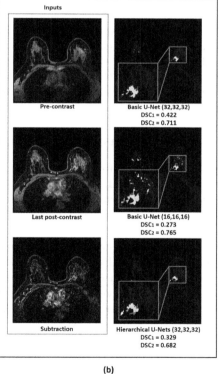

(a)   (b)

Fig. 3. Obtained segmentations of two example cases using basic U-Net with two different patch sizes compared to using a two hierarchical U-Nets approach. (a) is case A0E0 and (b) is case A18I. GT is represented in red and obtained segmentation is represented in white. (Color figure online)

(proposed in Sect. 3.3) for both stages as well as our proposed pre-processing steps (proposed in Sect. 3.2) instead of the pre-processing and U-Net architecture proposed in [15]. The obtained results are reported in Table 5.

As observed from Table 5, results obtained using our proposed approach (basic U-Net) were comparable to those obtained using the other approach (two hierarchical U-Nets). As we can see, using a basic U-Net with patch size of (32, 32, 32) outperformed the other method in terms of general mean dice (DSC_1) that is 0.508 compared to 0.482, while in terms of segmenting main lesions (DSC_2) the performance was slightly lower with a mean dice of 0.576 compared to 0.581. Hence, in general the two performances were comparable. On the other hand, using a basic U-Net with patch size of (16, 16, 16) outperformed the other method in terms of segmenting main lesions achieving a mean dice (DSC_2) of 0.630 compared to 0.581 which indicates substantial improvement. However, it achieved a slightly lower general dice (DSC_1) which indicates more FPs. Therefore, our results prove that using a basic U-Net with a binary cross-entropy loss function and investigating the optimal configuration of other aspects (such as patch size, optimizer, etc.) have the potential to outperform other more complex approaches from state-of-the-art methods.

Figure 3 shows qualitative and quantitative results obtained for two example cases using both our proposed architecture (with both patch sizes of 32, 32, 32 and 16, 16, 16) and the two hierarchical U-Nets approach. As we can see in both Fig. 3(a) and Fig. 3(b), basic U-Net with the smaller patch size shows improved segmentation of small, irregular and low enhanced lesions. However, it detected more FPs in some cases as we can see in Fig. 3(b).

5   Conclusions and Future Works

In this work an automated method has been proposed for segmenting breast lesions in DCE-MRI. Our proposed method is a 3D patch based U-Net framework in which we perform a ROI restricted, balanced patch extraction in order to address both the class imbalance and confounding regions problems. Differently from most existing works on this topic, 3D segmentation was performed instead of 2D. Additionally we utilized two temporal volumes (pre-contrast and last post-contrast) along with the difference between them as inputs. Moreover, different patch sizes, optimizers, loss functions were investigated in order to find the configuration that yields the best results.

Experiments were performed on 46 cases and DSC was used to evaluate the obtained segmentation. We obtained promising results considering the complex dataset used and the fact that GT of only main lesions were provided. We compare results of our proposed method to another method from a recent study, and results showed better performance of our proposed method on the dataset we used.

Further improvements could be achieved by incorporating larger dataset with a complete annotation for those cases with multiple lesions. Moreover, further investigation of the inputs and utilizing information from more temporal volumes could also potentially alleviate the results.

Finally, the deployment of architectures other than the simple U-Net such as a deeper or modified architecture could also improve the performance.

Acknowledgments. This work was partially supported by the project ICEBERG: Image Computing for Enhancing Breast Cancer Radiomics (RTI2018-096333-B-I00, Spanish Ministry). We would also like to thank the TCGA Breast Phenotype Research Group for providing the computer-extracted lesion segmentation data used in this study, which comes from the University of Chicago lab of Maryellen Giger.

References

1. Badrinarayanan, V., Kendall, A., Cipolla, R.: SegNet: a deep convolutional encoder-decoder architecture for image segmentation. IEEE Trans. Pattern Anal. Mach. Intell. **39**(12), 2481–2495 (2017)
2. Bria, A., Karssemeijer, N., Tortorella, F.: Learning from unbalanced data: a cascade-based approach for detecting clustered microcalcifications. Med. Image Anal. **18**(2), 241–252 (2014)
3. Chen, M., Zheng, H., Lu, C., Tu, E., Yang, J., Kasabov, N.: A spatio-temporal fully convolutional network for breast lesion segmentation in DCE-MRI. In: Cheng, L., Leung, A.C.S., Ozawa, S. (eds.) ICONIP 2018. LNCS, vol. 11307, pp. 358–368. Springer, Cham (2018). https://doi.org/10.1007/978-3-030-04239-4_32
4. Clark, K., et al.: The Cancer Imaging Archive (TCIA): maintaining and operating a public information repository. J. Digit. Imaging **26**(6), 1045–1057 (2013). https://doi.org/10.1007/s10278-013-9622-7
5. Degani, H., Gusis, V., Weinstein, D., Fields, S., Strano, S.: Mapping pathophysiological features of breast tumors by MRI at high spatial resolution. Nat. Med. **3**(7), 780–782 (1997)
6. DeSantis, C.E., et al.: Breast cancer statistics, 2019. CA Cancer J. Clin. **69**(6), 438–451 (2019)
7. El Adoui, M., Mahmoudi, S., Larhmam, A., Benjelloun, M.: MRI breast tumor segmentation using different encoder and decoder CNN architectures. J. Comput. **8**, 52 (2019)
8. Gubern-Mérida, A., et al.: Automated localization of breast cancer in DCE-MRI. Med. Image Anal. **20**(1), 265–274 (2014)
9. Long, J., Shelhamer, E., Darrell, T.: Fully convolutional networks for semantic segmentation. In: 2015 IEEE Conference on Computer Vision and Pattern Recognition (CVPR), pp. 3431–3440 (2015)
10. Piantadosi, G., Marrone, S., Galli, A., Sansone, M., Sansone, C.: DCE-MRI breast lesions segmentation with a 3TP U-Net deep convolutional neural network. In: 2019 IEEE 32nd International Symposium on Computer-Based Medical Systems (CBMS), pp. 628–633. IEEE (2019)
11. Ronneberger, O., Fischer, P., Brox, T.: U-Net: convolutional networks for biomedical image segmentation. In: Navab, N., Hornegger, J., Wells, W.M., Frangi, A.F. (eds.) MICCAI 2015. LNCS, vol. 9351, pp. 234–241. Springer, Cham (2015). https://doi.org/10.1007/978-3-319-24574-4_28
12. Subbhuraam, V.S., Ng, E., Acharya, U.R., Faust, O.: Breast imaging: a survey. World J. Clin. Oncol. **2**(4), 171–178 (2011)
13. Vignati, A., et al.: Performance of a fully automatic lesion detection system for breast DCE-MRI. J. Magn. Reson. Imaging JMRI **34**(6), 1341–1351 (2011)

14. Zhang, J., Gao, Y., Park, S.H., Zong, X., Lin, W., Shen, D.: Structured learning for 3-D perivascular space segmentation using vascular features. IEEE Trans. Biomed. Eng. **64**(12), 2803–2812 (2017)
15. Zhang, J., Saha, A., Zhu, Z., Mazurowski, M.A.: Hierarchical convolutional neural networks for segmentation of breast tumors in MRI with application to radiogenomics. IEEE Trans. Med. Imaging **38**, 435–447 (2019)
16. Zhang, L., Luo, Z., Chai, R., Arefan, D., Sumkin, J., Wu, S.: Deep-learning method for tumor segmentation in breast DCE-MRI. In: Chen, P.H., Bak, P.R. (eds.) Medical Imaging 2019: Imaging Informatics for Healthcare, Research, and Applications, vol. 10954, pp. 97–102. International Society for Optics and Photonics, SPIE (2019)
17. Zheng, Y., Baloch, S., Englander, S., Schnall, M.D., Shen, D.: Segmentation and classification of breast tumor using dynamic contrast-enhanced MR images. In: Ayache, N., Ourselin, S., Maeder, A. (eds.) MICCAI 2007. LNCS, vol. 4792, pp. 393–401. Springer, Heidelberg (2007). https://doi.org/10.1007/978-3-540-75759-7_48
18. Çiçek, Ö., Abdulkadir, A., Lienkamp, S.S., Brox, T., Ronneberger, O.: 3D U-Net: learning dense volumetric segmentation from sparse annotation. In: Ourselin, S., Joskowicz, L., Sabuncu, M.R., Unal, G., Wells, W. (eds.) MICCAI 2016. LNCS, vol. 9901, pp. 424–432. Springer, Cham (2016). https://doi.org/10.1007/978-3-319-46723-8_49

Fall Detection and Recognition from Egocentric Visual Data: A Case Study

Xueyi Wang$^{(\boxtimes)}$ (ID), Estefanía Talavera(ID), Dimka Karastoyanova(ID),
and George Azzopardi(ID)

University of Groningen, Nijenborgh 9, 9747 AG Groningen, The Netherlands
xueyi.wang@rug.nl

Abstract. Falling is among the most damaging events for elderly people, which sometimes may end with significant injuries. Due to fear of falling, many elderly people choose to stay more at home in order to feel safer. In this work, we propose a new fall detection and recognition approach, which analyses egocentric videos collected by wearable cameras through a computer vision/machine learning pipeline. More specifically, we conduct a case study with one volunteer who collected video data from two cameras; one attached to the chest and the other one attached to the waist. A total of 776 videos were collected describing four types of falls and nine kinds of non-falls. Our method works as follows: extracts several uniformly distributed frames from the videos, uses a pre-trained ConvNet model to describe each frame by a feature vector, followed by feature fusion and a classification model. Our proposed model demonstrates its suitability for the detection and recognition of falls from the data captured by the two cameras together. For this case study, we detect all falls with only one false positive, and reach a balanced accuracy of 93% in the recognition of the 13 types of activities. Similar results are obtained for videos of the two cameras when considered separately. Moreover, we observe better performance of videos collected in indoor scenes.

Keywords: Fall detection · Fall recognition · Wearable camera · Egocentric vision · Health monitoring · Well-being

1 Introduction

Owing to improved quality of life and advancement of medical technologies, there is a trend of extending life expectancy, resulting in an increasing elderly population across the world [1]. From the data given by the Department of Economic and Social Affairs Population Dynamics of the United Nations, it can be observed that the world population older than 60 years old almost doubled, from 8.0% to 13.5% between 1950 and 2020 [1]. This expectation indicates that the aging population process will accelerate in the next decades. Previous reports from the World Health Organization (WHO) have shown that falling is the second reason for unintentional injury death. It has defined fall as an event,

A. Del Bimbo et al. (Eds.): ICPR 2020 Workshops, LNCS 12661, pp. 431–443, 2021.
https://doi.org/10.1007/978-3-030-68763-2_33

which results in a person coming to rest unintentionally on the ground or floor or other lower level. Reports show that 28% to 35% of people older than 65 have suffered at least one fall [2]. Moreover, falling is even more severe among people older than 70, which accounts to 32% to 42% of the population in that age group.

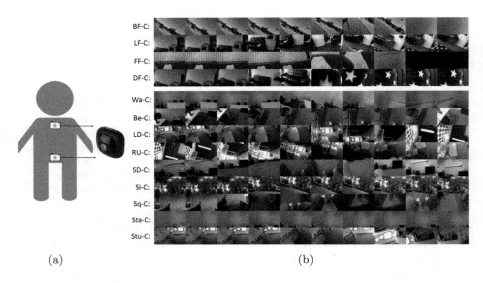

(a)   (b)

Fig. 1. (a) Illustration of the two body locations (chest and waist) that we use to collect data. (b) Examples of frames extracted from different collected activities of falls and non-falls considered in this work. The 13 abbreviations represent the type of activities which are described in Sect. 3. The '-C' indicates that the images were collected from the camera attached to the chest.

In [3] it was identified that fear of falling is an independent risk factor for reduced quality of life, activity restriction, loss of independence and fall-risk. Moreover, falls among the elderly have also an economic impact on society. Although there are various challenges in terms of fall detection, such as user acceptance, the rarity of actual data, and concerns about violation of privacy [4], there is an increasing interest in the development of more effective fall detection systems.

In this work, we study the detection and recognition of human falls through the analysis of egocentric videos collected by wearable cameras, something that goes one step forward beyond the literature. The decision of using wearable cameras stems out from the broader topic of visual lifelogging, which has attracted a lot of interest, mainly in terms of creating visual diaries of the life of people [5]. Egocentric images captured by wearable cameras show an objective and first-person view description of the activities that the user experiences daily. An example is the quantification of social interaction on daily basis [6]. In contrast to other wearable devices, the visual information captured by images/videos offer to gather context information that we believe is helpful when studying and understanding such event. Our proposed model is a conceptually simple pipeline with a lightweight and effective algorithm. Here we conduct a case study with data collected from one volunteer and address three *research questions*: a) Can falls be detected and recognized from egocentric visual data? b) Which is the best location of the wearable device, between the chest and the waist? c) Does an indoor or outdoor environment affect the performance of our proposed approach for fall detection?

In order to address the above questions, we collect two data sets from one male student volunteer, one from a camera attached to his chest and the other set from a camera attached to his waist. The data sets contain examples from four types of falls and nine kinds of non-fall events.

The contributions of this work are three-fold. On one hand, we demonstrate that video segments contain sufficient information to detect falls and the specific type of fall. On the other hand, we propose a computer vision/machine learning pipeline that is effective for fall detection and recognition. Furthermore, we contribute and make publicly available the new data set of 776 videos collected by one individual.

The rest of the paper is organized as follows. In Sect. 2, we give an account of related works. Section 3 reports the details of the data set that we collected. We describe our proposed model for fall detection and recognition in Sect. 4. In Sect. 5 and Sect. 6 we present the experimental results and discussion, respectively. Finally, we draw conclusions in Sect. 7.

2   Related Works

The literature of fall detection techniques is abundant. In our recent work, we give an overview of the challenges and recently proposed methods [7]. In that survey, among others, we identified that typical sensors used for fall detection are usually divided into three categories, namely wearable, visual, and ambient. Here we focus on the literature that concerns fixed visual sensors, regular wearable sensors and wearable cameras.

2.1   Fall Detection by Fixed Visual Sensors

Fall detection by fixed visual sensors have been widely explored. For instance, a sensor network was organised in a retirement residential home in Columbia, Missouri, to acquire real falls of the elderly. The sensing network was active for 3339 days and continuously collected daily activities of 16 elderly. During such a long period, however, only 9 falls were recorded [8,9] leading to an insufficiently representative data set for fall detection research purposes.

In order to counter for the difficulty to collect real falls, research reported in [10] hired stunt actors to simulate various falls and non-falls activities. Other attempts included the hiring of middle-age [11] and young [12,13] volunteers for that purpose. The performance of systems relying on fixed RGB cameras heavily depends on environmental conditions, such as changes in illumination. Moreover, fixed RGB cameras tend to cause a higher false alarm rate of deliberate actions such as lying on the floor, sleeping or sitting down abruptly, because they share similar movements to real falls. While the collection of daily activities can lead to effective methods, it is restricted to controlled environments, such as cameras monitoring living rooms or other parts of an indoor place. This can be problematic when aiming to detect falls in the outdoors. Wearable sensors thus play an important role for capturing every moment.

2.2   Fall Detection by Wearable Devices

In order to address the challenges mentioned above, non-vision wearable devices, such as accelerometers, gyroscopes, pressure sensors, and ECG, have also been investigated. One can distinguish an anomaly through the detection of critical physiological variations of the concerned individual. Because of the advantages of mobility and portability, wearable sensors have received popularity and have become among the prominent types of sensors used in this field. Wearable non-visual sensors, however, cannot distinguish the type of fall nor the exact location within an indoor area, information that can be very useful to paramedics.

2.3   Fall Detection by Wearable Cameras

In [14] wearable cameras embedded in spectacles were proposed for the classification of daily activities. Also, in [15], more than 100 h of video data were collected from 20 persons performing in total 18 activities using a GoPro. The authors used different representations as features and trained SVM classification models. They suggested that real-world activities of daily living recognition are all about the objects being interacted with and obtained a classification accuracy of 77%. Visual wearable devices worn as necklaces have shown their potential for the description of behavioural patterns [5].

The study in [16] used multiple data sets designed for egocentric actions and activity recognition. The authors combined motion compensation, trajectory selection, Fisher encoding and finally used a SVM for classification. The authors identified three key components for performance: motion compensation, object features over foreground regions and the use of an attention point to guide feature extraction. The research reported in [17] collected over 600 events of falls, sitting, and lying down by wearable cameras attached to the waist. A method based on the Histogram of Gradients was proposed and achieved 91% fall detection rate.

A Microsoft LifeCam camera attached to the waist was used in [18,19] for collecting a data set with fall and non-fall events. A hierarchy classification model to recognize different types of falls and non-falls was applied in [18]. Firstly, a modified histograms of edge orientations and edge strengths were used to distinguish falls from non-falls. If a given even resulted in a non-fall event, optical flow was subsequently calculated to specifically determine which of the non-fall events occurred. Moreover, they tested the algorithm in a smart platform

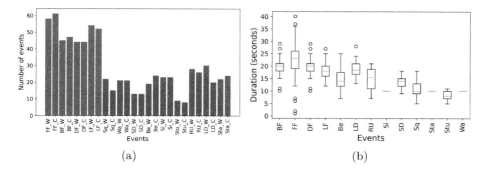

Fig. 2. (a) Number of samples per each activity. The abbreviations are given in full in Sect. 3 and Appendix. The suffixes "_W" and "_C" refer to the waist and chest, respectively, according to where the camera was attached. (b) Distributions of the duration of the collected clips for the 13 types of falls, which shows the averaged, maximum, minimum seconds of duration for each category of events. The abbreviations are described in Table 1.

embedded camera, which features a microprocessor and a wireless transmission module, and achieved 87.84% accuracy for the detection of falls.

In [19] it was proposed a modified version of the histogram of oriented gradients (HOG) approach together with the gradient local binary patterns (GLBP). It turned out that the GLBP feature is more descriptive and discriminative than the other approaches investigated in their research. With their approach the authors achieved an accuracy of 93.78% for indoor falls and 89.8% for outdoor falls. The study in [20,21] proposed a fall detection system including a portable camera, a communication module, and an embedded processor. Their algorithm was based on HOG combined with optical flow and reported up to a sensitivity of 95%. The few studies which applied wearable cameras, either deployed web cameras [20,21] or GoPros [15], which are not very convenient portable devices.

Fall detection studies, especially those that use vision-based approaches, have been shifting to machine/deep learning during the past years. Previous works indicated the suitability of deep learning to fall detection [22–24]. In this work, we advance further and analyze the appropriateness of a supervised approach for the recognition of falls from a first-person view, i.e. through the analysis of egocentric photo-streams collected by wearable cameras.

3   Data Set

We collect a new data set from one volunteer for testing our hypothesis with the evaluation of our method described below. The collection of events is recorded with two Onreal G1 wearable cameras. OnReal G1 is a portable mini action camera with dimensions $420 \times 420 \times 200$ mm that captures videos with a resolution of up to 1080P and 30 fps. For this case study, the male student participant was asked to record fall- and non-fall related events by wearing both cameras attached to the chest area of his t-shirts and to his belt in the waist area as shown in Fig. 1a. Events were collected in indoor and outdoor scenes. Indoor scenes consist of events recorded in the volunteer's bedroom, living room, and kitchen, while outdoor scenes are represented by events in parks and city streets.

In particular, the volunteer collected a total of 776 events from both cameras together. They include four types of falls and nine types of non-falls. In order to simulate real scenarios, the volunteer starts each recording while walking or standing. The volunteer was instructed to wait for several seconds before stopping the recording of an event. Table 1 contains the description of all types of falls and non-falls that we consider in this study, with the fourth column showing the instructions given to the volunteer.

Table 1. Description of the collected fall- and non-fall events. The last column indicates the instructions given to the volunteer.

	No.	Name	Symbol	Description
Falls	1	Front-falls	FF	From a standing position falling forward to the floor with arm protection and lying down
	2	Backward-falls	BF	From a standing position falling backwards and lying on the floor
	3	Lateral-falls	LF	From a standing position falling in the right-lateral and left-lateral direction ending lying on the floor
	4	Downside-falls	DF	From a standing position following a vertical trajectory ending lying on the floor
Non-falls	5	Lying	LD	From a standing position lying on the bed and keeping the position for several seconds
	6	Rising-up	RU	From lying to sitting or standing
	7	Sitting-down	SD	From a standing position to sitting on a sofa or a chair
	8	Bending	Be	From a standing position to bending in any direction from the waist
	9	Stumbling	Stu	From a standing position momentarily losing balance; almost falling
	10	Squatting	Sq	From a standing position bending low on the knees and standing up again
	11	Walking	Wa	Walking naturally
	12	Standing	Sta	Standing with natural movement
	13	Sitting	Si	Maintaining a sitting position

In Fig. 1b, we can observe examples of collected fall- and non-fall events. Each row is composed of sample frames equally spaced in time of a collected video. Most of the falls last 10–20 s as shown in Fig. 2b. Figure 2a shows the distribution of the number of examples per class that the volunteer collected. Due to some errors in data recording, we ended up with few differences between the number videos collected from the chest and waist in most of the classes. To the best of our knowledge, this represents the first public fall data set collected by egocentric cameras[1].

4   Method

In this section, we depict our proposed pipeline for fall detection and recognition from egocentric videos. In Fig. 3 we illustrate our proposed pipeline that consists of extraction of frames, feature extraction and fusion, and classification model. We elaborate on these components below.

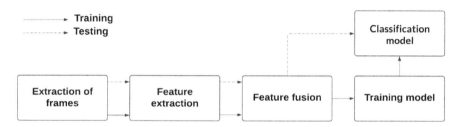

Fig. 3. Flowchart depicting our proposed approach. The model is learned through the training pipeline indicated with the solid arrows, and evaluated via the test pipeline as specified by the dashed arrows. Both pipelines take video clips as input.

4.1   Extraction of Frames

Instead of using all frames from the recorded videos we only extract a subset of frames equally spaced in time. This decision is motivated by our overarching goal of having a lightweight system that can be effective with few frames, and thus using as little computational resources as possible. For this work, an adapted frame rate is calculated to extract 10 frames from each video. Moreover, in order to keep computational power to a minimum, we do not do any preprocessing operations to the extracted frames.

---

[1] The data set can be downloaded from https://doi.org/10.34894/3DV8BF.

4.2   Feature Extraction

The extracted frames are described using a global representation of the scene. To do so, we extract the 2048-element feature vector from the fully connected layer of a ConvNet. More specifically, we rely on the residual network of 50 layers called ResNet50 [25], which is pre-trained on the ImageNet data set. The alternative of training a neural network from scratch or training a classification model with handcrafted features is not yet possible due to the limited amount of collected data.

It is to be highlighted that the deep residual network and its variants have been widely proven to be one of the most groundbreaking ConvNets. It can achieve compelling performance because of the strong representational capacity even for deep networks with many layers. The performance of some computer vision tasks have been improved dramatically by such ConvNets, as for instance shown in [25].

4.3   Fusion of Features and Classification Model

Each event is then described by concatenating the 2048-element feature vectors of the ten frames into one long vector of 20,480 elements. We perform an ablation study and evaluate different kinds of classifiers, including Linear SVM [26], Nearest Neighbors [27], Decision Tree [28], and a Neural Network [29] for fall detection and recognition in this case study.

5   Experiments and Results

5.1   Experimental Design

In order to address the proposed research questions we conduct three different experiments. On one side, we evaluate the performance for the different classifiers for the task of (1) fall detection, (2) the determination of the best location to attach the camera, and (3) performance comparison of indoor and outdoor environments. We carry out all experiments with a 10-fold cross validation and report average performance measurements.

5.2   Performance Measurements

For each experiment we first determine the confusion matrix and then quantify the performance in terms of macro weighted recall, precision, and F1-score, along with the balanced-accuracy and accuracy.

5.3   Results

In Table 2 we show the results of the first experiment that evaluates different classifiers and that uses the whole data set composed of 776 falls collected by both cameras in a 10-fold cross validation.

Table 2. Results of different classifiers for the entire data set of 13 classes.

Classifier	Weighted recall	Weighted precision	Weighted F1-score	Balanced accuracy	Accuracy
Linear SVM	0.93 (±0.04)	0.93 (±0.06)	0.92 (±0.05)	0.93 (±0.04)	0.94 (±0.03)
3-NN	0.88 (±0.06)	0.87 (±0.09)	0.87 (±0.07)	0.88 (±0.06)	0.90 (±0.05)
Decision tree	0.34 (±0.06)	0.33 (±0.06)	0.32 (±0.05)	0.34 (±0.06)	0.46 (±0.08)
Neural network	0.93 (±0.06)	0.90 (±0.09)	0.91 (±0.10)	0.89 (±0.15)	0.93 (±0.05)

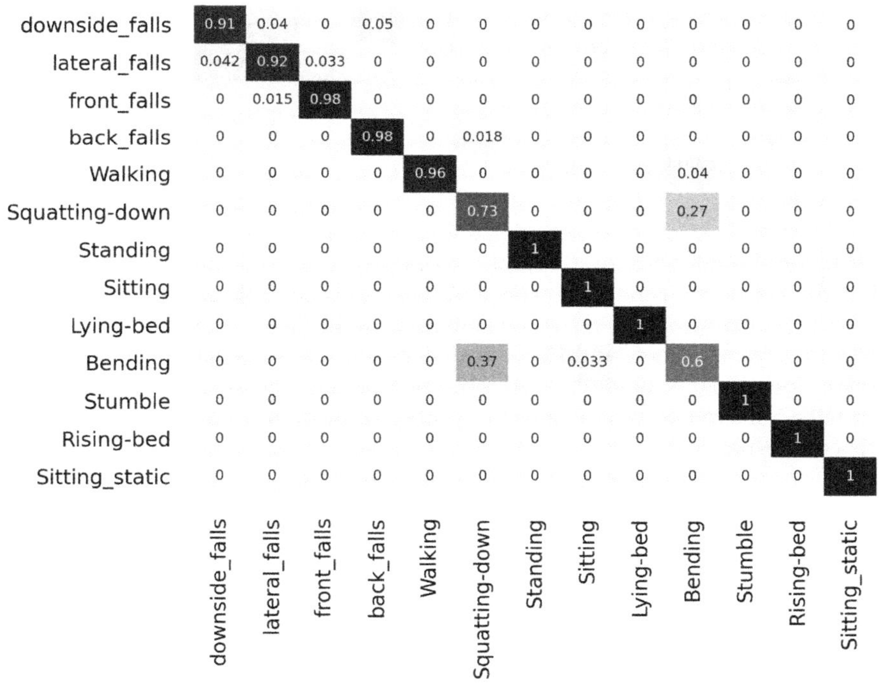

	downside_falls	lateral_falls	front_falls	back_falls	Walking	Squatting-down	Standing	Sitting	Lying-bed	Bending	Stumble	Rising-bed	Sitting_static
downside_falls	0.91	0.04	0	0.05	0	0	0	0	0	0	0	0	0
lateral_falls	0.042	0.92	0.033	0	0	0	0	0	0	0	0	0	0
front_falls	0	0.015	0.98	0	0	0	0	0	0	0	0	0	0
back_falls	0	0	0	0.98	0	0.018	0	0	0	0	0	0	0
Walking	0	0	0	0	0.96	0	0	0	0	0.04	0	0	0
Squatting-down	0	0	0	0	0	0.73	0	0	0	0.27	0	0	0
Standing	0	0	0	0	0	0	1	0	0	0	0	0	0
Sitting	0	0	0	0	0	0	0	1	0	0	0	0	0
Lying-bed	0	0	0	0	0	0	0	0	1	0	0	0	0
Bending	0	0	0	0	0	0.37	0	0.033	0	0.6	0	0	0
Stumble	0	0	0	0	0	0	0	0	0	0	1	0	0
Rising-bed	0	0	0	0	0	0	0	0	0	0	0	1	0
Sitting_static	0	0	0	0	0	0	0	0	0	0	0	0	1

Fig. 4. The aggregated and normalized confusion matrix of the results obtained with the linear SVM.

As can observed, the SVM classifier with a linear kernel achieves the best performance in terms of weighted F1-score and balanced-accuracy. Figure 4 shows the normalised and aggregated confusion matrix across the 10 experiments of the 10-fold cross validation using SVM for the classification of the 13 concerned events. The lowest performance is achieved for two non-fall events, namely bending and squatting-down. When we consider the application as a two-class problem (fall or non-fall) we detect all falls with one false positive in the 10-fold cross-validation setting with the linear SVM classifier. Based on the fact that the SVM classifier yielded the best results above, in the following we evaluate the experiments that concern the location (chest and waist) and environment (indoor and outdoor) using only this classifier.

In the second experiment we treated the videos from the chest- and waist-attached cameras as two separate data sets, for which we report the results with the linear SVM in Table 3. The results show that the location where the wearable camera is attached does not influence the performance.

Table 3. Performance for the 13-class classification task for each of the two camera locations – waist and chest – and the linear SVM as classifier.

Location	Weighted recall	Weighted precision	Weighted F1-score	Balanced accuracy	Accuracy
Chest	0.94 (±0.06)	0.93 (±0.08)	0.93 (±0.06)	0.94 (±0.06)	0.95 (±0.04)
Waist	0.95 (±0.07)	0.93 (±0.11)	0.94 (±0.09)	0.95 (±0.07)	0.96 (±0.06)

Finally, the influence of different environments, indoor and outdoor, is studied in the third experiment. To this end, falls and non-falls are collected in both indoor (e.g. bedroom, living room, kitchen, and office), and outdoor environments (e.g. park, street, and the University campus) in order to cover as many realistic locations as possible. The obtained results shown in Table 4 indicate that falls collected in indoor environments are more accurately classified than their counterparts.

Table 4. Performance for the 13-class classification task of our model when analysing falls recorded in indoor and outdoor environments and the linear SVM as classifier.

Environment	Weighted recall	Weighted precision	Weighted F1-score	Balanced accuracy	Accuracy
Indoor	0.95 (±0.08)	0.94 (±0.10)	0.94 (±0.09)	0.95 (±0.08)	0.96 (±0.05)
Outdoor	0.91 (±0.13)	0.89 (±0.15)	0.89 (±0.14)	0.91 (±0.13)	0.96 (±0.07)

6   Discussion

From the results of our case study, it seems that the proposed approach by wearable cameras is able to recognise fall- and non-fall events effectively. Besides the effectiveness of this approach, the main advantage of wearable cameras is that they are light and portable and therefore events of interest can be detected and recognized everywhere, not only in controlled indoor environments. Moreover, egocentric visual data has a broader potential use beyond the fall/non-fall problem that we consider here. For instance, such content can be investigated to model the detection of early signs of mobility and cognitive problems in the elderly.

The results also indicate that there is comparable performance on the data collected from the chest and from the waist. Our initial hypothesis was that the camera attached to the waist would suffer from occlusions, especially for certain activities, such as sitting, bending, downside falls, and squatting-down. The occlusions in such occasions could cause dark frames, that negatively impact the classification of events. However, the obtained results indicate that the location of the camera does not affect the detection and recognition of the fall. This can be due to the fact that the volunteer paid attention and collected good quality videos from both locations. This might not be the most realistic scenario, but allows the analysis and study of the effect of the location of the camera.

Moreover, the results reveal that the type of environment affect slightly the performance of the proposed methodology. Indoor events are more easily recognized than the ones collected outdoors. The reason for such a result is still debatable. With further experiments that we plan to conduct on a bigger data set from several participants we will be in a position to draw more robust conclusions.

So far this work is a case study with the data of one volunteer. As a natural follow-up, we plan to extend our data set with multiple volunteers so that we will evaluate the generalization ability across different users. Moreover, we aim to investigate the fusion of non-visual sensors, such as accelerometers, with the wearable cameras we used in this study. In that work, we will investigate a two-tier approach where first we will use the accelerometer to detect an event and then we use the egocentric frames to recognize the exact type of event.

7   Conclusions

We propose a novel approach for fall detection and recognition with wearable egocentric cameras. Here we conducted a case study with the data collected by two cameras from one volunteer, one attached to his chest and the other to his waist.

For the total of 776 events collected by both cameras together, with the proposed approach we detected all falls with only one false positive across the 10-fold cross validation. When we attempted to specifically label the events with four types of falls and nine types of non-falls we achieved a balanced accuracy of 93% with 10-fold cross validation. In particular, when the images of both cameras were treated as two separate data sets, it turned out that the location of camera does not influence the performance in this case study. Better performance was, however, achieved for indoor activities.

References

1. United Nations: Data query: Percentage of total population by broad age group (2019). https://population.un.org/wpp/dataquery/
2. World Health Organization: Ageing and Life Course Unit. WHO global report on falls prevention in older age. World Health Organization (2008)
3. Hadjistavropoulos, T., Delbaere, K., Fitzgerald, T.D.: Reconceptualizing the role of fear of falling and balance confidence in fall risk. J. Aging Health **23**(1), 3–23 (2011)
4. Igual, R., Medrano, C., Plaza, I.: Challenges, issues and trends in fall detection systems. Biomed. Eng. Online **12**(1), 66 (2013). https://doi.org/10.1186/1475-925X-12-66
5. Talavera, E., Wuerich, C., Petkov, N., Radeva, P.: Topic modelling for routine discovery from egocentric photo-streams. Pattern Recogn. **104**, 107330 (2020)
6. Talavera, E., Cola, A., Petkov, N., Radeva, P.: Towards egocentric person re-identification and social pattern analysis. In: 1st Applications of Intelligent Systems (APPIS), vol. 310, no. 5, pp. 203–211 (2019)
7. Wang, X., Ellul, J., Azzopardi, G.: Elderly fall detection systems: a literature survey. Front. Robot. AI **7**, 71 (2020)
8. Stone, E.E., Skubic, M.: Capturing habitual, in-home gait parameter trends using an inexpensive depth camera. In: 2012 Annual International Conference of the IEEE Engineering in Medicine and Biology Society, pp. 5106–5109. IEEE (2012)
9. Banerjee, T., Keller, J.M., Skubic, M.: Resident identification using kinect depth image data and fuzzy clustering techniques. In: 2012 Annual International Conference of the IEEE Engineering in Medicine and Biology Society, pp. 5102–5105. IEEE (2012)
10. Li, Y., Banerjee, T., Popescu, M., Skubic, M.: Improvement of acoustic fall detection using kinect depth sensing. In: 2013 35th annual international conference of the IEEE Engineering in medicine and biology society (EMBC), pp. 6736–6739. IEEE (2013)
11. Kangas, M., Konttila, A., Lindgren, P., Winblad, I., Jämsä, T.: Comparison of low-complexity fall detection algorithms for body attached accelerometers. Gait Posture **28**(2), 285–291 (2008)
12. Bourke, A.K., O'brien, J.V., Lyons, G.M.: Evaluation of a threshold-based tri-axial accelerometer fall detection algorithm. Gait Posture **26**(2), 194–199 (2007)
13. Ma, X., Wang, H., Xue, B., Zhou, M., Ji, B., Li, Y.: Depth-based human fall detection via shape features and improved extreme learning machine. IEEE J. Biomed. Health Inform. **18**(6), 1915–1922 (2014)
14. Zhan, K., Ramos, F., Faux, S.: Activity recognition from a wearable camera. In: 2012 12th International Conference on Control Automation Robotics & Vision (ICARCV), pp. 365–370. IEEE (2012)
15. Pirsiavash, H., Ramanan, D.: Detecting activities of daily living in first-person camera views. In: 2012 IEEE Conference on Computer Vision and Pattern Recognition, pp. 2847–2854. IEEE (2012)
16. Li, Y., Ye, Z., Rehg, J.M.: Delving into egocentric actions. In: Proceedings of the IEEE Conference on Computer Vision and Pattern Recognition, pp. 287–295 (2015)
17. Casares, M., Ozcan, K., Almagambetov, A., Velipasalar, S.: Automatic fall detection by a wearable embedded smart camera. In: 2012 Sixth International Conference on Distributed Smart Cameras (ICDSC), pp. 1–6. IEEE (2012)

18. Ozcan, K., Mahabalagiri, A.K., Casares, M., Velipasalar, S.: Automatic fall detection and activity classification by a wearable embedded smart camera. IEEE J. Emerg. Sel. Top. Circuits Syst. **3**(2), 125–136 (2013)
19. Ozcan, K., Velipasalar, S., Varshney, P.K.: Autonomous fall detection with wearable cameras by using relative entropy distance measure. IEEE Trans. Hum.-Mach. Syst. **47**(1), 31–39 (2016)
20. Boudouane, I., Makhlouf, A., Saadia, N., Ramdane-Cherif, A.: Wearable camera for fall detection embedded system. In: Proceedings of the 4th International Conference on Smart City Applications, pp. 1–6 (2019)
21. Boudouane, I., Makhlouf, A., Harkat, M.A., Hammouche, M.Z., Saadia, N., Ramdane Cherif, A.: Fall detection system with portable camera. J. Ambient Intell. Humaniz. Comput. **11**(7), 2647–2659 (2019). https://doi.org/10.1007/s12652-019-01326-x
22. Adhikari, K., Bouchachia, H., Nait-Charif, H.: Activity recognition for indoor fall detection using convolutional neural network. In: 2017 Fifteenth IAPR International Conference on Machine Vision Applications (MVA), pp. 81–84. IEEE (2017)
23. Kong, Y., Huang, J., Huang, S., Wei, Z., Wang, S.: Learning spatiotemporal representations for human fall detection in surveillance video. J. Vis. Commun. Image Represent. **59**, 215–230 (2019)
24. Han, Q., et al.: A two-stream approach to fall detection with MobileVGG. IEEE Access **8**, 17556–17566 (2020)
25. He, K., Zhang, X., Ren, S., Sun, J.: Deep residual learning for image recognition. In: Proceedings of the IEEE Conference on Computer Vision and Pattern Recognition, pp. 770–778 (2016)
26. Hearst, M.A., Dumais, S.T., Osuna, E., Platt, J., Scholkopf, B.: Support vector machines. IEEE Intell. Syst. Appl. **13**(4), 18–28 (1998)
27. Cover, T., Hart, P.: Nearest neighbor pattern classification. IEEE Trans. Inf. Theory **13**(1), 21–27 (1967)
28. Quinlan, J.R.: Induction of decision trees. Mach. Learn. **1**(1), 81–106 (1986). https://doi.org/10.1007/BF00116251
29. Bishop, C.M., et al.: Neural Networks for Pattern Recognition. Oxford University Press, Oxford (1995)

Deep Attention Based Semi-supervised 2D-Pose Estimation for Surgical Instruments

Mert Kayhan[1], Okan Köpüklü[1]([✉]), Mhd Hasan Sarhan[1,2], Mehmet Yigitsoy[2], Abouzar Eslami[2], and Gerhard Rigoll[1]

[1] Technical University of Munich, Munich, Germany
okan.kopuklu@tum.de
[2] Carl Zeiss Meditec AG, Munich, Germany

Abstract. For many practical problems and applications, it is not feasible to create a vast and accurately labeled dataset, which restricts the application of deep learning in many areas. Semi-supervised learning algorithms intend to improve performance by also leveraging unlabeled data. This is very valuable for 2D-pose estimation task where data labeling requires substantial time and is subject to noise. This work aims to investigate if semi-supervised learning techniques can achieve acceptable performance level that makes using these algorithms during training justifiable. To this end, a lightweight network architecture is introduced and mean teacher, virtual adversarial training and pseudo-labeling algorithms are evaluated on 2D-pose estimation for surgical instruments. For the applicability of pseudo-labelling algorithm, we propose a novel confidence measure, total variation. Experimental results show that utilization of semi-supervised learning improves the performance on unseen geometries drastically while maintaining high accuracy for seen geometries. For RMIT benchmark, our lightweight architecture outperforms state-of-the-art with supervised learning. For Endovis benchmark, pseudo-labelling algorithm improves the supervised baseline achieving the new state-of-the-art performance.

Keywords: 2D pose estimation · Surgical instruments · Convolutional neural networks

1 Introduction

It has been shown that deep learning algorithms can achieve human- or super-human- level performance on variety of tasks by utilizing large amounts of labeled data. However, these achievements come at a cost: Creating these massive annotated datasets usually require a great deal of time investment, sometimes also expertise and is prone to human errors. For many practical problems and applications, it is not feasible to create such a vast and accurately labeled dataset, which restricts the application of deep learning in many areas.

© Springer Nature Switzerland AG 2021
A. Del Bimbo et al. (Eds.): ICPR 2020 Workshops, LNCS 12661, pp. 444–460, 2021.
https://doi.org/10.1007/978-3-030-68763-2_34

A possible solution to this problem may be semi-supervised learning (SSL). Unlike supervised learning algorithms, which require all the examples to be labeled, SSL algorithms can improve performance by also leveraging unlabeled data. SSL algorithms generally enable the learning system to learn the structure of the data.

This work investigates if the need for labels can be reduced by using semi-supervised learning in 2D-pose estimation setting. To the best of our knowledge, so far, there has not been any investigation of the usage and performance of SSL for surgical instrument tracking, where data labeling requires substantial time, and therefore, amount of unlabeled data is large compared to the labeled ones. However, this poses some fundamental challenges. In particular for 2D-pose estimation where there is no proposed method to measure the confidence of the network outputs. This is a big setback for the pseudo-labeling method where a confidence threshold is utilized to select samples where the network is certain of the answer. This study introduces total variation as a confidence measure for 2D-pose estimation task to enable the usage of pseudo-labeling.

In this work, we have applied 2D-pose estimation on surgical instruments. For this purpose, a lightweight deep attention based network architecture is proposed. On this architecture, three SSL algorithms are investigated: Mean teacher, virtual adversarial training and pseudo-labeling. Detailed experimental analysis is conducted on single-instrument Retinal Microsurgery Instrument Tracking (RMIT) dataset and multi-instrument EndoVis challenge dataset. As there is no unlabeled data for RMIT dataset, hyper parameter search is done using supervised learning. For this dataset, proposed network architecture achieves superior performance compared to state-of-the-art. For Endovis dataset, supervised learning is taken as baseline and SSL algorithms are benchmarked, where pseudo-labelling algorithm outperforms the previous state-of-the-art results.

2   Related Work

Operations Requiring Surgical Tools. Retinal microsurgery is a very challenging field for surgeons. In a typical vitreoretinal surgery, the surgeon has to manipulate retinal layers that are very delicate and less than $10\,\mu$m thick [9]. A surgical precision in the order of tens of microns is required for this operation. Furthermore, the resistance applied by the retinal tissue to the instruments is exceedingly small [9], which limits the haptic feedback. Therefore, it is very difficult to estimate the precise location of the instruments. However, knowing where exactly the instruments are can provide vital information which can help avoid injuries inside the eye, e.g. broken blood vessel.

Another category of surgery that can benefit from knowing exact instrument location is robotic laparoscopic surgery. Laparoscopy is a surgical procedure which examines the organs inside the abdomen to check for signs of disease. During laparoscopic surgery, small incisions are made in the wall of the abdomen and a laparoscope (a thin, lighted tube) is inserted into one of the incisions. During robotic laparoscopic surgery, surgeons receive visual information about the instruments using the cameras embedded on the robotic device [21]. Utilizing this information, the robotic master handles are used to move the robot to the desired position. Since the surgeons are limited to the visual information collected by a rod-like instrument where left and right channels are closely embedded, estimating the depth and precise locations of instruments are very challenging. Therefore, a real-time knowledge of the instruments' position with respect to anatomical structures is a key component to improve the assistive or autonomous capabilities of surgical robots [4].

Approaches for Surgical Tool Pose Estimation. Recent developments in computer vision have resulted in advanced approaches for vision-based tracking of surgical tools. The work prior to deep-learning era relies on handcrafted features, such as Haar wavelets [22], gradient [14,29] or color features [19,31]. These approaches are not robust enough for real life scenarios due to strong illumination changes and motion blur that occur during surgeries.

With the surge of deep learning the focus has shifted towards instrument localization and/or segmentation through CNNs. However, most of these approaches focus only on segmentation of the image, localization of keypoints on the instrument tip or bounding box detection [6,7,11,16,17]. The method proposed by I. Laina and N. Rieke et al. [11] focuses on the interdependency between instrument segmentation and tip localization. This is the first attempt to combine these two tasks into one pipeline. By jointly optimizing for these two objectives, they improve the state of the art by a clear margin. The reported network runtime for this work is 56 ms on Nvidia TITAN X. The major shortcoming of this work is that it cannot represent the full pose of the instrument or include articulation. In response to these challenges, Du et al. [4] provide the first work on articulated pose estimation for surgical instruments. They base their approach on the methods proposed by [1,2] which consist of two stages. First, joints and joint connections are segmented, and then these are refined to come up with the final output heatmaps. These heatmaps represent the confidence of the network about the presence of a joint or joint connection at any given pixel location. Final pose of the instrument is inferred using bipartite graph matching after non-maximum suppression as post-processing step. They report a network runtime of 24 ms and post-processing runtime of 89 ms on Nvidia TITAN X GPU. Although their approach provides good generalization performance, the biggest challenge remains to be achieving real time performance while maintaining low localization error.

3   Methodology

In this section, we initially give the details of the network architecture. Then we explain the proposed confidence measure, total variation, which is needed for pseudo-labeling algorithm. Finally, we mention the training details.

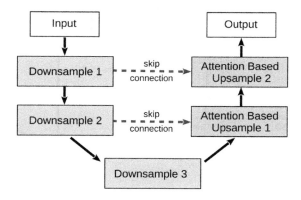

Fig. 1. The modified U-Net architecture which is used in all experiments. For visual clarity, the downsample, attention based upsample and attention blocks are illustrated in Fig. 2 (a), Fig. 2 (b) and Fig. 3, respectively.

3.1 Network Architecture

For surgical tool pose estimation, a modified U-Net [15] architecture is used, where each joint location is found via a separate heatmap output channel. Our architecture makes use of attention mechanism intensively. Accordingly we have named our architecture DAU-Net referring to Deep Attention based U-Net. DAU-Net diverges from U-Net in the following regards: Downsampling operation is applied for 3 times, ReLU activation function is replaced with RLReLU activation [27], 2D attention module is added to upsampling blocks at each concatenation point, group normalization [26] is used before each activation function in the main network, whereas it is omitted in the attention module. The final output maps are generated using a 1×1 convolution to scale the output channels to the number of joints and joint associations of interest.

The final model that is used for all experiments is illustrated in Fig. 1. The details of downsample and attention based upsample blocks are also illustrated in Fig. 2(a) and Fig. 2(b), respectively. Skip connections are applied from downsample block (before maxpooling) to attention based upsample blocks after deconvolution.

2D Attention Mechanism for Pose Estimation. Girshick et al. [8] have shown that by cropping relevant locations from feature maps, we can detect bounding boxes and classify the corresponding object. The biggest drawback of this method is that we need bounding box annotations to learn the correct answers.

To eliminate the need for bounding box annotations, 2D attention module turns on/off elements in the feature maps. The turn on/off effect is achieved by elementwise multiplication after sigmoid activation. In other words, for each element in the feature map, the attention mechanism tries to decide if this element contains information about the joints and/or connections between joints.

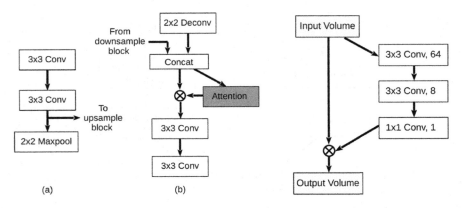

Fig. 2. Architectures of downsample (a) and attention based upsample (b) blocks. Each convolution and deconvolution is followed by group normalization and RLReLU activation. ⊗ stands for elementwise multiplication.

Fig. 3. Attention mechanism applied in Fig. 2, where ⊗ refers to elementwise multiplication. Output of the attention mechanism has 1 channel with input volume size and it is broadcasted across channels during elementwise multiplication.

This leads to a drastic reduction in search space for the network because only relevant elements are propagated further. The applied attention architecture is depicted in Fig. 3. A visualization of the learned attention maps and the corresponding images can be seen in Fig. 4. As can be seen, the attention mechanism successfully concentrates on the important parts of the input image.

3.2   Post-processing

For single instrument localization only the joint probability maps are predicted, whereas for multi-instrument localization the connection probability maps are predicted as well. The following procedure is used to retrieve the final joint locations.

Fig. 4. Visualization of the attention mechanism for multi-instrument case.

For single instrument detection, Gaussian filter is applied to the output, and then, for each channel of the output the pixel location that contains the maximum value is found.

For multiple instrument detection, Gaussian filter is applied to the joint probability maps which is followed by thresholded non-maximum suppression to retrieve the joint candidates. Then, if total variation measure of the output maps are below a certain threshold high-boost filter is applied to the connection probability maps. Finally, line integral [2,4] is utilized to find joint pairs and the instrument is parsed.

3.3   Total Variation as a Confidence Measure for Pose Estimation

In mathematics, total variation is a measure that describes the local and global structure of functions [18]. Furthermore, in the context of image processing, it is often assumed that signals with high total variation have excessive detail. Following this notion, this study proposes total variation of probability maps as a way of assessing the confidence of the inferred pose estimates.

Formally, the *anisotropic* version of total variation is shown as

$$V(y) = \sum_c \sum_{ij} |y_{i+1,j,c} - y_{i,j,c}| + |y_{i,j+1,c} - y_{i,j,c}|$$

for multi-channel images [18]. As can be seen in the above given formulation, total variation is the sum of the local discrete gradients in x and y direction. In other words, images with high total variation have large value differences between neighboring pixels. This is often assumed to be noise and irrelevant information, and therefore, *total variation denoising* [25] has been proposed to eliminate the noise from the images. However, in the context of CNN based 2D pose estimation, the global structure of the output maps match the instrument location because during training MSE objective is minimized. Exploiting this information, total variation of output maps can be used to evaluate the local properties of the output maps. As it can be seen in the autoencoder literature [24], two images may have low MSE but look quite different because MSE does not necessarily address the sharpness of the image. In this study, by using total variation, the sharpness of the output maps is evaluated. In other words, if an output map has low total variation, this translates to a flat output distribution which represents a low confidence prediction. Thus, total variance measure can be used as a post-processing step to evaluate the quality of predictions and if necessary, enable a decision mechanism which can be used to evaluate the need for further processing. Furthermore, this measure complements the pseudo-labeling method for pose estimation because this method requires a confidence threshold to be used effectively.

3.4 Training Details

Learning: Throughout the training Adam solver is used with default parameters [10]. The training lasted 50k iterations. Following Du et al. [4], input resolution is set to 288×384 pixels and 256×320 pixels for RMIT and EndoVis datasets respectively. DAU-Net kernels are initialized from a truncated Gaussian distribution and kernels in attention module is initialized using Xavier initialization. Target labels are created by heatmaps, where each joint annotation corresponds to a 2D Gaussian density map centred at the labelled point location and the annotation for joint association corresponds to a Gaussian distribution along the joint pair center line. Following Du et al. [4], the standard deviation of 20 pixels is used for Gaussian distributions.

Regularization: The network is regularized using dropout [20] with dropping rate of 30% and 10% for RMIT and EndoVis, respectively. Also, noisy labels are applied by sampling a random variable uniformly between -0.01 and 0.01, and adding to each pixel of the target heatmap.

Augmentation: Since both datasets contain very limited data, heavy data augmentation is used to avoid overfitting. For RMIT dataset, random flipping, random translation (5 px), random rotation ($10°$), Gaussian noise, random brightness, random contrast, random saturation, histogram equalization, random blurring, pepper noise, salt noise, speckle noise and random erasing [30] are used. For EndoVis dataset, random flipping, random translation (5 px), random rotation ($20°$), random swapping are used.

Random Swapping Data Augmentation: EndoVis dataset contains very limited annotated samples. Furthermore, a large fraction of these samples consist of frames where only a single instrument is visible. This makes it very difficult to learn models with good generalization across single and multi-instrument cases. To deal with this issue, *Random Swapping* is introduced as a data augmentation strategy.

Inspired from [3,5], *Random Swapping* is a method that uses keypoint annotation to generate semantically meaningful mixtures of images and simulate occlusion. In this study, the clasper annotations are used to split the frames into 2 parts. Afterwards another image is sampled from the training set and again a split is formed depending on the clasper annotation. Finally, two cropped parts from these two training images are fused together. If the sum of the crop sizes do not correspond to the original frame size, the final image is either zero-padded from the middle or cropped from the edges. The same operations are performed on the target heatmaps as well to generate labels for training. An illustration of the output images can be seen in Fig. 5.

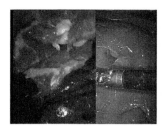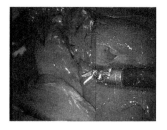

Fig. 5. The resulting frames from random swapping is depicted in the figure. To make it visually more comprehensible, parts that come from different images are visualized using BGR and RGB color formats respectively.

Implementation: The whole training setup and network is implemented using Tensorflow. For reproduciblity of results, we make our code publicly available[1].

4   Experiments

In this section, we share the obtained results from our experiments on two publicly available datasets: RMIT[2] and Endovis[3]. First, RMIT dataset is used to develop the *deep attention U-Net* (DAU-Net) model. Since RMIT dataset does not contain any unlabeled samples we do not investigate semi-supervised learning on this dataset. Next, EndoVis dataset is utilized to evaluate the performance of the developed network architecture. Furthermore, the unlabeled training data is used to evaluate the effectiveness of mean teacher, virtual adversarial learning and pseudo labeling algorithms.

4.1   Datasets

RMIT Dataset: Retinal Microsurgery Instrument Tracking (RMIT) dataset consists of three surgical sequences which are recorded during *in vivo* retinal microsurgery where only a single instrument is visible during recording. The original frames extracted from the videos have a resolution of 640 × 480 pixels. Following Du et al. [4], the dataset was split into training and test datasets where the training set consists of the first halves of each sequence and rest of the data was used for testing. A detailed distribution of the data can be seen in Table 1. For most of the frames 4 keypoints (tip1 - tip2 - shaft - end) are annotated. An example annotation can be seen in Fig. 6(a).

Endovis Dataset: EndoVis challenge dataset is a multi-instrument dataset that contains 6 video sequences from endoscopic surgeries where in fraction of

---

[1] https://github.com/mertkayhan/SSL-2D-Pose.

[2] https://sites.google.com/site/sznitr/code-and-datasets.

[3] https://endovissub-instrument.grand-challenge.org.

Table 1. The distribution of the data across different sequences for RMIT and Endovis datasets. Each row contains number of labeled images/number of total images for corresponding sequence. It should be noted that Sequence 5 and 6 are only present in the test set for Endovis Dataset.

	EndoVis dataset		RMIT dataset	
	Training	Testing	Training	Testing
Seq 1	210/1107	80/370	201/201	201/201
Seq 2	240/1125	76/375	111/111	111/111
Seq 3	252/1124	76/375	265/271	266/276
Seq 4	238/1123	76/375	–	–
Seq 5	–	301/1500	–	–
Seq 6	–	301/1500	–	–
Total	940/4479	910/4495	577/583	578/588

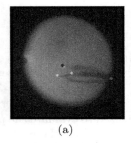 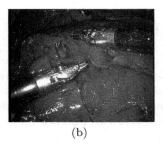

(a)   (b)

Fig. 6. Example training labels for RMIT (a) and Endovis (b) datasets. For RMIT dataset, the tips (cyan, blue), shaft (green) and end (red) of the instrument are annotated. For Endovis dataset, the claspers (red, blue), head (green), shaft (yellow) and end (cyan) joints are annotated. (Color figure online)

the sequences, 2 instruments are present in the frame. The training set consists of four 45 s *ex vivo* video sequences of surgeries whereas the test set consists of four 15 s video sequences which are complementary to the training set as well as two additional 1 min recorded interventions. A detailed distribution of the data can be seen in Table 1. The frame resolution for each of the videos is 720 × 576 pixels. Since the sparse annotations proposed by Du et al. [4] are used, as done by Du et al., the entire training set is used for training which differs from the leave-one-surgery-out training strategy requirement of the original challenge. For semi-supervised learning, the unlabeled training data is used as well. Du et al. construct a high quality multi-joint annotation which consists of Left Clasper, Right Clasper, Head, Shaft and End joint positions. An example annotation can be seen in Fig. 6(b).

Table 2. A compact summary of the results obtained by varying one component at a time to find the right architecture and training pipeline for RMIT dataset. Augmentation refers to only geometric transformations while heavy augmentation also includes color space transformations.

Pixel error rates (MAE)				
	Shaft	Tip 1	Tip 2	Avr
U-Net + augmentation	5.9	7.12	5.57	6.2
U-Net + augmentation + attention	3.79	6.67	4.72	5.06
U-Net + heavy augmentation + attention	3.73	5.98	**4.12**	4.61
U-Net + heavy augmentation + attention + L2 regularization	4.72	6.63	4.98	5.44
U-Net + heavy augmentation + attention + dropout	3.81	5.71	4.4	4.64
U-Net + heavy augmentation + attention + dropout + noisy labels	3.19	5.59	4.23	4.34
U-Net + heavy augmentation + attention + dropout + noisy labels + lrelu	3.1	6.59	4.49	4.73
U-Net + heavy augmentation + attention + dropout + noisy labels + rlrelu	**2.8**	**4.82**	4.17	**3.93**

4.2   Results Using RMIT Dataset

For the experiments shown in Table 2, the network is trained on the groundtruth bounding boxes to enable faster experimentation and simulate an object detection based localization system. Bounding boxes are extracted using 3-point annotation as shown in Fig. 6(a) excluding end point. A resolution of 128×128 is used for all experiments. In Table 2, the pixel error rate corresponds to mean absolute error since the groundtruth bounding boxes are used for training which eliminates the possibility of false detection.

First, a vanilla U-Net is trained using only the geometric augmentations. It is observed that the network produces very coarse output maps which lead to high pixel error. In response to this observation, attention mechanism is introduced to help the network to concentrate on the important parts of the image. Following this modification, it is observed that the network trains a lot faster and produces more finegrained outputs. However, it is also observed that the network is highly prone to overfitting, and therefore, more data augmentation is introduced to deal with this. Even with the additional augmentation, it is observed that the network overfits, thus, regularization is added in the following experiments. It can be seen that dropout yields superior performance compared to L2 regularization, and therefore, dropout with 30% drop rate is used in the following experiments. Because increasing the drop rate does not increase the generalization performance, more creative ways of regularizing the network are investigated. It is observed that the combination of heavy data augmentation and

Table 3. Comparison of DAU-Net-64-3 with the state of the art for 4-point annotation and end-to-end training on RMIT dataset.

Precision/recall/pixel error (RMSE)		
	DAU-Net-64-3	Du et al. [4]
Tip1	96/96/4.44	**99.13/99.13/5.26**
Tip2	**98.3/98.3/5.13**	97.58/97.58/4.61
Shaft	**99.5/99.5/4.01**	94.12/94.12/4.93
End	**92.4/92.4/5.68**	86.51/86.51/4.68
Avr	**96.6/96.6/4.82**	94.3/94.3/4.87

noise injection to the labels simulates new data points more convincingly and leads to a better generalization performance. The structure of the injected noise is described in Subsect. 3.4. Finally, an investigation over the activation functions is conducted to see if generalization performance can be improved. It is observed that RLReLU activation function [27] improves the generalization performance furthermore. All in all, one can see that by increasing the input and network level stochasticity (random data augmentation, dropout and RLReLU), the generalization performance is improved drastically. This model is used throughout this study and represented by DAU-Net-<*base_feature_maps*>-<*depth*> which corresponds to DAU-Net-32-3 in this case.

In order to make a fair comparison with state-of-the-art, the proposed system is scaled up and trained on 4-point annotations in end to end manner. Except increasing the number of trainable parameters, no other modifications are made and same input resolution as Du et al. [4] is used. As can be seen in Table 3, DAU-Net-64-3 improves the state of the art while using fewer parameters ($\sim$2.1M) for a detection threshold of 15 pixels on the original frame. It should be noted that in Table 3, the pixel error does not correspond to mean absolute error but to root mean squared error computed for the detected joints.

Table 4. A compact summary of the results obtained by varying one component at a time to find the right amount of regularization and data augmentation strategies for EndoVis dataset.

Experiments (Test set loss (MSE))	
	Avr. loss
30% dropout	0.002337
Dilated Conv	0.003029
10% dropout	0.002357
Random Swap	**0.002288**
Elastic Disp.	0.002302

4.3   Results Using Endovis Dataset

For all the experiments given in Table 4, *DAU-Net-64-3* is used because it was shown to deliver very accurate pose estimates for single instrument cases. The main idea of these experiments is to test the performance on multi-instrument cases and measure the effectiveness of semi-supervised learning in 2D-pose estimation setting. Since finding the exact poses of multiple instruments require a post-processing procedure based on thresholded non-maximum suppression and graph matching, test set loss is compared to find models with better performance.

First, the network is trained with the exact setup from the previous section. However, it is observed that the generalization performance is not very good. At the beginning it is speculated that this is caused by the larger receptive field requirement for the EndoVis dataset. Therefore, dilated convolutions with dilation rate 2 are introduced. As can be seen in the Table 4, this does not improve the performance. After analysing the output maps, it is observed that network produces flat outputs to minimize MSE which is interpreted as underfitting. In response to that, dropout rate is reduced to 10%. Furthermore, the color space augmentations are removed because in EndoVis the lighting does not vary between sequences. Next, random swapping data augmentation is introduced to generate more data. Introduction of random swapping reduced the test set error below 0.0023. Afterwards, to see the effectiveness of random swap, it is removed from the augmentation pipeline and elastic displacement is introduced. However, this model performs slightly worse.

Table 5 shows the precision, recall, f1-scores and the RMSE of the network for seen and unseen instruments. As can be seen, the network delivers very accurate pose estimates for seen instruments compared to unseen instruments since the network has difficulty extrapolating to an unknown geometry. Except for the left clasper, it can be seen that the detected joints are mostly within the 20 pixel threshold, whereas for left clasper, detections are not very accurate. After analysing the output maps, it is seen that the network produces low confidence predictions which get thresholded away. It is speculated that this is the main reason for the low recall for most of the joints. To counter that, our proposed total variation confidence measure is utilized. More information about this method can be found in Sect. 3.3. Using the steps given in Sect. 3.2, an improvement from 73.9 to 76.1 in average f1-score is observed. A detailed report of the results with this new post-processing pipeline can be seen in Table 6.

After establishing the right data augmentation strategies and post-processing pipeline, the unlabeled training data is utilized in semi-supervised learning context to see if further performance improvement is possible. To this end, mean teacher [23], pseudo-labeling [28] and VAT [12] algorithms are implemented and evaluated. It should be noted that for pseudo-labeling, the confidence threshold is set to be above 1000 total variation for multi-instrument cases and above 400 total variation for single instrument cases. For the mean teacher algorithm, $\alpha = 0.95$ is used for EMA. For VAT, the distance metric to compute the virtual adversarial loss is chosen to be MSE. In Table 7, ξ represents the maximum consistency coefficient for the mean teacher algorithm and ϵ is the magnitude of the

Table 5. Performance of the supervised baseline on the seen and unseen instruments after post-processing.

Keypoint	Sequence 1–4 (Seen instruments)				Sequence 5–6 (Unseen instruments)			
	Precision	Recall	F1-score	Pixel error (RMSE)	Precision	Recall	F1-score	Pixel error (RMSE)
Left clasper	95.6	100	97.8	4.44	58.0	83.5	68.5	8.13
Right clasper	99.7	100	99.9	2.83	90.7	63.5	74.7	5.85
Head	99.7	100	99.9	4.23	95.1	65.1	77.3	4.92
Shaft	100	100	100	2.86	99.4	66.1	79.4	8.11
End	100	100	100	5.93	91.9	56.1	69.7	7.13
Avr	99.1	100	99.5	4.06	87.0	68.7	73.9	6.83

Table 6. Performance of the supervised baseline on the unseen instruments with the modified post-processing which utilizes total variation measure.

Sequence 5–6 (Unseen instruments)				
	Precision	Recall	F1-score	Pixel error (RMSE)
Left clasper	61.6	90.2	73.2	7.89
Right clasper	86.0	75.8	74.7	6.31
Head	83.4	67.9	74.9	5.32
Shaft	94.8	71.5	81.5	8.25
End	90.3	64.0	74.9	7.70
Avr	82.8	72.2	76.1	7.09

virtual adversarial noise. The maximum consistency coefficient is reached after 20k iterations for mean teacher algorithm, whereas there is no ramp-up for VAT as it was the case for the original paper as well [12]. The sigmoid schedule that was used by Oliver et al. [13] is utilized for these experiments to determine the value of ξ throughout the training. As can be seen in Table 7, 3 candidates with lower test set loss is selected for post-processing to enable a thorough comparison of the algorithms.

As can be seen on Table 8, semi-supervised learning methods consistently improve the ability to extrapolate to unseen geometries while maintaining high accuracy for seen instruments. It is observed that the network trained with pseudo-labeling method is more consistent across seen and unseen instruments, and therefore, this model has been selected as the final semi-supervised model. Furthermore, in Table 9, a comparison of the supervised baseline, final semi-supervised model and state of the art in terms of f1-score and root mean squared pixel error provided. It should be noted that following Du et al. [4], for all the experiments a pixel threshold of 20 pixels on the original frame is used. Table 9 shows that semi-supervised learning improves the supervised baseline in average f1-score and pixel error. Plus, the state of the art is improved in terms of average f1-score and pixel error while only using ∼2.1M trainable parameters which goes to show the usefulness of semi-supervised learning and the strength of the designed network architecture. The runtime of DAU-Net-64-3 is measured as 35 ms on Nvidia TITAN X GPU.

Table 7. An overview of the experiments and the respective test set losses. Test set loss is used to only find the better performing hyperparameters but not to compare algorithms.

Experiments (Test set loss (MSE))	
SSL Algorithms	Avr. loss
VAT ($\epsilon = 1$)	0.002319
VAT ($\epsilon = 0.1$)	**0.002295**
VAT ($\epsilon = 10$)	0.002361
Pseudo-labeling	**0.002335**
Mean teacher ($\xi = 1$)	0.002428
Mean teacher ($\xi = 0.1$)	**0.002335**

Table 8. An exhaustive comparison of different semi-supervised learning algorithms for seen and unseen instruments.

Keypoint	F1-score/pixel error (RMSE)					
	Sequence 1–4 (Seen instruments)			Sequence 5–6 (Unseen instruments)		
	VAT	Pseudo-labeling	Mean teacher	VAT	Pseudo-labeling	Mean teacher
Left clasper	95.6/4.48	**96.1/3.97**	95.8/5.34	74.8/9.43	77.8/7.57	**80.5/8.87**
Right clasper	**98.8/2.94**	97.9/2.22	95.6/6.99	**82.5/6.15**	68.8/6.39	71.0/6.28
Head	99.7/3.43	**100/3.54**	97.1/3.58	72.0/4.50	**81.3/4.89**	71.5/5.15
Shaft	100/3.61	**100/3.28**	96.0/2.90	81.4/7.98	87.2/8.24	**88.9/9.48**
End	**100/5.24**	99.9/6.05	99.1/5.23	83.0/8.25	82.3/8.40	**85.6/8.66**
Avr	**98.8/3.94**	98.8/3.81	96.7/4.81	78.7/7.26	**79.5/7.10**	**79.5/7.69**

Table 9. A comparison of f1-score and root mean squared pixel error for the supervised baseline, selected semi-supervised model and the state of the art.

All sequences (F1-score/pixel error (RMSE))			
	Supervised	Pseudo-labeling	Du et al. [4]
Left clasper	80.6/6.67	82.8/6.63	**86.4/5.03**
Right clasper	81.7/5.58	76.2/5.39	**85.7/5.40**
Head	80.9/5.19	**85.6/4.56**	76.3/6.55
Shaft	85.2/7.25	90.1/7.32	**91.0/8.63**
End	81.4/7.26	**86.4/7.84**	77.3/9.17
Avr	82.0/6.39	**84.2/6.35**	83.3/6.96

5 Conclusion

This study encompasses an evaluation of semi-supervised learning for 2D-pose estimation for surgical instruments where data labeling is prone to human errors and requires a lot of time investment. All in all, it is observed that utilization of the attention mechanism improves the performance drastically and eliminates the need for a 2-stage pipeline that consists of detection and refinement. Furthermore, it has been shown that semi-supervised learning improves the performance for unseen instruments while maintaining high accuracy for seen ones. More specifically, it is recognized that the combination of pseudo-labeling and total variation is more consistent and easier to use, whereas VAT and mean teacher algorithms require extensive hyperparameter search and additional computational overhead during training. Furthermore, the introduced confidence measure, total variation, is shown to be very useful in many aspects. Our experiments indicate that the utilization of total variation as a post-processing step and/or as a part of pseudo-labeling algorithm can yield serious performance improvement.

References

1. Bulat, A., Tzimiropoulos, G.: Human pose estimation via convolutional part heatmap regression. In: Leibe, B., Matas, J., Sebe, N., Welling, M. (eds.) ECCV 2016. LNCS, vol. 9911, pp. 717–732. Springer, Cham (2016). https://doi.org/10.1007/978-3-319-46478-7_44
2. Cao, Z., Simon, T., Wei, S.E., Sheikh, Y.: Realtime multi-person 2D pose estimation using part affinity fields. In: Proceedings of the IEEE Conference on Computer Vision and Pattern Recognition, pp. 7291–7299 (2017)
3. DeVries, T., Taylor, G.W.: Improved regularization of convolutional neural networks with cutout. arXiv preprint arXiv:1708.04552 (2017)
4. Du, X., et al.: Articulated multi-instrument 2-D pose estimation using fully convolutional networks. IEEE Trans. Med. Imaging **37**(5), 1276–1287 (2018)
5. Dvornik, N., Mairal, J., Schmid, C.: Modeling visual context is key to augmenting object detection datasets. In: Ferrari, V., Hebert, M., Sminchisescu, C., Weiss, Y. (eds.) ECCV 2018. LNCS, vol. 11216, pp. 375–391. Springer, Cham (2018). https://doi.org/10.1007/978-3-030-01258-8_23
6. García-Peraza-Herrera, L.C., et al.: ToolNet: holistically-nested real-time segmentation of robotic surgical tools. In: 2017 IEEE/RSJ International Conference on Intelligent Robots and Systems (IROS), pp. 5717–5722. IEEE (2017)
7. García-Peraza-Herrera, L.C., et al.: Real-time segmentation of non-rigid surgical tools based on deep learning and tracking. In: Peters, T., et al. (eds.) CARE 2016. LNCS, vol. 10170, pp. 84–95. Springer, Cham (2017). https://doi.org/10.1007/978-3-319-54057-3_8
8. Girshick, R.: Fast R-CNN. In: Proceedings of the IEEE International Conference on Computer Vision, pp. 1440–1448 (2015)
9. Gupta, P.K., Jensen, P.S., de Juan, E.: Surgical forces and tactile perception during retinal microsurgery. In: Taylor, C., Colchester, A. (eds.) MICCAI 1999. LNCS, vol. 1679, pp. 1218–1225. Springer, Heidelberg (1999). https://doi.org/10.1007/10704282_132
10. Kingma, D.P., Ba, J.: Adam: a method for stochastic optimization. arXiv preprint arXiv:1412.6980 (2014)
11. Laina, I., et al.: Concurrent segmentation and localization for tracking of surgical instruments. In: Descoteaux, M., Maier-Hein, L., Franz, A., Jannin, P., Collins, D.L., Duchesne, S. (eds.) MICCAI 2017. LNCS, vol. 10434, pp. 664–672. Springer, Cham (2017). https://doi.org/10.1007/978-3-319-66185-8_75

12. Miyato, T., Maeda, S.I., Koyama, M., Ishii, S.: Virtual adversarial training: a regularization method for supervised and semi-supervised learning. IEEE Trans. Pattern Anal. Mach. Intell. **41**(8), 1979–1993 (2018)
13. Oliver, A., Odena, A., Raffel, C.A., Cubuk, E.D., Goodfellow, I.: Realistic evaluation of deep semi-supervised learning algorithms. In: Advances in Neural Information Processing Systems, pp. 3235–3246 (2018)
14. Rieke, N., et al.: Real-time localization of articulated surgical instruments in retinal microsurgery. Med. Image Anal. **34**, 82–100 (2016)
15. Ronneberger, O., Fischer, P., Brox, T.: U-Net: convolutional networks for biomedical image segmentation. In: Navab, N., Hornegger, J., Wells, W.M., Frangi, A.F. (eds.) MICCAI 2015. LNCS, vol. 9351, pp. 234–241. Springer, Cham (2015). https://doi.org/10.1007/978-3-319-24574-4_28
16. Sahu, M., Mukhopadhyay, A., Szengel, A., Zachow, S.: Addressing multi-label imbalance problem of surgical tool detection using CNN. Int. J. Comput. Assist. Radiol. Surg. **12**(6), 1013–1020 (2017)
17. Sarikaya, D., Corso, J.J., Guru, K.A.: Detection and localization of robotic tools in robot-assisted surgery videos using deep neural networks for region proposal and detection. IEEE Trans. Med. Imaging **36**(7), 1542–1549 (2017)
18. Scherzer, O., Grasmair, M., Grossauer, H., Haltmeier, M., Lenzen, F.: Variational Methods in Imaging. AMS, vol. 167. Springer, New York (2009). https://doi.org/10.1007/978-0-387-69277-7
19. Speidel, S., et al.: Automatic classification of minimally invasive instruments based on endoscopic image sequences. In: Medical Imaging 2009: Visualization, Image-Guided Procedures, and Modeling, vol. 7261, p. 72610A. International Society for Optics and Photonics (2009)
20. Srivastava, N., Hinton, G., Krizhevsky, A., Sutskever, I., Salakhutdinov, R.: Dropout: a simple way to prevent neural networks from overfitting. J. Mach. Learn. Res. **15**(1), 1929–1958 (2014)
21. Sung, G.T., Gill, I.S.: Robotic laparoscopic surgery: a comparison of the da Vinci and Zeus systems. Urology **58**(6), 893–898 (2001)
22. Sznitman, R., Richa, R., Taylor, R.H., Jedynak, B., Hager, G.D.: Unified detection and tracking of instruments during retinal microsurgery. IEEE Trans. Pattern Anal. Mach. Intell. **35**(5), 1263–1273 (2012)
23. Tarvainen, A., Valpola, H.: Mean teachers are better role models: weight-averaged consistency targets improve semi-supervised deep learning results. In: Advances in Neural Information Processing Systems, pp. 1195–1204 (2017)
24. Tschannen, M., Bachem, O., Lucic, M.: Recent advances in autoencoder-based representation learning. arXiv preprint arXiv:1812.05069 (2018)
25. Vogel, C.R., Oman, M.E.: Iterative methods for total variation denoising. SIAM J. Sci. Comput. **17**(1), 227–238 (1996)
26. Wu, Y., He, K.: Group normalization. In: Ferrari, V., Hebert, M., Sminchisescu, C., Weiss, Y. (eds.) ECCV 2018. LNCS, vol. 11217, pp. 3–19. Springer, Cham (2018). https://doi.org/10.1007/978-3-030-01261-8_1
27. Xu, B., Wang, N., Chen, T., Li, M.: Empirical evaluation of rectified activations in convolutional network. arXiv preprint arXiv:1505.00853 (2015)
28. Yalniz, I.Z., Jégou, H., Chen, K., Paluri, M., Mahajan, D.: Billion-scale semi-supervised learning for image classification. arXiv preprint arXiv:1905.00546 (2019)
29. Ye, M., Zhang, L., Giannarou, S., Yang, G.-Z.: Real-time 3D tracking of articulated tools for robotic surgery. In: Ourselin, S., Joskowicz, L., Sabuncu, M.R., Unal, G., Wells, W. (eds.) MICCAI 2016. LNCS, vol. 9900, pp. 386–394. Springer, Cham (2016). https://doi.org/10.1007/978-3-319-46720-7_45

30. Zhong, Z., Zheng, L., Kang, G., Li, S., Yang, Y.: Random erasing data augmentation. arXiv preprint arXiv:1708.04896 (2017)
31. Zhou, J., Payandeh, S.: Visual tracking of laparoscopic instruments. J. Autom. Control Eng. **2**(3), 234–241 (2014)

Development of an Augmented Reality System Based on Marker Tracking for Robotic Assisted Minimally Invasive Spine Surgery

Francesca Pia Villani[1](✉), Mariachiara Di Cosmo[1],
Álvaro Bertelsen Simonetti[2], Emanuele Frontoni[1], and Sara Moccia[1]

[1] Department of Information Engineering, Università Politecnica delle Marche,
Ancona, Italy
francesca.pia.v@gmail.com, dicosmo.mariachi@gmail.com,
{e.frontoni,s.moccia}@univpm.it
[2] eHealth and Biomedical Applications, Vicomtech, San Sebastián, Spain
abertelsen@vicomtech.org

Abstract. Spine surgery is nowadays performed for a great number of spine pathologies; it is estimated that 4.83 million surgeries are carried out globally each year. This prevalence led to an evolution of spine surgery into an extremely specialized field, so that traditional open interventions to the spine were integrated and often replaced by minimally invasive approaches. Despite the several benefits associated to robotic minimally invasive surgeries (RMIS), loss of depth perception, reduced field of view and consequent difficulty in intraoperative identification of relevant anatomical structures are still unsolved issues. For these reasons, Augmented Reality (AR) was introduced to support the surgeon in surgical applications. However, even though the irruption of AR has promised breakthrough changes in surgery, its adoption was slower than expected as there are still usability hurdles. The objective of this work is to introduce a client software with marker-based optical tracking capabilities, included into a client-server architecture that uses protocols to enable real-time streaming over the network, providing desktop rendering power to the head mounted display (HMD). Results relative to the tracking are promising (Specificity $= 0.98 \pm 0.03$; Precision $= 0.94 \pm 0.04$; Dice $= 0.80 \pm 0.07$) as well as real-time communication, which was successfully set.

Keywords: Augmented Reality · Marker tracking · Spine surgery

1 Introduction

The incidence of spinal disorders has undergone a huge increase in the last few years, reaching epidemic extensions. It is estimated that globally 4.83 million spinal operations are annually performed [6]. This growing trend was related to

© Springer Nature Switzerland AG 2021
A. Del Bimbo et al. (Eds.): ICPR 2020 Workshops, LNCS 12661, pp. 461–475, 2021.
https://doi.org/10.1007/978-3-030-68763-2_35

the aging population, greater disease prevalence, improved diagnostic modalities, development of new surgical techniques, and an increased number of spine surgeons [15]. Over the past few decades, spine surgery has become an extremely specialized field; highly complex procedures are more and more performed, across all age groups, and often through minimally invasive approaches [19]. Traditional open interventions to the spine, although familiar to surgeons, are associated with morbidity, increased blood loss, increased postoperative pain, longer recovery time, and impaired spinal functions. Thus, less invasive techniques that can provide equivalent or better outcomes compared with conventional spine surgery, while limiting approach-related surgical morbidity, are desirable [16].

Minimally invasive surgeries (MIS) procedures are characterized by small surgical incisions, minimal disruption of musculature, intraoperative monitoring and imaging modalities. The use of small surgical incisions was associated with less surgical-related morbidity, better long-term postoperative outcomes, and decreased costs mostly due to shorter postoperative hospital stays [20]. Under this scenario, surgical robots emerged during the 90s [10] and from then, progresses to optimize the use of robotic technology were made. Robotic minimally invasive surgeries (RMIS) in fact, increase surgeons ability with tremor compensation, allowing the use of more sophisticated control strategies (e.g., virtual fixture) [12]. Nevertheless, as spine surgeons are familiar with the patient anatomy when it can be directly visualized and MIS generally limits the area of surgical interest, certain key anatomic landmarks can be lost [17]. Moreover, RMIS is associated with reduced field of view and consequent difficulty in intraoperative identification of relevant anatomical structures. For these reasons, RMIS is more technically demanding; however operative times and complications are reduced as the surgeon becomes more experienced with the technique [11].

A solution for these problems can be found in augmented reality (AR), an imaging technology which provides digital contents that augment information directly on the real world. AR creates opportunities for new medical treatments: in fact, various imaging methods can be used to guide surgical instruments through the body without the physician direct sight [5]. Thanks to AR, sensitive structures placed in the surgical field can be identified in the pre-operative plan, and their intra-operative position can be retrieved in order to avoid the interaction of the robot with these structures [1]. Moreover, AR enables the surgeon direct sight on the surgical area, without the need to switch between screen and patient, and it is associated with increased safety and accuracy, and reduced amount of intraoperative radiation (as it happens when using fluoroscopy) [23].

Although AR is not a new technology and it has made progresses in the past years, with considerable benefits for both patient care and surgical performance, its adoption in the surgical field is still impeded by a set of technological barriers regarding handling, feasibility, hardware limitations, and the high cost of the instruments, which reduces the possibility of a wider development of this surgery [21]. One of the greatest limitations of AR is the low frame rate achieved by the head mounted display (HMD). Another problem is the need of real-time patient motion tracking, which is required to accurately position the instruments.

This is usually solved by positioning markers on the patient body or on the robot end-effector, whose position in space is measured by tracking devices. The marker to be placed is printed and then attached to the patient skin or to the robot end-effector. In the first case it is fixed using any kind of existing bio-compatible transparent tape or glue, paying attention to the placement of the marker in a smooth and planar site; in the second one, it is attached to the robot and then covered with a sterile transparent foil. The marker usually does not affect the intervention but problems could arise due to occlusion, which can occur if the marker is partially covered, and the augmented scene is suppressed or visualized on top of real objects (e.g. surgical instruments or surgeon hands) [7].

Multiple tracking technologies were proposed but they are characterized by different drawbacks: optical tracking requires direct line of sight between a set of stereo cameras and the markers -which is difficult to achieve in a crowded operating room (OR)- while electromagnetic tracking precision is reduced by the proximity of metallic objects. Optical tracking normally achieves tracking errors of several millimeters [22], which is not sufficient for high-precision interventions such as spine surgery. However, previous studies made with electromechanical tracking show the potential to achieve tracking errors $< 1\,mm$, which is a great improvement over existing technology [2].

In this work, a marker-based optical tracking is proposed, in which two-dimensional open source markers were used. It was tested and evaluated with different metrics and then integrated in a client-server architecture, on which computationally intensive tasks are performed on remote servers, leaving the wearable devices in charge of rendering the final frames transmitted as a video stream.

2   Methods

2.1   Marker System Selection

For the client software implementation, open-source libraries were used as a starting point for the development of a marker detection and tracking algorithm and for the integration of this algorithm on the HoloLens 1[1]. The marker tracking algorithm was developed taking as reference OpenCV[2], an open source Computer Vision library, which offers infrastructures for real time applications. In OpenCV the ArUco module, based on the ArUco library [8,13], was used to implement the tracker application. ArUco library was chosen among the many fiducial marker detection systems available, as it is the most popular and reliable one. In fact, ArUco is robust and able to detect and correct binary code errors, it is characterized by a good performance at a wide range of marker orientations and great adaptability to non-uniform illumination conditions [13,14]. The algorithm and the libraries were mainly implemented in C++.

---

[1] https://docs.microsoft.com/it-it/hololens/.
[2] https://opencv.org/.

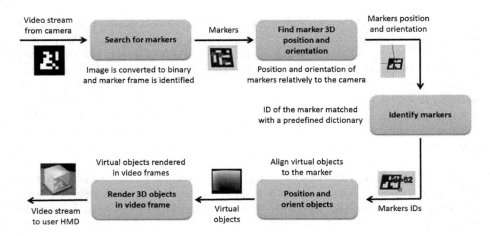

Fig. 1. Phases of ArUco marker tracking.

Experimental Design: The marker tracking algorithm was firstly tested on a desktop application acquiring video of markers with a smartphone, later Adobe After Effect [4] was used to simulate an intraoperative scenario and finally it was adapted to be used as Universal Windows Platform (UWP) application for HoloLens in the context of server-client communication. The diagram in Fig. 1 shows the phases of the tracking algorithm based on fiducial bitonal markers. ArUco markers are synthetic square markers composed by a black border and an inner binary matrix which determines their identifier (ID). The marker black border facilitates its fast detection in the image and the binary codification allows its identification and the application of error detection and correction techniques [8].

The marker size defines the dimension of the internal matrix (such as, a marker size of 4×4 is composed by 16 bits); markers can be found rotated in the environment, as the detection process is able to determine the original rotation, so that each corner is identified unequivocally. A dictionary of markers is the set of markers that are considered in a specific application, it is the list of binary codifications of each of its markers. The marker ID is the marker index within the dictionary it belongs to [7]. Starting from an image containing ArUco markers, the detection process must return a list of detected markers. Each detected marker includes the position of its four corners in the image (in their original order) and the ID of the marker. In this work a 4×4 dictionary was used.

Calibration of the System: Camera calibration is the process of obtaining intrinsic and extrinsic camera parameters which allows to determine where a 3D point in the space projects in the camera sensor (pose estimation). In this work the OpenCV routine was used [3,24]. OpenCV uses the pinhole camera model in which a scene view is formed by projecting 3D points into the image plane through a perspective transformation. The camera parameters can be divided into intrinsics and extrinsics. Intrinsic parameters include focal length of the camera lens in both axes, optical center of the sensor and distortion coefficients. The calibration was done by targeting the camera on a known structure, a flat pattern of alternating black and white squares (chessboard) [24].

By viewing this structure from various angles, it is possible to obtain the (relative) location and orientation of the camera for each image in addition to the intrinsic parameters of the camera. To provide multiple views, the board was rotated and translated while keeping the camera fixed to acquire the images (80 images of a 9×6 chessboard with square dimension of 24 mm). At the end of the calibration process, results were saved into an XML file (which contains intrinsics and extrinsics parameters, and camera matrix), and it was used in the routine to estimate the pose and to track ArUco markers.

2.2   Server-Client Communication

Once obtained a working desktop application it was adapted to be used with HoloLens 1 and included in the client-server architecture. DirectX[3] and WebRTC[4] (Web Real-Time Communications) were used to deliver desktop rendering power to HoloLens, so that the entire computation is done on the server side and HoloLens becomes a viewer. The proposed visualization architecture includes three interconnected applications, running at the same time: the HoloLens Client, the Windows Desktop Server, and a Signaling Server which manages the communication and connection between the first two. This architecture was built on the 3DStreamingToolkit[5] which uses the WebRTC protocols, as well as the NVEncode hardware encoding library from NVIDIA[6]. The hardware architecture used to establish the communication includes three components: a router, a desktop Windows server (hosting the rendering server and the signaling server[7]), and the HoloLens 1 running the DirectX HoloLens Client. A local network was used for communication as it enables control, reliability, transmission speed and latency. The peers interact with the signaling server to share the handshakes and start a direct peer-to-peer transmission. After this, data are sent directly between client and server.

2.3   Evaluation Protocol

The following metrics were used to qualitatively analyze the marker-based optical tracking system:

– *Localization accuracy of the marker pose:* it is important, in spine surgery, to test how accurately the position and orientation of the marker were determined by the localization algorithm.

[3] https://docs.microsoft.com/it-it/windows/mixedreality/.
[4] https://webrtc.org/.
[5] https://3dstreamingtoolkit.github.io/docs-3dstk/.
[6] https://www.nvidia.com/.
[7] https://github.com/anastasiiazolochevska/signaling-server.

– *Runtime performance:* to measure how long it takes to process a frame is an important parameter to consider: in fact, the algorithm being part of a real time application needs to have a fast processing time. A timer was integrated in the algorithms to get the time the system needs to process one frame. The running time was measured at a distance of 40 cm between the marker and the camera, a marker size of 4 cm and a static scene with constant lighting conditions. Furthermore, to ensure consistent results, the measurements were performed several times and finally the average of the detection rate for 100 frames was determined.

– *Robustness:* to test how the system behaves in different environment conditions. It is important to consider the environment in which a marker system is used, in fact parameters as illumination conditions and partial occlusion of the marker play an important role [9]. For these tests, a marker grid was used. The detection rate was first determined with three different light conditions, from low to strong light (typical condition in an OR). Moreover, in the OR it is often required to cover the marker with a protective transparent foil, which can lead to light reflection and therefore to partial masking of the marker. To simulate this scenario the marker grid was coated firstly with a transparent smooth foil, and then with a transparent crumpled foil.

All these metrics were evaluated by recording a set of videos containing a variable number of markers (1 to 35), with a Huawei P20 camera, using an image resolution of 1080×1920 pixels. All tests were performed using an Intel Core i5-7200U 2.50 GHz x 4-core processor with 12 GB RAM running Windows10 (10.0.18363).

The correct detection of markers is a critical aspect that must be analyzed to verify that the proposed algorithm is able to obviate redundant information present in the scene, extracting exclusively marker information. To assess the quality of the tracked marker pose, it is necessary to know the marker pose as ground truth. The ground truth used was extracted from the thresholding process involved in the detection of the marker. Then indexes were calculated in MATLAB 2018a[8]: multiple frames containing the marker in gray scale were analyzed and compared with a mask. The mask was created using the function roipoly, which creates an interactive polygon tool associated with the image displayed in the current figure and returns the mask as a binary image, setting pixels inside the Region Of Interest to 1 and pixels outside to 0. The segmented image is then confronted with the ground truth.

The quality of the proposed algorithm was assessed calculating the following spatial overlap-based metrics:

Accuracy: assesses the extent to which a binary segmentation method correctly identifies or excludes a condition. It is defined by: $Accuracy = \frac{TP+TN}{TP+FP+TN+FN}$, where TP, TN, FP, FN mean true positive, true negative, false positive and false negative, respectively.

---

[8] https://www.mathworks.com/products/matlab.html.

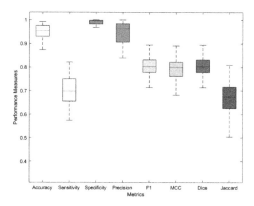

Fig. 2. Boxplot of the different metrics used to evaluate the localization accuracy of the pose estimation.

Sensitivity: also known as True Positive Rate (*TPR*) or Recall, defines the portion of positive voxels in the ground truth which are also identified as positive by the evaluated segmentation. It is defined by: $Sensitivity = \frac{TP}{TP+FN}$.

Specificity: or True Negative Rate (*TNR*), measures the portion of negative voxels (background) in the ground truth segmentation that are also identified as negative by the evaluated segmentation. It is defined by: $Specificity = \frac{TN}{TN+FP}$.

Precision: or Positive Predictive Value (*PPV*), is not usually used in validation of medical images, but it is used to calculate the F-Measure. It is defined by: $Precision = \frac{TP}{TP+FP}$.

F1-Measure: Fβ-Measure is a balance between precision and recall. Fβ-Measure is defined by: $FMS_\beta = \frac{(\beta^2+1)\cdot PPV \cdot TPR}{\beta^2 \cdot PPV + TPR}$. When $\beta = 1.0$ (precision and recall are equally important), it becomes F1-Measure (*FMS1*). It is also known as harmonic mean, and it is defined by: $FMS = \frac{2\cdot PPV \cdot TPR}{PPV + TPR}$.

MCC: or Matthew Correlation Coefficient, is used to assess performances, has a range of -1 (completely wrong binary classifier) to 1 (completely right binary classifier). It is defined by: $MCC = \frac{TP \cdot TN - FP \cdot FN}{\sqrt{(TP+FP)\,(TP+FN)\,(TN+FP)\,(TN+FN)}}$.

Dice: or Dice Similarity Index, evaluates the similarity between prediction and ground truth, by measuring the *TP* found and penalizing the *FP* found. It is defined by: $Dice = \frac{2\cdot TP}{2\cdot TP + FP + FN}$.

Jaccard: the Jaccard index or Jaccard similarity coefficient, evaluates the similarity and diversity of sample sets. It has a relation with Dice, and it is defined by: $Jaccard = \frac{TP}{TP + FP + FN}$.

3   Results

3.1   Localization Accuracy of the Pose Estimation

The establishment of how accurately the position and orientation of the marker is performed by the localization algorithm is particularly important. It was found that augmenting the distance between the marker and the camera the accuracy decreases, while with a fixed distance accuracy improves with increasing marker size. For these reasons all the tests were performed at a distance of 40–60 cm from the sensor to the marker, using a marker size of 3–5 cm.

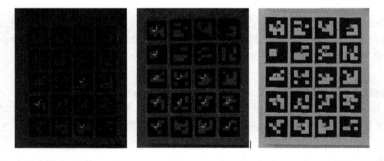

Fig. 3. Detection of an ArUco marker grid under three different light conditions. From left: low light, medium light and bright light.

Table 1. Average time of detection and pose estimation.

Process	Runtime: 1 marker ($\frac{ms}{frame}$)	Runtime: 5 × 4 grid ($\frac{ms}{frame}$)
Marker detection	224.74	502.68
Pose estimation	231.07	552.65

The performance was assessed through several spatial overlap-based metrics calculated on individual frames from video sensor data. All the items were individually tested to verify the presence of a match between the frame under test and the ground truth, for each video frame. The performance on each individual frame was then averaged over the total to develop performance scores. The statistics of the computed performance measures are reported in Fig. 2 which shows the relative boxplots; while mean values and standard deviation (*SD*) are listed in Table 2.

Table 2. Mean value and standard deviation of the metrics used to evaluate the localization accuracy of the pose estimation.

Metric	Mean	SD
Accuracy	0.94	±0.04
Sensitivity	0.70	±0.10
Specificity	0.98	±0.03
Precision	0.94	±0.07
F1	0.80	±0.07
MCC	0.78	±0.08
Dice	0.80	±0.07
Jaccard	0.67	±0.10

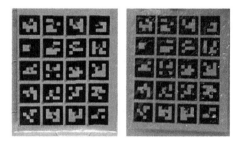

Fig. 4. Samples of the detection of ArUco marker grid covered with largely smooth foil (left) and covered with a crumple-rich foil (right).

Specificity which indicates the ability to correctly generate a negative result when the marker is not present in the scene (high TNR) has shown the highest value among the indexes.

3.2 Runtime

Results of the experiments done to determine the time required to process a frame to detect and estimate the pose of a single marker of size 4 cm and of 20 markers arranged on a 5×4 grid, at a camera distance of 40 cm in a stationary scene with constant illumination conditions, are presented in Table 1.

3.3 Robustness to External Influences

The detection rates of the markers for each of the following conditions were calculated dividing the number of markers correctly identified by the total number of markers in the grid. Figure 3 shows a picture of the camera detecting the marker grid at the three different light conditions (dark, medium and bright), while Fig. 4 shows the influence of covering on marker detection. Detection rates of each trial are shown in Table 3. Even with medium lighting the detection of ArUco is possible with 42.7% in almost half of all images, while with a very low lighting the rate decreases at 3.5%.

Table 3. Detection rates under different lighting and covering conditions.

Condition	Detection rate
Low light	3.5%
Medium light	42.7%
Bright light	100%
Smooth foil	98%
Crumpled foil	47%

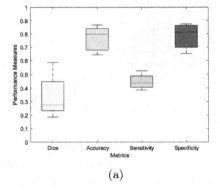

(a)

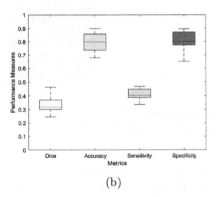

(b)

Fig. 5. Localization accuracy metrics. (a) Boxplot of the metrics used to evaluate the marker detection ability in condition of medium light. (b) Boxplot of the metrics used to evaluate the marker detection ability in presence of a crumpled covering foil.

Results obtained covering the marker grids with transparent foils to simulate the sterile coating of the OR are dependent on the degree of crumpling: the higher the folds, the stronger the generated light reflection and the lower the detection rate.

In Fig. 5 the boxplot of metrics used to evaluate the localization accuracy in presence of dark light and in presence of a crumpled foil covering the marker are shown. Significant differences were observed in *Dice* index and the *Sensitivity* values if compared with the ones of the detection performance in optimal conditions. Reduced marker detection rates in these conditions can be also observed in the reduction of these values. *Accuracy* and *Specificity* have similar values both in the optimal condition and in case of external disturbances.

3.4 Communication and 3D Visualization

Communication was successfully set between the rendering server and two different DirectX clients (desktop and HoloLens). Once launched the signaling server, the rendering server and the client were connected to it and started to exchange information.

As a first trial to test the communication, a spinning cube was remotely rendered and visualized on a desktop client in the 3DStreamingToolkit environment. Then, the same desktop client was used to receive a rendered frame implemented on a VTK server. These tests were conducted on a computer receiving the frames from a remote host running both signaling and rendering servers; 60 frames per second (FPS) were obtained almost all the time.

Later, communication with the HoloLens client was verified. The client was developed in Visual Studio 2017 as UWP application and then deployed on HoloLens. An application that renders the model of a vertebra developed on a Unity rendering server was transmitted and effectively visualized on HoloLens as can be seen in Fig. 6.

Fig. 6. Picture of the HoloLens client showing the model of a vertebra that was previously remotely rendered on a Unity server and then transmitted to the headset through 3DStreamingToolkit communication architecture.

4 Discussion

Results of spatial overlap-based metrics are promising: among the indexes *Specificity* shows the highest value (mean $= 0.98 \pm 0.03$), thus the algorithm rarely gives positive results in absence of marker. This is most likely due to the small dimension of the marker and so to the small portion occupied in the scene, which leads to the identification of a lot of *TN*. This finding is further strengthened by the result of the *FPR* as function of the marker size in the image, which resulted to be zero in all cases tested.

Accuracy (mean $= 0.94 \pm 0.04$) and *Precision* (mean $= 0.94 \pm 0.07$) have the highest values after *Specificity*. *Accuracy* is a measure of the system performance in relation to both correctly detecting and correctly rejecting targets, so a high value can be interpreted as the capability of the algorithm to consider only *TP*, rejecting *FP*. This is also confirmed by the high resultant value of *Precision*, which is the fraction of detected items that are correct, and the high value of the *F1-measure* (mean $= 0.80 \pm 0.07$) which gives an estimate of the accuracy of the system under test.

The *Dice* coefficient is the most used statistical metric in validating segmentations. Besides the direct comparison between manual and ground truth segmentations, usually the *Dice* is used to measure reproducibility (repeatability) and accuracy of manual segmentations and the spatial overlap accuracy [25]. Results show a high value of the *Dice* coefficient (mean $= 0.80 \pm 0.07$), suggesting that the outcomes match the ground truth with a high extent, thus the marker is detected in the correct position. The *F1-measure* is mathematically equivalent to *Dice* [18], in fact their resultant values are the same.

The *MCC* index shows how the manually segmented image is correlated with the annotated ground truth. The promising resultant value of the index (mean $= 0.79 \pm 0.08$) indicates the consistency and capability of the proposed algorithm in correctly identifying, tracking and estimating the pose of markers in the scene.

In this study, the optimal size of the marker was determined based on the detection rate, resulting in a marker dimension of 3–5 cm at a distance of 40–60 cm from the sensor. It was also observed that the dimension of the marker and the distance from the camera influence the computation speed: the higher is the marker size and the smaller is the distance from the camera, the faster is the detection. This finding is in accordance with the literature [13].

Regarding the runtime, the obtained results (224.74 ms for single marker detection and 231.07 ms for pose estimation) were found to be a bit higher than in the literature [7]. However, as the selection of the camera influences the runtime of the marker detection, the obtained runtime is supposed to be influenced by the used hardware (both camera and computer used to process the frames). It was also observed that increasing the number of markers in the scene the runtime increases.

About findings on the capability of the algorithm to correctly identify markers in worse conditions like partial occlusion, results show that noise resilience decreases (detection rate $= 47\%$) when covering the markers with a crumpled foil: this is due to the higher reflection that is generated, thus the inability of the algorithm to find the corners of the markers and estimate their IDs. While for the illumination criteria, detection rate decrease up to 3.5%, suggesting the inability of the algorithm to detect markers in condition of reduced illumination. Results from the boxplots of metrics used to evaluate the algorithm performance in these conditions show that the match with the ground truth is low (*Dice*), so the marker is often detected in the wrong position. On the other hand, *Accuracy* and *Specificity* have similar values both in the optimal condition and in case of external disturbances, and this is due to the fact that even with worse conditions a smaller percentage of markers is correctly identified.

Results related to the communication and 3D visualization are still partial. If on one side the communication between the rendering server and the DirectX clients was successfully set, on the other side the client needs to be completed integrating the tracking algorithm to send information regarding the marker pose to the robot, in order for the server to read the last transform messages coming from the glasses and tracker, and to upload its position. To do so, the tracking applications already adapted for this work need to be fused together to obtain a final one capable to access the camera frame and use the OpenCV libraries.

5   Conclusion

This paper is part of a project which was developed starting from the idea to provide assistance to the surgeon during spine surgery, by visualizing the area of interest using an AR device. More practically, the proposed system will help the surgeon both to develop pre-operative plans (to study the patient's anatomy through different imaging techniques used to generate the AR scene to be visualized on the HMD and overlaid on specific anatomical sites) and to visualize patient structures without cutting or disrupting tissues, to perform low-risk surgeries, and minimize side effects and operational time.

To reach this goal a marker tracking algorithm was developed to detect ArUco markers attached to the patient's skin or to the robot end effector to track movements. ArUco markers characteristics (reliability, robustness, ability to detect and correct errors, good performance, adaptability to non-uniform illumination conditions) led to the choice of this system among the many available [13].

To use the developed algorithm directly on HoloLens and integrate it in an AR application, it was included in a system which permits real time communication between server and client through the WebRTC protocol. The HoloLens in this architecture was used as client to receive frames remotely rendered on a desktop server, via a signaling server. The use of remote rendering allows the offloading of heavy GPU tasks from the HoloLens client, increasing the possibility to achieve a real-time framerate of 30 FPS.

At present the client-server system is still at an early stage, the integration of the tracking algorithm directly on the headset system is essential to transmit the marker pose to the robot allowing it to adjust its position accordingly. Nevertheless, the current state of the application provides an evidence that this architecture and current materials may be implemented with positive outcomes. In fact, with current tools, the tested application shows the 3DStreamingToolkit desktop client receiving the rendered frame, with 60 FPS obtained almost all the time. This result is promising as the final goal for the use of AR in the surgical world is the achievement of a real-time framerate of 30 FPS at least.

As a next step, deep learning techniques could also be included in the marker tracking to improve the detection process and provide better performances for pose estimation. However, to avoid delays and keep the real-time characteristics needed for this system, this step should be offloaded on the server side.

To conclude, it is acknowledged that additional research is required to improve the proposed architecture so that, once attained the required adjustments, the presented system has the potential to be used in the medical field.

References

1. Bernhardt, S., Nicolau, S.A., Soler, L., Doignon, C.: The status of augmented reality in laparoscopic surgery as of 2016. Med. Image Anal. **37**, 66–90 (2017)
2. Bertelsen, Á., et al.: Collaborative robots for surgical applications. In: Ollero, A., Sanfeliu, A., Montano, L., Lau, N., Cardeira, C. (eds.) ROBOT 2017. AISC, vol. 694, pp. 524–535. Springer, Cham (2018). https://doi.org/10.1007/978-3-319-70836-2_43
3. Bradski, G., Kaehler, A.: Camera models and calibration, Chapter 11, pp. 370–403. O'REILLY Media (2008)
4. Christiansen, M.: Adobe After Effects CC Visual Effects and Compositing Studio Techniques. Adobe Press, San Francisco (2013)
5. De Paolis, L.T., Aloisio, G.: Augmented reality in minimally invasive surgery. In: Mukhopadhyay, S.C., Lay-Ekuakille, A. (eds.) Advances in Biomedical Sensing, Measurements, Instrumentation and Systems. LNEE, vol. 55, pp. 305–320. Springer, Heidelberg (2010). https://doi.org/10.1007/978-3-642-05167-8_17
6. Fiani, B., et al.: Impact of robot-assisted spine surgery on health care quality and neurosurgical economics: a systemic review. Neurosurg. Rev. **43**(1), 17–25 (2018)
7. Garrido-Jurado, S., Muñoz-Salinas, R., Madrid-Cuevas, F., Marín-Jiménez, M.: Automatic generation and detection of highly reliable fiducial markers under occlusion. Pattern Recogn. **47**(6), 2280–2292 (2014)
8. Garrido-Jurado, S., Muñoz-Salinas, R., Madrid-Cuevas, F., Medina-Carnicer, R.: Generation of fiducial marker dictionaries using mixed integer linear programming. Pattern Recogn. **51**, 481–491 (2016)
9. Kunz, C., Genten, V., Meissner, P., Hein, B.: Metric-based evaluation of fiducial markers for medical procedures. In: Medical Imaging 2019: Image-Guided Procedures, Robotic Interventions, and Modeling (2019)
10. Kwoh, Y., Hou, J., Jonckheere, E., Hayati, S.: A robot with improved absolute positioning accuracy for CT guided stereotactic brain surgery. IEEE Trans. Biomed. Eng. **35**(2), 153–160 (1988)
11. Lau, D., Han, S.J., Lee, J.G., Lu, D.C., Chou, D.: Minimally invasive compared to open microdiscectomy for lumbar disc herniation. J. Clin. Neurosci. **18**(1), 81–84 (2011)
12. Moccia, S., et al.: Toward improving safety in neurosurgery with an active handheld instrument. Ann. Biomed. Eng. **46**(10), 1450–1464 (2018)
13. Romero-Ramirez, F.J., Muñoz-Salinas, R., Medina-Carnicer, R.: Speeded up detection of squared fiducial markers. Image Vis. Comput. **76**, 38–47 (2018)
14. Sagitov, A., Shabalina, K., Lavrenov, R., Magid, E.: Comparing fiducial marker systems in the presence of occlusion. In: 2017 International Conference on Mechanical, System and Control Engineering (ICMSC) (2017)
15. Salzmann, S.N., et al.: Cervical spinal fusion: 16-year trends in epidemiology, indications, and in-hospital outcomes by surgical approach. World Neurosurg. **113**, e280–e295 (2018)
16. Schwender, J., Holly, L., Transfeldt, E.: Minimally Invasive Posterior Surgical Approaches to the Lumbar Spine, 5th edn. Saunders/Elsevier, London (2006)

17. Syed, O.N., Foley, K.T.: History and Evolution of Minimally Invasive Spine Surgery. In: Phillips, F.M., Lieberman, I.H., Polly, D.W. (eds.) Minimally Invasive Spine Surgery. AISC, pp. 3–13. Springer, New York (2014). https://doi.org/10.1007/978-1-4614-5674-2_1

18. Taha, A.A., Hanbury, A.: Metrics for evaluating 3D medical image segmentation: analysis, selection, and tool. BMC Med. Imaging **15**(1), 29 (2015)

19. Tandon, M.: Spinal surgery, Chapter 24, pp. 399–439. Hemanshu Prabhakar (2017)

20. Topcu, O., Karakayali, F., Kuzu, M., Aras, N.: Comparison of long-term quality of life after laparoscopic and open cholecystectomy. Surg. Endosc. **17**(2), 291–295 (2003)

21. Vadalà, G., De Salvatore, S., Ambrosio, L., Russo, F., Papalia, R., Denaro, V.: Robotic spine surgery and augmented reality systems: a state of the art. Neurospine **17**(1), 88–100 (2020)

22. Vávra, P., et al.: Recent development of augmented reality in surgery: a review. J. Healthcare Eng. **2017**, 1–9 (2017). https://doi.org/10.1155/2017/4574172. Article ID 4574172

23. Yoo, J.S., Patel, D.S., Hrynewycz, N.M., Brundage, T.S., Singh, K.: The utility of virtual reality and augmented reality in spine surgery. Ann. Transl. Med. **7**(S5), S171 (2019)

24. Zhang, Z.: A flexible new technique for camera calibration. IEEE Trans. Pattern Anal. Mach. Intell. **22**(11), 1330–1334 (2000)

25. Zou, K.H., et al.: Statistical validation of image segmentation quality based on a spatial overlap index. Acad. Radiol. **11**(2), 178–189 (2004)

Towards Stroke Patients' Upper-Limb Automatic Motor Assessment Using Smartwatches

Asma Bensalah[1]([✉])(iD), Jialuo Chen[1]([✉])(iD), Alicia Fornés[1]([✉])(iD),
Cristina Carmona-Duarte[2]([✉])(iD), Josep Lladós[1]([✉])(iD),
and Miguel Ángel Ferrer[2]([✉])(iD)

[1] Computer Vision Center, Computer Science Department,
Universitat Autònoma de Barcelona, Barcelona, Spain
{abensalah,jchen,afornes,josep}@cvc.uab.es
[2] Instituto Universitario para el Desarrollo Tecnológico y la Innovación en
Comunicaciones, Universidad de Las Palmas de Gran Canaria,
Las Palmas de Gran Canaria, Spain
ccarmona@idetic.eu, miguelangel.ferrer@ulpgc.es

Abstract. Assessing the physical condition in rehabilitation scenarios is a challenging problem, since it involves Human Activity Recognition (HAR) and kinematic analysis methods. In addition, the difficulties increase in unconstrained rehabilitation scenarios, which are much closer to the real use cases. In particular, our aim is to design an upper-limb assessment pipeline for stroke patients using smartwatches. We focus on the HAR task, as it is the first part of the assessing pipeline. Our main target is to automatically detect and recognize four key movements inspired by the Fugl-Meyer assessment scale, which are performed in both constrained and unconstrained scenarios. In addition to the application protocol and dataset, we propose two detection and classification baseline methods. We believe that the proposed framework, dataset and baseline results will serve to foster this research field.

Keywords: Human activity recognition · Stroke rehabilitation · Fugl-Meyer assessment · Gesture spotting · Smartwatches

1 Introduction

Neuromuscular diseases (e.g. multiple sclerosis, Parkinson's disease) and strokes (cerebrovascular accident) involve a loss in the motor control system. In the particular case of stroke patients, the rehabilitation stage is crucial for minimizing, as much as possible, their deficits or motor disabilities towards their social reintegration. During the rehabilitation process, which mainly consists in drug therapy and rehabilitation exercises, the patient's neuromotor condition and progress must be evaluated. But above all, a continuous and accurate estimation is necessary during the early rehabilitation stages (e.g. first weeks) so that the neurologist can monitor the patient's improvement and adapt the rehabilitation therapy (e.g. modify the medication doses) before the patient's motor

© Springer Nature Switzerland AG 2021
A. Del Bimbo et al. (Eds.): ICPR 2020 Workshops, LNCS 12661, pp. 476–489, 2021.
https://doi.org/10.1007/978-3-030-68763-2_36

impairment becomes irreversible (the most notable progress is usually achieved during the first weeks). Unfortunately, the probability that the patient fully recovers the upper-limb mobility is very low (<15%) [1].

Monitoring the patient's neuromotor conditions involves Human Activity Recognition (HAR) tasks, preferably in a continuous unconstrained scenario. Methods for HAR use input data from video images [2] or from time series signals acquired with on-body sensors [3]. In the last fourteen years, most HAR systems have either focused on entire action recognition within a constrained scenario [4,5] or repetitive movements in an unconstrained scenario [6]. HAR in a constrained scenario refers to recognizing an action among a set of, solely, well defined actions (namely, target actions), in terms of action's content and performance style. Contrary, HAR in an unconstrained scenario means recognizing an action in a melange of well defined actions (like in a constrained scenarios) that are performed together with other actions either loosely defined or not defined at all (namely, non-target actions).

An action in HAR is a composition of body movements. In that sense, actions split into two categories: Actions with repetitive movements (e.g. walking/running are actions that involve the lifting foot movement repetitively), and actions with non-repetitive movements (e.g. grabbing something). Although it is difficult to segment actions and therefore recognize them in an unconstrained scenario, it is even more difficult when the (target) actions to recognize are compound of non-repetitive movements. The main reason is that the repetition can serve as context (like objects vs background in an image), hence, the classification and segmentation are context-aware. However, that context is absent in non-repetitive movements scenarios. This is the case of the upper-limb movements used for the Fugl-Meyer assessment (FMA) [7], one of the most frequently used metric scales for stroke patients.

Therefore, our motivation is to design an upper-limb assessment framework for stroke patients. This work has been developed in the context of the *3D kinematics for remote patient monitoring* (RPM3D) project[1]. The main goal of this project is to derive an objective estimator of the improvement of the patients' motor abilities during rehabilitation through the analysis of the 3D movements captured with smartwatches (worldwide affordable and non-intrusive technology). On the basis of the context of our study and the target population, we opted for "non-intrusive" sensors. Our choice went to Apple Watch Series 4, which is an FDA-cleared class 2 medical device and less expensive than existing high-end clinical devices. Moreover, in order to deploy a real assessment on the stroke patient's stated amid the rehabilitation process, we have designed an unconstrained data experimentation scenario, similar to the real conditions outside of a lab or therapy rooms, towards a continuous (24/7) patient monitoring.

Within this general objective in mind, in this paper we focus on the first part of this pipeline. We have simulated in the lab the gesture capture with smartwatch and the subsequent analysis conditions for stroke patients. This framework is exportable to 24/7 patient monitoring in daily life conditions. Thus, the first

---

[1] http://dag.cvc.uab.es/patientmonitoring/.

contribution of this work is the design of an evaluation protocol based on the Fugl-Meyer scale for constrained and unconstrained scenarios with non-repetitive movements. It consists of a set of target actions acquired from the movements of a study population. We got inspired from the FMA to outline the well defined target actions, to which we appended a set of loose (non-target) defined actions. In this way we simulate a real use case scenario, in which the patient wears the smartwatch all day (so, continuous recording). The dataset contains samples from healthy subjects and stroke patients and has been manually annotated. The dataset will be made available for public use to foster the HAR research for stroke rehabilitation purposes.

The second contribution of this work consists of an Activity Recognition Chain (ARC) for detecting and classifying gestures in the constrained and unconstrained FMA inspired scenario. Since the input data recorded by the sensors is a continuous time series data, actions must be detected as subsequences. We propose two segmentation approaches: in the first one, namely *action segmentation*, the subsequence covers the entire action, whereas in the second one, namely *gesture spotting*, the subsequence only covers a part of it (the gesture). We also propose two classification methods: the first one is based on Support Vector Machines (SVM), whereas the second is based on Convolutional Neural Networks (CNN). These methods can serve as baseline results. The correct detection and segmentation of these subsequences is important, so that they can be properly analyzed by the kinematic model [8], estimating the improvement of the neuromotor control system of the patient.

The rest of this paper is organized as follows. In Sect. 2 we overview the existing methods related to our work. Section 3 describes the experimentation protocol, based on the Fugl-Meyer Assessment. Section 4 describes our methodology in detail, including the data capturing, preprocessing and the gesture spotting. Section 5 shows the experimental baseline results, and Sect. 6 draws the conclusions and future work.

2   State of the Art

Efficient methods for HAR have to tackle with the traditional pattern recognition problems, namely intraclass variability (performance differences within the same individual) and interclass similarities (performance similarities between individuals) [9]. When gesture spotting is faced, the NULL class problem arises. When the objective is to spot a certain number of prototype (target) activities in the input signal, the rest of non-spotted (non-target) activities fall in the NULL class. The diversity in the NULL class makes it difficult to model. Moreover, there are specific issues related to the nature of the activity recognition problem and the data itself, for instance, the loose definition of a physical activity, the data labelling or the experiment design and setup [10].

Clarkson Patrick [11] approached the feasibility of computationally structuring human daily activities, based on the raw sponsors' data. In addition, they addressed the challenging task of structures' similarity, perplexity, prediction and classification. The picked sensors aim to reproduce the natural insect senses: the eyes (two cameras), the hearing (microphone) and gyros for orientation. As an extension of this work, a first algorithm that explores the efficiency of human activity recognition algorithm deployed with five biaxial accelerometers was proposed in [12]. Following the above cited works, HAR witnessed an enhance in the number contributions, mainly focusing on the segmentation and recognition tasks.

The signal segmentation is applied before the recognition step. This segmentation step is often addressed while designing the experimentation scenario. For example, for facilitating the ground-truthing and labelling process, users were asked to stand still for five seconds in [13]. Other works use Discrete wavelet transforms to segment the data [14] and split the input signal into approximations. One of the most perpetual approaches to face annotation scarcity in HAR is sliding windows [15–17]. A small sliding window can discard crucial information, while larger ones can contain action transactions. Thus, ascertaining the sliding window size is a vital step for bettering off an ARC. In another work [18], Convolutional Neural Networks (CNN) are employed to attribute each label timestep, instead of labeling an entire sliding window [15].

Concerning the recognition task, several methods were proposed. The Support Vector Machine's (SVM) efficiency and ease incited its wide use in HAR applications [19–21]. SVM performs the classification task via separating classes by linear decision border (hyperplane) in the feature space [22]. In tandem, sparse signal representations have also been popular in HAR [23,24]. Other statistical learning algorithms were broadly used, like Random forest [25,26]. In the interest of extracting more robust and scalable features to improve the recognition task, deep learning was introduced to HAR [27,28].

Clearly, one of the HAR field applications is health [6,29], inter alia Neurorehabilitation. Cognate to our work study case, in [5] an ARC was implemented to track long-term tremor activities and the treatment effect. In [30] authors provided a proof-of-principle regarding the identification of a set of daily life activities within stroke patients. In [31], inertial sensors from high-end clinical devices were used for evaluating the functional improvement of stroke patients (in lieu of relying on diaries and self-questionnaire which does not bespeak the patient's real condition). Anyway, the above methods present several limitations: in [6,29], the data was collected from perfectly healthy subjects, while in [31] the work's aim was to classify the movements into purposeful and non-purposeful solely movements rather than recognizing them.

In summary, and from the state of the art review, we observe that there is still the need to design suitable HAR approaches for Neurorehabilitation in unconstrained and continuous scenarios using affordable and consumer electronic devices such as smartwatches.

3   Experimentation Protocol

This section is devoted to describe our experimental setup. As explained earlier, we are focusing in non-repetitive actions inspired by the Fugl-Meyer Assessment scale, an index to assess the sensorimotor impairment (i.e. the motor functioning, balance, sensation and joint functioning) in stroke patients. Concretely, we have defined four target (or key) movements $\mathcal{M}_i$ based on the following joint movements:

- Movement $\mathcal{M}_1$: shoulder extension/flexion.
- Movement $\mathcal{M}_2$: shoulder abduction/abduction.
- Movement $\mathcal{M}_3$: external/internal shoulder rotation.
- Movement $\mathcal{M}_4$: elbow flexion/extension

a)   b)   c)   d)

Fig. 1. Target (key) movements based on the Fugl-Meyer Assessment. a) Movement 1; b) Movement 2; c) Movement 3; d) Movement 4.

These movements are illustrated in Fig. 1. In order to analyze the performance of the detection and classification methods, we have recorded these movements both in constrained and unconstrained scenarios. Thus, we designed two scenarios, namely L1 and L2, as follows:

- Scenario L1: It is a constrained scenario which consists in performing the same type of target movement in a sequence, but alternating the arm (left, right or both). Thus, the user performs the movement $\mathcal{M}_i, i \in [1,4]$, as follows:
  1. Perform movement $\mathcal{M}_i$ with the dominant hand;
  2. Perform movement $\mathcal{M}_i$ with the non-dominant hand;
  3. Perform movement $\mathcal{M}_i$ with both hands, simultaneously;
  Between each movement, the user is asked to rest calm for 5 s.
- Scenario L2: It is an unconstrained scenario, in which the user is performing target $\mathcal{M}_i$ movements in between of longer sequences of non-target $\mathcal{R}_j$ movements. It requires carrying out a movement $\mathcal{M}_i$, $i \in [1,4]$, along with a movement $\mathcal{R}_j$, $j \in [1,19]$. The movements $\mathcal{R}_j$ have a loose definition in terms of the action content and the performing style (so they could be seen as background/noise), although they are common daily life activities. Examples of these kind of non-target but realistic movements include: eating, pouring water into a glass, drinking, brushing your teeth, aiming to an object with your arm, getting up, sitting on a chair, applauding, scratching the ear/shoulder, etc. In order to mimic real world conditions, we randomly alternate between target/key $\mathcal{M}_i$ movements and non-target $\mathcal{R}_j$ ones.

As it can be noted, the scenario L2 is more difficult than the L1 one because the sequence of movements is completely random (both the target and non-target ones), so the system can not benefit from information on previous actions.

4   Methodology

The first step of our ARC consists in the data capturing using two smartwatches, one wrist each. This data is recorded in the smartwatch and sent to the mobile phone and the cloud service. The following step consists in the preprocessing and segmentation. The action is classified either as a whole (sliding window), or only analyzing the relevant trimmed parts. The classification task is accomplished via an SVM or a CNN model. All these steps are described next.

4.1   Data Capture and Preprocessing

The data collection consists of recording sequences of movements while wearing two Apple Watch 4 (series 4), one on the left wrist and another one on the right wrist. We record data in both arms because stroke patients usually have one side of the body more affected than the other. The user-generated acceleration (without gravity) for all three axes of the device, unbiased gyroscope (rotation rate), magnetometer, altitude (Euler angles) and temporal information data have been recorded 100 Hz sampling rate and labelled in the smartwatch's internal memory. Once the data has been recorded, it is transmitted to the mobile phone and the cloud service.

We have developed an application for the smartwatch, as shown in Fig. 2, that allows selecting the recording time and the user's number. Once the user is ready to start recording, he/she can tap the corresponding button. When the two smartwatches are synchronized, they emit an audio and visual signal to inform that the recording has started. In this way, the activities and the data captured by the two watches are aligned and synchronized.

Fig. 2. Developed smartwatch application for data capturing.

Once the data is recorded, we load the data from the different sensors. In case of using the raw data from the IMU (accelerometer, gyroscope, magnetometer and attitude), the angular acceleration has to be transformed to linear one using quaternions (for instance with the AHRS algorithm[2]), obtaining also the Euler

---

[2] https://x-io.co.uk/open-source-imu-and-ahrs-algorithms/.

angles. Since the Apple Watch also gives the linear acceleration, we do not need to convert the angular to linear acceleration. Thus, we only have to preprocess the acceleration to minimize the sensor drift, which often leads to inaccurate measures.

4.2 Data Labelling

We have manually labeled the captured data for training the classification and gesture spotting approach. Thus, we isolate all movements and label them with the corresponding movement ($\mathcal{M}_i$ and $\mathcal{R}_j$). In this way, with the groundtruth timestamps from the user recordings, we can get the exact positions of the target movements and the time where the user was resting calm.

4.3 Segmentation

The segmentation step aims to obtain the subsequences that are candidates of being a target movement. These subsequences will be later classifed, whereas the rest of the sequence will be discarded. In order to detect a target movement, we explored two options: considering the entire action or only a part of it (gesture). Since L1 is a constraint scenario, it is easier to segmented because users make a pause between movements. Contrary, L2 is an unconstrained continuous stream signal, so it is more difficult to automatically segment given that L2 was designed to simulate real life conditions. Consequently, the segmentation is held differently in each scenario, as described next.

Scenario L1. In the constrained continuous scenario L1, we use the following segmentation options:

– *Action segmentation.* In this case, the sequences in L1 are segmented thanks to the very short rest time between the sequence of target movements. So, whenever an inappreciable movement is recorded by the sensors, the sequence is segmented.
– *Gesture spotting.* In order to speed-up the detection and classification time, we propose gesture spotting. Since the peak of the signal is widely employed as a classification feature in activity recognition [32,33], we also explore this possibility. Thus, instead of classifying the entire action, we only segment the relevant parts of the action. In our case, the relevant part is the positive peak and a small part of the motionless linear acceleration signal before and after that peak, as shown in Fig. 3.

Scenario L2. In the unconstrained continuous scenario L2, we opt for these two segmentation options:

– *Action segmentation with Non-overlapping Sliding windows.* Sliding windows have been traditionally used to exhaustively analyse sequential data, although they imply a high computational cost. Sliding windows are commonly used [15] in two forms: overlapping or non-overlapping windows. After various experiments, we experienced that non-overlapping windows are preferable. The optimal "size" of the sliding window had been experimentally set using the training data.

– *Gesture spotting.* In this scenario we also try to speed-up the detection using gesture spotting. Thus, as in L1, we segment the part around the positive peak of the sliding window, as shown in Fig. 3.

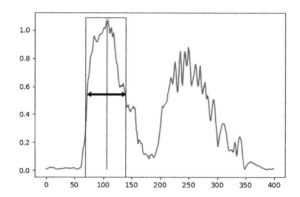

Fig. 3. Gesture Spotting illustration. The peak is shown in a vertical red line. The relevant part is the region covered by the rectangular bounding box shown in black color. (Color figure online)

4.4   Classification

Given the particularities and the few available labelled data, we have explored two different classification methods. The first one is a classical machine learning approach (SVMs), whereas the second one is a deep learning model (CNN).

Support Vector Machines (SVM). This first choice is motivated by the fact that SVM perform well in small datasets [34]. In addition, it has also been reported that SVMs are frequently used in classification medical task: decision-making, estimation of drug synergy, therapy synergy [35]. As explained in Sect. 2, Support Vector Machines have been typically used in HAR because of their efficiency in data classification and classes separation. The Apple Watch provides the following information: acceleration, rotation, yaw, pitch, roll. For classification, we do take into account all the provided sensors' information. In our case, we have evaluated different sets of feature vectors, and we have experimentally found that the most suitable minimalist feature set is the mean, the minimum, the maximum and the standard variation of a window.

Convolutional Neural Networks (CNN). The typical signal classification pipelines usually start with a pre-processing step, and subsequently, a feature extraction stage. Obviously, a good choice of the feature descriptors is important to avoid omitting relevant signal features that could affect the classification. So, to palliate the above mentioned issue, and contrary to the SVMs approach described above that uses a defined feature vector set, we alternatively opt to use the preprocessed raw signal as the input of the Convolutional Neural Networks model. In this classification model, we use all the time points of the window or gesture as input.

We propose a CNN model inspired from EEGNet [36], a compact CNN architecture intended to classify and interpret electroencephalography-based brain computer interfaces. The original architecture has been modified (concretely, the convolution dimensions) because the signal nature is different, both in terms of frequency and length. The input of in EEG is defined by (C,T), being C the number of channels and T the number of time points. Both C and T change in our case, since the recording frequency 100 Hz 128 Hz and the number of channels is 12. Accordingly, the first filter convolution size is set to be half of the sampling rate (50 in our case). In the first part of the architecture, two convolutions are carried out, in sequence. Next, we have a wise separable convolution, so that we reduce the number of parameters and computations while scaling up representational efficiency. Finally, the resulted features are passed to a softmax for the final classification. The proposed architecture is shown in Fig. 4.

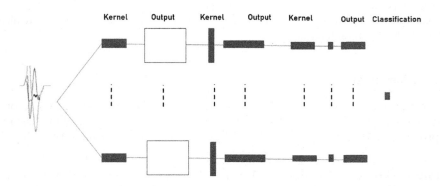

Fig. 4. CNN-based model classification architecture.

5   Results

In this section we describe the dataset and discuss the experimental results.

5.1   Dataset

The dataset is collected using the Apple Watch integrate sensors. We have recorded 25 healthy subjects and 4 patients in the L1 and L2 scenarios described before. The healthy population's age distribution is shown in Fig. 5a). The gender percentages are 48% women, 52% men. Concerning the patients, there are 3 men and 1 woman. The patients' age distribution is shown in Fig. 5b). This amount and distribution of users (in terms of age and gender) aims to provide enough variation in the performing style of each movement, and thus, ease the training of the classification algorithms.

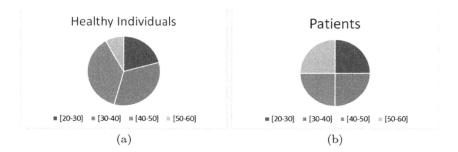

Fig. 5. Population statistics of healthy individuals (a) and patients (b).

In scenario L1, each user is recorded multiple times while performing each one of the four key target movements $[\mathcal{M}_1....\mathcal{M}_4]$. Afterwards, the user performs three L2 sessions. An L2 session consists of a random sequence of target $\mathcal{M}_i$ and non-target $\mathcal{R}_j$ actions. Obviously, all sessions are different since the sequence movements is randomly selected. This means that no user repeats the same sequence of movements.

The dataset will be available the project's website[3].

5.2   Results

The baseline results are presented in this subsection. For the CNN classifier, we randomly split our data into 60% for training, 20% for validation and 20% for testing. In the case of the SVM classifier, we use the same 20% for testing, whereas the remaining 80% is used for training (no validation set).

The performance results of the two approaches are shown in Table 1. Concerning the evaluation of healthy individuals' data, we observe that, in general, the SVM classifier obtains better results. The SVM classifier reaches an accuracy of 84% in L1. However, the random sequences and the size of the NULL class in the L2 scenario makes it hard to achieve similar classification results, so the SVM accuracy decreases to 61%. The CNN classifier obtains lower results than

---

[3] Dataset available at http://dag.cvc.uab.es/patientmonitoring/.

Table 1. Classification accuracies of the SVM and CNN-based classifiers in the test set. The higher the value, the better.

Scenario	Healthy subjects				Patients	
	Action segm.		Gesture spotting		Action segm.	Gesture spotting
	SVM	CNN	SVM	CNN	SVM	SVM
L1	84%	65%	55%	60%	56%	41%
L2	61%	59%	51%	53%	41%	35%

the SVM classifier. We believe that the small size of the dataset plays a major role in the lessening of the performance, because deep learning methods usually need more training data than classical machine learning approaches. As in the SVM classifier, the CNN's accuracy is slightly lower in the L2 scenario.

Regarding gesture spotting, we observe that classifying the entire action using sliding windows obtains better accuracies. However, the classification via gesture spotting highly reduces both the number of signals and also the length of the signal to evaluate. This suggests that it is more suitable for real-time applications running in smartwatches. Anyway, it must be noted that when classifying via gesture spotting, the results obtained by the SVM and CNN classifiers are quite similar, with a difference of 5 points in the L1 scenario (55% versus 60%) and only 2 points in the L2 scenario (51% versus 53%).

Concerning the evaluation of the patients' data, and given the few amount of training data and the results obtained with healthy subjects, here we only present the results related to the SVMs classifiers. We can notice a decrease in classification accuracy by more than 20%, in scenario L1, compared to healthy individuals. The gesture spotting reaches only 35% in the L2 scenario. The main reason behind this performance decrease is the fact that the patients experience hemiparesis (weakness of one side of the body), so the target movements are poorly performed. In consequence, it is extremely difficult to detect these target movements in the affected arm, especially in the first weeks of rehabilitation.

These results suggest that, given the difficulties in spotting the target movements in the impaired arm in patients, whenever the movements are symmetric (performed by the two arms at the same time), the gesture spotting might be based on the healthy arm solely.

6   Conclusion

In this work we have proposed an upper-limb assessment framework for assessing the neuromotor status of stroke patients. This application protocol is particularly designed for unconstrained scenarios and based on non-repetitive movements inspired on the Fugl-Meyer scale, with the aim to simulate more realistic evaluation scenarios. We have constructed an experimental database consisting of gesture recordings of healthy subjects and stroke patients, with the corresponding ground truth. In addition of this protocol and dataset, we have also proposed an Activity Recognition baseline (SVMs and CNNs). We do expect that this protocol, dataset and baseline results will foster the research in the rehabilitation assessment field.

Future work will focus on exploring data augmentation techniques for increasing the few available training data as well as transfer learning techniques for benefiting from similar HAR datasets. In the near future, we plan to integrate the spotting method in the full motor assessment pipeline, so that the automatic segmentation of the target movements will be the input of the kinematic analysis algorithm.

Acknowledgment. This work has been partially supported by the H2020 ATTRACT EU project (Grant Agreement 777222, TPPA 773, RPM3D), the Spanish project RTI2018-095645-B-C21, the FI fellowship AGAUR 2020 FI-SDUR 00497 (with the support of the Secretaria d'Universitats i Recerca of the Generalitat de Catalunya and the Fons Social Europeu), the Ramon y Cajal Fellowship RYC-2014-16831 and the CERCA Program/ Generalitat de Catalunya. C. Carmona-Duarte was supported by a Viera y Clavijo contract from the Universidad de Las Palmas de Gran Canaria. The authors would like to thank Oriol Ramos and Ángel Sánchez for fruitful discussions.

References

1. Lee, K.B., et al.: Six-month functional recovery of stroke patients: a multi-time-point study. Int. J. Rehabil. Res. **38**(2), 173 (2015)
2. Zunino, A., et al.: Video gesture analysis for autism spectrum disorder detection. In: 24th International Conference on Pattern Recognition (ICPR), pp. 3421–3426. IEEE (2018)
3. Rueda, F.M., Fink, G.A.: Learning attribute representation for human activity recognition. In 24th International Conference on Pattern Recognition (ICPR), pp. 523–528. IEEE (2018)
4. Zinnen, A., van Laerhoven, K., Schiele, B.: Toward recognition of short and non-repetitive activities from wearable sensors. In: Schiele, B., et al. (eds.) AmI 2007. LNCS, vol. 4794, pp. 142–158. Springer, Heidelberg (2007). https://doi.org/10.1007/978-3-540-76652-0_9
5. Kim, J., Parnell, C., Wichmann, T., DeWeerth, S.P.: Longitudinal wearable tremor measurement system with activity recognition algorithms for upper limb tremor. In: 38th Annual International Conference of the IEEE Engineering in Medicine and Biology Society (EMBC), pp. 6166–6169 (2016)
6. Morris, D., Saponas, T.S., Guillory, A., Kelner, I.: Recofit: using a wearable sensor to find, recognize, and count repetitive exercises. In: Proceedings of the SIGCHI Conference on Human Factors in Computing Systems, pp. 3225–3234 (2014)
7. Oña, E.D., Jardón, A., Monge, E., Molina, F., Cano, R., Balaguer, C.: Towards automated assessment of upper limbs motor function based on fugl-meyer test and virtual environment. In: Masia, L., Micera, S., Akay, M., Pons, J.L. (eds.) ICNR 2018. BB, vol. 21, pp. 297–301. Springer, Cham (2019). https://doi.org/10.1007/978-3-030-01845-0_60
8. Schindler, R., Bouillon, M., Plamondon, R., Fischer, A.: Extending the sigma-lognormal model of the kinematic theory to three dimensions. In: Proceedings of the International Conference on Pattern Recognition and Artificial Intelligence (2018)

9. Akila, K., Chitrakala, S.: Highly refined human action recognition model to handle intraclass variability & interclass similarity. Multimedia Tools Appl. **78**(15), 20877–20894 (2019). https://doi.org/10.1007/s11042-019-7392-z

10. Bulling, A., Blanke, U., Schiele, B.: A tutorial on human activity recognition using body-worn inertial sensors. ACM Comput. Surv. **46**(3), 1–33 (2013)

11. Clarkson, B.P.: Life patterns: structure from wearable sensors. PhD thesis, Massachusetts Institute of Technology (2002)

12. Bao, L., Intille, S.S.: Activity recognition from user-annotated acceleration data. In: Ferscha, A., Mattern, F. (eds.) Pervasive 2004. LNCS, vol. 3001, pp. 1–17. Springer, Heidelberg (2004). https://doi.org/10.1007/978-3-540-24646-6_1

13. He, Z., Jin, L.: Activity recognition from acceleration data based on discrete consine transform and SVM. In: IEEE International Conference on Systems, Man and Cybernetics, pp. 5041–5044. IEEE (2009)

14. Bhat, G., Deb, R., Chaurasia, V.V., Shill, H., Ogras, U.Y.: Online human activity recognition using low-power wearable devices. In: IEEE/ACM International Conference on Computer-Aided Design (ICCAD), pp. 1–8. IEEE (2018)

15. Dehghani, A., Sarbishei, O., Glatard, T., Shihab, E.: A quantitative comparison of overlapping and non-overlapping sliding windows for human activity recognition using inertial sensors. Sensors **19**(22), 5026 (2019)

16. Zhang, Y., Zhang, Y., Zhang, Z., Bao, J., Song, Y.: Human activity recognition based on time series analysis using U-net. arXiv preprint arXiv:1809.08113 (2018)

17. Rastegari, E., Ali, H.: A bag-of-words feature engineering approach for assessing health conditions using accelerometer data. Smart Health **16**, 100116 (2020)

18. Yao, R., Lin, G., Shi, Q., Ranasinghe, D.C.: Efficient dense labeling of human activity sequences from wearables using fully convolutional networks. Pattern Recogn. **78**, 252–266 (2017)

19. Ahmed, N., Rafiq, J.I., Islam, M.R.: Enhanced human activity recognition based on smartphone sensor data using hybrid feature selection model. Sensors **20**(1), 317 (2020)

20. Garcia-Gonzalez, D., Rivero, D., Fernandez-Blanco, E., Luaces, M.R.: A public domain dataset for real-life human activity recognition using smartphone sensors. Sensors **20**(8), 2200 (2020)

21. Souza, W., Kavitha, R.: Human activity recognition using accelerometer and gyroscope sensors. Int. J. Eng. Technol. pp. 1171–1179 (2017)

22. Ayumi, V., Fanany, M.I.: A comparison of SVM and RVM for human action recognition. Internetworking Indonesia J. **8**(1), 29–33 (2016)

23. Zhang, M., Sawchuk, A.A.: Human daily activity recognition with sparse representation using wearable sensors. IEEE J. Biomed. Health Inform. **3**, 553–560 (2013)

24. Xu, W., Zhang, M., Sawchuk, A.A., Sarrafzadeh, M.: Robust human activity and sensor location corecognition via sparse signal representation. IEEE Trans. Biomed. Eng. **11**, 3169–3176 (2012)

25. Mehrang, S., Pietilä, J., Korhonen, I.: An activity recognition framework deploying the random forest classifier and a single optical heart rate monitoring and triaxial accelerometer wrist-band. Sensors **18**(2), 613 (2018)

26. Xu, L., Yang, W., Cao, Y., Li, Q.: Human activity recognition based on random forests. In: Liu, Y., Zhao, L., Cai, G., Xiao, G., Li, K., Wang, L., eds. 13th International Conference on Natural Computation, Fuzzy Systems and Knowledge Discovery, ICNC-FSKD 2017, Guilin, China, July 29–31, 2017, pp. 548–553. IEEE (2017)

27. Ha, S., Choi, S.: Convolutional neural networks for human activity recognition using multiple accelerometer and gyroscope sensors. In: International Joint Conference on Neural Networks (IJCNN), pp. 381–388 (2016)
28. Ordóñez, F., Roggen, D.: Deep convolutional and lstm recurrent neural networks for multimodal wearable activity recognition. Sensors 16(1), 115 (2016)
29. Tian, Y., Zhang, J., Chen, L., Geng, Y., Wang, X.: Selective ensemble based on extreme learning machine for sensor-based human activity recognition. Sensors 19(16), 3468 (2019)
30. Ryanne, J.M., et al.: Recognizing complex upper extremity activities using body worn sensors. PLoS One 10(3), e0118642 (2015)
31. Butt, A.H., et al.: Assessment of purposeful movements for post-stroke patients in activites of daily living with wearable sensor device. In: IEEE Conference on Computational Intelligence in Bioinformatics and Computational Biology (CIBCB), pp. 1–8 (2019)
32. Rosati, S., Balestra, G., Knaflitz, M.: Comparison of different sets of features for human activity recognition by wearable sensors. Sensors 18(122), 4189 (2018)
33. Pires, I.M., et al.: Pattern recognition techniques for the identification of activities of daily living using mobile device accelerometer. Electronics 9(3), 509 (2017)
34. Cervantes, J., Garcia-Lamont, F., Rodríguez, L., Lopez, A.: A comprehensive survey on support vector machine classification: applications, challenges and trends. Neurocomputing 408, 189–215 (2020)
35. Banegas-Luna, A.J., et al.: When will the mist clear? on the interpretability of machine learning for medical applications: a survey. arXiv preprint arXiv:2010.00353 (2020)
36. Lawhern, V.J., Solon, A.J., Waytowich, N.R., Gordon, S.M., Hung, C.P., Lance, B.J.: EEGNet: a compact convolutional network for EEG-based brain-computer interfaces. J. Neural Eng. 15(5), 056013 (2016)

Multimodal Detection of Tonic–Clonic Seizures Based on 3D Acceleration and Heart Rate Data from an In-Ear Sensor

Jasmin Henze[1,2(✉)], Salima Houta[1], Rainer Surges[3], Johannes Kreuzer[4], and Pinar Bisgin[1]

[1] Fraunhofer Institute for Software and Systems Engineering, Emil-Figge-Straße 91, 44227 Dortmund, Germany
jasmin.henze@isst.fraunhofer.de
[2] University of Bremen, Bibliotheksstraße 1, 28359 Bremen, Germany
[3] Department of Epileptology, University of Bonn Medical Center, Venusberg-Campus 1, 53127 Bonn, Germany
[4] Cosinuss GmbH, Kistlerhofstr. 60, 81379 München, Germany

Abstract. Patients with epilepsy suffer from recurrently occurring seizures. To improve diagnosis and treatment as well as to increase patients' safety and quality of life, it is of great interest to develop reliable methods for automated seizure detection. In this work, we evaluate a first trial of a multimodal approach combining 3D acceleration and heart rate data acquired with a mobile In-Ear sensor as part of the project EPItect. For the detection of tonic–clonic seizures (TCS), we train different classification models (Naïve Bayes, K-Nearest-Neighbor, linear Support Vector Machine and Adaboost.M1) and evaluate cost-sensitive learning as a measure to address the problem of highly imbalanced data. To assess the performance of our multimodal approach, we compare it to a unimodal approach, which only uses the acceleration data. Experiments show that our method leads to a higher sensitivity, lower detection latency and lower false alarm rate compared to the unimodal method.

Keywords: Multimodal seizure detection · Classification · Imbalanced data · Cost-sensitive learning · Heart rate data · 3D acceleration data · Tonic–clonic seizures · In-Ear sensor · EPItect

1 Introduction

Epilepsy is one of the most common neurological diseases: 0.4–1% of the world's population is affected [1, 2]. One of the disease's symptoms is the recurrent occurrence of epileptic seizures. Automated detection of these seizures could be beneficial in two ways: as a tool for seizure documentation, it could improve diagnosis and thereby treatment for patients, which highly depends on accurate information about the seizures that occur [3]. As a tool for alarming, it could notify caregivers when a seizure occurs. This way, severe injuries or even sudden unexpected death in epilepsy (SUDEP) could be prevented

© Springer Nature Switzerland AG 2021
A. Del Bimbo et al. (Eds.): ICPR 2020 Workshops, LNCS 12661, pp. 490–502, 2021.
https://doi.org/10.1007/978-3-030-68763-2_37

[2, 4, 5]. The gold standard used in clinical practice for seizure detection, a combination of video and electroencephalography (Video-EEG), is not practicable for the usage at patients' homes [6, 7]. Therefore, research aims at developing a mobile solution using other biomarkers for detection.

Within the project EPItect, an In-Ear sensor (see Fig. 1), developed by cosinuss°, forms the basis for mobile seizure detection. It is capable of measuring 3D acceleration and temperature. Additionally, it uses photoplethysmography (PPG) to calculate the patient's heart rate.

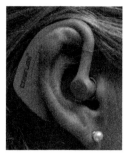

Since the different forms of epileptic seizures can vary greatly in the accompanying symptoms, research generally focuses on one specific seizure type or a group of similar types [8]. This work focuses on the detection of tonic–clonic seizures (TCS), since these are associated with a comparatively high risk of injuries, SUDEP and other complications [9]. As the name suggests, a TCS consists of tonic contractions of the whole body (stiffening of all muscles) followed by clonic convulsions (jerking movements of all limbs and head). TCS usually last

Fig. 1. In-Ear sensor, developed by cosinuss°, Copyright cosinuss°.

for 1–2 min (mostly up to 30 s for the tonic phase and 30–60 s for the clonic phase). However, if a TCS does not stop after 5 min, or if spontaneous breathing after cessation of the TCS fails, the patient needs medical attention as soon as possible [6, 10–12].

Preliminary work within the EPItect project used the acquired 3D acceleration data for classification of TCS [13], exploiting that these seizures lead to a stereotypical pattern in the 3D acceleration signal [14–16]. The K-Nearest Neighbor algorithm used obtained a sensitivity of 65.1%. One possibility to improve these results is to add another modality [5, 8]. Heart rate (HR) is especially promising since most of the heart rate changes caused by epileptic seizures occur at the start of a seizure [17]. Within the acceleration signal, the tonic phase is not as prominent as the clonic phase [16], hindering the detection of the TCS' start.

In this work, we present a multimodal approach, combining acceleration and HR data acquired by the In-Ear sensor. To evaluate this effect, we compare our method to an equivalent unimodal method, which only uses acceleration data. Additionally, we examine the influence of cost-sensitive learning, to evaluate its potential to improve results in this scenario of highly imbalanced data.

The paper is organized as follows: Sect. 2 presents the related works on seizure detection based on acceleration and HR data; Sect. 3 explains our method for detection of TCS; Sect. 4 presents our experimental results and a discussion. Finally, we draw a conclusion and outline future work in Section 5.

2 Related Work

Recently, the research on seizure detection with mobile devices has increased significantly. Pearl et al. [8] provide a literature review of seizure detection devices and their effectiveness for different seizure types. Movement is seen as one of the main pillars for the automated detection of seizures with predominant motor component like TCS [5, 6,

15, 16, 18]. In addition, the monitoring of autonomic dysfunctions (via cardiac, respiratory or other autonomic body signals), in particular with view to preventing SUDEP, is also considered relevant [5, 6, 18]. Various studies have also shown that a higher sensitivity and a lower false alarm rate can be achieved when several modalities are combined [4, 5]. Combining acceleration (as a modality for movement) and HR (as a modality for autonomic dysfunctions) is regarded to be promising [5, 8, 15, 18]. However, there are little efforts using these modalities in combination so far.

Van Andel et al. [19] have developed a system for the detection of nocturnal motor seizures (including TCS) based on 3D acceleration and ECG-based HR data. They acquired data using a shimmer bracelet from 23 patients who had 86 motor seizures in a total measurement time of 402 h. The system achieved a sensitivity of 71% to 87% with a false alarm rate of 2.3 to 5.7 per night (8 h). In a further approach, the same research group [20] used 3D acceleration with PPG-based heart rate acquired with a wristband on the upper arm (night watch). They recorded data from 28 patients in 1,826 nights who had 809 seizures. However, no Video-EEG was used as reference standard, but video recordings and reports (e.g. nursing reports). Overall, the median sensitivity per participant was 86% (95% confidence interval 77%–93%) with a false alarm rate of 0.03 per night (95% confidence interval 0.01–0.05).

For a broader review of non-EEG seizure detection, including works using 3D acceleration alone or in combination with other modalities and works using heart rate, see the literature review of Van de Vel et al. [5].

Despite the high number of publications regarding automated seizure detection, design and reporting of the corresponding studies differ greatly, e.g. regarding the daytime of data acquisition (day/night), patient groups, seizure types, reference standard (Video-EEG/no Video-EEG) and evaluation metrics. In addition, the definitions of true positives and false positives (false alarms), which build the basis for the different evaluation metrics that are used, can be very different or even unknown. For example, in [19], a detection counts as true positive if it occurs within 5 min before and after a seizure and false positives are counted as one false positive if they are less than 5 min apart. In [20], a detection counts as true positive if it occurs within 3 min before and 5 min after the start of a seizure and false positives are counted as one if they are less than 3 min apart. This makes the determination of the state of the art and a comparison of results very difficult. To improve this situation, Beniczky and Ryvlin [21] defined standards for testing and clinical validation of seizure detection devices.

Notwithstanding of all research recently published, there is still a need to improve seizure detection and to combine it with a device that patients accept for usage in their daily life. Our work contributes to seizure detection research with a multimodal approach, combining 3D acceleration and heart rate acquired with a novel In-Ear sensor. Different to the approaches mentioned above that combine these two modalities, we use Machine Learning methods for seizure detection. Additionally, we investigate the impact of cost-sensitive learning in this scenario of highly imbalanced data.

3   Method

3.1   Data Preparation

Data Acquisition. The data was acquired from epilepsy patients at the University Hospital Bonn (Germany) after informed consent (Ethikkommission der Medizinischen Fakultät der Rheinischen Friedrich-Wilhelms-Universität Bonn, No. 355/16). They were under continuous Video-EEG monitoring, which the physicians of the Department of Epileptology used to label start and end of every seizure that occurred during their stay. In addition, the patients were wearing the In-Ear sensor. It measures 3D acceleration (ACC) with a sampling rate of approximately 50 Hz. Additionally, it calculates the heart rate (HR) once per second based on the previous 6 s of PPG-signal. The device also provides a quality indicator for the calculated HR. Figure 2 and 3 show an example of ACC and HR measurements taken during a TCS within the EPItect project, showing the stereotypical pattern caused by this seizure type.

Data Preprocessing. Before feature calculation, we used the device's HR quality indicator to remove low quality HR data. Afterwards, we adjusted both ACC and HR data to a consistent sampling rate and interpolated missing values. In addition, the ACC data was filtered with a first order low-pass filter with a cut-off frequency of 0.5 Hz (as in [22]), splitting this data into parts of high and low frequencies. We calculated features using a sliding window of 10 s length and 50% overlap. Aside from standard statistical features (like mean and variance of the values within one window), we chose features from the literature used for the detection of TCS (from [7, 20, 23–27]). Additionally, we chose features used for the detection of tonic seizures in literature (from [22]) to increase the detection capabilities regarding the seizure's first phase and features used in activity recognition for better differentiation between seizure and similar non-seizure activities (from [28, 29]). We also considered experiences made at the University Hospital Bonn with seizure detection based on HR data, which include the calculation of features based on broader window sizes in addition to the 10-s-window. Thus, for each sample, some HR features are calculated based on a window of one minute and five minutes before and after the center of the 10-s-window. This is possible, since we only worked on retrospective data with a focus on documentation purposes for this first trial. For an alarming system, of course no data "from the future" could be used. In total, we obtained 208 ACC features and 110 HR features. Result of the feature calculation process is one feature vector (sample) per window. This gets the label "TCS" if at least 5 s (50%) of the window belong to a TCS and "no-TCS" otherwise.

3.2   Learning Process

For the learning process, we split the acquired data into three datasets: a training, a validation and a test set. To be representative for the whole dataset, each subset contains approximately 1/3 of the data, 1/3 of the TCS and 1/3 of the other seizures included in the dataset. Since the TCS greatly differ in length (between one minute and nine minutes), we also ensure that each subset contains 1/3 of the feature vectors labeled as TCS. Since we want the resulting model to generalize about different patients, the data of each patient is only contained in one of these sets.

Afterwards, we use feature selection and extraction methods based on the training set for the removal of features without a merit and the reduction of the resulting amount of features. On these features, we train different learning schemes (for both the unimodal and the multimodal approach): Naïve Bayes (NB), K-Nearest Neighbor (KNN), Support Vector Machines (SVM) and AdaBoost.M1 based on Decision Stumps (ABM1). These schemes are evaluated in different parameter combinations using the validation set. For each learning scheme, we choose the best parameter combination (see paragraph 'Determination of the "best model"' below) and train it again on the combined training and validation set. The final evaluation is conducted using the remaining test set.

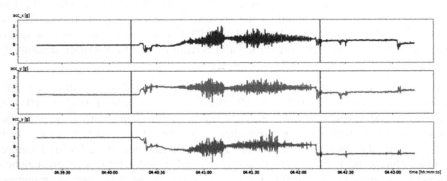

Fig. 2. Raw data of 3D acceleration recorded during the EPItect project using the In-Ear sensor (see Fig. 1). The y-axis represents the acceleration (acc_) of the x-, y-, and z- axes in gravity units, while the x-axis depicts the time of the recording. Within the two black vertical lines is the recording of a TCS (the same as in Fig. 3), showing the stereotypical pattern of this seizure type as it can be found in the literature [14, 16]

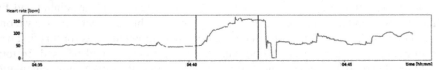

Fig. 3. Raw heart rate calculated using the PPG signal recorded during the EPItect project using the In-Ear sensor (see Fig. 1). The y-axis represents the heart rate in beats per minute (bpm), while the x-axis depicts the time of the recording. Within the two black vertical lines is the recording of a TCS (the same as in Fig. 2), showing the typical pattern of heart rate often found at the start of TCS (also see [6]). Since for the heart rate, features using sliding windows of maximal 5 min are used, there are 5 min plotted before and after the seizure

The Problem of Imbalanced Data. Since most classification algorithms internally assume the class ratio to be balanced, they tend to deliver suboptimal results if it is not. That is because the learning process if often guided by metrics like accuracy, which leads to a tendency to predict the majority class (the class for that more examples are given) to minimize the overall error. This is especially problematic if the cost for misclassification of the minority class (the class for that less examples are given) is higher than the cost for misclassification of the majority class. Cost-sensitive learning is an approach to include the costs of the different types of misclassifications into the learning process, which leads to a classifier that minimizes the overall costs instead of the overall error [30, 31, 31].

To evaluate if cost-sensitive learning can improve results in this scenario of highly imbalanced data, we add a cost-sensitive variant for each parameter combination of each learning scheme to the parameter optimization process.

Evaluation Metrics. Comparisons of different approaches to seizure detection are quite difficult because of the big differences in study design and reports [5, 16, 21]. To address this problem, Beniczky and Ryvlin [21] developed a standard for testing and clinical validation of seizure detection devices. For clarity of results and better comparability with future works, we use the evaluation metrics recommended by them:

- *Sensitivity*: Number of all detected TCS / Number of all TCS.
- *False Alarm Rate*: Number of false alarms per 24 h.
- *Mean Detection Latency*: Mean of the time from seizure onset to the detection time over all TCS.

In our work, a TCS counts as detected if at least one of the corresponding windows is correctly classified as "TCS". We use the first of these windows to calculate the detection latency. To determine the number of false alarms, we divide the samples labeled with "no-TCS" into segments with the median of the duration of TCS (2 min) defining the length of these segments. For the calculation of false alarms, the "no-TCS" segments that include at least one window classified as "TCS" are counted. This approach is taken from the work of Bender et al. [25].

For a more detailed insight into the detection abilities of our (final) algorithm, we calculate additional parameters based on the samples themselves:

- *Positive Predictive Value (PPV)*: Number of samples correctly classified as TCS / Number of samples classified as TCS
- *Mean Sensitivity over all TCS based on the first 1/3 of the samples belonging to a seizure (Sens first 1/3)*
- *Mean Sensitivity over all TCS based on the last 2/3 of the samples belonging to a seizure (Sens last 2/3)*

The split of the samples belonging to a seizure serves as an estimation of the tonic and clonic phase respectively, used because no labels for these are given. Since usually the tonic phase is much shorter than the clonic phase, we assume that it is located within the first 1/3 of a TCS, while the last 2/3 mainly consists of the clonic phase.

Determination of the "Best Model". Naturally, for seizure detection, it is desirable to achieve a sensitivity as high as possible, while keeping false alarm rate and detection latency as low as possible. We define a set of rules to determine the "best model" of a learning scheme for our application as follows: first, we look at all the models that achieve a mean detection latency below 30 s, the maximal latency that is considered as adequate by Beniczky and Ryvlin [21]. Of those models, we only regard the one / those with the highest sensitivity. Of the remaining models, we chose the one with the lowest false alarm rate.

4   Experiments

In this section, we describe our experiments, including the dataset used and the steps performed. Additionally, we present and discuss the experimental results.

4.1   Dataset

The data used within the experiments only contains measurements from 17 patients who had at least one TCS during the EPItect study. The corresponding recording time per patient varies between 5 and 250 h (mean: 80 h). These recordings contain 23 TCS (1–3 per patient) and 22 other seizures. In total, there are 2,059 h of measurements of which approximately 1 h belongs to TCS. This data leads to 966,978 samples labeled as "no-TCS" and 736 labeled as "TCS".

4.2   Experimental Setup

For the experiments, the open source software Weka [32] was used in version 3.8.3.

We used the feature selection method GainRatioAttributeEval and the filter PrincipalComponents for feature extraction. In the end, 27 features remain for the unimodal method and 44 for the multimodal method. For classification, we use the Weka classifiers NaiveBayes (no hyperparameters), IBk (for KNN, hyperparameter "KNN" was optimized), SGD (for SVM, hyperparameters "Epochs" and "learningRate" were optimized) and AdaBoostM1 (hyperparameter "numIterations" was optimized).

To add cost-sensitive learning as an additional hyperparameter to optimize for each classifier, we use Weka's CostSensitiveClassifier. For most of the learning schemes, misclassification costs are integrated directly into the learning process. Therefore, the CostSensitiveClassifier reweights each sample depending on the corresponding costs of misclassification. For KNN, since there is no actual learning process, the costs are applied during the classification process: it returns the class with the lowest misclassification costs. Since no misclassification costs are known for this domain, we start with the imbalance ratio between "TCS" and "no-TCS" data for this first trial (as is recommended as a starting point by [30]). This way, the misclassification costs for the class "no-TCS" is set to 1 and the misclassification costs for the class "TCS" is set to 1,300 (966,978 / $736 \approx 1,300$).

We use a separate script to get our chosen evaluation metrics from the classification result ("TCS" or "no-TCS") of each sample, since these are not available in Weka.

4.3   Results

Influence of Cost-Sensitive Learning. Table 1 contains an excerpt of the parameter optimization of the multimodal ABM1 with Decision Stumps, which (as an example) shows the influence of cost-sensitive learning to the results. Without it, sensitivity is relatively low (under 60%, not more than 3 of 7 TCS are detected), latency is pretty high (mostly around 2 min) while the false alarm rate is very low (below 1 false alarm per 24 h). Using cost-sensitive learning, sensitivity is very high (100%, all 7 seizures are detected, no matter how many iterations were performed) with a latency much lower than without cost-sensitive learning. On the contrary, false alarm rate goes up very strongly, leading to 34 to 175 false alarms per 24 h. We observe the same effect for SVM and KNN, while the influence on NB is very low.

Table 1. Excerpt of parameter optimization of multimodal AdaBoost.M1 with DecisionStumps

Cost-sensitive	#Iterations	Sens	Latency [s]	FA/24 h
No	50	0.286	37	< 1
	100	0.429	128	< 1
	500	0.571	111	< 1
	1,000	0.571	132	< 1
	5,000	0.571	142	< 1
Yes	50	1	24	175
	100	1	27	142
	500	1	38	98
	1,000	1	88	69
	5,000	1	138	34

Model Evaluation. Table 2 shows the results of the unimodal method, while Table 3 shows those of the multimodal method. Each table contains one line for each of the learning schemes (with the chosen "best" parameter combination) and the value for each performance metric (as explained in Sect. "3.2 Learning process"). The TCS related sensitivity is left out since all the methods were able to detect all TCS included in the test set. Additionally, there is one line describing the mean of the performance metrics over all learning schemes.

The mean detection latency of the unimodal results varies between 17 s (SVM) and 22 s (KNN) with a mean of 20 s. False alarm rate varies between 180 FA/24 h (NB) and 516 FA/24 h (SVM) with a mean of 359 FA/24 h. The mean sensitivity based on the first third of the TCS is generally lower than the mean sensitivity based on the last two-thirds: While the first varies between 0.551 (NB) and 0.815 (SVM) with a mean of 0.681, the second varies between 0.809 (NB) and 0.983 (SVM) with a mean of 0.913. The window related PPV is overall very low with values between 0.002 (SVM) and 0.012 (NB) with a mean of 0.008.

On the contrary, the mean detection latency of the multimodal methods varies between 8 s (KNN) and 19 s (ABM1) with a mean of 13 s. The false alarm rate varies between 138 FA/24 h (NB and KNN) and 348 (SVM) with a mean of 192. Again, the

Table 2. Results of the unimodal approach

Unimodal	Seizure related		Window related		
	Latency [s]	*FA/ 24 h*	*Sens first 1/3*	*Sens last 2/3*	*PPV*
NB	21	180	0.551	0.809	0.012
KNN	22	398	0.650	0.938	0.006
SVM	17	516	0.815	0.983	0.002
ABM1	21	341	0.709	0.953	0.009
Ø	**20**	**359**	**0.681**	**0.913**	**0.008**

Table 3. Results of the multimodal approach

Multimodal	Seizure related		Window related		
	Latency [s]	*FA/ 24 h*	*Sens first 1/3*	*Sens last 2/3*	*PPV*
NB	10	138	0.919	0.922	0.025
KNN	8	138	0.812	0.895	0.017
SVM	14	348	0.869	0.914	0.004
ABM1	19	142	0.823	0.934	0.019
Ø	13	192	0.856	0.91	0.016

mean sensitivity based on the first third of the TCS is generally lower than the mean sensitivity based on the last two-thirds: While the first varies between 0.812 (KNN) and 0.919 (NB) with a mean of 0.856, the second varies between 0.895 (KNN) and 0.934 (ABM1) with a mean of 0.91. The window related PPV is, again, overall very low with values between 0.004 (SVM) and 0.025 (NB) with a mean of 0.016.

4.4 Discussion

While both the unimodal and the multimodal approach can detect all the TCS within the test set (leading to a sensitivity of 100%), values of the other performance metrics differ between the two approaches. The mean detection latency is lower on average (13 s vs. 20 s) over all learning schemes for the multimodal approach. Additionally, it is lower for the multimodal variant of each learning model compared to its unimodal variant (e.g. 10 s vs. 21 s for NB). The same effect applies to the false alarm rate: It is lower in average over all learning models (192 FA/24 h vs. 359 FA/24 h) and lower for the multimodal variant of each model compared to its unimodal variant (e.g. 138 FA/24 h vs. 180 FA/24 h for NB). The comparison of the mean sensitivity on the first third of the TCS and the last two-thirds shows the same effect for both unimodal and multimodal result: It is higher on the last two-thirds for each of the learning models and variants. This indicates that all the models perform better detecting the clonic compared to the tonic phase of a TCS. While the mean sensitivity on the last two-thirds is very similar between all models (around 0.91 in average), the sensitivity on the first third is clearly higher for the multimodal methods. On average, it reaches a value of 0.856 compared to 0.681, indicating that the multimodal approach allows a better detection of samples belonging to the tonic phase of the seizure. Again, the value is also better for the multimodal variant of each learning model compared to its unimodal variant (e.g. 0.919 vs. 0.551 for NB). While the PPV approximately doubles its value from the unimodal to the multimodal methods, it is still very low, matching the corresponding false alarm rate. These results show that the multimodal approach outperforms the unimodal one. It allows better detection of TCS with a lower false alarm rate. As best method, we see the multimodal Naïve Bayes, which uses cost-sensitive learning and reaches a sensitivity of 100%, a mean detection latency of 10 s and a false alarm rate of 138 FA/24 h.

While these results are promising regarding sensitivity and detection latency, the false alarm rate is still much too high (the PPV is much too low) for real life applications. One reason for the very high false alarm rate lies in the focus on the evaluation criteria sensitivity and detection latency inducted by the rules defined in '3.2 Learning process' in the paragraph 'Determination of the "best model"'. Therefore, in most of the cases, a cost-sensitive variant of the learning scheme is chosen which improves detection (higher sensitivity and lower detection latency) but increases false alarm rate greatly. Since no appropriate cost values are known from the domain, the initial cost for misclassification of TCS samples was set to a very high value of 1,300 (in comparison to 1 for the misclassification of non-TCS samples), matching the class ratio of "non-TCS" and "TCS". Further experiments with varying cost values could reveal better fitting cost values that lead to a lower false alarm rate, while keeping sensitivity and mean detection latency within an appropriate range.

Another factor that probably influences the results is the availability of the HR data and its quality. In total, nearly 1/3 of the HR data was removed due to low quality. Especially during TCS, the HR data was often missing or of a quality below the threshold that led to removal. Since not all of the removed data could be interpolated, the frequency domain features calculated for the HR contained too many missing values to be useful. Since the calculation of the HR data is based on PPG measurements, it is of great importance that the sensor sits in the right position all the time. Due to the strong movements during a TCS, the sensor can get out of place, though, leading to missing HR values or low quality of those calculated. Since the experiments showed that a combination of acceleration and HR data from the In-Ear sensor leads to better results than the unimodal approach, even with the quality problems of HR data, improving availability and quality of HR data via adaptations in the technical setting might lead to better results.

A direct comparison of these results to the works from van Andel et al. (see "2 Related Work") is not advisable. While we focused on the detection of TCS during 24 h, they work on the nightly (8 h) detection of motor [19] and various kinds of seizures of major concern to the patient's safety [20] respectively. Also, the patient groups are different: They use data from patients in a residential care setting, while we use data from patients who visit the University Hospital Bonn for diagnosis purposes. They also do not report about the detection latency. As already outlined, this shows how difficult it is to compare different approaches to seizure detection.

5   Conclusion and Future Work

In this work, we developed a multimodal approach for the detection of TCS based on 3D acceleration and heart rate data acquired with an In-Ear sensor. We found that our proposed method achieves high sensitivity in combination with a low detection latency. Experiments show that it outperforms a comparable unimodal approach, which only uses the 3D acceleration data, in terms of sensitivity, mean detection latency and false alarm rate. However, the false alarm rate produced by the method is still too high for a device usable in patient's daily life. Therefore, future work should focus on lowering the false alarm rate.

The high sensitivity and low mean detection latency partly result from the application of cost-sensitive learning, which also leads to the high false alarm rate. Thus, further approaches should consider a broader range of cost values to find out if this way, a similar sensitivity and mean detection latency can be reached with a reasonable false alarm rate. Another starting point is the data base used for the feature calculation. Improvements in the technical setting might lead to a better availability and quality of the heart rate data, which might in conclusion improve the seizure detection. Also, the addition of further modalities, like a mobile version of EEG, could help to improve the results. Future work should also include other seizure types (which might also increase the amount of seizure data available to the algorithm and provide a better class ratio between "seizure" and "no-seizure") and potentially real-time processing. It is expected that the algorithm has to be adapted iteratively since the models are based on data from patients sitting or lying at the hospital. In addition, it should be examined whether individualizing the models for certain patients (groups) achieves better results.

The promising multimodal approach will be pursued in a follow-up project. It is planned to consider additional modalities in the In-Ear sensor, such as a mobile EEG, and to follow up on experiments with cost-sensitive learning and/or other approaches to the handling of highly imbalanced data.

Acknowledgements. The authors acknowledge the financial support by the Federal Ministry of Education and Research of Germany in the framework of EPItect (project number 16SV7482).

References

1. Picot, M.-C., Baldy-Moulinier, M., Daurs, J.-P., Dujols, P., Crespel, A.: The prevalence of epilepsy and pharmacoresistant epilepsy in adults: A population-based study in a Western European country. Epilepsia **49**(7), 1230–1238 (2008). https://doi.org/10.1111/j.1528-1167.2008.01579.x
2. Ramgopal, S., et al.: Seizure detection, seizure prediction, and closed-loop warning systems in epilepsy. Epilepsy Behav. **37**, 291–307 (2014). https://doi.org/10.1016/j.yebeh.2014.06.023
3. Hoppe, C., Poepel, A., Elger, C.E.: Epilepsy: Accuracy of patient seizure counts. Arch. Neurol. **64**(11), 1595–1599 (2007)

4. Bidwell, J., Khuwatsamrit, T., Askew, B., Ehrenberg, J.A., Helmers, S.: Seizure reporting technologies for epilepsy treatment: a review of clinical information needs and supporting technologies. Seizure **32**, 109–117 (2015). https://doi.org/10.1016/j.seizure.2015.09.006
5. Van de Vel, A., et al.: Non-EEG seizure detection systems and potential SUDEP prevention: State of the art. Seizure **41**, 141–153 (2016). https://doi.org/10.1016/j.seizure.2016.07.012
6. Baumgartner (hrsg.), C., et al.: Handbuch der Epilepsien: Klinik, Diagnostik, Therapie und psychosoziale Aspekte. Wien: Springer, Wien (2001)
7. De Cooman, T., Carrette, E., Boon, P., Meurs, A., Van Huffel, S.: Online seizure detection in adults with temporal lobe epilepsy using single-lead ECG. In: 22nd European Signal Processing Conference (EUSIPCO), pp. 1532–1536. IEEE (2014)
8. Pearl, P.L., Loddenkemper, T., Ulate-Campos, A., Coughlin, F., Gaínza-Lein, M., Fernández, I.S.: Automated seizure detection systems and their effectiveness for each type of seizure. Seizure **40**, 88–101 (2016). https://doi.org/10.1016/j.seizure.2016.06.008
9. Halford, J.J., et al.: Detection of generalized tonic–clonic seizures using surface electromyographic monitoring. Epilepsia **58**(11), 1861–1869 (2017). https://doi.org/10.1111/epi.13897
10. Schneble, H.: Epilepsie. Erscheinungsbilder - Ursachen - Behandlung, Originalau. München: Beck (Beck'sche Reihe; 2047 : C.H. Beck Wissen) (1996)
11. Matthes, A., Schneble, H.: Epilepsien: Diagnostik und Therapie für Klinik und Praxis, 6., Neubea. Stuttgart: Georg Thieme Verlag (1999)
12. Wolf (Hrsg.), P.: Praxisbuch Epilepsien: Diagnostik - Behandlung - Rehabilitation. Stuttgart: W. Kohlhammer (2003)
13. Houta, S., Bisgin, P., Dulich, P.: Machine learning methods for detection of Epileptic seizures with long-term wearable devices. In: Eleventh International Conference on eHealth, Telemedicine, and Social Medicine (2019)
14. Nijsen, T.M.E., Arends, J.B.A.M., Griep, P.A.M., Cluitmans, P.J.M.: The potential value of three-dimensional accelerometry for detection of motor seizures in severe epilepsy. Epilepsy Behav. **7**(1), 74–84 (2005). https://doi.org/10.1016/j.yebeh.2005.04.011
15. Gutierrez, E.G., Crone, N.E., Kang, J.Y., Carmenate, Y.I., Krauss, G.L.: Strategies for non-EEG seizure detection and timing for alerting and interventions with tonic-clonic seizures. Epilepsia **59**, 36–41 (2018). https://doi.org/10.1111/epi.14046
16. Arends, J.B.A.M.: Movement-based seizure detection. Epilepsia **59**(February), 30–35 (2018). https://doi.org/10.1111/epi.14053
17. Zijlmans, M., Flanagan, D., Gotman, J.: Heart rate changes and ECG abnormalities during epileptic seizures: Prevalence and definition of an objective clinical sign. Epilepsia **43**(8), 847–854 (2002). https://doi.org/10.1046/j.1528-1157.2002.37801.x
18. Leijten, F.S.S., et al.: Multimodal seizure detection: a review. Epilepsia **59**(S1), 42–47 (2018). https://doi.org/10.1111/epi.14047
19. van Andel, J., et al.: Multimodal, automated detection of nocturnal motor seizures at home: is a reliable seizure detector feasible? Epilepsia Open **2**(4), 424–431 (2017). https://doi.org/10.1002/epi4.12076
20. Arends, J., et al.: Multimodal nocturnal seizure detection in a residential care setting: a long-term prospective trial. Neurology **91**(21), e2010–e2019 (2018). https://doi.org/10.1212/WNL.0000000000006545
21. Beniczky, S., Ryvlin, P.: Standards for testing and clinical validation of seizure detection devices. Epilepsia **59**, 9–13 (2018). https://doi.org/10.1111/epi.14049
22. Nijsen, T.M.E., Aarts, R.M., Arends, J.B.A.M., Cluitmans, P.J.M.: Automated detection of tonic seizures using 3-D accelerometry. IFMBE Proceedings **22**, 188–191 (2008). https://doi.org/10.1007/978-3-540-89208-3_47

23. De Cooman, T., Van De Vel, A., Ceulemans, B., Lagae, L., Vanrumste, B., Van Huffel, S.: Online detection of tonic-clonic seizures in pediatric patients using ECG and low-complexity incremental novelty detection. In: Proceedings Annual International Conference IEEE Engineering Medical Biology Social EMBS, vol. 2015–Novem, pp. 5597–5600 (2015). doi: https://doi.org/10.1109/EMBC.2015.7319661.

24. Vandecasteele, K., et al.: Automated epileptic seizure detection based on wearable ECG and PPG in a hospital environment. Sensors 17(10), 2338 (2017). https://doi.org/10.3390/s17102338

25. Bender, D., et al.: Multicenter clinical assessment of improved wearable multimodal convulsive seizure detectors. Epilepsia 58(11), 1870–1879 (2017). https://doi.org/10.1111/epi.13899

26. Poh, M.Z., et al.: Convulsive seizure detection using a wrist-worn electrodermal activity and accelerometry biosensor. Epilepsia 53(5), 93–97 (2012). https://doi.org/10.1111/j.1528-1167.2012.03444.x

27. De Cooman, T., Kjær, T., Van Huffel, S., Sorensen, H.: Adaptive heart rate-based epileptic seizure detection using real-time user feedback. Physiol. Measur. 39(1), 014005 (2018). https://doi.org/10.1088/1361-6579/aaa216

28. Mannini, A., Sabatini, A.M.: Machine learning methods for classifying human physical activity from on-body accelerometers. Sensors 10(2), 1154–1175 (2010). https://doi.org/10.3390/s100201154

29. Bao, L., Intille, S.: Activity recognition from user-annotated acceleration data. In: Ferscha, A., Mattern, F. (eds.) Pervasive 2004. LNCS, vol. 3001, pp. 1–17. Springer, Heidelberg (2004). https://doi.org/10.1007/978-3-540-24646-6_1

30. Haixiang, G., Yijing, L., Shang, J., Mingyun, G., Yuanyue, H., Bing, G.: Learning from class-imbalanced data: review of methods and applications. Expert Syst. Appl. 73(December), 220–239 (2017). https://doi.org/10.1016/j.eswa.2016.12.035

31. Kumar, M.N.A., Sheshadri, H.S.: On the classification of imbalanced datasets. Int. J. Comput. Appl. 44(8), 1–7 (2012). http//doi.org.https://doi.org/10.5120/6280-8449

32. Sonak, A., Patankar, R.A.: A survey on methods to handle imbalance dataset. Int. J. Comput. Sci. Mob. Comput. 4(11), pp. 338–343 (2015). https://ijcsmc.com/docs/papers/November2015/V4I11201573.pdf.

33. Hall, M., Frank, E., Holmes, G., Pfahringer, B., Reutemann, P., Witten, I.H.: The WEKA data mining software. ACM SIGKDD Explor. Newsl. (2009). https://doi.org/10.1145/1656274.1656278

Deep Learning Detection of Cardiac Akinesis in Echocardiograms

Alessandro Bitetto[1,2]([envelope]) [ID], Elena Bianchi[2] [ID], Piercarlo Dondi[1] [ID],
Luca Bianchi[2] [ID], Janos Tolgyesi[2] [ID], Diego Ferri[3] [ID], Luca Lombardi[1] [ID],
Paola Cerchiello[4] [ID], Azzurra Marceca[5] [ID], and Alberto Barosi[5] [ID]

[1] Department of Electrical, Computer and Biomedical Engineering,
University of Pavia, Via Ferrata 5, 27100 Pavia, Italy
{alessandro.bitetto,piercarlo.dondi,luca.lombardi}@unipv.it
[2] Neosperience SpA, Via Gaspare Gozzi 1/A, 20129 Milano, Italy
{elena.bianchi,luca.bianchi,janos.tolgyesi}@neosperience.com
[3] Looptribe Srl, Viale Italia, 8, 25126 Brescia, Italy
diego.ferri@looptribe.com
[4] Department of Economics and Management, University of Pavia, Via San Felice 5,
27100 Pavia, Italy
paola.cerchiello@unipv.it
[5] Department of Cardiology, high specialties, Luigi Sacco Hospital, Via Giovanni
Battista Grassi, 74, 20157 Milano, Italy
{marceca.azzurra,barosi.alberto}@asst-fbf-sacco.it

Abstract. Heart diseases are still among the main causes of death in
the world population. The use of tools able to discriminate early this type
of problem, even by non-specialized medical personnel on an outpatient
basis, would put a decrease in health pressure on hospital centers and a
better patient prognosis. This paper focuses on the problem of cardiac
akinesis, a condition attributable to a very large number of pathologies, and a possible serious complication for SARS-Covid19 patients. In
particular, we considered echocardiographic images of both akinetic and
healthy patients. The dataset, containing echocardiograms of around 700
patients, has been supplied by Sacco hospital of Milan (Italy). We implemented a modified ResNet34 architecture and we tested the model under
various combinations of parameters. The final best performing model was
able to achieve a F1-score of 0.91 in the binary classification Akinetic vs.
Normokinetic.

Keywords: Deep learning · CNN · Echocardiography · Cardiac
akinesis

1 Introduction

The heart is one of the main organs of our body. It is considered a discontinuous volumetric pump whose functional cycle consists of a relaxation phase

This work was partially granted by the project DIMASDIA-COVID19, co-founded by
Italy and POR FESR Regione Lombardia (2014–2020).

(diastolic), responsible for filling the ventricle, and a contraction phase (systolic), during which the blood is expelled from the ventricles. Thanks to the contraction of the heart muscle, generated by a change in the electrical potential of the myocyte membrane (autorhythmic contraction, nervous command independent), it helps the blood flow (cardiac output) and its propagation in all systems by providing oxygenation essential for the biochemical processes underlying the main physiological activities. This aspect must be kept in mind in a holistic and systemic vision of the main diseases and pathologies of the human organism. The vital importance of the heart explains the numerous studies in the cardiology field, and the continuous search for innovative diagnostic techniques in the aim of an ever through knowledge of the organ.

Today, the most commonly used diagnostic tools for the discrimination of cardiac pathologies are: electrocardiogram; coronary angiography and cardiac characterization; electron beam computed tomography (EBCT); MR cardio and echocardiography. The present study focuses on two-dimensional transthoracic echocardiography, one of the most widespread and widely used instruments in the medical environment. It is a non-invasive test which allows to quickly have a complete view of the organ in all its parts and to simultaneously study the heart (anatomical and physiological) and the flow of blood through the valves by means of ultrasound. Thanks to the use of ultrasound probes positioned on the chest wall, it is in fact possible to obtain a tomogram of the mediastinum (middle and lower) within a fan chart (30–90°) that circumscribes the area under examination [17].

Through this examination it is possible to obtain a large amount of information, and a qualitative and quantitative evaluation (ventricular function as well as structural pathologies of heart): heart valve diseases; movements of the heart walls and its anomalies; congenital heart diseases and myocardial damages in diseases with high social interest and with a significant incidence of the population (e.g., arterial hypertension, myocardial infarction, diabetes).

Our analysis focused on the detection of alterations in the movement of the heart muscle (binary akinetic vs normokinetic discrimination). Cardiac akinesia refers to the absence of deformation of the myocardium visible as a lack of myocardial thickening. This condition is attributable to a very large number of pathologies including coronaropathy, cardiomyopathy and myocarditis. The last ones are inflammatory condition in response to pathogenic agents including virus agents. In recent 2020 SARS-Covid19 pandemia, myocarditis has been described as possible complication of the infection, capable of worsening the prognosis of patients. The presence of dyspnea and asthenia, often preceded by a febrile episode, together with the finding of repolarization anomalies on electrocardiographic examination and elevated enzymatic values of troponin (enzyme released by myocyte necrosis) guide the Clinician in suspecting myocarditis. The echocardiographic examination is in this case the first and most used diagnostic imaging method for the evaluation of possible involvement of the myocardium, highlighted precisely as a diffuse or segmental alteration of the contractility of the left ventricle. Furthermore, a pre-existing heart disease in the patient affected by SARS-Covid19 infection has been shown to be a negative prognostic risk factor. For this reason, the echocardiographic evaluation of the myocardial function and the rapid recognition of its alteration are extremely important in the clinical management of the patient [2].

To reach this goal, we used a modified ResNet34 architecture, adapted to the specific characteristic of echocardiography images. As dataset we used a series of echocardiograms of healthy and akinetic patients supplied by Luigi Sacco Hospital of Milan (Italy). We tested various combinations of parameters obtaining promising results. The best performing model was able to reach 0.91 as F1-score.

The paper is structured as follow: Sect. 2 provides a brief overview of previous works related to the automatic analysis of the echocardiograms; Sect. 3 describes the dataset and the proposed approach; Sect. 4 presents and discusses the experimental results; finally, Sect. 5 draws the conclusions and proposes possible future steps.

2   Related Works

Cardiovascular image analysis is a widely studied topic. In the last years, the rapid growth of machine learning and deep learning techniques lead to new solutions to automatically analyze different kinds of cardiac images, obtained, for example, by magnetic resonance, tomography or echocardiography [1,6,11]. Focusing in particular on echocardiograms, many machine learning and deep learning studies have been conducted to date [3]. Madani et al. designed a CNN able to classify 15 standard echocardiographic views [12], then, they extended their work to identify left ventricular hypertrophy testing both a supervised and a semi-supervised network [13]. Other alternative solutions for the problem of echocardiographic views classification include the ad-hoc deep learning model proposed by Kununose et al. [8], and the knowledge distillation approach adopted by Vaselli et al., who started from three commonly used CNNs (VGG-16, DenseNet, and Resnet) to train an accurate lightweight deep learning model [18].

Ghorbani et al. introduced EchoNet, a deep learning model able to identify local cardiac structures, estimate cardiac function, and predict systemic phenotypes [4]. Leclerc et al., instead, studied the problem of segmentation of 2D echocardiographic images comparing the performances of various deep learning and non-deep learning methods [9]. Other researchers focused on more specific tasks, such as detecting the cardiac phase using a combination of CNNs and RNNs [16], discriminate between the hypertrophic cardiomyopathy (HCM) and the physiological hypertrophy seen in athletes [14], or detecting regional wall motion abnormalities (RWMAs) [7].

An overview of the most recent applications of machine and deep learning applied to the analysis of echocardiograms can be found in [19].

3   Proposed Method

3.1   Dataset

The dataset contains 732 echocardiograms of patients with age ranging from 30 to 90 years and with a sex distribution of 33% female. Each echocardiogram is composed by different frames, ranging from 23 to 291 (see Fig. 1). We selected a minimum number of frames, set to 40, for being able to capture at least one full cardiac cycle, as suggested by doctors. After this first selection, we dropped 54 clips ending with a dataset of 678 observation. For each observation we had the label Akinetic or Normokinetic, target of our analysis, for a total of 199 Akinetic and 479 Normokinetic samples.

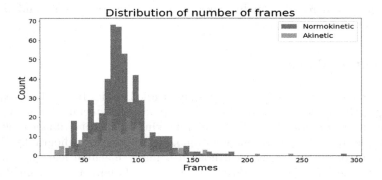

Fig. 1. Distribution of frames by class.

Each echocardiogram had additional information (such as patient personal data, the date of the exam or machine specifications) hard printed on each frame. Thus, we created a heuristic algorithm to automatically remove these unwanted parts of the image and maintain only the area that changes over time. Firstly, we identify the interest region, i.e., the central triangular shape, by using the difference of consecutive frames: in this way the static objects in the frame are cancelled out whilst the moving parts are kept. Then, we span a vertical scanner to record the minimum and maximum y-value and we evaluate the resulting convex hull that identifies the mask. The procedure is repeated for all consecutive pairs of frames and the final mask is obtained as average of all masks. A sample of image cleaning is reported in Fig. 2.

Original frame 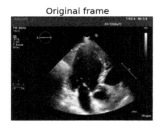   Mask 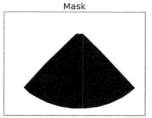   Masked frame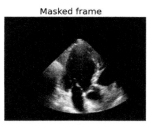

Fig. 2. Example of frame cleaning.

3.2 Network Specifications

For the classification task we used a modified ResNet34 [5] architecture. Firstly, given the binary nature of the task, we substituted the last fully connected Softmax layer with a Sigmoid output layer. Then, due to the characteristics of echocardiographic images, we decided to input the frames of each clip as separate channels of a single image. Thus, we changed the standard 3-channel input layer of ResNet34 with a n-channel one, where n is the number of frames. We tested different values of n from 40 to 100 and different frames sampling approaches from each clip. In particular, we tried to take:

(a) first n frames.
(b) n equally spaced frames.
(c) first n consecutive frames difference, resulting in $n - 1$ channels;
(d) n equally spaced consecutive frames difference.

Approach (a) with $n = 50$ performed best. Moreover, given the unbalanced nature of our dataset, we trained four different versions of the model using all combinations of Binary Cross-Entropy Loss versus Focal Loss [10] and target labels with 1 (Akinetic) and 0 (Normokinetic) versus inverted labels.

In order to have robust predictions we cross-validated our models with a 5-fold stratified (on target label) approach, thus, each model version consisted of 5 fold-models, trained on a 4-fold training set $T_{i,k}$ and tested on 1-fold validation set $V_{i,k}$ for i-th model version ($i \in [1,4]$), and k-th fold ($k \in [1,5]$). The predicted probabilities of each validation fold $V_{i,.}$, that match the full dataset, were used to feed a 2nd-level learner with four inputs from each model version resulting in a staking of models. The 2nd-level learner was trained with a 5-fold stratified approach but with a different random seed from the one used to generate the CNN folds, thus, the learner resulted in five fold-models with T_k^{2nd} and V_k^{2nd} analogous train and validation sets. The training procedure is showed in Fig. 3.

As the stacked model produces five probabilities from each fold-model, an aggregation function is needed to get a single probability, to be converted into the final output label. We tested three different aggregation functions: (i) average, (ii) median and (iii) majority vote. For the first two cases, the average and the median of the probabilities are evaluated and then converted into a label, given a certain threshold th. For majority vote, instead, all the probabilities are firstly

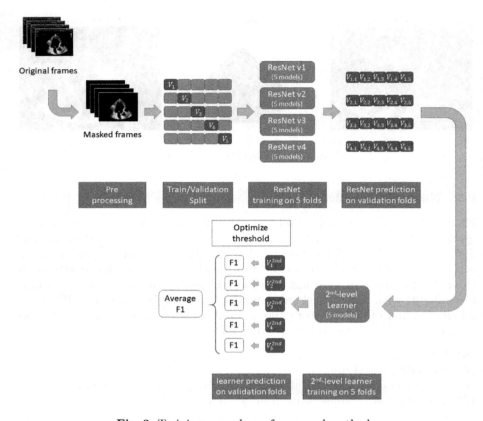

Fig. 3. Training procedure of proposed method

converted into a label given the same th and then, the most frequent one is taken as final outcome. The threshold th has been selected by testing different values, from 0 to 1 by 0.01, for all folds and maximizing the resulting average F1-score. The prediction procedure is showed in Fig. 4.

4   Experimental Results

As described in Sect. 3.2, we trained four different versions of our modified ResNet34 architecture. Each model has been trained with a batch size of 32 using a Stochastic Gradient Descent (SGD) optimizer with 0.9 momentum and 0.0001 weight decay and with a learning rate scheduler every 34 iterations for each epoch with a γ decay of 0.9. In order to avoid convergence problems, we used regularization clipping gradient norm to 1. We used accuracy on predicted label and loss value as early stopping criteria. Each model training lasted 20 min for 25 epochs for all the five folds on a workstation with two NVidia GeForce GTX 1080 Ti using PyTorch framework.

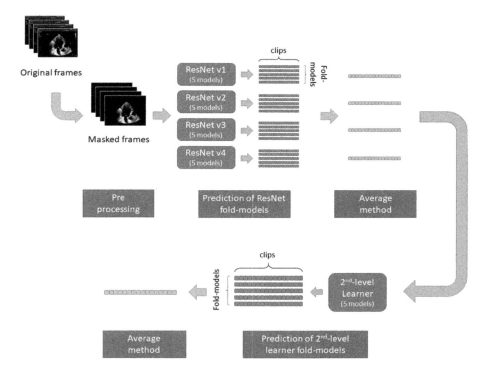

Fig. 4. Prediction procedure of proposed method

Results after 25 epochs of training can be found in Tables 1 (train fold) and 2 (validation fold), where accuracy (ACC), F1-score for both classes and Matthews correlation coefficient (MCC) are reported. Average confusion matrix for train and validation folds are showed in Fig. 5 for the best performing model, i.e., the one with BCE loss and no inverted class. Figures 6 shows how the predicted probabilities, used as input of 2nd-level learner, are polarized. We can notice that most of the probabilities are correctly distributed, whilst the remaining ones leave room for improvement for the 2nd-level learner.

For the 2nd-level learner we tested the following classifiers: the three simple averaging methods described in Sect. 3.2 (average, majority vote and

Table 1. Training performance of the four version of ResNet34 model. Akinetic (AK) and Normokinetic (NK). Best result highlighted in green.

Loss	Inv. Class	ACC	F1 (AK)	F1 (NK)	MCC
BCE	no	0.99 ± 0.01	0.99 ± 0.03	0.99 ± 0.01	0.98 ± 0.04
BCE	yes	0.98 ± 0.01	0.98 ± 0.02	0.98 ± 0.03	0.98 ± 0.03
FocLos	no	0.97 ± 0.01	0.97 ± 0.03	0.97 ± 0.02	0.98 ± 0.03
FocLos	yes	0.98 ± 0.02	0.98 ± 0.02	0.98 ± 0.01	0.98 ± 0.03

Table 2. Validation performance of the four version of ResNet34 model. Akinetic (AK) and Normokinetic (NK). Best result highlighted in green.

Loss	Inv. Class	ACC	F1 (AK)	F1 (NK)	MCC
BCE	no	0.88 ± 0.02	0.77 ± 0.05	0.92 ± 0.01	0.70 ± 0.06
BCE	yes	0.87 ± 0.01	0.78 ± 0.02	0.91 ± 0.01	0.70 ± 0.03
FocLos	no	0.86 ± 0.03	0.76 ± 0.06	0.91 ± 0.02	0.67 ± 0.07
FocLos	yes	0.87 ± 0.02	0.76 ± 0.05	0.91 ± 0.02	0.68 ± 0.06

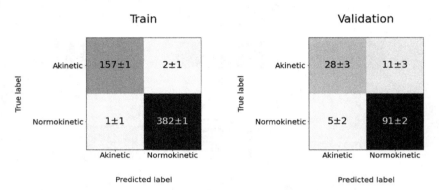

Fig. 5. Average confusion matrix for train and validation folds for model with BCE loss and no inverted class.

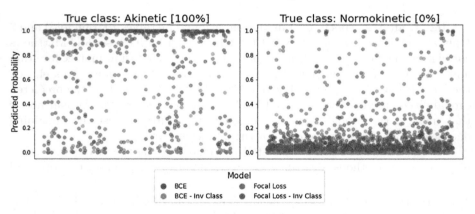

Fig. 6. Predicted probabilities using BCE and Focal loss, with and without inverted class.

median), Ordinary Logistic Regression, Polynomial Regression, Elastic Net Regression, Elastic Net Linear Perceptron, Passive-Aggressive encoder, K-Neighbors, Support-Vector Machine (SVM), Random Forest, Gradient Boosting

(GBM) and Multi-layer Perceptron (MLP). All classifiers hyperparameters were tuned with 5-fold stratified cross-validation with average validation F1-score as performance metric. Moreover, before converting the predicted probabilities to class labels, different thresholds, from 0 to 1 by 0.01, were tested in order to optimize the same metric. Results of tuned models can be found in Table 3. We can notice the improvement with respect to the best performing ResNet34 used alone. In particular, Gradient Boosting performed best, increasing the F1-score of 4%. Average confusion matrix for train and validation folds are showed in Fig. 7 for GBM model.

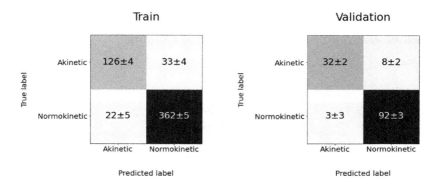

Fig. 7. Average confusion matrix for train and validation folds for GBM model.

Table 3. Training performance for 2nd-level learner and corresponding binary threshold maximizing average F1-score on validation set. Highlighted in green the best result.

Learner	Avg Valid F1-score	Binary threshold
ResNet34 - BCE	0.877	0.50
Average	0.902	0.36
Majority vote	0.903	0.18
Median	0.902	0.26
GBM	0.910	0.42
Random Forest	0.898	0.66
KNeighbors	0.904	0.29
SVM	0.902	0.29
Passive-aggressive	0.897	0.50
ENet-perceptron	0.882	0.50
Polynomial Regression	0.877	0.66
Logistic Regression	0.896	0.56
Elastic Net Regression	0.902	0.50
MLP	0.904	0.35

Finally, we visualized the activation functions of the last convolution layer before the fully-connected one by the mean of heatmaps in order to identify which part of the image the network was focusing on. We used an approach similar to Grad-CAM [15], where the gradient value of each channel is averaged and then passed through a ReLU function. We decided to exponentially scale both positive and negative values into a $[-1, 1]$ range. Figure 8 shows the obtained heatmaps for some samples of both classes. You can see how the network mainly focuses on the same parts of the frame, regardless of the predicted class. A majority of positive values (in purple) leads to an Akinetic prediction, while a majority of negative values (in yellow) to a Normokinetic one. Obviously, the areas highlighted are those deemed more meaningful by the model, and not a detection of the exact positions of akinetic and normokinetic regions of the heart, that will be demanded to a future extension of the work.

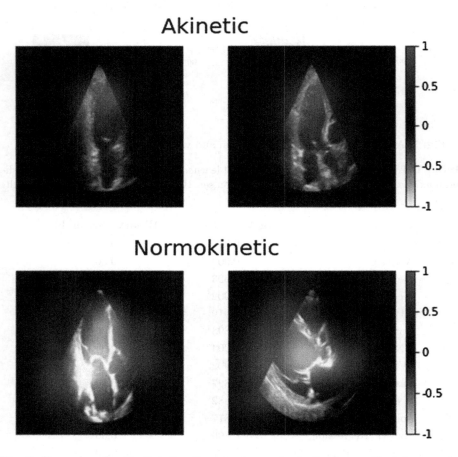

Fig. 8. Examples of activation functions heatmaps for both classes. First frame only is displayed.

5   Conclusions

In this work we have presented a study about the use of deep learning techniques for the automatic discrimination between akinetic and healthy patients. We implemented a modified ResNet34 architecture and we tested the model on a dataset composed by 678 echocardiograms, achieving a F1-score of 0.91.

The creation of a binary discrimination model for the early diagnosis of heart diseases is a fundamental starting point and a first step towards a completely new approach to medical diagnosis. Today, heart diseases are still among the main causes of death in the world population. Thus, the use of tools able to discriminate early this type of problems, even by non-specialized medical personnel on an outpatient basis, would put a decrease in health pressure on hospital centers and a better patient prognosis. This type of approach also opens up interesting prospects in the research of new therapies and drugs thanks to a more in-depth knowledge of the disease, prediction of risk levels and patient predisposition to possible complications and decentralization of care with better home care.

Next steps will include additional tests (when new data will be made available by the hospital) to further evaluate the effectiveness of our approach. A comparison with other state-of-the art classification methods will be considered, too. Regarding the structure of the network, we will also consider the use of additional CNN architectures as input of 2nd-level learner and (given the sequential nature of the clips) the introduction of recurrent and attention layers. To date, the focus has shifted to different new data related to the patients under examination (blood gas analysis, blood tests, lung ultrasounds), which will be the basis for training future models; the interaction between the different types of models will lead to a deeper understanding of the pathology and physiology of the human organism.

Acknowledgement. We would like to thank the team of the Department of Cardiology of Luigi Sacco hospital, Echocardiography Laboratory in particular Maria Michela Caracciolo, Manfredo Cerchiello, Simone Colombo, Stefano De Vita, Alessandra Giavarini, Maria Isabella Tagliasacchi, for supplying us with the dataset.

References

1. Al'Aref, S.J., et al.: Clinical applications of machine learning in cardiovascular disease and its relevance to cardiac imaging. Eur. Heart J. **40**(24), 1975–1986 (2019). https://doi.org/10.1093/eurheartj/ehy404
2. Capotosto, L., Nguyen, B.L., Ciardi, M.R., Mastroianni, C., Vitarelli, A.: Heart, covid-19, and echocardiography. Echocardiography **37**(9), 1454–1464 (2020). https://doi.org/10.1111/echo.14834
3. Gandhi, S., Mosleh, W., Shen, J., Chow, C.M.: Automation, machine learning, and artificial intelligence in echocardiography: a brave new world. Echocardiography **35**(9), 1402–1418 (2018). https://doi.org/10.1111/echo.14086
4. Ghorbani, A., et al.: Deep learning interpretation of echocardiograms. NPJ Digit. Med. **3**(1), 1–10 (2020). https://doi.org/10.1038/s41746-019-0216-8

5. He, K., Zhang, X., Ren, S., Sun, J.: Deep residual learning for image recognition. In: Proceedings of the IEEE Conference on Computer Vision and Pattern Recognition, pp. 770–778 (2016). https://doi.org/10.1109/CVPR.2016.90
6. Kilic, A.: Artificial intelligence and machine learning in cardiovascular health care. Ann. Thorac. Surg. **109**(5), 1323–1329 (2020). https://doi.org/10.1016/j. athoracsur.2019.09.042
7. Kusunose, K., et al.: A deep learning approach for assessment of regional wall motion abnormality from echocardiographic images. Cardiovasc. Imaging **13**(2 Part 1), 374–381 (2020). https://doi.org/10.1016/j.jcmg.2019.02.024
8. Kusunose, K., Haga, A., Inoue, M., Fukuda, D., Yamada, H., Sata, M.: Clinically feasible and accurate view classification of echocardiographic images using deep learning. Biomolecules **10**(5), 665 (2020). https://doi.org/10.3390/biom10050665
9. Leclerc, S., et al.: Deep learning for segmentation using an open large-scale dataset in 2D echocardiography. IEEE Trans. Med. Imaging **38**(9), 2198–2210 (2019). https://doi.org/10.1109/TMI.2019.2900516
10. Lin, T.Y., Goyal, P., Girshick, R., He, K., Dollar, P.: Focal loss for dense object detection. In: Proceedings of the IEEE International Conference on Computer Vision (ICCV), pp. 2980–2988 (2017). https://doi.org/10.1109/ICCV.2017.324
11. Litjens, G., et al.: State-of-the-art deep learning in cardiovascular image analysis. Cardiovasc. Imaging **12**(8, Part 1), 1549–1565 (2019). https://doi.org/10.1016/j. jcmg.2019.06.009
12. Madani, A., Arnaout, R., Mofrad, M., Arnaout, R.: Fast and accurate view classification of echocardiograms using deep learning. NPJ Digit. Med. **1**(1), 1–8 (2018). https://doi.org/10.1038/s41746-017-0013-1
13. Madani, A., Ong, J.R., Tibrewal, A., Mofrad, M.R.: Deep echocardiography: data-efficient supervised and semi-supervised deep learning towards automated diagnosis of cardiac disease. NPJ Digit. Med. **1**(1), 1–11 (2018). https://doi.org/10.1038/ s41746-018-0065-x
14. Narula, S., Shameer, K., Salem Omar, A.M., Dudley, J.T., Sengupta, P.P.: Machine-learning algorithms to automate morphological and functional assessments in 2D echocardiography. J. Am. Coll. Cardiol. **68**(21), 2287–2295 (2016). https://doi.org/10.1016/j.jacc.2016.08.062
15. Selvaraju, R.R., Cogswell, M., Das, A., Vedantam, R., Parikh, D., Batra, D.: Grad-cam: visual explanations from deep networks via gradient-based localization. In: IEEE International Conference on Computer Vision (ICCV), pp. 618–626 (2017). https://doi.org/10.1109/ICCV.2017.74
16. Taheri Dezaki, F., et al.: Cardiac phase detection in echocardiograms with densely gated recurrent neural networks and global extrema loss. IEEE Trans. Med. Imaging **38**(8), 1821–1832 (2019). https://doi.org/10.1109/TMI.2018.2888807
17. Tanaka, N., et al.: Transthoracic echocardiography in models of cardiac disease in the mouse. Circulation **94**(5), 1109–1117 (1996). https://doi.org/10.1161/01.CIR. 94.5.1109
18. Vaseli, H., et al.: Designing lightweight deep learning models for echocardiography view classification. In: Medical Imaging 2019: Image-Guided Procedures, Robotic Interventions, and Modeling. International Society for Optics and Photonics, vol. 10951, p. 109510F (2019). https://doi.org/10.1117/12.2512913
19. Zamzmi, G., Hsu, L., Li, W., Sachdev, V., Antani, S.: Harnessing machine intelligence in automatic echocardiogram analysis: Current status, limitations, and future directions. IEEE Rev. Biomed. Eng. press (2020). https://doi.org/10.1109/RBME. 2020.2988295

Prediction of Minimally Conscious State Responder Patients to Non-invasive Brain Stimulation Using Machine Learning Algorithms

Andrés Rojas[1], Eleni Kroupi[1], Géraldine Martens[2], Aurore Thibaut[2], Alice Barra[2], Steven Laureys[2], Giulio Ruffini[1], and Aureli Soria-Frisch[1]([⊠])

[1] Starlab Barcelona SL, Av Tibidabo 47 bis, Barcelona, Spain
`aureli.soria-frisch@starlab.es`
[2] Coma Science Group, GIGA-Consciousness, University and University Hospital of Liege, Liège, Belgium

Abstract. The right matching of patients to an intended treatment is routinely performed by doctor and physicians in healthcare. Improving doctor's ability to choose the right treatment can greatly speed up patient's recovery. In a clinical study on Disorders of Consciousness patients in Minimal Consciousness State (MCS) have gone through transcranial Electrical Stimulation (tES) therapy to increase consciousness level. We have carried out the study of MCS patient's response to tES therapy using as input the EEG data collected before the intervention. Different Machine Learning approaches have been applied to the Relative Band Power features extracted from the EEG. We aimed to predict tES treatment outcome from this EEG data of 17 patients, where 4 of the patients sustainably showed further signs of consciousness after treatment. We have been able to correctly classify with 95% accuracy the response of patients to tES therapy. In this paper we present the methodology as well as a comparative evaluation of the different employed classification approaches. Hereby we demonstrate the feasibility of implementing a novel informed Decision Support System (DSS) based on this methodological approach for the correct prediction of patients' response to tES therapy in MCS.

Keywords: Artificial intelligence · Machine learning · Decision support systems

1 Introduction

Non-Invasive Brain Stimulation - NIBS (Vosskuhl et al. 2018), which employ the application of electromagnetic stimulation to modulate brain activity, has become a field of increasing importance in research and clinical applications. NIBS is gaining relevance on the treatment of neurological and psychiatric diseases (Kuo et al. 2014; Lefaucheur et al. 2017), for which pharmacological treatments have demonstrated difficult to achieve optimal performance either in terms of efficacy or side effects.

© Springer Nature Switzerland AG 2021
A. Del Bimbo et al. (Eds.): ICPR 2020 Workshops, LNCS 12661, pp. 515–525, 2021.
https://doi.org/10.1007/978-3-030-68763-2_39

There is an increasing understanding that patients do not homogeneously respond to treatments, especially in neurology and mental health (Wu et al. 2020). Hence, one of the roles of neuroimaging biomarkers is the prediction of treatment outcome as recently proposed (Woo et al. 2017). In the case of NIBS-based treatments, personal biophysical characteristics of brain tissue are responsible among other factors for the subject variability in the response to treatments. Given the influence of tissue biophysical characteristics in electrophysiological recordings, we hypothesize that electroencephalography (EEG) recordings of patients are able to characterize the potential response to treatments based on both invasive, as recently shown in (Scangos et al. 2019), and non-invasive stimulation. An analogous rationale is followed in a recent opinion paper, where the employment of EEG in the prediction of NIBS response is proposed in the concrete case of stroke rehabilitation (Ovadia-Caro et al. 2019). This last paper not only advocates for the utilization of EEG but moreover of machine learning techniques for the prediction of NIBS outcomes in stroke rehabilitation. In a previous study with healthy subjects (Hordacre et al. 2017) found out that functional connectivity as measured on EEG could be used as a predictor of the neuroplastic response to transcranial Electrical Stimulation (tES), which constitutes a particular NIBS modality. The statement is based on objective response characterization of tES response through motor evoked potentials but not on spontaneous EEG as we propose herein. It is worth mentioning that this line of research is currently being investigated in some clinical trials[1,2].

We have recently investigated the treatment of Disorders of Consciousness based on transcranial direct current stimulation (tDCS), a form of tES (Martens et al. 2020). In this study only a small percentage of Minimal Conscious State (MCS) patients positively responded to the therapeutic intervention. Clinical partners at the University of Liege required to optimize the work on tES in the case of DOC patients because of the enormous costs associated with their treatment. Hence, they requested whether it would be possible to apply any type of analysis technique to avoid long treatments with patients who would have a low probability of success. In a recent multisite study these same clinical partners have analyzed markers in different modalities that can facilitate such a forecast on clinical recovery in this type of patients (Estraneo et al. 2020). We aim to predict treatment outcome in patients suffering from DOC based on spontaneous EEG, an easy-to-use and cost-effective brain monitoring technique, whose features can therefore enormously facilitate its clinical translation. We propose in this paper the application of Machine Learning techniques on spontaneous EEG data for the prediction of tES treatment outcome, which we are convinced constitutes a development of great value for supporting decisions in the DOC clinical domain.

The paper is organized as follows. Section 1 introduces the context, the description of the experiment and the interest of our study, explains the data set, the methods and the metrics that were employed in this study. Section 2 presents the results obtained for the prediction of responder patients to non-invasive brain stimulation and the discussion. Section 3 present the conclusions and future work.

---

[1] https://clinicaltrials.gov/ct2/show/NCT03293316.

[2] https://ichgcp.net/clinical-trials-registry/NCT03221413.

1.1 Methods

We have used an EEG dataset collected by the Coma Science Group in Liege that includes data from Disorders of Consciousness (DOC) patients with their corresponding Coma Recovery Scale-Revised (CRS-R) scores (Martens et al. 2020). Specifically, forty-six patients were included in a randomized double-blind sham-controlled crossover study (17 Unresponsive Wakefulness Syndrome - UWS, 23 Minimally Conscious State - MCS and 6 emerged from MCS). All patients received multifocal active or sham transcranial direct current stimulation (tDCS) for 20 min using 4 anodes and 4 cathodes in a fronto-parietal montage (see Fig. 5) with 1 mA per electrode. The resting-state EEG signals of 42 out of 46 patients were acquired before and after the stimulation, during 10 min. We have focused this study on MCS patients who went through the tDCS intervention since no UWS patient recovered any sign of consciousness. Below we describe the data subset used in this study:

- 21 MCS patients, who went through tDCS and sham.
- From these, data from 4 patients were discarded due to the bad quality of the EEG recordings.
- From the 17 remaining patients, 4 patients showed an improvement in consciousness signs after receiving tES.

For this study, we only used the resting state EEG data acquired before each stimulation session, as our goal is to predict the treatment response based on data acquired before the therapeutic intervention in order to simulate the operational conditions of such a system. The physicians, who followed up the patients after tDCS was applied, provided the labels as well as indicated if a patient was a responder or non-responder to tDCS, i.e. if they show respectively an increase or a decrease in their CRS-R scores after stimulation. As already commented, given the small sample size of the available artefact-free EEG data, we have additionally used bootstrapping for data augmentation. We compare in the following the performance of both methodologies.

Data Analysis Pipeline. The acquired EEG signals go through a standard processing pipeline. The signals were demeaned and detrended as well as re-referenced to the common average. They were initially band-pass filtered into the delta (1–4 Hz), theta (4–8 Hz), alpha (8–13 Hz), low beta (13–23 Hz) and high beta (23–35 Hz) bands using an IIR Butterworth filter. The data were segmented into 5-sec epochs with 50% overlap. Epochs with amplitude larger than 75 μV as well as epochs where the maximum value was below 10 μV were considered artefacts and excluded from further analysis.

Relative band power (RBP) features were extracted and used as input features of the classifiers. RBP is computed as the power per band divided by the total power in the broadband (1–35 Hz). In order to better understand the discrimination capability of the extracted features, we have visualized our feature space by applying different visualization techniques. First we use the well-known histograms and scatter plots of feature pairs (see Fig. 1). Furthermore, we have applied Principal Component Analysis (PCA) (Wold et al. 1987) and t-distributed Stochastic Neighbor Embedding (TSNE) (Maaten and Hinton 2008) to project the feature space in a two-dimensional plot. TSNE provided a better visualization, probably because it considers the distances between the points in the original space within the projection procedure. TSNE presents some parameters. We concretely evaluated different perplexity parameters and fixed a perplexity value of 40 with 1000 thousand iterations and with a fixed seed value. Figure 2 shows the EEG epoch plots with the dimensionality projection performed with TSNE. Alternatively, we have used as feature vector the projection of the RBP values through the TSNE, i.e. we also explored the use of TSNE components as input features to our classifiers as TSNE can capture much of the local structure of the high-dimensional data.

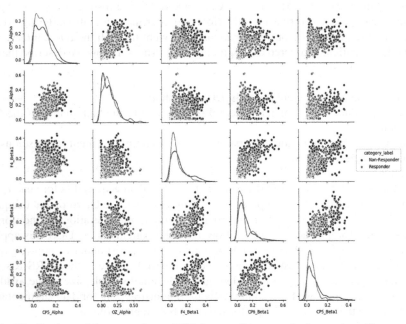

Fig. 1. Distributions of the most relevant RBP features for responder (orange) vs. Non-responder (blue) patients. These features were selected after checking the most relevant algorithm features found by the RF classifier. (Color figure online)

Data Pre-processing and Augmentation. The ULG data set presents a very reduced amount of artefact-free data due to the existence of numerous nursery interventions during data collection. Moreover, several epochs present a signal level of extreme low amplitude due to bad electrode contacts. On the other hand, the data set in highly unbalanced, i.e. presents a larger number of epochs corresponding to non-responding patients than these of positively responding patients. In order to tackle these problems, we have used Bootstrapping for data augmentation. Bootstrapping is a simple Monte-Carlo-based resampling technique used to approximate a probability distribution. It can be implemented by constructing a particular number of resamples with replacement of the observed data set (and of equal size to the observed dataset) (Efron and Tibshirani 1994).

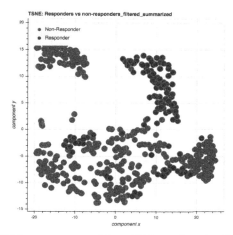

Fig. 2. Projection of RBP features extracted from EEG epochs using TSNE. *Responder (green) vs. Non-responder (red) patients.* (Color figure online)

Machine Learning Classifier Training. The Support Vector Machine (SVM) and the Random Forest (RF) algorithms were selected for solving the classification problem described herein. An SVM is a discriminative classifier formally defined by a separating hyperplane in a projection of the feature space of larger dimensionality than the original one implemented by means of kernel functions (Cortes and Vapnik 1995). The main advantage of this projection is the transformation of non-linear classification problems into linear ones. Given the distribution of the feature points in the TSNE-projected feature space, which presents a circular area of one of the classes surrounded by the samples of the other one (see Fig. 2), we thought the SVM methodology may be a good choice for solving the classification problem.

Random forest (RF) is a classification ensemble formed by decision tree predictors such that the structure of each tree depends on the values of a randomly sampled subset of the overall data set. The generalization error of RF converges to a limit as the number of trees in the forest becomes large. The generalization error of a forest of tree classifiers depends on the strength of the individual trees in the forest and the correlation between them (Breiman 2001). This methodology has been selected given the existence of associated techniques that facilitate its interpretability, an important feature for applications in the clinical domain (El Shawi et al. 2019).

Cross-Validation Scheme and Performance Measures for Model Evaluation. Given the small sample size of our data set, we validate our model using a leave one subject out cross validation (LOSOCV) scheme, i.e. leaving the epochs of one of the patients for test and training the algorithm with the data of the remaining ones. This validation scheme allows us both to estimate the generalization capability of the algorithm with a small data set and to mimic the operational conditions of a potential system for predicting the treatment outcome in a *de novo* patient, whose data had not been included in the existing data set. The average of the performance measures calculated over each of the subjects left out as test data set is calculated and delivered as performance measure of the predicting system. Cross-validation with leave one out can also be carried out with random grid search, which has provided very close to optimal results as demonstrated by (Bergstra and Bengio 2012).

We use the AUC-ROC at epoch level and the accuracy of the classifier at patient level to measure its performance. Hence, we have calculated the AUC-ROC on the EEG epochs in the test set. Additionally, we calculated the accuracy of correctly classifying each of the patients (using the majority voting for all of the patient epochs), which delivers the performance metric in operational conditions. This is important given the enormous variability in the number of epochs among the different patients, a fact that may be easily reproduce in operational conditions. Given the epoch fusion algorithm, i.e. majority voting, we can't evaluate the performance at patient level through the AUC-ROC, which requires real-valued scores and not categorical ones as the ones delivered by majority voting.

2   Results

We present in the following sections the performance using the available data set and the one through bootstrapping. Moreover, we present the analysis of outperforming features, which can be used by clinicians to interpret classification results.

2.1   Pre-EEG (Stimulation and Sham)

Using the RBP features previously described, the RF classifier achieved an AUC-ROC of 80% classifying EEG epochs and an accuracy of 76% for the right classification of the patients (Fig. 3), whereas the SVM perform with the same accuracy (76%) at subject level. This performance figures have been achieved by classifying the feature space projected through TSNE with both applied classification approaches, which outperforms the classification of the non-projected RBP features. Given the size of the data set, our SVM classifier presents some overfitting at epoch level, i.e. it has a very high value of the AUC-ROC 99%. The dissimilarity in performance at epoch and subject level is explained by the fact that subjects with the smaller number of epochs, which do not therefore affect a lot the epoch level performance metric, are the ones that make decrease the overall subject level accuracy because they present worse performance of right classification than subjects with more data.

It is worth mentioning that the variability of the number of epochs for each patient and the number of patients for each class made the training data set unbalanced, i.e. the training set presents more samples of the non-responder class than smaples of the responder one. While the SVM classifier offers a methodological parameter to correct for this unbalance, the RF does not. Bootstrapping has therefore been applied in order to balance the dataset besides augmenting the number of EEG epochs of each patient. It is worth mentioning that bootstrapping was applied at subject level to keep the inter-subject variability.

The RF classifiers trained with RBP features provided very valuable information regarding the decision flow of the algorithm and the importance of the input features.

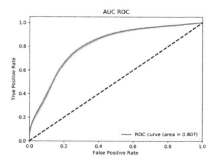

Fig. 3. RF achieved an AUC-ROC of 80% for the classification of EEG Epochs using TSNE components. The subject classification accuracy was of 76%.

RF is a decision tree ensemble. Hence, it is possible to visualize the classification flow in each of the trees that form the ensemble. An example of such a visualization is given in Fig. 4.

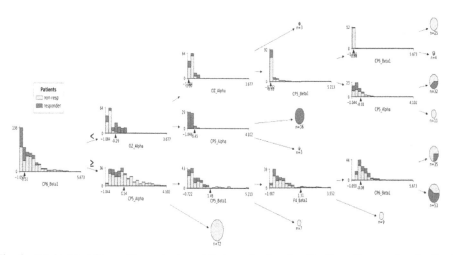

Fig. 4. RF decision flow with most relevant features for the classification of responders (yellow) vs. Non-responders (green). The labels of the feature used in each level for decision is given with its distribution histograms at each node of the tree. (Color figure online)

Feature importance was calculated using the Gini index in the random forest. the Gini index uses information gain to provide a measure of quality of the split between the two target classes. The average of the Gini index across the forest of trees provides therefore a global measure of feature importance that can be used to rank them. In the context of translational neuroscience, feature importance of a ML classifier such as RF, provides additional information that can help in the decision analysis for each patient within a clinical setting (Fig. 4 and 5). The feature importance provides a methodology to understand the inference logic behind the model as commented in (Woo et al. 2017). In

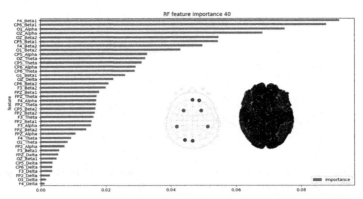

Fig. 5. RF most relevant features for the classification of responders with tDCS montage and target areas as ranked by the average Gini Index over the tree.

case of the MCS patients taken into account in this study, the bar plot in Fig. 5 allows to identify low beta power in frontal and parietal areas, and low alpha in parietal-occipital area as the main contributors to response to tDCS. In this context it is worth mentioning that the localization of these features overlaps with the position of the stimulation electrodes, which offers a plausible explanation of the relevance of the specific feature locations (see tDCS montage and target areas in Fig. 5).

2.2 Pre-EEG (Stimulation and Sham) Augmented with Bootstrap

As previously explained, we have used Bootstrapping for both increasing the sample size of the epoch data set and balancing the number of positive and negative samples in it. We did not create any new subjects in order to keep the inter-subject variability stable, but instead we augmented the number of epochs of the subjects to balance the number of epochs for the patients of each class included in the training set.

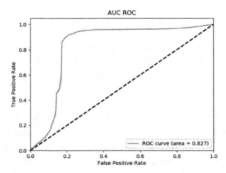

Fig. 6. SVM achieved an AUC-ROC of 82% classifying of EEG epochs using TSNE components with an accuracy of 94% for subject classification.

With the Bootstrapped dataset our SVM classifier achieved an AUC-ROC of 82% and an accuracy of 94% (see Fig. 6) for the right classification at patient level. This provides the best performance of our classifiers as it provides the largest accuracy for patient prediction of treatment outcome.

2.3 Discussion

Table 1 summarises the performance metrics of the classifiers in the different analyzed set-ups of the classification system.

Table 1. Summarized performance results for the prediction of tCS treatment outcome in MCS patients. Outperforming classifier in bold. Bold italics indicate overfitting of the classification system.

Data set	Method	Features	AUC	ACC subject
Original	RF	RBP	0.88	0.64
	RF	TSNE	0.80	0.76
	SVM	RBP	0.84	0.59
	SVM	TSNE	*0.99*	0.76
Bootstrap	RF	RBP	0.76	0.58
	RF	TSNE	0.82	0.67
	SVM	RBP	0.82	0.53
	SVM	**TSNE**	**0.82**	**0.94**

As it can be observed, the classification approach based on the TSNE projection of RBP EEG features, bootstrapping for epoch sample size augmentation and balancing, and a SVM classifier outperforms the other tested approaches in the prediction of positive responding MCS patients. Although we have not applied any interpretability technique for the SVM (which in spite of its difficulty we aim to realize in the future) our feature analysis on RF elucidates oscillatory rhythms in the alpha and beta bands localized close to the electrical stimulation positions as the ones most relevant for the classification performance. This confirms that brain state as characterized by electrophysiological markers are good information cues for the prediction of stimulation response. A similar rationale has been reported in (Bočková and Rektor 2019) in the context of Deep Brain Stimulation and Parkinson's' Disease, where electrophysiological markers in the stimulation area, i.e. sub-thalamic nucleus, are conferred predictive value of the stimulation outcome.

We do not have a clear hypothesis for the predominance of the alpha and beta bands over other bands in the prediction performance. However, it is worth pointing out, that patients with UWS, who present a lower consciousness level than patients with MCS and do not respond to the tDCS therapeutic intervention at all, present in general lower power in alpha and beta bands than patients with MCS. We would need further analysis, which we will attain in the future, to formulate a more elaborated rationale on the link between the two observed facts. Moreover this further analysis will be realized with a larger data set than the one used herein.

One justified criticism of the results presented herein is the fact that TSNE projection is not trainable, i.e. we have to run the TSNE on the training and the test data sets. Although in principle TSNE has been proposed to learn a non-parametric mapping, i.e. it is not possible to embed validation samples in a learned projection, recent works in the literature propose to use a multivariate regressor to minimize the TSNE loss function in order to overcome this problem (van der Maaten 2009). We plan to apply such a methodology in the future to allow the translation of our predictive approach based on the TSNE projection into operational conditions. It is noteworthy though that avoiding the usage of the TSNE projection the current system achieves a performance of 0.88 AUC at epoch level and 64% patient level accuracy with a RF classifying the RBP features without bootstrapping (see Table 1). With this purpose it may be worth as well further extending the methodologies for balancing the original data set.

3 Conclusions

We have proven the efficacy and the feasibility of using ML algorithms for the prediction of MCS patient response to tCS therapies. With the current available data from 17 patients our outperforming classifier achieved 82% of the AUC-ROC at epoch level and accuracy of 94% at patient level, i.e. only one out of 17 MCS patients did not get a right prediction on the outcome of the tES intervention. The use of bootstrapping has improved the results of the classifiers as it avoided the classifier to specialize on the class with the largest number of epochs, i.e. the non-responder class.

We believe that the use of such models could be improved with a larger sample size in terms of subjects, a goal which is fortunately hindered by the small prevalence of Disorders of Consciousness (DOC). The further development of such a Decision Support System (DSS) will increase the available information for a clinician to select the right treatment for DOC patients. Besides being able to identify MCS patient response to tCS therapies, the classifiers provided a good insight into the interpretation of the most relevant features selected by the models. As shown, model feature importance is a useful resource for providing not only model explainability, but also identification of EEG markers of consciousness sign recovery. In the case of MCS patients we have identified low beta in frontal and parietal areas, and alpha in the parietal-occipital area as the most important features. Interesting enough these areas correspond to the brain stimulation targets.

We have applied machine learning in a very innovative application that provides clinicians with a Decision Support System (DSS) to predict tES outcome. The developed system accurately predicts the outcome in 16/17 patients. The clinical usage of such a DSS system could save clinicians time and allow patients to skip a tedious therapeutic intervention when its success probability is very low. The innovation potential of such an application goes far beyond the treatment of DOC patients as we plan to further develop in the mid-term and constitutes a very interesting application field for machine learning approaches.

References

Vosskuhl, J., Struber, D., Herrmann, C.S.: Non-invasive brain stimulation: a paradigm shift in understanding brain oscillations. Front. Hum. Neurosci. **12**, 211 (2018)

Kuo, M.F., Paulus, W., Nitsche, M.A.: Therapeutic effects of non-invasive brain stimulation with direct currents (tCS) in neuropsychiatric diseases. Neuroimage **85**, 948–960 (2014)

Woo, C.W., Chang, L.J., Lindquist, M.A., Wager, T.D.: Building better biomarkers: brain models in translational neuroimaging. Nat. Neurosci. **20**(3), 365 (2017)

Lefaucheur, J.P., et al.: Evidence-based guidelines on the therapeutic use of transcranial direct current stimulation (tDCS). Clin. Neurophysiol. **128**(1), 56–92 (2017)

Martens, G., et al.: Behavioral and electro-physiological effects of network-based frontoparietal tDCS in patients with severe brain injury: a randomized controlled trial. NeuroImage. Clin. **28**, 102426 (2020). https://doi.org/10.1016/j.nicl.2020.102426

Wu, W., et al.: An electroencephalograph-ic signature predicts antidepressant response in major depression. Nat Biotechnol. **38**(4), 439–447 (2020). https://doi.org/10.1038/s41587-019-0397-3

Scangos, K.W., Weiner, R.D., Coffey, E.C., Krystal, A.D.: An electrophysio-logical biomarker that may predict treatment response to ECT. J ECT. **35**(2), 95–102 (2019). https://doi.org/10.1097/YCT.0000000000000557

Ovadia-Caro, S., Khalil, A.A., Sehm, B., Villringer, A., Nazarova, M.: Predicting the response to non-invasive brain stimulation in stroke. Front. Neurol. **10**, 302 (2019)

Hordacre, B., Moezzi, B., Goldsworthy, M.R., Rogasch, N.C., Ridding, M.C.: Resting state functional connectivity measures correlate with the response to anodal transcranial direct current stimulation. Eur J Neurosci **45**, 837–845 (2017). https://doi.org/10.1111/ejn.13508

Estraneo, A., et al.: Multicenter prospective study on predictors of short-term outcome in disorders of consciousness. Neurology **95**(11), e1488–e1499 (2020)

Maaten, L.V.D., Hinton, G.: Visualizing data using t-SNE. J. Mach. Learn. Res. 9, 2579–2605 (2008)

Wold, S., Esbensen, K., Geladi, P.: Principal component analysis. Chemometr. Intell. Lab. Syst. **2**(1–3), 37–52 (1987)

Efron, B., Tibshirani, R.J.: An introduction to the bootstrap. CRC Press, Boca Raton (1994)

Cortes, C., Vapnik, V.: Support-vector networks . Mach. Learning **20**(3), 273–297 (1995)

Breiman, L.: Random forest. Mach. Learn. **45**(1), 5–32 (2001)

El Shawi, R., Sherif, Y., Al-Mallah, M., Sakr, S.: Interpretability in healthcare a comparative study of local machine learning inter-pretability techniques. In: IEEE 32nd International Symposium on Computer-Based Medical Systems (CBMS), Cordoba, Spain, vol. 2019, 275–280 (2019). https://doi.org/10.1109/CBMS.2019.00065

Bergstra, J., Bengio, Y.: Random search for hyper-parameter optimization. J. Mach. Learn. Res. **13**(1), 281–305 (2012)

Bočková, M., Rektor, I.: (2019) Impairment of brain functions in Parkinson's disease reflected by alterations in neural connectivity in EEG studies: a viewpoint. Clin. Neurophysiol. **130**(2), 239–247 (2019). https://doi.org/10.1016/j.clinph.2018.11.013. Epub 2018 Dec 3 PMID: 30580247

van der Maaten, L.J.P.: Learning a parametric embedding by preserving local structure. In: Proceedings of the Twelfth International Conference on Artificial Intelligence & Statistics (AI-STATS), JMLR W&CP, vol. 5, pp. 384–391 (2009)

Sinc-Based Convolutional Neural Networks for EEG-BCI-Based Motor Imagery Classification

Alessandro Bria[1]([envelope]) [iD], Claudio Marrocco[1] [iD], and Francesco Tortorella[2] [iD]

[1] University of Cassino and Southern Latium, 03043 Cassino, FR, Italy
a.bria@unicas.it
[2] University of Salerno, 84084 Fisciano, SA, Italy

Abstract. Brain-Computer Interfaces (BCI) based on motor imagery translate mental motor images recognized from the electroencephalogram (EEG) to control commands. EEG patterns of different imagination tasks, e.g. hand and foot movements, are effectively classified with machine learning techniques using band power features. Recently, also Convolutional Neural Networks (CNNs) that learn both effective features and classifiers simultaneously from raw EEG data have been applied. However, CNNs have two major drawbacks: (i) they have a very large number of parameters, which thus requires a very large number of training examples; and (ii) they are not designed to explicitly learn features in the frequency domain. To overcome these limitations, in this work we introduce Sinc-EEGNet, a lightweight CNN architecture that combines learnable band-pass and depthwise convolutional filters. Experimental results obtained on the publicly available BCI Competition IV Dataset 2a show that our approach outperforms reference methods in terms of classification accuracy.

Keywords: Motor imagery · Brain computer interface · Convolutional neural networks

1 Introduction

A Brain-Computer Interface (BCI) translates brain signals into messages or commands for an interactive task. This enables a wide range of applications from clinic to industry for both patients and healthy users, such as rehabilitation devices for stroke patients [22], controllable wheelchairs and prostheses [35], new gaming input devices [8], to name a few. Among different brain activity monitoring modalities, noninvasive approaches based on electroencephalography (EEG) use multiple electrodes placed on the skull surface to record the activity of cerebral cortical neurons [5] and are widely used in many BCI studies thanks to

This work was supported by MIUR (Minister for Education, University and Research, Law 232/216, Department of Excellence).

A. Del Bimbo et al. (Eds.): ICPR 2020 Workshops, LNCS 12661, pp. 526–535, 2021.
https://doi.org/10.1007/978-3-030-68763-2_40

their ease of implementation, reduced costs and high availability [20]. The most popular EEG signals used to control BCI systems are P300 evoked potentials, steady-state visual evoked potentials (SSVEP) and motor imagery (MI) which is the focus of our work. Specifically, MI refers to the imagination of moving certain body parts without actual movement [28]. Different MI tasks result into discriminable patterns observed from the oscillatory activities in the sensorimotor cortex region of the brain [21]. Imagination of left hand, right hand, foot and tongue movements are the most investigated MI tasks in the BCI literature [15].

Handcrafted feature extraction methods coupled with conventional classifiers like Linear Discriminant Analysis (LDA), Support Vector Machines (SVM), Bayesian classifiers, and Nearest Neighbor classifiers have been used in a number of studies for MI task recognition [15]. A widely used approach is to extract and combine band power features from different channel(electrode) signals to capture connectivity patterns among different regions of the sensorimotor cortex and, ultimately, their interaction and engagement with each other. This is thought to play a fundamental role in accomplishing movement imaginations [14]. Common spatial patterns (*CSP*) were introduced to this end in [23] and received a large share of research in the field [4,16,25,26,34], but their effectiveness depended on subject-specific frequency bands. This problem was alleviated by the popular filter bank CSP (*FBCSP*) [1] that decomposes the EEG into multiple frequency pass bands prior to spatial filtering, feature selection and classification. This method also won the BCI Competition IV [33] for 4-class motor imagery recognition (Dataset 2a) and was since used as a reference method for comparison.

Given their effectiveness in other fields [9,29], deep learning methods, and in particular Convolutional Neural Networks (CNNs) [13], have the potential to learn both effective features and classifiers simultaneously from raw EEG data. Several studies have recently explored deep learning for MI classification [12,17,27,31,32]. Notably, [27] showed that their *Shallow ConvNet* (one temporal convolution, one spatial convolution, squaring and mean pooling) could outperform their *Deep ConvNet* (temporal convolution, spatial convolution, then three layers of standard convolution) as well as *FBCSP*. A similar result was achieved by [12] with *EEGNet*, a compact lightweight network (one temporal convolution, one depthwise convolution, one separable convolution, and a fully connected layer) that compared favorably with *Deep ConvNet* and performed on par with *Shallow ConvNet*. These results indicate that shallow networks having a small number of parameters are beneficial for MI applications that are characterized by very small numbers of training examples because of the difficulty in performing millions or even thousands of mental commands during training sessions.

In this paper we propose *Sinc-EEGNet*, a 4-layer CNN architecture that combines the benefits of both EEG frequency band decomposition of classical methods, such as *FBCSP*, and automatic feature learning and extraction of lightweight CNN models, such as *EEGNet*. In particular, the first convolutional layer of our network is restricted to use parameterized sinc functions that implement band pass filters. The subsequent depthwise and separable convolution

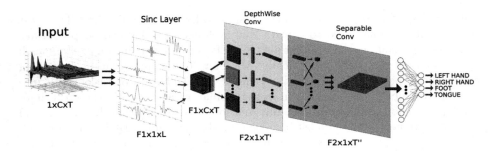

Fig. 1. An overview of the proposed *Sinc-EEGNet* architecture.

layers learn a spatial filter and combine the features from the different frequency bands previously selected, which are then inputted to the final classification layer. An overview of the proposed architecture is shown in Fig. 1.

2   Sinc Layer

A standard CNN convolution layer applied on a one-dimensional discrete time-domain signal $s[t]$ performs convolutions with F one-dimensional filters $h_1, ..., h_F$ each having K learnable weights. Conversely, the Sinc layer performs convolutions with F predefined functions $g_1, ..., g_F$ each implementing a learnable band-pass filter G as the difference between two low-pass filters in the frequency domain:

$$G[f] = rect\left(\frac{f}{2f_2}\right) - rect\left(\frac{f}{2f_1}\right) \tag{1}$$

where f_1 and $f_2 > f_1$ are the learnable low and high cutoff frequencies. Using the inverse Fourier transform, the time-domain filter g is obtained as:

$$g[t] = 2f_2 sinc(2\pi f_2 t) - 2f_1 sinc(2\pi f_1 t) \tag{2}$$

where the sinc function is defined as $sinc(x) = sin(x)/x$. The cutoff frequencies are initialized by sampling from a Gaussian distribution with mean and variance equal to $f_s/4$, where f_s represents the sampling frequency of the input signal. The constraint $f_2 > f_1$ is implemented by using in Eq. 2 the following cutoff frequencies f_1^{abs} and f_2^{abs}:

$$f_1^{abs} = |f_1| \tag{3}$$

$$f_2^{abs} = f_1 + |f_2 - f_1|. \tag{4}$$

Because of the discrete approximation of g, the resulting bandpass filter is non-ideal and may present ripples in the passband and limited attenuation in the stopband. To alleviate this problem, we multiply g with the popular Hamming window w [18] defined as:

$$w[t] = 0.54 - 0.46 \cdot \cos\left(\frac{2\pi t}{L}\right) \tag{5}$$

where L is the number of discrete samples used to approximate g. The sinc convolutional layer transforming the input signal $s[t]$ into the band-decomposed output signal $o_1, ..., o_F$ is then defined by:

$$o_i[t] = s[t] * (g_i[t] \cdot w[t]) \,. \tag{6}$$

3   The Sinc-EEGNet Architecture

The proposed Sinc-EEGNet is a combination and adaptation of the Sinc convolution layer originally proposed by [24] for speech recognition with *SincNet*, and *EEGNet* [12] for what concerns the spatial filtering implemented with depthwise convolution. Specifically, the architecture of Sinc-EEGNet (see Fig. 1 and Table 1) consists of four blocks described as follows:

1. *Sinc Convolution.* The first block takes in input a signal having C channels and T time samples, and performs convolution with F_1 sinc filters having L time samples. Compared to the first standard convolution layer used in other CNN architectures such as *EEGNet*, here the sinc filters are explicitly designed to learn the optimal band decomposition for the MI classification task and, when the CNN is trained with data from a single BCI user, this will reflect the peculiarities of the EEG oscillatory activity of that user. Another advantage is the reduced number of parameters, from $K \times F_1$ of the standard convolution to $2 \times F_1$ of the sinc convolution. This also implies faster convergence and better generalization capabilities especially when using small training sets as in the case of MI applications. Computational efficiency also is improved since the filters are symmetric, thus the convolution can be performed on one side of the filter and inheriting the result for the other half.
2. *Depthwise Convolution.* Similarly to *EEGNet* [12], we use a Depthwise Convolution layer [6] of size $(C, 1)$ to learn D spatial filters for each of the F_1 inputted feature maps across the channel dimension, for a total of $F_2 = D \times F_1$ filters. Combined with the first layer that performs optimal band decomposition, this two-step sequence can be considered a 'learnable' version of the well known *FBCSP* [1] approach.
3. *Separable Convolution.* Similarly to *EEGNet*, we summarize each feature map individually using a Depthwise Convolution of size $(1, 16)$, and then merge the outputs using F_2 $(1, 1)$ Pointwise Convolutions. This allows optimal combination of the information within and across feature maps.
4. *Classification.* The last layer is a fully connected layer that receives the flattened features from the previous layer and maps them to 4 decision classes (left hand, right hand, foot, tongue).

At the end of blocks 1–3 we apply Average Pooling of size $(1, 4)$ for dimensionality reduction, Layer Normalization [2], Dropout regularization [30], and CELU activation [3]. Layer Normalization, as opposed to Batch Normalization [10] used in other architectures (*EEGNet, Deep ConvNet, Shallow ConvNet*), calculates the mean and variance across channels instead than batches. This

Table 1. Sinc-EEGNet architecture, where C = number of channels, T = number of time points, L = number of sinc samples, F_1 = number of temporal filters, D = number of spatial filters, F_2 = number of pointwise filters, and N = number of classes.

Block	Layer	Filters	Size	Params	Output	Activation
1	Input				(C, T)	
	Reshape				$(1, C, T)$	
	Sinc convolution	F_1	$(1, L)$	$2 \times F_1$	(F_1, C, T)	
	Average pooling		$(1, 4)$		$(F_1, C, \frac{T}{4})$	
	Layer normalization			$2 \times F_1$	$(F_1, C, \frac{T}{4})$	CELU
	Dropout				$(F_1, C, \frac{T}{4})$	
2	Depthwise convolution	$D \times F_1$	$(C, 1)$	$C \times D \times F_1$	$(D \times F_1, 1, \frac{T}{4})$	
	Average pooling		$(1, 4)$		$(D \times F_1, 1, \frac{T}{16})$	
	Layer normalization			$2 \times D \times F_1$	$(D \times F_1, 1, \frac{T}{16})$	CELU
	Dropout				$(D \times F_1, 1, \frac{T}{16})$	
3	Depthwise convolution	$D \times F_1$	$(1, 16)$	$16 \times D \times F_1$	$(D \times F_1, 1, \frac{T}{16})$	
	Layer normalization			$2 \times D \times F_1$	$(D \times F_1, 1, \frac{T}{16})$	CELU
	Dropout				$(D \times F_1, 1, \frac{T}{16})$	
	Pointwise convolution	F_2	$(1, 1)$	$F_2 \times (D \times F_1)$	$(F_2, 1, \frac{T}{16})$	
	Average pooling		$(1, 4)$		$(F_2, 1, \frac{T}{64})$	
	Layer normalization			$2 \times F_2$	$(F_2, 1, \frac{T}{64})$	CELU
	Dropout				$(F_2, 1, \frac{T}{64})$	
4	Flatten				$F_2 \times \frac{T}{64}$	
	Fully connected			$N \times F_2 \times \frac{T}{64}$	N	Softmax

is especially useful for BCI datasets characterized by a high number of channels(electrodes) and small batch sizes resulting from the scarcity of training data. As to the CELU activation, it is an improvement over the ELU activation [7] used in other architectures (*EEGNet, Deep ConvNet, Shallow ConvNet*) since its derivative does not diverge and it contains both the linear transfer function and ReLU [19] activation as special cases.

4 Experiments

The EEG data used in this study comes from the BCI Competition IV Dataset 2A [33]. The data consists of four classes of imagined movements of left and right hands, feet and tongue recorded from 9 subjects during two separate sessions, each composed by 288 trials. The EEG data were originally recorded using $C = 22$ Ag/AgCl electrodes(channels), sampled 250 Hz and bandpass filtered between 0.5 and 100 Hz. We applied a further bandpass filtering to suppress frequencies 64 Hz and resampled the timeseries 128 Hz as in [12]. Z-score standardization was used to normalize the signals within each trial.

Table 2. Comparison of classification accuracies between our method and reference methods on the BCI Competition IV-2A.

Method	Accuracy
FBCSP	68.0%
Deep ConvNet	70.9%
Shallow ConvNet	73.7%
Sinc-EEGNet	75.39%

EEG data were splitted for training and testing according to three different paradigms:

1. *Competition-based.* The training and test sets were the same as indicated in the BCI Competition. This allowed to compare our method with reference methods from the literature that reported their results using the same data split, namely *FBSCP* [1], *Deep ConvNet* [27], and *Shallow ConvNet* [27] as well as all other participants to the original challenge.
2. *Within-subject.* For each subject, a dedicated experiment was performed using only data from that subject from the BCI Competition training and test sets.
3. *Cross-subject.* For each subject, a dedicated experiment was performed using only data from other subjects from the BCI Competition training set, and only data from that subject from the BCI Competition test set.

In all the experiments, we performed a four-class classification using accuracy as the summary measure. In the within- and cross-subject experiments, we also trained and tested an *EEGNet* with $F_1 = 8$ and $D = 2$, which was the best performing CNN reported in [12]. As to our *Sinc-EEGNet*, we chose $D = 2$ for a fair comparison with *EEGNet*, but we set $F_1 = 32$ since our Sinc layer is specifically designed for frequency band decomposition and thus can benefit from learning a wide variety of bandpass filters. This can be seen in Fig. 2 that shows 32 distinct filters learnt by *Sinc-EEGNet* in the competition-based experiment. The number of samples L used to discretize the sinc functions was set to 64 that resulted from a trade-off between approximation precision and computational complexity.

All the CNNs were trained using backpropagation and Adam optimizer [11] with weight updates that proceeded in batches of 20 samples for 100 epochs. The base learning rate was set to 10^{-3}. Momentum and weight decay were set respectively to 0.9 and 2×10^{-2}. Following [12], for the Dropout layers we chose $p = 0.5$ for within-subject experiments, and $p = 0.25$ for competition-based and cross-subject experiments that used more training data and thus required less regularization. The loss function was categorical cross-entropy.

5 Results

The comparison between *Sinc-EEGNet* and the reference methods from the literature on the competition-based data split are reported in Table 2. Remarkably,

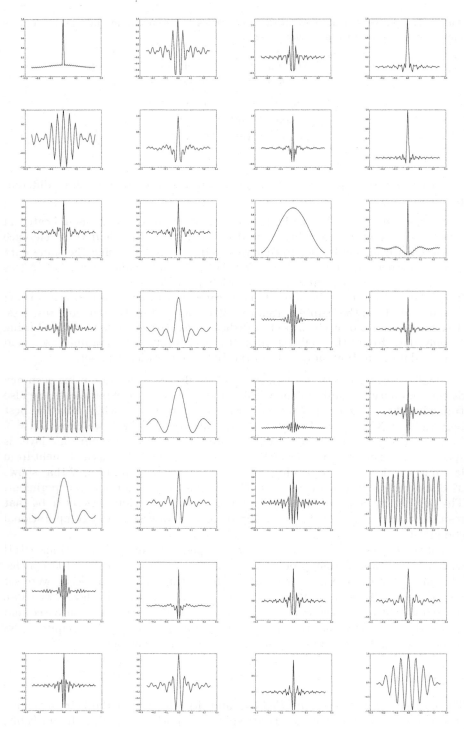

Fig. 2. The 32 sinc filters learnt by *Sinc-EEGNet* on the BCI Competition IV Dataset 2A.

Sinc-EEGNet outperforms all other methods in terms of accuracy and sets a new state-of-the-art on the BCI Competition IV-2A with an accuracy of 75.39% that improves *FBCSP* by 17.39%. As to the within- and cross-subject experiments, *EEGNet* yielded an average accuracy of 60.99% and 58.75%, respectively, and *Sinc-EEGNet* of 70.56% and 58.98%, respectively. Also in this case, our method exhibited superior performance, with an improvement of almost 10% accuracy in the more practically adopted within-subject classification.

6   Conclusions

In this work we proposed *Sinc-EEGNet*, a lightweight convolutional neural network for EEG-BCI-based motor imagery classification that learns optimal band decomposition and spatial filtering, mimicking the behavior of the well-known *FBCSP* but learning the filters directly from the raw EEG data. Our method outperformed reference methods from the literature, including *FBCSP* and *EEG-Net*, on the publicly available BCI Competition IV-2A dataset. To the best of our knowledge, this is the first work that validated the use of learnable band-pass filters in the first layer of a CNN for EEG signal classification. Future work will investigate alternative frequency filters, such as Difference of Gaussian (DoG) filter, that are less subject to discrete approximation issues, and architecture variants that explore different spatial filtering and feature map combination approaches.

References

1. Ang, K.K., Chin, Z.Y., Wang, C., Guan, C., Zhang, H.: Filter bank common spatial pattern algorithm on BCI competition iv datasets 2a and 2b. Front. Neurosci. **6**, 39 (2012)
2. Ba, J.L., Kiros, J.R., Hinton, G.E.: Layer normalization. arXiv preprint arXiv:1607.06450 (2016)
3. Barron, J.T.: Continuously differentiable exponential linear units. arXiv pp. arXiv-1704 (2017)
4. Blankertz, B., Tomioka, R., Lemm, S., Kawanabe, M., Muller, K.R.: Optimizing spatial filters for robust EEG single-trial analysis. IEEE Sig. Process. Mag. **25**(1), 41–56 (2007)
5. Britton, J.W., et al.: Electroencephalography (EEG): An introductory text and atlas of normal and abnormal findings in adults, children, and infants. American Epilepsy Society, Chicago (2016)
6. Chollet, F.: Xception: deep learning with depthwise separable convolutions. In: Proceedings of the IEEE Conference on Computer Vision and Pattern Recognition, pp. 1251–1258 (2017)
7. Clevert, D.A., Unterthiner, T., Hochreiter, S.: Fast and accurate deep network learning by exponential linear units (elus). arXiv preprint arXiv:1511.07289 (2015)
8. Coyle, D., Principe, J., Lotte, F., Nijholt, A.: Guest editorial: brain/neuronal-computer game interfaces and interaction. IEEE Trans. Comput. Intell. AI games **5**(2), 77–81 (2013)

9. He, K., Zhang, X., Ren, S., Sun, J.: Delving deep into rectifiers: Surpassing human-level performance on imagenet classification. In: Proceedings of the IEEE International Conference on Computer Vision, pp. 1026–1034 (2015)
10. Ioffe, S., Szegedy, C.: Batch normalization: accelerating deep network training by reducing internal covariate shift. arXiv preprint arXiv:1502.03167 (2015)
11. Kingma, D.P., Ba, J.: Adam: a method for stochastic optimization. arXiv preprint arXiv:1412.6980 (2014)
12. Lawhern, V.J., et al.: Eegnet: a compact convolutional neural network for EEG-based brain-computer interfaces. J. Neural Eng. 15(5), 056013 (2018)
13. LeCun, Y., Bengio, Y., Hinton, G.: Deep learning. Nature 521(7553), 436–444 (2015)
14. Liu, T., et al.: Cortical dynamic causality network for auditory-motor tasks. IEEE Trans. Neural Syst. Rehabil. Eng. 25(8), 1092–1099 (2016)
15. Lotte, F., et al.: A review of classification algorithms for EEG-based brain-computer interfaces: a 10 year update. J. Neural Eng. 15(3), 031005 (2018)
16. Lotte, F., Guan, C.: Regularizing common spatial patterns to improve BCI designs: unified theory and new algorithms. IEEE Trans. Biomed. Eng. 58(2), 355–362 (2010)
17. Lu, N., Li, T., Ren, X., Miao, H.: A deep learning scheme for motor imagery classification based on restricted Boltzmann machines. IEEE Trans. Neural Syst. Rehabil. Eng. 25(6), 566–576 (2016)
18. Mitra, S.K.: Digital Signal Processing. McGraw-Hill Science/Engineering/Math (2005)
19. Nair, V., Hinton, G.E.: Rectified linear units improve restricted Boltzmann machines. In: ICML (2010)
20. Nicolas-Alonso, L.F., Gomez-Gil, J.: Brain computer interfaces, a review. Sensors 12(2), 1211–1279 (2012)
21. Pfurtscheller, G., Da Silva, F.L.: Event-related EEG/MEG synchronization and desynchronization: basic principles. Clin. Neurophysiol. 110(11), 1842–1857 (1999)
22. Pichiorri, F., et al.: Brain-computer interface boosts motor imagery practice during stroke recovery. Ann. Neurol. 77(5), 851–865 (2015)
23. Ramoser, H., Muller-Gerking, J., Pfurtscheller, G.: Optimal spatial filtering of single trial EEG during imagined hand movement. IEEE Trans. Rehabil. Eng. 8(4), 441–446 (2000)
24. Ravanelli, M., Bengio, Y.: Interpretable convolutional filters with sincnet. arXiv preprint arXiv:1811.09725 (2018)
25. Rivet, B., Cecotti, H., Phlypo, R., Bertrand, O., Maby, E., Mattout, J.: EEG sensor selection by sparse spatial filtering in p300 speller brain-computer interface. In: 2010 Annual International Conference of the IEEE Engineering in Medicine and Biology, pp. 5379–5382. IEEE (2010)
26. Samek, W., Kawanabe, M., Müller, K.R.: Divergence-based framework for common spatial patterns algorithms. IEEE Rev. Biomed. Eng. 7, 50–72 (2013)
27. Schirrmeister, R.T., et al.: Deep learning with convolutional neural networks for EEG decoding and visualization. Hum. Brain Map. 38(11), 5391–5420 (2017)
28. Schuster, C., et al.: Best practice for motor imagery: a systematic literature review on motor imagery training elements in five different disciplines. BMC Med. 9(1), 75 (2011)
29. Silver, D., et al.: Mastering the game of go with deep neural networks and tree search. Nature 529(7587), 484 (2016)

30. Srivastava, N., Hinton, G., Krizhevsky, A., Sutskever, I., Salakhutdinov, R.: Dropout: a simple way to prevent neural networks from overfitting. J. Mach. Learn. Res. **15**(1), 1929–1958 (2014)
31. Sturm, I., Lapuschkin, S., Samek, W., Müller, K.R.: Interpretable deep neural networks for single-trial EEG classification. J. Neurosci. Meth. **274**, 141–145 (2016)
32. Tabar, Y.R., Halici, U.: A novel deep learning approach for classification of EEG motor imagery signals. J. Neural Eng. **14**(1), 016003 (2016)
33. Tangermann, M., et al.: Review of the BCI competition IV. Front. Neurosci. **6**, 55 (2012)
34. Yger, F., Lotte, F., Sugiyama, M.: Averaging covariance matrices for EEG signal classification based on the CSP: an empirical study. In: 2015 23rd European Signal Processing Conference (EUSIPCO), pp. 2721–2725. IEEE (2015)
35. Zhang, R., et al.: Control of a wheelchair in an indoor environment based on a brain-computer interface and automated navigation. IEEE Trans. Neural Syst. Rehabil. Eng. **24**(1), 128–139 (2015)

An Analysis of Tasks and Features for Neuro-Degenerative Disease Assessment by Handwriting

Vincenzo Dentamaro[(⊠)] ⬥, Donato Impedovo ⬥, and Giuseppe Pirlo ⬥

University of Bari "Aldo Moro", Via Orabona 4, Bari, Italy
Vincenzo.dentamaro@uniba.it

Abstract. Neurodegenerative disease assessment with handwriting has been shown to be effective. In this exploratory analysis, several features are extracted and tested on different tasks of the novel HAND-UNIBA dataset. Results show what are the most important kinematic features and the most significant tasks for neurodegenerative disease assessment through handwriting.

Keywords: Hand-uniba · Neurodegenrative disease · Handwriting · Kinematic theory · Velocity-based features

1 Introduction

Neurodegenerative diseases such as Alzheimer disease (AD) and Parkinson's disease (PD) are the most common neurodegenerative disorders.

These diseases are characterized by a progressive decline of cognitive, functional and behavioural areas of the brain [1, 2]. At moment, several behavioural biometrics techniques can be used for assessing neurodegenerative diseases, such as speech [4], showing promising accuracies in binary classification (healthy/unhealthy). It is important to state that these techniques are non-invasive.

Another non-invasive technique which has been well studied in neurodegenerative diseases assessment is handwriting. Nonetheless, it is well known that handwriting problems are related to the majority of neurodegenerative diseases and their severity, so handwriting changes are considered an important biomarker [1, 2]. On its own, handwriting, is a complex activity entailing kinesthetic, cognitive and perceptual-motor related tasks [4], whose are used for the evaluation of several neurodegenerative diseases such as PD and AD [3, 5–7, 20–22].

Here, handwriting acquisition is performed online: a tablet is used to acquire the x, y coordinates, as well as azimuth, pressure, altitude, in air movements and the timestamps of each acquisition.

Thus, the acquired trait is a sequence $\{S(n)\}_{n=0, 1,...,N}$, where $S(n)$ is the signal value sampled at time $n\Delta t$ of the writing process ($0 \leq n \leq N$), Δt being the sampling period (in this experiments the sampling frequency is strictly set to 200 Hz).

© Springer Nature Switzerland AG 2021
A. Del Bimbo et al. (Eds.): ICPR 2020 Workshops, LNCS 12661, pp. 536–545, 2021.
https://doi.org/10.1007/978-3-030-68763-2_41

In this paper, a subset of a novel dataset, called HAND-UNIBA dataset, has been used for assessing neurodegenerative diseases trough handwriting. In this paper, 8 different tasks are presented and classical features, as well as velocity-based features are investigated. Some of these features include the Maxwell-Boltzmann distribution and transform based features.

This is a preliminary study on this dataset and accuracies are reported only on a subset of tasks of this dataset, as it is currently under development.

The paper is organized as follows. Section 2 sketches classic velocity-based features, Sect. 3 illustrates additional kinematic-based features. In Sect. 4 experiments and results are presented. Section 5 sketches conclusions and future remarks.

2 Classic Velocity-Based Features

Neurodegenerative diseases show some important motor deficits such as bradykinesia (slowness of movement), akinesia (impairment of voluntary activity), micrographia (reduction in writing size), and rigidity and tremor [2].

In order to model these symptoms, velocity-based features have shown to be effective when writing meanders, circle, star, sentence/name, spirals as well as on copying tasks [3, 8–10] and [12].

Other tasks, such as meanders, horizontal, straight forward and backward slanted lines, circles drawing and sentence writing have demonstrated to model the Tremor/Jerk [11, 12] and [13].

Here, the velocity is meant as the derivative of the displacement. Tremor/Jerk is evaluated in terms of Number of Changes in Velocity (NCV) and/or in Acceleration (NCA) and/or as the derivative of the acceleration signal. Since the result are vectors of values, statistical parameters such as mean, median, standard deviation, 1st percentile, 99th percentile are used to synthetize the previously computed features.

3 Additional Kinematic-Based Features

The Selected Kinematic Based Features Are the Maxwell Boltzmann Distribution and the Discrete Fourier Transformation.

3.1 Maxwell-Boltzmann Distribution

Maxwell-Boltzmann distribution has been already used to model handwriting velocity profiles and handwritten digit recognition [14].

The Maxwell-Boltzmann distribution used in this work, is used for determining a set of parameters according to the following formula:

$$mb_j = v_j^2 e^{-v_j^2}.$$

Where mb_j means Maxwell-boltxman at time j and v is the velocity profile.

3.2 Discrete Transformations

The Discrete Fourier Transform (DFT) was used for computing the coefficients necessary to represent the velocity profile of the handwritten pattern. [15] It is expected that healthy control subjects have different coefficients with respect to patients with some form of neurodegenerative disease.

For sake of completeness, the real cepstrum of the velocity profile is computed using the following formulation:

$$rcep = IDFT\{log[|DFT(v_j)|]\},$$

The Inverse Discrete Fourier Transform (IDFT) is the spectrum containing harmonics whose magnitude is inversely proportional to the frequency. [16] The natural logarithm of the spectrum allows to re-organize the frequencies by re-organizing the dynamic range. In this way, components with low variations, are approximated close to 0. Intuitively, if the velocity profile is composed by an underling periodic pattern (tremor, jerks), this pattern is represented as various, but repeated peaks in the cepstrum at higher frequencies.

In addition to the Inverse Discrete Fourier Transform, the Discrete Cosine Transform was also implied.

4 Experiment

The raw data was captured by the device by using the x and y coordinates of the pen position and their timestamps, pen inclination (tilt-x and tilt-y) and pen pressure. Finally, also the so-called button status was captured, which is a binary variable evaluating 0 for pen-up state (in-air movement) and 1 for pen-down state (on-surface movement). All the features have the same length, varying from execution to execution. Therefore, the execution of a task can be described by a matrix $X = (x, y, p, t, tilt\_x, tilt\_y, b)$, where each column is a vector of length N, where M equals to the number of sampled points.

The tasks are presented in Table 2. For the check copying task, the user is asked to copy a check as shown in Fig. 1.

Other tasks are matrices, where the user is asked to find and mark one or more predefined numbers as shown in Fig. 2.

It is clear that the trail test in Fig. 3 is made by someone with a neurodegenerative disease.

Specifically, the subset used in this study is composed by 42 subjects in total: 21 subjects with a neurodegenerative disease in mild, assessed, severe or very severe state and 21 healthy control subjects. Age and sex of the subjects, in this first exploratory analysis, is not kept into consideration. The choice of these task was driven by the fact that no other authors used these new tasks, and an initial accuracy investigation was required. Patients suffering of neurodegenerative disease were assessed by neurologists and psychologists using standardized medical tests. The tablet used is a Wacom mobile studio pro with pen support and Microsoft Windows 10. This tablet has a pen and matte screen surface that gives similar user experience of writing with pen and paper.

Table 1. Features

Feature name	Description
Position	Position in terms of s (x,y)
Button Status	Movement in the air: b(t) = 0 Movement on the pad: b(t) = 1
Pressure	Pressure of the pen on the pad
Azimuth	Angle between the pen and the vertical plane on the pad
Altitude	Angle between the pen and the pad plane
Displacement	$d_i \begin{cases} \sqrt[2]{(x_{i+1} - x_i)^2 + (y_{i+1} - y_i)^2}, 1 \leq i \leq n-1 \\ d_n - d_{n-1}, i = n \end{cases}$
Velocity	$v_i = \begin{cases} \frac{d_i}{t_{i+1} - t_i}, 1 \leq i \leq n-1 \\ v_n - v_{n-1}, i = n \end{cases}$
Acceleration	$a_i = \begin{cases} \frac{v_i}{t_{i+1} - t_i}, 1 \leq i \leq n-1 \\ a_n - a_{n-1}, i = n \end{cases}$
Jerk	$j_i = \begin{cases} \frac{a_i}{t_{i+1} - t_i}, 1 \leq i \leq n-1 \\ j_n - j_{n-1}, i = n \end{cases}$
x/y displacement	Displacement in the x/y direction
x/y velocity	Velocity in the x/y direction
x/y acceleration	Acceleration in the x/y direction
x/y jerk	Jerk in the horizontal/vertical direction
NCV	Number of Changes in Velocity, NCV has been also normalized to writing duration
NCA	Number of Changes in Acceleration, NCA has been also normalized to writing duration
Kinematic Features	
Maxwell Boltzmann	$mb_j = v_j^2 e^{-v_j^2}$
IDFT Real Cepstrum	$rcep = IDFT\{log[|DFT(v_j)|]\}$
Discrete Cosine Transform	$F(u) = \left(\frac{2}{N}\right)^{\frac{1}{2}} \sum_{i=0}^{N-1} \Lambda(i) \cdot cos\left[\frac{\pi \cdot u}{2.N}(2i+1)\right] f(i)$

Features extracted were standardized (z-scored). In addition, Random Forest [17] ensemble learning algorithm with ordered feature importance was used as feature selection criteria [18] with a pre-pruning parameter of maximum tree depth of 10 and 50 trees, in order to prevent overfitting and balance accuracies.

Fig. 1. check copying task performed by a patient with dementia.

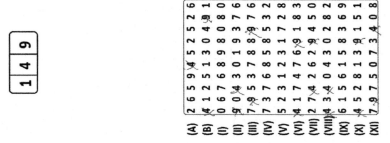

Fig. 2. Matrix M3 task.

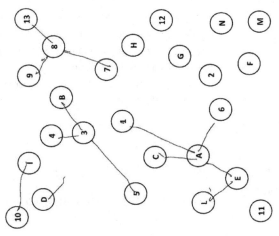

Fig. 3. Trail test 2 mixing numbers and letters, the patient is requested to connect numbers and letters respecting the order in an alternate fashion.

Table 2. Tasks.

Task name	Task description
Check	Check copying
M1	Matrix 1
M2	Matrix 2
M3	Matrix 3
Tmt1	Trail 1 (connecting path)
Tmt2	Trail 2 (connecting path)
Tmtt1	Trail test 1 (connecting path)
Tmtt2	Trail test 2 (connecting path)

For classification purposes, the Random Forest [17] algorithm was used. Its maximum depth was 10 and the number of trees was defined dynamically by inspecting the validation curve. An example can be seen in Fig. 4, the number of trees (estimators) used for this specific task is 5, but this depends on the task. Accuracies reported are based on randomized (shuffled) 10-Fold cross validation, where the entire procedure has been repeated ten times, until each fold is used as test set.

Thus, Random Forest algorithm was used in first instance for selecting the most important features and then for performing the final classification in 10-Fold cross validation fashion.

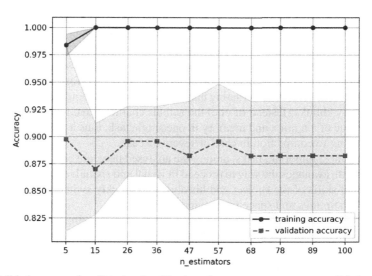

Fig. 4. Validation curve for all tasks classification, the green area represent validation standard deviation. (Color figure online)

Table 1 summarizes the features adopted used in this work. As mentioned earlier, for each feature, mean, median, standard deviation, 1st percentile and 99th percentile are used to synthetize the previously computed features. In this work, all the features reported in Table 1 have been implemented and represent the baseline on tasks on Table 2 with the amount of data currently analysed.

Table 3. Accuracy performances.

Task name	Accuracy	Standard deviation
Check copying	85.33%	10.4%
M1	67.69%	14.3%
M2	70.20%	12.5%
M3	70.38%	7.3%
Tmt1	79.91%	8.5%
Tmt2	72.62%	10.7%
Tmtt1	77.39%	9.4%
Tmtt2	85.83%	8.8%
All tasks	92.33%	7.4%
Selected tasks (check & tmtt2)	89.66%	6.5%

Performances on various tasks are shown in Table 3. In 10-Fold cross validation, and with data currently available, trail test 2(connecting path with medium/high difficulty) shown in Fig. 3 seems to be a prominent biomarker for neurodegenerative disease assessment, followed by Check copying task shown in Fig. 1.

The difference between Trail (1 and 2) and Trail Test, is that trail is simpler, and the patient should connect paths of number in order. Instead in Trail Tests, patient is required to connect paths in order but alternating numbers and letters. Doing so, the patient stores in two memory chunks (instead of one) the actuals character and number. This process brings evidence of attention and memory in one single task, thus it is more complete but difficult to bring to completion in case of severe disease.

Thus, the most important tasks, among the analysed here, are check copying and the trail tasks. Both, evaluates the way to proceed in visual and spatial research, investigating the attentional skills of the subject and his ability to quickly switch from a numeric to an alphabetic stimulus and space management [19].

Merging, for each patient, all features from all tasks and padding with zeroes the tasks that were not performed by the analysed subject, increased the accuracy considerably. In this case, merging all tasks the accuracy is 92.33%, instead using only check and tmtt2 tasks the overall accuracy is 89.66%. This result confirms our hypothesis of using ensemble of tasks. This is because an ensemble of tasks could help finding certain patterns not raised when using one single task alone, especially for tasks that are widely used in medicine for assessing certain type of neurodegenerative disease.

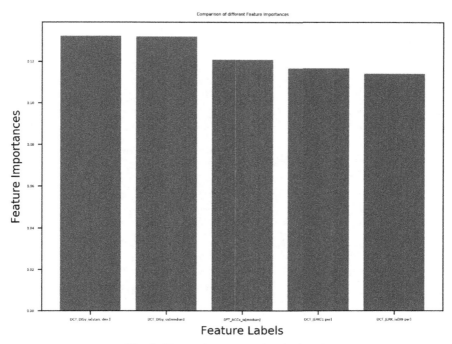

Fig. 5. Feature importance for check task

Ranking, for each task, the top 5 most important features using the Random Forest algorithm using Gini Index as internal metric and as reported in Fig. 5 and 6, it is possible to see that both the Discrete Cosine Transformation, as well as the Discrete Fourier Transformation on the displacement and acceleration of the y coordinate as well as the acceleration on both axis are among the top features in all the tasks. This finding reinforces once more that velocity-based features play a crucial role in detecting subjects with some kind of neurodegenerative disease from an online handwriting perspective.

Although the work proposed show solid background in terms of signal processing and accuracies in performing healthy/unhealthy classification, the main limitation of this work relies in the amount of data analyzed at moment. The dataset HAND-UNIBA will offer a wide higher range of subjects with various kinds of neurodegenerative disease and in various severity stages kept in 2 sessions with at least 6 months of distance from the first session for the same subject.

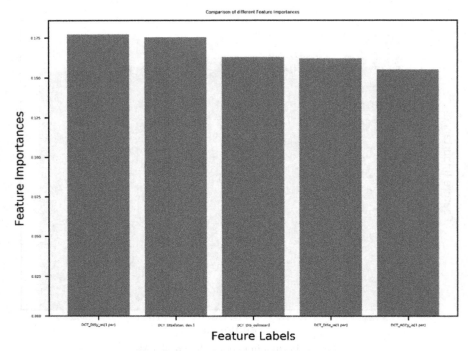

Fig. 6. Feature importance for tmtt2 task.

5   Conclusions

In this work, classic and kinematic based features have been employed to classify healthy/unhealthy subjects belonging to the new HAND-UNIBA dataset. This is an exploratory analysis on a subset of tasks of this dataset. Despite its numerosity, the results on this new dataset are encouraging and in line with other works on different datasets [15].

In future, new tasks will be evaluated and new features will be integrated with the aim to, not only perform binary classification healthy/unhealthy, but also predict the disease se-verity level and, since the dataset supports multiple sessions for same patients, also infer if the severity has increased with time or, if when some medication is taken, its severity has slowed down.

References

1. Impedovo, D., Pirlo, G.: Dynamic handwriting analysis for the assessment of neurodegenerative diseases: a pattern recognition perspective. IEEE Rev. Biomed. Eng. **12**, 209–220 (2019)
2. De Stefano, C., Fontanella, F., Impedovo, D., Pirlo, G., di Freca, A.S.: Handwriting analysis to support neurodegenerative diseases diagnosis: a review. Pattern Recogn. Lett. **121**, 37–45 (2019)

3. Rosenblum, S., Samuel, M., Zlotnik, S., Erikh, I., Schlesinger, I.: Handwriting as an objective tool for Parkinson's disease diagnosis. J. Neurol. **260**(9), 2357–2361 (2013)
4. Astrom, F., Koker, R.: A parallel neural network approach to prediction of Parkinson's disease. Expert Syst. Appl. **38**(10), 12470–12474 (2011)
5. O'Reilly, C., Plamondon, R.: Development of a sigma–lognormal representation for on-line signatures. Pattern Recogn. **42**(12), 3324–3337 (2009)
6. Pereira, C.R., et al.: A step towards the automated diagnosis of Parkinson's disease: analyzing handwriting movements. In: IEEE 28th International Symposium on Computer Based Medical Systems (CBMS), pp. 171–176 (2015)
7. Kahindo, C., El-Yacoubi, M.A., Garcia-Salicetti, S., Rigaud, A., Cristancho-Lacroix, V.: Characterizing early-stage Alzheimer through spatiotemporal dynamics of handwriting. IEEE Sig. Process. Lett. **25**(8), 1136–1140 (2018)
8. Caligiuri, M.P., Teulings, H.L., Filoteo, J.V., Song, D., Lohr, J.B.: Quantitative measurement of handwriting in the assessment of drug-induced Parkinsonism. Hum. Mov. Sci. **25**(4), 510–522 (2006)
9. Drotár, P., Mekyska, J., Rektorová, I., Masarová, L., Smékal, Z., Faun-dez-Zanuy, M.: Decision support framework for Parkinson's disease based on novel handwriting markers. IEEE Trans. Neural Syst. Rehabil. Eng. **23**(3), 508–516 (2015)
10. Ponsen, M.M., Daffertshofer, A., Wolters, E.C., Beek, P.J., Berendse, H.W.: Impairment of complex upper limb motor function in de novo Parkinson's disease. Parkinsonism Relat. Disord. **14**(3), 199–204 (2008)
11. Smits, E.J., et al.: Standardized handwriting to assess bradykinesia, micrographia and tremor in Parkinson's disease. PLoS ONE **9**(5), e97614 (2014)
12. Broderick, M.P., Van Gemmert, A.W., Shill, H.A.: Hypometria and bradykinesia during drawing movements in individuals with Parkinson disease. Exp. Brain Res. **197**(3), 223–233 (2009)
13. Kotsavasiloglou, C., Kostikis, N., Hristu-Varsakelis, D., Arnaoutoglou, M.: Machine learning-based classification of simple drawing movements in Parkinson's disease. Biomed. Sig. Process. Control **31**, 174–180 (2017)
14. Li, G., et al.: Temperature based restricted Boltzmann Machines. Sci. Rep. **6**(1), 1–12 (2016)
15. Impedovo, D.: Velocity-based signal features for the assessment of Parkinsonian handwriting. IEEE Sig. Process. Lett. **26**(4), 632–636 (2019)
16. Rao, K.R., Yip, P.: Discrete Cosine Transform: Algorithms, Advantages. Applications. Academic press, Cambridge (2014)
17. Breiman, L.: Random forest. Mach. Learn. **45**(1), 5–32 (2001)
18. Baraniuk, R.G.: Compressive sensing [lecture notes]. IEEE Sig. Process. Mag. **24**(4), 118–121 (2007)
19. Reitan, R.M.: Validity of the trail making test as an indicator of organic brain damage. Percept. Mot. Skills **8**(3), 271–276 (1958)
20. Cilia, N.D., De Stefano, C., Fontanella, F., Molinara, M., Scotto Di Freca, A.: Handwriting analysis to support alzheimer's disease diagnosis: a preliminary study. In: Vento, M., Percannella, G. (eds.) CAIP 2019. LNCS, vol. 11679, pp. 143–151. Springer, Cham (2019). https://doi.org/10.1007/978-3-030-29891-3_13
21. Cilia, N.D., De Stefano, C., Fontanella, F., Molinara, M., Di Freca, A.S.: Using handwriting features to characterize cognitive impairment. In: International Conference on Image Analysis and Processing, September 2019, pp. 683–693. Springer, Cham. https://doi.org/10.1007/978-3-030-30645-8_62
22. Cilia, N.D., De Stefano, C., Fontanella, F., Di Freca, A.S.: An experimental protocol to support cognitive impairment diagnosis by using handwriting analysis. Proc. Comput. Sci. **141**, 466–471 (2018)

A Comparative Study on Autism Spectrum Disorder Detection via 3D Convolutional Neural Networks

Kaijie Zhang[1,2], Wei Wang[1,2,3], Yijun Guo[2], Caifeng Shan[4,5], and Liang Wang[1,2,3]

[1] School of Artificial Intelligence, University of Chinese Academy of Sciences, Beijing, China
[2] Center for Research on Intelligent Perception and Computing, National Laboratory of Pattern Recognition, Beijing, China
{kaijie.zhang,yijun.guo}@cripac.ia.ac.cn,
{wangwei,wangliang}@nlpr.ia.ac.cn
[3] Center for Excellence in Brain Science and Intelligence Technology, Institute of Automation, Chinese Academy of Sciences, Beijing, China
[4] College of Electrical Engineering and Automation, Shandong University of Science and Technology, Qingdao, China
caifeng.shan@gmail.com
[5] Artificial Intelligence Research, Chinese Academy of Sciences, Beijing, China

Abstract. The prevalence of Autism Spectrum Disorder (ASD) in the United States has increased by 178% from 2000 to 2016. However, due to the lack of well-trained specialists and the time-consuming diagnostic process, many children are not able to be promptly diagnosed. Recently, several research have taken steps to explore automatic video-based ASD detection systems with the help of machine learning and deep learning models, such as support vector machine (SVM) and long short-term memory (LSTM) model. However, the models mentioned above could not extract effective features directly from raw videos. In this study, we aim to take advantages of 3D convolution-based deep learning models to aid video-based ASD detection. We explore three representative 3D convolutional neural networks (CNNs), including C3D, I3D and 3D ResNet. In addition, a new 3D convolutional model, called 3D ResNeSt, is also proposed based on ResNeSt. We evaluate these models on an ASD detection dataset. The experimental results show that, on average, all of the four 3D convolutional models can obtain competitive results when compared to the baseline using LSTM model. Our proposed 3D ResNeSt model achieves the best performance, which improves the average detection accuracy from 0.72 to 0.85.

Keywords: ASD detection · 3D convolution · 3D ResNeSt

© Springer Nature Switzerland AG 2021
A. Del Bimbo et al. (Eds.): ICPR 2020 Workshops, LNCS 12661, pp. 546–558, 2021.
https://doi.org/10.1007/978-3-030-68763-2_42

1   Introduction

Autism Spectrum Disorder (ASD) is a developmental disorder, which could impair communication abilities and cause psychological and physical abnormalities. Recent research has shown that the prevalence of ASD was 18.5 per 1,000 (1 in 54) children aged 8 years across all 11 sites of the United States in 2016, while the prevalence was 6.7 per 1000 (1 in 150) in 2000, which indicates that the prevalence has increased by 178% in 16 years [12]. However, due to the lack of well-trained specialists and the time-consuming diagnostic process, many children cannot be diagnosed as early as possible. It is essential for children with ASD to receive early diagnosis since the importance of timely treatment for this kind of disease.

Machine learning and deep learning methods have achieved remarkable progress in many areas, such as image classification [4,10,15,16] and action recognition [1,3,8,13,19,20]. Recently, several research have taken steps to explore automatic video-based ASD detection systems with the help of these methods. Tariq et al. [17] adopted support vector machine (SVM) and logistic regression (LR) to identify possible ASD subjects by feeding them behavioral features assessed by non-expert raters from home videos. Zunino et al. [23] proposed an automated objective method using LSTM [5] model to discriminate between ASD and typically developing (TD) subjects. However, these models could not accept raw videos directly to extract effective features from both spatial and temporal dimensions.

In this study, we aim to take advantages of deep learning models to aid video-based ASD detection and achieve higher detection accuracy. In particular, we mainly consider 3D convolutional models, which can accept raw videos as input to extract effective features from both spatial and temporal dimensions. In our study, we explore three representative 3D convolutional neural networks, including C3D [19], 3D ResNet [3] and I3D [1]. In addition, we also propose a new 3D convolutional model by inflating all the 2D convolution and pooling kernels in the ResNeSt [22] model into 3D kernels, which is called 3D ResNeSt. These models are evaluted on the ASD detection dataset proposed in [23], which contains video clips of 40 subjects performing reach-to-grasp action with four different intentions, and to the best of our knowledge, this is the only publicly available video-based ASD detection dataset. Similar to [23], we adopt leave-one-out cross-validation strategy to evaluate and compare the performance of these 3D convolutional models. Our experimental results show that, on average, all of the four 3D convolutional models can achieve higher accuracy than [23], which means 3D convolutional models are indeed more suitable for this video-based ASD detection task. Our proposed 3D ResNeSt model outperforms the other three 3D CNNs when considering accuracy, f1 score and AUC. The average detection accuracy is improved from 0.72 to 0.85.

In summary, this paper has two major contributions: (1) We explore three representative 3D CNNs for ASD detection and the experimental results show that 3D convolutional models are more suitable for video-based ASD detection task. (2) A new 3D convolutional model is proposed based on ResNeSt, which achieves the best performance on the ASD detection dataset proposed in [23]. The average detection accuracy is improved from 0.72 to 0.85.

2   Related Work

2.1   ASD Detection

The conventional diagnostic process of ASD needs well-trained specialists and it is also time-consuming. To reduce dependence on well-trained specialists, Tariq et al. [17] adopted machine learning models to identify possible ASD subjects by feeding them behavioral features assessed by non-expert raters from home videos. Zunino et al. [23] applied LSTM network to process video clips of children performing the same action to discriminate between ASD and TD subjects. Different from the methods mentioned above, Tian et al. [18] proposed a model called Temporal Pyramid Network to detect ASD typical actions and determine if repetitive behaviors appeared in videos to identify ASD and TD children. Liang et al. [11] proposed an unsupervised online learning model for ASD classification, which makes the classification system more scalable. Sun et al. [14] proposed a spatial attentional bilinear 3D convolutional network with LSTM model for fine-grained video analysis, which has achieved significant improvement on one class of the ASD detection dataset proposed in [23]. Besides video-based ASD detection methods, visual attention data are also proved to be able to provide effective features for ASD detection. Jiang et al. [9] analyzed the difference of eye fixations between ASD and TD subjects when viewing images and adopted deep learning model to extract features to distinguish between ASD and TD subjects. Chen et al. [2] presented a novel framework for automated and quantitative screening of ASD, a photo-taking task was introduced that subjects were asked to freely explore the environment and take some photos of the scene they are interested in. Then these photos were combined with the data collected in image-viewing task to train the ASD screening models.

In this study, we mainly focus on 3D convolutional models for video-based ASD detection task.

2.2   3D Convolutional Neural Networks (CNN)

3D CNN model was proposed for action recognition tasks, which can accept raw videos as input and has the advantage of extracting effective features from both spatial and temporal dimensions [8]. Based on 3D convolution operation, Tran et al. [19] proposed a deep 3D CNN model called C3D, which contains eight 3D convolution, five max-pooling, two fully connected layers and a softmax output layer, and it has achieved impressive results on action recognition tasks. The inception architecture was introduced in [15], which adopts 1×1 convolutions to reduce the parameters of neural networks without a significant performance penalty. Based on [15], Carreira et al. [1] proposed a new 3D convolutional model called Inflated 3D ConvNet (I3D) by inflating all the filters and pooling kernels of the model proposed in [15]. Residual learning framework has been proved to be able to achieve excellent performance when training very deep neural networks [4]. Inspired by [4], Hara et al. [3] proposed a deeper 3D convolutional model by changing the 2D convolution operation of the ResNet [4] model into 3D convolution operation and achieved better performance than relatively shallow networks.

In our experiments, we explore three 3D convolutional neural networks, including C3D [19], 3D ResNet [3] and I3D [1]. In addition, we also propose a new 3D convolutional model based on ResNeSt [22]. The structure and implementation details of these models will be shown in Sect. 3 and 4.

3   3D CNN for ASD

The abnormal behaviors linked to ASD can be well recorded in videos. As 3D CNNs can accept raw videos as input and have the advantage of extracting effective features from both spatial and temporal dimensions, it is a good choice to apply 3D CNNs for video-based ASD detection task. The overall detection procedure of our method is shown in Fig. 1. As depicted in Fig. 1, when given a video, Gaussian smoothing is applied to each frame first, and then we will randomly sample 16 consecutive frames n times from the video. Specifically, during the training process, n is 1, and during the validation process, n is 10. These clips are then fed to 3D convolutional models. The outputs of these clips will be averaged to form the final result. In this study, we consider three representative 3D CNNs in our experiments, including C3D [19], 3D ResNet [3] and I3D [1]. Recently, a new variant of ResNet model, called ResNeSt, was proposed in [22], which achieves impressive results in object detection, instance segmentation and semantic segmentation tasks. Based on ResNeSt model, we propose a new 3D convolutional model called 3D ResNeSt. We will introduce the detailed structure of these models in the following subsections.

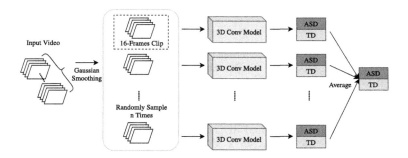

Fig. 1. The detection procedure of our method.

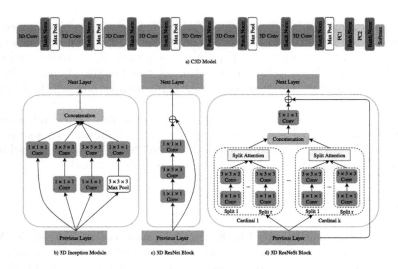

Fig. 2. The structure of the models used in our experiments. a) C3D model, b) 3D Inception module, c) 3D ResNet block, d) 3D ResNeSt block of our proposed model, all kernels of the convolution and the polling operation in the ResNeSt [22] block are inflated from N × N to N × N × N

3.1   C3D

C3D model was proposed in [19], which contains eight 3D convolution, five max-pooling, two fully connected layers and a softmax output layer, and it has achieved impressive results on action recognition tasks. In our experiments, we make a small change to the original model. A batch normalization layer is added after all the convolution and fully connected layers, which could solve the internal covariate shift problem and accelerate the training process [7]. The overview of the C3D model structure is shown in Fig. 2. a), and the batch normalization layer is added explicitly in Fig. 2. a) to distinguish from the original C3D model.

3.2   I3D

Compared to 2D CNNs, 3D CNNs always have more parameters due to the additional kernel dimension, which makes the model harder to train. To handle this problem, Carreira et al. [1] proposed the I3D model by inflating all the filters and pooling kernels of the model proposed in [15]. Figure 2. b) shows the crucial architecture of I3D called 3D Inception Module, $1 \times 1 \times 1$ convolutions are applied before the expensive $3 \times 3 \times 3$ convolutions, which reduces the number of parameters and allows the model to increase in both width and depth without getting into computational difficulties. In our paper, as the size of the input frames are set to $16 \times 112 \times 112$ (time × height × width), we implemented a small variation of I3D model, the kernel size of the first convolution layer is changed from $7 \times 7 \times 7$ to $3 \times 3 \times 3$ with a stride of $2 \times 1 \times 1$, the kernel size of the last average pooling layer is changed from $2 \times 7 \times 7$ to $2 \times 5 \times 5$ with a stride of $1 \times 1 \times 1$, and the last convolution layer is replaced with 2 fully connected layers to get the final outputs.

3.3   3D ResNet

Residual learning framework, which introduces shortcut connections that bypass a signal from one layer to the next, has been proved to be able to achieve excellent performance when training very deep neural networks [4]. Inspired by [4], Hara et al. [3] proposed a deeper 3D convolutional model by changing the 2D convolution operation of the ResNet [4] model into 3D convolution operation and achieved better performance than relatively shallow networks. The 3D ResNet model has various versions with different total layers. Due to the time consuming training process, in this study, we only consider the 50-layers model. Figure 2. c) shows the residual block of the 50-layers 3D ResNet model, which contains three convolution layers, including two $1 \times 1 \times 1$ and one $3 \times 3 \times 3$ convolution layers.

3.4   The Proposed 3D ResNeSt

Multi-path representation, group convolution and channel-attention mechanism have been proved to be successful in many computer vision tasks [6,15,21]. Inspired by these methods, Zhang et al. [22] proposed the ResNeSt model, which generalizes the channel-wise attention into feature-map group representation. Based on ResNeSt, we propose a new 3D convolutional model called 3D ResNeSt. Figure 2. d) shows the key block of the proposed model. Our model preserves the structure of ResNeSt. Outputs from previous layer are divided into several cardinal groups and finer-grained splits when fed to the 3D ResNeSt blocks. We also adopt the split attention operation to aggregate all the splits in each cardinal group like [22]. In our experiments, the number of cardinal groups and splits are set to 1 and 2 respectively, which has been proved to be a good trade-off between speed, accuracy and memory usage in [22]. All the kernels of the convolution and the polling operation are inflated from $N \times N$ to $N \times N \times N$, except the kernel of the optional average pooling layer, the kernel of this layer is inflated from 3×3 to $1 \times 3 \times 3$. To ensure comparability, we also only consider 50-layers 3D ResNeSt model in this study.

3.5   Dataset

The ASD detection dataset [23] used in our experiments is down-loaded from https://pavis.iit.it/datasets/autism-spectrum-disorder-detection-dataset with the authors' authorization. This dataset contains video clips of 40 subjects performing reach-to-grasp action with four different intentions. Among the 40 subjects, 20 are ASD children without accompanying intellectual impairment and 20 are TD children. The reach-to-grasp action mentioned above refers

Fig. 3. Sample frames from the dataset after applying Gaussian smoothing.

to grasping an object (a bottle), all subjects are asked to perform the same action with four intentions, including 1) to place it into a box (grasp-to-place), 2) to pour some water into a glass (grasp-to-pour), 3) to pass the bottle to a co-actor, who would then place the bottle into the box (pass-to-place), 4) to pass the bottle to a co-actor, who would then pour some water (pass-to-pour). And for short, we use class1, class2, class3, class4 to represent the above four classes of reach-to-grasp actions respectively.

3.6 Data Preprocessing

Similar to [23], we apply Gaussian smoothing over all the frames to reduce details of visual appearance. The original resolution of the video frames is 1280×720 pixels. However, some frames may contain subjects' head or body. In order to remove this information, the right part of all the frames are cropped a width of 150 pixels, and then the resolution of the remaining parts of these frames becomes 1130×720 pixels. Figure 3 shows some sample frames from the dataset after applying Gaussian smoothing.

Table 1. Setup of learning rate and learning rate decay of the four 3D convolutional models.

	C3D	I3D	3D ResNet	3D ResNeSt
Base learning rate	0.0001			
Epoch of learning rate decay	80	90	100	90

Table 2. Performance of the models used in our experiments and the LSTM model used in [23] evaluated on the ASD detection dataset.

		[23]	C3D	I3D	3D ResNet	3D ResNeSt
Class1	Accuracy	0.67	0.69	0.74	**0.79**	0.77
	F1	0.65	0.67	0.74	**0.80**	0.74
	Sensitivity	0.63	0.63	0.74	**0.84**	0.68
	Specificity	0.70	0.75	0.75	0.75	**0.85**
	AUC	0.74	0.82	0.79	**0.84**	0.79
Class2	Accuracy	0.77	0.72	0.72	0.69	**0.79**
	F1	**0.77**	0.69	0.69	0.68	0.76
	Sensitivity	**0.79**	0.63	0.63	0.68	0.68
	Specificity	0.75	0.80	0.80	0.70	**0.90**
	AUC	**0.86**	0.79	0.80	0.79	0.84
Class3	Accuracy	0.69	0.79	**0.85**	0.79	**0.85**
	F1	0.67	0.79	0.83	0.79	**0.82**
	Sensitivity	0.63	**0.79**	**0.79**	**0.79**	0.74
	Specificity	0.75	0.80	0.90	0.80	**0.95**
	AUC	0.76	0.89	0.88	0.86	**0.91**
Class4	Accuracy	0.59	0.77	0.74	0.77	**0.82**
	F1	0.53	0.71	0.74	0.78	**0.81**
	Sensitivity	0.47	0.58	0.74	**0.84**	0.79
	Specificity	0.70	**0.95**	0.75	0.70	0.85
	AUC	0.75	0.84	0.87	0.86	**0.90**
Average	Accuracy	0.72	0.79	0.79	0.79	**0.85**
	F1	0.70	0.76	0.78	0.80	**0.82**
	Sensitivity	0.68	0.68	0.74	**0.84**	0.74
	Specificity	0.75	0.90	0.85	0.75	**0.95**
	AUC	0.84	0.87	0.88	0.86	**0.90**

4 Experiments and Results

4.1 Implementation Details

As the ASD detection dataset only contains 40 subjects, for better evaluating and comparing the performance of these 3D convolutional models, we also adopt leave-one-out cross-validation strategy like [23], which is more challenging than the usual cross-validation strategy. The four classes of videos in the ASD detection dataset are processed separately, which means we will perform leave-one-out cross-validation procedure on the four different classes of videos respectively. This leads to a total number of 160 models to be trained when evaluate one 3D Convolutional model on this dataset, which is very time consuming. All of our models are trained on a single GPU. We adopt adaptive moment estimation (Adam) to optimize our model. The cropped frames are resized to 112×112 pixels to form the input. The base learning rate of these models is all 0.0001 and is divided by 10 after specific epochs (shown in Table 1).

Table 3. Leave-one-out cross-validation results compared with the results reported in [23]. In the average column, probabilities greater than 0.5 are highlighted in bold.

		Class1		Class2		Class3		Class4		Average	
		[23]	3D ResNeSt	[23]	3D ResNeSt	[23]	3D ResNeSt	[23]	3D ResNeSt	[23]	3D ResNeSt
ASD	1	0.67	0.68	0.80	1.00	0.73	0.49	0.27	0.05	**0.62**	**0.55**
	2	0.09	0.94	1.00	1.00	0.08	0.75	0.92	0.98	**0.52**	**0.92**
	3	–	–	–	–	–	–	–	–	–	–
	4	0.83	0.72	0.64	0.52	0.00	0.92	0.08	0.01	0.39	**0.54**
	5	0.17	0.71	0.67	0.24	1.00	0.93	0.45	0.92	**0.57**	**0.70**
	6	0.00	0.29	1.00	0.71	0.08	0.67	0.08	0.97	0.29	**0.66**
	7	0.25	0.32	0.00	0.49	0.83	0.36	0.08	0.22	0.29	0.35
	8	0.08	0.01	0.08	0.00	0.42	0.00	0.25	0.68	0.21	0.17
	9	0.92	1.00	1.00	0.99	1.00	1.00	1.00	1.00	**0.98**	**1.00**
	10	0.92	0.99	1.00	0.98	0.58	1.00	1.00	1.00	**0.88**	**0.99**
	11	1.00	1.00	0.92	1.00	1.00	1.00	1.00	0.99	**0.98**	**1.00**
	12	1.00	0.98	1.00	0.99	0.92	1.00	0.42	1.00	**0.84**	**0.99**
	13	1.00	0.94	0.83	0.98	0.83	0.90	1.00	1.00	**0.92**	**0.96**
	14	1.00	1.00	0.75	1.00	1.00	1.00	0.50	1.00	**0.81**	**1.00**
	15	1.00	1.00	1.00	1.00	1.00	1.00	1.00	1.00	**1.00**	**1.00**
	16	0.33	0.07	0.42	0.27	0.17	0.12	0.45	0.57	0.34	0.26
	17	0.17	0.06	0.00	0.16	0.09	0.81	0.17	0.75	0.11	0.44
	18	1.00	0.03	1.00	0.13	0.83	0.44	1.00	0.38	**0.96**	0.24
	19	0.91	1.00	1.00	1.00	0.50	1.00	1.00	1.00	**0.85**	**1.00**
	20	0.75	1.00	1.00	1.00	1.00	1.00	0.92	1.00	**0.92**	**1.00**
TD	21	0.90	1.00	0.75	0.76	0.55	0.56	0.58	0.84	**0.70**	**0.79**
	22	0.33	0.92	0.50	0.69	0.67	0.53	0.08	0.56	0.40	**0.67**
	23	0.42	0.56	0.75	0.67	0.00	0.64	0.00	0.62	0.29	**0.62**
	24	0.58	0.53	0.40	0.82	0.36	0.40	0.42	0.97	0.44	**0.68**
	25	0.64	0.67	0.92	0.92	0.83	0.88	0.50	0.93	**0.72**	**0.85**
	26	1.00	0.76	1.00	0.79	1.00	0.75	0.83	0.44	**0.96**	**0.68**
	27	0.91	0.83	0.75	0.94	1.00	0.70	1.00	0.42	**0.92**	**0.72**
	28	0.67	0.23	1.00	0.57	1.00	0.89	0.92	0.65	**0.90**	**0.59**
	29	0.67	1.00	0.33	1.00	1.00	1.00	0.92	1.00	**0.73**	**1.00**
	30	1.00	1.00	0.75	1.00	0.83	1.00	0.50	1.00	**0.77**	**1.00**
	31	0.92	0.96	0.83	0.94	1.00	0.99	0.92	1.00	**0.92**	**0.97**
	32	0.75	0.98	0.92	0.96	0.91	1.00	1.00	0.99	**0.90**	**0.98**
	33	0.33	1.00	1.00	1.00	0.92	1.00	0.75	1.00	**0.75**	**1.00**
	34	0.50	1.00	1.00	1.00	1.00	1.00	1.00	1.00	**0.88**	**1.00**
	35	1.00	1.00	1.00	1.00	1.00	0.98	1.00	1.00	**1.00**	**0.99**
	36	0.45	0.00	0.25	0.00	0.08	0.51	0.67	0.04	0.36	0.14
	37	0.82	0.82	1.00	0.78	0.82	0.64	0.20	0.75	**0.71**	**0.75**
	38	0.18	0.89	0.50	0.83	0.36	0.98	0.83	0.97	0.47	**0.92**
	39	0.64	0.23	0.67	0.91	0.45	0.96	1.00	0.98	**0.69**	**0.77**
	40	1.00	0.56	1.00	0.07	0.83	0.95	1.00	0.95	**0.96**	**0.63**
Accuracy (p > 0.5)		0.67	0.77	0.77	0.79	0.69	0.85	0.59	0.82	0.72	0.85

4.2 Experimental Results

As mentioned above, in our experiments, the four classes of videos in the ASD detection dataset are separately processed and these 3D convolutional models perform leave-one-out cross-validation on the four classes of videos respectively. In this paper, we mainly consider the average performance on all classes, and as

[14] only report the results of one class, we did not include [14] in our comparison. As for the average performance, [23] is currently state-of-the-art method. Therefore, we mainly compare our results with [23]. We use detection accuracy, f1 score, sensitivity, specificity, and area under the receiver operating characteristic curve (AUROC/AUC) as the metrics to evaluate our models. We report the ASD detection performances measured by these metrics in Table 2. As [23] did not contain the results of these metrics, we use the data reported in [23] to calculate them. As for the average results of these metrics, we first calculate the average ASD and TD probabilities of the leave-one-out cross-validation results on the four classes, and then use the average probabilities to calculate these metrics. From Table 2, we can find that, on average, all of the four 3D convolutional models can achieve higher accuracy and f1 score than [23], which means 3D convolutional models are indeed more suitable for this task. Our proposed 3D ResNeSt model achieves the best performance when considering accuracy, f1 score and AUC and the average detection accuracy is improved from 0.72 to 0.85. If we explore the results class by class, we can draw the following conclusions. For class1, the 3D ResNet model is the best choice among the five models, which acquires the highest f1 score, accuracy and AUC. For class2, [23] may be more suitable for this class of videos, as it achieves the highest f1 score and AUC, although the 3D ResNeSt model achieves higher accuracy. For class3 and class4, our proposed model is the best choice among the five models, which achieves much better performance than [23]. The detection accuracy of class3 is improved from 0.69 to 0.85 and class4 is improved from 0.59 to 0.82.

In order to make a more detailed comparison between our proposed 3D ResNeSt model that achieves the best performance in our experiments and the published research in [23], we report the leave-one-out cross-validation results in Table 3. Each line in Table 3 refers to the outputs of a different subject left out. The first half (subject 1–20) represents the results with ASD subjects left out and the rest with TD ones left out (subject 21–40). For subject 1–20, the value in cell represents the probability of being predicted as ASD, and for subject 21–40, it represents the probability of being predicted as TD. From Table 3, we can find that, on average, [23] and our model both achieve better performance in TD group than in ASD group, which means both achieve higher specificity than sensitivity. Similar to [23], some subjects could be perfectly classified with our model in all classes of the ASD detection dataset, like subject 14, 15, 19 and 20 in the ASD group and subject 29, 30, 33 and 34 in the TD group. However, for some subjects, our model could not classify them in any class of the dataset, like subject 7 and 18 in the ASD group. Globally, our proposed 3D ResNeSt model achieves much better performance than [23].

To further evaluate the performance of our model, we report the average detection accuracy of the 3D ResNeSt model and the LSTM model used in [23] when the threshold varies from 0.5 to 0.95 with a step of 0.05 in Fig. 4. We can find that when the threshold is greater than 0.7, our model is much more robust than [23], and even when the threshold is 0.95, our model still can achieve an accuracy of 0.41, while the accuracy of LSTM model has reduced to 0.18.

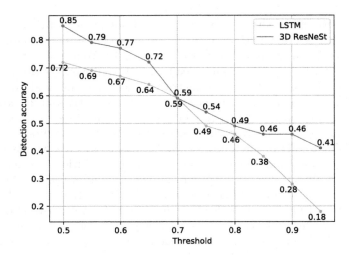

Fig. 4. Average detection accuracy acquired by 3D ResNeSt and LSTM [23] with different threshold.

5   Conclusion

In this paper, we explore three representative 3D CNNs for ASD detection task, including C3D, I3D and 3D ResNet, our experimental results show that 3D convolutional models are more suitable for video-based ASD detection task. And we also proposed a new 3D convolutional model based on ResNeSt, which achieves the best performance on the ASD detection dataset reported in [23]. However, when compared to other action recognition tasks, the ASD detection dataset is still too small. If we want better evaluation of these models, we still need larger datasets. Meanwhile, we should also take computational efficiency into consideration when video datasets become larger. In addition, we did not explore how these models make predictions, as for the future work, studying on how deep learning models make predictions may provide more meaningful information for diagnosis of ASD.

Acknowledgments. This work is jointly supported by the National Natural Science Foundation of China (NO. 61976214, 61972188), and Shandong Provincial Key Research and Development Program (Major Scientific and Technological Innovation Project) (NO. 2019JZZY010119).

References

1. Carreira, J., Zisserman, A.: Quo vadis, action recognition? a new model and the kinetics dataset. In: proceedings of the IEEE Conference on Computer Vision and Pattern Recognition, pp. 6299–6308 (2017)

2. Chen, S., Zhao, Q.: Attention-based autism spectrum disorder screening with privileged modality. In: Proceedings of the IEEE International Conference on Computer Vision, pp. 1181–1190 (2019)
3. Hara, K., Kataoka, H., Satoh, Y.: Learning spatio-temporal features with 3d residual networks for action recognition. In: Proceedings of the IEEE International Conference on Computer Vision Workshops, pp. 3154–3160 (2017)
4. He, K., Zhang, X., Ren, S., Sun, J.: Deep residual learning for image recognition. In: Proceedings of the IEEE Conference on Computer Vision and Pattern Recognition, pp. 770–778 (2016)
5. Hochreiter, S., Schmidhuber, J.: Long short-term memory. Neural Comput. **9**(8), 1735–1780 (1997)
6. Hu, J., Shen, L., Sun, G.: Squeeze-and-excitation networks. In: Proceedings of the IEEE Conference on Computer Vision and Pattern Recognition, pp. 7132–7141 (2018)
7. Ioffe, S., Szegedy, C.: Batch normalization: Accelerating deep network training by reducing internal covariate shift. arXiv preprint arXiv:1502.03167 (2015)
8. Ji, S., Xu, W., Yang, M., Yu, K.: 3d convolutional neural networks for human action recognition. IEEE Trans. Pattern Anal. Mach. Intell. **35**(1), 221–231 (2012)
9. Jiang, M., Zhao, Q.: Learning visual attention to identify people with autism spectrum disorder. In: Proceedings of the IEEE International Conference on Computer Vision, pp. 3267–3276 (2017)
10. Krizhevsky, A., Sutskever, I., Hinton, G.E.: Imagenet classification with deep convolutional neural networks. In: Advances in Neural Information Processing Systems, pp. 1097–1105 (2012)
11. Liang, S., Loo, C.K., Md Sabri, A.Q.: Autism spectrum disorder classification in videos: a hybrid of temporal coherency deep networks and self-organizing dual memory approach. In: Kim, K.J., Kim, H.-Y. (eds.) Information Science and Applications. LNEE, vol. 621, pp. 421–430. Springer, Singapore (2020). https://doi.org/10.1007/978-981-15-1465-4_42
12. Maenner, M.J., Shaw, K.A., Baio, J., et al.: Prevalence of autism spectrum disorder among children aged 8 years-autism and developmental disabilities monitoring network, 11 sites, united states, 2016. MMWR Surveill. Summ. **69**(4), 1 (2020)
13. Simonyan, K., Zisserman, A.: Two-stream convolutional networks for action recognition in videos. In: Advances in Neural Information Processing Systems, pp. 568–576 (2014)
14. Sun, K., Li, L., Li, L., He, N., Zhu, J.: Spatial attentional bilinear 3d convolutional network for video-based autism spectrum disorder detection. In: ICASSP 2020–2020 IEEE International Conference on Acoustics, Speech and Signal Processing (ICASSP), pp. 3387–3391. IEEE (2020)
15. Szegedy, C., et al.: Going deeper with convolutions. In: Proceedings of the IEEE Conference on Computer Vision and Pattern Recognition, pp. 1–9 (2015)
16. Szegedy, C., Vanhoucke, V., Ioffe, S., Shlens, J., Wojna, Z.: Rethinking the inception architecture for computer vision. In: Proceedings of the IEEE Conference on Computer Vision and Pattern Recognition, pp. 2818–2826 (2016)
17. Tariq, Q., Daniels, J., Schwartz, J.N., Washington, P., Kalantarian, H., Wall, D.P.: Mobile detection of autism through machine learning on home video: a development and prospective validation study. PLoS Med. **15**(11), e1002705 (2018)
18. Tian, Y., Min, X., Zhai, G., Gao, Z.: Video-based early asd detection via temporal pyramid networks. In: 2019 IEEE International Conference on Multimedia and Expo (ICME), pp. 272–277. IEEE (2019)

19. Tran, D., Bourdev, L., Fergus, R., Torresani, L., Paluri, M.: Learning spatiotemporal features with 3d convolutional networks. In: Proceedings of the IEEE International Conference on Computer Vision, pp. 4489–4497 (2015)
20. Wang, L., et al.: Temporal segment networks: towards good practices for deep action recognition. In: Leibe, B., Matas, J., Sebe, N., Welling, M. (eds.) ECCV 2016. LNCS, vol. 9912, pp. 20–36. Springer, Cham (2016). https://doi.org/10.1007/978-3-319-46484-8_2
21. Xie, S., Girshick, R., Dollár, P., Tu, Z., He, K.: Aggregated residual transformations for deep neural networks. In: Proceedings of the IEEE Conference on Computer Vision and Pattern Recognition, pp. 1492–1500 (2017)
22. Zhang, H., et al.: ResNeSt: split-attention networks. arXiv preprint arXiv:2004.08955 (2020)
23. Zunino, A., et al.: Video gesture analysis for autism spectrum disorder detection. In: 2018 24th International Conference on Pattern Recognition (ICPR), pp. 3421–3426. IEEE (2018)

A Multi Classifier Approach for Supporting Alzheimer's Diagnosis Based on Handwriting Analysis

Giuseppe De Gregorio[2(✉)], Domenico Desiato[1], Angelo Marcelli[2], and Giuseppe Polese[1]

[1] Department of Computer Science, University of Salerno,
via Giovanni Paolo II n. 132, 84084 Fisciano, SA, Italy
{ddesiato,gpolese}@unisa.it
[2] NCLab, Department of Electrical and Information Engineering and Applied
Mathematics, University of Salerno, Via Giovanni Paolo II 132,
84084 Fisciano, SA, Italy
{gdegregorio,amarcelli}@unisa.it

Abstract. Nowadays, the treatments of neurodegenerative diseases are increasingly sophisticated, mainly thanks to innovations in the medical field. As the effectiveness of care, strategies is enhanced by the early diagnosis, in recent years there has been an increasing interest in developing reliable, non-invasive, easy to administer, and cheap diagnostics tools to support clinicians in the diagnostic processes. Among others, Alzheimer's disease (AD) has received special attention in that it is a severe and progressive neurodegenerative disease that heavily influence the patient's quality of life, as well as the social costs for proper care. In this context, a large variety of methods have been proposed that exploit handwriting and drawing tasks to discriminate between healthy subjects and AD patients. Most, if not all, of these methods adopt a single machine learning technique to achieve the final classification. We propose to tackle the problem by adopting a multi-classifier approach envisaging as many classifiers as the number of tasks, each of whom produces a binary output. The outputs of the classifiers are eventually combined by a majority vote to achieve the final decision. Experiments on a dataset involving 175 subjects executing 25 different handwriting and drawing tasks and 6 different machine learning techniques selected among the most used ones in the literature show that the best results are achieved by selecting the subset of tasks on which each classifier perform best and then combining the outputs of the classifier on each task, achieving an overall accuracy of 91% with a sensitivity of 83% and a specificity of 100%. Moreover, this strategy reduces the meantime to complete the test from 25 minutes to less than 10.

Keywords: Alzheimer's disease · Handwriting · Machine learning · Multi classifier system

ⓒ Springer Nature Switzerland AG 2021
A. Del Bimbo et al. (Eds.): ICPR 2020 Workshops, LNCS 12661, pp. 559–574, 2021.
https://doi.org/10.1007/978-3-030-68763-2_43

1   Introduction

Neurodegenerative diseases (NDs) affect millions of people worldwide, and among them, Alzheimer's and Parkinson's diseases are the most common ones. Both are age-related, and therefore the increment of the lifespan due to the continuous improvement in the medical field will make their impact on both individuals and society even greater. In particular, Alzheimer's disease produces a slow and progressive decline in mental functions such as memory, thought, judgment, and learning ability. In the early stages of the disease, the sole or predominant symptom is the episodic memory impairment that is indicative of ventromedial temporal lobe dysfunction [1]. After that, it is followed by progressive amnesia and deterioration in other cognitive domains, expressing pathological involvement of more widespread neural systems. Individuals affected by Alzheimer's patients lose the ability to handle themselves, and with the evolution of the disease, they become dependent on caregivers. Although there is currently no cure for NDs, an early diagnosis strongly improves the available treatments' effectiveness.

In this context, the scientific community has shown an increasing interest in developing and adopting AI methodologies for supporting both the diagnosis and the treatments of these diseases. Several methods have been proposed for the early diagnosis of both Parkinson's and Alzheimer's disease [2]. One of the approaches exploits biomarkers useful for characterising the specific neurodegenerative disorder. Clinical, imaging, biochemical, and genetic are four categories of biomarkers that have been suggested for the early diagnosis of neurodegenerative diseases. However, by exploiting different predicting values of biomarkers, few of them have been found useful for this purpose [3,4]. Olfactory dysfunction [5], and α-synuclein biopsy [6] could be biomarkers useful with the early diagnosis, but they need further revisions to be exploited [7,8]. Additionally, other studies have proposed that combining different biomarkers could yield improvements in formulating an early diagnosis of the neurodegenerative disease [4,8]. Another approach exploits the deterioration of motor processes involved in handwriting and drawing in subjects affected by neurodegenerative diseases [9–14]. With respect to the previous approach, the handwriting analysis might provide a cheap and non-invasive method for evaluating the disease progression [15]. Moreover, it has been observed that the application of machine learning methods to motor function has shown promise in decreasing the time taken to perform clinical assessments [2]. The methods proposed in the literature adopts a variety of tasks, features and classifiers to discriminate between healthy subjects and AD patients. Still, they all adopt a single machine learning method to build the classifier.

Departing from state of the art, we introduce a multi classifier approach for discriminating between healthy subjects and AD patients. We propose a different architecture of the multi classifier system by type of classifiers to be combined, as well as their number. As machine learning tools to build the classifiers, we adopt the Random Forest, the Logistic Regression, the k-Nearest Neighbor, the Linear Discriminant Analysis, the Gaussian Naive Bayes, and the Support Vector

Machine with linear kernel, as they are representative of the methods adopted in the literature for automatic diagnosis of NDs.

The paper is organised as follows. In Sect. 2, we discuss previous works specifically designed to deal with AD patients, highlighting the features and the tool adopted to build the classifier and report the main findings. In Sect. 3, we describe the architectures of the multi classifier system we have designed and in Sect. 4 illustrate the results of several experiments that we performed to evaluate the effectiveness of the proposed architectures. Finally, conclusions and future research directions are discussed in Sect. 5.

2   Related Work

One of the early attempts to look at handwriting for discriminating AD and patients affected by Mild Cognitive Impairment (MCI) from healthy controls is reported in [16], where kinematic measures of the handwriting process across different functional tasks are exploited for the purpose. The authors asked participants to perform five functional writing tasks: copying a phone number, copying a grocery list (five words), copying the details of a check into the appropriate places, copying the alphabet sequence, and copying a paragraph (107 characters). They performed evaluations on 31 persons with MCI, 22 with mild Alzheimer's disease, and 41 healthy controls made functional tasks while using a computerised system. By complementing kinematic measures with cognitive functioning tests, and adopting a discriminant analysis for the classification, the authors achieved 72% accuracy.

More recently, in [17], handwritten signatures are exploited for the early diagnosis of AD. The authors used Plamondon's Sigma Normal model to map patients' signatures by extracting twelve features. In particular, features depicted the maximum speed of the signing divided by the time of writing, the number of Log-Normal divided by the time, and the number of peaks of the speed/time graph. Authors have used CART, bagging CART, and SVM with the linear kernel to classify Alzheimer patients, and the best performance was obtained by the bagging CART, whose achieved accuracy, sensitivity, and specificity were 96.7%, 96.5% and 96.8% respectively.

The target of the work reported in [18] was to discriminate AD patients, MCI patients, and control subjects by comparing their handwriting kinematics. Authors have adopted a protocol consisting of copying a sentence, writing a dictated sentence and an own sentence, coping two and-three dimensions drawings, and executing the clock drawing test. By using discriminant analysis as a classification algorithm, they have analysed the most discriminating features and the best-distinguished groups for the same task, and figured out that discriminatory features depended on the type of group to be discriminated, and some tasks, such as the clock drawing test, allowed some groups, e.g. AD vs MCI, to be well discriminated.

In [19], an approach for characterising early Alzheimer's is proposed. Authors exploit the loop velocity trajectory (full dynamics) in an unsupervised way,

562   G. De Gregorio et al.

through a temporal clustering based on K medoids by discovering clusters that give new insights on the problem. Classification is performed by utilising a Bayesian formalism that aggregates the clusters' contributions by probabilistically combining the discriminative power of each. Authors extrapolate information from a dataset consisting of two cognitive profiles, 27 early-stage Alzheimer's disease, and 27 healthy persons. They report an overall accuracy of 74% with a specificity of 72.2% and a sensitivity of 75.6% as the best performance.

In [20], preliminary results concerning the evaluation of an experimental handwriting protocol (including the copy of words, letters and sentence) are presented. Authors aim to evaluate the kinematic properties of the movements performed during the handwriting activity. In particular, they exploit data related to the on-air features, data concerning the on paper features, and the overall data for training two different classifiers: the Random Forest and the Decision Tree. Authors evaluate obtained results in terms of accuracy by reaching an overall score greater than 70% in classifying AD patients.

In [21], authors extended the work presented in [20]. In particular, they improve their analysis by introducing other additional experiments by exploiting different classifiers: The random Forest, the Decision tree, the Neural Network, and the Support Vector Machine. They compare obtained results by showing that on-air features have the greatest weight in the classification of patients by contributing to increase the Recognition Rate of the classification phase.

In [22], results concerning the analysis of two copy tasks of regular words and non-words are presented. Authors aim to investigate kinematic and pressure properties of handwriting by extracting some standard features proposed in the literature for evaluating the discriminative power of non-words task in discriminating AD patients. They perform experimental result by using two classification methods: the Random Forest and the Decision Tree. In particular, authors evaluate obtained results in term of accuracy by reaching an overall score greater than 80% in discriminating AD patients exploiting Random Forest over non-words task.

Finally, in [23], five representative tasks used in neuropsychological tests, namely spontaneous writing, trail marking test with numbers and characters, crossed pentagons, and clock drawing, were investigated for extracting meaningful features to classify AD and mild cognitive impairment subjects (MCI). Data were collected from 71 senior, including MCI, AD, and control subjects. Using a three-class classification model based on a generalised linear model with a logit link function and combining the features of multiple tasks, they obtain an overall accuracy of 74.6%.

3   The Multi Classifier Architecture

While there is a general agreement on which aspects of handwriting execution are mostly affected by AD and the features to be used for capturing them, the tasks that the subjects have to execute during the test are still an open and challenging issue. The methods proposed in the literature range from requiring the execution of simple tasks, e.g. drawing a spiral or writing a few letters or bigrams, to more complex ones involving many different tasks to execute. In this study, we adopted the protocol proposed in [24], as it adopts a set of 25 tasks, including most of those used in previous studies, as well as tasks that have been derived from recent findings in neuroscience and motor control of handwriting. This choice will allow us to evaluate the performance of the proposed system by varying both the machine learning tool adopted to build the basic classifiers and the tasks to be considered, as it is described later in this Section.

As different tasks can elicit different handwriting alterations, the approach followed in previous work is that of merging the features extracted form each task into a unique representation that is eventually used by the machine learning tool to build the classifier, as depicted in Fig. 1).

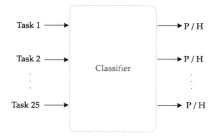

Fig. 1. Single classifier working on features set obtained by merging each task features value.

On the contrary, we propose to merge the output of many classifiers, each processing the features obtained from the samples resulting from the execution of a single task, as depicted in Fig. 2.

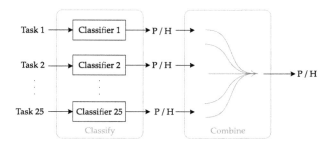

Fig. 2. Combined classifications for each handwriting task.

This general architecture has been implemented in different ways. In the first case, each classifier is built by using one of the machine learning tools we have considered, leading to 6 implementations. In the second case, we select the top-performing classifiers for each task among those provided by the machine learning tools, leading to 1 implementation, which will be indicated from now on with *BestForTask*. Eventually, in the third case, for each machine learning tool, we sorted the tasks in descending order according to the accuracy exhibited by the classifier. By computing the cumulative accuracy incrementally, we were able to select the subset of tasks corresponding to the best performance for each type of classifier, leading to 6 more implementations, each one with a different number of classifiers to be combined. In all the implementations, the outputs of the classifier are combined by using the majority vote.

4 Experimental Results

In this Section, we report the results of the experiments we have designed to evaluate the performance of the different implementations of the multi classifier architecture we have developed. To provide a baseline for assessing the improvement, we report preliminarily the single classifiers' performance working on the feature vector obtained by merging all features of all 25 tasks.

4.1 Implementation Details

We adopt different machine learning tools for building the classifier that either has been adopted in previous works or exhibited good performance on a wide range of classification problems. As mentioned in the Introduction, we have chosen Random Forest [25], Logistic Regression [26], K-Nearest Neighbor (KNN) [27], Linear Discriminant Analysis (LDA) [28], Gaussian Naive Bayes [29], and Support Vector Machine (SVM) [30]. The architecture implementations have been written in Python, using the functionality of the Scikit-Learn library. The tuning of the various classifiers' parameters has been performed following a grid search approach, and then classifiers have been trained using 5-fold cross-validation.

4.2 Dataset

The dataset consists of 175 subjects, of which 89 affected by Alzheimer's disease and 86 healthy control subjects. The two populations show similar mean values and standard deviations for age, sex and years of education. To carry out the experiments, the dataset was divided into a training set composed of 80% of the data and a test set containing the remaining 20%. The features computed on each sample resulting from the execution of the tasks are summarised in Table 1.

4.3 Tasks Characterisation

The tasks are grouped into four categories, in increasing order of difficulty:

Table 1. Features set used in the experiment. Features are grouped in on-paper and on-air depending on whether they are extracted when the pen touches the paper or not. Feature names terminating with P denote the former, while those terminating with A denote the latter

Feature	Name	Description
Total time	TT	Total time required to perform the entire task
Air time	AT	Time spent near the sheet, with the tip of the pen not in contact with the sheet
Paper time	PT	Time spent on the sheet, with the tip of the pen in contact with the sheet
Mean speed on-paper	MSP	Average speed recorded on paper
Mean speed in-air	MSA	Average of the speeds recorded near the sheet
Mean acceleration on-paper	MAP	Average of accelerations recorded on paper
Mean acceleration in-air	MAA	Average of the accelerations recorded near the sheet
Mean jerk on-paper	MJP	Average of the jerk recorded on the sheet
Mean jerk in-air	MJA	Average of the jerk recorded near the sheet
Pressure mean	PM	Average of the pressure levels exerted on the sheet
Pressure var	PV	Variance of pressure levels exerted on the sheet
GMRT on-paper	GMRTP	Generalization of the Mean Relative Tremor defined in [31] computed on in-air movements. It considers the top left corner of the sheet as the center for the computation
GMRT in-air	GMRTA	Generalization of the Mean Relative Tremor defined in [31] computed on on-paper movements. It considers the top left corner of the sheet as the center for the computation
Mean GMRT	GMRT	Average of GMRTP and GMRTA
Pendowns number	PWN	The number of pendowns
Max X extension	XE	Maximum extension recorded along the X axis
Max Y extension	YE	Maximum extension recorded along the Y axis
Dispersion index	DI	It measures the dispersion of the drawing on the sheet; a fully covered sheet will correspond to an index equal to one while a completely empty sheet will have an index equal to zero

- Graphic tasks; for testing the skill in writing elementary traits, joining points, and drawing simple figures.
- Copy and Reverse Copy tasks; aimed at evaluating the ability in replaying elaborate graphic gestures, such as letters, words, and numbers.
- Memory tasks; its purpose is to test the variation of the graphic section, keeping in memory a word, a letter, a graphic gesture, or a motor plan.
- Dictation; it tests the patient's ability to use the working memory during the variation of writing tasks.

The 25 handwriting tasks used in the experiments described below are described in detail in [24].

4.4 Baseline Evaluation Session

In the preliminary experiment, we evaluated the performance of the six implementations of the baseline classifiers, classifiers using as feature the union of the features computed from the execution of each of the 25 tasks. Table 2 shows the accuracy achieved by each classifier, and Table 3 the corresponding confusion matrices. All together, the data reported in the tables show that the Gaussian NB outperforms the others in terms of accuracy, sensitivity and specificity.

Table 2. Accuracy of the baseline classifiers.

	Random forest	Logistic regression	KNN	LDA	Gaussian NB	SVM
Accuracy	80.00%	68.57%	51.43%	62.86%	85.71%	68.57%

Table 3. Confusion matrices of the baseline classifiers.

	Random forest	Logistic regression	KNN
Actual	Predicted	Predicted	Predicted
	H P	H P	H P
H	12 5	11 6	14 3
P	2 16	5 13	14 4

	LDA	Gaussian NB	SVM
Actual	Predicted	Predicted	Predicted
	H P	H P	H P
H	12 5	14 3	11 6
P	8 10	2 16	5 13

4.5 The Basic Classifiers

The basic classifiers to be combined were obtained by using the features extracted from each task to build as many classifiers as the number of tasks. Table 4 shows the accuracy achieved by each classifier on each task.

4.6 Combining All

To obtain a single classification label for each subject, the output of the basic classifiers were combined by using a majority vote [32]. We considered two different ways for combining them. The first one combines the outputs of the 25 basic classifiers produced by a given machine learning tool, while the second combines

Table 4. Accuracy achieved by the classifiers on each task. The best performance achieved on each task is highlighted in bold.

	Random forest	Logistic regression	KNN	LDA	Gaussian NB	SVM
Task 1	63%	57%	51%	58%	**66%**	60%
Task 2	63%	69%	63%	69%	63%	**74%**
Task 3	69%	66%	71%	**71%**	71%	63%
Task 4	66%	**71%**	66%	63%	71%	66%
Task 5	71%	71%	60%	71%	**74%**	66%
Task 6	63%	66%	**69%**	69%	60%	66%
Task 7	**74%**	71%	51%	69%	71%	71%
Task 8	60%	60%	60%	60%	66%	**66%**
Task 9	69%	57%	54%	57%	**71%**	60%
Task 10	**63%**	60%	51%	60%	60%	54%
Task 11	66%	66%	54%	57%	**69%**	60%
Task 12	57%	57%	**60%**	57%	57%	54%
Task 13	54%	54%	43%	49%	57%	**60%**
Task 14	**63%**	51%	60%	54%	54%	57%
Task 15	**74%**	71%	66%	66%	69%	66%
Task 16	57%	63%	54%	60%	63%	**71%**
Task 17	**71%**	66%	60%	69%	51%	66%
Task 18	57%	57%	43%	60%	**60%**	60%
Task 19	74%	74%	**77%**	69%	57%	71%
Task 20	**69%**	69%	54%	69%	60%	69%
Task 21	**77%**	69%	57%	66%	63%	60%
Task 22	60%	66%	**74%**	54%	66%	57%
Task 23	**71%**	71%	57%	60%	71%	71%
Task 24	60%	66%	60%	57%	**69%**	66%
Task 25	66%	71%	66%	**77%**	71%	63%

Table 5. Accuracy achieved by combining all the basic classifiers.

	Random forest	Logistic regression	KNN	LDA	Gaussian NB	SVM	BestForTask
Accuracy	82.86%	74.29%	74.29%	74.29%	71.43%	68.57%	85.71%

the outputs of the 25 top performing basic classifiers for each task, leading to seven multiclassifier systems. In the following, we will denote the first 6 systems by the acronym of the machine learning tool adopt to build the single task classifiers, while will refer to the last implementation as the *BestForTask* one. Table 5 reports the results achieved by the seven multiclassifier systems in terms of accuracy, and Table 6 lists the confusion matrices. From Table 5 we can see that the

BestForTask multiclassifier overperforms the others in terms of accuracy, and the RF multiclassifier is the best among all the other ones. The confusion matrices of Table 6, moreover, show that the *BestForTask* multiclassifier achieves the same specificity of the RF multiclassifier, but better sensitivity. This represents a critical point as the primary objective is precisely that of detecting patients as early as possible, as mentioned in the Introduction.

By comparing the results in Table 5 and Table 2 it is possible to notice that the *BestForTask* multiclassifier achieves the same accuracy as the Gaussian NB classifier, better specificity and worse sensitivity. For the same reason as before, the former performs better than the latter.

4.7   Combining the Best

To improve the overall multiclassifier performance, we have combined only the best classifiers, as it follows. We sorted the tasks in descending order depending on the accuracy achieved by the basic classifiers on that task. Starting with the top performing task, the remaining tasks are considered and the corresponding basic classifiers added to the set of classifiers to be combined. The results obtained in terms of accuracy were recorded as the number of tasks considered increases.

Table 6. Confusion matrices achieved by combining all the basic classifiers.

		Random Forest		**Logistic Regression**		**KNN**	
		predicted		predicted		predicted	
		H	P	H	P	H	P
actual	H	16	1	15	2	15	2
	P	5	13	7	11	7	11
		LDA		**Gaussian NB**		**SVM**	
		predicted		predicted		predicted	
		H	P	H	P	H	P
actual	H	16	1	16	1	16	1
	P	8	10	9	9	10	8
		BestForTask					
		predicted					
		H	P				
actual	H	16	1				
	P	4	14				

Table 7 reports the best accuracy achievable, the number of selected tasks and the average total time to execute them, while Table 8 shows the corresponding confusion matrices. Figure 3 shows, for each multiclassifier, how the accuracy varies as the number of classifier increases.

Table 7. Accuracy, total time and number of selected tasks of the multiclassifier combining the top basic classifiers.

	Random forest	Logistic regression	KNN	LDA	Gaussian NB	SVM	Best for task
Accuracy	91.43%	88.57%	85.71%	85.71%	77.14%	80.00%	88.57%
Time	09:20	10:26	04:59	15:32	02:23	17:38	07:54
Number of tasks	9	7	5	13	3	17	7

Table 8. Confusion matrices of the multiclassifier combining the top basic classifiers.

	Random Forest		**Logistic Regression**		**KNN**	
	predicted		predicted		predicted	
	H	P	H	P	H	P
actual H	17	0	15	2	16	1
P	3	15	2	16	4	14
	LDA		**Gaussian NB**		**SVM**	
	predicted		predicted		predicted	
	H	P	H	P	H	P
actual H	17	0	16	1	16	1
P	5	13	7	11	6	12
	BestForTask					
	predicted					
	H	P				
actual H	16	1				
P	3	15				

Finally, similarly to the procedure reported in Subsect. 4.4, for each machine learning model, we have merged the features extracted from the respective top-performing tasks as reported in Table 7 into a single feature vector and used it to train and test a single classifier. Table 9 reports the accuracy achieved by each classifier while Table 10 reports confusion matrices.

The experimental results reported in the tables above show that when a single classifier is used, providing the classifier with the features extracted from the subset of tasks leading to the top performance is beneficial for all the machine learning tool, except that in the case of Random Forest and Gaussian NB, whose accuracy drops, and with the KNN showing the largest improvement. They also show that combining as many classifiers as the number of tasks leads to a substantial improvement of the accuracy with respect to a single classifier for all the machine learning tool. On the contrary, when as many classifiers as the number of tasks on which the classifiers achieve the top performance are combined, better performances are achieved with respect to the single classifier for all the machine learning tool, with the only exception of the Gaussian NB, but in this case, the drop is less than 10%. The implementation of the multi classifier envisaging as

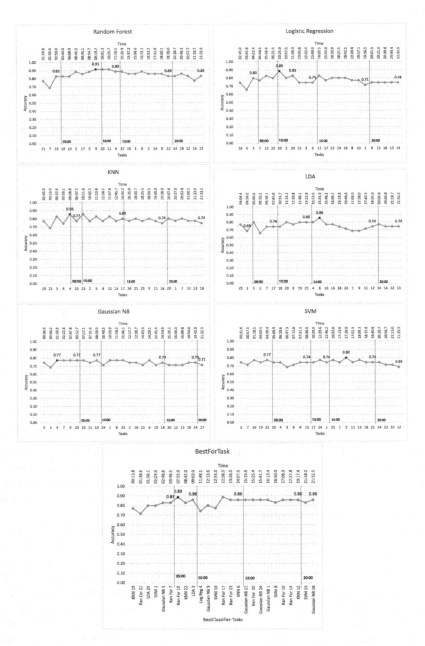

Fig. 3. Accuracy achieved by incrementally combining the basic classifiers. The ordered tasks are shown on the abscissa, while the average total time required to execute the tasks is shown on the upper part. Red bars are placed every 5 min of the average total time. (Color figure online)

Table 9. Accuracy achieved using a single classifier merging the features from the best tasks.

	Random forest	Logistic regression	KNN	LDA	Gaussian NB	SVM
Accuracy	77.14%	71.43%	71.43%	68.57%	74.29%	71.43%

Table 10. Confusion matrices using a single classifier merging the features from the best tasks.

	Random forest	Logistic regression	KNN
Actual	Predicted	Predicted	Predicted
	H P	H P	H P
H	11 6	12 5	13 4
P	2 16	5 13	6 12

	LDA	Gaussian NB	SVM
Actual	Predicted	Predicted	Predicted
	H P	H P	H P
H	12 5	14 3	13 4
P	6 12	6 12	6 12

many classifiers as the number of tasks leads to the top accuracy when, for each task, the top-performing classifiers is included in the pool. On the contrary, this is not true in case the number of classifiers equals the number of tasks to be considered for achieving the top performance, where the Random Forest performs slightly better in terms of accuracy and specificity.

5   Conclusions

Handwriting activity can be an innovative way of characterising the peculiarities of neurodegenerative diseases. It can be exploited to extrapolate features useful to train machine learning models to help the physicians in early diagnosing and monitoring the effects of the treatments, pursuing patient-centred care aimed at improving the patient's quality of life and the social cost of their impairments.

In this work, departing from the current trends in the field, we have proposed a multi classifier system for discriminating between AD patients and healthy controls by using the samples produced during the execution of handwriting and drawing tasks. We have proposed different implementations of the multi classifier system, varying the machine learning tool adopted to build the basic classifiers and adopting different strategies to build the pool of classifiers to be combined.

The experimental results, obtained on a dataset including 175 subjects, have shown that combining many classifiers leads to better performance with respect to a single classifier and that selecting the number of classifiers to be included in the pool depending on their performance on each task, leads to the top performance, with an accuracy bigger the 91%, a specificity of 100% and a sensitivity bigger than 83% when the Random Forest is adopted to build the basics classifiers. Moreover, reducing the number of tasks to be performed by the subjects also leads to reduce more than 50% the time required to perform the test. We believe that the combination of the performance with the short time needed to execute the test, may favour the introduction of the test by physicians, particularly family doctors and neurologists, for both an early diagnosis and continuous monitoring of the effects of the treatments.

Eventually, we did not report any comparison with the performance presented in [16–19, 23] as they have been obtained on different datasets, so that a direct comparison is meaningless. Simialry, the experiments reported in [20–22] use the same dataset, but different features/classifiers and just a few tasks set. We believe that the lack of large and publicly available datasets is one of the reasons why there has been much less research on AD with respect to other NDs, as for instance PD for whom there are a few datasets publicly available. However, their size is small in terms of both the number of subjects who contributed to the data collection and the number of collected samples. For this reason, we have started to collect samples from patients suffering from other NDs, as PD and MCI, and our next step will be that of completing the procedure to make our dataset publicly available. From a technical point of view, we plan to investigate the role played by the size of the training set on the performance we have reported before, searching for the smallest size needed to achieve satisfactory performance.

References

1. Armstrong, M.J., et al.: Criteria for the diagnosis of corticobasal degeneration. Neurology **80**(5), 496–503 (2013)
2. Myszczynska, M.A.: Applications of machine learning to diagnosis and treatment of neurodegenerative diseases. Nature Rev. Neurol. **16**(8), 1–17 (2020)
3. Le, W., Dong, J., Li, S., Korczyn, A.D.: Can biomarkers help the early diagnosis of parkinson's disease? Neurosci. Bull. **33**(5), 535–542 (2017)
4. Li, T., Le, W.: Biomarkers for parkinson's disease: how good are they? Neurosci. bull. **36**(2), 183–194 (2020)
5. Morley, J.F., et al.: Optimizing olfactory testing for the diagnosis of parkinson's disease: item analysis of the university of pennsylvania smell identification test. NPJ Parkinson's Dis. **4**(1), 1–7 (2018)
6. O'Hara, D.M., Kalia, S.K., Kalia, L.V.: Methods for detecting toxic α-synuclein species as a biomarker for parkinson's disease. Critical Rev. Clin. Lab. Sci. **57**(5), 1–17 (2020)
7. Chang, C.-W., Yang, S.-Y., Yang, C.-C., Chang, C.-W., Wu, Y.-R.: Plasma and serum alpha-synuclein as a biomarker of diagnosis in patients with parkinson's disease. Frontiers Neurol. **10**, 1388 (2020)
8. Schapira, A.H.: Recent developments in biomarkers in parkinson disease. Current Opin. Neurol. **26**(4), 395 (2013)
9. Broderick, M.P., Van Gemmert, A.W., Shill, H.A., Stelmach, G.E.: Hypometria and bradykinesia during drawing movements in individuals with parkinson's disease. Exp. Brain Res. **197**(3), 223–233 (2009)

10. Van Gemmert, A., Adler, C.H., Stelmach, G.: Parkinson's disease patients undershoot target size in handwriting and similar tasks. J. Neurol. Neurosurg. Psychiatry **74**(11), 1502–1508 (2003)
11. Senatore, R., Marcelli, A.: A paradigm for emulating the early learning stage of handwriting: performance comparison between healthy controls and parkinson's disease patients in drawing loop shapes. Hum. Mov. Sci. **65**, 89–101 (2019)
12. Teulings, H.-L., Contreras-Vidal, J.L., Stelmach, G.E., Adler, C.H.: Parkinsonism reduces coordination of fingers, wrist, and arm in fine motor control. Exp. Neurol. **146**(1), 159–170 (1997)
13. Teulings, H.-L., Stelmach, G.E.: Control of stroke size, peak acceleration, and stroke duration in parkinsonian handwriting. Hum. Mov. Sci. **10**(2–3), 315–334 (1991)
14. Jankovic, J.: Parkinson's disease: clinical features and diagnosis. J. Neurol. Neurosurg. Psychiatry **79**(4), 368–376 (2008)
15. Impedovo, D., Pirlo, G., Vessio, G.: Dynamic handwriting analysis for supporting earlier parkinson's disease diagnosis. Information **9**(10), 247 (2018)
16. Werner, P., Rosenblum, S., Bar-On, G., Heinik, J., Korczyn, A.: Handwriting process variables discriminating mild alzheimer's disease and mild cognitive impairment. J. Gerontol. Ser. B Psychol. Sci. Soc. Sci. **61**(4), P228–P236 (2006)
17. Pirlo, G., Diaz, M., Ferrer, M.A., Impedovo, D., Occhionero, F., Zurlo, U.: Early diagnosis of neurodegenerative diseases by handwritten signature analysis. In: Murino, V., Puppo, E., Sona, D., Cristani, M., Sansone, C. (eds.) ICIAP 2015. LNCS, vol. 9281, pp. 290–297. Springer, Cham (2015). https://doi.org/10.1007/978-3-319-23222-5_36
18. Garre-Olmo, J., Faúndez-Zanuy, M., López-de-Ipiña, K., Calvó-Perxas, L., Turró-Garriga, O.: Kinematic and pressure features of handwriting and drawing: preliminary results between patients with mild cognitive impairment, alzheimer disease and healthy controls. Current Alzheimer Res. **14**(9), 960–968 (2017)
19. Kahindo, C., El-Yacoubi, M.A., Garcia-Salicetti, S., Rigaud, A.-S., Cristancho-Lacroix, V.: Characterizing early-stage alzheimer through spatiotemporal dynamics of handwriting. IEEE Signal Proc. Lett. **25**(8), 1136–1140 (2018)
20. Cilia, N.D., De Stefano, C., Fontanella, F., Molinara, M., Scotto Di Freca, A.: Handwriting analysis to support alzheimer's disease diagnosis: a preliminary study. In: Vento, M., Percannella, G. (eds.) CAIP 2019. LNCS, vol. 11679, pp. 143–151. Springer, Cham (2019). https://doi.org/10.1007/978-3-030-29891-3_13
21. Cilia, N.D., De Stefano, C., Fontanella, F., Molinara, M., Scotto Di Freca, A.: Using handwriting features to characterize cognitive impairment. In: Ricci, E., Rota Bulò, S., Snoek, C., Lanz, O., Messelodi, S., Sebe, N. (eds.) ICIAP 2019. LNCS, vol. 11752, pp. 683–693. Springer, Cham (2019). https://doi.org/10.1007/978-3-030-30645-8_62
22. Cilia, N.D., De Stefano, C., Fontanella, F., di Freca, A.S.: How word choice affects cognitive impairment detection by handwriting analysis: a preliminary study. In: Cicirelli, F., Guerrieri, A., Pizzuti, C., Socievole, A., Spezzano, G., Vinci, A. (eds.) WIVACE 2019. CCIS, vol. 1200, pp. 113–123. Springer, Cham (2020). https://doi.org/10.1007/978-3-030-45016-8_12
23. Ishikawa, T. et al.: Handwriting features of multiple drawing tests for early detection of alzheimer's disease: a preliminary result. In: MedInfo, pp. 168–172 (2019)
24. Cilia, N.D., De Stefano, C., Fontanella, F., Di Freca, A.S.: An experimental protocol to support cognitive impairment diagnosis by using handwriting analysis. Procedia Comput. Sci. **141**, 466–471 (2018)

25. Sarica, A., Cerasa, A., Quattrone, A.: Random forest algorithm for the classification of neuroimaging data in alzheimer's disease: a systematic review. Frontiers Aging Neurosci. **9**, 329 (2017)
26. Abdullah, M.N., Wah, Y.B., Zakaria, Y., Majeed, A.B.A., Huat, O.S.: Discovering potential blood-based cytokine biomarkers for alzheimer's disease using firth logistic regression. Epidemiology, Biostatistics Pub. Health 16(4), 2019
27. El Mehdi Benyoussef, B., Elbyed, A., El Hadiri, H.: 3d MRI classification using KNN and deep neural network for alzheimer's disease diagnosis. Advanced Intelligent Systems for Sustainable Development (AI2SD 2018): vol. 4: Advanced Intelligent Systems Applied to Health, vol. 914, p. 154 (2019)
28. Ghazi, M.M., et al.: Training recurrent neural networks robust to incomplete data: application to alzheimer's disease progression modeling. Med. Image Anal. **53**, 39–46 (2019)
29. Kruthika, K., Maheshappa, H., Initiative, A.D.N., et al.: Multistage classifier-based approach for alzheimer's disease prediction and retrieval. Inf. Med. Unlocked **14**, 34–42 (2019)
30. Battineni, G., Chintalapudi, N., Amenta, F.: Machine learning in medicine: performance calculation of dementia prediction by support vector machines (svm). Inf. Med. Unlocked **16**, 100200 (2019)
31. Pereira, C.R., et al.: A step towards the automated diagnosis of parkinson's disease: Analyzing handwriting movements. In: 2015 IEEE 28th International Symposium on Computer-Based Medical Systems, pp. 171–176 (2015)
32. Kittler, J., Hatef, M., Duin, R.P., Matas, J.: On combining classifiers. IEEE Trans. Pattern Anal. Mach. Intell. **20**(3), 226–239 (1998)

A Lightweight Spatial Attention Module with Adaptive Receptive Fields in 3D Convolutional Neural Network for Alzheimer's Disease Classification

Fei Yu, Baoqi Zhao, Qingqing Ge, Zhijie Zhang, Junmei Sun, and Xiumei Li[✉]

Hangzhou Normal University, Hangzhou, 311121, Zhejiang, China
lixiumei@hznu.edu.com

Abstract. The development of deep learning provides powerful support for disease classification of neuroimaging data. However, in the classification of neuroimaging data based on deep learning methods, the spatial information cannot be fully utilized. In this paper, we propose a lightweight 3D spatial attention module with adaptive receptive fields, which allows neurons to adaptively adjust the receptive field size according to multiple scales of input information. The attention module can fuse spatial information of different scales on multiple branches, so that 3D spatial information of neuroimaging data can be fully utilized. A 3D-ResNet18 based on our proposed attention module is trained to diagnose Alzheimer's disease (AD). Experiments are conducted on 521 subjects (254 of patients with AD and 267 of normal controls) from Alzheimer's Disease National Initiative (ADNI) dataset of 3D structural MRI brain scans. Experimental results show the effectiveness and efficiency of our proposed approach for AD classification.

Keywords: Alzheimer's disease · Deep learning · Attention mechanism · Receptive field

1 Introduction

Alzheimer's disease (AD) is an irreversible progressive neurodegenerative disorder that is the most common form of dementia in elderly person worldwide [1]. The disease slowly destroys memory, reduces thinking ability and leads to difficulty in communication and performing daily activities such as speaking and walking. There are approximately 47 million people with dementia world-widely. As the problem of population aging is getting worse, this number is expected to rise to 75 million people globally by 2030 and estimated to triple by 2050 [2]. In addition, the cost of taking care for patients with AD is expected to increase dramatically, seriously affecting the quality of life of patients and their families and social development [3]. Therefore, effective and accurate diagnosis of AD is highly demanded.

The traditional machine learning methods have been widely used in the study of neuroimaging data. In the past decade, a large number of studies on AD classification

© Springer Nature Switzerland AG 2021
A. Del Bimbo et al. (Eds.): ICPR 2020 Workshops, LNCS 12661, pp. 575–586, 2021.
https://doi.org/10.1007/978-3-030-68763-2_44

have used traditional machine learning algorithms, such as support vector machine, decision tree or random forest, to classify AD medical images [4–7]. Classification based on traditional machine learning methods requires complex data pre-processing, such as feature extraction, feature selection and dimensionality reduction [8]. The classification accuracy of this method depends strongly on effective pre-processing, and the pre-processing work consumes a lot of manpower and material resources [1, 8].

With the advent of artificial intelligence technology, there are several studies using deep learning for the AD classification. The difference between using deep learning methods and traditional machine learning methods for AD classification is that deep learning methods require little or no data pre-processing, and can automatically extract features of 3D spatial information from neuroimaging data, so it is a more objective method with less error [8, 9]. Korolev et al. [10] showed how similar performance can be achieved skipping these feature extraction steps with the residual and plain 3D convolutional neural network architectures. Yang et al. [11] developed three approaches for producing visual explanations from 3D-convolution neural networks (CNNs) for Alzheimer's disease classification. Jin et al. [12] proposed a 3D-ResNet architecture based on single-branch spatial attention to diagnose AD and explore potential biological markers. Although the previous studies based on deep learning method achieve great classification performance, they still cannot make full use of the 3D spatial information of neuroimaging data.

Inspired by the attention mechanism, we propose a lightweight 3D spatial attention module with adaptive receptive fields, which allows each neuron to adaptively adjust the size of receptive fields by weighted fusion of multi-scale information from different branches, and fully utilize the 3D spatial information of the neuroimaging data. We examine the performance of a 3D residual neural network (ResNet) [13] based on our attention module for AD diagnosis using brain MRI data. Our attention module can increase accuracy on AD classification at a small extra computational cost. The proposed approach provides technical support for the automatic diagnosis of AD disease, and can also be applied to other diseases classifications where MRI data is available.

In summary, the main contributions of this paper are as follows:

1. We propose a lightweight 3D spatial attention module with adaptive receptive fields, which fuse the weighted multi-scale information from multiple branches with different kernel sizes and fully utilize the information in 3D space;
2. We introduce dilated convolution into the proposed attention module, which can be computationally lightweight and impose only a slightly increase in parameter and computational cost;
3. We conduct a series of experiment using 3D-ResNet based on our 3D spatial attention module for AD classification and achieve competitive performance with low complexity.

2   Related Work

2.1   Deep Learning Methods for AD Classification

CNNs are the most successful deep learning methods for image analysis and have been designed to better utilize spatial information by taking images as input [1]. In AD classification using deep learning methods, researchers used to train 2D CNNs for AD classification [14, 15, 16]. With the development of convolutional neural networks, 3D CNNs have been proposed, which can capture 3D information from the 3D volume of a brain scan and has shown better performance compared with 2D CNNs [17]. Korolev et al. [10] proposed a residual and plain CNN for classification of brain MRI scans without manual feature generation. Yang et al. [11] proposed three efficient approaches for generating visual explanations from 3D CNNs for AD classification. These previous studies have shown the advantages of capturing 3D information. Therefore, we also use 3D CNNs for AD classification in this paper.

2.2   Attention Mechanism

Attention mechanism, first introduced for machine translation [18], has now become an essential component of deep learning. In recent years, the benefits of attention mechanism have been shown in many practical applications, such as image recognition [19, 20], image segmentation [21, 22] and natural language processing [23]. Wang et al. [24] proposed a residual attention network to generate attention-aware features. SENet [19] adaptively recalibrated channel-wise feature responses to boost the representational power of the network, and won first place on ILSVRC 2017. CBAM [25] further introduced spatial attention mechanism to achieve considerable performance improvement with low computational complexity. SKNet [20] brought an effective lightweight channel attention mechanism, which was the first to explicitly focus on the adaptive receptive field size of neurons. In addition, there are also a number of studies for attention mechanism [26, 27]. All of the above methods on attention mechanism is based on 2D image datasets. Different from the mentioned research, our approach aims at spatial attention in 3D space.

Based on the idea in [12], we propose a 3D spatial attention module for AD classification. Our approach differs from exiting methods in that: (i) our method uses multiple branches to fuse weighted multi-scales information. (ii) we propose a 3D spatial attention module to perform accurate AD accuracy classification with low computational cost.

2.3   Dilated Convolution

Dilated convolution was originally developed in an algorithm for wavelet decomposition [28, 29], which can extract dense feature in networks by inserting "holes" between pixels in convolutional kernels to increase image resolution. Dilated convolution is also used to enlarge receptive field without loss of coverage. For example, a $3 \times 3 \times 3$ convolution with dilation 2 can approximately over the receptive field of a $5 \times 5 \times 5$ convolution, while using less parameters and memory. Wang et al. [30] used a decomposition of dilated convolution to improve the performance of dense prediction tasks. Yu et al. [31]

utilized dilated convolution to design a new network structure that reliably increases accuracy when combined into exiting semantic segmentation system. In other tasks, such as machine translation [32], audio generation [33] and object detection [34], dilated convolutions are employed to replace standard convolutions to enlarge the receptive fields of outputs.

3   Method

3.1   3D Spatial Attention Module with Adaptive Receptive Fields

To enable the network to obtain more 3D spatial information from neuroimaging data, we propose a lightweight spatial attention module with adaptive receptive fields, as illustrated in Fig. 1, where a two-branch case is shown. In this example, there are only two branches with two different kernels, but it is convenient to extend to multiple branches cases. Each branch of the attention module distributes weights to feature map through convolution operations with different kernel sizes, and then fuse the weighted attention map of each branch, which allows neurons to adaptively adjust receptive field size, so that the 3D spatial information of neuroimaging data can be fully utilized.

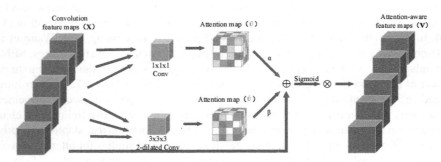

Fig. 1. Diagram of attention module.

For any given feature map $X \in \mathbb{R}^{C' \times H' \times W' \times D'}$, by default we first conduct two transformations $\widetilde{\mathcal{F}} : X \rightarrow \tilde{U} \in \mathbb{R}^{C \times H \times W \times D}$ and $\widehat{\mathcal{F}} : X \rightarrow \hat{U} \in \mathbb{R}^{C \times H \times W \times D}$ with kernel size 1 and 5, respectively. Both $\widetilde{\mathcal{F}}$ and $\widehat{\mathcal{F}}$ are composed of convolutions and reduce the channel C of feature map to 1. For efficiency, the conventional convolution with a $5 \times 5 \times 5$ kernel is replaced by the dilated convolution with $3 \times 3 \times 3$ kernel and dilation size 2. To allow neurons to adaptively adjust their receptive field size, the attention module fuses the weighted information of different scales from each branch. In the processing of weighted fusion, the weight distributed by attention module to the multi-scale information of each branch is obtained during end-to-end training. Further, the fused information is nonlinearly activated by the activation function, and the final feature map $V_{i,c}$ is obtained through attention weights on various convolutions with different kernels:

$$V_{i,c} = \sigma(\alpha \cdot \tilde{U}_i + \beta \cdot \hat{U}_i) * X_{i,c} \tag{1}$$

where i denotes the spatial position of the voxel in H, W and D dimensions, σ is the Sigmoid function, α and β is the weight distributed to attsention maps $\tilde{U}$ and $\hat{U}$, respectively. Similar to 3D SENet, in the case of single-branch, by default we conduct transformation: $\widetilde{\mathcal{F}}:X \rightarrow \tilde{U} \in \mathbb{R}^{C \times H \times W \times D}$ with kernel size 1. The final feature map $V_{i,c}$ is obtained through the attention weight:

$$V_{i,c} = \sigma(\tilde{U}_i) * X_{i,c} \qquad (2)$$

Experiments in this paper mainly use single-branch and two-branch attention module, so we provide formulas for the single-branch case and the two-branch case. It can be easily extended to situations with more branches by extending (1).

We integrate the attention module with each ResBlock in 3D-ResNet18 network for AD classification, as shown in Fig. 2. Table 1 shows the architecture of 3D-ResNet18 with the single-branch attention module and the two-branch attention module. After end-to-end training, the attention module in the network distributes weights to voxels by fusing information from different branches with different kernels, which can automatically extract features and improve the classification performance of the network. The network can be used not only for AD classification, but also for 3D neuroimaging data of other brain diseases.

Table 1. Architecture of 3D-ResNet18 with attention module.

Layers	Single-branch	Two-branch
Conv 3D	$7 \times 7 \times 7$, 64, stride 1,2,2	
Maxpool 3D	$3 \times 3 \times 3$, stride 2	
Residual Block_1	$\begin{bmatrix} 3 \times 3 \times 3, & 64 \\ 3 \times 3 \times 3, & 64 \\ 5 \times 5 \times 5, & 64 \end{bmatrix} \times 2$	$\begin{bmatrix} 3 \times 3 \times 3, & 64 \\ 3 \times 3 \times 3, & 64 \\ 1 \times 1 \times 1 \quad 5 \times 5 \times 5, & 64 \end{bmatrix} \times 2$
Residual Block_2	$\begin{bmatrix} 3 \times 3 \times 3, & 128 \\ 3 \times 3 \times 3, & 128 \\ 5 \times 5 \times 5, & 128 \end{bmatrix} \times 2$	$\begin{bmatrix} 3 \times 3 \times 3, & 128 \\ 3 \times 3 \times 3, & 128 \\ 1 \times 1 \times 1 \quad 5 \times 5 \times 5, & 128 \end{bmatrix} \times 2$
Residual Block_3	$\begin{bmatrix} 3 \times 3 \times 3, & 256 \\ 3 \times 3 \times 3, & 256 \\ 5 \times 5 \times 5, & 256 \end{bmatrix} \times 2$	$\begin{bmatrix} 3 \times 3 \times 3, & 256 \\ 3 \times 3 \times 3, & 256 \\ 1 \times 1 \times 1 \quad 5 \times 5 \times 5, & 256 \end{bmatrix} \times 2$
Residual Block_4	$\begin{bmatrix} 3 \times 3 \times 3, & 512 \\ 3 \times 3 \times 3, & 512 \\ 5 \times 5 \times 5, & 512 \end{bmatrix} \times 2$	$\begin{bmatrix} 3 \times 3 \times 3, & 512 \\ 3 \times 3 \times 3, & 512 \\ 1 \times 1 \times 1 \quad 5 \times 5 \times 5, & 512 \end{bmatrix} \times 2$
Avgpool, 2-d fc, Softmax		

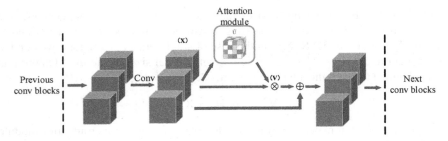

Fig. 2. Attention module integrated with ResBlock.

3.2 Data and Preprocessing

The T1 structural MRI scans from the Alzheimer's Disease Neuroimaging Initiative (ADNI, https://adni.loni.usc.edu/) are used to examine the performance of our approach. Since each subject may have more than one MRI scan in ADNI dataset, we only use the earliest MRI scan associated with each subject to avoid the possibility of information leakage between the training and testing dataset. As a result, the dataset includes 521 subjects, of which 254 patients with AD (119 females, age: 75.35 ± 7.75, MMSE: 23.58 ± 2.58) and 267 normal controls (NCs) (133 females, age: 75.48 ± 5.6, MMSE: 29.04 ± 1.14).

In our experiment, to investigate valuable information about regional changes in gray matter for network model, structural MRI images were all preprocessed with the standard steps in the Cat12 toolbox (https://www.neuro.uni-jena.de/cat/index.html). All images were preprocessed with bias-correction, skull-stripping, segmentation to gray matter (GM), white matter (WM) and cerebrospinal fluid (CSF), registration to Montreal Neurological Institute (MNI) space using affine transformation (global scaling) and non-linear warping (local volume change) and modulation. The gray matter images were resliced to 2 mm cubic size resulting in a volume size of 91 × 109 × 91, as shown in Fig. 3.

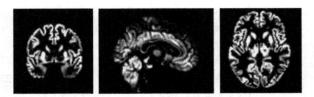

Fig. 3. Example of image after preprocessing.

3.3 Experiment Setup

To get better and more objective classification performance, we run stratified 5-fold cross-validations with 5 different fold splits each time. The evaluation metrics include effectiveness (accuracy, sensitivity and specificity) and efficiency (network parameters, floating point operations per second (FLOPs)). The parameters of networks are optimized by Adam with cosine annealing learning rate decay. The initial learning rate is set to 3e−4 and batch size is 8. All models are trained within 70 epochs from scratch on a TITAN V GPU.

4   Result and Discussion

4.1   Comparisons Using Different Single-Branch Cases

In this section, we evaluate effect of kernel size on the single-branch attention module. We compare 3D-ResNet18 model and four 3D-ResNet18 models based on single-branch attention module with different kernels by setting kernel size to be $1 \times 1 \times 1$, $3 \times 3 \times 3$, $5 \times 5 \times 5$ and $7 \times 7 \times 7$, respectively.

The results are given in Table 2, #. Param. Denotes the number of network parameters. We can observe that, all four 3D-ResNet18 models based on single-branch attention module improve accuracy and sensitivity performance over 3D-ResNet18, demonstrates that the single-branch attention module can further improve the discriminative ability of network. As the convolutional kernel size in attention module increases, the complexity of the network model also increases. Remarkably, the 3D-ResNet18 based on single-branch attention module with kernel of 1 shares almost the same model complexity with 3D-ResNet18, while achieving 0.3% gains in accuracy, which demonstrates efficiency of the former model. As shown in Fig. 4, single-branch attention module with kernel size of $5 \times 5 \times 5$ and $7 \times 7 \times 7$ outperform the one with kernel size of $1 \times 1 \times 1$ and $3 \times 3 \times 3$, and it obtains best result 92.11% at kernel size of $5 \times 5 \times 5$ for 3D-ResNet18. The reason is that the convolution of larger receptive field is more sensitive to obtain the important lesion information about AD. It is shown that the network based on single-branch attention module can capture information in 3D space, and improve the performance of AD classification.

Table 2. Comparisons of using different single-branch cases.

Method	Kernel	Accuracy	Sensitivity	Specificity	#. Param	FLOPs
3D-ResNet18		0.9154 ± 0.0160	0.8831 ± 0.0416	0.9426 ± 0.0211	33.16M	29.15G
Single-branch	$1 \times 1 \times 1$	0.9184 ± 0.0262	0.9107 ± 0.0386	0.9224 ± 0.0472	33.16M	29.16G
Single-branch	$3 \times 3 \times 3$	0.9188 ± 0.0215	0.8988 ± 0.0512	0.9350 ± 0.0434	33.21M	29.29G
Single-branch	$5 \times 5 \times 5$	0.9211 ± 0.0171	0.9120 ± 0.0477	0.9262 ± 0.0452	33.40M	29.79G
Single-branch	$7 \times 7 \times 7$	0.9192 ± 0.0176	0.9057 ± 0.0444	0.9301 ± 0.2852	33.82M	30.91G

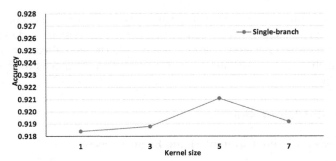

Fig. 4. Results of 3D-ResNet18 based on single-branch attention module with various numbers of kernel size.

4.2   Comparisons Using Different Two-Branch Cases

We compare five 3D-ResNet18 models based on different two-branch attention modules. The dilation rate is crucial to control the receptive field size. Since the 3D-ResNet18 based on single-branch attention module with kernel of $1 \times 1 \times 1$ has better classification performance with low model complexity, we compare the 3D-ResNet18 with two-branch cases attention module and fix the setting $1 \times 1 \times 1$ kernel size in the first branch. Under the constraint of similar model complexity, we can increase the dilation rate to enlarge receptive field of the second branch. The five 3D-ResNet18 models based on two-branch attention module with different kernel by setting kernel size to be $3 \times 3 \times 3$ with dilation rate 3, $3 \times 3 \times 3$ with dilation rate 2, $3 \times 3 \times 3$ with dilation rate 1, $5 \times 5 \times 5$ with dilation rate 1 and $7 \times 7 \times 7$ with dilation rate 1 in the second branch, respectively. The receptive field of the second branch of kernel size $3 \times 3 \times 3$ with dilation rate 3 is equal to the one with kernel size $7 \times 7 \times 7$ with dilation rate 1, and the receptive field of kernel size $3 \times 3 \times 3$ with dilation rate 2 equals to the one of kernel size $5 \times 5 \times 5$ with dilation rate 1.

The results are given in Table 3, D denotes dilation rate. We can observe that, comparing with 3D-ResNet18 with two-branch attention module of kernel size $7 \times 7 \times 7$ with dilation rate 1, the 3D-ResNet18 with two-branch attention module of kernel size $3 \times 3 \times 3$ with dilation rate 3 obtains competitive classification performance with lower model complexity. We also note that 3D-ResNet18 with two-branch attention module of kernel size $3 \times 3 \times 3$ with dilation rate 2 achieves best classification accuracy 92.72% and better or comparable performance than the one of kernel size $5 \times 5 \times 5$ with dilation rate 1 with fewer parameters. We note that the 3D-ResNet18 with two-branch attention module of kernel size $7 \times 7 \times 7$ and the one of kernel size $5 \times 5 \times 5$ outperform the one of kernel size $3 \times 3 \times 3$ with dilation rate 1. This indicates the potential of sensitivity of larger receptive field kernel to important information for AD classification.

As shown in Fig. 5 and Table 3, we empirically find that the series of $3 \times 3 \times 3$ kernels with various dilation rates is moderately superior to the corresponding counterparts with the same receptive field in both performance and model complexity.

Table 3. Comparisons of using different two-branch cases.

Settings		Accuracy	Sensitivity	Specificity	#. Param	FLOPs	Resulted kernel
Kernel	D						
$3 \times 3 \times 3$	3	0.9264 ± 0.0190	0.9094 ± 0.0469	0.9338 ± 0.0380	33.21M	29.30G	$7 \times 7 \times 7$
$3 \times 3 \times 3$	2	0.9272 ± 0.0215	0.9055 ± 0.0345	0.9449 ± 0.0354	33.21M	29.30G	$5 \times 5 \times 5$
$3 \times 3 \times 3$	1	0.9240 ± 0.0217	0.8951 ± 0.0414	0.9486 ± 0.0262	33.21M	29.30G	$3 \times 3 \times 3$
$5 \times 5 \times 5$	1	0.9254 ± 0.0176	0.9015 ± 0.0349	0.9364 ± 0.0297	33.40M	29.80G	$5 \times 5 \times 5$
$7 \times 7 \times 7$	1	0.9261 ± 0.0150	0.9096 ± 0.0389	0.9258 ± 0.0386	33.82M	30.91G	$7 \times 7 \times 7$

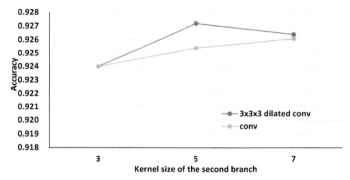

Fig. 5. Results of 3D-ResNet18 based on two-branch attention module with various number of kernel size.

4.3 Comparisons Using Different Single-Branch and Two-Branch Cases

Then we compare the above four 3D-ResNet18 models with single-branch attention module and the above five 3D-ResNet18 models with two-branch attention module. The latter one all consistently improve accuracy performance over the former one. Remarkably, the two-branch case of kernel size $3 \times 3 \times 3$ with dilation rate 2 obtains 1.18% absolute improvement over the baseline and outperforms the single-branch of kernel size $5 \times 5 \times 5$ by above 0.61%, although the former has fewer parameters. This demonstrates that our attention module is very efficient and shows the superiority of adaptive fusion for multiple branches.

4.4 Comparisons with Related Studies

We compare the proposed approach in this paper with related studies. As presented in Table 4, these recent AD classification studies all use deep learning methods based on

MRI neuroimaging data, and they all use datasets from ADNI and different data processing methods. Comparing with the previous studies, the proposed approach achieves better performance. It shows that our approach is efficient and can capture valuable information of brain areas for AD classification.

Table 4. Performance comparison with previous related work.

Methods	Sample Size	Accuracy
Yang et al. [11]	47 AD, 56 NC	0.794
Aderghal et al. [16]	188 AD, 228 NC	0.914
Korolev et al. [10]	50 AD, 61 NC	0.800
Suk et al. [35]	186 AD, 226 NC	0.903
Huang et al. [36]	288 AD, 272 NC	0.911
Jin et al. [12]	227 AD, 205 NC	0.921
The proposed	254 AD, 257 NC	0.927

5 Conclusion

In this paper, we propose a lightweight 3D spatial attention module, which allows neurons to adaptively adjust the size of receptive fields by weighted fusion of multi-scale information from different branches. Experimental results demonstrate that the 3D-ReNet18 with our proposed attention module can improve the performance of AD classification based on the MRI neuroimaging data. We show that the proposed approach achieves better performance than previous studies. It should also be noted that our attention module can be combined into other 3D networks and can be easily transferred to classification of other brain diseases based on MRI neuroimaging data.

Acknowledgment. This research work is supported by the National Natural Science Foundation of China (grant numbers 61571174 and 61801159).

References

1. Ebrahimighahnavieh, M.A., Luo, S., Chiong, R.: Deep learning to detect Alzheimer's disease from neuroimaging: a systematic literature review. Comput. Methods Programs Biomed. 187, 105242 (2020)
2. Ulep, M.G., Saraon, S.K., McLea, S.: Alzheimer disease. J. Nurse Pract.14, 129-135 (2018)

3. Bron, E.E., et al.: Standardized evaluation of algorithms for computer-aided diagnosis of dementia based on structural MRI: the CADDementia challenge. NeuroImage **111**, 562–579 (2015)
4. Long, Z., et al.: A support vector machine-based method to identify mild cognitive impairment with multi-level characteristics of magnetic resonance imaging. Neuroscience **331**, 169–176 (2016)
5. Proitsi, P., et al.: Association of blood lipids with Alzheimer's disease: a comprehensive lipidomics analysis. Alzheimer's & Dementia **13**(2), 140–151 (2017)
6. Cai, K., et al.: Identification of early-stage Alzheimer's disease using Sulcal morphology and other common neuroimaging indices. PLoS ONE **12**(1), e0170875 (2017)
7. Li, M., Qin, Y., Gao, F., Zhu, W., He, X.: Discriminative analysis of multivariate features from structural MRI and diffusion tensor images. Magn. Reson. Imaging **32**(8), 1043–1051 (2014)
8. Rathore, S., Habes, M., Iftikhar, M.A., Shacklett, A., Davatzikos, C.: A review on neuroimaging-based classification studies and associated feature extraction methods for Alzheimer's disease and its prodromal stages. NeuroImage **155**, 530–548 (2017)
9. LeCun, Y., Bengio, Y., Hinton, G.: Deep learning. Nature **521**(7553), 436–444 (2015)
10. Korolev, S., Safiullin, A., Belyaev, M., Dodonova, Y.: Residual and plain convolutional neural networks for 3D brain MRI classification. In: IEEE 14th International Symposium on Biomedical Imaging (ISBI 2017), pp. 835–838 (2017)
11. Yang, C., Rangarajan, A., Ranka, S.: Visual explanations from deep 3D convolutional neural networks for Alzheimer's disease classification. In: AMIA Annual Symposium Proceedings, p. 1571 (2018)
12. Jin, D., et al.: Attention-based 3D convolutional network for Alzheimer's disease diagnosis and biomarkers exploration. In: IEEE 16th International Symposium on Biomedical Imaging (ISBI 2019), pp. 1047–1051 (2019)
13. Hara, K., Kataoka, H., Satoh, Y.: Learning spatio-temporal features with 3D residual networks for action recognition. In: Proceedings of the IEEE International Conference on Computer Vision Workshops, pp. 3154–3160 (2017)
14. Farooq, A., Anwar, S., Awais, M., Rehman, S.: A deep CNN based multi-class classification of Alzheimer's disease using MRI. In: IEEE International Conference on Imaging Systems and Techniques (IST), pp. 1–6 (2017)
15. Islam, J., Zhang, Y.: A novel deep learning based multi-class classification method for Alzheimer's disease detection using brain MRI data. In: Zeng, Yi., et al. (eds.) BI 2017. LNCS (LNAI), vol. 10654, pp. 213–222. Springer, Cham (2017). https://doi.org/10.1007/978-3-319-70772-3_20
16. Aderghal, K., Benois-Pineau, J., Afdel, K.: Classification of sMRI for Alzheimer's disease diagnosis with CNN: single Siamese networks with 2D+? approach and fusion on ADNI. In: Proceedings of the 2017 ACM on International Conference on Multimedia Retrieval, pp. 494–498 (2017)
17. Ji, S., Xu, W., Yang, M., Yu, K.: 3D convolutional neural networks for human action recognition. IEEE Trans. Pattern Anal. Mach. Intell. **35**(1), 221–231 (2012)
18. Bahdanau, D., Cho, K., Bengio, Y.: Neural machine translation by jointly learning to align and translate. arXiv preprint arXiv:1409.0473 (2014).
19. Hu, J., Shen, L., Sun, G.: Squeeze-and-excitation networks. In: Proceedings of the IEEE Conference on Computer Vision and Pattern Recognition, pp. 7132–7141 (2018)
20. Li, X., Wang, W., Hu, X., Yang, J.: Selective kernel networks. In: Proceedings of the IEEE Conference on Computer Vision and Pattern Recognition, pp. 510–519 (2019)

21. Roy, A.G., Navab, N., Wachinger, C.: Concurrent spatial and channel 'squeeze & excitation' in fully convolutional networks. In: Frangi, A., Schnabel, J., Davatzikos, C., Alberola-López, C., Fichtinger, G. (eds.) Medical Image Computing and Computer Assisted Intervention – MICCAI 2018. MICCAI 2018. Lecture Notes in Computer Science, vol 11070. Springer, Cham (2018). https://doi.org/https://doi.org/10.1007/978-3-030-00928-1_48

22. Lin, T.-Y., Dollár, P., Girshick, R., He, K., Hariharan, B., Belongie, S.: Feature pyramid networks for object detection. In: Proceedings of the IEEE Conference on Computer Vision and Pattern Recognition, pp. 2117–2125 (2017)

23. Vaswani, A., et al. Attention is all you need. In: Advances in Neural Information Processing Systems, pp. 5998–6008 (2017)

24. Wang, F., et al.: Residual attention network for image classification. In: Proceedings of the IEEE Conference on Computer Vision and Pattern Recognition, pp. 3156–3164 (2017)

25. Woo, S., Park, J., Lee, J.-Y., Kweon, I.S.: CBAM: convolutional block attention module. In: Ferrari, V., Hebert, M., Sminchisescu, C., Weiss, Y. (eds.) ECCV 2018. LNCS, vol. 11211, pp. 3–19. Springer, Cham (2018). https://doi.org/10.1007/978-3-030-01234-2_1

26. Wang, Q., Wu, B., Zhu, P., Li, P., Zuo, W., Hu, Q.: ECA-net: efficient channel attention for deep convolutional neural networks. In: Proceedings of the IEEE/CVF Conference on Computer Vision and Pattern Recognition, pp. 11534–11542 (2020)

27. Park, J., Woo, S., Lee, J.-Y., Kweon, I.S.: Bam: bottleneck attention module. arXiv preprint arXiv:1807.06514 (2018)

28. Holschneider, M., Kronland-Martinet, R., Morlet, J., Tchamitchian, P.: A real-time algorithm for signal analysis with the help of the wavelet transform. In: Combes, J.-M., Grossmann, A., Tchamitchian, P. (eds.) Wavelets, pp. 286–297. Springer Berlin Heidelberg, Berlin, Heidelberg (1990). https://doi.org/10.1007/978-3-642-75988-8_28

29. Shensa, M.J.: The discrete wavelet transform: wedding the a trous and Mallat algorithms. IEEE Trans. Signal Process. **40**(10), 2464–2482 (1992)

30. Wang, Z., Ji, S.: Smoothed dilated convolutions for improved dense prediction. In: Proceedings of the 24th ACM SIGKDD International Conference on Knowledge Discovery & Data Mining, pp. 2486–2495 (2018)

31. Yu, F., Koltun, V.: Multi-scale context aggregation by dilated convolutions. arXiv preprint arXiv:1511.07122 (2015)

32. Kalchbrenner, N., Espeholt, L., Simonyan, K., Oord, A.v.d., Graves, A., Kavukcuoglu, K.: Neural machine translation in linear time. arXiv preprint arXiv:1610.10099 (2016)

33. Oord, A.v.d., et al.: Wavenet: a generative model for raw audio. arXiv preprint arXiv:1609.03499 (2016)

34. Dai, J., Li, Y., He, K., Sun, J.: R-FCN: object detection via region-based fully convolutional networks. arXiv preprint arXiv:1605.06409 (2016)

35. Suk, H.-I., Lee, S.-W., Shen, D., Initiative, A.S.D.N.: Deep ensemble learning of sparse regression models for brain disease diagnosis. Med. Image Anal. **37**, 101–113 (2017)

36. Huang, Y., Jiahang, X., Zhou, Y., Tong, T., Zhuang, X.: Diagnosis of Alzheimer's disease via multi-modality 3D convolutional neural network. Frontiers in Neuroscience **13**, 509 (2019). https://doi.org/10.3389/fnins.2019.00509

Handwriting-Based Classifier Combination for Cognitive Impairment Prediction

Nicole Dalia Cilia, Claudio De Stefano, Francesco Fontanella[✉],
and Alessandra Scotto di Freca

Department of Electrical and Information Engineering (DIEI), University of Cassino
and Southern Lazio, Via G. Di Biasio, 43, 03043 Cassino, FR, Italy
{nicoledalia.cilia,destefano,fontanella,a.scotto}@unicas.it

Abstract. Cognitive impairments affect areas such as memory, learning, concentration, or decision making and range from mild to severe. Impairments of this kind can be indicators of neurodegenerative diseases such as Alzheimer's, that affect millions of people worldwide and whose incidence is expected to increase in the near future. Handwriting is one of the daily activities affected by this kind of impairment, and its anomalies are already used for the diagnosis of neurodegenerative diseases, such as, for example, micrographia in Parkinson's patients. Classifier combination methods have proved to be an effective tool for increasing the performance in pattern recognition applications. The rationale of this approach follows from the observation that appropriately diverse classifiers, especially when trained on different types of data, tend to make uncorrelated errors. In this paper, we present a study in which the responses of different classifiers, trained on data from graphic tasks, have been combined to predict cognitive impairments. The proposed system has been trained and tested on a dataset containing handwritten traits extracted from some simple graphic tasks, e.g. joining two points or drawing circles. The results confirmed that a simple combination rule, such as the majority vote rule, performs better than single classifiers.

Keywords: Handwriting · Classifier combination · Cognitive impairments

1 Introduction

Cognitive impairment is when individuals have cognitive deficits that are greater than those that would be statistically expected for their age and education, but which do not significantly interfere with their daily activities. It is seen as the transition state between normal aging and dementia and often it may evolve into dementia [11]. The amnestic subtype of cognitive impairments has a high risk of progression to Alzheimer's disease (AD). For this reason, identifying this kind of impairments can help to an early diagnosis of AD, which is crucial

© Springer Nature Switzerland AG 2021
A. Del Bimbo et al. (Eds.): ICPR 2020 Workshops, LNCS 12661, pp. 587–599, 2021.
https://doi.org/10.1007/978-3-030-68763-2_45

in slowing its progression as well as alleviating its symptoms. To date, brain imaging, cerebrospinal fluid tests and cognitive tests such as the Minimental State Examination (MMSE) or Montreal Cognitive Assessment (MOCA) test may be performed to determine whether the person's cognitive impairment is due to Alzheimer's.

Handwriting is among the perceptive-motor skills affected by cognitive impairments [13,22–24], and spatial disorganization and poor control of movements cause it to be altered in patients with AD [17]. Some aspects of the writing process are more vulnerable than others and, for example, dysgraphia may be a diagnostic sign of Parkinson's disease. For this reason, many medical studies have been done to investigate how cognitive impairments affect handwriting. Typically these studies use statistical tools, e.g. ANOVA and T-test analysis, to investigate the relationship between the disease under investigation and each of the features used to characterize the handwriting [16,20,25,31]. More recently, with the aim of developing tools to support an early diagnosis of this kind of impairment, machine learning based algorithms have been used to determine the complex interactions that may co-exist between these features and the diseases to be diagnosed [1,2,18,19,26]. The statistical studies mentioned-above typically involve a few dozens participants. These numbers are sufficient to achieve statically significant results for the tools used in those studies, but may limit the effectiveness of classification algorithms, such as neural networks, SVMs and decision trees [12,29]. To try to overcome this problem, in [7] we have proposed a protocol consisting of twenty-five handwriting tasks. These tasks require the participants to, for example, copy letters, words, or even a paragraph as well as to draw simple shapes. The protocol was used to acquire data from about one hundred eighty participants, equally split between cognitively impaired and a healthy control group. Preliminary results obtained from this data, by using widely used and well-known classifiers like, for example, decision trees or SVM, can be found in [3–5].

Ensemble techniques have been widely and successfully used in the last few years to improve the performance of classification algorithms [8–10]. They try to combine the responses provided by a set of classifiers in such a way that improves the overall classification accuracy. Such techniques rely on a procedure for the selection or the training of a set of sufficiently diverse classifiers, as well as a voting mechanism, to combine the responses provided by the learned classifiers. If the classifiers are sufficiently diverse, then the majority vote rule ensures an improvement of the performance achieved by the single classifiers making up the whole.

In this paper, we present an ensemble-based approach. The responses provided by a set of classifiers trained on the data from the graphic tasks of the protocol mentioned above are combined using the majority vote rule, with the aim of predicting the cognitive status of the participant performing the tasks. In order to reduce classification errors, our combination rule implements a reject option: the classifier responses with probability below a fixed threshold are ignored and

do not contribute to the voting providing the final response for a given participant. Only graphic tasks were chosen as:

- From the literature we know that brain damages due to ND dementia (e.g.,
  brain atrophy, neuronal loss, cellular or synaptic dysfunction) may cause
  both cognitive and motor dysfunctions or affect the performance of previously learned motor skills [21]. The analysis of the changes in learned movements caused by MCI and AD facilitates the understanding of brain-body
  functional relationships and allows the identification of patterns of sensory-
  motor dysfunctions associated with MCI and AD. In [30], for example, the
  authors observe unique movement characteristics that are related to cognitive aging (motor speed, smoothness, coordination, timing, and profiles of
  movement trajectory, velocity, or acceleration). In a point-to-point task, the
  controls and MCI were significantly faster and smoother than AD patients.
  Also Schroter et al. [25] found that from graphic tasks, kinematic results
  of circular and quick handwriting movements performed by AD and MCI
  patients, and control groups, show greater variability in movement velocity
  of AD and MCI. Furthermore, graphical tasks are excellent candidates for
  use with deep learning techniques [6].
- In our previous studies we analyzed the influence of a subset of copy tasks in
  the diagnosis of AD [4,5]. Moreover, in [3], we tested the cognitive deterioration from mild to moderate AD, starting from the meaning of two regular
  words, two non-regular words and two non words. This paper can help complete the picture of the different cognitive aspects underlying the different
  types of tasks compromised by AD.

The paper is organized as follows: Sect. 2 illustrates the tasks used to acquire
handwriting of the participants involved in this study, and Sect. 3 details the
data used and features extracted. Section 4 describes the proposed approach,
whereas Sect. 5 reports the experimental results. Finally, concluding remarks
are discussed in Sect. 6.

2   The Tasks

As mentioned in the Introduction, in this study we analyzed the handwriting of
subjects performing some graphic tasks to predict their cognitive status. The six
tasks used are detailed in below (Fig. 1 shows examples of tasks performed by
participants in the experiments).

The first two tasks consist of joining two points 3cm apart with a straight
continuous horizontal (task #1) or vertical (task #2) line four times. This kind
of tasks investigate elementary motor functions [31]. Horizontal movements, primarily require movements of the wrist joint. Vertical movements however require
fine finger movements. In addition, drawing a single continuous line four times
requires the execution of long-term motor planning, which is a typically compromised function in individuals with cognitive impairments.

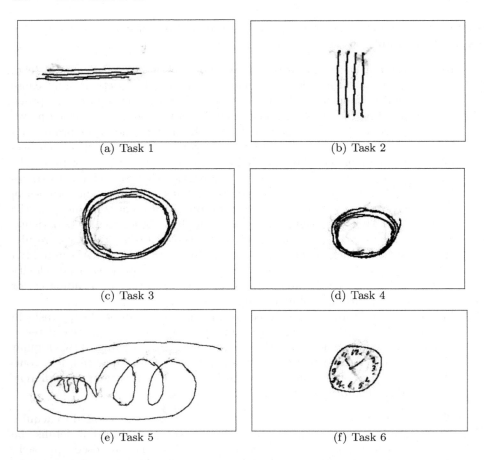

(a) Task 1   (b) Task 2

(c) Task 3   (d) Task 4

(e) Task 5   (f) Task 6

Fig. 1. Examples of tasks performed by a subject involved in the experiments. Green lines represent the in-air traits. (Color figure online)

The third and fourth tasks consist of retracing a 3cm (task #3) or 6 cm (task #4) wide circle four times. These tasks highlight the continuity of the line by repeatedly retracing a circular shape of various dimensions. The continuity and distance from the background shape to be traced are indicative of cognitive deterioration. These tasks make it possible to check the automaticity of movements and the regularity and coordination of the sequence of movements [25].

The fifth task, consists of retracing a complex form specifically devised to test the subject's motor control skills. This task investigates the alteration of the handwritten traits independent of any letter, word or related semantic usage. The handwriting movements needed to retrace the shape requires a constant motor remodulation. The shape consists of a continuous line with different curvature radii with the aim of testing both fine control and long-term motor motion planning [14,15].

Table 1. Feature list.

#	Name	Description
1	Peak vertical velocity	Maximum value of vertical velocity among the points of the stroke
2	Peak vertical acceleration	Maximum value of vertical acceleration among the points of the stroke
3	Average absolute velocity	Average absolute velocity computed across all the samples of the stroke
4	Normalized y jerk	Dimensionless as it is normalized for stroke duration and size
5	Normalized jerk	Dimensionless as it is normalized for stroke duration and size
6	Pen pressure	Average pen pressure computed over the points of the stroke
7	#strokes	Total number of strokes of the task
8	Age	Subject's age
9	Instruction	Subject's education level, expressed in years

Finally, the sixth task is the well-known Clock drawing test: the subject is asked to draw a clock face, included the numbers and then to draw the hands at five past eleven. The clock-drawing test (CDT) is used to screen for cognitive impairments and dementia. It is also used to assess subjects' spatial dysfunction and lack of attention. It was originally used to evaluate visuo-constructive abilities but it has been shown that abnormal clock drawing occurs in other cognitive impairments. The test requires verbal understanding and, memory and spatially coded knowledge, in addition to constructive skills [27]. Moreover, in [28] the authors found that the CDT is highly sensitive to mild Alzheimer's disease.

3   Data Collection and Feature Extraction

The data used in this study were collected from one hundred and eighty-one subjects, ninety cognitively impaired and ninety-one healthy controls. They were recruited with the support of the Alzheimer unit of the geriatric ward at the "Federico II" hospital in Naples (Italy). As cutoff criteria, physicians took into account clinical tests such as PET, TAC and enzymatic analyses as well as standard cognitive tests (MMSE and MOCA). We also acquired people educational level, age, and type of job. Finally, we ensured that the participants were not using psychotropic drugs or any other drug that could influence their cognitive abilities.

The data were collected using the Wacom bamboo folio graphic tablet. This records both the on-paper and in-air pen movements used to write on A4 white paper arranged on the tablet. The in-air movements are acquired when the pen is lifted from the sheet, but remains within a distance of three centimeters.

Table 2. Values of the classifier parameters used in the experiments. Note that as for the number of hidden neurons of the NN we applied, it derives from the following formula: (#features + #classes)/2.

Classifier	Parameter	Value
DT	Confidence factor	0.25
	Minimum #instances per leaf	2
NN	Learning rate	0.3
	Momentum	0.2
	Hidden Neurons	6
	Epochs	500
SVM	Kernel	RBF
	C	1.0
	γ	0.5

The handwritten traces acquired were processed using the MovAlyzer tool[1]. This tool segments the traces acquired into elementary strokes by using two types of segmentation points: (i) pen-up/pen-down; (ii) zero-crossing of the vertical velocity. The first represents points in which the pen is lifted from/resting on the sheet, whereas the second represent direction changes along the vertical axis. From each stroke we extracted the features listed in Table 1. We computed the values of each of the first six features shown in Table 1 by averaging the strokes of that task, per participant, per task. At the end of this process we obtained a data file containing one hundred and eighty one samples, each consisting of nine numerical values plus the label (healthy or cognitively impaired), for each task.

4   The Proposed Approach

Once the features described above were extracted and the data available for each task, our system was built by training a classifier for each task and then combining the responses provided to get a final prediction, according to the majority vote rule. This rule, given a set of responses for a given participant, gave the highest number of occurrences among those in the set as a final prediction. The basic idea of this approach is that the combination of the responses provided by several classifiers, each trained on the data from one of the six tasks used, provides a final prediction for the cognitive state of the participant that is better than that provided by each of the single classifiers. This idea is based on the assumption that the single classifier errors are uncorrelated. Therefore, the errors of the single classifiers present in the set of responses provided for a given participant, can be canceled out by the correct responses of the remaining classifiers.

---

[1] https://neuroscript.net/movalyzer.php.

Table 3. Decision tree results, expressed in percentages. For each category (healthy, patient and average) the best result achieved is in bold.

Features	Thresh.	Healthy	Patients	Average	Rejected
All	0.5	82.9	72.8	77.9	10
	0.6	84.7	75.6	80.2	11
	0.7	90.5	76.6	83.6	12
	0.8	91.0	76.9	84.0	14
	0.9	**91.8**	77.6	84.7	15
On Air	0.5	75.5	73.8	74.7	10
	0.6	77.0	74.1	75.6	12
	0.7	78.3	77.9	78.1	12
	0.8	81.7	78.0	79.9	17
	0.9	81.9	78.6	80.3	19
On paper	0.5	86.0	75.1	80.6	12
	0.6	87.0	75.2	81.1	12
	0.7	88.0	75.6	81.8	13
	0.8	88.3	81.1	84.7	14
	0.9	90.1	**81.9**	**86.0**	15

In the proposed system, for each task, a person is classified as cognitively impaired or normal. The trained classifiers also provide a reliability value (the probability of belonging to the aforementioned classes). The higher the probability, the more reliable the prediction. This value is taken into account by the majority vote rule: responses that have a reliability (probability) lower than a pre-set threshold Tr are ignored.

The proposed system also takes into account missing predictions (due to data loss because of communication problems between the tablet and the PC or incapacity of the participant to perform the task) from one or more tasks for a given participant.

5   Experiments and Results

We tested our approach on three types of feature, the on-paper and in-air features mentioned above as well as those computed without distinguishing between in-air and on-paper traits. In practice, for each task, these features were extracted by averaging both in-air and on-paper traits, allowing us to merge the information contained in these in-air and on-paper features. These features will be described in the following as "all".

We used three well-known and widely-used classification algorithms, namely Decision Tree (DT), Neural Networks (NN), and Support Vector Machines (SVM). The values of the parameters used in the experiments are shown in

Table 4. Neural network results, expressed in percentages. For each category (healthy, patient and average) the best result achieved is in bold.

Features	Thresh.	Healthy	Patients	Average	Rejected
All	0.5	75.5	74.5	75.0	11
	0.6	76.2	75	75.6	12
	0.7	79.8	77.2	78.5	15
	0.8	81.9	77.5	79.7	17
	0.9	**83.1**	**80.2**	**81.7**	21
On air	0.5	69.6	67.9	68.8	10
	0.6	71.3	70.1	70.7	12
	0.7	72	74.3	72.0	14
	0.8	73.2	75	72.9	17
	0.9	76.9	75.6	76.3	22
On paper	0.5	75.3	70.8	73.1	8
	0.6	77.3	73.6	75.5	10
	0.7	78	74.1	76.1	15
	0.8	78.2	75	76.6	18
	0.9	80.4	76	76.6	24

Table 2. The classification results reported below have been computed by using the five-fold cross-validation strategy.

The classification results are detailed in Tables 3, 4 and 5. These tables report the accuracy achieved by the three classifiers used as a function of the threshold value used to ignore the response provided by a single classifier (see Sect. 4). These results have been computed separately for control-group participants and patients: the aim of any system for medical diagnosis is to minimize misclassification errors for persons affected by the pathology in question. The tables also report the percentage of participants rejected, i.e. those for whom no response was given by the single classifiers, because the associated probabilities were below the fixed threshold or missing. From the tables we can observe that, as expected, the threshold significantly affects the classification performance of both categories, with higher threshold values achieving a better performance. This suggests that the training data allowed a good estimation of the class probabilities. Furthermore, the rejection rate was never too high for all the classifiers and feature categories, especially for the higher threshold values. Indeed, the highest rejection rate was 24% (NN, on paper, thresh=0.9), whereas in most cases these rates are below 15%.

To summarize to results shown in the mentioned above tables, Table 6 shows the best performance achieved for each threshold value. From it we can observe that DT and SVM always outperformed NN, with SVM always achieving the best performance for the patient category. As concerns the healthy controls, DT always achieved the best performance, except for threshold 0.9, where SVM was

Table 5. SVM results, expressed in percentages. For each category (healthy, patient and average) the best result achieved is in bold.

Features	Thresh.	Healthy	Patients	Average	Rejected
All	0.5	71.9	71.5	71.7	13
	0.6	75.2	72.9	74.1	15
	0.7	82.8	75.1	79.0	18
	0.8	84.5	76.3	80.4	20
	0.9	85	79.2	82.1	23
On air	0.5	79.7	76.5	78.1	10
	0.6	81.1	78	79.6	12
	0.7	86.2	78	82.1	15
	0.8	89.5	81.3	85.4	19
	0.9	**95**	85.8	90.4	21
On paper	0.5	76.7	76	76.4	13
	0.6	77	78.3	77.7	15
	0.7	85.9	82.5	84.2	15
	0.8	89.6	86	87.8	18
	0.9	90.3	**87.3**	**88.8**	21

Table 6. Summary results. P and A stands for "on paper" and "on air", respectively.

Thresh.	Healthy			Patient			Average		
	Acc.	Feat.	Class.	Acc.	Feat.	Class.	Acc.	Feat.	Class.
0.5	86.0	P	DT	76.5	A	SVM	80.6	P	DT
0.6	87.0	P	DT	78.3	P	SVM	81.1	P	DT
0.7	90.5	All	DT	82.5	P	SVM	84.2	P	SVM
0.8	91.0	All	DT	86.0	P	SVM	87.8	P	SVM
0.9	95.0	A	SVM	87.3	P	SVM	90.4	A	SVM

able to classify correctly 95% of the accepted participants. Regarding the average performances SVM outperformed DT for threshold values greater than 0.6, meaning that, on average, high probability values of SVM imply more reliable responses than those provided by DT and NN. Finally, from the table we can also observe that on paper features achieve the best performance in ten out of the fifteen cases analyzed. This suggests that these features are the most suitable to distinguish handwritten traits of healthy people from those of the cognitively impaired.

To test the effectiveness of our approach (the combination of the responses provided by the classifiers trained on the single tasks), we compared our results with those achieved by the single tasks only. These results are shown in Table 7. From the table we can observe that our approach outperformed the single clas-

Table 7. Single task results, expressed in percentages. For each classifier and feature category the best result achieved is in bold.

Features	Task	Classifier		
		DT	NN	SVM
All	1	**69.3**	63.7	**69.8**
	2	63.0	**65.2**	69.6
	3	65.6	53.3	60.6
	4	59.1	61.9	64.1
	5	64.1	62.4	68.0
	6	64.6	64.6	62.4
On Air	1	**69.6**	62.4	**68.1**
	2	64.1	62.3	62.4
	3	68.5	54.1	61.9
	4	60.8	57.5	60.8
	5	66.8	**64.1**	66.9
	6	64.6	62.4	63.0
On paper	1	62.4	61.9	60.8
	2	66.3	**68.0**	63.0
	3	61.3	57.5	59.1
	4	60.2	63.0	63.5
	5	63.5	63.0	**65.7**
	6	**66.9**	58.0	62.4

sifiers for each feature category and classifier. Furthermore, this improvement is visible right from the lowest threshold value.

6   Conclusions

Cognitive impairments are one the first signs of neurodegenerative diseases such as Alzheimer's and Parkinson's. The prevalence of these kind of diseases is expected to increase worldwide in the near future, and as such, the availability of tools for their early diagnosis is crucial.

In this paper, we have presented a novel approach for the prediction of cognitive impairments through the analysis of handwriting movements. To this end, we first trained a set of classifiers on data representing the movements of people while performing simple tasks like joining two points or retracing circles. The responses provided by these classifiers were combined according to majority vote rule. We also implemented a reject option to reduce the classification error rates.

In the experiments performed we tested our approach by using three classifiers (decision trees, neural networks, and SVM). To assess how the implemented reject option affected the classification performance and the rejection rate, we analyzed the overall accuracy as a function of the threshold value used to ignore the response provided by a single classifier. The results confirmed that the data allowed a good estimation of the class probabilities, thus allowing the reject option to improve the classification performance of our system. The reject rates were never too high, even for the higher threshold values. These results also proved that: (i) decision trees and SVM always outperform neural networks; (ii) the simple majority vote rule allows a significant improvement of the results achieved by the single classifiers.

Future work will focus on investigating two aspects. Firstly, other categories of tasks such as copy tasks: copying simple letters or words which requires different skills from the graphic tasks considered here. Secondly, we will investigate stacked classification techniques for implementing the combination rule: these techniques are based on the idea that effective combination rules can be obtained by a second-level classifier, trained on the set of responses provided by the single classifiers making up the ensemble.

Acknowledgements. This work was supported by MIUR (Minister for Education, University and Research), Law 232/216, Department of Excellence.

References

1. Bevilacqua, V., D'Ambruoso, D., Mandolino, G., Suma, M.: A new tool to support diagnosis of neurological disorders by means of facial expressions. In: 2011 IEEE International Symposium on Medical Measurements and Applications, pp. 544–549 (2011)
2. Cavaliere, F., Cioppa, A.D., Marcelli, A., Parziale, A., Senatore, R.: Parkinson's disease diagnosis: towards grammar-based explainable artificial intelligence. In: 2020 IEEE Symposium on Computers and Communications (ISCC), pp. 1–6 (2020). https://doi.org/10.1109/ISCC50000.2020.9219616
3. Cilia, N., De Stefano, C., Fontanella, F., Scotto di Freca, A.: How word choice affects cognitive impairment detection by handwriting analysis: a preliminary study. Commun. Comput. Inf. Sci. (CCIS) **200**, 113–123 (2020)
4. Cilia, N.D., De Stefano, C., Fontanella, F., Molinara, M., Scotto di Freca, A.: Handwriting analysis to support Alzheimer's disease diagnosis: a preliminary study. In: Vento, M., Percannella, G. (eds.) CAIP 2019. LNCS, vol. 11679, pp. 143–151. Springer, Cham (2019). https://doi.org/10.1007/978-3-030-29891-3_13
5. Cilia, N.D., De Stefano, C., Fontanella, F., Molinara, M., Scotto di Freca, A.: Using handwriting features to characterize cognitive impairment. In: Ricci, E., Rota Bulò, S., Snoek, C., Lanz, O., Messelodi, S., Sebe, N. (eds.) ICIAP 2019. LNCS, vol. 11752, pp. 683–693. Springer, Cham (2019). https://doi.org/10.1007/978-3-030-30645-8_62
6. Cilia, N.D., De Stefano, C., Fontanella, F., Marrocco, C., Molinara, M., Scotto di Freca, A.: Deep transfer learning for Alzheimer's disease detection. In: 25th International Conference on Pattern recognition (ICPR 2020), pp. 1–7 (2020)
7. Cilia, N.D., De Stefano, C., Fontanella, F., Scotto di Freca, A.: An experimental protocol to support cognitive impairment diagnosis by using handwriting analysis. Procedia Comput. Sci. **141**, 466–471 (2018)

8. De Stefano, C., Fontanella, F., Folino, G., Scotto di Freca, A.: A Bayesian approach for combining ensembles of GP classifiers. In: Sansone, C., Kittler, J., Roli, F. (eds.) MCS 2011. LNCS, vol. 6713, pp. 26–35. Springer, Heidelberg (2011). https://doi.org/10.1007/978-3-642-21557-5_5

9. De Stefano, C., Fontanella, F., Marrocco, C., Scotto di Freca, A.: A hybrid evolutionary algorithm for Bayesian networks learning: an application to classifier combination. In: Di Chio, C. (ed.) EvoApplications 2010. LNCS, vol. 6024, pp. 221–230. Springer, Heidelberg (2010). https://doi.org/10.1007/978-3-642-12239-2_23

10. De Stefano, C., Fontanella, F., Scotto di Freca, A.: A novel naive bayes voting strategy for combining classifiers. In: Proceedings - International Workshop on Frontiers in Handwriting Recognition, IWFHR, pp. 467–472 (2012)

11. Elbaz, A., Carcaillon, L., Kab, S., Moisan, F.: Epidemiology of parkinson's disease. Revue Neurologique **172**(1), 14–26 (2016)

12. Garre-Olmo, J., Faundez-Zanuy, M., de Ipiña, K.L., Calvo-Perxas, L., Turro-Garriga, O.: Kinematic and pressure features of handwriting and drawing: Preliminary results between patients with mild cognitive impairment, alzheimer disease and healthy controls. Curr. Alzheimer Res. **14**, 1–9 (2017)

13. Impedovo, D., Pirlo, G., Sarcinella, L., Stasolla, E., Trullo, C.A.: Analysis of stability in static signatures using cosine similarity. In: 2012 International Conference on Frontiers in Handwriting Recognition, pp. 231–235 (2012). https://doi.org/10.1109/ICFHR.2012.180

14. Marcelli, A., Parziale, A., Santoro, A.: Modelling visual appearance of handwriting. In: Petrosino, A. (ed.) ICIAP 2013. LNCS, vol. 8157, pp. 673–682. Springer, Heidelberg (2013). https://doi.org/10.1007/978-3-642-41184-7_68

15. Marcelli, A., Parziale, A., Senatore, R.: Some observations on handwriting from a motor learning perspective. In: 2nd International Workshop on Automated Forensic Handwriting Analysis (2013)

16. Müller, S., Preische, O., Heymann, P., Elbing, U., Laske, C.: Diagnostic value of a tablet-based drawing task for discrimination of patients in the early course of alzheimer's disease from healthy individuals. J. Alzheimer's Dis. **55**(4), 1463–1469 (2017)

17. Neils-Strunjas, J., Groves-Wright, K., Mashima, P., Harnish, S.: Dysgraphia in Alzheimer's disease: a review for clinical and research purposes. J. Speech Lang. Hear. Res. **49**(6), 1313–30 (2006)

18. Parziale, A., Senatore, R., Cioppa, A.D., Marcelli, A.: Cartesian genetic programming for diagnosis of parkinson disease through handwriting analysis: performance vs. interpretability issues. Artif. Intell. Med. p. 101984 (2020). https://doi.org/10.1016/j.artmed.2020.101984

19. Parziale, A., Della Cioppa, A., Senatore, R., Marcelli, A.: A decision tree for automatic diagnosis of Parkinson's disease from offline drawing samples: experiments and findings. In: Ricci, E., Rota Bulò, S., Snoek, C., Lanz, O., Messelodi, S., Sebe, N. (eds.) ICIAP 2019. LNCS, vol. 11751, pp. 196–206. Springer, Cham (2019). https://doi.org/10.1007/978-3-030-30642-7_18

20. de Paula, J.J., Albuquerque, M.R., Lage, G.M., Bicalho, M.A., Romano-Silva, M.A., Malloy-Diniz, L.F.: Impairment of fine motor dexterity in mild cognitive impairment and Alzheimer's disease dementia: association with activities of daily living. Revista Brasileira de Psiquiatria **38**, 235–238 (2016)

21. Pennanen, C., et al.: Hippocampus and entorhinal cortex in mild cognitive impairment and early ad. Neurobiol. Aging Physiol. Rev. **25**, 303–10 (2004)

22. Pirlo, G., Impedovo, D.: Adaptive membership functions for handwritten character recognition by voronoi-based image zoning. IEEE Trans. Image Proc. **21**(9), 3827–3837 (2012)
23. Pirlo, G., Impedovo, D.: A new class of monotone functions of the residue number system. Int. J. Math. Models Methods Appl. Sci. **9**(9), 802–809 (2013)
24. Pirlo, G., Trullo, C.A., Impedovo, D.: A feedback-based multi-classifier system. In: 2009 10th International Conference on Document Analysis and Recognition, pp. 713–717 (2009)
25. Schröter, A., Mergl, R., Bürger, K., Hampel, H., Möller, H.J., Hegerl, U.: Kinematic analysis of handwriting movements in patients with Alzheimer's disease, mild cognitive impairment, depression and healthy subjects. Dement. Geriatr. Cogn. Disord. **15**(3), 132–42 (2003)
26. Triggiani, A.I., et al.: Classification of healthy subjects and Alzheimer's disease patients with dementia from cortical sources of resting state eeg rhythms: A study using artificial neural networks. Frontiers Neurosci. **10**, 604 (2017)
27. Tseng, M.H., Cermak, S.A.: The influence of ergonomic factors and perceptual-motor abilities on handwriting performance. Am. J. Occup. Ther. **47**(10), 919–926 (1993)
28. Vyhnálek, M., et al.: Clock drawing test in screening for Alzheimer's dementia and mild cognitive impairment in clinical practice. Int. J. Geriatr. Psychiatry **32**(9), 933–939 (2017)
29. Werner, P., Rosenblum, S., Bar-On, G., Heinik, J., Korczyn, A.: Handwriting process variables discriminating mild alzheimer's disease and mild cognitive impairment. J. Gerontol. Psychol. Sci. **61**(4), 228–36 (2006)
30. Yan, J.: The effects of aging on linear and curvilinear arm movement control. Exp. Aging Res. **26**, 393–407 (2000)
31. Yan, J.H., Rountree, S., Massman, P., Doody, R.S., Li, H.: Alzheimer's disease and mild cognitive impairment deteriorate fine movement control. J. Psychiatr. Res. **42**(14), 1203–1212 (2008)

CADL2020 - Workshop on Computational Aspects of Deep Learning

Preface

Deep Learning has been the most significant breakthrough in the past 10 years: it has radically changed the research methodology towards a data-oriented approach, in which learning involves all steps of the prediction pipeline. In this context, optimization and careful design of neural architectures play an increasingly important role which directly affects the research pace, the effectiveness of state-of-the-art models and their applicability in production scale.

The ICPR workshop on "Computational Aspects of Deep Learning" (CADL) collects research works that focus on the development of optimized deep neural network architectures and on the optimization of existing ones, also onto highly scalable systems. This includes the training on large-scale or highly-dimensional datasets, the design of novel architectures and operators for increasing the efficacy or the efficiency in feature extraction and classification, the optimization of hyperparameters to enhance model's performance, solutions for training in multi-node systems such as HPC clusters.

The workshop targets any research field related to pattern recognition, ranging from computer vision to natural language processing and multimedia, in which data and computationally intensive architectures are needed to solve key research issues. The workshop favors positive criticism on the current data-intensive trends in machine learning and encourages new perspectives and solutions on the matter. The collected papers address computationally intensive scenarios from the point of view of architectural design, data processing, operator design, training strategies, distributed and large-scale training.

The first edition of the International Workshop on Computational Aspects of Deep Learning (CADL 2020) was organized within the 25th International Conference on Pattern Recognition (ICPR2020), and was established in cooperation with NVIDIA AI Technology Center. The format of the workshop included keynotes from researchers, industry and supercomputing centers, followed by technical presentations. This year we received 19 submissions for reviews: after an accurate and thorough peer-review and single-blind process, we selected 10 papers for presentation at the workshop. Each paper was reviewed by three reviewers, and the review process focused on the quality of the papers, their scientific novelty and applicability to existing problems and frameworks. The acceptance rate was 52.6%. The accepted articles represent an interesting mix of techniques and solutions to address data-intensive problems and contain novel architectural and methodological proposals for modeling and training large-scale Deep Learning algorithms.

November 2020

Organization

General Chairs

Lorenzo Baraldi   University of Modena and Reggio Emilia, Italy
Claudio Baecchi   University of Florence, Italy
Iuri Frosio   NVIDIA, USA
Frederic Pariente   NVIDIA, France

Program Committee

Idan Azuri   The Hebrew University of Jerusalem, Israel
Ishan Bhatnagar   University of Illinois Chicago, USA
Shubhang Bhatnagar   Qualcomm, India
Silvia Cascianelli   Università di Modena e Reggio Emilia, Italy
Marcella Cornia   University of Modena and Reggio Emilia, Italy
Ranjita Das   National Institute of Technology Mizoram, India

Giuseppe Fiameni   NVIDIA, Italy
Oscar Fontenla-Romero   University of A Coruña, Spain
Antonio Greco   University of Salerno, Italy
Adam Grzywaczewski   NVIDIA, UK
Krishnam Gupta   Mfine, India
Jian Han   University of Amsterdam, Netherlands
Andrew Hellicar   CSIRO Computational Informatics, Australia
Luanxuan Hou   Institute of Automation, Chinese Academy of Sciences
Emmanouil Hourdakis   Foundation for Research and Technology, Greece
Zhiqi Huang   Peking University, China
Sezer Karaoglu   University of Amsterdam, Netherlands
Taranjit Kaur   Indian Institute of Technology, Delhi, India
Oswald Lanz   Fondazione Bruno Kessler, Italy
Matt Poyser   Durham University, UK
Chetan Ralekar   Indian Institute of Technology, Delhi, India
Antonio Rapuano   University of Salerno, Italy
Shintaro Takenaga   Kindai University, Japan
Matteo Tomei   University of Modena and Reggio Emilia, Italy
Dat Tran   Tampere University, Finland
Duc Hoa Tran   École Polytechnique Montréal, Canada

Shaochen Wang   University of Science and Technology
                         of China, China
Jin Hyeok Yoo   Hanyang University, South Korea
Julio Zamora   Intel, California
Peilin Zhou   Peking University, China
Hao Zhu   Anhui University, China

WaveTF: A Fast 2D Wavelet Transform for Machine Learning in Keras

Francesco Versaci[✉]

Distributed Computing Group CRS4, Cagliari, Italy
`francesco.versaci@crs4.it`

Abstract. The wavelet transform is a powerful tool for performing multiscale analysis and it is a key subroutine in countless applications, from image processing to astronomy. Recently, it has extended its range of users to include the ever growing machine learning community. For a wavelet library to be efficiently adopted in this context, it needs to provide transformations which can be integrated seamlessly in already existing machine learning workflows and neural networks, being able to leverage the same libraries and run on the same hardware (e.g., CPU vs GPU) as the rest of the machine learning pipeline, without impacting training and evaluation performance. In this paper we present WaveTF, a wavelet library available as a Keras layer, which leverages TensorFlow to exploit GPU parallelism and can be used to enrich already existing machine learning workflows. To demonstrate its efficiency we compare its raw performance against other alternative libraries and finally measure the overhead it causes to the learning process when it is integrated in an already existing Convolutional Neural Network.

Keywords: Discrete wavelet transforms · Machine learning · Neural networks

1 Introduction

The wavelet transform [18] is a powerful tool for multiscale analysis. It produces a mix of time/spatial and frequency data and has countless applications in many areas of science, including image compression, medical imaging, finance, geophysics, and astronomy [2]. Recently, the wavelet transform has also been applied to machine learning, for instance to extract the feature set to be used by a standard learning workflow [3,16] and to enhance Convolutional Neural Networks (CNNs) [4,12,15,21]. For many of these applications, and machine learning in particular, parallel execution on GPGPU accelerators is of critical importance to ensure the tractability of real-world problems. Therefore, a library that provides wavelet transform functionality for this context must efficiently integrate into existing computational pipelines, mitigating the loss of performance due to the cost of exchanging data between memories in different phases of the computation – e.g., if our pipeline runs on a GPU we would like to execute the wavelet on

© Springer Nature Switzerland AG 2021
A. Del Bimbo et al. (Eds.): ICPR 2020 Workshops, LNCS 12661, pp. 605–618, 2021.
https://doi.org/10.1007/978-3-030-68763-2_46

the same device, without the need to repeatedly move data between the GPU and the main memory.

In this work we present WaveTF, a library providing a fast 1D and 2D wavelet implementation that provides scalable parallel execution on CPU and GPU devices. WaveTF enables full GPU execution of computational pipelines including wavelet transforms. The library is built on top of the popular Tensor-Flow framework and is exposed as a Keras layer, making it easy to integrate into existing Python workflows based on these widely adopted frameworks. Our evaluation shows that WaveTF improves upon the state of the art by providing faster routines and by adding only a negligible overhead to machine learning applications.

The rest of this manuscript is structured as follows. In Sect. 2 we provide a description of wavelet transforms, followed by a discussion of the related work in Sect. 3. Section 4 describes the implementation of the WaveTF library, while an evaluation of its performance is presented in Sect. 5. Finally, Sect. 6 points the reader to the software and Sect. 7 concludes the manuscript.

2   Background

2.1   Wavelet Transform

Wavelet transforms are a family of invertible signal transformations that, given an input signal evolving in time, produce an output which mixes time and frequency information [8]. This paper will only focus on discrete transformations.

Haar Transform. The simplest wavelet transform is the Haar transform, which, given in input a signal $x = (x_0, \ldots, x_{n-1})$ (with n even) produces as output

$$H(x) := (l_0, \ldots, l_{\frac{n}{2}-1}, h_0, \ldots, h_{\frac{n}{2}-1}) = (l(x), h(x)) \,,$$

where

$$l_i := \frac{x_{2i} + x_{2i+1}}{\sqrt{2}} \,, \qquad\qquad h_i := \frac{x_{2i} - x_{2i+1}}{\sqrt{2}} \,, \qquad (1)$$

with l_i and h_i containing low and high frequency components localized at times $2i$ and $2i + 1$ of the original signal. Note that when the input size is not even, the signal must be extended using some form of padding. The wavelet transform is often iterated on the low components to carry out a multiscale analysis:

$$H^d(x) := \left(H^{d-1}(l(x)), h(x) \right), \qquad\qquad \text{with } H^0(x) := x \,. \qquad (2)$$

Daubechies Wavelet. The Haar transform can be extended so that l_i and h_i are linear functions of more than two terms, as done by the following Daubechies-$N = 2$ (DB2) transform (see [7] for details):

$$l_i = \lambda_0 x_{2i-1} + \lambda_1 x_{2i} + \lambda_2 x_{2i+1} + \lambda_3 x_{2i+2},$$
$$h_i = \mu_0 x_{2i-1} + \mu_1 x_{2i} + \mu_2 x_{2i+1} + \mu_3 x_{2i+2},$$

where

$$\lambda_0 = \frac{1+\sqrt{3}}{2\sqrt{2}} \quad \lambda_1 = \frac{3+\sqrt{3}}{2\sqrt{2}} \quad \lambda_2 = \frac{3-\sqrt{3}}{2\sqrt{2}} \quad \lambda_3 = \frac{1-\sqrt{3}}{2\sqrt{2}}$$
$$\mu_0 = \lambda_3 \qquad \mu_1 = -\lambda_2 \qquad \mu_2 = \lambda_1 \qquad \mu_3 = -\lambda_0,$$

(3)

and vectors $\boldsymbol{\lambda} := (\lambda_0, \lambda_1, \lambda_2, \lambda_3)$ and $\boldsymbol{\mu} := (\mu_0, \mu_1, \mu_2, \mu_3)$ being orthonormal.

When working with larger kernels (4×2 in this case, where Haar was 2×2) the border of the signal must always be extended with padding to be able to invert the transformation.

Multidimensional Transform. The wavelet transform is extended to multidimensional signals by executing it orderly in all the dimensions. For instance, in the two-dimensional case the input is a matrix and the output is obtained by first transforming the rows and then the columns; it is thus formed by 4 matrices (conventionally called LL, LH, HL, and HH), containing the low and high components for the horizontal and vertical directions (an example can be seen in Fig. 1). As with the 1D case, the multidimensional transformations can also be iterated for perform a multilevel analysis (see Fig. 2). When the input is a multichannel image (e.g., RGB or HSV), transformations are performed independently for each channel.

WaveTF supports batched, multichannel inputs, i.e., for the two-dimensional case it accepts a tensor of shape [batch_size, dim_x, dim_y, channels], and returns a tensor of shape [batch_size, new_x, new_y, 4×channels].

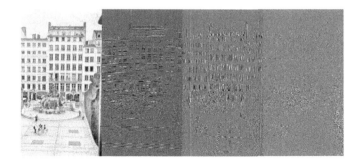

Fig. 1. The four components (LL, LH, HL and HH) of a two-dimensional Daubechies-$N = 2$ wavelet transform. LH, HL and HH have been contrasted to emphasize their structure.

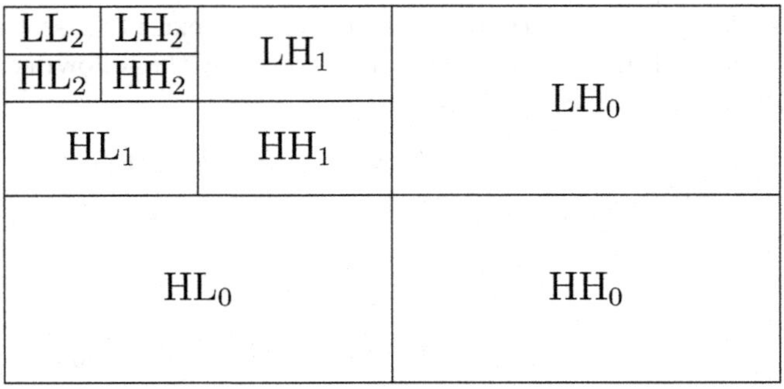

LL$_2$	LH$_2$	LH$_1$	LH$_0$
HL$_2$	HH$_2$		
HL$_1$		HH$_1$	
HL$_0$			HH$_0$

Fig. 2. Recursive structure of a 2D multilevel wavelet transform: each new level is obtained by transforming the LL component of the previous level (which can be preserved or discarded, as in this case).

2.2 TensorFlow and Keras

TensorFlow [1] is a powerful framework for efficiently manipulating multidimensional arrays (i.e., tensors) in parallel, and it provides APIs for Python, C++, Java and JavaScript. It has been developed as a fast and scalable framework for machine learning, and for this purpose it is complemented by the higher level Keras library [6]. However, TensorFlow offers many powerful algebraic routines which can be used independently of the application and its Python API can be seen as a parallel, GPU-enabled version of NumPy [23], with which it shares many similarities in the syntax and names of its methods. Note that TensorFlow supports a wide variety of computing hardware: it can run on multiple CPUs, GPUs and also on specialized ASICs known as TPUs [13], which are now available for end-users as part of the Google Cloud infrastructure.

We have chosen to implement WaveTF leveraging TensorFlow's rich API and scalability, so that it can easily exploit available parallelism, be easily and efficiently integrated with other programs that use TensorFlow and Keras and provide its functions to the growing machine learning community.

3 Related Work

In this section we briefly describe three alternative wavelet libraries available for Python and published as open source software: PyWavelets, pypwt and TF-Wavelets. In Sect. 5.1 we will compare their raw performance to our library.

3.1 PyWavelets

PyWavelets [14] is probably the most widely used Python library for wavelet transforms. Its core routines are written in C and made available to Python through Cython. It supports 1D and 2D transformations and provides over 100 built-in wavelet kernels and 9 signal extension modes. Unlike WaveTF, it is a sequential library and runs exclusively on CPUs.

3.2 pypwt

pypwt [20] is a Python wrapper of PDWT, which in turn is a C++ wavelet transform library, written using the parallel CUDA platform and running on NVIDIA GPUs. It implements 1D and 2D transforms (though it does not support batched 2D transforms) supports 72 wavelet kernels and adopts periodic padding for signal extension.

3.3 TF-Wavelets

TF-Wavelets [10,17] is a Python wavelet implementation which, like WaveTF, leverages the TensorFlow framework. It features two wavelet kernels (Haar and DB2) and implements periodic padding for signal extension. It is the library more conceptually similar to ours, allowing, for instance, both input and output to reside in GPU memory, and it is thus the best match for a raw performance comparison against WaveTF. However, it lacks support of batched, multichannel, 2D transforms, which are typically required for machine learning applications in Keras. As a consequence, it does not provide a network layer for that framework.

4 Implementation

WaveTF is written in Python using the TensorFlow API. It exposes its functions via a Keras layer which can either be called directly or can be plugged easily into already existing neural networks. The library currently implements the Haar (Eq. (1)) and DB2 (Eq. (3)) wavelet kernels – which are the two most commonly used ones. To handle border effects, anti-symmetric-reflect padding (known as *asym* in MATLAB) has been implemented, which extends the signal by preserving its first-order finite difference at the border. WaveTF supports both 32- and 64-bit floats transparently at runtime.

4.1 Direct Transform

In order to efficiently implement the wavelet transform in TensorFlow we first reshape it as a matrix operation. Let us consider, as an example, the 1D DB2 transform with input size n, where n is a multiple of 4. The original formulation of the transform presented in Sect. 2.1 can be rewritten as a matrix multiplication in the following form:

$$
\begin{pmatrix} l_0 & h_0 \\ l_1 & h_1 \\ l_2 & h_2 \\ l_3 & h_3 \\ \vdots & \vdots \\ l_{\frac{n}{2}-1} & h_{\frac{n}{2}-1} \end{pmatrix} = \begin{pmatrix} 2x_0 - x_1 & x_0 & x_1 & x_2 \\ x_1 & x_2 & x_3 & x_4 \\ x_3 & x_4 & x_5 & x_6 \\ x_5 & x_6 & x_7 & x_8 \\ \vdots & \vdots & \vdots & \vdots \\ x_{n-3} & x_{n-2} & x_{n-1} & 2x_{n-1} - x_{n-2} \end{pmatrix} \begin{pmatrix} \lambda_0 & \mu_0 \\ \lambda_1 & \mu_1 \\ \lambda_2 & \mu_2 \\ \lambda_3 & \mu_3 \end{pmatrix}.
$$

In order to generate the data matrix above we need to group the data vector by 4 and interleave it with a copy of itself, shifted left by two (plus some constant operations for the padding at the border). This operation can be implemented with the `reshape`, `concat` and `stack` methods provided by TensorFlow. Alternatively, the specialized `conv1d` method can be employed instead of the standard matrix multiplication, somewhat simplifying the data rearrangement. We have implemented both the variants and we have seen that the convolution one is faster in all considered cases, except for the 1D-Haar transform (for which we have thus adopted the matrix multiplication algorithm).

Note that when n is not a multiple of 4, the border values are arranged slightly differently, but the procedural steps remain the same.

4.2   Inverse Transform

In this section we show how to properly invert the DB2 wavelet transform, taking into account the border effects while keeping the padding as small as possible. This is done both to justify the exact algorithmic steps we adopted and to offer a future reference for alternative implementations by other authors. To the best of our knowledge the following derivation, at this level of detail, is original, though it is likely that it might be already present, at least implicitly, in the vast literature on Wavelet transform.

To better understand how to properly handle the border effect when computing the inverse, let us reshape the transformation above in a slightly different way: i.e., as $\boldsymbol{w} = W\boldsymbol{x} = KP\boldsymbol{x}$, with K being the $n \times (n+2)$ kernel matrix and P the $(n+2) \times n$ (anti-symmetric-reflect) padding matrix:

$$
\underbrace{\begin{pmatrix} l_0 \\ h_0 \\ l_1 \\ h_1 \\ \vdots \\ l_{\frac{n}{2}-1} \\ h_{\frac{n}{2}-1} \end{pmatrix}}_{\boldsymbol{w}} = \underbrace{\begin{pmatrix} \lambda_0 \ \lambda_1 \ \lambda_2 \ \lambda_3 \\ \mu_0 \ \mu_1 \ \mu_2 \ \mu_3 \\ \quad \lambda_0 \ \lambda_1 \ \lambda_2 \ \lambda_3 \\ \quad \mu_0 \ \mu_1 \ \mu_2 \ \mu_3 \\ \quad\quad \ddots \ \ddots \ \ddots \ \ddots \end{pmatrix}}_{K} \underbrace{\begin{pmatrix} 2 \ -1 \\ 1 \\ \quad 1 \\ \quad\quad \ddots \\ \quad\quad\quad 1 \\ \quad\quad\quad\quad 1 \\ \quad\quad\quad\quad -1 \ 2 \end{pmatrix}}_{P} \underbrace{\begin{pmatrix} x_0 \\ x_1 \\ \vdots \\ x_{n-1} \end{pmatrix}}_{\boldsymbol{x}}.
$$

We can then decompose K, P and W in (non-square) blocks (with each block shape shown between parentheses):

$$
K = \begin{pmatrix} K_{00} & K_{01} & 0 \\ {\scriptstyle (4\times3)} & {\scriptstyle (4\times n-4)} & {\scriptstyle (4\times3)} \\ 0 & K_{11} & 0 \\ {\scriptstyle (n-8\times3)} & {\scriptstyle (n-8\times n-4)} & {\scriptstyle (n-8\times3)} \\ 0 & K_{21} & K_{22} \\ {\scriptstyle (4\times3)} & {\scriptstyle (4\times n-4)} & {\scriptstyle (4\times3)} \end{pmatrix}, \quad P = \begin{pmatrix} P_{00} & 0 & 0 \\ {\scriptstyle (3\times2)} & {\scriptstyle (3\times n-4)} & {\scriptstyle (3\times2)} \\ 0 & \mathbb{I}_{n-4} & 0 \\ {\scriptstyle (n-4\times2)} & {\scriptstyle (n-4\times n-4)} & {\scriptstyle (n-4\times2)} \\ 0 & 0 & P_{22} \\ {\scriptstyle (3\times2)} & {\scriptstyle (3\times n-4)} & {\scriptstyle (3\times2)} \end{pmatrix},
$$

$$W = KP = \begin{pmatrix} \begin{array}{c|c|c} K_{00}P_{00} & K_{01} & 0 \\ \text{\scriptsize(4×2)} & \text{\scriptsize(4×n−4)} & \text{\scriptsize(4×2)} \\ \hline 0 & K_{11} & 0 \\ \text{\scriptsize(n−8×2)} & \text{\scriptsize(n−8×n−4)} & \text{\scriptsize(n−8×2)} \\ \hline 0 & K_{21} & K_{22}P_{22} \\ \text{\scriptsize(4×2)} & \text{\scriptsize(4×n−4)} & \text{\scriptsize(4×2)} \end{array} \end{pmatrix}.$$

To invert W we first note that K_{11} has orthonormal rows and thus admits its transpose as a right inverse: $K_{11}K_{11}^t = \mathbb{I}_{n-4}$. Furthermore, $W_{00} := K_{00}P_{00}$ and $W_{22} := K_{22}P_{22}$ have linearly independent columns and thus admit a (Moore–Penrose) left inverse: $W_{00}^+ W_{00} = W_{22}^+ W_{22} = \mathbb{I}_2$. Finally, because of the choice of coefficients in Eq. (3), we have

$$W_{00}^+ K_{01} = K_{01}^t W_{00} = W_{22}^+ K_{21} = K_{21}^t W_{22} = 0,$$
$$K_{01}^t K_{01} + K_{11}^t K_{11} + K_{21}^t K_{21} = \mathbb{I}_{n-4}.$$

We can now verify that W is inverted by

$$W^{-1} = \begin{pmatrix} \begin{array}{c|c|c} W_{00}^+ & 0 & 0 \\ \text{\scriptsize(2×4)} & \text{\scriptsize(2×n−8)} & \text{\scriptsize(2×4)} \\ \hline K_{01}^t & K_{11}^t & K_{21}^t \\ \text{\scriptsize(n−4×4)} & \text{\scriptsize(n−4×n−8)} & \text{\scriptsize(n−4×4)} \\ \hline 0 & 0 & W_{22}^+ \\ \text{\scriptsize(2×4)} & \text{\scriptsize(2×n−8)} & \text{\scriptsize(2×4)} \end{array} \end{pmatrix},$$

and that we can compute its non-border elements similarly to the direct transform case:

$$\begin{pmatrix} x_1 & x_2 \\ x_3 & x_4 \\ \vdots & \vdots \\ x_{n-3} & x_{n-2} \end{pmatrix} = \begin{pmatrix} l_0 & h_0 & l_1 & h_1 \\ l_1 & h_1 & l_2 & h_2 \\ \vdots & \vdots & \vdots & \vdots \\ l_{\frac{n}{2}-3} & h_{\frac{n}{2}-3} & l_{\frac{n}{2}-2} & h_{\frac{n}{2}-2} \\ l_{\frac{n}{2}-2} & h_{\frac{n}{2}-2} & l_{\frac{n}{2}-1} & h_{\frac{n}{2}-1} \end{pmatrix} \begin{pmatrix} \lambda_2 & \lambda_3 \\ \mu_2 & \mu_3 \\ \lambda_0 & \lambda_1 \\ \mu_0 & \mu_1 \end{pmatrix}$$

and its border values as:

$$\begin{pmatrix} x_0 \\ x_1 \end{pmatrix} = W_{00}^+ \begin{pmatrix} l_0 \\ h_0 \\ l_1 \\ h_1 \end{pmatrix}, \qquad \begin{pmatrix} x_{n-2} \\ x_{n-1} \end{pmatrix} = W_{22}^+ \begin{pmatrix} l_{\frac{n}{2}-2} \\ h_{\frac{n}{2}-2} \\ l_{\frac{n}{2}-1} \\ h_{\frac{n}{2}-1} \end{pmatrix}.$$

4.3   Correctness

In addition to the formal derivation given above, we have tested our implementation for consistency against PyWavelets, and we have composed direct and inverse transforms to verify that they result in an identity map (up to numerical precision errors). The randomized test code is included with the source code and is runnable with the *pytest* framework [19].

Note that, contrary to PyWavelets, WaveTF always uses a minimal padding when transforming: e.g., WaveTF's output for an input vector of size 10 is a 2×5 matrix, whereas PyWavelets produces a 2×6 matrix when using the DB2 kernel and a 2×5 one when using the Haar kernel.

Table 1. Hardware configuration of the test machine.

CPU	Intel(R) Xeon(R) CPU E5-2650 v4 @ 2.20 GHz (24 SMT cores)
RAM	250 GiB
GPU	GeForce RTX 2080 Ti (11 GB GDDR6)

Table 2. Versions of the software used in this work.

Package	Version	Source
WaveTF	0.1	https://github.com/crs4/WaveTF
PyWavelets	1.1.1	https://github.com/PyWavelets/pywt
pypwt	d225e09	https://github.com/pierrepaleo/pypwt
TF-Wavelets	ac4f357	https://github.com/UiO-CS/tf-wavelets
TensorFlow	2.1.0	https://www.tensorflow.org/install
CUDA	V10.1.243	https://developer.nvidia.com/cuda-downloads
NVIDIA driver	435.21	https://www.nvidia.com/Download/Find.aspx

5 Performance Results

The performance of WaveTF has been tested in two ways:

- By executing raw signal transforms, leaving the output data available for the user either in RAM or in the GPU memory;
- As a Keras layer, integrated in a simple neural network for a training task.

In the first test, we also computed the same transformations with the PyWavelets, pypwt and TF-Wavelets libraries to compare their performance to WaveTF's.

In order to better exploit the computation power provided by the GPU [5], the tests have been run with single-precision floating-point types: np.float32 for PyWavelets, tf.float32 for WaveTF and TF-Wavelets, and pypwt compiled to use 32-bit floats.

The hardware and software used in the tests are detailed in Tables 1 and 2.

5.1 Raw Transformation

PyWavelets operates in RAM and pypwt uses RAM for input and output but runs its computation in the GPU. On the other hand, WaveTF and TF-Wavelets operate on TensorFlow tensors which, when GPUs are available and used, reside in the GPU memory. We expect to see this difference reflect on the runtimes, because of the overhead of moving data between GPU and RAM.

We have recorded the wall clock time of one- and two-dimensional Haar and DB2 wavelet transforms using WaveTF, PyWavelets and pypwt and TF-Wavelets. For WaveTF, we have measured both the time required when leaving the data in the GPU memory and when input and output are required to be in main memory. For TF-Wavelets we have instead focused on the fastest case of working only on GPU memory, to offer a fair comparison for WaveTF. The test procedure for the one-dimensional case is as follows:

– A random array of n elements is created, with n ranging from $5 \cdot 10^6$ to 10^8,
– For the non-batched case the array is used as is (i.e., shape $= [n]$), for the batched case it is reshaped to $[b, n/b]$, with $b = 100$,
– The transform, on the same input array, is executed from a minimum of 500 up to a maximum of 10000 times for smaller data size; the total time is measured and the time per iteration is recorded.

For the two-dimensional case, the input matrix is chosen to be as square as possible given the target total size of n elements, i.e., shape $= [\lfloor \sqrt{n} \rfloor, \lceil \sqrt{n} \rceil]$.

Note that we have not measured the time to execute a single transformation, but instead the time to execute many of them grouped together (up to 10000), because the single execution time when working in GPU memory would have been completely overshadowed by the setup time required for the library calls. The standard deviations for these grouped measures are all well below 1%, so they are not shown in the plots.

Table 3. Runtimes, for the largest tested size, i.e., 10^8 elements, normalized against WaveTF.

Operation	WaveTF	TF-Wavelets	PyWavelets	pypwt
1D Haar	1	2.98	74.81	73.55
1D DB2	1	1.58	42.91	36.04
1D Haar, batched	1	3.21	73.69	72.37
1D DB2, batched	1	1.62	39.85	33.63
2D Haar	1	2.58	45.59	14.30
2D DB2	1	2.30	44.61	12.27
2D Haar, batched	1	n.a	42.55	n.a.
2D DB2, batched	1	n.a	41.08	n.a

Discussion. As can be seen from the data in Fig. 3 and Table 3, there is a huge gap in performance between PyWavelets and pypwt and the TensorFlow programs. The performance of PyWavelets is explained by the fact that it is a serial program and that it does not exploit the parallelism available in the GPU. pypwt, on the other hand, does use the GPU but incurs a big overhead caused by the data movement between GPU and main memory – as demonstrated by the similar performance achieved by WaveTF when it is forced to have both input and output in RAM.

When working directly in GPU memory WaveTF and TF-Wavelets have a big performance advantage over the other evaluated libraries, with WaveTF being about 70x faster than PyWavelets and pypwt on 1D Haar and 30–40x on 1D DB2. For the 2D cases WaveTF has a speedup greater than 40x over PyWavelets and a 12–14x one over pypwt. This test scenario mirrors the common situation in TensorFlow-based machine learning workflows using wavelet transforms.

The speedup of WaveTF against TF-Wavelets is still quite impressive, considered that both libraries adopt the same general strategy, and it ranges from 1.6x up to 3.2x. This improvement is mainly due to a careful algorithmic implementation as to avoid redundant computations.

5.2 Machine Learning

In this section we quantify the overhead of integrating WaveTF in machine learning workflows. For this purpose we consider a classification problem on a standard image dataset solved by a simple CNN. In our experiment we measure the training and evaluation times before and after enriching the CNN with wavelet layers.

For this test we have adopted the Imagenette2-320 dataset [11] – a subset of 10 classes from ImageNet [22] – consisting of 9469 training and 3925 validation RGB images. For the classification task we used a basic CNN network featuring 5 levels of convolution, followed by downscaling which halves the spatial feature dimensions at each level (i.e., $320 \times 320 \rightarrow 160 \times 160 \rightarrow 80 \times 80 \rightarrow 40 \times 40 \rightarrow 20 \times 20$). To enrich this network with the wavelet transform, each newly downscaled layer is concatenated with the corresponding level from the output of WaveTF (see Fig. 4), launched iteratively as shown in Eq. (2). This approach has been used, e.g., for improving texture classification [9].

Since the objective of our experiment is only to quantify the computational overhead of adding wavelet features via WaveTF to the network, we disabled all forms of data augmentation for the training – these procedures would add their own considerable overhead which would confound our results. To compute the training overhead, we measured the wall clock time required to train the model for 20 epochs, with and without enriching the network with the wavelet features. We repeated this training process 20 times (after a first, unmeasured run, used to set the memory buffering to a stationary state). On the other hand, to measure the overhead incurred in evaluation we used the trained network to evaluate all the images in the dataset and repeated the process 20 times.

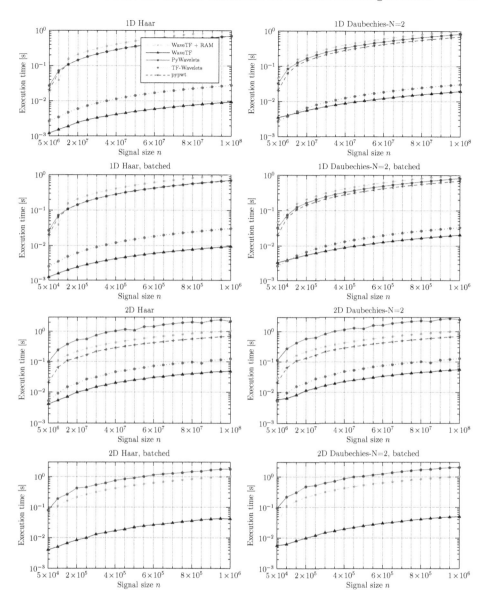

Fig. 3. Runtime of wavelet transforms: WaveTF vs. PyWavelets vs. pypwt vs. TF-Wavelets – Wall time of execution, for Haar and Daubechies-$N = 2$ kernels, one- and two-dimensional, batched and non-batched. For WaveTF we show two runtimes: i) when working directly in GPU memory, ii) when input and output are required to be in RAM. Standard deviation is below 1% in all cases.

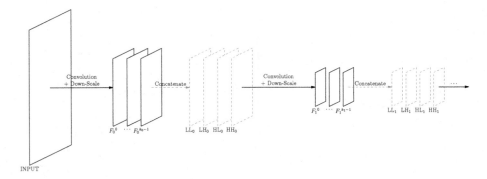

Fig. 4. The first steps of a wavelet-enriched CNN: after down-scaling at level l, the k_l output features $(F_l^0, \ldots, F_l^{k_l-1})$ are concatenated with the wavelet components (LL$_l$, LH$_l$, HL$_l$, HH$_l$,) at the corresponding level of scale, before the following convolution is performed.

Table 4. Running times (with standard deviation) of a 5-level CNN on the Imagenette dataset, with and without enriching the network with wavelet features computed by the WaveTF Keras layer.

Operation	Baseline	With wavelet	Overhead
Training time [s]	1581 ± 18	1593 ± 14	<1%
Evaluation time [s]	78.5 ± 0.5	78.7 ± 0.8	<1%

Discussion. As can be seen from the results shown in Table 4, the overhead of adding wavelet features to the existing 5-level CNN is below 1%, both in training and evaluation, thus allowing its use at an almost negligible cost.

6   Software Availability

WaveTF is released under the open source Apache License Version 2.0. Its source code is available for download from the GitHub platform, together with accompanying documentation and some usage examples, which also include the CNN used in this paper. The link to the GitHub repository is shown in Table 2.

7   Conclusion and Future Work

In this work we have presented an efficient wavelet library which leverages TensorFlow and Keras to exploit GPU parallelism and allows for easy integration in already existing machine learning workflows. Since the wavelet transform is characterized by high parallelism and low computational complexity (time complexity being $O(n)$ for an input of size n), minimizing communication is pivotal to achieve good performance, and in this work we have shown how to do it by limiting the transfer between GPU and memory whenever is possible.

In future we plan to extend the library to include other popular wavelet kernels and padding extensions, as well as extending it to 3D signals.

Acknowledgments. I'd like to thank G. Busonera and L. Pireddu for reviewing the draft and S. Leo for his suggestions on structuring the Python code. This work has been funded by the European Commission under the H2020 program grant DeepHealth (n. 825111).

References

1. Abadi, M., et al.: Tensorflow: a system for large-scale machine learning. In: 12th USENIX Symposium on Operating Systems Design and Implementation (OSDI 16), pp. 265–283 (2016)
2. Addison, P.S.: The Illustrated Wavelet Transform Handbook: Introductory Theory and Applications in Science, Engineering, Medicine and Finance. CRC Press, Boca Raton (2017)
3. Amin, H.U., et al.: Feature extraction and classification for eeg signals using wavelet transform and machine learning techniques. Australas. Phys. Eng. Sci. Med. **38**(1), 139–149 (2015)
4. Bruna, J., Mallat, S.: Invariant scattering convolution networks. IEEE Trans. Pattern Anal. Mach. Intell. **35**(8), 1872–1886 (2013)
5. Burgess, J.: Rtx on-the nvidia turing gpu. IEEE Micro **40**(2), 36–44 (2020)
6. Chollet, F., et al.: Keras: the python deep learning library. Astrophysics Source Code Library (2018)
7. Daubechies, I.: Orthonormal bases of compactly supported wavelets. Commun. Pure Appl. Math. **41**(7), 909–996 (1988)
8. Daubechies, I.: Ten Lectures on Wavelets, vol. 61. Siam, Thailand (1992)
9. Fujieda, S., Takayama, K., Hachisuka, T.: Wavelet convolutional neural networks for texture classification (2017)
10. Haug, K.M.: Stability of Adaptive Neural Networks for Image Reconstruction. Master's thesis (2019)
11. Howard, J.: Fastai's imagenette and imagewoof datasets (2020). https://github.com/fastai/imagenette
12. Huang, H., He, R., Sun, Z., Tan, T.: Wavelet-srnet: a wavelet-based cnn for multi-scale face super resolution. In: The IEEE International Conference on Computer Vision (ICCV) (2017)
13. Jouppi, N., Young, C., Patil, N., Patterson, D.: Motivation for and evaluation of the first tensor processing unit. IEEE Micro **38**(3), 10–19 (2018)
14. Lee, G., Gommers, R., Waselewski, F., Wohlfahrt, K., O'Leary, A.: Pywavelets: a python package for wavelet analysis. J. Open Source Softw. **4**(36), 1237 (2019)
15. Liu, P., Zhang, H., Lian, W., Zuo, W.: Multi-level wavelet convolutional neural networks. IEEE Access **7**, 74973–74985 (2019)
16. Livani, H., Evrenosoglu, C.Y.: A machine learning and wavelet-based fault location method for hybrid transmission lines. IEEE Trans. Smart Grid **5**(1), 51–59 (2013)
17. Lohne, M.: Parseval Reconstruction Networks. Master's thesis (2019)
18. Mallat, S.G.: A theory for multiresolution signal decomposition: the wavelet representation. IEEE Trans. Pattern Anal. Mach. Intell. **11**(7), 674–693 (1989)
19. Oliveira, B.: pytest Quick Start Guide: Write Better Python Code with Simple and Maintainable Tests. Packt Publishing Ltd., Birmingham (2018)

20. Paleo, P.: pypwt, parallel discrete wavelet transform (2020). https://github.com/pierrepaleo/pypwt
21. Rodriguez, M.X.B., et al.: Deep adaptive wavelet network. In: The IEEE Winter Conference on Applications of Computer Vision, pp. 3111–3119 (2020)
22. Russakovsky, O., et al.: ImageNet large scale visual recognition challenge. Int. J. Comput. Vis. (IJCV) **115**(3), 211–252 (2015)
23. Walt, S.V.D., Colbert, S.C., Varoquaux, G.: The NumPy array: a structure for efficient numerical computation. Comput. Sci. Eng. **13**(2), 22–30 (2011)

Convergence Dynamics
of Generative Adversarial Networks:
The Dual Metric Flows

Gabriel Turinici$^{(\boxtimes)}$ (iD)

CEREMADE, Université Paris Dauphine - PSL, Paris, France
`Gabriel.Turinici@dauphine.fr`
`http://www.turinici.com`

Abstract. Fitting neural networks often resorts to stochastic (or similar) gradient descent which is a noise-tolerant (and efficient) resolution of a gradient descent dynamics. It outputs a sequence of networks parameters, which sequence evolves during the training steps. The gradient descent is the limit, when the learning rate is small and the batch size is infinite, of this set of increasingly optimal network parameters obtained during training. In this contribution, we investigate instead the convergence in the Generative Adversarial Networks used in machine learning. We study the limit of small learning rate, and show that, similar to single network training, the GAN learning dynamics tend, for vanishing learning rate to some limit dynamics. This leads us to consider evolution equations in metric spaces (which is the natural framework for evolving probability laws) that we call dual flows. We give formal definitions of solutions and prove the convergence. The theory is then applied to specific instances of GANs and we discuss how this insight helps understand and mitigate the mode collapse.

Keywords: GAN · Metric flow · Generative network

1 Introduction

Deep generative models are of high interest and used in many applications of deep learning. Among them, the GANs have been one of the most efficient in terms of practical results. The GANs and their convergence are the object of a huge quantity of research papers (4′861 arxiv results mid-October 2020 for "generative adversarial network", 26′110 Google Scholar results). Nevertheless, only very few works concern the behavior of solutions in the general framework of metric spaces or the meaning to be given to the learning trajectory in the limit of a small learning rate. On the other hand, the GANs are known to exhibit unstable convergence behavior (see [17]) and several procedures have been proposed to cure this drawback, among which [4,8,11,18,29]. In order to contribute to a fundamental understanding of the objects involved, we give in this work a rigorous definition of the concept of solution of the evolution equation

© Springer Nature Switzerland AG 2021
A. Del Bimbo et al. (Eds.): ICPR 2020 Workshops, LNCS 12661, pp. 619–634, 2021.
https://doi.org/10.1007/978-3-030-68763-2_47

associated to a GAN that we call a *dual metric flow*. We identify the hypothesis that guarantee that the discrete solutions converge, when the learning rate τ tends to 0, to a dual metric flow and apply this insight to understand and mitigate the mode collapse phenomena. Finally we give examples that show that the dual flows correspond indeed to procedures used in GAN practice.

1.1   Motivation: W-GANs

The goal of (deep) generative models such as the GANs is to generate new data from some (unknown) distribution given a list of samples drawn from that distribution. To simplify the presentation, we suppose that the distribution to be learned is a set of images. Two objects are important in a GAN: the *Generator* and the *Discriminator*; both are deep networks with fixed, but rich enough, architecture capable of representing a very large class of transformations. For instance, in a Wasserstein-GAN (see [4]), the training has the following form (see Fig. 1 for an illustration): after initializing (randomly) both the Generator and the Discriminator, the Discriminator is trained first. It takes as input images generated by the Generator (with label "fake") and images from the real database with label "true". It is trained for (one or possibly several) steps in order to achieve good discrimination efficiency between the "fake" and "real" labels. In the next step the discriminator is kept constant and the generator is trained in order to create images which, when run through the (fixed) discriminator obtain as much labels "real" as possible. Then the procedure is repeated till convergence.

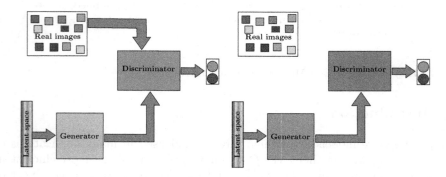

Fig. 1. Illustration of the dynamics of a GAN. Color code: in green the part that is active (under training) and in grey the part that is fixed. **Left:** the discriminator is active. **Right:** the generator is active. This is repeated till convergence. (Color figure online)

A very natural question is whether such a procedure can converge to a satisfactory solution i.e., if the Generator samples from the right distribution and the Discriminator is able to tell with high precision the quality of any sample.

The answer is not always yes, as illustrated by the following simple situation: consider a target distribution which is a Dirac mass centered in some constant x_r. The generator is described by a vector of two real parameters $x \in \mathbb{R}^2$ and the discriminator y has the same format. In the framework of integral probability metrics (see [26]) used in GANs, this simple situation has the following transcription: if the current parameter of the generator is x_n then the next parameter y_{n+1} of the discriminator will be updated to maximize the distance from x_n to x_r, i.e. $y_{n+1} = y_n + \tau(x_n - x_r)$, where τ is the learning rate. The generator itself will take into account this new discriminator and will move towards the unknown value x_r by taking a step: $x_{n+1} = x_n - \tau y_{n+1}$, where τ is the learning rate. These equations can be also written as

$$\frac{y_{n+1} - y_n}{\tau} = x_n - x_r$$
$$\frac{x_{n+1} - x_n}{\tau} = y_{n+1}. \tag{1}$$

When $\tau \to 0$ the limit evolution will be

$$y'(t) = x(t) - x_r$$
$$x'(t) = y(t). \tag{2}$$

However, except for very special initial conditions, the system (2) does not have the property that $x(t) \to x_r$ because $x(t)$ will have a periodic evolution around x_r, see Fig. 2.

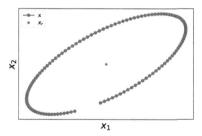

Fig. 2. Illustration of the oscillations dynamics of a GAN, see Eq. (2).

Prompted by this example we aim to analyze in this paper the intrinsic constraints coming from the GAN training in the form of an alternative adversary evolution. More precisely, given the discrete Generator/Discriminator dynamics (similar to Eq. (1)) we want to write the equivalent limit Eq. (2).

To do so, we suppose that the architectures of the Generator and Discriminator networks are rich enough so that the Generator can reach with satisfactory precision any target distribution μ_r and the discriminator can realize any mapping that separates an arbitrary pair of distinct distributions in the integral probability metrics sense, i.e. for any distinct distributions the Discriminator can propose a mapping whose averages under the two distributions are different. Of course this is an ideal setting but we take this view in order to better distinguish the effects due to network architectures from those intrinsically included in the GAN convergence protocol.

Let us now introduce the mathematical objects involved in the GAN training. The Generator is a mapping from a given distribution (e.g. the multi-dimensional Gaussian distribution) on some base space (called Latent space) to the space of objects of interest, denoted Ω; for instance in Fig. 1 Ω are images). Thus in general the Generator can construct probability distributions on Ω; denote by $\mathcal{P}_1(\Omega)$ the set of all probability laws on Ω with finite first order moment. This set can be given the structure of a metric space by introducing a distance; many distances exists and have been used but a popular choice, used by W-GANs is the 1-Wasserstein distance (see [3] for a definition) denoted $d_{W,1}$. Thus formally we work in the metric space $(\mathcal{P}_1(\Omega), d_{W,1})$.

On the other hand the Discriminator constructs a Lipschitz mapping to label the generated samples as fake or real. Mathematically the object is a Lipschitz function $\ell : \Omega \to \mathbb{R}$. The Discriminator works best when the average $\mathbb{E}_\mu(\ell)$ is as different as possible from the average $\mathbb{E}_{\mu_r}(\ell)$. Again, ℓ lives in a metric space $\mathcal{Y}$ (as opposed to a Hilbert space) with the distance being the Lipschitz distance.

The GAN update of the Generator will move μ_n (n indexes now the learning steps) to some μ_{n+1} along the gradient of the mapping $\mu \mapsto \mathbb{E}_\mu(\ell) - \mathbb{E}_{\mu_r}(\ell)$ (to be minimized, here ℓ being the current Discriminator state). In practice the update is performed with a stochastic descent algorithm (that we take in this work to be the SGD). We will not inquire about the stochastic oscillations but only consider the average state. In full rigor the update rule is difficult to write in the formal, metric space setting: for instance, for the Generator update, the intuitive formula would be $\mu_{n+1} = \mu_n - \tau \nabla_\mu [\mathbb{E}_{\mu_n}(\ell_{n+1}) - \mathbb{E}_{\mu_r}(\ell_{n+1})]$. This formulation has several problems: first the space of probability laws is not a vector space thus the addition and substractions operator are not well defined. Secondly, the differential structure on the same space is not straightforward to manipulate, i.e., ∇_μ is not easy to work with. For these reasons, we will replace the real dynamics with another, close, one and we model the update by the requirement that μ_{n+1} is the minimizer of

$$\mu \mapsto \frac{d_{\mathcal{X}}(\mu_n, \mu)^2}{2\tau} + [\mathbb{E}_\mu(\ell) - \mathbb{E}_{\mu_r}(\ell)]. \tag{3}$$

The intuitive justification for this formula (very classic in metric space evolution Eqs. [3]) is the following: in a Hilbert space, $d_{\mathcal{X}}(\mu_n, \mu)^2 = \|\mu_n - \mu\|^2$ and taking a general functional $F(\mu)$ in (3) (here $F(\mu) = \mathbb{E}_\mu(\ell) - \mathbb{E}_{\mu_r}(\ell)$) the critical point equations derived from (3) can be written as $\mu_{n+1} = \mu_n - \tau \nabla F(\mu_{n+1})$ which is an implicit gradient descent of step τ starting from μ_n. The advantage of the implicit formulation is that μ_{n+1} defined through (3) can be written for any abstract objects in a metric space (only $d_{\mathcal{X}}(\mu_n, \mu)^2$ and $F(\cdot)$ are required). Same model is used for the Discriminator update steps; all this leads us to consider the main discrete equation that will model the GAN training dynamics[1]

$$\ell_{n+1} = \text{argmin}_{\ell \in \mathcal{Y}} \frac{d(\ell, \ell_n)^2}{2\tau} - [\mathbb{E}_{\mu_n}(\ell) - \mathbb{E}_{\mu_r}(\ell)] \tag{4}$$

$$\mu_{n+1} = \text{argmin}_{\mu \in \mathcal{X}} \frac{d(\mu, \mu_n)^2}{2\tau} + [\mathbb{E}_{\mu}(\ell_{n+1}) - \mathbb{E}_{\mu_r}(\ell_{n+1})], \tag{5}$$

with $\tau > 0$ the learning rate and $\mathcal{X}, \mathcal{Y}$ two metric spaces. The goal of this paper is to clarify whether, when $\tau \to 0$, the discrete curves $(\mu_n)_{n\geq 0}$, $(\ell_n)_{n\geq 0}$, converge to some limit continuous curves; we also want to give a formal definition of the dynamics satisfied by the limit curves.

The GAN protocol described above is not the only one used in the literature. Many other procedures aim to improve convergence, generation quality, computing speed, etc. For instance in [11] the authors add a penalty on the gradient in order to make convergence better and the new type of GAN is called WGAN-GP. A full zoology of GAN versions appeared: the Deep Convolutional Generative Adversarial Network (DCGAN, [23]) use deep convolution networks which are better adapted to images, the Coupled GANs proposal (coGAN [20]) uses two generators and two discriminators in order to improve convergence and generation properties, Progressive Growing Generative Adversarial Network (Progressive GAN [15]) improve the generation quality by gradually increasing image resolution (size), Style-Based Generative Adversarial Network (StyleGAN, [16]) better control the Latent space distribution and are able to generate content with given characteristics; other contributions include Cycle-Consistent Generative Adversarial Network (CycleGAN, [30]), Big Generative Adversarial Network (BigGAN, [6]), Pix2Pix [12], and the research is still advancing.

In [9] the authors use even more abstract objects which lead to a loss functional called "Wasserstein of Wasserstein loss"; that is, the most basic objects that are here the images (with our notations elements $\omega \in \Omega$) are not given the usual Euclidian distance, but instead are immersed in a metric space and the Wasserstein distance $d_{W,1}(\omega_1, \omega_2)$ is used to measure the distance (dissimilarity) between two (elementary) images $\omega_1, \omega_2 \in \Omega$. The Wasserstein distance $d_{W,1}(\mu_1, \mu_2)$ is then used a second time in order to discriminate between probability laws $\mu_1, \mu_2 \in \mathcal{P}_1(\Omega)$.

Similar abstraction for the ground distance are to be found in [1] that present Banach space GANs.

All these examples enforce even more the need for an abstract formulation of GAN convergence, that we give below. Finally, see also [13] for implicit procedures relevant to GANs.

---

[1] See Lemma 1 in appendix for information on the relationship between explicit and implicit numerical schemes.

1.2   Mathematical Setting

We consider $\mathcal{X}$, $\mathcal{Y}$ two (Polish geodesic) metric spaces (see [7] for an introduction to metric spaces) and $\mathcal{C}(\cdot,\cdot) : \mathcal{X} \times \mathcal{Y} \to \mathbb{R} \times \mathbb{R}$ a functional (that will stand for the loss functional). Note that $\mathcal{C}(\cdot,\cdot)$ is vector valued, we will denote by $\mathcal{C}^x(\cdot,\cdot)$ and $\mathcal{C}^y(\cdot,\cdot)$ its components. Note that in a GAN we will have

$$
\begin{aligned}
\mathcal{C}(\ell,\mu) &= (\mathcal{C}^x(\ell,\mu), \mathcal{C}^y(\ell,\mu)) \\
&= (-\mathbb{E}_\mu(\ell) + \mathbb{E}_{\mu_r}(\ell), \mathbb{E}_\mu(\ell) - \mathbb{E}_{\mu_r}(\ell)).
\end{aligned}
\tag{6}
$$

We investigate the equation:

$$
\partial_t \begin{pmatrix} x_t \\ y_t \end{pmatrix} + \begin{pmatrix} \nabla_x \mathcal{C}^x(x_t, y_t) \\ \nabla_y \mathcal{C}^y(x_t, y_t) \end{pmatrix} = 0, \quad \begin{pmatrix} x_0 \\ y_0 \end{pmatrix} = \begin{pmatrix} \bar{x} \\ \bar{y} \end{pmatrix}.
\tag{7}
$$

Such an equation will be called a *dual flow*. The discrete version is defined by the recurrence:

$$
x_0^\tau = \bar{x}, \quad x_{k+1}^\tau \in argmin_{x \in \mathcal{X}} \frac{d(x, x_k^\tau)^2}{2\tau} + \mathcal{C}^x(x, y_k^\tau), \quad k \geq 0.
\tag{8}
$$

$$
y_0^\tau = \bar{y}, \quad y_{k+1}^\tau \in argmin_{y \in \mathcal{Y}} \frac{d(y, y_k^\tau)^2}{2\tau} + \mathcal{C}^y(x_{k+1}^\tau, y), \quad k \geq 0.
\tag{9}
$$

These numerical schemes are a distant cousin of some other evolution on metric spaces, namely the evolution flows, see [5, 27]).

From the theoretical point of view, these results are not available with previous techniques from [2, 10, 10, 19, 21, 22, 24]).

2   Theoretical Results

2.1   Motivation and Literature Review

Note that when $\mathcal{C}^x$ is independent of the second argument, i.e.,

$$
\mathcal{C}^x(x,y) = E(x),
\tag{10}
$$

the relation (8) becomes the celebrated implicit Euler-type scheme of Jordan, Kinderlehrer and Otto [14] for the definition of gradient flows in metric spaces

$$
\partial_t y_t + \nabla E(y_t) = 0, \quad y_0 = \bar{y},
\tag{11}
$$

and received considerable attention (see [3, 25, 28] for instance). However, the situation when E has dependence on other variables has not been treated to the same extent and the related contributions involve gradient flows of time dependent functionals $\mathcal{E}(t, u)$ with a known dependence on time (see [10, 19, 21, 22, 24]). Of course, formally one can set $\mathcal{E}(t, u) = \mathcal{C}(u, y_t)$, and hope to analyze the (x_t, y_t) dynamics in this way. This is not possible for technical reasons (see for instance the discussion in [27]); in particular doing so supposes the knowledge of the dynamics y_t (which is not available) and moreover the dynamics may not be differentiable with respect to time (but remains absolute continuous).

2.2   Basic Reminders

The absence of a vector operations in a metric space does no allow to develop fully a differential calculus and requires adaptation of notions of derivative. Accordingly the definition of evolution equations have to use alternative properties.

We recall below the main ideas of such an alternative formulation (see [2]) for the particular case (10)–(11); suppose for a moment that $\mathcal{X}$ is an Euclidian space and E a smooth (C^1 or above) function; then:

$$\frac{d}{dt}E(x_t) = \langle \nabla E(x_t), x'_t \rangle \geq -|\nabla E(x_t)| \cdot |x'_t|$$

$$\geq -\frac{1}{2}|x'_t|^2 - \frac{1}{2}|\nabla E|^2(x_t),$$

or equivalently,

$$\frac{d}{dt}E(x_t) + \frac{1}{2}|x'_t|^2 + \frac{1}{2}|\nabla E|^2(x_t) \geq 0 \; \forall t, \tag{12}$$

with equality only if x is solution of (11). Therefore asking that

$$\frac{d}{dt}E(x_t) + \frac{1}{2}|x'_t|^2 + \frac{1}{2}|\nabla E|^2(x_t) \leq 0 \; \forall t, \tag{13}$$

is an equivalent characterization of (11) (more precisely called the EDI formulation). Its integral form is:

$$\forall \; 0 \leq a \leq b:$$

$$E(x_b) - E(x_a) + \int_a^b \left(\frac{1}{2}|x'_t|^2 + \frac{1}{2}|\nabla E|^2(x_t) \right) dt \leq 0. \tag{14}$$

The advantage of formulation (14) is that it only uses quantities that can be defined in a metric space (see below for definition of $|x'_t|$ and $|\nabla E|$). The corresponding computation for a bi-variate functional $\mathcal{C}$ is:

$$\forall \; 0 \leq a \leq b: \quad \int_a^b \left(\frac{d}{dt}\mathcal{C}^x(x_t, \nu) \Big|_{\nu=y_t} \right) dt$$

$$+ \int_a^b \left(\frac{1}{2}|x'_t|^2 + \frac{1}{2}|\nabla_1 \mathcal{C}^x|^2(x_t, y_t) \right) dt$$

$$+ \int_a^b \left(\frac{d}{dt}\mathcal{C}^y(\nu, y_t) \Big|_{\nu=x_t} \right) dt$$

$$+ \int_a^b \left(\frac{1}{2}|y'_t|^2 + \frac{1}{2}|\nabla_2 \mathcal{C}^y|^2(x_t, y_t) \right) dt \leq 0. \tag{15}$$

However this formulation poses specific problems as in general the solution $(x_t, y_t)_{t \geq 0}$ is only absolutely continuous (with respect to time) while, for instance, the manipulation of the term $\frac{d}{dt}\mathcal{C}^x(x_t, \nu)\Big|_{\nu=y_t}$ requires additional assumptions. This will be made precise later.

2.3   Definition of (EDI Style) Equilibrium Flows

Let us recall the following definition:

Definition 1. *A curve* $x : [0, T] \to (\mathcal{X}, d)$ *is called absolutely continuous if there exists* $f \in L^1(0, T)$ *such that*

$$d(x_{t_1}, x_{t_2}) \leq \int_{t_1}^{t_2} f(t)dt, \ \forall t_1 < t_2, \ t_1, t_2 \in [0, T]. \tag{16}$$

For an absolutely continuous curve $(x_t)_{t \in [0,T]}$ the metric derivative of x at r defined by

$$|x'_r| = \lim_{h \to 0} \frac{d(x_{r+h}, x_r)}{|h|}, \tag{17}$$

exists a.e., belongs to $L^1(0, T)$ and is the smallest L^1 function that verifies (16).

We suppose from now on that $\mathcal{C}$ satisfies the assumption:

($\mathbf{A_1}$) There exists $C_1 < \infty$ such that $\mathcal{C}^x(y, x), \mathcal{C}^y(y, x) \geq -C_1, \forall x, y \in \mathcal{X} \times \mathcal{Y}$.

For any $\alpha, \beta \in \mathbb{R}$, $\alpha \leq \beta$, we denote by $\mathcal{S}(\alpha, \beta)$ the set of divisions of the interval $[\alpha, \beta]$. Let $z = (x, y) = (x_t, y_t)_{t \in [0,T]}$ be an absolutely continuous curve in $\mathcal{X} \times \mathcal{Y}$; define for $0 \leq a \leq b \leq T$ and a division $\Delta = \{a = t_0 < t_1 < \dots t_{N_\Delta} = b\} \in \mathcal{S}(a, b)$:

$$\Upsilon^x(\Delta; z, a, b) = \sum_k \mathcal{C}^x(x_{t_{k+1}}, y_{t_k}) - \mathcal{C}^x(x_{t_k}, y_{t_k}). \tag{18}$$

$$\Upsilon^x(z, a, b) = \liminf_{\Delta \in \mathcal{S}(a,b), \ |\Delta| \to 0} \Upsilon^x(\Delta; z, a, b). \tag{19}$$

Similar definitions are introduced for $\Upsilon^y(z, a, b)$ (summing the variations of $\mathcal{C}^y$ along the curve z). Furthermore we denote

$$\Upsilon(\Delta; z, a, b) = \Upsilon^x(\Delta; z, a, b) + \Upsilon^y(\Delta; z, a, b). \tag{20}$$

Remark 1. When $\mathcal{X}$ is e.g., Euclidian and under regularity assumptions on $\mathcal{C}$ it is easy to check that $\Upsilon^x(x, a, b) = \int_a^b \frac{d}{dt} \mathcal{C}^x(x_t, \nu) \big|_{\nu = y_t} dt$ and the same for Υ^y.

We are now ready to state the formal definition of a solution of (7) in the abstract setting of metric spaces. The particular flavor we use is the so-called "EDI" solution, see [3] for details.

Definition 2 (EDI equilibrium flow).   *An absolutely continuous curve* $z = (x_t, y_t)_{t \in [0,T]}$ *is called an EDI-equilibrium flow starting from* $(\bar{x}, \bar{y})$ *if*

$\lim_{t \to 0}(x_t, y_t) = (\bar{x}, \bar{y})$ *and:*

$$\forall s \geq 0, \ \Upsilon(z, 0, s) + \frac{1}{2} \int_0^s |x_r'|^2 + |y_r'|^2 \, \mathrm{d}r$$

$$+\frac{1}{2} \int_0^s |\nabla_1 \mathcal{C}^x|^2 (x_r, y_r) + |\nabla_2 \mathcal{C}^y|^2 (x_r, y_r) \, \mathrm{d}r \leq 0, \tag{21}$$

a.e. $t > 0, \ \forall s \geq t, \ \Upsilon(x, t, s) + \frac{1}{2} \int_t^s |x_r'|^2 + |y_r'|^2 \, \mathrm{d}r$

$$+\frac{1}{2} \int_t^s |\nabla_1 \mathcal{C}|^2 (x_r, x_r) + |\nabla_2 \mathcal{C}^y|^2 (x_r, y_r) \, \mathrm{d}r \leq 0,$$

$$\tag{22}$$

where the slope $|\nabla_1 \mathcal{C}^x| (x, y)$ *of* $\mathcal{C}^x(\cdot, \cdot)$ *with respect to the first argument evaluated at* (x, y) *is:*

$$|\nabla_1 \mathcal{C}^x| (x, y) = \limsup_{u \to x} \frac{(\mathcal{C}^x(x, y) - \mathcal{C}^x(u, y))^+}{d(x, u)}, \tag{23}$$

and similarly for $|\nabla_2 \mathcal{C}^y| (x, y)$.

Remark 2. For the particular case of a Hilbert space the definition above coincides with the usual definition of an evolution Eq. (7).

2.4   Convergence of Numerical Schemes

Let us denote

$$\mathcal{M}^x(x, y, \tau) = argmin_{u \in \mathcal{X}} \frac{d(u, x)^2}{2\tau} + \mathcal{C}^x(u, y) \tag{24}$$

$$\mathcal{M}^y(x, y, \tau) = argmin_{u \in \mathcal{Y}} \frac{d(u, y)^2}{2\tau} + \mathcal{C}^y(x, u). \tag{25}$$

With this definition the numerical scheme in Eqs. (8)–(9) can be written as

$$x_{k+1}^\tau \in \mathcal{M}^x(x_k^\tau, y_k^\tau, \tau), y_{k+1}^\tau \in \mathcal{M}^y(x_{k+1}^\tau, y_k^\tau, \tau). \tag{26}$$

The goal of this contribution is to investigate whether when $\tau \to 0$ the set $\{(x_k^\tau, y_k^\tau), k \geq 1\}$ converges to a solution of (7) as defined in (21)–(22).

In order to work with meaningful objects, we introduce the following assumption which is the analogue of [2, Assumption 4.8 page 67]:

(A$_2$) There exists $\bar{\tau} > 0$ such that for any $\tau \leq \bar{\tau}$ and $(x, y) \in \mathcal{X} \times \mathcal{Y}$:

$$\mathcal{M}^x(x, y, \tau) \neq \emptyset, \mathcal{M}^y(x, y, \tau) \neq \emptyset. \tag{27}$$

Assuming that assumption $(\mathbf{A_2})$ is satisfied, we can define the interpolation à la de Giorgi which is a curve $t \in [0,T] \mapsto (x_t^\tau, y_t^\tau)$ such that $(x_0^\tau, y_0^\tau) = (\bar{x}, \bar{y})$ and $\forall t \in]k\tau, (k+1)\tau]$:

$$x_t^\tau \in \mathcal{M}^x(x_{k\tau}^\tau, y_{k\tau}^\tau, t - k\tau), y_t^\tau \in \mathcal{M}^y(x_{(k+1)\tau}^\tau, y_{k\tau}^\tau, t - k\tau). \tag{28}$$

We will need some additional hypothesis:

$(\mathbf{A_3})$ For any $c \in \mathbb{R}$, $r > 0$ and $(x,y) \in \mathcal{X} \times \mathcal{Y}$ the sets $\{u \in \mathcal{X} | \mathcal{C}^x(u,y) \leq c, d(u,x) \leq r\}$ and $\{u \in \mathcal{Y} | \mathcal{C}^y(x,u) \leq c, d(u,u) \leq r\}$ are both compact.

$(\mathbf{A_4})$ The slopes $|\nabla_1 \mathcal{C}^x|$ and $|\nabla_2 \mathcal{C}^y|$ are lower semicontinuous.

$(\mathbf{A_5})$ The function $\mathcal{C}^x$ is Lipschitz with respect to the second argument and $\mathcal{C}^y$ is Lipschitz with respect to the first argument.

$(\mathbf{A_6})$ For any absolutely continuous curve $z = (x_t, y_t)_{t \in [a,b]}$:

$$\Upsilon(x,a,b) \leq \begin{array}{c} \liminf \\ |\Delta_n| \to 0 \\ z_n = (x_n, y_n) \to z \\ \sup_n \int_a^b |\dot{x}_n(t)| + |\dot{y}_n(t)| \, dt < \infty \end{array} \quad \Upsilon(\Delta_n; z_n, a, b), \tag{29}$$

where the convergence of the curves z_n to z is in the uniform (on compacts) norm.

$(\mathbf{A_7})$ There exists $C_L < \infty$ such that for any x, y, u, w:

$$|\mathcal{C}^x(u,v) + \mathcal{C}^x(u,y) - \mathcal{C}^x(w,v) - \mathcal{C}^x(w,y)| \leq C_L d(u,w) d(v,y). \tag{30}$$

and the same for $\mathcal{C}^y(u,v)$.

Remark 3. The assumption $(\mathbf{A_7})$ implies $(\mathbf{A_6})$ (see [27, Lemma 2]).

With these provisions, the properties of the curves obtained by the numerical scheme (8) are detailed in the Theorem 1.

Theorem 1. *Let $\mathcal{C}$ satisfying assumptions $(\mathbf{A_1})$, $(\mathbf{A_2})$, $(\mathbf{A_3})$, $(\mathbf{A_4})$, $(\mathbf{A_5})$ and $(\mathbf{A_6})$. Then the set of curves $\{(x_t^\tau, y_t^\tau)_{t \in [0,T]}; \tau \leq \bar{\tau}\}$ defined in (28) is relatively compact in the set of curves in $\mathcal{X} \times \mathcal{Y}$ with local uniform convergence and any limit curve is an EDI equilibrium flow in the sense of Definition 2.*

Proof. The proof is somehow technical but is a adaptation of the proof of Theorem 1 in [27]: first we show that the map $\tau \mapsto \frac{d(x_\tau, x)^2}{2\tau} + \mathcal{C}^x(x_\tau, y)$ is locally Lipshitz. Then the discrete identity is obtained as in [27, formula (32)] and then estimations similar to [27, formulas (35) and (36)] allow to conclude.

Similar results hold for the convex case (see [27, Theorem 2]).

3   Applications

Using Lemma 1 we conclude that if in some circumstances there are ways to use explicit numerical schemes (like for GANs), the convergence is also ensured for the explicit schemes, once the implicit ones converge.

Let us now inquire what are the consequences of the theoretical results for WGAN training. Because the Discriminator is trained first one can consider the variable x to be the Discriminator network parameters that will result in a Lipschitz function $\ell = \ell(x)$ and y to be the Generator parameters that will generate a distribution $\mu = \mu(y)$. Functions $\mathcal{C}^x$ and $\mathcal{C}^y$ are given by (6) thus in particular $\mathcal{C}^x = -\mathcal{C}^y$. With these notations we can apply the Theorem 1 and obtain that, in the limit of a vanishing learning rate, the WGAN training will tend to some evolution curve, both in the space $\mathcal{X} \times \mathcal{Y}$ of parameters, but also in the space of the distributions (where μ belongs) and Lipschitz function (where ℓ belongs).

As a further application, we can investigate the conditions under which the GAN training give rise to a mode collapse. The discussion below is not a mathematical proof but oriented towards a practical understanding. A mode collapse describes, e.g.., the situation when a strong Discriminator pushes the Generator to only produce a limited number of samples with a loss in diversity. With our notations, this means that the evolution (x_t, y_t) will be close to a constant (x^∞, y^∞) but the corresponding distribution $\mu(y^\infty)$ is far from μ_r but can be expressed (at least approximately) as a finite sum of Dirac masses $\sum_{a=1}^{A} p_a \delta_{i_a}$ where $i_a \in \Omega$ are given images. Using the insight from Lemma 2 and under assumption that the generator network is locally injective (i.e., does not generate redundant probability laws) the point $\mu(y^\infty)$ is a critical point of the loss function. But, denoting l^∞ the Lipschitz function corresponding to the Discriminator network, the loss function for the Generator will be $\mathbb{E}_\mu(\ell^\infty) - \mathbb{E}_{\mu_r}(\ell^\infty)$ and the loss of the Discriminator will be $\ell \mapsto \mathbb{E}_{\mu_r}(\ell) - \mathbb{E}_{\mu^\infty}(\ell)$. For such a loss function, the information that μ is a sum of Dirac masses and also a critical point of $\mu \mapsto \mathbb{E}_\mu(\ell^\infty) - \mathbb{E}_{\mu_r}(\ell^\infty)$ implies that moving (in the space of probability laws endowed with the 1-Wasserstein metric) towards any other Dirac mass does not change (decrease) the loss value (to the first order). Therefore the images i_a in the support of the measure μ are necessarily of lowest possible loss value i.e., if the discriminator is good enough, are members of the original "real" image values (in mathematical terms are members of the support of μ_r). On the other hand, if the dynamics of the Discriminator is also blocked in some point ℓ^∞, this means again that, to the first order, $\mathbb{E}_{\mu^\infty}(\ell) - \mathbb{E}_{\mu_r}(\ell)$ cannot be increased locally when ℓ is slightly perturbed around ℓ^∞. Or, since μ and μ_r are different we obtain a contradiction. Therefore the mode collapse is **not** a legitimate limit dynamics. We can therefore conclude that if mode collapse happens this is due to a too large time step, to a not strong enough Generator architecture or to numerical traps that can be removed by perturbating slightly the dynamics.

4   Discussion and Conclusion

When averaging out the steps of a SGD one obtains the gradient flow of the loss functional. The question that we ask in this paper is what is obtained when one averages out the generator-discriminator dynamics encountered in GANs. To answer the question we notice that in GANs the ground metric is not always of L^2 type but can be arbitrary (Wasserstein metric as in [9], Banach norm as in [1], etc.). Thus we re-formulate the question: when the learning rate becomes smaller and smaller, is there any limit for the curves obtained during the GAN training ? Does this correspond to a dynamical system? We first give sufficient conditions for this convergence in general metric space when the learning process is composed of implicit steps. On the other side we recall that under mild conditions explicit and implicit steps will be arbitrary close thus converge to the same limit. Therefore the dynamics of GAN training will in general follow the solution of a evolution equation whose details are given explicitly in Eq. (7). The knowledge of such a fact can help better understand the GAN optimization dynamics and the mode collapse phenomena.

Acknowledgements

1 Explicit and Implicit Numerical Schemes in Hilbert Spaces

We recall below a standard result on the relationship between explicit and implicit numerical schemes in Hilbert spaces.

Lemma 1. *Let H be a Hilbert space, $f : H \to \mathbb{R}$ a bounded Lipschitz function with Lipschitz constant L and two numerical schemes defined by the recurrences:*

$$x_{n+1}^E = x_n^E + \tau f(x_n^E), \quad x_0^E = \bar{x} \tag{31}$$

$$x_{n+1}^I = x_n^I + \tau f(x_{n+1}^I), \quad x_0^I = \bar{x} \tag{32}$$

Then for τ small enough:

1. *the implicit scheme (32) has a unique solution for any step $n \geq 0$.*
2. *let $T = N\tau$ for some fixed N, then $\|x_N^I - x_N^E\| \leq C\tau$, with the constant C depending only on f, $\bar{x}$ and T.*

Remark 4. Note that point 2 implies in particular that if, for $\tau \to 0$, the implicit curves $(x_n^I)_{n\geq 0}$ converge to some limit curve then the explicit curves $(x_n^E)_{n\geq 0}$ converge to the same. However in order to avoid technicalities we will not state precisely what the full curves are and what kind of convergence is obtained.

Proof. Point 1 is obtained by a Picard procedure after observing that the mapping $x \mapsto x_n^E + \tau f(x)$ is a contraction for τ small enough. For the point 2 we make use of the Lipschitz constant of f:

$$\|x_{n+1}^I - x_{n+1}^E\| \leq \|x_n^I - x_n^E\| + \tau L\|x_{n+1}^I - x_n^E\|$$
$$\leq \|x_n^I - x_n^E\| + \tau L\left(\|x_n^I - x_n^E\| + \tau f(x_{n+1}^I)\right) \tag{33}$$

Thus, denoting by C_f an upper bound on f:

$$\|x_{n+1}^I - x_{n+1}^E\| \le (1 + \tau L)\|x_n^I - x_n^E\| + \tau^2 \, LC_f. \tag{34}$$

If suffices now to use the discrete version of the Gronwall lemma to obtain $\|x_{n+1}^I - x_{n+1}^E\| \le e^{\tau L}(n+1)\tau^2 LC_f$, and the conclusion follows from:

$$\|x_N^I - x_N^E\| \le \tau e^{\tau L} T L C_f. \tag{35}$$

2 Critical Points of Gradient Flows on Intermediary Spaces

We investigate in this section a simple situation of a gradient flow of a composed function. Suppose thus an initial space $X_p = \mathbb{R}^n$ (for a GAN the neural network parameter space), an object space $X_o = \mathbb{R}^m$ (for a GAN this will be the space of probability measures where μ belongs and that of Lipschitz functions where ℓ belongs). Consider also two functions $g : X_p \to X_o$, $f : X_o \to \mathbb{R}$ and the gradient flow:

$$x_t' = -\nabla_x(f \circ g)(x_t), \tag{36}$$

where for any function we denote by ∇ its differential; for instance $\nabla_o f(o)$ is the gradient of f at the point o, taken as a row vector, $\nabla_x g(x)$ is the $m \times n$ Jacobian matrix of g at x (entry i, j being $\partial g_i/\partial x_j$).

This dynamics in parameter space X_p defines a dynamics $o_t = g(x_t)$ in the object space X_o. We want to investigate the relationship between the dynamics x_t and o_t when the evolution (36) ends up in a stationary point i.e., stalls at some given point $x^\infty \in X_p$ and $o^\infty = g(x^\infty) \in X_o$.

Lemma 2. *Suppose that the functions f and g are of C^1 class (i.e. with continuous derivatives). Then:*

1. *denoting $o_t = g(x_t)$ the dynamics in parameter space can also be written*

$$x_t' = -(\nabla_o f)(o_t) \cdot (\nabla_x g)(x_t). \tag{37}$$

2. *the dynamic in object space X_o is:*

$$o_t' = -(\nabla_o f)(o_t) \cdot (\nabla_x g)(x_t) \cdot (\nabla_x g)(x_t)^T. \tag{38}$$

   In particular the dynamics in object space is not in general a gradient flow (but will be when $(\nabla_x g) \cdot (\nabla_x g)^T = Id$).
   Suppose now that the dynamics (36) is such that for some $t \ge t_1$ we have $x_t = x^\infty$. Then:
3. *$o^\infty = g(x^\infty)$ is a critical point of f (i.e., $\nabla_o f(o^\infty) = 0$) as soon as $\nabla_o g^T$ is locally injective around o^∞ (which implies that g is locally injective around o^∞).*

Proof. Formulas (37) and (38) are derived from (36) using the chain rule. Suppose now x^∞ is a critical stationary point of the dynamics (36). This of course implies that $o_t = g(x_t)$ will also be constant but is not enough to conclude that o^∞ is a critical point of f. But, since the time derivative x'_t in the evolution equation is zero for the constant dynamics $x_t = x^\infty$, we have that $(\nabla_o f)(o^\infty) \cdot (\nabla_x g)(x^\infty) = 0$, which, when $(\nabla_x g)^T(x^\infty)$ is injective will imply that $(\nabla_o f)(o^\infty) = 0$. ∎

Note that by the rank theorem the local injectivity of $(\nabla_x g)^T(x^\infty)$ and of g are related.

References

1. Adler, J., Lunz, S.: Banach Wasserstein GAN. In: Bengio, S., Wallach, H., Larochelle, H., Grauman, K., Cesa-Bianchi, N., Garnett, R. (eds.) Advances in Neural Information Processing Systems 31, pp. 6754–6763. Curran Associates, Inc. (2018). http://papers.nips.cc/paper/7909-banach-wasserstein-gan.pdf
2. Ambrosio, L., Gigli, N.: A user's guide to optimal transport. In: Piccoli, B., Rascle, M. (eds.) Modelling and Optimisation of Flows on Networks: Cetraro, Italy 2009, pp. 1–155. Springer, Heidelberg (2013)
3. Ambrosio, L., Gigli, N., Savaré, G.: Gradient Flows in Metric Spaces and in the Space of Probability Measures, 2nd edn. Birkhäuser, Basel (2008)
4. Arjovsky, M., Chintala, S., Bottou, L.: Wasserstein GAN. arXiv preprint arXiv:1701.07875 (2017)
5. Blanchet, A., Carlier, G.: Remarks on existence and uniqueness of Cournot-Nash equilibria in the non-potential case. Math. Fin. Econ. **8**(4), 417–433 (2014). https://doi.org/10.1007/s11579-014-0127-z, http://dx.doi.org/10.1007/s11579-014-0127-z
6. Brock, A., Donahue, J., Simonyan, K.: Large Scale GAN Training for High Fidelity Natural Image Synthesis. arXiv:1809.11096 [cs, stat], February 2019, http://arxiv.org/abs/1809.11096, arXiv: 1809.11096
7. Burago, D., Burago, Y., Ivanov, S.: A course in metric geometry, Graduate Studies in Mathematics, vol. 33. American Mathematical Society, Providence, RI (2001). https://doi.org/10.1090/gsm/033, http://dx.doi.org/10.1090/gsm/033
8. Deshpande, I., et al.: Max-Sliced Wasserstein Distance and its use for GANs. arXiv preprint arXiv:1904.05877 (2019)
9. Dukler, Y., Li, W., Lin, A.T., Montúfar, G.: Wasserstein of Wasserstein loss for learning generative models. In: Chaudhuri, K. (ed.) Proceedings of the 36th International Conference on Machine Learning, 9–15 June 2019, Long Beach, California, USA, Proceedings of machine learning research, vol. 97, pp. 1716–1725. PMLR, Long Beach, California (2019)
10. Ferreira, L.C.F., Valencia-Guevara, J.C.: Gradient flows of time-dependent functionals in metric spaces and applications to pdes. Monatshefte für Mathematik, pp. 1–38 (2017). https://doi.org/10.1007/s00605-017-1037-y, http://dx.doi.org/10.1007/s00605-017-1037-y
11. Gulrajani, I., Ahmed, F., Arjovsky, M., Dumoulin, V., Courville, A.C.: Improved training of Wasserstein GANs. In: Advances in Neural Information Processing Systems, pp. 5767–5777 (2017)

12. Isola, P., Zhu, J.Y., Zhou, T., Efros, A.A.: Image-to-image translation with conditional adversarial networks. arXiv:1611.07004 [cs], November 2018. http://arxiv.org/abs/1611.07004, arXiv: 1611.07004
13. Iwaki, R., Asada, M.: Implicit incremental natural actor critic algorithm. Neural Networks **109**, 103–112 (2019). https://doi.org/10.1016/j.neunet.2018.10.007, http://www.sciencedirect.com/science/article/pii/S0893608018302922
14. Jordan, R., Kinderlehrer, D., Otto, F.: The variational formulation of the Fokker-Planck equation. SIAM J. Math. Anal. **29**(1), 1–17 (1998). https://doi.org/10.1137/S0036141096303359, http://dx.doi.org/10.1137/S0036141096303359
15. Karras, T., Aila, T., Laine, S., Lehtinen, J.: Progressive growing of GANs for improved quality, stability, and variation. In: International Conference on Learning Representations (2018). https://openreview.net/forum?id=Hk99zCeAb
16. Karras, T., Laine, S., Aila, T.: A Style-Based Generator Architecture for Generative Adversarial Networks. arXiv:1812.04948 [cs, stat], March 2019. http://arxiv.org/abs/1812.04948, arXiv: 1812.04948
17. Kodali, N., Abernethy, J., Hays, J., Kira, Z.: On convergence and stability of GANs. arXiv preprint arXiv:1705.07215 (2017)
18. Kolouri, S., Pope, P.E., Martin, C.E., Rohde, G.K.: Sliced-Wasserstein autoencoder: an embarrassingly simple generative model. arXiv preprint arXiv:1804.01947 (2018)
19. Kopfer, E.: Gradient flow for the Boltzmann entropy and Cheeger's energy on time-dependent metric measure spaces. ArXiv e-prints, November 2016
20. Liu, M.Y., Tuzel, O.: Coupled Generative Adversarial Networks. arXiv:1606.07536 [cs], September 2016, http://arxiv.org/abs/1606.07536, arXiv: 1606.07536
21. Mielke, A., Rossi, R., Savaré, G.: Variational convergence of gradient flows and rate-independent evolutions in metric spaces. Milan J. Math. **80**(2), 381–410 (2012). https://doi.org/10.1007/s00032-012-0190-y, http://dx.doi.org/10.1007/s00032-012-0190-y
22. Mielke, A., Rossi, R., Savaré, G.: Nonsmooth analysis of doubly nonlinear evolution equations. Calc. Var. Partial Differential Equations **46**(1–2), 253–310 (2013). https://doi.org/10.1007/s00526-011-0482-z, http://dx.doi.org/10.1007/s00526-011-0482-z
23. Radford, A., Metz, L., Chintala, S.: Unsupervised representation learning with deep convolutional generative adversarial networks. arXiv:1511.06434 [cs], January 2016, http://arxiv.org/abs/1511.06434, arXiv: 1511.06434
24. Rossi, R., Mielke, A., Savaré, G.: A metric approach to a class of doubly nonlinear evolution equations and applications. Ann. Sc. Norm. Super. Pisa Cl. Sci. (5) **7**(1), 97–169 (2008)
25. Santambrogio, F.: Optimal transport for applied mathematicians. In: Progress in Nonlinear Differential Equations and their Applications, 87, Birkhäuser/Springer, Cham (2015). https://doi.org/10.1007/978-3-319-20828-2, http://dx.doi.org/10.1007/978-3-319-20828-2, calculus of variations, PDEs, and modeling
26. Sriperumbudur, B.K., Gretton, A., Fukumizu, K., Schölkopf, B., Lanckriet, G.R.G.: Hilbert space embeddings and metrics on probability measures. J. Mach. Learn. Res. **11**, 1517–1561 (2010). http://www.jmlr.org/papers/v11/sriperumbudur10a.html
27. Turinici, G.: Metric gradient flows with state dependent functionals: the Nash-MFG equilibrium flows and their numerical schemes. Nonlinear Anal. **165**, 163–181 (2017). https://doi.org/10.1016/j.na.2017.10.002, http://www.sciencedirect.com/science/article/pii/S0362546X17302444

28. Villani, C.: Optimal transport. Old and new, Grundlehren der mathematis-
chen Wissenschaften, vol. 338. Springer (2009). https://doi.org/10.1007/978-3-
540-71050-9

29. Wu, J., Huang, Z., Acharya, D., Li, W., Thoma, J., Paudel, D.P., Gool, L.V.:
Sliced Wasserstein generative models. In: Proceedings of the IEEE Conference on
Computer Vision and Pattern Recognition, pp. 3713–3722 (2019)

30. Zhu, J.Y., Park, T., Isola, P., Efros, A.A.: Unpaired image-to-image translation
using cycle-consistent adversarial networks. In: 2017 IEEE International Conference on Computer Vision (ICCV), pp. 2223–2232 (2017)

Biomedical Named Entity Recognition at Scale

Veysel Kocaman$^{(\boxtimes)}$ and David Talby

John Snow Labs Inc., 16192 Coastal Highway, Lewes, DE 19958, USA
veysel@johnsnowlabs.com

Abstract. Named entity recognition (NER) is a widely applicable natural language processing task and building block of question answering, topic modeling, information retrieval, etc. In the medical domain, NER plays a crucial role by extracting meaningful chunks from clinical notes and reports, which are then fed to downstream tasks like assertion status detection, entity resolution, relation extraction, and de-identification. Reimplementing a Bi-LSTM-CNN-Char deep learning architecture on top of Apache Spark, we present a single trainable NER model that obtains new state-of-the-art results on seven public biomedical benchmarks without using heavy contextual embeddings like BERT. This includes improving BC4CHEMD to 93.72% (4.1% gain), Species800 to 80.91% (4.6% gain), and JNLPBA to 81.29% (5.2% gain). In addition, this model is freely available within a production-grade code base as part of the open-source Spark NLP library; can scale up for training and inference in any Spark cluster; has GPU support and libraries for popular programming languages such as Python, R, Scala and Java; and can be extended to support other human languages with no code changes.

Keywords: Named entity recognition · Apache Spark · Biomedical NLP · Deep learning

1 Introduction

Electronic health records (EHRs) are the primary source of information for clinicians tracking the care of their patients. Information fed into these systems may be found in structured fields for which values are inputted electronically (e.g. laboratory test orders or results) [21] but most of the time information in these records is unstructured making it largely inaccessible for statistical analysis [25]. These records include information such as the reason for administering drugs, previous disorders of the patient or the outcome of past treatments, and they are the largest source of empirical data in biomedical research, allowing for major scientific findings in highly relevant disorders such as cancer and Alzheimer's disease [30]. Unlocking this information can bring a significant advancement to biomedical research.

The widespread adoption of EHRs and the growing wealth of digitized information sources about patients are opening new doors to uncover previously

© Springer Nature Switzerland AG 2021
A. Del Bimbo et al. (Eds.): ICPR 2020 Workshops, LNCS 12661, pp. 635–646, 2021.
https://doi.org/10.1007/978-3-030-68763-2_48

unidentified associations and accelerating knowledge discovery via state-of-the-art Machine Learning (ML) algorithms and new statistical methods. Due to innate obstacles in extracting information from unstructured text data and the high level of preciseness dictated in healthcare domain, manual abstraction has been prevalent in the industry. As the manual abstraction is highly expensive, time consuming and error prone process, there has been a growing trend in natural language processing (NLP) applications in clinical and biomedical domain to automate the abstraction process as well as making the EHR data available through high-performant and fail-safe pipelines.

As the key ingredient of any NLP system, named entity recognition (NER) is regarded as the first building block of question answering, topic modelling, information retrieval, etc. [42]. In the medical domain, NER plays the most crucial role by giving out the first meaningful chunks of a clinical note, and then feeding them as an input to the subsequent downstream tasks such as clinical assertion status [39], clinical entity resolvers [37] and de-identification of the sensitive data [38]. However, segmentation of clinical and drug entities is considered to be a difficult task in biomedical NER systems because of complex orthographic structures of named entities [22].

ML methods formulate the clinical NER task as a sequence labeling problem that aims to find the best label sequence (e.g., BIO format labels) for a given input sequence (individual words from clinical text) [41]. Many top-ranked NER systems applied the Conditional Random Fields (CRFs) model [18], which is the most popular solution among conventional ML algorithms. A typical state-of-the-art clinical NER system usually utilizes features from different linguistic levels, including orthographic information (e.g., capitalization of letters, prefix and suffix), syntactic information (e.g. POS tags), word n-grams, word embeddings, and semantic information (e.g., the UMLS concept unique identifier) [41]. These features are usually utilized in LSTM [14] based neural network frameworks [7,15,23] and gained popularity among researchers due to their effectiveness of modeling the sequential patterns.

In the last few months, pretraining large neural language models and rich contextual embeddings, such as BERT [8] and ELMO [31], have also led to impressive gains on NER systems and many clinical variants of BERT models such as BioBert [19], ClinicalBert [2], BlueBert [28], SciBert [5] and Pubmed-Bert [12] have been crafted to address biomedical and clinical NER tasks with state-of-the-art results. However, since these methods require significant computational resources during both pretraining and getting prediction, using them in production is impractical under the restricted computational resources compared to classical pretrained embeddings (e.g. Glove). A recent study [4] empirically shows that classical pretrained embeddings can match contextual embeddings on industry-scale data, and often perform within 5 to 10% accuracy (absolute) on benchmark tasks.

Despite the growing interest and all these ground breaking advances in NER systems, easy to use production ready models and tools are scarce and it is one of the major obstacles for clinical NLP researchers to implement the latest algorithms into their workflow and start using immediately. On the other hand, NLP tool kits specialized for processing biomedical and clinical text, such as MetaMap [3] and cTAKES [35] typically do not make use of new research innovations such as word representations or neural networks discussed above, hence producing less accurate results [26,44]. In the last year, two new libraries, Stanza [44] and SciSpacy [26] took the stage to find a solution to the issues discussed above and released Python-based, de facto language of data science, production grade libraries. Both libraries offer out of the box clinical and biomedical pretrained NER models utilizing state-of-the-art deep learning frameworks mentioned above. However, none of these libraries or tools can scale up in clusters in terms of distributed data processing principles and do not support in-memory distributed data processing solutions such as Spark.

In this study, we show through extensive experiments that our NER module in Spark NLP library, one of the most widely used NLP libraries in industry, exceeds the biomedical NER benchmarks reported by Stanza in 7 out of 8 benchmark datasets and in every dataset reported by SciSpacy. Using the modified version of the well known BiLSTM-CNN-Char NER architecture [7] into Spark environment, Spark NLP's NER module can also be extended to other spoken languages with zero code changes and can scale up in Spark clusters.

The specific novel contributions of this paper are the following:

- Delivering the first production-grade scalable NER model implementation.
- Delivering a state-of-the-art NER model that exceeds the biomedical NER benchmarks reported by Stanza and SciSpaCy.
- Comparing the effectiveness of domain specific clinical word embeddings with general purpose GloVe embeddings inside the same NER architecture.
- Explaining the NER model implementation in Spark NLP which is the only NLP library that can scale up in Spark clusters while supporting popular programming languages (Python, R, Scala and Java).

The remainder of the paper is organized as follows: Sect. 2 introduces Spark NLP and explains the NER model framework implemented in Spark NLP. Section 3 elaborates the implementation details, datasets and settings for our experiments and presents results for Spark NLP, Stanza and SciSpacy on the same benchmark datasets. Section 4 concludes this paper by pointing out key points and future directions.

2   NER Model Implementation in Spark NLP

The deep neural network architecture for NER model in Spark NLP is BiLSTM-CNN-Char framework, a slightly modified version of the architecture proposed by Chiu et al. [7]. It is a neural network architecture that automatically detects word and character-level features using a hybrid bidirectional LSTM and CNN architecture, eliminating the need for most feature engineering steps.

In the original framework, the CNN extracts a fixed length feature vector from character-level features. For each word, these vectors are concatenated and fed to the BLSTM network and then to the output layers. They employed a

stacked bi-directional recurrent neural network with long short-term memory
units to transform word features into named entity tag scores. The extracted
features of each word are fed into a forward LSTM network and a backward
LSTM network. The output of each network at each time step is decoded by a
linear layer and a log-softmax layer into log-probabilities for each tag category.
These two vectors are then simply added together to produce the final output [7].
The detailed architecture of the proposed framework in the original paper is
illustrated at Fig. 1. In sum, 50-dimensional pretrained word embeddings is used
for word features, 25-dimension character embeddings is used for char features,
and capitalization features (*allCaps, upperInitial, lowercase, mixedCaps, noinfo*)
are used for case features. They also made use of lexicons as a form of external
knowledge as proposed in [34].

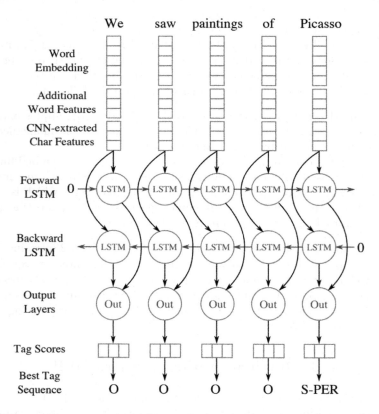

Fig. 1. Overview of the original BiLSTM-CNN-Char architecture [7].

In Spark NLP, we modified this framework as follows:

- [13] compared the performance of LSTM-CRF approach on 33 data sets
  covering five different entity classes with that of best-of-class NER tools and

an entity-agnostic CRF implementation. On average, F1-score of LSTM-CRF is 5% above that of the baselines, using WikiPubMed-PMC word embeddings. Using a similar neural network architecture, we trained our own biomedical word embeddings with skip-gram model on PubMed abstracts and case studies, as described in [24], for learning distributed representations of words using contextual information. The trained word embeddings has 200-dimensions and a vocabulary size of 2.2 million. In order to compare the effectiveness of this embeddings, we also used 300-dimension pretrained GloVe embeddings with 6 billion tokens, trained on Wikipedia and Gigaword-5 dataset [29]. Both embeddings are ported into Spark through an annotator concept specifically designed for Spark NLP. The average word coverage of our implementation of domain specific word embeddings (we call it Spark-Biomedical embeddings in this study) is 99.5% and the coverage of Glove6B embeddings is 96.1% on the biomedical datasets used in this study (see Table 1).

- Even though better results were reported by [11] through robust lexical features, after experimenting with different parameters and components, we decided to remove lexical features in order to reduce the complexity and relied on pretrained biomedical embeddings, casing features and char features through CNN. As sentences are represented through 2 nested sequences (words & chars), a CNN is applied in a way that each character is embedded in a character embedding matrix, of dimension 25. Then, a 1D Convolution layer processes the sequence of embedded char vectors, followed by a Max-Pooling operation. This way, each word gets a vector representation. We used 25 filters and kernel size of 3. It is worth to mention that char features are proved to be highly useful in NER models and had provided a level of immunity to typos and spelling errors.
- We built a modified version of the framework [7] in Tensorflow (TF) and used LSTMBlockFusedCell. This is an extremely efficient LSTM implementation based on [43], that uses a single TF operation for the entire LSTM. Our experiments show that it is both faster and more memory-efficient than LSTMBlockCell. Then we implemented this framework in Scala using TensorFlow API. This setup is ported into Spark and let the driver node run the entire training using all the available cores on the driver node. We also added CuDA version of each TF component to be able to train our models on GPU when available.

Due to architectural design choices by Tensorflow implementation in JVM at the time of writing this paper, distributing the model training over the worker nodes in the cluster was not viable and effective, and putting the burden of entire training process on the driver node mandated some limitations in terms of training speed and computational resources. Nevertheless, being able to get predictions on scale from voluminous data with state-of-the-art accuracy would overwhelm the aforementioned disadvantage.

Table 1. Word embeddings coverage ratios on biomedical datasets. Our domain specific embeddings have near-perfect word coverages. The average word coverage of our implementation of domain specific word embeddings (we call it Spark-Biomedical Embeddings in this study) is 99.5% and the average word coverage of Glove6B embeddings is 96.1% on the biomedical datasets used in this study)

Dataset	Spark-Biomedical Embeddings		Spark-Glove6B Embeddings	
	Training set	Test set	Training set	Test set
NBCI-disease	99.700	99.695	96.703	96.710
BC5CDR	99.171	99.106	96.059	95.795
BC4CHEMD	99.571	99.551	96.409	96.434
Linnaeus	99.162	99.181	96.801	96.867
Species800	99.350	99.345	95.909	96.258
JNLPBA	99.530	99.496	92.566	92.690
AnatEM	99.580	99.623	96.992	96.945
BioNLP-CG	99.859	99.814	97.750	96.663

3   Implementation Details and Experimental Results

In this section, we describe the datasets, evaluation metrics, and provide an overview of experimental setup.

3.1   Datasets

In this study, we trained individual NER models on 8 publicly available biomedical NER datasets provided by [40]: AnatEM [32], BC5CDR [20], BC4CHEMD [17], BioNLP13CG [33], JNLPBA [16], Linnaeus [10], NCBI-Disease [9] and S800 [27]. These models cover a wide variety of entity types in domains ranging from anatomical analysis to genetics and cellular biology. For the sake of brevity, we didn't include details about the nature of the data sets and readers can refer to cited papers for more information. We trained several other clinical and biomedical NER models in Spark NLP, but we just report metrics on these 8 biomedical data sets as Stanza and SciSpacy also reported their benchmarks on these data sets that are freely available without any restrictions.

3.2   Overview of Experimental Setup

Biomedical NER datasets provided by [40] are already in BIO and BIOES schemes for encoding entity annotations as token tags. IOB (or BIO) stands for Begin, Inside and Outside. Words tagged with O are outside of named entities and the I-XXX tag is used for words inside a named entity of type XXX. Whenever two entities of type XXX are immediately next to each other, the first word of the second entity will be tagged B-XXX to highlight that it starts another entity. On the other hand, BIOES (also known as BIOLU) is a little bit sophisticated annotation method that distinguishes between the end of a named entity and single entities. BIOES stands for Begin, Inside, Outside, End, Single. In this scheme, for example, a word describing a gene entity is tagged with "B-Gene" if it is at the beginning of the entity, "I-Gene" if it is in the middle of the entity, and "E-Gene" if it is at the end of the entity. Single-word gene entities are tagged with "S-Gene". All other words not describing entities of interest are tagged as 'O'.

BIOES scheme was also used in the original implementation of our NER architecture and considerable performance improvements over BIO are reported [7]. [34] also showed that the minimal BIO scheme was more difficult to learn than the BIOES scheme, which explicitly marks boundary tokens. However, we experienced various performance issues when we used BIOES schema (converging very fast in the early epochs but then fail to generalize further and stuck at local minima), and then decided to use BIO scheme.

In terms of hyperparameter tuning, we run experiments by tuning the hyperparamaters with the following parameter ranges through Random Search [6] and found out that the following parameters would produce the best results (figures within the parenthesis represent the parameter ranges tested):

- LSTM state size: 200 (200, 250)
- Dropout rate: 0.5 (0.3, 0.7)
- Batch size: 8 (4, 256)
- Learning rate: 0.001 (0.01, 0.0003)
- Epoch: 10–15 (10, 100)
- Optimizer: Adam
- Learning rate decay coefficient (po) (*real learning rate = lr/(1 + po * epoch*) (36): 0.005 (0.001, 0.01))

3.3 Experiment Results

We run our experiments on Colab[1] server provided by Google (2vCPU @ 2.2 GHz, 13 GB RAM) and used Apache Spark in local mode (no cluster). We present our results at Table 2 and Fig. 2. As the only NLP library that scales up for training and inference in any Spark cluster, Spark NLP NER architecture obtains new state-of-the-art results on seven public biomedical benchmarks without using heavy contextual embeddings like BERT. This includes improving BC4CHEMD to 93.72% (4.1% gain), Species800 to 80.91% (4.6% gain), and JNLPBA to 81.29% (5.2% gain). Given that Stanza already claims that its NER performance is on par with or superior to the strong performance achieved by BioBERT, our proposed NER model can get better results despite using considerably more compact model. Moreover, this model is available within a production-grade code base as part of the open-source Spark NLP library and a new NER model can be trained with a single line of code as presented in Appendix A.

---

[1] https://colab.research.google.com/.

Table 2. NER performance across different datasets in the biomedical domain. All scores reported are micro-averaged test F1 excluding O's. Stanza results are from the paper reported in [44], SciSpaCy results are from the scispacy-medium models reported in [26]. The official training and validation sets are merged and used for training and then the models are evaluated on the original test sets. For reproducibility purposes, we use the preprocessed versions of these datasets provided by [40] and also used by Stanza. Spark-x prefix in the table indicates our implementation. Bold scores represent the best scores in the respective row.

Dataset	Entities	Spark - Biomedical	Spark - GloVe 6B	Stanza	SciSpacy
NBCI-disease	Disease	**89.13**	87.19	87.49	81.65
BC5CDR	Chemical, disease	**89.73**	88.32	88.08	83.92
BC4CHEMD	Chemical	**93.72**	92.32	89.65	84.55
Linnaeus	Species	86.26	85.51	**88.27**	81.74
Species800	Species	**80.91**	79.22	76.35	74.06
JNLPBA	5 types in cellular	**81.29**	79.78	76.09	73.21
AnatEM	Anatomy	**89.13**	87.74	88.18	84.14
BioNLP13-CG	16 types in cancer genetics	**85.58**	84.3	84.34	77.6

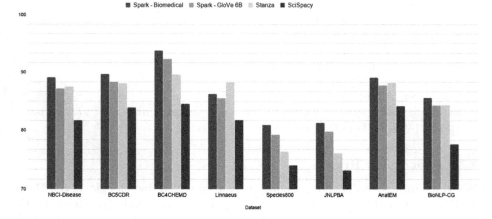

Fig. 2. NER performance across different biomedical benchmark datasets. Our implementation of NER model with domain specific embeddings exceeds Stanza in 7 out of 8 datasets and exceeds SciSpacy in all the benchmarks. The same implementation with general purpose GloVe embeddings is also better than SciSpacy in every dataset and exceeds Stanza in 4 out of 8 datasets.

As you can see on the leaderboard given at Table 3, our NER model with pretrained biomedical embeddings produces better results than Stanza in 7 out of 8 biomedical datasets and exceeds SciSpacy in all the benchmarks. It is also surprising to see that our NER model with GloVe6B embeddings, despite being a general purpose embeddings, can also exceed Stanza's (also using domain specific embeddings, CharLM - character-level language model [1]) benchmarks in half of the benchmarks and again exceeds SciSpacy in all the benchmarks.

Table 3. Biomedical NER benchmarks leaderboard. Spark-x prefix indicates our implementation.

Dataset	Best		2nd best		3rd best	
	Model	Score	Model	Score	Model	Score
NBCI-disease	Spark-Biomedical	89.13	Stanza	87.49	Spark-GloVe6B	87.19
BC5CDR	Spark-Biomedical	89.73	Spark-GloVe6B	88.32	Stanza	88.08
BC4CHEMD	Spark-Biomedical	93.72	Spark-GloVe6B	92.32	Stanza	89.65
Linnaeus	Stanza	88.27	Spark-Biomedical	86.26	Spark-GloVe6B	85.51
Species800	Spark-Biomedical	81.29	Spark-GloVe6B	79.78	Stanza	76.09
AnatEM	Spark-Biomedical	89.13	Stanza	88.18	Spark-GloVe6B	87.74
BioNLP-CG	Spark-Biomedical	85.58	Stanza	84.34	Spark-GloVe6B	84.3

4 Conclusion

Despite the growing interest and ground breaking advances in NLP research and NER systems, easy to use production ready models and tools are scarce in Biomedical domain and it is one of the major obstacles for clinical NLP researchers to implement the latest algorithms into their workflow and start using immediately.

In this study, we show through extensive experiments that NER module in Spark NLP library, one of the most widely used NLP libraries in industry, exceeds the biomedical NER benchmarks reported by Stanza in 7 out of 8 benchmark datasets and in every dataset reported by SciSpacy without using heavy contextual embeddings like BERT. Using the modified version of the well known BiLSTM-CNN-Char NER architecture [7] into Spark environment, we also presented that even with a general purpose GloVe embeddings (GloVe6B) and with no lexical features, we were able to achieve state-of-the-art results in biomedical domain and produces better results than Stanza in 4 out of 8 benchmark datasets. Given that Stanza also uses domain specific clinical embeddings, exceeding its benchmarks with general purpose embeddings is also another important observation.

Spark NLP's NER module can also be extended to other spoken languages with zero code changes and can scale up in Spark clusters. In addition, this model is available within a production-grade code base as part of the Spark NLP library; can scale up for training and inference in any Spark cluster; has GPU support and libraries for popular programming languages such as Python, R, Scala and Java; and is already extended to support other human languages with no code changes.

A   Appendices

```python
from pyspark.ml import Pipeline
import sparknlp
from sparknlp.training import CoNLL
from sparknlp.annotator import *

spark = sparknlp.start()

training_data = CoNLL().readDataset(spark, 'BC5CDR_train.conll')

word_embedder = WordEmbeddings.pretrained('wikiner_6B_300', 'xx'
    ) \
 .setInputCols(["sentence",'token'])\
 .setOutputCol("embeddings")

nerTagger = NerDLApproach()\
   .setInputCols(["sentence", "token", "embeddings"])\
   .setLabelColumn("label")\
   .setOutputCol("ner")\
   .setMaxEpochs(10)\
   .setDropout(0.5)\
   .setLr(0.001)\
   .setPo(0.005)\
   .setBatchSize(8)\
   .setValidationSplit(0.2)\

pipeline = Pipeline(
    stages = [
    word_embedder,
    nerTagger
  ])

ner_model = pipeline.fit(training_data)
```

References

1. Akbik, A., Blythe, D., Vollgraf, R.: Contextual string embeddings for sequence labeling. In: Proceedings of the 27th International Conference on Computational Linguistics, pp. 1638–1649 (2018)
2. Alsentzer, E., et al.: Publicly available clinical bert embeddings. arXiv preprint arXiv:1904.03323 (2019)
3. Aronson, A.R., Lang, F.M.: An overview of MetaMap: historical perspective and recent advances. J. Am. Med. Inform. Assoc. **17**(3), 229–236 (2010)
4. Arora, S., May, A., Zhang, J., Ré, C.: Contextual embeddings: when are they worth it? arXiv preprint arXiv:2005.09117 (2020)
5. Beltagy, I., Lo, K., Cohan, A.: SciBERT: a pretrained language model for scientific text. arXiv preprint arXiv:1903.10676 (2019)

6. Bergstra, J., Bengio, Y.: Random search for hyper-parameter optimization. J. Mach. Learn. Res. **13**(1), 281–305 (2012)
7. Chiu, J.P., Nichols, E.: Named entity recognition with bidirectional LSTM-CNNs. Trans. Assoc. Comput. Linguist. **4**, 357–370 (2016)
8. Devlin, J., Chang, M.W., Lee, K., Toutanova, K.: BERT: pre-training of deep bidirectional transformers for language understanding. arXiv preprint arXiv:1810.04805 (2018)
9. Doğan, R.I., Leaman, R., Lu, Z.: NCBI disease corpus: a resource for disease name recognition and concept normalization. J. Biomed. Inform. **47**, 1–10 (2014)
10. Gerner, M., Nenadic, G., Bergman, C.M.: LINNAEUS: a species name identification system for biomedical literature. BMC Bioinformatics **11**(1), 85 (2010)
11. Ghaddar, A., Langlais, P.: Robust lexical features for improved neural network named-entity recognition. arXiv preprint arXiv:1806.03489 (2018)
12. Gu, Y., et al.: Domain-specific language model pretraining for biomedical natural language processing. arXiv preprint arXiv:2007.15779 (2020)
13. Habibi, M., Weber, L., Neves, M., Wiegandt, D.L., Leser, U.: Deep learning with word embeddings improves biomedical named entity recognition. Bioinformatics **33**(14), i37–i48 (2017)
14. Hochreiter, S., Schmidhuber, J.: Long short-term memory. Neural Comput. **9**(8), 1735–1780 (1997)
15. Huang, Z., Xu, W., Yu, K.: Bidirectional LSTM-CRF models for sequence tagging. arXiv preprint arXiv:1508.01991 (2015)
16. Kim, J.D., Ohta, T., Tsuruoka, Y., Tateisi, Y., Collier, N.: Introduction to the bio-entity recognition task at JNLPBA. In: Proceedings of the International Joint Workshop on Natural Language Processing in Biomedicine and Its Applications, pp. 70–75. Citeseer (2004)
17. Krallinger, M., et al.: The CHEMDNER corpus of chemicals and drugs and its annotation principles. J. Cheminform. **7**(1), 1–17 (2015). https://doi.org/10.1186/1758-2946-7-S1-S2
18. Lafferty, J., McCallum, A., Pereira, F.C.: Conditional random fields: Probabilistic models for segmenting and labeling sequence data (2001)
19. Lee, J., et al.: BioBERT: a pretrained biomedical language representation model for biomedical text mining. arXiv preprint arXiv:1901.08746 (2019)
20. Li, J., et al.: BioCreative V CDR task corpus: a resource for chemical disease relation extraction. Database **2016**, baw068 (2016)
21. Liede, A., Hernandez, R.K., Roth, M., Calkins, G., Larrabee, K., Nicacio, L.: Validation of international classification of diseases coding for bone metastases in electronic health records using technology-enabled abstraction. Clin. Epidemiol. **7**, 441 (2015)
22. Liu, S., Tang, B., Chen, Q., Wang, X.: Effects of semantic features on machine learning-based drug name recognition systems: word embeddings vs. manually constructed dictionaries. Information **6**(4), 848–865 (2015)
23. Ma, X., Hovy, E.: End-to-end sequence labeling via bi-directional LSTM-CNNs-CRF. arXiv preprint arXiv:1603.01354 (2016)
24. Mikolov, T., Chen, K., Corrado, G., Dean, J.: Efficient estimation of word representations in vector space. arXiv preprint arXiv:1301.3781 (2013)
25. Murdoch, T.B., Detsky, A.S.: The inevitable application of big data to health care. JAMA **309**(13), 1351–1352 (2013)
26. Neumann, M., King, D., Beltagy, I., Ammar, W.: ScispaCy: fast and robust models for biomedical natural language processing. arXiv preprint arXiv:1902.07669 (2019)

27. Pafilis, E., et al.: The species and organisms resources for fast and accurate identification of taxonomic names in text. PLoS ONE **8**(6), e65390 (2013)
28. Peng, Y., Yan, S., Lu, Z.: Transfer learning in biomedical natural language processing: An evaluation of BERT and ELMo on ten benchmarking datasets. arXiv preprint arXiv:1906.05474 (2019)
29. Pennington, J., Socher, R., Manning, C.D.: GloVe: global vectors for word representation. In: Proceedings of the 2014 Conference on Empirical Methods in Natural Language Processing (EMNLP), pp. 1532–1543 (2014)
30. Perera, G., Khondoker, M., Broadbent, M., Breen, G., Stewart, R.: Factors associated with response to acetylcholinesterase inhibition in dementia: a cohort study from a secondary mental health care case register in London. PLoS ONE **9**(11), e109484 (2014)
31. Peters, M.E., et al.: Deep contextualized word representations. arXiv preprint arXiv:1802.05365 (2018)
32. Pyysalo, S., Ananiadou, S.: Anatomical entity mention recognition at literature scale. Bioinformatics **30**(6), 868–875 (2014)
33. Pyysalo, S.: Overview of the cancer genetics and pathway curation tasks of BioNLP shared task 2013. BMC Bioinformatics **16**(S10), S2 (2015)
34. Ratinov, L., Roth, D.: Design challenges and misconceptions in named entity recognition. In: Proceedings of the Thirteenth Conference on Computational Natural Language Learning (CoNLL 2009), pp. 147–155 (2009)
35. Savova, G.K., et al.: Mayo clinical Text Analysis and Knowledge Extraction System (cTAKES): architecture, component evaluation and applications. J. Am. Med. Inform. Assoc. **17**(5), 507–513 (2010)
36. Smith, L.N.: A disciplined approach to neural network hyper-parameters: Part 1-learning rate, batch size, momentum, and weight decay. arXiv preprint arXiv:1803.09820 (2018)
37. Tzitzivacos, D.: International classification of diseases 10th edition (ICD-10): main article. CME Your SA J. CPD **25**(1), 8–10 (2007)
38. Uzuner, Ö., Luo, Y., Szolovits, P.: Evaluating the state-of-the-art in automatic de-identification. J. Am. Med. Inform. Assoc. **14**(5), 550–563 (2007)
39. Uzuner, Ö., South, B.R., Shen, S., DuVall, S.L.: 2010 i2b2/VA challenge on concepts, assertions, and relations in clinical text. J. Am. Med. Inform. Assoc. **18**(5), 552–556 (2011)
40. Wang, X., et al.: Cross-type biomedical named entity recognition with deep multi-task learning. Bioinformatics **35**(10), 1745–1752 (2019)
41. Wu, Y., Jiang, M., Xu, J., Zhi, D., Xu, H.: Clinical named entity recognition using deep learning models. In: AMIA Annual Symposium Proceedings, vol. 2017, p. 1812. American Medical Informatics Association (2017)
42. Yadav, V., Bethard, S.: A survey on recent advances in named entity recognition from deep learning models. arXiv preprint arXiv:1910.11470 (2019)
43. Zaremba, W., Sutskever, I., Vinyals, O.: Recurrent neural network regularization. arXiv preprint arXiv:1409.2329 (2014)
44. Zhang, Y., Zhang, Y., Qi, P., Manning, C.D., Langlotz, C.P.: Biomedical and clinical English model packages in the Stanza Python NLP library. arXiv preprint arXiv:2007.14640 (2020)

PyraD-DCNN: A Fully Convolutional Neural Network to Replace BLSTM in Offline Text Recognition Systems

Jonathan Jouanne, Quentin Dauchy, and Ahmad Montaser Awal[✉]

Research Departement, ARIADNEXT, Rennes, France
`montaser.awal@ariadnext.com`

Abstract. We present in this paper a fast and efficient multi-task fully convolutional neural network (FCNN). The proposed architecture uses a multi-resolution Pyramid of Densely connected Dilated Convolution (PyraD-DCNN). Our design also implements optimized convolutional building blocks that enable large dimensional representation with a low computational cost. Besides its ability to perform semantic image segmentation by itself as an auto-encoder, it may also be coupled with a signal encoder to build an end-to-end signal-to-sequence system without the help of recurrent layers (RNN). In the current work, we present the PyraD-DCNN through an application on Optical Character Recognition task and how it holds the comparison with Bidirectional Long Short-Term Memory (BLSTM) RNN. The pyramid-like structure using dilated kernels provides short and long term context management without recurrence. Thus we managed to improve inference time on CPU up to three times faster on our own datasets compared to a classical CNN-LSTM, with slight accuracy improvements in addition to faster training cycles (up to 24 times faster). Furthermore, the lightness of this structure makes it naturally adapted to mobile applications without any accuracy loss.

Keywords: OCR · FCNN · Dilated convolutions · Multi-resolution pyramid · RNN · Deep learning

1 Introduction

Offline text recognition consists in transcribing printed or handwritten text lines into a string. It is a challenging task due to the high variability of writing styles and backgrounds. The systems that provide state-of-the-art performance on those tasks are usually hybrid neural networks built as a stack of two systems: an optical features extractor, based on convolutional layers (CNN), and a sequence modelling part, based on recurrent neural networks (RNN) that produces a sequence of characters probabilities, interpreted by a Connectionist Temporal Classification heuristic [10]. Grounded on the analogy between the time

This work was realized within MOBILAI Project.

A. Del Bimbo et al. (Eds.): ICPR 2020 Workshops, LNCS 12661, pp. 647–661, 2021.
https://doi.org/10.1007/978-3-030-68763-2_49

axis and the reading axis of text lines, the RNN models have led to great accuracy improvements [11, 12] with the trade-off that they are not easily parallelizable.

In order to design OCR models for embedded systems, such as smartphones, neural networks need to be minimized in terms of weights and computational cost. For this specific context, traditional CNN-BLSTM seems inappropriate as each BLSTM neuron has the same cost as 4 dense neurons and the recurrence means sequential computing through the text-line axis. These constraints have consequently motivated research to get rid of RNN by replacing them with CNN.

A simple straight CNN could be a trivial solution to get rid of recurrence layers to manage short strings of characters as a multi-class classification problem. A first approach consists in providing the network with as many outputs as the longest string it may encounter [9]. While providing a straight and efficient way to build OCR system, it does not scale well to larger contexts as it requires to train specific weights for each output. A generalization of this approach consists in building a CNN with variable length outputs through a sliding shared output layer. Given an estimated or known number of characters to recognize, the system squeeze the input image so that the reduction operators in the OCR produce the expected number of outputs [16, 18]. The downside of this solution is its need to build a second system: the estimator of the sequence length.

Gated Convolutional Neural Networks (GCNN) based models [2] replicate the attention mechanism observed in LSTMs [3]. Attention heat-maps are generated through convolutions and help the network to focus on the right features at the right moment. The GCNN has shown good ability to provide the attention mechanism when used in the optical features extraction part, but failed to convince when implemented without any RNN layers as output layers[6].

On the other hand, Recurrent Convolutional Neural Networks (RCNN) implement a recurrence mechanism by sharing weights among a batch of stacked convolutional layers, thus these convolutional layers get their own outputs as inputs. The recurrence depth is consequently limited by the depth of the network itself instead of the input length. Such convolutional layers are called Recurrent Convolution Layers (RCL)[14].

Mixed together, GCNN and RCNN give the GRCNN [19]. The attention modelling provided by GCNN allows a more intelligent management of recursive connections in the RCL by filtering non pertinent contextual features. It has been designed as an analogue to the Gated Recurrent Units (GRU) which are themselves a simplification of the LSTM layers. Unfortunately, the GRCNN presented by Wang and Hu [19] still use BLSTM layers for sequence modelling and so convey the same disadvantages.

Breaking with the aforementioned designs, our model implements a Pyramid of Densely connected Dilated Convolutional Neural Network (PyraD-DCNN) as the sequence modeller instead of recurrent layers. This design aims to replicate the ability of LSTM layers to manage long and short term spatial dependencies while minimizing the footprint of the sequence modeling. An ablation study is conducted to validate our design choices compared a similar shaped CNN-LSTM as a benchmark. It has been shown that: a) dilated convolutions provide long term dependencies, demonstrated empirically by large accuracy improvements; b) skip connections are required to train an architecture this deep and perform better than residual connections; c) combining a downscale and an upscale cascade of dilated convolutions performs better than any other combination.

The paper is organized as follows. In Sect. 2 we present related works from other fields that mostly inspired this work. Section 3 details the main architectural principles that guided the design of the PyraD-DCNN and its full specification. Section 4 exposes the experiments held to validate our design choices, and Sect. 5 compiles the results. Finally, Sect. 6 concludes this paper.

2   Related Work

Optical Character Recognition (OCR) of text lines is the task of transcribing an input image into a string of characters. It is at the crossroad between pure 2D signal processing such as image semantic segmentation, and sequence processing such as language modelisation. Recent works in both fields shared a common denominator: the use of dilated convolution neural networks (DCNN).

Semantic image segmentation consists in labelling images at the pixel level, it requires large contextual information and precise generative layers to precisely identify objects in natural scenes. It is in this context that DCNN have been first introduced as a mean to expand observational windows on the convolutions while keeping a high resolution on the processed features [20]. Its high versatility allowed it to be used in broader applications and with wide variations such as: the aggregated multicolumn DCNN in [7] for counting objects in real scenes, where convolutions with various dilation factor are stacked in parallel branches to analyze the features on multiple scales at once; the 3D Dilated Multi Fiber Network for real-time brain tumor segmentation [5], it takes the same approach of parallelization on two levels: the 3D dilated convolutions are mounted in parallel in blocks which are nested in parallel "fibers"; or more closely to the OCR field of research, the text detection system in [17] where a stack of dilated convolutions provides a precise heatmap of handwritten text line locations in a scanned document.

In Sequence Processing, DCNN have also been widely used, as for modelling DNA sequence in [13], here convolutions are applied on the sequence axis, which make them be 1D-DCNN layers. As well as for text classification in [15], dilated convolutions has shown good ability to manage very large sequences. To further demonstrate its effectiveness, a generic evaluation of DCNN for sequence modelling is proposed in [1], they propose a residual dilated convolution block for time series management and evaluate it on a large range of tasks with success.

Inspired by both fields we also found great insights in [8] on how to properly manage dilated networks to build a coherent multiresolution approach. Their work on cellular automaton demonstrated the need of progressive merge layers when building a pyramid of dilated networks to avoid non-desired artifacts produced by the inherent dilations subsampling.

Finally, a similar approach to ours but in Voice Activity Detection [4] uses Gated Residual Dilated Convolutions instead of our Densely connected Dilated

Convolutions or in the self-supervised dense DCNN for image despeckling in [21], which follows a very similar design. The main difference relies on the use of skip connections and bottlenecks layers, there they are used to reconstruct a significant depth of abstractions from reduced inputs, whereas here the bottlenecks are used to reduce the outputs of the densely connected stack of DCNN.

3   PyraD-DCNN Model

3.1   Design Principles

Dilated Convolutions. Sequence modeling is generally processed with the use of LSTM recurrent networks. Such artificial networks provide Long and Short Term context management through recurrent connections and memory gates, see Fig. 1a. On the other hand, convolutions naturally work with forward and backward context but are limited by the size of their kernels (also called vanilla convolutional layers) (Fig. 1b). The introduction of dilated kernels in convolutional layers (also called atrous convolutions) allowed processing of very large windows with relatively shallow stacks of convolutional layers (Fig. 1c).

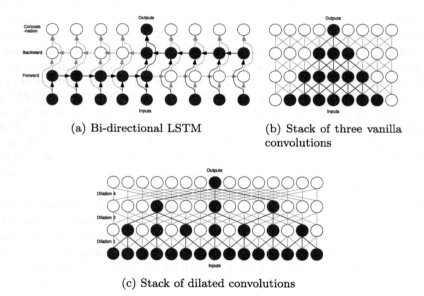

(a) Bi-directional LSTM

(b) Stack of three vanilla convolutions

(c) Stack of dilated convolutions

Fig. 1. A graphical comparison of BLSTM, CNN an DCNN fieldviews' width.

The receptive field of dilated 1D-convolution stack can be computed by:

$$R = 1 + \sum_{i=0}^{n}(k_i - 1) * d_i$$

with n the number of layers, d_i and k_i respectively the dilation factor and the width of the kernel applied at the i_{th} layer. It is easily generalizable to 2D or 3D kernels by elevating the result R to its square R^2 or cube R^3. In our case, the kernel is 1D of width 3, which gives the simplified formula of:

$$R' = 1 + 2 * \sum_{i=0}^{n} d_i$$

Multi-Resolution Pyramid with Dilated Networks. A dilated kernel is equivalent to a vanilla kernel enlarged with 0-value spacing between the weights. It can also be seen as the application of dense convolutional kernels on every subset of features that a pooling operator would give from a feature map when sliding the starting point, the different colored nodes highlight this effect in Fig. 2. Hence, the neighbouring outputs of a dilated networks are decorrelated as they are produced from different sets of pooled features. This particular aspect has been demonstrated to produce non-desired artifacts and has been solved with the use of fusion layers [8].

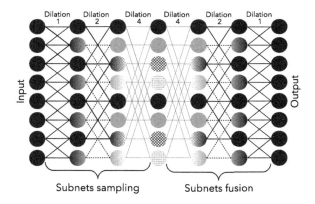

Fig. 2. Sub-networks in a multi-resolution pyramid

Similarly to [8], we designed our multi-resolution pyramid of dilated convolutions to be symmetrical. Thus we stack dilated convolutions in increasing order of dilation (1-2-4), then in decreasing order (4-2-1) for them to operate smooth fusion of the highly dilated features produced in the first half. We expect this design to help produce accurate and robust features by making the best use of the DCNN.

Skip Connections. Skip connections consist in forwarding the concatenation of the input and the output of a layer, see Fig. 3. It allows the following layers to work with both features which represent different level of abstraction or different widths of visual field. Such networks are said to be densely connected.

Without skip connections our pyramid of dilated convolutions is forced to manage larger and larger observational windows. On the other hand making the pyramid densely connected allows it to compose features using the different upstream steps of dilation. We hypothesize that it helps to manage both short and long term dependencies, the core ability of LSTM-RNN.

Bottlenecks. The counterpart of using skip connections is that it incrementally increases the number of channels as we stack skipped layers of artificial neurons. The growing number of features may cause the network to require an unaffordable number of weights. To address this matter, dilated convolutions blocks are built as follows: a) a 1×1 convolutional layer (*Pointwise*) operates as a bottleneck on the input features by reducing the number of channels to a fixed number, the *conv_depth*; b) a 1×3 dilated channelwise convolutional that produces the spatial analysis of the signal, here a row; c) a ReLU layer as activation; and d) a dropout layer. Figure 3 presents the Dilated Convolutional Block (*DCB*).

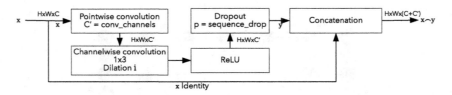

Fig. 3. A skipped optimized Dilated Convolution Block with dilation i (*DCB-i*)

To furtherly limit the channels expansion, bottlenecks are also introduced in the middle and at the end of the multi-resolution pyramid. These layers compress the features down to a fixed number of channels, the *feature_depth*.

3.2 Overall Architecture

This section details the overall architecture of the PyraD-DCNN, which is composed of: 1) an Optical Feature Extractor that produces a vector of features out of two-dimensional image; 2) a Sequence Modeller network that transcribes optical features into character probabilities; and 3) a Connectionist Temporal Classifier for character alignment.

Optical Feature Extractor. Two Vanilla convolution layers are used with 3×3 kernels, each followed by a MaxPooling layer of kernel and stride 2×2 to reduce height and width dimensions by a factor of 4. LReLU activation with an *alpha* parameter set to 0.3, batch normalization and dropout are also applied at the output of each convolution. The dropout rate has been searched empirically to give best accuracy with the proposed PyraD-DCNN architecture. Finally, the features are reshaped so that height dimensions are merged into channels dimension which are then reduced to match the *feature_depth* using a *Bottleneck* layer, see Sect. 3.1 (Table 1).

Table 1. Details of the optical feature extractor

Layer	Hyper-parameter
Convolution 3×3	$channels = 32$
MaxPool 2×2	
LReLU	$alpha = 0.3$
DropOut	$probability = 0.05$
BatchNorm	
Convolution 3×3	$channels = 64$
MaxPool 2×2	
LReLU	$alpha = 0.3$
DropOut	$probability = 0.05$
BatchNorm	
Reshape merge channels with height	
Bottleneck Convolution 1×1	$channels = feature\_depth$
ReLU	

PyraD-DCNN Sequence Modeler. Following our design principles, the multi-resolution pyramid is built symmetrically using three dilation stages with two Dilated Convolution Blocks (DCB-i, see Fig. 1c) at each. Thus, the receptive field at the end of the pyramid covers up to 57 optical features, which, as the OFE reduces input dimensions by a factor of 4, gives an observational window over 200 pixels wide. This may represent up to 25 characters in our datasets. The full architecture of the PyraD-DCNN module is observable in Fig. 5.

CTC. As the last layer, a Connectionist Temporal Classification (CTC) method is used to interpret the output per-frame predictions and compute a loss that bridges the spatially aligned prediction to its dense label sequence.

4   Experiments

4.1   Data

Text field images from various European identity documents are extracted to compose two data-sets, Small-ID and Big-ID. Six main categories of fields are considered: dates (in the DD MM YYYY format), document numbers (composed of letters and digits mixed together), names (usually in capital characters with diacritics), genders (single letter F or M), nationalities (a 2 or 3 letter code) and addresses (a mix of digits, letters and punctuation), see Fig. 4. Each data-set is split as follows: 60% for training, 20% for validation and the last 20% for evaluation. No data augmentation has been used in this work.

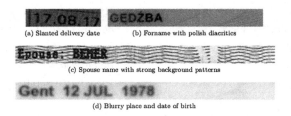

(a) Slanted delivery date   (b) Forname with polish diacritics

(c) Spouse name with strong background patterns

(d) Blurry place and date of birth

Fig. 4. Examples of challenging text sequences found in the dataset

Both perfect match rate (*accuracy*) and character error rate (*CER*) are considered. The trained model from the training epoch that produces the best *accuracy* on the validation set is kept and then evaluated on the test set.

A Small Data Set (Small-ID) is created from Portuguese and Spanish documents. Eight accented letters and four punctuation characters are considered, for a total of fifty classes including digits and blank space. Totaling 40 000 samples, this data-set is a good candidate for rapid comparison of various architectures as it is easy to fit and fast to train.

A Big Data Set (Big-ID) is composed of 600,000 images of text fields from Belgium, French, German, Polish, Portuguese, Romanian and Spanish documents. It is used for advanced comparison of the PyraD-DCNN against its benchmark competitors. It has 115 different characters to classify and a much larger variability in field formats, fonts and backgrounds.

4.2   Implementation Details

The architecture described in Sect. 3.2 is used. The input images are gray-scale, resized to 32 pixels in height, and padded to 800 pixels in width. The output features have 144 frames with depth related to the dataset characters dictionary. The batch size is set to 16 and the training is stopped at the 50th epoch. At each epoch the network is tested against the validation set, the best of them in term of *accuracy* is then evaluated on a test set to get the final scores.

Dropout in the Optical Feature Extractor is set to 0.5 and in the Sequence Modeler to 0.2. We use the SGD algorithm to regress the loss. Learning rate evolves between a minimum value of 0.0001 and a maximum of 0.01 using a periodic triangular profile.

4.3   Ablation Study

To validate the design choices of our PyraD-DCNN we explore different families of derived architectures for the sequence modeling part. All of them share the same Optical Feature Extractor (OFE, Sect. 3.2) and have the same output layer, the stepwise dense layer, that provides output character probabilities. The different architectures of sequence modeler are represented in Fig. 5 and 6.

Benchmark is provided by a BLSTM network using a stack of two BLSTM layers with 128 neurons each way to provide Sequence Modeling.

Pyramid Height is chosen through comparison to shallower and deeper networks. The ShallowPyraD-DCNN implements dilated convolutions up to a factor of 2 while the DeepPyraD-DCNN increases dilation to 8.

Variable Dilation Factor in convolutions is tested against a flat model that only has standard convolutional kernels (1-Flat-DCNN), another flat model with dilated convolutions by a factor of 2 (2-Flat-DCNN), and one last model with dilated factor of 4 (4-Flat-DCNN), as shown in Fig. 5. All of these models have exactly the same number of weights as our PyraD-DCNN and the same bottleneck pointwise convolutions.

Up-Down Architecture of the stacked dilated convolutions is compared to different approaches: a) a simple up-way stack of dilated convolutions (Up-DCNN); b) its inverse, a down-way pyramid (Down-DCNN); c) a doubled up-way stack of dilated convolutions with a bottleneck in between (UpUp-DCNN); d) again the reverse is also evaluated (DownDown-DCNN); e) and finally a reverse pyramid of stacked dilated convolutions (DownUp-DCNN) is also considered.

Bottleneck Pointwise Convolutions' positions and amounts are validated against three PyraD-DCNN derived models: a) one with none of them (Free PyraD-DCNN); b) another one with a bottleneck after each pair of convolutional blocks that share the same dilation factor (Block PyraD-DCNN); c) and one with a bottleneck after each skip connections (Full PyraD-DCNN). All the introduced bottlenecks squeeze the features to the same number of channels.

Skip connections in the PyraD-DCNN are compared to a straight stack of dilated convolutions (Straight-DCNN) and an equivalent network using residual connections (PyraR-DCNN). Both of these last two networks do not implement bottleneck pointwise convolutions, as they are not required to avoid channels' depth over-growth.

5   Results

5.1   Experiment on Small-ID

In Sect. 4.3 we proposed evaluating a set of different networks to validate our design choices. They all have been evaluated on the Small-ID dataset with a limited number of neurons. The *feature_depth* is set to 64 and the *channels_depth*

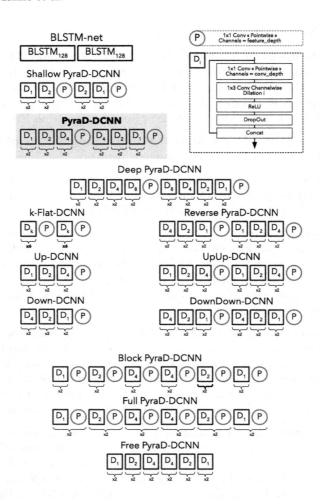

Fig. 5. Architectures of the different PyraD-DCNN based sequence modellers

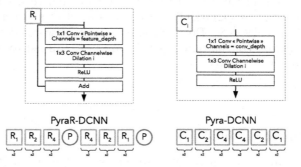

Fig. 6. Architectures of PyraR-DCNN and the Pyra-DCNN sequence modellers.

to 32. With 50 different characters to learn, the networks have to deal with low representativeness margins. In these conditions, the differences between the models are accentuated.

The results obtained on SmallID shown in Table 2 lead to several observations:

1. training time is greatly reduced on GPU using fully convolutional networks such as the PyraD-DCNN compared to classical BLSTM-RNN;
2. PyraD-DCNN achieves competitive scores on accuracy and CER while dividing inference time by three on CPU;
3. dilation depth, from the Shallow to the Deep PyraD-DCNN has a positive impact on the results but increases the number of weights and, slightly, the computation cost;
4. Flat designs, especially with dilated kernels (2-Flat-DCNN and 4-Flat-DCNN), failed to reach good performance which confirms the need to use different levels of dilation;
5. the use of skip or residual connections is confirmed to be an improvement above standard *Pyra-DCNN*;
6. while UpUp and DownDown DCNN seem to be possible alternatives to PyraD-DCNN, the Down-Up failed to achieve good performances.

This first experiment has shown that the use of densely connected dilated convolutional layers is competitive in terms of training and inference time compared to RNN while maintaining comparable accuracy on the OCR task. Still, the legitimity of the PyraD-DCNN specifically is not fully established, which is why we proceeded to another experiment on a larger dataset: the Big-ID.

5.2 Experiment on Big-ID

For the Big-ID experiment, $features\_depth$ and $channels\_depth$ have been doubled up to 128 and 64 respectively, as this task is expected to be harder (the networks now have to learn 115 characters). Furthermore, with 15 times more samples the models have much more time to converge. This tougher task has been chosen to break the tie between the best candidates given by Small-ID.

This time the training of the BLSTM network has been early-stopped due to over-time. The results given in Table 3 show that: 1) on large datasets the training time of BLSTM-RNN is prohibitive compared to FCNN; 2) enlarging the network to enable more complex tasks had a lower impact on CPU inference time for the DCNN networks than for the RNN; and 3) the Up-Down design of the PyraD-DCNN is superior to others excepted the UpUp and DownDown.

5.3 Discussion

While Up-Down design of the PyraD-DCNN has not been proved to be obviously superior to others approaches such as Up-Up architecture, it has the benefit to be closely related to auto-encoder like the U-Net, where the symmetry between

Table 2. Results of experiment on Small-ID

Model	Accuracy (%)	CER	Inference time on CPU (in ms/U)	Number of weights (×1000)	Training time on GPU
PyraD-DCNN	*97.3*	*0.39*	*11*	*144*	*41 min*
LSTM-64	***97.4***	***0.36***	*30*	*120*	*16 h*
Deep PyraD-DCNN	**97.6**	**0.36**	12	187	46 min
Shallow PyraD-DCNN	97.0	0.44	11	109	38 min
PyraR-DCNN	97.1	0.43	11	106	48 min
Pyra-DCNN	92.0	1,11	11	106	1 hour
1-Flat-DCNN	97.0	0.44	11	144	55 min
2-Flat-DCNN	96.4	0.55	11	144	36 min
4-Flat-DCNN	94.2	0.64	11	144	35 min
Free PyraD-DCNN	97.0	0.42	11	177	42 min
Block PyraD-DCNN	97.3	0.39	11	136	43 min
Full PyraD-DCNN	97.0	0.41	12	154	46 min
Reverse PyraD-DCNN	96.7	0.45	11	144	42 min
Up-DCNN	96.8	0.46	11	99	33 min
UpUp-DCNN	97.2	0.41	11	144	42 min
Down-DCNN	96.8	0.46	11	99	33 min
DownDown-DCNN	**97.5**	**0.36**	11	144	42 min

Table 3. Results of experiment on Big-ID. *The BLSTM network has been stopped after 10 epochs and 50 h of training.

Model	Accuracy (%)	CER	Inference time (in ms on CPU)	Number of weights (×1000)	Training time on GPU
PyraD-DCNN	***94.65***	***0.81***	*13*	*454*	*13 h 20*
LSTM-128	*94.20*	*0.84*	*44*	*360*	*50 h**
Deep PyraD-DCNN	**94.99**	**0.74**	14	627	14 h 50 m
Shallow PyraD-DCNN	93.97	0.91	12	109	12 h 10 m
PyraR-DCNN	92.83	1.11	13	300	16 h 20 m
1-Flat-DCNN	93.68.0	0.97	13	454	20 h 30 m
Block PyraD-DCNN	93.82	0.95	12	421	13 h 30 m
UpUp-DCNN	94.51	0.82	13	454	13 h 40 m
DownDown-DCNN	94.37	0.85	13	454	13 h 20 m

down-sampling and up-sampling is one of the core design principles. Thus, this network is also compatible with other tasks such as described in Sect. 2 using 1D to 3D dilated convolutional layers.

To give an example we conducted an experiment on document localization using a PyraD-DCNN with 2D kernels. It is trained to locate the borders of a document as well as inner segments that should help identifying vanishing points and out of field borders. Has shown on Fig. 7 the network achieves to produce quite good but perfectible results on the task, which tends to support that our design is effectively an auto-encoder that can be used as a sequence modeller.

Fig. 7. Examples of results obtained on document localization using a PyraD- DCNN

6   Conclusion

In this paper, we have shown that using a dilated convolutions based auto-encoder network: the PyraD-DCNN, it is possible to replace traditional BLSTM-RNN layers in some OCR systems. The proposed architecture is easy to tune by expanding the layers width or adding dilation steps thus making it a versatile network. Using only convolutional layers allows for much shorter training time to get to comparable, if not better, results than with RNN. Furthermore, it is also lightweight and more computational efficient on CPU which opens opportunities for mobile applications. Finally, we can notice that the network can be applied to a wide range of fields using 2D or even 3D kernels such as for end-to-end scene text detection and recognition, sound processing or video processing. Future works may be focused on evaluating the PyraD-DCNN design on public datasets such as RIMES or IAM datasets for handwritten text recognition to settle a stronger benchmark.

References

1. Bai, S., Kolter, J.Z., Koltun, V.: An empirical evaluation of generic convolutional and recurrent networks for sequence modeling (2018)
2. Bluche, T., Messina, R.: Gated convolutional recurrent neural networks for multilingual handwriting recognition. In: 2017 14th IAPR International Conference on Document Analysis and Recognition (ICDAR), vol. 01, pp. 646–651, November 2017. https://doi.org/10.1109/ICDAR.2017.111
3. Bluche, T., Louradour, J., Messina, R.O.: Scan, attend and read: end-to-end handwritten paragraph recognition with MDLSTM attention. CoRR abs/1604.03286 (2016). http://arxiv.org/abs/1604.03286
4. Chang, S.Y., et al.: Temporal modeling using dilated convolution and gating for voice-activity-detection. In: 2018 IEEE International Conference on Acoustics, Speech and Signal Processing (ICASSP), pp. 5549–5553. IEEE (2018)
5. Chen, C., Liu, X., Ding, M., Zheng, J., Li, J.: 3D dilated multi-fiber network for real-time brain tumor segmentation in MRI. In: Shen, D., et al. (eds.) MICCAI 2019. LNCS, vol. 11766, pp. 184–192. Springer, Cham (2019). https://doi.org/10.1007/978-3-030-32248-9_21
6. Coquenet, D., Soullard, Y., Chatelain, C., Paquet, T.: Have convolutions already made recurrence obsolete for unconstrained handwritten text recognition? In: 2019 International Conference on Document Analysis and Recognition Workshops (ICDARW), pp. 65–70. IEEE, Sydney, September 2019. https://doi.org/10.1109/ICDARW.2019.40083, https://hal.archives-ouvertes.fr/hal-02420313
7. Deb, D., Ventura, J.: An aggregated multicolumn dilated convolution network for perspective-free counting. CoRR abs/1804.07821 (2018). http://arxiv.org/abs/1804.07821
8. Devillard, F., Heit, B.: Multi-scale filters implemented by cellular automaton for retinal layers modelling. Int. J. Parallel Emergent Distrib. Syst., 1–24 (2018). https://doi.org/10.1080/17445760.2018.1495206
9. Goodfellow, I.J., Bulatov, Y., Ibarz, J., Arnoud, S., Shet, V.: Multi-digit number recognition from street view imagery using deep convolutional neural networks (2013)
10. Graves, A., Fernández, S., Gomez, F.J., Schmidhuber, J.: Connectionist temporal classification: labelling unsegmented sequence data with recurrent neural networks. In: ICML 2006 (2006)
11. Graves, A., Schmidhuber, J.: Offline handwriting recognition with multidimensional recurrent neural networks. In: Koller, D., Schuurmans, D., Bengio, Y., Bottou, L. (eds.) Advances in Neural Information Processing Systems 21, pp. 545–552. Curran Associates, Inc. (2009). http://papers.nips.cc/paper/3449-offline-handwriting-recognition-with-multidimensional-recurrent-neural-networks.pdf
12. Grosicki, E., El Abed, H.: ICDAR 2009 handwriting recognition competition. In: 2009 10th International Conference on Document Analysis and Recognition, pp. 1398–1402. IEEE (2009)
13. Gupta, A., Rush, A.M.: Dilated convolutions for modeling long-distance genomic dependencies (2017)
14. Liang, M., Hu, X.: Recurrent convolutional neural network for object recognition. In: The IEEE Conference on Computer Vision and Pattern Recognition (CVPR), June 2015
15. Lin, J., Su, Q., Yang, P., Ma, S., Sun, X.: Semantic-unit-based dilated convolution for multi-label text classification. CoRR abs/1808.08561 (2018). http://arxiv.org/abs/1808.08561

16. Ptucha, R., Such, F.P., Pillai, S., Brockler, F., Singh, V., Hutkowski, P.: Intelligent character recognition using fully convolutional neural networks. Pattern Recogn. **88**, 604–613 (2019)
17. Renton, G., Soullard, Y., Chatelain, C., Adam, S., Kermorvant, C., Paquet, T.: Fully convolutional network with dilated convolutions for handwritten text line segmentation. Int. J. Doc. Anal. Recogn. (IJDAR) **21**(3), 177–186 (2018). https://doi.org/10.1007/s10032-018-0304-3
18. Such, F.P., Peri, D., Brockler, F., Paul, H., Ptucha, R.: Fully convolutional networks for handwriting recognition. In: 2018 16th International Conference on Frontiers in Handwriting Recognition (ICFHR), pp. 86–91. IEEE (2018)
19. Wang, J., Hu, X.: Gated recurrent convolution neural network for OCR. In: Guyon, I., et al. (eds.) Advances in Neural Information Processing Systems 30, pp. 335–344. Curran Associates, Inc. (2017). http://papers.nips.cc/paper/6637-gated-recurrent-convolution-neural-network-for-ocr.pdf
20. Yu, F., Koltun, V.: Multi-scale context aggregation by dilated convolutions (2015)
21. Yuan, Y., Guan, J., Sun, J.: Blind SAR image despeckling using self-supervised dense dilated convolutional neural network (2019)

Learning Sparse Filters in Deep Convolutional Neural Networks with a l_1/l_2 Pseudo-Norm

Anthony Berthelier[1]([✉])(iD), Yongzhe Yan[1](iD), Thierry Chateau[1](iD),
Christophe Blanc[1], Stefan Duffner[2](iD), and Christophe Garcia[2](iD)

[1] Universite Clermont Auvergne, Institut Pascal, Clermont-Ferrand, France
anthony.berthelier@etu.uca.fr
[2] INSA Lyon, LIRIS, Lyon, France

Abstract. While deep neural networks (DNNs) have proven to be efficient for numerous tasks, they come at a high memory and computation cost, thus making them impractical on resource-limited devices. However, these networks are known to contain a large number of parameters. Recent research has shown that their structure can be more compact without compromising their performance.

In this paper, we present a sparsity-inducing regularization term based on the ratio l_1/l_2 pseudo-norm defined on the filter coefficients. By defining this pseudo-norm appropriately for the different filter kernels, and removing irrelevant filters, the number of kernels in each layer can be drastically reduced leading to very compact Deep Convolutional Neural Networks (DCNN) structures. Unlike numerous existing methods, our approach does not require an iterative retraining process and, using this regularization term, directly produces a sparse model during the training process. Furthermore, our approach is also much easier and simpler to implement than existing methods. Experimental results on MNIST and CIFAR-10 show that our approach significantly reduces the number of filters of classical models such as *LeNet* and *VGG* while reaching the same or even better accuracy than the baseline models. Moreover, the trade-off between the sparsity and the accuracy is compared to other loss regularization terms based on the $l1$ or $l2$ norm as well as the SSL [1], NISP [2] and GAL [3] methods and shows that our approach is outperforming them.

Keywords: Deep learning · Compression · Neural networks · Architecture

1 Introduction

Since the advent of *Deep Neural Networks* (DNNs) and especially *Deep Convolutional Neural Networks* (DCNNs) and their massively parallelized implementations [4,5], deep learning based methods have achieved state-of-the-art

This work has been sponsored by the Auvergne Regional Council and the European funds of regional development (FEDER).

© Springer Nature Switzerland AG 2021
A. Del Bimbo et al. (Eds.): ICPR 2020 Workshops, LNCS 12661, pp. 662–676, 2021.
https://doi.org/10.1007/978-3-030-68763-2_50

performance in numerous visual tasks such as face recognition, semantic segmentation, object classification and detection, etc. [4,6–9]. Accompanied with the high performance, also high computation capabilities and large memory resources are needed as these models usually contain millions of parameters. These issues prevent them from running on resource-limited devices such as smartphones or embedded devices. Network compression is a common approach in this context, i.e. to reduce the inherent redundancy in the parameters and thus in the computation.

Numerous methods have been developed to obtain compact DNNs. Since a large number of these networks are built upon convolutional layers and since the convolution operations are the most computationally demanding, we are focusing on the reduction of these layers. A simple reduction strategy consists in removing non-relevant filters using pruning methods. For example, Li *et al.* [10] proposed to remove filters that are identified as having a small effect on the output accuracy. Another approach by Luo *et al.* [11] is evaluating information at the filter level using statistical and optimization methods.

Our approach is motivated and inspired by (1) previous works demonstrating the redundancy among the weights of a DCNN [12]; (2) numerous sparsity methods proposed in the literature [13] and (3) the fact that these sparsity methods have rarely been used to remove unimportant weights during training [1]. We therefore propose a new strategy, based on l_1/l_2-norm, to obtain a subset of kernels with all weights equal to zero (such as that the associated filters can be removed). The main idea is to express the filter reduction problem by introducing sparsity on a set of pseudo-norms computed on each kernel but not directly on the kernels actual values. Figure 1 illustrates the general idea of our method. Each kernel of the network is transformed to a single value using a pseudo-norm. All these values are concatenated into a global vector (its size being the number of filters) called kernel norm vector. Our global kernel-sparsity is defined by the sparsity on this vector and is estimated by a l_1/l_2-norm ratio. Since a kernel with all weights equal to zero produces a pseudo-norm of zero, the number of filters can be reduced by enforcing sparsity on the kernel norm vector. In this paper, we propose the l_1/l_2-norm for two reasons: (1) the so-called l_1/l_2-norm is a simple group norm to implement and (2) the use of the l_1-norm can increase the performance, interpretability and sparsity of a model [14–16] combined with the l_2-norm allows to converge to stable solution and maintain sparsity at a good level.

We propose a l_1/l_2-norm computed on the global vector (vector of kernel pseudo-norms) such that adding this sparsity term to minimize to the global loss will reduce the number of (non-zero) filters of a DCNN. Compared to other approaches, our method presents several advantages:

1. All steps are done during training, i.e. no additional fine-tuning operations are needed.
2. Our method being based on simple l_1 and l_2 norms, is straightforward to implement and compute compared to other methods that remove weights during training.

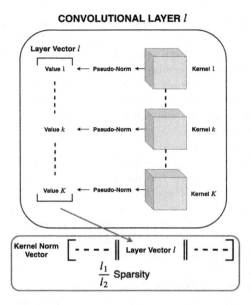

Fig. 1. Visual representation of our method and the computation of the kernel norm vector using a pseudo-norm.

3. As we are keeping track of the evolution of the network at every step during training, it is possible to choose the best model based on a trade-off between compression and accuracy.

In the following, we will first present existing work related to network pruning and weight sparsity, in Sect. 2. In Sect. 3, we describe our l_1/l_2 pseudo-norm method. Finally, in Sect. 4, we show experimental results of our method with *LeNet* and *VGG* network architectures trained on the MNIST and CIFAR-10 datasets. We demonstrate that our method is able to significantly improve the sparsity among convolutional layers in these DCNNs without significant drops in accuracy.

2   Related Work

Many studies have been done on DNN compression. Knowledge distillation [17,18] tackles the problem of transferring the encoded information from a bigger model into a smaller one. Lowering numerical precision is also an extensive field [19–21]. Many works, are focused on designing compressed and optimal models architectures. SqueezeNet [22] and MobileNets [23] both propose structures of convolutional layers to improve memory and computation time. Some Neural Architecture Search (NAS) [24–26] methods use reinforcement learning and genetic algorithms to search the best possible networks designs for a given task. Depending on the size of the search space, finding an optimized model with these methods can be enormously time-consuming. However, the most promising approaches try to reduce the model redundancy and among them: parameter quantization [27,28] and network pruning [10,11,29–31]. Our method can be classified in this last category.

2.1 Network Pruning

Pruning methods are aiming to remove unimportant parameters of a neural network. Han *et al.* [27,29] proposed to prune parameters of *AlexNet* and *VGG* with connection pruning by setting a threshold and removing any parameters under it. As opposed to our method, most of the reduction is done on fully connected layers and not on convolutional layers. However, compression of convolutional layers is essential nowadays as new DNNs are mostly DCNNs with fewer fully connected layers *e.g.,* only 3.99% parameters of *Resnet* [9]. Closer to our approach, structured pruning methods are removing directly structured parts e.g., kernels or layers, to compress CNNs. Li *et al.* [10] used l_1-norm to remove filters. He *et al.* [32] used a LASSO regression based channel selection to prune filters. Channel pruning methods are preferred on widely-used DCNNs. For example, the selection of unimportant feature maps can be done using l_1-regularization [33].

These past few years, numerous networks compression algorithms using pruning methods and achieving state-of-the-art results have emerged. Yu *et al.* [2] proposed a neurons importance score propagation (NISP) method based on the response of the final layers to evaluate the pruning impact of the prior layers. Zhuang *et al.* [34] developed discrimination-aware losses in order to determine the most useful channels in intermediate layers. Some methods such as Filter Pruning Via Geometric Median (FPGM) [35] are not focused on pruning filters with less importance but only by evaluating their redundancy. Similarly, Lin *et al.* [3] tackled the problem of redundant structures by proposing a generative adversarial learning method (GAL) (not only to remove filters, but also branches and blocks).

Still, standard pruning methods usually construct non structured and irregular connectivity in a network, leading to irregular memory access. In most of these approaches, the DNN is trained first. Then each parameter is evaluated to understand if it brings information to the network. If not, the parameter is removed. Therefore, a fine-tuning needs to be performed afterwards to restore the model accuracy. These steps take time. Most of them are done offline and need costly reiterations of decomposing and fine-tuning to find an optimal weight approximation maintaining high accuracy and high compression rate. Unlike these methods, our approach is able to directly increase the sparsity of the network during training, identifying which kernels to prune without any considerable extra computational overhead.

2.2 Weight Sparsity

An important factor for the compression of a model is its sparsity *i.e.* the number of parameters set to zero. However, this sparsity must be structured in order to be memory-efficient and time-efficient. Liu *et al.* [36] obtained a sparsity of 90% on *AlexNet* with only 2% accuracy loss using sparse decomposition and a sparse matrix multiplication algorithm. This method also employed group Lasso [37], an efficient regularization to learn sparse structures. It is also used by Wen *et al.* [1] to regularize the structure of a DNN at different levels (*i.e.* filters, channels, filter shapes and layer depth). This approach leads to DNNs with reduced computational cost and efficient acceleration due to the structured sparsity induced by the method. We propose to use a different type of regularization based on the norm ratio l_1/l_q [13,38]. It allows to dynamically maximize the sparsity of a model with one hyper-parameter (q) without additional iterations and severe drops in accuracy while being straightforward to implement.

3 Training with Kernel-Sparsity

We mainly focus on inducing sparsity on convolutional layers to regularize and compress the structure of DCNNs during the training steps. We propose a generic method to regularize DCNNs using the l_1/l_2 pseudo-norm.

3.1 Kernel-Sparsity Regularization

Let $\mathcal{N}$ be a DCNN with L convolutional layers. We define $W^{l,k}$ as the $k^{th} \in \{1,..N_k^l\}$ 3d-tensor (kernel) associated with the lth convolutional layer. Thus, a weight of kernel k in the convolutional layer l is defined as: and $W_{w,h,c}^{l,k} \in \mathbb{R}^{N_w^l, N_h^l, N_c^l}$ the (width, height, channel) weight of kernel k of layer l.

$$W_{w,h,c}^{l,k} \in \mathbb{R}^{N_w^l, N_h^l, N_c^l} \tag{1}$$

Here, $w \in \{1,..N_w^l\}$ is the column, $h \in \{1,..N_h^l\}$ is the row and $c \in \{1,..N_c^l\}$ is the channel index of the kth kernel matrix in the convolutional layer l. The key idea is to express sparsity on pseudo-norms of kernels. Let n_k^l be the pseudo-norm defined by the l_1-norm of the flattened kernel $W^{l,k}$:

$$n_k^l \doteq \sum_{w=1}^{N_w^l} \sum_{h=1}^{N_h^l} \sum_{c=1}^{N_c^l} \frac{|W_{w,h,c}^{l,k}|}{N_k^l} \tag{2}$$

The vector $\vec{N}^l$ concatenates, for layer l, the N_k^l norms n_k^l:

$$\vec{N}^l \doteq \mathop{\|}_{k=1}^{N_k^l} n_k^l \tag{3}$$

We introduce kernel-sparsity for a layer as a value linked to the number of kernels of this layer with all weights equal to zeros. Therefore, the kernel-sparsity of layer l can be linked with the number of values of the vector $\vec{N}^l$ equal to zero. Global kernel-sparsity can be expressed from the concatenation of vectors $\vec{N}^l$ for each layer:

$$\vec{N} \doteq \overset{L}{\underset{l=1}{\|}} \vec{N}^l \tag{4}$$

For better understanding, we visualize these operations in Fig. 2. In order to normalize the value of N, each of its component is divided by the number of values (or norms) that it contains. Finally, the global kernel-sparsity is defined by the sparsity of $\vec{N}$ and can be estimated by a l_1/l_2 ratio function:

$$\mathcal{L}_s \doteq \frac{\vec{N}_1}{\vec{N}_2} \tag{5}$$

Minimizing this term will encourage zero-valued coefficients (numerator), corresponding to the different kernels, while keeping the remaining coefficients at large values (denominator), thus producing convolution layers with few non-zero kernels.

3.2   Training with Kernel-Sparsity Regularization

Let $\mathcal{L}_\mathcal{N}$ be the loss function that is minimized to find the optimal weight configuration for a given task (e.g. cross entropy). We propose to simply add the kernel-sparsity regularization term weighted by the coefficient $\lambda \in \mathbb{R}$:

$$\mathcal{L}_{all} = \mathcal{L}_\mathcal{N} + \lambda \mathcal{L}_s . \tag{6}$$

We will discuss how to set an appropriate values of λ in the experimental section.

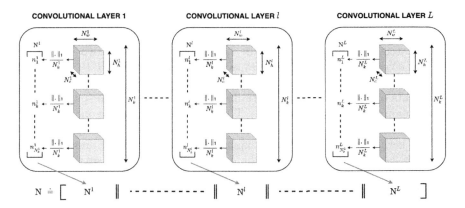

Fig. 2. Visualization of the computation of the kernels pseudo-norm and how the global kernel norm vector $\vec{N}$ is obtained.

3.3   Setting Kernels to Zero

Our method induces sparsity in a DCNN, i.e. the pseudo-norm regularization pushes some kernels to have only zero-valued coefficients. However, in practice, during optimization, the actual values of these kernels will not be exactly zero but very small. Thus, to compress the network effectively, our approach identifies these kernels during training and forces them to be zero in order to remove them.

More specifically, the algorithm works as follows: each pseudo-norm of the kernels is contained in the global kernel pseudo-norm vector $\vec{N}$. Thus, at each epoch, we normalize the values of $\vec{N}$ so that $\sum_{i=1}^{K} \vec{N}_i = 1$. Sorting these vectors in ascending order will allow us to objectively determine which pseudo-norms are the smallest. We then define a percentage (or a threshold) under which the cumulative sum of these sorted values is judged too small to be kept, i.e. the corresponding filters are considered unimportant and set to zero. Once the weights of a kernel are set to zero, they are keeping this value until the end of the training, and these parameters are no longer updated. This ensures that the potential errors and imprecision introduced by removing these kernels can be compensated by the remaining kernels during the training converging to a stable solution with high accuracy.

To summarize, our approach consists of two steps at each epoch:

1. The l_1/l_2 pseudo-norm is computed on each kernel of the model and is integrated to the loss function. Thus the training stage is minimizing the loss function and inducing sparsity at the kernel level, pushing some weights to have a near zero value.
2. Sort kernels according to their ascending normalized pseudo-norm and compute a cumulative sum vector from the sorted normalized pseudo-norm vector. The kernels participating to the cumulative sum under a threshold t are removed. This set of operations aims at keeping kernels that produce more than $t\%$ of the global norm.

4   Experiments

We evaluated the performance of the l_1/l_2 pseudo-norm on two classification models (*LeNet* and *VGG*) and two datasets: MNIST and CIFAR-10. Our method is implemented in *Pytorch*, running on various Nvidia GPUs using CUDA. The weights of the networks are initialized randomly and hyper-parameters are selected manually for optimal results. The chosen λ value is the one allowing the model to have an accuracy close to its baseline accuracy while sparsifying the most the kernels norms. In all the experiments, the threshold under which the kernels are removed by evaluating the cumulative sum of the smallest norms is set to 1%. We found that this value was the best trade-off between a converging accuracy of the models and a slow removal of the kernels during the training phase.

EPOCH	KERNELS	$\mathcal{L}_s$
0	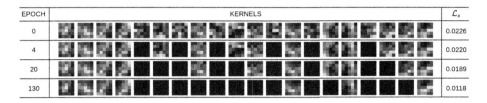	0.0226
4		0.0220
20		0.0189
130		0.0118

Fig. 3. Evolution of the 20 kernels of the first convolutional layer of *LeNet* and the global kernel-sparsity regularization term $\mathcal{L}_s$ during a training on the MNIST dataset. For a better visualization, each kernel is flatten from 3 dimensions to 2 dimensions.

4.1 Experiments on LeNet

In the experiments with *LeNet* [39], we investigate the effectiveness of the l_1/l_2 pseudo-norm on the MNIST and CIFAR-10 datasets. In order to compare our results with state-of-the-art methods such as SSL [1], NISP [2] and GAL [3], we decide to chose the *LeNet* model implemented by *Caffe*. All these methods are using evaluation and regression at different level i.e Lasso-group regression at different level of a convolutional layer in the SSL method, which makes it more complex to implement than our method. There is no data augmentation for the training on both datasets.

LeNet on MNIST: As previously described, the l_1/l_2 pseudo-norm is applied on the filters of a DCNN to penalize them. Hence our method is inducing sparsity among the filters of the convolutional layers in *LeNet*. To visualize the effect on our approach on the kernels, Fig. 3 shows the evolution of the kernels of the first convolutional layer of *LeNet* during a training on MNIST with our kernel-sparsity regularization. We see that the kernel-sparsity term $\mathcal{L}_s$ is decreasing epoch after epoch and that the number of filters in the layer is also decreasing with it. The complete evolution of the kernel-sparsity $\mathcal{L}_s$ can be seen on Fig. 4. $\mathcal{L}_s$ being computed on the pseudo-norm of the kernels and kernels weights being set to zero over time: this result shows the effectiveness of our method.

Table 1 summarizes the results on MNIST of different methods. In the best case scenario that we have tested, the l_1/l_2 pseudo-norm with a λ value set to 0.5 is able to achieve an accuracy better than the baseline by 0.2%. Furthermore the number of filters is dropping drastically in both convolutional layers respectively from 20 to 5 and from 50 to 18. Compared to the other state-of-the-art methods, the l_1/l_2 pseudo-norm is able to achieve a better accuracy while penalizing more filters too. We also compare our method to the l_1-norm and l_2-norm. During our evaluations, both of these norms were able to reach a higher level of sparsity by setting to zero more kernels. However they were never able to reach the same or a better level of accuracy than the baseline.

To visualize the effect of our method on the parameters, we show the learned filters of the first convolutional layer in Fig. 5. For $\lambda = 0.5$ and for different level of sparsity, it can be seen that the number of remaining filters can be set to only 2 or 4. Furthermore between the baseline and our method, the accuracy is the same

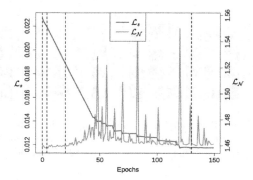

Fig. 4. Evolution of the cross-entropy loss function $\mathcal{L}_{\mathcal{N}}$ and the global kernel-sparsity regularization term $\mathcal{L}_s$ during training with $\lambda = 0.5$. Evaluations are done on *LeNet* on the MNIST dataset. Vertical lines show which epochs were taken to construct Fig. 3.

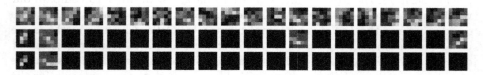

Fig. 5. Learned filters of the first convolutional of *LeNet* on MNIST. Top is *LeNet* baseline, middle and bottom are l_1/l_2-norm with $\lambda = 0.5$ and different level of sparsity.

or is increased. This shows that there is effectively a large amount of redundancy between filters and that most of them are not required. Moreover, compared to the baseline, it seems that the remaining filters are more structured, with more regular patterns. This assumption seems especially true when only two filters are remaining. Thus, we arrive at the same conclusion than [1]: the baseline has a high freedom in the parameter space and our method is able to obtain the same accuracy by optimizing the filters into more regularized patterns.

LeNet on CIFAR-10: In order to test the l_1/l_2 pseudo-norm and visualize its effect on a more difficult classification task than MNIST, we decided to use the CIFAR-10 dataset with the same *LeNet* model. The results are summarized in Table 2. The baseline *LeNet* is not performing as well on CIFAR-10 than it is performing on MNIST, i.e. the classification accuracy is only around 70%. As a result, the accuracy of our approach also drops but the l_1/l_2 pseudo-norm is still able to perform well on this model, even for this classification task. With a λ value set to 0.7, we are able to decrease the number of filters in the first and the second convolutional layers respectively from 20 to 10 and from 50 to 25, which means that half of the filters of *LeNet* are removed. With this configuration, our method performs 1.7% worse than the baseline. We were able to remove up to 80% of the filters in our experiments, but the resulting accuracy was too low to be interesting (more than 20% behind the baseline). Hence, more filters

Table 1. Results after penalizing unimportant filters in *LeNet* on MNIST. Baseline is the simple *LeNet* Caffe model. l_1 and l_2 are the best results found by using the l_1-norm and l_2-norm regularization on the kernels. SSL, NISP and GAL are the pruning methods respectively from [1–3]. l_1/l_2 is our method with $\lambda = 0.5$.

Method	λ	Error	Conv1 filter # (Sparsity)	Conv2 filter # (Sparsity)	Total sparsity
Baseline	–	**0.9%**	20	50	**0%**
l_1	0.5	1.2%	4 (80%)	5 (90%)	87.1%
l_2	0.5	1.2%	3 (85%)	5 (90%)	88.6%
SSL 1	–	**0.8%**	5 (75%)	19 (62%)	**65.7%**
SSL 2	–	1.0%	3 (85%)	12 (76%)	78.6%
NISP	–	**0.8%**	10 (50%)	25 (50%)	**50.0%**
GAL	–	1.0%	2 (90%)	15 (70%)	75.7%
l_1/l_2	0.5	**0.7%**	5 (75%)	18 (64%)	**67.1%**

are needed in order to classify correctly the CIFAR-10 dataset compared to the MNIST dataset. The best trade-off between filters and accuracy that we found was still with a value of λ set to 0.7. In both convolutional layers, the number of filters is dropping respectively from 20 to 14 and from 50 to 30. This means that our method is able to zero out more than a third of the filters with only a drop of 0.9% in accuracy. Compared to the l_1-norm and the l_2-norm, the l_1/l_2 pseudo-norm also shows good results. Indeed, both the l_1-norm and l_2-norm where unable to reach the same level of accuracy and setting to zero as many filters as the l_1/l_2 pseudo-norm can do.

As previously done with the MNIST dataset, we visualize the learned filters of the first convolutional layer in Fig. 6. From this visualization, we can draw the same conclusion than with the MNIST dataset. The more we are removing filters, the more the remaining ones seems to have a defined structure, as opposed to the baseline where each of the filters seems blurry. It is even more remarkable when we let our algorithm run until only a couple of filters are remaining. Even if the model does not reach a satisfactory accuracy, the two remaining filters have learned remarkable patterns. Thus, the l_1/l_2 pseudo-norm is still able to smooth a high freedom of parameter space into fewer filters with more regularized patterns.

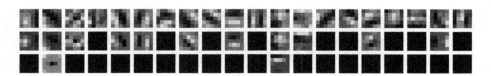

Fig. 6. Learned filters of the first convolutional layer of *LeNet* on CIFAR-10. Top is *LeNet* baseline, middle and bottom are l_1/l_2-norm with $\lambda = 0.7$ and different level of sparsity.

Table 2. Results after penalizing unimportant filters in *LeNet* on CIFAR-10. Baseline is the simple *LeNet* Caffe model. l_1/l_2 is our method with different coefficient of regulation $\lambda = 0.7$.

Method	λ	Error	Conv1 filter # (Sparsity)	Conv2 filter # (Sparsity)	Total sparsity
Baseline	-	**28.4%**	20	50	**0%**
l_1	0.7	**35.4%**	7 (65%)	14 (72%)	**70.0%**
l_2	0.7	29.8%	12 (40%)	24 (52%)	48.6%
l_1/l_2	0.7	30.1%	10 (50%)	25 (50%)	50.0%
l_1/l_2	0.7	**29.3%**	14 (30%)	30 (40%)	**37.1%**

4.2   VGG on CIFAR10

To demonstrate the generalization of our method on larger DNNs, we evaluate the performance of our method on the well-known *VGG* [6], a deeper model than *LeNet*, with several convolutional layers. A *VGG* model can have different sizes, notably depending on the number of layers. We chose the *VGG11* model with a total of 8 convolutional layers. We implemented it using *Pytorch*, running on various Nvidia GPUs using CUDA. The model is trained without data augmentation and evaluated on the CIFAR-10 dataset. In this experiment, the kernels pseudo-norms are not normalized on the full network, which explains why the λ values are smaller than the ones used with *LeNet*.

With *LeNet*, the l_1/l_2 pseudo-norm method was applied on only 2 convolutional layers, with 50 filters at most in the second convolutional layer. In *VGG11* our method is applied on 8 different convolutional layers with a number of filters set to 64 in the first convolutional layer and a maximum of 512 filters in the last four convolutional layers. The results are shown in Table 3. The baseline model, with all the filters and a classical loss function (cross-entropy), obtains an error of 17.6% on the test dataset. Using the l_1/l_2 pseudo-norm with a λ set to 0.005, the model achieves a classification accuracy roughly 1% inferior to the baseline. However the number of filters is vastly reduced. Moreover, it seems that the deeper we go in the network, the more the proportion of filter sets to zero is important. For example, the second convolutional layer has around 10% of its filters set to zero while the last convolutional layer has over 65% of filters set to zero. Thus we could deduce that the last convolutional layers keep less important information for the model than the first ones or that there is more redundancy in the last layers. However, the first convolutional layer seems to be an exception as approximately half of its filters can be removed. We suppose that the shapes learned in the first layer are not decisive for the model and can be balanced by the following layers and the more defined shapes that they have assimilated.

By decreasing the λ coefficient to 0.001, we confirm the results that the last convolutional layers seem to contain more filters with non decisive or redundant information than the first ones. Indeed, only the last two layers have filters set to zero. But more importantly, the removal of a few filters in the last two convolutional layers leads to a classification error of only 16.8%, which is 0.8% less than the baseline. Thus, our method, by only removing a few filters, is able to achieve a better accuracy than the baseline model. Compared to the l_1-norm and the l_2-norm, the l_1/l_2 pseudo-norm is also performing well. The l_1-norm is able to zero out numerous filters but is unable to achieve a correct level of accuracy, always performing worse than the baseline or our approach. Nearly the same conclusions can be drawn from the l_2-norm. Under certain conditions, the l_2-norm is able to zero out slightly more filters than our method in the last convolution layers. However, the models are not able to obtain a satisfying accuracy, always around 1% behind the baseline.

In order to conclude this study, we visualize in Fig. 7 the evolution of the accuracy of the model against the number of kernel set to zero in the first and second convolutional layers for different coefficient of regularization λ. When $\lambda = 0$, the l_1/l_2 pseudo-norm is not taken into account, resulting into the baseline model. The order that the filters are set to zero is determined by the filters

Table 3. Results after penalizing unimportant filters in *VGG11* on CIFAR-10. Baseline is the *VGG11* network baseline. l_1/l_2 is our method with different coefficient of regulation λ.

Method	λ	Error	Conv1 to conv 8 filter #	Total sparsity
Baseline	-	**17.6%**	64 - 128 - 256 - 256 - 512 - 512 - 512 - 512	**0%**
l_1	0.0001	19.3%	52 - 128 - 255 - 256 - 175 - 147 - 97 - 123	55.2%
l_2	0.005	**18.2%**	64 - 128 - 256 - 256 - 511 - 474 - 434 - 299	**12%**
l_1/l_2	0.005	18.8%	35 - 115 - 238 - 176 - 354 - 195 - 190 - 175	46.3%
l_1/l_2	0.001	**16.8%**	64 - 128 - 256 - 256 - 512 - 512 - 510 - 380	**5%**

pseudo-norm arranged by ascending order. These tests are done at a single convolutional layer level. Meaning that during training, the only filters that are evaluated and set to zero are the ones belonging to the studied layer. The other layers are remaining untouched. We visualize that for both layers, we are able to set numerous filters to zero without a noticeable decrease of the accuracy, even when our method is not active. This result shows that there is unimportant information in the layer and that it is possible to remove it, even if there are no methods that are defined to emphasize this phenomenon. With the implementation of the l_1/l_2 pseudo-norm ($\lambda > 0$), we see that (1) more kernels are set to zero before the beginning of the accuracy drop compared to the baseline and (2) a greater λ value means that more kernels are zeroed-out but at the price of an inferior accuracy. Based on these conclusions, our method is increasing the sparsity of the filters within a layer, shifting information between them in order to centralize the information. However this sparsity has its limits. The more we force it (with a significant λ value), the more we increase the chances to lose important information that could be never recovered.

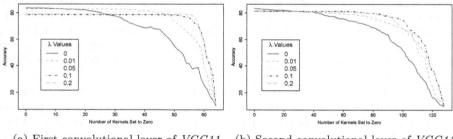

(a) First convolutional layer of *VGG11*   (b) Second convolutional layer of *VGG11*

Fig. 7. Visualization of the effect of setting kernels to zero in the first two convolutional layers of *VGG11* against the accuracy of the network. Each line represents a different value for the coefficient of regulation λ of the l_1/l_2 pseudo-norm method.

5   Conclusion

In this work, we proposed a new regularization approach for inducing kernel sparsity in DCNNs based on the l_1/l_2 pseudo-norm. This method reorganizes the weights of the convolutional layers in order to learn more compact structures during training. These compact DCNNs can reach almost the same accuracy as the original models and in some cases even perform better. Our experiments have demonstrated the benefits of our approach and its generalization to deep structures: it is straightforward to implement, it operates during the training process and it is possible to choose between the compactness and the accuracy of the model. So far, we have only applied our method to classification problems. To go beyond, in the future, the method needs to be applied on deeper models such as Resnet [9] and bigger datasets. Autoencoders, fully convolutional networks and segmentation problems are also an important focus. Furthermore, it would be interesting to generalize the l_1/l_2-norm to the l_1/l_q-norm to study its properties in more detail and improve on different model structures and learning problems.

References

1. Wen, W., Wu, C., Wang, Y., Chen, Y., Li, H.: Learning structured sparsity in deep neural networks. arXiv preprint arXiv:1608.03665 (2016)
2. Yu, R., et al.: NISP: pruning networks using neuron importance score propagation. In: Proceedings of the IEEE Conference on Computer Vision and Pattern Recognition, pp. 9194–9203 (2018)
3. Lin, S., et al.: Towards optimal structured CNN pruning via generative adversarial learning. In: Proceedings of the IEEE/CVF Conference on Computer Vision and Pattern Recognition, pp. 2790–2799 (2019)
4. Krizhevsky, A., Sutskever, I., Hinton, G.E.: Imagenet classification with deep convolutional neural networks. Adv. Neural Inf. Process. Syst. **25**, 1097–1105 (2012)
5. LeCun, Y., Bengio, Y., Hinton, G.: Deep learning. Nature **521**(7553), 436–444 (2015)
6. Simonyan, K., Zisserman, A.: Very deep convolutional networks for large-scale Image recognition. arXiv preprint arXiv:1409.1556 (2015)
7. Szegedy, C., et al.: Going deeper with convolutions. In: Proceedings of the IEEE Conference on Computer Vision and Pattern Recognition, pp. 1–9 (2015)
8. He, K., Sun, J.: Convolutional neural networks at constrained time cost. In: Proceedings of the IEEE Conference on Computer Vision and Pattern Recognition, pp. 5353–5360 (2015)
9. He, K., Zhang, X., Ren, S., Sun, J.: Deep residual learning for image recognition. In: Proceedings of the IEEE Conference on Computer Vision and Pattern Recognition, pp. 770–778 (2016)
10. Li, H., Kadav, A., Durdanovic, I., Samet, H., Graf, H.P.: Pruning filters for efficient ConvNets. arXiv preprint arXiv:1608.08710 (2017)
11. Luo, J. H., Wu, J., Lin, W.: Thinet: a filter level pruning method for deep neural network compression. In: Proceedings of the IEEE International Conference on Computer Vision, pp. 5058–5066 (2017)
12. Jaderberg, M., Vedaldi, A., Zisserman, A.: Speeding up convolutional neural networks with low rank expansions. arXiv preprint arXiv:1405.3866 (2014)
13. Bach, F., Jenatton, R., Mairal, J., Obozinski, G.: Optimization with sparsity-inducing penalties. arXiv preprint arXiv:1108.0775 (2012)
14. Huang, J., Zhang, T.: The benefit of group sparsity. Ann. Statist. **38**(4), 1978–2004 (2010)
15. Turlach, B., Venables, W., Wright, S.: Simultaneous variable selection. Technometrics **47**(3), 349–363 (2000)
16. Yuan, M., Lin, Y.: Model selection and estimation in regression with grouped variables. J. Roy. Stat. Soc. B (Stat. Methodol.) **68**(1), 49–67 (2006)
17. Dauphin, Y.N., Bengio, Y.: Big neural networks waste capacity. arXiv preprint arXiv:1301.3583 (2013)
18. Ba, L.J., Caruana, R.: Do deep nets really need to be deep? arXiv preprint arXiv:1312.6184 (2014)
19. Gupta, S., Agrawal, A., Gopalakrishnan, K., Narayanan, P.: Deep learning with limited numerical precision. In: International Conference on Machine Learning, pp. 1737–1746 (2015)

20. Courbariaux, M., Bengio, Y., David, J.P.: Training deep neural networks with low precision multiplications. arXiv preprint arXiv:1412.7024 (2014)
21. Williamson, D.: Dynamically scaled fixed point arithmetic. In: IEEE Pacific Rim Conference on Communications, Computers and Signal Processing Conference Proceedings, pp. 315–318 (1991)
22. Iandola, F.N., Han, S., Moskewicz, M.W., Ashraf, K., Dally, W.J., Keutzer, K.: SqueezeNet: alexnet-level accuracy with 50x fewer parameters and ¡0.5 mb model size. arXiv preprint arXiv:1602.07360 (2016)
23. Howard, A.G., et al.: Mobilenets: efficient convolutional neural networks for mobile vision applications. arXiv preprint arXiv:1704.04861 (2017)
24. Miikkulainen, R., et al.: Evolving deep neural networks. In: Artificial Intelligence in the Age of Neural Networks and Brain Computing, pp. 293–312 (2017)
25. Tan, M., Chen, B., Pang, R., Vasudevan, V., Le, Q.V.: MnasNet: platform-aware neural architecture search for mobile. In: Proceedings of the IEEE/CVF Conference on Computer Vision and Pattern Recognition, pp. 2820–2828 (2019)
26. He, Y., Lin, J., Liu, Z., Wang, H., Li, L.J., Han, S.: AMC: autoML for model compression and acceleration on mobile devices. In: Proceedings of the European Conference on Computer Vision (ECCV), pp. 784–800 (2018)
27. Han, S., Mao, H., Dally, W. J.: Deep compression: compressing deep neural networks with pruning, trained quantization and huffman coding. arXiv preprint arXiv:1510.00149 (2016)
28. Choi, Y., El-Khamy, M., Lee, J.: Towards the limit of network quantization. arXiv preprint arXiv:1612.01543 (2017)
29. Han, S., Pool, J., Tran, J., Dally, W.J.: Learning both weights and connections for efficient neural network. arXiv preprint arXiv:1506.02626 (2015)
30. Anwar, S., Hwang, K., Sung, W.: Structured pruning of deep convolutional neural networks. ACM J. Emerg. Technol. Comput. Syst. **13**(3), 1–18 (2017)
31. Molchanov, P., Tyree, S., Karras, T., Aila, T., Kautz, J.: Pruning convolutional neural networks for resource efficient transfer learning. arXiv preprint arXiv:1611.06440, 3 (2017)
32. He, Y., Zhang, X., Sun, J.: Channel pruning for accelerating very deep neural networks. In: Proceedings of the IEEE International Conference on Computer Vision, pp. 1389–1397 (2017)
33. Liu, Z., Li, J., Shen, Z., Huang, G., Yan, S., Zhang, C.: Learning efficient convolutional networks through network slimming. In: Proceedings of the IEEE International Conference on Computer Vision, pp. 2736–2744 (2017)
34. Zhuang, Z., et al.: Discrimination-aware channel pruning for deep neural networks. arXiv preprint arXiv:1810.11809 (2018)
35. He, Y., Liu, P., Wang, Z., Hu, Z., Yang, Y.: Filter pruning via geometric median for deep convolutional neural networks acceleration. In: Proceedings of the IEEE/CVF Conference on Computer Vision and Pattern Recognition, pp. 4340–4349 (2019)
36. Liu, B., Wang, M., Foroosh, H., Tappen, M., Pensky, M.: Sparse convolutional neural networks. In: Proceedings of the IEEE Conference on Computer Vision and Pattern Recognition, pp. 806–814 (2015)
37. Yuan, M., Lin, Y.: Model selection and estimation in regression with grouped variables. J. Roy. Stat. Soc. B (Stat. Methodol. **68**(1), 49–67 (2006)
38. Liu, J., Ye, J.: Efficient l1/lq norm regularization. arXiv preprint arXiv:1009.4766 (2010)
39. LeCun, Y., Bottou, L., Bengio, Y., Haffner, P.: Gradient-based learning applied to document recognition. Proc. IEEE **86**(11), 2278–2324 (1998)

Multi-node Training for StyleGAN2

Niki A. Loppi[1(✉)] and Tuomas Kynkäänniemi[2]

[1] NVIDIA AI Technology Center, Helsinki, Finland
nloppi@nvidia.com
[2] Aalto University, Helsinki, Finland
tuomas.kynkaanniemi@aalto.fi

Abstract. StyleGAN2 is a Tensorflow-based Generative Adversarial
Network (GAN) framework that represents the state-of-the-art in generative image modelling. The current release of StyleGAN2 implements
multi-GPU training via Tensorflow's device contexts which limits data
parallelism to a single node. In this work, a data-parallel multi-node
training capability is implemented in StyleGAN2 via Horovod which
enables harnessing the compute capability of larger cluster architectures.
We demonstrate that the new Horovod-based communication outperforms the previous context approach on a single node. Furthermore, we
demonstrate that the multi-node training does not compromise the accuracy of StyleGAN2 for a constant effective batch size. Finally, we report
strong and weak scaling of the new implementation up to 64 NVIDIA
Tesla A100 GPUs distributed across eight NVIDIA DGX A100 nodes,
demonstrating the utility of the approach at scale.

Keywords: GAN · StyleGAN2 · GPU · Massively parallel
architectures · Multi-node training

1 Introduction

The emergence of deep learning has directly led to tremendous improvements
in generative modeling. In recent years, generative methods, such as generative
adversarial networks (GAN) [1–5], variational-autoencoders (VAE) [6–8], autore-
gressive models [9,10], and likelihood-based models [11,12], have been applied
to a wide range of tasks from image generation to drug discovery. GANs, in particular, have been at the forefront in the efforts to generate high-quality images
that are indistinguishable from real images. However, the success of GANs is
not only limited to generation of high-fidelity images – they have been successfully applied in image-to-image translation [13–16], super-resolution [17–19], and
video synthesis [20].

Typical GAN architectures contain a large number of learnable parameters
and they need to be trained with large data sets, which makes the process computationally very expensive and time-consuming. Moreover, despite recent advances
in GAN research [2,4,21–24], almost every aspect of the GAN training, such as
model architecture, loss function, optimizer, is sensitive to hyperparameter and

© Springer Nature Switzerland AG 2021
A. Del Bimbo et al. (Eds.): ICPR 2020 Workshops, LNCS 12661, pp. 677–684, 2021.
https://doi.org/10.1007/978-3-030-68763-2_51

design choices [3]. One way to decrease training time and ease design experimentation with GANs is to scale up the process to harness more GPUs. In this paper, we present a multi-node training extension to the state-of-the-art generative image modelling framework StyleGAN2. This work has relevance to both production and research applications as it can significantly decrease turnaround time of GAN training.

The paper is structured as follows. Section 2 provides an overview of our multi-node StyleGAN2 implementation and details the modifications introduced to the original StyleGAN2 codebase. In Sect. 3, the new multi-node implementation is validated and its performance is measured against the original implementation. Section 4 presents strong and weak scaling studies to demonstrate the utility of the approach at scale. Finally, conclusions are drawn in Sect. 5.

2   Multi-node Training via Horovod

GAN training consist of alternately optimizing a generator network, whose task is to generate images from a noise input, and a discriminator network, whose task is to recognize reals from generated images in order to guide the generator in producing more realistic images.

The original StyleGAN2 training program is launched as a single process where all available GPU devices are visible to the host. In the program, GPUs receive a copy of the networks and the optimizers to train the model in parallel. Parallel operations are designated to the individual GPUs using Tensorflow's device contexts. The common gradients for the global model update are averaged using Tensorflow's `nccl_ops.all_sum` method which outsources the reduction to the NVIDIA Collective Communications Library (NCCL) to leverage very fast NVLink interconnects. The majority of earlier work on StyleGAN2 have been undertaken using an NVIDIA DGX node with eight GPUs.

We implemented the multi-node training capability for StyleGAN2 using Horovod [25]. Horovod is a distributed deep learning training framework whose foundations are in Message Passing Interface (MPI). In contrast to the original StyleGAN2 context-based parallelism, the new Horovod-based implementation leverages parallel processes to distribute workloads. This makes the approach completely agnostic to the underlying system architecture. In this section, we detail the changes to the original StyleGAN2 to allow multi-node training via Horovod.

2.1   Process Parallelism

A setup of a single GPU per process is adopted. After importing Horovod, parallel processes can by launched using Horovod's initializer, as shown in Fig. 1. Processes can be bound to unique GPU devices by setting the `CUDA_VISIBLE_DEVICES` environment variable as the local rank in the `run_training.py` module. Horovod's helper functions `hvd.rank` and `hvd.local_rank` return the ID of a process globally and within a node, respectively.

```
import horovod.tensorflow as hvd

hvd.init()
os.environ['CUDA_VISIBLE_DEVICES'] = str(hvd.local_rank())
run(**vars(args))
```

Fig. 1. Initialising Horovod processes and binding them to unique GPU devices.

```
dset = tf.data.TFRecordDataset(tfr_file, compression_type='',
                               buffer_size=buffer_mb<<20)
if self._sharding:
    dset = dset.shard(num_shards=hvd.size(), index=hvd.rank())
```

Fig. 2. TFRecord dataset sharding.

Since GANs heavily build upon random number generators to draw samples from the latent space, it is important to initialise all processes with a unique random seed. In StyleGAN2, this can be done by perturbing the default seed with the global rank IDs in the run_training.py module as tf_config ={'rnd.np_random_seed': 1000 + hvd.rank()}. Note that different random seeds also affect random initialisers, causing differences in the initial states across ranks. Before the start of the training process in the training_loop.py module, all global variables must be broadcasted from the root rank (0) using hvd.broadcast_global_variables(0) to ensure that training starts from the same initial state.

2.2 Data Sharding

Sharding is a term used to describe the process where the input dataset is split into smaller partitions to ensure that all parallel copies train with unique data. By default, StyleGAN2 uses the TFRecord binary format to load the data from disk and the data loader can automatically split the data for multiple GPUs within a single process. However, as we now deal with multiple processes, and hence also with multiple copies of the data loader, we need to explicitly tell each process to use its own shard. Figure 2 illustrates the sharding implementation in the dataset.py module, where the dset.shard(num_shards=hvd.size(), index=hvd.rank()) takes every nth sample into the process-specific shard, with n being the global rank.

2.3 Gradient Averaging

A common practice with Horovod is to use a distributed optimizer class which abstracts all communication. StyleGAN2 uses a custom optimizer class and therefore the communication was implemented using Horovod's reduction primitive wrappers. Specifically, gradients can be summed using hvd.allreduce (grad, average=False) in the apply_updates method in the optimizer.py module, which replaces the `nccl_ops.all_sum` method. In contrast to the original `nccl_ops.all_sum` method which takes all device arrays as an input argument, `hvd.allreduce` takes only the unique tensor available to the process. This makes communication completely agnostic to the system configuration as Horovod formulates the reduction pattern using the local and global rank hierarchy. The default allreduce operator is based on the ring-allreduce approach that is bandwidth optimal [25]. After the reduction operation has been executed, the model updates occur efficiently per device.

To ensure that Horovod is performing the reduction operations efficiently using NCCL, using a clean containerised environment is recommended. In this work, we run the `nvcr.io/nvidia/tensorflow:20.08-tf1-py3` container cloned from the NVIDIA NGC registry which contains Horovod.

2.4 Multi-node Metrics

StyleGAN2 uses Fréchet Inception Distance (FID) [23] metric to assess the quality of generated images. Multi-node acceleration for the computation of this metric in the `frechet_inception_distance.py` module was enabled as follows.

First, the Inception network [26] activations for the real images need to be computed only once and therefore it is unnecessary to distribute this one-off task. These activations are stored as a pickled Python object onto disk during the first metric evaluation step. It is important to consider that the activations are computed using the entire dataset, not the process-specific data shards. Second, all processes load the pickled object as well as the Inception network to compute the activations for synthetic images. Third, all processes take part in generation of synthetic images using rank-specific random seeds. Subsequently, these are run through the Inception network and the activation results from all processes are gathered using `hvd.allgather`. Finally, the FID metric between the activations of real and synthetic images is computed using NumPy on the CPU.

3 Validation

Three training runs were performed to validate that:

- New implementation does not deteriorate single-node performance.
- New implementation does not compromise the quality of the generated images.

We used StyleGAN2 configuration-f and Flickr-Faces-HQ (FFHQ) dataset, in 256×256 resolution, to train our models. FFHQ is a dataset of human faces, containing 70,000 unique images. StyleGAN2 constructs the network and sets the hyperparameters automatically based on the given configuration identifier. For StyleGAN2 configuration details, see [5]. Table 1 describes the run configurations and reports their performance in wall-time seconds per thousand images. An effective batch size (batchsize × number of nodes) of 32 was used throughout

Table 1. Run configurations and their performance in wall-time seconds per thousand images.

Case	N_{GPU}	Performance (s/kimgs)
Standard single-node	4	30.8
New single-node	4	28.5
New multi-node	16	9.3

the study. All cases were run on CSC's Puhti-AI cluster, each node containing four NVIDIA Tesla V100 GPUs connected via NVLink. The nodes are connected with Mellanox HDR100 InfiniBand links. From the performance numbers, it can be seen that Horovod-based training outperforms the standard device context-based implementation by a factor 1.08x on a single node. Using four nodes the speed-up factor relative to the standard single-node implementation goes as high as 3.3x. Figure 3 shows the FID metric, computed using 50,000 real and generated images, for the 4 GPU single-node and 16 GPU multi-node setting. The models were trained until 25×10^6 real images had been processed. The multi-node implementation does not have any negative effect on the training dynamics and the model convergences to a level comparable to that of standard StyleGAN2 [5].

Figure 3b shows synthetic images generated using the multi-node-trained model. These images do not show any signs of quality issues relative to the standard single-node implementation. On the whole, the evolution of the FID50k metric and visual quality of the images demonstrate that multi-node training with the new Horovod-based implementation does not compromise the accuracy of StyleGAN2.

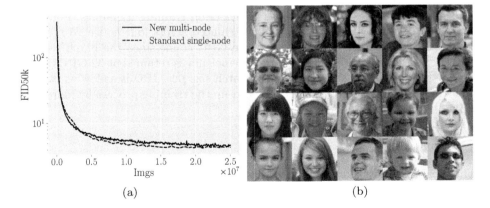

(a)   (b)

Fig. 3. (a) Evolution of FID for the new multi-node StyleGAN2 case, together with reference data obtained with single-node StyleGAN2. (b) Images generated using the model that was trained with 16 GPUs across four nodes.

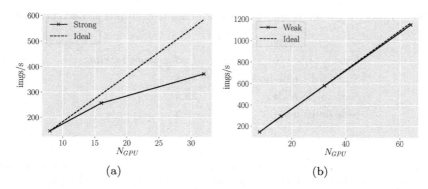

Fig. 4. (a) Strong scaling up 32 GPUs on NVIDIA DGX A100 nodes, using an effective batch size of 64. (b) Weak scaling up 64 GPUs on NVIDIA DGX A100 nodes, using an effective batch size of 64 × the number of nodes.

4   Scaling Tests

In addition to the validation tests, strong and weak scaling of the multi-node StyleGAN2 implementation was studied using state-of-the-art hardware. All results presented in this section were run on NVIDIA's Selene supercomputer with DGX A100 nodes, each containing eight NVIDIA Tesla A100 GPUs. We used StyleGAN2 configuration-f and FFHQ dataset, in 256 × 256 resolution, to train the models for strong and weak scaling tests.

4.1   Strong Scaling

The strong scaling study was undertaken with a constant effective batch size of 64. Keeping the effective batch size constant ensures that increasing the GPU and node count does not have adverse effects on training dynamics. Figure 4a shows the strong scaling up 32 GPUs distributed across four nodes. We can see that parallel efficiency decreases with the GPU count since the batch size per GPU decreases. In this case, 63% parallel efficiency is retained at 32 GPUs which is still substantial, considering that the batch size per GPU is as low as two. By quadrupling the GPU count one can speed-up the training process by more than 2.5x.

4.2   Weak Scaling

The weak scaling study was undertaken with an effective batch size of 64 × the number of nodes. Scaling the batch size with the number of nodes allows significantly more images to be processed in parallel. Figure 4b shows the weak scaling up to 64 GPUs across eight nodes. In this case, the scaling is nearly linear and 98% parallel efficiency is retained at 64 GPUs. However, increasing the effective batch size can change the underlying training dynamics and cause instabilities. In [3], it was shown that GANs can benefit from large batch sizes when stabilization techniques such as spectral normalisation [24] and R_1 gradient penalty [27] for the discriminator are being are used. Training dynamics in the context of very large batch sizes has been identified as an avenue for future work.

5   Conclusion

Typical GAN architectures contain a large number of learnable parameters and they need to be trained with large data sets, which makes the process computationally very expensive and time-consuming. We implemented a data-parallel multi-node training capability to StyleGAN2 via Horovod to allow effective utilisation of larger system architectures. We demonstrated that the new Horovod-based multi-node implementation can outperform the previous device context-based multi-GPU implementation approach on a single node. Furthermore, we demonstrated that multi-node training does not compromise the accuracy of StyleGAN2 for a constant effective batch size. Finally, we reported strong and weak scaling of the new implementation on NVIDIA Tesla A100 GPUs. In a weak scaling sense i.e. keeping the effective batch size constant, the implementation achieves 63% parallel efficiency up to 32 GPUs. In a strong scaling sense i.e. scaling the batch size with the number of nodes, the implementation achieves more than 98% parallel efficiency up to 64 GPUs. On the whole, these results demonstrate the utility of the new multi-node training approach at scale.

Acknowledgment. The authors would like to thank Associate Professor Jaakko Lehtinen and Tero Karras for help with the StyleGAN2 codebase, and CSC – IT Center for Science for the GPU resources on Puhti-AI via project ID 2002415.

References

1. Goodfellow, I., et al.: Generative adversarial nets. In: Advances in Neural Information Processing Systems 27, Ghahramani, Z., Welling, M., Cortes, C., Lawrence, N.D., Weinberger, N.Q., (Eds.), Curran Associates Inc, pp. 2672–2680 (2014). http://papers.nips.cc/paper/5423-generative-adversarial-nets.pdf
2. Karras, T., Aila, T., Laine, S., Lehtinen, J.: Progressive growing of gans for improved quality, stability, and variation, CoRR.abs/1710.10196 (2017). http://arxiv.org/abs/1710.10196
3. Brock, A., Donahue, J., Simonyan, K.: Large scale GAN training for high fidelity natural image synthesis. In: Proceedings of ICLR (2019)
4. Karras, T., Laine, S., Aila, T.: A style-based generator architecture for generative adversarial networks. In: Proceedings of the IEEE/CVF Conference on Computer Vision and Pattern Recognition (CVPR), June 2019
5. Karras, T., Laine, S., Aittala, M., Hellsten, J., Lehtinen, J., Aila, T.: Analyzing and improving the image quality of stylegan. In: Proceedings of the IEEE/CVF Conference on Computer Vision and Pattern Recognition (CVPR), June 2020
6. Kingma, D.P., Rezende, D.J., Mohamed, S., Welling, M.: Semi-supervised learning with deep generative models, CoRR.abs/1406.5298 (2014). http://arxiv.org/abs/1406.5298

7. van den Oord, A., Vinyals, O., Kavukcuoglu, K.: Neural discrete representation learning. In: Proceedings of NIPS (2017)
8. Razavi, A., van den Oord, A., Vinyals, O.: Generating diverse high-fidelity images with vq-vae-2. In: Proceedings of NeurIPS (2019)
9. van den Oord, A., Kalchbrenner, N., Kavukcuoglu, K.: Pixel recurrent neural networks. In: ICML, pp. 1747–1756 (2016)
10. van den Oord, A., Kalchbrenner, N., Vinyals, O., Espeholt, L., Graves, A., Kavukcuoglu, K.: Conditional image generation with PixelCNN decoders, CoRR.abs/1606.05328 (2016)
11. Dinh, L., Sohl-Dickstein, J., Bengio, S.: Density estimation using Real NVP. CoRR. abs/1605.08803 (2016)
12. Kingma, D.P., Dhariwal, P.: Glow: generative flow with invertible 1x1 convolutions, CoRR.abs/1807.03039 (2018)
13. Zhu, J., Park, T., Isola, P., Efros, A.A.: Unpaired image-to-image translation using cycle-consistent adversarial networks, CoRR.abs/1703.10593 (2017)
14. Choi, Y., Choi, M. Kim, M., Ha, J.-W., Kim, S., Choo, J.: Stargan: Unified generative adversarial networks for multi-domain image-to-image translation, CoRR.abs/1711.09020 (2018)
15. Choi, Y., Uh, Y., Yoo, J., Ha, J.-W.: Stargan v2: Diverse image synthesis for multiple domains, CoRR.abs/1912.01865 (2019)
16. Kim, V., Kim, M., Kang, H., Lee, K.: U-gat-it: Unsupervised generative attentional networks with adaptive layer-instance normalization for image-to-image translation, CoRR.abs/1907.10830 (2019)
17. Ledig, C.: Photo-realistic single image super-resolution using a generative adversarial network, CoRR.abs/1609.04802 (2016)
18. Shaham, T.R., Dekel, T., Michaeli, T.: Singan: learning a generative model from a single natural image. In: Proceedings of ICCV (2019)
19. Bell-Kligler, S., Shocher, A., Irani, M.: Blind super-resolution kernel estimation using an internal-gan. In: Proceedings of NeurIPS (2019)
20. Clark, A., Simonyan, K., Donahue, J.: Adversarial video generation on complex datasets, CoRR.abs/1907.06571 (2019)
21. Arjovsky, M., Chintala, S., Bottou, L.: Wasserstein GAN, CoRR.abs/1701.07875 (2017)
22. Gulrajani, I., Ahmed, F., Arjovsky, M., Dumoulin, V., Courville, A.C.: Improved training of Wasserstein GANs, CoRR.abs/1704.00028 (2017)
23. Heusel, M., Ramsauer, H., Unterthiner, T., Nessler, B., Hochreiter, S.: GANs trained by a two time-scale update rule converge to a local Nash equilibrium. In: NIPS, pp. 6626–6637 (2017)
24. Miyato, T., Kataoka, T., Koyama, M., Yoshida, Y.: Spectral normalization for generative adversarial networks, CoRR.abs/1802.05957 (2018)
25. Sergeev, A., Balso, M.D.: Horovod: fast and easy distributed deep learning in TensorFlow, arXiv preprint arXiv:1802.05799 (2018)
26. Szegedy, C., Vanhoucke, V., Ioffe, S., Shlens, J., Wojna, Z.: Rethinking the inception architecture for computer vision. In: Proceedings of CVPR (2016)
27. Mescheder, L., Geiger, A., Nowozin, S.: Which training methods for GANs do actually converge? CoRR.abs/1801.04406 (2018)

Flow R-CNN: Flow-Enhanced Object Detection

Athanasios Psaltis[1(✉)], Anastasios Dimou[1,2], Federico Alvarez[2],
and Petros Daras[1]

[1] Centre for Research and Technology Hellas, Thessaloniki, Greece
{at.psaltis,dimou,daras}@iti.gr
[2] Universidad Politécnica de Madrid, Madrid, Spain
fag@gatv.ssr.upm.es

Abstract. This work addresses the problem of multi-task object detection in an efficient, generic but at the same time simple way, following the recent and highly promising studies in the computer vision field, and more specifically the Region-based Convolutional Neural Network (R-CNN) approach. A flow-enhanced methodology for object detection is proposed, by adding a new branch to predict an object-level flow field. Following a scheme grounded on neuroscience, a pseudo-temporal motion stream is integrated in parallel to the classification, bounding box regression and segmentation mask prediction branches of Mask R-CNN. Extensive experiments and thorough comparative evaluation provide a detailed analysis of the problem at hand and demonstrate the added value of the involved object-level flow branch. The overall proposed approach achieves improved performance in the six currently broadest and most challenging publicly available semantic urban scene understanding datasets, surpassing the region-based baseline method.

Keywords: Flow field · Object detection · Deep learning

1 Introduction

Object detection and recognition is a fundamental task for the human visual system. It has been proved that the human brain uses multiple object properties to achieve the required recognition performance. Appearance features such as shape, structure, color, and texture comprise essential information for this purpose. Therefore, most object representation methods have concentrated on single frame cues for recognition.

However, the vast majority of objects are not stationary. The motion characteristics of an object constitute a unique signature that can be used for recognition of the object. Intuitively, exploiting the motion characteristics of an object can improve our object recognition capabilities. The role of motion information in object recognition has been already examined by a number of studies [15]. Both rigid and non-rigid motion, have been studied for their role in different tasks.

© Springer Nature Switzerland AG 2021
A. Del Bimbo et al. (Eds.): ICPR 2020 Workshops, LNCS 12661, pp. 685–700, 2021.
https://doi.org/10.1007/978-3-030-68763-2_52

As it has been highlighted, object recognition involves a number of heterogeneous modalities, namely appearance, shape and motion. Specialized neural networks have been developed to model each one of them. However, these modalities are strongly interconnected and it has been shown in the literature that employing a multi-target learning technique to address them all in parallel can have important advantages. It drastically reduces the overhead between the networks and it allows the network to generalize better.

Given the lack of motion information in single frames, only appearance-related features have been employed until now in multi-target learning methods. The shape of an object has been shown to be correlated with its motion characteristics. This is further confirmed by recent literature that has shown it is possible to predict the flow of an object [8] from a single frame. This pseudo-flow information can be used as a substitute for the actual motion information.

In this paper, a neuroscience-inspired scheme is proposed to improve object detection by introducing to the Mask R-CNN architecture an additional pseudo-temporal stream (branch) for motion prediction from still images. An object-level flow field is incorporated in the object recognition process. In particular, the proposed pseudo-temporal information is effectively incorporated into the proposed detection framework by penalizing the global loss computation with an optical flow loss factor. For this purpose, a dense pseudo-flow estimation branch is added that achieves satisfactory motion prediction accuracy at a relatively low computational cost, since the latter is applied solely at the RoI level. Specifically, the resulting network detects object bounding boxes with instance segmentation masks and estimates the object flow predictions for each candidate object.

The remainder of the paper is organized as follows: Related work is reviewed in Sect. 2. The proposed approach is detailed in Sect. 3. Experimental results are discussed in Sect. 4 and conclusions are drawn in Sect. 5.

2   Related Work

Over the past few years, a broad number of techniques have been proposed, targeting object detection from still images or videos, while combining and integrating different approaches. This section analyses the different methodologies available in the literature for object detection from still images and videos, focusing on Deep Learning (DL) techniques. DL methods can be roughly divided in a) region-based and b) regression-based ones, depending on the number of processing steps/phases they employ.

2.1   Region-Based Methods

Current region-based methods perform detection by carrying out a classification on different regions, sub-windows or patches extracted from the image. This is the most popular category of methods, where the aim is to produce region proposals at first and then classifying each proposal into different object categories [3, 10–13, 28]. Most of the approaches vary on the type of methodology used for choosing the regions, trying to find the balance between an exhaustive search and a fixed number of region proposals. One of the first attempts to utilize Convolutional Neural Networks (CNNs) in object detection was the Region-based CNN (R-CNN) [11] in which a number of class-agnostic candidate regions are proposed and fed to a CNN to extract a fixed-length feature descriptor for each region. Thereafter, a unique linear Support Vector Machine (SVM) for each class classifies these regions based on their extracted descriptors. In [13], a Spatial Pyramid Pooling (SPP) layer is introduced, in order to remove the fixed-size constraint of the network. The latter computes a convolutional feature map from the entire image only once and then pools features in arbitrary regions to generate fixed-length representations for training the detectors.

Built upon R-CNN success, the Fast R-CNN [10] targets the inefficiency of having to pass each of the candidate regions individually through the CNN by forward passing the input image to the network once, generating its feature map and applying Region of Interest (RoI) pooling for each of the candidate regions to extract their feature representations. Based on the previously mentioned methods, Faster R-CNN [28] introduced a trainable mechanism for the purpose of proposing candidate regions called Regional Proposal Network (RPN). Given a number of uniformly generated anchors across the image, the RPN distinguishes them between foreground and background before passing the former to the classifier. Moreover, Mask R-CNN [12] extended the Faster R-CNN by adding an extra head for segmentation and replaced the RoI-pooling with RoI-align resulting in higher accuracy predictions. In [20], T.-Y. Lin et al. proposed Feature Pyramid Networks (FPN) on the basis of Faster R-CNN. The latter presented a top-down architecture with lateral connections for building high-level semantics at all scales. Later, a variety of improvements have been proposed, including Region-based Fully Convolutional Networks (R-FCNs) [3] and Light-head R-CNN [19].

In contrast to previous Region-based detectors, such as Fast/Faster R-CNN [10,28], that apply a costly per-region sub-network hundreds of times, the proposed Region-based detector in [3] is fully convolutional with almost all computations shared on the entire image, while also improves speed by reducing the amount of work needed for each RoI. The latter introduces position-sensitive score maps to address a dilemma between translation-invariance in image classification and translation-variance in object detection. Additional classifiers are added in [1] aiming at progressively increasing the Intersection over Union's (IoU) of the proposed regions with the ground truth objects which results in improved predictions.

2.2   Regression-Based Methods

In contrary to the R-CNN family methods where region proposal and region classification are done by discrete modules, in one-stage methods the regions are generated and classified in a single forward pass. Methods belonging at this category try to map directly from image pixels to bounding box coordinates and class probabilities [6, 14, 23, 25–27]. In particular, Liu et al. [23] describe a method

FlowNet   Im2Flow

Fig. 1. Optical flow estimation architectures: a) FlowNet architecture: including the refinement part, is trained in an end-to-end manner, b) Im2Flow architecture: an encoder-decoder model that infers flow given a single image

for detecting objects in images, using a single deep neural network. The approach, named Single shot multi-box detector (SSD), discretizes the output space of bounding boxes into a set of default boxes over different aspect ratios and scales per feature map location. At prediction time, the network generates scores for the presence of each object category in each default box and produces adjustments to the box to better match the object shape. Additionally, the network combines predictions from multiple feature maps with different resolutions to naturally handle objects of various sizes. In [25], a CNN-based technique is proposed, which models the problem of object detection as an iterative search in a multi-scale grid-space of all possible bounding boxes.

The You Only Look Once (YOLO) [26] and the SSD [23] algorithms are the most representative one-stage/regression object detection approaches. Later, R. Joseph has made a series of improvements on the basis of YOLO and has proposed its v2 and v3 editions [27], which further improve the detection accuracy while keeps a very high detection speed. Moreover, an approach for introducing addition context into the SSD model is described in [6], where a state-of-the-art feature extractor (Residual-101 [14]) is combined with the aforementioned detection framework [23]. The proposed SSD+Residual-101 architecture is augmented with a set of deconvolution layers in order to introduce additional large-scale context in object detection.

Although this category of methods offers faster performance compared to the RPN based one, they are limited in terms of prediction accuracy due to the high imbalance between positive and negative regions fed to the classifier (the positive and negative terms refer to the presence and the absence of ground truth object, respectively). Lin *et al.* [21] addresses the imbalance by having the ambiguous regions contribute more in the loss calculation, thus valuing the hard examples more than the easily classified ones. To this end, the authors introduced a novel loss function named 'focal loss' by reshaping the standard cross-entropy loss so that the detector will put more focus on hard misclassified examples during training. Focal Loss enables the one-stage detectors to achieve comparable accuracy of two-stage detectors while maintaining a very high detection speed.

2.3   Flow-Based Object Detection

Optical flow techniques have been applied to video-based object detection tasks over the years, as the incorporation of temporal information in the object detection task can improve the feature quality and recognition accuracy. The majority of them incorporate optical flow vectors obtained after applying an Optical Flow algorithm in the visual analysis loop for marking the detected object in the video frame. In [17], a DL framework, called Tube-CNN (T-CNN), which incorporates temporal and contextual information from tubelets/boxes obtained in videos is presented, by propagating detection results across adjacent frames according to pre-computed optical flows. Zhu *et al.* [31] propose a flow-guided feature aggregation, an accurate and end-to-end learning framework for video object detection, which leverages temporal coherence on feature-level. The later enhances the visual features by employing an optical flow network to estimate the motions between the nearby frames and the reference frame. Recently, a unified approach is introduced, which is based on the principle of multi-frame end-to-end learning of features and cross-frame motion. It belongs to the category of feature-level methods, and introduces a *Spatially-adaptive Partial Feature Updating* to fix the inaccurate feature propagation caused by inaccurate optical flow.

From the above analysis, it can be deduced that despite the fact that optical flow features have been extensively applied in video object detection task, the current study is the first study, to the best of authors knowledge, that addresses the problem of object detection from still images, by incorporating object flow predictions of each detected object. In addition, object detection-related literature has in principle concentrated on appearance and contextual information analysis, while the respective pseudo-temporal information has not been examined yet, *i.e.* leaving great potential for further performance improvement unexplored.

3   Flow R-CNN

Objects inherently have motion characteristics, the capturing and encoding of which could be of paramount importance for achieving robust detection performance. According to recent neuroscience reports [18,24], the cerebral cortex can predict the path of a moving object (visual motion), even in cases where the object is traveling faster than the brains' visual processing rate, in order to adapt human behavior to surrounding objects moving in real-time. Neuroscientists conclude that there is a specific part, called the Medial Superior Temporal (MST) area, in the cerebral cortex, which lies in the dorsal/parietal stream of the visual area of the primate brain where the whole visual processing takes place. The MST cooperates with the Middle Temporal (MT) area, in order to estimate the motion field of each moving object in a scene. In other words, that specific part is responsible for estimating the final or close to the final location of a moving object. Therefore, it is evident that the human brain can reveal the implied motion using a single still image. Given a single static image, the brain's ventral stream interprets the instantaneous semantic content, and at the same time the dorsal stream predicts what is going to happen based on scene spatial configuration, *e.g.* the ventral stream detects a car, while the dorsal stream anticipates that the car is moving forward. In this section, Flow R-CNN is thoroughly presented, including a detailed analysis of the new object-based motion branch.

3.1 Object-Based Motion Analysis

CNNs have been extensively employed for optical flow estimation, achieving a huge improvement in prediction quality. In the current study, the literature approach of [5] is selected (Fig. 1a), where the information included in a pair of successive images is first spatially compressed in a contractive part of the CNN and then refined in an expanding part. However, for small displacement, *FlowNet* is not reliable. Thus, the authors proposed an extension of their previous model, called *FlowNetSD* [16], where they replaced several network parameters including kernel size and window stride of selected layers. Despite the very good results of these methods, they pose an impermeable constraint, as they require a pair of images as input to obtain satisfactory results. On the contrary, inspired by the aforementioned neuro-scientific notion of visual dynamics, Gao *et al.* have introduced an encoder-decoder CNN (refer to Fig. 1b) equipped with a novel optical flow encoding scheme that is able to translate a single static image into an accurate flow field. Their main idea is to learn a motion prior over short-term dynamics from a large set of videos and transfer the learned motion from videos to static images to infer their motion. The current study adopts the findings of Gao *et al.* [8] for object-level flow estimation.

Fig. 2. An example of a computed flow field given a static image. The flow field color coding can be found in [16]. Smaller vectors are lighter and color represents the direction (Color figure online)

3.2 Mask R-CNN

The baseline of this work is Mask R-CNN that belongs, as briefly stated in Sect. 2, to the Region-based/two-stage approaches. The latter is equipped with an RPN mechanism in the first stage in order to propose candidate RoIs. In the second stage, another part of the network takes the proposed RoIs and locates the relevant areas of the feature map by utilizing a RoI-Align layer.

The extracted features are further processed in parallel to perform classification, bounding box regression and instance-level semantic segmentation. Both stages are connected to the backbone. Backbone could be any Convolution network, but usually, Residual Neural Network (ResNet) or Very Deep Convolutional Networks (VGG) are used to extract raw images.

3.3 Proposed Architecture

In the current work, the proposed approach mimics the visual perception procedures that take place in the human brain, following an appropriate deep neurophysiologically grounded architecture. The primary visual cortex is emulated by the backbone of the network (the encoder part), generating high-level feature representations, while the dorsal ('where') and ventral ('what') stream are incarnated by the flow-estimation, denoted as OF, and object classification, denoted as CL, branches respectively, predicting object categories with each respective motion in a collaborative way.

The introduced Flow R-CNN exhibits the following advantageous characteristics: a) it enhances the two-stage detector by introducing an additional pseudo-temporal stream, and b) it incorporates the aforementioned stream in a multi-task learning process. In particular, the current study adopts the findings of Gao et al. [8] while moving their concept one step further, utilizing the pseudo-temporal object-level motion patterns combined with the appearance/contextual information to distinguish objects in still images. To this end, an object detection architecture is designed that takes into account the implied movement estimation.

The proposed Flow R-CNN model is built upon the Mask R-CNN model, estimating a per RoI flow field given a single static in image an Im2Flow inspired branch (OF). As a feature extractor (encoder) the ResNet-50 variant is selected for its simplicity and relatively short training time. In the decoder, the three existing branches of the baseline model (object classification, bounding box prediction, and mask prediction) remain intact and a 4th sub-network (OF) is integrated to the RoI head, in an end-to-end manner, to estimate a flow field for each predicted region proposal. The flow branch is inspired by the encoder-decoder logic of the Im2Flow model, where a motion prior-learned from videos in the form of a two-dimensional vector, taken from several urban scene understanding datasets, is transferred to images, bridging the still-image detection with video object motion understanding. In particular, a deep network is trained to learn a motion prior from a large set of unlabeled videos, and then transfer the learned motion from videos to static images to hallucinate their motion. Then, given a static image, the system translates the observed RGB image into a flow map, encoding the inferred motion for the static image. By encoding motion as a 3-channel image makes its usage efficient, convenient, and suitable for the framework.

Prior to the application of the proposed Flow R-CNN, optical flow estimation is realized for each dataset described in Sect. 4. More specifically, videos from several datasets were used to model the motion patterns of objects and people in

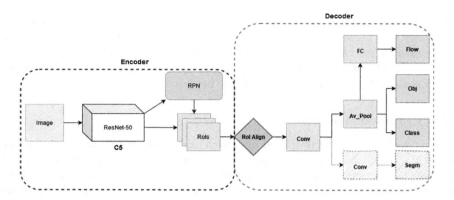

Fig. 3. Overall Flow R-CNN architecture: a composite region-based object detection model, the backbone of the network is used for the image encoding, while the object-level flow estimation branch is used to infer the optical flow field. Sketched part of the network, i.e. the segmentation branch, remains intact during training.

the scene, then embed the resulting knowledge into a representation for individual images (*i.e.* a two dimensional vector as can be seen in Fig. 2). Finally, the proposed Flow R-CNN combines, in a way, the appearance information from the static image and the predicted motion dynamics from the introduced 4th branch in order to improve the detection accuracy. A graphical representation of the developed Flow R-CNN model is illustrated in Fig. 3. It needs to be highlighted that in the current implementation a modified version of the Im2Flow was used, where the encoder part was replaced by a region-based model backbone (ResNet) and the decoder part with the object-level flow estimation branch (OF). The developed CNN part of the OF branch consists of one convolutional layer, which models the correlations among the RoI features, an average pooling layer, and two fully connected layers, denoted as FC, for computing the respective flow field. Experimentation with additional configurations, regarding the number of convolutional and fully connected layers (as well as their parameterization), did not lead to improved recognition performance.

In the training phase, a multi-task loss L_{total} is defined on each sampled proposal, as shown in (1). The classification loss L_{class}, the bounding-box loss L_{bbox} and the instance segmentation loss L_{seg} are identical to the ones define in Mask R-CNN model.

$$L_{total} = L_{class} + L_{bbox} + L_{seg} + L_{of} \tag{1}$$

For each RoI, an additional object-level flow loss L_{of} is computed to supervise the per-object motion by penalizing the predicted m x m x 2 optical flow output. This requires optical flow data for every image in the database, and in some cases, the authors of this study have extracted such info using state-of-the-art optical flow estimators [16]. The predicted object-level flow fields were compared with the cropped and resized region from the ground truth motion fields, penalized with an $l1$ loss function. It is assumed that the loss of the optical flow estimation branch enhances the learning process of the composite model while retaining key parts of the baseline model unaffected.

4 Experimental Results

4.1 Object Detection Datasets

Major research efforts have been made in the field of computer vision to understand the complex urban scenarios. The respective progress is bonded with the availability of vast amounts of annotated training data (*e.g.* cars, bicycles, pedestrians *etc.*) under varying conditions. In this section, experimental results, as well as comparative evaluation from the application of the proposed object detection method, are presented. For the evaluation, the 'KITTI' [9], 'V-KITTI' [7], 'Visdrone' [30], 'Cityscapes' [2], 'Berkeley Deep Drive' [29] as well as the 'UDacity' [4] datasets were used.

- **KITTI dataset** [9]: The KITTI object detection benchmark consists of 7481 training images and 7518 test images, comprising a total of 80.256 labeled objects. All images are color and the goal of the challenge is to detect objects from three common urban categories, namely *Car*, *Pedestrian*, and *Cyclist*. For evaluation, an Average Precision (AP) is computed.
- **V-KITTI dataset** [7]: The Virtual KITTI dataset contains 50 photo-realistic high-resolution synthetic videos for a total of approximately 21.000 frames, generated from 5 different virtual worlds in urban settings under different imaging and weather condition. These worlds were created using the Unity game engine and a novel real-to-virtual cloning method. These photo-realistic synthetic videos are automatically, exactly, and fully annotated for 2D and 3D multi-object tracking and at the pixel level with category, instance, flow, and depth labels. For the particular task of object detection the V-KITTI contains detailed class annotation for the objects of interest (*Car*, *Van*).
- **Visdrone dataset** [30]: The Visdrone benchmark dataset consists of 288 video clips formed by 261.908 frames and 10.209 static images, captured by various drone-mounted cameras, covering a wide range of aspects including location, environment (urban and country), objects, and density (sparse and crowded scenes). The dataset was collected using various drone platforms, in different scenarios, and under various weather and lighting conditions. From those only 8.559 images are used for the object detection task, with more than 540k bounding boxes in ten predefined categories, such as *Pedestrians*, *Cars*, *Bicycles*, and *Tricycles*. The dataset is further divided into training, validation and testing sets, having 6.471, 548 and 1580 images, respectively.
- **Cityscapes dataset** [2]: The Cityscapes dataset contains a diverse set of stereo video sequences recorded in street scenes from 50 different cities, with high-quality pixel-level annotations of 5.000 frames in addition to a larger set

of 20.000 weakly annotated frames. A number of 30 visual classes for annotation were defined, which are further grouped into eight categories: flat, construction, nature, vehicle, sky, object, human, and void. However, instance-level labeling is available only for humans and vehicles (*Person, Rider, Car, Truck, Bus, Train, Motorcycle,* and *Bicycle*). Around 3000 images are used for the training, 500 for the validation, as well as 1500 images with annotation being held for benchmarking purposes.

- **Berkeley Deep Drive (BDD) dataset** [29]: The BDD dataset is a new driving dataset comprised of over 100K videos with diverse kinds of annotations including image-level tagging, object bounding boxes, drivable areas, lane markings, and full-frame instance segmentation. The dataset possesses geographic, environmental, and weather diversity, which is useful for training models so that they are less likely to be surprised by new conditions. The latter contains 10 object categories (*bus, traffic light, traffic sign, person, bike, truck, motor, car, train,* and *rider*) spread over 100.000 images with over 1.8M object instance labeled bounding boxes, making it suitable for robust object detection and semantic instance segmentation. The dataset is divided further into 3 domains, namely 'clear weather', 'city street' and 'daytime'. The current study selects only the 'city street' as a training domain which has a number of around 36.000 images in the training set.
- **Udacity dataset** [4]: The UDacity dataset contains over 600K urban objects in a variety of outdoor urban videos involving *Pedestrians, Cars, Bicycles* and other objects moving in the scene. It has been divided into two groups: traffic objects and traffic signs. Part of the data was collected using an HD camera mounted in a vehicle. Around 375.000 annotated traffic objects for 100k images are used for training purposes. The train/validation and test splits are 40%, 40% and 20%, respectively.

4.2 Experimental Environment

In order to define the experimental protocol a set of parameters should be initialized as follows:

- The R-CNN part of the model was pre-trained using the COCO [22] dataset, while for the fine-tuning, the training and validation sets from each dataset were used.
- The ResNet-50 variant is selected for its simplicity and relatively short training time.
- Images were resized such that their scale (longer edge) is 512 pixels.
- The RPN anchors span 5 scales and 3 aspect ratios, and the IoU threshold of positive and negative anchors was 0.7 and 0.3 respectively.
- As in Mask R-CNN, a RoI was considered positive if it has IoU with a ground-truth bounding box of at least 0.5, otherwise it was discarded as negative.

Fig. 4. Object detection results obtained from the application of the Mask R-CNN (a) and Flow R-CNN (b) models to the supported datasets [4,29,30]

- The optical flow loss L_{of} was defined only on positive RoIs. During training, a set of 64 samples was selected for each input image, while at test time the proposal number was set 300 followed by an Non-Maximum Suppression (NMS) mechanism. The NMS process was performed twice, at the RPN results as well as at the predicted classes (class-specific NMS).
- The training phase is divided into two stages: a) only the flow branch being trained, b) all layers from ResNet stage 4 and up being fine-tuned.
- The 'Keras 2' deep learning framework with 'Tensorflow' backend was used for experimentation on two Nvidia GeForce GTX TITAN X GPUs. Ubuntu 18.04.
- The model was trained using Stochastic Gradient Decent (SGD) algorithm, utilizing batches of 2 images with learning rate (lr), initially set equal to $1e^{-3}$.
- Momentum was set to 0.9 and weight decay to 0.0001.

4.3   Comparative Evaluation

In Tables 1, 2, 3, 4, 5 and 6, quantitative object detection results are given in the form of the mean Average Precision (mAP), *i.e.* computes the average precision value for recall value over 0 to 1. The current study follows the evaluation protocol defined by COCO challenge and adopts the primary challenge metric mAP that computes mAP over all classes and over 10 IoU thresholds. Averaging over the 10 IoU thresholds rather than only considering one general threshold of $mAP^{IoU=.5}$ tends to reward models that are better at precise localization. For providing a better insight, indicative object detection results obtained by the application of the proposed approach against the baseline one are presented in Fig. 4. It can be observed that the proposed scheme exhibits improved recognition performance (especially in the case of moving cars) over the baseline in varying urban scenarios (night-view, top-view, car-view).

Table 1. Comparative results on KITTI dataset

	Easy mask	Flow	Moderate mask	Flow	Hard mask	Flow
Car	0.893	0.905	0.843	0.849	0.733	0.736
Pedestrian	0.804	0.812	0.672	0.677	0.619	0.622
Cyclist	0.739	0.746	0.635	0.638	0.554	0.556
mAP	0.812	0.821	0.717	0.721	0.635	0.638

Table 2. Comparative results on V-KITTI dataset

Class	Mask R-CNN	Flow R-CNN
Car	0.932	0.958
Van	0.917	0.940
mAP	0.924	0.949

From the first group (Table 1) of the provided results (*i.e.* KITTI dataset), it can be seen that the introduced Flow R-CNN model slightly improved the results of the respective Mask R-CNN model in all categories (Car, Pedestrian, Cyclist) as well as in every application scenario (Easy, moderate, hard). However, there was a significant improvement for the 'Car' category, about 1.2%, that supports the initial claim. The latter demonstrates the increased discrimination capabilities of the flow information stream. The same applies to the V-KITTI experiments (Table 2), where the proposed architecture surpasses the baseline by a large margin (over 2% improvement).

Table 3. Comparative results on visdrone dataset

Class	Mask R-CNN	Flow R-CNN
Pedestrian	0.205	0.223
People	0.071	0.064
Bicycle	0.029	0.033
Car	0.406	0.428
Van	0.208	0.232
Truck	0.148	0.181
Tricycle	0.132	0.148
Awn	0.091	0.085
Bus	0.216	0.253
Motor	0.153	0.151
mAP	0.166	0.180

Concerning the Visdrone experiments (Table 3), it can be observed that the introduced scheme perform reasonably well in categories where the motion is evident ('Car', 'Van', 'Track', *etc.*), while fails to recognize those that have complex structure or cover small portion of the image due to camera positioning (*e.g.* based on drone footage).

Table 4. Comparative results on cityscapes dataset

Class	Mask R-CNN	Flow R-CNN
Person	0.345	0.364
Rider	0.271	0.307
Car	0.488	0.505
Truck	0.296	0.306
Bus	0.401	0.387
Train	0.302	0.252
Motorcycle	0.237	0.256
Bicycle	0.182	0.204
mAP	0.315	0.323

The exhibited results of the Cityscapes dataset (Table 4) suggest that incorporating the flow stream into the learning process of an R-CNN architecture may have a positive impact in the detection and recognition of moving objects, such as 'Cars', 'Motorcycles' and 'Trucks', by 1.7%, 1.9% and 1%, respectively. Moreover, regarding the BDD experiments (Table 5) the influence of the motion branch to the R-CNN scheme is evident in the presented results, as most classes have superior recognition performance, whereas a slight increase is reported for

Table 5. Comparative results on BDD dataset

Class	Mask R-CNN	Flow R-CNN
Bike	0.383	0.391
Bus	0.481	0.489
Car	0.732	0.746
Motor	0.194	0.198
Person	0.531	0.537
Rider	0.349	0.352
Traffic-light	0.479	0.473
Traffic-sign	0.558	0.547
Truck	0.506	0.514
mAP	0.421	0.424

the overall mAP (0.3%), as static objects ('traffic-light' and 'traffic-sign') over-shade the performance. Udacity dataset (Table 6) has quite similar content and category types to the previous one, and due to the lack of optical flow training data for this group, as Udacity is composed of still images, it was decided to transfer the acquired knowledge from the previous set (*i.e.* the BDD). This limitation has led the model to fail in most cases, except in the case of cars, that hold a significant portion of the dataset, demonstrating the need for data but also highlighting the cumulative capabilities that the introduced model offers to the moving objects. An evaluation of the proposed Flow R-CNN in six different datasets using various backbones is shown in Table 7. It can be observed that the introduced model achieves improved performance in all datasets using deeper ResNet architectures, while also benefiting from advanced schemes such as the FPN-variant; highlighting the generalizability of the proposed design. It should be noted that given the initialization of the R-CNN part with a dataset comprised of static images, it further affects the overall result.

Table 6. Comparative results on udacity dataset

Class	Mask R-CNN	Flow R-CNN
Bike	0.625	0.629
Bus	0.949	0.951
Car	0.724	0.736
Motorbike	0.738	0.736
Person	0.747	0.752
Traffic-light	0.502	0.498
Traffic-sign	0.701	0.696
mAP	0.712	0.714

Table 7. Comparative results on six datasets using different backbone architectures

Backbone	KITTI	V-KITTI	Visdrone	Cityscapes	BDD	Udacity
ResNet-50	0.724	0.949	0.180	0.323	0.424	0.714
ResNet-101	0.731	0.956	0.185	0.329	0.430	0.720
ResNet-50-FPN	0.735	0.961	0.194	0.334	0.432	0.725
ResNet-101-FPN	0.742	0.967	0.207	0.340	0.438	0.731

5   Conclusions

In this paper, the problem of multi-task object detection using DL techniques was investigated following the recent and highly promising studies in the computer vision field, and more specifically the R-CNN approach. A methodology for incorporation of pseudo-temporal information in Region-based CNN object detection schemes was presented, in contrast to the vast majority of literature methods that rely only on the use of appearance information and semantic knowledge. Additionally, following a neuro-scientifically grounded scheme, the pseudo-temporal stream was integrated parallel to the classification, bounding box regression and segmentation mask prediction branches of Mask R-CNN, and it was effectively incorporated into the learning process by penalizing the global loss computation with an optical flow loss factor. Extensive experiments and thorough comparative evaluation were reported, which provide a detailed analysis of the problem at hand and demonstrate the added value of the involved instance-level motion branch. The overall proposed approach achieved improved performance in the six currently broadest and most challenging publicly available semantic urban scene understanding datasets, surpassing the baseline method. Future work includes the investigation of re-adjusting the proposed pseudo-temporal branch utilizing a more sophisticated optical flow estimation methodology.

Acknowledgment. The work presented in this paper was supported by the European Commission under contract H2020-787061 ANITA.

References

1. Cai, Z., Vasconcelos, N.: Cascade R-CNN: high quality object detection and instance segmentation. IEEE Trans. Pattern Anal. Mach. Intell. (2019). https://doi.org/10.1109/TPAMI.2019.2956516
2. Cordts, M., et al.: The cityscapes dataset for semantic urban scene understanding. In: Proceedings of the IEEE Conference on CVPR, pp. 3213–3223 (2016)
3. Dai, J., Li, Y., He, K., Sun, J.: R-fcn: object detection via region-based fully convolutional networks. In: Advances in NIPS, pp. 379–387 (2016)
4. Dominguez-Sanchez, A., Cazorla, M., Orts-Escolano, S.: A new dataset and performance evaluation of a region-based CNN for urban object detection. Electronics **7**(11), 301 (2018)
5. Dosovitskiy, A., et al.: Flownet: Learning optical flow with convolutional networks. In: The IEEE ICCV (December 2015)
6. Fu, C.Y., Liu, W., Ranga, A., Tyagi, A., Berg, A.C.: Dssd: Deconvolutional single shot detector. arXiv preprint arXiv:1701.06659 (2017)
7. Gaidon, A., Wang, Q., Cabon, Y., Vig, E.: Virtual worlds as proxy for multi-object tracking analysis. In: Proceedings of the IEEE conference on CVPR, pp. 4340–4349 (2016)
8. Gao, R., Xiong, B., Grauman, K.: Im2flow: motion hallucination from static images for action recognition. In: Proceedings of the IEEE Conference on CVPR, pp. 5937–5947 (2018)
9. Geiger, A., Lenz, P., Stiller, C., Urtasun, R.: Vision meets robotics: the kitti dataset. IJRR **32**(11), 1231–1237 (2013)
10. Girshick, R.: Fast R-CNN object detection with caffe. Microsoft Research (2015)
11. Girshick, R., Donahue, J., Darrell, T., Malik, J.: Rich feature hierarchies for accurate object detection and semantic segmentation. In: Proceedings of the IEEE conference on CVPR, pp. 580–587 (2014)

12. He, K., Gkioxari, G., Dollar, P., Girshick, R.: Mask R-CNN. In: The IEEE ICCV (October 2017)
13. He, K., Zhang, X., Ren, S., Sun, J.: Spatial pyramid pooling in deep convolutional networks for visual recognition. IEEE Trans. PAMI **37**(9), 1904–1916 (2015)
14. He, K., Zhang, X., Ren, S., Sun, J.: Deep residual learning for image recognition. In: Proceedings of the IEEE conference on CVPR, pp. 770–778 (2016)
15. Hill, H., Johnston, A.: Categorizing sex and identity from the biological motion of faces. Current Biol. **11**(11), 880–885 (2001)
16. Ilg, E., Mayer, N., Saikia, T., Keuper, M., Dosovitskiy, A., Brox, T.: Flownet 2.0: evolution of optical flow estimation with deep networks. In: Proceedings of the IEEE Conference on CVPR, pp. 2462–2470 (2017)
17. Kang, K., et al.: T-cnn: Tubelets with convolutional neural networks for object detection from videos. IEEE Trans. CSVT **28**(10), 2896–2907 (2017)
18. Kourtzi, Z., Kanwisher, N.: Activation in human mt/mst by static images with implied motion. J. Cogn. Neurosci. **12**(1), 48–55 (2000)
19. Li, Z., Peng, C., Yu, G., Zhang, X., Deng, Y., Sun, J.: Light-head R-CNN: In defense of two-stage object detector. arXiv preprint arXiv:1711.07264 (2017)
20. Lin, T.Y., Dollár, P., Girshick, R., He, K., Hariharan, B., Belongie, S.: Feature pyramid networks for object detection. In: Proceedings of the IEEE conference on CVPR, pp. 2117–2125 (2017)
21. Lin, T.Y., Goyal, P., Girshick, R., He, K., Dollár, P.: Focal loss for dense object detection. In: Proceedings of the IEEE ICCV, pp. 2980–2988 (2017)
22. Lin, T.Y., et al.: Microsoft COCO: common objects in context. In: Fleet, D., Pajdla, T., Schiele, B., Tuytelaars, T. (eds.) ECCV 2014. LNCS, vol. 8693, pp. 740–755. Springer, Cham (2014). https://doi.org/10.1007/978-3-319-10602-1_48
23. Liu, W., et al.: SSD: single shot multiBox detector. In: Leibe, B., Matas, J., Sebe, N., Welling, M. (eds.) ECCV 2016. LNCS, vol. 9905, pp. 21–37. Springer, Cham (2016). https://doi.org/10.1007/978-3-319-46448-0_2
24. Maus, G.W., Ward, J., Nijhawan, R., Whitney, D.: The perceived position of moving objects: transcranial magnetic stimulation of area mt+ reduces the flash-lag effect. Cereb. Cortex **23**(1), 241–247 (2013)
25. Najibi, M., Rastegari, M., Davis, L.S.: G-CNN: an iterative grid based object detector. In: The IEEE Conference on CVPR (June 2016)
26. Redmon, J., Divvala, S., Girshick, R., Farhadi, A.: You only look once: unified, real-time object detection. In: Proceedings of the IEEE Conference on CVPR, pp. 779–788 (2016)
27. Redmon, J., Farhadi, A.: Yolo9000: better, faster, stronger. In: Proceedings of the IEEE conference on CVPR, pp. 7263–7271 (2017)
28. Ren, S., He, K., Girshick, R., Sun, J.: Faster R-CNN: Towards real-time object detection with region proposal networks. In: Advances in NIPS, pp. 91–99 (2015)
29. Yu, F., et al.: Bdd100k: A diverse driving video database with scalable annotation tooling. arXiv preprint arXiv:1805.04687 (2018)
30. Zhu, P., et al.: Visdrone-vdt2018: the vision meets drone video detection and tracking challenge results. In: Proceedings of the ECCV (2018)
31. Zhu, X., Wang, Y., Dai, J., Yuan, L., Wei, Y.: Flow-guided feature aggregation for video object detection. In: The IEEE ICCV (October 2017)

Compressed Video Action Recognition Using Motion Vector Representation

Chenghui Zhou[1], Xiaolei Chen[2], Pei Sun[2], Guanwen Zhang[1(✉)], and Wei Zhou[1]

[1] School of Electronics and Information, Northwestern Polytechnical University,
Xi'an, China
{guanwen.zh,zhouwei}@nwpu.edu.cn
[2] CNPC Logging Co., Ltd., Xi'an, China

Abstract. Action recognition is an important task for video understanding. Due to expensive time consumption, the conventional approaches employing the optical flow are difficult to be used for real-time purpose. Recently, the Motion Vector (MV), which can be directly extracted from the compressed video, has been introduced for action recognition. In this paper, we propose a novel approach by utilizing motion vector representation for action recognition. On the one hand, we use the motion vector information to select key information sequences for recognition. On the other hand, we further use the motion vector to formulate the representation of the selected sequences. We evaluate the proposed approach on UCF101 and HMDB51 datasets. The experimental results demonstrate that the proposed approach is able to achieve competitive recognition performance, and is able to maintain a 461.5 fps end-to-end processing rate at the same time.

Keywords: Action recognition · Motion vector · Real-time

1 Introduction

The video action recognition is an important area in computer vision for understanding real-world video data, and it has received much attention in recent years due to the rapid growth of deployed smart devices. Generally, the performance of action recognition greatly depends on whether the temporal information of the entire video can be fully utilized. The state-of-the-art deep learning methods for action recognition use convolutional neural networks (CNNs) on the basis of the pre-computed optical flow features. Those methods densely sample the video frames in a short time range and optical flow to characterize the temporal information [13,15].

However, optical flows computation is still inefficient and costs over 90% of the whole run-time both at training and testing phases because of the dense estimation between pixels. Besides, those methods are lack of the capability to incorporate long-range temporal information. Since the videos have very low information density, the video data is supposed to be compressed to meet the

A. Del Bimbo et al. (Eds.): ICPR 2020 Workshops, LNCS 12661, pp. 701–713, 2021.
https://doi.org/10.1007/978-3-030-68763-2_53

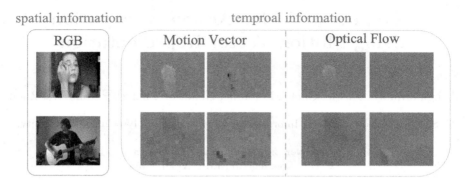

Fig. 1. Visualization of the motion vector and optical flow. Although motion vector contains some noise, it still represents motion information similar to optical flow to a certain content.

limit requests of bandwidth and storage media before transmission and storage. The video encoding algorithms and implementations, such as MPEG [10], H.264 [24], and H.256 [2] standards, have been built-in the smart devices. In video encoding, one similar criterion as that of the optical flow for describing temporal information of video is the Motion Vector (as shown in Fig. 1). Motion vector is designed to represent the motion information of two consecutive frames. It is able to represent local motion patterns of image blocks, and is able to remove the redundant content. Compared with optical flow, the motion vector has already been calculated on the smart devices, and saved in the video stream. Therefore, utilizing the motion vector as the feature representation for action recognition will be much more efficient and faster compared with that of the video decompression and optical flow computation for optical flow. DTMV-CNN [26] has explored to use motion vector as temporal information to train the deep neural network. This work apply distillation to transfer knowledge from an optical flow network to a motion vector network. However, unlike our approach, it still densely sample the video frames in a short time range and optical flow to characterize the temporal information and has risks of missing key information in video. Meanwhile, it still requires optical flow as an additional supervision.

In this paper, we propose a novel approach for compressed video action recognition using motion vector representation. On the one hand, we formulate the motion information on the basis of motion vector to describe motion intensity. The sequences with high motion intensity indicate the sequences with more information, which are selected as key information sequences. On the other hand, we introduce a two-stream deep convolutional neural network (CNN) to perform feature learning on the basis of motion vector. The network consists of a spatial and a temporal CNN, which are finial fused as an end-to-end manner for action recognition. We evaluate the proposed method on UCF101 [17] and HMDB51

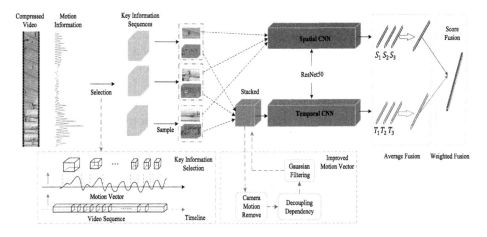

Fig. 2. Overview of our approach. A video, according to its motion vector features, is divided into L sequences. During these sequences, the key sequences contain the most abundant characterization information. Accurate and efficient video-level action prediction can be achieved by extracting the high performance representation of key sequence and designing a reasonable fusion function.

[9] datasets. The experimental results demonstrate that the proposed method significantly outperforms the-state-of-art methods on the two datasets.

2   Related Works

Action recognition has been widely studied in recent years. Extracting and applying discriminative features from videos is the most important step in action recognition. The research can be roughly divided into two groups: deeply-learned features and temporal sampling strategy.

Deeply-Learned Features. The latest developments in deep neural networks have greatly improved the effect of video understanding. A lot of studies designed effective CNN architectures to extract deep features for action recognition [15,19–21]. Zisserman et al. proposed two-stream architecture that exploits two CNNs to model RGB and optical flow respectively [15]. This method achieved excellent performance in recognition accuracy. Zhang et al. developed the deeply transferred motion vector CNN, which applied distillation to transfer knowledge from an optical flow network to a motion vector network [26]. Wang et al. proposed a two-stream 3D CNN fusion technology, which uses spatial-temporal pyramid pools (STPP) and LSTM models to extract multi-size descriptions and learn the global representation of each input video [23]. Several works [6,12] tried to use recurrent neural networks (RNNs) to model the temporal evolution of frame features for action recognition. Almost all these methods need to extract the extra temporal features such as optical flow, that results in introducing excessive computational cost. Different from those methods, we leverage motion vector as the temporal feature, which can be extracted directly from standard compressed video with very low computational cost.

Temporal Sampling Strategy. Many research works have been devoted to modeling the long-temporal sampling structure for action recognition [5, 7]. Fernando et al. postulated that a function, which is capable of ordering the frames of a video temporally, would capture well the evolution of the appearance within the video via a ranking machine [7]. Shi et al. proposed a long-term motion descriptor called sequential Deep Trajectory Descriptor (sDTD), which was introduced into a three-stream framework so as to identify actions from a video sequence [14]. Song et al. introduced a simple yet effective temporal-spatial mapping (TSM) for capturing the temporal evolution of the frames by jointly analyzing all the frames of a video [16]. Zhu et al. presented a CNN architecture that implicitly captured motion information between adjacent frames, which only took raw video frames as input and directly predicted action classes without explicitly computing optical flow [27]. However, those methods would be time consuming when applied to long video sequences and have risks of missing key information in video. In order to tackle this issue, we propose a key information sequence detection algorithm and a sparse temporal sampling strategy to enable learning key motion information efficiently.

3 Proposed Approach

The proposed approach exploits motion vectors to learn temporal information for action recognition. Due to the dependency of motion vectors and interference of camera movement, the motion vector can not be used directly as input for feature learning. We first select the key information sequences based on output motion vector and then formulate the motion information by decoupling the dependency and camera movement. The motion vector representation is finally learning by using a two-stream CNN. As discussed in above sections, the motion vectors have already been calculated and saved in video stream, which will introduce no extra computation. The proposed method can achieve extremely fast processing speed. The overview of the proposed method is summarized in Fig. 2.

3.1 Motion Vector

Motion vectors are criterion of the degree of contents intensity. It is designed for describing macro blocks movement between two successive frames. The video compression algorithms or implementation generally utilize motion vectors to leverage the redundancy of similar contents in videos. Those algorithms exploit a famous search algorithm "Three Step Search" [11] to achieve great balance between search times and preferable result. If there exists displacement (i, j) that makes Mean Absolute Difference (MAD) get minimal value, this displacement is the motion vector of current block (MV_{block}) as:

$$MAD_{block}(i,j) = \frac{1}{MN} \sum_{m=1}^{M} \sum_{n=1}^{N} |f_c(m,n) - f_{c+1}(m+i,n+j)|, \qquad (1)$$

where (i,j) is displacement, M and N are the height and width of a block. In Eq. 1, the $f_c(m,n)$ is the pixel value of point (m,n).

The video frames are split into I-frames (intra-coded frames), P-frames (predictive frames), and B-frames (bi-directional frames) as in H.264 or H.265 standard. The I-frames are coded using only information from the current frame. The P-frames and B-frame are referring to other frames, and they only encode the changed content parts. For each P-frame, only the change corresponding to the reference frame is stored.

3.2   Key Information Selection

Due to the continuity of action, the effective information density of video is very sparse. We have designed a new key information sequence selection algorithm based on motion vectors to extract key information sequences.

We exploit motion vector as an objective criteria to detect key information sequences in video. The core part of the key information selection algorithm is locating active parts of motion vector curve. The sum of motion vector blocks in a frame indicates how fast the content changes as:

$$MV_a = \sum_{t=0}^{N} MV_t, \qquad (2)$$

where, N is the total number of macro blocks in a frame and MV_a is the sum of all motion vectors value within the frame a. Due to the consideration of camera movement, we exploit a normalized metric as:

$$MV_a^r = \frac{MV_a}{max(MV_{frames})}, \qquad (3)$$

In Eq. 3, MV_{frames} is a matrix containing MV values of all frames within current video and the MV_a^r is a normalized result of frame a, which can offset the adverse effects of background movement to a certain extent. In order to detect the boundary of the key information sequence in the video, we use the absolute value of the motion vector difference between two consecutive frames to evaluate the degree of fluctuation. The residual of MV can be represented as:

$$MV\_residual = |MV_a^r - MV_{a+1}^r|, \qquad (4)$$

where MV_a^r and MV_{a+1}^r represents the normalized motion vector of frame a and next frame. $MV\_residual$ represents the degree of fluctuation of motion state at

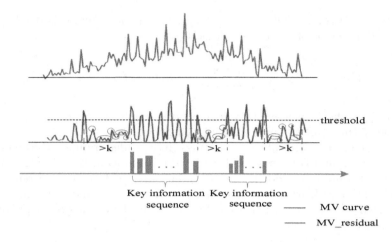

Fig. 3. Visualization of the key information sequence selection algorithm.

two continuous frames. We use $MV_{residual}$ as a measure rather than MV_{frame} because MV_{frame} is just a representation of the speed at which video content changes. If there is a continuous high MV_{frame} value without significant difference, no fluctuation will occur. In order to ensure motion integrity and reduce redundancy, we locate the key information sequence boundary by matching the pattern of weakly continuous high $MV_{residual}$ values. As shown in Fig. 3, weakly continuous patterns allow the appearance of continuous frames with low $MV_{residual}$, in which the length is less than k. In this manner, we can divide a video into several sequences based on motion vector and its residual. We assume that when the number of consecutive low $MV_{residual}$ exceeds the threshold k, the current region is the segmentation edge of the key sequence.

3.3   Motion Vector Representation

During video coding, motion vectors are mainly composed of two factors: the object motion and camera motion. Moving objects usually attract more visual attention than background. It is thus necessary to remove the interference caused by camera movement. Furthermore, it has been pointed out in [25] that the motion vectors in P-frames do not contain the full information and have strong interdependence, because the reference frame of P-frame may be a P-frame again. In order to relieve those problems, we firstly propose a voting algorithm based on the motion angle to remove the camera motion. In video coding, macro block is the basic coding unit, which has sizes ranging from 8×8 to 16×16. In other words, the splitting depth is 1 (= 8×8 block size) and 0 (= 16×16 block size) [18]. Generally speaking, the split depth of background is always smaller than object. To this end, the background region R_b can roughly be calculated as:

$$R_b = \{(x, y) \| D_{xy} < \frac{1}{|N|} \sum_{(x', y') \in N} D_{x'y'}\}, \tag{5}$$

here D_{xy} is the split depth at location (x, y) in current frame. $|N|$ is the total number of macro blocks. As for camera motion, assuming that $M_{x,y}$ is the two-dimensional motion vector of pixel (x, y) and the dominant camera motion M_c in this frame can be determined via voting all motion vectors angles in the background R_b as:

$$max \; hist(\bigcup_{x, y \in R_b} A(M_{x,y})), \tag{6}$$

here $A(M_{x,y})$ is the azimuth for MVs and $hist(.)$ is the azimuth histogram of all MVs. Considering that the motion vector is a two-dimensional vector, we can calculate the angle of the motion vector in the Cartesian coordinate system through a trigonometric function. In this paper, 12 bins with equal angle width ($\frac{360°}{12} = 30°$) are applied for the histogram $A(M_{x,y})$, radius $r(M_{x,y})$ for the camera motion needs to be calculated via averaging over all MVs from the selected bin of $A(M_{x,y})$. Hence, the camera motion of each frame can be achieved upon $A(M_{x,y})$ and $r(M_{x,y})$. Secondly, in order to break the dependency between consecutive P-frames, we accumulate the motion vectors and residual. According to statistics, the first P-frame after the I-frame often contains the most complete motion structure information, so we use the first P-frame closest to the current frame as the basis of the entire time stream. Let $\mathcal{R}_{f-1} = L_f - M_f$ be reference location in previous frame. L_f and M_f represents the location and motion vector of a pixel at current frame respectively. The location traced back to frame l is formed as:

$$\mathcal{R}_l = L_f - M_f - ... - M_l, \tag{7}$$

Then the corrected motion vector $\mathcal{C}_P$ at current P-frame are

$$\mathcal{C}_P^{(t)} = L_P^{(t)} - T_{P\_first}^{(t)} + M_{P\_first}^{(t)}, \tag{8}$$

here $L_P^{(t)}$ is the location of pixel t in current P-frame and $T_{P\_first}^{(t)}$ is the location traced back to the first P-frame. $M_{P\_first}^{(t)}$ represents the motion vector information in the first P-frame. This corrected approach can be efficiently implemented by simple recursive algorithm in linear time.

3.4   Baseline Model

Our baseline module is based on the classical two-stream structure and uses motion vectors to capture temporal information. We adopt the cross modality pre-training and partial BN [22] to mitigate the risk of over-fitting. In terms

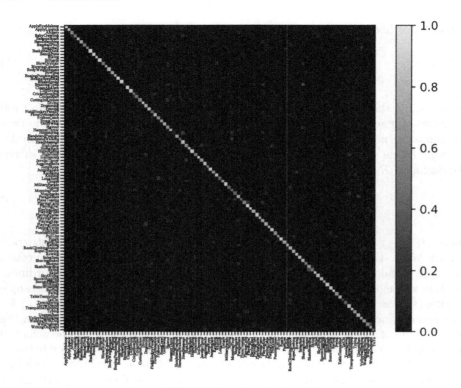

Fig. 4. Confusion matrix for MVR-AR based on high performance motion vectors of 101 classes on UCF101 (split1).

of network architecture, we use Resnet-50 which is pre-trained in ImageNet [4] to formulate spatial and temporal networks. As shown in experiments, it could achieve a good balance between recognition speed and accuracy.

We design a multi-input network model. As for the spatial stream CNN, we randomly sampled one frame of RGB image as feature for network learning in sequences with relatively low motion intensity. In the critical stage of the action, because the motion information is more abundant, we sample two frames for the feature learning. The design of such a sampling strategy helps the network to better learn the key parts of the motion in the video, and only needs four frames to learn the action. We obtain 10 stacked motion vectors in the x and y directions respectively as the temporal features by removing camera motion, decoupling between P-frames, as well as gaussian filtering.

As explained in [22], the fusion function of the network has a crucial impact on the recognition results. In this paper, we utilize average fusion without any other supervision. As shown in the experiments, the baseline model can still achieve competitive results.

4 Experiments

In this section, we first introduce the test datasets and the implementation details of experimental. Then we validate that high performance motion vector can be a good replacement for optical flow for action recognition. At the same time, we also experimentally demonstrate that key information sequences can improve the recognition accuracy of network (Table 2).

Table 1. Improved recognition accuracy when replacing original motion vectors with improved motion vectors on ucf-101 [17] and hmdb-51 [9]. r-mv: original motion vectors. h-mv: high performance motion vectors. '+' represents the fusion scores of models. K is the number of key information sequences.

$K = 3$	RGB	R-MV	H-MV	R-MV+RGB	H-MV+RGB
UCF-101					
Average	**82.2**	**73.5**	**76.0**	**90.5**	**91.8**
HMDB-51					
Average	**50.6**	**34.9**	**37.1**	**58.2**	**58.4**

Table 2. Compared result of the algorithm of key information sequence and average segmentation. kis: key information selection.

$K = 3$	RGB	R-MV	H-MV	R-MV+RGB	H-MV+RGB
UCF-101					
Average	81.2	73.5	76.0	89.5	90.8
KIS	**82.8**	**75.8**	**77.6**	**91.2**	**92.1**
HMDB-51					
Average	50.6	34.9	37.1	58.2	58.4
KIS	**51.8**	**36.9**	**38.0**	**59.6**	**60.3**

4.1 Datasets and Experimental Details

We evaluate our method Motion Vector Representation based Action Recognition (MVR-AR) on two action recognition datasets, UCF101 [17] and HMDB51 [9]. The UCF101 dataset contains 101 action classes and 13,320 video clips. HMDB51 contains 6,766 videos from 51 action categories. Each dataset has 3 training/testing splits for evaluation. Unless otherwise stated, we report the average effect of the 3 testing splits. During testing, we uniformly sample 25 RGB frames or motion vectors stacks from the action videos following [22]. Meanwhile,

Table 3. The speed of extracting motion and vector optical flow under the same video resolution.

Dataset	Spatial-resolution	TV-L1 Flow(GPU)(FPS) (RTX 1080 Ti)	High performance MV(CPU)(FPS)
UCF101	320 * 240	28.2	676.7
HMDB51	320 * 240	28.2	676.7

we crop 4 corners and 1 center, and their horizontal flipping from the sampled frames. We use average pooling before Softmax to aggregate the predictions of different crops and snippets. For the fusion of spatial and temporal stream networks, we take a weighted average of them. We give more credits to the temporal stream by setting its weight as 1.5 and that of spatial stream as 1. As for training details, our models are pre-trained on the ImageNet [4] and fine-tuned using Adam [8] with a batch size of 64. For spatial networks, the initial learning rate is set to 0.001. The learning rate is divided by 10 at epoch 25, epoch 50 respectively. There are total 60 epochs for the training phase. For temporal network, the initial learning rate is set to 0.001. The learning rate is divided by 10 at epoch 180, epoch 270 respectively. And there are total 300 epochs for the training phase. For data augmentation, we apply color jittering, random cropping to 224×224 and horizontal flipping for training set during training. To speed up training, we employ a data-parallel strategy with multiple GPUs, implemented with our modified version of PyTorch. The whole training time on UCF101 is around 1.5 h for spatial network and 6 h for temporal network with 2 GeForce RTX 1080 Ti.

4.2 Accuracy and Efficiency

In this section, we study the benefits of motion vectors representation and key sequences selection for action recognition. Table 1 shows the experimental results of our algorithm on these two datasets. When motion vector is combined with RGB, the algorithm results are more ideal, and the accuracy on the UCF101 and HMDB51 datasets is increased by 18.3% and 23.5%, respectively.

And then, we experimentally verified the improvement of the key information sequence selection compared with the average division. In order to achieve a balance in recognition accuracy and efficiency, we divide the video into 3 as indicated in [22]. Differently, we sparsely sample features within the key information sequence selection.

The proposed method is very efficient because all features can be directly extracted from the video stream. We calculated the time required to generate the motion vector and optical flow. The comparison results are shown in Table 3. The computation speed of motion vectors is 676 FPS on CPU, while the computation speed of optical flows is only 28.2 FPS on GPU.

We compare the performance of our proposed method with several state-of-the art methods. The results are summarized in Table 4. The proposed method has a greater performance in recognition rate. Compared with the DTMV + RGB-CNN algorithm [26], which uses motion vector as the temporal feature

Table 4. Comparison of speed and accuracy with state-of-the-art on ucf101.

UCF-101	Accuracy	FPS[1]
MDI + RGB [1]	76.9%	<131
C3D(1 net)(GPU) [19]	82.3%	313.9
DTMV + RGB-CNN [26]	86.4%	390
Two-stream CNNs(GPU) [15]	88.0%	14.3
Two-stream I3D (RGB + Flow) [3]	93.4%	< 14
TSN (RGB + Optical Flow) (GPU) [22]	94.0%	14
TSN (RGB + RGBDiff) (GPU) [22]	91.0%	340
MVR-AR (RGB + Motion Vector)	**92.1%**	**461.5**

[1] The comparison results in the table are extracted from the original papers

and relies on additional supervision from an optical flow, MVR-AR still outperforms 5.8%. The main difference between DTMV + RGB-CNN and MVR-AR is the different sampling strategy. DTMV + RGB-CNN algorithm based classical two-stream network chooses the dense sampling strategy in a short time range to characterize the temporal information with the risks of missing key information in video. However, MVR-AR utilizes sparse sampling strategy in key information sequences and has a great capacity to incorporate long-range temporal information.

Compared with other optical flow based algorithms [3,15,22], our proposed method is about 14 times faster.

4.3   Ablation Studies

We first analyze the parameter sensitivity. There is one important parameter in our approach: the threshold k used to locate the key information sequence boundary. Considering the frames-per-second(fps) of videos is 24, we test three different parameter settings by setting k to 6, 12, 18. The accuracy of temporal CNN on UCF101 grows up from 75.6% to 75.8% when k 6 to 12 and goes down to 75.5% at k 18. According to this study, we set $k = 12$ in all experiments.

4.4   Visualizations

We show the confusion matrix for MVR-AR on UCF101 in Fig. 4. It can be shown that MVR-AR performs well in most videos for Human action category like **Billiards** and **CleanAndJerk**. However, MVR-AR performs worse in class **HeadMassage** and **Hammering**. For **HeadMassage**, MVR-AR always misclassifies into **Hammering**. It is possible that the action in **HeadMassage** is similar to the one in **Hammering**.

5   Conclusions

In this paper, we propose to train deep networks directly on compressed video representation. We use motion vectors to replace the optical flows as temporal features. Motion vectors can be extracted directly from video without extra calculation and represent the true and interesting signal. However, due to the dependency of motion vectors and interference from camera movement, training CNNs with motion vectors directly is extremely challenging. In order to mitigate this issue, we propose high performance motion vectors for network learning. At the same time, in order to reduce the high temporal redundancy and capture the key information in video, we propose a key information sequence detection algorithm to extract key sequences in the video for network learning. In general, our network has very good performance in recognition accuracy and efficiency and has very good practical application potential.

References

1. Bilen, H., Fernando, B., Gavves, E., Vedaldi, A., Gould, S.: Dynamic image networks for action recognition. In: Proceedings of the IEEE Conference on Computer Vision and Pattern Recognition, pp. 3034–3042 (2016)
2. Bross, B., Han, W.J., Ohm, J.R., Sullivan, G.J., Wang, Y.K., Wiegand, T.: High efficiency video coding (hevc) text specification draft 10 (for fdis & final call). Joint Collaborative Team on Video Coding (JCT-VC) of ITU-T SG16 WP3 and ISO/IEC JTC1/SC29/WG11, JCTVCL1003. v34 (2013)
3. Carreira, J., Zisserman, A.: Quo vadis, action recognition? a new model and the kinetics dataset. In: proceedings of the IEEE Conference on Computer Vision and Pattern Recognition, pp. 6299–6308 (2017)
4. Deng, J., Dong, W., Socher, R., Li, L.J., Li, K., Fei-Fei, L.: Imagenet: a large-scale hierarchical image database. In: 2009 IEEE Conference on Computer Vision and Pattern Recognition, pp. 248–255. IEEE (2009)
5. Diba, A., Sharma, V., Van Gool, L.: Deep temporal linear encoding networks. In: Proceedings of the IEEE Conference on Computer Vision and Pattern Recognition, pp. 2329–2338 (2017)
6. Du, Y., Wang, W., Wang, L.: Hierarchical recurrent neural network for skeleton based action recognition. In: Proceedings of the IEEE Conference on Computer Vision and Pattern Recognition, pp. 1110–1118 (2015)
7. Fernando, B., Gavves, E., Oramas, J.M., Ghodrati, A., Tuytelaars, T.: Modeling video evolution for action recognition. In: Proceedings of the IEEE Conference on Computer Vision and Pattern Recognition, pp. 5378–5387 (2015)
8. Kingma, D.P., Ba, J.: Adam: a method for stochastic optimization. arXiv preprint arXiv:1412.6980 (2014)
9. Kuehne, H., Jhuang, H., Garrote, E., Poggio, T., Serre, T.: HMDB: a large video database for human motion recognition. In: 2011 International Conference on Computer Vision, pp. 2556–2563. IEEE (2011)
10. Le Gall, D.: Mpeg: a video compression standard for multimedia applications. Commun. ACM **34**(4), 46–58 (1991)
11. Li, R., Zeng, B., Liou, M.L.: A new three-step search algorithm for block motion estimation. IEEE Trans. Circ. Syst. Video Technol **4**(4), 438–442 (1994)

12. Liu, J., Shahroudy, A., Xu, D., Wang, G.: Spatio-temporal LSTM with trust gates for 3D human action recognition. In: Leibe, B., Matas, J., Sebe, N., Welling, M. (eds.) ECCV 2016. LNCS, vol. 9907, pp. 816–833. Springer, Cham (2016). https://doi.org/10.1007/978-3-319-46487-9_50

13. Lu, T., Ai, S., Jiang, Y., Xiong, Y., Min, F.: Deep optical flow feature fusion based on 3D convolutional networks for video action recognition. In: 2018 IEEE SmartWorld, Ubiquitous Intelligence & Computing, Advanced & Trusted Computing, Scalable Computing & Communications, Cloud & Big Data Computing, Internet of People and Smart City Innovation (SmartWorld/SCALCOM/UIC/ATC/CBDCom/IOP/SCI), pp. 1077–1080. IEEE (2018)

14. Shi, Y., Tian, Y., Wang, Y., Huang, T.: Sequential deep trajectory descriptor for action recognition with three-stream CNN. IEEE Trans. Multimedia **19**(7), 1510–1520 (2017)

15. Simonyan, K., Zisserman, A.: Two-stream convolutional networks for action recognition in videos. In: Advances in Neural Information Processing Systems, pp. 568–576 (2014)

16. Song, X., Lan, C., Zeng, W., Xing, J., Sun, X., Yang, J.: Temporal-spatial mapping for action recognition. IEEE Trans. Circ. Syst. Video Technol. **30**, 748–759 (2019)

17. Soomro, K., Zamir, A., Shah, M.: Ucf101-action recognition data set (2017)

18. Sullivan, G.J., Baker, R.L.: Efficient quadtree coding of images and video. In: Proceedings ICASSP 91: 1991 International Conference on Acoustics, Speech, and Signal Processing (2002)

19. Tran, D., Bourdev, L., Fergus, R., Torresani, L., Paluri, M.: Learning spatiotemporal features with 3D convolutional networks. In: Proceedings of the IEEE International Conference on Computer Vision, pp. 4489–4497 (2015)

20. Tran, D., Ray, J., Shou, Z., Chang, S.F., Paluri, M.: Convnet architecture search for spatiotemporal feature learning. arXiv preprint arXiv:1708.05038 (2017)

21. Varol, G., Laptev, I., Schmid, C.: Long-term temporal convolutions for action recognition. IEEE Trans. Pattern Anal. Mach. Intell. **40**(6), 1510–1517 (2017)

22. Wang, L., et al.: Temporal segment networks: towards good practices for deep action recognition. In: Leibe, B., Matas, J., Sebe, N., Welling, M. (eds.) ECCV 2016. LNCS, vol. 9912, pp. 20–36. Springer, Cham (2016). https://doi.org/10.1007/978-3-319-46484-8_2

23. Wang, X., Gao, L., Wang, P., Sun, X., Liu, X.: Two-stream 3-D convnet fusion for action recognition in videos with arbitrary size and length. IEEE Trans. Multimedia **20**(3), 634–644 (2017)

24. Wiegand, T., Sullivan, G.J., Bjontegaard, G., Luthra, A.: Overview of the h. 264/avc video coding standard. IEEE Trans. Circ. Syst. Video Technol. **13**(7), 560–576 (2003)

25. Wu, C.Y., Zaheer, M., Hu, H., Manmatha, R., Smola, A.J., Krähenbühl, P.: Compressed video action recognition. In: Proceedings of the IEEE Conference on Computer Vision and Pattern Recognition, pp. 6026–6035 (2018)

26. Zhang, B., Wang, L., Wang, Z., Qiao, Y., Wang, H.: Real-time action recognition with deeply transferred motion vector CNNs. IEEE Trans. Image Process. **27**(5), 2326–2339 (2018)

27. Zhu, Y., Lan, Z., Newsam, S., Hauptmann, A.: Hidden two-stream convolutional networks for action recognition. In: Jawahar, C.V., Li, H., Mori, G., Schindler, K. (eds.) ACCV 2018. LNCS, vol. 11363, pp. 363–378. Springer, Cham (2019). https://doi.org/10.1007/978-3-030-20893-6_23

Introducing Region Pooling Learning

Jesus Adan Cruz Vargas, Julio Zamora Esquivel$^{(\boxtimes)}$, and Omesh Tickoo

Intel Labs, Guadalajara, Mexico
{jesus.a.cruz.vargas,julio.c.zamora.esquivel,omesh.tickoo}@intel.com

Abstract. In recent years, the advancement of convolutional neural network (CNN) topologies have been constantly evolving at an increasingly fast pace, with current novel proposals like Inception, ResNet, MobileNet, etc., pushing the performance results on available benchmarks, and optimizing towards smaller models with lower number of trainable parameters capable of achieving comparable results to the known state of the art. To this day, most of these novel approaches either rely on the use of pooling layers or the use of strided convolutions as one of the main building blocks of a CNN, i.e., the traditional max pooling and average pooling layers, as a way to reduce spatial dimensionality of features progressively through the network and focusing on obtain a value that not necessarily contains valuable information of the position of the object of interest. The selection between these two layers is typically based on the experience of the Neural Network architect, were several training procedures have to be evaluated to guarantee the best accuracy. In this work, we introduce the concept of the region pooling learning, in which an optimal pooling behavior is learned through training. Additionally, the knowledge of the region pooling layers can be leveraged by deeper layers. The region pooling layer could learn to behave as a max-pooling or an average-pooling, or it might learn to pool the most convenient value based on training. The experimental results presented in this work over two available image datasets suggest that the use of the region pooling layer improves the performance of a Resnet18 CNN network, outperforming in some cases a typical ResNet110 CNN.

Keywords: Feature pooling · Convolutional neural network · Image classification

1 Introduction

Neural network topologies are mainly composed of a coding step, that outputs features with desirable properties by passing an input image through a set of convolutional layers, together with a pooling step that transforms the features of the previous step into a more compact representation. Pooling helps to reduce the amount of computations and provides invariance to image transformations, while preserving relevant details robust to noise and clutter [2].

Typically, there are two commonly used pooling operations. The first one is the average pooling, where the idea of this operator is to perform a local

© Springer Nature Switzerland AG 2021
A. Del Bimbo et al. (Eds.): ICPR 2020 Workshops, LNCS 12661, pp. 714–724, 2021.
https://doi.org/10.1007/978-3-030-68763-2_54

averaging and a sub-sampling, reducing the resolution of the feature maps and adding some level of invariance to distortions and translations [14]. The second one is the max pooling, that operates in a similar way as the average pooling, but instead it uses the maximum value in the neighborhood to sub-sample the feature map.

New types of topologies focused on object recognition tasks [9,20,22] have succeeded in the production of better features representations during the coding steps; these features can be then pooled by a kernel that operates in a local spatial neighborhood or use strided convolutions that can reduce the dimension of the output features. The issue with these approaches is that the neighborhoods could contain heterogeneous vectors that may result in a considerable loss of information [1], limiting the generalization of the network.

The focus of this work is to define a smart pooling kernel able to define by itself a region at a sub-pixel precision, in which it can apply its own pooling operation, minimizing the loss of information.

To better describe the introduction of the smart pooling layer, we organized this manuscript as follows: Sect. 2 describes the related work in regards to novel proposed pooling operations; Sect. 3 explains in detail the methodology followed in our experimentation; Sect. 4 presents how the training of the smart pool layer is done; and Sect. 5 presents the results obtained and the conclusions observed, respectively.

2   Related Work

There has been some recent proposals around the use of different pooling layers. Some of these use attention mechanisms in order to compute the pooling operation; an example of this is presented in Natural Language Processing applications [19], where the pooling methodology is focused on an answer selection problem, where given a Question q of size M, and a Candidate Answer a of size L, the algorithm passes each input through a convolutional neural network (CNN) that outputs a feature map $Q \epsilon R^{c \times M}$ and $A \epsilon R^{c \times L}$ respectively. After this process, a Matrix G is defined as $G = \tanh(Q^T U A)$, where $U \epsilon R^{c \times c}$ is the matrix of parameters to be learned; the matrix G now contains a soft alignment between the hidden vectors of q and a. Taking into account this, a column-wise and a row-wise max pooling is applied, resulting in g^q and g^a that are used to compute $r_q = Q * softmax(g^q)$ and $r_a = Q * softmax(g^a)$ that are the pooled vectors.

Other works proposing different pooling operations are described in fractional max pooling [6]. In the reported work, given a 2×2 pooling operation, the disjoint nature of the pooling regions can limit the generalization of the network. Additionally, as this layer reduces very quickly the size of the feature maps by a factor of 2, stacks of back to back convolutional layers are used to build deeper networks [20]. This method proposes the reduction factor α of the pooling between $1 < \alpha 2$, and at the same time adding randomness to the pooling process. The max pooling process can be seen as $P_{i,j} \subset \{1, 2, \ldots, N_{in}\}^2$

for each $(i,j)\epsilon\{1,\dots,N_{out}\}^2$, where $P_{i,j}$ is the pooling region, N_{in} and N_{out} are the height of the input and output matrix respectively, and the maximum value is used in each region $P_{i,j}$. This methodology generates a square grid in the input feature map, and using two increasing series of integers $(a_i)_{i=0}^{N_{out}}$ and $(b_i)_{i=0}^{N_{out}}$ starting at 1 and ending with $N_i n$, the pooling regions are defined by $P_{i,j} = [a_{i-1}, a_i - 1] \times [b_{j-1}, b_j - 1]$.

In the CoordConv approach [16] the authors propose to concatenate extra channels to the input features with shape $h \times w \times c$, where h, w and c are the height, width and number channels, resulting in new feature maps with shape $h \times w \times c + n$, where n corresponds to the number of channels added, in their most basic version the added channels correspond to the i and j coordinates, respectively, although it could have a third channel for an r coordinate, where $r = \sqrt{(i - h/2)^2 + (j - w/2)}$. Thus the number of parameters in each Coord-Conv layer will contain $(c + d) \times c' \times k^2$. Although this approach was able to achieve good results in Generative Modeling tasks, it was not able to significantly improve the Top-5 accuracy in the ImageNet [4] challenge using a ResNet50 topology.

The Global Second-order Pooling (GSoP) [3] techniques have shown successful results in different tasks, such as object recognition, object detection and video classification, one of the ways to extract second-order features using pooling layers is by computing a covariance matrix $X^\mathsf{T} X$, then applying a tangent space mapping using the matrix logarithm which can be computed using singular value decomposition, thus this layer has the form $X_{l+1} = \log(X^\mathsf{T} X + \epsilon I)$ [11], this layer, although only used at the last convolutional layer, it has shown promising results [15] and the idea of using it at earlier layers has been borded in [5], where they not only introduce GSoP at the last convolutional layer but also into intermediate layers of deep convolutional networks.

3   Region Pooling Learning

The idea behind the Region Pooling Learning or smart pooling approach proposed in this work is the usage of a neural network, as described in Fig. 3, that takes a sub-image as the input and generates the coordinates (x, y) at the network's output. This output represent the location of the most representative pixel from the image to be pooled. It is important to remark that the x and y coordinates are floating point values that allow for sub-pixel precision, with these coordinates a weighted average is applied in the same way the texture sampler works in a GPU. The details of implemented procedure will be covered in this section.

In the first stage, the input image I with size (W_i, H_i) is cropped removing the last $W_i \bmod w_k$ columns and the last $H_i \bmod h_k$ rows, where (w_k, h_k) represent the size of the pooling kernel. Removing these columns and rows, the dimension of the output image is given by the ratio of the sizes as:

$$d_x = (W_i - \delta_x)/w_k \tag{1}$$
$$d_y = (H_i - \delta_y)/h_k \tag{2}$$

where $\delta_x = W_i \bmod w_k$, and $\delta_y = H_i \bmod h_k$, representing the residual columns and rows, respectively. An illustration of this can be observed in Fig. 1.

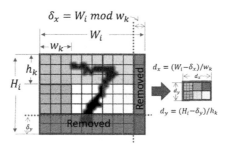

Fig. 1. The input image is cropped, removing rows and columns that allows the entire division in the ratio of W_i/w_k.

In order to process the cropped image, every sub-image will be batched, generating a one-dimensional array of images of (w_k, h_k). The length of this array is given by $d_x \times d_y$ as shows Fig. 2.

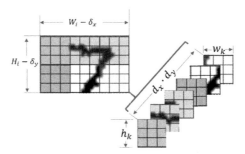

Fig. 2. The cropped image is sliced in an array of sub-images, where each sub-image has the size of the pooling kernel, and the stride is equal to the size of the kernel.

Finally, every image in the generated batch is evaluated by a small neural network composed by four layers: two convolutional layers of 8 filters with sizes of 5×1; one fully connected layer of 20 units fed by 1-dimensional kernels from the output of the first convolutional layers; and the output layer with 2 units in order to generate the x and y coordinates, thus the output of this network will be of size $(d_x \times d_y, 2)$. These coordinates are scaled to the size of the kernel w_k and h_k respectively, and represent the location of the pooled pixel in the sub-image coordinate frame.

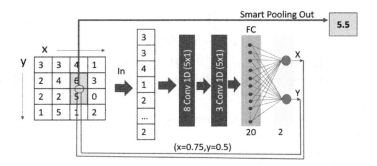

Fig. 3. The smart pooling sub neural network, designed to provide the (x, y) coordinates for pooling a sample from the input image.

Since these values are floating point type, one simple idea could be to take the nearest value to the pixel, but this ignores all the other pixels in the sub-image, and does not weight their contribution, instead we use the bilinear interpolation.

4   Experiments and Results

In order to test the concept of the region pooling learning in CNNs, three sets of experiments were implemented. The first one is a toy example that shows that our proposed pooling method can behave as Max Pooling or Average Pooling, the second one consists of training a CNN over the CIFAR-10 dataset, and the third one is a CNN over the ImageNet dataset. All the implementations use the PyTorch framework.

4.1   Average-Max Pooling Behavior

The first task we considered in order to show that our layer can act as max-pooling or average-pooling was to learn to behave as these poolings methods, here a training dataset composed of random matrices was used, during these tests the smart pooling layer had 16 neurons in its first convolution layer and 8 neurons in the second convolutional layer. For the max-pooling task, only two layers were used, a max-pooling layer with a 3×3 kernel size, serving as the target output, and the smart pooling layer, which was trained for 3 epochs, where datasets of 50,000 30×30 matrices with a range of $[0, 1]$ were randomly generated. An initial learning rate of 0.1, divided by 10 each epoch and weight decay of 0.0001 using Stochastic Gradient Descent (SGD), our method was able to predict the x, y coordinates of the maximum value with a 95% of accuracy over a 1000 30×30 random matrices. For the mean-pooling task a similar setup was employed, with the difference that the mean pooling layer produced the target output, the results showed that our layer had a maximum pixel difference of 0.06 between the predicted and the target output, the output of this task can be seen in Fig. 4.

As the purpose of our method is not to imitate the max or average pooling. Instead, is to compute the coordinates of the pixel that best represents the kernel, and in order to reduce the computation requirements, the number of neurons was reduced resulting in the topology depicted in Fig. 3.

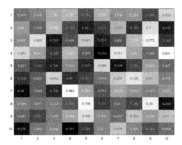
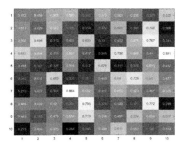

Target mean pooling   Predicted mean pooling

Fig. 4. Result of the smart pooling layer trained as mean pooling.

4.2   CIFAR-10

The CIFAR-10 [13] is a public data set that consists of 60,000 32 × 32 color images in 10 classes, with 6,000 images per class. There are 50,000 training images and 10,000 test images in the official release. In this context, the CIFAR-10 has been widely used for testing and benchmarking the state of the art models with the use of traditional pooling layers.

For this work, we modified ResNet18 [9] and PyramidNet [7] replacing their pooling method with the smart pooling layer, in this use case, only the global average pooling layer was replaced with our approach, for the ResNet18 topology a batch size of 128 was used, a weight initialization as in [8], a weight decay of 0.0001, a momentum of 0.9, an initial learning rate of 0.1 that is divided by 10 at 25 and 50 epochs, and terminating the training at 75 epochs. The training rule used during the experiments was SGD.

The ResNet18 topology is described in Table 1, it is important to highlight that there are two ResNet versions, the one that has up to 1.7M of parameters, that is described in Table 1, and the other version that has more than 11M of parameters and uses a similar topology as described in Table 4, with the difference that the first convolutional layer has a kernel size of 3 × 3, a stride of 1 and the last layer has an output size of 10.

In the case of the PyramidNet topology, it was trained for 300 epochs, depths of 110 and 18 were considered, an $alpha = 84$, the training settings were the same as in [7].

Table 1. ResNet18* topology with a smart pooling layer added, trained over CIFAR-10

Name	Output size	ResNet-18
Conv1	$32 \times 32 \times 16$	3×3, 16 stride 1
Conv2	$32 \times 32 \times 16$	$\begin{bmatrix} 3 \times 3, 16 \\ 3 \times 3, 16 \end{bmatrix} \times 2$
Conv3	$16 \times 16 \times 32$	$\begin{bmatrix} 3 \times 3, 32 \\ 3 \times 3, 32 \end{bmatrix} \times 2$
Conv4	$8 \times 8 \times 64$	$\begin{bmatrix} 3 \times 3, 64 \\ 3 \times 3, 64 \end{bmatrix} \times 2$
Smart pooling	$1 \times 1 \times 64$	8×8 **(Fig.** 3)
Fully connected	10	64×10

We have observed that the new versions of the topologies over-performed the originals, and in the case of ResNet18 topology (0.27M) achieves higher accuracy than the ResNet110 (44.5M parameters) with a marginal increment in the number of trainable parameters this represents 164X less number of parameters, and results in a model with better accuracy. These experimental results are detailed in Table 2, where there is also a comparison with other methods.

In order to compare against the related work described before, some of the latest topologies used for CIFAR-10 pattern recognition problem are included (limiting our analysis to those having less than 2.5M number of trainable parameters). Our intention is not to outperform the accuracy of these topologies. Instead, the idea is to achieve similar results with a significantly smaller model. This approach can potentially enable us to target an efficient implementation into embedded systems. Table 3 shows a summary of results from the smallest models recently reported for the CIFAR-10 classification problem.

While there is no simple way to determine the efficiency of a NN, our target is the highest accuracy with the least amount of memory as shown in Table 3. Comparing with All-CNN [21] our solution represents a 6X memory reduction with an improvement in accuracy; comparing with MobileNetV2, we have 11X compression with 2% increase in accuracy.

4.3   ImageNet

ImageNet is an image database organized according to the WordNet hierarchy, in which each node of the hierarchy is depicted by hundreds and thousands of images [17]. This dataset contains 1.2 million of images approximately. For this experiment, an image size of 224×224 was used and our neural network

Table 2. Results for different reported topologies with smart pooling and with other methods

Neural network	Depth	#Parameters	Accuracy%
ResNet18	18	0.27M	91.25
ResNet18 + CoordConv	18	0.27M + 4288	91.91
ResNet18 + GSoP	18	0.27M + 24384	92.68
ResNet56	56	0.85M	93.03
ResNet110	110	1.7M	93.57
ResNet18	18	11M	93.02
ResNet56	50	25.6M	93.62
ResNet110	100	44.5M	93.75
ResNet18 + Smart pooling	**18**	**0.27M + 3310**	**94.08**
PyramidNet-18 + CoordConv	18	0.21M + 4288	90.49
PyramidNet-18 + GSoP	18	0.21M + 24384	91.4
PyramidNet-18	18	0.21M	91.48
PyramidNet-18 + Smart pooling	**18**	**0.21M + 4095**	**92.17**
PyramidNet-110 + GSoP	18	3.9M + 49629	95.2
PyramidNet-110 + CoordConv	18	3.9M + 6205	95.55
PyramidNet-110	110	3.9M	95.81
PyramidNet-110 + Smart pooling	**18**	**3.9M + 4095**	**95.96**

Table 3. CIFAR-10 Classification error vs Number of parameters

Neural network	Depth	#Parameters	Error%
All-CNN [21]	9	1.3M	7.25
MobileNetV2 [18]	54	2.24M	7.22
SqueezeNet [10]	14	1.2M*	6.23
ShuffleNet 8G [23]	10	0.91M	7.71
ShuffleNet 1G [23]	10	0.24M	8.56
ResNet18 [12]	20	0.27M	8.75
Smart pooling	20	**0.2M**	5.92

topology was based on ResNet18 [9], replacing the average pooling layer with the smart pooling layer as described in the Table 4. The weight initialization is as in [8]. We used a batch size of 128, a learning rate that starts from 0.1 and is divided by 10 every 30 epochs and stopped at 90 epochs. A weight decay of 0.0001 was used and a momentum of 0.9, with SGD as training rule, yielding a 1.57% improvement for the top-1 error, these results are detailed in Table 5.

Table 4. ResNet18* topology with a smart pooling layer added, trained over ImageNet

Name	Output size	ResNet-18
Conv1	$112 \times 112 \times 64$	$7 \times 7{,}64$ stride 2
Conv2	$56 \times 56 \times 64$	$\begin{bmatrix} 3 \times 3, 64 \\ 3 \times 3, 64 \end{bmatrix} \times 2$
Conv3	$28 \times 28 \times 128$	$\begin{bmatrix} 3 \times 3, 128 \\ 3 \times 3, 128 \end{bmatrix} \times 2$
Conv4	$14 \times 14 \times 256$	$\begin{bmatrix} 3 \times 3, 256 \\ 3 \times 3, 256 \end{bmatrix} \times 2$
Conv5	$7 \times 7 \times 512$	$\begin{bmatrix} 3 \times 3, 512 \\ 3 \times 3, 512 \end{bmatrix} \times 2$
Smart pooling	$1 \times 1 \times 512$	7×7 **(Fig. 3)**
Fully connected	1000	512×1000

Table 5. Accuracy results for ResNet18* with smart pooling vs reported ResNet topologies for ImageNet

Neural network	#Param	Top1%	Top5%
ResNet18	11M	69.76	89.08
ResNet50	25.6M	76.15	92.87
ResNet101	44.5M	77.37	93.56
ResNet18*	**11M**	**71.33**	**90.07**

5   Conclusion

When implementing CNN, the most simple and widely used operations for feature compression are the pooling layers. Not many works scrutinize their performance since their main objective is to perform a sub-sampling of the input images into a smaller spatial representation. Typical pooling layers do not have any additional tunable parameters, and the decision of their usage, e.g. between max pooling or average pooling, is heuristically set by the neural network architect. There is not a strict definition on which one of these layers will yield better results, so traditionally the model is trained two times, one for each type of pooling layer, selecting at the end the model with better performance. In our proposal, the pooling layers can adjust their behaviour, automating the process of selecting the best pooling factor. The smart pooling layer learns how to imitate the max or the average pooling, but beyond this behavior, it learns new pooling strategies to improve the accuracy, defining the pooling location (x, y) on the fly based on the input image. The smart pool layer enables sub-pixel precision for pooling, creating CNN models 164X more efficient in terms of accuracy Vs memory. The usage of this smart pooling layer resulted in a ResNet18 with

270K number of trainable parameters, over-performing a Resnet110 with 44.5 Million parameters, i.e. 94.08% Vs 93.75%, over the CIFAR-10 dataset. Similar behavior was seen in a more challenging task, which is the ImageNet dataset, where the replacement of a traditional pooling layer for the proposed method improved the accuracy in a 1.57%.

References

1. Boureau, Y., Le Roux, N., Bach, F., Ponce, J., LeCun, Y.: Ask the locals: multi-way local pooling for image recognition. In: 2011 International Conference on Computer Vision, pp. 2651–2658, November 2011. https://doi.org/10.1109/ICCV.2011.6126555
2. Boureau, Y.L., Ponce, J., LeCun, Y.: A theoretical analysis of feature pooling in visual recognition. In: Proceedings of the 27th International Conference on International Conference on Machine Learning. ICML 2010, Omnipress, USA, pp. 111–118 (2010). http://dl.acm.org/citation.cfm?id=3104322.3104338
3. Carreira, J., Caseiro, R., Batista, J., Sminchisescu, C.: Semantic segmentation with second-order pooling. In: Fitzgibbon, A., Lazebnik, S., Perona, P., Sato, Y., Schmid, C. (eds.) ECCV 2012. LNCS, vol. 7578, pp. 430–443. Springer, Heidelberg (2012). https://doi.org/10.1007/978-3-642-33786-4_32
4. Deng, J., Dong, W., Socher, R., Li, L.J., Li, K., Fei-Fei, L.: ImageNet: a large-scale hierarchical image database. In: CVPR09 (2009)
5. Gao, Z., Xie, J., Wang, Q., Li, P.: Global second-order pooling convolutional networks (2018)
6. Graham, B.: Fractional max-pooling. CoRR abs/1412.6071 (2014). http://arxiv.org/abs/1412.6071
7. Han, D., Kim, J., Kim, J.: Deep pyramidal residual networks. CoRR abs/1610.02915 (2016). http://arxiv.org/abs/1610.02915
8. He, K., Zhang, X., Ren, S., Sun, J.: Delving deep into rectifiers: surpassing human-level performance on ImageNet classification. In: Proceedings of the IEEE International Conference on Computer Vision, pp. 1026–1034 (2015)
9. He, K., Zhang, X., Ren, S., Sun, J.: Deep residual learning for image recognition. In: Proceedings of the IEEE Conference on Computer Vision and Pattern Recognition, pp. 770–778 (2016)
10. Iandola, F.N., Moskewicz, M.W., Ashraf, K., Han, S., Dally, W.J., Keutzer, K.: SqueezeNet: Alexnet-level accuracy with 50x fewer parameters and <1mb model size. CoRR abs/1602.07360 (2016). http://arxiv.org/abs/1602.07360
11. Ionescu, C., Vantzos, O., Sminchisescu, C.: Matrix backpropagation for deep networks with structured layers. In: 2015 IEEE International Conference on Computer Vision (ICCV), pp. 2965–2973 (2015)
12. He, K., Zhang, X., Ren, S., Sun, J.: Deep residual learning for image recognition. arXiv:1512.03385 (2015)
13. Krizhevsky, A.: Learning multiple layers of features from tiny images. Technical report (2009)
14. LeCun, Y., et al.: Handwritten digit recognition with a back-propagation network. In: Touretzky, D.S. (ed.) Advances in Neural Information Processing Systems 2, pp. 396–404. Morgan-Kaufmann (1990). http://papers.nips.cc/paper/293-handwritten-digit-recognition-with-a-back-propagation-network.pdf

15. Li, P., Xie, J., Wang, Q., Zuo, W.: Is second-order information helpful for large-scale visual recognition? CoRR abs/1703.08050 (2017). http://arxiv.org/abs/1703.08050

16. Liu, R., et al.: An intriguing failing of convolutional neural networks and the Coord-Conv solution (2018)

17. Russakovsky, O., et al.: ImageNet large scale visual recognition challenge. CoRR abs/1409.0575 (2014). http://arxiv.org/abs/1409.0575

18. Sandler, M., Howard, A., Zhu, M., Zhmoginov, A., Chen, L.C.: MobileNetV2: inverted residuals and linear bottlenecks. In: Proceedings of the IEEE Conference on Computer Vision and Pattern Recognition, pp. 4510–4520 (2018)

19. dos Santos, C.N., Tan, M., Xiang, B., Zhou, B.: Attentive pooling networks. CoRR abs/1602.03609 (2016). http://arxiv.org/abs/1602.03609

20. Szegedy, C., et al.: Going deeper with convolutions. CoRR abs/1409.4842 (2014). http://arxiv.org/abs/1409.4842

21. Tobias, J., Dosovitskiy, A., Brox, T., Riedmiller, M.A.: Striving for simplicity: the all convolutional net. CoRR abs/1412.6806 (2014). http://dblp.uni-trier.de/db/journals/corr/corr1412.html#SpringenbergDBR14

22. Zagoruyko, S., Komodakis, N.: Wide residual networks. CoRR abs/1605.07146 (2016). http://arxiv.org/abs/1605.07146

23. Zhang, X., Zhou, X., Lin, M., Sun, J.: ShuffleNet: an extremely efficient convolutional neural network for mobile devices. In: Proceedings of the IEEE Conference on Computer Vision and Pattern Recognition, pp. 6848–6856 (2018)

Second Order Bifurcating Methodology for Neural Network Training and Topology Optimization

Julio Zamora Esquivel$^{(\boxtimes)}$, Jesus Adan Cruz Vargas, and Omesh Tickoo

Intel Labs, Guadalajara, Mexico
{julio.c.zamora.esquivel,jesus.a.cruz.vargas,omesh.tickoo}@intel.com

Abstract. This work proposes a second-order methodology that minimizes the global loss error over a neural network (NN) training process of fully connected layers, based on the usage of vertical and horizontal tangent parabolas to the error derivative. This methodology expands the search area of zero-crossings in the error derivative function without restrictions, therefore quantifying the need for a larger or a smaller number of neurons in a given fully connected layer in order to optimally converge to the solution of a given training database. During training, the number of neurons in a layer converges to the number of roots of the derivative of the error function, e.g. when two neurons converge to the same root, both will merge into a single neuron; additionally, every neuron improves its position to better cover the training data distribution, or otherwise, it will be split into two neurons of needed, depending on its derivative function on each training iteration. The proposed routine removes neurons that are not in the error's minimum value neighborhood, reducing computational costs and therefore optimizing the model architecture, since it adjusts the NN topology embedded in the same training process, without the cost of having to train multiple topologies over an exhaustive trial-and-error approach.

Keywords: Topology optimization · Kernel surface bifurcating methods

1 Introduction

In fundamental math, the root of a real valued function f is a member x in the domain of f such that $f(x)$ vanishes at x, i.e., x is a solution of the equation $f(x) = 0$. There are many approaches to find the roots. The main goal of those methods is to find the roots using a lower number of iterations. Some methods like [6,8] and [5] require the user to specify the initial interval where the root is located. Some others like [7] need to start with an initial point close to the root in order to efficiently converge. In general these methods only provide one root; to compute all existing roots, it is needed to run the methodology multiple

© Springer Nature Switzerland AG 2021
A. Del Bimbo et al. (Eds.): ICPR 2020 Workshops, LNCS 12661, pp. 725–738, 2021.
https://doi.org/10.1007/978-3-030-68763-2_55

times staring with different intervals or different initialization. Here a second-order method to find the existing roots of a function, based on the usage of vertical and horizontal tangent parabolas is proposed. This method expands the area of search, creating more possible threads and finding more local roots. The proposed methodology requires less number of iterations to converge in a wider range of functions and starting points. Additionally, it can be used to find the roots of a function, but it can also be used to find the maxima and minima values of a function if its derivative is available, which is the application this work is focused on, basically finding the minimal error that a Radial Basis Function (RBF) neural network produces on the evaluation of the database, by finding the roots of its error derivative. The weights on the hidden layer will be located or moved towards its closes singular point (root in the NN error derivative).

2   Related Work

In machine learning, a topology is defined by specifying the number of layers, the number of neurons on each layer, the type of layers, etc. such values are know as hyper-parameters. This work focus in just one of those hyper-parameters: the number of neurons in a hidden layer. The typical procedure is to define the number of neurons manually, and to use a trial-and-error process with multiple trainings, until the user obtains a satisfactory balance between the number of neurons and the expected accuracy performance.

Some existing techniques like AutoML, try to automatically tune the hyper-parameters with applications like Talos (Hyperparameter Scanning for Keras and Tensorflow [3]), HyperAS (the Keras + Hyperopt: A very simple wrapper for convenient hyper-parameter optimization [1]), Auto-keras: An efficient neural architecture search system [11], Auto-PyTorch: Automatic architecture search and hyperparameter optimization for PyTorch [13]. Performing multiple trainings through brute force, until the combination of hyper-parameters that yields the best performance is found. There are some improvements on the naive search for instance NASNet—Neural Architecture Search Network [17], but the computational cost is high using 500GPUs.

Another technique is to use genetic algorithms. In this method, every model represents an element of the population and new models are generated combining the previous generations, and for each combination a new training is performed in order to identify the best topologies in the new population. For instance DEvol (DeepEvolution) is a basic proof of concept for genetic architecture search in Keras [2] and [10].

Another more related technique was introduced in [9] with a growing neural gas network learns topologies. In which an incremental network model is introduced which is able to learn the important topological relations in a given set of input vectors by means of a simple Hebb-like learning rule. Our work follows a different method to grow the topology (Fig. 1).

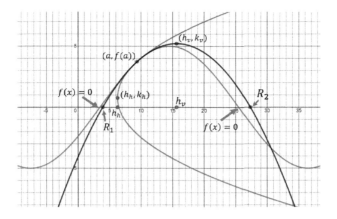

Fig. 1. Vertical and horizontal tangent parabolas

3   Method

Our method is based on the horizontal and vertical tangent parabola, because the roots of the tangent vertical parabola approximate the location of the function roots, then before describing the general algorithm, the method we use to compute the horizontal and vertical parabola will be described.

3.1   Horizontal Tangent Parabola (HTP)

The General equation of the x-axis aligned parabola is given by:

$$x = h_h + p_h(y - k_h)^2 \tag{1}$$

where $(h_h, k_h) \in \Re$ is the vertex of the parabola and p_h is proportional to the focal length. This parabola is tangent to the function f only if satisfies $y(a) = f(a)$, $y(a)' = f'(a)$ and $y(a)' = f'(a)$. Then the values of h_h, k_h, p_h should be computed in terms of f, f' and f'' in order to generate the Horizontal tangent parabola. Using the derivative horizontal parabola (1)

$$1 = 2p_h(y - k)y' \tag{2}$$

While second derivative gives

$$0 = 2p_h(y - k)y'' + 2p_h(y')^2 \tag{3}$$

Solving for k_h in the Eq. 3

$$k_h = y + \frac{y'^2}{y''} \tag{4}$$

Replacing Eq. 4 in 2

$$p_h = -\frac{y''}{2y'^3} \tag{5}$$

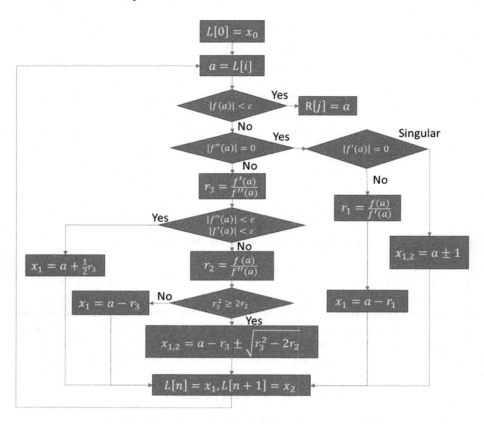

Fig. 2. The method finds the roots of a function based on different ratios of the function and its first and second derivative (r_1, r_2 and r_3). The algorithm selects a candidate from a set of candidates L and generates one or two new candidates (x_1 and x_2). The new candidates are added to L at its last position n (and $n+1$ when two point are generated). The candidates that are found to be roots are added to R.

Finally, replacing Eq. 4 and Eq. 5 in 1

$$h_h = x + \frac{y'}{2y''} \tag{6}$$

It means, for a function f the horizontal tangent parabola at point a is given by

$$h_h = a + \frac{f'(a)}{2f''(a)}, k_h = f(a) + \frac{f'(a)^2}{f''(a)}, p_h = -\frac{f''(a)}{2f'(a)^3} \tag{7}$$

Replacing those values on 1 the HTP gets defined.

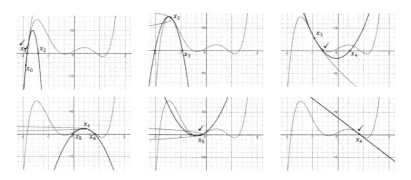

Fig. 3. Different iterations to find the roots of an example root using the methodology. Here it starts with x_0, generating x_1 (a root) and x_2. x_2 is not a root but it helps to generate x_3, in the next iteration it finds another root and also x_4, x_4 helps to find the root x_6 and so on.

3.2   Vertical Tangent Parabola (VTP)

Following the same methodology used for the horizontal parabola, the general equation of the y-axis aligned parabola is given by:

$$y = k_v + p_v(x - h_v)^2 \tag{8}$$

Computing the first and second derivative:

$$y' = 2p_v(x - h_v) \tag{9}$$

$$y'' = 2p_v \tag{10}$$

From the Eq. 10 the value of p is used to get h from 9.

$$h_v = x - \frac{y'}{y''} \tag{11}$$

Replacing the 11 and 10 in 8 the value of k_v is determined by

$$k_v = y - \frac{y'^2}{2y''} \tag{12}$$

In summary the vertical tangent parabola to the function f at point a

$$h_v = a - \frac{f'(a)}{f''(a)}, k_v = f(a) - \frac{f'(a)^2}{2f''(a)}, p_v = \frac{f''(a)}{2} \tag{13}$$

Then, replacing all those coefficients in the Eq. 8 the VTP is given by:

$$y = f(a) - \frac{f'(a)^2}{2f''(a)} + \frac{f''(a)}{2}\left(x - a + \frac{f'(a)}{f''(a)}\right)^2 \tag{14}$$

Once the vertical parabola is defined, its roots R_1 and R_2 can be computed doing:

$$R_1 = \left(a - \frac{f'(a)}{f''(a)}\right) - \sqrt{\left(\frac{f'(a)}{f''(a)}\right)^2 - 2\frac{f(a)}{f''(a)}} \tag{15}$$

$$R_2 = \left(a - \frac{f'(a)}{f''(a)}\right) + \sqrt{\left(\frac{f'(a)}{f''(a)}\right)^2 - 2\frac{f(a)}{f''(a)}} \tag{16}$$

Since the VTP approximates f at a, at least one of its roots R_1 or R_2 approximates one of the roots of f, then the next value of a could be R_1 or R_2 or both creating two threads for root finding. It is clear that the function f not always has roots. There are many conditions in which the VTP does not intersects the x-axis, in this case the next value for a should be a vertex of the VTP, it means that $a_{n+1} = h_v$. There are some function like $y = tanh(x)$ where the newton method fails, but also for that function if the initial point a is far form the root, it means that $a > \pi$, then the VTP will produce roots even farther, here is where the HTP takes place. If the $|f'(a)| < \epsilon$ and $|f''(a)| < \epsilon$ the next value of a should be the vertex of the HTP $a_{n+1} = h_h$. A detailed diagram of the algorithm is shown in Fig. 2 and explained in the next section.

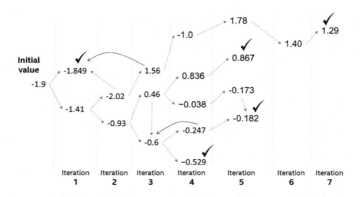

Fig. 4. 7 iterations performed in an example function to successfully find all roots.

3.3 Algorithm

The algorithm proposed in this paper is multi-threaded, it requires at least an initial value (a thread) to start the exploration of the local function. The method is based in the derivative ratios r_1, r_2, r_3 generated by the derivatives of the function $f(x)$, defined as:

$$r_1 = \frac{f(a)}{f'(a)}, r_2 = \frac{f(a)}{f''(a)}, r_3 = \frac{f'(a)}{f''(a)} \tag{17}$$

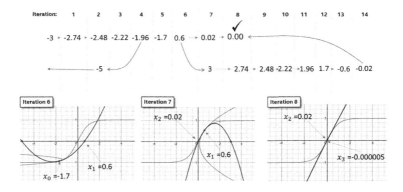

Fig. 5. Illustration of the 8 iterations of our method used to obtain the roots of the *tanh* function.

Depending on the values of $f'(a)$ and $f''(a)$ there are four different scenarios as described in the flow diagram in 2.

Each thread (initial value) generates a refinement of the one or two new candidates to continue the exploration. In the flow diagram in 2, if $r_3^2 < 2r_2$, then the square root is considered zero. In this case, only a candidate point is generated with $x_1 = a - r_3$.

To prove the feasibility of our method, we provide the next results obtained from different examples.

3.4   Example 1

As an initial illustration of the method, consider the following function:

$$f(x) = 5x^5 + 2x^4 - 15x^3 + 6x + 1 \tag{18}$$

The graphs of Fig. 3 and the diagram of Fig. 4 show the sequence of values calculated by each thread during the iterations of our method. In this case, the longest thread performed seven iterations, where the algorithm was able to successfully find all roots of the example function. The algorithm can be stopped once it finds the first root, or after a specified number of iterations. For this function in this scenario the method used 7 iterations to find 5 roots. This is less than 5 iterations per root in average. In general our method will not be able to find all roots, but if the initial point is close to the root it will converge to the closest root. As Fig. 3 shows at every iteration the algorithm could generate up to two new points for each candidate, some times one of the new candidates is actually the root and sometimes it returns back to a previously analyzed point (Fig. 5).

3.5   Example 2

For this example, the function $f(x) = tanh(x)$ is used. In this case, the Newton-Raphson method diverges while the bisections method requires to have a priory two point in opposite side of the root. In contrast, our method does converge requiring only 8 iterations to obtain the roots of *tanh*.

In this experiment the method combined the horizontal and vertical parabola in order to find the root. The only limitation identified of the algorithm is present when the initial point or thread is in the proximity of a local minimum without roots; in this particular case, the methodology will converge to the local minimum. This is not unique to our methodology, since all other numerical methods used to obtain the roots of a function suffer from the same limitation. However, if other initial points are tested, our system is expected to reach all the possible roots in less iterations than other numerical methods.

We have shown that our method finds in a efficient way the roots of a function, but how it connects with the training of a neural network? Basically because the all error minimization methods moves the weights of a given neural network trying to find a local global or minima for a given topology in a database, and the minimum value (combinations of weights) is actually a root in the error derivative of the function defined by the model in an specific dataset. In the following section a small example will be used in order to better explain the idea.

4 Training a Radial Basis Function NN

For our experiments, we used a Radial Basis Function (RBF) NN, but any other type of network can be used. The following diagram shows the basic architecture in which the number of neurons in the hidden layer is k. Our method will increase and decrease the number of neurons depending of the number of roots detected in the derivative of the error function.

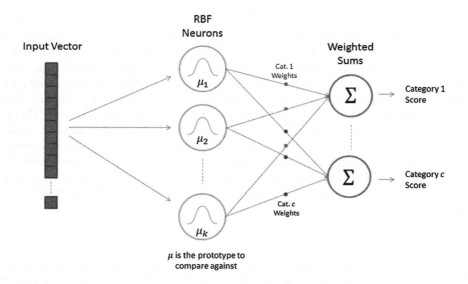

Fig. 6. Radial Basis Function neural network topology

Radial basis function based fully connected layers (in Fig. 6), μ represents the centroid of the hyper-spheroid (a Gaussian for 2D), w represents the weights of the output layer, a represents the outputs from the Gaussian neurons and o is the output of the final layer. For This network the total error is given by:

$$E = \frac{1}{2} \sum_{i=1}^{N} (d_i - o_i) \tag{19}$$

where o_i is given by:

$$o_i = \sum_{j}^{k} w_j a_{ij} \tag{20}$$

And a_{ij} is defined as:

$$a_{ij} = e^{-\sum_{l=1}^{D} (x_{il} - \mu_{jl})^2} \tag{21}$$

Then, the error E partial derivative is:

$$f(\mu_{il}) = \frac{\partial E}{\partial \mu_{jl}} = 2 \sum_{i=1}^{N} (d_i - o_i) \, w_j a_{ij} \, (x_{il} - \mu_{jl}) \tag{22}$$

Since we define our function as the derivative of the error:

$$f(\mu_{il}) = \frac{\partial E}{\partial \mu_{jl}} \tag{23}$$

Then, the derivative is denoted as:

$$f'(\mu_{jl}) = \sum_{i=1}^{N} \left(\frac{f(\mu_{jl})^2}{(d_i - o_i)^2} + 2p \, (x_{il} - \mu_{jl}) - \frac{f(\mu_{jl})}{x_{il} - \mu_{jl}} \right)$$

And $f''(\mu_{jl}) =$

$$\frac{2f(\mu_{jl}) \, f'(\mu_{jl}) \, (d_i - o_i) + 4f(\mu_{jl})^2 \, w_j a_j \, (x_{il} - \mu_{jl})}{(d_i - o_i)^3} + s$$

Where S is:

$$s = \sum_{n=0}^{3} (x_{il} - \mu_{jl})^{(1-n)} V_n \tag{24}$$

And:

$$V = [2f'(u_{jl}), -2f(u_{jl}), -f'(u_{jl}), -f(u_{jl})] \tag{25}$$

Now we can compute the ratios in the Eq. 17 that allow us to follow the algorithm described in 2 to find the roots of the derivative of the error function. The roots found are proportional to the number of neurons needed by the NN to solve the problem. Instead of showing the performance of the algorithm highlighting the accuracy, our experiments were designed to visualize internally the motion of the neurons and the reduction of them across the time, a couple of two dimensional experiments were used, the method scales two high dimensions, but the visualization in a two dimensional scenario is much easier.

5   Experiments

The following set of experiments highlight the adaptation of the NN topology functionality, by reducing the number of neurons; these are not intended to show accuracy performances.

5.1   Interpolation of a 2D Surface

The scenarios consist on a set of features in a 2D space for visualization purposes; the number of randomly initialized neurons is set intentionally high for the task (60 neurons which are more than needed to solve the problem). The experiments were selected to be simple in the first test scenario as shown in Fig. 7, where we have a set of points (ones) surrounded by points zeroes. The system started with sixty units and ended with only seven and correctly classifying all the patterns. In the second test scenario, as shown in Fig. 8 the NN is trained to classify between the red dots and the black dots (see plots below). White circles represent each 2D RBF neuron distribution. As can be seen in the sequence of plots, the number of neurons decreases while the NN is being trained and the error decreases, based on merging the neurons on the same E' root. In this test after (b) we added data on the fly and the network continues refining and removing units and adjusting the position of each one as Fig. 8 shows.

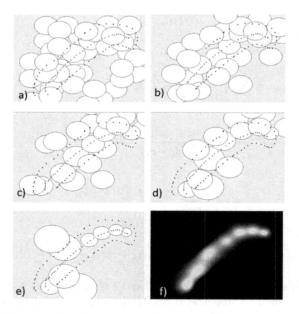

Fig. 7. Evolution of the network size (number of units in the hidden layer) across iterations all units that converge to the same value are merged producing a reduction in the number of units.

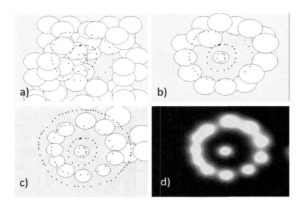

Fig. 8. a) Initial state with 60 units, b) End of removing mos of the unneeded units, c) adding extra data to force the system to Adapt, d) Final solution with only one unneeded unit.

5.2 Learning the Kernel Surface

Our proposed approach can be used efficiently in deep learning, based on the fact that every filter is represented by a two dimensional surface. Traditional convolutional kernels present n^2 degrees of freedom, but the surfaces generated on the filters can be approximated in most of the cases with less parameters (saving memory), e.g. a Sobel filter with only two Gaussians. In this section, a RBF neural network with 2 inputs and 1 output will be used per convolutional Kernel. During the training, the RBF adjust its weights to generate the surface of the filter, and reduce or increase the number of units used for this purpose (to better approximate the filter); each of the units in the RBF have only 3 degrees of freedom having as limit eight units per kernel. This restriction is defined by eight units representing 24 degrees of freedom or trainable parameters, which represents one less parameter than the ones present in a 5x5 filter, and the purpose is to compress the number of parameters. In this way, the total number of weights in a layer becomes dynamic and does not depend on the size of the kernel, but instead it depends on the complexity of the required filter. In order to test our approach, we trained a basic Sobel filter used as an example.

The popular Sobel filter, represented by the 1st derivative of a Gaussian filter (DoG), is approximated by using the difference of two Gaussians. This derivate filter is identical to the well-known Sobel filter (used normally for edge detection in classic image processing) multiplied by a factor of -1. Likewise, it is typically used to detect the sharp borders or edges of the image by removing the low frequency components, i.e. passing only the high frequency components.

The mask of this filter is given by the equation:

$$\frac{\partial G(x,y)}{\partial x} = xe^{-\frac{x^2+y^2}{2\sigma^2}} \tag{26}$$

The shape of this filter on the frequency domain is also a Sobel-like function. The Fig. 9 summarizes its shape in $2D$ along with the numerical representation

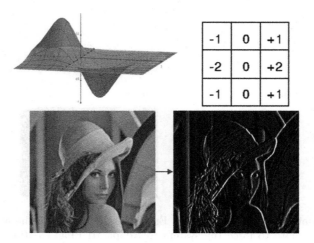

Fig. 9. Derivative of Gaussian (DOG) filter, its mask and the effect on the input image.

of the mask (Fig. 9, top right) and the effect it produces on an input image (Fig. 9 bottom right). During the training, the Gaussians move to interpolate the filter; originally, this filter is generated by the difference of two filters, but with our approach, we used more Gaussians to interpolate a sampled area, shown in this work only for illustration purposes (Fig. 10).

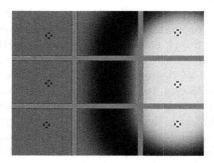

Fig. 10. Filter surface generated by the RBF NN.

5.3   Application in Convolutional Neural Networks

In order to benchmark our approach in a real use case scenario, the MNIST dataset was used to train a convolutional neural network (CNN) to classify handwritten numbers from 0 to 9. The MNIST is a public dataset that consists of 60,000 28×28 gray scale images in group into 10 classes (handwritten numbers), with 6000 images per class [15]. There are 50,000 training images and 10,000 test images provided in the official dataset split. The topology used in this work as the baseline for comparison comprises 6 convolutional filters in the first layer, 10 convolutional units in the second layer, 15 in the third layer, and a fully connected layer with 240 inputs and 10 outputs for classification. The number of parameters per layer is: 150, 1,500, 3,750, and 2,400, respectively, for a total of 7,800 parameters (ignoring biases). It can be noted that the biggest number of parameters are in the third convolutional layer; for this experiment, we replaced this third layer with our proposed methodology and allow each kernel inside this layer to define its resources and optimize the number of parameters needed without scarifying the accuracy of the CNN.

Once trained, the CNN resulted in only 1,350 parameters in the third convolutional layer, instead of the 3,750 present in the original baseline. In terms of performance, the accuracy drooped from 99.31% to 99.20%, i.e a small reduction when considering the $2.7X$ compression in the number of parameters for the tested layer (results shown in Table 1).

Table 1. MNIST Accuracy vs Memory

Neural network	#Parameters	Accuracy
LeNet [4]	431K	99.4%
LetNet5 [16]	64K	99.24%
50-50-200-10NN [12]	226K	99.51%
Best Practices [14]	132.5K	99.5%
6-10-15-10	7.8K	99.31%
Our method	**5.4K**	99.20%

6 Conclusions

This work presents a novel methodology to train a NN by not only adjusting it weights, but also automatically adjusting the number of neurons inside a fully connected layer during the training process. This is achievable by means of quadratic functions (e.g. the tangent vertical and Horizontal parabola).

By implementing this methodology, we demonstrate that it is possible to converge faster and more robustly to the roots of the derivative of the error function. At each of the roots found, a neuron is located, and when two neurons converge into the same root, these get merged into one neuron to avoid redundancy. This constitutes the base mechanism to optimize the number of neurons needed by the final NN topology. In the same fashion, if the algorithm detects the presence of a large number of roots, it is possible to generate additional neurons by splitting the existing ones in the layer (similar to the biological behavior found in the mitosis process). These two processes guarantee the optimal number of neurons will be obtained at the end of the training stage.

This work constitutes a mean to help encounter the optimal topology of a NN model in order to save computing resources during training, and guarantee an expected performance when deployed into an inference engine. For this work, we placed special attention to the visualization of the method as a way to show the performance benefits.

Our experiments on the MNIST dataset show a $2.7X$ compression of the number of parameters in the tested convolutional layer, resulting in a drop impact of 0.1% in the accuracy. Our technique gets the optimal topology in a single training, as compared to other commonly available techniques, e.g. the AutoML, that require a large number of trainings, typically around 22,000GPU hours.

References

1. Hyperas. http://maxpumperla.com/hyperas/
2. Devol (2019). https://github.com/joeddav/devol
3. Autonomio: Autonomio talos (2019). http://github.com/autonomio/talos
4. BAIR/BVLC: Lenet architecture in caffe tutorial. Github (2018). https://github.com/BVLC/caffe/blob/master/examples/mnist/lenet.prototxt
5. Brent, R.P.: An algorithm with guaranteed convergence for finding a zero of a function. Comput. J. **14**, 422–425 (1971)
6. Burden, R.L., Faires, D.J.: Numerical analysis, 3rd edn. PWS Publishing Company, Boston (1985)
7. Bussotti, P.: Differential calculus: The use of newton's methodus fluxionum et serierum infinitarum in an education context. Problems of Education in the 21st Century 65, Discontinuous (June 2015). http://journals.indexcopernicus.com/abstract.php?icid=1163179
8. Ford, J.A.: Improved algorithms of Illinois-type for the numerical solution of non-linear equations (1995)
9. Fritzke, B.: A growing neural gas network learns topologies. Adv. Neural Inf. Proc. Syst. **7**, 625–632 (1995)
10. Gómez, A.B., Sáez, Y., Viñuela, P.I.: Evolutionary convolutional neural networks: an application to handwriting recognition. Neurocomputing **283**, 38–52 (2017)
11. Jin, H., Song, Q., Hu, X.: Efficient neural architecture search with network morphism. CoRR abs/1806.10282 (2018). http://arxiv.org/abs/1806.10282
12. Ranzato, M., Poultney, C., Chopra, S., LeCun, Y.: Efficient learning of sparse representations with an energy-based model. NIPS2006, 1137–1144 (2006)
13. Mendoza, H., et al.: Towards automatically-tuned deep neural networks. In: Hutter, F., Kotthoff, L., Vanschoren, J. (eds.) Automated Machine Learning. TSSCML, pp. 135–149. Springer, Cham (2019). https://doi.org/10.1007/978-3-030-05318-5_7
14. Simard, P.Y., Steinkraus, D., Platt, J.C.: Best practices for convolutional neural networks applied to visual document analysis. In: ICDAR 2003 (2003)
15. Yann, L., Corinna, C.: MNIST handwritten digit database (2010). http://yann.lecun.com/exdb/mnist/
16. LeCun, Y., Bottou, L., Bengio, Y., Haffner, P.: Gradient-based learning applied to document recognition. Proc. IEEE **86**(11), 2278-2324 (1998)
17. Zoph, B., Vasudevan, V., Shlens, J., Le, Q.V.: Learning transferable architectures for scalable image recognition. CoRR abs/1707.07012 (2017). http://arxiv.org/abs/1707.07012

Author Index

Printed in the United States
By Bookmasters